TO MY FAMILY
Roger, Kristin, Karen, and Karla

About the Author

Laura A. Freberg is Professor of Psychology at California Polytechnic State University, San Luis Obispo, where she teaches courses in Introductory Psychology, Biological Psychology, and Sensation and Perception. With John Cacioppo of the University of Chicago, Laura is the co-author of two editions of *Discovering Psychology: The Science of Mind* for Cengage Learning.

Laura completed her undergraduate and graduate studies at UCLA, where her thinking about psychology was shaped by Eric Holman, John Garcia, O. Ivar Lovaas, Larry Butcher, Jackson Beatty, John Libeskind, Donald Novin, Frank Krasne, and F. Nowell Jones. She was privileged to study neuroanatomy with Arnold Scheibel, and investigated the effects of psychoactive drugs on learning and memory under the direction of Murray Jarvik and Ronald Siegel in the UCLA Neuropsychiatric Institute. As a capstone to her education, Laura completed her dissertation with Robert Rescorla, then at Yale University.

Laura's teaching career began when she taught her first college course at Pasadena City College at the age of 23 while still a graduate student at UCLA. Recently, to better understand the needs of the online education community, she also began teaching for Argosy University Online, including courses in Social Psychology, Sensation/Perception, Cognitive Psychology, Statistics, Research Methods, and Writing in Psychology. She has received Faculty Member of the Year recognition from Cal Poly Disabilities Resource Center three times (1991, 1994, and 2009) for her work with students with disabilities. She enjoys using technology and social media in the classroom and is a Google Glass Explorer. Laura serves as the Content Expert Writer for Psychology for Answers.com. and enjoys collaborating with daughters Kristin Saling (Systems Engineering—U.S. Military Academy at West Point) and Karen Freberg (Communications—University of Louisville) on a variety of research projects in crisis management and public relations as well as in psychology. She serves as the Bylaws and Archives Committee Chair for the Society for Social Neuroscience and is a member of the editorial board for *Leadership Quarterly*.

In her spare time, Laura enjoys family time with her husband, Roger, their youngest daughter Karla, who has autism spectrum disorder, and an active menagerie including an Australian shepherd, two cats, and three parakeets. She usually writes while consuming vast quantities of Gevalia coffee and listening to the Rolling Stones (which might be apparent in the book's writing style), and she has been known to enjoy college football, Harley Davidsons, episodes of *Game of Thrones* that do not feature weddings, and *Sherlock*. Her ringtone is from Nintendo's *Legend of Zelda*.

About the Cover

If you are familiar with the first and second editions of this textbook, you know that we like to pick colorful visuals that portray the biology behind the behavior. For this third edition, we selected an image of a "brainbow" of the hippocampus of a transgenic mouse. Brainbows are constructed by promoting the expression of different ratios of red, green, and blue fluorescent proteins by individual neurons. This imaging process has assisted researchers interested in mapping the connectome, or the neural connections of the brain. The brainbow technique was developed in 2007 by researchers under the direction of Joshua Sanes and Jeff Lichtman.

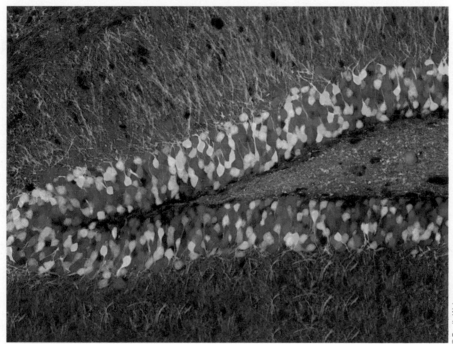

© Tamily Weissman

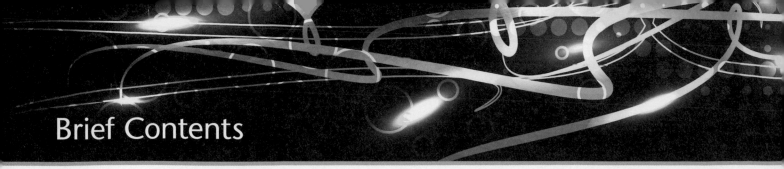

Brief Contents

Contents

3   Neurophysiology: The Structure and Functions of the Cells of the Nervous System   63

Psychopharmacology   101

7   Nonvisual Sensation and Perception   215

8   Movement   253

9 Homeostasis and Motivation   289

10 Sexual Behavior   325

11   Sleep and Waking   363

12 Learning and Memory 399

13   Hemispheric Asymmetry, Language, and Intelligence   443

14   Emotion, Reward, Aggression, and Stress   477

15   Neuropsychology   511

16   Psychopathology   543

Preface

"… in teaching, you must simply work your pupil into such a state of interest in what you are going to teach him that every other object of attention is banished from his mind; then reveal it to him so impressively that he will remember the occasion to his dying day; and finally fill him with devouring curiosity to know what the steps in connection with the subject are."

—William James (1899, p. 10)

James's goals for the classroom instructor might seem lofty to some, but many of us who teach neuroscience have enjoyed the peak experience of seeing students "turn on" to the material in just the way James describes.

This is an exciting time to be a neuroscientist. Every day, science newsfeeds announce some new and dramatic breakthroughs in our knowledge about the nervous system and the human mind. Important questions raised in the past now have definitive answers. In 1890, James commented that "blood very likely may rush to each region of the cortex according as it is most active, but of this we know nothing" (vol. 1, p. 99). With today's technology, it is safe to say we now know much more than "nothing" about this phenomenon James described.

Much has changed in the field of neuroscience since our first edition of this textbook in 2006. More than half of the four-year universities in the United States now offer bachelors degrees in neuroscience, and most offer at least a minor in the discipline. Neuroscience reflects a general academic trend of the 21st century, in which the walls separating specializations are giving way to new, transdisciplinary research teams, courses, and educational programs. In recognition of these changes, we have decided to modify the title of the third edition of this textbook from *Discovering Biological Psychology* to *Discovering Behavioral Neuroscience: An Introduction to Biological Psychology*. A greater emphasis on the neurosciences in general is also achieved by renaming some chapter titles. Psychology, of course, still provides a foundation for the study of behavioral neuroscience, as without the ability to ask the right questions about behavior and mental processes, all of the technology on the planet wouldn't do us much good. Our current behavioral neuroscience students, however, are just as likely to be preparing for careers in the health professions, biomedical engineering, or even scientific journalism as they are in psychology.

A major reflection of the transdisciplinary approach exemplified by the neurosciences is the inclusion of psychology and behavioral neuroscience content in the revised edition of the Medical College Admission Test (MCAT) beginning in 2015. One hundred years ago, the leading killers of humans were infectious diseases. Today's top killers—heart disease, diabetes, and cancer—have far stronger relationships with behavior, not only in their causes but also in their treatments. A simple five-minute conversation with a health professional about the need to quit smoking is sufficient to lead to abstention for one year by 2 percent of patients (Law & Tang, 1995). This might not sound like much, but given the 20 percent or so of American adults who smoke and the billions of dollars their healthcare and lost productivity represent, the stakes are very high. Imagine what could be accomplished by healthcare providers who have a deep understanding of learning, motivation, and social influences on behavior. In response to these and similar trends, the current edition of the textbook explores relevant applications to students pursuing fields of study other than psychology whenever these are relevant.

This third edition continues and expands upon the goals of the previous two:

► To provide challenging, very current content in a student-friendly, accessible form.

► To stimulate critical thinking about neuroscience by presenting controversial and cutting-edge material.

► To promote active student engagement and excitement about the neurosciences.

► To integrate across chapters rather than treating them as stand-alone modules; to encourage students to see the connections among the topics. For example, connections are made between glutamate as a chemical messenger, its role in learning, the effects of psychoactive drugs on glutamate, its role in psychosis, and its importance to the causes and treatments of stroke and epilepsy.

Pedagogical Features

We realize that a course in behavioral neuroscience can be challenging for many students, particularly those who are underprepared for science courses. To make the process of mastering behavioral neuroscience concepts easier, we have included the following features:

► **Accessible Writing Style** Many textbooks are classified by "level," but it is my opinion that the most complex topics can be mastered by students across a wide range of preparation if the writing style is clear. Students and instructors from the community college through the top R1 universities have kindly complimented me on the accessible writing style used in this textbook. The textbook is also widely adopted in non-English-speaking countries, which suggests that the writing style is manageable for those for whom English is not a first language.

► **Clear, Large, Carefully Labeled Illustrations** Our medical-quality anatomical illustrations help students visualize the structures and processes discussed in each part of the textbook. Behavioral neuroscience is similar to geography in its highly visual nature, and both fields require more visual aids than most other courses. The illustrations in the textbook are augmented by a set of online animations that help the student grasp processes over time, such as the propagation of action potentials down the length of an axon.

► **Learning Objectives and Chapter Outlines** Each chapter begins with a concise set of learning objectives designed to tap into higher levels of Bloom's taxonomy, as well as an outline of the chapter's content. These features assist students in planning their learning and in becoming familiar with main terms and concepts to be covered.

► **Margin Glossaries** We regularly provide margin definitions for many difficult terms. Unlike many textbooks, we do not restrict margin definitions to keyterms only. In the electronic forms of the book, these take the form of pop-up definitions, with which students are familiar from their online searching experience.

► **Keyterms** We provide a concise list of keyterms to help students focus their learning. Behavioral neuroscience can often seem more like a foreign language course than a science course, and students benefit from guidance regarding which terms should be prioritized.

► **Interim Summaries** Each chapter features two to three interim summaries where students can catch their breath and check their mastery of the material before proceeding. These summaries feature summary points keyed to the learning objectives listed at the beginning of each chapter as well as review questions. Most interim summaries also include a helpful table that pulls together key concepts from the previous section in one convenient place.

▶ **Chapter Integration** To emphasize how the material fits together and to promote elaborative rehearsal, we make references to other chapters relevant to the topic at hand. In the electronic form of the textbook, these will take the form of hyperlinks. This will allow the reader to refer to other parts of the book as review if necessary before proceeding to new material.

▶ **Chapter Review** At the end of each chapter, the student will find some thought questions that can also serve as essay or discussion prompts. The Chapter Reviews also include the list of keyterms.

▶ **Practice Tests** In the electronic version of the textbook (see the description of MindTap), practice tests will be available for each main heading with a comprehensive practice test at the end of each chapter.

New Features for the Third Edition

Students have told me that the narrative of the textbook is "packed," and that skimming paragraphs is usually a recipe for disaster, as each sentence "counts." In defense, I respond that we have so much to say and so little room to say it in that there is little space for "fluff." At the same time, psychological science shows that spaced learning is superior to massed learning, so it is a good idea to provide regular breaks in the narrative to allow students to catch their breath and digest what they have read. We like to think of these breaks as cool stepping-stones in the flow of lava.

One type of break that we used in the previous editions and continue here in the third is the use of interim summaries that include section summary points and review questions. Most also feature tables that pull together chunks of material in a way that makes it easy to learn. Any complex field like the neurosciences entails a bit of simple, rote memorization to form a foundation for later analysis and critical thinking. The more quickly we can bring students up to speed on the basics, the faster we can move on to higher levels of discussion. Chapter summaries include thought questions designed to push students to think more actively and deeply about what they have read.

In addition to the interim and chapter summaries, each chapter of the third edition includes four types of features. We recognize that "boxing" material often encourages students to overlook content unless expressly instructed to read the boxes, but we trust instructors to use these in ways consistent with their personal style. Obviously, we hope that the content is sufficiently engaging that students will read the material regardless of "what's on the test."

▶ **Thinking Ethically** features introduce controversial, contemporary questions that require the students to use the information in the chapter in critical ways. Our students will graduate to become community leaders, and they need to be able to think ethically about future cultural choices related to the neurosciences. For example, this feature in Chapter 1 follows a discussion of brain imaging technology with questions about the potential use of brain imaging as a "lie detection" technology.

▶ **Connecting to Research** features highlight either classic or very contemporary single studies in behavioral neuroscience. This provides students with a "soft" segue into the scholarly literature, which might otherwise seem somewhat intimidating. The feature emphasizes the type of critical thinking and creativity required to advance science. For example, this feature in Chapter 2 describes the re-analysis of Phineas Gage's brain damage using a connectome approach.

▶ **Behavioral Neuroscience Goes to Work** features expose students to some of the many real-world career paths that relate to behavioral neuroscience. In my experience, many students are unaware of a number of these options. They love the material but have no idea how they can meld this passion with their need to find employment. In this feature in Chapter 5, we describe the role of the genetics counselor, whose insights will be increasingly important as the public obtains more information about personal genotypes. As a bridge between biological sciences and the counseling professions, this career has become increasingly popular with my students. At least half a dozen who are now enrolled or who have completed genetics counseling master's degrees attribute their career choice to my "selling" this concept in class.

▶ **Building Better Health** features provide an additional opportunity for students to think critically about behavioral neuroscience in the context of real-world health problems. Do gluten-free diets relieve symptoms of autism spectrum disorder? How well do smartphone sleep apps work? How do you recognize the signs of a stroke?

New Content for the Third Edition

This new edition contains many hundreds of new citations to reflect the advances in the field that have occurred since the previous edition went to press. One of the major sources of change was the publication of DSM-5 in May 2013. The discussion of movement disorders, neurocognitive disorders, and psychological disorders has been updated to match changes made by DSM-5 in terminology and organization.

Illustrations have also been updated to reflect the new content. Because space is so precious, illustrations are viewed as "teachable moments" that expand on or further explain the narrative rather than redundant, "pretty" placeholders. We are especially proud of our medical-quality anatomical illustrations, which have been the source of much positive feedback through the previous editions.

Space does not permit me to provide an exhaustive list of the updates, but here are some of the chapter-by-chapter highlights:

Chapter 1 What Is Behavioral Neuroscience?

▶ Updated definitions of neuroscience and behavioral neuroscience

▶ Updated methods section including a description of optogenetics

▶ Added description of the analysis of epigenetics

Chapter 2 Functional Neuroanatomy and the Evolution of the Nervous System

▶ Clarified use of anatomical directional terms

▶ Expanded discussion of embryological divisions of the brain, including organizational table

▶ Expanded discussion of the parts of the basal ganglia

▶ Added section on the enteric nervous system

▶ Added section on the endocrine system

Chapter 3 Neurophysiology: The Structure and Function of the Cells of the Nervous System

▶ Re-ordered discussion of glia and neurons to improve transition from discussions of neural structure to neural function

▶ Introduction of concept of axonal varicosities.

▶ Introduction of distinction between directed and nondirected synapses

Chapter 4 Psychopharmacology

► Clarified use of neurotransmitter, neuromodulator, and neurohormone terms in conjunction with directed and nondirected synapses

► Updated discussion of gasotransmitters

► Added discussion of histamine to the indoleamines

► Expanded discussion of dopaminergic pathways to include the mesostriatal and mesolimbocortical pathways and pathways originating in the hypothalamus

► Expanded discussion of receptor subtypes

► Added discussion of glycine

► Updated discussion of mode of action of methamphetamine and MDMA

Chapter 5 Genetics and the Development of the Human Brain

► Added discussion of copy-number variations (CNVs)

► Added section on epigenetics, including discussion of histone modification and DNA methylation

► Updated discussion of role of astrocytes in synapse formation and pruning

► Expanded discussion of enriched environments

► Expanded section on the brain in adolescence and adulthood, emphasizing healthy brain aging

Chapter 6 Vision

► Added general section introducing concepts of sensation, perception, transduction, and top-down/bottom-up processing

► Distinguished between diffuse and midget bipolar cells in the retina

► Added section on cortical mapping of the visual field

► Added description of akinetopsia

Chapter 7 Nonvisual Sensation and Perception

► Updated and expanded discussion of loudness perception

► Updated section on cochlear implants

► Expanded and clarified discussion of the gate theory of pain

► Expanded discussion of the chemical senses

Chapter 8 Movement

► Added subtypes of muscle spindle fibers and their relationships with Ia and group II sensory fibers

► Updated section on planning of movement

► Updated discussion of mirror systems

► Updated discussion of the causes and treatments for movement disorders, and in particular Parkinson's disease and Huntington's disease

Chapter 9 Homeostasis and Motivation

► Increased coverage of hyperthermia related to MDMA and serotonin syndrome

► Expanded explanation of the preoptic area and temperature regulation

▶ Updated information about why we stop drinking
▶ Updated discussion of obesity
▶ Updated discussion of disordered eating to be consistent with DSM-5, including section on new binge-eating disorder

Chapter 10 Sexual Behavior

▶ Updated discussion of sex chromosome variations, including mosaic karyotypes
▶ Expanded discussion of intersex and gender dysphoria
▶ Increased emphasis on organizing and activating roles of sex hormones in development
▶ Updated discussion of biomarkers for prenatal hormone environment
▶ Updated discussion of sexual dimorphism in the brain
▶ Expanded section on gender differences in behavior and cognition
▶ Added section on gender identity and transsexuality
▶ Expanded discussion on sexual orientation
▶ Updated section on male contraception
▶ Updated section on attraction, romantic love, and sexual desire
▶ Updated section on sexual dysfunction and its treatment

Chapter 11 Biorhythms

▶ Expanded discussion of the effects of artificial lighting on circadian rhythms
▶ Added discussion of gamma band activity
▶ Added discussion of default mode network (DMN) and its relationship to levels of consciousness
▶ Updated section on sleep–wake disorders to conform to DSM-5

Chapter 12 Learning and Memory

▶ Reorganized chapter material into sections on learning at the synapse and learning involving brain structures and circuits
▶ Updated information about short-term and long-term learning at the synapse
▶ Added information on operant conditioning in *Aplysia*
▶ Added information about extinction learning
▶ Expanded and updated section on long-term potentiation (LTP)
▶ Expanded and updated section on the biochemistry of memory
▶ Updated sections on the effects of stress and healthy aging on memory

Chapter 13 Hemispheric Asymmetry, Language, and Intelligence

▶ Updated discussion of lateralization to include lateralization "hubs"
▶ Expanded discussion of the advantages and development of lateralization
▶ Added section on lateralization, psychological disorders, and disease
▶ Updated and expanded discussion of gesture and language
▶ Updated and expanded discussion of multilingualism, including its contribution to cognitive reserve

▶ Added discussion of dual stream models of language

▶ Updated discussion of epigenetics and intelligence

Chapter 14 Emotion, Reward, Aggresssion, and Stress

▶ Expanded discussion of somatic markers

▶ Updated discussion of roles of amygdala, insula, basal ganglia, and anterior cingulate cortex to emotional processing

▶ Updated and expanded discussion of mesostriatal pathway, reward, and addiction

▶ Expanded and updated discussion of epigenetics and aggression

▶ Distinguished between roles of the sympathetic adrenal-medullary (SAM) system and the HPA axis in responses to stress

▶ Added section on epigenetics and stress

▶ Updated section on stress and health

Chapter 15 Neuropsychology

▶ Reorganized chapter to begin with a discussion of neuropsychology

▶ Updated and expanded section on neuropsychological assessment

▶ Updated terms such as neurocognitive disorder to maintain consistency with DSM-5

▶ Updated and greatly expanded coverage of Alzheimer's disease, which was moved here from Chapter 5 in 2e

▶ Expanded coverage of traumatic brain injury (TBI) to differentiate between combat-related blast injuries and other types of TBI

▶ Updated discussion of treatment of TBI

▶ Added section on substance/medication-induced neurocognitive disorder

▶ Updated section on HIV-associated neurocognitive disorder

▶ Updated and expanded section on recovery and treatment of neurocognitive disorders, including discussion of cognitive reserve and "Wii-hab"

Chapter 16 Psychopathology

▶ Updated the ordering of topics, new terminology, and new diagnostic criteria for all disorders to maintain consistency with DSM-5

▶ Discussed new research identifying common susceptibility genes for schizophrenia, bipolar disorder, autism spectrum disorder, attention deficit disorder, and major depressive disorder

▶ Updated discussion of the prevalence, causes, and brain correlates of autism spectrum disorder and attention deficit hyperactivity disorder

▶ Updated discussion of genetic, biochemical, and brain correlates of schizophrenia

▶ Introduced the concept of oxidative stress as a correlate of bipolar disorder

▶ Expanded the discussion of biochemical correlates of major depressive disorder

▶ Expanded and updated section on posttraumatic stress disorder (PTSD) and the roles of the hippocampus and anterior cingulate cortex in particular

▶ Discussed the relationship between psychopathy and antisocial personality disorder within the context of DSM-5

▶ Expanded discussion of biological correlates and treatment of antisocial personality disorder

MindTap

MindTap Psychology for Freberg's *Discovering Behavioral Neuroscience: An Introduction to Biological Psychology,* 3rd edition, is a personalized teaching experience with relevant assignments that guide students to analyze, apply, and improve thinking, allowing you to measure skills and outcomes with ease.

The *Discovering Behavioral Neuroscience* MindTap:

▶ Delivers assessment and content that moves students into higher-order thinking

▶ Provides evidence of student performance and a targeted delivery of assets to better engage and further demonstrate concepts both in and out of class

▶ Provides secure online testing comprised of evidence-based, standard assessment items to ensure students are performing based on their whole learning experience

▶ Provides first-rate animations and simulated lab experiences that illustrate biological processes

While other publishers offer homework-based solutions that focus on knowledge and comprehension, the *Discovering Behavioral Neuroscience* MindTap learning path includes resources that move students through Bloom's taxonomy utilizing formative and summative assessment and first-class videos, animations, and virtual labs.

Instructor Ancillaries

To further serve the needs of faculty, I have paid close attention to the production of useful ancillaries. As tempting as it was to farm these out in the interests of time and sanity, I have been personally involved with the production of animations as well as the construction of more than 3,000 questions for the Test Bank. Many of these questions have been piloted in my own classes. My questions reflect past collaboration with consultants who specialize in test construction for higher education, and I think you will find them a refreshing change from the usual test banks supplied with textbooks. The following ancillaries give instructors the tools to present course materials according to individual preference:

▶ *Instructor's Resource Manual:* Save time, streamline your course preparation, and get the most from the text by preparing for class more quickly and effectively. The Instructor's Resource Manual contains sample lecture outlines, ideas for classroom demonstrations and handouts, and suggestions for using outside resources in the classroom.

▶ *Cengage Learning Testbank Powered by Cognero:* This is a flexible, online system that allows you to: import, edit, and manipulate content from the text's test bank or elsewhere, including your own favorite test questions; create multiple test versions in an instant; and deliver tests from your LMS, your classroom, or wherever you want.

▶ *PowerPoints*: This one-stop lecture and class preparation tool contains ready-to-use Microsoft PowerPoint slides and allows you to assemble, edit, publish, and present custom lectures for your course. Our PowerPoints let you bring together text-specific lecture outlines along with videos, animations based on the art program, or your own materials—culminating in a powerful, personalized, media-enhanced presentation.

▶ *The Instructors' Website:* Log on to the password-protected site to access a wide range of resources, such as electronic versions of the instructor's manual, PowerPoint slides, and more.

Acknowledgments

I view this text as a work in progress. Please take a moment to share your thoughts and suggestions with me: lfreberg@calpoly.edu. You can also find me on Facebook and on my blog: http://www.laurafreberg.com/blog.

I am enormously grateful for the team that Cengage assembled to help make this book a reality. First, I would like to thank my professional colleagues who reviewed the many drafts of the current edition:

Aileen Bailey *St. Mary's College of Maryland*
Steve Bradshaw *Bryan College*
Deborah Carroll *Southern Connecticut State University*
James Chrobak *University of Connecticut, Storrs*
Cynthia Cimino *University of South Florida*
Sherry Dingman *Marist College*
Joyce Jadwin *Ohio University*
Joshua Karelitz *Pennsylvania State University, New Kensington*
Katrina Kardiasmenos *Bowie State University*

Melinda Meszaros *Clarke College*
Irene Nielsen *Bethany College, Lindsborg*
Terry Pettijohn *Ohio State University, Marion*
Ronald Ruiz *Riverside City College*
Royce Simpson *Spring Hill College*
Don Smith *Everett Community College*
Barbara Vail *Rocky Mountain College*
Rachael Volokhov *Kent State University, Salem*
Dana Wallace *Jamestown College*
Kimberly Wear *High Point University*
Yeuping Zhang *Lewis and Clark College*
Phillip Zoladz *Ohio Northern University*

I would also like to thanks the reviewers of the previous two editions:

John Agnew *University of Colorado at Boulder*
James E. Arruda *Mercer University*
Giorgio Ascoli *George Mason University*
Jeffrey S. Bedwell *University of Central Florida*
Virginia Bridwell *Bellevue College*
Gayle Brosnan-Watters *Slippery Rock University*
John P. Bruno *Ohio State University*
Allen E. Butt *Indiana State University*
David A. Cater *John Brown University*
James R. Coleman *University of South Carolina*
Bob Ferguson *Buena Vista University*
Aaron Ettenberg *University of California, Santa Barbara*
Thomas M. Fischer *Wayne State University*
John P. Galla *Widener University*
Ben Givens *Ohio State University*
Karen Glendenning *Florida State University*
C. Hardy *Columbia College*
James G. Holland *University of Pittsburgh*
Richard Howe *College of the Canyons*
Robert A. Jensen *Southern Illinois University*

Camille Tessitore King *Stetson University*
Norman E. Kinney *Southeast Missouri State University*
Paul J. Kulkosky *Colorado State University Pueblo*
Gloria Lawrence *Wayne State College*
Simon Levay Charles F. Levinthal *Hofstra University*
David R. Linden *West Liberty State College*
Michael R. Markham *Florida International University*
Richard Mascolo *El Camino College*
Robert Matchock *Penn State University, Altoona*
Janice E. Mcphee *Gulf Coast University*
Jody Meerdink *Nebraska Wesleyan University*
Maura Mitrushina *California State University Northridge*
Robert R. Mowrer *Angelo State University*
Mark Nawrot *North Dakota State University*
David W. Pittman *Wofford College*
Jerome L. Rekart *Rivier College*
John C. Ruch *Mills College*

Lawrence J. Ryan *Oregon State University*

Carl Samuels *Glandale Community College*

Anthony C. Santucci *Manhattanville College*

Virginia F. Saunders *San Francisco State University*

Sheralee Tershner *Western New England College*

C. Robin Timmons *Drew University*

Linda L. Walsh *University of Northern Iowa*

Frank M. Webbe *Florida Institute of Technology*

Stephen P. Weinert *Cuyamaca College*

Margaret H. White *California State University Fullerton*

Xiojuan Xu *Grand Valley State University*

Robert M. Zacharko *Carleton University*

Ronald Baenninger *Temple University*

Joseph H. Porter *Virginia Commonwealth University*

Cynthia Gibson *Creighton University*

Marcello Spinella *Richard Stockton College of New Jersey*

The many instructors who responded to market research surveys and interviews over the past several years have also contributed greatly to the text and its ancillaries.

I would like to give a special thank you to several colleagues. **Skirmantis Janusonis** of the University of California, Santa Barbara, has provided not only encouragement but gentle suggestions for improved accuracy. Skirmantis kindly provided me with an opportunity to photograph some of his human brains (one appears in Chapter 1) and he shared an image of his fantastic dissection of the hippocampus for us to use in Chapter 2. **Simon LeVay** is not only a gifted researcher but a truly elegant writer. His careful review of the chapter on sexual behavior for the first edition is deeply appreciated. I am indebted to Simon for pointing out many important studies included in the sections on sexual orientation and gender differences in cognition. **Marie Banich** at the University of Colorado at Boulder provided her expert opinions on the art program, and **Gayle Brosnan-Watters** at Arizona Christian University contributed many helpful suggestions as a reviewer and while working with me on the third edition of the Test Bank. **John Cacioppo** of the University of Chicago generously shared his considerable insight into the social aspects of neuroscience. **Konstantinos Priftis** of the University of Padova supplied several helpful corrections to the second edition. **Robert Matchock** of the University of Pennsylvania, Altoona, has been a friendly voice of encouragement beginning with the first edition. The late **Larry Butcher** of UCLA, one of my former professors, provided valuable assistance in the fine-tuning of my cholinergic pathway image in Chapter 4. **Rick Howe** and the students and faculty of the psychology department at College of the Canyons in California not only took the time to meet with me to share their reactions to the first edition but fed me cookies as well.

At Cengage, Tim Matray, product team manager for psychology, has championed my text through this edition. Bob Jucha, my content developer for the third edition, was my sounding board and partner every step of the way. Michelle Clark, senior project manager, guided the production of the text and coordinated innumerable aspects of the art and text program. Photo researcher Veerabhagu Nagarajan tenaciously pursued the photos that enliven the text. Vernon Boes, art director, guided our design to new heights in appeal and usability. I would also like to thank the many other capable and creative professionals at Cengage who contributed to this project in ways large and small over the years of its development.

Finally, I would like to thank my family for their patience and support. Roger, my husband of 43 years, read every word, helped me choose photos, and even contributed some of our original sketches when I had trouble articulating what I wanted to show. My daughters, Kristin, Karen, and Karla, frequently offered their encouragement and perspectives. I am very much indebted to all.

Laura A. Freberg

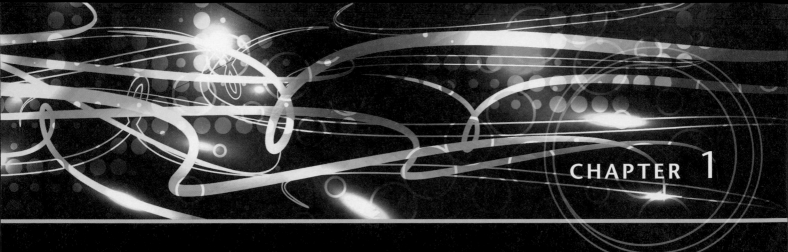

CHAPTER 1

What Is Behavioral Neuroscience?

LEARNING OBJECTIVES

L01 Classify the subfields of neuroscience, and explain how behavioral neuroscience fits within the field.

L02 Interpret the significance of the major historical highlights in the study of the nervous system.

L03 Differentiate the brain imaging technologies, including CT, PET, SPECT, MRI, fMRI, and DTI.

L04 Assess the use of histological, recording, stimulation, lesion, optogenetics, and biochemical methods in behavioral neuroscience.

L05 Discuss the relative strengths and weaknesses of twin studies, adoption studies, and the investigation of epigenetics for understanding behavior.

L06 Evaluate the ethical standards used to protect human and animal research participants.

CHAPTER OUTLINE

Neuroscience as an Interdisciplinary Field

Historical Highlights in Neuroscience

Ancient Milestones in Understanding the Nervous System

The Dawn of Scientific Reasoning

Modern Neuroscience Begins

Interim Summary 1.1

Behavioral Neuroscience Research Methods

Histology

Autopsy

Imaging

Recording

Brain Stimulation

Lesion

Biochemical Methods

Genetic Methods

Stem Cells

Interim Summary 1.2

Research Ethics in Behavioral Neuroscience

Human Participant Guidelines

Animal Subjects Guidelines

Interim Summary 1.3

Chapter Review

BEHAVIORAL NEUROSCIENCE GOES TO WORK: What Can I Do with a Degree in Neuroscience?

CONNECTING TO RESEARCH: Social Pain and the Brain

THINKING ETHICALLY: Can We Read Minds with Brain Imaging?

BUILDING BETTER HEALTH: When Is It Appropriate To Use Placebos?

Neuroscience as an Interdisciplinary Field

Neuroscience is the scientific study of the brain and nervous system, in health and in disease (UCLA, 2008). Neuroscientists strive to understand the functions of the brain and nervous system across a number of levels of analysis, using molecular, cellular, synaptic, network, computational, and behavioral approaches. You might think of this field as analogous to Google Earth. We can zoom in to see the tiniest detail and then zoom back out again to see the "big picture."

Beginning at the most microscopic level, the molecular neuroscientist explores the nervous system at the level of the molecules that serve as its building blocks. We will cover their work in our chapters on neural cell physiology (Chapter 3) and psychopharmacology (Chapter 4). Starting with DNA and RNA and the proteins resulting from gene expression, the molecular neuroscientist attempts to understand the chemicals that build the system and make neural functioning possible.

Zooming out just a bit from the molecular level of analysis, we find the cellular neuroscientist hard at work outlining the structure, physiological properties, and functions of single cells found within the nervous system. These isolated cells would be of no use unless they could forge connections, which they do at junctions we call synapses. Synaptic neuroscience examines the strength and flexibility of neural connections, which underlie complex processes such as learning and memory.

Beyond the single synapse, we find that interconnected neurons form pathways or networks. In contemporary neuroscience, we are seeing a move away from the idea that "this structure engages in this function" to ideas that more accurately reflect neural networks that have been identified. We are more likely to say that "this structure participates in a network connecting these other structures to engage in this type of processing."

Zooming out perhaps to the most global point of view, we find **behavioral neuroscience**, also known as **biological psychology**, which is the primary focus of this textbook. Behavioral neuroscientists use all of the previous levels of analysis, from the molecular up through the network, in their efforts to understand the biological correlates of behavior. Like the neurosciences in general, behavioral neuroscience looks at the activity of the nervous system in health and in cases of illness or injury. Subspecialties within behavioral neuroscience include cognitive neuroscience, or the study of the biological correlates of information processing, learning and memory, decision making, and reasoning. Social neuroscience explores the interactions between the nervous system and our human social environment and behavior.

Computational neuroscience runs parallel to the types of neuroscience described so far, but draws from computer science, electrical engineering, mathematics, and physics to produce models of the nervous system from the molecular up through the behavioral levels of analysis. The predictions from these computational models can then be tested against living systems, forming a cooperative symbiosis with researchers in other areas of neuroscience.

These different levels of analysis complement each other rather than compete with one another. Because of the diversity of skills needed to pursue each of these approaches, neuroscience is an essentially interdisciplinary field of study, reaching across traditional academic departments of biology, chemistry, psychology, medicine, mathematics, physics, engineering, and computer science.

The need for better understanding of the nervous system has never been greater. The Society for Neuroscience (2012) reported that neurological illnesses impact one out of

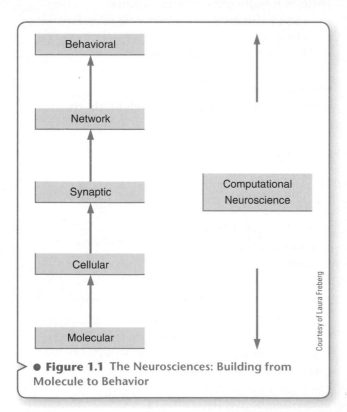

Courtesy of Laura Freberg

● **Figure 1.1** The Neurosciences: Building from Molecule to Behavior

neuroscience The scientific study of the brain and nervous system in health and in disease.

behavioral neuroscience/ biological psychology The study of the biological foundations of behavior, emotions, and mental processes.

••• Behavioral Neuroscience GOES TO WORK

WHAT CAN I DO WITH A DEGREE IN NEUROSCIENCE?

One of the pleasures of teaching courses in behavioral neuroscience occurs when a student suddenly falls in love with the field. "This is for me," the student might say, but the question that usually follows is "But how can I make a living doing this?" The answers to this question are as diverse as the field. Because neuroscience is so broad, opportunities can be found down many different paths.

Like many other fields, neuroscience has more opportunities for people with more education. Many practicing neuroscientists have medical degrees, PhDs, or even both. This does not mean that jobs are unavailable for students with undergraduate degrees, however. Students with undergraduate degrees can be employed as research assistants in pharmaceutical firms, universities, and government agencies. Some neuroscience graduates work in substance abuse counseling or in mental health facilities. Neuroscience is used in some unexpected places as well. A growing trend in advertising agencies is to use brain imaging and other technologies to gauge public reactions to advertising. Web designers use eye-tracking technology to assess whether a person "sees" and processes the important features of a webpage.

The ongoing burst in neuroscience technologies is likely to continue to shape the field, and additional opportunities are likely to emerge. In the meantime, any student interested in neuroscience would benefit from gaining the best possible skills in general science, research methods, mathematics, and statistics.

six Americans annually at a cost of more than $500 billion for treatment, which does not include the cost of disability. Delaying the onset of Alzheimer's disease on an average of five years would save the United States $50 billion in annual health care costs. Connections between biology and behavior are not just relevant to neurological disease, but inform our understanding of health in general. Compared to 100 years ago, when most people died from infectious diseases, today's killers (cancer, diabetes, heart disease) are tightly linked to behavior. Reflecting recognition of the role of behavior in illness, the standardized Medical College Admission Test (MCAT) for medical school applicants contains a significant number of questions about psychology and behavioral neuroscience.

Illness is only part of the human equation. We also need to understand how the nervous system responds in typical ways to promote well-being, including better relationships, better parenting, better child development, and better thinking and learning. Through improved understanding of the nervous system and its interactions with behavior, scientists and practitioners will be more thoroughly prepared to tackle the significant challenges to health and well-being faced by contemporary world populations.

Historical Highlights in Neuroscience

The history of neuroscience parallels the development of tools for studying the nervous system. Early thinkers were limited in their understanding of the structures and functions of the nervous system by lack of scientific methods and technologies and by religious prohibitions regarding autopsy.

Ancient Milestones in Understanding the Nervous System

Our earliest ancestors apparently had at least a rudimentary understanding about the brain's essential role in maintaining life. Archaeological evidence of brain surgery suggests that as long as 7,000 years ago, people tried to cure others by drilling holes in the skull, a process known as trephining or trepanation. Because some skulls have been located that show evidence of healing following the drilling procedure, we can assume that the patient lived through the procedure and that this was not a

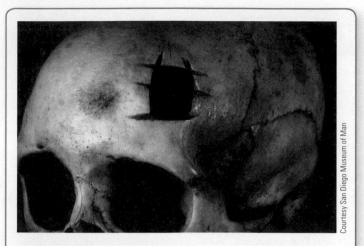

Courtesy San Diego Museum of Man

● **Figure 1.2** Prehistoric Brain Surgery As far back in history as 7,000 years ago, people used trepanation (trephining), or the drilling of holes in the skull, perhaps to cure "afflictions" such as demonic possession. Regrowth around some of the holes indicates that at least some of the patients survived the procedure. More recently, trephining has resurfaced as a DIY (do it yourself) process, possibly as a type of self-injurious behavior.

postmortem ritual. What is less clear is the intent of such surgeries. Possibly, these early surgeons hoped to release demons or relieve feelings of pressure (Clower & Finger, 2001).

The *Edwin Smith Surgical Papyrus* represents the oldest known medical writing in history, yet features many sophisticated observations (Breasted, 1930). The Egyptian author of the *Papyrus* clearly understood that paralysis and lack of sensation in the body resulted from nervous system damage. Cases of nervous system damage were usually classified as "an ailment not to be treated," indicating the author's understanding of the relatively permanent damage involved.

Building on the knowledge taken from ancient Egypt, the Greek scholars of the fourth century BCE proposed that the brain was the organ of sensation. Hippocrates (460–379 BCE) correctly identified epilepsy as originating in the brain, although the most obvious outward signs of the disorder were muscular convulsions (see Chapter 15). Galen (130–200 CE), a Greek physician serving the Roman Empire, made careful dissections of animals (and we suspect of the mortally wounded gladiators in his care as well). Galen believed erroneously that the ventricles played an important role in transmitting messages to and from the brain, an error that influenced thinking about the nervous system for another 1,500 years (Aronson, 2007).

The Dawn of Scientific Reasoning

The French philosopher René Descartes (1596–1650) argued in favor of **mind–body dualism**. For Descartes and other dualists, the mind is neither physical nor accessible to study through the physical sciences. In contrast, the modern neurosciences are based on **monism** rather than dualism. The monism perspective proposes that the mind is the result of activity in the brain, which can be studied scientifically. Descartes's ideas were very influential, and even today some people struggle with the idea that factors such as personality, memory, and logic simply represent the activity of neurons in the brain. Later in the chapter, the discussion of research ethics presents another legacy of Descartes's ideas. Because many shared his view of animals as mechanical, not sentient, beings, experiments were carried out on animals that seem barbaric to many modern thinkers.

Between 1500 and 1800, scientists made considerable progress in describing the structure and function of the nervous system. The invention of the light microscope by Anton van Leeuwenhoek in 1674 opened up a whole new level of analysis. Work by Luigi Galvani and Emil du Bois-Reymond established electricity as the mode of communication used by the nervous system. British physiologist Charles Bell (1774–1842) and French physiologist François Magendie (1783–1855) demonstrated that information traveled in one direction, not two, within sensory and motor nerves.

Modern Neuroscience Begins

As late as the beginning of the 20th century, many scientists, including Italian researcher Camillo Golgi, continued to support the concept of the nervous system as a vast, interconnected network of continuous fibers. Others, including the Spanish anatomist Santiago Ramón y Cajal, argued that the nervous system was composed of an array of separate, independent cells. Cajal's concept is known as the Neuron Doctrine. Golgi

mind–body dualism A philosophical perspective put forward by René Descartes in which the body is mechanistic, whereas the mind is separate and nonphysical.

monism A philosophical perspective characteristic of the neurosciences in which the mind is viewed as the product of activity in the brain.

● **Figure 1.3** Luigi Galvani Demonstrated a Role for Electricity in Neural Communication This engraving illustrates the basement laboratory of Luigi Galvani, where his experiments with frogs helped establish understanding of the electrical nature of neural communication.

and Cajal shared the Nobel Prize for their work in 1906. Ironically, Cajal used a stain invented by Golgi to prove that Golgi was incorrect.

The road to our current understanding of the nervous system has not been without its odd turns and dead ends. The notion that certain body functions are controlled by certain areas of the brain, called localization of function, began with an idea proposed by Franz Josef Gall (1758–1828) and elaborated by Johann Gasper Spurzheim (1776–1832). These otherwise respectable scientists proposed a "science" of **phrenology** that maintained that the structure of an individual's skull could be correlated with his or her individual personality characteristics and abilities. A phrenologist could "read" a person's character by comparing the bumps on his or her skull to a bust showing the supposed location of each trait. Although misguided, Gall and Spurzheim's work did move us away from the metaphysical, nonlocalized view of the brain that had persisted from the time of Descartes. Instead, Gall and Spurzheim proposed a more modern view of the brain as the organ of the mind, composed of interconnected, cooperative, yet relatively independent functional units.

Further evidence in support of localization of function in the brain began to accumulate. In the mid-1800s, a French physician named Paul Broca correlated the damage he observed in patients with their behavior and concluded that language functions were localized in the brain (see Chapter 13). Gustav Theodor Fritsch and Eduard Hitzig (1870/1960) described how electrically stimulating the cortex of a rabbit and a dog produced movement on the opposite side of the body. Localization of function in the brain became a generally accepted concept.

The founding of modern neuroscience has often been attributed to the British neurologist John Hughlings Jackson (1835–1911). Hughlings Jackson proposed that the nervous system was organized as a hierarchy, with simpler processing carried out by lower levels and more sophisticated processing carried out by the higher levels, such as the cerebral cortex. We meet Hughlings Jackson again in Chapter 15, in which his contributions to the understanding of epilepsy will be discussed.

Progress in the neurosciences over the past 100 years accelerated rapidly as new methods became available for studying the nervous system. Charles Sherrington not only coined the term *synapse* (defined as the point of communication between two neurons), but also conducted extensive research on reflexes and the motor systems of the brain (see Chapter 8). Otto Loewi demonstrated chemical signaling at the synapse (see Chapter 3),

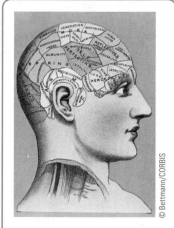

● **Figure 1.4** Phrenology Bust Franz Josef Gall and his followers used busts like this one to identify traits located under different parts of the skull. Bumps on the skull were believed to indicate that the underlying trait had been "exercised." Although Gall's system was an example of very bad science, the underlying principle that functions could be localized in the brain turned out to be valuable.

phrenology The misguided effort to correlate character traits with bumps in the skull.

using an elegant research design that he claims came to him while asleep. Sir John Eccles, Bernard Katz, Andrew Huxley, and Alan Hodgkin furthered our understanding of neural communication. You will meet many more contemporary neuroscientists as you read the remainder of this text. The ranks of neuroscientists continue to grow, with membership in the Society for Neuroscience expanding from 500 members in 1969 to more than 42,000 members in 90 countries as of 2014 (Society for Neuroscience).

INTERIM SUMMARY 1.1

Highlights in the Neuroscience Timeline

Historical Period	Significant Highlights and Contributions
Ca. 3000 BCE	• Egyptians discard brain during mummification process; however, published case studies indicate accurate observations of neural disorders.
Ca. 400 BCE–200 CE	• Hippocrates recognizes that epilepsy is a brain disease. • Galen makes accurate observations from dissection; however, he believed erroneously that fluids transmitted messages.
1600–1800	• René Descartes suggests mind-body dualism. • Anton van Leeuwenhoek invents the light microscope. • Galvani and du Bois-Reymond discover that electricity transmits messages in the nervous system.
1800–1900	• Bell and Magendie determine that neurons communicate in one direction and that sensation and movement are controlled by separate pathways. • Gall and Spurzheim make inaccurate claims about phrenology, but their notion of localization of function in the nervous system is accurate. • Paul Broca discovers localization of speech production. • Fritsch and Hitzig identify localization of motor function in the cerebral cortex.
1900–Present	• Ramón y Cajal declares that the nervous system is composed of separate cells; he shares the 1906 Nobel Prize with Camillo Golgi. • John Hughlings Jackson explains brain functions as a hierarchy, with more complicated functions carried out by higher levels of the brain. • Otto Loewi demonstrates chemical signaling at the synapse. • Charles Sherrington coins the term *synapse*; he wins the Nobel Prize in 1932. • Sir John Eccles, Andrew Huxley, and Alan Hodgkin share the 1963 Nobel Prize for their work in advancing our understanding of the way neurons communicate. • Bernard Katz receives the 1970 Nobel Prize for his work on chemical transmission at the synapse. • Society for Neuroscience counts more than 42,000 members in 2012.

Summary Points

1. Neuroscience is the field that explores the structures, functions, and development of the nervous system in illness and in health. Behavioral neuroscience is

the branch of the neurosciences that studies the correlations between the nervous system and behavior. **(LO1)**

2. Although some periods of enlightenment regarding the relationship between the nervous system and behavior emerged among the Egyptians and Greeks, the major advances in biological psychology have been relatively modern and recent. **(LO2)**

3. Highlights in the neuroscience timeline include discoveries regarding the electrical and chemical nature of neural communication, the control of sensation and motor functions by separate nerves, the role of single cells as building blocks for the nervous system, and the localization of functions in the brain. **(LO2)**

‖ Review Questions

1. How would you describe the goals and methods of the interdisciplinary field of neuroscience?

2. What historical discoveries contributed to our modern understanding of the brain and behavior? Which concepts actually led us in the wrong direction?

Behavioral Neuroscience Research Methods

The methods described in this section have helped neuroscientists discover the structure, connections, and functions of the nervous system and its components. From the level of single nerve cells to the operation of large parts of the nervous system, we now have the ability to make detailed observations that would likely astonish the early pioneers of neuroscience.

Histology

Histology refers to the study of microscopic structures and tissues. Histological methods provide means for observing the structure, organization, and connections of individual cells. As mentioned earlier, the first investigation of nerve tissue under a microscope was conducted by Anton van Leeuwenhoek in 1674. However, due to the technical challenges of viewing structures as small and complex as those found in the nervous system, most of the advances in microscopy occurred following the development of stronger, clearer lenses during the 1800s.

Tissue to be studied under the microscope must be prepared for viewing in a series of steps. Tissue must be made thin enough to allow light to pass through it. Brain tissue is fragile and somewhat watery, which makes the production of thin enough slices impossible without further treatment. To solve this problem, the first step in the histological process is to "fix" the tissue, either by freezing it or by treating it with formalin, a liquid containing the gas formaldehyde. Formalin not only hardens the tissue, making it possible to produce thin slices, but it also preserves the tissue from breakdown by enzymes or bacteria. Freezing the tissue accomplishes these objectives as well.

Once tissue is fixed, it is sliced by a special machine known as a **microtome**. A microtome typically looks and works like a miniature version of the meat slicers found in most delicatessens. The tissue is pushed forward while a sliding blade moves back and forth across the tissue, producing slices. For viewing tissue under the light microscope, tissue slices between 10 and 80 µm (micrometers) thick are prepared. A micrometer is one one-millionth of a meter or one one-thousandth of a millimeter. Electron microscopes require slices of less than 1 µm. The fragile slices are mounted on slides for viewing. Sectioning a single rat brain produces several thousand slides.

Even when fixed and mounted on slides, nerve tissue would appear nearly transparent under the microscope if it were not for a variety of specialized stains. Researchers select particular stains depending on the features they wish to examine. For example,

histology The study of cells and tissues at the microscopic level.
microtome A device used to make very thin slices of tissue for histology.

● **Figure 1.5** Using a Microtome to Section Patient H.M.'s Brain Researchers at UC San Diego broadcast the careful sectioning of the brain of the late Henry Molaison, otherwise known as the famous amnesic patient H.M., via streaming video on the Internet. Molaison's temporal lobe surgery and the resulting memory deficits he experienced are familiar to all students of psychology.

The Brain Observatory

to make a detailed structural analysis of a small number of single cells, the best choice is a **Golgi silver stain**, named after its discoverer, Camillo Golgi. On the other hand, you might be more interested in identifying clusters of cell bodies, the major bulk of the nerve cell, within a sample of tissue. In this case, you would select a **Nissl stain**. A **myelin stain** would allow you to follow pathways carrying information from one part of the brain to another by staining the insulating material that covers many nerve fibers. If you know where a pathway ends but would like to discover its point of origin, you should use **horseradish peroxidase**. When this enzyme is injected into the end of a nerve fiber, it travels backward toward the cell body. Antibodies, proteins normally produced by the immune system to identify invading organisms, can be combined with a variety of dyes to highlight particular proteins found in cells in a process known as immunohistochemistry (IHC). In particular, antibodies are helpful in identifying the activity of the c-Fos gene in the brain, which in turn is a reliable indicator of brain activity in response to a wide variety of stimuli such as administration of methamphetamine (Cornish, Hunt, Robins, & McGregor, 2012).

Once tissue is appropriately prepared, it can be viewed under either a light or electron microscope. Electron microscopes, first developed in Germany in the 1930s, use short, highly concentrated electron beams rather than light to form images. Modern electron microscopes produce magnifications of up to one million times. Using an electron microscope, Sanford Palay and George Palade (1955) provided the first clear images of the synapse (see Chapter 3).

Autopsy

Researchers have frequently relied on observations made during an **autopsy**, or examination of the body following death. The word *autopsy* means "to view for oneself." Although autopsy for research purposes has been largely replaced by modern imaging methods, it remains a useful technique. Simon LeVay (1991) used autopsy to examine an area of the brain known as INAH-3 (see Chapter 10). LeVay believed that the size of INAH-3 might be used to differentiate between homosexual and heterosexual males. Because this structure was too small to see well with existing imaging techniques, LeVay studied the brains of deceased individuals. Autopsies, like other correlational methods, must be interpreted carefully and precisely. Although LeVay's data indicate that differences in brain structure are correlated with sexual orientation, we cannot conclude on the basis of these correlational data that brain structure either causes or is caused by sexual orientation.

Golgi silver stain A stain developed by Camillo Golgi used to observe single neurons.
Nissl stain A stain used to view populations of cell bodies.
myelin stain A stain used to trace neural pathways.
horseradish peroxidase A stain used to trace axon pathways from their terminals to points of origin.
autopsy The examination of body tissues following death.

Imaging

New imaging techniques provide significant advantages over autopsy. With current imaging technologies, we can watch the living brain as it engages in processes such as reading (Chapter 13) or emotional response (Chapter 14). We can identify differences in the ways the brains of serial murderers function compared with the brains of typical people (Chapter 16).

COMPUTERIZED TOMOGRAPHY (CT) The groundwork for brain imaging was laid by German physicist Wilhelm Röntgen, who discovered X-rays in 1896. Röntgen was astonished to learn that X-rays could move through the human body and that they would produce a negative photographic image of the body's major structures. The first X-ray ever taken was an image of Röntgen's wife's hand.

Normal X-rays do not do a very good job of imaging soft tissue. If you have ever seen an X-ray of your head taken by your dentist or orthodontist, you probably saw bones and teeth, but not much brain. However, with adaptations made possible by more modern computers, X-rays can be used to image previously unseen anatomical structures. **Computerized tomography (CT)** was invented in 1972 by Godfrey Hounsfield and Allan Cormack. "Tomography" comes from the Greek words *tomos,* or slice, and *graphia,* to write or describe. CT technology provided the first high-resolution look at a living brain. More modern CT technology allows for the construction of highly detailed three-dimensional images.

However useful CT scanning may be for medical imaging, the technology does have drawbacks for research purposes. Although it provides excellent structural information, a CT scan cannot distinguish between a living brain and a dead one. In other words, the CT scan provides no information regarding activity levels in the brain. This limits the usefulness of CT in helping us answer questions about behavior.

POSITRON EMISSION TOMOGRAPHY (PET) The next major breakthrough in imaging technology was the development of the **positron emission tomography**, or **PET**, scan, which allowed researchers to observe brain activity for the first time. PET scans were made possible by the invention of the gamma camera, which is used to detect radiation released by radioactive atoms that are decaying or breaking up. Beginning in the mid-1970s, Michael Phelps and Edward Hoffman of Washington University began to apply this basic technique to the study of brain function (Hoffman, Phelps, Mullani, Higgins, & Ter-Pogossian, 1976; Phelps, Hoffman, Mullani, Higgins, & Ter-Pogossian, 1976).

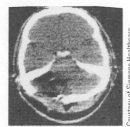
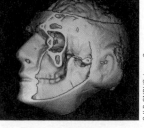

● **Figure 1.6** CT Scans Hounsfield's original machine took several hours to obtain data for a single slice (above). Modern scanning equipment is much faster, and can produce detailed 3-D images (bottom).

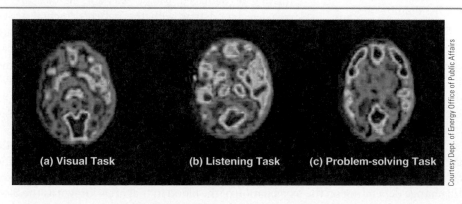

(a) Visual Task   (b) Listening Task   (c) Problem-solving Task

● **Figure 1.7** PET Scans Show Patterns of Brain Activation PET scans do not provide much structural detail, but they do offer a clear picture of brain activity. Red and yellow areas are most active, whereas blue and black areas are least active. These three images show different patterns of brain activity during a visual task, a listening task, and a problem-solving task.

computerized tomography (CT) An imaging technology in which computers are used to enhance X-ray images.

positron emission tomography (PET) An imaging technique that provides information regarding the localization of brain activity.

PET brain studies combine radioactive tracers with a wide variety of molecules, including oxygen, water, and drugs. Each gamma ray resulting from the breakdown of the tracer is recorded by detectors and fed to a computer, by which the data are reconstructed into images. Typically, programmers have assigned red and yellow to areas of high activity and green, blue, and black to areas of low activity. Newer PET machines can take images of adjacent slices at the same time, which allows for three-dimensional reconstruction of brain activity. A closely related procedure, single photon emission computed tomography (SPECT), is less expensive than PET but provides less visual detail.

MAGNETIC RESONANCE IMAGING (MRI) **Magnetic resonance imaging**, or **MRI**, has become a standard medical diagnostic tool and a valuable research asset. Raymond Damadian, Larry Minkoff, and Michael Goldsmith produced the first MRI image in 1977. This imaging technology uses powerful magnets to align hydrogen atoms within a magnetic field. Next, radio frequency (RF) pulses are directed at the part of the body to be imaged, producing "resonance," or spinning, of the hydrogen atoms. When the RF pulses cease, the hydrogen atoms return to their natural alignment within the magnetic field. As the atoms "relax," each becomes a miniature radio transmitter, emitting a characteristic pulse that is detected by the scanner. To construct the image, each small area of tissue is assigned a **voxel**, which is a three-dimensional version of a pixel. The darkness or coloration of each voxel represents the level of pulse activity in an area.

Functional MRI (fMRI) is used to assess brain activity. The first fMRI of the brain was conducted by Belliveau et al. (1991). Functional MRI takes advantage of the fact that active neurons require more oxygen than less active neurons, and that variations in blood flow to a particular area will reflect this need.

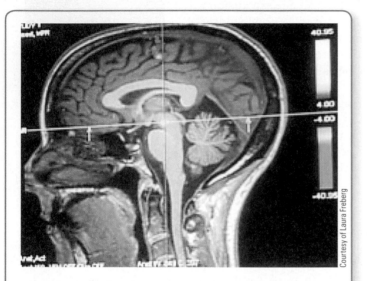

Courtesy of Laura Freberg

● **Figure 1.8 Functional Magnetic Resonance Imaging (fMRI) Tracks Cerebral Blood Flow** This image demonstrates the use of fMRI to identify parts of the brain (the red and yellow areas) that became selectively active when the author engaged in a "finger tap" exercise (touching each digit of her right hand one by one with her thumb).

The use of fMRI to track blood flow in the brain was previewed in the 19th century by America's first official psychologist, William James, who was impressed by the observations of Italian physiologist Angelo Mosso on patients with head injuries. Due to the nature of these injuries, in which some of the patients' skull bones were missing or damaged, Mosso was able to measure and correlate blood flow with the patients' mental activity (Mosso, 1881). James's reflections on Mosso's work sound very contemporary: "Blood very likely may rush to each region of the cortex according as it is most active, but of this we know nothing" (James, 1890, vol. 1, p. 99). Mosso's observations were confirmed by Roy and Sherrington (1890), who reported the existence of "an automatic mechanism by which the blood supply of any part of the cerebral tissue is varied in accordance with the activity of the chemical changes which underlie the functional action of that part" (p. 105).

How does fMRI track cerebral blood flow? Hemoglobin, the protein molecule that carries oxygen within the blood, has different magnetic properties when combined with oxygen or not (Ogawa, Lee, Kay, & Tank, 1990). Consequently, signals from a voxel will change depending on the oxygenation of the blood in that area, known as the Blood Oxygenation Level Dependent (BOLD) effect. Let's look at an example of the author's own results of a standard demonstration conducted at the Brain Imaging Laboratory at the University of California, Santa Barbara. Scans were taken as the author alternated 20 second intervals of remaining very still with 20 second intervals of touching her right thumb to each of the other digits of her right hand one at a time. The image highlights the voxels that showed changes in activity correlated with movement and stimulation.

magnetic resonance imaging (MRI) An imaging technique that provides very high resolution structural images.

voxel Short for "volume pixel." A pixel is the smallest distinguishable square part of a two-dimensional image. A voxel is the smallest distinguishable box-shaped part of a three-dimensional image.

functional MRI (fMRI) A technology using a series of MRI images taken one to four seconds apart in order to assess the activity of the brain.

diffusion tensor imaging (DTI) Use of MRI technology to trace fiber pathways in the brain by tracking the flow of water.

MRI technology has significant advantages over both CT and PET. It can provide images taken at any angle without any movement of the individual. In tracking brain activity, fMRI is considered superior in both spatial and temporal resolution to PET scans (Cohen & Bookheimer, 1994).

The same machinery used for MRI and fMRI can also produce images using **diffusion tensor imaging (DTI)**. This technique allows researchers to track the movement of water in the fiber pathways of the nervous system (Le Bihan & Breton, 1985; Moseley et al., 1990). Using this technique, the negative effects of occasional binge drinking episodes on brain fiber integrity in adolescents becomes all too apparent (McQueeny et al., 2009).

Recording

Although perhaps less dramatic than the imaging techniques, methods that allow researchers to record the electrical and magnetic output from the brain continue to be useful. As we will see in greater detail in Chapter 3, nerve cells are capable of generating small electrical charges across their membranes, much like miniature batteries. Although small in scale, this electrical activity can be recorded using electrodes either on the surface of the skull or brain or imbedded within the brain tissue itself.

Parkinson Research Foundation

● **Figure 1.9 Diffusion Tensor Imaging (DTI)** Using MRI technology, the flow of water down the length of nerve fibers can be imaged to construct maps of the fiber pathways of the brain.

●●● Connecting to **Research**

SOCIAL PAIN AND THE BRAIN

Nobel Laureate Konrad Lorenz wrote that "It is a good morning exercise for a research scientist to discard a pet hypothesis every day before breakfast. It keeps him young." This is often easier said than done, but with the rapid changes we experience in the world of neuroscience, being able to update your thinking is an essential skill.

One of the most "fun" results that many instructors of behavioral neuroscience have shared with students is the work of Naomi Eisenberger and her colleagues (2003), in which a Cyberball game was used to initiate feelings of social isolation. Brain imaging of the 13 participants indicated that the brain's "pain matrix," which included a structure known as the anterior cingulate cortex (ACC), was activated by this experience of social pain. In other words, the brain had appeared to co-opt the system responsible for responding to physical pain for use in responding to social pain. Publication by Eisenberger et al. (2003) was followed by a long string of positive replications.

One of the challenges of using fMRI is the statistical analyses involved. Brains come in rather different sizes and shapes, and to make any conclusions, the researcher must demonstrate that activity in a voxel in one brain is analogous to activity in a voxel in a completely different brain. The methods used to conduct these analyses have continued to evolve along with the technology. So 10 years after Eisenberger et al. (2003) published their original report, Stephanie Cacioppo and her colleagues (2013) used multilevel kernel density analysis (MKDA) to conduct a meta-analysis of Cyberball imaging studies featuring 244 participants. This analysis failed to support the attractive notion that social and physical pain activate the same network. Instead, Cacioppo et al. (2013) argue that the "neural correlates of social pain are more complex than previously thought" (p. 1).

One of the common themes of study in the neurosciences is that things always seem to become "more complex than previously thought" as technologies improve. While this can be occasionally frustrating, as we all tend to prefer straightforward answers instead of "it depends," good science requires that we continue to modify our thinking to be as accurate as possible.

••• THINKING *Ethically*

CAN WE READ MINDS WITH BRAIN IMAGING?

In the 2002 film *Minority Report*, Tom Cruise plays a police officer who arrests people for crimes they have not yet committed. How close are we to knowing what people are planning to do before they actually do it? Perhaps closer than you think.

Current imaging technologies, such as fMRI, do not exactly allow us to "read" the human mind, but we are getting ever closer to that ability (Tong & Pratte, 2012). For example, researchers were able to use fMRI recordings taken while a participant watched Steve Martin playing Inspector Clouseau in the movie *The Pink Panther* to reconstruct the image (Nishimoto et al., 2011).

Of even greater importance for society is the fact that researchers are closing in on the ability to use fMRI to detect deception (Langleben, Willard, & Moriarty, 2012). As we will see in our discussion of emotion in Chapter 14, typical lie detection technologies, which rely on indirect measures of arousal, are so poor that they are not admissible as court evidence in the United States. The ability to detect deception directly through brain imaging promises enormous benefits to criminal justice and national security, but raises equally substantial concerns about ethics. Not only can we envision the legislative need to expand our constitutional right to privacy to include "mental privacy," but legislators will also have to consider that the new technology may acquire information from brain scans that is irrelevant to the purpose of the investigation in the first place.

THE ELECTROENCEPHALOGRAM (EEG) The first recordings of the human brain's electrical activity, measured through electrodes placed on the scalp, were made by a German psychiatrist, Hans Berger, in 1924. Berger noted that the recordings varied during wakefulness, sleep, anesthesia, and epilepsy. Chapter 11 investigates the relationship between the EEG and these states of consciousness in greater detail.

For many years, EEG technology did not change much. Although it was useful in the study of sleep and the diagnosis of epilepsy, EEG did not offer anything further to our understanding of brain function. With the advent of more powerful computers, however, new quantitative methods for analyzing EEG recordings became possible. Computerized EEG brain tomography can be used to generate maps of activity, making it possible to pinpoint the source of abnormal activity. EEG brain tomography can be used to follow a patient through withdrawal from psychoactive drugs or during a coma. The technique can aid in diagnoses of many disorders, including schizophrenia, dementias, epilepsy, and attention deficit hyperactivity disorder (see Chapters 5, 15, and 16). Computerized analysis of EEG recordings can be used to generate animations of activity over time and for the construction of three-dimensional maps of brain activity. These analysis tools have breathed new life into EEG technology.

EVENT-RELATED POTENTIALS (ERPS) An application of basic EEG technology used to assess sensation is the recording of **event-related potentials (ERPs)**. This technique allows researchers to correlate the activity of cortical sensory neurons recorded through scalp electrodes with stimuli presented to the participant. The brain's electrical activity in response to a stimulus, such as a tone, is quite small compared to the activity normally recorded in an EEG, so responses to many presentations of a stimulus are averaged. This type of analysis can be helpful in cases in which a person's behavior does not provide a clear indication of whether a particular stimulus has been perceived. For example, young children with autism spectrum disorder (see Chapter 16) often behave as though their hearing were impaired. When spoken to by parents or others, a child with autism spectrum disorder often shows no reaction at all. Through observations of event-related potentials to sound, we can determine whether the child can actually hear.

electroencephalogram (EEG) The recording of the brain's electrical activity through electrodes placed on the scalp.

event-related potential (ERP) An alteration in the EEG recording produced in response to the application of a particular stimulus.

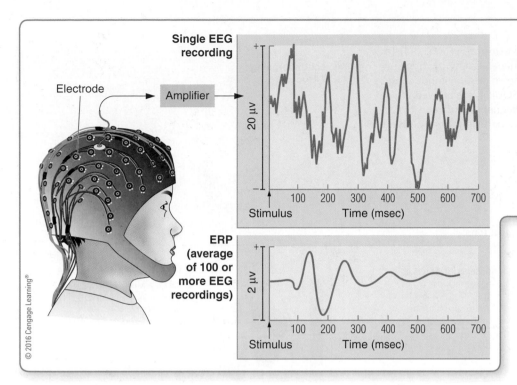

Single EEG recording

ERP (average of 100 or more EEG recordings)

© 2016 Cengage Learning®

● **Figure 1.10** Event-Related Potentials (ERPs) The analysis of event-related potentials allows researchers to map the brain's EEG response to environmental stimuli. In this example, a characteristic waveform emerges when responses to the presentation of a tone are averaged over 100 trials.

MAGNETOENCEPHALOGRAPHY (MEG)

Magnetoencephalography (MEG) allows researchers to record the brain's magnetic activity (Cohen, 1972). Active neurons put out tiny magnetic fields. By "tiny," we mean that the fields generated by neural activity are about one billion times smaller than Earth's magnetic field and about 10,000 times smaller than the field surrounding a typical household electric wire. The major advantage of recording magnetism rather than electrical activity from the brain relates to the interference of the skull bones and other tissues separating the brain from the electrodes, which prevents a large amount of the brain's electrical activity from being recorded using EEG. In contrast, the skull bones and tissues allow magnetism to pass through without any reduction. In addition, recordings of the magnetic fields produced by the brain can be taken much faster than either fMRI or PET scans, providing a moment-by-moment picture of brain activity. MEG has the added advantage of being silent, as opposed to the loud hammering sound produced by the magnets used in MRI. Consequently, MEG provides researchers with an important technique for studying brain responses to sound.

MEG utilizes sensors known as superconducting quantum interference devices, or SQUIDs, that convert magnetic energy into electrical impulses that can be recorded and analyzed. Because MEG does not provide any anatomical data, researchers superimpose MEG recordings on three-dimensional images obtained with MRI. This combination provides simultaneous information about brain activity and anatomy. Not only does MEG allow researchers to localize cognitive functions such as language, but it also provides precise localization of the source of the abnormal electrical activity that characterizes a seizure (see Chapter 15).

SINGLE-CELL RECORDINGS

The activity of single neurons can be assessed using tiny microelectrodes surgically implanted in the area of interest. Electrodes can be permanently implanted, allowing animals free range of movement during stimulation.

The use of single-cell recordings was pioneered by Vernon Mountcastle, David Hubel, and Torsten Wiesel for use in their investigations of the visual system. More recently, this technique was used to identify mirror neurons, or neurons that fire in response to an action, like reaching for a banana, whether the reaching is done by a monkey or an experimenter (Caggiano et al., 2011; Pellegrino, Fadiga, Fogassi, Gallese, & Rizzolatti, 1992).

magnetoencephalography (MEG) A technology for recording the magnetic output of the brain.

single-cell recording The recording of the activity of single neurons through microelectrodes surgically implanted in the area of interest.

● **Figure 1.11** Magnetoencephalograpy (MEG) (a) To record the tiny magnetic fields generated by the brain, a series of supercooled sensors known as superconducting quantum interference devices (SQUIDs) are arrayed around the participant's head. (b) This sequence illustrates the process of using MEG to record a participant's response to a tone.

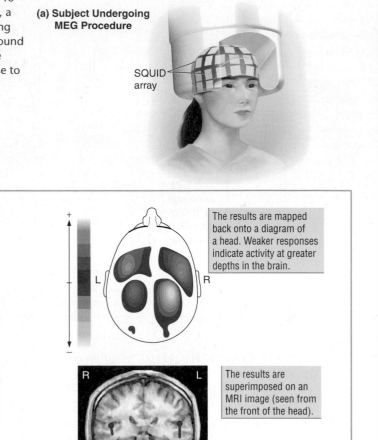

(a) Subject Undergoing MEG Procedure

SQUID array

(b) MEG Analysis of a Response to a Tone

L   R

Changes in magnetic fields, recorded by 143 SQUIDS in the array (seen from the top of the head).

L   R

The results are mapped back onto a diagram of a head. Weaker responses indicate activity at greater depths in the brain.

Superimposing all the channels establishes that the maximum response occurs 97 ms after the onset of the tone.

R   L

The results are superimposed on an MRI image (seen from the front of the head).

0   97   600
Time (msec)

© 2016 Cengage Learning®

Brain Stimulation

One of the important questions raised in behavioral neuroscience relates to the localization of functions within the brain and nervous system. Although this question can be approached with a number of techniques, we can begin by artificially stimulating the area in question and watching for resulting behavior. Interpretation of the results of stimulation research must be done with great caution. Because brain structures are richly connected with other areas of the brain, stimulating one area will also affect other areas to which it is connected.

Electrical stimulation of the brain can be applied during neurosurgery. As unpleasant as it may sound to you, most neurosurgery is conducted under local, as opposed to general, anesthesia. The tissues of the brain itself lack receptors for pain. Once the bone and the tissues covering the brain are anesthetized, the surgeon can work on the brain of the conscious patient without causing pain. Why would we put people through such an unpleasant experience? Although brains are similar in many ways from person to person, individual differences frequently do occur. By stimulating an area with a small amount of electricity and assessing any changes in behavior, the surgeon can identify whether the area participates in a particular type of behavior.

Considerable knowledge regarding the mapping of the functions of the cortex has been derived from this technique. Neurosurgeon Wilder Penfield investigated the brains of more than a thousand patients undergoing surgery for the treatment of epilepsy (see Chapter 15). Penfield's work contributed significantly to our understanding of the mapping of movement, memory, and language (Penfield, 1958). Penfield's stimulation was restricted to the surface of the cortex. Others have investigated stimulation of deeper structures through implanted electrodes. Robert Heath (1963) implanted electrodes in a patient who suffered from the sleep disorder narcolepsy (see Chapter 11) and allowed the patient to push a button that administered a brief electrical stimulus. The patient was able to describe his reactions to stimulation of each of the 14 electrodes implanted in his brain. One of the electrodes, which the patient activated most frequently, elicited sexual arousal.

Encouraged by the improvements provided by brain stimulation in patients with the movement disorder Parkinson's disease, discussed in Chapter 8, physicians have begun to surgically implant electrodes in areas of the brain believed to participate in feelings of reward to treat individuals with depression (Bewernick et al., 2010).

Repeated transcranial magnetic stimulation (rTMS) consists of magnetic pulses delivered through a single coil of wire encased in plastic that is placed on the scalp. Low frequency rTMS (about one pulse per second) provides an interesting technique for temporarily changing brain activity immediately below the stimulation site (Hoffman et al., 2003). This technique has shown promise in the treatment of auditory hallucinations associated with schizophrenia and of depression (Slotema, Blom, Koek, & Sommer, 2010). Repeated TMS has also been shown to temporarily produce unusual calculation skills, like those occasionally found in people with autism spectrum disorder, in healthy participants (Snyder, 2006).

Optogenetics (Boyden, 2011) involves the use of molecules genetically inserted in specific neurons in the brain, which then allows neural function to be modified by light. In other words, light can be used to turn living neurons on and off. Stimulation is provided through optical fibers attached to the skull or surgically implanted. In one study, optogenetics was used to confirm a role for the chemical messenger glutamate (see Chapter 4) in pathways involved with reward and addiction (Tecuapetla et al., 2010).

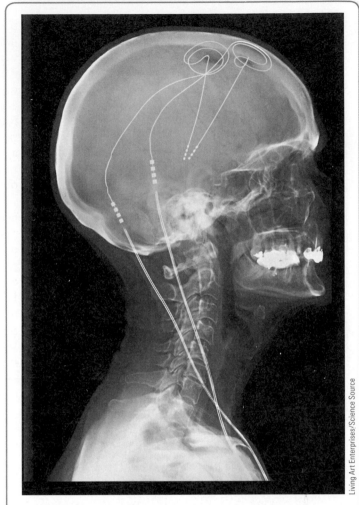

Living Art Enterprises/Science Source

● **Figure 1.12** Deep Brain Stimulation In research, brain stimulation is typically used to identify the possible functions of a part of the brain. Recently, brain stimulation has been used to treat Parkinson's disease and, less frequently, major depressive disorder.

Lesion

A **lesion** is an injury to neural tissue and can be either naturally occurring or deliberately produced. As was the case with stimulation, the primary purpose of lesion analysis is to assess the probable function of an area. Behavior observed prior to the lesion can be compared with behavior occurring after the lesion, with changes

repeated transcranial magnetic stimulation (rTMS) A technique for stimulating the cortex at regular intervals by applying a magnetic pulse through a wire coil encased in plastic and placed on the scalp.
optogenetics The genetic insertion of molecules into specific neurons that allows the activity of the neurons to be controlled by light.
lesion Pathological or traumatic damage to tissue.

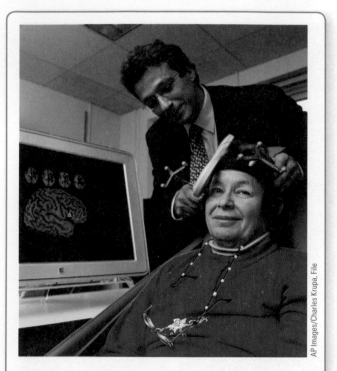

● **Figure 1.13** Repeated Transcranial Magnetic Stimulation (rTMS) Repeated TMS changes the activity of the cortex underlying the stimulator. The technique is used for research purposes and potentially could be used for treating hallucination, depression, and migraine headaches.

attributed to the area that was damaged. Once again, interpretation must be done very carefully. Lesions not only damage a particular area of the brain but also damage any nerve fibers passing through that area.

Neuropsychologists (see Chapter 15) evaluate naturally occurring lesions that result from injury or disease, gaining a great deal of information about the function of the brain. Many examples of this type of analysis will be discussed in the remainder of the text. The ability to perform an autopsy allowed Paul Broca to make the previously mentioned correlations between the damage he observed and the clinical observations he made during the patient's lifetime.

Deliberate lesions are generally performed in research using laboratory animals, as opposed to human participants. However, as we will see in Chapter 15, lesions are occasionally used to treat cases of epilepsy that do not respond to medication. The technique of producing deliberate lesions in research animals originated with Pierre Flourens in the 1800s. A classic example of lesion work using animals identified a role for the ventromedial hypothalamus (VMH) in satiety (Hoebel & Teitelbaum, 1966). When this area is electrically stimulated, an animal will stop eating. When this area is lesioned, the animal eats so much that its body weight can double or even triple (see Chapter 9).

Deliberate lesions are performed in a number of ways. In some studies, large areas of brain tissue are surgically removed. In this case, we might refer to the procedure as **ablation** rather than lesion. Lesions are experimentally produced when an electrode is surgically inserted into the area of interest. The electrode is insulated except at the very tip, to prevent damage to cells lining the entire pathway of the electrode. Heat is generated at the tip of the electrode, effectively killing a small population of cells surrounding the tip. Small lesions can also be produced by applying neurotoxins, chemicals that specifically kill neurons, into the area of interest through a surgically implanted micropipette. Chemically produced lesions have the advantage of harming only the cell bodies of neurons while leaving the nerve fibers traveling through the area intact. Conversely, fiber pathways can be chemically lesioned while sparing adjacent cell bodies. Obviously, both heat-produced and chemically produced lesions result in permanent damage to the brain. A reversible type of lesion can be produced by cooling

ablation The surgical removal of tissue.

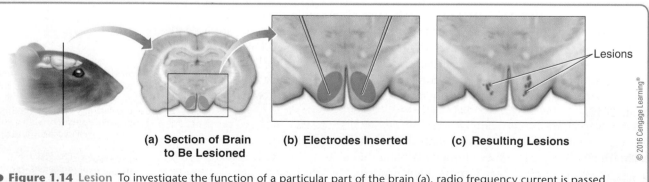

(a) **Section of Brain to Be Lesioned** (b) **Electrodes Inserted** (c) **Resulting Lesions** Lesions

● **Figure 1.14** Lesion To investigate the function of a particular part of the brain (a), radio frequency current is passed through the tips of insulated electrodes that have been surgically implanted (b). Resulting changes in behavior are correlated with the lesions produced (c).

an area using a probe. When the area is chilled, the neurons are unable to function. However, when the area returns to normal temperatures, normal behavioral function is restored.

Biochemical Methods

As we will see in Chapters 3 and 4, the brain and nervous system are unusually well protected, compared with other organs in the body, from circulating toxins. As a result, if a researcher wishes to investigate the effects of chemical stimulation in the brain, these normal protective mechanisms often must be bypassed. Obviously, some chemicals naturally gain access to the brain, resulting in psychoactive effects. Many other chemicals are blocked from exiting the blood supply into neural tissue. For example, most agents used for cancer chemotherapy simply circulate through the brain without leaving the blood supply, adding to the challenges of treating brain tumors (see Chapter 15).

Different methods used to administer drugs to a subject include eating, inhaling, chewing, and injecting the drug (see Chapter 4). These methods result in the delivery of very different concentrations of a drug into the blood supply within a given period. For research purposes, chemicals can be directly administered to the brain through the surgical implantation of micropipettes. This technique allows researchers to observe the effects of chemicals administered in an awake, freely moving animal.

On occasion, it is desirable to be able to identify the chemicals that naturally exist in a particular location. Using implanted micropipettes, small amounts of extracellular fluid are filtered from the area of the brain surrounding the tip of the pipette for analysis. This technique is known as **microdialysis**. Microdialysis allows researchers to identify which neurochemicals are active in a precise location, as well as the approximate quantity of these chemicals.

Genetic Methods

Many researchers strive to identify the interactions between hereditary and environmental variables on a particular behavior. In general, we wish to avoid either—or thinking in these analyses. Heredity and environment always work together to produce the ultimate outcome.

TWIN STUDIES The natural comparison between monozygotic (identical) and dizygotic (fraternal) twins provides some insight into the relative contributions of heredity and environment. Monozygotic twins share an identical set of genes, whereas fraternal twins average about 50 percent of their genes in common, just like any other pair of non-identical siblings.

As is discussed in Chapter 16, some psychological disorders, such as bipolar disorder and schizophrenia, seem to be influenced more by heredity than others, like major depressive disorder. The contribution of heredity to these conditions is often stated in the form of a **concordance rate**, a type of statistical probability. Given the existence of a trait in one twin, the concordance rate for the remaining twin estimates the probability of the other twin having the trait. For example, in the case of bipolar disorder, we see concordance rates as high as 71–77 percent (Edvardsen et al., 2008). If one identical twin has the disorder, the other has a 71–77 percent likelihood of also being diagnosed with the disorder. Note that this is not 100 percent. In contrast, the concordance rate for identical twins in regard to major depressive disorder is usually reported to be about 40 percent (Shi et al., 2011). This indicates that environmental variables play a more significant role in depression than in bipolar disorder. However, it is important to remember that "environmental variables" might still include biological components such as prenatal environment and exposure to infection.

microdialysis A technique for assessing the chemical composition of a very small area of the brain.

concordance rate The statistical probability that two cases will agree; usually used to predict the risk of an identical twin for developing a condition already diagnosed in his or her twin.

ADOPTION STUDIES Another approach to investigating the influences of heredity and environment is to compare the similarities of an adopted individual to his or her biological and adoptive parents. Similarities to the biological parents suggest a stronger role for heredity, whereas similarities to the adoptive parents suggest a stronger role for the environment. Adoption studies have been used to assess the relative contributions of heredity and environment to such characteristics as intelligence and criminality. Interpretation of such studies remains controversial, because adoptive families are often quite similar to one another, which in turn magnifies genetic influences. **Heritability**, or the amount that a trait varies in a population due to genetics, is still influenced by the environment. For example, if you planted seeds under ideal conditions (good soil, lots of sunlight, regular watering), the differences you observe among your mature plants are largely due to genetics. In contrast, if you planted seeds under more variable conditions, the resulting plants would reflect contributions of both genetic and environmental factors. Like the ideal conditions for our plants, genetic influences may be magnified by the similar environments provided by adoptive parents.

STUDIES OF GENETICALLY MODIFIED ANIMALS We review a number of studies in this text that use a relatively new genetic technique in which specially engineered, defective versions of genes are inserted into the chromosomes of animals, usually mice. The normal version of these knockout genes encodes for a specific protein. The **knockout genes** take the place of the normal genes but fail to produce the specific protein. By using this method, researchers can assess the roles of particular genes and the proteins they encode.

One example of this method is found in the work of H. W. Matthes and his colleagues (1996). As we will see in Chapter 4, many drugs have effects on behavior because they are chemically similar to normally occurring chemicals found in the nervous system. Opoids, such as morphine and heroin, activate receptors for naturally occurring substances known as endorphins. Matthes et al. (1996) bred mice that lacked the genes for producing some of the endorphin receptors. Their general behavior seemed unaffected, but they did not experience any pain relief when given morphine. They were incapable of becoming addicted to morphine, and they showed no withdrawal symptoms when morphine administration was discontinued. We can therefore conclude that certain aspects of an animal's normal reaction to morphine are dependent on the existence of endorphin receptors. Without these receptors, pain reduction, addiction, and withdrawal related to opioids do not occur.

EPIGENETICS The production of proteins by a particular gene can be influenced by a whole host of external factors, including diet, whether or not a person smokes, or stress. **Epigenetics** describes the development of traits by factors that influence the performance of genes without changing the underlying genes themselves (see Chapter 5). For example, baby rats that were licked frequently by their mothers (the rat version of a hug from mom) were calmer in the face of stress later in life than rats that received less nurture (Champagne, Francis, Mar, & Meaney, 2003). This type of interaction helps to explain why identical twins become less and less similar to each other over the course of their lifetimes. Their different choices in lifestyle and accumulated experience can change the way their genes behave (Fraga, 2005).

Stem Cells

One of the most promising approaches to understanding neural development, regeneration, and disease is the use of stem cells (Vunjak-Novakovic & Scadden, 2011). A **stem cell** is a cell that can divide and differentiate into other types of cells (see Chapter 5). If provided with the appropriate laboratory environment, a stem cell line,

heritability The amount that a trait varies in a population due to genetics.

knockout gene A gene used to replace a normal gene that does not produce the protein product of the normal gene.

epigenetics The development of traits by factors that influence the performance of genes without changing the underlying genes themselves.

stem cell A cell that can divide and differentiate into other types of cells.

or culture, can replicate indefinitely. Currently, researchers can derive stem cell lines from a number of sources, including adult stem cells, stem cells from umbilical cord blood, and embryonic stem cells.

The various types of stem cells offer different sets of advantages and disadvantages. Embryonic stem cells are usually obtained from embryos in the blastocyst stage, or about five days after conception in humans. These cells are pluripotent, meaning that they can differentiate into any type of tissue. In addition, embryonic cells are virtually immortal, as they can divide endlessly in the laboratory. On the other hand, these cells will provoke an immune reaction in a recipient, just like any other transplanted tissue. Adult stem cells have been retrieved from blood, nerve cells, muscle, the cornea and retina of the eye, some internal organs, and skin. Typically, these cells are less flexible than the embryonic cells and can only differentiate into cells similar to their source. They lack the immortality of the embryonic cells, but they are less likely to cause rejection by a tissue recipient.

Researchers are very excited about the potential of using stem cells to repair damage to the nervous system. For example, stem cells derived from human tooth pulp reestablished the ability to move in mice whose spinal cords had been completely severed (Sakai et al., 2012).

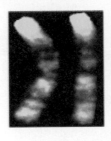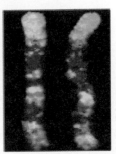

Cacioppo/Freberg

● **Figure 1.15 Epigenetics** Epigenetics, or changes in the performance of genes without any underlying changes in the genes themselves, explains why identical twins become "less identical" as they age. The twins' individual experiences, including diet, stress, smoking, and so on, produce epigenetic change. Compared with 3-year-old identical twins on the left, the 50-year-old twins on the right show much greater amounts of red and green, which indicate areas of less and more methylation respectively. The yellow areas indicate equal levels of methylation. Methylation, or the addition of a methyl group to a molecule like DNA, is one of several mechanisms capable of epigenetic change that are discussed further in Chapter 5.

INTERIM SUMMARY 1.2

Methods in Behavioral Neuroscience

Method	Function
Histology	Studying the microscopic structure of the nervous system
Autopsy	Studying the structure of the nervous system following death
Computerized tomography (CT)	Studying structure and diagnosing structural damage
Positron emission tomography (PET)	Studying the relative activity of nervous system structures
Magnetic resonance imaging (MRI)	Studying structure in very fine detail
Functional MRI (fMRI)	Studying the activity of nervous system structures
Diffusion Tensor Imaging (DTI)	Studying fiber pathways in the nervous system
Electroencephalogram (EEG)	Studying brain activity, primarily during sleep and waking or seizures
Event-related potential (ERP) recording	Studying the brain's response to specific stimuli using an adapted EEG
Magnetoencephalography (MEG)	Studying brain activity

(continued)

Method	Function
Single-cell recordings	Identifying the stimulus responsible for activating an individual neuron
Electrical stimulation and lesion	Identifying behavior linked to a particular location in the nervous system
Optogenetics	Using light to initiate neural activity
Repeated transcranial magnetic stimulation (rTMS)	Producing long-lasting changes in cortical activity; linking behavior to a particular location in the cortex
Microdialysis	Identifying particular chemicals in a very small location
Twin and adoption studies	Studying contributions of genetic and nongenetic factors to behavior
Genetically modified animals (knockout genes)	Studying the role of particular genes and the proteins they produce
Epigenetics	Studying changes in the performance of genes
Stem cells	Growing replacement tissue for repairing damaged organs, including the brain and spinal cord

Summary Points

1. Improvements in histology provided the means for examining the nervous system at the microscopic level. **(LO4)**

2. Imaging technologies, including CT scans, PET scans, MRI, fMRI, and DTI have built on knowledge gained through autopsy regarding the structure and function of the brain. **(LO3)**

3. Recording techniques include measurements of the brain's overall electrical and magnetic outputs. In addition, recordings can also be made of the activity of single cells. **(LO3)**

4. Stimulation and lesion techniques can be used to assess the function of particular areas of the brain. Magnetic stimulation can enhance or reduce the activity of the brain. **(LO3)**

5. Biochemical methods allow for the artificial stimulation of the nervous system with chemicals as well as the assessment of the biochemical environment in an area of particular interest within the nervous system. **(LO3)**

6. Genetic methods, including twin studies, adoption studies, and the analysis of epigenetics, allow researchers to assess the role of our genetic inheritance in the relationship between the nervous system and behavior. **(LO5)**

Review Questions

1. What are the relative strengths and weaknesses of the major imaging methods?

2. What are the challenges involved with the interpretation of data from stimulation and lesion research?

Research Ethics in Behavioral Neuroscience

The Greek physician and scholar Hippocrates set a standard for ethical behavior in the sciences that has certainly stood the test of time. Hippocrates wrote in the *Epidemics*: "As to diseases, make a habit of two things—to help, or at least do no harm." As you have seen in this chapter, we have developed a wealth of technology in the neurosciences that has moved our understanding forward quite rapidly. In our rush for knowledge, what controls are in place to ensure that Hippocrates' rule of "do no harm" is respected by those entrusted with the lives and welfare of research participants?

Protection for research participants in the United States begins with the federal government and the Common Rule, a set of standards shared by seventeen federal agencies (Center for Science, Technology, and Congress, 2001). These standards apply to any researcher obtaining federal funds or conducting research at an institution that receives federal funds, which includes most universities. In addition, guidance is provided by professional societies, such as the American Psychological Association (APA) and the Society for Neuroscience (SfN). To evaluate compliance with ethical standards, each university maintains institutional review boards (IRBs) for human research and institutional animal care and use committees (IACUCs) for animal research. These committees are composed of faculty members with expertise in the appropriate areas, plus at least one faculty member from a nonscience discipline. In addition, the boards include a community member, so that the university is not simply policing itself behind closed doors.

Human Participant Guidelines

Thinking about the protection of human participants has changed dramatically over the past 30 years. Today's scientific community is far more protective of the safety and well-being of research participants. As an undergraduate student in introductory psychology, I was compelled to serve as a research participant in a fixed number of experiments to pass the course. I found myself acting as the confederate in a Milgram-type obedience experiment in which the real participant was supposed to administer a punishment to me in the form of increasingly potent electrical shocks. As in Milgram's original experiment (1963), I received no shocks, but the real participant (a girl from my floor in the dorm) believed that I was being shocked. After she "administered" the maximum levels of shock to me, I never quite trusted her again, and she avoided me for the remainder of our undergraduate days.

Today, coercing people into serving as research participants, either for course credit or any other incentive, is unacceptable. Although we recognize as psychologists that people who volunteer for research are probably quite different from people who don't volunteer, the resulting limitations on our abilities to generalize are a reasonable price to pay for ethical practice. Benefits for participation, including money, should not be "excessive or inappropriate" (American Psychological Association, 1992). Participants must be informed at the outset that they can leave the experiment at any point in time without penalty. In this text, you will read about research conducted with human participants who are not able to volunteer freely to participate. For example, individuals may not be capable of fully understanding the nature of the experiment or of their participation due to conditions such as schizophrenia or Alzheimer's disease. In these situations, legal permission must be obtained from a third party. The university-level review boards play an essential role in deciding these gray areas on a case-by-case basis.

To freely volunteer, a participant must be told enough about the experiment to make an informed decision about participating. This disclosure is accomplished through a carefully worded informed consent form prepared by the researchers and reviewed by the campus IRB. The form provides information about the general purpose of the experiment and any risks that may be involved. Participants are provided with contact

● **Figure 1.16** Human Research Ethics One of the studies that provoked today's concerns with the safety of human research participants was the Tuskegee Syphilis Study, in which men infected with syphilis were not made aware that effective treatments were available, among other ethical lapses.

Centers for Disease Control and Prevention

information in case they have further questions regarding the study. Participants are assured that their data will be confidential and that they can choose to receive information about the outcomes and conclusions of the experiment.

Animal Subjects Guidelines

According to the American Psychological Association (APA, 2005), 90 percent of animals used in research are rodents and birds, and monkeys and other primates are used in 5 percent or less of all studies. The use of dogs and cats in behavioral neuroscience is exceedingly rare.

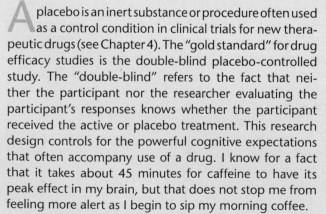

●●● Building Better
HEALTH

WHEN IS IT APPROPRIATE TO USE PLACEBOS?

A placebo is an inert substance or procedure often used as a control condition in clinical trials for new therapeutic drugs (see Chapter 4). The "gold standard" for drug efficacy studies is the double-blind placebo-controlled study. The "double-blind" refers to the fact that neither the participant nor the researcher evaluating the participant's responses knows whether the participant received the active or placebo treatment. This research design controls for the powerful cognitive expectations that often accompany use of a drug. I know for a fact that it takes about 45 minutes for caffeine to have its peak effect in my brain, but that does not stop me from feeling more alert as I begin to sip my morning coffee.

Miller et al. (2010) identify two ethical issues with placebo use. First, placebo research is inherently deceptive to some degree. Participants are commonly misled about the purpose of the study and are not aware of the deception until they are debriefed at the end. In only a few cases, "authorized deception" is used, in which the participants are told in advance that the study involves deception that will be revealed to them at the conclusion of the study. Second, placebo use in clinical practice is not uncommon. Although "only" 5 percent of a random sample of 1,200 US physicians prescribed true placebos (sugar pills or saline injections), close to a majority used some "alternative" approaches such as vitamins specifically to boost "patient expectations."

The fact that placebos might result in true physical changes, such as the release of our body's natural opiates or endorphins, further complicates the situation. These are topics for which accurate research is vital, yet are truly complicated when it comes to ethical constraints.

The first provision for the protection of animal subjects relates to necessity. The American Psychological Association (2008) stipulates that animal research should have a clear scientific purpose, such as increasing our knowledge of behavior or improving the health and welfare of humans or other animals. In other words, the research needs to do more than build a scientist's résumé for tenure and promotion. The knowledge gained should balance and justify the use of animals. The species used should be appropriate to the task. If the same questions can be asked without using animals, the alternate method should be used.

A second provision relates to basic care and housing of the animals. Animal research is expensive, but there are no alternatives to excellent care. When I was a graduate student in the 1970s, a furnished apartment near UCLA cost about $165 per month. In that same period, housing a single rhesus monkey for research purposes cost approximately $650 per month. Regular checkups by veterinarians and inspections occurred. We were extensively trained regarding the typical behavior of the animals (more for our own safety, in this case, as adult rhesus can be quite dangerous to humans).

Finally, experimental procedures should cause as little pain and distress as possible. Consider, however, that animals are generally used when procedures are not acceptable for human participants. The American Psychological Association guidelines include provisions related to the use of pain, surgery, stress, and deprivation with animal subjects, as well as to the termination of the animal's life. Some individuals and groups object to the notion that research that is considered unethical with humans is acceptable when animal subjects are used. Nonetheless, this is the primary rationale for the use of animal subjects, and we can expect a continued lively debate on the topic.

INTERIM SUMMARY 1.3

Ethical Principles

Participants	Ethical Principles
Human participants	No coercion Informed consent Confidentiality
Animal subjects	Necessity Excellent food, housing, vet care Avoidance of pain and distress

Summary Points

1. Research ethics agreed upon by government agencies, universities, and individual researchers are designed to protect both human participants and animal subjects from harm. (LO6)

2. In addition to being protected from physical and psychological harm, human participants must not be coerced into participation, and their confidentiality must be strictly maintained. (LO6)

3. Animal subjects must be protected from unnecessary pain and suffering. Researchers must establish the necessity of using animal subjects and are obligated to provide excellent housing, food, and veterinary care. (LO6)

Review Question

1. What are the major considerations for the protection of human participants and animal research subjects?

Chapter Review

THOUGHT QUESTIONS

1. How have societal factors influenced scientific discovery in the past? What aspects of our current environment act to enhance or hinder scientific understanding in behavioral neuroscience?
2. Which of the methods outlined in this chapter have the greatest potential for producing further advancements in our understanding of brain and behavior?

KEY TERMS

autopsy (p. 8)

behavioral neuroscience/biological psychology (p. 2)

computerized tomography (CT) (p. 9)

concordance rate (p. 17)

diffusion tensor imaging (DTI) (p. 11)

electroencephalogram (EEG) (p. 12)

epigenetics (p. 18)

event-related potential (ERP) (p. 12)

functional MRI (fMRI) (p. 10)

heritability (p. 18)

histology (p. 7)

lesion (p. 15)

magnetic resonance imaging (MRI) (p. 10)

magnetoencephalography (MEG) (p. 13)

mind-body dualism (p. 4)

neuroscience (p. 2)

optogenetics (p. 15)

positron emission tomography (PET) (p. 9)

repeated transcranial magnetic stimulation (rTMS) (p. 15)

single-cell recording (p. 13)

stem cell (p. 18)

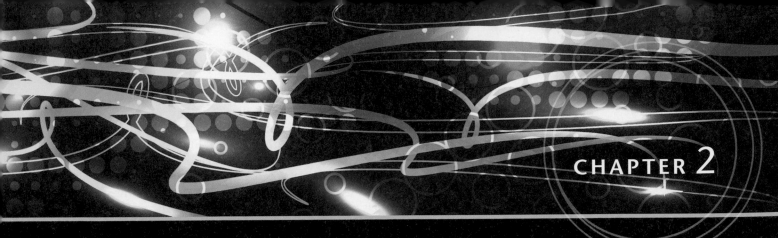

CHAPTER 2

Functional Neuroanatomy and the Evolution of the Nervous System

LEARNING OBJECTIVES

L01 Distinguish among the major anatomical directional terms and planes of section.

L02 Describe the locations and functions of the meninges, cerebrospinal fluid, and cerebral arteries.

L03 Identify the major divisions and functions of the spinal cord.

L04 Explain the functions of the major structures found in the hindbrain, midbrain, and forebrain.

L05 Describe the structure and functions of the cerebral cortex.

L06 Identify the structures and functions of the peripheral nervous and endocrine systems.

L07 Discuss the evolution of the human nervous system.

CHAPTER OUTLINE

BEHAVIORAL NEUROSCIENCE GOES TO WORK: Treating Hydrocephalus

CONNECTING TO RESEARCH: The Connectome and Phineas Gage

THINKING ETHICALLY: Can We Localize Intelligence in the Brain?

BUILDING BETTER HEALTH: Do Gluten-Free Diets Have Benefits for People with Autism Spectrum Disorder?

Anatomical Directions and Planes of Section

Navigating around the three-dimensional human brain is similar to describing the geography of our three-dimensional earth. Without a vocabulary to describe the location of one area relative to others, we would quickly get lost. Instead of north, south, east, or west, anatomists have their own sets of directional terms. Although it might seem to be a lot of work to memorize these terms, the payoff comes when you can locate structures easily by their names. The ventromedial hypothalamus could simply be memorized, but knowing that *ventral* means toward the belly side of an animal and *medial* means toward the midline, you will know exactly where to look in the hypothalamus for this structure.

Because anatomical directions for human beings are complicated by the fact that we walk on two legs, we'll start off with the simpler case of the four-legged animal. Structures that are located toward the head end of the animal are **rostral**. In other words, the head of a dog is rostral to its shoulders. Structures located toward the tail end of the animal are **caudal**. For example, the dog's ears are caudal to its nose, and its hips are caudal to its shoulders. Structures located toward the belly side are **ventral**, whereas structures toward the back are **dorsal**. If you have trouble keeping these last two straight, it might help to remember that scary dorsal shark fin cutting through the water in the film *Jaws*. Like geographical terms, these anatomical terms are relative to another place. Just as New York is north of Florida but south of Canada, the dog's ears are caudal to its nose but rostral to its shoulders.

Why are anatomical directions different in people? As shown in ●Figure 2.1, our two-legged stance puts a bend in the **neuraxis**, an imaginary line that runs the length of the spinal cord through the brain. In the four-legged animal, the neuraxis forms a straight line running parallel to the ground. The dorsal parts of the animal's brain are in line with the dorsal parts of the spinal cord. In humans, the dorsal parts of our brain form an 80-degree angle with the dorsal parts of the spinal cord, so that the dorsal part of the brain is on the top of your head, but the dorsal part of the spinal cord runs

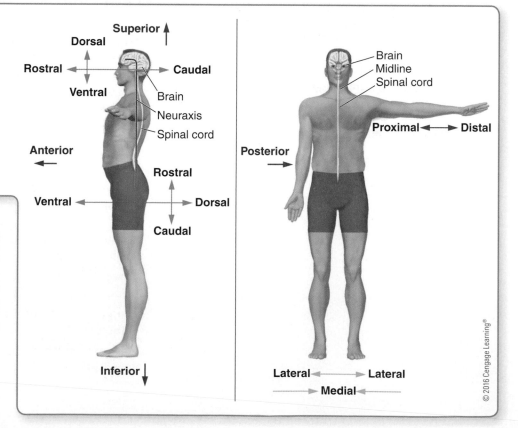

● **Figure 2.1** Anatomical Directions Anatomists use directional terms to name and locate brain structures. Because standing upright puts an 80-degree angle in the human neuraxis, the dorsal surface of the human brain also forms an 80-degree angle with the dorsal spinal cord.

rostral A directional term meaning toward the head of a four-legged animal.
caudal A directional term meaning toward the tail of a four-legged animal.
ventral A directional term meaning toward the belly of a four-legged animal.
dorsal A directional term meaning toward the back of a four legged animal.
neuraxis An imaginary line that runs the length of the spinal cord to the front of the brain.

along your back. In contrast, a second set of anatomical terms (**anterior–posterior**, **superior–inferior**) does not change with the bending of the neuraxis. You can think of the ceiling as superior, the floor as inferior, the front wall of your classroom as anterior, and the back wall of the classroom as posterior. Using this set of terms, the rostral part of your brain and the ventral part of your spinal cord would both be referred to as "anterior."

Additional directional terms refer to the **midline**, an imaginary line that divides us into approximately equal halves. If two structures are **ipsilateral**, they are both on the same side of the midline. My left arm and left leg are ipsilateral. If structures are on opposite sides of the midline, we say they are **contralateral**. My right arm and left leg are contralateral to each other. Structures close to the midline are referred to as **medial**, and structures to the side of the midline are called **lateral**. My heart is medial to my arms, whereas my ears are lateral to my nose. Similar terms include **proximal**, which means close to the center, and **distal**, which means far away from the center. Usually, we use these two terms to refer to limbs. My toes are distal relative to my knees, and my shoulders are proximal relative to my elbows.

Although directional terms help us find our way around the nervous system, we also need a way to view three-dimensional structures as flat images on a page. Anatomists have found it useful to make particular cuts or sections in the nervous system to view the structures in two rather than three dimensions. The choice of how to make the section can be arbitrary. Different structures are often more easily viewed with one section than with others. My graduate neuroanatomy professor, the esteemed Dr. Arnold Scheibel, was fond of using his favorite diagonal sections during exams. Traditionally, we use the coronal, sagittal, and horizontal sections, which can be seen in ● Figure 2.2. **Coronal sections**, also known as **frontal sections**, divide the nervous system from front to back. **Sagittal sections** are parallel to the midline, allowing us a side view of brain structures. The special section that divides the brain into two relatively equal halves is known as a **midsagittal section**. The third type of section is the

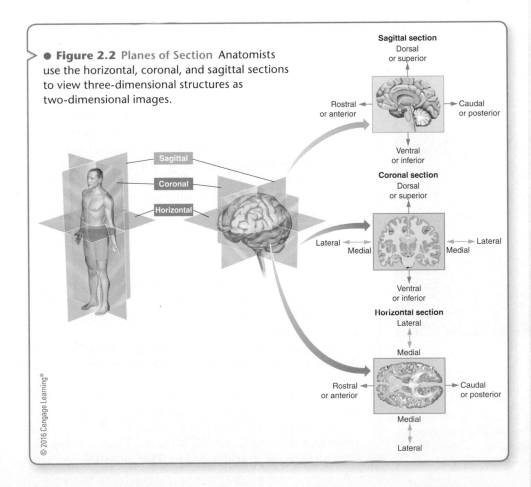

> ● **Figure 2.2** Planes of Section Anatomists use the horizontal, coronal, and sagittal sections to view three-dimensional structures as two-dimensional images.

© 2016 Cengage Learning®

anterior A directional term meaning toward the front.

posterior A directional term meaning toward the rear.

superior A directional term meaning toward the top.

inferior A directional term meaning toward the bottom.

midline An imaginary line dividing the body into two equal halves.

ipsilateral A directional term referring to structures on the same side of the midline.

contralateral A directional term referring to structures on opposite sides of the midline.

medial A directional term meaning toward the midline.

lateral A directional term meaning away from the midline.

proximal A directional term that means closer to center; usually applied to limbs; opposite of distal.

distal A directional term meaning farther away from another structure, usually in reference to limbs.

coronal/frontal section An anatomical section dividing the brain front to back, parallel to the face.

sagittal section An anatomical section that is parallel to the midline.

midsagittal section A sagittal section that divides the brain into two approximately equal halves.

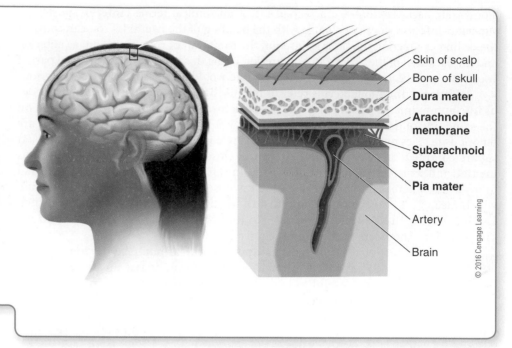

● **Figure 2.3** The Skull and Three Layers of Membrane Protect the Brain In addition to the protection provided by the skull bones, the brain and spinal cord are covered with three layers of membranes known as meninges. Going from the skull to the brain, we find the dura mater, the arachnoid layer, and the pia mater. Between the arachnoid and pia mater layers is the subarachnoid space, which contains cerebrospinal fluid (CSF). In the peripheral nervous system (PNS), only the dura mater and pia mater layers cover the nerves. There is no CSF in the PNS.

Skin of scalp
Bone of skull
Dura mater
Arachnoid membrane
Subarachnoid space
Pia mater
Artery
Brain

© 2016 Cengage Learning

horizontal/axial/transverse An anatomical section that divides the brain from top to bottom.

meninges The layers of membranes that cover the central nervous system (CNS) and the peripheral nerves.

dura mater The outermost of the three layers of meninges; found in both the central and peripheral nervous systems (PNS).

arachnoid layer The middle layer of the meninges covering the central nervous system (CNS).

horizontal section also known as an **axial** or **transverse section**, which divides the brain from top to bottom. You will see many examples of each type of section in this chapter and in the remainder of the text.

Protecting and Supplying the Nervous System

Because of the obvious importance of the brain, it is one of the most protected organs in your body. The bony skull protects the brain from all but the most serious blows. It is important to note, however, that the skull bones are not fully mature in infants. The infant is born with skull bones that can overlap each other, somewhat like the tectonic plates of the earth. This design aids the movement of the baby's head through the birth canal. In a young baby with very light or no hair, you can often see a pulse at the top of the head between the skull bones, known as a soft spot, or fontanel. It takes about 18 months for human skull bones to fuse completely.

Meninges

Although the bones offer the best defense, even the baby with a soft spot enjoys substantial protection of its brain provided by three layers of membranes, or **meninges**, that surround the nervous system.

The outermost layer of the meninges is known as the **dura mater**, which literally means "hard mother" in Latin. Our word *durable* comes from the same root. The reference to "mother" might have originated from early comparisons between the protective membranes and the blankets used to swaddle infants. The dura mater is composed of leatherlike tissue that follows the outlines of the skull bones. Below the dura mater is the **arachnoid layer**. This more delicate layer

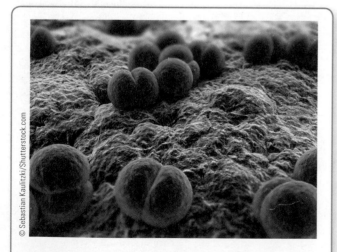

© Sebastian Kaulitzki/Shutterstock.com

● **Figure 2.4** Meningitis Results from Infection of the Meninges Viruses and bacteria can invade the layers of the meninges, causing meningitis. Meningitis causes headache and stiffness of the neck, which can be followed by incoherence, drowsiness, coma, and death. This photo shows a fatal case of meningitis with large areas of pus within the meninges.

gets its name from the fact that its structure looks like a spider's web in cross-section. The innermost layer is the **pia mater**, or "pious mother." This nearly transparent membrane sticks closely to the outside of the brain. Between the arachnoid and pia mater layers is the **subarachnoid space**, with "sub" meaning below. All three of these layers cover the brain and spinal cord. Once nerves leave the bony protection of the skull bones and vertebrae of the back, they are referred to as peripheral nerves and are protected by only the dura mater and pia mater. There is no arachnoid layer or subarachnoid space surrounding these peripheral nerves.

Cerebrospinal Fluid

Cerebrospinal fluid (CSF) is secreted within hollow spaces in the brain known as **ventricles**. Within the lining of the ventricles, the **choroid plexus** converts material from the nearby blood supply into CSF. CSF is very similar in composition to the clear plasma of the blood. Because of its weight and composition, CSF essentially floats the brain within the skull. This has several advantages. If you bump your head, the fluid acts like a cushion to soften the blow to your brain. In addition, nerve cells (neurons) respond to appropriate input, not to pressure on the brain. Pressure can often cause neurons to fire in maladaptive ways, such as when a tumor causes seizures by pressing down on a part of the brain. By floating the brain, the CSF prevents neurons from responding to pressure and providing false information.

CSF circulates through the **central canal** of the spinal cord and four ventricles in the brain: the two lateral ventricles, one in each hemisphere, and the third and fourth ventricles in the brainstem. The fourth ventricle is continuous with the central canal of the spinal cord, which runs the length of the cord at its midline. The ventricles and the circulation of CSF are illustrated in ● Figure 2.5. Below the fourth ventricle, there

pia mater The innermost of the layers of meninges, found in both the CNS and the peripheral nervous system(PNS).

subarachnoid space A space filled with cerebrospinal fluid (CSF) that lies between the arachnoid and pia mater layers of the meninges in the central nervous system (CNS).

cerebrospinal fluid (CSF) The special plasma-like fluid circulating within the ventricles of the brain, the central canal of the spinal cord, and the subarachnoid space.

ventricle One of four hollow spaces within the brain that contain cerebrospinal fluid (CSF).

choroid plexus The lining of the ventricles, which secretes the cerebrospinal fluid (CSF).

central canal The small midline channel in the spinal cord that contains cerebrospinal fluid (CSF).

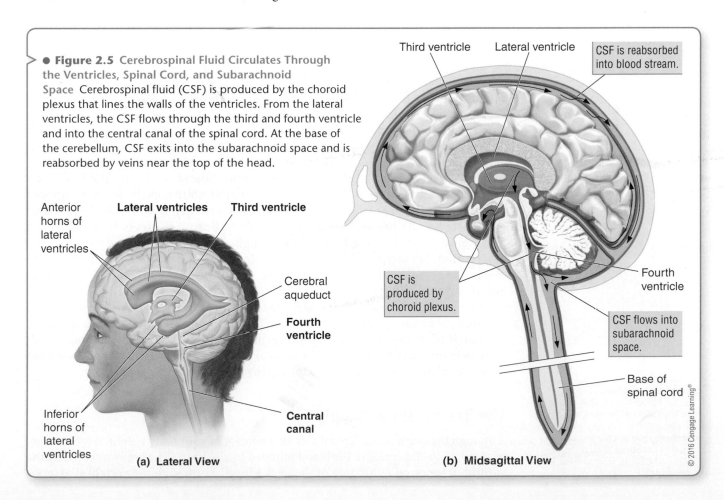

● **Figure 2.5** Cerebrospinal Fluid Circulates Through the Ventricles, Spinal Cord, and Subarachnoid Space Cerebrospinal fluid (CSF) is produced by the choroid plexus that lines the walls of the ventricles. From the lateral ventricles, the CSF flows through the third and fourth ventricle and into the central canal of the spinal cord. At the base of the cerebellum, CSF exits into the subarachnoid space and is reabsorbed by veins near the top of the head.

Third ventricle   Lateral ventricle

CSF is reabsorbed into blood stream.

Anterior horns of lateral ventricles

Lateral ventricles   **Third ventricle**

Cerebral aqueduct

Fourth ventricle

CSF is produced by choroid plexus.

Fourth ventricle

CSF flows into subarachnoid space.

Inferior horns of lateral ventricles

Central canal

Base of spinal cord

(a) Lateral View   **(b) Midsagittal View**

© 2016 Cengage Learning®

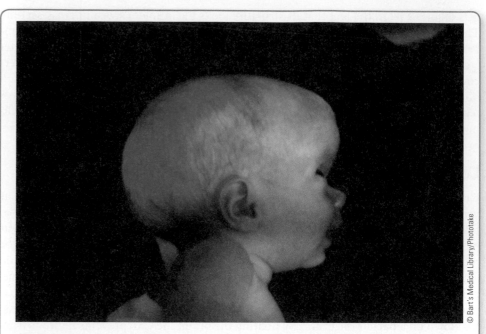

● Figure 2.6 Hydrocephalus Results from Blockage in the Circulation of Cerebrospinal Fluid This photograph shows a baby born with the condition of hydrocephalus, which results when the normal circulation of cerebrospinal fluid (CSF) is blocked. Note the large size of the baby's head, which has expanded to accommodate all of the CSF. Untreated, hydrocephalus causes intellectual disability, but, today, shunts installed to drain off the excess fluid can prevent any further damage to the child's brain.

is a small opening that allows the CSF to flow into the subarachnoid space that surrounds both the brain and spinal cord. New CSF is made constantly, with the entire supply being turned over about three times per day. The old CSF is reabsorbed into the blood supply at the top of the head.

Because there are several narrow sections in this circulation system, blockages sometimes occur. This condition, known as hydrocephalus, is apparent at birth in affected infants. Hydrocephalus literally means water on the head. Left untreated, hydrocephalus can cause intellectual disability, as the large quantity of CSF prevents the normal growth of the brain. Currently, however, hydrocephalus can be treated by the installation of a shunt to drain off excess fluid, as shown in ● Figure 2.7. When the baby is old enough, surgery can be used to repair the obstruction. Some adults also experience blockages of the CSF circulatory system due to the growth of tumors or scar tissue. They, too, must be treated with shunts and/or surgery.

CSF moves through a completely self-contained and separate circulation system that never has direct contact with the blood supply. Because the composition of the CSF is often important in diagnosing diseases, a spinal tap is a common, though extremely unpleasant, procedure. In a spinal tap, the physician withdraws some fluid from the subarachnoid space surrounding the spinal cord through a needle.

The Brain's Blood Supply

Although the brain makes up only about 2 percent of your body weight, it is the target of about 15 to 20 percent of the blood pumped by the heart. The brain is served by the **carotid arteries** on either side of the neck as well as through the **vertebral arteries**

carotid artery One of the two major blood vessels that travel up the sides of the neck to supply the brain.

vertebral artery One of the important blood vessels that enters the brain from the back of the skull.

••• Behavioral Neuroscience GOES TO WORK

TREATING HYDROCEPHALUS

Hydrocephalus affects both newborns and adults. Obstructions, poor reabsorption, and overproduction can lead to symptoms of head enlargement, headache, nausea and vomiting, loss of bladder control, poor balance and coordination, and cognitive impairment. Because these symptoms can be caused by a number of different conditions, the diagnosis of hydrocephalus is made on the basis of neurological exams and brain imaging. Some cases of hydrocephalus are noted in prenatal ultrasounds.

The typical treatment for hydrocephalus involves surgery. Most commonly, a shunt is placed within one of the ventricles of the brain. Tubing is inserted under the skin, allowing the excess fluid to be redirected to the abdomen or a chamber of the heart, where it will be reabsorbed by the body without doing further harm. A valve controls the rate and direction of flow, so there is limited danger of too much fluid being drained away from the system. A less typical surgical treatment is the ventriculostomy, which involves making a small hole in the bottom of the floor of the third ventricle or between two ventricles to improve circulation of CSF.

In addition to neurologists and neurosurgeons, teams treating hydrocephalus usually include occupational therapists, developmental therapists for children, special education teachers, social workers, and mental health providers, who help the patient and family cope with a serious, potentially disabling disorder.

---

that travel up through the back of the skull. Once inside the skull, these major arteries branch to form the anterior, middle, and posterior cerebral arteries, which serve most of the brain. (see ● Figure 2.8).

Because the brain is unable to store energy, any interruption of the blood supply produces damage very quickly (see Chapter 15). Significant brain damage occurs less than three minutes after the stopping of a person's heart. Other structures in the body will not be affected so quickly. With life support, other organs are able to continue almost indefinitely. That is why we currently view brain death as our working definition of death.

VP SHUNT

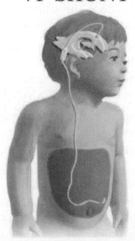

VA SHUNT

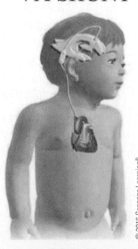

© 2016 Cengage Learning®

● **Figure 2.7** Shunt for Hydrocephalus Hydrocephalus in newborns used to be a major cause of intellectual disability. Contemporary treatment consisting of shunts inserted into the ventricle that drain excess cerebrospinal fluid (CSF) to the abdomen or heart has reduced the damage done to the brains of individuals with this condition.

● **Figure 2.8** The Brain Has a Generous Supply of Blood Blood reaches the brain either through the carotid arteries on either side of the neck or through the vertebral arteries entering through the base of the skull. Once in the brain, these arteries branch into the anterior cerebral artery, the middle cerebral artery, and the posterior cerebral artery.

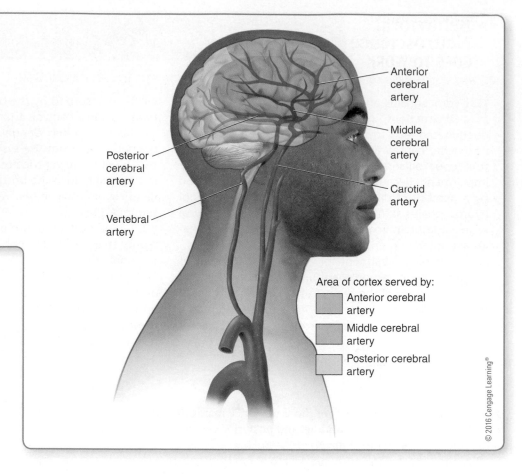

Anterior cerebral artery

Middle cerebral artery

Carotid artery

Posterior cerebral artery

Vertebral artery

Area of cortex served by:

Anterior cerebral artery

Middle cerebral artery

Posterior cerebral artery

© 2016 Cengage Learning®

INTERIM SUMMARY 2.1

‖ Summary Points

1. Anatomical directions help us locate structures in the nervous system. In four-legged animals, rostral structures are located toward the head, caudal structures are located toward the tail, dorsal structures are located toward the back, and ventral structures are located toward the belly. In humans, the dorsal parts of our brain form an 80-degree angle with the dorsal parts of the spinal cord. Additional terms that do not vary with the body's orientation in space include *anterior* (toward the front), *posterior* (toward the back), *superior* (top), and *inferior* (bottom). **(LO1)**

2. Ipsilateral structures are on the same side of the midline, and contralateral structures are on opposite sides of the midline. Structures near the midline are medial, and structures away from the midline are lateral. In limbs, proximal structures are closer to the body center, and distal structures are farther away. **(LO1)**

3. Coronal or frontal sections divide the brain from front to back. Sagittal sections are parallel to the midline and give us a side view of the brain. Horizontal (or axial or transverse) sections divide the brain from top to bottom. **(LO1)**

4. Three layers of meninges protect the central nervous system: the dura mater, the arachnoid, and the pia mater. Only the dura mater and pia mater layers are present in the peripheral nervous system. Cerebrospinal fluid (CSF) floats and cushions the brain. CSF circulates through the four ventricles of the brain, the central canal of the spinal cord, and the subarachnoid space. **(LO2)**

5. The brain is supplied with blood through the carotid and vertebral arteries. **(LO2)**

Review Questions

1. When considering your nervous system and that of your dog or cat, what anatomical direction terms would be the same or different?

2. Why do we have cerebrospinal fluid (CSF), and where in the nervous system is it found?

The Central Nervous System

We divide the entire nervous system into two components: the **central nervous system (CNS)** and the **peripheral nervous system (PNS)**. The CNS includes the brain and **spinal cord**. The PNS contains all the nerves that exit the brain and spinal cord, carrying sensory and motor messages to and from the other parts of the body. The tissue of the CNS is encased in bone, but the tissue of the PNS is not. ● Figure 2.9 summarizes the general organization of the central and peripheral nervous systems.

Although the neurons in both the CNS and PNS are essentially similar, there are some differences between the two systems. As we saw previously, the CNS is covered by three layers of membranes, whereas the PNS is covered by only two. CSF circulates within the layers covering the CNS but not within the PNS. In addition, damage to the CNS is considered permanent, whereas some recovery can occur in the PNS.

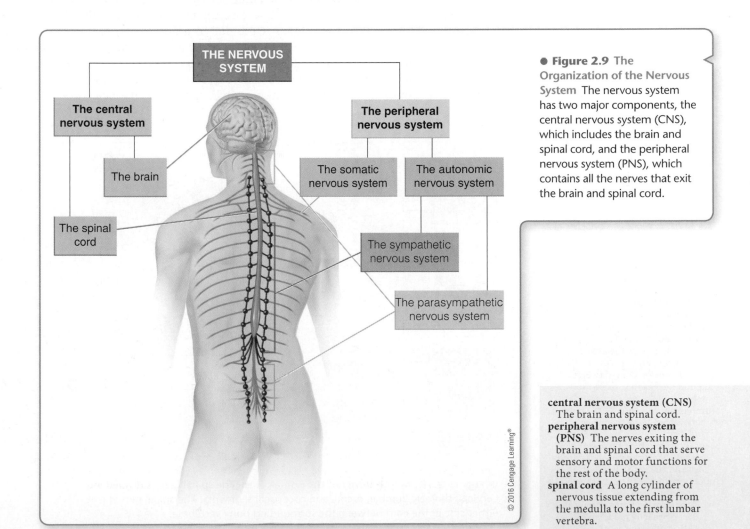

● **Figure 2.9** The Organization of the Nervous System The nervous system has two major components, the central nervous system (CNS), which includes the brain and spinal cord, and the peripheral nervous system (PNS), which contains all the nerves that exit the brain and spinal cord.

© 2016 Cengage Learning®

central nervous system (CNS) The brain and spinal cord.
peripheral nervous system (PNS) The nerves exiting the brain and spinal cord that serve sensory and motor functions for the rest of the body.
spinal cord A long cylinder of nervous tissue extending from the medulla to the first lumbar vertebra.

The Spinal Cord

The spinal cord is a long cylinder of nerve tissue that extends like a tail from the medulla, the most caudal structure of the brain, down to the first lumbar vertebra (a bone in the spine, or vertebral column). The neurons making up the spinal cord are found in the upper two thirds of the vertebral column. The spinal cord is shorter than the **vertebral column** because the cord itself stops growing earlier in a child's development than the bones in the vertebral column do. Running down the center of the spinal cord is the central canal.

The spinal nerves exit between the bones of the vertebral column. The bones are cushioned from one another with disks. If any of these disks degenerate, pressure is exerted on the adjacent spinal nerves, producing a painful pinched nerve. Based on the points of exit, we divide the spinal cord into 31 segments, as shown in ● Figure 2.10. Starting closest to the brain, there are 8 **cervical nerves** that serve the area of the head, neck, and arms. We refer to the neck brace used after a whiplash injury as a cervical collar. Below the cervical nerves are the 12 **thoracic nerves**, which serve most of the torso. You may have heard the term *thoracic surgeon* used to identify a surgeon who specializes in operations involving the chest, such as heart or lung surgeries. Five **lumbar nerves** come next, serving the lower back and legs. If somebody complains of lower back pain, this usually means he or she has lumbar problems. The 5 **sacral nerves** serve the backs of the legs and the genitals. Finally, we have the single **coccygeal nerve**. We will discuss these nerves in greater detail in relation to touch in Chapter 7.

Although the spinal cord weighs only 2 percent as much as the brain, it is responsible for several essential functions. The spinal cord is the original information superhighway. When viewed in a horizontal section, much of the cord appears white. **White matter** is made up of nerve fibers known as axons, the parts of neurons that carry signals to other neurons. The tissue looks white due to a fatty material known as myelin, which covers most human axons. When the tissue is preserved for study, the myelin repels staining and remains white, looking much like the fat on a steak. These large bundles or tracts of axons are responsible for carrying information to and from the brain. Axons from sensory neurons that carry information about touch, position,

vertebral column The bones of the spinal column that protect and enclose the spinal cord.

cervical nerve One of eight spinal nerves that serve the area of the head, neck, and arms.

thoracic nerve One of twelve spinal nerves that serve the torso.

lumbar nerve One of five spinal nerves that serve the lower back and legs.

sacral nerve One of five spinal nerves that serve the backs of the legs and the genitals.

coccygeal nerve The most caudal of the spinal nerves.

white matter An area of neural tissue primarily made up of myelinated axons.

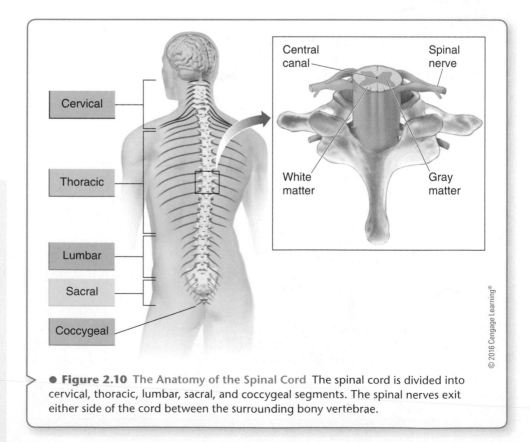

© 2016 Cengage Learning®

● **Figure 2.10** The Anatomy of the Spinal Cord The spinal cord is divided into cervical, thoracic, lumbar, sacral, and coccygeal segments. The spinal nerves exit either side of the cord between the surrounding bony vertebrae.

pain, and temperature travel up the dorsal parts of the spinal cord. Axons from motor neurons, responsible for movement, travel in the ventral parts of the cord. (Axons will be discussed in more detail in Chapter 3.)

There appears to be a gray butterfly or letter H shape in the center of the cord. **Gray matter** consists of areas primarily made up of cell bodies (see Chapter 3). The tissue appears gray because the cell bodies absorb some of the chemicals used to preserve the tissue, which stains them a pinkish gray. The neurons found in the **dorsal horns** of the H receive sensory input, whereas neurons in the **ventral horns** of the H pass motor information on to the muscles. These ventral horn cells participate in either voluntary movement or spinal **reflexes**.

Without any input from the brain, the spinal cord neurons are capable of some important reflexes. The knee jerk, or **patellar reflex**, that your doctor checks by tapping your knee, is an example of one type of spinal reflex. This reflex is managed by only two neurons. One neuron processes sensory information coming to the cord from muscle stretch receptors (see Chapter 8). This neuron communicates with a spinal motor neuron that responds to input by contracting a muscle, causing your foot to kick. Spinal reflexes also protect us from injury. If you touch something hot or step on something sharp, your spinal cord produces a withdrawal reflex. You immediately pull your body away from the source of the pain. This time, three neurons are involved: a sensory neuron, a motor neuron, and an interneuron between them. Because so few neurons are involved, the **withdrawal reflex** produces very rapid movement. The spinal cord also manages a number of more complex postural reflexes that help us stand and walk. These reflexes allow us to shift our weight automatically from one leg to the other.

Damage to the spinal cord results in loss of sensation (of both the skin and internal organs) and loss of voluntary movement in parts of the body served by nerves located below the damaged area. Some spinal reflexes are usually retained. Muscles can be stimulated, but they are not under voluntary control. A person with cervical damage, such as the late actor Christopher Reeve (Superman), is a quadriplegic (quad meaning "four," indicating loss of control over all four limbs). All sensation and ability to move the arms, legs, and torso are lost. A person with lumbar-level damage is a paraplegic. Use of the arms and torso is maintained, but sensation and movement in the lower torso and legs are lost. In all cases of spinal injury, bladder and bowel functions are no longer under voluntary control, as input from the brain to the sphincter muscles does not occur. Currently, spinal damage is considered permanent, but significant progress is being made in repairing the spinal cord (see Chapters 5 and 15).

Embryological Divisions of the Brain

Early in embryological development, the brain divides into three parts: the **hindbrain** (rhombencephalon), **midbrain** (mesencephalon), and **forebrain** (prosencephalon). Together, the hindbrain and midbrain make up the **brainstem**. Later in embryological development, the midbrain makes no further divisions, but the hindbrain divides into the myelencephalon, or **medulla**, and the metencephalon, which includes the **pons** and **cerebellum**. The forebrain divides further into the diencephalon and telencephalon. *Cephalon*, by the way, refers to the head. Table 2.1 outlines these divisions and the major structures we will find in each.

The Hindbrain

The structures of the brainstem are illustrated in ● Figure 2.11. We will begin our exploration of the brainstem in the hindbrain, located just above the spinal cord, which contains both myelencephalon and metencephalon.

THE MEDULLA (MYELENCEPHALON) The gradual swelling of tissue above the cervical spinal cord marks the most caudal portion of the brain, the **medulla**, or **myelencephalon**. The medulla, like the spinal cord, contains large quantities of white

gray matter An area of neural tissue primarily made up of cell bodies.

dorsal horns Gray matter in the spinal cord that contains sensory neurons.

ventral horns Gray matter in the spinal cord that contains motor neurons.

reflex An involuntary action or response.

patellar reflex The knee-jerk reflex; a spinal reflex in which tapping below the knee produces a reflexive contraction of the quadriceps muscle of the thigh, causing the foot to kick.

withdrawal reflex A spinal reflex that pulls a body part away from a source of pain.

hindbrain The most caudal division of the brain, including the medulla, pons, and cerebellum.

midbrain The division of the brain lying between the hindbrain and forebrain, including the superior and inferior colliculi, periaqueductal gray, red nucleus, and substantia nigra.

forebrain The division of the brain containing the diencephalon and the telencephalon.

brainstem The hindbrain and midbrain.

medulla/myelencephalon The most caudal part of the hindbrain.

pons A structure located in the metencephalon between the medulla and midbrain that participates in the management of states of consciousness.

cerebellum A structure located in the metencephalon that participates in balance, muscle tone, muscle coordination, some types of learning, and possibly higher cognitive functions in humans.

TABLE 2.1 | Embryological Divisions of the Brain

Division	Subdivision	Ventricle	Structures
Forebrain	Telencephalon	Lateral ventricles	Cerebral cortex Hippocampus Amygdala Basal ganglia
	Diencephalon	Third ventricle	Thalamus Hypothalamus
Midbrain	Mesencephalon	Cerebral aqueduct	Tectum Tegmentum
Hindbrain	Metencephalon	Fourth ventricle	Cerebellum Pons
	Myelencephalon		Medulla

matter. The vast majority of all information passing to and from higher structures of the brain must still pass through the medulla.

Instead of the butterfly appearance of the gray matter in the spinal cord, the medulla contains a number of **nuclei**, or collections of cell bodies with a shared function. These nuclei are suspended within the white matter of the medulla. Some of these nuclei contain cell bodies whose axons make up several of the cranial nerves serving the head and neck area. Other nuclei manage essential functions such as breathing,

● **Figure 2.11** **Structures of the Brainstem** (a) This sagittal section displays many of the important structures found in the brainstem. (b) With the cerebral hemispheres removed, we can see spatial relationships between the major structures of the brainstem. The key-to-slice allows us to view a horizontal section of the medulla and several of the important structures found at this level of the brain.

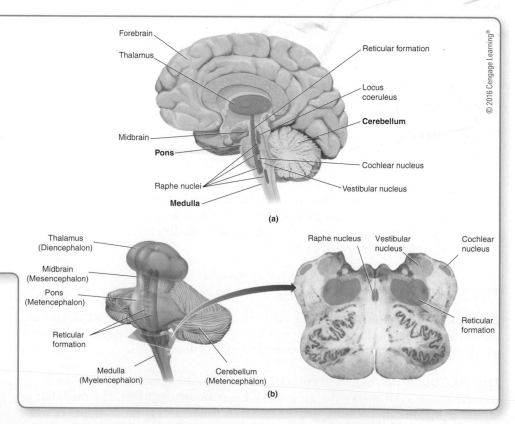

© 2016 Cengage Learning®

nuclei Collections of cell bodies that share a function.

heart rate, and blood pressure. Damage to the medulla is typically fatal due to its control over these vital functions.

Along the midline of the upper medulla, we see the caudal portion of a structure known as the **reticular formation**. The reticular formation, shown in ● Figure 2.11, is a complex collection of nuclei that runs along the midline of the brainstem from the medulla up into the midbrain. Contemporary neuroanatomists are more likely to refer to particular collections of nuclei within the reticular formation, such as the raphe nuclei, than to the reticular formation as a whole. The structure gets its name from the Latin *reticulum*, or network. Nuclei and circuits within the reticular formation play important roles in the regulation of consciousness and arousal (see Chapter 11), movement, and pain.

THE PONS AND CEREBELLUM (METENCEPHALON) The **metencephalon** contains two major structures, the **pons** and the **cerebellum**. The pons, which also appears in ● Figure 2.11, lies immediately rostral to the medulla. *Pons* means "bridge" in Latin, and one of the roles of the pons is to form connections between the medulla and higher brain centers as well as with the cerebellum.

As in the medulla, large fiber pathways with embedded nuclei are found in the pons. Among the important nuclei found at this level of the brainstem are the **cochlear nucleus** and the **vestibular nucleus**. The fibers communicating with these nuclei arise in the inner ear (see Chapter 7). The cochlear nucleus receives information about sound, and the vestibular nucleus receives information about the position and movement of the head. This vestibular input helps us keep our balance (or makes us feel motion sickness on occasion).

The reticular formation, which begins in the medulla, extends through the pons and on into the midbrain. Nuclei located within the pons are necessary for the production of rapid-eye-movement (REM) sleep, which is discussed in greater detail in Chapter 11. The **raphe nuclei** and the **locus coeruleus** project widely to the rest of the brain and influence mood, states of arousal, and sleep.

The second major part of the metencephalon, the cerebellum, is also shown in ● Figure 2.11. The cerebellum looks almost like a second little brain attached to the dorsal surface of the brainstem. Its name, *cerebellum*, actually means "little brain" in Latin. The use of "little" is misleading because the cerebellum actually contains more neurons than the rest of the brain combined. When viewed with a sagittal section, the internal structure of the cerebellum resembles a tree. White matter, or axons, forms the trunk and branches, while gray matter, or neural cell bodies, forms the leaves.

A traditional view of the cerebellum emphasized its role in coordinating voluntary movements, maintaining muscle tone, and regulating balance. Input from the spinal cord tells the cerebellum about the current location of the body in three-dimensional space. Input from the cerebral cortex, by way of the pons, tells the cerebellum about the movements you intend to make. The cerebellum then processes the sequences and timing of muscle movements required to carry out the plan. Considerable data support this role for the cerebellum in movement. Damage to the cerebellum affects skilled movements, including speech production. Because the cerebellum is one of the first structures affected by the consumption of alcohol, most sobriety tests, such as walking a straight line or pointing in a particular direction, are actually tests of cerebellar function. Along with the previously mentioned vestibular system, the cerebellum contributes to the experience of motion sickness.

More contemporary views see the cerebellum as responsible for much more than balance and motor coordination. In spite of its lowly position in the hindbrain, the cerebellum is involved in some of our most sophisticated processing of information, including executive functions and emotional processing (Schmahmann, 2010). In the course of evolution, the size of the cerebellum has kept pace with increases in the size of the cerebral cortex. One of the embedded nuclei of the cerebellum, the dentate nucleus, has become particularly large in monkeys and humans. A part of the dentate

reticular formation A collection of brainstem nuclei, located near the midline from the rostral medulla up into the midbrain, that regulate sleep and arousal.
metencephalon The division of the hindbrain containing the pons and cerebellum.
cochlear nucleus A nucleus found in the pons that receives information about sound from the inner ear.
vestibular nucleus A group of cell bodies in the pons that receive input about the location and movement of the head from sensory structures in the inner ear.
raphe nuclei Nuclei located in the pons that participate in the regulation of sleep and arousal.
locus coeruleus A structure in the pons that participates in arousal.

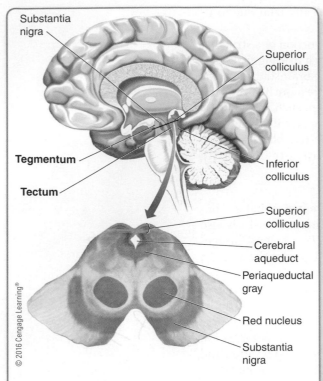

● **Figure 2.12** **The Internal Structure of the Midbrain** Important structures in the midbrain include the superior and inferior colliculi, the cerebral aqueduct, the periaqueductal gray, the substantia nigra, and the red nucleus.

mesencephalon Another term for midbrain, the division of the brain lying between the hindbrain and forebrain.

tectum The "roof," or dorsal half, of the midbrain.

tegmentum The "covering," or ventral half of the midbrain.

cerebral aqueduct The small channel running along the midline of the midbrain that connects the third and fourth ventricles.

periaqueductal gray Gray matter surrounding the cerebral aqueduct of the midbrain that is believed to play a role in the sensation of pain.

red nucleus A structure located within the reticular formation that communicates motor information between the spinal cord and the cerebellum.

substantia nigra Midbrain nuclei that communicate with the basal ganglia of the forebrain.

superior colliculi A pair of bumps on the dorsal surface of the midbrain that coordinates visually guided movements and visual reflexes.

inferior colliculi A pair of bumps on the dorsal surface of the midbrain that processes auditory information.

nucleus, known as the neodentate, is found only in humans. In addition to language difficulties, patients with cerebellar damage also experience subtle deficits in cognition and perception. As we will see in Chapter 12, the cerebellum also participates in learning (Albus, 1971; Marr, 1969). In cases of autism spectrum disorder, in which language, cognition, and social awareness are severely afflicted, abnormal development of the cerebellum is frequently observed (Scott, Schumann, Goodlin-Jones, & Amaral, 2009). Although neuroscientists do not agree on its exact function, most theories propose a cerebellum that can use past experience to make corrections and automate behaviors, whether they involve motor systems or not.

The Midbrain

The midbrain, or **mesencephalon**, shown in ● Figure 2.12, has a dorsal or top half known as the **tectum**, or "roof," and a ventral, or bottom half, known as the **tegmentum**, or "covering." In the midbrain, CSF is contained in a small channel at the midline known as the **cerebral aqueduct**. The cerebral aqueduct separates the tectum from the tegmentum and links the third and fourth ventricles.

Although the midbrain is relatively small compared with the other portions of the brainstem, it still contains a complex array of nuclei. Surrounding the cerebral aqueduct are cell bodies known as **periaqueductal gray** (*peri* means around). Periaqueductal gray appears to play an important role in our perception of pain, discussed more fully in Chapter 7. There are large numbers of receptors in the periaqueductal gray that respond to opiates such as morphine and heroin. Electrical stimulation of this area provides considerable relief from pain.

The midbrain also contains the most rostral portion of the reticular formation and a number of nuclei associated with cranial nerves. Several important motor nuclei are also found at this level of the brainstem, including the **red nucleus** and the **substantia nigra**. The red nucleus, which is located within the reticular formation, communicates motor information between the spinal cord and the cerebellum. It gives rise to the rubrospinal tract, which is an alternate pathway for voluntary movement commands that seems more important in other animals than in humans (see Chapter 8). The substantia nigra, whose name literally means "black stuff" due to the pigmentation of the structure, is closely connected with the basal ganglia of the forebrain (see the next section). Degeneration of the substantia nigra occurs in Parkinson's disease, which is characterized by difficulties in initiating movement.

On the dorsal surface of the midbrain are four prominent bumps. The upper pair is known as the **superior colliculi**. The superior colliculi receive input from the optic nerves leaving the eye. Although the colliculi are part of the visual system, they are unable to tell you what you're seeing. Instead, these structures allow us to make visually guided movements, such as pointing in the direction of a visual stimulus. They also participate in a variety of visual reflexes, including changing the size of the pupils of the eye in response to light conditions (see Chapter 6).

The other pair of bumps is known as the **inferior colliculi**. These structures are involved with hearing, or audition. The inferior colliculi are one stop along the pathway from the ear to the auditory cortex. These structures are involved with auditory reflexes such as turning the head in the direction of a loud noise. The inferior colliculi also participate in the localization of sounds in the environment by comparing the timing of the arrival of sounds at the two ears (see Chapter 7).

TABLE 2.2 | Important Structures in the Brainstem

Brainstem Location	Important Structures	Functions
Medulla	Reticular formation	Arousal
	Cranial nerve nuclei	Various
Pons	Reticular formation (continuing)	Arousal
	Cranial nerve nuclei	Various
	Cochlear nucleus	Audition
	Vestibular nucleus	Balance, position
	Raphe nucleus	Sleep and arousal
	Locus coeruleus	Sleep and arousal
Cerebellum		Balance, motor coordination, cognition
Midbrain	Reticular formation (continuing)	Arousal
	Cranial nerve nuclei	Various
	Periaqueductal gray	Pain
	Red nucleus	Motor
	Substantia nigra	Motor
	Superior colliculi	Vision
	Inferior colliculi	Audition

The Forebrain

The forebrain contains many of the most advanced and most recently evolved structures of the brain. Like the hindbrain, the forebrain divides again later in embryological development. The two resulting divisions are the **diencephalon** and the **telencephalon**. The diencephalon contains the thalamus and hypothalamus, which are located at the midline just above the mesencephalon or midbrain. The telencephalon contains the bulk of the left and right **cerebral hemispheres**.

THE THALAMUS AND HYPOTHALAMUS The diencephalon, depicted in ● Figure 2.13, is located at the rostral end of the brainstem. The upper portion of the diencephalon consists of the **thalamus**, often referred to as the "gateway to the cortex." We actually have two thalamic nuclei, one on either side of the midline. These structures appear to be just about in the middle of the brain, as viewed in a midsagittal section. The thalamus receives two types of information from other parts of the brain: sensory input and regulatory input. Most of our sensory systems (with the exception of olfaction, or smell) converge on the thalamus, which then forwards the information to the cerebral cortex for further processing. It appears that the thalamus does not change the nature of sensory information, so much as it filters the information delivered to the cortex depending on the organism's state of arousal (Alexander et al., 2006; Sherman & Guillery, 2002). The reticular formation of the brainstem and the cortex form large numbers of connections with the thalamus that regulate its sensitivity during stages of sleep and wakefulness (see Chapter 11). Damage to the thalamus typically results in coma, and disturbances in circuits linking the thalamus and cerebral cortex are involved in some seizures (see Chapter 15). The thalamus also participates in learning and memory (see Chapter 12).

diencephalon A division of the forebrain made up of the hypothalamus and the thalamus.
telencephalon The division of the brain comprising the cerebral hemispheres.
cerebral hemispheres One of the two large, globular structures that make up the telencephalon of the forebrain.
thalamus A structure in the diencephalon that processes sensory information, contributes to states of arousal, and participates in learning and memory.

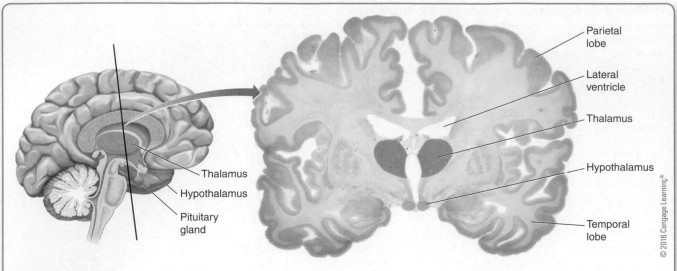

● **Figure 2.13** **The Thalamus and Hypothalamus of the Diencephalon** The thalamus lies close to the center of the brain, and the hypothalamus is located rostrally and ventrally relative to the thalamus. Directly below the hypothalamus is the pituitary gland, which is an important part of the endocrine system.

hypothalamus A structure found in the diencephalon that participates in the regulation of hunger, thirst, sexual behavior, and aggression; part of the limbic system.

pituitary gland A gland located just above the roof of the mouth that is connected to the hypothalamus and serves as a major source of hormones.

basal ganglia A collection of nuclei within the cerebral hemispheres that participate in the control of movement. Also known as the corpus striatum.

caudate nucleus One of the major nuclei that make up the basal ganglia.

putamen One of the nuclei contained in the basal ganglia.

globus pallidus One of the nuclei making up the basal ganglia.

subthalamic nucleus A small nucleus, located ventral to the thalamus, that is part of the basal ganglia.

nucleus accumbens A small nucleus associated with the basal ganglia known to be important in reward and addiction. Also known as the ventral striatum.

Just below the thalamus is the **hypothalamus**. The name hypothalamus literally means "below the thalamus." The hypothalamus is a major regulatory center for such behaviors as eating, drinking, sex, biorhythms, and temperature control. Rather than being a single, homogeneous structure, the hypothalamus is a collection of nuclei. For example, the aforementioned ventromedial nucleus of the hypothalamus (VMH) participates in the regulation of feeding behavior. The suprachiasmatic nucleus receives input from the optic nerve and helps set daily rhythms according to the rising of the sun. The hypothalamus plays an important role in regulating the endocrine system and is directly connected to the **pituitary gland**, from which many important hormones are released (see Chapter 10). Finally, the hypothalamus directs the autonomic nervous system, the portion of the PNS that controls our glands and organs.

THE BASAL GANGLIA Several nuclei make up the **basal ganglia**, which participate in motor control. A ganglion (*ganglia* is plural) is a general term for a collection of cell bodies. These nuclei, illustrated in ● Figure 2.14, include the **caudate nucleus**, the **putamen**, the **globus pallidus**, the **subthalamic nucleus** (which gets its name from its location "sub," or below, the thalamus), and the **nucleus accumbens**. This group of structures is also known as the corpus striatum, because of its "striated" or striped appearance. The nucleus accumbens is often referred to as the ventral striatum, because of its position relative to the rest of these structures. In primates, there are no functional differences between the caudate nucleus and putamen, so they are often referred to collectively as a single structure known as the striatum. Because these structures are so closely connected with the substantia nigra of the midbrain, the substantia nigra is usually considered to be part of the basal ganglia.

The basal ganglia are an important part of our motor system, although their exact role in motor control is not completely understood. Voluntary movement is initiated by the cortex, but without healthy functioning in the basal ganglia, it appears that cortical commands do not reach the lower parts of the motor system that actually implement these commands. In other words, the basal ganglia can be viewed as selecting and enabling the execution of motor programs stored by the cortex. Degeneration of the basal ganglia, which occurs in Parkinson's disease and in Huntington's disease, produces characteristic disorders of movement (see Chapter 8). The basal ganglia have also been implicated in a number of psychological disorders, including attention deficit hyperactivity disorder (ADHD) and obsessive-compulsive disorder (OCD; see Chapter 16).

The basal ganglia might perform similar functions during cognitive tasks as they do during motor tasks, namely selecting and enabling programs that are stored in other locations such as the cortex. Research animals that have learned simple maze-running tasks very well show activity in the striatum at the beginning of the task (initiating the program) and at the end of the task (evaluating reward; Jog et al., 1999). In humans, the basal ganglia are also involved with forming and using implicit, or unconscious, memories (see Chapter 12).

THE LIMBIC SYSTEM The **limbic system**, illustrated in ● Figure 2.15, is often referred to as the "limbic or sixth lobe" of the cortex, although it is not a true lobe. *Limbic* means border and describes the location of these structures on the margins of the cerebral cortex. Limbic structures play significant roles in learning, motivated behavior, and emotion.

The **hippocampus**, named after the Greek word for "seahorse," curves around within the cerebral hemispheres from close to the midline out to the tip of the temporal lobe as seen in ● Figure 2.16. The hippocampus participates in learning and memory, and it is vulnerable to damage as a result of stress (see Chapters 14 and 16). Damage to the hippocampus in both hemispheres produces a syndrome known as anterograde amnesia (see Chapter 12). People with this type of memory loss have difficulty forming new long-term declarative memories, which are memories for facts, language, and personal experience. In studies of patients with hippocampal damage, it was found that memories formed prior to the damage remained relatively intact; however, the patients were able to learn and remember procedures for solving a puzzle requiring multiple steps, like the Tower of Hanoi (see Chapter 12).

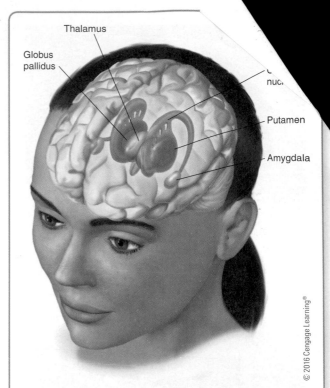

© 2016 Cengage Learning®

● **Figure 2.14 The Basal Ganglia** The basal ganglia include the caudate nucleus, putamen, globus pallidus, subthalamic nucleus, and nucleus accumbens. (The subthalamic nucleus and nucleus accumbens cannot be seen from this point of view). The substantia nigra of the midbrain is usually considered to be a part of this system.

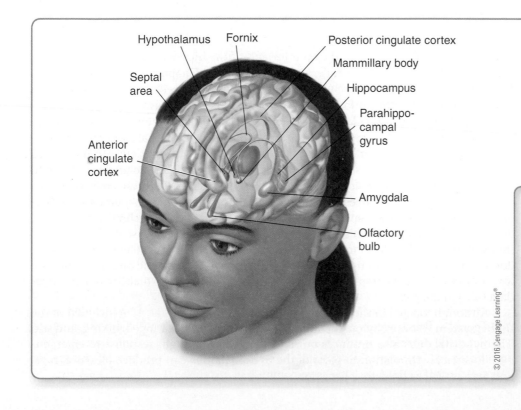

© 2016 Cengage Learning®

● **Figure 2.15 The Limbic System Participates in Learning and Emotion** A number of closely connected forebrain structures are included in the limbic system, which participates in many emotional, learning, and motivated behaviors.

limbic system A collection of forebrain structures that participate in emotional behavior, motivated behavior, and learning.

hippocampus A structure deep within the cerebral hemispheres that is involved with the formation of long-term declarative memories; part of the limbic system.

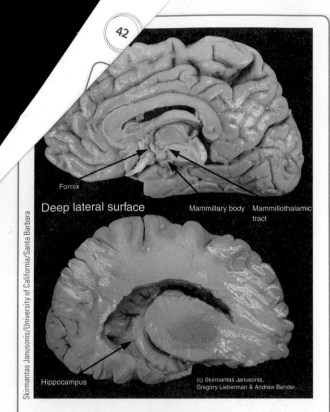

Skirmantas Janusonis/University of California/Santa Barbara

● **Figure 2.16** **The Hippocampus** The hippocampus curves away from the midline out towards the rostral temporal lobe. This structure plays important roles in learning, memory, and stress.

Bettmann/Corbis

● **Figure 2.17** **Amygdala Abnormalities Can Lead to Irrational Violence** In very rare cases, abnormalities of the amygdala are correlated with uncharacteristic, totally irrational violence. Charles Whitman, who led a previously unremarkable life, killed several family members and then climbed a clock tower at the University of Texas, Austin, in 1966. He methodically opened fire on the people below, killing 15 and injuring 31. Whitman, who was killed by police, was later found to have a tumor pressing on his amygdala.

The **amygdala**, located at the anterior end of the hippocampus, plays important roles in emotion, notably fear, rage, and aggression (see Chapter 14) as well as motivation. The amygdala receives input from all of the senses as well as from the viscera. In turn, the amygdala sends information to other limbic structures.

Electrical stimulation of the amygdala normally produces intense fear and aggressiveness. Damage to the amygdala leads to an abnormal emotional calmness and specifically interferes with an organism's ability to respond appropriately to dangerous situations. In laboratory studies, rats with damaged amygdale were unable to learn to fear tones that reliably predicted electric shock (LeDoux, 2000). Rhesus monkeys with damaged amygdale were overly friendly with unfamiliar monkeys, a potentially dangerous way to behave in a species that enforces strict social hierarchies (Emery et al., 2001). Stimuli that normally elicit fear in monkeys, such as rubber snakes or unfamiliar humans, failed to do so in monkeys with lesions in their amygdalas (Mason et al., 2006). Autism spectrum disorder, which produces either extreme and inappropriate fear and anxiety or a complete lack of fear, might involve abnormalities of the amygdala (see Chapter 16).

Although located in the diencephalon, the hypothalamus is often included in the limbic system. We are obviously emotional when it comes to eating, drinking, and sex. The hypothalamus also produces our so-called fight-or-flight response to emergencies. Electrical stimulation to parts of the hypothalamus can produce pleasure, rage, and fear as well as predatory behavior.

amygdala An almond-shaped structure in the rostral temporal lobes that is part of the limbic system.

The **cingulate cortex** is a fold of cortical tissue on the inner surface of the cerebral hemispheres. *Cingulum* means "belt" in Latin. The cingulate cortex contains an unusual and possibly recently evolved class of nerve cells known as von Economo or "spindle" neurons (see Chapter 3). Von Economo neurons are found only in the great apes, elephants, whales, dolphins, and humans and might, therefore, have considerable significance for the recent evolution of intelligent and social behavior (Nimchinsky, 1999; Seeley et al., 2012). Observations of patients with damage to areas containing Von Economo neurons indicate they play significant roles in empathy, social awareness, and self-control (Allman et al., 2011).

The cingulate cortex is further divided into anterior and posterior sections. The anterior cingulate cortex (ACC) exerts some influence over autonomic functions but has received the greatest attention from neuroscientists for its apparent roles in decision making, error detection, emotion, anticipation of reward, and empathy. For example, ACC activation increased when participants believed they had lost money while performing a decision task (Taylor et al., 2006). In addition, the ACC processes emotional information about pain (see Chapter 7). Although early research suggested that social pain associated with feelings of exclusion had co-opted the ACC and other parts of the pain matrix (Eisenberger, Lieberman, & Williams, 2003), suggesting that the human physical pain system had evolved to manage complex social interactions, this conclusion was not supported by a recent meta-analysis (Cacioppo et al., 2013). The posterior cingulate cortex (PCC) participates in a variety of functions, including eye movements, spatial orientation, and memory (Vogt, Finch, & Olson, 1992). The PCC is one of the first structures in the brain to be affected by Alzheimer's disease (Valla, Berndt, & Gonzalez-Lima, 2001; see Chapter 15).

The **septal area** is located anterior to the thalamus and hypothalamus and participates in reward (see Chapter 14). Electrical stimulation of this area is usually experienced as pleasurable, whereas lesions in this area produce uncontrollable rage and attack behaviors. On one unforgettable occasion, a rat with a septal lesion jumped at my face when I leaned over to pick it up (my apologies to those of you who are phobic about rodents).

Other structures often included in the limbic system are the **olfactory bulbs**, which are located at the base of the forebrain. These structures receive and process information about olfaction, or smell (see Chapter 7). If our sense of smell were not at all emotional, the perfume industry would probably go out of business. Also included in many descriptions of the limbic system are the **parahippocampal gyrus**, a fold of tissue near the hippocampus; the **mammillary bodies** of the diencephalon; and the **fornix**, a fiber pathway connecting the mammillary bodies and the hippocampus. These diverse structures are actually tightly connected with one another and participate in memory processes.

THE CORTEX   The outer covering of the cerebral hemispheres is known as the cortex, from the Latin word for "bark." Like the bark of a tree, the cerebral cortex is a thin layer of gray matter that varies from 1.5 mm to 4 mm in thickness in different parts of the brain. Unlike the spinal cord, the cerebral hemispheres are organized with gray matter on the outside and white matter on the inside. Below the thin layers of cortical cell bodies are vast fiber pathways that connect the cortex with the rest of the nervous system. The average 20-year-old human brain features about 100,000 miles (162,500 km) of fiber pathways (Marner, Nyengaard, Tang, & Pakkenberg, 2003).

The cerebral cortex has a wrinkled appearance somewhat like the outside of a walnut. The hills of the cortex are referred to as **gyri** (plural of gyrus), and the valleys are known as **sulci** (plural of sulcus). A particularly large sulcus is usually called a **fissure**. Why is the cerebral cortex so wrinkled? This feature of the cortex provides more surface area for cortical cells. We have limited space within the skull for brain tissue, and the wrinkled surface of the cortex allows us to pack in more neurons than we could otherwise. If stretched out flat, the human cortex would cover an area of about 2½ square feet. Just as we ball up a piece of paper to save space in our wastebasket, the sulci and gyri of the brain allow us to fit more tissue into our heads. The degree of

cingulate cortex A segment of older cortex just dorsal to the corpus callosum that is part of the limbic system.

septal area An area anterior to the thalamus and hypothalamus that is often included as part of the limbic system.

olfactory bulb A structure extending from the ventral surface of the brain that processes the sense of smell; part of the limbic system.

parahippocampal gyrus A fold of tissue near the hippocampus that is often included in the limbic system.

mammillary body One of two bumps on the ventral surface of the brain that participate in memory and are included in the limbic system.

fornix A fiber pathway connecting the hippocampus and mammillary bodies that is often included in the limbic system.

gyrus/gyri One of the "hills" on the convoluted surface of the cerebral cortex.

sulcus/sulci A "valley" in the convoluted surface of the cerebral cortex.

fissure A large sulcus.

granule cell A small type of cell found in layers II and IV of the cerebral cortex.

pyramidal cell A large, triangular cell found in layers III and V of the cerebral cortex.

lobe One of the four major areas of the cerebral cortex: frontal, parietal, temporal, and occipital.

frontal lobe The most rostral lobe of the cerebral cortex, separated from the parietal lobe by the central sulcus and from the temporal lobe by the lateral sulcus.

central sulcus The fissure separating the frontal and parietal lobes of the cerebral cortex.

parietal lobe One of the four lobes of the cerebral cortex; located between the frontal and occipital lobes.

temporal lobe The lobe of the cerebral cortex lying ventral and lateral to the frontal and parietal lobes and rostral to the occipital lobe.

lateral sulcus The fissure separating the temporal and frontal lobes of the cortex.

occipital lobe The most caudal lobe of the cortex; location of primary visual cortex.

insula The cortex located within the lateral sulcus between the frontal/parietal and temporal lobes. Referred to as "the fifth lobe."

longitudinal fissure The major fissure dividing the two cerebral hemispheres on the dorsal side of the brain.

sensory cortex An area of the cortex that is devoted to the processing of sensory information.

TABLE 2.3 | Structures of the Limbic System

Structure	Function
Hippocampus	Declarative memory formation, stress
Amygdala	Fear, aggression, memory, motivation
Hypothalamus	Aggression; regulation of hunger, thirst, sex, temperature, circadian rhythms, hormones
Anterior cingulate cortex (ACC)	Decision making, error detection, emotion, anticipation of reward, pain, and empathy
Posterior cingulate cortex (PCC)	Eye movements, spatial orientation, and memory
Septal area	Reward
Olfactory bulbs	Olfaction (smell)
Parahippocampal gyrus	Memory
Mammillary bodies	Part of the hypothalamus; memory
Fornix	Connects the hippocampus to mammillary bodies and other parts of the brain

wrinkling, or convolution, is related to how advanced a species is. ● Figure 2.18 shows that human brains are much more convoluted than a sheep's brain, for example, and the sheep's brain is more convoluted than a rat's brain.

The cells of the cerebral cortex are organized in layers, illustrated in ● Figure 2.19. The number, organization, and size of the layers vary somewhat throughout the cortex. In most parts of the cortex, there are six distinct layers, which are numbered from the outermost layer toward the center of the brain. Layer I has no cell bodies at all. Instead, it is made up of the nerve fibers of cells forming connections with other layers. Layers II and IV contain large numbers of small cells known as **granule cells**. Layers III and V are characterized by large numbers of the triangular-shaped **pyramidal cells**. These layers usually provide most of the output from an area of cortex to other parts of the nervous system. Layer VI has many types of neurons, which merge into the white matter that lies below the cortical layers.

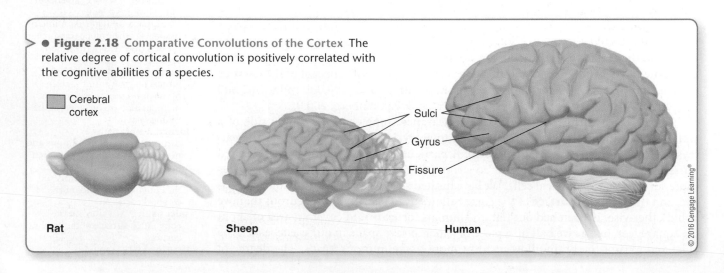

● **Figure 2.18** Comparative Convolutions of the Cortex The relative degree of cortical convolution is positively correlated with the cognitive abilities of a species.

Cerebral cortex

Sulci

Gyrus

Fissure

Rat

Sheep

Human

© 2016 Cengage Learning®

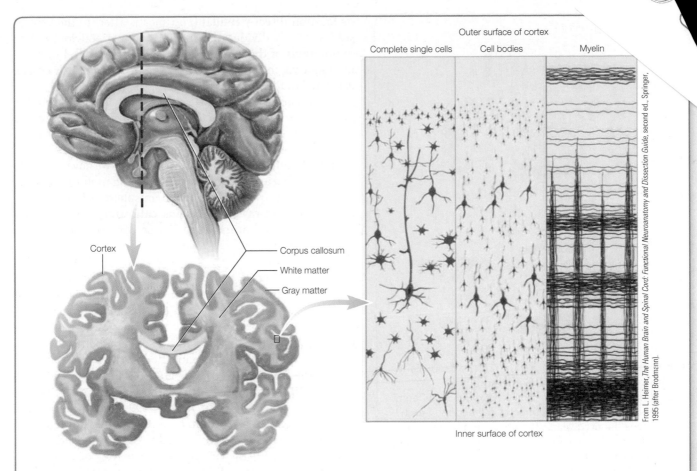

From L. Heimer, *The Human Brain and Spinal Cord: Functional Neuroanatomy and Dissection Guide*, second ed., Springer, 1995 (after Brodmann).

● **Figure 2.19** **The Layers of the Cerebral Cortex** The cerebral cortex covers the outer surface of the brain. Six distinct layers are apparent in most areas of the cortex. Three different views of these layers are shown here. The Golgi stain highlights entire neurons, and the Nissl stain highlights cell bodies. Note the large pyramidal cells shown by the Nissl stain in layer V. The Weigert stain highlights pathways formed by myelinated axons through the cortex.

There are a number of systems for dividing the cerebral cortex. As shown in ● Figure 2.20, Korbinian Brodmann used the distribution of cell bodies within the six layers of the cortex to distinguish between 52 separate areas (Brodmann, 1909/1994). A simpler approach divides the cortex into four sections known as **lobes**, as shown in ● Figure 2.21. The lobes are actually named after the skull bones that lie above them. The most rostral of the lobes is the **frontal lobe**. The caudal boundary of the frontal lobe is marked by the **central sulcus**. On the other side of the central sulcus, we find the **parietal lobe**. In the ventral direction, the frontal lobe is separated from the **temporal lobe** by the **lateral sulcus**. At the very back of the cortex is the **occipital lobe**. Within the lateral sulcus, which separates the frontal and temporal lobes, we find an area known as the **insula**, which is sometimes referred to as the insula lobe or "fifth lobe." Like the cingulate cortex, the insula contains von Economo neurons. Separating the two cerebral hemispheres along the dorsal midline is the **longitudinal fissure**.

These areas of the cortex are so large that many different functions are located in each lobe. In general, we can divide the functional areas of the cortex into three categories: **sensory cortex**, **motor cortex**, and **association cortex**. The sensory cortex processes incoming information from the sensory systems. Different areas of the sensory cortex are found in the occipital, temporal, and parietal lobes. The occipital lobe contains the **primary visual cortex**. The **primary auditory cortex** is located in the temporal lobe. The **postcentral gyrus** of the parietal lobe contains the **primary somatosensory cortex**, which is the highest level of processing for information about touch, pain, position, and skin temperature. The postcentral gyrus gets its name from

motor cortex An area of the cortex that is devoted to the processing of movement.
association cortex An area of the cortex that does not process sensory or motor information directly but rather serves as a bridge between areas that do process these functions.
primary visual cortex An area of the sensory cortex located within the occipital lobe that provides the initial cortical processing of visual information.
primary auditory cortex An area of the sensory cortex located within the temporal lobe that provides the initial cortical processing of sound information.
postcentral gyrus The fold of parietal lobe tissue just caudal to the central sulcus; the location of the primary somatosensory cortex.
primary somatosensory cortex An area of the sensory cortex located within the parietal lobe that provides the highest level of processing for body senses such as touch, position, skin temperature, and pain.

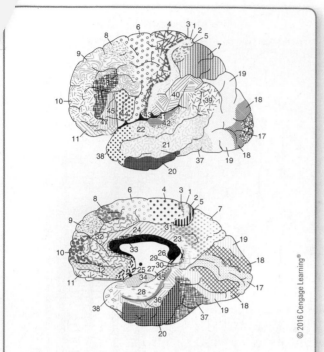

● **Figure 2.20** Brodmann's Map of the Brain Early 20th-century German neurologist Korbinian Brodmann divided the cerebral cortex into 52 different areas, based on the distribution of cell bodies in each area. One hundred years after Brodmann's system was first published, it remains the most widely used system for describing cortical architecture.

© 2016 Cengage Learning®

its location directly caudal (*post* means after) to the central sulcus, which divides the frontal and parietal lobes. The motor areas of the cortex provide the highest level of command for voluntary movements. The **primary motor cortex** is located in the **precentral gyrus** of the frontal lobe.

Some areas of the cortex have neither specific motor nor specific sensory functions. These areas are known as **association cortex** and are located primarily in the frontal, temporal, and inferior parietal lobes. *Association* means connection. In other words, these are the areas we have available for connecting and integrating sensory and motor functions.

The right and left cerebral hemispheres are linked by two major pathways, the **corpus callosum** and the much smaller **anterior commissure**. These commissures may be seen in ● Figure 2.22.

LOCALIZATION OF FUNCTION IN THE CORTEX In addition to the sensory and motor functions identified earlier, we can localize a number of specific functions in areas of the cerebral cortex. In many cases, these functions appear to be managed by cortex on either the left or right hemisphere.

In addition to being the location of the primary motor cortex, the frontal lobe participates in a number of higher-level cognitive processes such as the planning of behavior, attention, and judgment (Fuster, 1997). Two important structures within the frontal lobes are the **dorsolateral prefrontal cortex (DLPC)**, located to the top and side of the frontal lobes, and the **orbitofrontal cortex**, located above and behind the eyes. These areas of the frontal lobes, illustrated in ● Figure 2.21, maintain extensive, reciprocal connections with the limbic system, the basal ganglia, and other

● **Figure 2.21** The Lobes of the Cerebral Cortex The cortex is traditionally divided into the frontal, parietal, temporal, and occipital lobes.

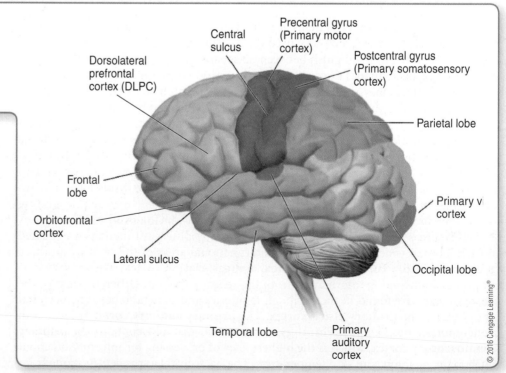

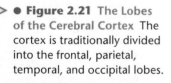

primary motor cortex An area of the cortex located within the frontal lobe that provides the highest level of command to the motor systems.
precentral gyrus The fold of frontal lobe tissue just rostral to the central sulcus; the location of the primary motor cortex.
association cortex Areas of the cortex that link and integrate sensory and motor information.

© 2016 Cengage Learning®

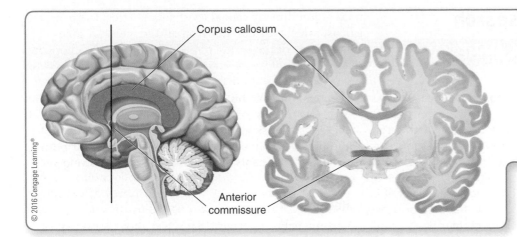

● **Figure 2.22 The Corpus Callosum and the Anterior Commissure** Two fiber bundles, the very large corpus callosum and the much smaller anterior commissure, connect the right and left cerebral hemispheres.

parts of the cortex. The DLPC is involved in executive functions such as attention and working memory and in the planning of behavior (see Chapter 12), whereas the orbitofrontal cortex is involved in impulse control and delayed gratification.

One of the classical methods for identifying brain functions is to consider cases in which the area of interest has been damaged. Possibly the most dramatic case of frontal lobe damage is that of the unfortunate Phineas Gage, a railroad worker in the mid-1800s. While Gage was preparing to blow up some rock, a spark set off his gunpowder and blew an iron tamping rod through his head, entering below his left eye and exiting through the top of his skull. Miraculously, Gage survived the accident. He was not the same man, however, according to his friends. Prior to his accident, Gage appears to have been responsible, friendly, and polite. After his accident, Gage had difficulty holding a job and was profane and irritable. His memory and reason were intact, but his personality was greatly changed for the worse.

Gage's results are consistent with modern findings of frontal lobe damage. People with damage to the DLPC experience apathy, personality change, and the lack of ability

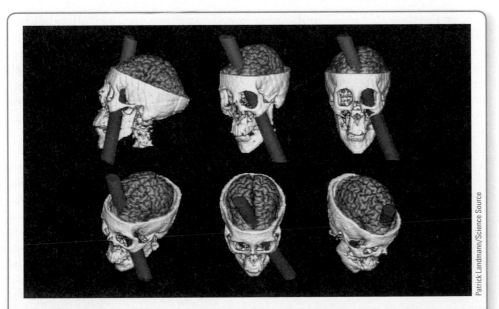

Patrick Landmann/Science Source

● **Figure 2.23 The Case of Phineas Gage** Mid-19th-century railroad worker Phineas Gage suffered an accident in which an iron rod was shot through the frontal lobe of his brain. Although Gage survived, he was described by his friends as a "changed man." Gage's case illustrates the localization of higher-order cognitive functions in the frontal lobe.

corpus callosum A wide band of axons connecting the right and left cerebral hemispheres.

anterior commissure A small bundle of axons that connects structures in the right and left cerebral hemispheres.

dorsolateral prefrontal cortex (DLPC) An area located at the top and sides of the frontal lobe that participates in executive functions such as attention and the planning of behavior.

orbitofrontal cortex An area of the frontal lobe located just behind the eyes involved in impulse control; damage to this area can produce some antisocial behavior.

••• Connecting to **Research**

THE CONNECTOME AND PHINEAS GAGE

Reconstructions of the damage to Phineas Gage's brain focus on the loss of gray matter in his left frontal cortex due to the violent passage of the iron tamping rod, and interpretation of his symptoms correlates them with the activity in the frontal lobes of the brain (Damasio, Grabowski, Frank, Galaburda, & Damasio, 1994). With new technologies, however, it is now possible to reconstruct not only the area of damage, but the damage to the connectome, or the connections between the damaged areas and other parts of the brain (Van Horn et al., 2012).

THE QUESTION: *What effects did Gage's injury have on the white matter connecting his left frontal cortex with the rest of his brain?*

Methods

The authors obtained existing CT images of Gage's skull and the Gage life-mask. They note that it is unlikely that further medical scans of the skull will be possible due to its fragile state. To provide a baseline of normal connectivity, the authors conducted MRI and diffusion tensor imaging using 110 right-handed male participants between the ages of 25 and 36 (Gage was 25 at the time of his accident and died at the age of 36). For further comparison, the authors simulated the effects of similarly sized lesions in other parts of the brain. A connectogram was constructed for both healthy participants and Phineas Gage following his accident.

Results

Reconstructions suggest that while about 4 percent of Gage's cerebral cortex was intersected by the passage of the tamping iron, 11 percent of the total white matter was damaged. While the location of Gage's damage probably contributed to the disruption of several network hubs, the overall damage to the networking of Gage's brain is likely to be similar to that seen in the "average" brain lesion of the same size occurring in other locations.

Conclusions

The authors argue that consideration of the pattern of Gage's white matter damage does a better job of explaining his cognitive and emotional deficits than a simple discussion of the gray matter damage he sustained in the left frontal lobe.

to plan. People with damage to the orbitofrontal cortex experience emotional disturbances and impulsivity. As we will see in our discussion of mental disorders (Chapter 16), several types of psychopathology involve the frontal lobes. Some people with schizophrenia show lower than normal activity in the frontal lobe. Because children with attention deficit hyperactivity disorder are usually very impulsive and have short attention spans, it has been suggested that they, too, suffer from underactivity of the frontal lobes. Finally, people who show extreme antisocial behavior, including serial murderers, frequently show damage to the orbitofrontal cortex.

Further evidence of the importance of the frontal lobes comes from the unfortunate experiment in **frontal lobotomies** during the mid-20th century. In 1935, Yale researchers Carlyle Jacobsen and John Fulton reported evidence indicating that chimpanzees with frontal lobe damage experienced a reduction in negative emotions. After listening to a presentation by Fulton, Portuguese neurologist Egaz Moniz advocated the use of frontal lobotomies with human patients to reduce negative outbursts. During the 1940s and 1950s, more than 10,000 frontal lobotomies were performed to reduce fear and anxiety in mental patients and in some people without major disorders. The lobotomy, discussed in greater detail in Chapter 14, consisted of a surgical separation of the most rostral parts of the frontal lobe from the rest of the brain. Without any remaining connections, the functions of this area of cortex would be lost. Moniz received the Nobel Prize in 1949 for advocating the procedure. Walter Freeman, an American doctor, performed many such operations, either in his office or even in his car, which he nicknamed his "lobotomobile." Initially, the operation was restricted to psychotic patients, but by the 1950s in the United States, depressed housewives and other people without major disorders were victims of the procedure. I would like

frontal lobotomy A surgical procedure in which a large portion of the frontal lobe is separated from the rest of the brain.

••• THINKING *Ethically*

CAN WE LOCALIZE INTELLIGENCE IN THE BRAIN?

Few topics elicit as much discomfort and controversy as the idea that "intelligence" can be localized in the brain. At the same time, neuropsychologists working with patients who have experienced brain damage require the best scientific evidence for understanding how the locations and extent of the damage are likely to influence intelligent behavior.

Psychologists have difficulty agreeing on definitions of intelligence and about whether intelligence is a single entity or collection of abilities. The idea of general intelligence (*g*) is based on observed correlations between multiple cognitive tasks and real-world success (see Chapter 13). At the level of analysis used in the neurosciences, we need to know if *g* reflects the "whole brain" activity or if some subset of systems contributes to success in cognitive tasks.

One approach to this problem is the use of data from many patients who have experienced brain lesions (Gläscher et al., 2010). Which areas of damage were most likely to be correlated with cognitive deficits? Would the amount of brain damage be more important, as proposed by Karl Lashley in his theories

of "mass action" and "equipotentiality," or would the specific areas of damage be predictive of intellectual functioning?

Gläscher et al. (2010) carefully mapped brain damage in 241 patients and correlated measures of *g*. Features that were apparently important to *g* included white matter association tracts connecting the frontal and parietal lobes along with the gray matter of the left frontal lobe itself (probably due to the importance of verbal abilities in most cognitive tasks and the statistical likelihood for verbal processing to be lateralized to the left hemisphere). The authors concluded that general intelligence is based on connections between regions that integrate executive processes with verbal, visuospatial, and working memory.

If localizing areas of the brain associated with general intelligence is possible, it leads to the further possibility that individual differences in the workings of these circuits could also be assessed. This could certainly avoid the criticisms of contemporary IQ tests as being culturally insensitive, but it might raise entirely new sets of ethical concerns.

---

to be able to say that physicians stopped doing lobotomies (very few are done today) because they recognized the tremendous negative side effects of the procedure, but that would not be entirely accurate. Lobotomies were largely discontinued when major antipsychotic medications were discovered. With the new drugs, the lobotomies were no longer considered necessary.

The frontal lobe is also home to an important area of the motor cortex known as **Broca's area**. Broca's area is necessary for speech production. Damage to this area produces difficulty speaking but has relatively less effect on a person's understanding or comprehension of speech. For most people, language functions appear to be controlled by cortex on the left hemisphere rather than on the right hemisphere. We will explore the lateralization of the language function in more detail in Chapter 13.

In addition to speech, other cognitive functions appear to show lateralization to one hemisphere or the other. For the vast majority of people, the left hemisphere manages logical thought and basic mathematical computation. You might think of the left hemisphere as the rational, school side of your brain. In contrast, the right hemisphere appears to be more emotional and intuitive. Our appreciation for art and music, as well as our ability to think three-dimensionally, are typically located in the right hemisphere. Please try to forget any pop psychology you have read previously about accessing your right brain to become a better artist. With the corpus callosum constantly relaying messages from one hemisphere to the other, you are already using your right hemisphere as much as you can.

BRAIN CIRCUITS AND THE CONNECTOME Before we leave the discussion of the CNS to explore the PNS, we need to ensure that our discussion of the functions of certain parts of the brain has not led to a misunderstanding about the nature of neural

Broca's area An area near the primary motor cortex in the frontal lobe that participates in speech production.

functioning. Neurons do not behave in isolation, but rather participate in circuits. Parts of the brain, such as the ventromedial hypothalamus, do not "run" a function like satiety, but rather participate in circuits that influence satiety.

The mapping of the connectome, or the neural connections in the brain, is a major contemporary research initiative. The U.S. National Institutes of Health (NIH) has launched the Human Connectome Project with the goal of completely mapping the connections of the healthy, adult human brain. Connectomes are investigated at both the cellular level and at the more macro level, which is the level of analysis used in this chapter. New technologies, such as diffusion tensor imaging (see Chapter 1) are making this work more feasible.

INTERIM SUMMARY 2.2

⏸ Summary Table: Major Structures of the Central Nervous System

Division	Major Structures	Functions
Hindbrain	Medulla	Breathing, heart rate, and blood pressure; contains nuclei serving several cranial nerves
	Reticular formation (extends into midbrain)	Arousal and attention
	Pons	Sleep/waking cycles; contains nuclei serving several cranial nerves
	Cerebellum	Motor control, balance, cognition
Midbrain	Superior colliculi	Visual reflexes
	Inferior colliculi	Auditory reflexes
	Substantia nigra	Motor control
	Periaqueductal gray	Pain
Forebrain	Thalamus	Sensory processing, states of arousal, learning, and memory
	Hypothalamus	Regulation of hunger, thirst, aggression, sexual behavior, and the autonomic nervous system
	Amygdala	Recognition of danger, or aggression and motivation
	Hippocampus	Memory formation, stress
	Cerebral cortex	Highest level of sensory and motor processing; highest cognitive activity
	Corpus callosum	Connects the two cerebral hemispheres

Summary Points

1. The spinal cord is divided into cervical, thoracic, lumbar, sacral, and coccygeal segments. In addition to carrying messages to and from the brain, the spinal cord provides a variety of protective and motor reflexes. **(LO3)**

2. The hindbrain consists of the medulla, pons, and cerebellum. Running through the medulla and pons at the midline is the reticular formation, which helps control arousal. The midbrain contains the remaining section of the reticular formation, the periaqueductal gray, the red nucleus, the superior colliculi, the inferior colliculi, and the substantia nigra. The forebrain is divided into the diencephalon and the telencephalon. The diencephalon contains the thalamus and hypothalamus. The telencephalon contains the cerebral cortex, basal ganglia, and limbic system structures. **(LO4)**

3. The cerebral cortex is made up of six layers that cover the outer surface of the cerebral hemispheres. The hills of the cortex are referred to as gyri, and the valleys are referred to as sulci, or fissures. **(LO5)**

4. The cerebral cortex is divided into four lobes: the frontal lobe, the parietal lobe, the temporal lobe, and the occipital lobe. **(LO5)**

5. The two cerebral hemispheres are connected by the corpus callosum and the anterior commissure. Some functions, such as language, appear to be localized on one hemisphere or the other. **(LO5)**

6. The cortex also can be divided into sensory, motor, or association cortex based on its function. **(LO5)**

Review Questions

1. What are the major structures and functions found in the hindbrain, midbrain, and forebrain?

2. What functions can be localized in particular areas of cortex?

The Peripheral Nervous System

For all its power, the brain still depends on the PNS to enable it to perceive the outside world and to tell the body to carry out its commands. The role of the PNS is to carry sensory information from the body to the spinal cord and brain and bring back to the body commands for appropriate responses. The PNS contains three structural divisions: the cranial nerves, the spinal nerves, and the autonomic nervous system.

Together, the cranial nerves and spinal nerves make up the **somatic nervous system**. The somatic nervous system brings sensory input to the brain and spinal cord and returns commands to the muscles. The **autonomic nervous system** controls the actions of many glands and organs. The glands of the **endocrine system** coordinate arousal, metabolism, growth, and sex by releasing chemical messengers directly into the bloodstream.

The Cranial Nerves

As shown in ● Figure 2.24, 12 pairs of **cranial nerves** enter and exit the brain directly. Three of the cranial nerves carry only sensory information. These are the **olfactory nerve (I)**, the **optic nerve (II)**, and the **auditory nerve (VIII)**. Five of the nerves carry only motor information. The muscles of the eyes are controlled by the **oculomotor nerve (III)**, the **trochlear nerve (IV)**, and the **abducens nerve (VI)**. The **spinal accessory nerve (XI)** controls the muscles of the neck, and the **hypoglossal nerve (XII)** controls movement of the tongue. The remaining nerves have mixed sensory and motor functions. The **trigeminal nerve (V)** controls chewing movements but

somatic nervous system The peripheral nervous system (PNS) division that brings sensory input to the brain and spinal cord and returns commands to the muscles.

autonomic nervous system The division of the peripheral nervous system (PNS) that directs the activity of the glands, organs, and smooth muscles of the body.

endocrine system Glands that secrete hormones directly into the blood supply.

cranial nerves Twelve pairs of nerves that exit the brain as part of the peripheral nervous system (PNS).

olfactory nerve (I) A cranial nerve carrying information about smell to the brain.

optic nerve (II) A cranial nerve carrying information from the eyes to the brain.

auditory nerve (VIII) A cranial nerve that carries information from the inner ear to the brain.

oculomotor nerve (III) A cranial nerve that controls muscles of the eye.

trochlear nerve (IV) A cranial nerve that controls the muscles of the eye.

abducens nerve (VI) A cranial nerve that controls the muscles of the eye.

spinal accessory nerve (XI) A cranial nerve that controls the muscles of the neck.

hypoglossal nerve (XII) A cranial nerve responsible for movement of the tongue.

trigeminal nerve (V) A cranial nerve that controls chewing movements and provides feedback regarding facial expression.

● **Figure 2.24 The Twelve Pairs of Cranial Nerves** Twelve pairs of cranial nerves leave the brain directly to carry sensory and motor information to and from the head and neck areas. The red lines represent sensory functions, and the blue lines show motor control. Some cranial nerves are sensory only, some are motor only, and some are mixed.

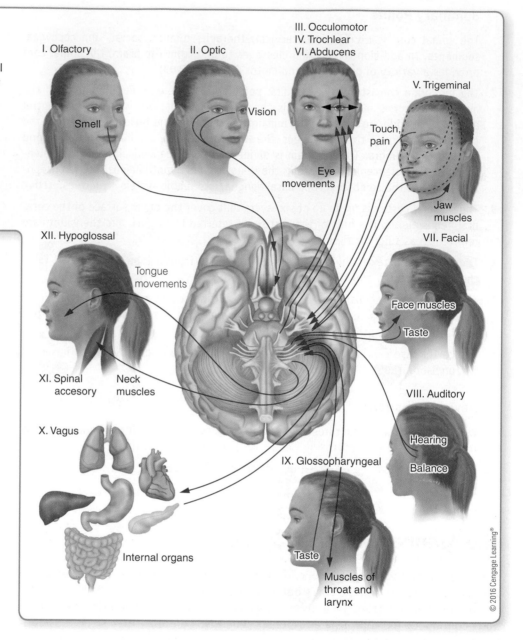

facial nerve (VII) A cranial nerve that produces muscle movement in facial expressions and that carries taste information back to the brain.
glossopharyngeal nerve (IX) A cranial nerve that manages both sensory and motor functions in the throat.
vagus nerve (X) A cranial nerve that serves the heart, liver, and digestive tract.
mixed nerve Spinal nerves that carry both sensory and motor information.
afferent nerve A nerve that carries sensory information to the CNS.
efferent nerve A nerve that carries motor commands away from the CNS.

also provides some feedback regarding facial expression. The **facial nerve (VII)** produces facial expressions and carries the sensation of taste. The **glossopharyngeal nerve (IX)** performs both sensory and motor functions for the throat. Finally, the long-distance fibers of the **vagus nerve** (vagus comes from the same Latin root as our word "vagabond") **(X)** provide input and receive sensation from the heart, liver, and digestive tract.

The Spinal Nerves

As mentioned earlier, 31 pairs of spinal nerves exit the spinal cord to provide sensory and motor pathways to the torso, arms, and legs. Each spinal nerve is also known as a **mixed nerve** because it contains a sensory, or **afferent**, **nerve** (the "a" means toward the CNS in this case, as in *access*) and a motor, or **efferent**, **nerve** (the "e" means away from the CNS, as in *exit*). The mixed nerves travel together to the part of the body they serve. This makes a great deal of practical sense. The nerves that are bringing you sensory information from your hand are adjacent to the nerves that tell your hand to

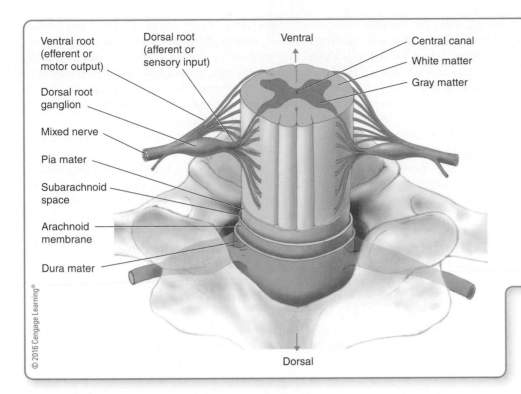

Ventral root (efferent or motor output)

Dorsal root (afferent or sensory input)

Ventral

Central canal

White matter

Gray matter

Dorsal root ganglion

Mixed nerve

Pia mater

Subarachnoid space

Arachnoid membrane

Dura mater

Dorsal

© 2016 Cengage Learning®

● **Figure 2.25** The **Structure of the Spinal Cord** This cross-section of the spinal cord shows a number of important anatomical features. Three layers of meninges surround the cord. The gray matter of the cord is located in a butterfly shape near the central canal, which contains cerebrospinal fluid (CSF). The dorsal afferent (sensory) nerves join the ventral efferent (motor) nerves beyond the spinal ganglion to form a mixed nerve.

move. Damage to a mixed nerve is likely to reduce both sensation and motor control for a particular part of the body.

● Figure 2.25 shows the spinal nerves exiting a segment of the spinal cord. Upon leaving the spinal cord itself, the spinal nerves enjoy the protection of only two layers of meninges: the dura mater and pia mater. CSF does not surround the spinal nerves. Afferent roots arise from the dorsal part of the spinal cord, whereas efferent roots arise from the ventral part. Once outside the cord, the dorsal afferent root swells into the **dorsal root ganglion**, which contains the cell bodies of the afferent nerves that process information about touch, temperature, and other body senses from the periphery. Beyond the dorsal root ganglion, the dorsal and ventral roots join to form a mixed nerve.

Afferent (sensory) nerves contain both myelinated and unmyelinated fibers, whereas efferent (motor) nerves are all myelinated in the human adult. As discussed in Chapter 3, myelin is a substance that insulates nerve fibers and increases the speed with which they can transmit messages. Myelinated fibers in both systems tend to be very large and very fast. Among the sensations carried by myelinated afferent fibers is the first, sharp experience of pain. Small unmyelinated afferent fibers are responsible for that dull, achy feeling that follows injury.

The Autonomic Nervous System

The autonomic nervous system was first described as cells and fibers that pass to tissues other than the skeletal muscle (Langley, 1921). Your heart, lungs, digestive system, and other organs are commanded by the autonomic nervous system. The autonomic nervous system participates in a large number of critical regulatory functions, including blood circulation, secretion, digestion, urination, and defecation. In addition, many reflexive behaviors are carried out with the assistance of autonomic neurons. These reflexes include respiration, pupil dilation, sneezing, coughing, swallowing, vomiting, and genital responses.

You might think of this system as the automatic, or "cruise control," nervous system. It manages many vital functions without conscious effort or awareness. You wouldn't have much of a social life if you had to consciously command your lungs to inhale and exhale and your heart to beat. This doesn't mean that you are incapable of

dorsal root ganglion A collection of cell bodies of afferent nerves located just outside the spinal cord.

taking voluntary control of autonomic functions. We do this all the time, but it takes attention. For example, breathing normally continues whether we are awake or asleep. However, when we swim, it's vital that we take conscious control of our breathing patterns, or we'll end up swallowing a lot of water. Through specialized training in **biofeedback**, people can learn to control a number of autonomic processes, such as lowering blood pressure and reducing blood flow to the brain to avoid migraine head-aches. Once they shift attention, however, the effect may not last.

The brain structure that plays the greatest role in managing the autonomic nervous system is the hypothalamus. The pathways to and from the hypothalamus are exceedingly complex. Many structures involved with emotion have the potential to affect the hypothalamus and, indirectly then, the autonomic nervous system. As a result, the responses of our internal organs are tightly connected with our emotional behaviors, leading to the many common physical symptoms we experience as a result of our emotions, such as feeling like you have butterflies in your stomach.

The hypothalamus, in turn, connects with the midbrain tegmentum and to the reticular formation in particular. Damage to the midbrain in the vicinity of the red nucleus produces a wide variety of autonomic disturbances, probably due to interruptions to large fiber pathways that descend from these areas to the autonomic neurons of the lower brainstem and spinal cord.

The autonomic nervous system is divided into three main parts: the **sympathetic** and **parasympathetic nervous systems** and the **enteric nervous system**. The sympathetic and parasympathetic systems transmit commands to the glands and organs from the CNS. The enteric nervous system consists of neurons embedded in the lining of the gastrointestinal system, extending its entire length from the esophagus to the anus. Although the organs of the gastrointestinal system receive sympathetic and parasympathetic input as well, the enteric nervous system can act independently to control the functions of the gastrointestinal tract.

The action of the sympathetic and parasympathetic systems on their target organs is illustrated in ● Figure 2.26. These two systems usually have opposite effects on the same set of organs, so we traditionally view them as working like a toggle switch. Turning one system on can inhibit the other. It's difficult to imagine being aroused and resting at the same time. Nonetheless, it is overly simplistic to view these systems as mutually exclusive. There are many instances in which both systems operate cooperatively and simultaneously. A good example of the cooperation between the systems is sexual behavior. The parasympathetic system stimulates erection of the penis, and the sympathetic system stimulates ejaculation.

The parasympathetic division is typically activated by internal stimuli such as the arrival of food in the digestive system. In contrast, the sympathetic nervous system is activated by external environmental cues such as the sensing of danger.

THE SYMPATHETIC NERVOUS SYSTEM The sympathetic nervous system copes with emergencies by preparing the body for action. Human beings have two basic ways of dealing with an emergency. We can run, or we can fight. As a result, the sympathetic nervous system is known as our *fight-or-flight* system. You probably know all too well what this feels like because you probably have had a close call or two while driving your car. In this type of emergency, our hearts race, our breathing is rapid, the palms of our hands get sweaty, our faces are pale, and we are mentally alert and focused. All of these behaviors have been refined through millions of years of evolution to keep you alive when faced with an emergency.

The sympathetic nervous system prepares the body for fighting or fleeing by shutting down low-priority systems and putting blood and oxygen into the most necessary parts of the body. Salivation and digestion are put on standby. If you're facing a hungry lion on the Serengeti Plain, you don't need to worry about digesting your lunch unless you survive the encounter. Your heart and lungs operate to provide extra oxygen, which is fed to the large-muscle groups. Blood vessels near the skin's surface are constricted to channel blood to the large-muscle groups. Aside from giving you

biofeedback A set of techniques that enable people to control typically unconscious or involuntary functions such as blood pressure.
sympathetic nervous system The division of the autonomic nervous system that coordinates arousal.
parasympathetic nervous systems The division of the autonomic nervous system responsible for rest and energy storage.
enteric nervous system A division of the autonomic nervous system consisting of neurons embedded in the lining of the gastrointestinal system.

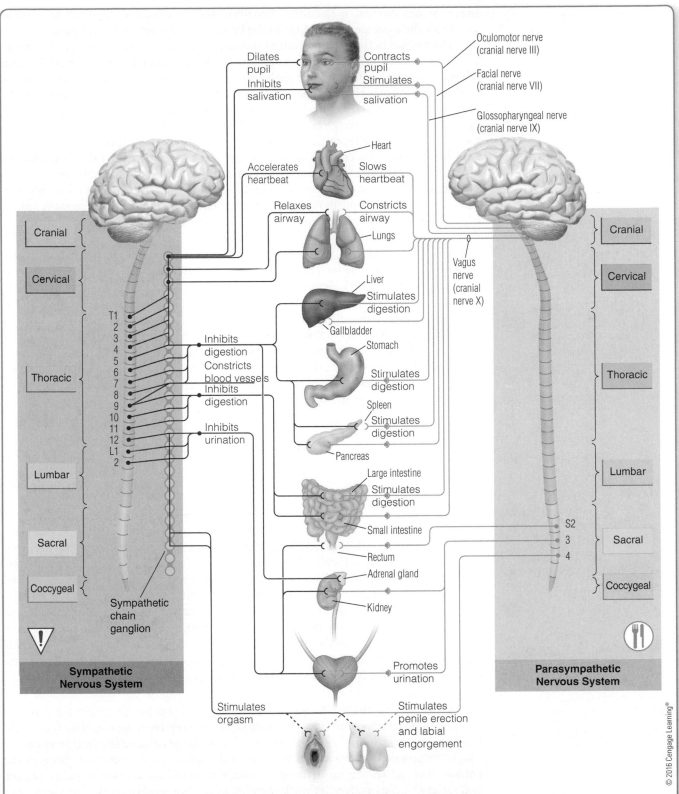

Dilates pupil
Inhibits salivation
Contracts pupil
Stimulates salivation

Oculomotor nerve (cranial nerve III)
Facial nerve (cranial nerve VII)
Glossopharyngeal nerve (cranial nerve IX)

Heart
Accelerates heartbeat
Slows heartbeat

Relaxes airway
Constricts airway
Lungs

Vagus nerve (cranial nerve X)

Liver
Stimulates digestion
Gallbladder

Inhibits digestion
Constricts blood vessels
Inhibits digestion

Stomach
Stimulates digestion

Spleen
Stimulates digestion

Inhibits urination

Pancreas

Large intestine
Stimulates digestion

Small intestine

Rectum

Adrenal gland

Kidney

Promotes urination

Stimulates orgasm
Stimulates penile erection and labial engorgement

Cranial
Cervical
Thoracic
Lumbar
Sacral
Coccygeal

T1
2
3
4
5
6
7
8
9
10
11
12
L1
2

Sympathetic chain ganglion

Cranial
Cervical
Thoracic
Lumbar
Sacral
Coccygeal

S2
3
4

Sympathetic Nervous System

Parasympathetic Nervous System

● **Figure 2.26** **The Autonomic Nervous System** The sympathetic and parasympathetic divisions of the autonomic nervous system often have opposite effects on target organs. To carry out their respective tasks, sympathetic neurons form their first synapse in the sympathetic chain, whereas parasympathetic neurons synapse on ganglia close to the target organs. In addition, the systems use different neurotransmitters at the target organ.

that pale look, you enjoy the added benefit of not bleeding very badly should you be cut. With the increased blood flow to the brain, mental alertness is at a peak.

The sympathetic nervous system is configured for a simultaneous, coordinated response to emergencies. Axons from neurons in the thoracic and lumbar segments of the spinal cord communicate with a series of ganglia just outside the cord known as the **sympathetic chain**. Fibers from cells in the sympathetic chain then communicate with target organs. Because the messages from the spinal neurons reach the sympathetic chain through fibers of equal length, they arrive at about the same time. Consequently, input from the sympathetic chain arrives at all of the target organs simultaneously. This coordinated response is essential for survival. It wouldn't be efficient for the heart to get a delayed message in the case of an emergency.

Because the same organs receive input from both the sympathetic and parasympathetic systems, it is important for the organs to have a way to identify the source of the input. This is accomplished through the types of chemical messengers used by the two systems. Both the sympathetic and parasympathetic systems communicate with cells in ganglia outside the spinal cord, which then form a second connection with a target organ. Both systems use the chemical messenger acetylcholine (ACh) to communicate with their ganglia (see Chapter 3). At the target organ, the parasympathetic nervous system continues to use ACh. The sympathetic nervous system, however, switches to another chemical messenger, norepinephrine, to communicate with target organs. The only exception is the connection between the sympathetic nerves and the sweat glands, where ACh is still used. This system of two chemical messengers provides a clear method of action at the target organ. If the heart, for instance, is stimulated by ACh, it will react by slowing. If it receives stimulation from norepinephrine, it will speed up. Survival depends on not having any ambiguities, mixed messages, or possibility of error.

THE PARASYMPATHETIC NERVOUS SYSTEM During times of sympathetic nervous system activity, the body is expending rather than storing energy. Obviously, the sympathetic nervous system can't run continuously, or the body would run out of resources. The job of the parasympathetic nervous system is to provide rest, repair, and energy storage.

Whereas the neurons for the sympathetic nervous system are found in the thoracic and lumbar regions of the spinal cord, the neurons for the parasympathetic nervous system are found above and below these regions, in the brain and sacral divisions of the spinal cord, specifically. This is the origin of the name *parasympathetic. Para* means around, and the neurons of the parasympathetic nervous system are around those of the sympathetic nervous system, like brackets or parentheses.

After exiting the brain and sacral spinal cord, parasympathetic axons do not synapse with a chain, as was the case with the sympathetic axons. Instead, they travel some distance to locations near their target organs, where the parasympathetic ganglia are located. Because timing is not as important to parasympathetic activity as it is to sympathetic activity, the coordination provided by a chain is not necessary.

THE ENTERIC NERVOUS SYSTEM Because of the number of neurons it contains along with its relative autonomy, the enteric nervous system, shown in ● Figure 2.27, has been referred to as "a second brain." The number of neurons in this system is roughly equivalent to the number found in the spinal cord. Some functions of the enteric nervous system contribute to conscious sensations, such as pain, hunger, and satiety, while much of its work remains below the level of conscious awareness.

The enteric nervous system communicates with endocrine cells that release a variety of hormones essential to digestion. A large number of gut endocrine cells associated with the enteric nervous system release the chemical messenger serotonin (see Chapter 4). Ninety-five percent of the serotonin in the body is released by the enteric nervous system, typically to control reflexes that move food through the system. Too much serotonin causes nausea and vomiting. It is interesting to note that not only do individuals with autism spectrum disorder (see Chapter 16) show higher than normal

sympathetic chain A string of cell bodies outside the spinal cord that receive input from sympathetic neurons in the central nervous system (CNS) and that communicate with target organs.

••• Building Better HEALTH

DO GLUTEN-FREE DIETS HAVE BENEFITS FOR PEOPLE WITH AUTISM SPECTRUM DISORDER?

Parents of children with autism spectrum disorder have often been vulnerable to "magic bullets" for improving their children's well-being, whether that is treatment in hyperbaric chambers or avoidance of vaccinations or other fads. One of the more popular fads has been the use of gluten-free and casein-free diets in an effort to improve the symptoms of autism spectrum disorder.

Why would diet be a possible target? Some evidence suggests that digestion is somewhat disrupted in individuals with autism spectrum disorder, as discussed in the section on the enteric nervous system. Theoretically, if you combine inadequate digestive enzymes to break down the proteins gluten and casein with a permeable gut, peptides can leak into the bloodstream, cross the blood–brain barrier, and interact with the nervous system, leading to symptoms of autism spectrum disorder.

As a result of publicity regarding this possibility, approximately 30 percent of children with autism spectrum disorder have been placed by their parents on a gluten-free and casein-free diet (Green et al., 2006). The diet is not without risks, as it can cause nutritional deficiencies leading to reduced bone development.

Very few studies on the gluten-free and casein-free diet use the optimum double blind-placebo controlled design, due to the inherent difficulties of providing a placebo diet that is not detectable. As a result, the positive results of some studies must be considered suspect on the basis of observer bias. A systematic review of the existing literature did not find empirical support for any benefits of the gluten-free and casein-free diet in autism spectrum disorder (Mulloy et al., 2010). Given the side effects of the diet, the authors recommend its use only when other objective testing has indicated an allergy or intolerance to gluten and casein.

---

levels of serotonin in their blood (Janusonis, 2008), but many experience gastrointestinal distress (Kazek et al., 2013).

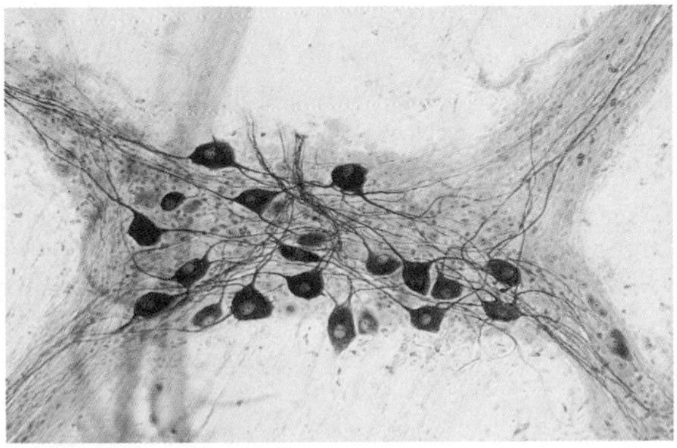

The Endocrine System

The hypothalamus directly controls the release of hormones by the glands making up the endocrine system, including the pineal gland, the pituitary gland, the thyroid gland, the adrenal glands, the islets of Langerhans in the pancreas, and the ovaries of females and testes of males.

The pineal gland plays an important role in the maintenance of our sleep–waking cycles, discussed in greater detail in Chapter 11. The pituitary gland is often referred to as the body's "master gland," because the hormones it releases activate many other glands. Pituitary activity can stimulate the release of sex hormones by the ovaries and testes (see Chapter 10) or the release of cortisol by the adrenal glands at times of stress (see Chapter 14). Other pituitary products include oxytocin and vasopressin, which contribute to bonding and parenting (see Chapter 10), and growth hormone. The islets of Langerhans produce a number of hormones essential to digestion, including insulin (see Chapter 9).

● **Figure 2.27** The Enteric Nervous System The enteric nervous system serves the gastrointestinal tract. Activity in this system is related to digestion, hunger, and satiety.

Biophoto Associates/Science Source

The Evolution of the Human Nervous System

The human genome, the set of DNA instructions for building a human being, is the result of millions of years of evolution. Brains are a relatively recent addition among living things, and our modern *Homo sapiens* brain may be only 100,000 to 200,000 years old.

● **Figure 2.28** Timeline for the Evolution of the Brain When compared with the entire time scale of evolution, nervous systems represent a very new development, appearing for the first time in the form of simple neural nets about 700 million years ago. Advanced brains, such as the human brain, are more recent still.

The first single-cell organisms would have emerged 18 hours ago.

The first nervous systems would have emerged about 3 hours and 45 minutes ago.

The first true brain would have emerged about 2 hours and 40 minutes ago.

The first hominin brain would have emerged less than 2.5 minutes ago.

And the current version of the human brain would have emerged less than 3 seconds ago.

© 2016 Cengage Learning®

Natural Selection and Evolution

As outlined in his 1859 *On the Origin of the Species,* Charles Darwin proposed that species evolve, or change from one version to the next, in an orderly manner. Modern biologists define evolution as "descent with modification from a common ancestor."

Darwin was well aware of the artificial selection procedures used by farmers to develop animals and plants with particular desirable traits. If a farmer's goal was to raise the strongest oxen, it was advisable to breed the strongest available oxen to each other. In these cases, the farmer makes the determination of which individuals have the opportunity to produce offspring. In **natural selection**, Darwin suggested that the pressures of survival and reproduction in the wild would take the place of the farmer. Natural selection favors the organism with the highest degree of **fitness**, or likelihood of reproducing successfully compared with others of the same species. Fitness is not some static characteristic, such as being strongest or fastest. Instead, fitness describes the successful interaction between an organism's characteristics and the environment in which it exists. An organism that succeeds during an ice age might be at a significant disadvantage during more temperate times.

Combining our modern understanding of genetics (see Chapter 5) with Darwin's work provides a basis for understanding the progression of species and their behavior. As Richard Dawkins (1982) reminds us, genes can replicate themselves but not without a lot of help from their friends. All genes in a single individual share the same fate. If that individual survives and reproduces, his or her genes will become more frequent in the next generation. At the same time, an individual's ability to survive and reproduce will be a function of the characteristics encoded by his or her genes.

Evolution of the Nervous System

Nervous systems are a rather recent development belonging only to animals. To begin our evolution timeline, illustrated in ● Figure 2.28, current estimates place the origin of Earth at about 4.5 billion years ago. Single-cell organisms appeared about 3.5 billion years ago,

natural selection The process by which favorable traits would become more common and unfavorable traits would become less common in subsequent generations due to differences among organisms in their ability to reproduce successfully.
fitness The ability of an organism with one genetic makeup to reproduce more successfully than organisms with other types of genetic makeup.

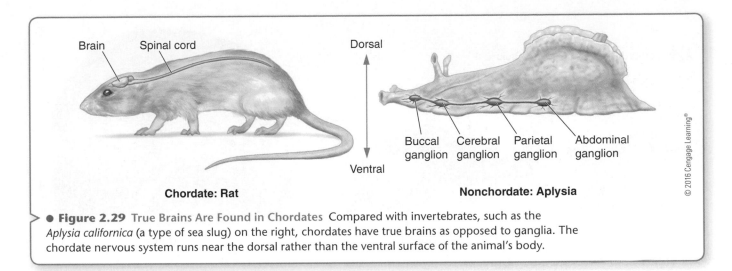

Chordate: Rat

Nonchordate: Aplysia

• **Figure 2.29** **True Brains Are Found in Chordates** Compared with invertebrates, such as the *Aplysia californica* (a type of sea slug) on the right, chordates have true brains as opposed to ganglia. The chordate nervous system runs near the dorsal rather than the ventral surface of the animal's body.

and animals with very simple nerve nets first developed about 700 million years ago. More complex animals, with the first rudimentary brains, appeared about 250 million years ago, and the first **hominin** brain probably appeared about 7 million years ago (Calvin, 2004).

The neural networks that developed early, such as those found in snails, consist of collections of cells, or ganglia, that control certain aspects of the animal's behavior in a particular region of the body. Although some of these ganglia are located in the head, they do not perform the central executive functions we normally attribute to a brain. The abdominal ganglia may perform behaviors that are just as crucial to the animal's survival as behaviors managed by ganglia in the head. In addition, most of these primitive nervous systems are located in the more vulnerable ventral, or belly side, of the animal where they are easily damaged or attacked. Because they lack a spinal column, such animals are referred to by biologists as invertebrates.

Animals with spinal columns and real brains are referred to as vertebrates, or **chordates** (see • Figure 2.29). Brains provide a number of advantages for chordates compared with the neural networks found in more primitive species. Unlike the ganglia of the invertebrate, the brain and spinal cord coordinate all of the animal's activity. The brain exerts this executive control from its vantage point in the head, close to the major sensory systems that provide information from the eyes, ears, nose, and mouth. With its centralized functions and ability to integrate sensory input, the brain of the first chordates to appear on the scene many millions of years ago enabled those animals to respond consistently and rapidly. The brains and spinal cords of the chordates enjoyed much more protection than the ganglia of the invertebrates. Not only were these important structures now encased in bone, but their location on the dorsal, or back, surface of the animal's body was easier to defend.

As shown in • Figure 2.30, the brains of chordates continued to develop, culminating in the very large brains found in mammals and birds. Early brains differ from more advanced brains in both size and degree of convolution, or folding, of the cortex. In addition, the size of the forebrain and cerebellum increased in more advanced chordate species.

Evolution of the Human Brain

Human beings are members of the primate order, a biological category that includes some 275 species of apes, monkeys, lemurs, tarsiers, and marmosets. We are further classified as being in the suborder of apes, the family of hominids, and the species of ***Homo sapiens***. The first modern *Homo sapiens* appeared between 100,000 and 200,000 years ago. By this point, early humans had migrated extensively throughout Europe and Asia. Their tool use appeared quite sophisticated, they hunted efficiently, and their culture, which included the ritual burial of their dead, was cooperative and social.

hominin A primate in the family Hominidae, of which *Homo sapiens* is the only surviving member.

chordates The phylum of animals that possess true brains and spinal cords. Also known as vertebrates.

Homo sapiens The species of modern humans.

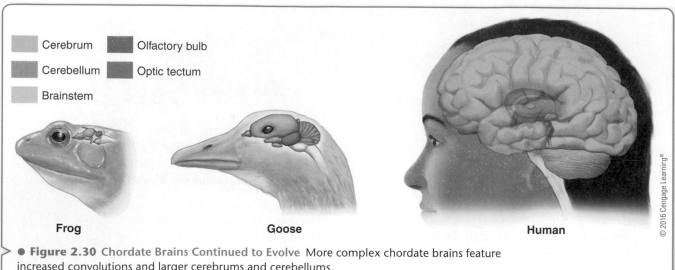

Cerebrum
Cerebellum
Brainstem
Olfactory bulb
Optic tectum

Frog   **Goose**   **Human**

© 2016 Cengage Learning®

> ● **Figure 2.30 Chordate Brains Continued to Evolve** More complex chordate brains feature increased convolutions and larger cerebrums and cerebellums.

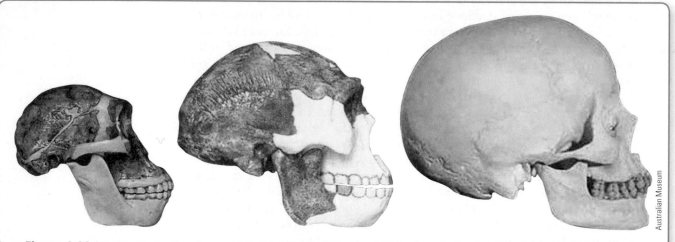

Australian Museum

> ● **Figure 2.31 Human Brain Development Proceeded Swiftly** Hominin brains advanced rapidly from those of the early australopithecines, shown on the left, who had brains about the size of modern chimpanzees, to *Homo erectus* (700 cm³; shown in the center), to *Homo sapiens* (1,400 cm³; shown on the far right). Brain development then appears to have leveled off. You are reading this text with essentially the same size brain that has worked for *Homo sapiens* for the past 200,000 years.

During the 7 million years since the first hominin species appeared, brain development appears to have occurred very quickly (see ● Figure 2.31). The early tool-using australopithecines had brains that were about the same size as that of a modern chimpanzee, around 400 cubic cm. *Homo erectus* had a brain of about 700 cubic cm, and modern human brains are around 1,400 cubic cm. Interactions among multiple factors, including body size, the long period of dependency in children, long life-spans, the need to adapt to changing climates, and the complexity of social life probably contributed to the rapid increase in hominin brain size (Charvet & Finlay, 2012). However, since the initial appearance of *Homo sapiens*, brain size has not changed much. What is unclear is why major cultural changes such as agriculture, urbanization, and literacy have not produced additional changes in brain size. Further increases in brain size might simply be too costly in terms of greater difficulties in childbirth and the need for more resources. Unless we experience a reduction in costs or pressure for even greater intelligence, we might have reached a balance between the advantages and disadvantages of large brains.

INTERIM SUMMARY 2.3

Summary Table: Major Structures of the Peripheral Nervous System

Structure	Function
Cranial nerves	Carry sensory and motor information between the brain and regions of the head and neck
Spinal nerves: cervical, thoracic, lumbar, sacral, coccygeal	Carry sensory and motor information between the spinal cord and the remainder of the body
Autonomic nervous system	Provides input to the glands and organs
Sympathetic division	Arousal
Parasympathetic division	Rest and repair
Enteric system	Moves food through digestive tract and provides feedback from gut to brain
Endocrine system	Releases hormones into the circulation under the direction of the hypothalamus

Summary Points

1. The PNS includes the cranial nerves, the spinal nerves, and the autonomic nervous system. The 12 pairs of cranial nerves exit the brain and provide sensory and motor functions to the head, neck, and internal organs. The 31 pairs of spinal nerves perform the same functions for the rest of the body. **(LO6)**

2. The autonomic nervous system processes sensory and motor information to and from glands, organs, and smooth muscle. The sympathetic nervous system operates during times of arousal and prepares the body for fight-or-flight reactions. The parasympathetic nervous system operates during times of rest and restoration. The enteric nervous system moves food through the gut and provides feedback to the CNS. **(LO6)**

3. The endocrine system consists of glands that release important hormones into the blood that regulate arousal, growth, metabolism, and sex. **(LO6)**

4. True brains evolved relatively recently. Hominin brain evolution featured very rapid increases in brain size. **(LO7)**

Review Questions

1. How are the spinal nerves organized once they exit the cord?

2. How are the structures of the sympathetic and parasympathetic nervous systems well suited to their functions?

Chapter Review

THOUGHT QUESTIONS

1. Given your understanding of the functions of the basal ganglia, why are these structures suspected of playing a role in attention deficit hyperactivity disorder (ADHD) and obsessive-compulsive disorder (OCD)?
2. Given your understanding of frontal lobe functions, what objectionable side effects might result from a frontal lobotomy?
3. What types of challenges facing human populations today might result in natural selection?

KEY TERMS

amygdala (p. 42)
anterior (p. 27)
anterior commissure (p. 47)
arachnoid layer (p. 28)
association cortex (p. 45)
autonomic nervous system (p. 51)
basal ganglia (p. 40)
brainstem (p. 35)
caudal (p. 26)
central canal (p. 29)
central nervous system (CNS) (p. 33)
central sulcus (p. 44)
cerebellum (p. 35)
cerebral aqueduct (p. 38)
cerebral hemisphere (p. 39)
cerebrospinal fluid (CSF) (p. 29)
chordates (p. 59)
cingulate cortex (p. 43)
contralateral (p. 27)
coronal/frontal section (p. 27)
corpus callosum (p. 47)
cranial nerve (p. 51)
diencephalon (p. 39)
distal (p. 27)
dorsal (p. 26)
dorsolateral prefrontal cortex (DLPC) (p. 47)
dura mater (p. 28)
enteric nervous system (p. 54)

forebrain (p. 35)
frontal lobe (p. 44)
gray matter (p. 35)
gyrus/gyri (p. 43)
hindbrain (p. 35)
hippocampus (p. 41)
hominin (p. 59)
Homo sapiens (p. 59)
horizontal/axial/transverse section (p. 28)
hypothalamus (p. 40)
inferior (p. 27)
ipsilateral (p. 27)
lateral (p. 27)
limbic system (p. 41)
locus coeruleus (p. 37)
medial (p. 27)
medulla/myelencephalon (p. 35)
meninges (p. 28)
mesencephalon (p. 38)
metencephalon (p. 37)
midbrain (p. 35)
midline (p. 27)
nucleus accumbens (p. 40)
occipital lobe (p. 44)
orbitofrontal cortex (p. 47)
parasympathetic nervous system (p. 54)
parietal lobe (p. 44)

periaqueductal gray (p. 38)
peripheral nervous system (PNS) (p. 33)
pia mater (p. 29)
pituitary gland (p. 40)
pons (p. 35)
postcentral gyrus (p. 45)
posterior (p. 27)
precentral gyrus (p. 46)
proximal (p. 27)
raphe nuclei (p. 37)
reflex (p. 35)
reticular formation (p. 37)
rostral (p. 26)
sagittal section (p. 27)
somatic nervous system (p. 51)
spinal cord (p. 33)
subarachnoid space (p. 29)
substantia nigra (p. 38)
sulcus/sulci (p. 43)
superior (p. 27)
sympathetic nervous system (p. 54)
telencephalon (p. 39)
temporal lobe (p. 44)
thalamus (p. 39)
ventral (p. 26)
ventricle (p. 29)
white matter (p. 34)

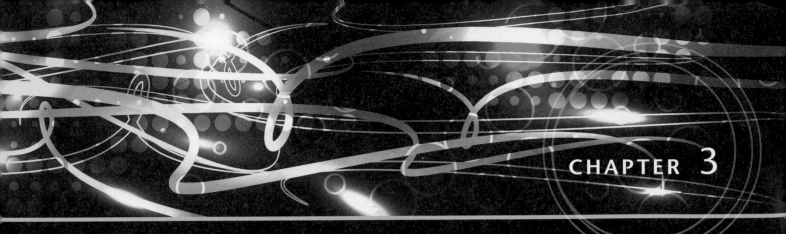

CHAPTER **3**

Neurophysiology: The Structure and Functions of the Cells of the Nervous System

LEARNING OBJECTIVES

L01 Differentiate between glia and neurons.

L02 Identify the major types, structures, and functions of the glia.

L03 Describe the structural features and functions of the cell membrane, cytoskeleton, cell body, axons, and dendrites.

L04 Differentiate between the structural and functional types of neurons.

L05 Explain the processes responsible for electrical and chemical signaling.

L06 Differentiate between EPSPs and IPSPs, and explain the process of neural integration.

L07 Summarize the processes used by some neurons to modulate activity of other neurons.

CHAPTER OUTLINE

CONNECTING TO RESEARCH: Astrocytes, HIV, and the Blood–Brain Barrier

THINKING ETHICALLY: Lethal Injection

BEHAVIORAL NEUROSCIENCE GOES TO WORK: What Are We Reading in an ECG or EEG?

BUILDING BETTER HEALTH: Eradicating Tetanus Worldwide

Glia and Neurons

The great architect Frank Lloyd Wright was fond of saying that "form follows function." That same wisdom applies not only to good architecture, but also to biology. The structure of our nervous system has been shaped through the course of evolution to carry out functions essential to survival and reproduction.

The nervous system is made up of two types of cells, **glia** and **neurons**. The glia, whose name comes from the Greek word for *glue*, serve a variety of support functions for neurons. The neuron is specialized to carry out the functions of information processing and communication. The neurons and glia cooperate to carry out nervous system functions. First, we will consider the supportive glia, followed by a detailed discussion of the structure and function of neurons.

Glia

Glia are cells in the nervous system that support the activities of neurons. These cells are generally categorized by size. The **macroglia** are the largest varieties of glial cells, and the **microglia** are the smaller varieties.

MACROGLIA There are three primary types of macroglia: astrocytes, oligodendrocytes, and Schwann cells. The **astrocytes** provide a variety of support functions to neurons, whereas the **oligodendrocytes** and **Schwann cells** supply the myelin covering that insulates axon fibers.

Astrocytes get their name from their starlike shape, which is evident in ● Figure 3.1. Astrocytes are the most common type of glia in the brain. One of the primary functions of the astrocytes is to provide a structural matrix for the neurons. Otherwise,

glia Cells in the nervous system that support the activities of neurons.

neuron A cell of the nervous system that is specialized for information processing and communication.

macroglia Large glial cells, including astrocytes, oligodendrocytes, and Schwann cells.

microglia Tiny, mobile glial cells that migrate to areas of damage and digest debris.

astrocyte A large, star shaped glial cell of the central nervous system (CNS), responsible for structural support, isolation of the synapse, control of the extracellular chemical environment at the synapse, and possibly communication.

oligodendrocyte A glial cell that forms the myelin on central nervous system (CNS) axons.

Schwann cell A glial cell that forms the myelin on axons in the peripheral nervous system (PNS).

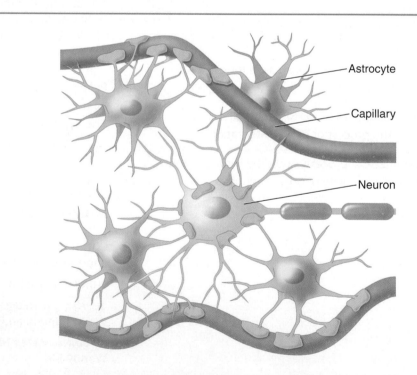

© 2016 Cengage Learning®

> ● **Figure 3.1 Astrocytes** Astrocytes have several support functions. Through their close association with the blood supply, astrocytes help transfer nutrients to neurons and block the movement of some circulating toxins into neural tissue. Astrocytes also provide a structural matrix for neurons, holding them in place.

the neurons would be literally floating around in the extracellular fluid. In reality, neurons occupy a cramped space controlled by the adjacent astrocytes.

Astrocytes form close connections with the capillary cells of the brain, making what is known as "neurovascular units." The close association of astrocytes with the capillary cells allows these glia to transfer glucose and other nutrients to the neurons. Astrocytes contribute to the protective **blood–brain barrier**. The blood–brain barrier prevents most toxins circulating in the blood from entering the brain. Astrocytes help form the blood–brain barrier by literally covering the outer surface of capillaries with their endfeet, large structures at each end of the astrocyte's branches.

Astrocytes surround and isolate the area of the synapse. Neurochemicals are very active, and it is not in our best interests to have them floating every which way. The astrocytes keep the neurochemicals from moving outside a restricted area. In addition, astrocytes can clear molecules from the synaptic gap. As we will see shortly, neurons release potassium ions when they send messages, and the astrocytes have the important ability to remove excess potassium from the extracellular fluid.

On occasion, astrocytes behave in ways that are far from helpful. When central nervous system (CNS) neurons are damaged, astrocytes form scar tissue that fills the area previously occupied by the now dead neurons and release chemicals that inhibit neural regrowth. Although the response of the astrocytes to injury may be helpful in the overall healing process, it also interferes with the repairing of damaged connections. A major area of glial research is focused on preventing these outcomes in cases of brain or spinal injury (Davies et al., 2006; Jurynec et al., 2003).

The astrocytes' role may be even more important than previously thought. Neurons grown in Petri dishes along with astrocytes are 10 times more responsive than neurons grown alone (Pfrieger & Barres, 1997). Follow-up research showed that the astrocytes were signaling the neurons to build synapses (Ullian, Sapperstein, Christopherson, & Barres, 2001). This suggests an important role for astrocytes in the development of the brain and in learning and memory, which involve the reorganization of synaptic connections between neurons (Min & Nevian, 2012; see Chapter 12).

Astrocytes also play an important and active role in the chemical signaling that occurs in the brain. Astrocytes influence adjacent neurons and other astrocytes by releasing the amino acid glutamate and the energy molecule adenosine triphosphate (ATP) (Fellin et al., 2006). Glutamate serves as an important excitatory chemical messenger in the brain, while a byproduct of ATP, adenosine, exerts inhibitory effects (see Chapter 4). Consequently, astrocytes have the ability to both excite and suppress the activity of neighboring neurons and other astrocytes.

An improved understanding of this signaling role of astrocytes will be very helpful in managing many brain diseases. Although glutamate is an important neurochemical, too much glutamate kills neurons (Farber, Newcomer, & Olney, 1998). If glial cells release too much glutamate in response to damage, such as a stroke, many nearby neurons will die. Medical treatments limiting the release of glutamate by astrocytes should reduce the loss of neurons associated with many common brain disorders (Hines & Haydon, 2013).

The other types of macroglia, oligodendrocytes and Schwann cells, provide the myelin covering that insulates some nerve fibers or axons (Peters, Palay, & Webster, 1991). Oligodendrocytes form myelin in the CNS, and Schwann cells supply the myelin for the peripheral nervous system (PNS). As shown in ● Figure 3.2, a single oligodendrocyte puts out a number of branches that wrap themselves around the axons of adjacent neurons. Because a single oligodendrocyte can myelinate axons from an average of 15 different neurons, these macroglia contribute to the structural stability of the brain and spinal cord. In contrast, a single Schwann cell provides a single myelin segment on one peripheral axon. It takes large numbers of Schwann cells to myelinate a peripheral nerve.

blood-brain barrier An impediment to the transfer of molecules from the circulation into the brain formed by the astrocytes.

● **Figure 3.2**
Oligodendrocytes and Schwann Cells (a) Each oligodendrocyte in the central nervous system (CNS) sends out branches that form myelin segments on an average of 15 different axons. (b) The Schwann cells perform a similar function in the peripheral nervous system (PNS), although each Schwann cell forms only one segment of myelin.

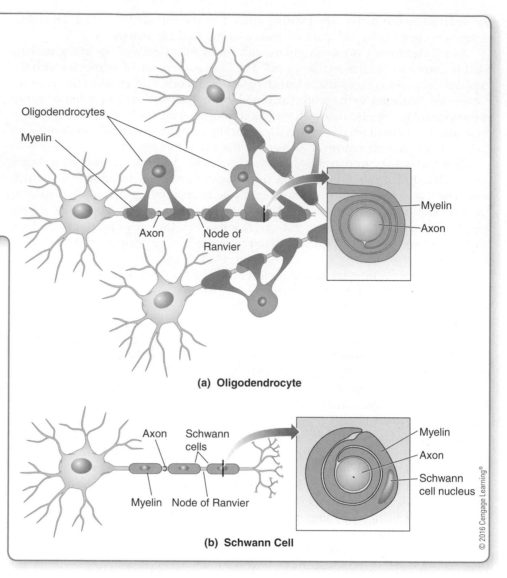

(a) **Oligodendrocyte**

(b) **Schwann Cell**

© 2016 Cengage Learning®

© Kai Forsterling/epa/Corbis

● **Figure 3.3** Regrowth of Peripheral Axons Makes Body Part Transplants Possible Alba Lucia Cardona of Columbia lost both arms 30 years ago in a laboratory explosion. Spanish doctors recently transplanted two cadaver arms onto Cardona's body, a process that would not make sense without the ability of peripheral nerves to regenerate and reestablish some movement and sensation in the attached body parts. Unfortunately, duplicating this success in the central nervous system (CNS) remains a challenge for scientists attempting to repair damage to the spinal cord and brain.

We can see the importance of myelin by studying conditions in which it is damaged. The disease multiple sclerosis (MS) involves a progressive demyelination of the nervous system (see Chapter 15). The end result is neural signaling that may not work properly, leading to a range of symptoms from mild (increased fatigue) to more severe (vision and mobility problems) to death.

Oligodendrocytes and Schwann cells differ in their reactions to injury. Schwann cells actually help guide the regrowth of damaged axons, whereas the oligodendrocytes lack this capacity. If axon regrowth were impossible in the PNS, we would not bother to re-attach severed fingers or limbs (see ● Figure 3.3). Surgeons are even transplanting hands and faces from cadavers to living people, which would be pointless unless nerve growth eventually provided some sensation and motor control (Petit, Minns, Dubernard, Hettiaratchy, & Lee, 2003).

MICROGLIA You may not particularly like the idea of having "brain debris," but like any cells, neurons and glia do die. Rather than leave the debris lying around where it might interfere with neural function, microglia serve as the brain's cleanup crew. At rest, the branches of microglia reach out and sample their immediate environments (Nimmerjahn, Kirchhoff, & Helmchen, 2005). Should they detect any one of the many types of molecules related to cell damage, whether from head injury, stroke, or other sources, these tiny cells travel to the location of the injury, where they digest the debris.

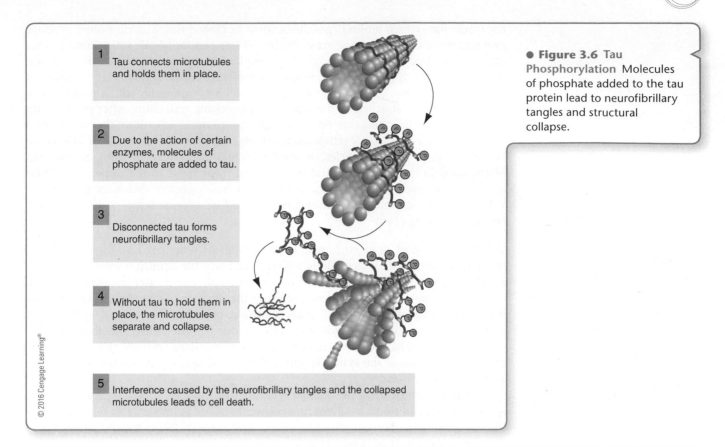

1 Tau connects microtubules and holds them in place.

2 Due to the action of certain enzymes, molecules of phosphate are added to tau.

3 Disconnected tau forms neurofibrillary tangles.

4 Without tau to hold them in place, the microtubules separate and collapse.

5 Interference caused by the neurofibrillary tangles and the collapsed microtubules leads to cell death.

● **Figure 3.6** Tau Phosphorylation Molecules of phosphate added to the tau protein lead to neurofibrillary tangles and structural collapse.

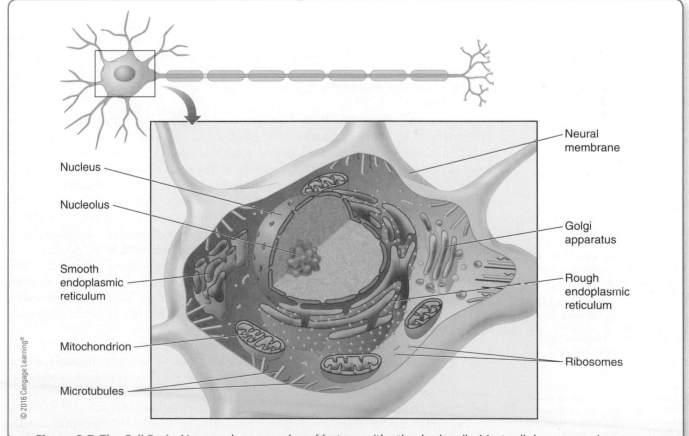

Neural membrane

Nucleus

Nucleolus

Golgi apparatus

Smooth endoplasmic reticulum

Rough endoplasmic reticulum

Mitochondrion

Ribosomes

Microtubules

> ● **Figure 3.7** The Cell Body Neurons share a number of features with other body cells. Most cells have a membrane, a nucleus, a nucleolus, mitochondria, ribosomes, smooth and rough endoplasmic reticuli, and Golgi apparati.

the **nucleolus**, which builds organelles known as **ribosomes**. The ribosomes produce proteins either on their own or in association with the **endoplasmic reticulum**, another organelle located in the cell body. The endoplasmic reticulum may be divided into rough and smooth portions. The rough endoplasmic reticulum has many ribosomes bound to its surface, giving it the bumpy appearance responsible for its name. There are no ribosomes attached to the smooth endoplasmic reticulum. After proteins are constructed by the ribosomes on the rough endoplasmic reticulum, they are moved by the smooth endoplasmic reticulum to a **Golgi apparatus**. This organelle inserts the completed proteins into vesicles, or small packages made out of membrane material. **Mitochondria** extract oxygen and pyruvic acid from sugar in the intracellular fluid and construct and release molecules of ATP, the major energy source for the neuron. Wherever you see many mitochondria, you can be sure activities requiring much energy are taking place.

DENDRITES Most neurons have a large number of branches known as dendrites, from the Greek word for *tree*. Along with the cell body, the dendrites serve as locations at which information from other neurons is received. The greater the surface area of dendritic membrane a neuron has, the larger the number of connections or synapses it can form with other neurons. At each synapse on a dendrite, special ligand-gated ion channels serving as receptor sites are embedded in the neural membrane. These receptor sites interact with molecules of **neurotransmitter** released by adjacent neurons that float across the **synaptic gap**, a fluid-filled space between the transmitting and receiving neurons.

Some dendrites form knobs known as **dendritic spines**. As illustrated in ● Figure 3.8, spines provide additional locations for synapses to occur. Spines are able to change their shape based on the amount of activity occurring at the synapse, which contributes to the processes of learning and memory (see Chapter 12).

THE AXON Although a neuron may have large numbers of dendrites, it typically has only one axon, as shown in ● Figure 3.8. The axon is responsible for carrying messages to other neurons. The cone-shaped segment of axon that lies at the junction of the axon and the cell body is known as the **axon hillock**. Electrical signals known as **action potentials** arise in the axon hillock and are then reproduced down the length of the axon.

Axons vary substantially in diameter. In vertebrates, including humans, axon diameters range from less than 1 micrometer (μm, or 10^{-6} meter) to about 25 micrometers. In invertebrates, such as the squid, axon diameter can be as large as 1 mm, or over 1000 times larger than the smallest vertebrate axons. Axon diameter is crucial to the speed of signaling. Larger diameter axons are much faster than smaller diameter axons. Does this mean that the squid thinks faster than we do? Not at all. As we mentioned in the section on macroglia, many vertebrate axons are insulated by **myelin**, a material that allows for rapid signal transmission in spite of smaller axon diameter.

In addition to varying in diameter, axons also vary in length. Some neurons have axons that barely extend from the cell body to communicate with adjacent cells. These neurons are referred to as **local circuit neurons**. Other neurons, known as **projection neurons**, have very long axons. Consider for a moment that you have neural cell bodies in your spinal cord with axons that extend as far as your big toe. Depending on your height, these axons can be three feet long or more.

A neuron with only one axon can still communicate with a large number of other cells. The ends of many axons are divided into branches, known as **collaterals**. At the very end of each axon collateral is a swelling known as the **axon terminal**. Additional swellings, or **axonal varicosities**, occur at intervals along the length of unmyelinated segments of axon. Axon terminals and axonal varicosities contain both mitochondria and synaptic vesicles, from which neurochemicals can be released. **Synaptic vesicles** are made from the same double-lipid molecule structure as the cell membrane and are approximately 40 nm in diameter.

nucleolus A substructure within a cell nucleus where ribosomes are produced.

ribosome An organelle in the cell body involved with protein synthesis.

endoplasmic reticulum An organelle in the cell body that participates in protein synthesis.

Golgi apparatus An organelle in the cell body that packages proteins in vesicles.

mitochondria Organelles that provide energy to the cell by transforming pyruvic acid and oxygen into molecules of adenosine triphosphate (ATP).

neurotransmitter A chemical messenger that transfers information across a synapse.

synaptic gap The tiny fluid-filled space between neurons at a synapse.

dendritic spine A knob on the dendrite that provides additional membrane area for the formation of synapses with other neurons.

axon hillock The cone-shaped segment of axon located at the junction of the axon and cell body that is specialized for the generation of action potentials.

action potential The nerve impulse arising in an axon.

myelin The fatty insulating material covering some axons that boosts the speed and efficiency of electrical signaling.

local circuit neuron A neuron that communicates with neurons in its immediate vicinity.

projection neuron A neuron with a very long axon that communicates with neurons in distant areas of the nervous system.

collateral One of the branches near the end of the axon closest to its targets.

axon terminal The swelling at the tip of an axon collateral specialized for the release of neurochemicals.

axonal varicosity A swelling in an unmyelinated segment of axon containing mitochondria and in some cases, synaptic vesicles.

synaptic vesicles A small structure in the axon terminal that contains neurochemicals.

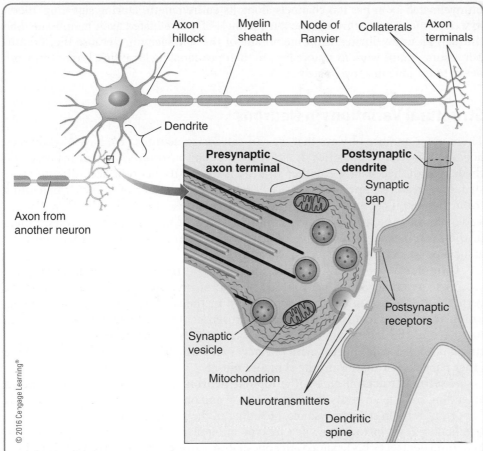

● **Figure 3.8** Axons and Dendrites Action potentials originate in the axon hillock and then travel the length of the axon to the axon terminal. The arrival of action potentials at the axon terminal signals the release of neurotransmitters from the synaptic vesicles. Molecules of neurotransmitter diffuse across the synaptic gap, where they interact with receptors embedded in the dendrite of the adjacent neuron.

Many, but not all, axons in vertebrate nervous systems are covered by myelin. In the adult human, the vast majority of CNS neurons and peripheral motor neurons are myelinated. Peripheral sensory nerves may or may not be myelinated, with the smallest diameter fibers less likely to be so (see Chapter 7). Myelin does not cover the entire length of an axon. The axon hillock is completely uncovered and between each myelin segment there is a bare space of axon membrane known as a **node of Ranvier**. Nodes of Ranvier are about 1 micrometer long (1 millionth of a meter) and occur somewhere between 0.2 mm and 2.0 mm apart down the length of the axon, depending on both the diameter and length of the axon. Large diameter axons have thicker myelin and greater distances between nodes of Ranvier.

There are a number of important advantages to myelin. First of all, as mentioned earlier, myelin allows human axons to be smaller in diameter without sacrificing transmission speed. Space is a precious commodity in the nervous system. The smaller the diameter of our axons, the more neural tissue we can pack into our skulls, and the more information we can process. In addition, myelin reduces the energy requirements of neurons by decreasing the amount of work done by sodium-potassium pumps. Myelin segments wrap so tightly around axons that there is little to no extracellular fluid between the myelin and the axon membrane. As a result, there is no need for ion channels under a myelin sheath. The only places on a myelinated axon that have large numbers of ion channels are the axon hillock and the nodes of Ranvier. In contrast, an

node of Ranvier The uncovered section of axon membrane between two adjacent segments of myelin.

unmyelinated axon has ion channels along its entire length. During signaling, therefore, fewer ions move through the ion channels of a myelinated axon membrane than through an unmyelinated axon membrane of the same length. Because the sodium-potassium pumps work to restore ions to their presignaling locations, less of this work needs to be done in a myelinated axon.

Structural Variations in Neurons

There are a number of ways that we can categorize neurons. We have already seen how neurons can be classified as either local circuit or projection neurons based on the length of their axons. Another strategy is to classify neurons according to other structural features. Specifically, we will look at the number of branches extending from the neural cell body. As we said earlier, form usually does follow function, so understanding the form of a neuron provides insight into the possible roles it plays in the nervous system. A sample of different structural types of neurons and their associated functions can be seen in ● Figure 3.9.

Unipolar neurons have a single branch extending from the cell body, as indicated by the name. These neurons are typical of invertebrate nervous systems. In vertebrates like us, unipolar cells are found in the sensory systems. For example, unipolar cells are involved with the somatosenses (touch, temperature, and pain). Just beyond the cell body of a unipolar neuron in the somatosensory system, the single branch divides in two, with one part extending back toward the CNS and the other part extending toward the skin and muscle.

A second structural type is the **bipolar neuron**. These cells have two branches extending from the neural cell body: one axon and one dendrite. Bipolar neurons play important roles in sensory systems, including in the retina of the eye (see Chapter 6). In Chapter 2, we introduced a special type of bipolar cell known as a spindle or von Economo neuron (VEN), named after one of its discoverers (von Economo & Koskinas, 1929). These cells occur in the anterior cingulate cortex (ACC), in the junction of the frontal lobe and insula area of the temporal lobe, and in the dorsolateral prefrontal cortex in humans, great apes, elephants, and members of the whale family. Although their exact function is not well understood, the VENs appear to be specifically designed to provide fast, intuitive assessments of complex situations (Allman, Watson, Tetreault, & Hakeem, 2005). It is possible that these cells are particularly important to assessing and performing the complex social behaviors that characterize the very intelligent species that possess them.

The most common structural type of neuron in the vertebrate nervous system is the **multipolar neuron**. Multipolar neurons have many branches extending from the cell body. Usually, this means that the cell has one axon and numerous dendrites. Multipolar neurons may be further classified according to shape. For example, pyramidal cells in the cerebral cortex and the hippocampus have cell bodies that are shaped like pyramids. The Purkinje cells of the cerebellum have dramatic dendritic trees that allow a single cell to form as many as 150,000 synapses.

Functional Variations in Neurons

Neurons can be classified according to the roles they play within the nervous system. **Sensory neurons** are specialized to receive information from the outside world and from within our bodies. Our senses of vision, hearing, touch, taste, smell, and pain all depend on specialized receptor neurons. These neurons can translate many types of information, such as light or sound waves, into neural signals that the nervous system can process. **Motor neurons** transmit commands from the CNS (the brain and spinal cord) directly to muscles and glands. The vast majority of neurons are known as **interneurons**. Interneurons are not specialized for either sensory or motor functions but act as bridges between the sensory and motor systems.

unipolar neuron A neuron with one branch that extends a short distance from the cell body then splits into two branches.

bipolar neuron A neuron with two branches extending from the cell body: one axon and one dendrite.

multipolar neuron A neuron that has multiple branches extending from the cell body, usually one axon and numerous dendrites.

sensory neuron A specialized neuron that translates incoming sensory information into electrical signals.

motor neuron A specialized neuron that communicates with muscles and glands.

interneuron A neuron that serves as a bridge between sensory and motor neurons.

Type	Appearance	Location	Examples of Some Functions
Unipolar neuron	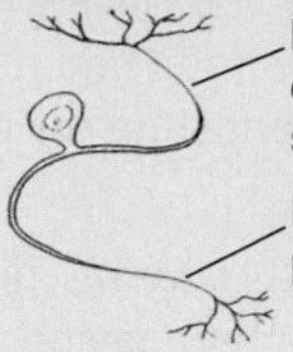 Branch to the central nervous system / Branch to the periphery	Near spinal cord, with processes extending to skin, muscle, organs, and glands	Transmits information about touch, skin temperature, and pain
Bipolar neuron	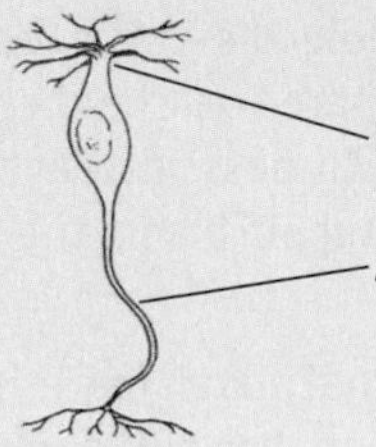 Dendrite / Axon	Retina Cochlea Olfactory bulb Tongue	Transmits information in several sensory systems
	Dendrite / Axon — Von Economo neuron (VEN)	Anterior cingulate cortex (ACC) Insula	Provides fast, intuitive assessments of complex situations
Multipolar	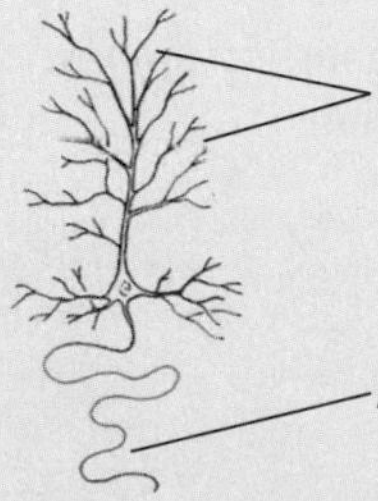 Dendrites / Axon — Pyramidal cell	Cerebral cortex	Participates in movement and cognition
	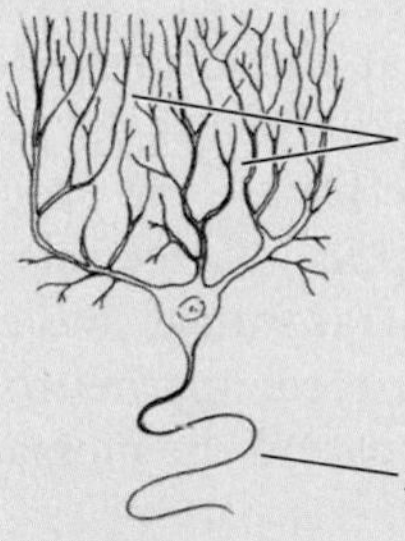 Dendrites / Axon — Purkinje cell	Cerebellum	Participates in movement
	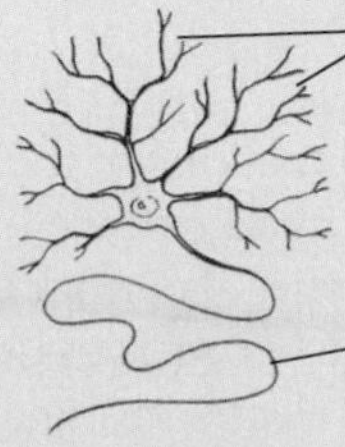 Dendrites / Axon — Motor neuron	Spinal cord, with axons extending to muscles and glands	Carries commands to muscles and glands

● **Figure 3.9 Structural and Functional Classification of Neurons** Unipolar and bipolar neurons are usually found in vertebrate sensory systems, where they encode and transmit information from the outside world or from within the body. Multipolar neurons typically serve as motor neurons, carrying commands to glands and muscles, or interneurons, serving as bridges between sensory and motor neurons.

INTERIM SUMMARY 3.1

Summary Points

1. The nervous system is made up of two types of cells, glia and neurons. Glia perform a variety of support functions and neurons are responsible for processing and communicating information. **(LO1)**

2. Macroglia provide a variety of support functions to neurons, including the formation of myelin. Microglia remove debris resulting from damage to neurons. **(LO2)**

3. The neural membrane is composed of a two-molecule-thick layer of phospholipids. Embedded within the phospholipid membrane are ion channels and pumps, which are specialized proteins that allow chemicals to pass into and out of the neuron. The neural cytoskeleton provides structural support and the ability to transport needed substances within the neuron. **(LO3)**

4. The cell body contains important organelles that participate in the basic metabolism and protein synthesis of the cell. In addition, the cell body is a site of synapses with other neurons. **(LO3)**

5. Neurons communicate with other cells through special branches known as axons and dendrites. **(LO3)**

6. Neurons may be classified according to the number of branches extending from their cell bodies and by their functions. **(LO4)**

Review Questions

1. What are the different functions carried out by the macroglia and microglia?

2. What are the roles of the dendrites and dendritic spines, and what structural features enable them to carry out these functions?

Generating Action Potentials

Now that we know the major structures involved in neural communication, we are ready to talk about how the process actually works. The first step in neural communication is the development of an electrical signal, the action potential, in the axon hillock of the neuron that is sending information, known as the presynaptic neuron. When the action potential arrives at the axon terminal, the process switches from electrical to chemical signaling. The presynaptic neuron releases molecules of neurotransmitter from its terminal. The neurotransmitter molecules float across the synaptic gap to the waiting postsynaptic, or receiving neuron. It is then up to the postsynaptic neuron to determine whether to send the message along.

The Ionic Composition of the Intracellular and Extracellular Fluids

In our discussion of the neural membrane, we found that one of the important responsibilities of the membrane is to keep the intracellular and extracellular fluids apart. In addition, the sodium-potassium pumps discussed earlier also work to maintain the differences between these two fluids. It is the difference between these two types of fluid that provides the neuron with a source of energy for electrical signaling.

The intracellular and extracellular fluids share a common ingredient, water, but differ from each other in the relative concentrations of ions they contain. When certain chemicals are dissolved in water, they take the form of ions. For example, table salt (sodium chloride, or NaCl) dissolves in water, forming separate sodium ions (Na⁺) and chloride ions (Cl⁻). The ions remain separate rather than rejoining to form salt because their attraction to water is stronger than their attraction to each other. The plus and minus signs associated with each type of ion indicates its electrical charge. This, in turn, is a function of the ion's relative numbers of protons and electrons. A negatively charged ion has more electrons than protons, whereas a positively charged ion has fewer electrons than protons.

As shown in ● Figure 3.10, extracellular fluid is characterized by large concentrations of sodium and chloride ions and a relatively small concentration of potassium (K⁺) ions. If you have difficulty remembering which ions go where, keep in mind that extracellular fluid is very similar to seawater. Single cell organisms interacted directly with seawater. As organisms became more complex, they essentially packaged some seawater within their bodies, such that their individual cells remained in the same environment as before.

Intracellular fluid is quite different from extracellular fluid. The intracellular fluid of the resting neuron contains large numbers of potassium ions and relatively few sodium and chloride ions. In addition, within the intracellular fluid there are some large proteins in ion form that are negatively charged.

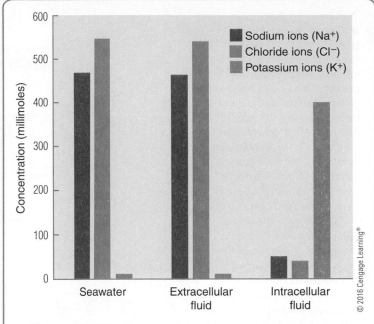

● **Figure 3.10** **The Composition of Intracellular and Extracellular Fluids** Extracellular fluid is similar to seawater, with large concentrations of sodium and chloride but small concentrations of potassium. Intracellular fluid has a large concentration of potassium but relatively little sodium and chloride.

Source: Data from Doumin (2004) and Smock (1999).

Because of the distribution of ions and other charged particles, particularly the large, negatively charged proteins, the electrical environment inside the neuron is more negative than it is on the outside. How do we know? As shown in ● Figure 3.11, we can actually record the difference between the two environments by inserting a tiny glass microelectrode through the membrane of the neuron itself. We can use a voltmeter to measure the difference between the microelectrode and a wire placed in the extracellular fluid adjacent to our cell. We use the same process when measuring the amount of charge left in a battery. The difference between the positive and negative terminals in a car battery is 12 volts. In contrast, the difference between the inside and outside of a neuron is approximately 70 millivolts (mV). A millivolt is one one-thousandth of a volt, so your neurons definitely work on a different scale of electricity than that of your car. It is conventional to assign the extracellular environment a value of 0; thus, we speak of this 70mV difference across the membrane as negative, or –70mV. Because this difference is measured when the cell is not processing a message, it is known as the **resting potential** of the cell.

The Movement of Ions

Electrical signals in an axon, or action potentials, result from the movement of ions. To understand the development of these signals, we need to review the forces that cause ions to move.

Diffusion is the tendency for molecules to distribute themselves equally within a medium such as air or water. In other words, like city dwellers seeking the quiet countryside, molecules will move from a crowded location to a less crowded location. In more formal terms, diffusion pressure moves molecules along a **concentration gradient** from areas of high concentration to areas of low concentration. Another important cause of movement of molecules is **electrostatic pressure**. As you may

resting potential The measurement of the electrical charge across the neural membrane when the cell is not processing information.
diffusion The force that moves molecules from areas of high concentration to areas of low concentration.
concentration gradient An unequal distribution in the concentration of molecules across a cell membrane.
electrostatic pressure The force that moves molecules with like electrical charges apart and molecules with opposite electrical charges together.

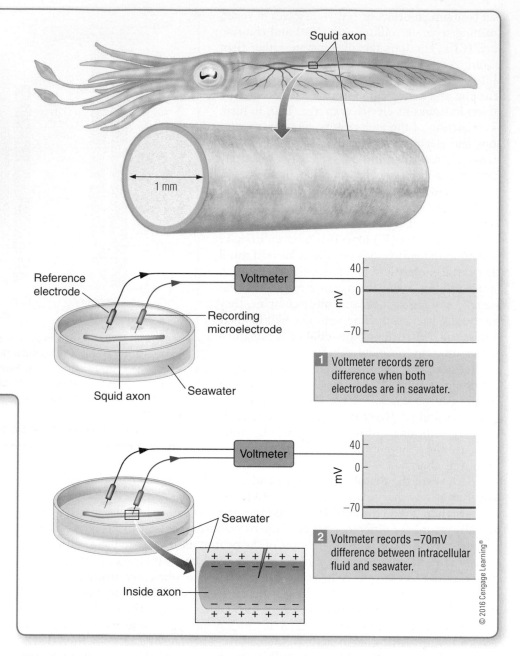

● **Figure 3.11** Measuring the Resting Potential of Neurons Axons from invertebrates like the squid can be dissected and maintained in a culture dish for study. Because these axons are so large in diameter, electrodes can be inserted into the intracellular fluid. If we compare the recordings from two electrodes, one located in the intracellular fluid of the axon and the other in the extracellular fluid, our recording shows that the inside of the cell is negatively charged relative to the outside. The relatively larger number of negatively charged molecules in the intracellular fluid compared with the extracellular fluid is responsible for this difference.

Squid axon

1 mm

Reference electrode

Voltmeter

Recording microelectrode

Squid axon — Seawater

40
mV
0
−70

1 Voltmeter records zero difference when both electrodes are in seawater.

Voltmeter

Seawater

40
mV
0
−70

Inside axon

2 Voltmeter records −70mV difference between intracellular fluid and seawater.

© 2016 Cengage Learning®

already know from playing with magnets, opposite signs attract and like signs repel. Ions work the same way. Table salt forms readily when it dries out because the positively charged sodium is highly attracted to the negatively charged chloride.

With diffusion and electrical force in mind, let's revisit the distribution of ions on either side of the neural membrane in the resting cell, illustrated in ● Figure 3.12. For the purposes of this exercise, assume that the neural membrane allows ions to move freely back and forth (which it doesn't do in the real world). Potassium is found in larger concentrations on the inside of the cell than on the outside. Diffusion would move the potassium ions along their concentration gradient from the inside (the area of higher concentration) to the outside (the area of lower concentration). However, diffusion is balanced by electrostatic pressure in this case. Potassium is a positively charged ion. As such, it is content to stay in the negative environment on the inside of the cell and reluctant to venture into the relatively positive environment outside the cell. The net distribution of potassium reflects a balance, or *equilibrium,* between diffusion pressure and electrostatic pressure.

Chloride is the mirror image of potassium. Chloride, a negatively charged ion, is more concentrated outside the cell than inside it. Therefore, diffusion works to push

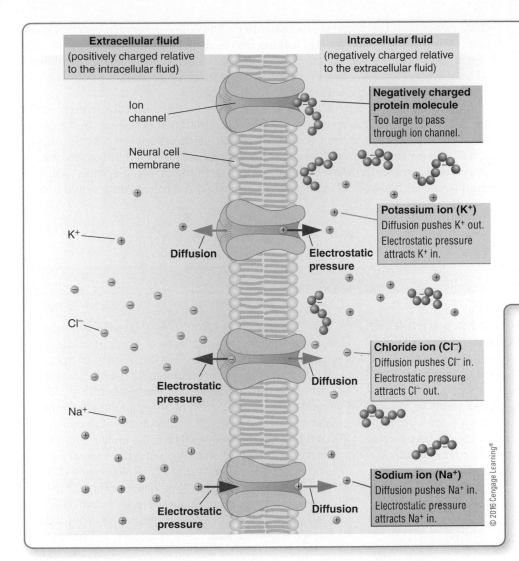

Extracellular fluid
(positively charged relative to the intracellular fluid)

Intracellular fluid
(negatively charged relative to the extracellular fluid)

Ion channel

Neural cell membrane

Negatively charged protein molecule
Too large to pass through ion channel.

K⁺

Diffusion   Electrostatic pressure

Potassium ion (K⁺)
Diffusion pushes K⁺ out.
Electrostatic pressure attracts K⁺ in.

Cl⁻

Electrostatic pressure   Diffusion

Chloride ion (Cl⁻)
Diffusion pushes Cl⁻ in.
Electrostatic pressure attracts Cl⁻ out.

Na⁺

Electrostatic pressure   Diffusion

Sodium ion (Na⁺)
Diffusion pushes Na⁺ in.
Electrostatic pressure attracts Na⁺ in.

© 2016 Cengage Learning®

● **Figure 3.12** Diffusion and Electrostatic Pressure In a resting neuron, diffusion and electrostatic pressure balance each other to determine an equilibrium for potassium and chloride. In contrast, both diffusion and electrostatic pressure act to push sodium into the neuron. The large protein molecules found in the intracellular fluid cannot move through the membrane due to their size. Because of their negative charge, they contribute to the relative negativity of the intracellular fluid.

chloride into the cell. Once again, diffusion is counteracted by electrostatic pressure. The negative interior of the cell repels the negatively charged chloride ions, whereas the relatively positive exterior attracts them. Chloride finds its equilibrium.

Now we come to the interesting case of sodium. Sodium is found in greater concentration on the outside of the cell. By now, you know that means that diffusion will work to push sodium into the cell. But unlike the cases of potassium and chloride, electrostatic pressure is not working against diffusion but rather in the same direction. The positive sodium ions should be very attracted to the negative interior of the cell. With both diffusion pressure and electrostatic pressure pushing sodium into the cell, how do we account for the fact that most of the sodium is found on the outside? The answer lies in the nature of our very important neural membrane.

So far, we have assumed that the neural membrane allows ions to move freely. In the real world, it does not. Although the membrane contains sodium channels, most of these are closed when the cell is at rest. Some sodium leaks into the cell, but most is removed by the sodium-potassium pumps. The net result is that sodium concentrations within the neuron are maintained at low levels in spite of the actions of diffusion and electrostatic pressure.

The Resting Potential

The resting neural membrane allows potassium to cross freely. In other words, we would say that the membrane is permeable to potassium. If the membrane were permeable to potassium and no other ions, the resting potential of the cell would be about

–93mV rather than the actual measurement of –70mV. The difference between these figures is the result of some sodium leaking into the cell. Because sodium is positively charged, the interior of the cell moves in a positive direction from –93mV to –70mV. This is an average figure. In reality, the resting potentials of different types of neurons may range between –40mV and –80mV.

Because the resting potential in a neuron is so dependent on the movement of potassium, the importance of controlling the concentration of potassium in the extra-cellular fluid becomes quite clear. We mentioned earlier that astrocytes have the important task of collecting excess potassium in the vicinity of neurons. If the concentration of potassium increases in the extracellular fluid, the resting potential is wiped out. The neuron would act like a battery that had lost its charge, and no signaling would occur.

••• THINKING *Ethically*

LETHAL INJECTION

Understanding the methods used to perform lethal injections for use in capital punishment is important because we are called on as members of a democracy to participate thoughtfully in ethical decisions.

Lethal injection is now the most common form of capital punishment used in the United States. As shown in ● Figure 3.12a, the procedure uses a combination of three drugs, administered intravenously: a barbiturate that induces coma, a muscle paralysis agent, and potassium chloride (Human Rights Watch, 2006).

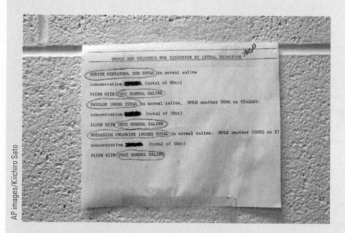

● **Figure 3.12a** **Three Drugs Are Combined in Lethal Injection** The current standard approach to lethal injection is to administer sodium thiopental, a barbiturate anesthetic; pancuronium bromide, a curare derivative that causes muscle paralysis and respiratory arrest; and potassium chloride, which blocks electrical signaling in the heart, causing cardiac arrest. The use of another combination, the sedative midazolam and the painkiller hydromorphone, took more than 25 minutes to kill convicted Ohio murderer Dennis McGuire, raising new challenges to the idea of lethal injection as well as concerns about the methods used.

It is the potassium chloride that actually produces death, typically within one minute of administration. As we mentioned in this chapter, the distribution of potassium across the neural membranes (and the membranes of heart cells, too) is essential for electrical signaling. By increasing the concentration of potassium in the extracellular fluid, the resting potential of cells is increased. This renders the cell inactive. The cell is unable to signal again until the its normal resting potential is regained.

The effects of potassium chloride alone would be extremely painful, so it is never given without other anesthesia. The barbiturate provides this pain relief, and it is given before the other drugs and in doses that far exceed those normally used in surgery. These doses would also produce death alone, but not for one half hour or so. The muscle paralysis agent is much more controversial, as it plays no essential role in the death of the condemned prisoner. Instead, it prevents any movements in response to the effects of the potassium chloride. As such, it is administered more for the benefit of those who must witness the procedure and who might be upset by the prisoner's involuntary movements occurring during the dying process.

Lethal injection remains a highly controversial issue, above and beyond capital punishment itself, due to concerns about the training of prison personnel, the possibility of conscious awareness that cannot be expressed due to paralysis, and other humane concerns. The current drugs have been used for over thirty years, in spite of advancements in the field of anesthesia.

Regardless of your thoughts on capital punishment itself, what is your position on the use of lethal injection? What further information do you need to inform your opinions? What recommendations would you make for further research? Are there other methods that you believe are more humane? Why or why not?

AP images/Kiichiro Sato

The Action Potential

Our next step is to describe the changes that take place when the cell signals by producing an action potential. We will explore the technique used by Nobel Laureates Alan Hodgkin and Andrew Huxley to identify the ionic basis of action potentials (Hodgkin & Huxley, 1952).

To understand the sequence of events responsible for the action potential, we need first to clarify how one is measured. A favorite source of axons for study has been the squid. Squid, like many other large invertebrates, have long, large diameter axons. Squid can grow to lengths of 10–15 feet, and unmyelinated invertebrate axons must be large in diameter to achieve sufficient signaling speed. These characteristics make it easy for researchers to insert electrodes into the intracellular fluid of a dissected squid axon. An axon dissected out of a squid will remain active for many hours when placed in a trough containing seawater, which substitutes for the extracellular fluid due to its similar ionic composition. During this time, researchers can stimulate the axon and record its activity. To measure action potentials, we would need to insert a recording electrode into the intracellular fluid of the squid axon, and another into the extracellular fluid (or its experimental equivalent). We should now be able to read a resting potential of approximately –70mV.

THRESHOLD Because there is no natural input to the disembodied squid axon we are studying, we need to employ a stimulating electrode in addition to the recording electrodes. Normally, a neuron reacts either to sensory input or to chemical messages from other neurons. In the squid axon experiment, we duplicate the effects of these natural inputs with a tiny, depolarizing electrical shock. Whether we're discussing politics or electricity, polarization means that we're on opposite ends of a continuum. Conversely, **depolarization** means that we're moving closer together. In response to a depolarizing shock to the squid axon, the interior of the cell will become more similar to the exterior of the cell; that is, it will be relatively less negative than before.

Shocks that produce a depolarization of less than 5mV to 10mV have no further effects on the axon, which quickly returns to the resting potential. However, if we apply a shock that results in a depolarization of at least 5mV to 10mV, we begin a chain of events that will lead to the production of an action potential. In other words, when our recording reaches about –65mV, we have reached the cell's **threshold** for producing an action potential. Reaching the threshold for an action potential is similar to pulling the trigger of a gun. As you squeeze the trigger, nothing happens until you reach a critical point. At that point, a sequence of events begins that leads to the firing of the gun, and no actions will stop the sequence once it is initiated. The sequence of events that characterizes an action potential is shown in ● Figure 3.13.

CHANNELS OPEN AND CLOSE DURING AN ACTION POTENTIAL The first consequence of reaching a cell's threshold is the opening of voltage-dependent sodium channels. Once the sodium gates open, sodium is free to move into the cell, and both diffusion and electrostatic pressure ensure that it does so rapidly.

The rush of sodium ions into the neuron is reflected in the recording, which rises from a threshold of around –65mV up to a peak of about +40mV. In other words, at the peak of the action potential, the inside of the neuron is now positively charged relative to the extracellular fluid, a complete reversal of the resting state. The peak of the action potential is similar to sodium's equilibrium of about +60mV. In other words, if the membrane allowed sodium to move freely, the inside of the cell would be positive relative to the extracellular fluid.

Voltage-dependent potassium channels are also triggered at threshold, but their response is much slower than the sodium channels. Toward the peak of the action potential, potassium begins to leave the cell, and the recording drops back to resting levels. Why does potassium move out of the cell toward the peak of the action potential? Recall that potassium is positively charged. In the resting cell, potassium is attracted to the negatively charged interior of the cell and relatively repulsed by the positive exterior. At the peak of the action potential, however, the positive potassium ions find

depolarization A change in a membrane potential in a more positive direction.
threshold The level of depolarization at which an action potential is initiated.

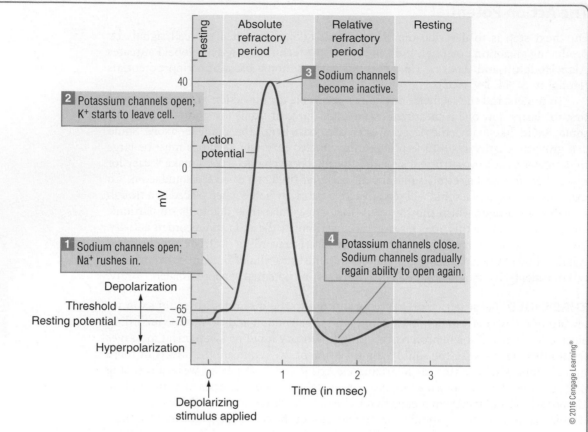

● **Figure 3.13 The Action Potential** Once a cell's threshold is reached, an action potential will be generated by a sequential opening and closing of ion channels in the neural membrane. Voltage-dependent sodium and potassium channels are triggered at the threshold. The sodium channels open and close very rapidly, allowing sodium to rush into the cell. As a result, the cell is depolarized. The potassium channels open near the peak of the action potential and close more slowly than the sodium channels. Potassium leaves the now positive intracellular environment, which brings the cell back to its original negative state. Because the sodium channels will not open again until the cell is close to its negative resting state, there is an absolute refractory period in which the cell cannot fire again. Due to remaining hyperpolarization during the relative refractory period, a larger than normal stimulus is necessary for the production of an action potential.

themselves in a more positive environment within the neuron. The exterior looks relatively attractive. As a result, potassium diffuses outside. As these positively charged ions leave the neuron, the interior of the cell becomes negative again, as shown in the downward slope of the recording.

Once the cell returns to the resting level, it actually **hyperpolarizes**, or overshoots its target and becomes even more negative than when at rest. The cell slowly returns to its normal resting level. Throughout the process, the sodium-potassium pumps are hard at work to return sodium ions to the extracellular fluid.

There are several important differences between the sodium and potassium voltage-dependent channels that are involved with action potentials. First of all, the sodium channels open very rapidly, whereas the potassium channels open slowly. This difference accounts for the rapid rise in our recording of the action potential. Second, the sodium channels remain open only briefly and are then inactivated until the cell nearly reaches its resting potential again. The potassium channels remain open for a longer period of time.

Understanding the importance of the sodium channels in electrical signaling helps to explain the dangers of consuming puffer fish sushi, or *fugu*. In spite of tight regulations, as many as 200 Japanese die each year from consuming this delicacy (see ● Figure 3.14). The *fugu* toxin (tetrodotoxin, or TTX) specifically blocks

hyperpolarization A change in membrane potential in a more negative direction.

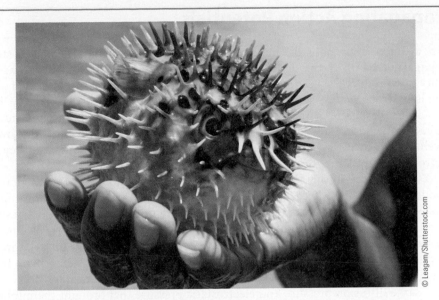

> ● **Figure 3.14** **Hundreds Die Each Year from Puffer Fish Poisoning** In spite of their intimidating appearance, hundreds of thousands of pounds of puffer fish, or fugu, are consumed each year in Japan. Unfortunately, certain species of puffer contain tetrodotoxin. In very small amounts, tetrodotoxin can cause death by blocking voltage-dependent sodium channels in the membranes of nerve fibers. When sodium is unable to enter the neuron, no signaling can occur, and death soon follows.

the voltage-dependent sodium channels responsible for the rising phase of the action potential. Without the movement of sodium at this point, there is no signaling. With no signaling, of course, life-sustaining processes stop.

REFRACTORY PERIODS The frequency with which neurons can fire is limited. Once the voltage-dependent sodium channels have been activated, they cannot be opened a second time until the membrane is repolarized to nearly resting levels. This interval, in which no stimulus whatsoever can produce another action potential, is known as the **absolute refractory period**.

While the cell is relatively hyperpolarized following an action potential, it can respond, but only to larger than normal input. We refer to this period as the **relative refractory period**. Because the recording is repolarized to at least –50mV, the sodium channels gradually regain the ability to open again. However, due to the hyperpolarized state of the membrane following an action potential and the relatively smaller numbers of active sodium channels, more depolarization than normal (10 to 15mV as opposed to 5mV or so) is needed to reach threshold.

THE ACTION POTENTIAL IS ALL-OR-NONE We do not encode information by producing fat or thin or tall or short action potentials. An action potential is either produced or it is not. Consequently, we speak of action potentials as being all-or-none.

If our neurons can make this one type of signal, how do we respond to different levels of stimulation? The rate of neural firing can vary to reflect stimulus intensity. Large amounts of stimulation produce rapid neural firing, whereas less intense input produces slower rates of firing. Firing rate does have physical limits, however. Because each action potential lasts about 1 msec, the maximum theoretical neural firing rate is about 1,000 action potentials per second (in reality about 800 per second). In addition to firing rate, the number of active neurons can vary with stimulus intensity. Intense input will recruit action potentials from many neurons, whereas lower levels of stimulation will activate fewer neurons.

absolute refractory period The period in which an action potential will not occur in a particular location of an axon regardless of input.
relative refractory period The period following an action potential in which larger than normal input will produce a second action potential but in which normal input will be insufficient.

Propagating Action Potentials

Once a single action potential has been formed at the axon hillock, the next step is **propagation**, by which the signal reproduces itself down the length of an axon. This ability to reproduce the original signal ensures that the signal reaching the end of the axon is as strong as the signal formed at the axon hillock.

Earlier, we measured an action potential by using one recording electrode toward one end of the squid axon and another in the extracellular environment. To follow the traveling signal, we now add more electrodes and record action potentials as they pass electrodes down the length of the axon as shown in ● Figure 3.15.

As we can see in ● Figure 3.16, the movement of an action potential along an axon is influenced by whether the axon is myelinated. When we last saw our unmyelinated squid axon, the generation of an action potential at the axon hillock resulted in the entry of sodium ions into the cell. Now that they are inside, these ions will behave like water in a leaky hose. Some of these sodium ions will exit the cell through the sodium-potassium pumps and other ion channels, and others will remain inside the cell membrane, or hose. Where are the remaining sodium ions likely to go? Due to the same diffusion pressure and electrostatic pressure that brought them into the cell, the sodium ions will drift to the adjacent axon segment, where there are many additional sodium channels. At the same time, incoming positive sodium ions will also push positive potassium ions ahead into adjacent axon segments due to their like electrical charges. The arrival of these positively charged ions depolarizes the next segment. If this depolarization is sufficient to reach threshold, the events leading to an action potential will be reproduced. A recording electrode in this segment will indicate another action potential identical to the one we recorded at the axon hillock.

Can the action potential move backward toward the cell body, too? Technically, if an action potential were produced for the first time in the middle of an axon as a result of an experimental shock, there's no reason why it couldn't go in either or both directions. In reality, however, the prior segment will still be in refractory period and won't be able to fire. Because refractory periods prevent an immediate reoccurrence of an

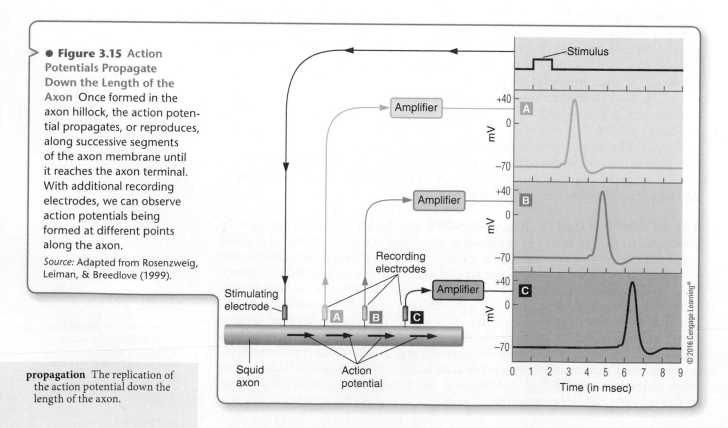

● **Figure 3.15** Action Potentials Propagate Down the Length of the Axon Once formed in the axon hillock, the action potential propagates, or reproduces, along successive segments of the axon membrane until it reaches the axon terminal. With additional recording electrodes, we can observe action potentials being formed at different points along the axon.

Source: Adapted from Rosenzweig, Leiman, & Breedlove (1999).

propagation The replication of the action potential down the length of the axon.

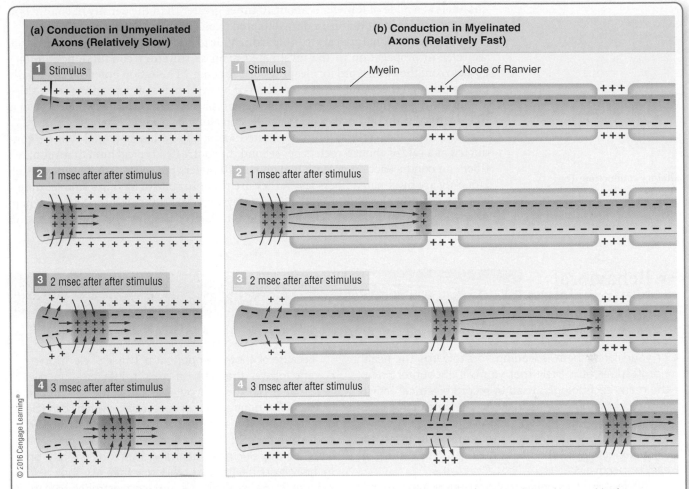

(a) Conduction in Unmyelinated Axons (Relatively Slow)

1 Stimulus

2 1 msec after after stimulus

3 2 msec after after stimulus

4 3 msec after after stimulus

(b) Conduction in Myelinated Axons (Relatively Fast)

1 Stimulus — Myelin — Node of Ranvier

2 1 msec after after stimulus

3 2 msec after after stimulus

4 3 msec after after stimulus

● **Figure 3.16** Propagation in Unmyelinated and Myelinated Axons In conduction in unmyelinated axons (a), the action potential must be replicated at each successive segment. Salutatory conduction in myelinated axons (b) is much faster because action potentials occur only at the nodes of Ranvier.

action potential in previous segments, action potentials move in one direction, from cell body to axon terminal. At the axon hillock, site of the first action potential, there is no previous segment in refractory period. As a result, current does appear to flow backward into the cell body and dendrites. Currently, the significance of this backward current remains unknown. Once the axon hillock has regained its resting potential, it can initiate a second action potential that will follow the first down the length of the axon. If an axon couldn't have multiple action potentials following one another in this manner, a neural firing rate of up to 800 times per second would be impossible.

Now we are ready to consider the propagation of action potentials in myelinated axons. To produce action potentials, we need ion channels. Numerous channels are located along the length of the unmyelinated axon, but in the myelinated axon, channels appear only at the nodes of Ranvier, the bare spaces of axon membrane between adjacent segments of myelin. Under the myelin segment itself, there is no contact between the membrane and extracellular fluid at all.

How does myelin produce the faster, more efficient propagation of action potentials? The myelinated axon is like a leaky hose that has been patched. The patches, or myelin, prevent leakage of the sodium ions, at least until they reach a node of Ranvier. Just as water moves faster through the patched hose, so do the sodium ions move faster in the myelinated axon. Once the sodium ions reach a node of Ranvier, they produce another action potential due to the presence of voltage-dependent channels in that area. The nodes are especially rich in these channels. The density of channels at a node of Ranvier is about 10 times greater than the density of channels at any comparable location on an unmyelinated axon (Rasband & Shrager, 2000).

Because the signal appears to jump from node to node down the length of the axon, we refer to propagation in the myelinated axon as **saltatory conduction**. *Saltatory* comes from the Latin word for "leaping" or "dancing." The action potential essentially passes through the segments of axon covered by myelin, just as an express train skips all but the most important stops. In contrast, propagation in the unmyelinated axon is like the local train that makes every single stop along its route.

In a typical invertebrate unmyelinated axon, the action potential will be conducted at a rate of about 5 meters per second. In contrast, a typical human myelinated fiber can conduct action potentials at about 120 meters per second, or 24 times faster. Not only are myelinated fibers faster, they are faster in spite of having a smaller diameter. As fast as we are, however, the nervous system does not communicate anywhere near the speed of light, as was once believed. Part of the delay in communication occurs between neurons, at the synapse.

saltatory conduction The movement of an action potential from node of Ranvier to node of Ranvier, down the length of a myelinated axon.

●●● Behavioral Neuroscience GOES TO WORK

WHAT ARE WE READING IN AN ECG OR EEG?

If your career path is leading you towards the health professions, it is likely that you will encounter one of the many technologies used to record electrical activity in the body. You may be asked to use an electrocardiogram (ECG), electroencephalogram (EEG), electromyogram (EMG), or electroretinogram (ERG) to assess the electrical activity of the heart, brain, skeletal muscle, or eye, respectively.

While it isn't essential that you understand exactly what you're recording, as your focus is likely to be on whether the recorded pattern is normal or not, grasping the basic principles behind these technologies might prepare you better for coping with the inevitable improvements in technology during the lifetime of your career.

We have just finished a discussion of the propagation of action potentials down the length of an axon, a process that depends on what physiologists label as *local circuit currents*. Without stopping here for an entire treatise on electrical engineering, we'll explain briefly how this works. Current flows between two areas that are at different potentials. Let's assume we're looking at a segment of an axon where an action potential is taking place. At the peak of that action potential, the interior of the axon segment is going to be positive compared to the adjacent and inactive axon segment downstream. In other words, the two areas are at different potentials, one relatively positive and the other relatively negative. Current will flow within the axon from the active to the inactive region, which of course is then likely to reach threshold and become active itself. Current also flows across the membrane into the extracellular fluid in the inactive region and back into the cell at the active region, completing the loop. So you have current flowing both within the axon and outside in the extracellular fluid.

Because of another important principle of electricity—current follows the path of least resistance—the current that is outside the cell will cause the skin above it to show differences in potential, which can be detected through the use of electrodes stationed in strategic locations. It is these differences that form the basis for the electrical recording methods we rely on so heavily in health care and research. As shown in ●Figure 3.16a, we can use surface electrodes to capture a snapshot of the electrical activity occurring in the tissues below.

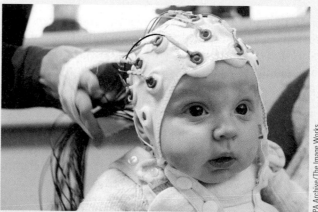

PA Archive/The Image Works

● **Figure 3.16a** Current Follows the Path of Least Resistance Because current follows the path of least resistance, current outside the cell will cause the skin above it to show differences in potential, which can be detected through the use of electrodes stationed in strategic locations on the surface of the body. These differences in potential form the basis for the electrical recording methods we rely on so heavily in health care and research.

Summary Table: Major Features of Electrical Signaling

Event	Location	Mechanisms of Action
Resting potential	Inactive segments of axon	• Equilibrium between diffusion and electrostatic pressure exists for K^+ and Cl^-. • Na^+ is actively prevented from entering the neuron.
Action potential	Begins at the axon hillock and propagates down the length of the axon	• Depolarization to threshold triggers opening of Na^+ channels. • Entering Na^+ ions make voltage inside neuron more positive. • Opening of K^+ channels near peak of action potential allows K^+ to leave the neuron. • Loss of K^+ returns neuron to the resting potential.
Absolute refractory period	Segments of axon during an action potential	• Na^+ channels are unable to open a second time until neuron nearly reaches the resting potential.
Relative refractory period	Segments of axon that have just experienced an absolute refractory period	• Return to resting potential resets Na^+ channels. Hyperpolarization makes an action potential less likely.
Propagation of action potential	Entire length of axon, beginning at axon hillock	• Drift of Na^+ and K^+ ions to adjacent segments of axon causes segments to reach threshold, triggering replication of the action potential. • Existence of refractory period in the preceding segment prevents backward propagation.

Summary Points

1. The intracellular fluid contains large amounts of potassium and smaller amounts of sodium and chloride. The extracellular fluid contains large amounts of sodium and chloride and smaller amounts of potassium. **(LO5)**

2. The resting potential of neurons averages about −70mV. In other words, the interior of the cell is negatively charged relative to the exterior. An action potential is a reversal of this polarity. **(LO5)**

3. Absolute and relative refractory periods, during which further action potentials are either impossible or less likely, result from the nature of the sodium and potassium channels. **(LO5)**

4. Action potentials move much more rapidly down the length of myelinated axons than in unmyelinated axons due to the process of saltatory conduction. **(LO5)**

Review Questions

1. How do diffusion and electrostatic pressure account for the chemical composition of intracellular and extracellular fluids when the neuron is at rest?

2. How do neurons signal stimulus intensity given that the action potential is all-or-none?

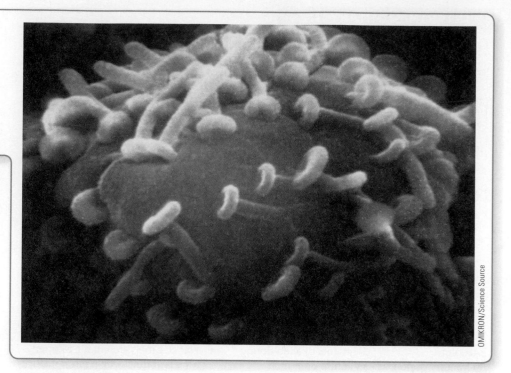

● **Figure 3.17** Neurons Communicate at the Synapse This colored electron micrograph shows the axon terminals from many neurons forming synapses on a cell body.

OMIKRON/Science Source

The Synapse

The birth and propagation of the action potential within the presynaptic neuron makes up the first half of our story of neural communication. The second half begins when the action potential reaches the axon terminal and the message must cross the synaptic gap to the adjacent postsynaptic neuron (see ● Figure 3.17).

The human brain contains about 100 billion neurons, and the average neuron forms something on the order of 1,000 synapses. Remarkably, these numbers suggest that the human brain has more synapses than there are stars in our galaxy (Kandel & Siegelbaum, 1995). In spite of these large numbers, synapses take one of only two forms. At **chemical synapses**, neurons stimulate adjacent cells by sending neurotransmitters across the synaptic gap (see ● Figure 3.18). At **electrical synapses**, also known as gap junctions, neurons directly stimulate adjacent cells by sending ions across the gap through channels that actually touch.

chemical synapse A type of synapse in which messages are transmitted from one neuron to another by chemical neurotransmitters.

electrical synapse A type of synapse in which a neuron directly affects an adjacent neuron through the movement of ions from one cell to the other.

Electrical Synapses

Electrical synapses between two cells, illustrated in ● Figure 3.19, are found not just in animals but in plants as well, which suggests that they are very ancient in terms of evolution. Not only do we retain small numbers of electrical synapses in the human nervous system, but electrical communication also occurs in the heart and liver.

TABLE 3.2 | A Comparison of Electrical and Chemical Synapses

Type of Synapse	Width of Synaptic Gap	Speed of Transmission	Method of Transmission	Type of Message	Types of Cells Involved
Electrical	3.5 nm	Nearly instantaneous	Direct movement of ions from one cell to the other	Excitatory only	Requires large presynaptic neuron to influence small postsynaptic neurons
Chemical	20 nm	Up to several milliseconds	Release of chemical neurotransmitters	Excitatory or inhibitory	Small presynaptic neurons can influence large postsynaptic neurons

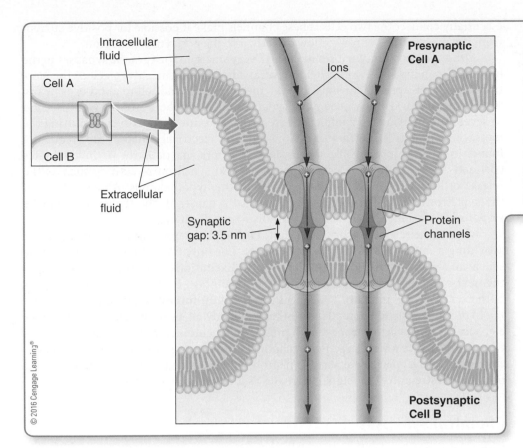

Intracellular fluid

Cell A

Cell B

Extracellular fluid

Ions

Presynaptic Cell A

Synaptic gap: 3.5 nm

Protein channels

Postsynaptic Cell B

● **Figure 3.18 The Electrical Synapse** In electrical synapses, channels connecting the two neurons across a synaptic gap of only 3.5 hm allow for the direct movement of ions from one cell to the other. Electrical synapses have the advantage of nearly instantaneous communication between neurons.

In contrast to chemical synapses, the gap between two neurons in an electrical synapse is quite small. The average gap between the presynaptic and postsynaptic neurons at a chemical synapse is about 20 nm wide, whereas the gap between cells at an electrical synapse is only 3.5 nm wide. Because of this tiny gap, the presynaptic and postsynaptic cells at an electrical synapse are joined by special protein channels that

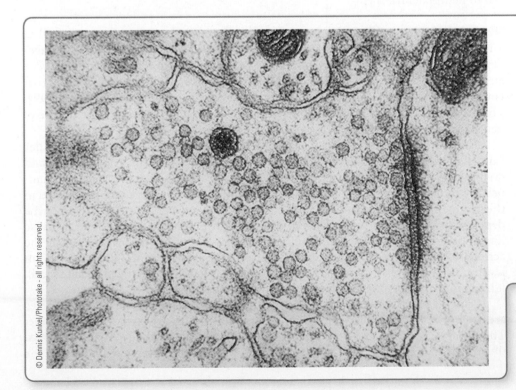

● **Figure 3.19 The Chemical Synapse** In chemical synapses, neurotransmitter substance released by the presynaptic neuron floats across the synaptic gap (the vertical line) to receptor molecules embedded in the membrane of the postsynaptic cell. Although this takes more time than transmission at an electrical synapse, it allows neurons to send a much greater variety of information. This image shows an electron microscopic image of a synapse.

essentially connect the two cells. These channels make it possible for positive current from the presynaptic neuron to flow directly into the postsynaptic neuron.

Although electrical synapses make up a very small minority of the synapses in the brains of mammals, they do provide several advantages. One advantage of the electrical synapse is speed. Transmission of a message from one cell to another is nearly instantaneous. In contrast, chemical synapses take anywhere from 0.3 millisecond to several milliseconds to complete the series of steps involved with transmitting the message from one cell to the next. Consequently, electrical synapses are frequently found in circuits responsible for escape behaviors, particularly in invertebrates (Bennett & Zukin, 2004). Electrical synapses also synchronize activity such as the release of hormones in response to activity in the hypothalamus. Abnormalities in the synchrony typically produced by electrical synapses in the thalamus might be responsible for some seizure activity (Landisman et al., 2002).

Although electrical synapses are fast, chemical synapses have the advantage of providing a much greater variety of messages. The only type of message that can be sent at an electrical synapse is an excitatory one. **Excitation** means that one cell can tell the next cell to produce an action potential. In contrast, chemical synapses allow for both excitatory and inhibitory messages to be sent. In **inhibition**, the next cell is told *not* to produce an action potential. Another major advantage of chemical synapses over electrical synapses is that a very small presynaptic neuron using chemical messengers can still influence a very large postsynaptic neuron. In the case of the electrical synapse, it takes a very large presynaptic neuron to influence a tiny postsynaptic neuron, because the strength of the signal decreases as it moves from one cell to the next.

Chemical Synapses

Chemical synapses can be either directed (affecting a nearby cell) or nondirected (affecting more distant cells). As we will see in Chapter 4, the term *neurotransmitter* is usually used in discussing directed synapses. While much of our discussion refers to directed synapses, we will use the more general term of neurochemical in this context.

Signaling at chemical synapses occurs in two steps. The first step is release of the neurochemicals by a presynaptic cell. The second step is the reaction of a postsynaptic cell to neurochemicals.

NEUROCHEMICAL RELEASE In response to the arrival of an action potential at a terminal, a new type of voltage-dependent channel will open. This time, voltage-dependent calcium (Ca^{2+}) channels will play the major role in the cell's activities. The amount of neurochemical released is a direct reflection of the amount of calcium that enters the presynaptic neuron (Heidelberger, Heinemann, Neher, & Matthews, 1994; Von Gersdorff & Mathews, 1994). A large influx of calcium triggers a large release of neurochemical.

Calcium is a positively charged ion (Ca^{2+}) that is more abundant in the extracellular fluid than in the intracellular fluid. Therefore, its situation is very similar to sodium, and it will move under the same circumstances that cause sodium to move. Calcium channels are rather rare along the length of the axon, but there are a large number located in the axon terminal membrane. Calcium channels open in response to the arrival of the depolarizing action potential. Calcium does not move immediately, however, because it is a positively charged ion and the intracellular fluid is positively charged during the action potential. As the action potential recedes in the axon terminal, however, calcium is attracted by the relatively negative interior. Once calcium enters the presynaptic cell, it triggers the release of neurochemicals within about 0.2 msec.

Prior to release, neurochemicals are stored in synaptic vesicles. These vesicles are anchored by special proteins near release sites on the presynaptic membrane. The process by which these vesicles release their contents is known as **exocytosis**, illustrated in ●Figure 3.20. Calcium entering the cell frees the vesicles from their

excitation A neural message that increases the likelihood that a receiving cell will produce an action potential.

inhibition A neural message that decreases the likelihood that a receiving cell will produce an action potential.

exocytosis The process in which vesicles fuse with the membrane of the axon terminal and release neurochemicals into the synaptic gap.

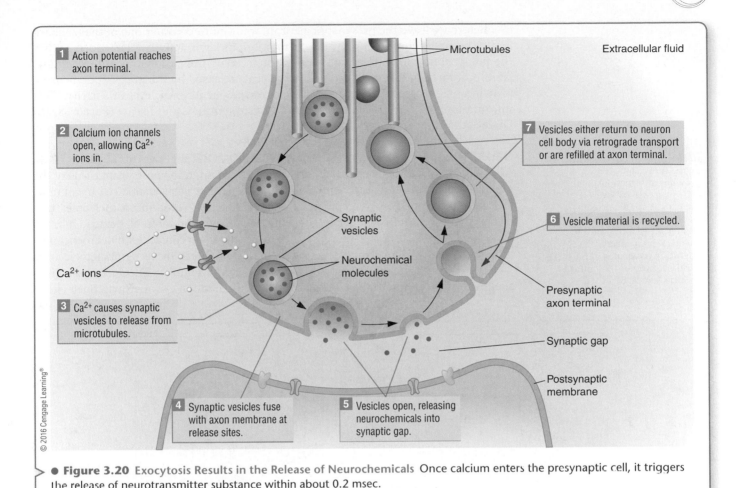

1 Action potential reaches axon terminal.

2 Calcium ion channels open, allowing Ca²⁺ ions in.

Ca²⁺ ions

3 Ca²⁺ causes synaptic vesicles to release from microtubules.

Microtubules

Extracellular fluid

7 Vesicles either return to neuron cell body via retrograde transport or are refilled at axon terminal.

6 Vesicle material is recycled.

Synaptic vesicles

Neurochemical molecules

Presynaptic axon terminal

Synaptic gap

Postsynaptic membrane

4 Synaptic vesicles fuse with axon membrane at release sites.

5 Vesicles open, releasing neurochemicals into synaptic gap.

© 2016 Cengage Learning®

● **Figure 3.20** **Exocytosis Results in the Release of Neurochemicals** Once calcium enters the presynaptic cell, it triggers the release of neurotransmitter substance within about 0.2 msec.

protein anchors, which allows them to migrate toward the release sites. At the release site, calcium stimulates the fusion between the membrane of the vesicle and the membrane of the axon terminal, forming a channel through which the neurochemicals escape.

A long-standing assumption regarding exocytosis is that each released vesicle is fully emptied of neurochemical. However, some researchers have suggested the possibility that there are instances of partial release, which they have dubbed "kiss and run" (Ceccarelli, Hurlbut, & Mauro, 1973). In kiss and run, vesicles are only partially emptied of neurochemical molecules before closing up again and returning to the interior of the axon terminal. If vesicles did indeed have the ability to kiss and run, the process of neurotransmission would be much faster than if they had to be filled from scratch after each use. In addition, kiss and run raises the possibility that the vesicles themselves control the amount of neurochemical released to some extent (Harata, Aravanis, & Tsien, 2006).

Following exocytosis, the neuron must engage in several housekeeping duties to prepare for the arrival of the next action potential. Calcium pumps return calcium to the extracellular fluid. Otherwise, neurochemicals would be released constantly rather than in response to the arrival of an action potential. Because the vesicle membrane fuses with the presynaptic membrane, something must be done to prevent a gradual thickening of the membrane that would interfere with neurochemical release. The solution to this unwanted thickening is the recycling of the vesicle material. Excess membrane material forms a pit, which is eventually pinched off to form a new vesicle.

Before we leave the presynaptic neuron, we need to consider one of the feedback loops the presynaptic neuron uses to monitor its own activity. Embedded within the presynaptic membrane are special protein structures known as **autoreceptors**. Autoreceptors bind some of the neurochemicals released by the presynaptic neuron, providing feedback to the presynaptic neuron about its own level of activity. This information may affect the rate of neurochemical synthesis and release (Parnas, Segel, Dudel, & Parnas, 2000).

autoreceptor Receptor site located on the presynaptic neuron that provides information about the cell's own activity levels.
receptors A special protein structure embedded in a neural membrane that responds to chemical messengers.
recognition molecules A molecule within a receptor that binds to specific neurochemicals.

NEUROCHEMICALS BIND TO POSTSYNAPTIC RECEPTOR SITES The newly released neurochemicals diffuse across the synaptic gap. On the postsynaptic side of the synapse, we find new types of proteins embedded in the postsynaptic cell membrane, known as **receptors**. The receptors are characterized by **recognition molecules** that respond only to certain types of neurochemicals. Recognition molecules extend into the extracellular fluid of the synaptic gap, where they come into contact with neurochemical molecules. These function as keys that fit into the locks made by the recognition molecules.

Two major types of receptors are illustrated in ● Figure 3.21. Once the neurochemicals have bound to recognition sites, ligand-gated ion channels will open either

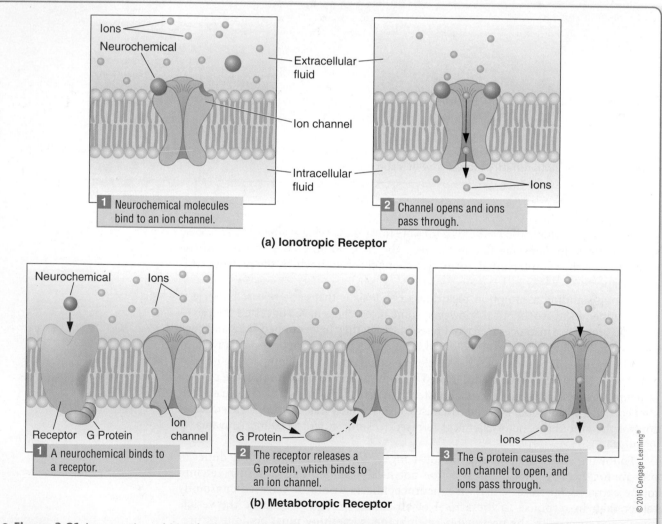

(a) Ionotropic Receptor

1 Neurochemical molecules bind to an ion channel.

2 Channel opens and ions pass through.

(b) Metabotropic Receptor

1 A neurochemical binds to a receptor.

2 The receptor releases a G protein, which binds to an ion channel.

3 The G protein causes the ion channel to open, and ions pass through.

© 2016 Cengage Learning®

● **Figure 3.21** **Ionotropic and Metabotropic Receptors** Ionotropic receptors, shown in (a), feature a recognition site for molecules of neurochemical located on an ion channel. These one-step receptors provide a very fast response to the presence of neurochemicals. Metabotropic receptors, shown in (b), require additional steps. Neurochemical molecules are recognized by the receptor, which in turn releases internal messengers known as G proteins. G proteins initiate a wide variety of functions within the cell, including opening adjacent ion channels and changing gene expression.

directly (fast) or indirectly (slowly). In the direct, or fast, case, known as an **ionotropic receptor**, the recognition site is located on the channel protein. As soon as the receptor captures molecules of neurochemical, the ion channel opens. These one-step receptors are capable of very fast reactions to neurochemicals. In other cases, however, the recognition site does not have direct control over an ion channel (Birnbaumer, Abramowitz, & Brown, 1990). These receptors, known as **metabotropic receptors**, have a recognition site that extends into the extracellular fluid and a special protein called a **G protein** located on the receptor's intracellular side. When molecules of neurochemical are bound at the recognition site, the G protein separates from the receptor complex and moves to a different part of the postsynaptic cell. G proteins can open ion channels in the nearby membrane or activate additional chemical messengers within the postsynaptic cell known as **second messengers**. (The neurochemicals bound by the metabotropic receptors are the first messengers.) Because of the multiple steps involved, the metabotropic receptors respond more slowly, in hundreds of milliseconds to seconds, than the ionotropic receptors, which respond in milliseconds. In addition, the effects of metabotropic activation can last much longer than those produced by the activation of ionotropic receptors.

What is the advantage to an organism of evolving a slower, more complicated receptor system? The answer is that the metabotropic receptor provides the possibility of a much greater variety of responses to the binding of neurochemicals. The activation of metabotropic receptors can result not only in the opening of ion channels, but also in a number of additional functions. Different types of metabotropic receptors influence the amount of neurochemicals released, help maintain the resting potential, and initiate changes in gene expression (Pan et al., 2008). Unlike the ionotropic receptor, which affects a very small, local part of a cell, a metabotropic receptor can have wide-ranging and multiple influences within a cell due to its ability to activate a variety of second messengers.

TERMINATION OF THE CHEMICAL SIGNAL Before we can make a second phone call, we need to end the first call. If we want to send a second message across a synapse, it's necessary to have some way of ending the first message.

Neurochemicals bind very briefly to receptors, after which they are released back into the synaptic gap. In the gap, neurochemicals are deactivated in three different ways, illustrated in ● Figure 3.22. The particular method used depends on the type of neurochemical involved (see Chapter 4). The first method is simple diffusion away from the synapse. Like any other molecule, neurochemicals diffuse away from areas of high concentration to areas of low concentration. Recall, however, that the astrocytes surrounding the synapse influence the diffusion of neurochemicals away from the synapse, so there are limits to this process. In the second method for ending chemical transmission, neurochemical molecules are deactivated by enzymes in the synaptic gap. In the third process, **reuptake**, the presynaptic membrane uses its own set of receptors known as **transporters** to recapture molecules of neurochemical and return them to the interior of the axon terminal. In the terminal, the neurochemicals can be repackaged in vesicles for subsequent release. Unlike the cases in which enzymes deactivate neurochemicals, reuptake spares the cell the extra step of reconstructing the molecules out of component parts.

POSTSYNAPTIC POTENTIALS When molecules of neurochemical bind to postsynaptic receptors, they can produce one of two outcomes, illustrated in ● Figure 3.23. One outcome, excitation, increases the likelihood that the postsynaptic cell will generate an action potential. The other outcome, inhibition, decreases the likelihood that the postsynaptic cell will fire.

Excitation results from the depolarization of the postsynaptic membrane, known as an **excitatory postsynaptic potential**, or **EPSP**. EPSPs result from the opening of ligand-gated rather than voltage-dependent sodium channels in the postsynaptic membrane. The inward movement of positive sodium ions produces the slight

ionotropic receptor A receptor protein in the postsynaptic membrane in which the recognition site is located on the same structure as the ion channel.

metabotropic receptor A protein structure embedded in the postsynaptic membrane containing a recognition site and a G protein. Neurochemicals binding to these receptors do not directly open ion channels.

G protein A protein found on the intracellular side of a metabotropic receptor that separates in response to the binding of a neurochemical and travels to adjacent areas of the cell to affect ion channels or second messengers.

second messenger A chemical within the postsynaptic neuron that is indirectly activated by synaptic activity and interacts with intracellular enzymes or receptors.

reuptake A process for ending the action of neurochemicals in the synaptic gap in which the presynaptic membrane recaptures the molecules of neurotransmitter.

transporter A receptor in the presynaptic membrane that recaptures released molecules of neurochemical in the process of reuptake.

excitatory postsynaptic potential (EPSP) A small depolarization produced in the postsynaptic cell as a result of input from the presynaptic cell.

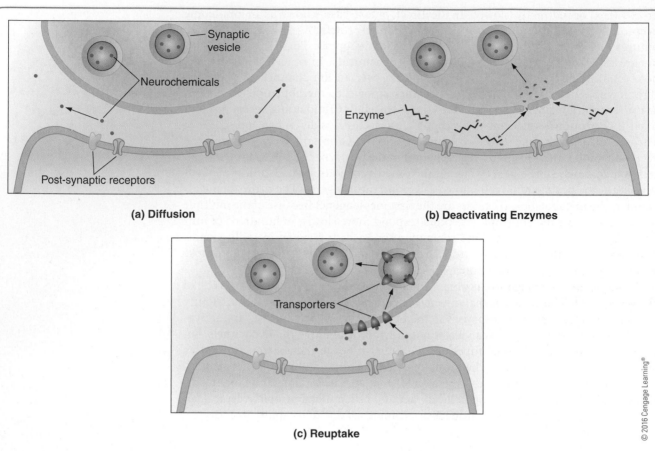

(a) Diffusion

(b) Deactivating Enzymes

(c) Reuptake

● **Figure 3.22** Methods for Deactivating Neurochemicals Neurochemicals released into the synaptic gap must be deactivated before additional signals are sent by the presynaptic neuron. Deactivation may occur through (a) diffusion away from the synapse, (b) the action of special enzymes, or (c) reuptake. Deactivating enzymes break the neurochemical molecules into their components. The presynaptic neuron collects these components and then synthesizes and packages more neurochemical molecules. In reuptake, presynaptic transporters "recapture" released neurochemicals and repackage them in vesicles.

© 2016 Cengage Learning®

depolarization of the EPSP. In addition to opening a different type of channel, EPSPs differ from action potentials in other ways. We have described action potentials as being all-or-none. In contrast, EPSPs are known as **graded potentials**, referring to their varying size and shape. Action potentials last about 1 msec, but EPSPs can last up to 5 to 10 msec.

The second possible outcome of the binding of neurochemicals to a postsynaptic receptor is the production of an **inhibitory postsynaptic potential**, or **IPSP**. The IPSP reduces the likelihood that the postsynaptic cell will produce an action potential. Like the EPSP, the IPSP is a graded potential that can last 5 to 10 msec. IPSPs are produced by the opening of ligand-gated channels that allow for the inward movement of chloride (Cl^-) or the outward movement of potassium (K^+). The movement of negatively charged chloride ions into the postsynaptic cell would add to the cell's negative charge. The loss of positively charged potassium cells would also increase a cell's negative charge. IPSPs usually produce a hyperpolarizing current. To be completely accurate, however, we must note that IPSPs can also have depolarizing effects in some less typical situations. The effects of these depolarizing IPSPs remain inhibitory. A complete explanation of these odd circumstances is beyond the scope of this textbook, but we can say that the outcomes depend on the relationship

graded potentials An electrical signal that can vary in size and shape.
inhibitory postsynaptic potential (IPSP) A small hyperpolarization produced in the postsynaptic cell as a result of input from the presynaptic cell.

••• Building Better HEALTH

ERADICATING TETANUS WORLDWIDE

In the United States, there have been an average of 29 cases of tetanus per year since 1996, due to the widespread availability of effective vaccines (Centers for Disease Control and Prevention [CDC], 2013). Nearly all of these cases occur among people who have not been vaccinated or have not obtained a booster shot once every ten years. A small number of cases occur due to contaminated heroin, and those who inject the drug are more particularly at risk.

Worldwide, tetanus statistics look very different than in the United States (see • Figure 3.22a). Over one million deaths per year still occur due to tetanus, and about one fourth of these deaths occur in newborns. Tetanus accounts for 14 percent of neonatal deaths and 5 percent of maternal deaths worldwide, and yet it is easily one of the more preventable diseases. Among the countries with the highest rates of newborn deaths due to tetanus are India, Nigeria, Pakistan, Ethiopia, Bangladesh, Somalia, Niger, and Chad (World Health Organization [WHO], 2004).

Tetanus occurs when spores of the bacterium *Clostridium tetani* enter the body through a wound. Spores are common in the feces of many domestic animals, including dogs, cats, rats, guinea pigs, chickens, horses, sheep, and cattle. Human adults in heavily agricultural areas might also harbor spores. In the absence of oxygen, as in a dirty wound or umbilical cord cut with an unsterilized instrument, the spores produce a neurotoxin called tetanospasmin.

Tetanospasmin cannot cross the blood–brain barrier to affect the CNS. Instead, the toxin hitches a ride from the wound site to the spinal cord, using the retrograde transport system within axons (Schwab, Suda, & Thoenen, 1979). Once in the CNS, the toxin binds to receptor sites for a major inhibitory neurochemical, gamma-aminobutyric acid (GABA), and can't be dislodged. If you have any remaining doubts about the need for IPSPs, the effects of tetanospasmin will probably

• **Figure 3.22a Vaccinations for Tetanus Reduce Risks for Mothers and Newborns** Although this Haitian mother and her child seem distressed by the tetanus vaccination provided by the World Health Organization (WHO), vaccination programs targeting mothers and newborns have eliminated tetanus cases in more than 30 high-risk nations as of 2013. Due to unsanitary birth conditions in many parts of the world, tetanus remains a major killer of new mothers and their babies.

erase them. Without normal inhibition, muscles begin to go into sudden, involuntary contractions, or spasms. Spasms occur first in the jaw and neck, giving tetanus its other popular name, "lockjaw." As the disease progresses, muscles rip apart and the vertebrae of the spine suffer compression fractures. The later stages of the disease often lead to respiratory or cardiac arrest. Even with intensive care, 30 to 40 percent of patients will die.

War, poverty, and lack of health education continue to be barriers to the eradication of preventable diseases worldwide. By specifically targeting women of child-bearing age in areas with high risk of infection, the World Health Organization (WHO) is attempting to achieve the best results with its limited access and resources.

between a neurochemical's effects and the particular cell's threshold for producing an action potential.

NEURAL INTEGRATION Neurons in the human brain can receive input from thousands of other neurons. Some of that input will be in the form of EPSPs, and some in the form of IPSPs. The task faced by the neuron receiving this input is to determine whether to produce an action potential. You may have had the experience of asking friends and family members for help with a moral dilemma. Some of your advisors give you an excitatory "go for it" message, and others give you an inhibitory "don't even

neural integration The determination of whether to fire an action potential, based on the summation of inputs to a neuron.

TABLE 3.3 | A Comparison of the Characteristics of Action Potentials, EPSPs, and IPSPs

	Action Potential	EPSPs	IPSPs
Role	Signaling within neurons	Signaling between neurons	Signaling between neurons
Duration	1 to 2 msec	5 to 10 msec up to 100 msec	5 to 10 msec up to 100 msec
Size	About 100mV	Up to 20mV	Up to 15mV
Character	All-or-none	Graded depolarization	Graded hyperpolarization or depolarization
Channels involved	Voltage-dependent sodium and potassium channels	Ligand-gated sodium channels	Ligand-gated potassium or chloride channels

think about it" message. After reviewing the input, it is your task, like the neuron's, to consider all of the advice you've received and decide whether to go forward (although you have the luxury of disagreeing with your input, and the neuron does not). This decision-making process on the part of the neuron is known as **neural integration**, illustrated in ● Figure 3.23.

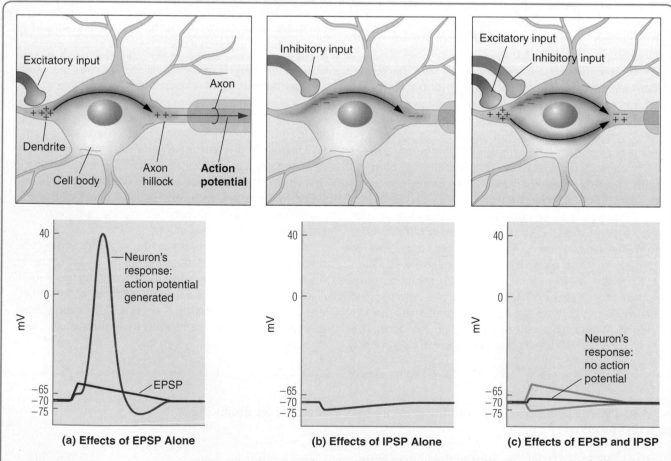

(a) Effects of EPSP Alone

(b) Effects of IPSP Alone

(c) Effects of EPSP and IPSP

> ● **Figure 3.23** **Neural Integration Combines Excitatory and Inhibitory Input** These graphs illustrate the effects of excitatory postsynaptic potentials (EPSPs) and inhibitory postsynaptic potentials (IPSPs) alone and together on the overall response by the postsynaptic neuron. In (a), the EPSP alone depolarizes the postsynaptic cell to threshold and initiates an action potential. In (b), the IPSP alone hyperpolarizes the postsynaptic neuron. In (c), the EPSP and IPSP essentially cancel each other out, and no action potential occurs.

Source: Data from Kandel (1995).

In vertebrates, cells receive their excitatory and inhibitory advice in different locations. The dendrites and their spines are the major locations for excitatory input. In contrast, most of the inhibitory input occurs at synapses on the cell body. Because the dendrites and cell body contain few voltage-dependent channels, they do not typically produce action potentials. Instead, EPSPs from the dendrites and IPSPs from the cell body spread passively but very rapidly until they reach the axon hillock.

The only time the cell will produce an action potential is when the area of the axon hillock is depolarized to threshold. This may occur as a result of **spatial summation**, in which inputs from all over the cell converge at the axon hillock. The cell adds up all the excitatory inputs and subtracts all the inhibitory inputs. If the end result at the axon hillock is about 5mV in favor of depolarization, the cell will fire. Spatial summation is analogous to adding up all of your friends' votes and following the will of the majority.

Because EPSPs and IPSPs last longer than action potentials, they can build on one another at a very active synapse, leading to **temporal summation**. Although it typically takes substantial excitatory input to produce an action potential in the postsynaptic cell, temporal summation provides a means for a single, very active synapse to trigger the postsynaptic cell. One particularly persistent (and noisy) friend can definitely influence our decisions.

Neuromodulation

The synapses we have discussed so far involve an axon terminal or axonal varicosity as the presynaptic element and either a dendrite or a cell body as the postsynaptic element. In addition, we can observe synapses between an axon terminal and another axon fiber, as illustrated in ● Figure 3.24. These **axo-axonic synapses** have a modulating effect on the release of neurochemical by the target axon. If the presynaptic neuron increases the amount of neurochemical released, **presynaptic facilitation** has occurred. If the presynaptic neuron decreases the amount of neurochemical released by the target axon, we say that **presynaptic inhibition** has occurred. This type of modulation occurs quite frequently in sensory systems and during some types of learning (see Chapter 12).

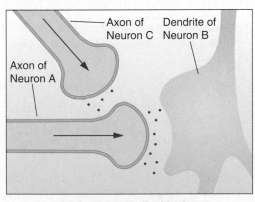
(a) Presynaptic Facilitation

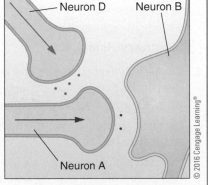
(b) Presynaptic Inhibition

© 2016 Cengage Learning®

> ● **Figure 3.24** Synapses Between Two Axons Modulate the Amount of Neurochemical Released In presynaptic facilitation, input from neuron C will increase the amount of neurochemical released by neuron A onto neuron B. In presynaptic inhibition, input from neuron D will decrease the amount of neurochemical released by neuron A, onto neuron B.

spatial summation Neural integration in which the combined inputs from many synapses converge on the axon hillock, where an action potential will result if threshold is reached.

temporal summation Neural integration in which excitation from one active synapse is sufficient to initiate the formation of an action potential.

axo-axonic synapse A synapse in which both the presynaptic and postsynaptic elements are axons.

presynaptic facilitation At a synapse between two axons, the increase of neurochemical release by the postsynaptic axon as a result of input from the presynaptic axon.

presynaptic inhibition At a synapse between two axons, the decrease of neurochemical release by the postsynaptic axon as a result of input from the presynaptic axon.

INTERIM SUMMARY 3.3

Summary Table: Communication at the Synapse

Event	Location	Mechanism of Action
Exocytosis	Axon terminal or axonal varicosity	• Ca2+ enters the cell. • Vesicles fuse with the axon terminal membrane. • Neurochemicals are released. • Vesicles are returned to the terminal interior and refilled.
Postsynaptic receptors bind neurochemical molecules	Postsynaptic membrane	• Receptors bind available neurochemical molecules in the gap. • Ion channels are directly opened in ionotropic receptors. • G proteins are released by metabotropic receptors, opening nearby ion channels.
Neurochemical deactivation	Synaptic gap	• Neurochemicals may diffuse away from the synapse, be deactivated by enzymes, or be transported back across the presynaptic membrane.
Postsynaptic potentials	Postsynaptic membrane	• EPSPs result from the opening of ligand-gated Na^+ channels. • IPSPs result from the opening of ligand-gated K^+ or Cl^- channels.
Integration or summation	Axon hillock of postsynaptic cell body	• Drifting positive and negative currents converge at the axon hillock. • If sufficient depolarization occurs at the axon hillock, the postsynaptic cell will generate an action potential.

Summary Points

1. Chemical synapses involve the release of neurochemicals by the presynaptic cell. Electrical synapses are characterized by very tiny synaptic gaps crossed by ion channels from the presynaptic and postsynaptic neurons. **(LO5)**

2. Receptor proteins on the postsynaptic cell can be either ionotropic or metabotropic. **(LO5)**

3. The action of neurochemicals in the synaptic gap may be terminated through diffusion away from the gap, by deactivation by enzymes, or by reuptake by the presynaptic neuron. **(LO5)**

4. Postsynaptic potentials are small, local, graded potentials that can last 5–10 msec. Excitatory postsynaptic potentials (EPSPs) produce slight depolarizations by opening channels that allow sodium to enter the cell. Inhibitory postsynaptic potentials (IPSPs) produce slight hyperpolarizations by opening channels that allow either chloride to enter or potassium to exit the cell. **(LO6)**

5. In spatial summation, the input from many synapses is added together to determine whether an action potential will be produced. In temporal summation, a single, very active synapse may provide sufficient input to produce an action potential. **(LO6)**

6. The release of neurochemicals at a synapse can be facilitated or inhibited by the activity at axo-axonic synapses. **(LO7)**

‖ Review Questions

1. Why would presynaptic neurons benefit from having autoreceptors?

2. What are the advantages to presynaptic inhibition and facilitation?

Chapter Review

THOUGHT QUESTIONS

1. If you were designing a neural system that had to respond very quickly over long distances, what characteristics would you want your axons to have?

2. If two equally active synapses are located on a distant dendrite and on the cell body, which will have the greatest effect on the axon hillock, and why? What is the likelihood that this cell will produce an action potential?

3. In multiple sclerosis, axons that were meant to be myelinated lose their myelin. In what ways would signaling in these axons be even less effective than in axons designed to be unmyelinated?

KEY TERMS

absolute refractory period (p. 83)
action potential (p. 72)
astrocyte (p. 64)
autoreceptor (p. 92)
axon (p. 67)
axon hillock (p. 72)
axon terminal (p. 72)
axon varicosity (p. 72)
bipolar neuron (p. 74)
cell body/soma (p. 67)
cytoskeleton (p. 69)
dendrite (p. 67)
dendritic spine (p. 72)
depolarization (p. 81)
diffusion (p. 77)
electrostatic pressure (p. 77)
excitatory postsynaptic potential (EPSP) (p. 94)
exocytosis (p. 90)
extracellular fluid (p. 68)
glia (p. 64)
G protein (p. 93)

hyperpolarization (p. 82)
inhibition (p. 90)
inhibitory postsynaptic potential (IPSP) (p. 94)
interneuron (p. 74)
intracellular fluid (p. 68)
ion (p. 69)
ion channel (p. 69)
ionotropic receptor (p. 93)
ion pump (p. 69)
ligand-gated channel (p. 69)
macroglia (p. 64)
metabotropic receptor (p. 93)
microfilament (p. 70)
microglia (p. 64)
microtubule (p. 67)
motor neuron (p. 74)
multipolar neuron (p. 73)
myelin (p. 72)
neural integration (p. 95)
neurochemical (p. 72)
neurofilament (p. 70)

neuron (p. 64)
node of Ranvier (p. 73)
oligodendrocyte (p. 64)
presynaptic facilitation (p. 97)
presynaptic inhibition (p. 97)
relative refractory period (p. 83)
resting potential (p. 77)
reuptake (p. 93)
saltatory conduction (p. 86)
Schwann cell (p. 64)
sensory neuron (p. 74)
sodium–potassium pump (p. 69)
spatial summation (p. 97)
synapse (p. 69)
synaptic gap (p. 72)
synaptic vesicle (p. 72)
temporal summation (p. 97)
threshold (p. 81)
unipolar neuron (p. 74)
voltage-dependent channel (p. 69)

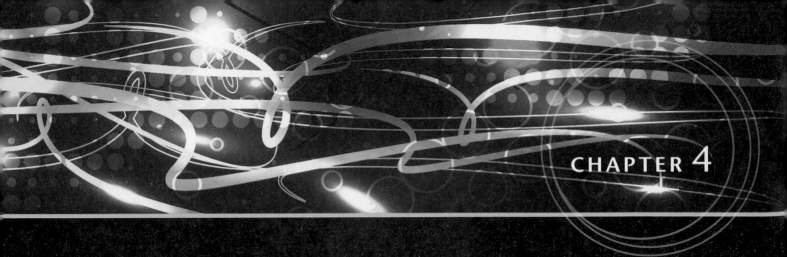

CHAPTER 4

Psychopharmacology

LEARNING OBJECTIVES

LO1 Differentiate among neurotransmitters, neuromodulators, and neurohormones.

LO2 Identify the major locations, functions, synthesis pathways, receptor characteristics, and process of deactivation for acetylcholine, dopamine, norepinephrine, epinephrine, serotonin, glutamate, GABA, glycine, and adenosine triphosphate.

LO3 Identify the major differences among small molecule, neuropeptide, and gasotransmitters.

LO4 Differentiate between agonists and antagonists.

LO5 Provide examples of drugs that produce effects by influencing neurochemical production, neurochemical storage, neurochemical release, receptor activity, reuptake, and enzymatic degradation.

LO6 Review the major principles of drug effects, including the mode of administration, sources of individual differences in reactions to drugs, placebo effects, tolerance, withdrawal, and addiction.

LO7 Identify the major features and modes of action of stimulants, opioids, marijuana, LSD, and alcohol.

CHAPTER OUTLINE

CONNECTING TO RESEARCH: Otto Loewi and "Vagus Stuff"

BEHAVIORAL NEUROSCIENCE GOES TO WORK: Substance Abuse Counselors

BUILDING BETTER HEALTH: Reducing Nicotine Use

THINKING ETHICALLY: Using Addictive Drugs Affects Future Generations

Neurotransmitters, Neuromodulators, and Neurohormones

Neurochemicals fall into three general categories: neurotransmitters, neuromodulators, and neurohormones. As we mentioned in Chapter 3, chemical synapses can be directed or nondirected. As shown in ● Figure 4.1, **neurotransmitters** participate in directed synapses by acting on neurons in their own immediate vicinity, generally at a synapse. **Neuromodulators** and **neurohormones** participate in nondirected synapses by acting on more distant neurons. Neuromodulators diffuse away from their site of release to influence diverse populations of neurons located at some distance from the releasing cell. This process is known as "volume transmission," because large volumes of the nervous system can be influenced. Neuromodulators remain in the cerebrospinal fluid for extended periods of time, during which they can continue to influence the activity of the central nervous system (CNS). Neurohormones travel in the blood supply to reach their final targets. Regardless of the distance traveled, these chemical messengers will interact only with other cells that have specialized receptor sites to receive them. As we will see later in this chapter, the same chemical can play more than one of these roles.

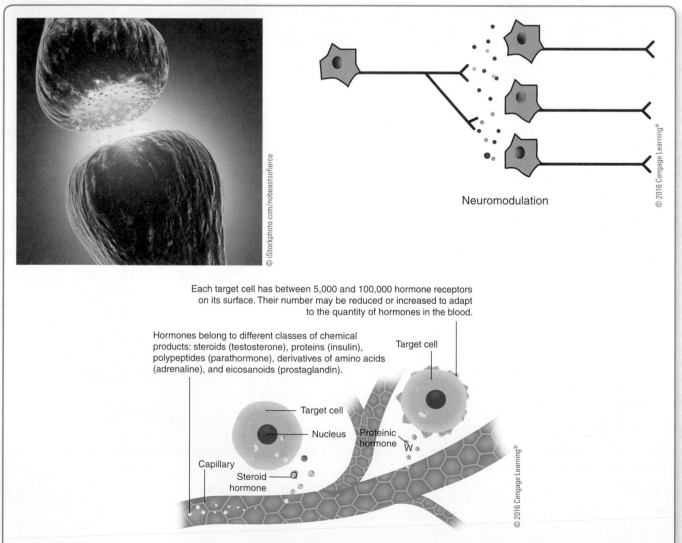

> ● **Figure 4.1** Neurotransmitters, Neuromodulators, and Neurohormones Neurotransmitters typically influence cells across a synaptic gap, while neuromodulators diffuse away after being released to affect cells at a distance. Neurohormones are often released into the bloodstream to travel to their ultimate destinations.

Identifying Neurochemicals

Our first step in understanding the biochemistry of the nervous system is to define the characteristics of neurochemicals. Because a single chemical can perform a wide variety of functions in a cell, it is challenging to determine when and where it is acting as a chemical messenger. Immunohistochemistry, which uses antibodies for particular neurochemicals, makes the identification process somewhat easier (see Chapter 1).

Neurochemicals are substances released by one cell that produce a reaction in a target cell. Beyond this basic definition, neuroscientists generally agree with the following additional criteria:

1. The substance must be present within a presynaptic cell.
2. The substance is released in response to presynaptic depolarization.
3. The substance interacts with specific receptors on a postsynaptic cell.

Types of Neurochemicals

As shown in ● Figure 4.2, neurochemicals fall into three classes, the **small molecules**, the **neuropeptides**, and the gasotransmitters. The small molecules can be further divided into **amino acids** and amines, which are derived from amino acids. Neuropeptides are chains of amino acids. Gases known as **gasotransmitters** (Sen & Snyder, 2010) have been shown to influence adjacent neurons in ways similar to more classical chemical messengers.

Small molecules and neuropeptides differ in several important ways. Small molecules are typically synthesized in the axon terminal, whereas neuropeptides are synthesized in the cell body and must be transported the length of the axon. Vesicles containing neuropeptides are used only once, in contrast to the recycling of vesicles possible with small molecules. Compared to the release of small molecules, the release of neuropeptide vesicles requires higher levels of calcium, which in turn requires a higher rate of action potentials reaching the axon terminal (Fulop & Smith, 2006).

small molecules One of a group of neurochemicals that includes amino acids and amines.
neuropeptide A peptide that acts as a neurotransmitter, a neuromodulator, or a neurohormone.
amino acid An essential component of proteins.
gasotransmitter A gas such as nitric oxide (NO) that performs a signaling function.

••• Connecting to **Research**

OTTO LOEWI AND "VAGUS STUFF"

Early physiologists realized that if electrical signaling was the only mode of communication in the nervous system, messages would be sent and received much faster than their observations were indicating. There must be another step involved, but what form did that step take?

German physiologist Otto Loewi (1873–1961) suspected, like many others, that some form of chemical communication was involved. In 1921, he succeeded in demonstrating he was correct. To test his hypothesis, he dissected hearts from two frogs and placed them in separate containers. Inserting a small cannula of saline solution maintained normal heart activity for several hours. When Loewi electrically stimulated the vagus nerve attached to one of the hearts, the heart slowed down. Loewi removed some of the liquid from the cannula inserted in this heart and applied it to the second heart, which also

slowed down. Loewi concluded correctly that a substance released by the vagus nerve was responsible for slowing the heart. He referred to the substance as "Vagusstoff" or "vagus stuff," but we know this substance today by the name of acetylcholine.

Loewi's discovery earned him the Nobel Prize in 1932, but he is almost more famous for his recollections of how his famous experiment came to mind (Loewi, 1953). After struggling with his research question, Loewi came up with the perfect design while asleep, but not necessarily while "dreaming" as is often reported (see Chapter 11). He wrote notes on paper on his nightstand and, much to his dismay, could not read the notes the next morning. While asleep the next night, Loewi once again thought of his design. This time, instead of writing it down, he went to his laboratory at 3 o'clock in the morning and immediately performed his experiment.

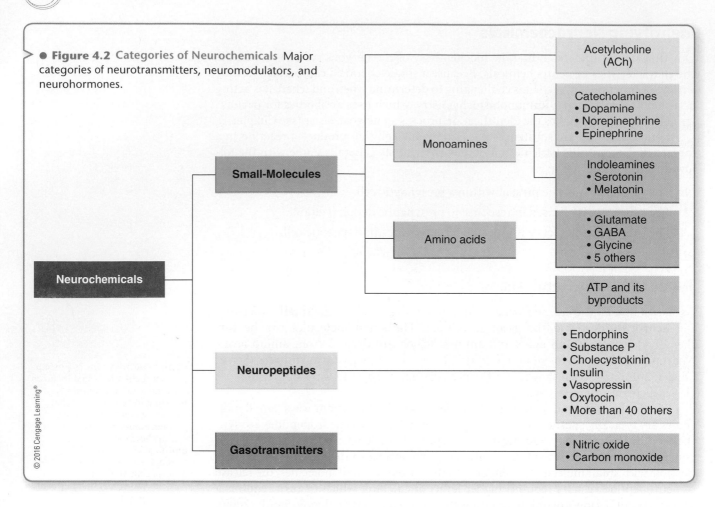

● **Figure 4.2** Categories of Neurochemicals Major categories of neurotransmitters, neuromodulators, and neurohormones.

© 2016 Cengage Learning®

Finally, neuropeptides diffuse away from the synapse or are broken down by enzymes, but unlike the small molecules, they are not deactivated by reuptake (see Chapter 3).

Early pharmacological pioneer Henry Dale proposed that a single neuron released one and only one type of chemical messenger. Using modern technology, we can see that Dale was incorrect. Many neurons release a small molecule along with a neuropeptide (Salio, Lossi, Ferrini, & Merighi, 2006) or a gasotransmitter. Further, studies of motor neurons show that the same neuron can release two small molecules in different locations. As we will see in a later section, motor neurons release acetylcholine onto muscle fibers and other neurons in the spinal cord but release glutamate only in the spinal cord and not onto muscle fibers (Nishimaru, Restrepo, Ryge, Yanagawa, & Kiehn, 2005).

TABLE 4.1 | Features of Small-Molecules and Neuropeptides

	Small-Molecules	Neuropeptides
Synthesis	In axon terminal	In cell body; requires transport
Recycling of Vesicles	Yes	No
Activation	Moderate action potential frequency	High action potential frequency
Deactivation	Reuptake or enzymatic degradation	Diffusion away from the synapse or enzymatic degradation

THE SMALL MOLECULES A number of small molecules meet all or most of the preceding criteria specified for neurochemicals and appear to play a vital role in neural signaling: acetylcholine, six monoamines, several amino acids, and the energy molecule adenosine triphosphate (ATP) and its byproducts.

Acetylcholine (ACh) was the very first chemical messenger to be discovered. Neurons that use ACh as their major neurochemical are referred to as cholinergic neurons. The cholingeric neuron obtains the building block choline from dietary fats and from the breakdown of existing ACh. A second building block, acetyl coenzyme A (acetyl CoA), results from the metabolic activities of mitochondria, so it is abundantly present in most cells. The enzyme choline acetyltransferase (ChAT) acts on these two building blocks, or precursors, to produce ACh. The presence of the enzyme ChAT provides a useful marker for identifying cholinergic neurons because ChAT is found only in neurons that produce ACh.

Cholinergic neurons also manufacture the enzyme **acetylcholinesterase (AChE)**. AChE is released into the synaptic gap, where it breaks down any ACh in that location. The choline resulting from the breakdown of ACh can then be recaptured by the presynaptic neuron and resynthesized into more ACh.

ACh is the primary neurotransmitter at the neuromuscular junction, the synapse between a neuron and a muscle fiber (see Chapter 8). ACh is also essential to the operation of the autonomic nervous system. All preganglionic synapses in the autonomic nervous system are cholinergic. Postganglionic synapses in the parasympathetic division of the autonomic nervous system are also cholinergic (see Chapter 2).

In addition to their importance in the peripheral nervous system (PNS), cholinergic neurons are widely distributed in the brain. As shown in ● Figure 4.3, major groups of cholinergic neurons located in the basal forebrain, septal area, and brainstem influence the cerebral cortex, hippocampus, and amygdala. As we will see in Chapter 15,

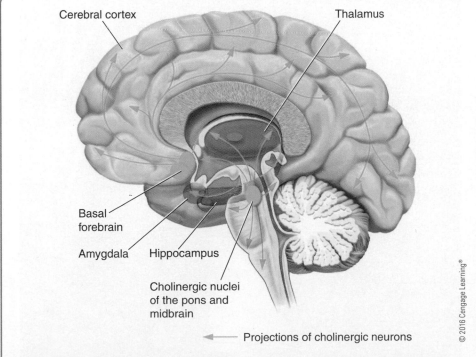

Cerebral cortex

Thalamus

Basal forebrain

Amygdala   Hippocampus

Cholinergic nuclei of the pons and midbrain

← — Projections of cholinergic neurons

© 2016 Cengage Learning®

> ● **Figure 4.3 The Distribution of Cholinergic Systems in the Brain** In addition to playing important roles at the neuromuscular junction and in the autonomic nervous system, cholinergic neurons are widely distributed in the brain. Important systems originate in the basal forebrain and brainstem and form projections to the limbic system and cerebral cortex. These systems participate in learning and memory and deteriorate in patients diagnosed with Alzheimer's disease.

acetylcholine (ACh) A major small-molecule neurochemical used at the neuromuscular junction, in the autonomic nervous system, and in the central nervous system (CNS).
acetylcholinesterase (AChE) An enzyme that breaks down acetylcholine (ACh).

these groups of neurons deteriorate as a result of Alzheimer's disease. Not too surprisingly, given the memory loss associated with Alzheimer's disease, these cholinergic neurons appear to participate in attention, wakefulness, learning, and memory.

Two major subtypes of cholinergic receptors, **nicotinic receptors** and **muscarinic receptors**, are found in the nervous system (Dani, 2001). These receptors take their names from substances other than ACh to which they also react. In other words, a nicotinic receptor responds to both ACh and to nicotine, found in all tobacco products, whereas the muscarinic receptor responds to both ACh and muscarine, a substance derived from the hallucinogenic (and highly poisonous) mushroom *Amanita muscaria*, shown in ● Figure 4.4.

Nicotinic and muscarinic receptors differ in their mechanisms of action and locations within the nervous system. As we observed in Chapter 3, receptors are either single-step ionotropic or multiple-step metabotropic in structure. Nicotinic receptors are fast ionotropic receptors. In contrast, muscarinic receptors are slower metabotropic receptors. Nicotinic receptors are found at the neuromuscular junction, which is logical given the need for speed in muscular responses. Muscarinic receptors are found in heart muscle and other smooth muscles (see Chapter 8). The CNS contains both nicotinic and muscarinic receptors, but the muscarinic are more common (Ehlert, Roeske, & Yamamura, 1995). Both types of receptors are also found in the autonomic nervous system.

The six **monoamines** are further divided into subgroups, the **catecholamines** (dopamine, norepinephrine, and epinephrine), the **indoleamines** (serotonin and melatonin), and histamine. All of the monoamines are subject to reuptake from the synaptic gap following release. Within the axon terminal, monoamines that are not encased in vesicles are broken down by the action of the enzyme **monoamine oxidase (MAO)**. Outside neurons, catecholamines are broken down by the enzyme **catechol-O-methyl-transferase (COMT)**.

nicotinic receptor A postsynaptic receptor that responds to nicotine and acetylcholine (ACh).

muscarinic receptor A postsynaptic receptor that responds to both acetylcholine (ACh) and muscarine.

monoamines One of a major group of biogenic amine neurotransmitters, including dopamine, norepinephrine, epinephrine, and serotonin.

catecholamines A member of a group of related biogenic amines that includes dopamine, epinephrine, and norepinephrine.

indoleamines One of a subgroup of monoamines, including serotonin and melatonin.

monoamine oxidase (MAO) An enzyme that breaks down monoamines.

catechol-O-methyl-transferase (COMT) An enzyme that breaks down catecholamines in the synaptic gap.

L-dopa A substance produced during the synthesis of catecholamines that is also administered as a treatment for Parkinson's disease.

© Vitaly Ilyasov/Shutterstock.com

● **Figure 4.4** *Amanita muscaria* Muscarinic cholinergic receptors get their name in recognition of their response to both acetylcholine (ACh) and muscarine, derived from the deadly *Amanita muscaria* mushroom.

Catecholamine synthesis begins with the amino acid tyrosine, as shown in ● Figure 4.5. All neurons containing a catecholamine also contain the enzyme tyrosine hydroxylase (TH). When TH acts on tyrosine, the end product is **L-dopa** (L-dihydroxyphenylalanine). The production of **dopamine** requires one step following the synthesis of L-dopa. The enzyme dopa decarboxylase acts on L-dopa to produce dopamine. Dopamine is converted to **norepinephrine** by the action of the enzyme dopamine β-hydroxylase (DBH). This last step takes place within the synaptic vesicles. Finally, the catecholamine **epinephrine** is produced by the reaction between norepinephrine and the enzyme phenylethanolamine N-methyl-transferase (PNMT). The synthesis of epinephrine is complicated. PNMT exists in the intracellular fluid of the axon terminal of neurons that use epinephrine. Once norepinephrine is synthesized within synaptic vesicles, it must be released back into the intracellular fluid, where it is converted by PNMT into epinephrine. The epinephrine is then transported back into vesicles.

Dopamine systems are involved with motivated behaviors and the processing of reward. As we will see later in the chapter, addiction to drugs (and also to some behaviors, such as gambling) is especially influenced by activity in circuits using dopamine. In addition, disruptions in dopamine function are suspected of playing a role in schizophrenia and attention deficit hyperactivity disorder (see Chapter 16).

As shown in ● Figure 4.6, cells releasing dopamine are located primarily in the midbrain and form connections with other parts of the brain along several major pathways. To make learning the names of neural pathways easier, remember that the order of the terms in a pathway name allows you to follow the pathway from its origin to any intermediary stops and to its final destination.

The first pathway, known as the **mesostriatal pathway** or **nigrostriatal pathway**, can be further divided into two parts (*meso* refers to mesencephanolon or midbrain, *nigro* refers to the substantia nigra, and *striatal* refers to structures within the basal ganglia). Both parts originate in the substantia nigra. The first part proceeds in a dorsal direction to communicate with the caudate nucleus, putamen, and globus pallidus of the basal ganglia. This circuit participates in voluntary motor activity. It appears to be particularly damaged in cases of Parkinson's disease, in which patients have great difficulties initiating movement (see Chapter 8). The second part travels in a ventral direction from the substantia nigra to form connections with the nucleus accumbens, the olfactory cortex, the caudate nucleus, and putamen. This system is very important to the processing of reward and incentive.

A second major dopaminergic pathway, the **mesolimbocortical system**, arises in the ventral tegmentum of the midbrain and projects to various parts of the limbic system and cortex, including the hippocampus, the amygdala, olfactory cortex, septal area, (the cingulate cortex, and the parahippocampal cortex (see Chapter 2). Connections between the midbrain and limbic system might influence motivated behavior, while connections between the midbrain and cortex participate in higher-level cognitive functioning, including the planning of behavior. As we will see in Chapter 16, disruption of this system appears to be involved in schizophrenia. Increased activity in dopaminergic neurons projecting from the midbrain to the

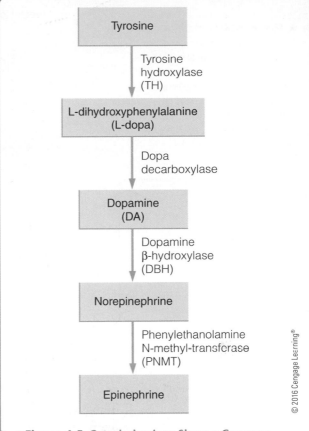

● **Figure 4.5 Catecholamines Share a Common Synthesis Pathway** The catecholamines, including dopamine, norepinephrine, and epinephrine, are synthesized from the substrate tyrosine. Tyrosine is converted into L-dopa by the action of tyrosine hydroxylase. L-dopa is converted into dopamine by dopa decarboxylase. The action of dopamine β-hydroxylase on dopamine produces norepinephrine. When norepinephrine reacts with phenylethanolamine N-methyl-transferase, epinephrine is produced.

© 2016 Cengage Learning®

dopamine A major monoamine and catecholamine neurotransmitter implicated in motor control, reward, and psychosis.

norepinephrine A major monoamine and catecholamine neurotransmitter.

epinephrine One of the monoamine/catecholamine neurotransmitters; also known as adrenaline.

mesostriatal pathway or **nigrostriatal pathway** A dopaminergic pathway originating in the substantia nigra and projecting to the basal ganglia; also known as the nigrostriatal pathway.

mesolimbocortical system A dopaminergic pathway originating in the ventral tegmentum of the midbrain and projecting to the limbic system and cortex.

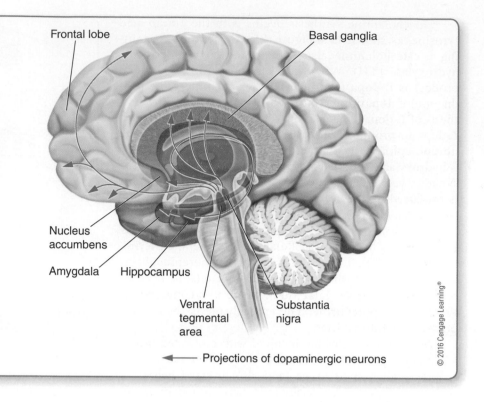

● Figure 4.6 Dopaminergic Systems in the Brain Dopaminergic neurons in the midbrain project to the basal ganglia, the limbic system, and the frontal lobes of the cerebral cortex. These systems appear to participate in motor control, reward, and the planning of behavior.

Frontal lobe

Basal ganglia

Nucleus accumbens

Amygdala

Hippocampus

Ventral tegmental area

Substantia nigra

← Projections of dopaminergic neurons

© 2016 Cengage Learning®

limbic system coupled with a decrease in activity in dopaminergic neurons projecting from the midbrain to the cortex might be responsible for some of the symptoms observed in this psychological disorder.

Two other dopaminergic pathways originate in the hypothalamus. The paraventricular dopamine system connects the hypothalamus to the thalamus and to sympathetic neurons in the spinal cord, helping to coordinate motivated behaviors such as appetite, sex, and thirst. A second hypothalamic dopaminergic pathway connects to the pituitary gland and controls milk production in mammals.

As we saw in the case of ACh receptors, multiple receptor subtypes also exist for dopamine, labeled D_1 through D_5 in order of their discovery. The receptors are grouped into two categories. One class includes the D_1 and D_5 receptors, and the other class includes the remaining D_2, D_3, and D_4 receptors. All of these receptors are of the slow metabotropic variety. The first class produces excitation while the second class produces inhibition. All of these receptor types are found in the basal ganglia and olfactory cortex, but the first-class receptors are also found in the hippocampus and hypothalamus while the second-class receptors are found in the frontal lobes of the cortex, the thalamus, and the brain stem.

Epinephrine and norepinephrine were formerly referred to as adrenalin and noradrenalin, respectively. We continue to refer to neurons releasing epinephrine as adrenergic and those releasing norepinephrine as noradrenergic.

Epinephrine is an important neurohormone, but plays a limited role as a CNS neurochemical. Two areas in the medulla contain cells that release epinephrine and participate in such basic functions as the coordination of eating and regulation of blood pressure. The "adrenalin rush" we associate with stress actually results from the release of epinephrine from the adrenal glands located above the kidneys in the lower back into the blood supply.

Neurons that secrete norepinephrine are found in the pons, medulla, and hypothalamus. Probably the most significant source of norepinephrine is the locus coeruleus of the pons, shown in ●Figure 4.7, in spite of the fact that this structure might contain as few as 4,000 cells. These cells make up for their small numbers, however, by having axons with as many as 100,000 collaterals each. Projections from the locus

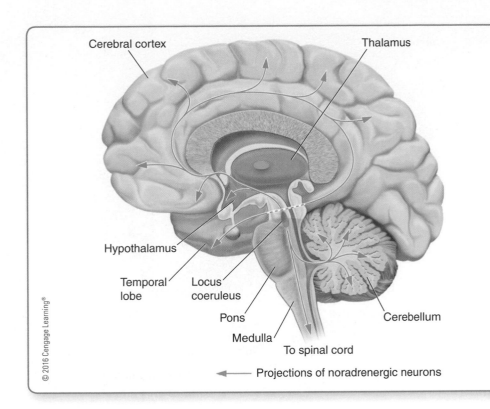

© 2016 Cengage Learning®

● **Figure 4.7** Noradrenergic Systems in the Brain Neurons releasing norepinephrine are found in the pons, medulla, and hypothalamus. Released norepinephrine goes to nearly every major part of the brain and spinal cord, producing arousal and vigilance.

coeruleus go to the spinal cord and nearly every major part of the brain. The primary result of activity in these circuits is to increase arousal and vigilance. In the PNS, norepinephrine is found at the postganglionic synapses of the sympathetic nervous system, which is also involved in arousal.

Receptor types that respond to either norepinephrine or epinephrine are classified as α or β receptors. These receptors are found in both the CNS and target organs that respond to sympathetic nervous system activity and neurohormones. All of these receptors are metabotropic, which might surprise you given the need for speedy responses associated with the fight-or-flight functions of the sympathetic nervous system.

Indoleamines, including **serotonin** and melatonin, are similar enough in chemical structure to the catecholamines to share the umbrella term of monoamine yet are different enough to warrant their own subheading. The synthesis of serotonin begins with the amino acid tryptophan. Tryptophan is obtained from dietary sources, including grains, meat, and dairy products. As shown in ● Figure 4.8, two chemical reactions are required to convert tryptophan into serotonin. The first is the action of the enzyme tryptophan hydroxylase, which converts tryptophan to 5-hydroxytryptophan (5-HTP). Second, the 5-HTP is converted to serotonin by the action of the enzyme 5-HTP decarboxylase.

In spite of their essential roles in behavior and their widespread projections, serotonergic neurons in the CNS are surprisingly few in number. We noted in Chapter 2 that 95 percent of the body's serotonergic neurons are located in the enteric nervous system. In contrast, estimates suggest there might be as few as 200,000 serotonergic neurons in the human brain (Baker et al., 1991). As shown in ● Figure 4.9, some serotonergic neurons are located in the medulla and cerebellum, but most are located in the raphe nuclei of the brainstem. Their projections travel to the spinal cord, the cerebellum, the limbic system, and the cerebral cortex. The more rostral serotonergic neurons form direct synapses, while the serotonergic neurons in the medulla form indirect synapses. At least 15 subtypes of serotonergic receptors have been identified, and all but one of these function as metabotropic receptors (Leonard, 1992). Several serve as autoreceptors.

Serotonergic activity has been implicated in a variety of behaviors, including appetite, sleep, mood, dominance, and aggression. Serotonin pathways influence our motivation to consume carbohydrates, leading to experimentation with reuptake blockers to

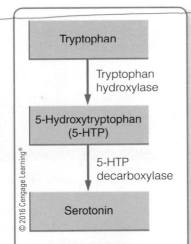

© 2016 Cengage Learning®

● **Figure 4.8** The Synthesis of Serotonin Serotonin synthesis begins with dietary tryptophan, which is converted into 5-HTP by the action of tryptophan hydroxylase. 5-HTP is converted into serotonin by the action of 5-HTP decarboxylase.

serotonin A major monoamine and indoleamine neurochemical believed to participate in the regulation of mood, sleep, aggression, social status, and appetite.

● **Figure 4.9** Serotonergic Pathways in the Brain Most serotonergic neurons are found in the raphe nuclei of the brainstem. Serotonin released by these neurons affects the spinal cord, cerebellum, limbic system, and cerebral cortex. These systems participate in the control of mood, sleep, social status, aggression, and appetite.

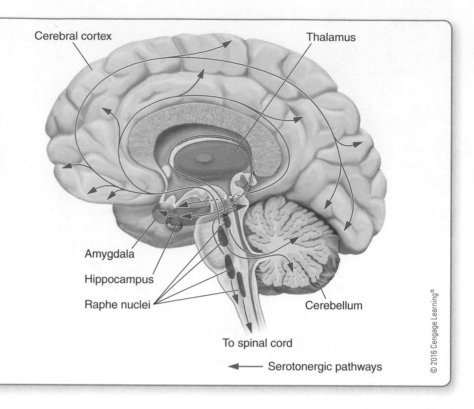

Cerebral cortex

Thalamus

Amygdala

Hippocampus

Raphe nuclei

Cerebellum

To spinal cord

← Serotonergic pathways

© 2016 Cengage Learning®

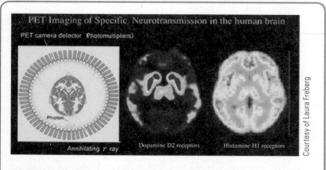

PET Imaging of Specific Neurotransmission in the human brain

PET camera detector Photomultipliers

Annihilating γ ray

Dopamine D2 receptors

Histamine H1 receptors

Courtesy of Laura Freberg

● **Figure 4.10** Location of Histamine Receptors in the Brain Histamine activity in the brain is associated with wakefulness. Older versions of antihistamines crossed the blood–brain barrier and produced drowsiness.

treat obesity. As we will see in Chapter 11, serotonin activity varies systematically with stages of wakefulness and sleep. Mood disorders, such as major depressive disorder (see Chapter 16), are often treated with medications that increase the activity of serotonin. Finally, low levels of serotonin activity are associated not just with depressed mood, but also with lower social rank, increased risk taking, and aggression (see Chapter 14).

Histamine results from the action of histidine decarboxylase on histidine in the presence of vitamin B6. Three types of histamine receptors are found in both the CNS and PNS, and all are metabotropic (see ● Figure 4.10). As we will see in Chapter 11, histamine activity is positively correlated with wakefulness, so antihistamines are the basis of most over-the-counter treatments for insomnia. Antihistamines are also used to reduce unpleasant symptoms of allergies. Newer versions that do not cross the blood–brain barrier manage to reduce peripheral symptoms like a runny nose without producing drowsiness.

After ACh and the monoamines, the next category of small molecules is the amino acids. Although as many as eight amino acids participate as chemical messengers, three are especially significant: **glutamate**, **gamma-aminobutyric acid (GABA)**, and **glycine**. Glutamate (also known as glutamic acid) and glycine are among the 20 basic amino acids that are used to build other proteins. GABA is not.

Glutamate is the most common excitatory neurochemical in the CNS (Schwartz, 2000). Glutamate is synthesized from α-ketoglutarate in the mitochondria. Once released, glutamate is taken up by both neurons and astrocytes. The synaptic area must be cleared of excess glutamate because extended action of glutamate on neurons can be toxic. Some people appear to be oversensitive to the common food additive monosodium glutamate (MSG), which consists of a combination of glutamate and sodium. Adverse reactions include chest pain, headache, nausea, and rapid heartbeat. However, the blood–brain barrier (see Chapter 3) drains dietary glutamate from

glutamate A major excitatory amino acid neurochemical.
gamma-aminobutyric acid (GABA) A major inhibitory amino acid neurochemical.
glycine An amino acid neurochemical having inhibitory effects in the spinal cord and excitatory effects in conjunction with the NMDA glutamate receptor.

entering the brain (Hawkins, 2009), and the Food and Drug Administration (FDA) views MSG as a safe food additive for most adults (Beyreuther et al., 2007; U.S. Food and Drug Administration [FDA], 2011).

Glutamate receptors can be either ionotropic or metabotropic. Three major types of ionotropic glutamate receptors are named after the external substances that also activate them, in the same manner that ACh receptors were named nicotinic or muscarinic. The three glutamate receptors are the N-methyl-D-aspartate (NMDA) receptor, the alpha-amino-3-hydroxy-5-methylisoxazole-4-proprionic acid (AMPA) receptor, and the kainate receptor. Both the AMPA receptor, which is the most common variety, and the kainate receptor operate by controlling a sodium channel. When these receptors bind molecules of glutamate, a sodium channel opens, and an EPSP is produced.

The NMDA receptor, shown in ● Figure 4.11, has received a tremendous amount of attention due to its unusual method of action. NMDA receptors are apparently unique in that they are both voltage-dependent and ligand-dependent. In other words, they will not open unless glutamate is present *and* the postsynaptic membrane is depolarized at the same time. At the typical negative resting potentials of the postsynaptic neuron, the ion channels of NMDA receptors are blocked by magnesium ions. However, because NMDA and AMPA receptors are usually found near one another on the same postsynaptic membrane, sodium moving through a nearby AMPA receptors will depolarize the postsynaptic cell. When the membrane becomes sufficiently depolarized, the magnesium ions will be ejected from the NMDA receptor, allowing it to open in response to the binding of glutamate.

NMDA receptors are also unusual in their ability to allow both positively charged sodium and calcium ions to enter the cell, which further depolarizes the cell. In addition, calcium activates enzyme sequences that result in structural and biochemical changes. Because of calcium's ability to trigger lasting changes in neurons, the NMDA receptor is thought to participate in functions such as long-term memory, which we will discuss in Chapter 12. The action of calcium upon entering the cell is also responsible for the toxicity of excess glutamate levels mentioned earlier. As more glutamate stimulates NMDA receptors, more calcium enters neurons. The resulting excess enzyme activity can literally digest and kill the affected neuron. This process might be responsible for much damage following strokes and in a number of brain diseases (Olney, 1994; see Chapter 15).

GABA serves as the major inhibitory neurochemical of the CNS. GABA is synthesized from glutamate through the action of the enzyme glutamic acid decarboxylase

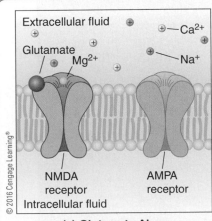
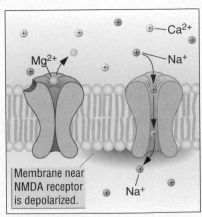
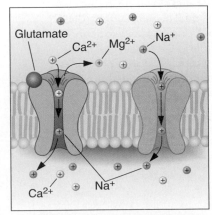

(a) Glutamate Alone   (b) Depolarization Alone   (c) Glutamate and Depolarization

● **Figure 4.11 The NMDA Glutamate Receptor** The NMDA receptor has two unusual qualities. First, it requires both the binding of glutamate and sufficient depolarization before it responds. At the resting potential, the ion channel is blocked by a molecule of magnesium (Mg^{2+}). Depolarization ejects the Mg^{2+}. If glutamate now binds with the receptor, the channel will open and ions will be allowed to pass. Second, the receptor allows both sodium and calcium ions to enter the neuron. These features make the NMDA glutamate receptor a prime candidate for having a significant role in learning at the cellular level.

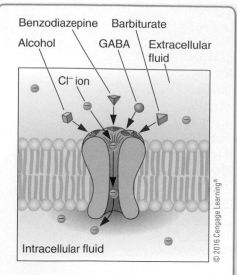

Benzodiazepine   Barbiturate
Alcohol   GABA   Extracellular
fluid
Cl⁻ ion
Intracellular fluid

© 2016 Cengage Learning®

● **Figure 4.12 The GABA_A Receptor Interacts with Several Drugs** In addition to binding sites for GABA itself, the GABA_A receptor also contains binding sites that interact with benzodiazepines, barbiturates, and ethanol (alcohol). These drugs depress nervous system activity by increasing the inhibition produced by GABA. Combining any of these drugs can produce a life-threatening level of neural inhibition.

(GAD). There are two types of GABA receptors, referred to as GABA_A and GABA_B. GABA_A receptors are ionotropic postsynaptic chloride channels, which allow negatively charged chloride ions to enter the cell. As shown in ● Figure 4.12, the GABA_A receptor interacts with a number of psychoactive substances, which we'll discuss in more detail later in the chapter. GABA_B receptors are metabotropic potassium channels, which allow positively charged potassium ions to leave the cell. Hyperpolarization occurs whenever negative ions enter the cell or when positive ions leave the cell.

Glycine acts directly as an inhibitory neurochemical, primarily in synapses formed by spinal cord interneurons but also in smaller numbers elsewhere in the nervous system (see ● Figure 4.13). It plays an excitatory role in conjunction with glutamate at the NMDA receptor described earlier. Glycine is synthesized when the enzyme serine transhydroxymethylase acts on serine in mitochondria. It is removed from the synaptic gap by reuptake. Ionotropic glycine receptors allow chloride to enter the cell, leading to hyperpolarization. These receptors are blocked by the poison strychnine. Strychnine kills by preventing the diaphragm muscles from relaxing. Because glycine also participates in the management of sleep-waking cycles, it is used occasionally as an unapproved alternative approach to treating insomnia.

Adenosine triphosphate (ATP) and its byproducts, particularly **adenosine**, act as neurochemicals in the CNS and in connections between autonomic neurons and the vas deferens, bladder, heart, and gut. ATP is involved with the perception of pain (see Chapter 7) and sleep–waking cycles (see Chapter 11). ATP frequently coexists in high concentrations in vesicles containing other chemical messengers, particularly the catecholamines. Adenosine, shown in ● Figure 4.14, inhibits the release of a wide range of classical neurochemicals (Dunwiddie, 2001).

● **Figure 4.13 Glycinergic Neurons** Glycine is a major inhibitory neurotransmitter in spinal cord interneurons and in smaller numbers of neurons located elsewhere in the central nervous system (CNS). Glycine plays an excitatory role at the NMDA glutamate receptor and also contributes to the management of sleep–waking cycles.

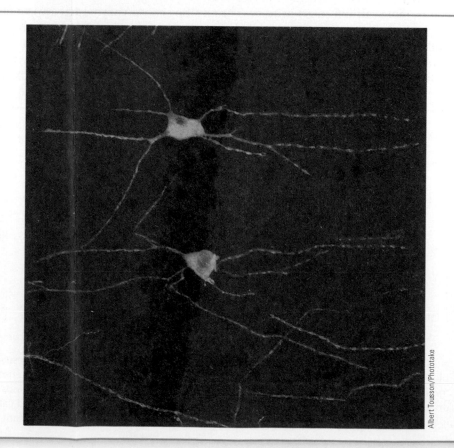

Albert Tousson/Phototake

adenosine A neurochemical that is a byproduct of adenosine triphosphate (ATP).

NEUROPEPTIDES There are at least 40 different peptides that act as neuromodulators and neurohormones. Neuropeptides, unlike the small molecules, are manufactured in the cell body and must be transported to the axon terminal, a process that could take as long as one day. Because of this, it is possible to "run out of" neuropeptides during periods of active signaling. Neuropeptides often coexist in the same neuron with a small-molecule messenger and modify its effect. A single neuron can contain and release several different neuropeptides. All receptors for neuropeptides are metabotropic (see Chapter 3). Deactivation of neuropeptides in the synapse occurs through diffusion or enzymatic degradation and is generally a very slow process.

Among the neuropeptides are substance P, which is involved in the perception of pain, and the endogenous morphines (endorphins), substances that act on the same receptors as opioids such as heroin. The distribution of receptors for endorphins may be seen in ● Figure 4.15. Peptides involved with digestion, including insulin and cholecystokinin (CCK), have neuromodulating and neurohormone functions in addition to their better-known impact on the processing of nutrients (see Chapter 9). Other peptides released from the pituitary gland, such as oxytocin and vasopressin, act as both neuromodulators and hormones.

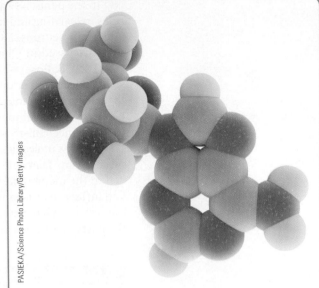

PASIEKA/Science Photo Library/Getty Images

● **Figure 4.14 Caffeine and Adenosine Share Similar Structure** Because of their similar structures, caffeine and adenosine (shown here) compete at binding sites of postsynaptic receptors for adenosine. Because adenosine activity is correlated with drowsiness, caffeine's ability to block adenosine at the receptor contributes to alertness.

GASOTRANSMITTERS Recent developments in the study of neural transmission have stretched the boundaries of our criteria for chemical messaging. Some gases, including **nitric oxide (NO)**, carbon monoxide (CO), and hydrogen sulfide (H_2S), transfer information from one cell to another (Wang, Li, Song, & Pang, 2014). NO is a very short-living free radical produced by actions of the enzyme nitric oxide synthase (NOS), which is found in a small number of neurons (between 1 and 2 percent of those in the cerebral cortex), on the amino acid arginine.

Prior to the 1990s, NO was best known as a precursor for acid rain. We now understand that NO is involved with neural communication, the maintenance of blood pressure, and penile erection (Furchgott & Vanhoutte, 1989; Snyder, 2000). The anti-impotence medication sildenafil citrate (Viagra) acts by boosting the activity of

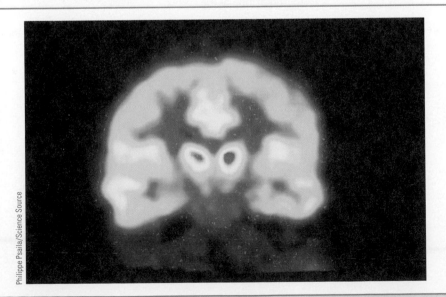

Philippe Psaila/Science Source

● **Figure 4.15** Distribution of Endorphin Receptors in the Human Brain This PET scan identifies areas of the brain rich in endorphin receptors, which appear in red and yellow. These receptors respond both to our naturally occurring endorphins and to externally supplied opioids, including heroin and morphine.

nitric oxide (NO) A gas that performs a type of signaling between neurons.

NO in the penis. NO activates second messengers within neurons, leading to probable roles in learning and memory, anxiety, and addiction. NO at high levels can have toxic effects on neurons. NO abnormalities may underlie a number of psychological disorders discussed in Chapter 16, including schizophrenia (Bernstein, Becker, Keilhoff, Grecksch, & Bogerts, 2011). NO appears to play a particularly important role in regulating communication between the thalamus and the cerebral cortex, which in turn influences the amount of sensory input processed by the highest levels of the brain (Alexander, Kurukulasuriya, Mu, & Godwin, 2006).

The mechanism for gasotransmission is unlike the processes we have discussed so far. Gaseous molecules diffuse through membranes without needing vesicles or a release mechanism. They act on receptors located within cells rather than on receptors embedded in the membrane. It is even possible for gasotransmitters to travel through one cell and influence its neighbors. Gasotransmitters break down very quickly without needing the action of enzymes. In addition, gasotransmitters appear to transfer information from the postsynaptic neuron to the presynaptic neuron, rather than the other way around.

INTERIM SUMMARY 4.1

‖ Summary Table: Characteristics of Selected Neurochemicals

Neurotransmitter	Locations	Functions
Acetylcholine (ACh)	• Neuromuscular junction • Preganglionic autonomic synapses • Postganglionic parasympathetic synapses • Basal forebrain projections to hippocampus and amygdala; the septum; the brainstem	• Movement • Autonomic function • Learning and memory
Dopamine	• Substantia nigra and basal ganglia • Ventral tegmentum projections to hippocampus, amygdala, and nucleus accumbens • Ventral tegmentum projections to frontal lobe of the cortex	• Movement • Reinforcement • Planning
Norepinephrine	• Pons (especially locus coeruleus, which projects widely to spinal cord and brain) • Medulla • Hypothalamus • Postganglionic sympathetic synapses	• Arousal and vigilance • Mood
Serotonin	Pons, particularly the raphe nucleus, projecting widely to the brain and spinal cord	• Sleep • Appetite • Mood • Aggression • Social rank

Neurotransmitter	Locations	Functions
Glutamate	Widely distributed in the central nervous system	• Excitation • Long-term memory
GABA	Widely distributed in the central nervous system	• Inhibition • Mood • Seizure threshold
Glycine	Spinal interneurons, lesser role in the central nervous system	• Inhibition • Excitation at the NMDA glutamate receptor • Sleep
Adenosine triphosphate (ATP) and byproducts	• Central nervous system • Autonomic nervous system • In some axons containing catecholamines	• Pain modulation • Inhibition
Endorphins	• Periaqueductal gray • Hypothalamus • Pituitary gland • Limbic system • Basal ganglia • Spinal cord • Ventral tegmentum	• Pain reduction • Feelings of well-being
Substance P	• Spinal cord	• Pain
Nitric oxide (NO)	• Central and peripheral nervous systems • Smooth muscle	• Relaxes smooth muscle cells in blood vessels • Erection • Possible retrograde signaling

‖ Summary Points

1. Affect adjacent cells across the synapse. Neuromodulators diffuse away from the synapse to target cells some distance away. Circulating neurohormones reach even more distant target cells. (LO1)

2. Neurochemicals exist within presynaptic neurons, are released in response to presynaptic depolarization, and interact with specific receptors on a postsynaptic cell. (LO2)

3. ACh is found at the neuromuscular junction, in the autonomic nervous system, and within the CNS. Dopamine is involved with systems controlling movement, reinforcement, and planning. Norepinephrine pathways increase arousal and vigilance. Serotonin participates in the regulation of mood, appetite, social status, aggression, and sleep. Glutamate is the most common excitatory neurotransmitter in the CNS. GABA and glycine generally produce inhibition. ATP and its byproducts appear to act as neurochemicals. (LO3)

4. Small-molecule neurochemicals include acetylcholine, dopamine, norepinephrine, epinephrine, serotonin, glutamate, GABA, glycine, and adenosine. **(LO4)**

5. Gasotransmitters diffuse through membranes and interact with internal receptors to transmit information. Gases can communicate from postsynaptic neurons to presynaptic neurons. **(LO4)**

6. Neuropeptides include substance P and endorphins, among at least 40 others. **(LO5)**

Review Questions

1. How are neurotransmitters, neuromodulators, and neurohormones similar to and different from one another?

2. What are some of the distinctive features of receptors for ACh, dopamine, glutamate, and GABA?

Drug Actions at the Synapse

Many drugs produce their psychoactive effects through actions at the synapse. Drugs can affect synthesis of neurochemicals, storage of neurochemicals within the axon terminal, release of neurochemicals, reuptake or enzyme activity following release, and interactions with either pre- or postsynaptic receptor sites.

Agonists and Antagonists

Drugs can boost or reduce the activity of a neurochemical. Drugs that enhance the activity of a neurochemical are known as **agonists**. Drugs that reduce the activity of a neurochemical are known as **antagonists**. Pharmacologists often limit the use of the terms agonist or antagonist to chemicals that act at receptor sites, but our broader use of the terms in behavioral neuroscience includes chemicals that influence activity in additional ways such as affecting the amount of neurochemical that is released.

It is important to avoid equating agonists with postsynaptic or behavioral excitation and antagonists with behavioral inhibition. The outcome of the action of an agonist or antagonist depends on the normal operation of a synapse. If a neurochemical generally has an inhibitory effect on a postsynaptic neuron, the action of an agonist would increase the amount of this inhibitory effect. The action of an antagonist at this same synapse, interfering with the inhibitory neurochemical, would result in less inhibition. Consider the case of caffeine. Caffeine, as you are probably well aware, produces alertness. As we will see later in the chapter, caffeine is an antagonist for adenosine, which means it reduces adenosine's effects. Because adenosine typically acts as an inhibitor at the synapse, reduced inhibition due to caffeine equates to increased neural activity.

Production of Neurochemicals

Manipulating the synthesis of a neurochemical will affect the amount available for release. Substances that promote increased production will act as agonists, whereas substances that interfere with production will act as antagonists.

The simplest way to boost the rate of neurochemical synthesis is to provide larger quantities of the basic building blocks, or precursors. Serotonin levels can be raised, making it available temporarily by eating high carbohydrate meals. This results in more tryptophan crossing the blood–brain barrier to be synthesized into serotonin (Wurtman et al., 2003).

agonist Substance that promotes the activity of a neurochemical.
antagonist Substance that reduces the action of a neurochemical.

Drugs can exert antagonistic effects by interfering with the synthesis pathways of neurochemicals. One example is the drug α-methyl-*p*-tyrosine (AMPT), which interferes with the activity of tyrosine hydroxylase (TH). As we observed earlier in the chapter, TH converts the substrate tyrosine into L-dopa. Consequently, AMPT interferes with the production of dopamine, norepinephrine, and epinephrine.

Neurochemical Storage

Certain drugs have an antagonistic effect by interfering with the storage of neurochemicals in vesicles within the neuron. For example, the drug **reserpine**, used to reduce blood pressure and psychosis (see Chapter 16), interferes with the uptake of monoamines into synaptic vesicles. As a result, abnormally small quantities of monoamines are available for release in response to the arrival of action potentials. Reserpine's interference with the monoamine serotonin often results in profound depression. As many as 15 percent of all patients who used reserpine to lower blood pressure also experienced severe depression (Sachar & Baron, 1979). As a result, reserpine is rarely prescribed today.

Neurochemical Release

Drugs often modify the release of neurochemicals in response to the arrival of an action potential. Some drugs affect release by interacting with presynaptic autoreceptors. Other drugs interact directly with the proteins responsible for exocytosis, which is the process responsible for the release of neurochemical molecules into the synapse (see Chapter 3). Exocytosis is promoted by agonists but blocked by antagonists.

Methamphetamine serves as a dopamine agonist in an interesting manner. Initially, the methamphetamine molecules are taken up by the dopamine transporters. Once inside the axon terminal, the methamphetamine displaces dopamine in the vesicles. Some dopamine is deactivated by monoamine oxidase (MAO), of course, but the higher concentration of dopamine in the intracellular fluid disturbs the actions of the transporters. Instead of moving dopamine from the synaptic gap back into the cell, the transporters reverse and start pumping dopamine into the gap, even in the absence of any action potentials. Because the transporters are malfunctioning, the released dopamine is trapped in the gap, where it can interact with postsynaptic receptors repeatedly.

Other drugs act as antagonists by preventing the release of chemical messengers. As illustrated in ● Figure 4.16, powerful toxins produced by *Clostridium botulinum* bacteria, found in spoiled food, prevent the release of ACh at the neuromuscular junction and at synapses of the autonomic nervous system. The resulting disease, **botulism**, leads rapidly to paralysis and death. Botox® is the trade name for one of the seven botulinum toxins. Botox is used to paralyze muscles to prevent the formation of wrinkles and to treat a variety of medical conditions involving excess muscle tension. Concerns have been raised about the ability of Botox to move from the injection site back to the brain using retrograde transport in neurons (Antonucci, Rossi, Gianfranceschi, Rossetto, & Caleo, 2008).

Receptor Effects

By far, the greatest number of drug interactions occur at the receptor. In some cases, drugs are similar enough in chemical composition to mimic the action of natural neurochemicals at the receptor site. In other cases, drugs can block synaptic activity by occupying a binding site on a receptor without activating the receptor. Finally, many receptors have multiple types of binding sites. Drugs that occupy one or more of these sites can indirectly influence the activity of the receptor. Using the lock-and-key analogy of receptor site activity, both chemical messengers and agonists at the receptor site can act like keys that can open locks. Antagonists act like a poorly made key that fits in

reserpine A substance derived from a plant that depletes supplies of monoamines by interfering with the uptake of monoamines into synaptic vesicles; used to treat high blood pressure and psychosis but often produces depression.

botulism A fatal condition produced by bacteria in spoiled food, in which a toxin produced by the bacteria prevents the release of acetylcholine (ACh).

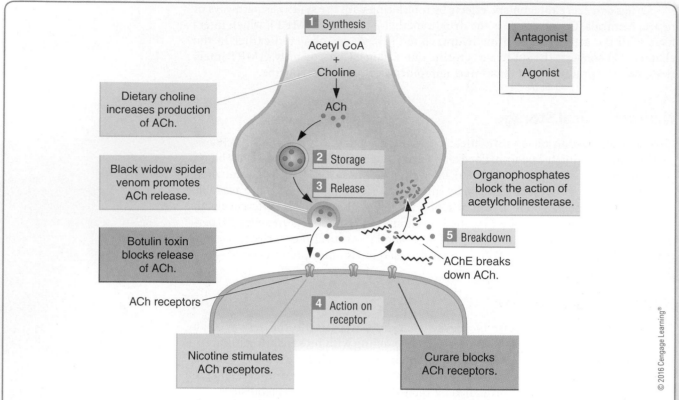

● **Figure 4.16** **Drug Interactions at the Cholinergic Synapse** Drugs can interact with many ongoing processes at a synapse. Agonists at the cholinergic synapse, which appear in green, include black widow spider venom, nicotine, and dietary choline. Spider venom enhances acetylcholine (ACh) release, and nicotine activates ACh receptors. Increased intake of dietary choline can increase production of ACh. Antagonists, which appear in red, include botulin toxin, curare, and organophosphates. Botulin toxin blocks the release of ACh, and curare blocks nicotinic ACh receptors. Organophosphates break down the enzyme acetylcholinesterase (AChE), so they technically serve as ACh agonists. Although a reduction in AChE activity might initially boost ACh activity, it eventually has a toxic effect on ACh receptors.

the lock but fails to open it. As long as the ineffective key is in the lock, real keys can't be used to open it either.

As we mentioned in our earlier discussion of ACh, the nicotinic and muscarinic receptors received their names due to their ability to respond to both ACh and nicotine or to both ACh and muscarine, respectively. Consequently, both nicotine and muscarine are classified as cholinergic agonists. Other drugs, such as **curare**, act by blocking nicotinic receptors. Curare is derived from plant species found in the Amazon region of South America. People in this region have historically used curare to tip their darts for hunting and warfare. Beginning in the 1940s, curare was used to relax muscles during surgery, but has since been replaced by more effective drugs. As shown in ● Figure 4.17, snake venom acts in much the same way as curare. Because curare and snake venom occupy the nicotinic receptors located at the neuromuscular junction without breaking down or being released, ACh is unable to stimulate muscle fibers. Inactivation of the muscles of the diaphragm, required for breathing, leads to paralysis and death.

A number of important drugs exert their influence on the $GABA_A$ receptor, which is a complicated receptor with a number of different binding sites. The purpose for these multiple binding sites is not currently understood. Although only one binding site is activated by GABA itself, there are at least five other binding sites on the $GABA_A$ receptor. These additional sites can be activated by the **benzodiazepines** (tranquilizers including diazepam Valium), alcohol, and **barbiturates**, which are

curare A substance derived from Amazonian plants that causes paralysis by blocking the nicotinic acetylcholine (ACh) receptor.

benzodiazepine A major tranquilizer that acts as a GABA agonist.

barbiturate A drug that produces strong sedation by acting as a GABA agonist

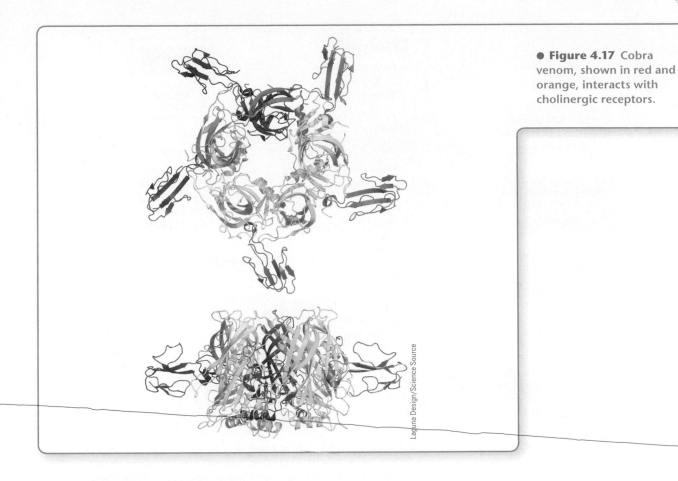

Laguna Design/Science Source

● **Figure 4.17** Cobra venom, shown in red and orange, interacts with cholinergic receptors.

used in anesthesia and in the control of seizures. Barbiturates can single-handedly activate the $GABA_A$ receptor without any GABA present at all (Bowery, Enna, & Olsen, 2004). Benzodiazepines and alcohol increase the receptor's response to GABA but only when they occupy binding sites at the same time GABA is present. Because GABA has a hyperpolarizing, or inhibitory, effect on postsynaptic neurons, GABA agonists enhance inhibition. The combined action of alcohol, benzodiazepines, or barbiturates at the same $GABA_A$ receptors can produce a life-threatening level of neural inhibition.

Reuptake and Enzymatic Degradation

Second only to drugs acting at receptor sites in terms of number and importance are drugs that affect the deactivation of neurochemicals. Some of these drugs influence the reuptake of neurochemicals, whereas others act on enzymes that break down released neurochemicals. Drugs that interfere with either reuptake or enzymatic degradation of chemical messengers are usually powerful agonists. They promote the effects of the neurochemical by allowing more of the released substance to stay active in the synapse for a longer period of time. This in turn provides more opportunities for the neurochemical to interact with receptors.

As shown in ● Figure 4.18, drugs that inhibit the reuptake of dopamine include cocaine, amphetamine, and methylphenidate (Ritalin). Consequently, each of these drugs is a powerful dopamine agonist. Another important class of **reuptake inhibitors** includes those that act on serotonin. This group includes the antidepressant medication fluoxetine (Prozac), shown in ● Figure 4.19. People who suffer from major depressive disorder (see Chapter 16) generally have lower than normal levels of serotonin activity. With slower reuptake, existing serotonin can remain more active in the synapse for a longer period of time, providing some relief from symptoms of depression.

reuptake inhibitor Substance that interferes with the transport of released neurotransmitter molecules back into the presynaptic terminal.

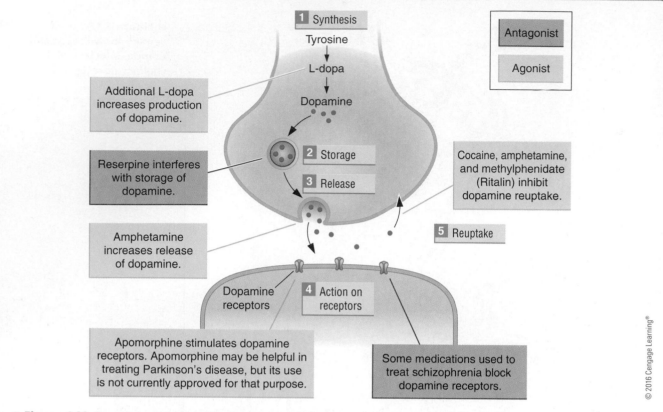

● **Figure 4.18** **Drug Interactions at the Dopaminergic Synapse** L-dopa, prescribed in cases of Parkinson's disease, serves as a dopaminergic agonist by promoting increased dopamine synthesis, and amphetamine increases the release of dopamine. Cocaine, amphetamine, and methylphenidate are dopamine reuptake inhibitors. Apomorphine activates dopaminergic receptors. Reserpine exerts an antagonistic effect by interfering with the uptake of monoamines into synaptic vesicles. Traditional medications used to treat schizophrenia, such as the phenothiazines, block dopaminergic receptors.

At the cholinergic synapse shown earlier in ● Figure 4.16, the enzyme acetylcholinesterase (AChE) deactivates ACh. Organophosphates, pesticides originally developed as chemical warfare agents, interfere with the action of AChE. Drugs that interfere with AChE boost ACh activity, which can be helpful in conditions like the muscular disorder myasthenia gravis (see Chapter 8). In a person with normal ACh activity, however, too much ACh can produce autonomic disruptions, involuntary movements, and eventually paralysis and death (Pope, Karanth, & Liu, 2005).

INTERIM SUMMARY 4.2

‖ Summary Points

1. Agonists boost the activity of a chemical messenger, whereas antagonists interfere with the action of a neurochemical. **(LO6)**

2. Drugs affect behavior by interacting with a variety of processes occurring at the synapse. **(LO7)**

‖ Review Question

1. What activities at the synapse are affected by drugs?

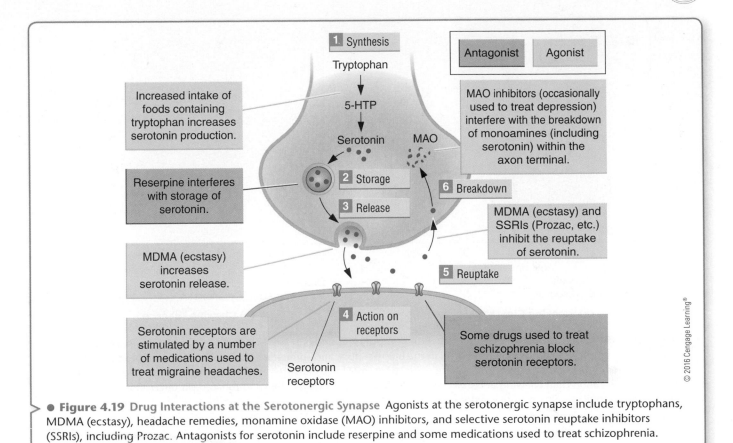

● **Figure 4.19 Drug Interactions at the Serotonergic Synapse** Agonists at the serotonergic synapse include tryptophans, MDMA (ecstasy), headache remedies, monamine oxidase (MAO) inhibitors, and selective serotonin reuptake inhibitors (SSRIs), including Prozac. Antagonists for serotonin include reserpine and some medications used to treat schizophrenia.

Basic Principles of Drug Effects

Before discussing specific types of drugs and their interactions with normal chemical signaling in the nervous system, we need to review basic concepts related to drug effects.

Administration of Drugs

Drugs have different effects on the nervous system depending on their method of administration. Once in the blood supply, a drug's effects are dependent on its concentration. Eating, inhaling, chewing, and injecting drugs deliver very different concentrations of the drug into the blood supply. ● Figure 4.20 shows how nicotine concentrations in the blood over time are influenced by using smoking or chewing to administer the drug.

Your body has several mechanisms designed to protect against toxins. The liver uses enzymes to deactivate substances in the blood. The blood–brain barrier, discussed in Chapter 3, prevents many toxins from entering the tissues of the nervous system. The **area postrema**, located in the medulla, reacts to the presence of circulating toxins by initiating a vomiting reflex (Miller & Leslie, 1994). In some cases involving ingested toxins, vomiting clears the stomach and prevents further damage.

Individual Differences in Responses to Drugs

Drug effects experienced by individuals are influenced by a number of factors, including body weight, gender, and genetics. Larger bodies have more blood than smaller bodies and therefore require larger quantities of a drug to reach an equivalent concentration. Gender effects can be seen in alcohol, which is diluted by the water in muscle

area postrema A brainstem area, in which the blood–brain barrier is more permeable, that triggers vomiting in response to the detection of circulating toxins.

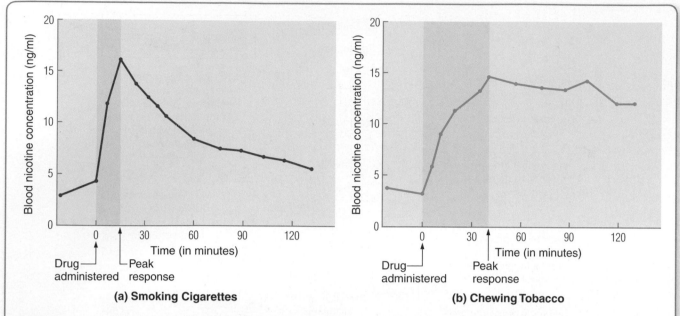

● **Figure 4.20** **Concentration of a Drug in the Blood Supply Depends on the Method of Administration** Drug effects are dependent on the concentration of the drug in the blood supply, and some methods of administration produce effective concentrations faster than others. In the case of nicotine, smoking a cigarette produces a much faster increase in blood nicotine concentration than chewing an equivalent dose of tobacco. However, chewing tobacco produces higher sustained concentrations of nicotine than smoking does.
Source: Adapted from Bennett (1983).

tissue. Because a man typically has more muscle than a woman of the same weight, the concentration of alcohol in his blood will be lower than in hers after consuming the same number of drinks. Genetic differences affect a liver enzyme, aldehyde dehydrogenase (ALDH), which participates in the metabolism of alcohol (Thomasson et al., 1991). With low levels of ALDH, alcohol byproducts build up and produce flushing, rapid heartbeat, muscle weakness, and dizziness. Many Asians lack genes for one type of ALDH and therefore experience more unpleasant symptoms associated with drinking (Li, Zhao, & Gelernter, 2011). It is not too surprising to find that alcohol consumption is lower among Asians than among members of other ethnicities, although cultural patterns undoubtedly contribute substantially to drinking rates.

Placebo Effects

Drug effects are often influenced by a user's expectations, experiences, and motivations (Finniss, Kaptchuk, Miller, & Benedetti, 2010). These indirect outcomes are known as **placebo effects**. A placebo, from the Latin for "I will please," is an inactive substance, and placebo effects are a person's observable reactions to the administration of a placebo. Placebo effects have been demonstrated across a wide variety of behaviors, including pain reduction, Parkinson's disease, depression, and anxiety.

The standard method for distinguishing between the effects of an active drug and placebo effects is the **double-blind experiment**. The first blind refers to the participant. If you agree to participate in such a study, you will not know whether you are receiving the active drug or the inactive substance (placebo). The second blind refers to the researcher. To prevent biased observations, the researcher will not know which participants are receiving a placebo and which are receiving an active drug until after the experiment is concluded. Not all drugs lend themselves to this type of research. For example, efforts to determine the relative benefits of using smoked marijuana for medical purposes (as opposed to traditional pharmaceuticals containing cannabinoids) are handicapped by the obvious difficulty of finding a believable placebo.

placebo effect Perceived benefit from inactive substances or procedures.
double-blind experiment A research design in which neither the participant nor the experimenter knows whether the participant is receiving a drug or a placebo until after the research is concluded.

Tolerance and Withdrawal

When a drug's effects are lessened as a result of repeated administration, **tolerance** has developed. To obtain the desired effects, the person needs to administer greater and greater quantities of the drug. Tolerance effects can occur due to changes in enzymes, changes at the level of the synapse such as increased receptor density, and learning. Not all effects of the same drug show equal levels of tolerance. For example, barbiturates produce both general feelings of sedation and depressed breathing. The sedative effect of barbiturates rapidly shows tolerance, but the depression of breathing does not. As the abuser of barbiturates takes more and more of the drug to achieve a sedative effect, he or she runs an increasing risk of death due to breathing problems.

Classical conditioning associated with drug use can also produce tolerance. The body's efforts to compensate for drug administration become conditioned, or associated, with the stimuli involved with drug administration. This learned component of tolerance might contribute to some cases of drug overdose. Siegel, Hinson, Krank, and McCully (1982) gave rats injections of heroin every day until they began to show signs of tolerance to the drug. At that point, the rats received overdoses of the drug. Half the rats received overdoses in their home cages, and the other half received their overdoses in an unfamiliar environment. Nearly all the rats receiving the overdose in the unfamiliar environment died, whereas only half of the rats receiving the drug in their familiar home cages died. The rats in the unfamiliar environment lacked the learned cues for triggering their bodies' compensations for the drug. Without the ability to compensate, they were quickly over-dosed. It is likely that similar factors influence the outcome of drug overdose for human beings. Addicts administering drugs to themselves in unfamiliar locations may be more prone to overdoses than addicts using drugs in a familiar environment (Siegel, Hinson, Krank, & McCully, 1982).

Withdrawal occurs when use of some substances is reduced or discontinued. In general, withdrawal effects are the opposite of the effects caused by the discontinued drug. A person in withdrawal from a sedative will become agitated, whereas a person in withdrawal from a stimulant will become lethargic. It is likely that most characteristics of a withdrawal syndrome reflect the same compensation mechanisms that are responsible for tolerance. Drug effects and compensatory mechanisms can cancel each other out, leading to fairly stable behavior. When the drug is no longer present, the compensation alone becomes apparent. Symptoms of withdrawal might motivate the addict to administer the drug again, but avoiding withdrawal symptoms is not the sole source of compulsive drug seeking and use.

Addiction

The traditional distinction made between physical and psychological dependence on a drug has probably outlived its usefulness. The defining feature of an **addiction** is the compulsive need to use the drug repeatedly in spite of negative consequences to the user (Kalant, 2010). Addiction overwhelms normal control of behavior, distorts typical systems of reward, and interferes with the recognition of problems.

CAUSES OF ADDICTION When people are addicted to drugs, they stop making logical choices on the basis of long-term outcomes (family, finances, avoiding jail) and persist in making impulsive choices on the basis of short-term outcomes (getting high). This reversal in normal, logical decision making results from changes in the relative strength of circuits involving reward, impulse control, and craving (Noël, Brevers, & Bechara, 2013).

Most addictive drugs have the ability to stimulate our natural neural systems of reward, which we experience as feelings of pleasure. These systems reward us for engaging in behaviors that are important either for our personal survival or for the survival of the species. When we eat due to hunger, drink due to thirst, or engage in sexual behavior, the same reward circuits of the brain are activated. Even the possibility of winning money activates the brain's reward circuits (Breiter, Aharon, Kahneman, Dale, & Shizgal, 2001).

tolerance The process in which more of a drug is needed to produce the same effect.

withdrawal The symptoms that occur when certain addictive drugs are no longer administered or are administered in smaller quantities.

addiction A compulsive craving for drug effects or other experience in spite of negative consequences.

These behaviors produce activity in dopamine circuits in the brainstem and, quite notably, in the mesolimbocortical system and in the nucleus accumbens. Addictive drugs produce a variety of behavioral effects, but many share the ability to stimulate more intense and longer-lasting dopamine release than we typically see in response to environmental events (Volkow, 2004). Drugs that do not influence either dopamine or the nucleus accumbens are often used habitually, but they do not seem to elicit the cravings and compulsive use associated with addiction. LSD seems to have little if any effect on dopamine circuits at recreational doses. People do not seem to be addicted to LSD, although they might choose to use it regularly.

Considerable research evidence shows that an interruption to the mesolimbocortical system, including the nucleus accumbens, reduces an animal's administration of addictive drugs. Animals can be addicted to drugs through regular injections. Once addicted, the animals will self-administer the drug by pressing a bar to activate an intravenous dose of the drug. Lesions of the nucleus accumbens reduce self-administration (Zito, Vickers, & Roberts, 1985). In addition, selective damage to dopaminergic neurons will also reduce self-administration (Bozarth & Wise, 1986). Because damage to dopaminergic neurons and to the nucleus accumbens reduces drug dependency, you might be wondering why these techniques are not used to assist human addicts as well. We do not treat addiction in this manner because damaging these general reward circuits could deprive addicts of all pleasure permanently. It's unlikely that addicts would choose such a course of action.

Dopamine is not only associated with the reward aspects of addiction but also plays a role in attention to stimuli and motivation. Based on imaging studies with addicts, Nora Volkow and her colleagues (2004) speculated that continued drug abuse reduces addicts' responses to normal environmental rewards. At the same time, addicts show a hyperactive response to stimuli associated with drug use such as the sight of drug paraphernalia.

These changes in the brain's reward system overwhelm the impulse control system managed by the frontal lobes (Noël, Brevers, & Bechara, 2013). These circuits normally weigh the pros and cons of a particular decision. In addition, a craving system involving the insula produces increased desire for a drug. Activity in the insula correlates with participants' ratings of their craving for their drug of choice, and strokes that damage the insula completely eliminate the urge to administer an addictive drug (Verdejo-Garcia, Clark, & Dunn, 2012). Increased activity in the impulsive reward circuits of the brain coupled with less influence of the frontal executive circuits and increased desire sets the stage for a long-term maintenance of compulsive, addictive behavior.

The use of addictive drugs can produce long-term, stable changes in gene expression in the brain (epigenetic change; see Chapter 5), leading to the maintenance of addictive behaviors (Robison & Nestler, 2011). Epigenetic explanations of addiction can also account for the roles of stress in adolescence and prenatal exposure to addictive drugs in increasing an individual's risk of addiction.

Although our interests center on the biological actions of drugs, we should not lose sight of environmental factors that cause and maintain addiction. As the Vietnam War began to wind down, the American health system braced for an anticipated epidemic of heroin addiction among the returning servicemen. Due to the obvious stress of war and the ready availability of heroin in Southeast Asia, many soldiers had used heroin habitually. However, their behavior on returning to the United States took health providers completely by surprise. Fewer than 10 percent of addicted veterans relapsed, in contrast to the 70 percent relapse rate among young civilian addicts (Robins, Helzer, & Davis, 1975). Changes in the veterans' environmental conditions had a tremendous impact on their motivation to use heroin.

TREATMENT OF ADDICTION Once an addiction has been established, it is remarkably difficult to end it. The large number of Hollywood celebrities who experience a revolving door between treatment and relapse appear to be not the exception but the rule.

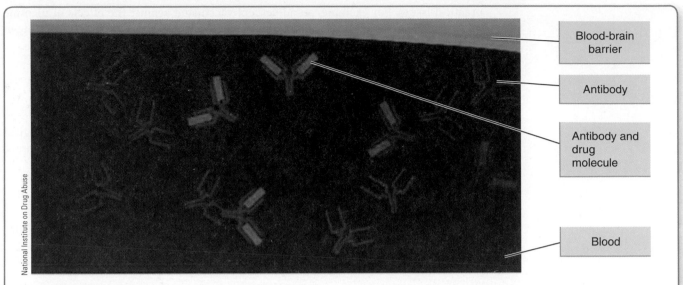

National Institute on Drug Abuse

> ● **Figure 4.21** **Vaccinations Against Drugs of Abuse** Psychoactive drugs would not be psychoactive at all if they were unable to cross the blood–brain barrier to interact with the central nervous system (CNS). By developing antibodies that link with molecules of particular drugs of abuse, the drugs can be prevented from passing through the blood–brain barrier.

A variety of medications have been used to assist addicts, and many more are under development. Methadone is used to wean heroin addicts away from their addiction. Methadone prevents withdrawal symptoms, yet it does not produce the major psychological effects of heroin. Alcoholics are treated with disulfiram, or Antabuse, which interferes with the activity of the enzyme ALDH in metabolizing alcohol. This medication produces a number of unpleasant symptoms when alcohol is consumed. Other medications prevent the behavioral effects of a drug altogether, reducing any incentive to administer the drug. Because these medications have not led to many successful recoveries, vaccinations that target nicotine, methamphetamine, cocaine, and heroin have been developed. As illustrated in ● Figure 4.21, these vaccinations work by stimulating the immune system to bind molecules of the problem drug, preventing or delaying its movement across the blood–brain barrier into the brain (Shen, Orson, & Kosten, 2011). If this turns out to be a feasible strategy, people at risk for addiction might choose to be immunized. However, vaccinations raise troubling ethical and

●●● **Behavioral Neuroscience GOES TO WORK**

SUBSTANCE ABUSE COUNSELORS

Recent changes in the legal management of substance abusers that favor treatment over incarceration have led to an increasing need for trained substance abuse counselors. The U.S. Bureau of Labor and Statistics projects a growth of 31 percent in substance abuse counselor positions during the next decade, fueled by new insurance coverage for addiction and counseling services.

Requirements for being a substance abuse counselor have been surprisingly low, given the state licensing requirements for psychotherapists in general and the significant challenges inherent in recovering from an addiction. It is possible to gain employment as a substance abuse counselor with a high school diploma, primarily because legal changes related to the treatment of addicts happened so quickly that there were not enough counselors initially to meet the need. As time passes, counselors are being required to obtain more education, with the master's degree becoming more common. Candidates are encouraged to obtain internships and other work experience in the counseling area.

For students who have the compassion needed for the helping professions and who relish the challenge of working with clients who often resist treatment, this profession might be just perfect.

practical issues. For example, an adolescent vaccinated against the effects of nicotine might use much higher quantities of the drug to overcome the vaccination, resulting in the ingestion of high levels of carcinogens (Shen et al., 2011).

Effects of Selected Psychoactive Drugs

Psychoactive drugs are usually administered to obtain a particular psychological effect. By definition, these drugs circumvent the protective systems of the blood–brain barrier to gain access to the CNS.

Stimulants

Stimulant drugs share the capacity to increase alertness and mobility. As a result, these drugs have been widely embraced among cultures such as our own, in which productivity and hard work are valued.

CAFFEINE As a graduate student, I participated in a research project on caffeine. The researchers calmly suggested to me that 20 cups of coffee a day (my reported intake) was "a bit much," and they suggested I cut back to 8 or so. What is the nature of the attraction many of us have to caffeine? For most people, **caffeine** increases blood pressure and heart rate, improves concentration, and wards off sleepiness. The substance is found in tea, coffee, cola and energy drinks, chocolate, and a number of over-the-counter pain relievers (see ● Figure 4.22).

Caffeine produces its behavioral effects by blocking adenosine receptors, reducing the normal inhibitory activity of adenosine. Caffeine's interference with adenosine's inhibition in the hippocampus and cerebral cortex probably accounts for the alertness associated with its use. Interference with normal adenosine activity in the basal ganglia produces improvements in reaction time.

Although many people consume caffeine without experiencing negative outcomes, others experience cardiac arrhythmias. Caffeine crosses the placenta easily, and the fetus and breastfed newborn are relatively unable to metabolize caffeine, leading to reduced rates of growth and other complications (Bakker et al., 2010). Caffeine produces a withdrawal syndrome featuring headache and fatigue. Because caffeine reduces blood circulation to the brain, withdrawal can produce severe headaches due to suddenly increased blood flow.

Caffeine use is correlated with lower rates of Parkinson's disease, particularly in men (Ross et al., 2000; Ross & Petrovich, 2001; see also Chapter 8). It is possible that personality or lifestyle factors associated with caffeine use are responsible for this correlation, but evidence for caffeine's ability to protect neurons from Parkinson's-like damage has been reported in animals (Joghataie, Roghani, Negahdar, & Hashemi, 2004). A Parkinson's-like syndrome can be artificially produced by injecting mice with a toxin known as MPTP, which reduces dopamine levels in the basal ganglia. If the MPTP injections are preceded by caffeine, little or no drop in dopamine occurs (Xu, Xu, Chen, & Schwarzschild, 2010).

NICOTINE After caffeine, the most commonly used stimulant in the United States is **nicotine**, usually delivered in the form of smoking or chewing tobacco. Nicotine increases heart rate and blood pressure, promotes the release of adrenaline into the circulation, reduces fatigue, and heightens cognitive performance. In the peripheral nervous system (PNS), nicotine produces muscular relaxation.

In spite of the known negative consequences of smoking, nicotine continues to be a widely used substance, particularly among American youth. One of the most remarkable statistics regarding nicotine is that about one-third of all nicotine products sold in the United States is used by the 7 percent of individuals who are diagnosed with both psychological disorders and nicotine dependence (Dani & Harris, 2005).

psychoactive drug A drug that produces changes in mental processes.

caffeine A stimulant drug found in coffee, tea, cola, and chocolate that acts as an antagonist to adenosine.

nicotine A stimulant drug that is the major active component found in tobacco.

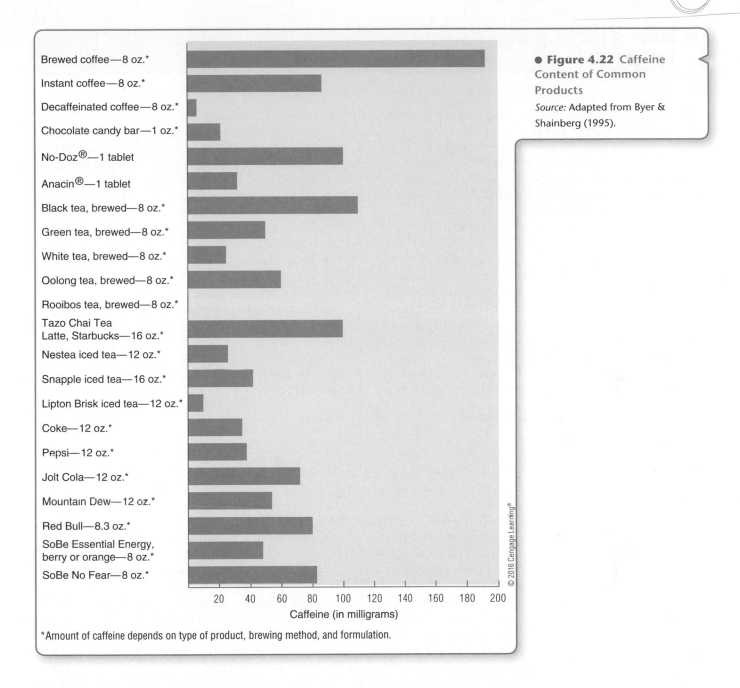

● Figure 4.22 Caffeine Content of Common Products

Source: Adapted from Byer & Shainberg (1995).

Brewed coffee—8 oz.*
Instant coffee—8 oz.*
Decaffeinated coffee—8 oz.*
Chocolate candy bar—1 oz.*
No-Doz®—1 tablet
Anacin®—1 tablet
Black tea, brewed—8 oz.*
Green tea, brewed—8 oz.*
White tea, brewed—8 oz.*
Oolong tea, brewed—8 oz.*
Rooibos tea, brewed—8 oz.*
Tazo Chai Tea Latte, Starbucks—16 oz.*
Nestea iced tea—12 oz.*
Snapple iced tea—16 oz.*
Lipton Brisk iced tea—12 oz.*
Coke—12 oz.*
Pepsi—12 oz.*
Jolt Cola—12 oz.*
Mountain Dew—12 oz.*
Red Bull—8.3 oz.*
SoBe Essential Energy, berry or orange—8 oz.*
SoBe No Fear—8 oz.*

20 40 60 80 100 120 140 160 180 200
Caffeine (in milligrams)

*Amount of caffeine depends on type of product, brewing method, and formulation.

© 2016 Cengage Learning®

Several explanations might account for these data. People with mental illnesses could be seeking to relieve their symptoms through the use of nicotine (Sacco, Termine, & Seyal, 2005). More troubling are suggestions that nicotine use actually contributes to the development of mental illnesses, especially depression (Husky, Mazure, Paliwal, & McKee, 2008). Nicotine serves as a true "gateway drug" by increasing the likelihood of a dependence on cocaine compared with cocaine users who do not use nicotine (Levine et al., 2011).

Nicotine has its primary effect as an agonist at the nicotinic cholinergic receptor. These receptors exist not only at the neuromuscular junction but also at several locations in the brain. Nicotine's action on the cholinergic system arising in the basal forebrain, described earlier, is probably responsible for increased alertness and cognitive performance. In addition to its effects on cholinergic systems, nicotine also stimulates dopaminergic neurons in the nucleus accumbens (Damsma, Day, & Fibiger, 1989; Levin & Rose, 1995). This action on the nucleus accumbens is the likely source

Building Better HEALTH

REDUCING NICOTINE USE

Smoking cigarettes remains the number one preventable cause of death in the United States, with direct responsibility for one out of five deaths each year (Centers for Disease Control and Prevention [CDC], 2010). Rates of smoking in developing countries are even higher than those in the United States. Two-thirds of current smokers live in developing countries, including 30 percent in China and 10 percent in India (World Health Organization [WHO], 2008). WHO (2013) reports that tobacco use kills 6 million people each year and causes half a trillion dollars of economic damage.

People do manage to quit smoking, although, as is the case with most addictions, the path is not easy. In the United States, the number of ex-smokers now exceeds the number of current smokers (47 million to 46 million; Chapman & MacKenzie, 2010). Prevention, however, is likely to have an even greater impact on tobacco use rates than improved treatment programs.

The WHO Framework Convention on Tobacco Control has identified six strategies that should allow policy makers to reduce tobacco use worldwide: monitor tobacco use and prevention policies (e.g., smoke-free environments); offer treatment; issue warnings; ban tobacco advertising, promotion, and sponsorships; and raise taxes on tobacco. France cut cigarette consumption in half between 1990 and 2005 by increasing tobacco taxes to levels above inflation (Jha & Peto, 2014). Jha and Peto (2014) argue that tripling current tobacco taxes would save 200 million lives by 2025. Because tobacco use cuts down people in midlife, especially in developing countries, saving the lives of these parents and experienced workers would have a significantly positive effect on the welfare of whole nations. Increased taxes might have their biggest benefits in discouraging adolescents from beginning to smoke.

of the addictive properties of nicotine. Symptoms of withdrawal include inability to concentrate and restlessness.

COCAINE AND AMPHETAMINE The behavioral effects of cocaine and amphetamine are quite similar to one another because both drugs are powerful dopamine agonists. These drugs are among the most addictive drugs known. A single recreational dose of cocaine is sufficient to produce addiction in mice (Grueter, Rothwell, & Malenka, 2011; Ungless, Whistler, Malenka, & Bonci, 2001).

In spite of the similarity in behavioral outcomes, the modes of action for these drugs are somewhat different. **Cocaine** acts as a dopamine reuptake inhibitor by blocking dopamine transporters, whereas amphetamine has a dual action at synapses that use dopamine and norepinephrine. **Amphetamine**, and its widely abused form known as **methamphetamine**, stimulate dopamine and norepinephrine release and inhibit their reuptake. The result of the use of these drugs is higher activity at dopaminergic synapses. At lower doses, these drugs produce alertness, elevated mood, confidence, and a sense of well-being. At higher doses, these drugs can produce symptoms that are similar to schizophrenia (see Chapter 16). Users often experience hallucinations, particularly in the form of tactile sensations such as feeling bugs on the skin. They frequently suffer from paranoid delusions, thinking that others wish to harm them. Methamphetamine users are at least 11 times more likely to experience psychotic symptoms than nonusers (McKetin, McLaren, Lubman, & Hides, 2006). In some cases, they show repetitive motor behaviors, particularly chewing movements or grinding of the teeth (see ● Figure 4.23).

Cocaine was originally used by the indigenous people of Peru as a mild stimulant and appetite suppressant. Sigmund Freud recommended cocaine as an antidepressant in his 1885 book, *Über Coca (On Coca)*. Freud became disenchanted with the drug after he became aware of its potential for addiction. Historically, many popular products contained some form of cocaine, as shown in ● Figure 4.24. The original formulation of Coca-Cola included extracts of the coca leaf. When cocaine was designated

cocaine A powerful, addictive dopamine agonist derived from the leaves of the coca plant of South America.

amphetamine A highly addictive drug that acts as a potent dopamine agonist.

methamphetamine A variation of amphetamine that is cheaply produced and widely abused in the United States.

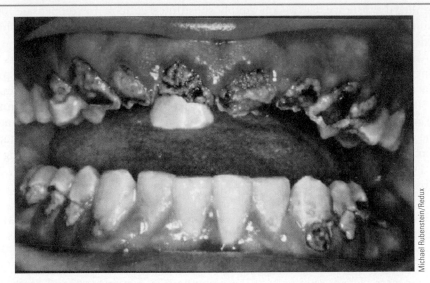

● **Figure 4.23 Methamphetamine Abuse Leads to Multiple Health Consequences** Not only does methamphetamine abuse frequently lead to hallucinations and delusions similar to those caused by schizophrenia, but users experience additional health issues, including a characteristic pattern of dental decay known as "meth mouth." This condition results from the mouth dryness and the clenching and grinding of teeth caused by the drug.

Michael Rubenstein/Redux

● **Figure 4.24 Cocaine Was an Ingredient in Many Widely Used Products** Prior to World War I, many commercial products contained cocaine. Sigmund Freud originally believed that cocaine was an effective antidepressant. The ability of cocaine to produce rapid addiction eventually changed people's minds about the safety of the drug.

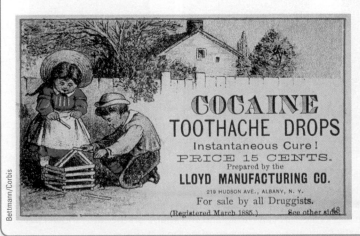

Bettmann/Corbis

Bettmann/Corbis

as an illegal substance, Coca-Cola simply substituted caffeine to compensate for the missing stimulant while retaining the remaining extracts of the coca leaf in its highly guarded secret formula.

Amphetamine was originally developed as a treatment for asthma. Inhalers containing amphetamine were sold without prescription throughout the 1940s in spite of the fact that people were opening the inhalers and ingesting the contents. During the past 50 years, amphetamine has been widely used by pilots and military personnel to ward off fatigue. In the 1960s, many Americans received prescriptions for amphetamine as a diet aid because it does suppress appetite. More recently, methamphetamine has emerged as a major drug of abuse, due to its cheap and easy manufacturing process. Long-term use in humans leads to extensive neural damage (Barr et al., 2006; Davidson, Gow, Lee, & Ellinwood, 2001).

ECSTASY (MDMA)   MDMA (3,4-methylenedioxymethamphetamine, or **ecstasy**) is a currently popular relative of amphetamine among youth. Structurally, MDMA is similar to both methamphetamine and the hallucinogen mescaline. MDMA increases heart rate, blood pressure, and body temperature for a period of about three to six hours. In some cases, dehydration, exhaustion, hypothermia, convulsions, and death occur (Pilgrim, Gerostamoulos, & Drummer, 2011). MDMA appears to produce increased sociability by stimulating the release of serotonin and the neurohormone oxytocin (Thompson, Callaghan, Hunt, Cornish, & McGregor, 2007). MDMA influences serotonin transporters in much the same way as methamphetamine influences dopamine transporters. MDMA is taken up by the transporters, causing them to reverse their action. Instead of removing serotonin from the synaptic gap, serotonin is pumped into the gap, where it is now trapped.

MDMA reduces the function of serotonergic neurons, although researchers continue to debate whether these changes represent neural death (which is permanent, as shown in ● Figure 4.25) or changes that can be reversed through abstinence (Biezonski & Meyer, 2011). Prior to its identification as a controlled substance, MDMA was used to supplement psychotherapy. Although results of MDMA's usefulness in therapy are usually viewed with skepticism (Parrott, 2007), a small (20 participant), placebo-controlled study demonstrated improvements in patients diagnosed with chronic posttraumatic stress disorder (PTSD; see Chapter 16) that had not responded to more typical therapies (Mithoefer, Wagner, Mithoefer, Jerome, & Doblin, 2011).

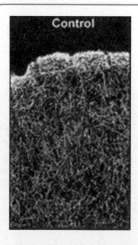  

Courtesy of Dr. GA Ricaurte, Johns Hopkins University School of Medicine

> ● **Figure 4.25** MDMA (Ecstasy) Damages Serotonergic Neurons Monkeys were given either MDMA twice per day for four days or saline (control). The image to the left shows the cortex of a control monkey, the middle image shows the cortex of one of the MDMA monkeys two weeks after the last dose, and the image on the right shows the cortex of one of the MDMA monkeys seven years after the last dose.

ecstasy (MDMA) A close relative of amphetamine that produces its behavioral effects by stimulating the release of serotonin and oxytocin.

Opioids

The term opioid is used to describe all substances that interact with endorphin receptors. The term opiate is restricted to substances derived from the sap of the opium poppy (*Papaver somniferum*), which include **morphine** and **codeine**. Heroin is synthesized from morphine. Opiates have legitimate medical purposes, including pain management, cough suppression, and the treatment of diarrhea. Before opiates became illegal in the United States around the time of World War I, many medicinal remedies, such as the opium-alcohol mix known as laudanum, were widely used by Americans in all walks of life. The United Nations estimates that about 15 million people use opiates illegally, with 85 percent of all heroin originating in Afghanistan (United Nations Office on Drugs and Crime, 2010) (see ● Figure 4.26).

Among the most frequently abused opioids in the United States is the painkiller Oxycodone hydrochloride (Oxycontin), used by over 8 percent of recent high school seniors (Johnston, O'Malley, Bachman, & Schulenberg, 2011). Oxycontin was reformulated in 2010 in an effort to reduce its abuse potential (U.S. Food and Drug Administration [FDA], 2010). The introduction of the new formulation was followed by a drop in Oxycontin abuse from 47.4 percent of opioid abusers to 30 percent, but this drop was accompanied by a doubling in heroin use by this same population (Cicero, Ellis, & Surratt, 2012).

At low doses, such as those typically used in medicine, opioids produce a sense of euphoria, pain relief, a lack of anxiety, muscle relaxation, and sleep. Higher doses characteristic of abuse produce a tremendous euphoria or rush. The physical mechanism for this response is unclear. With yet higher doses, opioids depress respiration, potentially leading to death.

Pert, Snowman, and Snyder (1974) identified three receptors in the brain that bind with opiates. At about the same time, John Hughes and Hans Kosterlitz (Hughes et al., 1975; Hughes, Kosterlitz, & Smith, 1977) identified neuropeptides produced within the body that activated receptors in the vas deferens of mice. The newly discovered neuropeptides were named endogenous morphines, shortened to **endorphins**. Why

Frank and Helen Schreider/National Geographic Creative

> ● **Figure 4.26** **Opium Is the Source of Several Psychoactive Substances** Opium is obtained from the opium poppy, *Papaver somniferum*. Afghanistan remains the world's leading supplier of opium, where the crop makes up at least 15 percent of the country's gross domestic product.

morphine A compound extracted from opium, used to treat pain.
codeine An opium derivative used medicinally for cough suppression and pain relief.
opioid A substance that interacts with endorphin receptors.
opiate An active substance derived from the opium poppy.
endorphins A naturally occurring neuropeptide that is very closely related to opiates.

would we have naturally occurring substances similar to opiates? These endorphins probably help us escape emergency situations in spite of extreme pain. Opioids mimic the effects of our bodies' own endorphins (see Chapter 7). Opioids are typically quite addictive, as one of the indirect consequences of their binding to endorphin receptors is to increase dopamine activity.

Marijuana

Cannabis, from the *Cannabis sativa*, or hemp plant, is another drug with a long human history. It was included in the pharmacy written by Chinese emperor Shen Neng nearly 5,000 years ago. Marco Polo's writings documented the rituals of the Hashashins, young men in the Middle East who used cannabis to prepare for war. The name of this group is the source of our English word, *assassins*. Cannabis first appeared in Europe when Napoleon's soldiers brought it back to Paris from Egypt. Marijuana, the smoked form of cannabis, came to the United States in the early 1900s. Marijuana experienced a huge increase in use during the 1960s and remains the most commonly used (federally) illegal substance in the United States today.

The behavioral effects of cannabis are often so subtle that many people report no changes at all in response to its use. Most individuals experience some excitation and mild euphoria, but others experience depression and social withdrawal. At higher doses, cannabis produces hallucinations, leading to its classification as a hallucinogen.

Cannabis contains over 50 psychoactive compounds, known as cannabinoids. Cannabinoids have been implicated in a wide variety of processes, including pain, appetite, learning, and movement. The most important of the cannabinoids in cannabis is **tetrahydrocannabinol (THC)**. THC produces some of its behavioral effects by serving as an agonist at receptors for endogenous cannabinoids, substances produced within the body that are very similar to THC in chemical composition. Two types of cannabinoid receptors have been identified, CB_1 and CB_2, that interact primarily with endogenous cannabinoids, **anandamide** and *sn*-2 **arachidonylglycerol (2-AG)**, respectively (Devane et al., 1992; Stella, Schweitzer, & Piomelli, 1997). CB_1 receptors are found in the basal ganglia, cerebellum, and cerebral cortex but are especially numerous in the hippocampus and prefrontal cortex.

The presence of cannabinoid receptors in the hippocampus and prefrontal cortex might explain why THC appears to have negative effects on memory formation (Bossong et al., 2012; Riedel & Davies, 2005). In addition to directly activating cannabinoid receptors in the hippocampus, THC might also adversely influence hippocampal activity and memory by inhibiting glutamate release (Maier et al., 2011). Marijuana is probably not a good choice for those who have a family history of schizophrenia (see Chapter 16). As shown in ●Figure 4.27, frequent use of cannabis by adolescents probably interacts with genetic factors to increase the risk of developing psychotic symptoms (Fergusson, Horwood, & Ridder, 2005; Henquet, Di Forti, Morrison, Kuepper, & Murray, 2008).

LSD

In 1938, the researcher Albert Hoffman reported some unusual sensations after absorbing the compound **lysergic acid diethylamide (LSD)** through his skin. LSD moved out of the laboratory and into the community after Timothy Leary and other investigators at Harvard University began experimenting with the drug. Hollywood embraced the new drug, and actor Cary Grant and others used LSD in psychotherapy (Regan, 2000). The glamour surrounding LSD didn't last long. It became associated with the infamous killing rampages of Charles Manson and his followers. Timothy Leary was sent to jail, and LSD was classified as a Schedule I drug, having no known medicinal value.

LSD is chemically similar to serotonin and, along with other hallucinogens, appears to act as a serotonergic agonist in the cerebral cortex (Gonzalez-Maeso et al.,

tetrahydrocannabinol (THC) The major psychoactive ingredient of cannabis.

anandamide A naturally occurring chemical that interacts with cannabinoid receptors.

***sn*-2 arachidonylglycerol (2-AG)** A naturally occurring chemical that interacts with cannabinoid receptors.

lysergic acid diethylamide (LSD) A hallucinogenic drug that resembles serotonin.

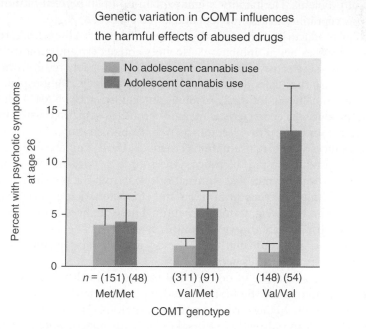

Genetic variation in COMT influences
the harmful effects of abused drugs

● Figure 4.27 Cannabis and Risk of Psychosis While the vast majority of people using cannabis will not experience psychosis, cannabis use, especially early, chronic use in adolescence, interacts with a person's genetics to influence risk of developing psychotic symptoms. The COMT gene, which produces an enzyme that breaks down catecholamines in the synaptic gap, features two alleles, "Met" and "Val." Individuals with the Val/Val genotype who use cannabis during adolescence are more likely to display psychotic symptoms. Among the catecholamines influenced by COMT is dopamine, which plays an important role in schizophrenia.

Source: Adapted from Caspi et al. (2005).

2007; 2008). However, LSD's ability to produce hallucination remains poorly understood. LSD produces tolerance but not withdrawal (Gresch, Smith, Barrett, & Sanders-Bush, 2005). It does not appear to cause addiction, although users might administer the drug habitually out of preference for the effects. A major but uncommon negative consequence of LSD use is the experience of flashbacks, intrusive and unwanted hallucinations, which can continue long after the person has stopped using the substance (Halpern & Pope, 2003). The occurrence of flashbacks suggests that LSD produces some long-term changes in brain function, but the nature of these changes is not currently understood.

Alcohol

Alcohol is one of the earliest drugs used by humans, dating back into our prehistory. Early humans possibly developed fermented drinks as a safety precaution against the ravages of contaminated water supplies.

At lower doses, alcohol dilates blood vessels, providing a warm, flushed feeling. It reduces anxiety, promotes assertiveness, and reduces behavioral inhibitions, causing people's behavior to be "silly" or "fun." At higher doses, however, assertiveness becomes aggression, and disinhibition can lead to overtly risky behaviors. Motor coordination drops, leading to alcohol-induced carnage on streets and highways. At very high doses, coma and death can result from suppression of respiration or aspiration of vomit. Approximately 14 percent of alcohol users meet criteria for dependence, including tolerance, withdrawal, inability to stop drinking, and continued drinking in spite of

alcohol A substance that has its main effect as an agonist at the $GABA_A$ receptor, but also stimulates dopaminergic pathways and antagonizes the NMDA glutamate receptor.

significant problems. Heritability might explain up to 80 percent of individual differences in susceptibility to alcohol dependence (Bierut et al., 2010).

Alcohol produces its main effects by acting as an agonist at the GABA$_A$ receptor, which normally produces neural inhibition. Alcohol's antianxiety and sedative effects, which are not unlike those caused by the benzodiazepines, probably result from action at this site. Alcohol also stimulates dopaminergic pathways, which might explain the euphoric and addictive qualities of the drug. Alcohol's antagonism at the NMDA glutamate receptor might produce the characteristic memory problems associated with alcohol. Alcohol appears to act on endorphin receptors as well. Administration of the opiate antagonist naloxone reduces alcohol consumption (Froehlich, Harts, Lumeng, & Li, 1987).

Alcohol produces rapid tolerance. One source of tolerance is an increase in the production of liver enzymes that eliminate alcohol from the system. Another source of tolerance is changes in receptor number and characteristics, especially at the GABA$_A$ receptor and the NMDA glutamate receptor. These changes can produce a dramatic and possibly life-threatening withdrawal syndrome. The person will experience sweating, nausea and vomiting, sleeplessness, and anxiety. In some cases, hallucinations and dangerous seizures occur.

Alcohol has a number of detrimental effects on health. Chronic use of alcohol damages several areas of the brain, including the frontal lobes, which are responsible for many of our higher-order cognitive functions (Harper & Matsumoto, 2005). Alcoholism can lead indirectly to Korsakoff's syndrome, in which the ability to form new memories is impaired. The lack of dietary thiamine (vitamin B$_1$) common among alcoholics leads to damage to the hippocampus (see Chapter 12). Alcohol can also have devastating effects on the developing fetus, which are explained more fully in Chapter 5. In addition, as little as a half ounce of alcohol per day significantly raises the risk of breast cancer for women with a genetic vulnerability for the disease (Hulka & Moorman, 2002). As shown in ● Figure 4.28, countering these health concerns are findings that light to moderate alcohol consumption (about the same amount per day that raises risk of breast cancer as mentioned above) is correlated with reduced risk for heart disease (Kloner & Rezkalla, 2007).

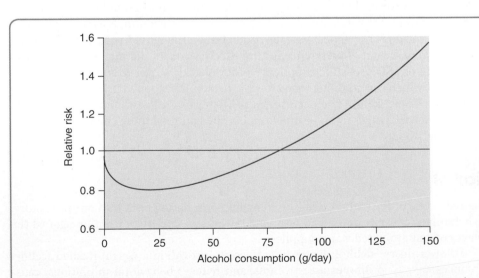

● **Figure 4.28** Alcohol and Mortality Large meta-analyses demonstrate that people who drink moderately (about 20 grams of alcohol per day or about 1.4 servings) experience a relatively lower risk of death than people who drink either no alcohol or more than 75 grams (about 5 servings) per day. The exact reasons for these correlations are not well understood, nor do these data distinguish between people who spread out their drinking over time or binge drink on occasion.

Source: Adapted from Corrao et al. (2000).

••• THINKING *Ethically*

USING ADDICTIVE DRUGS AFFECTS FUTURE GENERATIONS

Substance abuse disorders run in families, and cannot be explained by an either/or approach to the question of heredity and environment. The usual techniques of analyzing twins and adopted children indicate a genetic influence on substance abuse, but environmental influences are also well-supported by the data (Vassoler, Byrnes, & Pierce, 2014). Recent advances in our understanding of epigenetics, or changes in the way genes are expressed due to environmental factors, have led to possible explanations for these relationships. Somewhat more controversial is the idea of transgenerational heritability of epigenetic markers (see Chapter 5), although this is an active area of scientific investigation.

We are well aware that the use of many substances, even those that are quite benign in the adult such as aspirin, can have catastrophic effects in the fetus. However, emerging evidence suggests that drug use by either parent long before conception can also impact offspring. At least in animal studies, alcohol, tobacco, cannabinoids, opiates, and cocaine used prior to conception by either parent reduce fertility in the offspring (Vassoler et al., 2014). Increased levels of anxiety and depression in offspring are related to use of alcohol, opiates, and cocaine by the parents. Many drugs used by parents, including alcohol, cocaine, cannabinoids, and opiates, alter the offspring's own reaction to drugs of abuse (Vassoler et al., 2014).

It might seem frustrating to think that your own fertility, anxiety, depression, cognition, and response to drugs might be the result of somebody else's choices rather than your own. Thinking that choices made well in advance of becoming a parent, not just during a pregnancy, might impact your children in very real ways is also somewhat uncomfortable. Even more disturbing is evidence that transgenerational transmission might not stop at one generation. Your choices might have the potential to influence many generations of your family in the future, just as you might be feeling the influence of choices made by ancestors who died before you were even born. Will further evidence along these lines change the way we think about our health habits?

INTERIM SUMMARY 4.3

|| Summary Table: Some Commonly Used Drugs and Their Effects

Drug	Behavioral Effects	Mode of Action
Caffeine	Arousal; less need for sleep; reduces headache	Blocks adenosine receptor sites
Nicotine	Alertness; muscular relaxation	Stimulates nicotinic ACh receptors
Cocaine	Euphoria; excitement	Reuptake inhibitor for dopamine
Amphetamine	Alertness; appetite suppression; "rush"	Stimulates release of dopamine and norepinephrine; also a reuptake inhibitor for these neurotransmitters
Ecstasy (MDMA)	Excitement; endurance; increased intimacy	Stimulates release of serotonin and oxytocin
Opioids	Pain reduction; euphoria; relaxation	Stimulate endorphin receptors
Marijuana (cannabinoids)	Hallucination; vivid sensory experience; distortion of time and space; mild euphoria	Stimulates cannabinoid receptors

Drug	Behavioral Effects	Mode of Action
LSD	Hallucination	Unknown effects on serotonergic and noradrenergic systems
Alcohol	Reduced anxiety; mild euphoria; loss of motor coordination	Stimulates GABA$_A$ receptors; acts as an antagonist at the NMDA glutamate receptor; stimulates dopaminergic systems

Summary Points

1. Drugs have very different effects, depending on their mode of administration. Gender, size, and genetics influence individual differences in responses to drugs. **(LO8)**

2. Placebo effects occur when inactive substances appear to produce behavioral and cognitive effects. Continued use of some drugs can produce tolerance, withdrawal, and addiction. **(LO8)**

3. Stimulant drugs increase alertness and mobility. This class includes caffeine, nicotine, cocaine, amphetamine, and ecstasy (MDMA). Opioids produce profound pain relief and, in some forms, a remarkable sense of euphoria. **(LO9)**

4. Marijuana and LSD are classified as hallucinogens. **(LO9)**

5. Alcohol interacts with the GABA$_A$ receptor, where it boosts the inhibition normally provided by GABA, and antagonizes the NMDA glutamate receptor. **(LO9)**

Review Questions

1. What are the bases for individual responses to drugs?

2. Which drugs reverse the action of transporters?

Chapter Review

THOUGHT QUESTIONS

1. Amino acids, due to their simplicity and ready availability, probably served as the original chemical messengers. What advantages might have led to the evolution of more complex types of chemical messengers?

2. With further advances in our understanding of the human genome, we may be able to identify individuals with higher vulnerability to addiction to particular drugs. What ethical issues would face a society that had this ability? What policies, if any, would you recommend?

3. Which commonly used drug do you think is the safest? The most dangerous? State your reasons.

KEY TERMS

acetylcholine (ACh) (p. 105)
acetylcholinesterase (AChE) (p. 105)
addiction (p. 123)
adenosine (p. 112)
agonist (p. 116)
amphetamine (p. 128)
antagonist (p. 116)
barbiturate (p. 118)
benzodiazepine (p. 118)
caffeine (p. 126)
catecholamine (p. 106)
cocaine (p. 128)
dopamine (p. 107)
double-blind experiment (p. 122)
ecstasy (MDMA) (p. 130)
endorphin (p. 131)

epinephrine (p. 107)
gamma-aminobutyric acid (GABA) (p. 110)
gasotransmitter (p. 103)
glutamate (p. 110)
glycine (p. 110)
histamine (p. 00)
indoleamine (p. 106)
lysergic acid diethylamide (LSD) (p. 132)
methamphetamine (p. 128)
monoamine (p. 106)
monoamine oxidase (MAO) (p. 106)
neurohormone (p. 102)
neuromodulator (p. 102)
neuropeptide (p. 103)

neurotransmitter (p. 102)
nicotine (p. 126)
nitric oxide (NO) (p. 113)
norepinephrine (p. 107)
opiate (p. 131)
opioid (p. 131)
placebo effect (p. 122)
psychoactive drug (p. 126)
reuptake inhibitor (p. 119)
serotonin (p. 109)
small-molecule (p. 103)
tetrahydrocannabinol (THC) (p. 132)
tolerance (p. 123)
withdrawal (p. 123)

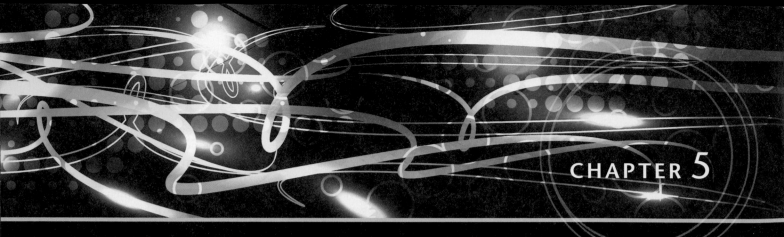

CHAPTER 5

Genetics and the Development of the Human Brain

LEARNING OBJECTIVES

LO1 Discuss the role of genes as the building blocks of human "nature," distinguishing between genotypes, gene expression, and phenotypes.

LO2 Describe the main sources of genetic diversity.

LO3 Assess the importance of heritability and epigenetics to our understanding of the interactions between genetics and environment.

LO4 Explain the processes of neurogenesis, migration, differentiation, apoptosis, synaptogenesis, and myelination.

LO5 Analyze the importance of critical periods of development.

LO6 Summarize the features and causes of developmental disorders affecting neural growth.

LO7 Describe the changes in the nervous system that accompany normal aging.

CHAPTER OUTLINE

The Genetic Bases of Behavior
  From Genome to Trait
  Sources of Genetic Variability
  Heritability
  Epigenetics
Interim Summary 5.1
Building a Brain
  Prenatal Development
  Effects of Experience on Development
  Disorders of Nervous System Development
Interim Summary 5.2
The Brain in Adolescence and Adulthood
  Brain Changes during Normal Aging
  Adult Neurogenesis
  Healthy Brain Aging
Interim Summary 5.3

CONNECTING TO RESEARCH: Epigenetics, Gene Expression, and Stress

BEHAVIORAL NEUROSCIENCE GOES TO WORK: Genetics Counseling

BUILDING BETTER HEALTH: Nutrition During Pregnancy

THINKING ETHICALLY: When Are Adolescents Responsible for Their Actions?

genotype The genetic composition of an individual organism.

phenotype The observable appearance of an individual organism.

gene A functional hereditary unit made up of DNA that occupies a fixed location on a chromosome.

gene expression The translation of the genotype into the phenotype of an organism.

The Genetic Bases of Behavior

There are about 19,000 protein-encoding genes in the human genome (Feero, Guttmacher, & Collins, 2010). It is somewhat humbling to consider that yeast cells have about 6,000 genes; flies have about 13,000; and plants have 26,000. Humans and other creatures differ substantially in the rate of expression of genes in the brain. The rate of human gene expression in the blood and in the liver is basically the same as in the chimpanzee, but human gene activity in the brain is much higher (Pääbo, 2001; Enard et al., 2002). We are also uniquely human due to our proteome, the set of proteins encoded and expressed by the genome.

You have the same DNA in each of the 100 trillion cells in your body, with the exception of red blood cells and sperm and egg cells. How does any single cell know how to become a muscle fiber in your heart or a neuron or a skin cell? The answer is that genes can be turned on or off. Genes that are not turned off are free to produce the proteins needed to build a particular type of cell. Each cell may contain the instructions for an entire human organism, but only a subset of instructions is expressed at any given time and location. Gene expression in a neuron is going to be very different than gene expression in a muscle cell.

Not only do genes turn on and off during development, but your ongoing interactions with the environment (what you eat, whether or not you smoke or drink, how much stress you experience) also influence the way your genes behave. This is why neuroscientists no longer argue about nature *versus* nurture. Instead, we view nature and nurture as intimately intertwining influences on the human body and mind (See ● Figure 5.1).

● **Figure 5.1** **Nature and Nurture Interact** When pregnant mice are fed a diet containing bisphenol-A or BPA, commonly found in plastics and food cans, they are more likely to give birth to obese offspring with yellow fur. It is likely that BPA affects the expression of the *Agouti* gene to produce these results. This situation illustrates the interaction between our nature (genetics) and our nurture (what we experience, or in this case, eat).

From Genome to Trait

Each cell of the body contains two complete copies of the human genome, a set of instructions for constructing a human being. Your personal set of genetic instructions is your **genotype**, which interacts with environmental influences to produce your **phenotype**, or your observable characteristics. Your genotype might include a gene for blonde hair and one for brown, whereas your phenotypical hair color is light brown. Your genotype consists of 23 matched pairs of chromosomes. One chromosome of each pair was donated by your mother via her egg and the other by your father via his sperm. The chromosomes are made up of molecules of deoxyribonucleic acid (DNA).

Smaller segments of DNA form individual **genes**. Genes are constructed from combinations of four biochemicals known as bases or nucleotides: adenine (A), cytosine (C), guanine (G), and thymine (T). Each gene contains instructions for making a particular type of protein. **Gene expression** occurs when these genetic instructions are converted into a feature of a living cell. As shown in ● Figure 5.3, sequences of bases in DNA are translated into proteins. A strand of DNA produces a copy of itself on a strand of ribonucleic acid (RNA). The bases along the DNA and RNA strands occur in groups of three, known as codons. Each codon provides instructions for the production of one of 20 amino acids, which are joined by ribosomes to form a chain. When complete, the chain folds into a shape based on its amino acid sequence and is now officially a protein.

Genotype	Phenotype
AA or AO	Type A Blood
BB or BO	Type B Blood
OO	Type O Blood
AB	Type AB Blood

● **Figure 5.2** **Three Alleles Give Rise to Four Types of Blood** The type A and type B alleles are dominant over type O, so a person with AO alleles will have type A blood and a person with BO alleles will have type B blood. Neither type A nor type B is dominant over the other, however, leading to the possibility of having type AB blood.

Different phenotypical traits result from the interactions between alternative versions of a particular gene, known as **alleles**. With two sets of chromosomes, an individual can have, at most, two versions of an allele. However, many more than two versions of an allele can exist within a population. As shown in ● Figure 5.2, there are three different alleles for blood type (A, B, and O). Because the alleles occur in pairs, with one allele from each parent, they give rise to four blood types: type A (AA or AO), type B (BB or BO), type AB (AB), or type O (OO).

If a person has two identical alleles at a given site, the individual is considered to be **homozygous** for that gene. If a person has two different alleles, such as one for type A blood and one for type O, he or she will be considered **heterozygous** for that gene. A **recessive allele** will produce its phenotype only when it occurs in a homozygous pair. The type O blood allele is recessive, which means that the only way a person can have the type O phenotype is if he or she receives a type O allele from each parent. A **dominant allele** produces a phenotypical trait regardless of whether its pair is homozygous or heterozygous.

Some genes do not show dominance. The serotonin transporter gene (SERT) has two alleles, long (L) and short (S). Neither of these dominates the other, so on behavioral measures such as a person's response to frequent bullying, people with the SL genotype fall midway between measures for people with the homozygous SS and LL genotypes (Sugden et al., 2010). If either the long or short version of SERT were

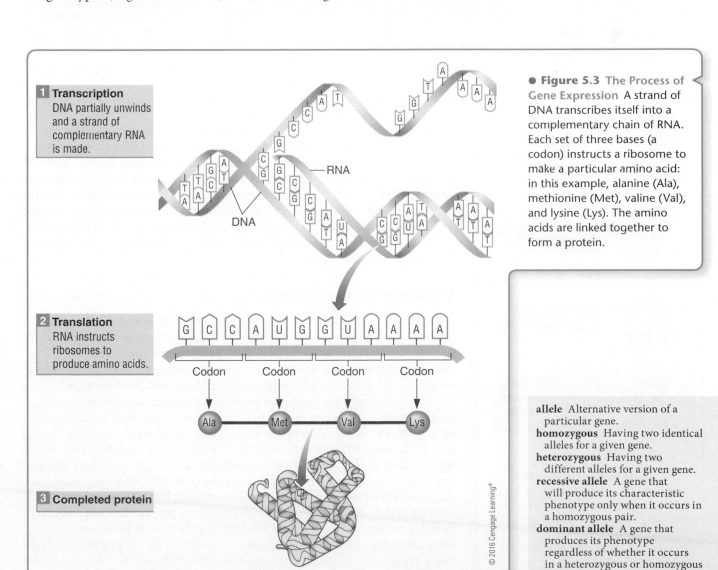

1 Transcription
DNA partially unwinds and a strand of complementary RNA is made.

RNA

DNA

2 Translation
RNA instructs ribosomes to produce amino acids.

Codon   Codon   Codon   Codon

Ala   Met   Val   Lys

3 Completed protein

● **Figure 5.3 The Process of Gene Expression** A strand of DNA transcribes itself into a complementary chain of RNA. Each set of three bases (a codon) instructs a ribosome to make a particular amino acid: in this example, alanine (Ala), methionine (Met), valine (Val), and lysine (Lys). The amino acids are linked together to form a protein.

© 2016 Cengage Learning®

allele Alternative version of a particular gene.
homozygous Having two identical alleles for a given gene.
heterozygous Having two different alleles for a given gene.
recessive allele A gene that will produce its characteristic phenotype only when it occurs in a homozygous pair.
dominant allele A gene that produces its phenotype regardless of whether it occurs in a heterozygous or homozygous pair.

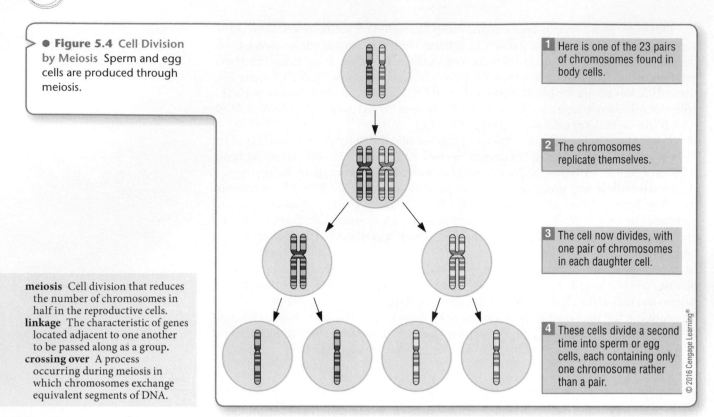

> ● **Figure 5.4** Cell Division by Meiosis Sperm and egg cells are produced through meiosis.

1 Here is one of the 23 pairs of chromosomes found in body cells.

2 The chromosomes replicate themselves.

3 The cell now divides, with one pair of chromosomes in each daughter cell.

4 These cells divide a second time into sperm or egg cells, each containing only one chromosome rather than a pair.

meiosis Cell division that reduces the number of chromosomes in half in the reproductive cells.
linkage The characteristic of genes located adjacent to one another to be passed along as a group.
crossing over A process occurring during meiosis in which chromosomes exchange equivalent segments of DNA.

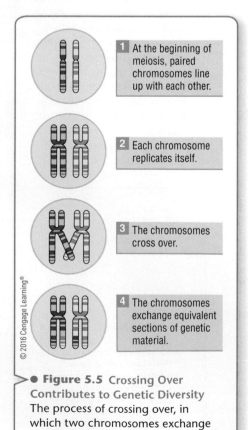

1 At the beginning of meiosis, paired chromosomes line up with each other.

2 Each chromosome replicates itself.

3 The chromosomes cross over.

4 The chromosomes exchange equivalent sections of genetic material.

> ● **Figure 5.5** Crossing Over Contributes to Genetic Diversity The process of crossing over, in which two chromosomes exchange equivalent segments of genetic material, adds to diversity by shuffling the parental genes that are inherited together.

dominant, individuals with the SL genotype would behave similarly to those with the homozygous dominant alleles.

Approximately 1 percent of mammals' genes are imprinted, which means that only one allele of a pair is expressed. The identity of the expressed gene depends on which parent supplied the allele. In other words, only the father's version is expressed in the case of some genes and only the mother's in others. Expression of imprinted genes appears to be especially prevalent in the brain (Wilkinson, Davies, & Isles, 2007), and imprinted genes have been implicated in the development of autism spectrum disorder (ASD), schizophrenia, and attention deficit disorder (ADHD) (see Chapter 16; Kopsida, Mikaelsson, & Davies, 2011).

Sources of Genetic Variability

Egg and sperm cells are formed through the process of **meiosis**. In meiosis, illustrated in ● Figure 5.4, the parental chromosome pairs are divided in half, leaving only one chromosome from each pair in an egg or sperm cell. When the egg and sperm cells from the two parents combine, the resulting zygote once again contains the full complement of 23 pairs of chromosomes.

Mathematically, the process of meiosis is analogous to shuffling a deck of cards. A meiotic division results in two egg or sperm cells, each containing one set of 23 chromosomes. As a result, a single human can produce eggs or sperm with 2^{23} (8,388,608) combinations of their chromosomes. Add this to the diversity provided by the other parent, and you can see why your brothers and sisters have some, but by no means all, features in common with you. Genes that are physically located close to one another on the same chromosome are often passed along to offspring as a group in a process known as **linkage**. However, linked genes are not automatically inherited together. In the process of **crossing over**, illustrated in ● Figure 5.5, chromosomes lining up prior to meiotic division physically cross one another and exchange equivalent sections of genetic material. This results in unique combinations of genes not seen in either parent.

MUTATIONS In the process of chromosome replication, errors, or **mutations**, happen. The average human baby is born with about 130 new mutations (Zimmer, 2009), but the vast majority of mutations have little effect. There is some overlap in the genetic encoding of amino acids. If a segment of DNA that normally encodes a particular amino acid is somehow switched with another segment that produces the same amino acid, there will be no effect. Mutations may occur in segments of DNA that do not appear to influence phenotypical traits, or a mutation may result in a recessive allele. Inheriting a dominant mutant allele or two copies of a recessive mutant allele will affect an organism's phenotype. If the mutant allele conveys some advantage to the organism, it is likely to spread within the population. On the other hand, a mutant allele may have negative, even fatal, consequences for the organism. In the latter case, it may disappear from the population.

THE SPECIAL CASE OF THE SEX CHROMOSOMES Most of the active genes on the Y chromosome are involved with male fertility (Jegalian & Lahn, 2001), whereas the X chromosome contains a wide variety of genes (see ● Figure 5.6). **Sex-linked characteristics** result from genes on the X chromosome that are not duplicated on the Y chromosome. For example, recessive genes resulting in the blood clotting disorder hemophilia, and genes resulting in some forms of red-green color deficiency, are located on the X chromosome. On chromosomes other than the X and Y, one would need two copies of a recessive gene or only one copy of a dominant gene to produce the trait in the organism. In the case of genes occurring on the X chromosome, however, a single recessive gene influences the phenotype when there is no corresponding gene on the Y chromosome. For this reason, males are far more likely to experience sex-linked disorders than females, who are likely to have a compensating dominant gene on their second X chromosome (see ● Figure 5.7).

The lack of matching pairs for most genes on the sex chromosomes has led to a phenomenon known as **X chromosome inactivation**. Because many genes on the X chromosome are not duplicated on the Y chromosome, females would produce double the amounts of some proteins compared to males. To compensate for this imbalance,

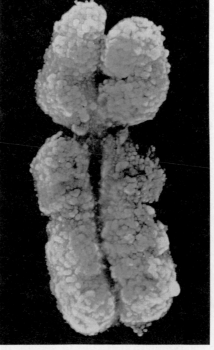

> ● **Figure 5.6** The X and Y Chromosomes Are Not a Matched Pair The X chromosome (right) resembles most of the other 22 in appearance, but the Y (left) is quite unusual. Not only is it much smaller, with only a few dozen genes compared with the X's 2,000 or so, but it has unusually high amounts of "junk" DNA that doesn't seem to encode anything useful.

© Biophoto Associates/Science Source

mutation A heritable alteration of genes.
sex-linked characteristic Phenotypical characteristics that result from expression of genes on the X chromosome that are not duplicated on the Y chromosome.
X chromosome inactivation The process by which one X chromosome in each female cell is silenced to equalize the amount of proteins produced by males and females.

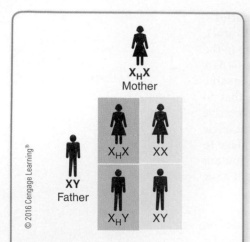

X_H X
Mother

XY
Father

X_H X   XX

X_H Y   XY

© 2016 Cengage Learning®

● **Figure 5.7** Probabilities of Hemophilia Hemophilia is a sex-linked condition in which blood fails to clot. If a mother carries the hemophilia gene on one of her X chromosomes (X_H) and the father has a typical X chromosome, each daughter will have a 50 percent chance of being typical and a 50 percent chance of being a carrier for the hemophilia gene. The couple's sons have a 50 percent chance of having hemophilia. Without a healthy X to counteract the X carrying the hemophilia gene, sons will have the condition if they inherit the hemophilia gene from their mothers.

most of the genes on one X chromosome in each female cell are silenced (Jegalian & Lahn, 2001). The actual identity of the silenced X chromosome genes (mother's or father's copy) varies from cell to cell, and a very small percentage escape silencing altogether.

An interesting example of this random X chromosome inactivation process is found in the coloring of calico cats (see ● Figure 5.8). Only female cats can be calicos because the genes for orange or black fur are located in the same area of the X chromosome. A male cat could have only orange or only black fur, but not both, because he has only one X chromosome. A female cat with an orange allele on one X and a black allele on the other X will be a calico. In each cell, the fur-color alleles on one X chromosome will be silenced. In cells with a silenced orange allele, the fur will be black. In cells with a silenced black allele, the fur will be orange. As a result, the cat will have a random pattern of orange and black fur.

On average, X inactivation should result in a woman's expressing 50 percent of X chromosome alleles from her father and 50 percent from her mother, but the exact ratio varies from woman to woman and forms an approximately normal curve for the population. Extreme skewing, in which 90 percent or more of a woman's alleles originate with one parent, has been associated with a number of diseases, and quite possibly might account for the larger number of women who are diagnosed with some conditions, including autoimmune diseases (Migeon, 2007).

SINGLE NUCLEOTIDE POLYMORPHISMS (SNPS) Genetics researchers are particularly interested in alleles whose genetic code differs in only one location. These alleles are known as **single nucleotide polymorphisms**, or SNPs (pronounced "snips"). A SNP occurs when a sequence of nucleotides making up one allele differs from the sequence of another at just one point, such as AAGGTTA to ATGGTTA. For example, the *APOE* gene on chromosome 19 produces a protein that helps keep cholesterol levels low. There are three alleles for the *APOE* gene, known as E^2, E^3, and E^4. Each *APOE* allele has 299 codons, or sets of three nucleotides. As shown in ● Figure 5.9, the 112th codon on this string encodes cystine in the E^2 and E^3 alleles but argenine in the E^4 alleles. The 158th codon encodes argenine in E^3 and E^4 but cystine in E^2. These are tiny differences when compared to the volume of DNA in our bodies, yet they have great significance in the development of diseases such as Alzheimer's disease, a degenerative, ultimately fatal condition marked initially by memory loss, discussed in Chapter 15. Alzheimer's disease is more likely to occur in individuals with two E^4 alleles than in individuals with one or two of the E^2 or E^3 alleles (Huang et al., 2011).

COPY-NUMBER VARIATIONS (CNVS) Increases or decreases in the number of copies of a single gene or series of genes are known as **copy-number variations (CNVs)** (Bassett, Scherer, & Brzustowicz, 2010). These variations can arise spontaneously or be inherited from a parent. Although the diagnostic criteria for ASD and schizophrenia are quite distinct (see Chapter 16), certain CNVs are much more common in people with either one of these disorders than in the general population (McCarthy et al., 2009; Sebat et al., 2007). Future systems of diagnostic criteria for psychological disorders are likely to place more emphasis on these types of shared underlying risk factors.

single nucleotide polymorphism Variation between alleles involving a single base.
copy-number variation (CNVs) Mutation resulting from duplication or deletion of sections of DNA.

Heritability

How do our genes and experience interact to produce the human mind and its behavior?

As noted in Chapter 1, heritability describes how much variation in a trait observed in a population is due to genetic differences. This is a concept that is frequently misunderstood. *Heritability always refers to populations, not to individuals.* If genes play no part in producing phenotypical differences between individuals, heritability is zero. For example, genes are responsible for building hearts, but there is no variation in the population in terms of the presence of a heart—we all have one. Therefore, heritability for having a heart is zero. In contrast, heritability for Huntington's disease, a fatal neurological condition discussed in Chapter 8, is 100 percent. If you inherit a defective gene from one parent, you will develop the condition. Heritability of most human traits typically falls between these extremes, in the range of 30 to 60 percent.

If we say that the heritability of ASD traits (see Chapter 16) is about 57 percent (Hoekstra, Bartels, Verweij, & Boomsma, 2007), this does not mean that 57 percent of a single individual's ASD traits are due to genetics and 43 percent are due to his or her environment. Instead, these findings mean that 57 percent of the variation we see in ASD traits in a population can be accounted for by genetic differences.

Heritability cannot be assessed without taking the environment into account, which is another source of confusion. If the environment is constant (everybody is treated exactly the same way), the heritability of a trait is likely to be high. For example, if you surveyed IQ in a population of children from the most affluent, well-educated families in a community, your results would be more influenced by heredity than if you sampled a group of children more representative of the diverse home environments in the community. In the affluent sample, many of the environmental influences we believe contribute to high IQ are likely to be present, such as good nutrition and health care, emphasis on education and achievement, and exposure to intellectually stimulating activities. With these environmental variables held at a fairly constant level, the differences you observe among the affluent children are likely to result from their heredity. The same can be said if you observed children from socially deprived circumstances, in which environmental influences related to high IQ were consistently lacking. Once again, the dif-

● **Figure 5.8** X Chromosome Inactivation Inactivation of most of the genes on one X chromosome takes place randomly in the cells of females. Because the genes for black and orange fur in cats exist at the same location on the X chromosome, a male cat will be either black or orange but not calico. The calico coloring of the female cat results from inactivation of the gene for orange and black fur by different cells.

ferences you observe in this homogeneous environment are likely to be due to genetic influences. In your sample of children from across the community, the environments vary more widely, thus heritability of IQ in this sample would be lower. Researchers assessing heritability of human traits attempt to do so within a "typical" range of environments, as in the previously cited work on ASD traits (Hoekstra et al., 2007).

Studies comparing identical, or monozygotic, and fraternal, or dizygotic, twins raised together or apart by adoptive parents can be useful in assessing the relative contributions of heredity and environment. Monozygotic (MZ) twins share the same genes, whereas dizygotic (DZ) twins share the same number of genes (about 50 percent) as ordinary siblings. All twins, however, share a similar environment, both before and after birth, whereas ordinary siblings who are born at different times experience greater variations in their environments.

The Minnesota Study of Twins Reared Apart (Bouchard, 1994; Bouchard, Lykken, McGue, Segal, & Tellegen, 1990) is an ongoing, large-scale study of twins. The pairs of identical twins in the study were quite similar, regardless of whether they were raised together. Some traits were highly correlated between identical twins, such as the number of ridges in a fingerprint. Other traits showed relatively low correlations, such as nonreligious social attitudes (e.g., political beliefs). The critical finding was that identical twins raised either apart or together were very similar, whether the correlation for a particular trait was high or low. However, it is important to note that adoptive families rarely represent as much diversity as the group of biological parents whose children they adopt. If all adoptive families provide a consistent environment, this could inflate the apparent heritability of characteristics examined in adopted children.

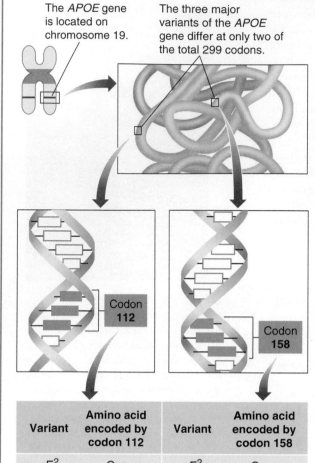

The *APOE* gene is located on chromosome 19.

The three major variants of the *APOE* gene differ at only two of the total 299 codons.

Codon 112

Codon 158

Variant	Amino acid encoded by codon 112	Variant	Amino acid encoded by codon 158
E^2	Cys	E^2	Cys
E^3	Cys	E^3	Arg
E^4	Arg	E^4	Arg

A person with two copies of the *APOE* E^4 variant has a 91 percent chance of developing Alzheimer's; average age at onset is 68 years.

© 2016 Cengage Learning®

● **Figure 5.9** SNPs and Disease Single nucleotide polymorphisms (SNPs) occur when a gene sequence differs from other variations by only a single nucleotide. Tiny variations in the *APOE* gene have dramatic consequences for a person's susceptibility to Alzheimer's disease.

epigenetics The reversible development of traits by factors that determine how genes perform.
histone modification Changes in the structure of histones that make it more or less likely that a segment of DNA will be transcribed.
DNA methylation Addition of a methyl group to a DNA molecule turns off the gene.

Epigenetics

Having identical genotypes, as is the case with identical twins, does not guarantee identical phenotypes. When factors other than the genotype itself produce changes in a phenotype, we say that an epigenetic change has occurred. *Epi* is Greek for "over" or "above," so **epigenetics** refers to the reversible development of traits by factors that determine how genes perform.

Two important processes that produce lasting but reversible changes in gene expression are **histone modification** and **DNA methylation** (see ● Figure 5.10). The DNA in each of your cells is tightly wound around protein structures known as histones. If the DNA were unwound, it would be nearly four feet in length (Grant, 2001). Histones have a core and a tail, both of which can be modified in ways that affect how a segment of DNA is transcribed. Some modifications make it more likely that a sequence of DNA will be transcribed, while other modifications essentially silence a section of DNA. DNA methlyation occurs when a methyl group is added to the DNA molecule. Genes that are methylated are essentially turned off. This process performs essential roles in cell differentiation and embryonic development, described in more detail later in this chapter. Abnormal DNA methylation is believed to contribute to a number of diseases. For example, methylation of tumor suppression genes promotes the spread of cancer. Each modification of the histones or DNA is known as an epigenetic tag. Epigenetic tags influence physical structure and behavior, but it is also important to recognize that behavior, such as smoking or the experience of stress, can also change epigenetic tags.

Several interesting examples of epigenetic change have been demonstrated. As we observed in ● Figure 5.1, a gene called *Agouti* produces yellow fur and obesity in mice when it is turned on, but brown fur and normal weight when it is turned off (Dolinoy, Huang, & Jirtle, 2007). Mother mice fed a diet containing bisphenol-A, or BPA (a common chemical found in food and beverage containers) produced more obese pups with yellow fur, suggesting that BPA exposure could turn on the *Agouti* gene. As discussed in more detail in a later section, infant rats that are licked by their mothers (the rat equivalent of a hug) were calmer in the face of later stress than rats that were not licked frequently (Champagne, Francis, Mar, & Meaney, 2003). By licking her pups, the mother rat changes the expression of genes related to the function of stress hormones. Similarly, as illustrated in ● Figure 5.11, children exposed to child abuse also show long-lasting changes in the expression of genes related to stress hormones (Neigh, Gillespie, & Nemeroff, 2009) and a number of gene locations associated with later medical problems and psychological disorders (Yang et al., 2013). Fortunately, some of these changes seem to be reversible as a result of responsive caregiving by foster parents (Fisher, Van Ryzin, & Gunnar, 2011).

Scientists are intrigued by the possibility that some epigenetic changes might be passed along to offspring. For this to be possible, the reprogramming (removal of epigenetic tags) that normally occurs in germ cells (precursors to sperm and egg cells) and in the zygote must be bypassed (Daxinger & Whitelaw, 2010). Without normal

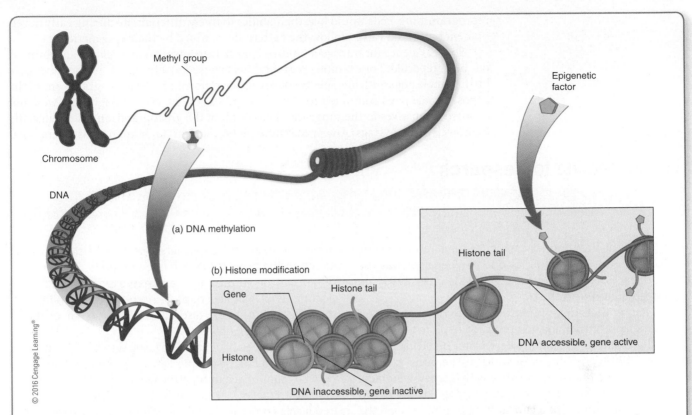

Chromosome

Methyl group

DNA

(a) DNA methylation

(b) Histone modification

Gene

Histone tail

Histone

DNA inaccessible, gene inactive

Epigenetic factor

Histone tail

DNA accessible, gene active

© 2016 Cengage Learning®

● **Figure 5.10** DNA Methylation and Histone Modification DNA methylation and histone modification are two major sources of epigenetic change. (a) When a methyl group is added to the DNA molecule, it essentially makes the DNA inaccessible, rendering the gene inactive. (b) When epigenetic tags interact with the histone structure as shown in the two boxes, nearby DNA may be more or less likely to be transcribed.

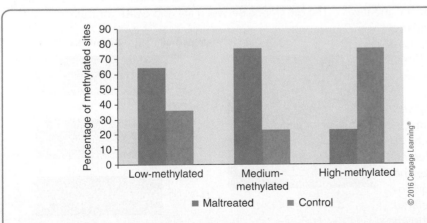

Percentage of methylated sites

Low-methylated   Medium-methylated   High-methylated

■ Maltreated   ■ Control

© 2016 Cengage Learning®

● **Figure 5.11** DNA Methylation and Child Maltreatment DNA methylation essentially silences a gene, so sites that are normally "low-methylated" are associated with genes that are expressed while sites that are normally "high-methylated" are not. In a comparison of children removed from their homes as a result of severe maltreatment with control children lacking a history of maltreatment, consistent differences were found in methylation across the genome, and in many sites known to contribute to medical disease and psychological disorder. Maltreated children showed increased methylation of sites that are normally less likely to be methylated and also showed reduced methylation at sites that are normally very likely to be methylated. These findings might explain why many people with a history of maltreatment as children experience higher risk for medical and psychological conditions later in life.

reprogramming, cells would lose their ability to freely differentiate during early development but would rather follow the pattern determined by their epigenetic tags.

Some evidence for transgenerational epigenetic transmission in plants and animals has been reported. For example, pregnant rats exposed to a fungicide in their diet gave birth to male pups with low sperm counts and poor fertility. The great-grandsons of the exposed male pups continued to show low sperm counts, even though they were not exposed themselves to the fungicide. The sperm of the great-grandsons had unusually high levels of methyl tags (Anway & Skinner, 2006). Support for human transgenerational

••• Connecting to **Research**

EPIGENETICS, GENE EXPRESSION, AND STRESS

One of the more dramatic demonstrations of the effects of epigenetics on later behavior was the work by Francis, Diorio, Liu, and Meaney (1999) on maternal nurture and stress.

Rat mothers differ in the amount of time they spend licking and grooming their pups. To explore the effects of these differences in nurture on later behavior, Francis et al. (1999) cross-fostered some of the pups to different types of mothers. In other words, they were able to compare the behavior of pups raised by their own biological mothers or a similar type of mother with the behavior of pups raised by a mother whose nurturant style differed from their own biological mother.

Tolerance for stress can be easily assessed in rodents by open-field tests. Stressed rodents will not stay out in the open (which is undeniably a dangerous place for a rodent to be) as long as a less-stressed rodent. Francis et al. (1999) found that all pups raised by an attentive mother (high licking and grooming) explored the open space longer than pups raised by an inattentive mother (low licking and grooming) no matter what type of biological mother they had.

What is the basis for this difference in behavior? Francis et al. (1999) further assessed the expression of glucocorticoid receptors in the hippocampus. Glucocorticoids, such as cortisol (see Chapters 11 and 14), are released in response to stress and help to mobilize the body for emergency responses. Higher glucocorticoid receptor gene expression is correlated with resilience to stress later in life. As shown in ● Figure 5.12, pups born to attentive mothers show greater expression of glucocorticoid receptors in the hippocampus (more resilience to stress) than pups born to low attentive mothers. However, Francis et al. (1999) were able to elicit more attentiveness from the normally less attentive mothers by handling their pups. When the handled pups are returned to the mother, she licks and grooms them more. Handling had no effect on the gene expression

of pups with attentive mothers, but it had a significant effect on the pups of low attentive mothers. The levels of glucocorticoid receptor gene expression in the hippocampus of handled pups of normally low attentive mothers could not be distinguished from that of the pups of attentive mothers.

Epigenetics provides a much faster way for the organism to respond to their immediate environment than the slow changes of evolution. Why would it ever be advantageous to make your offspring more reactive to stress? In our safe communities in the United States, we tend to view higher reactivity to stress as abnormal and undesirable. However, imagine a stressed mother living in a dangerous environment whose personal stress prevents her from providing attentive care to her children. Her children would enter the dangerous environment predisposed to react quickly to danger, which might make the difference between life and death for them.

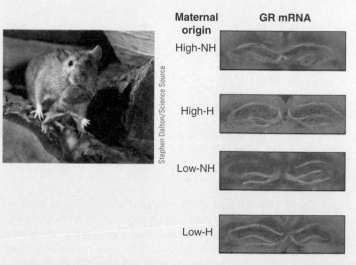

Stephen Dalton/Science Source

● **Figure 5.12** Nurture Affects Gene Expression The pups of nurturant (high) mothers showed high levels of glucocorticoid receptors (GR; shown in red) in the hippocampus regardless of whether they were handled (H) or not handled (NH). However, pups of non-nurturant (low) mothers showed nearly normal levels of gene expression when handled, but reduced levels when not handled.

Source: Adapted from Francis, Diorio, Liu, & Meaney (1999).

••• **Behavioral**
Neuroscience   **GENETICS COUNSELING**
GOES TO WORK

Along with the tremendous increase in our under-standing of the human genome has come an obvi-ous commercial bonanza in the form of genetic testing. Carrier screening for couples will tell them their odds of producing a child with a particular genetic disor-der. Analysis of amniocentesis and other prenatal tests are used by parents to either terminate pregnancy or prepare for the task of raising a child with a disabil-ity. Embryos to be used for assisted reproductive tech-nologies are screened for genetic abnormalities and, in some cases, for the desired sex of the child. Adults can be screened for their genetic vulnerability for certain cancers, for Huntington's disease (see Chapter 8), and for Alzheimer's disease. Acting on information about her genetic risk, actress Angelina Jolie made headlines for her preventive double mastectomy, raising cancer awareness on the one hand and the fear that women who would not benefit from the surgery might insist on it on the other hand.

In many cases, suppliers are offering direct-to-consumer tests, which are not regulated by the U.S. government. You can even buy a paternity test at your local drugstore (Antonucci, 2008). Simply send in a sample, and you get a result back in the mail. Although some corporations offer-ing these tests require a physician's consent, many do not (Williams, 2006). Even when physicians are involved, many lack sufficient training to provide genetic counseling.

As our knowledge and ability to test genetics improve, the public will face more and more sophisticated deci-sions of great importance to health and well-being. It is unlikely that most of us are prepared to make such deci-sions in thoughtful, informed ways. Consequently, we can expect a large increase in demand for trained genet-ics counselors. If you like both the science and the idea of being in one of the helping professions, you might consider investigating one of the graduate genetics counseling programs accredited by the American Board of Genetics Counselors (ABGC, 2014).

epigenetic transmission is much more controversial. In a large-scale Swedish study, early paternal smoking was associated with higher body weight in sons. The paternal grandfathers' diet in mid-childhood predicted grandsons' mortality while the paternal grandmothers' food supply predicted the mortality of granddaughters (Pembrey et al., 2005). However, given the lack of control inherent in human research, confounding variables such as cultural practices cannot be ruled out (Daxinger & Whitelaw, 2010).

INTERIM SUMMARY 5.1

‖ **Summary Table: Important Concepts in Genetics**

Concept	Definition	Significance
Genome	The complete set of chromosomes for a species	Identifies the characteristics that define a species. *Example:* The entire human genome.
Genotype	An individual's set of chromosomes	Identifies the genetic basis for individ-ual characteristics. *Example:* Having one allele for blue eyes and a second allele for brown eyes.
Phenotype	The observable characteris-tics of an individual	Identifies the end result of the inter-actions between genes and environ-ment. *Example:* Having hazel eyes or being six feet tall.
Chromosome	Bodies found within the nuclei of cells that are made up of DNA	Twenty-three pairs of chromosomes make up the entire human genome. *Example:* The X and Y sex chromosomes.

(continued)

Concept	Definition	Significance
Gene	A functional hereditary unit occupying a fixed location on a chromosome	Genes are responsible for the production of particular proteins. *Example:* Genes for eye color or for the production of dopamine receptors.
Allele	Alternative versions of a particular gene	Trait variations between individuals in a species. *Example:* The A, B, and O alleles for blood type.
Proteome	The set of proteins encoded by the genome	The identification of the set of proteins encoded by the genome of a species. *Example:* Analysis might identify proteins associated with vulnerability to diabetes, obesity, stroke, chronic pain, and Parkinson's disease.
Meiosis	Cell division that reduces the number of chromosomes to half in reproductive cells	Meiosis creates a huge number of possible genetic combinations. *Example:* A single human can produce eggs or sperm with 2^{23} (over 8 million) combinations of his or her chromosomes.
Mutation	A change on a gene or chromosome that can be passed to offspring	Results of mutation can be advantageous, neutral, or disadvantageous. *Example:* A mutation causes the disease cystic fibrosis, which causes premature death.
SNPs ("snips")	Variations that occur in a gene when a single base is changed from one version to the next	SNPs can be a major source of variation between individuals of a species. *Example:* APOE variants E^2, E^3, and E^4 that affect a person's chances of developing Alzheimer's disease.
Copy-Number Variations (CNVs)	Increases or decreases in the number of copies of a single gene or series of genes	CNVs can make the difference between a healthy genotype and an unhealthy one. *Example:* Although the diagnostic criteria for autism spectrum disorder and schizophrenia are quite distinct, certain CNVs are much more common in people with either one of these disorders than in the general population.

‖ Summary Points

1. The human genome contains two copies of 23 chromosomes, made up of DNA. DNA sequences, or genes, provide instructions for producing proteins. Alternative versions of a gene, or alleles, can be dominant or recessive. **(LO1)**

2. Genetic diversity is assured by meiosis, linkage, crossing over, and mutations. **(LO2)**

3. Heritability provides an estimate of the amount of variability in a trait across a population determined by genetics. Epigenetics is the reversible change in the ways genes perform. **(LO3)**

Review Questions

1. In what ways are the sex chromosomes different from the other 22 pairs of human chromosomes?
2. How do heredity and environmental factors interact to produce the phenotype of an individual?

Building a Brain

Beginning with the merger of a mother's egg and a father's sperm and the complex interactions of the genes they contain, we grow adult human bodies containing approximately 100 trillion cells (Sears, 2005). About 100 billion of those cells will be found in the brain. Although the process of development does not always proceed smoothly, we still enjoy a remarkable record of accuracy, considering the enormous complexity of the organism we are building.

Prenatal Development

The initial cell formed by the merger of egg and sperm is known as a **zygote**. From two to eight weeks following conception, the developing individual is known as an **embryo**. After the eighth week until birth, the individual is a **fetus**.

A week after conception, the human zygote has already formed three differentiated bands of cells known as germ layers. The outer layer is the **ectoderm**, which will develop into the nervous system, skin, and hair. The middle layer is the **mesoderm**, which forms connective tissue, muscles, blood vessels, bone, and the urogenital systems. The final layer is the **endoderm**, which will develop into many of the internal organs, including the stomach and intestines.

The third and fourth weeks following conception are a very important period in human nervous system development. During the third week, cells in the ectoderm located along the dorsal midline of the embryo begin to differentiate into a new layer known as the neural plate. Remaining cells in the ectoderm will form the skin. As the ectodermal cells begin to differentiate, a groove or depression forms along the midline of the **neural plate**. Further cell divisions produce two ridges of tissue on either side of the groove that eventually join to form the **neural tube**. This process is complete by the end of the fourth week. The interior of the neural tube will be retained in the adult brain as the system of ventricles and the central canal of the spinal cord (see Chapter 2). The surrounding neural tissue will form the brain and spinal cord.

Before the neural tube has even finished closing, it features three bulges or vesicles, the **prosencephalon** (future forebrain), the **mesencephalon** (future midbrain), and the **rhombencephalon** (future hindbrain). As shown in ● Figure 5.13, the neural tube bends twice, once at the junction of the rhombencephalon and what will be the spinal cord (this bend straightens out later) and again in the area of the mesencephalon. In the following week, the prosencephalon further differentiates into the **diencephalon** (thalamus, hypothalamus, and retina of the eye) and the **telencephalon** (remainder of the cerebral hemispheres). Around the same time, the rhombencephalon divides into the **myelencephalon** (medulla) and the **metencephalon** (pons and cerebellum). The mesencephalon does not undergo any further divisions.

Further development of the nervous system proceeds in a series of six distinct stages: (1) neurogenesis, or the continued birth of neurons and glia; (2) migration of cells to their eventual locations in the nervous system; (3) differentiation of neurons into distinctive types; (4) formation of connections between neurons; (5) death of particular neurons; and (6) rearrangement of neural connections.

zygote The cell formed by two merged reproductive cells.

embryo In humans, the developing individual between the second and eighth week following conception.

fetus The developing organism between the embryonic stage and birth.

ectoderm The germ layer that develops into the nervous system, skin, and hair.

mesoderm The germ layer that develops into connective tissue, muscle, blood vessels, bone, and the urogenital systems.

endoderm The germ layer that develops into internal organs, including the stomach and intestines.

neural plate A layer formed by differentiating neural cells within the ectoderm of the embryo.

neural tube A structure formed by the embryonic neural plate that will develop into the brain and spinal cord.

prosencephalon One of three early divisions of the neural tube that will develop into the forebrain.

mesencephalon One of three early divisions of the neural tube that will develop into the midbrain.

rhombencephalon One of the early three divisions of the neural tube that will develop into the hindbrain.

diencephalon A division of the prosencephalon that will contain the thalamus, hypothalamus, and retina of the eye.

telencephalon A division of the prosencephalon that develops into the bulk of the cerebral hemispheres.

myelencephalon A division of the rhombencephalon that develops into the medulla.

metencephalon A division of the rhombencephalon that develops into the pons and cerebellum.

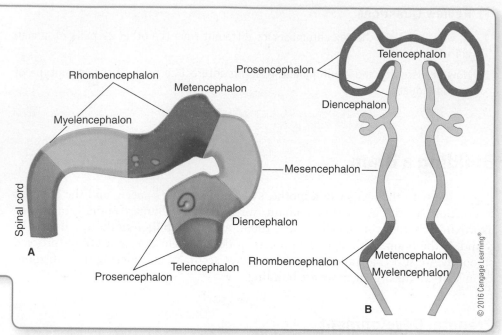

● **Figure 5.13** The Neural Tube Divides Before neural tube closure is complete, three bulges are apparent: the prosencephalon (forebrain), the mesencephalon (midbrain), and the rhombencephalon (hindbrain). In the following week, the prosencephalon divides once more to form the telencephalon and diencephalon, while the rhombencephalon divides to form the myelencephalon and metencephalon. The mesencephalon does not make an additional division.

© 2016 Cengage Learning®

••• Building Better HEALTH

NUTRITION DURING PREGNANCY

Researchers have known for decades that times of famine have long-reaching results for the offspring of women who were pregnant during times of food shortage. During the winter of 1945, food supplies in the Netherlands were dramatically reduced in the wake of World War II. The Dutch Famine Birth Cohort Study, carried out by the Academic Medical Centre in Amsterdam in cooperation with the University of Southampton, found that the children of women pregnant during this so-called Dutch Hunger Winter suffered a higher rate of a number of diseases, including diabetes, obesity, and cardiovascular disease. In addition, these children had higher rates of major depressive disorder and schizophrenia.

Although we often associate maternal malnutrition with developing countries characterized by food insecurity, moderate maternal malnutrition also occurs in industrialized nations due to maternal dieting and simple failure to improve diet during pregnancy. Should we worry about this? Ethical concerns as well as confounding variables such as poverty make studying maternal malnutrition in humans difficult. However, studies using other primates, such as baboons, show that even moderate maternal malnutrition suppressed neurotrophic factors, produced an imbalance between cell proliferation and apoptosis, impaired glial cell

maturation and axon growth, and distorted gene expression (Keenan et al., 2013). None of these outcomes bode well for the offspring's health and cognitive functioning later in life.

The American College of Obstetrics and Gynecology issues guidelines for healthy eating by pregnant women. Levels of iron, folic acid, calcium, and vitamin D that are adequate for most adults are insufficient for pregnant women and must be adjusted during pregnancy. Fish and shellfish provide an important source of Omega-3 fatty acids needed for healthy brain development, but pregnant women must also avoid fish contaminated by mercury, as this is a known neurotoxin. Following food safety guidelines to avoid consuming contaminated foods, such as milk products contaminated with bacteria, is especially important during pregnancy.

Caffeine intake should be sharply limited (one cup per day or less) or avoided completely.

Although it might seem inconvenient for pregnant women to change their preferred style of eating, this represents a nine-month commitment for the woman but a lifetime of benefits for her child. Many psychologists believe that rates of serious psychological disorders could be greatly reduced if each newborn had been exposed to the right nutrients during prenatal development.

NEUROGENESIS **Neurogenesis**, or the birth of new neurons and glia, occurs in the ventricular zone, a layer of cells lining the inner surface of the neural tube. These progenitor (reproducing) cells in the ventricular zone divide by mitosis, producing two identical "daughter" cells. Initially, both daughter cells remain and continue to divide in the ventricular zone, which thickens as a result. After about the seventh week following conception, many progenitors in the ventricular zone begin to produce a daughter cell that remains in the zone and a daughter cell that is destined to migrate outward to form a neuron or glial cell (Chan, Lorke, Tiu, & Yew, 2002). As shown in ● Figure 5.14, progenitor cells producing two additional progenitor cells divide along a cleavage line that lies perpendicular to the surface of the ventricular zone. In contrast, progenitor cells that produce an additional progenitor cell and a migrating cell divide along a cleavage line that is parallel to the ventricular zone surface. The parallel cleavage line means that the daughter cell to the outside will not be attached to the ventricular zone once the division is complete. This cell will be free to migrate. In humans, up to 250,000 new neural cells per minute might be born at the peak of this cell formation process. These cells are still somewhat immature, consisting of a cell body and a process that will become an axon later in development.

CELL MIGRATION **Migration** does not occur in a random manner. Instead, the journey for the majority of cells is guided by specialized progenitor cells known as **radial glia**, which grow out from the ventricular layer to the outer margins of the nervous system like the spokes of a wheel (Rakic, 1988). In addition to their critical role in cell migration, radial glia retain the ability to produce additional daughter cells (Weissman, Noctor, Clinton, Honig, & Kriegstein, 2003). Migrating cells wrap around the radial glia and move along them, as shown in ● Figure 5.15. The minority of cells that do not follow radial glia appear to move in a more horizontal (anterior-posterior) direction (Nadarajah & Parnavelas, 2002). Once migration is complete, most radial glia pull back their branches, although some remain in place throughout adulthood.

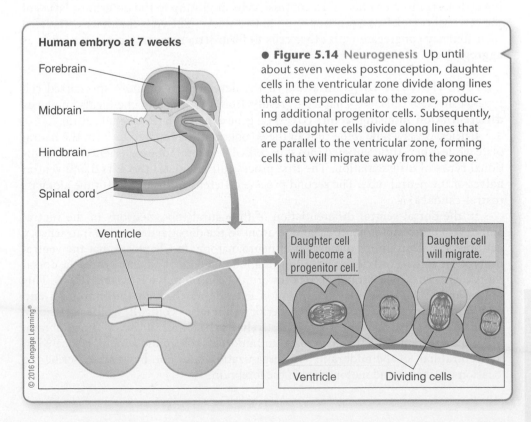

Human embryo at 7 weeks

Forebrain

Midbrain

Hindbrain

Spinal cord

Ventricle

Ventricle   Dividing cells

Daughter cell will become a progenitor cell.

Daughter cell will migrate.

● **Figure 5.14** Neurogenesis Up until about seven weeks postconception, daughter cells in the ventricular zone divide along lines that are perpendicular to the zone, producing additional progenitor cells. Subsequently, some daughter cells divide along lines that are parallel to the ventricular zone, forming cells that will migrate away from the zone.

© 2016 Cengage Learning®

neurogenesis The birth of new neurons and glia.
migration The movement of cells to their mature location.
radial glia Special glia that radiate from the ventricular layer to the outer edge of the cerebral cortex, serving as a pathway for migrating neurons.

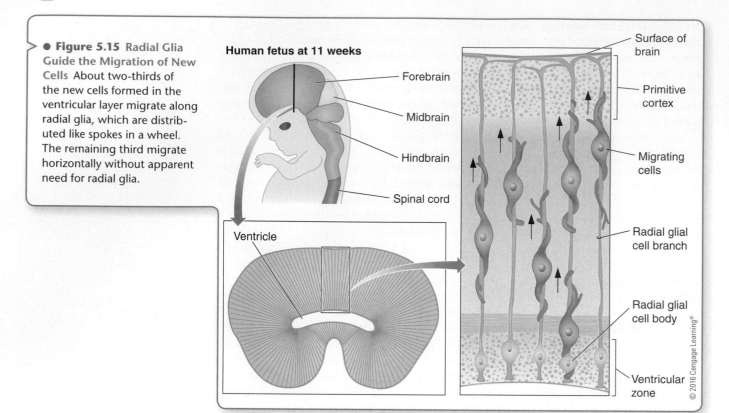

● **Figure 5.15** Radial Glia Guide the Migration of New Cells About two-thirds of the new cells formed in the ventricular layer migrate along radial glia, which are distributed like spokes in a wheel. The remaining third migrate horizontally without apparent need for radial glia.

Human fetus at 11 weeks

Forebrain

Midbrain

Hindbrain

Spinal cord

Ventricle

Surface of brain

Primitive cortex

Migrating cells

Radial glial cell branch

Radial glial cell body

Ventricular zone

© 2016 Cengage Learning®

Migrating cells form the cerebral cortex in an inside-out fashion. Cells destined for the outer cortical layers must somehow travel through the inner layers. In other words, a cell migrating to Layer IV of the cortex would have to bypass Layers VI and V en route to its final destination (see Chapter 2). The journey of early migrating cells lasts just a few hours. In contrast, cells migrating to the outermost layers of the cerebral cortex face a journey of up to two weeks. The cells that have completed their journey congregate with other cells to form structures in a process known as **aggregation**.

DIFFERENTIATION **Differentiation**, or the development of more specialized cell types from stem cells (see Chapter 1), results from the action of chemicals known as **differentiation-inducing factors (DIFs)** on gene expression (Patel et al., 2013).

Earlier, we saw how some cells in the ectoderm differentiated to form the neural plate while others differentiated into skin cells. The neural tube experiences two additional types of differentiation. The first process differentiates the dorsal and ventral halves of the neural tube. The second process differentiates the neural tube along its rostral-caudal axis.

In the dorsal-ventral differentiation of the neural tube, neurons in the ventral half develop into motor neurons, and neurons in the dorsal half develop into sensory neurons. Recall from our discussion of neuroanatomy in Chapter 2 that the ventral roots of the spinal cord carry motor information to muscles and glands and the dorsal roots carry sensory information back toward the central nervous system (CNS). This ventral-motor/dorsal-sensory organization extends up through the hindbrain and midbrain. For example, we find the superior and inferior colliculi, which participate in the senses of vision and hearing respectively, on the dorsal surface of the midbrain, while the substantia nigra, which plays an important role in movement, is located in the ventral half of the midbrain. This organization does not, however, describe the location of sensory and motor areas of the forebrain.

aggregation A process in which cells join others to form structures in the nervous system.
differentiation The development of stem cells into more specific types of cells.
differentiation-inducing factor (DIFs) Chemicals that stimulate changes in cell chemistry that produce cellular differentiation.

The second differentiation process occurs along the rostral-caudal axis of the neural tube, resulting in the division of the nervous system into the spinal cord, hindbrain, midbrain, and forebrain. The differentiation of the spinal cord and hindbrain appears to be controlled by DIFs encoded by *Hox* genes, the same types of genes that determine the correct placement of legs and wings on fruit flies (Bami, Episkopou, Gavalas, & Gouti, 2011). The midbrain does not show the same segmented organization found in the spinal cord and hindbrain, and *Hox* genes are not expressed this far in the rostral direction. Even less is known about the processes underlying the differentiation of the forebrain, although processes similar to those controlled by *Hox* genes are likely to exist.

The mature organization of the cerebral cortex also results from a combination of intrinsic (within the cell) and extrinsic (from outside the cell) influences. Studies in which cells from one part of the cerebral cortex are transplanted into other areas show that some transplanted cells continue to develop in their original pattern, indicating that their differentiation is largely controlled by intrinsic genetic factors. Others respond to input from adjacent cells in the form of released DIFs by taking on the characteristics of their new location. Of the two processes, intrinsic genetic factors probably play the more dominant role in human brain development (Rubenstein et al., 1999).

Christopher S. Cohan/Rockefeller University Press

● **Figure 5.16** Growth Cones Guide Axons to Their Targets Growth cones interact with the extracellular environment, guiding the growth of a nerve fiber to the target cell. Filopodia are the fingerlike extensions from the growth cone and lamellipodia appear as webbing or veils between the filapodia.

GROWTH OF AXONS AND DENDRITES Once the neurons are in place, they must form working connections with each other. This step begins with the development of processes or branches known as **neurites** that will mature to become axons and dendrites.

As shown in ● Figure 5.16, neurites end in **growth cones**, or swellings. The growth cones have both sensory and motor abilities that help the neurite find the right pathway. Growth cones have three basic structural parts: (1) a main body containing mitochondria, microtubules, and other organelles; (2) **filopodia**, or long, fingerlike extensions from the core; and (3) **lamellipodia**, additional flat, sheetlike extensions from the core, located between the filopodia. The filopodia and lamellipodia are capable of movement, and they have the ability to stick to elements of the extracellular environment, pulling the growing neurites along behind them. Microtubules from the main body of the cone move forward as the cone extends, forming a new segment of the neurite.

As shown in ●Figure 5.17, filopodia can signal the growth cone to move forward, move backward, or turn in a particular direction. The filopodia respond to both attracting and inhibiting chemicals released by guidepost cells along the way. Guidepost cells are glia that release chemicals that either attract or repel an approaching growth cone (Colón-Ramos & Shen, 2008). A dramatic example of this process can be observed in the growth of visual axons near the optic chiasm. In humans, the half of the visual axons closest to the nose cross the midline at the optic chiasm and continue contralaterally, whereas the half from the outer portion of each retina remain on the same side of the midline, proceeding ipsilaterally. When dye was applied to the retina and the course of the dyed axons to the optic chiasm was charted, the growing axons appeared to respond to a group of guidepost cells located at the midline of the optic chiasm (Godement, Wang, & Mason, 1994). The contralateral axons made

neurite An immature projection from a neuron.
growth cone The swelling at the tip of a growing axon or dendrite that helps the branch reach its synaptic target.
filopodia Long, fingerlike extensions from a growth cone.
lamellipodia Flat, sheetlike extensions from the core of a growth cone.

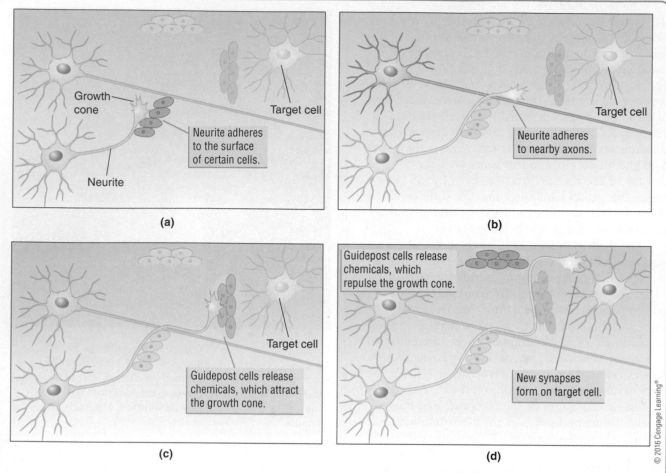

Growth cone

Neurite adheres to the surface of certain cells.

Neurite

Target cell

(a)

Neurite adheres to nearby axons.

Target cell

(b)

Guidepost cells release chemicals, which attract the growth cone.

Target cell

(c)

Guidepost cells release chemicals, which repulse the growth cone.

New synapses form on target cell.

(d)

© 2016 Cengage Learning®

● **Figure 5.17 Growth Cones Respond to a Variety of Cues** To reach their eventual targets, growth cones respond to the extracellular environment by (a) sticking to the surfaces of other cells, (b) sticking to other neurites traveling in the same direction, (c) growing toward chemical attractants, and (d) being repulsed by chemicals.

contact and passed these guidepost cells, whereas the ipsilateral axons appeared to be repelled by these cells.

Neurites that are growing in the same direction often stick together in a process known as fasciculation. Molecules on the surfaces of the neurites, known as cell adhesion molecules (CAMs), literally cause the neurites to stick together as they proceed in the same direction. As the growth cones approach their target, they begin to form either dendrites or axon collaterals (see Chapter 3). Now that the branches are in the correct general area, experience will interact with intrinsic factors to fine-tune the new connections.

FORMATION OF SYNAPSES The adult human brain features more than 100 trillion (10^{14}) synapses (Colón-Ramos & Shen, 2008). Any errors in the formation of these synapses during development can have profound effects on the ability of the nervous system to function. To complete the process of wiring the nervous system, the incoming neurite first identifies appropriate postsynaptic targets out of the many cells in the vicinity, a process known as **synaptic specificity**. Then, pre- and postsynaptic structures must mature.

One question about the development of synapses regards the determination of the type of neurotransmitter that will be used. At the sweat glands, which are relatively easy to study due to their peripheral location, mature sympathetic axons release

synaptic specificity The process by which a neurite identifies appropriate postsynaptic target cells from the many cells in the vicinity.

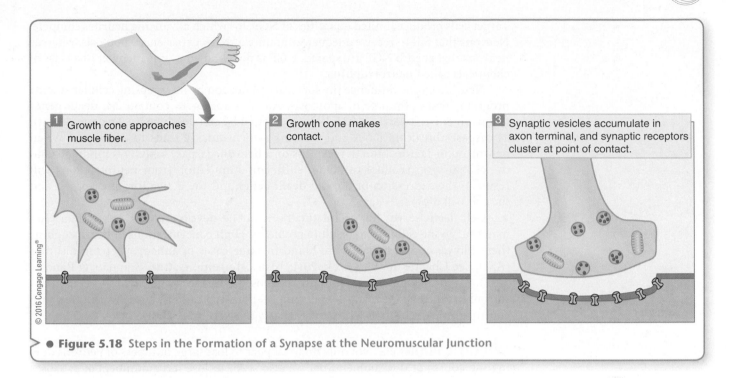

● **Figure 5.18** Steps in the Formation of a Synapse at the Neuromuscular Junction

acetylcholine (ACh) rather than norepinephrine, which is the typical neurotransmitter used by the sympathetic nervous system (see Chapters 2 and 4). Studies of cultured sympathetic neurons show that a switch from releasing norepinephrine to releasing ACh can be induced by exposure to chemical signals originating in the target cells, or the sweat glands in this case. We can conclude from these observations that the target cells determine the type of neurotransmitter released by the presynaptic cell (Apostolova & Dechant, 2009; Landis, 1990). How this process occurs in the CNS, where a single postsynaptic neuron responds to multiple types of neurotransmitter, is currently unknown.

The process of synapse formation can be observed easily at the neuromuscular junction (see ● Figure 5.18). Prior to any contact with a motor axon, a muscle fiber has already formed receptors for ACh, the neurotransmitter used at the neuromuscular junction. Initially, the receptors are evenly distributed within the membrane of the muscle fiber. Once the synapse is mature, however, the receptors are densely clustered at synaptic sites and rarely found in nonsynaptic motor fiber membrane areas.

A delicate sequence of chemical release by both the presynaptic and postsynaptic structures stimulates movement of the receptors to the synaptic site (Shi et al., 2010). Mutant strains of mice lacking essential presynaptic substances fail to develop normal clustering of ACh receptors, typically leading to death (DeChiara et al., 1996). Signals from the muscle fiber also affect the development of the approaching motor axon terminal. Relatively less is known about the process of synapse formation in the brain and spinal cord, but it is likely that similar processes occur. In the CNS, astrocytes play very important roles in synapse formation through the release of several types of DIFs (Eroglu & Barres, 2010).

CELL DEATH Following migration, as many as 40 to 75 percent of cells die in the process known as **apoptosis**, or programmed cell death. The term *apoptosis* comes from the Greek word for "falling leaves." Apoptosis during development was first described by Viktor Hamburger (1975), who observed that nearly half of the spinal motor neurons produced by chick embryos died before the birds hatched. Cohen, Levi-Montalcini, and Hamburger (1954) were able to isolate a substance they called nerve growth factor (NGF). Advancing neurites absorb NGF released by target cells.

apoptosis Programmed cell death.

Target cells produce limited quantities of NGF, for which advancing neurites compete. Neurons that fail to receive adequate amounts of NGF experience apoptosis, whereas neurons that absorb NGF are spared. NGF is now known as one member of a class of chemicals called **neurotrophins**.

Neurotrophins influence the survival of a neuron by interrupting cellular suicide programs that culminate in apoptosis. All cells appear to contain cell death genes (Johnson & Deckwerth, 1993). When activated by cell death genes, enzymes known as caspases break up DNA and proteins, which quickly leads to cell death. When neurotrophic factors bind to receptors on a neuron, caspase activity is inhibited, and the cell survives. Failure to obtain sufficient stimulation from neurotrophins will result in the expression of the cell death genes and the activation of caspases, and the cell will die.

Cell death serves important functions in the developing nervous system. Too many surviving cells might result in problems. High concentrations of neurotrophins (hence lower apoptosis rates) are found in some cases of autism spectrum disorder (ASD; See Chapter 16; Ratajczak, 2011; Tostes, Teixeira, Gattaz, Brandão, & Raposo, 2012). Children who were eventually diagnosed with ASD had higher levels of neurotrophins in their neonatal blood samples than typically developing children or a control group of children with cerebral palsy (Nelson et al., 2001).

SYNAPTIC PRUNING Not only do we appear to lose large numbers of neurons during the course of development, but we also seem to lose large numbers of synapses as well. Just as the brain initially overproduces neurons, followed by a refinement in their numbers, we experience a burst of synaptic growth followed by a period of **synaptic pruning**, in which the number of functional synapses is reduced. As shown in ● Figure 5.19, Huttenlocher (1994) suggested that pruning might eliminate significant

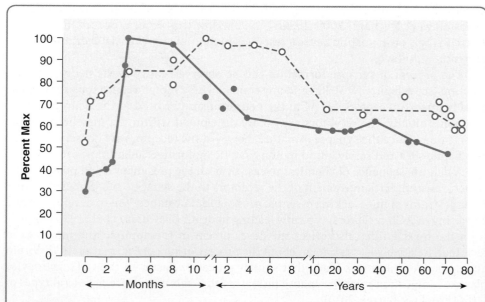

● **Figure 5.19** Synaptic Rearrangement over the Life Span In the human visual cortex (solid line), the number of synapses peaks at about the age of about four to eight months and decreases until about the age of four years. The number of synapses in the visual cortex remains relatively stable in adulthood. The number of synapses in the prefrontal cortex (dotted line) peaks around the age of one year, drops until about age 20, and then remains stable over the remainder of the life span.

Source: Adapted from Huttenlocher (1994).

neurotrophin Substance released by target cells that contributes to the survival of presynaptic neurons.

synaptic pruning The process in which functional synapses are maintained and nonfunctional synapses degenerate.

numbers of synapses in the visual cortex and in the prefrontal cortex. However, the time course of pruning differs between these two areas.

We have seen previously that competition for neurotrophins determines which neurons survive and which die. It is likely that a similar competition determines which synapses are retained. The nervous system clearly operates according to a "use it or lose it" philosophy. Changeux and Danchin (1976) suggested that only those synapses that participate in functional neural networks are maintained. A functional neural network is one in which the activity of presynaptic neurons reliably influence the activity of postsynaptic neurons. In addition, astrocytes appear to play significant roles in the regulation of synaptic pruning in the CNS. Secretions from astrocytes increase the production of neural chemical signals used to "tag" synapses for elimination (Eroglu & Barres, 2010). Tagged synapses are then digested by microglia (see Chapter 3). It is possible that distortions of this process also take place in the early stages of neurodegenerative diseases, such as Alzheimer's disease (see Chapter 15).

MYELINATION Myelination of the developing nervous system follows both a structural and a functional pattern of development. Structurally, myelination occurs in a rostral direction starting in the spinal cord, followed by successive myelination of the hindbrain, midbrain, and forebrain. Within the forebrain, myelination proceeds simultaneously from inferior to superior and from posterior to anterior. Functionally, the sensory parts of the cortex appear to be myelinated at an earlier time than the motor parts of the cortex.

The first human myelin can be observed in cranial and spinal nerves about 24 weeks after conception. Like many animals, human beings experience a burst of myelination around the time of birth, but the process is by no means complete at such an early age (see ● Figure 5.20). The last area to be myelinated is the prefrontal cortex, which is responsible for some of our most sophisticated cognitive functions. The prefrontal cortex is not completely myelinated until early adulthood (Sowell, Thompson, Holmes, Jernigan, & Toga, 1999). Differences in myelination might account for the fact that young adults in their early twenties were more accurate than teens in judging facial expressions (Baird et al., 1999). The teens showed greater activation in the amygdala, perhaps providing a "gut feeling" about the expressions they viewed, whereas the young adults showed greater activation of their more completely myelinated frontal lobes, producing a more reasoned response.

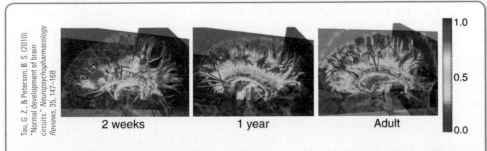

Tau, G. Z., & Peterson, B. S. (2010). "Normal development of brain circuits." *Neuropsychopharmacology Reviews, 35,* 147–168

2 weeks   1 year   Adult

1.0

0.5

0.0

● **Figure 5.20** **Human Myelination Continues into Adulthood** Although myelination is extensive early in life, the process of myelination is not complete in humans until young adulthood. These diffusion tensor images (DTI) indicate greater organization of white matter pathways resulting from myelination.

Source: Tau & Peterson (2010).

Effects of Experience on Development

By the time a human or other animal is born, much of the wiring of the nervous system is in place. However, throughout the life span, we retain the ability to rearrange our synaptic connections. Without this flexibility, or plasticity, it is unlikely that we would be able to learn and store new memories. In some cases, the time frame of plasticity is limited, in which case we refer to the window of time in which change can occur as a **critical period**. In other cases, it appears as though change can occur indefinitely.

These final adjustments to our neural wiring occurs as a result of the strengthening or weakening of existing synapses due to experience. In general, synapses are strengthened when the pre- and postsynaptic neurons are simultaneously active and weakened when their activity is not synchronized. The importance of correlated activity in strengthening synapses was first suggested in the 1940s by Donald Hebb. As a result, synapses strengthened by simultaneous activity are often referred to as Hebb synapses.

EXPERIENCE AND THE VISUAL SYSTEM ●Figure 5.21 shows the effects of grafting a third eye onto a frog embryo on the eventual organization of the frog's visual centers in the brain. Normally, the frog's right eye connects with the left optic tectum, its equivalent of the human superior colliculus, and the left eye connects with the right optic tectum. The frog's normal brain development is not prepared to manage input from a third eye. However, competition between axons originating from an original eye and the grafted eye for the same area of optic tectum results in a pattern of alternating connections from one eye and then the other. The experience of processing information from a third eye produces a rearrangement of the optic tectum.

We see this same type of process at work in the development of the human visual system. As we will see in Chapter 6, input from the retinas of the two eyes remains separate in both the lateral geniculate nucleus (LGN) of the thalamus and in the primary visual cortex of the occipital lobe. Early in development, the cells of the LGN and the primary visual cortex receive input from both eyes. The first axons to arrive at the LGN originate from the eye on the opposite (contralateral) side of the head. Shortly thereafter, axons from the eye on the same (ipsilateral) side of the head arrive at the LGN. During this initial period of development, input from the two eyes is not segregated in the layers of the LGN, as will be the case in the mature animal.

Segregation, in which LGN cells become selectively activated by input from one eye or the other, appears to proceed according to the process suggested by Hebb. As illustrated in ● Figure 5.22, input from the two eyes competes for the control of a given LGN cell. The input that is more highly correlated with activity in the LGN cell will be retained, whereas the input from the other eye, which is not as well correlated with activity in the LGN cell, will be weakened. When we say the input from one eye is "correlated" with the output of the LGN cell, this means that the synapse is active at the same time as many others influencing the same LGN cell. Eventually, a given LGN cell will be activated only by input originating in a single eye.

A similar process takes place as the LGN axons arrive in the primary visual cortex, located in the occipital lobe. Initially, LGN axons processing information from the two eyes are not segregated in the visual cortex. Later on, however, the cortex becomes organized in highly defined ocular dominance columns, or areas of cells that respond to only one eye or the other. Once again, simultaneous activity appears to be the critical factor responsible for segregation. In a

critical period A period of time during development in which experience is influential and after which experience has little to no effect.

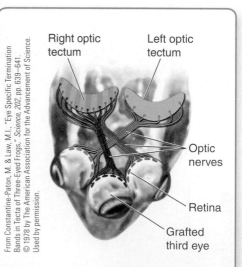

From Constantine-Paton, M. & Law, M.I., "Eye Specific Termination Bands in Tecta of Three-Eyed Frogs," *Science, 202,* pp. 639–641. © 1978 by The American Association for the Advancement of Science. Used by permission.

Right optic tectum

Left optic tectum

Optic nerves

Retina

Grafted third eye

● **Figure 5.21** Input Influences the Development of the Optic Tectum
(a) If a third eye is grafted onto a frog embryo, axons from the third eye compete with one of the original eyes for synapses in the frog's optic tectum.
(b) As a result of the competition, the axons from each competing eye connect with alternating bands of tectum.

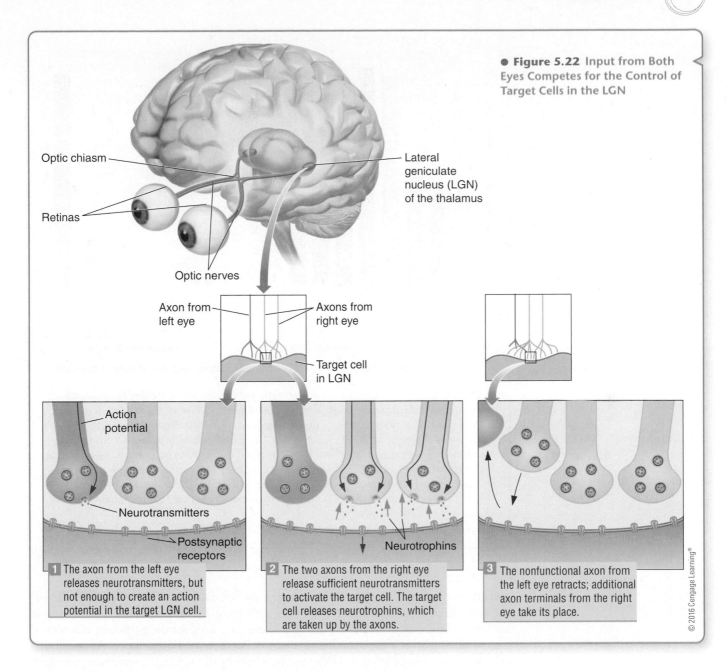

● **Figure 5.22** Input from Both Eyes Competes for the Control of Target Cells in the LGN

Optic chiasm

Lateral geniculate nucleus (LGN) of the thalamus

Retinas

Optic nerves

Axon from left eye

Axons from right eye

Target cell in LGN

Action potential

Neurotransmitters

Postsynaptic receptors

Neurotrophins

1 The axon from the left eye releases neurotransmitters, but not enough to create an action potential in the target LGN cell.

2 The two axons from the right eye release sufficient neurotransmitters to activate the target cell. The target cell releases neurotrophins, which are taken up by the axons.

3 The nonfunctional axon from the left eye retracts; additional axon terminals from the right eye take its place.

© 2016 Cengage Learning®

series of elegant experiments, David Hubel and Torsten Wiesel (1965, 1977) demonstrated how experience with the sensory environment could influence the segregation of inputs into ocular dominance columns in cats and rhesus monkeys. By suturing one eye of newborn kittens and monkeys closed and recording from cells in the visual cortex, Hubel and Wiesel (1965, 1977) were able to chronicle the effects of experience on the organization of ocular dominance columns in the cortex (see Chapter 6).

As shown in ● Figure 5.23, recordings from a normal cat demonstrated that most cells in the visual cortex responded to light falling in either eye. However, Hubel and Wiesel (1977) found other cells that responded to only one eye or the other. In the kitten subjected to monocular deprivation, the right eye was sutured closed for the first three months of life. Then the right eye was opened, and the left eye was sutured closed for the next three months. Subsequent recordings showed that the reversal of open eyes had little impact on the organization of the kitten's visual cortex. Most cells

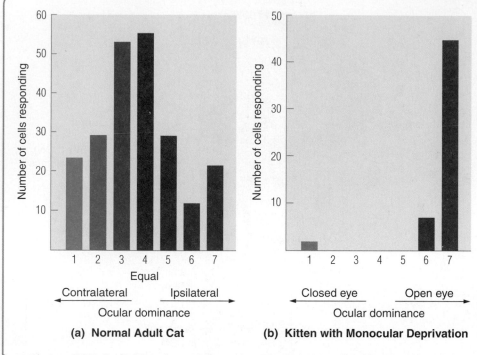

● **Figure 5.23** Early Experience Affects the Organization of Ocular Dominance Columns In a classic series of experiments by Hubel and Wiesel, manipulation of input during the critical period of visual development changed the organization of the primary visual cortex in cats. Cells labeled 1 or 2 respond primarily to input from the contralateral eye, whereas cells labeled 6 or 7 respond primarily to input from the ipsilateral eye. Cells labeled 3, 4, or 5 respond equally to either eye. Normal experience (a) results in a fairly equal distribution of cells responding to each eye. Suturing one eye closed for the first three months of life (b) reduces the number of cortical cells responding to the closed eye or to both eyes.

Source: Adapted from Hubel & Wiesel (1965).

continued to respond only to light falling in the left eye, which had been open during the first three months of life. None of the cells recorded responded to light falling in both eyes. Hubel and Wiesel argued that these data support the existence of a critical period during which the visual cortex can be modified by experience. Although the concept of suturing the eyes of baby animals may be disturbing to you, many children have benefited from the resulting knowledge that corrective surgery for vision must take place as early as possible.

EXPERIENCE AND SOCIAL BEHAVIOR Certain experiences might be necessary to refine the development of brain areas related to complex social behaviors as well as the sensory systems. Konrad Lorenz (1952) described the phenomenon of imprinting in several species of birds. If a newly hatched chick saw Lorenz right away instead of the mother bird, it persisted in treating Lorenz as its mother. As in the visual system, imprinting shows a critical period, a window of time in which experience will modify behavior.

Unfortunate conditions maintained in Romanian orphanages in the 1970s provided insight into the effects of social stimulation on human development. Children in these orphanages, like those shown in ●Figure 5.24, had very few opportunities to interact with other people or the environment. Elenor Ames (1997) followed the development of Romanian orphans adopted by Canadian parents. Children adopted prior to six months of age appear to have recovered from their earlier deprivation. Children

© Cynthia Johnson/Hulton Archive/Getty Images

● **Figure 5.24** Social Deprivation Affects Intellectual Development in Humans Romanian orphans adopted before the age of six months recovered from their earlier social deprivation, but those adopted at later ages did not make as good a recovery.

adopted later in life improved but did not make as good a recovery as the children adopted earlier. These findings suggest that human intellectual development is also subject to critical periods.

ENDING A CRITICAL PERIOD Critical periods for development have endpoints. Lorenz (1952) found that **imprinting** in baby geese would occur during the first two days of life but not at later ages. Very few people who learn a second language after puberty will be able to pass as native speakers. Several hypotheses have been proposed to account for the closing of critical periods of development. Growth spurts in myelin have been observed in parts of the brain involved with language and spatial relations between the ages of 6 and 13 years (Thompson et al., 2000). The conclusion of this growth period coincides with reduced abilities to learn additional languages. The presence or absence of neurotrophins might also influence the timing of critical periods (Berardi, Pizzorusso, & Maffei, 2000). Maturation of inhibitory pathways in the cerebral cortex that use the neurotransmitter GABA have been implicated in the closure of critical periods related to ocular dominance, and plasticity can be reestablished when this inhibition is chemically reduced (Harauzov et al., 2010).

Finally, epigenetic mechanisms might participate in the closure of critical periods (Sweatt, 2009). The development of ocular dominance, mentioned previously, is known to have a critical period. Experience following the end of the critical period does not change the way the visual cortex responds to input from each eye. Histone modification appears to be regulated differently before and after the time of closure, and application of enzymes that actively modify histones "re-opens" the ocular dominance cells to change (Medini & Pizzorusso, 2008).

THE BENEFITS OF AN ENRICHED ENVIRONMENT The conditions in the 1970s Romanian orphanages provided a tragic example of the importance of an enriched environment for cognitive development. Because of the obvious ethical concerns, most research on the effects of early enrichment have been conducted with animals (see ● Figure 5.25). Early work demonstrated that rats exposed to other rats, new toys, and other novel experiences experienced different brain development and

imprinting The process in which baby animals learn to follow their mother that usually coincides with the baby's mobility.

● **Figure 5.25** Enriched Environments Produce Long-lasting Effects on Cognitive Development Rats provided with opportunities to explore novel toys and interact with other rats develop heavier brains and demonstrate better learning abilities than rats raised in isolation in standard laboratory cages.

demonstrated better learning abilities than rats raised in conventional laboratory cages (Krech, Rosenzweig, & Bennett, 1960). More contemporary work suggests the observed advantages of the enriched environment result from two factors: higher connectivity in neural networks due to more synapses and enhanced flexibility due to more responsive dendritic spines (Jung & Herms, 2014). Enriched environments are not only beneficial to learning and memory. These environments seem to provide long-term protection against anxiety and exaggerated responses to stress (Baldini et al., 2013).

A number of psychological disorders, such as major depressive disorder and schizophrenia, appear to be more frequent in individuals in lower socioeconomic circumstances, where the environment could be characterized as impoverished as opposed to enriched (see Chapter 16). In addition, these disorders appear to be influenced by stress levels. The protection from stress effects enjoyed by people exposed to enriched environments during development might help explain why they are less likely to experience these disorders.

Disorders of Nervous System Development

Given the complexity of cell production, migration, differentiation, and connection, it seems to be a major miracle that most of us end up with a reasonably functional brain. Severe developmental errors usually result in miscarriage, or spontaneous abortion. A small percentage of children will be born with a variety of abnormal conditions due to errors in development.

NEURAL TUBE DEFECTS As we observed earlier, an important part of development is the closing of the neural tube. Two major types of neural tube defects are anencephaly and spina bifida.

Anencephaly, in which significant portions of the brain and skull fail to develop, occurs when the rostral neural tube does not develop properly. The majority of fetuses with anencephaly either die in utero or do not survive for more than a few hours after birth.

In **spina bifida**, the caudal portion of the neural tube fails to close normally. The condition can range from mild to life threatening. In the more serious forms of the

anencephaly Defect in the rostral closure of the neural tube resulting in incomplete development of brain and skull.
spina bifida Defect in caudal neural tube closure that results in mobility problems.

condition, in which a portion of the meninges and spinal cord form a sac protruding from the infant's back, surgery is typically used within the first 72 hours of life to correct the condition (Bowman & McLone, 2010). Efforts to repair the spinal damage prior to birth might be useful in some cases (Zambelli et al., 2007).

Although the exact causes of neural tube defects remain unknown, deficiencies of folic acid might be responsible for a large number of cases. Folic acid occurs naturally in dark green leafy vegetables, egg yolks, fruits, and juices. It is also added to fortified breakfast cereals and other products. However, the average American diet does not contain sufficient levels of folic acid to effectively prevent neural tube defects (Spina Bifida Association of America, 2001). Because neural tube closure occurs so early in development (around the third week following conception), before a woman might be sure she's pregnant, women with any probability of becoming pregnant are advised to maintain pregnancy levels of folic acid in their diets.

GENETIC DISORDERS A wide variety of genetic errors can occur in development, and it is beyond the scope of our current discussion to provide more than a sample.

Down syndrome, also known as trisomy 21, is characterized by an individual having three, rather than the normal two, copies of chromosome 21. Down syndrome occurs between 1 and 3 times out of 1,000 births (de Graaf et al., 2011). The major cause of trisomy 21 is abnormal division, or disjunction, of the mother's 21st chromosome during the final meiosis that results in a mature ovum or egg. Disjunction is related to maternal age rather than the inheritance of a faulty gene, so the risk of producing a child with Down syndrome is not higher in families that already have a member with this condition.

The relationship between the extra 21st chromosome and the physical and mental characteristics of Down syndrome is currently unknown. Individuals with Down syndrome usually function in the moderate range of intellectual disability, with IQs between 35 and 50. This level of intellect allows attainment of second-grade academic skills and requires living and working in a supervised setting. Physical features of Down syndrome include a small skull, large tongue, almond-shaped eyes, a flat nasal bridge, and abnormalities of the hands and fingers. Individuals with Down syndrome are subject to heart deformities, which contribute to shorter life expectancy. Down syndrome is also correlated with a high risk of Alzheimer's disease, which is discussed in detail in Chapter 15.

A common heritable condition is **fragile X syndrome**, which affects about 1 in 4,000 males and 1 in 8,000 females. More males are affected because the relevant gene is located on the X chromosome, making fragile X a sex-linked condition. Fragile X is also an example of a copy number variation (CNV) condition, discussed earlier in the chapter. The *FMR-1* gene on the X chromosome, shown in ●Figure 5.26, usually has between 6 and 50 codon repeats, or consecutive segments of the same codon along a strand of DNA. People with up to 200 repeats are healthy, but having more than 200 repeats leads to the fragile X condition. The large numbers of repeats interferes with the expression of the *fragile X mental retardation protein* (FMRP), which plays an important role in neural development. The intellectual consequences of the condition vary from typical intelligence to moderate intellectual disability. Physical characteristics include low-set ears and a large forehead and jaw. Males with the syndrome often show unusual social withdrawal, and about 30 percent meet the diagnostic criteria for autism spectrum disorder (Buxbaum & Baron-Cohen, 2010).

In other types of genetic abnormalities, the body is either unable to produce important chemicals or overproduces the chemicals. The best understood of these metabolic disorders is **phenylketonuria**, or PKU. This disorder occurs about once in 15,000 births in the United States, although 1 out of every 50 people is a carrier for the disorder (DiLella & Woo, 1987). PKU results from a recessive gene, leading to a lack of liver enzymes needed to convert the amino acid phenylalanine into

Down syndrome A condition associated with moderate intellectual disability resulting from having 3 copies of chromosome 21; also known as trisomy 21.

fragile X syndrome A heritable, sex-linked genetic disorder that produces physical and social deficits.

phenylketonuria A heritable condition characterized by the inability to metabolize phenylalanine.

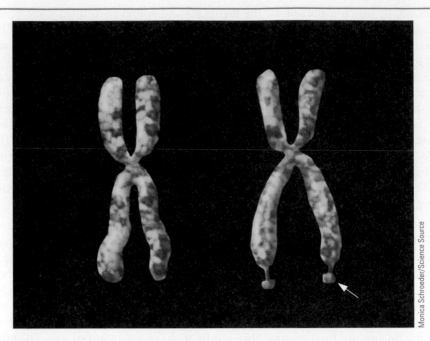

● **Figure 5.26** Fragile X Syndrome Because of an abnormally large number of codon repeats at the site of the *FMR-1* gene on the long arm of the X chromosome, the gene is not properly expressed during development. The arrow is pointing to the area of the X chromosome that is affected. The X chromosome on the left is normal.

tyrosine. Consequently, people with PKU produce an abnormal byproduct, phenyl-pyruvic acid, which damages the brain early in development. Intellectual disability can be prevented by avoiding foods containing phenylalanine. These foods include the artificial sweetener Aspartame and high-protein items such as milk, dairy products, meat, fish, chicken, eggs, beans, and nuts (University of Washington PKU Clinic, 2000). In the past, medical experts allowed individuals with PKU to abandon their special diets in late adolescence, but current advice is to remain on the diet throughout the lifetime.

ENVIRONMENTAL TOXINS One of the most thoroughly understood environmental causes of intellectual disability is maternal alcohol use, leading to **fetal alcohol syndrome**. Currently, there are no known safe levels of alcohol use during pregnancy, and pregnant women are strongly encouraged to abstain completely from alcohol. Alcohol use by pregnant women is the leading known nongenetic cause of intellectual disability (O'Leary et al., 2013). Children with fetal alcohol syndrome experience growth retardation, skin folds at the corners of the eyes, nose and mouth abnormalities, small head circumference, and reduced IQ (Streissguth et al., 1991). They are more likely to be diagnosed with attention deficits, poor impulse control, and severe behavioral problems. The impact of fetal alcohol syndrome on the brain is illustrated in ●Figure 5.27.

Alcohol can have direct effects on the developing fetus, and the malnutrition and poor health of the drinking mother might also have indirect effects (Steinhausen, 1993). In addition, pregnant women who use alcohol are also more likely to be using other drugs. Alcohol, tobacco, marijuana, or cocaine used singly during pregnancy can produce significant reductions in the gray matter in

fetal alcohol syndrome A set of physical and cognitive characteristics that result from maternal use of alcohol during pregnancy.

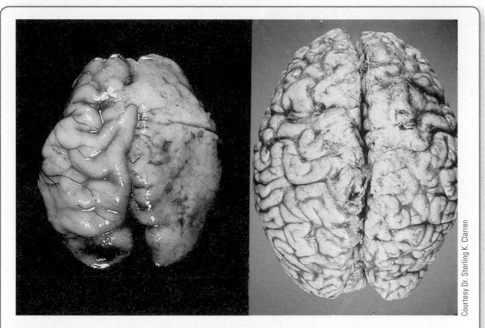

Courtesy Dr. Sterling K. Clarren

● **Figure 5.27** Fetal Alcohol Syndrome Produces Physical and Intellectual Abnormalities One of the most frequent preventable causes of mental retardation and behavioral problems is maternal use of alcohol and other drugs during pregnancy. These brains were taken from two fetuses of the same age. The one on the left had fetal alcohol syndrome, whereas the one on the right developed typically.

offspring, but combinations of two or more of these drugs produce even more dramatic results (Rivkin et al., 2008).

These are not short-term effects, either, as structural development and behavior in the offspring are affected well into adolescence and possibly beyond. When they reached 10–13 years of age, gray matter thickness and head circumference were still reduced in the children exposed prenatally to multiple drugs (Rivkin et al., 2008). Adolescents exposed prenatally to cocaine are nearly twice as likely to initiate early alcohol and marijuana use themselves, even after controlling for variables such as poverty, continued maternal substance use, and exposure to domestic violence (Richardson, Larkby, Goldschmidt, & Day, 2013).

Recreational drugs are not the only sources of risk for the developing fetus, of course. Simple over-the-counter aspirin can produce heart defects, slow growth, and intellectual disability. Exposure to mercury in fish and from industrial activity has known neurotoxic effects. Many thousands of new chemicals have been invented in the last two decades, and we know very little about their single or collective impacts on brain development and health.

A growing contemporary trend of prescribing medications for conditions where the health of the pregnant woman is not at risk (most painkillers are prescribed during pregnancy for "back pain") is a stark departure from medical practice decades ago, when any use of prescription or over-the-counter pharmaceuticals was viewed as highly undesirable. In a recent large-scale study, more than 14 percent of pregnant women were taking narcotic pain medications, such as Vicodin and Oxycontin (Bateman et al., 2014). As many as 8 percent of pregnant women on Medicaid continued to use SSRI antidepressants during pregnancy (Huybrechts et al., 2013). But like recreational alcohol, we know of no safe levels for these medications during pregnancy.

INTERIM SUMMARY 5.2

Summary Table: Milestones in Nervous System Development

Period of Life	Nervous System Development
Embryo	• Starting between two and three weeks following conception, billions of neurons are formed.
Prenatal period	• Neurons migrate to their appropriate locations. • Synapses begin forming and are influenced by fetal activity. • Myelination begins at about the sixth month following conception.
Birth	• The brain weighs 300 to 350 grams (about 0.75 lbs). • A period of rapid brain growth begins, extending into adolescence, primarily due to myelination. • Myelination of the auditory and visual systems is completed soon after birth. • Myelination of the corticospinal motor tract (see Chapter 8) is completed by the age of about 18 months.
Childhood	• Experience plays a significant role in the refinement and reorganization of synapses. • Adult brain weight of 1,300 to 1,500 grams (about 2.9–3.3 lbs) is achieved. • At puberty, a second burst of gray matter growth is followed by a period of synaptic pruning.

Summary Points

1. Within one week following conception, the human embryo divides into three germ layers. Differentiation-inducing factors (DIFs) guide the development of the ectoderm layer into skin and neural tissue. **(LO4)**

2. New neural cells are produced in the ventricular zone lining the neural tube. After migrating to their eventual location, they differentiate into neurons and glia. **(LO4)**

3. Growth cones respond to the chemical and physical properties of the extracellular environment to reach their destinations. Once neurites reach their destinations, pre- and postsynaptic structures and astrocytes influence synaptic development. **(LO4)**

4. Significant numbers of new neurons die during the development process. Synapses follow a similar pattern of overproduction followed by pruning. **(LO4)**

5. Although many parts of the brain retain the ability to change throughout the lifetime, some processes, including vision and language learning, have critical periods in which change and learning occur more readily. **(LO5)**

6. Abnormal development can occur due to neural tube defects, genetic disorders, and exposure to environmental toxins. **(LO6)**

Review Questions

1. What factors are responsible for the early differentiation of cells in the nervous system?

2. How do activity and experience fine-tune the connections of the developing brain?

The Brain in Adolescence and Adulthood

Prior to the availability of imaging technologies, researchers believed that the vast majority of human brain development took place prenatally and up to the age of about 18 months. Today, we do not consider the human brain mature until early adulthood.

Brain Changes in Normal Aging

A wave of gray matter development and pruning begins at puberty, with thickening of the cortex peaking at about age 11 for girls and age 12 for boys, followed by a gradual thinning (Giedd et al., 1999; Sowell et al., 1999). This burst of new growth especially affects the frontal lobes, influencing teens' abilities to plan, control impulses, and reason. Schizophrenia, a serious psychological disorder which we discuss in Chapter 16, is accompanied by four times the typical thinning of gray matter during this second major period of pruning (Rapoport et al., 1999).

As we noted previously, myelination of the brain also continues to develop and influence the behavior of teens and young adults. Because white matter is continuing to develop through adolescence, it seems to be especially vulnerable to disruption. White matter disruption is common among adult alcoholics, but ● Figure 5.28 shows that nonalcoholic teens with a history of binge drinking also experience significant white matter disruption (McQueeny et al., 2009).

Many parts of the brain that participate in processing emotion, such as the amygdala, mature earlier than the frontal lobes. This might account for some of the "risky" behaviors performed by many teens, such as drunk driving, experimenting with drugs, and having unprotected sex. The teen brain also responds more vigorously to pleasure compared to the adult brain, which means that immediate pleasures might overwhelm judgment (Galvan, Hare, Voss, Glover, & Casey, 2007).

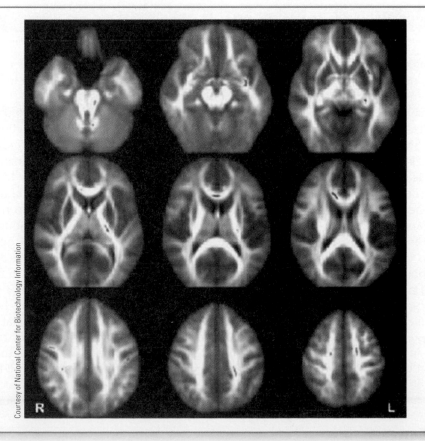

Courtesy of National Center for Biotechnology Information

● **Figure 5.28** White Matter Disruption and Binge Drinking The red areas indicate white matter affected by binge drinking in teens. In none of the samples did a teen with a history of at least one binge-drinking episode show better white matter integrity than nonbingeing teens.

Source: McQueeny et al. (2010) from http://www.ncbi.nlm.nih.gov/pmc/articles/PMC2825379/figure/F1/

The human brain is thought to have fully matured by the age of 25 years, and few changes occur from that point until about the age of 45 years. At that time, the weight of the brain begins to decrease significantly. These changes typically do not result in dramatic cognitive and behavioral changes in healthy adults. Results from the Baltimore Longitudinal Study of Aging (2000) show that aging produces very mild changes in speed of learning and problem solving, and that the changes occur rather late in life for most people.

Adult Neurogenesis

For many years, it was assumed that all neurogenesis was complete at birth in mammals. The only exception appeared to be neurons associated with the sense of smell.

The first suggestion that more extensive neurogenesis might occur in mature animals came from Barnea and Nottebohm (1994), who discovered that songbirds produced new neurons when they learned new songs. Elizabeth Gould and her colleagues (Gould, Reeves, Graziano, & Gross, 1999) showed not only that new neurons were being produced by adult rhesus monkeys but also that they migrated to the hippocampus and association areas of the cerebral cortex. Similar findings in the human brain and in mice were reported by Gage (2000). Contemporary neuroscientists believe that adult neurogenesis in humans results in small numbers of new neurons in the olfactory bulbs and in the dentate gyrus of the hippocampus (see Chapter 12).

Some cells arising through adult neurogenesis originate in the ventricular zone, just like the cells participating in prenatal neurogenesis as described earlier in this

••• THINKING *Ethically*

WHEN ARE ADOLESCENTS RESPONSIBLE FOR THEIR ACTIONS?

In 1843, Daniel M'Naghten attempted to assassinate British Prime Minister Sir Robert Peel, but shot his secretary, Mr. Drummond, instead. In the sensational trial that followed, M'Naghten's testimony about imaginary persecution he suffered at the hands of Mr. Peel's party led to his being "acquitted by reason of insanity." M'Naghten's legacy in British and American law is the "insanity defense," which means that a person must understand his or her act and the wrongfulness of that act before being held responsible for a crime (Mobbs, Lau, Jones, & Frith, 2007).

In 2005, the U.S. Supreme Court (*Roper vs. Simmons*) made it illegal for states to administer the death penalty to an offender whose crime was committed prior to the age of 18 years, partly in response to neuroscience evidence that showed that the prefrontal cortex continues to mature into a person's early 20s. In 2010, the Supreme Court struck down life-without-parole sentences for minors convicted of crimes other than murder (*Graham vs. Florida*) and is in the process of evaluating whether it should do so in the case of murder convictions as well. A number of states currently impose life sentences without parole on juveniles who participated in a felony murder (such as being a lookout) as well as on the actual murderers.

Complicating the issue is the frequent finding that teen murderers might have abnormal brain functioning. One 13-year-old murderer bludgeoned an 87-year-old to death with his skateboard, locked up the victim's mobile home to delay discovery of the crime, and took the victim's car for a joyride. Joseph Wu, director of the Brain Imaging Center at the University of California, Irvine, testified that the young murderer had "abnormally reduced activity in parts of his brain that govern a person's judgment" (Sneed, 2006, p. B1). We are assuming that Wu is comparing this 13-year-old to his age peers in making this statement.

If a person, and particularly a young person, has an immature or abnormally functioning brain, what is our best course of action? If you're curious about the court's actions regarding the 13-year-old, he was sentenced to a state juvenile facility from which he will be automatically freed at age 25 (Parilla, 2006).

chapter. These cells migrate in a rostral direction to the olfactory bulbs (Braun & Jessberger, 2014). Others develop within the dentate gyrus of the hippocampus itself. Although the numbers of neurons added to the mature brain are quite small compared with neurogenesis early in development, these new neurons may play very important roles in adult learning and memory (see ● Figure 5.29; Gould et al., 1999; Snyder et al., 2009, Gu et al., 2010), anxiety (Leuner & Gould, 2010), and stress (Snyder et al., 2011). Aging is associated with reduced adult neurogenesis in the hippocampus across a wide range of mammal species (Glasper & Gould, 2013). The rate of adult neurogenesis in the hippocampus slows in midlife, usually before any typical age-related changes in cognition become observable. This suggests that the slowing of neurogenesis in the hippocampus might possibly contribute to age-related cognitive decline.

Adult neurogenesis might also protect the mature brain from the effects of stress. The use of antidepressant medications appears to increase neurogenesis in the rat hippocampus, possibly contributing to the drugs' efficacy in treating stress-related depression (Malberg, Eisch, Nestler, & Duman, 2000). When neurogenesis was artificially inhibited through the use of radiation, antidepressant medications lost their ability to improve mood (Braun & Jessberger, 2014).

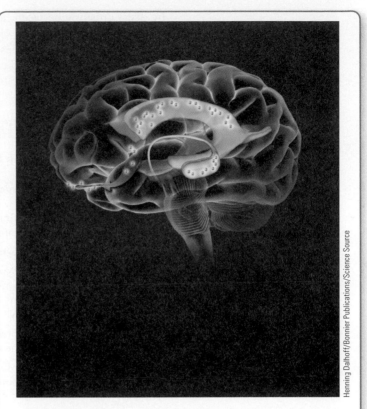

Henning Dalhoff/Bonnier Publications/Science Source

> ● **Figure 5.29** **Adult Neurogenesis** Neurogenesis in the adult human continues to occur in the ventricular zone and the hippocampus.

Healthy Brain Aging

Many variables seem to contribute to the maintenance of good cognition into later adulthood. Educational attainment and adult mental activity are negatively correlated with a person's risk for Alzheimer's disease (see Chapter 15). However, healthy brain activity is also associated with such diverse factors as heart, kidney, lung and other organ system health, being married, having strong social support, avoiding midlife depression, prayer, and physical fitness (Friedland, 2014). To account for these disparate contributions to healthy brain functioning in aging, a **multiple reserve hypothesis** has been proposed. According to this approach, the quality of life in later adulthood is a function of a person's "reserves," or resources that help him or her resist age-related loss of functioning (Friedland, 2014). These reserves can take many forms, including the cerebral, physical, social, psychological, and spiritual domains.

Most discussions of healthy brain aging are careful to distinguish between aging in healthy people and aging in those who are diagnosed with neurodegenerative disorders, such as Alzheimer's disease (see Chapter 15) and Parkinson's disease (see Chapter 8). This distinction might not be as clear as was previously believed. Healthy aging is accompanied by changes in medial temporal lobe areas involved with memory as well as changes in executive pathways connecting the basal ganglia and frontal lobes (Jagust, 2013). These are the exact same pathways that are involved with major neurodegenerative conditions. It is possible that these pathways are simply more vulnerable than other parts of the brain to disease states and to other damage-producing mechanisms. Brain aging may simply represent vulnerability to a number of harmful processes that accumulate over time (Jagust, 2013).

The conclusions of studies of brain aging often suggest that advances in our understanding and treatment of age-related brain conditions would be better served

multiple reserve hypothesis The resources a person possesses that offset age-related reductions in functioning.

by distinguishing between healthy functioning and the absence of disease. As noted by Friedland (2014), many older people do not have major illnesses, but nonetheless experience limited capacities for behavior. The generation and maintenance of good brain health is still less well understood than the mechanisms responsible for disease, especially among older adults.

INTERIM SUMMARY 5.3

Summary Table: The Brain in Adolescence and Adulthood

Period of Life	Nervous System Development
Adolescence	• Cortical thickening is followed by synaptic pruning, which is influenced by experience. • Synapses continue to develop and reorganize. • Synapse reorganization continues in some parts of the brain, whereas others experience critical periods of development.
Adulthood	• Myelination of the frontal lobes is completed. • Brain weight decreases after the age of 45, but cognition in healthy adults appears relatively unaffected. • Multiple reserves, both physical and psychological, help aging adults resist age-related loss of functioning.

Summary Points

1. Adolescence is accompanied by a burst of cortical thickening followed by pruning. The amygdala matures prior to the frontal lobes, and the adolescent brain is more vulnerable to damage by psychoactive substances than the adult brain. **(LO7)**

2. Healthy aging is associated with some loss of brain weight, but changes in learning speed and problem solving are mild and occur rather late in life. **(LO7)**

Review Questions

1. What aspect of adolescent brain development appears to be particularly abnormal in cases of schizophrenia?

2. What is the difference between healthy brain aging and the absence of disease?

Chapter Review

THOUGHT QUESTIONS

1. How would you respond to the following statement by neuroscientist Simon LeVay: "When we have gained the power to manipulate our own physical and mental traits and those of our offspring, society will have to wrestle with profound questions about what constitutes a normal human being, what kinds of human diversity are desirable or permissible, and who gets to make these decisions on behalf of whom."

2. Based on your knowledge of the timeline of embryonic and fetal brain development, what advice would you give to sexually active women of childbearing age?

KEY TERMS

allele (p. 144)
apoptosis (p. 157)
chromosome (p. 140)
critical period (p. 160)
deoxyribonucleic acid (DNA) (p. 140)
differentiation (p. 154)
DNA methylation (p. 146)
dominant allele (p. 141)
ectoderm (p. 151)
embryo (p. 151)
endoderm (p. 151)
epigenetics (p. 146)
fetal alcohol syndrome (p. 166)
fetus (p. 151)

filopodia (p. 155)
gene (p. 140)
gene expression (p. 140)
genotype (p. 140)
growth cone (p. 155)
heterozygous (p. 141)
histone modification (p. 146)
homozygous (p. 141)
lamellipodia (p. 155)
meiosis (p. 142)
mesencephalon (p. 151)
mesoderm (p. 151)
migration (p. 153)
multiple reserve hypothesis (p. 171)

mutation (p. 143)
neural tube (p. 151)
neurogenesis (p. 153)
neurotrophin (p. 158)
phenotype (p. 140)
prosencephalon (p. 151)
radial glia (p. 153)
recessive allele (p. 141)
rhombencephalon (p. 151)
ribonucleic acid (RNA) (p. 140)
sex-linked characteristics (p. 143)
synaptic pruning (p. 158)
zygote (p. 142)

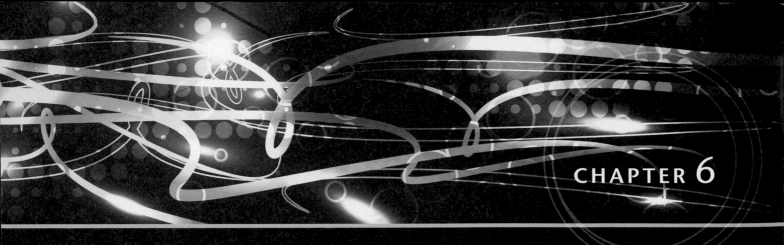

CHAPTER 6

Vision

LEARNING OBJECTIVES

L01 Discuss the major features of visible light as a stimulus.

L02 Explain the major features and functions of the eye, retina, and photoreceptors.

L03 Trace the pathways of information from the photoreceptors to the secondary visual cortex.

L04 Summarize the processes responsible for visual object perception, depth perception, and color vision.

L05 Describe the changes in the visual system than accompany normal aging.

L06 Differentiate between the major disorders that affect human vision.

CHAPTER OUTLINE

CONNECTING TO RESEARCH: Hubel and Wiesel Map the Visual Cortex

BEHAVIORAL NEUROSCIENCE GOES TO WORK: 3D Animation

THINKING ETHICALLY: Are There Sex Differences in Color Preferences?

BUILDING BETTER HEALTH: Does Eating Carrots Really Help Your Vision?

From Sensation to Perception

What is reality? This might seem to be a more fitting question for a philosophy course than a neuroscience course, but this question is very central to the study of sensation and perception. We believe that an objective physical reality does exist "out there," but we can only make educated guesses about its features using the human sensory systems we discuss in this chapter and the next.

The physical world provides many sources of information, from light waves to pressure to molecules suspended in the air. Over the course of evolution, organisms have developed sensory systems that **transduce** (translate) different types of information into the action potentials that the nervous system can process. Each organism has sensory capacities that enhance its survival within a particular niche. Ours is a uniquely human version of reality, providing us with just the right set of information we need to survive. We might not be able to sense odor as well as a dog, but we can see colors that dogs cannot see (see ● Figure 6.1). A single physical reality produces very different reactions in different organisms.

Sensation begins the process of building a model of reality by bringing relevant information to the central nervous system (CNS). Once the CNS has begun to interpret the information, the process of **perception** is underway. An important gateway to perception is the process of **attention**, which is a narrow focus of consciousness. Although we can consciously command ourselves to "pay attention" to a boring but necessary lecture, many aspects of attention are much more automatic. We naturally attend to unfamiliar, changing, and high-intensity stimuli, as these are likely to have significance for our safety and survival. We adapt to unchanging information like the hum of a computer by paying less attention to it over time.

The process of perception is often a two-way street, where incoming messages inform the brain at the same time the brain is imposing structure on those messages. Consider the following passage:

> All you hvae to do to mkae a snetnece raedalbe is to mkae srue taht the fisrt and lsat letrtes of ecah word saty the smae. Wtih prcatcie, tihs porcses becoems mcuh fsater and esaeir.

Clearly, the brain is receiving sensations resulting from the reflection of light from these letters on the page, which are then used to construct words and meanings. This pathway is known as **bottom-up processing**. At the same time, we use our knowledge and expectations to recognize words, even if they are misspelled. This pathway is

transduce To transform sensory information into neural signals.

sensation The process of obtaining information about the environment and transmitting it to the brain for processing.

perception The process of interpreting sensory signals sent to the brain.

attention A narrow focus of consciousness.

bottom-up processing The combining of simpler meanings to construct more complex meanings.

Courtesy of Laura Freberg

> ● **Figure 6.1** Sensory systems have evolved to enhance the survival of members of each species within their own niches. Human vision, seen in the photograph of the author's puppy on the left, is different than dog vision, simulated on the right. Do[gs] do a good job of distinguishing blue and yellow, but do not see reds and greens [the] way human beings do.

known as **top-down processing**. In many instances, the world we perceive is the world we expect to perceive (Neumeyer, 2012).

The Visual Stimulus: Light

Vision is one of the most important sensory systems in humans, with about 50 percent of our cerebral cortex responding to visual information but only 3 percent for hearing and 11 percent for touch and pain (Kandel & Wurtz, 2000; Sereno & Tootell, 2005). Whether we're searching for food or scanning the millions of colors displayed by a computer monitor, the process of vision begins with light energy reflected from objects.

Visible light, or the energy we can see, is one form of **electromagnetic radiation** produced by the sun. Electromagnetic radiation can be described as moving waves of energy (see ● Figure 6.2). **Wavelength**, or the distance between successive peaks of waves, is encoded by the visual system either as color or as shades of gray. The **amplitude** of light waves refers to the height of each wave, which is translated by the visual system as brightness. Large-amplitude waves are perceived as bright, and low-amplitude waves are perceived as dim.

Electromagnetic radiation can also be described as the movement of tiny, indivisible particles known as photons. **Photons** always travel at the same speed (the so-called speed of light), but they can vary in the amount of energy they possess. It is this variation in energy levels among photons that gives us waves with different wavelengths and amplitudes. You can think of a light wave as describing the movement of large numbers of photons, much as a wave in the ocean describes the movement of large numbers of water molecules.

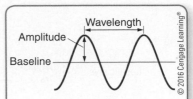

● **Figure 6.2** Dimensions of Electromagnetic Radiation The amplitude, or height, of light waves is encoded as brightness. Wavelength, or the distance between successive peaks, is encoded as color or shades of gray.

The Advantages of Light as a Stimulus

Why is electromagnetic energy, rather than some other feature of the environment, an effective stimulus for a sensory system? Electromagnetic energy, and visible light in particular, has features that make it a valuable source of information. First, electromagnetic energy is abundant in our universe. Second, because electromagnetic energy travels very quickly, there is no substantial delay between an event and an organism's ability to see the event. Finally, electromagnetic energy travels in fairly straight lines, minimizing the distortion of objects. What we see is what we get, literally.

The Electromagnetic Spectrum

The light from the sun contains a mixture of wavelengths and appears white to the human eye. Placing a prism in sunlight will separate individual wavelengths, which we see as different colors. Light shining through water droplets is affected the same way, producing the rainbows we enjoy seeing after a rainstorm.

As shown in ● Figure 6.3, light that is visible to humans occupies a very small part of the electromagnetic spectrum. The range of electromagnetic energy visible to humans falls between 400 and 700 **nanometers** (nm). A nanometer is 10^{-9} meters, or one billionth of a meter. When we say a light has a wavelength of 400 nanometers, this means that the peaks of the wave are 400 nanometers apart. Shorter wavelengths, approaching 400 nm, are perceived by humans as violet and blue, whereas longer wavelengths, approaching 700 nm, are perceived as red.

Gamma rays, X-rays, ultraviolet rays, infrared rays, microwaves, and radio waves lie outside the range of wavelengths the human eye can detect. These forms of energy have features that make them less desirable stimuli for a sensory system. Shorter wavelengths, such as ultraviolet rays, are typically absorbed by the ozone layer of Earth's atmosphere, leaving little energy left over for most organisms to sense. Nonetheless, some creatures, including insects and birds, are able to see parts of the ultraviolet spectrum. Longer wavelengths, such as microwaves, tend to penetrate objects rather

top-down processing The use of knowledge and expectation to interpret meanings.
electromagnetic radiation Radiation emitted in the form of energy waves.
wavelength The distance between successive peaks of a wave; determines color in visible light.
amplitude The height of a wave; in vision, the source of the subjective experience of brightness.
photons Individual, indivisible, very small particles that form waves of electromagnetic energy.
nanometers A unit of measurement equaling 10^{-9} m used to measure light wave frequency.

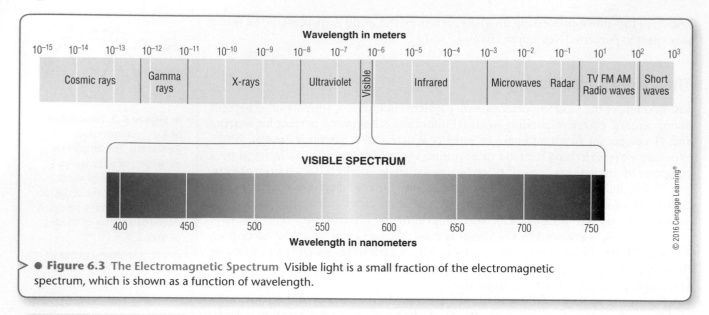

Wavelength in meters

| 10^{-15} | 10^{-14} | 10^{-13} | 10^{-12} | 10^{-11} | 10^{-10} | 10^{-9} | 10^{-8} | 10^{-7} | 10^{-6} | 10^{-5} | 10^{-4} | 10^{-3} | 10^{-2} | 10^{-1} | 10^{1} | 10^{2} | 10^{3} |

Cosmic rays | Gamma rays | X-rays | Ultraviolet | Visible | Infrared | Microwaves | Radar | TV FM AM Radio waves | Short waves

VISIBLE SPECTRUM

400   450   500   550   600   650   700   750

Wavelength in nanometers

© 2016 Cengage Learning®

● **Figure 6.3 The Electromagnetic Spectrum** Visible light is a small fraction of the electromagnetic spectrum, which is shown as a function of wavelength.

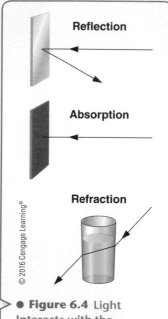

Reflection

Absorption

Refraction

© 2016 Cengage Learning®

● **Figure 6.4 Light Interacts with the Environment** Most of the light we see is reflected, or bent back, from objects. We do not see light that is absorbed by objects, although we can feel the energy as heat. Light is bent, or refracted, as it travels through air or water.

absorption The ability to retain something rather than reflect or transmit it to another location.
reflection The bending back of light toward its source.
refract The deflection, or changing of direction, of light at a boundary such as that between air and water.

than reflect back from them, a feature that is valuable in cooking but not in vision. However, some snakes, such as pit vipers, boas, and pythons, have developed the ability to "see" the body heat of prey and other predators by sensing infrared radiation.

Light Interacts with Objects

As shown in ● Figure 6.4, objects can absorb, reflect, or refract electromagnetic radiation. In some cases, an object's physical characteristics will absorb or retain certain wavelengths. In other cases, light is reflected from the surface of objects, or bent back toward the source. Most of the light energy entering the eye has been reflected from objects in the environment.

Absorption and **reflection** of light by objects determine the colors we see. The color of an object is not some intrinsic characteristic of the object but, rather, the result of the wavelengths of light that are selectively absorbed and reflected by the object. Instead of saying that my sweater is red, it is more accurate to say that my sweater has physical characteristics that reflect long wavelengths of visible light (perceived as red) and absorb shorter wavelengths. "Light-colored" clothing keeps us cooler because materials perceived as white or light-colored reflect more electromagnetic energy. "Dark" clothing keeps us warmer because these materials absorb more electromagnetic energy. You can easily demonstrate this concept by timing the melting of ice cubes in sunlight when one ice cube is covered by a white piece of cloth and the other by a black piece of cloth.

Air and water **refract**, or change the direction of, traveling waves of light in different ways. Because human eyes developed for use in air, they don't work as well underwater. To see clearly underwater, we need goggles or a face mask to maintain a bubble of air next to the eye. Consequently, even though our bodies are underwater, our eyes remain exposed to light that has been refracted by air, and they function normally. Fish eyes are perfectly adapted to a life underwater. To focus light properly as it is refracted by water, the outer surface of the fish eye is rippled, which reduces distortion or blurriness. In addition, the lens of the eye, which acts like a magnifying glass, is configured differently for viewing light through air or water. The human lens is shaped like an aspirin tablet, whereas the fish lens is shaped like a sphere. Some organisms, such as diving birds, move in and out of the water, which poses difficulty for either the human or fish eye. The cormorant solves the problem of blurry underwater vision with a special eyelid that closes when the bird dives after a fish. The nearly transparent eyelids act like built-in goggles and maintain the clarity of the bird's vision while underwater. The *Anableps anableps*

Zigmund Leszczynski/AGE Fotostock

● **Figure 6.5** To catch the waterborne insects that make up its diet and to avoid predators lurking below the surface, *Anableps anableps* must see both above and below the water. Normally, eyes that are designed to see in air will provide blurry images underwater. *Anableps* solves the dilemma with its unique eyes, each of which has two pupils—one above and one below the water. Locals refer to *Anableps* as "cuatros ojos," or "four eyes."

of Central and South America, shown in ● Figure 6.5, swims with its eyes half in and half out of the water to watch for its prey above the surface and predators below. Each eye has two pupils, one above and one below the water. The upper half of *Anableps*'s eye is designed to see light coming through air, whereas the lower half is adapted to light moving through the water. Local people refer to the fish as "cuatro ojos," or "four eyes."

INTERIM SUMMARY 6.1

‖ Summary Table: Features of Light as a Stimulus

Feature	Significance
Wavelength	Distance between peaks of the waves; determines the perceived color of objects.
Amplitude	Height of the wave; determines perception of brightness.
Absorption	Objects that absorb more visible light energy appear dark colored.
Reflection	Objects that reflect more visible light energy appear light colored. We perceive the reflected wavelengths as the color of an object.
Refraction	Refraction, as by air and water molecules, changes the direction of light.

‖ Summary Points

1. Human vision responds to the visible light portion of the electromagnetic radiation spectrum. Electromagnetic radiation can be described in terms of waves or as the movement of large numbers of particles known as photons. **(LO1)**

2. Visible light interacts with objects in the environment in ways that make light a useful source of information. Light is plentiful, travels in a fairly straight line, and reflects off many objects. **(LO1)**

Review Questions

1. What are the advantages of being able to see in the visible light spectrum as compared with other portions of the electromagnetic spectrum?

2. What do we mean by absorption, reflection, and refraction of light waves?

The Structure and Functions of the Visual System

We begin our discussion of visual processing at the eye. Animals have different solutions for the exact placement of the eyes in the head. Some have eyes in front like humans and cats, whereas others have eyes on the sides of the head, as do rabbits and horses. As we will see later in this chapter, having eyes in the front of the head provides superior depth perception that is advantageous for hunting, so this placement is characteristic of predators. The eyes-on-the-side placement is usually found in prey species and allows these animals to scan large areas of the environment for predators while feeding.

Protecting the Eye

A number of mechanisms are designed to support and protect the eye. Eyes are located in the bony **orbit** of the skull, which can deflect many blows. In addition, the eye is cushioned by fat. When people are starving, they show a characteristic hollow-eyed look due to the loss of this important fat cushion.

A second line of defense is provided by the eyelids. The eyelids can be opened and closed either voluntarily or involuntarily. Involuntary closure of the eyelids, or a **blink**, both protects the eye from incoming objects and moistens and cleans the front of the eye. Under most circumstances, we blink about once every four to six seconds (Burr, 2005). Surprisingly, we don't see these periods as mini-blackouts. Blinks are correlated with less activity in the prefrontal cortex and other areas believed to participate in consciousness (Bristow, Frith, & Rees, 2005). We might not respond to the sudden blackouts produced by a blink because parts of the brain that would normally provide awareness of such an event are also less active.

Tears, another feature of the eyes' protective system, are produced in the lacrimal gland at the outer corner of each eye. The fluid is composed primarily of water and salt but also contains proteins, glucose, and substances that kill bacteria. Tears flush away dust and debris and moisten the eye so that the eyelids don't scratch the surface during blinks. Tears that are shed in response to emotional events contain about 24 percent more protein than tears responding to irritants, such as onions, but the exact purposes of this difference remain unknown (Frey, DeSota-Johnson, Hoffman, & McCall, 1981).

The Functional Anatomy of the Eye

The human eye is roughly a sphere with a diameter of about 24 mm, just under one inch, and individual variations are very small, no more than 1 or 2 mm. Newborns' eyes are about 16–17 mm in diameter (about 6/10 of an inch) and attain nearly their adult size by the age of three years. The "white" of the eye, or **sclera**, provides a tough outer covering that helps the fluid-filled eyeball maintain its shape. The major anatomical features of the eye are illustrated in ● Figure 6.6.

Light entering the eye first passes through the outer layer, or **cornea**. Because the cornea is curved, it begins the process of bending or refracting light rays to form an image in the back of the eye. The cornea is actually a clear, blood vessel–free extension of the sclera. Special proteins on the surface of the cornea discourage the growth of

orbit The bony opening in the skull that houses the eyeball.
blink A rapid closing of the eyelids.
sclera The white outer covering of the eye.
cornea The transparent outer layer of the eye.

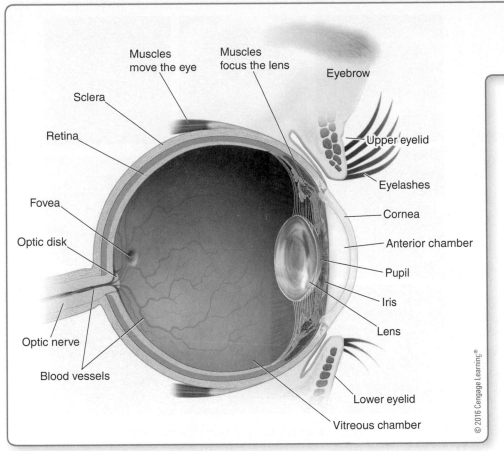

● **Figure 6.6** The Structure of the Eye

Muscles move the eye

Muscles focus the lens

Eyebrow

Sclera

Retina

Fovea

Optic disk

Optic nerve

Blood vessels

Upper eyelid

Eyelashes

Cornea

Anterior chamber

Pupil

Iris

Lens

Lower eyelid

Vitreous chamber

© 2016 Cengage Learning®

blood vessels (Cursiefen et al., 2006). The lack of a blood supply and the orderly alignment of the cornea's fiber structure make it transparent. As living tissue, the cornea still requires nutrients, but it obtains them from the fluid in the adjacent **anterior chamber** rather than from blood. This fluid is known as the **aqueous humor**. The cornea has the dubious distinction of having a greater density of pain receptors than nearly any other part of the body (see Chapter 7).

After light travels through the cornea and the aqueous humor of the anterior chamber, it next enters the **pupil**. The pupil is actually an opening formed by the circular muscle of the **iris**, which comes from the Greek word for "rainbow." The iris adjusts the opening of the pupil in response to the amount of light present in the environment. Pupil diameter is also affected by your emotional state through the activity of the autonomic nervous system (see Chapter 2). Under the influence of the sympathetic division of the autonomic nervous system, the pupil dilates. In times of less arousal during which the parasympathetic nervous system is active, the pupil becomes more constricted.

The color of the iris is influenced primarily by its amount of melanin pigment, which varies from brown to black, in combination with the reflection and absorption of light by other elements in the iris such as its blood supply and connective tissue (see ● Figure 6.7). The irises of people with blue or gray eyes contain relatively less melanin than the irises of people with brown eyes. Consequently, some wavelengths are reflected and scattered from the blue or gray iris in ways that are similar to light in the atmosphere, which is also perceived as blue. Green eyes contain a moderate amount of melanin, and brown or black eyes contain the greatest amounts. "Amber" eyes, brown eyes with a golden look, contain an additional yellowish pigment.

Directly behind the iris is the **lens**. The lens helps focus light on the retina in the back of the eye and functions very much like the lens of a camera. Like the cornea, the lens is transparent due to its fiber organization and lack of blood supply. It, too,

anterior chamber The area of the eye located directly behind the cornea, containing aqueous humor.

aqueous humor The fluid located in the anterior chamber that nourishes the cornea and lens.

pupil The opening in the front of the eye controlled by the iris.

iris The circular muscle in the front of the eye that controls the opening of the pupil.

lens The clear structure behind the pupil and iris that focuses light on the retina.

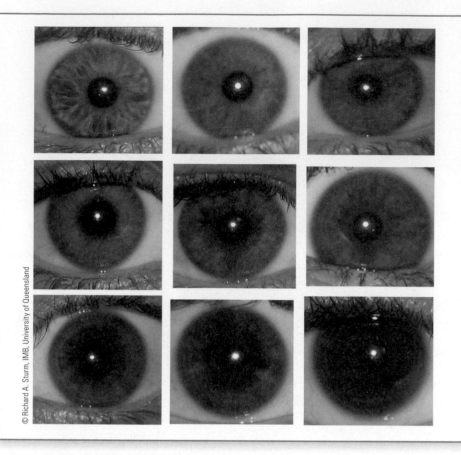

● **Figure 6.7** The color of the iris is influenced by the amount of melanin pigment, blood supply, and connective tissue. Each person's iris is as individual as a fingerprint.

© Richard A. Sturm, IMB, University of Queensland

accommodation The ability of the lens to change shape to adjust to the distance of the visual stimulus.

vitreous chamber The large inner cavity of the eyeball.

vitreous humor The jellylike substance in the vitreous chamber.

retina The elaborate network of photoreceptors and interneurons at the back of the eye that is responsible for sensing light.

photoreceptor Specialized sensory cell in the retina that responds to light.

optic disk The area in the retina where blood vessels and the optic nerve exit the eye.

depends on the aqueous humor for nutrients. Muscles attached to the lens allow us to adjust our focus as we look at objects near to us or far away. This process is called **accommodation**.

The major interior chamber of the eye, known as the **vitreous chamber**, is filled with a jellylike substance called **vitreous humor**. Unlike the aqueous humor, which circulates and is constantly renewed, the vitreous humor you have today is the same vitreous humor with which you were born. Under certain circumstances, you can see floaters, or debris, in the vitreous humor, especially as you get older.

Finally, light will reach the **retina** at the back of the eye. The image that is projected on the retina is upside down and reversed relative to the actual orientation of the object being viewed. You can duplicate this process by looking at your image in both sides of a shiny spoon. In the convex or outwardly curving side, you will see your image normally. If you look at the concave or inwardly curving side, you will see your image as your retina sees it. The visual system has no difficulty encoding this image to give us a realistic perception of the actual orientation of objects.

The retina is actually a part of the diencephalon that migrates outward during embryonic development (see Chapter 5). The word *retina* comes from the Latin word for "fisherman's net." As the name implies, the retina is a thin but complex network containing special light-sensing cells known as **photoreceptors**. The photoreceptors are located in the deepest layer of the retina. Before light can reach the photoreceptors, it must pass through the vitreous humor, numerous blood vessels, and a number of neural layers. We don't normally see the blood vessels and neural layers in our eyes due to an interesting feature of our visual system. Our visual system responds to change and tunes out stimuli that remain constant. Because the blood vessels and neural layers are always present, we don't "see" them.

The blood vessels serving the eye and the axons forming the optic nerve exit the back of the eye in a place known as the **optic disk**. This area does not contain any

● Figure 6.8 Demonstrating the Blind Spot There are no photoreceptors in the optic disk, essentially leaving a hole in our vision. Our brain "fills in the hole," so we don't normally notice it. Beginning with the image at arm's length, close one eye and focus on the dot. Move toward the image until the stack of money "disappears."

macula A 6 mm round area in the retina that is not covered by blood vessels and that is specialized for detailed vision.
central vision The ability to perceive visual stimuli focused on the macula of the retina.
peripheral vision The ability to perceive visual stimuli that are off to the side while looking straight ahead.
fovea A small pit in the macula specialized for detailed vision.
epithelium The pigmented layer of cells supporting the photoreceptors of the retina.

photoreceptors at all, which gives each eye a blind spot. Under normal conditions, we don't notice these blind spots, but you can find your own by following the directions in ● Figure 6.8.

Toward the middle of the retina, we can see a yellowish area about 6 mm in diameter that is lacking large blood vessels (see ● Figure 6.9). This area is known as the **macula**, from the Latin word for "spot." When we stare directly at an object, the image of that object is projected by the cornea and lens to the center of the macula. As a result, we say that the macula is responsible for **central vision** as opposed to **peripheral vision**. Peripheral vision is our ability to see objects that are off to the side while looking straight ahead.

In the very center of the macula, the retina becomes thin and forms a pit. The pit is known as the **fovea**, which is about 1.8 mm in diameter. In humans, the fovea is particularly specialized for detailed vision and contains only one type of photoreceptor, the cones, which permit vision in bright light. Primates, including humans, are the only mammals whose foveas contain only cones. Other mammals, such as cats, have retinal areas that are similar to a fovea, but these contain both cones and the photoreceptors known as rods, which allow vision in dim light.

The retina is embedded in a pigmented layer of cells called the **epithelium**. These cells support the photoreceptors and absorb random light. Because of this absorption of random light, the interior of the eye looks black when seen through the pupil. When a bright light source, such as a camera flash, is pointed directly at the eye, we see the reflection of the true red color of the retina that results from its rich blood supply. The shine we see reflected from the eyes of some animals at night has a different origin.

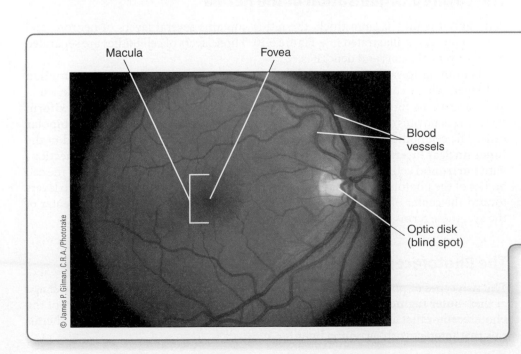

● Figure 6.9 Landmarks of the Retina Blood vessels serving the eye and the axons of the optic nerve exit the eye in the optic disk. The macula is an area of the retina not covered by blood vessels. Within the macula is a small pit, known as the fovea. Detailed vision is best for images projected onto the macula and fovea.

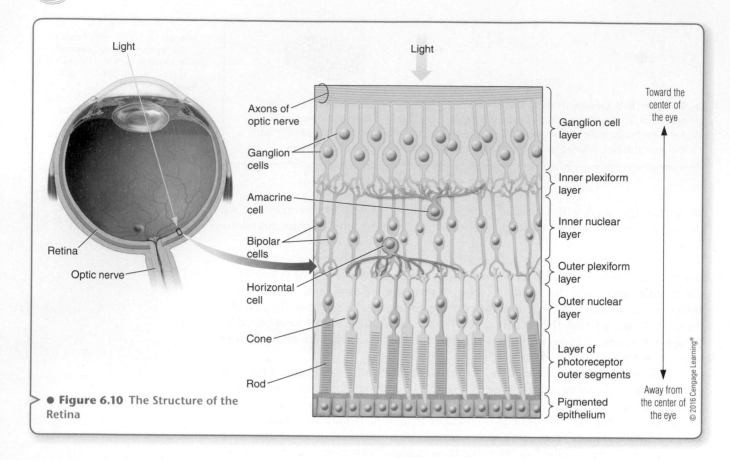

● Figure 6.10 The Structure of the Retina

Labels on figure:
- Light
- Axons of optic nerve
- Ganglion cells
- Amacrine cell
- Bipolar cells
- Horizontal cell
- Cone
- Rod
- Retina
- Optic nerve
- Light
- Toward the center of the eye
- Ganglion cell layer
- Inner plexiform layer
- Inner nuclear layer
- Outer plexiform layer
- Outer nuclear layer
- Layer of photoreceptor outer segments
- Pigmented epithelium
- Away from the center of the eye

© 2016 Cengage Learning®

ganglion cell layer The layer of retinal interneurons farthest from the photoreceptors, which contains ganglion cells and gives rise to the optic nerve.

ganglion cells Retinal cell in the ganglion cell layer whose axon leaves the eye as part of the optic nerve.

inner plexiform layer The location in the retina containing axons and dendrites that connect the ganglion, bipolar, and amacrine cells.

amacrine A retinal interneuron in the inner nuclear layer that integrates signals across adjacent segments of the retina.

bipolar cells A cell in the inner nuclear layer of the retina that forms part of the straight pathway between the photoreceptors and the ganglion cells.

inner nuclear layer The layer of retinal interneurons containing amacrine, bipolar, and horizontal cells.

outer plexiform layer The retinal layer containing axons and dendrites forming connections between bipolar cells, horizontal cells, and the photoreceptors.

horizontal cell A retinal interneuron located in the inner nuclear layer that integrates signals from across the surface of the retina.

Although it is normally advantageous to reduce reflection in the eye, the epithelium of some nocturnal animals, such as the cat, contains a white compound that acts more like a mirror. By reflecting light through the eye a second time, the odds of perceiving very dim lights at night are improved.

The Layered Organization of the Retina

Although it is only 0.3 mm thick, the retina contains several layers of neurons and their connections, illustrated in ● Figure 6.10. Three layers of cell bodies are separated by two layers of axons and dendrites.

Beginning toward the center of the eye, the retina's first layer is the **ganglion cell layer**, which contains the **ganglion cells**. Each ganglion cell has a single axon, and these axons form the optic nerve as it leaves the retina. In the **inner plexiform layer**, the dendrites of ganglion cells form connections with the **amacrine** and **bipolar cells**. The cell bodies of the bipolar, amacrine, and horizontal cells are located in the **inner nuclear layer**. In the **outer plexiform layer**, the bipolar cells form connections with **horizontal cells** and the photoreceptors. The **outer nuclear area** contains the cell bodies of the photoreceptors. If you remember that "inner" in this case refers to layers toward the center of the eye, whereas "outer" refers to layers away from the center of the eye, these terms become more reasonable.

The Photoreceptors

The two types of photoreceptors, **rods** and **cones**, are named according to the shape of their **outer segments**, shown in ● Figure 6.11. The outer segment is the part of the photoreceptor that absorbs light. The outer segment contains **photopigments**, chemicals that interact with incoming light.

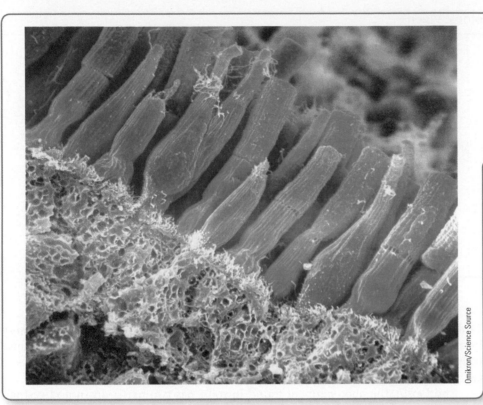

● **Figure 6.11** Rods and Cones The human eye contains approximately 90 million rods and between 4 and 5 million cones, named after the shapes of their outer segments.

Omikron/Science Source

Each human eye contains about 90 million rods. Rods have a long, cylinder-shaped outer segment containing large numbers of disks, like a large stack of pancakes. These disks contain a photopigment known as **rhodopsin**. Rods are responsible for **scotopic vision**, or the ability to see in dim light. Under ideal conditions, the human eye can see a single photon, or the equivalent of the light from a candle flame 30 miles away on a moonless night (Hecht, Shlaer, & Pirenne, 1942). The cost for this extraordinary sensitivity to light is in the clarity and color of the image provided by the rods. Rods do not provide any information about color, and they do not produce sharp images. At night under starlight, our vision is no better than 20/200. An object seen at night from a distance of only 20 feet would have the same clarity as the object viewed from a distance of 200 feet at high noon. It's a good idea to keep that fact in mind while driving at night.

There are only about 4 to 5 million cones in each human eye. Cones are responsible for **photopic vision**, or vision in bright light. Photopic vision is sensitive to color and provides images with excellent clarity. The outer segment of cones is shorter and more pointed than that of the rods. Cones store one of three different photopigments in a folded membrane rather than in disks, as the rods do. Because cones work best in bright light, we do not really see color at night. We might know that we're wearing a green sweater, and, in a sense, we may think it looks green as a result of that memory, but we require fairly bright light and the action of our cones to truly see the color.

As we move from the fovea to the outer margins of the primate retina, the concentration of rods increases and the number of cones decreases. As a result, the center is superior for seeing fine detail and color in the presence of bright light, periphery is superior for detecting very dim light. Because of this uneven rods and cones across the retina, we see better in dim light when we do at an object. Prior to the invention of night goggles, soldiers traveled to look slightly to the side of a location where they suspected rather than straight at the location. Stargazers know that if you star, it tends to disappear, but if you shift your vision a little to comes visible once again. Table 6.1 summarizes the differences photopic vision.

outer nuclear area The location in the retina containing the cell bodies of the photoreceptors.

rod A photoreceptor that responds to low levels of light but not to color.

cone A photoreceptor that operates in bright conditions and responds differentially to color.

outer segment The portion of a photoreceptor containing photopigments.

photopigment A pigment contained in the photoreceptors of the eye that absorbs light.

rhodopsin The photopigment found in rods.

scotopic vision The ability to perceive visual stimuli in near darkness due to the activity of rods.

photopic vision The ability to perceive visual stimuli under bright light conditions due to the activity of cones.

TABLE 6.1 | Scotopic and Photopic Vision

	Scotopic Vision (Dim Light)	Photopic Vision (Bright Light)
Photoreceptor used	**Rods**	**Cones**
Peak wavelength sensitivity	502 nm	420 nm (blue or short-wavelength cones) 530 nm (green or medium-wavelength cones) 560 nm (red or long-wavelength cones)
Ability to distinguish color	None	Color sensitive
Sensitivity to dim light	Excellent	Poor
Acuity	Poor	Excellent
Location of photoreceptors in the retina	Primarily in the periphery	Primarily in the fovea

TRANSDUCTION BY PHOTORECEPTORS Photoreceptors transduce light energy into electrical signals that can be sent to the brain for further processing. Because rods and cones transduce light energy in similar ways, we will focus on the process as carried out by rods.

Rhodopsin, the photopigment found in rods, has two parts, **opsin** and **retinal**. Opsin is a protein chain, and retinal is a chemical made from vitamin A. Vitamin A deficiencies can negatively affect your supply of rhodopsin, so eating carrots, which are rich sources of vitamin A, can truly improve your night vision. When retinal is bound with opsin, the resulting molecule of rhodopsin has a tail that bends at carbon atom number 11. Consequently, this is known as the **11-cis** form of the photopigment. When light enters the eye, photons are absorbed by rhodopsin molecules. As shown in ● Figure 6.12, the absorption of light energy changes the retinal from the 11-cis form to the **all-trans** form. This change in structure causes the rhodopsin molecule to break apart rapidly. To understand what happens next, we need to understand the normal resting state of the photoreceptors.

THE DARK CURRENT Photoreceptors operate differently from most neurons. In the generic neuron we discussed in Chapter 3, the membrane potential at rest was approximately −70 mV . In contrast, the resting potential of a rod outer segment in complete darkness is about −30 mV . In other words, photoreceptors are relatively depolarized (more positive) even when they are resting. Fesenko, Kolesnikov, and Lyubarsky (1985) discovered that rods are constantly depolarized by the inward movement of sodium ions through the outer-segment membrane. This movement of positive ions into the resting photoreceptor is known as the **dark current** because it occurs in the dark.

Sodium channels in neurons are typically kept closed when the cells are at rest. However, Fesenko and his colleagues (1985) showed that sodium channels in rods are kept open by a second messenger, **cyclic guanosine monophosphate (cGMP)**, which is constantly produced by the photoreceptor. When rhodopsin molecules break apart after absorbing light energy, enzymes that break down cGMP are released. With less cGMP available, fewer sodium channels remain open, and fewer positive sodium ions enter the cell. The photoreceptor becomes more negative, or hyperpolarized (Baylor, 1987).

When the rod returns to darkness, enzymes stimulate the molecules of retinal and opsin to rejoin as rhodopsin. Rhodopsin takes about 30 minutes to regenerate (Rushton, 1961). This relatively slow regeneration process explains the gradual improvement in vision that takes place when we move from bright sunlight into a darkened theater.

opsin A protein found in photopigments.

retinal A chemical contained in rhodopsin that interacts with absorbed light.

11-cis The form taken by retinal while it is bound to opsin in the absence of light.

all-trans The form taken by retinal after light is absorbed by the rod outer segment.

dark current The steady depolarization maintained by photoreceptors when no light is present.

cyclic guanosine monophosphate (cGMP) A second messenger within photoreceptors that is responsible for maintaining the dark current by opening sodium channels.

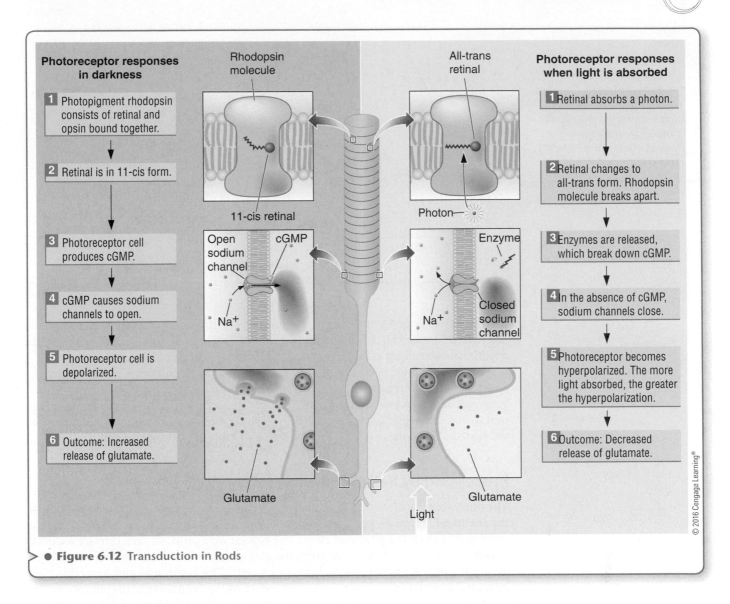

Photoreceptor responses in darkness

1 Photopigment rhodopsin consists of retinal and opsin bound together.

2 Retinal is in 11-cis form.

3 Photoreceptor cell produces cGMP.

4 cGMP causes sodium channels to open.

5 Photoreceptor cell is depolarized.

6 Outcome: Increased release of glutamate.

Rhodopsin molecule

11-cis retinal

Open sodium channel   cGMP

Na+

Glutamate

All-trans retinal

Photon

Enzyme

Closed sodium channel

Na+

Glutamate

Light

Photoreceptor responses when light is absorbed

1 Retinal absorbs a photon.

2 Retinal changes to all-trans form. Rhodopsin molecule breaks apart.

3 Enzymes are released, which break down cGMP.

4 In the absence of cGMP, sodium channels close.

5 Photoreceptor becomes hyperpolarized. The more light absorbed, the greater the hyperpolarization.

6 Outcome: Decreased release of glutamate.

© 2016 Cengage Learning®

● **Figure 6.12** Transduction in Rods

The end result is that photoreceptors are depolarized in the dark and hyperpolarized in the presence of light. Photoreceptors produce graded potentials (signals that vary in size) rather than action potentials. Bright light leads to greater hyperpolarization, whereas dim light leads to less hyperpolarization. Like ordinary neurons, photoreceptors release neurotransmitters (the excitatory neurotransmitter glutamate in this case) when depolarized. Photoreceptors release the largest amounts of glutamate while in the dark. When exposure to light produces hyperpolarization, the photoreceptor responds by releasing less glutamate. This might appear counterintuitive to you because stimulation by light is actually reducing the activity of the receptors. Rest assured that the cells upstream of the photoreceptors (bipolar and horizontal cells) are fully capable of sorting out this strange input.

Differences Between Rods and Cones

Rods and cones respond to a wide range of wavelengths, but their photopigments each have different peak sensitivities (see ● Figure 6.13). There are three classes of cones. The so-called blue or short-wavelength cones, which contain the photopigment cyanolabe, respond maximally to wavelengths of 419 nm (violet). The green, or middle-wavelength cones, containing chlorolabe, have peak responses to 531 nm (green), and

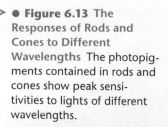

● **Figure 6.13** The Responses of Rods and Cones to Different Wavelengths The photopigments contained in rods and cones show peak sensitivities to lights of different wavelengths.

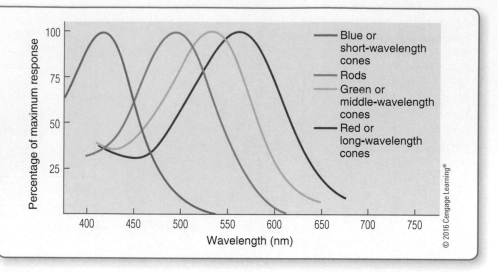

the red or long-wavelength cones, containing erythrolabe, peak at 558 nm (yellow) (Dartnall, Bowmaker, & Mollon, 1983; Wald & Brown, 1958). The rhodopsin in rods absorbs photons most effectively at wavelengths of 502 nm (a bluish-green).

Rods and cones need different amounts of light to respond. Rhodopsin breaks apart when relatively little light has been absorbed, which explains in part the rods' great sensitivity to low levels of light. The cone photopigments are much more resistant to breaking apart and will do so only in the presence of bright light. This is one of the reasons that cones are active in daylight rather than during the night.

Processing by Retinal Interneurons

The photoreceptors (rods and cones) are the only true receptor cells in the entire visual system. In ● Figure 6.10, we saw the four other types of cells in the retina that help process information from the photoreceptors. The bipolar and ganglion cells provide a direct, straight pathway for information from the photoreceptors to the brain that is modified by input from the horizontal and amacrine cells. The horizontal and amacrine cells integrate information across the surface of the retina. You can think of the photoreceptor-bipolar-ganglion connections as running perpendicular to the back of the eye, whereas the horizontal and amacrine connections run parallel to the back of the eye.

HORIZONTAL CELLS The horizontal cells are located in the inner nuclear layer. They receive input from the photoreceptors and provide output to another type of cell in the inner nuclear layer, the bipolar cell. The major task of horizontal cells is to integrate information from photoreceptors that are close to one another. The spreading structure of the horizontal cell is well suited to this task. Like the photoreceptors, horizontal cells communicate through the formation of graded potentials rather than of action potentials.

BIPOLAR CELLS Bipolar cells, also located in the inner nuclear layer, receive input from photoreceptors and from horizontal cells. In turn, bipolar cells communicate with the amacrine cells in the inner nuclear layer and with ganglion cells. Like the photoreceptors and horizontal cells, bipolar cells produce graded potentials rather than action potentials.

There are two major types of bipolar cells: diffuse and midget. Diffuse bipolar cells are more common in the periphery of the retina, where a single bipolar cell might receive input from as many as 50 rods. In contrast, midget bipolar cells located in the fovea might receive input from a single cone. This organization contributes to the trade-offs between photopic and scotopic vision discussed previously. A pinpoint of light falling on any of the 50 photoreceptors connected to a diffuse bipolar cell will influence that cell, making this system very sensitive to dim light. On the other hand, the diffuse bipolar cell is unable to tell the difference between one or several dots of light impacting the rods from which it receives information, reducing the bipolar cell's ability to process fine detail.

Rather than responding to the total amount of light present, bipolar cells begin the process of identifying contrast, or the relative amount of light falling on one area of the retina as opposed to that falling on another area. Bipolar cells accomplish this task by responding to light falling on photoreceptors located in the bipolar cells' **receptive fields**, a type of organization we will see repeated throughout the visual system as well as in the processing of touch, which is discussed in Chapter 7. Any single visual interneuron, such as a bipolar cell, receives input from a single set of photoreceptors located in a specific area on the retina. That area is referred to as the interneuron's receptive field (Hartline, 1938). You can think about the retina as a mosaic of receptive fields. If a pinpoint light is directed to the retina, it is possible to identify which interneurons are responding to the light by recording their activity. A light stimulus must fit within a cell's receptive field to influence its activity. The cell is "blind" to light falling outside its receptive field on the retina.

Let's imagine that we are doing a single-cell recording from one bipolar cell to map its receptive field. When we shine a pinpoint of light into our participant's eye, we find that our bipolar cell depolarizes. When we turn the light off, the cell returns to its normal resting status. If we move our light a little bit to the side, then the cell hyperpolarizes. We have discovered that our bipolar cell has three settings: a neutral resting potential in the absence of stimulation, an on when it depolarizes, and an off response when it hyperpolarizes. The on and off-response areas of the receptive field make up a doughnut shape on the retina, illustrated in ● Figure 6.14. If we shine light in the

receptive field A location on the retina at which light affects the activity of a particular visual interneuron.

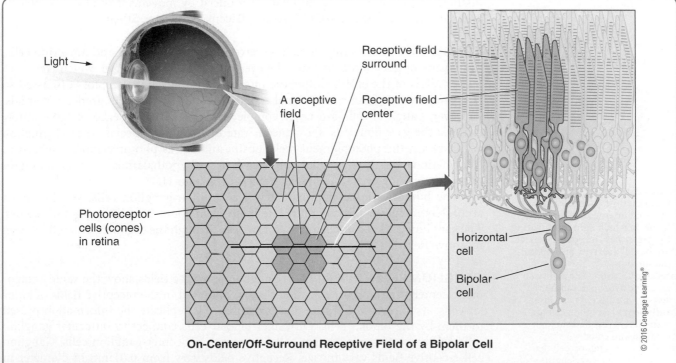

On-Center/Off-Surround Receptive Field of a Bipolar Cell

© 2016 Cengage Learning®

> ● **Figure 6.14 Retinal Bipolar Cells Have Receptive Fields** An on-center bipolar cell receives direct input from photoreceptors (purple) in the center of its receptive field and indirect input from photoreceptors (yellow) in its surround that communicate first with a horizontal cell that then communicates with the bipolar cell. Light falling on the center and surround of a receptive field always has opposite effects on a cell's activity. In this example, light falling on the center but not the surround depolarizes the cell, while light falling on the surround and not the center hyperpolarizes it. Light falling on both center and surround does not change the cell's activity.

center of the doughnut, the bipolar cell depolarizes. Shining a light on the doughnut surrounding the center hyperpolarizes the bipolar cell. A light that covers both center and surround creates an excitatory ("on") response in the center and an inhibitory ("off") response in the surround. These effects cancel each other out, and the cell remains neutral. About half the bipolar cells in the human retina are on-center, and the other half are off-center. On-center cells depolarize when light hits the center of their receptive field. Cells that hyperpolarize when light hits the center of their receptive field are called off-center.

This arrangement of receptive fields is referred to as an **antagonistic center-surround organization**. The response of a bipolar cell depends on the amount of light falling on its center relative to the amount of light falling on its surround. It is called antagonistic because light falling on the center of the receptive field always has the opposite effect on the cell's activity from light falling on the surround.

Photoreceptors and horizontal cells serving the center (doughnut hole) and surround (the doughnut) compete with each other to activate the bipolar cell in a process known as **lateral inhibition**. Lateral means that the process occurs across or parallel to the surface of the retina. In lateral inhibition, active photoreceptors and horizontal cells limit the activity of neighboring, less active cells. This produces a sharpening, or exaggeration, of the bipolar cells' responses to differences in light falling on adjacent areas. Through lateral inhibition, bipolar cells begin to identify the boundaries of a visual stimulus by making comparisons between light levels falling in adjacent areas of the retina. The message sent by the bipolar cells is "I see an edge or boundary."

AMACRINE CELLS Amacrine cells, also located in the inner nuclear layer, form connections with bipolar cells, ganglion cells, and other amacrine cells. In addition to integrating visual messages across the retina, amacrine cells process movement. Because the eyes are often moving themselves, the amacrine cells have the ability to distinguish between the retinal images produced by movement of observed objects and movement of the eye itself (Ölveczky, Baccus, & Meister, 2003).

GANGLION CELLS Ganglion cells receive input from bipolar and amacrine cells. The axons of ganglion cells leave the eye to form the optic nerve, which travels to higher levels of the brain. Unlike the interneurons and photoreceptors discussed so far, ganglion cells form conventional action potentials rather than graded potentials. However, ganglion cells are never completely silent. The presence of light simply changes the ganglion cells' spontaneous rate of signaling. Special types of ganglion cells contain the photopigment melanopsin, and act as photoreceptors themselves. Information from these ganglion cells travels to the hypothalamus and helps maintain our sleep–waking cycles, discussed further in Chapter 11.

The human eye has approximately 1.25 million ganglion cells, yet they must accurately integrate and communicate input from about 95 million photoreceptors. The ganglion cells accomplish this editing task through the organization of their own receptive fields.

GANGLION RECEPTIVE FIELDS Ganglion receptive fields show the same antagonistic center-surround organization that we observed in the receptive fields of bipolar cells. As shown in ● Figure 6.15, ganglion cells replicate the information passed to them by the bipolar cells. On-center bipolar cells connect to on-center ganglion cells, whereas off-center bipolar cells connect to off-center ganglion cells. Ganglion cell receptive fields vary in size. Receptive fields vary from 0.01mm in diameter in the macula to 0.5mm (50 times larger) in the periphery of the retina. Cells with small receptive fields respond best to fine detail.

THE THREE TYPES OF GANGLION CELLS About 70 percent of human ganglion cells are **P cells** (P stands for parvocellular, or small cells), 8–10 percent are **M cells** (M stands for magnocellular, or big cells), and the remainder are **K cells** (K stands for koniocellular).

antagonistic center-surround organization A characteristic of visual interneuron receptive fields, in which light illuminating the center has the opposite effect on the cell's activity as light in the surround.

lateral inhibition The ability of an active neuron to inhibit the activity of adjacent neurons.

P cell Retinal ganglion cell that is small and responds to high contrast and color.

M cell Large ganglion cell that responds to all wavelengths regardless of color, subtle differences in contrast, and stimuli that come and go rapidly.

K cell A small percentage of ganglion cells that do not fit the criteria for P or M cells exactly and respond to blue and yellow light.

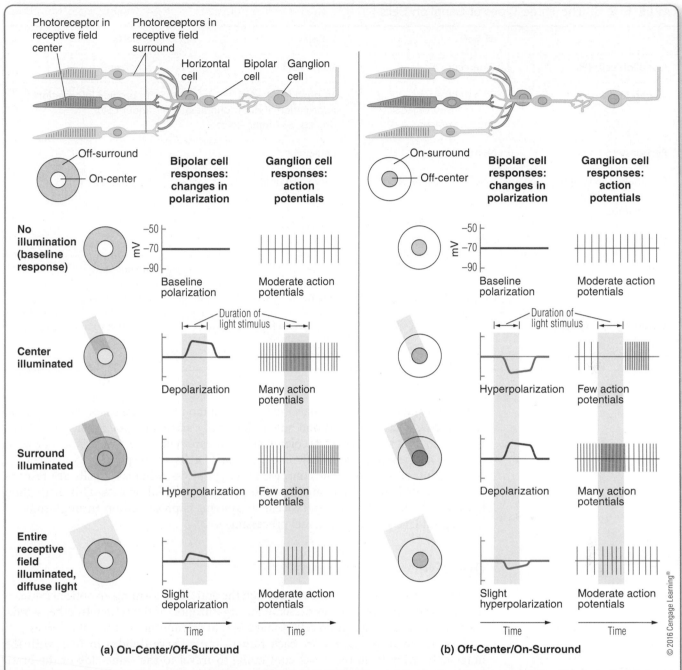

(a) On-Center/Off-Surround

(b) Off-Center/On-Surround

© 2016 Cengage Learning®

> ● **Figure 6.15** **Receptive Fields of Bipolar and Ganglion Cells** Observe the responses of an on-center bipolar cell and an off-center bipolar cell and the ganglion cells with which they communicate to lights falling in different parts of the receptive fields. (a) Light in the center excites the cells, whereas light in the surround inhibits their activity. (b) Light in the surround excites these cells, whereas light in the center inhibits them.

Differences among M, P, and K cells are summarized in Table 6.2. M cells are larger than P cells and have thicker, faster axons. M cells have larger receptive fields than P cells. M cells receive input from diffuse bipolar cells, while P cells receive input from midget bipolar cells. M cells respond to smaller differences in light between the center and surround, whereas P cells require a greater difference. This implies that M cells respond to subtle differences of contrast such as when viewing gray letters on a black background. P cells respond to larger differences in contrast such as when viewing black letters on a white background. M cells, but not P cells, respond to stimuli that are

TABLE 6.2 | The Three Types of Ganglion Cells

	M Cells	P Cells	K Cells
Ganglion cells (%)	5 percent	90 percent	5 percent
Apparent purpose	To detect large, low-contrast objects and movement	To provide detailed information about motionless objects, including color	To provide information about color
Response to color	None	Red-green	Blue-yellow
Destination in lateral geniculate nucleus (LGN) of thalamus	Magnocellular layers	Parvocellular layers	Koniocellular layers
Size	Large	Small	Small
Speed	Fast	Slower	Slower
Receptive field size	Large	Small	Small
Sensitivity to contrast	Sensitive to low contrast	Sensitive to high contrast	Sensitive to high contrast
Response to movement	Excellent	Poor	Poor

turned on and off rapidly, such as the flicker of a monitor or television screen. A final difference is that P cells respond only to lights of a particular color, whereas M cells respond to light regardless of its color. K cells share most of the characteristics of P cells.

The end result of these differences is that M cells are responsible for providing information about large, low-contrast, moving objects, whereas P cells are responsible for information about smaller, high-contrast, colorful objects. This distinction between magnocellular and parvocellular systems is preserved up through some of the highest levels of cortical visual processing.

Optic Nerve Connections

The ganglion cell axons exit the eye through the optic disk, forming an optic nerve leaving each eye. The optic nerves preserve the organization of the retina. In other words, axons from adjacent ganglion cells remain next to one another in the optic nerves.

As shown in ● Figure 6.16, each human optic nerve divides in half, with the outer half (away from the nose) continuing to travel to the same side of the brain (ipsilaterally) while the inner half (closest to the nose) crosses to the other side of the brain (contralaterally). This partial crossing ensures that information from both eyes regarding the same part of the visual field will be processed in the same places in the brain. If you hold your eyes steady by looking at a focal point straight ahead, information from the visual field to the left of the focal point will be transmitted to the right hemisphere. Information from the visual field to the right of the focal point will be transmitted to the left hemisphere. In humans, about 50 percent of the fibers from each eye cross to the opposite hemisphere. In rabbits and other animals with eyes placed on the side of the head, 100 percent of the fibers cross the midline to the opposite side. Because each of a rabbit's eyes sees a completely different part of the rabbit's visual field, there is no need for the rabbit's brain to reorganize the input.

The optic nerves cross at the **optic chiasm** (named after its X shape, or *chi* in Greek). The nerves continue past the optic chiasm as the **optic tracts**. Almost 90 percent of the axons in the optic tract proceed to the thalamus, which in turn projects to the primary visual cortex located in the occipital lobe of the brain. However, axons from

optic chiasm The area at the base of the brain where the optic nerves cross to form the optic tracts; the location of a partial decussation of the optic nerves in humans.

optic tracts The fiber pathways between the optic chiasm and destinations in the forebrain and brainstem.

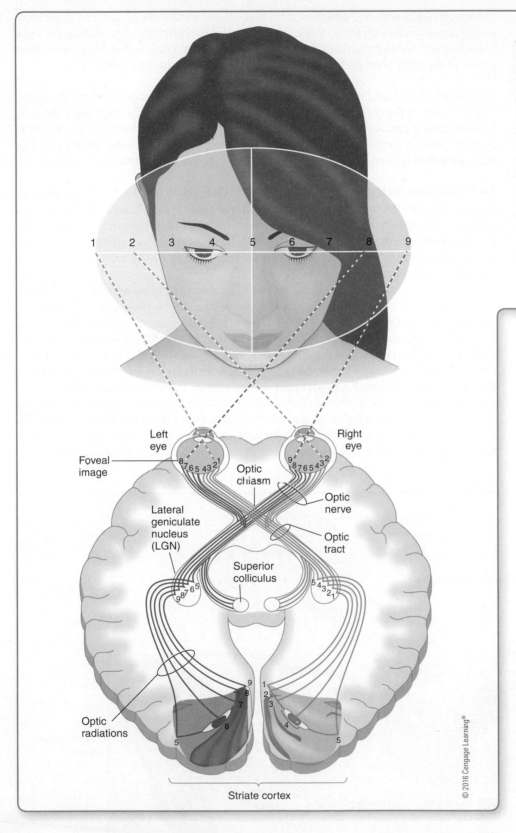

● **Figure 6.16** **The Pathways from Eye to Cortex** The optic nerves leaving the human eye partially cross at the optic chiasm. As a result, images in the left visual field seen by both eyes go to the right hemisphere, whereas images from the right visual field go to the left hemisphere. From the optic chiasm, most axons in the optic tracts synapse in the lateral geniculate nucleus (LGN) of the thalamus. The LGN sends visual information to the primary visual cortex of the occipital lobe.

superior colliculus A structure in the tectum of the midbrain that guides movements of the eyes and head toward newly detected objects in the visual field.

lateral geniculate nucleus (LGN) The nucleus within the thalamus that receives input from the optic tracts.

magnocellular layers The two ventral layers of the LGN that receive input from M cells in the ganglion layer of the retina.

parvocellular layers The four dorsal layers of the LGN that receive input from P cells in the ganglion layer of the retina.

koniocellular layers Layers of very small neurons between the larger six layers of the lateral geniculate nucleus that receive input from K cells in the ganglion layer of the retina.

the special light-sensitive ganglion cells that release melanopsin leave the optic tract and synapse in the suprachiasmatic nucleus of the hypothalamus, providing the light information used to regulate daily rhythms (see Chapter 11). Another 10 percent of the axons in the optic tract project to the **superior colliculus** in the midbrain.

THE SUPERIOR COLLICULUS In many species, including frogs and fish, the superior colliculus is the primary brain structure for processing visual information. Because humans have a cerebral cortex for this purpose, we use the superior colliculus to guide movements of the eyes and head toward newly detected objects in the visual field. The superior colliculus also receives input from the visual cortex, which moderates its activity.

THE LATERAL GENICULATE NUCLEUS OF THE THALAMUS Nearly 90 percent of optic tract axons form synapses in the **lateral geniculate nucleus (LGN)**, located in the dorsal thalamus. The LGN is a layered structure that is bent in the middle. The bend is the source of the name *geniculate*, which comes from the Latin for "bent knee" (as does the term *genuflect*, which describes the bending of the knee that Catholics perform prior to entering a pew to worship).

In primates, including humans, the LGN has about the same area as a credit card, but is about three times thicker. The LGN features six distinct stacked layers, numbered from ventral to dorsal. Each layer of the LGN processes a map of one half of the visual field. This mapping allows us to make connections between neural activity and the real world in front of our eyes. Layers 1 and 2 (the most ventral layers) contain larger neurons than the other four layers. These **magnocellular layers** receive input from the M cells in the retina. The other four are referred to as **parvocellular layers**, which receive input from the P cells. Between each of the six layers are very small neurons making up the **koniocellular layers**, which receive input from the K cells. The LGN keeps information from the two eyes completely separate. ●Figure 6.17 shows how alternating layers of the LGN receive input from the ipsilateral and contralateral eyes.

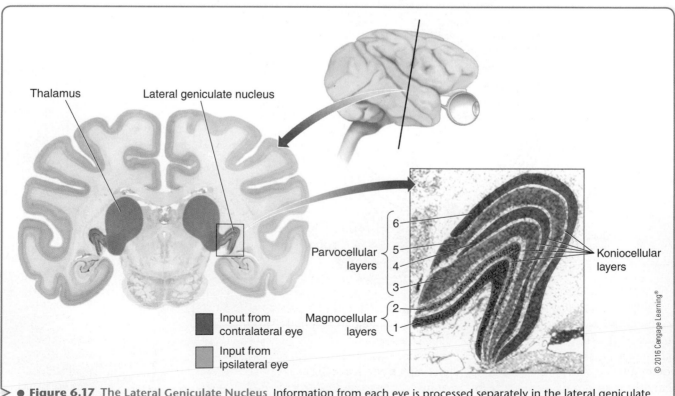

> ● **Figure 6.17 The Lateral Geniculate Nucleus** Information from each eye is processed separately in the lateral geniculate nucleus (shown here in the brain of a monkey). Layers 1 and 2 receive input from M ganglion cells in the retina, Layers 3 through 6 receive input from the P ganglion cells, and the koniocellular layers receive input from the K ganglion cells.

© 2016 Cengage Learning®

Neurons in the LGN show the same antagonistic center-surround organization of receptive fields that we observed in the retinal bipolar and ganglion cells. In LGN neurons, however, the lateral inhibition between center and surround is much stronger than we observed among retinal cells. This greater inhibition causes cells in the LGN to amplify or boost the contrast between areas of light and dark.

The exact role of the LGN in visual processing is not well understood, but this area is far from just a passive relay station in the flow of information to the cortex. The LGN receives much more information from the rest of the brain than it sends to the cortex. LGN activity changes in response to different levels of awareness and selective attention, suggesting that the LGN filters information before sending it along to the cortex (Saalmann & Kastner, 2011). The LGN also receives input from the brainstem reticular formation. This input from the cortex and the reticular formation modifies the flow of information to the cortex from the LGN based on levels of arousal and alertness (Saalmann & Kastner, 2011). For example, when you're asleep, someone could lift your eyelid, but you would not "see" (assuming you remained asleep).

The Striate Cortex

Primary visual cortex is often referred to as **striate cortex**, due to its striped appearance, or as simply V1 (visual area 1). Striate cortex, located in the occipital lobe, contains approximately 200 million neurons as opposed to the 2 million neurons found in the LGN.

The cortex in this area ranges from 1.5 to 2 mm in thickness, or about the height of the letter m on this page. Like other areas of cortex, the striate cortex has six distinct layers (see Chapter 2). Compared with other areas of cortex, striate cortex is relatively thicker in layers II and IV, which receive most of the input from other parts of the brain. Layer IV receives input from the LGN. Striate cortex is thinner than other areas of the cortex in layers III, V, and VI, which contain output neurons that communicate with other parts of the brain.

CORTICAL MAPPING OF THE VISUAL WORLD Earlier, we described how precisely the visual field was mapped by the LGN. The same thing is true of the striate cortex. Returning to ● Figure 6.16, you can trace the pathways from eye to striate cortex that are responding to reflected light from the woman's right eyebrow (numbers 3 and 4). This mapping allows us to use the location of neural activity to understand the position of an object in the visual field.

● Figure 6.16 demonstrates another feature of cortical mapping. The areas of the cortex that respond to input from the fovea of the retina (4, 5, and 6) are much larger than the areas responding to images seen in the periphery (1, 2, 3, 7, 8, and 9). Although the fovea contains 0.01 percent of the retina's total area, signals from the fovea are processed by 8 to 10 percent of the striate cortex (Van Essen & Anderson, 1995). This cortical magnification is yet another reason why focusing an image onto the fovea provides the greatest amount of fine detail.

CORTICAL RECEPTIVE FIELDS Although cortical neurons have receptive fields, these fields do not respond to the simple dots of light that activate bipolar and ganglion cells in the retina and cells within the LGN.

Based on a series of meticulous single-cell recording experiments, Hubel and Wiesel (1959) defined **simple cortical cells** as those cells that respond to stimuli shaped like bars or edges that have a particular slant or orientation in a particular location on the retina (see ● Figure 6.18). These cells probably help us respond to object shape. Simple cortical cell receptive fields maintain an antagonistic center-surround organization, but the shape of the receptive field is more elongated or racetrack-shaped than doughnut-like. Hubel and Wiesel defined **complex cortical cells** as cortical cells that share the simple cells' preference for stimulus size and orientation but without reference to the stimulus's location (see ● Figure 6.19).

Some complex cortical cells respond to lines moving in a particular direction. A cell might respond to a vertical line moving from right to left across the receptive

primary visual cortex The location in the occipital lobe for the initial cortical analysis of visual input. Also known as striate cortex or V1.

simple cortical cell A cortical interneuron that responds to stimuli in the shape of a bar or edge with a particular slant or orientation in a particular location on the retina.

complex cortical cell A cortical interneuron that shows a preferred stimulus size and orientation, and in some cases direction of movement, but not location within the visual field.

● **Figure 6.18** Simple Cortical Cells Simple cortical cells respond to bars of light at their preferred location and orientation (a vertical bar in this example).

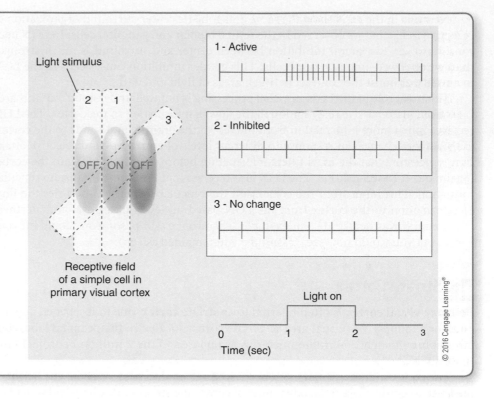

field but not to a line moving left to right. Consequently, complex cortical cells probably participate in the perception of movement (Regan, Beverley, & Cynader, 1979). Fatigue in these directional cells might be responsible for the waterfall illusion (Addams, 1934/1964). If you stare at a waterfall for a minute or two, then look away, the scene being viewed will appear to be moving in an upward direction. This phenomenon occurs due to the temporary fatigue of downward motion detectors (see ● Figure 6.20).

Some simple and complex cortical cells are also known as **end-stopped cells** (Hubel & Wiesel, 1962). These cells respond most vigorously to a stimulus that falls within their receptive field but not beyond. In other words, a bar of light that is too long for the receptive field would produce a smaller response than a bar that fit the receptive field perfectly. These cells participate in our detection of boundaries like the corners of the page of your textbook. Viewing corners and similar boundaries is essential to the recognition of familiar objects (Biederman, 1987).

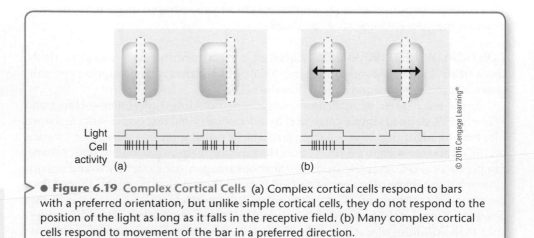

● **Figure 6.19** Complex Cortical Cells (a) Complex cortical cells respond to bars with a preferred orientation, but unlike simple cortical cells, they do not respond to the position of the light as long as it falls in the receptive field. (b) Many complex cortical cells respond to movement of the bar in a preferred direction.

end-stopped cells A cortical interneuron that responds most vigorously to a stimulus that does not extend beyond the boundaries of its receptive field.

CORTICAL COLUMNS If we moved a recording electrode perpendicular to the surface of the cortex, we would find that the neurons are organized in a cortical column. Neurons in cortical columns communicate with one another but do not form many connections with neighboring columns more than half a millimeter away (Mountcastle, 1978).

One type of column found in the striate cortex is known as an **ocular dominance column**. These are columns of cortex perpendicular to the cortical surface that respond to input from either the right eye or the left eye but not to both. These columns take advantage of the strict segregation of input from either eye that we observed in the LGN. The columns are about 1mm wide and alternate (right eye–left eye–right eye, etc.) across the surface of the visual cortex.

Orientation columns are much thinner than the ocular dominance columns. Each orientation column responds to lines of the same angle. Adjacent columns respond to angles shifted about 10 degrees. A set of these columns that responds to a complete rotation of 180 degrees, is referred to as a **hypercolumn**.

CYTOCHROME OXIDASE BLOBS **Cytochrome oxidase blobs** are named after an enzyme, cytochrome oxidase (Hubel & Livingstone, 1987; Livingstone & Hubel, 1984; Wong-Riley, 1989). Neurons in areas with high concentrations of cytochrome oxidase appear to process information regarding color.

CORTICAL MODULES We have seen how cortical neurons respond to line orientation, movement, and color. At some point, our visual system puts these separate characteristics back together to form coherent images. Hubel and Wiesel (1962) suggested that the unit responsible for this integration is the **cortical module**. As shown in ● Figure 6.20, cortical modules include two sets of ocular dominance columns,

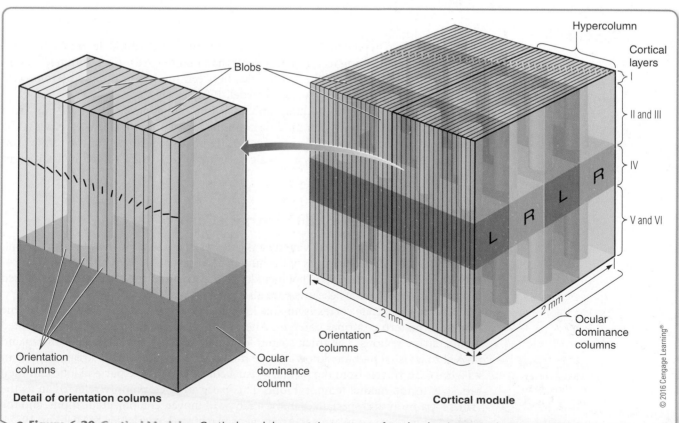

● **Figure 6.20 Cortical Modules** Cortical modules contain two sets of ocular dominance columns, 16 blobs, and two hypercolumns. These 2 mm × 2 mm chunks of primary visual cortex have all the types of neurons needed to analyze a complete image falling on their receptive field of the retina.

●●● Connecting to **Research**

HUBEL AND WIESEL MAP THE VISUAL CORTEX

Much of what we know about the organization of the visual cortex was discovered by David Hubel (1926–2013) and Torsten Wiesel (1924–). In a partnership that spanned decades, these researchers painstakingly explored the activity of single cells as they responded to visual stimuli. Their work culminated in their being awarded the 1981 Nobel Prize in Physiology or Medicine.

In one of their early experiments, Hubel and Wiesel observed the activity of single cells in 40 anesthetized cats that were maintained in a stage of "light sleep" according to their EEGs (Hubel & Wiesel, 1962). The cats faced a screen about 4 feet away, on which Hubel and Wiesel projected various patterns of white light. Microelectrodes were surgically inserted into the cats' striate cortex to a depth of about 3–4 mm. As the electrodes were advanced slowly, both moving and stationary stimuli were rapidly presented to see which type of stimulus produced the maximum response by cells near the recording electrode's tip.

Hubel and Wiesel knew from previous research that retinal cells and cells in the LGN had on and off-center receptive fields, yet no such organization had ever been demonstrated in the cerebral cortex. They set out to identify whatever organization might characterize this part of the visual system. In the course of this exploration, they found that "the great majority of fields seem to fall naturally into two groups, which we have termed 'simple' and 'complex'" (Hubel & Wiesel, 1962, p. 109). They classified 233 out of 303 cortical cells they evaluated as simple, and the remaining 70 as complex.

In this same report, Hubel and Wiesel discussed orientation columns and ocular dominance columns. Their article featured precise, handmade drawings of the paths of their electrodes and the resulting activity of the cells. They noted that much larger areas of cortex responded to light in the fovea compared to light in the periphery of the retina. This wide-ranging set of results continues to be relevant to our understanding of the visual system 50 years after it was published.

16 blobs, and two hypercolumns, each responding to the entire 180 degrees of line orientation. Newer mapping techniques suggest that modules are more accurately viewed as approximations because the boundaries between modules are much less precise than suggested by Hubel and Wiesel (Blasdel, 1992).

We have about 1,000 modules, and each one makes up a 2 mm × 2 mm area of primary visual cortex. Each module contains the neurons it needs to process the shape, color, and movement of an image falling on a specific part of the retina. You can think of the visual field as a mosaic with 1,000 tiles, each served by a different cortical module.

Visual Analysis Beyond the Striate Cortex

The striate cortex begins, but by no means finishes, the task of processing visual input. At least a dozen additional areas of the human cerebral cortex participate in visual processing. Because these areas are not included in the striate cortex, they are often referred to as extrastriate areas. These areas are also referred to as secondary visual cortex.

Next to the striate cortex is an area known as V2. If you stain V2 for cytochrome oxidase, a pattern of stripes emerges. Alternating thick and thin stripes are separated by interstripe regions. The thick stripes form part of the magnocellular pathway and project to a visual pathway known as the **dorsal stream**. The dorsal stream, shown in ● Figure 6.21, travels from the primary visual cortex toward the parietal lobe and then proceeds to the medial temporal lobe. This pathway is commonly referred to as the "where" pathway and specializes in the analysis of movement, object locations, and the coordination of eyes and arms in grasping or reaching (Ungerleider & Mishkin, 1982).

The thin stripes and interstripe regions of V2 project to another visual region known as V4, continuing the parvocellular pathway. Area V4 participates in a second major pathway, the **ventral stream**, which proceeds from the primary visual cortex to

dorsal stream A pathway leading from the primary visual cortex in a dorsal direction thought to participate in the perception of movement.

ventral stream A pathway of information from the primary visual cortex to the inferior temporal lobe that is believed to process object recognition.

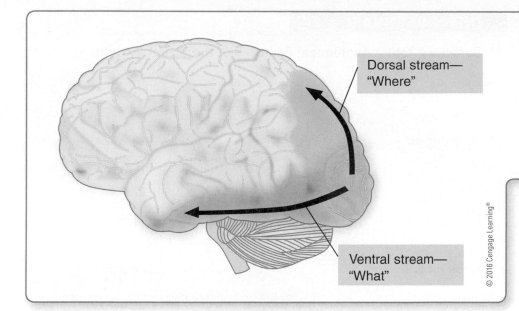

● **Figure 6.21** The Dorsal "Where" Pathway and the Ventral "What" Pathway Information in the dorsal stream contributes to our perception of movement. Information in the ventral stream helps us recognize objects.

Dorsal stream— "Where"

Ventral stream— "What"

© 2016 Cengage Learning®

the inferior temporal lobe. This second pathway, commonly referred to as the "what" pathway, specializes in object recognition (Ungerleider & Mishkin, 1982).

THE DORSAL STREAM **Area MT**, which stands for the medial temporal lobe, receives input from neurons along the dorsal stream and appears to play an important role in the processing of motion. Input to Area MT is primarily from the magnocellular pathways. Recall that the cells in this pathway have large receptive fields and often show responses to rapidly changing light conditions and direction of movement. Most of the cells in Area MT respond to movement in a particular direction. Unlike previous motion detectors, however, Area MT cells respond to movement across large regions of the visual field. Patients with damage to Area MT have a condition called *akinetopsia*, which results in their seeing the visual scene as a series of still photographs instead of an ongoing flow of information. These patients experience great difficulty with important tasks such as recognizing that a car is moving toward you (Rizzo, Nawrot, & Zihl, 1995).

Further processing of motion occurs adjacent to Area MT in **Area MST**, which stands for the medial superior temporal lobe. Tanaka and Saito (1989) found that Area MST neurons respond to stimulus rotation, stimulus expansion, and stimulus contraction. These are very large, global types of movement that do not produce consistent responses in other areas. Area MST helps us use vision to guide our movements.

Melvyn Goodale and his colleagues (Goodale & Humphrey, 2001; Milner & Goodale, 1995; Goodale & Milner, 1992) suggested that the dorsal stream would be more accurately characterized as a "how" stream than as a "where" stream. According to this view, not only does the dorsal stream tell us an object's location, but it also provides information about how to interact with an object. Patients with damage to the dorsal stream can judge the orientation of an object, such as lining up a card with a slot, but are unable to combine orientation and action to push the card through the slot.

THE VENTRAL STREAM As the information from the primary cortex and Area V2 travels ventrally toward the temporal lobe, we come to Area V4. The cells in this area respond to both shape and color. Cells in Area V4 project to the inferior temporal lobe, or **Area IT**. Cells in Area IT respond to many shapes and colors. In humans and monkeys, a small section of Area IT known as the **fusiform face area** (FFA) appears to respond most vigorously to faces and to members of learned categories, such as species of birds or models of cars (Gauthier, Skudlarski, Gore, & Anderson, 2000). Monkeys viewing blurred photographs are more likely to report "seeing" faces when their FFAs are stimulated (Afraz, Kiani, & Esteky, 2006).

Area MT An area in the medial temporal lobe believed to participate in motion analysis.

Area MST An area in the medial superior temporal lobe believed to participate in large-scale motion analysis.

Area IT An area in the inferior temporal lobe believed to participate in object recognition.

fusiform face area (FFA) An area in the inferior temporal lobe believed to participate in the recognition of familiar faces, especially in the right hemisphere.

INTERIM SUMMARY 6.2

Summary Table: Anatomical Features of the Visual System

Feature	Significance
Cornea	Bends light toward the retina
Anterior chamber	Contains fluid for nourishing the cornea and lens
Iris	Muscle that controls the amount of light entering the eye
Pupil	Opening in the iris
Lens	Focuses light onto the retina
Vitreous chamber	Fluid-filled chamber behind the lens
Retina	Contains photoreceptors and initial processing neurons
Macula	Responsible for central, as opposed to peripheral, vision
Fovea	Pit in the macula specialized for detailed vision
Optic nerves	Axons from retinal ganglion cells that exit the eye
Lateral geniculate nucleus (LGN)	Area of the thalamus that receives input from the optic nerves
Primary visual cortex	Receives input from the lateral geniculate nucleus; responsible for initial processing of an image
Dorsal stream	Analysis of movement
Ventral stream	Object recognition

Summary Points

1. Before reaching the retina, light travels through the cornea, the anterior chamber, the opening of the pupil controlled by the iris, the lens, and the vitreous chamber. (LO2)

2. The retina is a thin layer of visual interneurons and photoreceptors. (LO2)

3. The 90 million rods in the human eye are responsible for scotopic (dim light) vision, whereas the 4 to 5 million cones are responsible for photopic (bright light) vision. (LO2)

4. The human eye's 1.25 million ganglion cells integrate the input from about 95 million photoreceptors and send the information to the brain via action potentials in the optic nerves. The optic tracts proceed to the lateral geniculate nucleus (LGN) of the thalamus, with smaller branches connecting with the hypothalamus and superior colliculi. (LO3)

5. The primary visual cortex (striate cortex) is located in the occipital lobe. It contains simple cortical cells and complex cortical cells that participate in the encoding of shape and movement. Information about movement is processed further by the dorsal stream, whereas information about object recognition is processed further by the ventral stream. (LO3)

Visual Perception

How does the brain construct a model of visual reality out of the input it receives? Before objects can be recognized, information must be processed by the sensory receptors to be analyzed further, a process referred to previously as bottom-up processing. At the same time, the interpretation of this incoming data involves the memories, experiences, and expectations an observer has about an object, leading to top-down processing.

Hierarchies

The model of cortical visual processing proposed by Hubel and Wiesel implies a bottom-up, hierarchical organization in which simple cells contribute input to increasingly complex cells. At each level of processing, more complex responses are generated from simpler responses. The result of such a system would be a "grandmother cell," or a single cell that could combine all previous input to tell you that your grandmother was at the door to pay a visit.

The hierarchical model received considerable support from recordings of single cells in the temporal lobes of eight patients undergoing surgery for epilepsy (Quiroga, Reddy, Kreiman, Koch, & Fried, 2005; see ● Figure 6.22). One patient had a cell that fired in response to all images that included actress Jennifer Aniston, but not at all to images of other faces, landmarks, or objects. Another patient had a cell that responded to photos of actress Halle Berry, images of Berry in her Catwoman costume, caricatures of Berry, and even a letter sequence spelling her name.

Although the idea of a strict hierarchical structure is attractive in many ways, it does not fit perfectly with what we know about brain organization. First of all, we would need an immense number of "grandmother cells" to respond to the large numbers of objects and events that we can recognize. This extravagance in the use of cells is out of character for the highly efficient nervous system. Second, the ability of cortical visual neurons to respond equally to changes in more than one stimulus dimension (orientation and movement, for example) is not consistent with the hierarchical model. A true "grandmother cell" should respond only in the presence of its ideal stimulus and never in its absence. Finally, the hierarchical model would struggle to explain our response to the apparently random pattern of dots shown in ● Figure 6.23. Once you know that the image represents a Dalmatian dog, you can instantly pick out the shape of the dog. This requires top-down processing that includes knowledge and memory of the appearance of Dalmatian dogs. It is unlikely that a single cortical cell

> ● **Figure 6.22** Bottom-Up Processing? Recordings in patients awaiting brain surgery identified single cells that responded to all images of actress Jennifer Aniston, although the cell responded less when Aniston was pictured with her ex-husband Brad Pitt.

grating A striped stimulus used to study responses to spatial frequency.

spatial frequency analysis A way of describing visual processing as a basic mathematical analysis of the visual field.

contrast sensitivity function (CSF) The mapping of an individual's thresholds for contrast over a range of frequencies.

● **Figure 6.23** Problems for the Hierarchical Model of Vision Can you figure out what is in the picture? If I tell you that this is a picture of a Dalmatian dog, can you see the picture clearly? This visual experience would be difficult to explain in terms of bottom-up processing alone. The stimulus doesn't change when you learn the identity of the object, but the interpretation does.

From Richard L. Gregory, "The Medawar Lecture 2001 Knowledge for vision: vision for knowledge," Phil. Trans. R. Soc. B 2005 360, 1231-1251, © The Royal Society.

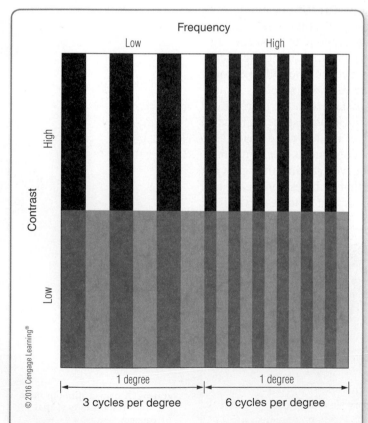

● **Figure 6.24** Spatial Frequencies It has been suggested that the visual system works by performing a mathematical analysis of spatial frequencies in the visual field. Gratings can be described in terms of frequency (number of bars in a given distance) or contrast (the difference in intensity between adjacent bars).

acting as a Dalmatian dog detector could incorporate such complex inputs from memory.

Spatial Frequencies

Striate cortex may not respond to isolated lines and bars but, rather, to patterns of lines. The simplest patterns of lines are known as **gratings**, as shown in ● Figure 6.24. A high-frequency grating has many bars in a given distance, whereas a low-frequency grating has relatively few bars. A high-contrast grating has a large amount of difference in intensity between bars, such as very bright white next to black. A low-contrast grating has a more subtle difference in intensity between bars, such as a dark gray next to black. The human visual system could perform a rough mathematical analysis, or **spatial frequency analysis**, of the gratings found in the visual field (De Valois & De Valois, 1980). This is very different from the hierarchical approach, which implies a reality built out of bars and edges.

Observing responses to gratings can give us a window into the visual world of other species. Thresholds for contrast can be identified over a range of frequencies. In other words, how much contrast is needed in adjacent bars of a grating before they can be distinguished from a uniform gray stimulus? The resulting graph is known as a **contrast sensitivity function**, or **CSF**. We can obtain CSFs from nonhuman species by training them to choose a grating rather than a uniformly colored stimulus to obtain

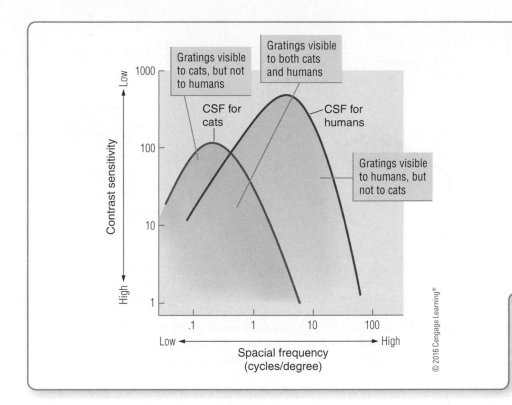

● **Figure 6.25** A Cat's View of the World A contrast sensitivity function (CSF) measures how much contrast is needed for a grating to look different from a uniformly colored disk as a function of spatial frequency. The resulting functions for cats and humans show significant overlap. However, you can see more fine detail (higher spatial frequencies) than your cat can. The cat can see better at lower spatial frequencies than you can.

food. When the animal's responses become no more accurate than chance, we can assume that the animal can no longer tell the difference between a grating and a uniformly colored stimulus. This determines the CSF for that animal.

●Figure 6.25 compares the CSFs of cats and humans. At higher spatial frequencies (lines in the grating get closer together), your vision is better than your cat's. This means that human beings see more fine detail than cats do. On the other hand, kitty has an advantage over you at low spatial frequencies. This means that a low-frequency (large), low-contrast (dark gray vs. black) shadow on the wall will get your cat's attention but not yours. You will think kitty is after ghosts again.

The Perception of Depth

The image projected on the retina is two-dimensional, so the visual system uses a number of cues to provide a sense of depth. Several of these cues are monocular, requiring the use of only one eye. Perspective, in which lines we expect to be parallel, such as the edges of a road, are made to converge or come together at the horizon, is a centuries-old artistic device to give the illusion of depth on a flat surface such as a painting. Texture, shading, and a comparison of the size of familiar objects can also provide a very realistic impression of depth in two dimensions.

The depth cues mentioned so far do not require the use of two eyes. We also have binocular (two-eye) depth cues that are even more effective. When eyes face front, as in humans and other predatory species, the two eyes produce overlapping, but slightly different, images of the visual field (as we saw earlier in ● Figure 6.16). The differences between the images projected onto the retinas of both eyes result in **retinal disparity**. Because retinal disparity increases with the distance of the object from the viewer, we can use the degree of disparity as a strong cue for depth. As shown in ●Figure 6.26, movies filmed with 3D technology take advantage of retinal disparity to give us the illusion of depth.

Binocular cells in the cortex respond most vigorously when both eyes are looking at the same features of a visual stimulus (Hubel & Wiesel, 1962). Binocular cells also respond to degrees of retinal disparity. Some cells fire more when their preferred features appear to be at an identical distance. Others fire more when the

retinal disparity The slightly different views of the visual field provided by the two eyes.
binocular cells A cell in the cerebral cortex that responds to input from both eyes.

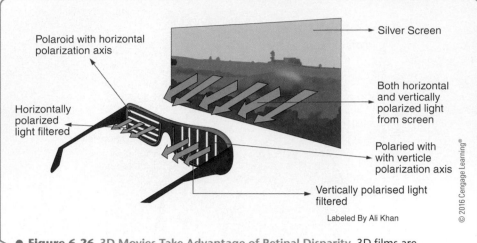

Polaroid with horizontal polarization axis

Horizontally polarized light filtered

Silver Screen

Both horizontal and vertically polarized light from screen

Polaried with with verticle polarization axis

Vertically polarised light filtered

Labeled By Ali Khan

© 2016 Cengage Learning®

● **Figure 6.26** **3D Movies Take Advantage of Retinal Disparity** 3D films are recorded by cameras with two lenses that are about as far apart as our eyes—two inches (about 5 cm). The recording is displayed by a projector also having two lenses, one with a horizontal polarizing filter and the other with a vertical polarizing filter. The images look blurry to the naked eye. Using 3D glasses, however, makes the experience similar to combining the images from both eyes in real life, which gives us a strong sense of depth.

preferred features are seen by different parts of the two eyes. These cells are known as **disparity-selective cells**. We coordinate the activity of these cells to judge retinal disparity. In areas of the anterior parietal lobe, information about retinal disparity is combined with judgments of how the shape of an object changes due to movement to construct the final impression of a three-dimensional object (Durand et al., 2007; Georgieva, Todd, Peeters, & Orban, 2008).

disparity-selective cell A binocular cortical cell that responds when its preferred features are seen by different parts of the two eyes.

••• Behavioral Neuroscience GOES TO WORK

3D ANIMATION

You might be among the millions of moviegoers who are willing to spend extra money to see a film in 3D. Our understanding of retinal disparity has made the development of this technology possible (Khan, 2013).

The 3D-movie experience begins with a special camera with two lenses, spaced about two inches (about 5 cm) apart. Scenes are recorded simultaneously by both lenses, mimicking the viewing of the scenes by your two eyes. The projector, like the camera, also has two lenses spaced closely together. The light from one of the lenses is vertically polarized, which means that particles of light oscillate in one plane only. Normal light oscillates in all directions. The other lens emits light that is horizontally polarized. Newer 3D projectors use a single lens that switches between the images recorded by each camera hundreds of times per second.

Viewing the projection on a screen would produce a blurry image. Special glasses are needed to sort the images out. Each lens of the glasses is coated with carbon filters that rotate light to be horizontally or vertically polarized, like the filters from the projector. More modern glasses have circular filters that also help reconstruct the images. The brain treats these separate images from each lens of the glasses similarly to the combining of images from our two eyes, resulting in a strong perception of depth.

If you are watching a rather boring 3D film and would like to explore the boundaries of the technology further, try tilting your head to see what happens to the image. If you are wearing linear polarizing glasses rather than circular ones, this will produce a distorted view of the scene. The brain is unable to interpret the resulting images properly. We usually are not aware of our staring straight ahead at a movie screen, but this is what most of us do.

Coding Color

Red, green, and blue lights can be mixed to generate all colors, and mixing them together will give you a white light (which can be separated with a prism or by water droplets that produce a rainbow). Consequently, red, green, and blue are considered to be the primary colors of light (see ● Figure 6.27).

THE TRICHROMATIC THEORY The **trichromatic theory** suggests that human color vision is based on our having three (tri) different color photopigments. As we discussed previously, the three photopigments are maximally responsive to lights of different wavelengths.

Based on a series of color-matching tasks with human participants, Thomas Young proposed his trichromatic theory of color vision in 1807, long before any knowledge was available regarding the types of human photoreceptors. Hermann von Helmholtz (1856–1866) expanded Young's theory by proposing three different color receptors in the retina. Both men are credited with the trichromatic theory, which is typically referred to as the Young-Helmholtz theory of color vision.

● **Figure 6.27 Mixing Lights** We might be accustomed to thinking of primary colors as red, yellow, and blue, but that works only for paint. In the world of light, red, green, and blue can be mixed to form all other colors. A mixture of all three colors of light looks white.

Although the trichromatic theory accounts for many of the phenomena related to color vision, it leaves other features unexplained. For instance, if you stare at the yellow, green, and white flag in ● Figure 6.28 and then focus on the dot in the white space below, you will get an afterimage of the flag in its more traditional red, white, and blue. Clearly, there is more to color vision than the trichromatic theory can explain.

OPPONENT PROCESSES Ewald Hering observed that mixing blue and yellow lights yielded the sensation of gray and that individuals with color deficiency seemed to lose the ability to discriminate between green and red rather than having difficulties seeing just one of the colors. These observations could not be explained in terms of the trichromatic theory. In his 1878 work, *On the Theory of Sensibility to Light*, Hering suggested an alternate theory of opponent processes based on three types of receptors: a red–green receptor, a blue–yellow receptor, and a black–white receptor.

Opponent process theory gains support from the organization of color receptive fields in the visual system (see ● Figure 6.29). P and K ganglion cells have center-surround receptive fields that respond differentially to color. P cells show red–green center-surround organization. In other words, we can locate receptive fields for P cells that have a center that responds maximally to red and a surround that responds to green. Other P cell receptive fields will have centers that respond maximally to green and surrounds that respond to red. The K cells show antagonistic center-surround organizations responding to blue and yellow. However, unlike the P cells, these blue–yellow ganglion cells come in only one variety. They always have blue centers and yellow surrounds but not the reverse.

You may be wondering how the input from three cone types can result in the opposition of four colors: green versus red and blue versus yellow. The green and red case is straightforward. These ganglion cells are receiving input from cones that respond maximally to red or green. The blue and yellow case is slightly different. These ganglion cells receive input from blue cones, of course, which they compare to a mixture of input from red and green cones, which in the world of light add up to yellow.

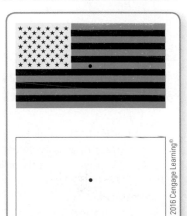

● **Figure 6.28 Color Afterimages Illustrate Opponency** If you stare at the dot in the center of the yellow, green, and white flag for a minute, then shift your gaze to the dot in the white space below, you should see the flag in its traditional red, white, and blue.

trichromatic theory The theory that suggests human color vision is based on our possessing three different color photopigments.
opponent process theory A theory of human color vision based on three antagonistic color channels: red-green, blue-yellow, and black-white.

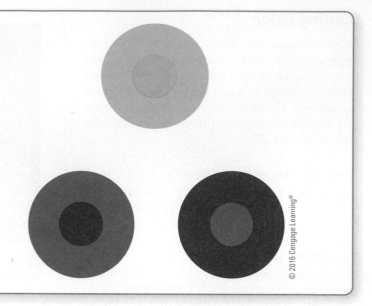

Figure 6.29 Opponent Process Theory
Opponent process theory is consistent with the finding that receptive fields of ganglion cells and LGN cells have antagonistic center-surround organizations for color. Cones maximally sensitive to red and green contribute to red–green receptive fields, which can take red-center green-surround or green-center red-surround forms. Cones sensitive to red and green (the combination in light produces yellow) contribute to the surround of the blue–yellow receptive field, while blue cones contribute to the center. We do not find evidence of yellow-center blue-surround receptive fields.

© 2016 Cengage Learning®

Which of the two theories of color vision is correct? It appears that both are correct but that they operate at different stages in the analysis of color. The Young-Helmholtz trichromatic theory provides an accurate framework for the functioning of the three types of cones in the retina. At levels of color analysis beyond the retina, Hering's opponent process theory seems to fit observed phenomena neatly.

••• THINKING *Ethically*

ARE THERE SEX DIFFERENCES IN COLOR PREFERENCES?

The idea that "pink is for girls and blue is for boys" seems hopelessly sexist to modern thinkers. Why shouldn't boys and girls enjoy whatever colors please them? Is there any real biological basis for color preferences?

One method for examining any biological contributions to color preferences is to look for cultural differences. If underlying biology plays a strong role in color preferences, we would not expect to see many strong differences across cultures. However, this is exactly what we do see. Urban Polish residents showed a strong preference for shades of blue, while Papuan participants who have had very little contact with outsiders show a strong preference for red and yellow (Sorokowski, Sorokowska, & Witzel, 2014). Both groups, however, chose yellow-orange as their least favorite color.

In an interesting twist, however, Sorokowski et al. (2014) reported that the degree of difference between men and women in both cultures was very similar in spite of their different overall preferences. As shown in ● Figure 6.30, the closer a color was to blue, the more men liked it and women disliked it. The closer a color was to red, the more women liked it and men disliked it. This does not necessarily imply a biological basis for

the different preferences, but more research is necessary to identify the sources of these preferences.

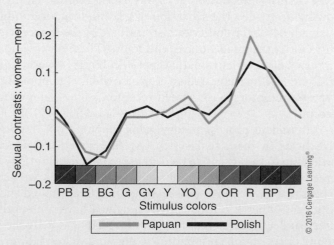

© 2016 Cengage Learning®

Figure 6.30 Sex Differences in Color Preference In spite of the overall preference for blue in Poland and red and yellow in Papua, the degree of difference between the sexes in color preference was very similar in both cultures. The closer a color was to blue, the more men preferred it. The closer a color was to red, the more women preferred it.

Original Image | Deuteranope Simulation

Courtesy of Laura Freberg

> ● **Figure 6.31** Looking Through the Eyes of a Dichromat This image shows your author and her husband as they appear to trichromats (left) and to dichromats (right) who are missing the medium (green) photopigment.

dichromacy Having eyes that contain two different cone photopigments.
monochromacy The ability to see in black and white only.
anomalous trichromacy A condition characterized by having three cone photopigments that respond to slightly different wavelengths than normal.
color contrast The fact that colors can look different depending on the surrounding colors.

COLOR DEFICIENCY Occasional errors occur in the genes that encode the cone photopigments. As a result, individuals with these genes show several kinds of atypical responses to color, known as color deficiency. The historical term *colorblindness* is somewhat misleading, as most of these individuals do see color, just somewhat differently than the majority of the population.

Dichromacy (having two cone photopigments) is the most common type of abnormality and results from a missing or abnormal cone pigment. Because genes for the red and green photopigments appear on the X chromosome, this type of dichromacy is sex-linked. Men are about 10 times more likely to experience this type of color deficiency than women (Hurvich, 1981). ● Figure 6.31 shows us what your author and her husband might look like to a dichromat.

There are very rare cases in which the blue photopigment is missing. The gene for the blue photopigment is located on chromosome 7 (Nathans, 1989), so these cases are not sex-linked and appear equally in males and females. Rarer still are cases of **monochromacy**. This condition occurs when a person has only one type of cone or a complete absence of cones. In either case, the person can't see color at all. Monty Roberts, who served as the inspiration for the film *The Horse Whisperer*, credits his unique ability to study animal motion and expression to his monochromacy (Roberts & Scanlan, 1999). Some individuals have three cone pigments, but their peak response occurs at slightly different wavelengths than is typical. This leads to a condition known as **anomalous trichromacy**. These individuals match colors in a slightly different way than most people, but they might not even know that they are unusual. Because of the process of x-inactivation (see Chapter 5), some mothers of anomalous trichromats might actually be tetrachromats (Jordan, Deeb, Bosten, & Mollon, 2010). These individuals match colors in a manner that would be predicted by their having four color photo pigments rather than three.

COLOR CONTRAST AND COLOR CONSTANCY Perception does not occur in a vacuum. In the case of **color contrast**, illustrated in ● Figure 6.32, colors can look very different depending on their context. Because of color contrast, Edwin Land (1959), the inventor of the Polaroid camera, could use red and green filters to give his photographs the appearance of a wide set of colors. Color contrast is primarily an effect of the opponency of color processing in the visual system.

© 2016 Cengage Learning®

> ● **Figure 6.32** Color Contrast Color contrast, or the differences in appearance when colors are viewed against different backgrounds, is a likely result of color opponency in the central nervous system (CNS). All letters in this image are really the same color.

Color constancy describes the fact that an object's colors do not appear to change much even as the light falling on that object changes. Your red sweater looks red outdoors at high noon, under indoor lights in the classroom, and on the way to the parking lot in twilight. Some of the color-constancy effect might be a result of adaptation. In any sensory process, adaptation occurs when prolonged stimulation reduces the response of neurons. In addition to adaptation, Semir Zeki (1983) has identified neurons in Area V4 of the visual cortex that might contribute to color constancy. When a green square was illuminated by white or red lights, the primary visual cortical cells of Zeki's monkeys responded differently. However, Zeki found cells in V4 that responded to green squares regardless of the light used to illuminate the squares. These cells could form the basis of higher-order color constancy.

The Life-Span Development of the Visual System

Although we can't ask young infants about what they can see, we can still establish the same types of contrast sensitivity functions (CSF) that we found earlier for adults and cats. Infants prefer to look at patterns rather than at uniform screens. We assume that if an infant looks at a grating longer than at a uniform circle, the infant must see a difference between the two. If we compare CSF curves for adults and for infants between the ages of one and three months, it becomes apparent that the infant cannot see fine detail at a distance (see ● Figure 6.33). In addition, the CSF curves show that the infant needs more contrast than an adult does to see. This probably relates to the preference most babies show for large, high-contrast, colorful objects.

As we age, predictable changes occur in our vision. In middle age, the lens accommodates more slowly to changes in focal distance. This condition is known as **presbyopia**, or "old sight." Older adults also have trouble responding quickly to changes in lighting, as when exiting a dark theater into the sunlight. The lens, which provides most of the focus of light onto the retina, continues to grow throughout the life span. As fibers are continually added to the structure of the lens, it takes on a yellow hue. Although this change in color provides more protection from ultraviolet rays that might otherwise harm the aging retina, the yellow lens will also distort the person's perception of blue and green. Aging is also associated with smaller pupils, probably due to the loss of elasticity in the muscles of the iris. Smaller pupils allow less light into the eye, negatively affecting the quality of vision.

Aging might have a negative effect on the cortical processing of visual information. Schmolesky, Wang, Pu, and Leventhal (2000) investigated the effects of aging on neurons responding to line orientation or motion in the primary visual cortex. In young monkeys, these researchers found that 90 percent of the measured neurons showed an orientation preference, whereas 70 percent showed a preference for

color constancy The concept that an object's color looks the same regardless of the type of light falling on the object.

presbyopia The reduced rate and extent of accommodation by the lens that results from aging.

| 1 month | 2 months | 3 months | adult |

© Felix Mizioznikov/Shutterstock.com

> ● **Figure 6.33** **The Development of Contrast Sensitivity** The infant cannot see the fine detail at a distance that the adult can see. Using the infant contrast sensitivity function (CSF), we can remove the spatial frequencies that the infant can't see. The resulting photographs provide insight into the visual world of young children.

a direction of movement. In aged monkeys, only 42 percent of the cells showed an orientation preference, and 25 percent showed a direction of movement preference. The aged neurons seemed to become less selective, firing at just about anything going on in the visual field.

Disorders of the Visual System

A variety of conditions can interfere with vision, ranging from the very mild and correctable to a complete loss of vision. Vision problems occur due to problems in the eye and retina as well as to central problems in the brain.

Amblyopia

Lazy eye, or **amblyopia**, occurs when one eye cannot focus on objects. If left untreated, the brain will learn to ignore the input from the less functional eye. Binocular depth perception will be permanently lost.

Cataracts

Cataracts result from clouding of the lens of the eye. Cataracts become more frequent with age. However, some ethnic populations, including Arabs and Sephardic Jews, have a high rate of cataracts at birth. Severe cataracts are usually treated by surgically removing the clouded lens. Following surgery, the person requires extremely strong glasses or the implant of an artificial lens. Removal of a lens can also negatively influence color vision. Following removal of a lens for cataracts, French impressionist painter Claude Monet saw nearly everything as blue.

Visual Acuity Problems

Some common visual acuity problems are illustrated in ● Figure 6.34. If the eyeball is slightly elongated, the image focused by the lens will fall short of the retina. This condition is known as **myopia**, or nearsightedness. The person can see well when looking at close objects, but the ability to see objects in the distance is impaired. If the eyeball is too short, the best image would be focused somewhere behind the retina. This condition is **hyperopia**, or farsightedness. Distance vision will be quite good, but close objects, including letters on the pages of books or newspapers, will be blurry. Unlike

amblyopia A condition also known as lazy eye, in which one eye does not track visual stimuli.
cataracts Clouding of the lens.
myopia An abnormal condition in which the eyeball is too long; also known as nearsightedness.
hyperopia An acuity problem resulting from a short eyeball; also known as farsightedness.

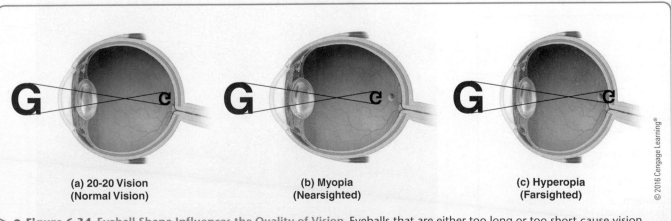

(a) 20-20 Vision
(Normal Vision)

(b) Myopia
(Nearsighted)

(c) Hyperopia
(Farsighted)

© 2016 Cengage Learning®

> ● **Figure 6.34 Eyeball Shape Influences the Quality of Vision** Eyeballs that are either too long or too short cause vision problems, because the focused image falls either short of the retina or beyond the retina.

myopia and hyperopia, **astigmatism** does not result from eyeball length. Instead, this condition results from unevenness in the shape of the cornea. These vision problems are typically addressed by the use of corrective lenses (eyeglasses or contact lenses) or laser surgery, which reshapes the cornea.

Blindness

Blindness, or the total loss of vision, can occur as a result of damage at many levels. Damage to the eye or optic nerves could prevent input to normally functioning visual cortical areas. Macular degeneration, in which the cells of the macula begin to die, is one of the leading causes of blindness among older adults. Macular degeneration results in the loss of central vision and a reduction in contrast sensitivity. Although the exact causes of macular degeneration are not known, smoking, high blood pressure, obesity, and exposure to short-wave light (as in many artificial lights) are believed to interact with genetic vulnerabilities.

Advances in treatment might make restoration of vision in some of these cases possible. Research with mice indicates that it may be possible to restore some vision through transplantation of rod precursor cells (Pearson et al., 2012). Gene therapy has produced promising results in six cases of a rare type of blindness (Huckfeldt & Bennett, 2014).

Other individuals are blind due to cortical damage. When the striate cortex is damaged, the patient has a **scotoma**, or region of blindness, that will depend on the exact location and amount of cortical damage (see ● Figure 6.35). These patients often demonstrate the very odd phenomenon of **blindsight** (Cowey & Stoerig, 1991). Although they claim they cannot see lights that are flashed in the area of their scotoma, these patients can point on command to the source of the light. It is likely that visual input to the extrastriate cortex, which does not result in conscious awareness of light, is responsible for these unusual effects (Silvanto, 2008). These findings suggest that processing by striate cortex is essential for conscious awareness of visual stimuli.

● **Figure 6.35** Scotoma Damage to the occipital cortex through stroke or traumatic brain injury produces an area where vision is poor or missing completely. *Scotoma* is Greek for "darkness."

© Susan Law Cain/Shutterstock.com

astigmatism A distortion of vision caused by the shape of the cornea.

scotoma An area in the visual field that can't be seen, usually due to central damage by stroke or other brain injury.

blindsight An abnormal condition in which parts of the visual field are not consciously perceived but can be subconsciously perceived by extrastriate cortex.

••• Building Better
HEALTH

DOES EATING CARROTS REALLY HELP YOUR VISION?

Your mother may have encouraged you to eat carrots "for your eyes," and as usual, mother is correct in suggesting that diet can be important to eye health. The American Optometric Association (2014) has listed a number of nutrients that reduce the risks of certain eye diseases, including the formation of cataracts and macular degeneration.

Lutien and zeaxanthin are found in green leafy vegetables and eggs. Consumption of these substances is negatively correlated with risk for cataracts and macular degeneration. Vitamin C from fruits and vegetables lowers cataract risk and can slow the progression of

other types of vision loss. Vitamin E, found in nuts, fortified cereals, and sweet potatoes, protects the eye from damage caused by free radicals. Omega-3 fatty acids, found in some fish, ensure normal development of the eye and help maintain retinal function. Finally, zinc participates in the movement of vitamin A from the liver to the retina. Zinc is usually found in very high concentrations in the eye, and deficits of zinc can cause visual problems.

Diet is not the only contributing factor to maintaining vision into older adulthood, but it can definitely be a good starting place.

Visual Agnosias

Visual agnosias are disorders in which a person can see a stimulus but has difficulty recognizing what is seen. The word *agnosia* comes from the Greek for "without knowledge." Responding to the image of a carrot, one patient with a visual agnosia said, "I have not the glimmerings of an idea. The bottom point seems solid and the other bits are feathery. It does not seem logical unless it is some sort of brush" (Humphreys & Riddoch, 1987, p. 59). The patient is attending to the major features of the stimulus (pointy end, leafy green part) but can't recognize the object.

In **prosopagnosia**, vision is retained, but the person cannot recognize the faces of people he or she knows (Barton, 2003). Patients with prosopagnosia can tell one face apart from another and can tell the gender of the people from pictures of their faces. In spite of these skills, these patients can't recognize faces as people they know, not even their own image in the mirror. As we mentioned earlier, the fusiform face area (FFA) is probably responsible for facial recognition. Prosopagnosia is usually associated with damage to this area due to stroke or other accidents, although other cases can run in families, indicating a genetic basis (Kennerknecht et al., 2006).

INTERIM SUMMARY 6.3

‖ Summary Table: Examples of Major Visual Disorders

Disorder	Symptoms	Causal Factors	Treatment
Cataracts	Mild blockage of light to complete blindness; distortion of color vision	Clouding of the lens	Surgical removal of the lens
Myopia (nearsightedness)	Difficulty seeing distant objects	Elongation of the eyeball	Corrective lenses, laser surgery
Hyperopia (farsightedness)	Difficulty seeing close objects, reading	Shortening of the eyeball	Corrective lenses, laser surgery

visual agnosia A disorder in which a person can see a stimulus but cannot identify what is seen.
prosopagnosia The inability to recognize known faces.

Disorder	Symptoms	Causal Factors	Treatment
Astigmatism	Difficulty seeing distant objects	Uneven cornea shape	Corrective lenses, laser surgery
Scotoma	Regions of blindness in visual field	Stroke, physical injury to visual cortex	None
Prosopagnosia	Inability to recognize familiar faces	Damage to the fusiform gyrus	None

‖ Summary Points

1. The cortex constructs a visual reality through either hierarchical processing or a basic mathematical analysis of contrast and frequencies. **(LO4)**

2. Depth perception results from monocular and binocular cues. **(LO4)**

3. The trichromatic theory of color perception is based on the fact that we have three types of cone photopigments that respond differentially to lights of different wavelengths. Our visual system also shows a pattern of red–green and blue–yellow opponency. **(LO4)**

4. Infants see less fine detail at a distance than adults do. Older adults experience less visual quality due to presbyopia, slow adaptation to changes in light, yellowing of the lens, smaller pupils, and less selectivity in cortical responses to visual input. **(LO5)**

5. Many conditions can interfere with vision, either at the level of the eye or the level of the brain. **(LO6)**

‖ Review Questions

1. How can contrast sensitivity functions (CSF) tell us what an organism can see?

2. What do cases of color deficiency teach us about the nature of color vision?

Chapter Review

THOUGHT QUESTIONS

1. If you had to lose either your scotopic or photopic vision, which would you choose to give up and why? What would be the consequences of your choice?
2. If increasing numbers of ultraviolet rays reaching the earth favor the evolution of a more yellow lens, what effect might this have on the colors we perceive?
3. Currently, very few states regularly test the vision of senior drivers. Based on your knowledge of the changes in vision typical of aging, what types of tests would you recommend?

KEY TERMS

amacrine cell (p. 184)
attention (p. 176)
bipolar cell (p. 184)
central vision (p. 183)
color constancy (p. 208)
color contrast (p. 207)
complex cortical cell (p. 195)
cone (p. 185)
contrast sensitivity function (CSF) (p. 201)
cornea (p. 180)
cortical module (p. 197)
cytochrome oxidase blob (p. 197)
dark current (p. 186)
dichromacy (p. 207)
dorsal stream (p. 198)
fovea (p. 183)

fusiform face area (FFA) (p. 199)
horizontal cell (p. 184)
hypercolumn (p. 197)
iris (p. 181)
lateral geniculate nucleus (LGN) (p. 194)
lateral inhibition (p. 190)
lens (p. 181)
ocular dominance column (p. 197)
opponent process theory (p. 205)
optic chiasm (p. 192)
optic disk (p. 182)
optic nerve (p. 182)
optic tracts (p. 192)
orientation column (p. 198)
perception (p. 176)
peripheral vision (p. 183)

photopic vision (p. 185)
photopigment (p. 185)
photoreceptor (p. 182)
pupil (p. 181)
receptive field (p. 189)
retina (p. 182)
rod (p. 185)
sclera (p. 180)
scotopic vision (p. 185)
sensation (p. 176)
simple cortical cell (p. 195)
striate cortex (p. 195)
transduction (p. 000)
trichromatic theory (p. 205)
ventral stream (p. 198)
vitreous chamber (p. 182)

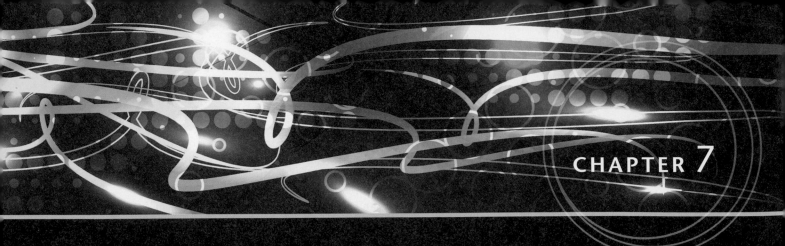

CHAPTER 7

Nonvisual Sensation and Perception

LEARNING OBJECTIVES

LO1 Identify the major features of sound as a stimulus.

LO2 Trace the process of hearing from the outer ear to the cerebral cortex.

LO3 Explain the perception of pitch, loudness, and the location of sounds.

LO4 Describe the structures and functions of systems responsible for the perception of body position and movement, touch, and pain.

LO5 Describe the structures and pathways responsible for olfaction and taste.

CHAPTER OUTLINE

Audition
  Sound as a Stimulus
  The Structure and Function of the Auditory System
  Auditory Perception
  Hearing Disorders
Interim Summary 7.1
The Body Senses
  The Vestibular System
  Touch
  Pain
Interim Summary 7.2
The Chemical Senses
  Olfaction
  Gustation
Interim Summary 7.3

BUILDING BETTER HEALTH: Earbuds and Hearing Loss

THINKING ETHICALLY: Cochlear Prosthetics and Deaf Culture

CONNECTING TO RESEARCH: Phantom Limbs, Mirrors, and Longer Noses

BEHAVIORAL NEUROSCIENCE GOES TO WORK: What Is a Perfumer?

Audition

When Helen Keller, who was both blind and deaf, was asked which disability affected her the most, she replied that blindness separates a person from things, whereas deafness separates a person from people. In addition to processing the speech of others, we use the sense of **audition**, or hearing, to identify objects in the environment and to determine where objects are in relation to our bodies.

Ours is a uniquely human auditory world (see ● Figure 7.1). Just as we can see a broad but limited range of the electromagnetic radiation spectrum, we can also hear a wide but limited range of sound. Your dog begins howling seconds before you hear the ambulance siren, because the dog's hearing is better than yours for these high-pitched sounds. Neither you nor your dog is likely to hear the even higher pitched vocalizations that bats use to locate food and navigate (see ● Figure 7.1) (Griffin, 1959).

Sound as a Stimulus

You may have heard the famous riddle by the philosopher George Berkeley, "If a tree falls in the forest and nobody is around to hear it, does it make a sound?" The neuroscientist's answer to this question is both yes and no. The answer is yes if we are asking whether the falling tree produces a physical sound stimulus, but the answer is no if we're talking about sound as result of the perceptual experience of hearing.

Sound as a physical stimulus begins with the movement of an object. Movement sets off waves of vibration in the form of miniature collisions between adjacent molecules that produce outwardly moving bands of high and low pressure, much like ripples in a pond (see ● Figure 7.2). Because sound waves require this jostling between molecules, sound cannot occur in a vacuum such as outer space. Those explosions we enjoy in Star Wars films may be good entertainment, but they are not great science.

audition The sense of hearing.

For humans, the medium that carries sound is usually air, but we can also sense sounds that travel through liquids and solids. Like light, sound interacts with the

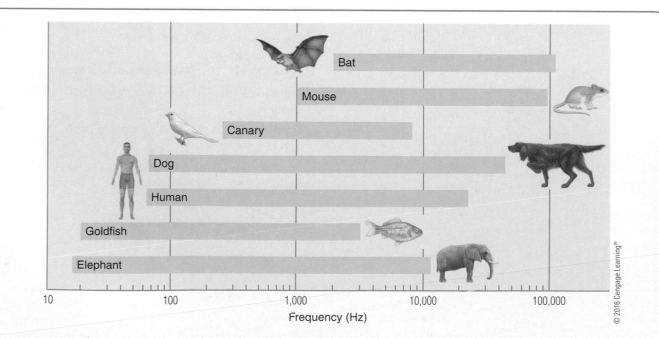

● **Figure 7.1** **The Auditory World Differs Across Species** This figure illustrates the range of frequencies that fall within the sensory capacities of several species, including humans.

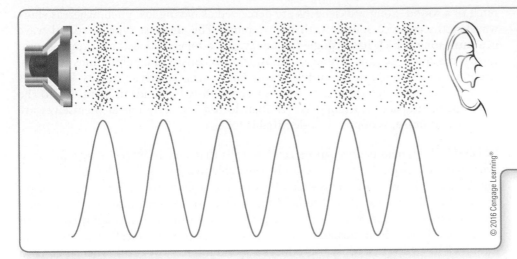

● **Figure 7.2** Sound Results from Collisions of Molecules Speakers produce alternating bands of high and low air pressure that move through the air like ripples in a pond. Sound waves travel through air at a rate of 340 meters (1,115.5 feet) per second.

© 2016 Cengage Learning®

environment as it travels from its source to the perceiver. Fabrics absorb sound waves and can be helpful in reducing noise. Sounds reflected from surfaces are used by a number of species, like bats, for echolocation. Although humans are not the best at using echolocation, we can improve with practice.

As shown in Table 7.1, sound energy, like electromagnetic energy, can be described in the form of waves. The height, or **amplitude**, of a wave, indicates the amount of vibration produced by the sound, which in turn is perceived as loudness by the listener. Low-amplitude waves are characteristic of soft sounds, and high-amplitude waves are perceived as loud. The **frequency** of the wave, or the number of cycles per unit of time, indicates wavelength. Wavelength usually corresponds to the perceived

amplitude The height of a wave; in audition, amplitude is perceived as loudness.
frequency The number of cycles of a periodic wave per unit of time; in audition, frequency is perceived as pitch.

TABLE 7.1 | Sounds Vary Along the Dimensions of Amplitude, Frequency, and Complexity

Wave Characteristic	Perception of Characteristic	Examples	
Amplitude (intensity)—Measures the height of the wave.	Loudness	High-amplitude waves are perceived as loud sounds.	Low-amplitude waves are perceived as soft sounds.
Frequency (wavelength)—Measures the number of wave cycles per unit of time.	Pitch	Low-frequency waves are perceived as low-pitched sounds.	High-frequency waves are perceived as high-pitched sounds.
Timbre (complexity)—The distinct quality or uniqueness of a sound.	The "color" or "quality" of tones having equal pitch and loudness.	Pure tones have a single frequency.	Complex tones are made up of several frequencies.

pitch of a sound. Long wavelengths are perceived as having low pitch, whereas short wavelengths produce sounds with higher pitch. The simplest type of sound wave is a **pure tone**, which has a single frequency like a tone produced by a tuning fork. Pure tones rarely exist in nature, and most sounds consist of combinations of waves. Complex tones combining multiple waves have a characteristic quality known as **timbre**. The same note played by a piano or violin will sound different due to the instruments' impact on timbre. Waves that do not regularly repeat themselves are perceived as **noise**, as opposed to identifiable tones.

INTENSITY Human beings can perceive sounds that vary in intensity by a factor of over 10 billion, from the quietest sounds detectable to a jet engine at takeoff. To manage such a wide range of intensities, a logarithmic scale of sound intensity based on the **decibel** (dB) is used. The threshold for hearing, or the least intense sound that a human can hear at least 50 percent of the time, is set at 0 dB. This is roughly equivalent to the sound made by a mosquito flying three meters (about 10 feet) away from you. As shown in Table 7.2, a whisper produces a sound intensity of 20 dB, whereas an iPod or iPhone turned up to maximum loudness can reach 120 dB. At 130 dB, we experience pain. This is a useful warning because exposure to sounds at this level of intensity might permanently damage our hearing.

FREQUENCY Frequency refers to the number of cycles per unit of time, or the wavelength, of a sound stimulus. The unit used to measure the frequency of sound is the **hertz (Hz)**. A 500 Hz sound completes 500 cycles in one second.

Human hearing ranges from approximately 20 Hz to 20,000 Hz (see ● Figure 7.1). **Infrasound** refers to frequencies below the range of human hearing. Many animals, including elephants and marine mammals, use infrasound for communication. **Ultrasound** refers to stimuli with frequencies beyond the upper range of human hearing. Ultrasound waves are used to clean objects or to produce noninvasive images for medical purposes.

TABLE 7.2 | Intensity Levels of Common Sounds

Source of Sound	Intensity Level
Threshold of hearing (TOH)	0 dB
Rustling leaves	10 dB
Whisper	20 dB
Normal conversation	60 dB
Busy street traffic	70 dB
Vacuum cleaner	80 dB
Water at the foot of Niagara Falls	90 dB
Power lawn mower	100 dB
Front rows of rock concert	110 dB
Propeller plane at takeoff	120 dB
Threshold of pain (e.g., machine-gun fire)	130 dB
Military jet at takeoff	140 dB
Instant perforation of eardrum	160 dB

pure tone Sound characterized by a single frequency.

timbre Distinct quality of a sound due to combinations of frequencies.

noise Unsystematic combinations of sound waves.

decibel (dB) A unit used to express a difference in intensity between two sounds, equal to 20 times the common logarithm of the ratio of the two levels.

hertz (Hz) A unit of sound frequency equal to one cycle per second.

infrasound Sound at frequencies below the range of human hearing, or lower than about 20 Hz.

ultrasound Sound at frequencies above the range of human hearing, or higher than about 20,000 Hz.

The Structure and Function of the Auditory System

The components that make up the ear are generally divided into three parts: the outer, middle, and inner ear.

THE OUTER EAR The major structures of the ear are illustrated in ● Figure 7.3. The outer ear consists of the structures visible outside the body: the pinna and the auditory canal. The **pinna** serves to collect and focus sounds, just like a funnel. The pinna also plays an important role in locating the source of sound. Movement of the pinna allows some species to further localize sound or to indicate emotional states, as when a dog puts its ears back while snarling. Sound collected by the pinna is channeled through the **auditory canal**, a tube-shaped structure about 3 cm long and about 7 mm wide.

THE MIDDLE EAR The **tympanic membrane**, or eardrum, forms the boundary between the outer ear and middle ear. The boundary between the middle ear and inner ear is formed by another membrane, the **oval window**.

pinna The visible part of the outer ear.
auditory canal A tube-shaped structure in the outer ear that leads to the tympanic membrane.
tympanic membrane The membrane separating the outer and middle ears; also known as the eardrum.
oval window The membrane separating the middle and inner ears.

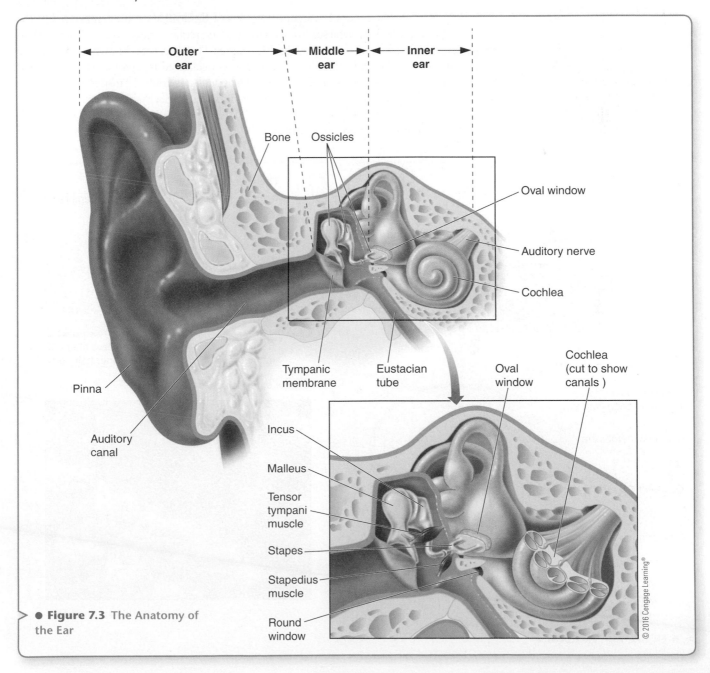

● **Figure 7.3** The Anatomy of the Ear

© 2016 Cengage Learning®

The three **ossicles** bridging the middle ear are the malleus (hammer), incus (anvil), and stapes (stirrup). Each of these tiny bones is about the size of a single letter of print in this text. The purpose of these bones is to transfer sound energy from the outside air to the fluid in the inner ear without losing too much of it. As you may have noticed when swimming, sounds waves originating in air lose much of their energy when they enter the water. If a friend calls out to you while you're under water, the sound is not very clear. The ear faces a similar problem, as sound energy must travel through the air of the outer and middle ears to the fluid of the inner ear.

The middle ear solves this transfer problem in two ways. First, the connections between the ossicles are hinged, which creates a lever action that increases the force of the vibration that the stapes bone delivers to the oval window. Second, force applied to the much smaller oval window produces much more pressure than the same force applied to the larger tympanic membrane. With both force and pressure increased at the oval window, the ear can recover about 23 dB of the 30 dB that would otherwise be lost when sound is transferred from the air in the middle ear to the fluid in the inner ear (Evans, 1982).

THE INNER EAR The inner ear contains two sets of fluid-filled cavities embedded in the temporal bone of the skull. One set, known as the semicircular canals, is part of the vestibular system, which will be discussed later in this chapter. The other set is known as the **cochlea** ("snail" in Greek). The fluid-filled cochlea contains specialized receptor cells that respond to the vibrations transmitted to the inner ear. The cochlea is about 32 mm long and 2 mm in diameter. When rolled up like a snail shell, the human cochlea is about the size of a pea.

The cochlea is divided into three parallel chambers, illustrated in ● Figure 7.4. Two of the chambers, the **vestibular canal** and the **tympanic canal**, are connected

ossicles The bones that span the middle ear, including the malleus, incus, and stapes.
cochlea The fluid-filled structure of the inner ear containing auditory receptors.
vestibular canal The upper chamber of the cochlea.
tympanic canal The lower chamber of the cochlea.

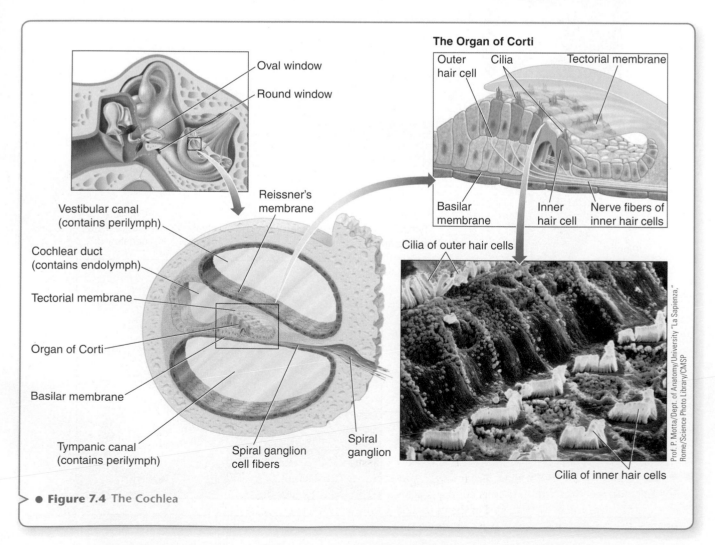

● **Figure 7.4** The Cochlea

to each other near the **apex**, which is the part of the cochlea most distant from the oval window. These two chambers contain a fluid known as **perilymph**, which is similar to cerebrospinal fluid (see Chapter 2). The third chamber, the **cochlear duct**, contains a very different type of fluid, known as **endolymph**. The endolymph is rich in potassium and low in sodium. The fluids (and chambers) are separated by two membranes. **Reissner's membrane** separates the vestibular canal and the cochlear duct. The **basilar membrane** separates the tympanic canal and the cochlear duct.

At the base of the cochlea, at the boundary between the middle and inner ears, the oval window covers the vestibular canal. The tympanic canal is covered by another membrane, known as the **round window**. Because the vestibular and tympanic canals are connected, pressure applied to the oval window by the stapes travels around the apex through the perilymph and pushes the round window out into the middle ear.

Within the cochlear duct is a specialized structure known as the **organ of Corti**, which is responsible for translating vibrations in the inner ear into neural messages. The organ of Corti, consisting of rows of hair cells, rests on the basilar membrane. Over the top of the hair cells, and actually attached to some of them, is the **tectorial (roof) membrane**. The tectorial membrane is attached to the cochlear duct at only one side and can move independently from the basilar membrane.

Several structural features of the basilar membrane are relevant to its response to sound. The membrane is about five times wider at its apex (farthest from the oval window) than at its base (next to the oval window). In addition, the basilar membrane is about 100 times stiffer at its base than at its apex. These structural differences are similar to the range of size and flexibility found in the different strings of a guitar. When vibration produces pressure changes within the cochlea, the basilar membrane responds with a wavelike motion, similar to the motion of a rope or whip that is snapped. It will move less at the stiff, smaller end near the base than at the wide, floppy end at the apex. As shown in ● Figure 7.5, high-frequency sounds will cause a peak vibration of the basilar membrane near its base, whereas low-frequency sounds will cause a peak vibration closer to its apex.

The movement of the basilar membrane is sensed by the hair cells attached to the organ of Corti. Out of the approximately 15,500 hair cells in each human inner ear, about 3,500 of them are known as **inner hair cells**, which are the actual auditory receptors. The inner hair cells are located near the connection between the tectorial membrane and cochlear duct. The remaining 12,000 hair cells are known as **outer hair cells**, which appear to amplify sound. Both types of cells have hairlike **cilia** extending from their tops. Although there are many more outer hair cells in the ear, only 5 percent of the **auditory nerve (cranial nerve VIII)** fibers connect with outer hair cells. The remaining 95 percent of auditory nerve fibers connect with the inner hair cells.

● Figure 7.6 shows how movement of the cilia back and forth within the endolymph alternately hyperpolarizes and depolarizes the hair cells away from their resting potential of $-70\,\text{mV}$. The amount of movement needed to produce a response in the hair cells is quite small. If cilia were the size of the Eiffel Tower in Paris, the movement required to produce a response would equate to only $1\,\text{cm}$ (about 0.4 inches; Hudspeth, 1983). The depolarization and hyperpolarization of the hair cells result from the opening and closing of mechanically gated potassium channels located in the tips of the cilia. When all of the cilia are straight up, as in a completely quiet environment, the channels are partially open. Small amounts of potassium will enter the cell. When the cilia bend one way, tension on the filaments connecting adjacent cilia opens the channels further, and greater amounts of potassium will enter the cell. Bending the cilia in the opposite direction releases the tension on the filaments, closing the channels.

Normally, when potassium channels are opened, potassium leaves a neuron, causing hyperpolarization (see Chapter 3). However, unlike most extracellular fluid, the endolymph surrounding the hair cells contains a higher concentration of potassium than is found in the intracellular fluid of the hair cells. Consequently, when potassium channels in hair cells open, potassium will move into the relatively negative internal

apex The part of the cochlea most distant from the oval window.

perilymph Fluid found in the vestibular and tympanic canals of the inner ear.

cochlear duct The middle of three chambers of the cochlea.

endolymph The fluid found in the cochlear duct.

reissner's membrane A membrane that separates the vestibular canal and cochlear duct.

round window A membrane covering the end of the tympanic canal.

organ of Corti A structure within the cochlear duct responsible for transducing vibrations in the inner ear into action potentials.

tectorial (roof) membrane A membrane that covers the organ of Corti.

inner hair cells Auditory receptor cells located near the junction of the tectorial membrane and cochlear duct.

outer hair cells Auditory receptor cells located on the Organ of Corti that amplify sound.

cilia Microscopic hair-like projections from a cell.

basilar membrane A structure in the cochlea that separates the tympanic canal and the cochlear duct.

auditory nerve (cranial nerve VIII) The nerve that makes contact with the hair cells of the cochlea; cranial nerve VIII.

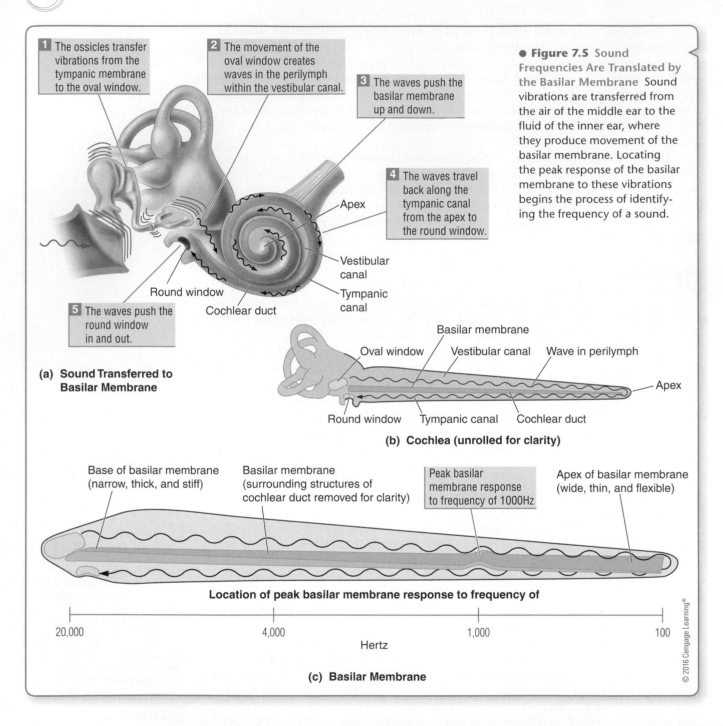

1 The ossicles transfer vibrations from the tympanic membrane to the oval window.

2 The movement of the oval window creates waves in the perilymph within the vestibular canal.

3 The waves push the basilar membrane up and down.

4 The waves travel back along the tympanic canal from the apex to the round window.

5 The waves push the round window in and out.

Apex

Vestibular canal

Tympanic canal

Round window

Cochlear duct

(a) Sound Transferred to Basilar Membrane

● Figure 7.5 Sound Frequencies Are Translated by the Basilar Membrane Sound vibrations are transferred from the air of the middle ear to the fluid of the inner ear, where they produce movement of the basilar membrane. Locating the peak response of the basilar membrane to these vibrations begins the process of identifying the frequency of a sound.

Basilar membrane

Oval window   Vestibular canal   Wave in perilymph

Apex

Round window   Tympanic canal   Cochlear duct

(b) Cochlea (unrolled for clarity)

Base of basilar membrane (narrow, thick, and stiff)

Basilar membrane (surrounding structures of cochlear duct removed for clarity)

Peak basilar membrane response to frequency of 1000Hz

Apex of basilar membrane (wide, thin, and flexible)

Location of peak basilar membrane response to frequency of

20,000   4,000   1,000   100

Hertz

(c) Basilar Membrane

© 2016 Cengage Learning®

environment of the cell due to both diffusion and electrostatic pressure. Potassium's positive charge depolarizes the hair cell, leading to the opening of voltage-dependent calcium channels and neurochemical release. Most hair cells release the excitatory neurochemical glutamate.

CENTRAL AUDITORY PATHWAYS As shown in ● Figure 7.7, **spiral ganglion neurons,** which are bipolar in structure, connect the hair cells of the cochlea with the brain. Cell bodies of the spiral ganglion neurons are located in the cochlea. One set of their fibers makes contact with the hair cells. The other set projects to the dorsal and ventral cochlear nuclei of the medulla as part of the auditory nerve (cranial nerve VIII). Input from both cochlear nuclei eventually reaches the inferior colliculus of the midbrain. However, axons from the ventral cochlear nuclei first synapse in the

spiral ganglion neuron Bipolar neuron found in the inner ear whose axons form the auditory nerve.

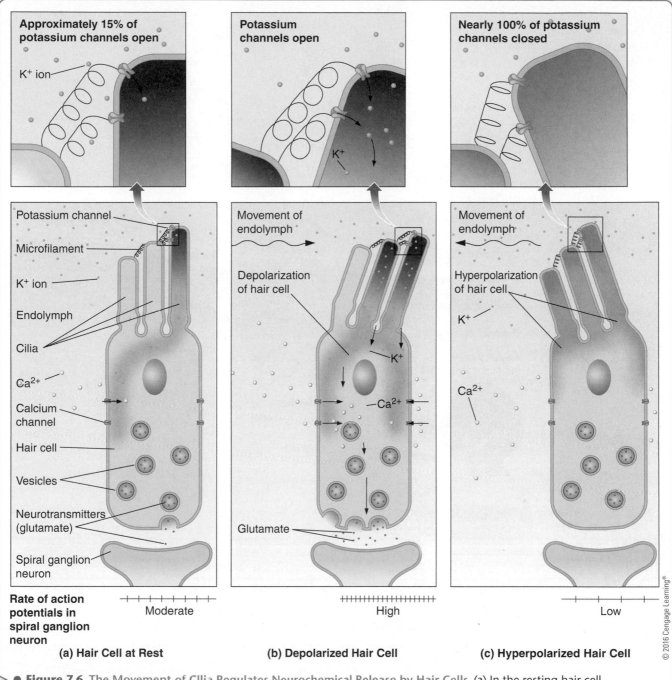

Approximately 15% of potassium channels open

K$^+$ ion

Potassium channels open

K$^+$

Nearly 100% of potassium channels closed

Potassium channel

Microfilament

K$^+$ ion

Endolymph

Cilia

Ca^{2+}

Calcium channel

Hair cell

Vesicles

Neurotransmitters (glutamate)

Spiral ganglion neuron

Movement of endolymph

Depolarization of hair cell

K$^+$

Ca^{2+}

Glutamate

Movement of endolymph

Hyperpolarization of hair cell

K$^+$

Ca^{2+}

Rate of action potentials in spiral ganglion neuron

Moderate

High

Low

(a) Hair Cell at Rest

(b) Depolarized Hair Cell

(c) Hyperpolarized Hair Cell

© 2016 Cengage Learning®

● **Figure 7.6** The Movement of Cilia Regulates Neurochemical Release by Hair Cells (a) In the resting hair cell, approximately 15 percent of the potassium (K$^+$) channels are open. The resulting influx of K$^+$ slightly depolarizes the cell, leading to the opening of calcium (Ca^{2+}) channels and the release of relatively small amounts of glutamate onto spiral ganglion neurons. Consequently, the spiral ganglion neurons form action potentials at a moderate rate. (b) When the moving endolymph displaces the cilia of the hair cell toward their tallest member, many more K$^+$ channels open. A greater influx of Ca^{2+} occurs, followed by an increase in the amount of glutamate released by the hair cell and a higher rate of action potentials in the spiral ganglion neurons. (c) When the moving endolymph displaces the cilia of the hair cell toward their shortest member, the K$^+$ channels close, and the cell hyperpolarizes. Less Ca^{2+} enters the cell, fewer molecules of glutamate are released, and the rate of action potentials in the spiral ganglion neurons is reduced.

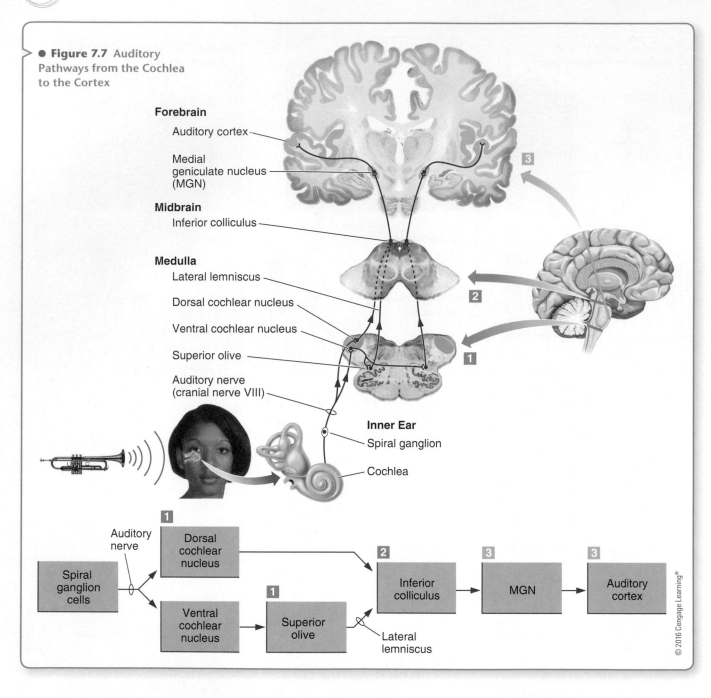

● **Figure 7.7** Auditory Pathways from the Cochlea to the Cortex

superior olive in the pons, which in turn forms connections via a pathway known as the lateral lemniscus with the inferior colliculus. Neurons from the inferior colliculus project to the **medial geniculate nucleus (MGN)** of the thalamus. In addition to auditory information, the MGN also receives input from the reticular formation of the brainstem. This input adjusts hearing sensitivity based on the organism's state of arousal. The MGN in turn projects to the primary auditory cortex located in the temporal lobe.

THE AUDITORY CORTEX **Primary auditory cortex,** also known as A1, is located in the temporal lobe, just below the lateral sulcus (see ● Figure 7.8).

Primary auditory cortex is organized in columns that respond to single frequencies. Lower frequencies produce a response in columns located rostrally in A1, whereas higher frequencies produce a response in columns located in the more caudal portions of the area. In some columns, input received by both ears produces

medial geniculate nucleus (MGN) Nucleus of the thalamus that receives auditory input.

primary auditory cortex (A1) Cortex located just below the lateral fissure in the temporal lobe that provides the initial cortical processing of auditory information.

a stronger response than input received by a single ear. In other columns, the opposite holds true: input received from a single ear produces a stronger response than input received by both ears. Other neurons within A1 respond to differences in intensity.

Surrounding A1 are areas known collectively as **secondary auditory cortex**. These areas appear to be activated by more complex types of stimuli such as clicks, general bursts of noise, and sounds with particular frequency patterns. Similar to observations in our discussion of vision, separate pathways originating in these areas process the quality of a sound ("what") and its location ("where") (Rauschecker, 2011; Rauschecker & Tian, 2000).

Auditory Perception

Now that we have an understanding of the structures involved with audition, we can turn our attention to the perception of pitch, loudness, and the localization of sounds.

PITCH PERCEPTION We associate pitch (the high or low quality of a sound) with frequency, although that is an overly simplistic view. Pitch can vary due to factors other than frequency, such as the intensity or context of a stimulus. For example, listeners perceive a bigger increase in pitch when comparing tones of 500 Hz and 1,000 Hz than they do when comparing tones of 3,000 Hz and 3,500 Hz , although the difference in frequency is the same in both cases.

Most frequencies are systematically encoded by the auditory system through **tonotopic organization**, which describes the fact that neurons responding to one frequency are located next to neurons responding to similar frequencies. Tonotopic organization is found throughout the auditory system, from the basilar membrane up through primary auditory cortex.

As a result of this tonotopic organization, one cue for assessing the frequency of a sound is the location of active neurons. Georg von Békésy's **place theory** explains the tonotopic organization of the basilar membrane. According to this theory, the peak of the wave traveling along the length of the basilar membrane is correlated with a sound's frequency. Place theory works well for sounds above 4,000 Hz. Below frequencies of 4,000 Hz, the response of the basilar membrane does not allow for precise localization. In these cases, **temporal theory**, in which patterns of neural firing match the actual frequency of a sound, provides a better model than place theory for the processing of sound.

LOUDNESS PERCEPTION Although the decibel level of a sound wave and its perceived loudness are related, they are not the same thing. Decibels describe the physical qualities of the sound stimulus, whereas loudness is the human perception of that stimulus. The perception of loudness does not change at the same rate as the decibels do. Loudness doubles with each 10 dB increase in stimulus intensity (Stevens, 1960). In other words, a stimulus that is 10 dB (or ten times) greater than another is perceived as only twice as loud.

Our ability to detect loudness varies with the frequency of a sound. By allowing participants to adjust the intensity of different tones until they sound equally loud, we can plot functions known as equal loudness contours (see ● Figure 7.9). To construct these curves, a 1,000 Hz tone (just above B5 or key 63 on a piano) is presented as a model. The 40 dB curve indicates how loud tones of other frequencies must be to be perceived as being as loud as the 40 dB 1,000 Hz comparison tone. Low frequencies are usually perceived as quieter than high frequencies at the same level of intensity. At very high intensities of 80 to 100 dB, you can see that all frequencies are perceived as being nearly equally loud.

Auditory neurons can respond to higher sound amplitudes by increasing their rate of response. However, the range of sound amplitudes we can hear is too broad to be completely encoded in this manner. Normally, a single neuron can respond to a range of about 40 dB, whereas at some frequencies, humans can perceive a range of

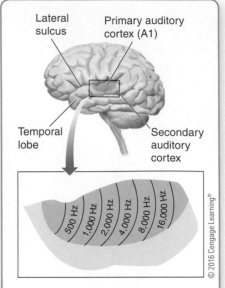

● **Figure 7.8** Tonotopic Organization Is Maintained by the Auditory Cortex Neurons responding to lower frequencies are located in the rostral portions of A1, and those responding to higher frequencies are located in the more caudal portions.

secondary auditory cortex Areas surrounding A1 in the temporal lobe that process complex sound stimuli.

tonotopic organization Neurons responding to one frequency are located next to neurons responding to similar frequencies.

place theory The peak response of the basilar membrane is correlated with a sound's frequency.

temporal theory For frequencies below 4000 Hz, the pattern of neural firing matches the frequency of a sound.

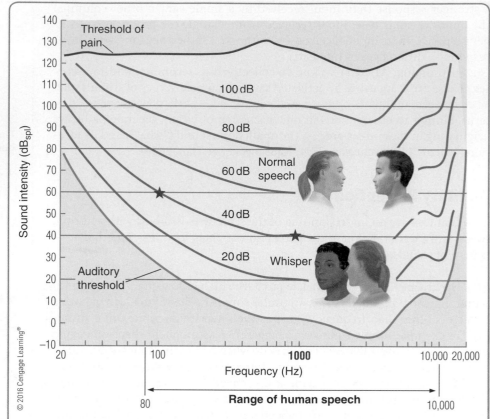

● **Figure 7.9** Equal Loudness Contours Perceived loudness is not the same thing as sound intensity, measured in dB and represented by the horizontal lines in this graph. Each curve in this graph represents the sound intensity (dB) at which tones of each frequency match the perceived loudness of a model 1,000 Hz tone at 40 dB. The red stars indicate that a 100 Hz tone at 60 dB sounds about as loud as a 1,000 Hz at 40 dB, because they fall along the same line. Sensitivity is best for sounds having the frequencies typical of speech, and rises on either side. This means that sounds with frequencies outside the range of speech must have more intensity to be perceived as well as speech sounds. At high levels of sound intensity, the curves flatten because all frequencies are perceived as being nearly equally loud.

130 dB. Although a single neuron might have a limited range of 40 dB, a population of neurons with different ranges can provide the coverage we require. In addition, although auditory neurons have a preferred frequency to which they respond, they will in fact respond to similar frequencies if amplitude is high enough. The recruitment of these additional neurons contributes to our perception of loudness.

Sounds that last longer are usually perceived as louder. This is due to temporal integration, or an addition of neural responses over time. In audition, temporal integration occurs for 100 to 200 milliseconds (msec). A tone lasting 50 msec will be perceived as softer than a tone with the same frequency and amplitude that lasts 300 msec. Tones lasting more than 300 msec, however, will not sound louder than the 300 msec tone.

LOCALIZATION OF SOUND One of our primary means of localizing sound in the horizontal plane (in front, behind, and to the side) is a comparison of the arrival times of sounds at each ear. The differences in arrival time are quite small, between 0 msec for sounds that are either straight ahead or behind you to 0.6 msec for sounds coming from a point perpendicular to your head on either side (see ● Figure 7.10). Because arrival times from sounds immediately in front or behind you are identical, these sounds are very difficult to localize accurately.

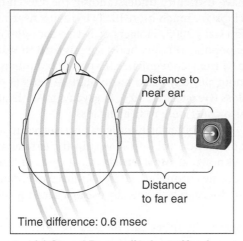
(a) Sound Perpendicular to Head

Distance to
near ear

Distance
to far ear

Time difference: 0.6 msec

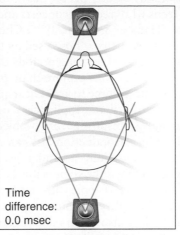
(b) Sound Directly in Front of
or Behind Head

Time
difference:
0.0 msec

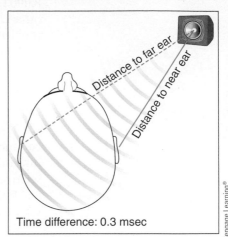
(c) Sound at 45 Degrees from Head

Distance to far ear

Distance to near ear

Time difference: 0.3 msec

© 2016 Cengage Learning®

Figure 7.10 We Localize Sound by Comparing Arrival Times at Both Ears (a) There will be a relatively large difference in the time of arrival of sound (0.6 msec) to the right and left ears, and the individual will have no difficulty localizing the source of the sound. (b) There is no difference between the arrival times to the two ears of sounds directly in front or behind the listener, and without additional cues, these sounds will be very difficult to localize accurately. (c) A 0.3 msec difference in arrival times would suggest a sound source of about 45 degrees from the head.

Distinctions between arrival times of sound at each ear are made by neurons in the superior olive. These neurons are known as binaural neurons because they receive input from both ears. Binaural neurons respond most vigorously when input from both ears reaches them simultaneously. If input from the two ears arrives at slightly different times, the cells will respond less vigorously.

In addition to using differences in arrival times to the two ears to localize sounds, we can also localize sound by assessing the differences in the intensities of sound reaching each ear. Because the head blocks some sound waves, a sound "shadow" is cast on the ear farthest away from the source of sound, producing a quieter signal to that ear. However, this system works only for high frequency sounds. Because of their larger wavelengths, lower-frequency sounds move around the head without producing a noticeable shadow.

The pinna of the ear is essential for localizing the elevation of sounds in the vertical plane (above or below). When different-shaped false pinnas were attached to human participants, sound localization was impaired. However, with practice wearing their new pinnas, the participants learned to localize sounds correctly (Hofman, Van Riswick, & Van Opstal, 1998). Sound localization also involves vision. While watching a movie, we perceive sound as originating from the actors' lips, in spite of the fact that the speakers producing the sound are typically above and to the sides of the screen (Alais & Burr, 2004).

Hearing Disorders

Hearing loss arises from a wide variety of causes and affects nearly 30 million Americans (Agrawal, Platz, & Niparko, 2008; NIDCD, 2006). A person is considered legally deaf when speech sounds of 82 dB or less cannot be heard. Typical speech occurs at about 60 dB.

Age-related hearing loss results from a variety of factors, including poor circulation to the inner ear or the cumulative effects of a lifetime of exposure to loud noise. After the age of 30, most people cannot hear frequencies above 15,000 Hz. After the age of 50, most people cannot hear sounds above 12,000 Hz, and people over 70 have difficulty with sounds over 6,000 Hz. Because speech normally ranges up to

8,000 Hz, many elderly people begin to have difficulty understanding the speech of others. Teens who frequent concerts and clubs are much more likely to report hearing problems (Hanson & Fearn, 1975; Chung et al., 2005; Holgers & Pettersson, 2005). Earbud devices, such as those used by the popular iPhone, boost signals 6 dB to 9 dB and tend to be used for long periods due to their convenience. Experts recommend using such devices for no more than an hour per day at no more than 60 percent of their maximum volume to avoid hearing loss (Garstecki, 2005). Everyday noises from vehicles, machinery, and appliances can also contribute to hearing loss.

Hearing loss resulting from problems in the outer or middle ear is referred to as **conduction loss**. Conduction loss can result from a buildup of wax in the ear canal, infections of the middle ear, and a disease known as **otosclerosis**. Most cases of otosclerosis occur when the stapes (stirrup) becomes immobilized by a buildup of abnormal bone at its base. People with conduction loss can be helped by use of a hearing aid, which acts by amplifying sound signals.

Hearing loss also occurs due to damage to the inner ear, the auditory pathways, or the auditory cortex. Medications, such as quinine and antibiotics, damage hair cells in sensitive individuals. Nicotine produces hearing loss by reducing blood supply to the ear (Zelman, 1973). Secondhand smoke exposure was sufficient to reduce hearing in adolescents (Lalwani, Liu, & Weitzman, 2011). Damage to the inner ear hair cells is often treated with **cochlear prosthetics**, or "cochlear implants." As shown in ● Figure 7.11, electrode arrays are threaded through the round window of the cochlea towards the apex of the basilar membrane. The electrode arrays receive radio signals from a small microphone positioned on the outside of the head behind the ear. In turn, the electrode arrays stimulate auditory nerve fibers. While not the equivalent of the hair cells, the cochlear prosthetics have improved the hearing of large numbers of people.

conduction loss Hearing loss due to problems in the outer or middle ears; treated with the use of hearing aids.

otosclerosis Hearing loss due to immobilization of the ossicles of the middle ear.

cochlear prosthetics Electrode arrays inserted in the cochlea to treat hearing loss due to damaged inner ear hair cells.

••• Building Better HEALTH

EARBUDS AND HEARING LOSS

Certain types of hearing loss are associated with cumulative noise exposure over a person's lifetime. Among the risk factors for hearing loss today is the use of headphones to listen to music. As mentioned previously in this chapter, the volume of an iPod or iPhone or similar device can easily exceed 120 dB, about the same level of sound intensity produced by a propeller plane at takeoff. This level is only 10 dB below the point at which a sound would be considered painful and can produce hearing loss in as little as 75 minutes. Experts recommend that consumers set the volume of their devices to about 60 percent of maximum and limit their use to about an hour per day (the 60/60 rule), but such recommendations are rarely heeded.

In one study of adolescents and young adults between the ages of 16 to 25 years, approximately 15 percent showed hearing threshold changes at high frequencies, indicative of the type of permanent hearing damage we usually associate with older adults (Dobrucki, Kin, & Kruk, 2013). These researchers also investigated the impact of the type of headphones used on changes in hearing. Headphones were described as closed, semi-open, open, and in-ear. "Openness" refers to the presence of openings in the back of the earphone, and these varieties are designed for their acoustic qualities rather than safety. Of the four types, use of the in-ear headphones (earbuds) appeared to produce the greatest changes in hearing thresholds.

Compounding the problem is the fact that we adapt rapidly to loudness. To experience the same subjective level of loudness over time, people tend to gradually increase the loudness of their electronic devices. How do you know when enough is enough? In general, if the listener cannot hear anything other than the sound from the device, the sound is far too loud. Symptoms such as ringing or buzzing in the ears, difficulty understanding speech in noisy places, sounds perceived as muffled or coming through a plugged ear, and awareness that television and other electronic device settings must be consistently higher than in the past could indicate early hearing loss and should be evaluated by a professional.

Using headphones other than earbuds, limiting listening time, and using device settings to cap maximum volume (in case we're tempted to adjust due to adaptation) can help preserve hearing.

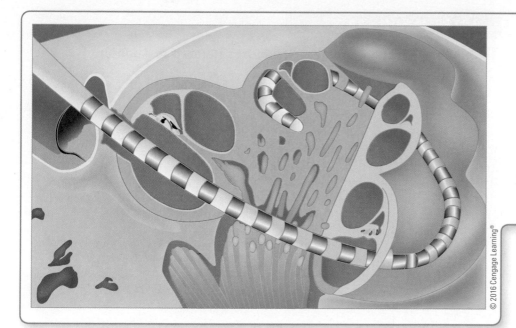

● **Figure 7.11** Cochlear Prosthetics The electrode array of the cochlear implant is threaded through the cochlea. Sounds picked up by an external microphone are encoded into electrical signals and sent to the electrode array. The signals from the array are picked up by the spiral ganglion fibers and transmitted to the brain.

© 2016 Cengage Learning®

••• THINKING *Ethically*

COCHLEAR PROSTHETICS AND DEAF CULTURE

It might come as a bit of a surprise to people who can hear that those who cannot hear did not welcome the discovery of cochlear prosthetics in the 1980s and 1990s with open arms (Sparrow, 2005). The choice by some hearing parents to have cochlear prosthetics inserted in their young children was viewed as particularly threatening. Debate over the use of cochlear prosthetics raises interesting questions about what it means to be "normal," and about the rights of minority cultures.

What is the basis for concerns about cochlear prosthetics? Critics of the cochlear prosthetic technology view this as an attempt to "cure" what they consider to be a culture, not a disability, and have even likened use of the technology to "genocide" (Sparrow, 2005). By ensuring that children grow up to use a spoken language instead of a visual (sign) language, the numbers of people with whom members of the deaf community could communicate in their first language would dwindle.

On the other side, supporters of the cochlear prosthetics argue that the technology provides the opportunity to communicate with hearing peers and does not necessarily mean that the child cannot also learn visual language and participate within the deaf community. Several decades of use of cochlear prosthetics has provided some perspective on the outcomes of the procedure. Evaluations of adolescents who received cochlear prosthetics at a very early age show that 30 percent identified with the deaf community, 32 percent identified with the hearing community, and 38 percent identified with both the hearing and deaf communities (Moog, Geers, Gustus, & Brenner, 2011). Youth identifying with the hearing community did not experience higher levels of adjustment problems. Nearly all youth with cochlear prosthetics reported having hearing friends, and a majority reported having deaf friends as well.

As we will see in a later chapter on sexuality (Chapter 10), people who are viewed by others as "different" often report wishing that they could have input into the choices made on their behalf as opposed to having these choices made for them during childhood by well-intentioned adults. The fact that language acquisition is subject to an apparent critical period (see Chapter 5) complicates the timing of these choices. It is likely that the best outcomes do not emerge from a one-size-fits-all approach, but instead from approaches that are tailored to the individuals in question.

INTERIM SUMMARY 7.1

‖ Summary Table: Important Structures Related to Audition

Structure	Location	Function
Pinna	Outer ear	Sound collection
Auditory canal	Outer ear	Resonating tube that conducts sound from the outer to middle ear
Tympanic membrane	Middle ear	Movement begins the process of transduction of sound waves to action potentials
Ossicles	Middle ear	Deliver vibration to the oval window of the cochlea
Cochlea	Inner ear	Fluid-filled structure containing auditory receptors
Inner hair cells	Inner ear	Frequency discrimination
Outer hair cells	Inner ear	Amplify responses to sound energy
Spiral ganglion	Inner ear	Source of fibers synapsing with hair cells; forms auditory nerve (cranial nerve VIII) that connects to the medulla
Dorsal cochlear nucleus; ventral cochlear nucleus	Medulla	Receives input from the spiral ganglion cells
Superior olive	Medulla	Transmits information from the ventral cochlear nucleus to the inferior colliculi; important for sound localization
Inferior colliculi	Midbrain	Sound localization; auditory reflexes
Medial geniculate nucleus of the thalamus	Diencephalon	Transmits sound information from the inferior colliculi to auditory cortex; may modulate output based on organism's level of arousal
Primary auditory cortex	A1 in the temporal lobe	Initial level of processing for auditory input
Secondary auditory cortex	Areas surrounding A1	Higher-level processing of auditory input

‖ Summary Points

1. Sound begins with the movement of an object in a medium, producing vibrations in surrounding media that can be described in terms of wavelength and amplitude. (LO1)

2. The outer ear contains the pinna and the auditory canal; the middle ear contains the tympanic membrane and ossicles. (LO2)

3. The cochlea of the inner ear is responsible for transducing sound waves into neural signals. These signals are carried centrally by the auditory nerve (cranial nerve VIII).

Subsequent processing of auditory information occurs in the cochlear nuclei, the superior olive, the inferior colliculi, the medial geniculate nucleus of the thalamus, and auditory cortex. **(LO2)**

4. Auditory perception involves the analysis of pitch, sound intensity, and localization. **(LO3)**

‖ Review Questions

1. What are the functions of the outer ear and the middle ear?

2. How does the auditory system process pitch and intensity?

The Body Senses

The **somatosensory system** provides us with information about the position and movement of our bodies and about touch, skin temperature, and pain. Although these senses might not seem as essential as vision or hearing, we are severely disabled by their loss (see ● Figure 7.12). You might think it would be a blessing to be born without a sense of pain. On the contrary, people who have impaired pain reception, typically die prematurely due to their inability to respond to injury.

The Vestibular System

The **vestibular system** provides information about the position and movements of our heads, which contribute to our sense of balance. When the vestibular system is impaired, perhaps by a bad head cold or by motion sickness, the result is usually an unpleasant period of nausea and dizziness.

MOVEMENT RECEPTORS The sensory organs of the vestibular system are found in the inner ear, adjacent to the structures responsible for audition (see ● Figure 7.13). The vestibular structures may be divided into two types, the **otolith organs** and the **semicircular canals**. The otolith organs consist of two separate structures, the **saccule** and the **utricle**.

The otolith organs provide information about the angle of the head relative to the ground, as well as information about **linear acceleration**. We sense linear acceleration when our rate of movement changes, such as when our car pulls away from a stop sign. Both the saccule and utricle contain hair cells similar to those we encountered earlier in our discussion of audition. The hair cells in the saccule are arranged along a vertical membrane, whereas the hair cells in the utricle are arranged along a horizontal membrane. Cilia extend from each hair cell into a gelatinous layer. Covering the gelatinous layer are **otoliths**, which are stones made of calcium carbonate. When the otoliths move due to the acceleration of the head, force is exerted on the hair cells. The hair cells either depolarize or hyperpolarize in response to this force, which in turn affects the firing rates of fibers in the auditory nerve (cranial nerve VIII). Individual hair cells have a preferred direction of head movement to which they respond. As a result of this organization, all possible movements and directions of the head will be encoded by a unique pattern of hair cell responses.

somatosensory system The system that provides information about the body senses, including touch, movement, pain, and skin temperature.

vestibular system The sensory system that provides information about the position and movement of the head.

otolith organ A structure in the inner ear vestibular system that provides information about the angle of the head relative to the ground and about linear acceleration.

semicircular canal One of three looping chambers found in the inner ear that provide information regarding the rotation of the head.

saccule One of the structures making up the otolith organs.

utricle One of the structures making up the otolith organs.

linear acceleration The force we perceive when our rate of movement increases.

otolith A stone made from calcium carbonate that is attached to hair cells in the otolith organs.

Jeff Riedel/Getty Images

> ● **Figure 7.12 The Consequences of Feeling No Pain** Ashlyn Blocker was born with a rare condition preventing her from feeling any pain. She went several days with a broken ankle without complaint after falling off her bicycle.

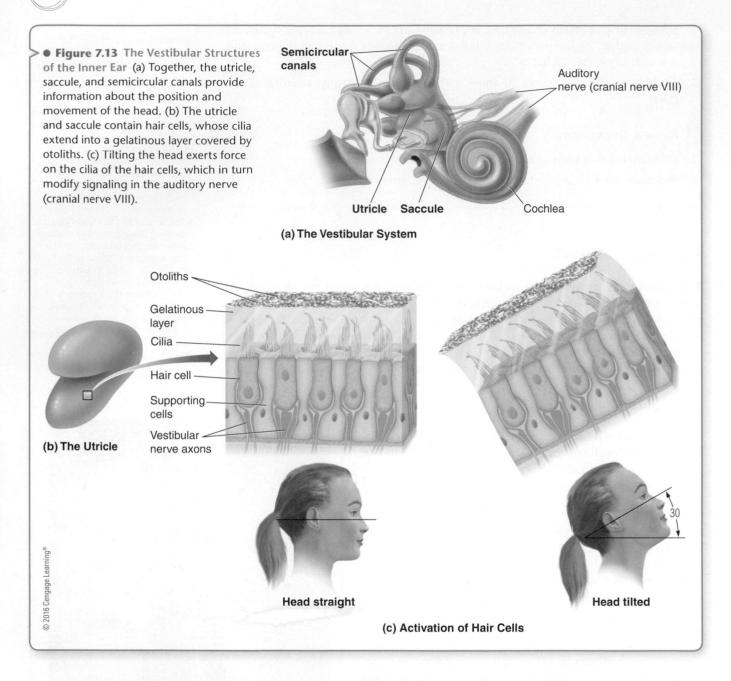

● **Figure 7.13** The Vestibular Structures of the Inner Ear (a) Together, the utricle, saccule, and semicircular canals provide information about the position and movement of the head. (b) The utricle and saccule contain hair cells, whose cilia extend into a gelatinous layer covered by otoliths. (c) Tilting the head exerts force on the cilia of the hair cells, which in turn modify signaling in the auditory nerve (cranial nerve VIII).

Semicircular canals

Auditory nerve (cranial nerve VIII)

Utricle   Saccule

Cochlea

(a) The Vestibular System

Otoliths

Gelatinous layer

Cilia

Hair cell

Supporting cells

Vestibular nerve axons

(b) The Utricle

30

Head straight

Head tilted

(c) Activation of Hair Cells

© 2016 Cengage Learning®

The semicircular canals consist of three looping chambers at approximately right angles to one another. These structures respond to rotational movements of the head and contribute to our ability to walk upright (Fitzpatrick, Butler, & Day, 2006). Rotating the head causes the endolymph within the canals to bend hair cells. When extensive movement stops (perhaps at the end of an amusement park ride), the endolymph reverses its course, and you may have the odd fleeting sensation that your head is moving now in the opposite direction.

CENTRAL PATHWAYS Axons originating in the otolith organs and semicircular canals form part of the auditory nerve (cranial nerve VIII). These axons synapse in the vestibular nuclei of the pons and medulla and in the cerebellum. The cerebellum also participates in maintaining balance and motor coordination (see Chapter 2). In turn, information from the cerebellum, the visual system, and the somatosensory systems converge on the vestibular nuclei. This allows us to coordinate information from the vestibular system with other relevant sensory input.

Axons from the vestibular nuclei make connections both in the spinal cord and in higher levels of the brain. Input to the spinal cord motor neurons provides a means to adjust our posture to keep our balance. Vestibular nuclei axons also form connections with the **ventral posterior (VP) nucleus** of the thalamus, which receives information regarding touch and pain as well. From the VP nucleus, information is sent to the **primary somatosensory cortex** in the parietal lobe and primary motor cortex in the frontal lobe.

Input from the vestibular system is highly integrated with visual processing. It is essential for accurate vision that we maintain a stable view of our surroundings regardless of what our body is doing. Rotations of the head result in reflexive movements of the eyes in the opposite direction. As a result of these reflexes, you maintain a steady view of the world while riding on the most extreme roller coaster. On the other hand, if your vestibular senses and your visual senses give conflicting information to your brain, you may feel nauseated or dizzy.

Touch

Our sense of touch begins with our skin, the largest and heaviest organ of the human body. Our skin provides a boundary separating what is inside from what is outside. It prevents dehydration and protects the body from dirt and bacteria. Human skin comes in two basic varieties, hairy skin and **glabrous**, or hairless, skin. Human glabrous skin is found on the lips, palms of the hands, and soles of the feet. When viewed in cross-section, as in ● Figure 7.14, the skin can be divided into the outer layer of **epidermis** and the inner layer of the **dermis**. The outermost layer of the epidermis is actually constructed of dead cells. Below the dermis, we find **subcutaneous tissue**,

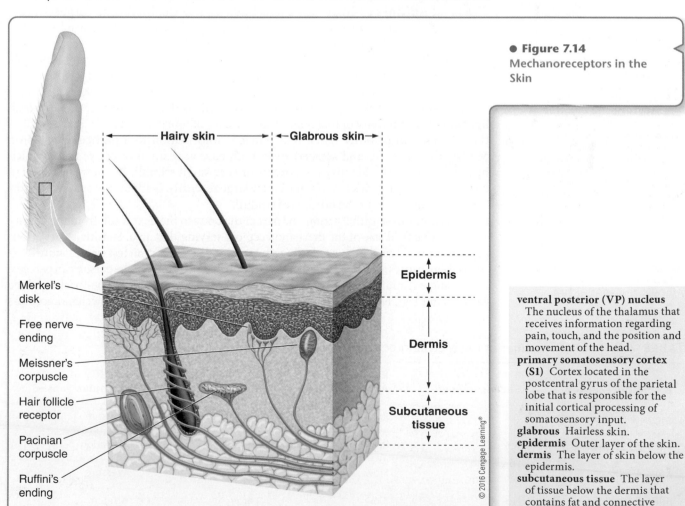

● **Figure 7.14**
Mechanoreceptors in the Skin

ventral posterior (VP) nucleus
The nucleus of the thalamus that receives information regarding pain, touch, and the position and movement of the head.

primary somatosensory cortex (S1) Cortex located in the postcentral gyrus of the parietal lobe that is responsible for the initial cortical processing of somatosensory input.

glabrous Hairless skin.

epidermis Outer layer of the skin.

dermis The layer of skin below the epidermis.

subcutaneous tissue The layer of tissue below the dermis that contains fat and connective tissue.

which contains connective tissues and fat. Human skin varies dramatically in thickness across different areas of the body, from about half a millimeter on your face to twenty times that thickness on the bottom of your foot.

TOUCH RECEPTORS The majority of the receptor cells for touch are referred to as **mechanoreceptors.** This term reflects the response of these receptor cells to physical displacement such as bending or stretching. In addition to their locations in the skin, mechanoreceptors are also found in our blood vessels, joints, and internal organs. Those unpleasant sensations of pressure from a too-full stomach or bladder are provided courtesy of mechanoreceptors in the walls of these organs.

Although mechanoreceptors come in a wide variety of shapes and sizes, they share a number of common features. Within each mechanoreceptor are unmyelinated axon fibers. The membranes of these axons contain sodium ion channels that respond to physical stretching or changes in membrane tension. When the membrane of the axon is stretched, the ion channels open, and sodium enters the cell. If sufficient amounts of sodium enter the cell, an action potential is generated.

Mechanoreceptors are categorized according to their structure, size of receptive field, rate of adaptation, and type of information that is processed. Structurally, mechanoreceptors are either encapsulated or not. In **encapsulated receptors**, the axon fibers are surrounded by a fluid-filled capsule formed of connective tissue. The two major types of encapsulated mechanoreceptors are the **Meissner's corpuscles** and the **Pacinian corpuscles**. The Meissner's corpuscles are found at the junction of the epidermis and dermis, whereas the Pacinian corpuscles are located deep in the skin, in the joints, and in the digestive tract. Nonencapsulated receptors include the **Merkel's disks** and **Ruffini's endings**. The Merkel's disks, like the Meissner's corpuscles, are located in the upper areas of the skin, whereas the Ruffini's endings are located at deeper levels. We also find free nerve endings distributed within the skin. As their name implies, these receptors do not have any specialized structure but are simply the unmyelinated nerve endings of sensory neurons. In addition, some receptors wrap themselves around hair follicles and respond to the bending of a hair (see Table 7.3).

In vision, we spoke of a neuron's receptive field as the area of the retina in which light affects the activity of that neuron. In the case of touch, a receptive field describes the area of skin or other tissue that provides information to a particular receptor. Meissner's corpuscles and Merkel's disks both have very small receptive fields, which means that they can identify the borders of very small stimuli. In contrast, Pacinian corpuscles and Ruffini's endings have very large receptive fields and provide only general information about the borders of stimuli.

Variations in sensitivity from one part of the body to the next result from the density and receptive field size of the mechanoreceptors serving that area. Sensitivity of various parts of the body can be assessed using a two-point discrimination test (see ● Figure 7.15). This test measures how close together two stimuli have to be before the person can perceive only a single stimulus. Our fingers and lips are far more sensitive than our backs and the calves of our legs. Not only do fingers and lips have a greater density of mechanoreceptors

mechanoreceptor A touch receptor that responds to physical displacement such as bending or stretching.

encapsulated receptors A receptor in which the axon terminal is surrounded by a fluid-filled capsule formed of connective tissue.

Meissner's corpuscles An encapsulated mechanoreceptor located near the surface of the skin that senses pressure.

Pacinian corpuscles An encapsulated mechanoreceptor located deeper in the skin, in joints, and in the digestive tract that senses pressure and vibration.

Merkel's disks A nonencapsulated mechanoreceptor located near the surface of the skin that senses pressure.

Ruffini's endings A nonencapsulated mechanoreceptor located deep in the skin that senses stretch.

TABLE 7.3 | Major Features of the Mechanoreceptors

Mechanoreceptor	Encapsulated?	Rate of Adaptation	Size of Receptive Field	Quality of Stimulus Sensed
Meissner's corpuscles	Yes	Rapid	Small	Pressure
Pacinian corpuscles	Yes	Rapid	Large	Vibration
Merkel's disks	No	Slow	Small	Pressure
Ruffini's endings	No	Slow	Large	Stretch

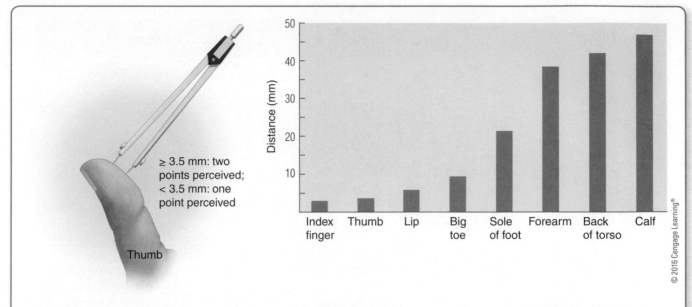

© 2016 Cengage Learning®

> ● **Figure 7.15** Two-Point Discrimination Thresholds The human body is not equally sensitive to touch. If you measure how close two points can be before a person perceives only one stimulus, you can map the sensitivity of different parts of the body. The calf is much less sensitive than the index finger.

overall than other areas of the body, but they also contain high concentrations of Merkel's disks and Meissner's corpuscles, with their small receptive fields.

A receptor's rate of adaptation refers to the length of time it will continue to respond to unchanging stimuli. A receptor that adapts rapidly will respond vigorously when stimulation begins or ends but will remain rather inactive while the stimulus is applied continuously. In contrast, a slow-adapting receptor will continue to respond steadily as long as the stimulus is present. We can classify our four major types of mechanoreceptors according to their rate of adaptation. Meissner's corpuscles and Pacinian corpuscles both demonstrate rapid adaptation, whereas Merkel's disks and Ruffini's endings are slow adapting.

A final feature of mechanoreceptors is the type of information processed. The relationship of mechanoreceptor type to the quality of the sensation is neither precise nor perfectly understood. In general, however, mechanoreceptors appear to be somewhat specialized in the type of information they provide. Free nerve endings typically supply information regarding pain, which we will discuss later in this chapter. Meissner's corpuscles, Merkel's disks, and Pacinian corpuscles all provide information about pressure. However, due to having larger receptive fields, the Pacinian corpuscles do not provide the fine spatial resolution that characterizes the Meissner's corpuscles and Merkel's disks. Pacinian corpuscles are superior to the others in detecting vibrating stimuli. The Ruffini's endings provide input regarding stretch.

TOUCH PATHWAYS We begin the journey from the mechanoreceptor in the skin back toward the brain by looking at the nerves that serve the receptors. As shown in ● Figure 7.16, the sensory fibers of the peripheral nervous system are classified into four categories based on diameter and speed. The largest fibers, called Aα (alpha-alpha), carry information from the muscles and will be discussed in Chapter 8. The smaller three sets of fibers serve the mechanoreceptors. The second-largest set, the Aβ (alpha-beta) class, carries information from the Meissner's corpuscles, Merkel's disks, Pacinian corpuscles, and Ruffini's endings toward the central nervous system (CNS). The smallest two groups, the myelinated Aδ (alpha-delta) fibers and the unmyelinated C fibers, carry information from the free nerve endings regarding pain and skin temperature.

Sensory fibers travel from the skin to join the dorsal roots of the spinal cord. The area of the skin surface served by the dorsal roots of one spinal nerve is known as a **dermatome**. As shown in ● Figure 7.17, dermatomes are easily identified in the disease

dermatome The area of skin surface served by the dorsal root of a spinal nerve.

Class of Axon		Diameter of Axon	Speed of Transmission	Receptor Types
Aα (Alpha-alpha) fibers		13–20 μm Axon Myelin	80–120 m/sec	Feedback from muscle fibers
Aβ (Alpha-beta) fibers		6–12 μm	35–75 m/sec	Mechanoreceptors of skin: Meissner's corpuscles Merkel's disks Pacinian corpuscles Ruffini's endings
Aδ (Alpha-delta) fibers		1–5 μm	5–30 m/sec	Pain, temperature receptors of skin: Free nerve endings
C fibers		0.2–1.5 μm	0.5–2 m/sec	Pain, temperature receptors of skin: Free nerve endings

● **Figure 7.16 The Four Classes of Sensory Axons Differ in Size and Speed** The largest, fastest afferent axons (Aα) serve the muscles and will be discussed in Chapter 8. The second-largest and fastest axons (Aβ) serve the mechanoreceptors. Fast, sharp pain and skin temperature are carried by the myelinated Aδ fibers, whereas the small, unmyelinated C fibers carry dull, aching pain and skin temperature.

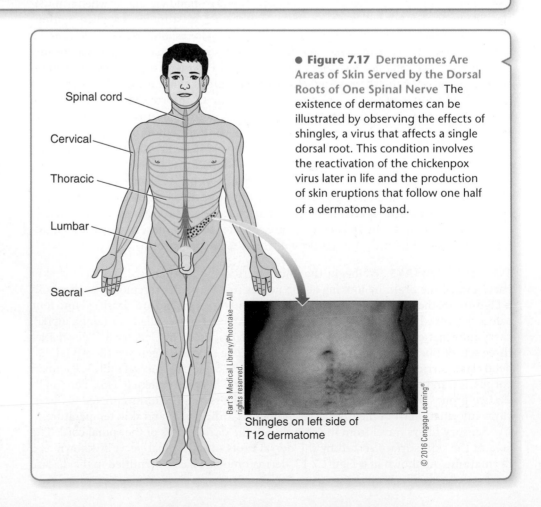

Spinal cord

Cervical

Thoracic

Lumbar

Sacral

● **Figure 7.17 Dermatomes Are Areas of Skin Served by the Dorsal Roots of One Spinal Nerve** The existence of dermatomes can be illustrated by observing the effects of shingles, a virus that affects a single dorsal root. This condition involves the reactivation of the chickenpox virus later in life and the production of skin eruptions that follow one half of a dermatome band.

Shingles on left side of T12 dermatome

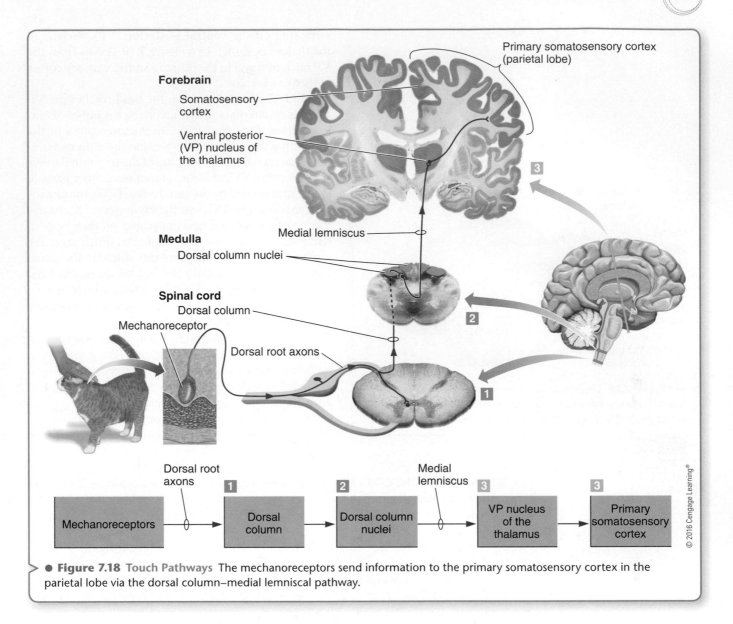

● **Figure 7.18 Touch Pathways** The mechanoreceptors send information to the primary somatosensory cortex in the parietal lobe via the dorsal column–medial lemniscal pathway.

known as shingles, which is caused by the same virus responsible for chickenpox (*herpes zoster*). In some people, the virus awakens decades after the original infection and produces skin eruptions. In addition, the virus increases the excitability of the sensory neurons, producing a burning, painful sensation along the dermatome. The reactivated virus appears to confine its mischief to a single dorsal root, leading to symptoms in one half of an individual dermatome. Fortunately, an effective vaccine for shingles is now available.

The pathways leading from the mechanoreceptors to the brain are illustrated in ●Figure 7.18. When the axons from the mechanoreceptors enter the spinal cord, they follow a route called the **dorsal column–medial lemniscal pathway**. As suggested by the pathway's name, axons join the white matter of the ipsilateral dorsal column and make their first synapse in the dorsal column nuclei of the medulla. The lack of synapses until this point greatly contributes to the speed of this system.

Axons from the dorsal column nuclei form a large band of white matter known as the medial lemniscus, which crosses the midline of the medulla. From this point forward, sensory information is processed contralaterally. In other words, the left side of the brain processes touch information from the right side of the body. The medial lemniscus continues to travel rostrally through the medulla, pons, and midbrain before

dorsal column–medial lemniscal pathway The pathway taken by touch information from the mechanoreceptors to the brain.

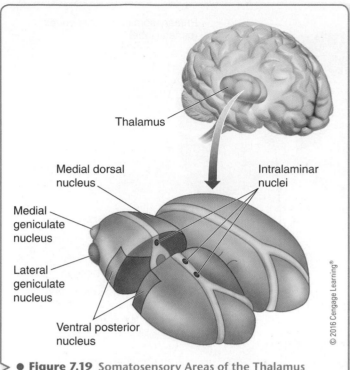

● **Figure 7.19** **Somatosensory Areas of the Thalamus**
Somatosensory information is processed by the ventral posterior (VP) and intralaminar nuclei of the thalamus.

© 2016 Cengage Learning®

synapsing on the **ventral posterior (VP) nucleus** of the thalamus, shown in ● Figure 7.19. Axons from the VP nucleus travel to the primary somatosensory cortex of the parietal lobe.

Touch information from the head reaches the VP nucleus by alternate routes involving a number of cranial nerves. Sensation from mechanoreceptors in the skin of the face, mouth, tongue, and the dura mater of the brain travels along branches of the trigeminal nerve (cranial nerve V). Additional input from other parts of the head is carried by the facial nerve (VII), the glosso-pharyngeal nerve (IX), and the vagus nerve (X). Axons forming these cranial nerves synapse on their respective ipsilateral nuclei in the brainstem, which serve the same purpose as the dorsal column nuclei in the spinal cord. From these cranial nerve nuclei, axons cross the midline and travel to the VP nucleus, which in turn passes the information to the primary somatosensory cortex in the parietal lobe.

You may be wondering what the dorsal column nuclei, cranial nerve nuclei, and the VP nucleus might be doing to the incoming sensory information. These synapses provide opportunities for the cortex to influence the input it receives through descending pathways. In addition, activity in one neuron inhibits its neighbor, leading to a sharpening or enhancement of its signal.

SOMATOSENSORY CORTEX Primary somatosensory cortex, also known as S1, is found in the postcentral gyrus of the parietal lobe, just caudal to the central sulcus that divides the parietal and frontal lobes. Secondary somatosensory cortex (S2) is located within the lateral sulcus.

Using single-cell recording, we can demonstrate that areas of the cortex serving the head and neck are located at the lower, ventral part of the postcentral gyrus, whereas areas serving the legs and feet extend over the top of the gyrus onto the medial surface of the parietal lobe. A map of the body's representation in the cortex is known as a *homunculus,* or "little man." An example of a homunculus is shown in ● Figure 7.20. Areas of the body receive cortical representation according to their need for precise sensory feedback. In humans, the hands and face are given a much larger portion of the cortex than their size would suggest. Rats devote a great deal of space to whiskers, whereas lips seem to have a very high priority in squirrels and rabbits.

PLASTICITY OF TOUCH The somatosensory cortex is capable of plasticity, which means it can rearrange itself in response to changes in the amount of input it receives. In adult monkeys who have had a finger surgically removed, the areas of the somatosensory cortex previously responsive to the missing finger now respond to stimulation of adjacent fingers (Kaas, Nelson, Sur, & Merzenich, 1981). In these cases, the brain is adapting to a reduction in input from a specific part of the body. Increased stimulation from a body part will also result in changes in the mapping of the somatosensory cortex. When monkeys were trained to use specific fingers to discriminate between tactile surfaces to earn a food reward, the area of the somatosensory cortex receiving input from the trained fingertips actually expanded (Wang, Merzenich, Sameshima, & Jenkins, 1995). This process represents a reorganization of synapses.

Plasticity occurs in the human somatosensory cortex as a result of both loss and enhancement of input. Amputation of a limb often causes **phantom pain**, in which pain is perceived as arising in the missing body part, or **referred sensations**, in

ventral posterior (VP) nucleus
  The part of the thalamus dedicated to the processing of information from the mechanoreceptors.
phantom pain Pain that is perceived as arising from a missing body part.
referred sensations The perception of touch of a body part as arising from a missing body part.

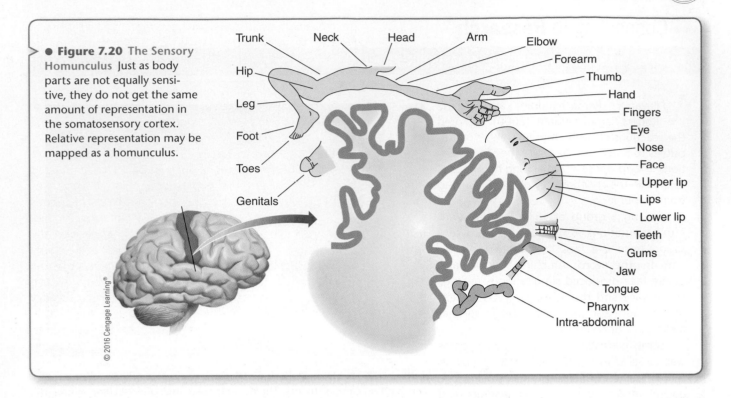

● **Figure 7.20** The Sensory Homunculus Just as body parts are not equally sensitive, they do not get the same amount of representation in the somatosensory cortex. Relative representation may be mapped as a homunculus.

© 2016 Cengage Learning®

which touching a body part such as the cheek is perceived as touch of the missing limb (Ramachandran, 2005). Brain imaging confirms that the part of somatosensory cortex previously responsive to an amputated arm subsequently responded to touching the face (Ramachandran & Rogers-Ramachandran, 2000). Other types of referred sensation occur as well. One patient was embarrassed to report that he experienced a sensation of orgasm in his missing foot. Such observations suggest that the brain rapidly reorganizes its representation of the body following amputation.

The increased representation due to training that was observed in monkeys has a parallel in the cortical organization of some musicians. Highly trained string musicians have a larger than normal area of somatosensory cortex representing touch in the fingers (Münte, Altenmüller, & Jäncke, 2002). A similar reorganization of somatosensory cortex occurs when blind individuals learn to read Braille (Pascual-Leone & Torres, 1993). Neural plasticity in the somatosensory system is quite flexible. Sighted participants who wore blindfolds initially activated only S1 while performing a Braille task (Pascual-Leone & Hamilton, 2001). After a few days, however, they began to recruit V1, or primary visual cortex, during the task. After no longer wearing blindfolds while reading Braille, they reverted to their initial pattern of S1 without V1 activity.

SOMATOSENSORY DISORDERS Damage to primary somatosensory cortex produces deficits in both sensation and movement of body parts served by the damaged area (Corkin, Milner, & Rasmussen, 1970). Damage to secondary somatosensory cortex, particularly on the right side of the brain, results in an odd phenomenon known as **neglect syndrome**. Patients with this syndrome have difficulty perceiving either a part of the body or a part of the visual field. Drawings by a patient with neglect syndrome may be seen in ● Figure 7.21. Oliver Sacks (1985) described a patient with neglect syndrome who believed that the hospital staff was playing a horrible joke on him by putting an amputated leg, which was actually his own very firmly attached leg, into his bed. While trying to remove the leg from his bed, the man frequently fell on the floor. Fortunately for Sacks's patient and others with neglect syndrome, the condition generally improves over time (see ● Figure 7.22).

neglect syndrome A condition resulting from secondary somatosensory cortex that produces difficulty perceiving a body part or part of the visual field.

••• Connecting to **Research**

PHANTOM LIMBS, MIRRORS, AND LONGER NOSES

Vilayanur Ramachandran and Diane Rogers-Ramachandran (2000) explored the reactions of both amputees and nonamputees to touch. As a result of their investigations, they propose a "remapping hypothesis" to explain the changes they observe resulting from amputation.

Among a group of 18 individuals with arm amputations, 8 perfectly referred sensation from the face to the now-missing limb. In other words, touching specific parts of the face produced simultaneous feelings of the face and the missing arm. The sensations were also modality specific, such as feeling hot or cold or massage.

Some patients experience movement as well as sensation in their phantom limbs. In some instances, this can result in pain. One patient examined by Ramachandran and Rogers-Ramachandran experienced the sensation of a tightly clenched hand that could not be relaxed. The phantom nails dug into the palm of the phantom hand, resulting in excruciating sensations of pain. Use of a mirror box to superimpose the reflection of the real hand on the felt location of the phantom left hand allowed the patient to gain relief by "unclenching" the phantom hand (see ●Figure 7.21).

Ramachandran and Rogers-Ramachandran (2000) argue that body image is remarkably flexible even in people who have not experienced amputation. You can try the "phantom nose" experiment yourself (Ramachandran & Hirstein, 1997). One person is blindfolded while seated. The second person sits to the side of the first person. The experimenter uses his or her left hand to take the blindfolded participant's left index finger and use it to tap or stroke the other person's nose in a random, unpredictable manner. Simultaneously, the experimenter uses his

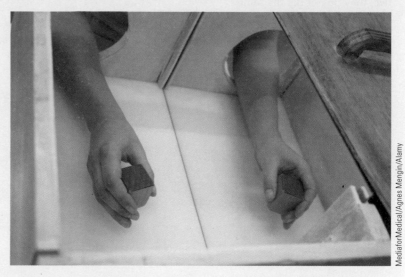

● **Figure 7.21 Mirror Boxes and Phantom Pain** Ramachandran's mirror box has two compartments. The patients place their affected limb in one side (covered) and their unaffected limb in the side with the mirror. The reflection gives the illusion of once again having two limbs, which relieves many symptoms of phantom limb.

or her right index finger to perform the same movements on the blindfolded person's nose. After only a few seconds, the blindfolded person begins to sense that his or her nose has been stretched or dislocated.

How can we account for these odd sensations? Ramachandran and Hirstein (1997) propose that the participant assumes that the matched tapping of nose and finger cannot be occurring by chance, resulting in the brain's use of the "simpler" explanation that the nose is displaced. The authors further argue that sensory systems have evolved to extract statistical regularities from the natural world around us. Most of the time, that works, but illusions can illustrate how tenuous the relationship between "reality" and our beliefs about reality can really be.

Pain

Pain combines sensation with emotion and cognition. No other sensory modality is as dramatically affected by culture, emotion, context, and experience as our sense of pain. The connection between culture and the experience of pain is vividly illustrated by the hook-swinging ritual practiced in India (Melzack & Wall, 1983). This ritual, designed to promote the health of children and crops, involves hanging a male volunteer from steel hooks embedded into the skin and muscles of his back. Instead of suffering excruciating pain, the volunteers appear to be in a state of exaltation.

A PURPOSE FOR PAIN Given the anguish experienced by chronic pain patients, it would seem initially miraculous to be able to do away with this sensory modality

pain The sense that provides information about tissue damage.

altogether. Research on those born without effective pain reception suggests otherwise. Patients who perceive no pain frequently die prematurely, due to injuries and degeneration of joints and the spine (Cox et al., 2006). We need pain to remind us to stop when we are injured, to assess a situation before proceeding, and to allow the body time to heal. Pain is not a perfect warning system. In many potentially fatal conditions, such as in some types of cancer, pain does not surface until the condition is quite advanced. In other cases, the pain people experience far exceeds the threat to their safety. The pain associated with many headaches, stomachaches, and backaches occurs in the absence of any tissue damage.

RECEPTORS FOR PAIN Free nerve endings that respond to pain are called **nociceptors**. Nociceptors respond to a variety of stimuli associated with tissue damage. Some nociceptors respond most vigorously to mechanical injury such as the damage caused by a sharp object. The pressure of the mechanical stimulus on the nociceptor membrane opens mechanically gated ion channels, leading to the generation of action potentials. Other nociceptors respond to extreme temperature. Some nociceptors appear to respond to both mechanical stimulation and temperature.

A variety of chemicals can also activate nociceptors. The unpleasant soreness we experience after exercising vigorously is produced by a buildup of lactic acid. Lactic acid produces an increase in hydrogen ions in the extracellular fluid. These ions activate nociceptors, which in turn send unpleasant messages of soreness to the brain. An interesting class of nociceptors responds to chemicals known as vanilloids, a group that includes capsaicin (Caterina et al., 1997). Capsaicin is best known as the ingredient found in hot peppers, and it is responsible for the heat sensations we enjoy while eating spicy foods. Chemicals released when a cell is damaged, such as potassium ions, enzymes, histamine, and adenosine triphosphate (ATP), also stimulate nociceptor activity.

PAIN PATHWAYS TO THE BRAIN Information from the nociceptors is carried toward the CNS by two types of nerve fiber. The faster, myelinated Aδ fibers are responsible for that quick, sharp "ouch." The slower, unmyelinated C fibers are responsible for dull, aching types of pain sensation. Both types of ascending pain fibers use glutamate as their primary neurotransmitter (Li & Tator, 2000; Jin, Nishioka, Wakabayashi, Fujita, & Yonehara, 2006).

As shown in ● Figure 7.23, pain fibers enter the spinal cord via the dorsal root. Once inside the cord, they synapse in the **substantia gelatinosa**, a group of cells in the outer gray matter of the dorsal horn. These cells also receive descending input from the brain. In addition to releasing glutamate, pain fibers are also capable of releasing **Substance P** in the dorsal horn of the spinal cord. Substance P stimulates changes in the dendrites of the cells in the substantia gelatinosa. These structural changes provide for adaptations to pain based on personal experience (Mantyh et al., 1997).

According to Melzack and Wall's (1965) influential **gate theory of pain**, a feedback loop in the dorsal horn determines which signals ultimately reach the brain. Excitatory signals from gate cells open the gate, allowing the message to continue. Chronic stress can make the opening of the gate more likely, and many people are more acutely aware of pain when stressed. Inhibitory signals from gate cells can close the gate, stopping the pain message from proceeding to the brain. High levels of arousal during emergencies can close the gate, making people unaware of how badly they have actually been injured.

Fibers originating in the substantia gelatinosa immediately cross the midline of the spinal cord to join the **spinothalamic pathway** that runs the length of the ventral surface of the spinal cord. These fibers travel up through the brainstem and finally synapse within the thalamus. Pain information from the head and neck is transmitted to the thalamus in a similar manner. This information travels first along the trigeminal nerve, which synapses in the spinal trigeminal nucleus of the brainstem. Fibers from the spinal trigeminal nucleus form the **trigeminal lemniscus**, which terminates in the thalamus.

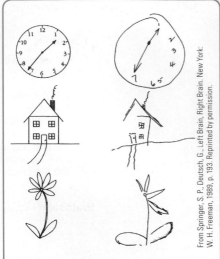

From Springer, S. P., Deutsch, G., Left Brain, Right Brain. New York: W. H. Freeman, 1989, p. 193. Reprinted by permission.

● **Figure 7.22** Drawings by a Patient with Neglect Syndrome Damage to the secondary somatosensory cortex, particularly on the right hemisphere, results in neglect syndrome. Patients with this syndrome have difficulty perceiving a part of the body or a part of the visual field. Because the patient attempting to copy the model cannot perceive the entire visual field, he or she draws only part of each object.

nociceptor A free nerve ending that responds to painful stimuli.
substantia gelatinosa A group of cells in the outer gray matter of the dorsal horn that receives input from pain fibers.
Substance P A neurochemical associated with the sense of pain.
gate theory of pain An explanation of the effects of context on the perception of pain.
spinothalamic pathway A pathway carrying pain information from the substantia gelatinosa to the thalamus.
trigeminal lemniscus A pathway for pain information from the head and neck that connects the spinal trigeminal nucleus and the thalamus.

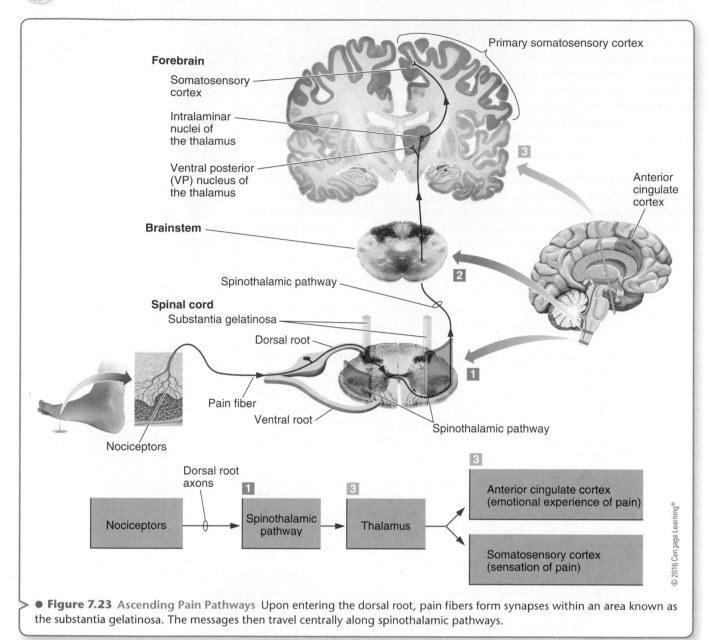

Forebrain

Somatosensory cortex

Intralaminar nuclei of the thalamus

Ventral posterior (VP) nucleus of the thalamus

Primary somatosensory cortex

Anterior cingulate cortex

Brainstem

Spinothalamic pathway

Spinal cord

Substantia gelatinosa

Dorsal root

Pain fiber

Ventral root

Nociceptors

Spinothalamic pathway

Nociceptors	Spinothalamic pathway	Thalamus	Anterior cingulate cortex (emotional experience of pain)
			Somatosensory cortex (sensation of pain)

Dorsal root axons

© 2016 Cengage Learning®

● **Figure 7.23** Ascending Pain Pathways Upon entering the dorsal root, pain fibers form synapses within an area known as the substantia gelatinosa. The messages then travel centrally along spinothalamic pathways.

The spinothalamic and trigeminal lemniscus fibers synapse in one of two locations in the thalamus. Some fibers synapse in the VP nucleus, which also receives information from touch receptors. However, input regarding pain remains separate in the VP nucleus from input regarding touch. Other fibers connect with the **intralaminar nuclei** of the thalamus, shown in ● Figures 7.19 and 7.23. Both areas of the thalamus then form connections with the anterior cingulate cortex (ACC) and, to a lesser degree, the somatosensory cortex. The ACC participates in our anticipation and emotional responses to pain. If participants are told to expect a mild amount of pain from placing their hands in hot water, the ACC is less active than when they are told to expect more pain (Rainville, Duncan, Price, Carrier, & Bushnell, 1997). People who chose an immediate but large electric shock over a delayed but smaller shock, demonstrating that they "dreaded" the upcoming shock, showed increased activity in the ACC (Berns et al., 2006). Remembering pain and anticipating further pain, perhaps when facing a second similar surgery for the same condition, activates the prefrontal cortex. Activity in the prefrontal cortex is correlated with cognition and executive control.

intralaminar nuclei Nuclei within the thalamus that receive pain information.

MANAGING PAIN   Although pain certainly has its purpose, we are also motivated to help those who face the challenges of chronic pain.

Although some of the individual differences in response to pain are due to culture and experience, a person's number of endogenous opioid receptors (see Chapter 4) also influences pain sensitivity (Zubieta et al., 2001). Researchers administered painful injections of saltwater into participants' facial muscles. Participants reported on their pain levels while undergoing PET scanning. Those with the highest amount of opioid activity as shown by the PET scans reported less pain.

In some cases, the pain signal can be modified by additional sensory input to the brain. Most of us spontaneously respond to bumping our elbow by rubbing it vigorously. Rubbing your elbow might actually lessen the ability of pain receptors to communicate with the brain. According to the gate theory discussed previously, input from touch fibers might compete with input from nociceptors for activation of cells in the substantia gelatinosa. Activation of the touch fibers effectively reduces the amount of pain information that can reach the brain.

In other cases, descending control from the brain has a dramatic influence on our perception of pain. As noted in Chapter 2, many higher-level brain structures form connections with the periaqueductal gray (PAG) of the midbrain, which also receives ascending pain signals (see ● Figure 7.24). The convergence of descending control and ascending pain information in the PAG provides an opportunity for the modification

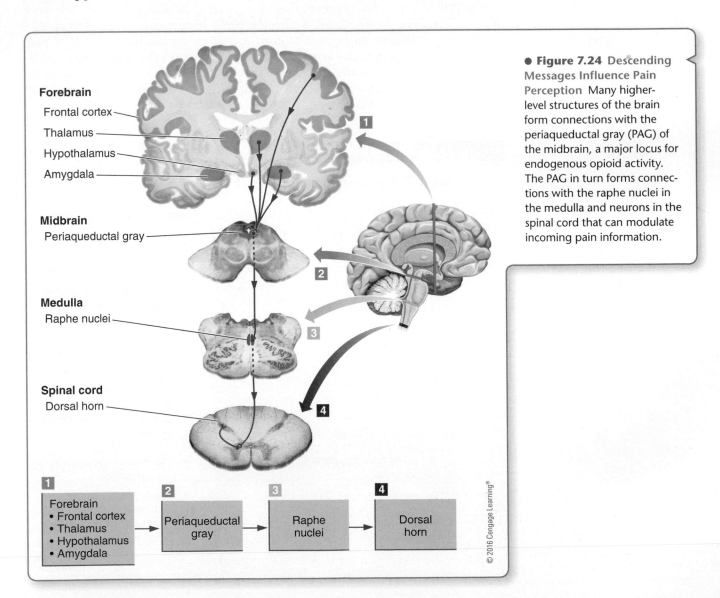

● **Figure 7.24** Descending Messages Influence Pain Perception   Many higher-level structures of the brain form connections with the periaqueductal gray (PAG) of the midbrain, a major locus for endogenous opioid activity. The PAG in turn forms connections with the raphe nuclei in the medulla and neurons in the spinal cord that can modulate incoming pain information.

Forebrain
Frontal cortex
Thalamus
Hypothalamus
Amygdala

Midbrain
Periaqueductal gray

Medulla
Raphe nuclei

Spinal cord
Dorsal horn

| 1 Forebrain • Frontal cortex • Thalamus • Hypothalamus • Amygdala | → | 2 Periaqueductal gray | → | 3 Raphe nuclei | → | 4 Dorsal horn |

© 2016 Cengage Learning®

of incoming pain messages by higher-level cognitive processes. Electrical stimulation of the PAG generally produces a significant reduction in pain (Barbaro, 1988). In addition, the PAG contains large numbers of endorphin receptors, which interact with opioids such as morphine. The pain relief achieved through the use of opioids probably occurs in large part due to the drugs' actions in the PAG.

One of the most troubling types of pain is chronic pain, which continues long after injuries have healed and affects nearly 10 percent of the U.S. population. Typical medications, such as aspirin and opioids, are relatively ineffective for managing this type of pain. Chronic pain is associated with increased activity in prefrontal areas, whereas physical pain (such as a burn) produces more activity in the thalamus (Millecamps et al., 2007). Researchers have suggested that chronic pain is more of a memory problem than a sensory problem, as if the brain has difficulty forgetting about the pain (ibid.).

Being disabled by pain during an emergency is not in the best interests of survival, so it should come as no surprise that extreme stress often reduces the perception of pain. Stress impacts the pain system at several levels. As discussed previously, the high arousal that occurs in stressful situations might act to close pain gates in the substantia gelatinosa. In addition, stress might produce analgesia, or pain relief, by promoting the release of endorphins in the brain.

Attitudes toward pain also play a significant role in our perceptions of the experience. Athletes and nonathletes share similar pain thresholds, or levels of stimulation identified as painful. However, these groups are quite different in their tolerance of pain (Sternberg, Bailin, Grant, & Gracely, 1998). In particular, athletes in contact sports such as boxing, rugby, and football appear to tolerate higher levels of pain before identifying a stimulus as painful. A sense of control can reduce the need for pain medication. Patients who are allowed to self-administer morphine for pain actually require less medication than patients who receive injections from hospital staff (Viscusi & Schechter, 2006).

INTERIM SUMMARY 7.2

Summary Table: Somatosensory Pathways

Sensory Modality	Receptor Types	Axon Types	Route to Somatosensory Cortex
Vestibular system	Hair cells within the saccule, utricle, and semicircular canals	Varied	• Fibers join the auditory nerve (cranial nerve VIII). • Axons synapse in cerebellum and vestibular nuclei. • Vestibular nuclei axons project to the spinal cord motor neurons and to the VP nucleus of the thalamus. • Information travels from the VP nucleus to primary somatosensory and motor cortex.
Touch	Mechanoreceptors	Aβ fibers	• Fibers enter spinal cord via dorsal root. • Axons join the dorsal column and synapse in the dorsal column nuclei of the medulla.

(continued)

Sensory Modality	Receptor Types	Axon Types	Route to Somatosensory Cortex
			• Axons from the dorsal column nuclei form the medial lemniscus and synapse in the VP nucleus of the thalamus. Cranial neurons V, VII, IX, and X carry touch information from the head to brainstem nuclei, which form connections with the VP nucleus of the thalamus. • The VP nucleus projects to primary somatosensory cortex in the parietal lobe.
Pain	Nociceptors (free nerve endings)	Aδ fibers and C fibers	• Fibers enter spinal cord via dorsal root. • Fibers synapse in substantia gelatinosa. • Pain information travels via the spinothalamic pathway and trigeminal lemniscus to the VP nucleus and intralaminar nuclei of the thalamus. • Information is transmitted to the anterior cingulate cortex, primary somatosensory cortex, and prefrontal cortex.

▌ Summary Points

1. The vestibular system provides information about the position and movement of the head. **(LO4)**

2. Major mechanoreceptors located within the skin include Meissner's corpuscles, Pacinian corpuscles, Merkel's disks, Ruffini's endings, and free nerve endings. **(LO4)**

3. Touch information travels along the dorsal column–medial lemniscal pathway to the dorsal column nuclei of the medulla, to the contralateral ventral posterior nucleus of the thalamus, and to the primary somatosensory cortex of the parietal lobe. **(LO4)**

4. Pain is sensed by free nerve endings called nociceptors. Ascending pain fibers synapse in the substantia gelatinosa, the thalamus, and the anterior cingulate and somatosensory cortices. Descending information regarding pain is transmitted to the periaqueductal gray (PAG). **(LO4)**

▌ Review Questions

1. How is the primary somatosensory cortex organized? How does experience change the organization of primary somatosensory cortex?

2. What factors modify an individual's perception of a painful stimulus?

The Chemical Senses

Philosopher Immanuel Kant (1798) considered olfaction, or the sense of smell, to be the "most dispensable" sense. Nonetheless, our chemical senses, olfaction and gustation, do provide warning of danger, such as smelling smoke from a fire or the taste of spoiled food. Contrary to Kant's view, people who have lost their sense of smell due to head injury often experience profound depression (Zuscho, 1983; Doty et al., 1997).

Olfaction

Olfaction begins with the detection of molecules suspended in the air. In addition to having the capacity to be suspended in air, olfactory stimuli must be small and water-repellant. We cannot sense every type of molecule suspended in the air. Natural gas, for example, has no detectable odor, so gas companies add an odorant so that we can sense potentially dangerous gas leaks in our homes.

Air containing olfactory stimuli is taken in through the nostrils and circulated within the nasal cavities connected to the nostrils. The congestion you experience during a bad cold limits this circulation, reducing your ability to smell.

Individuals vary in their sensitivity to smell. As we age, our sensitivity to smell decreases (Rawson, 2006). Females are generally more sensitive to smell than males (Koelega & Koster, 1974), and smokers are less sensitive to smell than nonsmokers (Ahlstrom, Berglund, Berglund, Engen, & Lindvall, 1987). Our ability to perceive a particular odor is also affected by how long we are exposed to the odor. Smell adapts rapidly, a fact to keep in mind when applying your favorite perfume.

OLFACTORY RECEPTORS The neural receptors for olfaction are contained in a thin sheet of cells within the nasal cavity known as the **olfactory epithelium**, illustrated in ● Figure 7.25. Unlike most other types of neurons, olfactory receptor cells regularly die and are replaced in a cycle lasting approximately four to six weeks. In addition to the receptor cells, the olfactory epithelium also contains glia-type support cells that produce mucus. Basal cells in the epithelium give rise to new receptors when needed.

The approximately 10,000 olfactory receptor cells in each nostril are bipolar, having two branches extending from the cell body. One branch reaches out to the surface of the epithelium. Cilia, or hairlike structures, extend from the end of this branch into the mucus that covers the epithelium. Molecules dissolved in the mucus bind and interact with these cilia. The binding of an odorant molecule to a receptor site on a cilium begins a process that results in an influx of sodium and calcium into the receptor neuron. If the resulting depolarization is large enough, it will produce action potentials sent along the branch of the receptor neuron that projects toward the olfactory bulb. These fibers collectively form the olfactory nerve (cranial nerve I), which makes its way centrally to the olfactory bulb.

Olfactory receptors must catalog the many thousands of different smells that we are able to discriminate. Buck and Axel (1991) suggested that mammals can have approximately 1,000 types of receptor cells to accomplish this task, although human beings have only about 350 to 400 (Spehr & Munger, 2009). The relatively lower sensitivity of humans and some other primates appears to be a trade-off for having trichromatic vision (Gilad, Wiebe, Przeworski, Lancet, & Pääbo, 2004). To make room in the brain for processing the amount of visual input available to primates, other systems must be given a lower priority.

How do such a small number of receptors encode information about a wide array of odorants? A shape-pattern theory suggests that odorant molecules interact with receptors like keys fitting into locks. A modification of this approach suggests that odorants can activate specific combinations of receptors. Overall patterns of receptor activity, as opposed to the response of a single type, could distinguish among many separate odorants. Other researchers believe that the olfactory system responds to the vibration of odorant molecules rather than to their shapes (Brookes, Hartoutsiou, Horsfield, & Stoneham, 2007; Turin, 2002).

olfaction The sense of smell.
olfactory epithelium The nasal cavity area containing olfactory receptors.

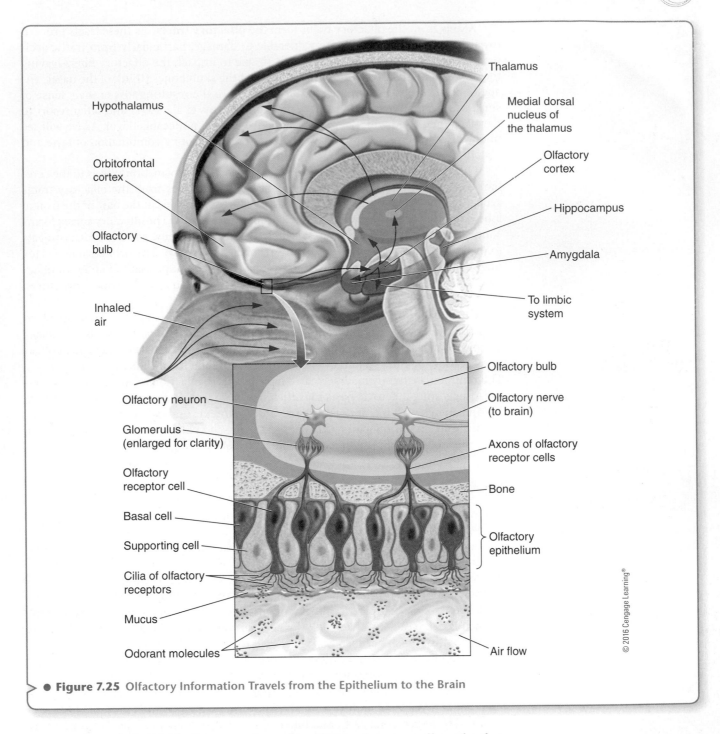

Thalamus

Medial dorsal
nucleus of
the thalamus

Olfactory
cortex

Hippocampus

Amygdala

To limbic
system

Hypothalamus

Orbitofrontal
cortex

Olfactory
bulb

Inhaled
air

Olfactory bulb

Olfactory nerve
(to brain)

Axons of olfactory
receptor cells

Bone

Olfactory
epithelium

Olfactory neuron

Glomerulus
(enlarged for clarity)

Olfactory
receptor cell

Basal cell

Supporting cell

Cilia of olfactory
receptors

Mucus

Odorant molecules

Air flow

© 2016 Cengage Learning®

● **Figure 7.25** Olfactory Information Travels from the Epithelium to the Brain

OLFACTORY PATHWAYS The axons from the olfactory receptor cells make their way to one of our two olfactory bulbs via the olfactory nerve (cranial nerve I). Receptor axons synapse within olfactory bulb structures known as **glomeruli**. In each glomerulus, approximately 25,000 olfactory receptor axons form synapses on about 100 olfactory neurons. Each glomerulus receives information from only one type of receptor cell. In this manner, precise information about the odorant stimulus is transmitted to the olfactory bulbs. It is likely that the bulbs also participate in some initial sorting of odorant categories, but further work is necessary before an odorant can actually be identified. The processing of components making up complex odors remains separate in the olfactory bulb, suggesting that the integration of these components and recognition of odors (the perfume of a rose, for example) occurs at even higher levels of processing in the brain (Lin, Shea, & Katz, 2006).

glomeruli Structures within the olfactory bulb where olfactory receptor axons form synapses with olfactory neurons.

Axons from the olfactory bulbs form the **olfactory tracts.** As these tracts proceed toward the brain, they are quite vulnerable to damage, particularly from traffic accidents. As the head is jerked back and forth due to impact, the olfactory fibers leaving the nose can be sheared by the nearby edges of the skull bones (think of the nasal "triangle" of the skeleton). People typically respond to the resulting loss of their sense of smell by developing symptoms of depression (Deems et al., 1991) and often resort to flavoring their food with pepper sauce to give it some noticeable flavor. As we will see in our discussion of taste, the flavor of a food results from a combination of taste and olfaction, with olfaction playing a leading role.

Olfaction is unique among the major senses in that information travels to the cerebral cortex without synapsing in the thalamus first. Axons from the olfactory tracts synapse in the **olfactory cortex.** The olfactory cortex is located at the base of the frontal lobe extending onto the medial surface of the temporal lobe. The olfactory cortex forms connections with the **medial dorsal nucleus** of the thalamus, which in turn projects to the insula and the orbitofrontal cortex (Sobel et al., 2000). The orbitofrontal cortex might participate in the identification of the pleasant or unpleasant qualities of olfactory stimuli. The olfactory cortex forms connections with many subcortical structures, including the amygdala and hypothalamus.

Olfactory information is widely distributed in the brain and is used by systems involved with odor identification, motivation, emotion, and memory. Olfaction is disturbed by a number of types of psychopathology. People with schizophrenia show deficits in olfaction, possibly due to general problems with frontal lobe functioning (see Chapter 16). Their immediate family members also show deficits in olfaction relative to healthy controls, suggesting a genetic basis for differences in olfactory function (Compton et al., 2006). Patients with major depressive disorder, anorexia nervosa, and alcoholism show specific patterns of olfactory deficits, illustrating the complex relationships between olfaction and emotion (Lombion-Pouthier, Vandel, Nezelof, Haffen, & Millot, 2006).

Gustation

The most likely original purpose of our sense of gustation, or taste, was to protect us from eating poisonous or spoiled food. Many bitter-tasting substances are actually poisonous, and we are attracted to tastes that boost our chances of survival. Gustation is actually a small part of the eating experience. When we eat, we perceive not only the taste of the food but also qualities such as temperature, texture, and consistency (Gibson, 1966). In addition, gustation interacts with olfaction to give us the flavor of a food. You have probably noticed that food just doesn't taste very good when your sense of smell is decreased by a bad cold. If you close your eyes and hold your nose, you are unable to distinguish between a slice of apple and a slice of raw potato.

Gustation begins with the dissolving of molecules in the saliva of the mouth. Saliva is similar in chemical composition to saltwater. Substances that do not dissolve in saliva cannot be tasted, although you can still obtain information about the size, texture, and temperature of objects in the mouth. Most of us are familiar with four major categories of taste: sweet, sour, salty, and bitter. However, you may not have heard of a fifth proposed type of taste, known by the Japanese term **umami**, which, roughly translated, means savory or meaty. Umami tastes are associated with proteins, especially glutamate. In addition, some taste receptors respond to free fatty acids, enabling us to detect the fats in food (Gilbertson, Fontenot, Liu, Zhang, & Monroe, 1997). Still other receptors alert us to the presence of carbohydrates (Turner, Byblow, Stinear, & Gant, 2014).

GUSTATORY RECEPTORS Receptors for taste are found not only on the tongue but also in other parts of the mouth and even in the gut (Egan & Margolskee, 2008). For our present purposes, we'll confine our discussion to the receptors of the tongue, shown in ● Figure 7.26.

Each bump on the surface of the tongue, known as a **papilla**, contains somewhere between 1 and 100 **taste buds**, which are too small to be seen with the naked eye (Bradley, 1979). Some papillae, such as those in the very center of the tongue, contain

---

olfactory tract A fiber pathway connecting the olfactory bulbs to the olfactory cortex.

olfactory cortex Cortex in the frontal and temporal lobes that responds to the sense of smell.

medial dorsal nucleus The area of the thalamus that processes olfactory information.

umami A proposed taste category associated with the presence of proteins.

papilla Bumps on the tongue that contain taste buds.

taste buds Structures that contain taste receptors.

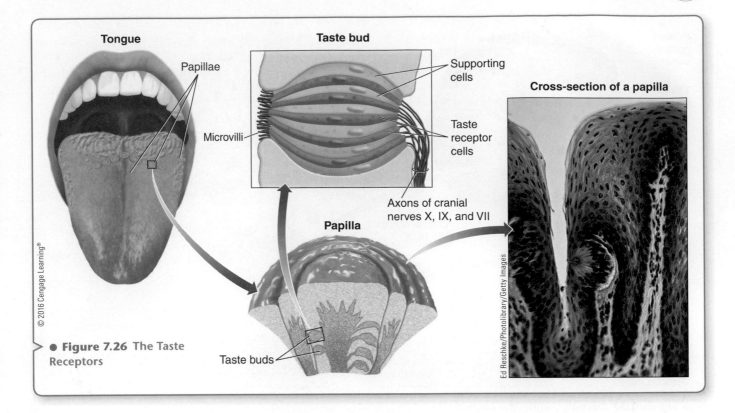

Tongue

Papillae

Microvilli

Taste bud

Supporting cells

Taste receptor cells

Cross-section of a papilla

Axons of cranial nerves X, IX, and VII

Papilla

Taste buds

Ed Reschke/Photolibrary/Getty Images

© 2016 Cengage Learning®

● **Figure 7.26** The Taste Receptors

no taste buds at all. Taste buds live for only about 10 days, after which time they are replaced. Burning your tongue on hot liquid reduces your sense of taste initially, but recovery occurs within a few days. In total, the average person has about 6,000 taste buds, although significant variation can occur from one person to the next (Miller & Reedy, 1990). Linda Bartoshuk (2000) has identified people with unusually high numbers of taste buds, whom she has named "supertasters." Not only do these individuals experience taste with greater intensity, giving them what Bartoshuk refers to as a "neon" sense of taste compared to the "pastels" experienced by others, but they also appear to be more sensitive to oral pain and to the texture of foods.

Most taste buds contain somewhere between 50 and 150 taste receptor cells. The taste receptor cells are not technically considered to be neurons, although they do have the capability of forming synapses. Each taste receptor has a number of thin fibers known as microvilli that extend into the saliva. Substances interact with the microvilli in different ways. Some molecules, such as sodium, pass through the cell's ion channels. Others bind to ion channels, either blocking them or opening them. Finally, some taste molecules bind to receptors on the taste cell and activate second messenger systems (see Chapter 4). The tongue also contains pain receptors that are sensitive to capsaicin, the main "hot" ingredient in peppers. Mice lacking capsaicin receptors happily consumed water containing capsaicin at levels that were rejected by normal mice (Caterina et al., 2000).

For many years, researchers believed that receptors for different taste qualities were located in different parts of the tongue. You probably have seen little maps showing where each taste was supposedly sensed. More recent research demonstrates that this earlier view is incorrect. Receptors for all taste qualities are found in all areas of the tongue (Huang et al., 2006).

GUSTATORY PATHWAYS Pathways linking the taste receptors to the brain are shown in ●Figure 7.27. Although taste receptors do not have a true axon, they are able to contact and influence taste fibers serving the tongue. These taste fibers form parts of cranial nerves VII, IX, and X. These nerves in turn form synapses with the **gustatory nucleus**, which is a part of the solitary nucleus of the medulla. Axons from the gustatory nucleus synapse in the **ventral posterior medial (VPM) nucleus of the thalamus**. Finally, axons from the VPM nucleus synapse in the **gustatory cortex** in the parietal

gustatory nucleus A location within the solitary nucleus that receives gustatory input from cranial nerves VII, IX, and X.
ventral posterior medial (VPM) nucleus of the thalamus The nucleus of the thalamus that receives information regarding taste.
gustatory cortex Area of the parietal lobe that processes gustatory information.

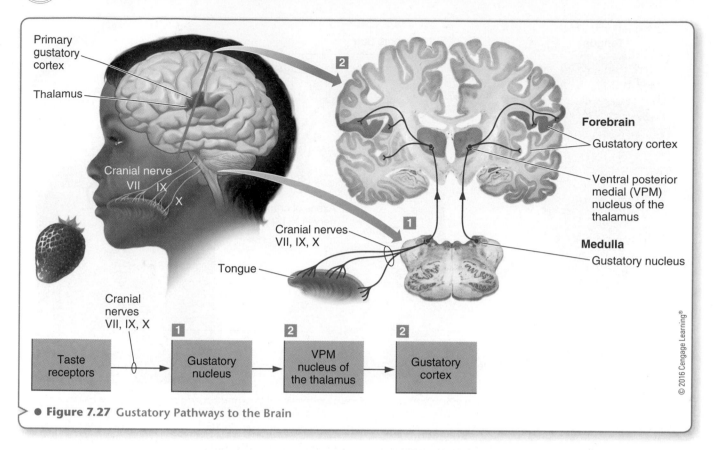

● Figure 7.27 Gustatory Pathways to the Brain

lobe, adjacent to areas of the somatosensory cortex serving the mouth and tongue. The recognition of a type of taste is probably determined at this level. Other fibers make their way to the orbitofrontal cortex. As in the case of olfaction, this input probably encodes the pleasantness, or emotional qualities, of taste.

INTERIM SUMMARY 7.3

‖ Summary Table: Major Features of the Chemical Sensory Systems

Sensory Modality	Receptor Types	Pathways and Connections
Olfaction	Bipolar cells embedded in the olfactory epithelium	• Axons from the receptors synapse in the glomeruli of the olfactory bulbs. • Axons from the olfactory bulbs form the olfactory tract and synapse in the olfactory cortex. • The olfactory cortex sends information to the thalamus, limbic system, insula, and orbitofrontal cortex.
Gustation	Taste buds on the tongue and elsewhere in the mouth	• Fibers serving the taste receptors join cranial nerves VII, IX, and X. • These axons synapse in the gustatory nucleus of the medulla. • Axons from the gustatory nucleus synapse in the ventral posterior medial (VPM) nucleus of the thalamus. • VPM axons synapse in somatosensory cortex and in the orbitofrontal cortex.

‖ Summary Points

1. Olfactory receptors lining the olfactory epithelium of the nasal cavity respond to airborne molecules by sending messages via the olfactory nerve to the olfactory bulb. The olfactory bulb axons project to the olfactory cortex, which forms widely distributed connections with the cerebral cortex and the limbic system. **(LO5)**

2. Interactions between taste receptors and dissolved chemicals activate parts of cranial nerves VII, IX, and X, which synapse with the gustatory nucleus of the medulla. Gustatory nucleus axons synapse in the ventral posterior medial nucleus of the thalamus, which in turn projects to the gustatory cortex and to the orbitofrontal cortex. **(LO5)**

‖ Review Questions

1. What are the major features of olfactory receptors?

2. What are the major types of taste stimuli?

••• Behavioral Neuroscience GOES TO WORK

WHAT IS A PERFUMER?

A quick tour of your home will reveal a large number of products containing scent, from your shampoo to your laundry detergent. Who designs these scents and what is their method?

A perfumer, often called "a nose," is responsible for creating fragrances to be used not just in perfume, but in many other household products as well. For many years, perfumers learned their craft as apprentices, but professional training schools have emerged in the past few decades. Entrance to these schools usually requires a background in chemistry. Training to become a perfumer begins with memorization of hundreds of both natural and synthetic materials, followed by learning how to combine "notes." ●Figure 7.28 shows a "nose" at work in front of his array of scents, known as an "organ." After further training, the perfumer will be tasked with creating new fragrances. Because of the complexity involved in the training, perfumers usually specialize in fine fragrances (perfumes), personal care fragrances, and household fragrances.

Do perfumers have a naturally superior sense of smell? According to brain imaging studies of student and

● **Figure 7.28 A Perfumer at Work** A perfumer, or "nose," works at his organ. Perfumers must develop the ability to remember very large numbers of scents.

expert perfumers, the answer to this question is probably "no" (Plailly, Delon-Martin, & Royet, 2012). Instead, the extensive training and experience of the expert perfumers appears to enhance their ability to generate olfactory mental images. Changes in the primary olfactory cortex, orbitofrontal cortex, and hippocampus are associated with improved memory for odors.

Chapter Review

THOUGHT QUESTIONS

1. If you had to give up one of your senses, which one would it be, and why?
2. What steps can you take to reduce environmental causes of hearing loss?
3. Why does the representation of pain information in the CNS make it difficult to treat chronic pain with surgery?
4. How might the gradual loss of olfactory sensitivity affect the eating habits of seniors?

KEY TERMS

audition (p. 216)

auditory nerve (cranial nerve VIII) (p. 221)

basilar membrane (p. 221)

cochlea (p. 220)

decibel (dB) (p. 218)

glomerulus/glomeruli (p. 247)

gustation (p. 000)

hertz (Hz) (p. 218)

mechanoreceptors (p. 234)

medial geniculate nucleus (p. 224)

nociceptor (p. 241)

olfaction (p. 246)

olfactory cortex (p. 248)

ossicles (p. 220)

otolith organs (p. 231)

pain (p. 218)

pinna (p. 219)

primary auditory cortex (p. 224)

primary somatosensory cortex (p. 233)

saccule (p. 231)

secondary auditory cortex (p. 225)

semicircular canals (p. 231)

somatosensory system (p. 231)

spiral ganglion neurons (p. 222)

tonotopic organization (p. 225)

tympanic membrane (p. 219)

umami (p. 248)

utricle (p. 231)

ventral posterior medial (VPM) nucleus of the thalamus (p. 249)

ventral posterior (VP) nucleus of the thalamus (p. 233)

vestibular system (p. 220)

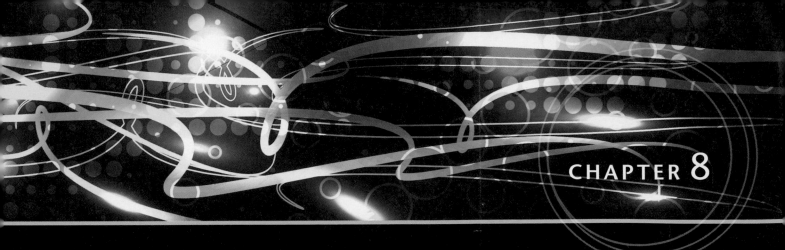

CHAPTER 8

Movement

LEARNING OBJECTIVES

L01 Describe the physical structure of muscle fibers and explain the process of muscle fiber contraction.

L02 Explain the processes responsible for the initiation and control of muscle contractions.

L03 Differentiate among the structures and processes responsible for providing feedback from muscles to the central nervous system.

L04 Describe the major motor reflexes.

L05 Explain the initiation and control of movement, and the ability to understand the movement of others.

L06 Identify the causes, symptoms, and treatments of major disorders of movement.

CHAPTER OUTLINE

THINKING ETHICALLY: Gene Doping for Strength

CONNECTING TO RESEARCH: Mirror Neurons

BUILDING BETTER HEALTH: When Vaccination Is Not Enough

BEHAVIORAL NEUROSCIENCE GOES TO WORK: Physical Therapy

smooth muscle A type of muscle found in the lining of the digestive tract, within arteries, and in the reproductive system; controlled by the autonomic nervous system.

striated muscle A type of muscle named for its striped appearance; including cardiac and skeletal muscles.

cardiac muscle A type of striated muscle found in the heart.

skeletal muscle A type of striated muscle that is attached to bones and is responsible for the majority of body movements.

Muscles

Muscles make up the majority of the human body's tissues and are responsible for the movement of the body and the movement of materials within the body. The human body contains somewhere between 640 and 850 skeletal muscles, depending on which anatomist you ask.

Types of Muscles

The muscles of the body, shown in ● Figure 8.1, can be divided into two types based on their appearance: smooth muscle and striated muscle. **Smooth muscle** is found in the lining of the digestive tract, within the arteries, and in the reproductive system. Smooth muscles move nutrients through the digestive tract, control blood pressure, and mix sperm with seminal fluid, among other tasks. The smooth muscles are controlled by the autonomic nervous system (see Chapter 2).

Striated muscle, named after its striped appearance, can be further divided into two types, cardiac muscle and skeletal muscle. **Cardiac muscle** produces the pumping action of the heart. The **skeletal muscles** attached to bones produce the majority of body movement. Other skeletal muscles are responsible for moving our eyes and

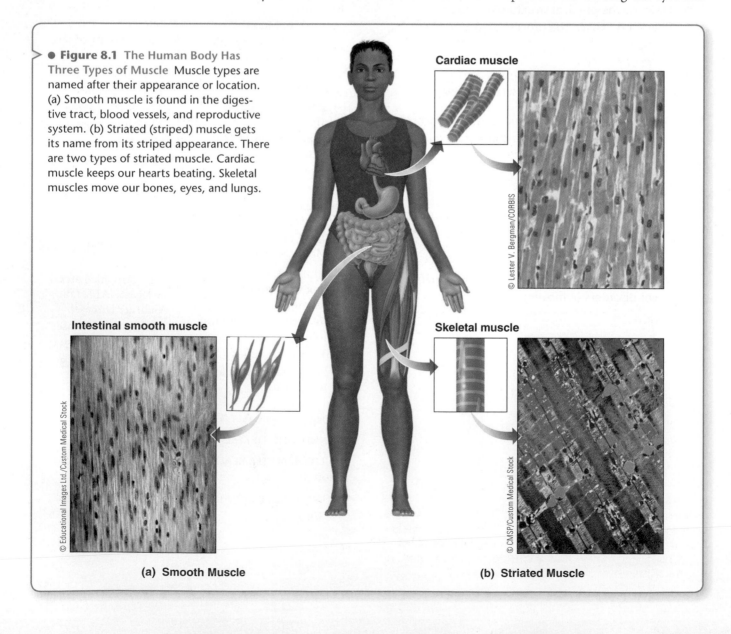

● **Figure 8.1 The Human Body Has Three Types of Muscle** Muscle types are named after their appearance or location. (a) Smooth muscle is found in the digestive tract, blood vessels, and reproductive system. (b) Striated (striped) muscle gets its name from its striped appearance. There are two types of striated muscle. Cardiac muscle keeps our hearts beating. Skeletal muscles move our bones, eyes, and lungs.

Cardiac muscle

© Lester V. Bergman/CORBIS

Intestinal smooth muscle

© Educational Images Ltd./Custom Medical Stock

Skeletal muscle

© CMSP/Custom Medical Stock

(a) Smooth Muscle

(b) Striated Muscle

lungs. Our discussion of movement will focus on the skeletal muscles because these are responsible for the majority of our behavior.

Muscle Anatomy and Contraction

Skeletal muscles, illustrated in ● Figure 8.2, are made up of long, very thin cells referred to as **muscle fibers**. Human muscle fiber cells usually extend the length of the muscle and are up to 30 cm long and from 0.05 mm to 0.15 mm wide.

THE MUSCLE FIBER The membranes encasing each muscle fiber are similar to the membranes of neurons. Like neural membranes, the muscle fiber membrane contains receptor sites, in this case for the neurotransmitter acetylcholine (ACh). When a molecule of ACh binds to a receptor site in the muscle fiber membrane, sodium channels open. Sodium rushing into the muscle fiber depolarizes the cell and triggers an action potential. In Chapter 3, we observed that action potentials in neurons travel in only one direction—from the axon hillock down the length of the axon. In contrast, the

muscle fiber An individual muscle cell.

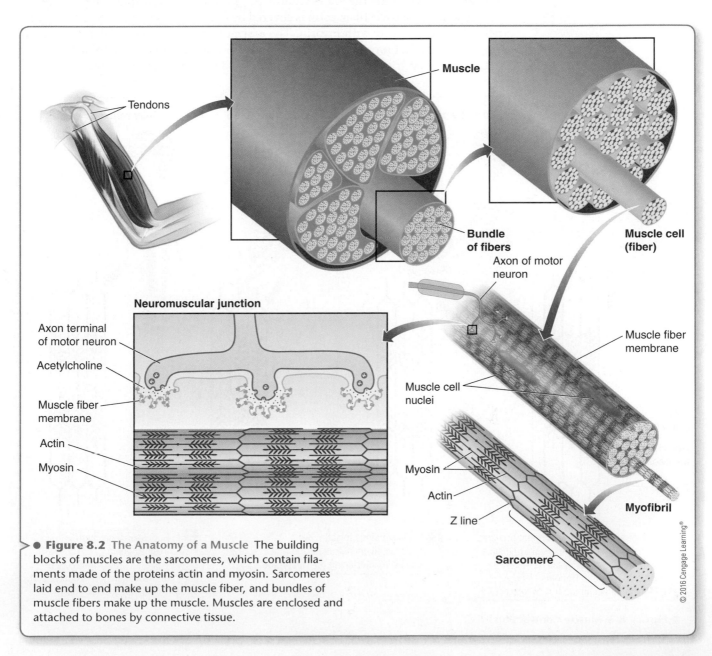

> ● **Figure 8.2** The Anatomy of a Muscle The building blocks of muscles are the sarcomeres, which contain filaments made of the proteins actin and myosin. Sarcomeres laid end to end make up the muscle fiber, and bundles of muscle fibers make up the muscle. Muscles are enclosed and attached to bones by connective tissue.

© 2016 Cengage Learning®

twitch The contraction of a single muscle fiber.

myofibril A long fiber strand running the length of a muscle fiber that is responsible for contraction.

sarcomere A myofibril segment bound on either side by a Z line and spanned by thin filaments.

Z line A boundary line for each sarcomere within a myofibril.

actin A protein that makes up the thin filaments of the myofibril.

myosin A protein that makes up the thick filaments of the myofibril.

troponin The protein covering of an actin molecule that prevents the molecule from binding with myosin when a muscle is in the resting state.

action potential in a muscle fiber spreads out in two directions on either side of the receptor site, which is located in the middle of the fiber. Each action potential produces a single contraction of the muscle fiber, known as a **twitch**.

THE STRUCTURE OF MYOFIBRILS The interior of the muscle fiber is made up of long strands of protein called **myofibrils**. The myofibrils run the length of the fiber and are responsible for producing fiber contractions.

Single segments of a myofibril are called **sarcomeres**, which are arranged end to end. The boundary of each sarcomere is known as a **Z line** because the boundary looks like a Z shape under a microscope. Attached to each Z line are a number of thin filaments made up of the protein **actin**. Lying between each pair of thin filaments is a thick filament made up of the protein **myosin**.

MUSCLE FIBER CONTRACTION Muscle contractions are caused by the movement of the thick myosin filaments along the length of the thin actin filaments. As the filaments slide by each other, the Z lines move closer together, and the sarcomere shortens. As the sarcomeres shorten, the muscle contracts. This process is illustrated in ● Figure 8.3.

In a resting muscle fiber, actin is covered by the protein **troponin**, which prevents actin from interacting with myosin. The arrival of an action potential at the muscle fiber is the catalyst for a series of events that allows actin and myosin to interact. The action potential triggers the release of calcium from internal organelles within the

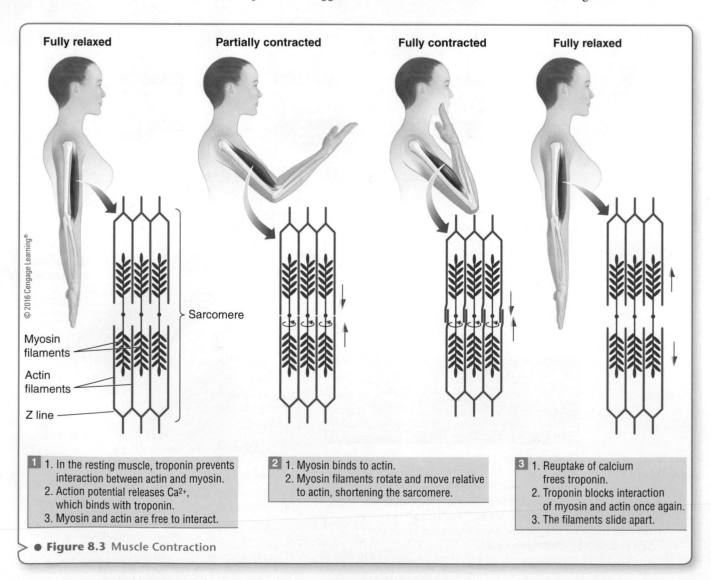

© 2016 Cengage Learning®

Fully relaxed   Partially contracted   Fully contracted   Fully relaxed

Sarcomere

Myosin filaments

Actin filaments

Z line

1. 1. In the resting muscle, troponin prevents interaction between actin and myosin.
   2. Action potential releases Ca²⁺, which binds with troponin.
   3. Myosin and actin are free to interact.

2. 1. Myosin binds to actin.
   2. Myosin filaments rotate and move relative to actin, shortening the sarcomere.

3. 1. Reuptake of calcium frees troponin.
   2. Troponin blocks interaction of myosin and actin once again.
   3. The filaments slide apart.

● **Figure 8.3** Muscle Contraction

muscle fiber. Calcium in turn binds with troponin, neutralizing troponin's blocking effect. Freed from troponin, actin binds with myosin.

As a result of the binding, the myosin molecules rotate, causing the thick myosin filaments to slide past the thin actin filaments. In a process requiring energy, the myosin molecules subsequently separate from the actin molecules. As long as calcium and energy are still present in the muscle fiber, the binding and unbinding process repeats itself, and the myosin filaments move step by step along the length of the actin filaments. Consequently, the muscle fiber gradually contracts.

In the absence of further action potentials, the muscle fiber will relax. Calcium is taken up again by the internal organelles, in a process similar to the reuptake of a neurochemical by a presynaptic neuron. When no longer bound by calcium, troponin once again blocks the interaction of myosin and actin, and the thin and thick filaments slide apart. The sarcomeres and the muscle fiber return to their resting length. If there is a shortage of energy in the cell, the detachment of myosin molecules from actin molecules can't take place, and the muscle becomes locked in its contracted state. This process accounts for the muscular stiffness, or rigor mortis, that occurs after death.

FIBER TYPES AND SPEED   In humans, the thick myosin filaments in muscle fibers come in three varieties. Type I fibers are known as **slow-twitch fibers**, and types IIa and IIb are known as **fast-twitch fibers**. Type IIa fibers are also known as fast-twitch, fatigue-resistant fibers, while type IIb are also known as fast-twitch, fatigable fibers. Type IIb fibers can contract up to 10 times faster than type I fibers. The contraction velocity of type IIa fibers falls somewhere between type I and type IIb (Scott, Stevens, & Binder–Macleod, 2001). Most skeletal muscles contain mixtures of all three types of fibers but in different proportions. The postural muscles of the back, neck, and legs are dominated by slow-twitch fibers. The muscles of the arms and shoulders contain higher proportions of fast-twitch fibers.

Fast- and slow-twitch fibers use energy differently. Slow-twitch fibers use **aerobic metabolism**, which requires oxygen, whereas the fast-twitch fibers use **anaerobic metabolism**, which occurs in the absence of oxygen. Endurance activities, such as distance running, rely primarily on aerobic slow-twitch fibers. Explosive, powerful movements, such as sprinting, jumping, and weightlifting, employ anaerobic fast-twitch fibers. Muscles dominated by fast-twitch fibers appear white (like the white meat of a turkey breast), whereas those containing slow-twitch fibers appear dark or red (like the dark meat of a turkey's legs and thighs). The red color reflects the presence of myoglobin, an iron-based muscle protein that stores the oxygen necessary for aerobic metabolism, and larger numbers of capillaries. Diving animals, such as seals and whales, owe part of their ability to remain submerged to the unusually high amounts of myoglobin contained in their muscles.

The average adult human has approximately equal numbers of fast- and slow-twitch fibers in the quadriceps muscle on the front of the thigh. However, people vary widely in the composition of their muscles. Jesper Andersen and his colleagues (Andersen, Schjerling, & Saltin, 2000) have observed some people with as few as 19 percent slow-twitch fibers in the quadriceps and other people with up to 95 percent slow-twitch fibers. This variation is probably the result of a single gene, *ACTN3*, which normally encodes a protein used by fast-twitch fibers (MacArthur & North, 2007). If a person receives two copies of a common mutation of the *ACTN3* gene, he or she will produce none of the fast-twitch protein at all and would likely excel at long-distance running and other endurance sports. The proportion of fast- and slow-twitch fibers in the quadriceps muscle of people engaged in different levels of activity is shown in ●Figure 8.4.

The Effects of Exercise on Muscle

We know that exercise can build muscles. In many cases, muscle enlargement is desirable. However, enlargement of the cardiac muscle often results in life-threatening heart disease. Muscle enlargement occurs in response to muscle fiber damage. When fibers are

slow-twitch fiber A muscle fiber containing type I myosin filaments and large numbers of mitochondria that contracts slowly using aerobic metabolism; primarily responsible for movement requiring endurance.

fast-twitch fiber A muscle fiber containing type IIa or type IIb myosin filaments that contains few mitochondria, uses anaerobic metabolism, and contracts rapidly; primarily responsible for movement requiring explosive strength.

aerobic metabolism A chemical process that requires oxygen.

anaerobic metabolism A chemical process that does not require oxygen.

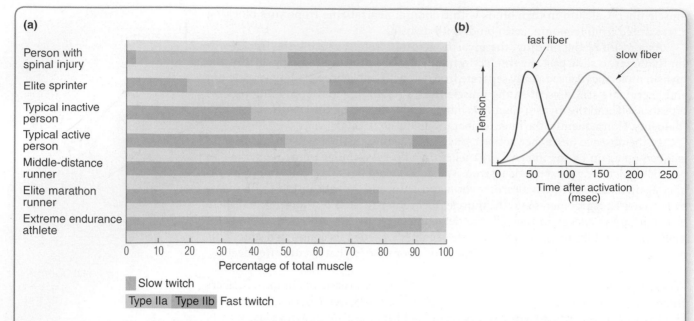

(a)

Person with spinal injury

Elite sprinter

Typical inactive person

Typical active person

Middle-distance runner

Elite marathon runner

Extreme endurance athlete

0 10 20 30 40 50 60 70 80 90 100

Percentage of total muscle

Slow twitch

Type IIa Type IIb Fast twitch

(b)

fast fiber

slow fiber

Tension

0 50 100 150 200 250

Time after activation (msec)

● **Figure 8.4 Human Fiber Types** (a) The average adult has approximately equal amounts of fast- and slow-twitch muscles. People who have spinal injury lose most of their slow-twitch fibers. Athletes involved in power events, such as sprinting, usually have a higher proportion of fast-twitch muscles than athletes involved with endurance sports. (b) Because fast fibers produce muscle tension very quickly, they are useful for explosive movements such as sprinting and weightlifting. The slower fibers can produce equal tension, but require a longer time to do so. Slower fibers are used in endurance activities such as long distance running and swimming.

Source: Data from Anderson, Schjerling, & Saltin (2000).

damaged due to weightlifting or other strenuous activity, more actin and myosin filaments are produced. Lack of activity reverses this process quickly because filament proteins are either broken down faster or synthesized more slowly when muscles are not used (Vandenburgh, Chromiak, Shansky, Del Tatto, & Lemaire, 1999). During space travel, in which lower gravity reduces the activity of major postural muscles, astronauts can lose as much as 20 percent of their muscle mass in as little as two weeks (Andersen et al., 2000).

Under certain circumstances, changes in muscle fiber type do occur. People who are paralyzed as a result of spinal cord injury experience a dramatic increase in fast-twitch fibers and a loss of slow-twitch fibers (see ● Figure 8.4). Apparently, neural input to the muscle, which is lacking in cases of spinal cord injury, is necessary for the maintenance of slow-twitch fibers.

Effects of Aging on Muscles

The loss of muscle mass as a result of aging begins as early as age 25 and accelerates through the remainder of the life span. By the age of 50, most people have lost at least 10 percent of the muscle mass they had at age 25, and that figure rises to 50 percent by the age of 80.

Age-related changes can be observed in both the muscles and the neurons that control them. When older adults move a muscle, the firing rates of the associated neurons are lower than the rates seen in younger adults, resulting in slower and weaker muscle responses (Knight & Kamen, 2007). As shown in ● Figure 8.5, the muscle fibers of young people seen in cross-section are angular, whereas in elderly people, the fibers are rounder. In addition, youthful muscles have a more even distribution of slow- and fast-twitch fibers. In the elderly muscle, the types appear clustered together. Elderly people appear to have a much higher proportion of hybrid muscles, neither slow nor fast, when compared with younger people, largely due to a selective atrophy of type II fibers. Although one cannot stop age-related changes in muscle fibers and neural firing rates, exercising can help offset this decline.

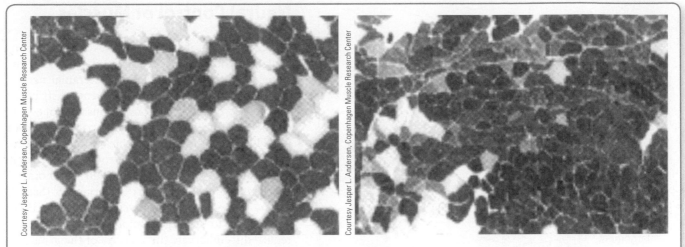

> ● **Figure 8.5 Aging Affects the Quantity, Shape, and Distribution of Muscle Fibers** As we age, we lose muscle fibers, which cannot be regrown. A comparison of the young muscle in the left photo with the aged muscle in the right photo shows other changes. The young muscle has angular-shaped fibers and a checkerboard distribution of fast- (light) and slow- (dark) twitch muscles. The aged muscle shows rounded fibers and clustering of fiber types.

●●● THINKING *Ethically*

GENE DOPING FOR STRENGTH

Athletics represents the very nature of competition, and athletes appear to be willing to go to great lengths to achieve a "competitive edge." The current use of performance-enhancing drugs, such as anabolic steroids, is likely to be eclipsed in the near future by new, genetically based methods. Among the targets for genetically based performance enhancing are myostatin, erythropoietin (EPO), insulin-like growth factor-1 (IGF-I), vascular endothelieal growth factor, fibroblast growth factor, peroxisome proliferator-activated receptor-delta (PPARó), and cytosolic phosphoenolpyruvate carboxykinase (PEPCK-C) (van der Gronde, de Hon, Haisma, & Pieters, 2013). Genetic treatments targeting diseases involving these substances, such as muscular dystrophy (described later in this chapter) could potentially be hijacked by athletes (Fischetto & Bermon, 2013). The strong likelihood that athletes would manipulate combinations of genes, not single genes, would further complicate detection (van der Gronde et al., 2013).

Myostatin is a protein that normally inhibits muscular growth. Inhibition of myostatin due to genetic mutation is associated with unusual musculature and strength. The remarkable musculature of Belgian blue cattle, like the one shown in ● Figure 8.6, results from a mutation in the myostatin gene. Increasing musculature on a frame that was not designed to support it, however, is risky. It is likely that athletes manipulating myostatin would suffer the same or even worse problems with damage to bones and connective tissue

● **Figure 8.6 Myostatin and Muscle Development** The replacement of typical genes with genes that enhance performance, or gene doping, is likely to replace the use of steroids and other drugs to improve athletic performance. One candidate for genetic modification is the gene for myostatin, a protein that limits muscular growth. Belgian Blue cattle have a mutation in the myostatin gene that produces unusual muscle development.

already experienced by those who use steroids to boost muscle growth.

Gene therapy is still in a very early stage of development, and patients in clinical trials have died during the administration of these types of treatments (Deakin, Alexander, & Kerridge, 2009). The risks, however, are unlikely to deter all athletes, who are already familiar with physical challenges.

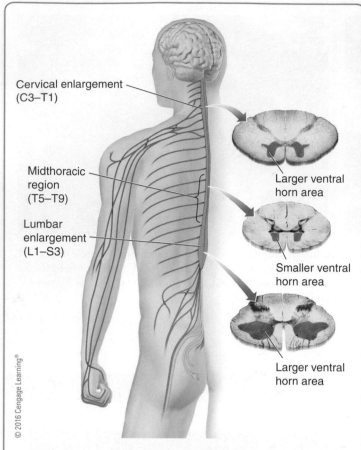

Cervical enlargement
(C3–T1)

Midthoracic
region
(T5–T9)

Lumbar
enlargement
(L1–S3)

Larger ventral
horn area

Smaller ventral
horn area

Larger ventral
horn area

> ● **Figure 8.7** **Distribution of Spinal Motor Neurons** The
spinal cord bulges in the segments that serve the arms and legs,
due to the large number of alpha motor neurons located in the
ventral parts of those segments. In comparison, relatively few
alpha motor neurons serve the torso.

Neural Control of Muscles

The contraction of skeletal muscles is directly controlled by motor neurons originating in either the
spinal cord or in the nuclei of the cranial nerves.
Just as skeletal muscles are not evenly distributed
throughout the body, motor neurons are not evenly
distributed throughout the spinal cord. As shown
in ● Figure 8.7, the ventral horns of the spinal cord,
which contain the motor neurons, appear large
in segments C (Cervical) 3 through T (Thoracic)
1 and again in L (Lumbar) 1 through S (Sacral)
3. The enlargement of the ventral horns in these
areas is due to the large number of motor neurons
required to innervate the muscles of the arms and
legs, respectively.

Alpha Motor Neurons

The spinal motor neurons directly responsible for
contracting muscles are known as **alpha motor neurons**. These are large myelinated neurons capable
of rapid signaling. The alpha motor neurons form
highly efficient connections with muscle fibers at a
location called the **neuromuscular junction**, shown
in ● Figure 8.8. Because of the efficiency of this
connection, a single action potential in the motor
neuron terminal is capable of producing an action
potential in the muscle fiber, leading to a single contraction, or twitch.

> ● **Figure 8.8** **The
Neuromuscular Junction**
This image shows alpha motor
neurons making contact with
individual muscle fibers. The
little dots at the end of each
motor neuron fiber are individual axon terminals.

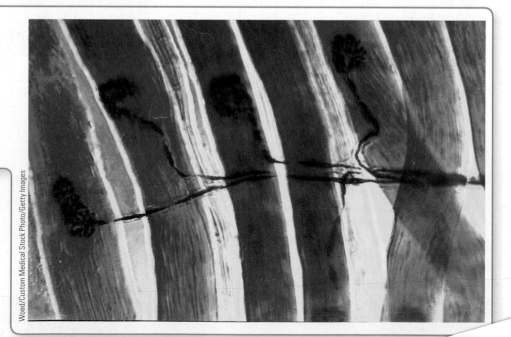

alpha motor neuron A spinal
motor neuron directly
responsible for signaling a muscle
fiber to contract.

neuromuscular junction A
synapse formed between an alpha
motor neuron axon terminal and
a muscle fiber.

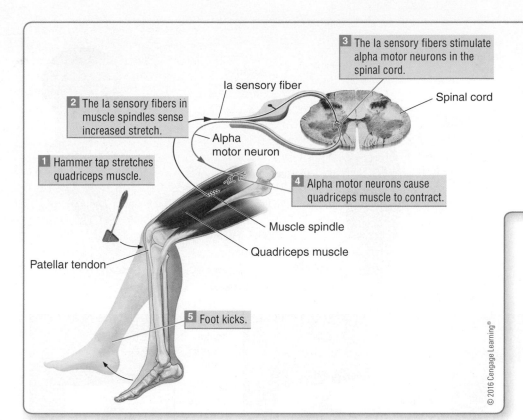

2 The Ia sensory fibers in muscle spindles sense increased stretch.

Ia sensory fiber

3 The Ia sensory fibers stimulate alpha motor neurons in the spinal cord.

Spinal cord

Alpha motor neuron

1 Hammer tap stretches quadriceps muscle.

4 Alpha motor neurons cause quadriceps muscle to contract.

Muscle spindle

Quadriceps muscle

Patellar tendon

5 Foot kicks.

● **Figure 8.10 The Patellar Tendon (Knee-Jerk) Reflex** The familiar patellar tendon or knee-jerk reflex tested by physicians in annual physicals is an example of a myotatic reflex. Myotatic reflexes occur when stretching of a muscle initiates a compensating contraction.

© 2016 Cengage Learning®

stretch, the quadriceps contracts and the foot kicks out. This test helps to determine whether a person's myotatic reflexes are in good working order. Some medical conditions, such as diabetes and Parkinson's disease, reduce or eliminate the reflex. Other medical conditions, such as meningitis (see Chapters 2 and 15), often produce exaggerated responses.

We have seen that the alpha motor neurons provide input to the extrafusal fibers. The intrafusal fibers have their own set of motor neurons, known as **gamma motor neurons**, shown in ● Figures 8.9 and 8.11. Why would the intrafusal fibers need input when they do not contribute to the overall contraction of a muscle? Without the gamma motor neurons, the intrafusal fibers could not provide accurate information about how far the muscle was stretched. When the extrafusal fibers contract, the intrafusal fibers would become limp if they did not also contract. This would cause the Ia and II sensory fibers to stop signaling, and the brain and spinal cord would not know how long the muscle was. To solve this problem, gamma motor neurons and alpha motor neurons are activated simultaneously by input from the brain. The gamma motor neurons cause a small contraction of the spindle at nearly the same time that the alpha motor neurons contract the extrafusal fibers. In this way, the spindle matches the length of the muscle, and the Ia and II fibers can provide continuous feedback.

FEEDBACK FROM GOLGI TENDON ORGANS The muscle spindles do a good job of providing the brain and spinal cord with information about muscle length, or the degree of stretch. However, we also need feedback regarding the degree of muscle contraction, or force. This information is provided by the **Golgi tendon organs**, which are located at the junction between a muscle and its tendon.

Like the muscle spindles, the Golgi tendon organs are innervated by sensory axons, the **Ib sensory fibers**. Ib fibers are a second type of Alpha-alpha (Aα) fiber

gamma (γ) motor neuron A small spinal neuron that innervates the muscle spindles.

Golgi tendon organ A structure located in the tendons of muscles that provides information about muscle contraction.

Ib sensory fiber A small, slower Alpha-alpha (Aα) sensory axon that connects the Golgi tendon organs to neurons in the spinal cord.

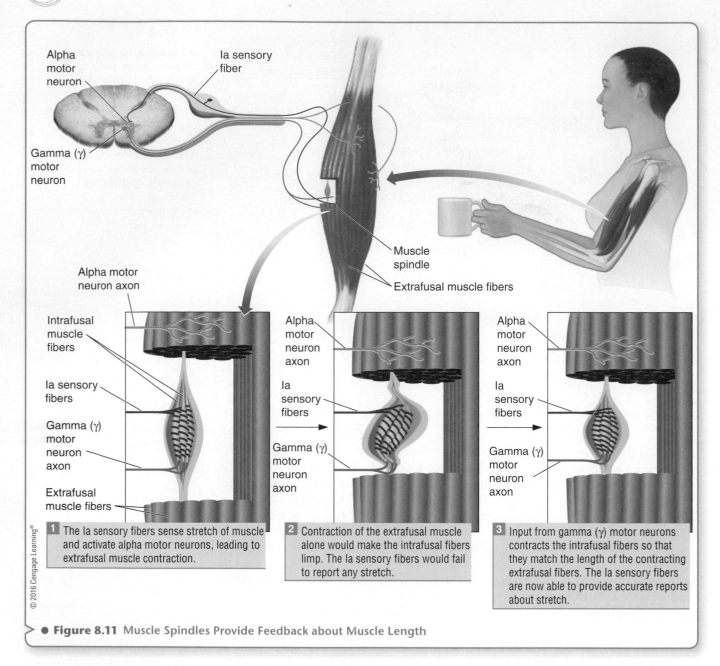

Alpha motor neuron

Ia sensory fiber

Gamma (γ) motor neuron

Alpha motor neuron axon

Muscle spindle

Extrafusal muscle fibers

Intrafusal muscle fibers

Ia sensory fibers

Gamma (γ) motor neuron axon

Extrafusal muscle fibers

Alpha motor neuron axon

Ia sensory fibers

Gamma (γ) motor neuron axon

Alpha motor neuron axon

Ia sensory fibers

Gamma (γ) motor neuron axon

1 The Ia sensory fibers sense stretch of muscle and activate alpha motor neurons, leading to extrafusal muscle contraction.

2 Contraction of the extrafusal muscle alone would make the intrafusal fibers limp. The Ia sensory fibers would fail to report any stretch.

3 Input from gamma (γ) motor neurons contracts the intrafusal fibers so that they match the length of the contracting extrafusal fibers. The Ia sensory fibers are now able to provide accurate reports about stretch.

● **Figure 8.11** Muscle Spindles Provide Feedback about Muscle Length

but are smaller and slower than the Ia fibers that innervate the spindles. The Ib fibers from the Golgi tendon organs enter the spinal cord and form synapses with spinal interneurons. In turn, these interneurons form inhibitory synapses on alpha motor neurons.

To understand how the Golgi tendon organ feedback loop works, we return to the example of holding a coffee cup steady. The Ia and II fibers from muscle spindles in your fingers and arm sense the stretch needed to hold the cup and activate the alpha motor neurons. The Golgi tendon organs respond to the resulting increase in muscle tension by sending signals to the spinal interneurons via the Ib sensory fibers. In response to this input, the interneurons inhibit the alpha motor neurons, and muscle contraction is reduced. However, the reduced muscle contraction results in less Golgi tendon organ activity, less input to the spinal interneurons, and less inhibition of the alpha motor neurons. The muscle contracts again. Not only does this system help prevent damage to the muscle fibers from too much contraction, but it also maintains the steady control over muscle tension that we need, particularly for fine motor movements. This process is illustrated in ● Figure 8.12.

FEEDBACK FROM JOINTS In addition to receiving feedback about muscle length and tension, we also receive information about position and movement from mechanoreceptors in the tissues surrounding each joint. These mechanoreceptors, which we discussed in Chapter 7, respond primarily to movement of the joint, and they are relatively quiet when the joint is at rest. Receptors located in the skin near joints also supply information about movement and position (Edin, 2001). Free nerve endings can signal pain resulting from extreme joint positions. It appears that joint receptors are not entirely necessary for judging the location of a joint. People who have undergone full hip or knee replacement surgery lose all of their joint receptors in the procedure, yet they can still describe the position of their joint without looking.

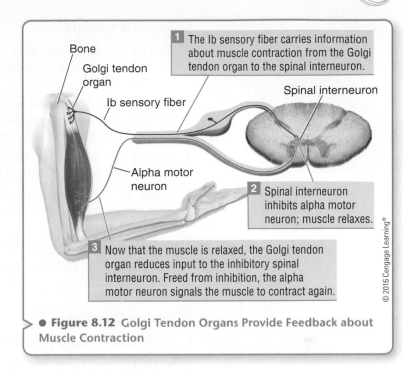

1 The Ib sensory fiber carries information about muscle contraction from the Golgi tendon organ to the spinal interneuron.

2 Spinal interneuron inhibits alpha motor neuron; muscle relaxes.

3 Now that the muscle is relaxed, the Golgi tendon organ reduces input to the inhibitory spinal interneuron. Freed from inhibition, the alpha motor neuron signals the muscle to contract again.

● **Figure 8.12** Golgi Tendon Organs Provide Feedback about Muscle Contraction

© 2016 Cengage Learning®

INTERIM SUMMARY 8.1

Summary Table: The Control of Spinal Motor Neurons

Cell Type	Location	Source of Input to These Cells	Fiber Type	Action Produced
Alpha motor neurons	Ventral horns of the spinal cord, some cranial nerve nuclei	Motor cortex, brainstem, muscle spindles, spinal interneurons		Alpha motor neurons produce action potentials in muscle fibers, leading to contraction.
Muscle spindles	Lie parallel to muscle fibers within a muscle	Respond to stretch of associated muscle fibers	Ia and II sensory fibers	Muscle spindles synapse with alpha motor neurons and spinal interneurons, allowing muscle contraction to adjust to muscle stretching.
Gamma motor neurons	Ventral horns of the spinal cord, some cranial nerve nuclei	Motor cortex, brainstem		Gamma motor neurons contract the muscle spindle to match spindle length to surrounding muscle fibers.
Golgi tendon organs	Junctions between muscles and tendons	Respond to tension in muscle	Ib sensory fibers	Golgi tendon organs synapse with spinal interneurons, inhibiting activity of alpha motor neurons, reducing contraction.

Summary Points

1. Muscles can be divided into three types: smooth muscles, cardiac muscles, and skeletal muscles. Together, the cardiac and skeletal muscles are known as striated muscles. (LO1)

2. Skeletal muscles are made up of individual muscle fibers surrounded by a membrane similar to that of a neuron. Muscle fiber contractions result from the movement of myosin filaments relative to actin filaments. (LO1)

3. Alpha motor neurons in the spinal cord or cranial nerve nuclei produce muscle contraction through their activity at the neuromuscular junction. (LO2)

4. Muscle spindles provide information about muscle stretch. Gamma motor neurons help the muscle spindle match the length of the muscle, providing continuous feedback. (LO3)

5. Golgi tendon organs located in the connective tissue between muscle and bone provide information regarding muscle contraction. Additional joint receptors provide information regarding the movement of joints. (LO3)

Review Questions

1. What is the sequence of events within the myofibril that leads to contraction?

2. What is a motor unit, and how do the units differ in terms of size, precision of movement, and muscle fiber type?

Reflex Control of Movement

The spinal cord is responsible for a number of reflex movements designed to protect us from injury, to maintain posture, and to coordinate the movement of our limbs. Most of these reflexes are examples of **polysynaptic reflexes**, or reflexes requiring more than one synapse. In contrast, the myotatic reflexes discussed previously are monosynaptic, or requiring only a single synapse between a sensory neuron and a motor neuron.

Reciprocal Inhibition at Joints

Muscles can do only one thing: contract. The contraction of a single muscle can either straighten or bend a joint, but not both. As a result, a muscle is able to pull a bone in a single direction but is unable to push it back. Relaxing the muscle will not necessarily cause a limb to move back to its original position.

To move a joint in two directions requires two muscles. Muscles are arranged at a joint in **antagonistic pairs**, as shown in ● Figure 8.13. Muscles that straighten joints are referred to as **extensors**, and muscles that bend joints are known as **flexors**. To bend the knee, the flexor muscles of the thigh must contract while the extensor muscles relax. To straighten the leg, the extensor muscles must contract while the flexors relax. Under most circumstances, flexors and extensors at the same joint are prevented from simultaneously contracting by a polysynaptic reflex known as **reciprocal inhibition**.

Coordinating this reciprocal inhibition requires inhibitory spinal interneurons. The Ia fibers branch in the spinal cord. As discussed previously, one branch communicates with the alpha motor neuron serving the muscle that is contracting to keep muscle tension steady. The other branch communicates with an inhibitory interneuron, which in turn synapses onto the alpha motor neuron serving the opposing muscle that needs to relax. Thus, information about contraction of the first muscle is transmitted by the Ia fiber to the inhibitory interneuron, which in turn prevents the alpha motor neuron from contracting the opposing muscle.

polysynaptic reflex A spinal reflex that requires interaction at more than one synapse.

antagonistic pair Two opposing muscles, one a flexor and one an extensor, arranged at a joint.

extensor A muscle that acts to straighten a joint.

flexor A muscle that acts to bend a joint.

reciprocal inhibition A polysynaptic reflex that prevents the simultaneous contraction of flexors and extensors serving the same joint.

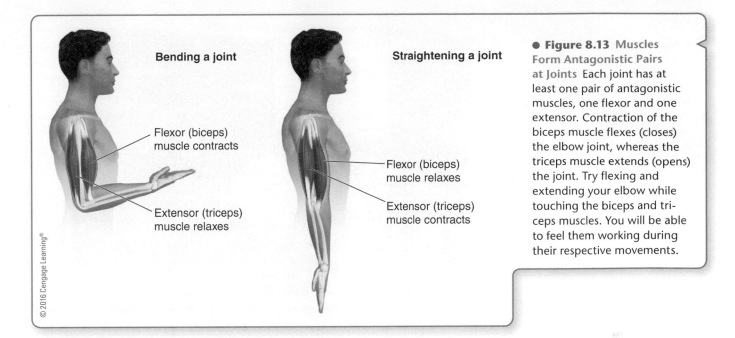

Bending a joint

Flexor (biceps) muscle contracts

Extensor (triceps) muscle relaxes

Straightening a joint

Flexor (biceps) muscle relaxes

Extensor (triceps) muscle contracts

● **Figure 8.13 Muscles Form Antagonistic Pairs at Joints** Each joint has at least one pair of antagonistic muscles, one flexor and one extensor. Contraction of the biceps muscle flexes (closes) the elbow joint, whereas the triceps muscle extends (opens) the joint. Try flexing and extending your elbow while touching the biceps and triceps muscles. You will be able to feel them working during their respective movements.

© 2016 Cengage Learning®

In some circumstances, such as when we stiffen our elbows while catching a ball, the stability provided by simultaneous contraction of antagonistic muscle pairs is actually desirable. Achieving simultaneous contraction rather than reciprocal inhibition requires descending control from the brain, which acts by changing the firing patterns of the inhibitory spinal interneurons.

The Flexor Reflex

Another familiar example of a polysynaptic reflex is the **flexor reflex**. We rely on flexor reflexes to protect us from further injury, such as when we jerk our hand away after touching a hot surface on the stove. It's a good thing that the spinal cord, rather than the brain, manages this function. By the time the brain perceived the problem, generated solutions, evaluated solutions, and implemented solutions, your hand would be in bad shape. The flexor reflex begins as sensory neurons transmit information about the painful stimulus to interneurons in the spinal cord. The interneurons excite the alpha motor neurons serving the flexor muscles of the affected limb. At the same time, alpha motor neurons serving the opposing muscle, the extensor, are inhibited. As a result, your hand is successfully pulled back from the heat source.

Spinal Reflexes Related to Walking

More complicated polysynaptic reflexes help coordinate the movement of several limbs at once. When we walk, we naturally balance our weight from side to side and swing our arms. These complex movements require many more synapses than the previous simple reflexes. In addition, there is growing evidence that the rhythm of movements such as walking is governed by spontaneously active central pattern generators within the spinal cord (Grillner et al., 1998; Marder & Bucher, 2001; Gordon & Whelan, 2006). In some patients, like the one shown in ● Figure 8.14, epidural stimulation of the central pattern generators of the spinal cord restored standing, voluntary movement, and assisted stepping in a patient with spinal cord injury (Harkema et al., 2011).

flexor reflex A polysynaptic spinal reflex that produces withdrawal of a limb from a painful stimulus.

● **Figure 8.14** The use of epidural stimulation to activate central pattern generators in the spinal cord has been used to restore some voluntary movement to patients with spinal cord damage.

University of Louisville

Reflexes over the Lifespan

The reflexes we have discussed so far are present throughout the human life span. Other types of reflexes are characteristic of young children but tend to diminish as the nervous system matures. These childhood reflexes are not lost by the nervous system, but they become inhibited or overwritten by other processes. When this normal inhibition of childhood reflexes fails due to brain damage or the use of alcohol and other drugs, the reflexes will reappear.

Among the normal childhood reflexes is the **Babinski sign**, a type of polysynaptic flexion reflex. When you stroke the bottom surface of the foot, infants will spread their toes with the big toe pointing up. The Babinski sign does not appear to confer any particular benefit to the infant. Instead, the reflex probably reflects the immaturity of the infant's motor system. In typical adults, stroking the bottom of the foot causes the toes to curl down, not up. Adults with damage to either the motor cortex or spinal motor pathways will show the infant's version of the reflex (Gardner, 1968). An illustration comparing the typical adult reaction with the infant's Babinski sign may be seen in ● Figure 8.15.

● **Figure 8.15** The Babinski Sign (a) Stroking the bottom of an infant's foot causes the toes to spread and the big toe to point upward, a movement known as the Babinski sign. (b) Stroking the bottom of an adult's foot results in the downward curling of the toes. In adults, the Babinski sign often indicates brain damage.

Babinski sign A polysynaptic reflex present in infants and in adults with neural damage, in which stroking the sole of the foot causes the toes to spread with the big toe pointing upward.

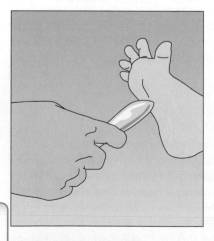

(a) Typical infant Version of Babinski Sign

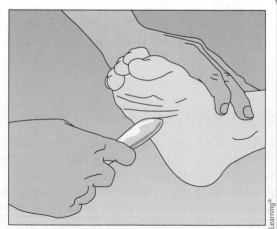

(b) Typical Reaction to the Stroking of the Foot in Subjects over Two Years Old

© 2016 Cengage Learning®

Motor Systems of the Brain

The alpha motor neurons that contract muscle fibers are at the lowest end of a chain of command for initiating movement. In addition to input from interneurons and stretch receptors, the alpha motor neurons receive direction from neurons located in the cerebellum, basal ganglia, red nucleus, brainstem, and cerebral cortex. As we will see, some of these motor pathways initiate voluntary movement, whereas others are responsible for subconscious, automatic movements.

The central motor system is not strictly hiearchical, however. Multiple parallel pathways communicate from one level of the motor system to the next. As a result, we usually observe complete paralysis only as a result of damage to the lowest levels of the hierarchy in the spinal cord. Damage to the brain itself, for example, can definitely impact movement in a negative way, but moving is still typically possible due to the ability of one pathway to compensate for damage to another.

Spinal Motor Pathways

Motor neurons in the spinal cord can be located according to their roles as serving flexors and extensors and whether they serve proximal or distal parts of the body (see Chapter 2). Motor neurons associated with flexors are located dorsally to those associated with extensors. Motor neurons associated with distal structures, such as your hands, are located laterally to those than serve more proximal structures, like your torso.

As shown in ● Figure 8.16, signals from the brain to the spinal alpha motor neurons travel along two routes. The first route, known as the **lateral pathway**, is located in the lateral part of the spinal column. This pathway originates primarily in the cerebral cortex and is the pathway through which the brain controls voluntary fine movements of the hands, feet, and outer limbs. You use this pathway to write notes, to drive your car, and to type on your keyboard.

The second route, known as the **ventromedial pathway**, travels along the ventromedial part of the spinal column. Most of the neurons that supply axons to this pathway are located in the brainstem rather than in the cerebral cortex. As a result, the ventromedial pathway carries commands from the brain for automatic movements in the neck, torso, and portions of the limbs close to the body. You use the ventromedial pathway for behaviors such as maintaining posture and muscle tone and moving the head in response to visual stimuli. The functions of these two pathways are easier to remember if you think of the lateral pathway as a long-distance system serving more distal structures (hands, feet, limbs) and the ventromedial pathway as a relatively local system serving more proximal structures (neck and torso.)

Cell bodies giving rise to the axons of the lateral pathway are located either in the primary motor cortex of the frontal lobe (the corticospinal tract) or in the red nucleus of the midbrain (the rubrospinal tract). As is true of most anatomical terms, the first part of each term refers to the origin of the pathway (*rubro* refers to red) and the last part of the term refers to the pathway's endpoint.

The fibers of the **corticospinal tract** are some of the fastest and longest in the central nervous system (CNS). This is the only descending system that makes direct synapses with alpha motor neurons. Humans and other primates have more of these directly synapsing corticospinal neurons than most other animals, and this feature probably accounts for our remarkable fine motor coordination of the hands and fingers.

The **rubrospinal tract** connects the red nucleus of the midbrain to the alpha motor neurons of the spinal cord. As you may recall from Chapter 2, the red nucleus receives substantial input from the motor cortex. Consequently, the motor cortex exerts both direct control (via the corticospinal tract) and indirect control (via the rubrospinal tract) on the alpha motor neurons of the spinal cord. However, the main source of input to the red nucleus is the cerebellum, so this pathway is probably one way that learned patterns of movement are communicated to the muscles.

lateral pathway A large collection of axons that originates in the cerebral cortex, synapses on either the red nucleus or alpha motor neurons, and controls voluntary movements.

ventromedial pathway A spinal motor pathway originating in the brainstem and carrying commands for subconscious, automatic movements of the neck and torso.

corticospinal tract A pathway connecting the motor cortex to alpha motor neurons in the spinal cord.

rubrospinal tract A pathway connecting the red nucleus of the midbrain to the alpha motor neurons of the spinal cord.

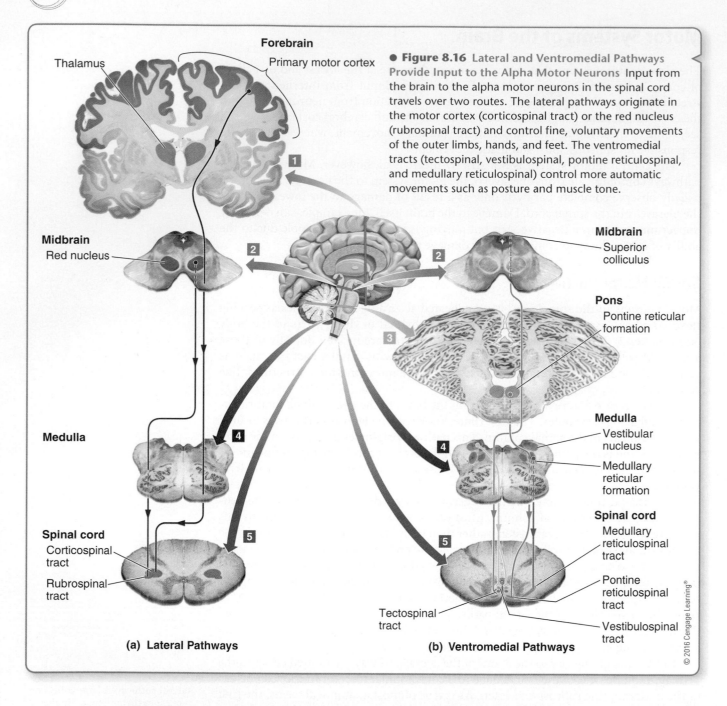

Forebrain

Thalamus

Primary motor cortex

● **Figure 8.16** Lateral and Ventromedial Pathways Provide Input to the Alpha Motor Neurons Input from the brain to the alpha motor neurons in the spinal cord travels over two routes. The lateral pathways originate in the motor cortex (corticospinal tract) or the red nucleus (rubrospinal tract) and control fine, voluntary movements of the outer limbs, hands, and feet. The ventromedial tracts (tectospinal, vestibulospinal, pontine reticulospinal, and medullary reticulospinal) control more automatic movements such as posture and muscle tone.

Midbrain
Red nucleus

Midbrain
Superior colliculus

Pons
Pontine reticular formation

Medulla

Medulla
Vestibular nucleus

Medullary reticular formation

Spinal cord
Corticospinal tract

Rubrospinal tract

Spinal cord
Medullary reticulospinal tract

Pontine reticulospinal tract

Tectospinal tract

Vestibulospinal tract

(a) Lateral Pathways

(b) Ventromedial Pathways

© 2016 Cengage Learning®

As these pathways travel from the cortex to the spinal cord, they decussate or cross the midline. The rubrospinal tract decussates immediately, and the corticospinal tract decussates at the junction of the medulla and the spinal cord. Crossing the midline means that the right hemisphere's motor cortex controls the left side of the body, whereas the left hemisphere's motor cortex controls the right side of the body. Although the advantages of this organization remain a mystery, the results are most obvious when a person has damaged either the motor cortex or the descending lateral pathways due to a stroke or other accident. If the damage occurs in the right hemisphere, the left side of the body will be weakened or paralyzed. If the damage occurs in the left hemisphere, the right side of the body will be weakened or paralyzed.

The four ventromedial pathways stimulate the alpha motor neurons to help maintain posture and carry out reflexive responses to sensory input such as moving the head and torso in coordination with our eye movements. The ventromedial pathways also assist in behaviors such as walking, in spite of the fact that these behaviors are largely under cortical control. These pathways originate in various parts of the brainstem, including the vestibular nuclei of the medulla, the superior colliculi of the midbrain, and the reticular formation in the pons and medulla. Once again, you can use the names of these tracts to remember their points of origin. The **tectospinal tract** originates in the tectum of the midbrain, primarily in the superior and inferior colliculi (see Chapter 2). The **vestibulospinal tract** originates in the vestibular nuclei of the medulla, and the **pontine** and **medullary reticulospinal tracts** originate in the reticular formation at the levels of the pons and medulla, respectively. The reticulospinal tract ensures that the flexor reflex described earlier will result from painful stimuli, but not other types of input.

The Cerebellum

The cerebellum participates in the maintenance of balance and coordination, as well as in the learning of motor skills (see Chapter 2). The cerebellum's role in movement is probably its best understood function, and most of its output connects with other motor systems, but it would be inaccurate to conclude that its functions are restricted to movement. The cerebellum also participates in language and other cognitive processes, discussed further in Chapter 12.

Although the cerebellum does not appear to initiate movement, it plays a very important role in the sequencing of complex movements. As you ride a bicycle or shoot a basket, your cerebellum is coordinating the contraction and relaxation of muscles at just the right time.

To understand the value of the cerebellum, it's helpful to see what happens when the cerebellum is not working. One common example of poor cerebellar function occurs when a person drinks alcohol. The cerebellum is one of the first structures in the brain to show the effects of alcohol, leading to a lack of balance and coordination. As a result, law enforcement personnel check the function of the cerebellum to assess drunkenness. Most sobriety tests, such as walking a straight line, are essentially the same as the tests a neurologist would use to diagnose lesions in the cerebellum.

How does the cerebellum help us coordinate sequenced movements? It appears that the cerebellum is able to inform the motor cortex about such factors as the direction, force, and timing required to carry out a skilled movement. In many cases, this process requires learning. The cerebellum is constantly comparing the cortex's intended movements with what actually happened. Adjustments as needed are made for future activity.

The Basal Ganglia

Moving rostrally through the motor hierarchy toward the cerebral cortex, we come next to the basal ganglia, a collection of large nuclei embedded within the white matter of the cerebral hemispheres. The location of the basal ganglia is illustrated in ● Figure 8.17. Among their many tasks, only some of which involve motor activity, the basal ganglia participate in the choice and initiation of voluntary movements.

As we saw in Chapter 2, the basal ganglia consist of the caudate nucleus, the putamen, the globus pallidus, the nucleus accumbens, and the subthalamic nucleus. Some anatomists include the substantia nigra of the midbrain in their discussion of the basal ganglia, due to the close linkages between these structures. Complex interactive loops connect the basal ganglia with the thalamus and with the motor cortex in the frontal lobe. The basal ganglia interact with the thalamus via two pathways, a direct pathway that excites the thalamus and an indirect pathway that inhibits the thalamus. As a result, you might think of the basal ganglia as a gate or filter for intentional activity, in which motor programs associated with reward will be carried out while competing motor programs unlikely to produce reward in the present circumstances

tectospinal tract A ventromedial pathway connecting the tectum of the midbrain to the alpha motor neurons in the spinal cord.

vestibulospinal tract A ventromedial pathway that connects the vestibular nuclei of the medulla to the alpha motor neurons of the spinal cord.

pontine reticulospinal tract A ventromedial pathway connecting the reticular formation in the pons to the alpha motor neurons of the spinal cord.

medullary reticulospinal tract A ventromedial pathway connecting the reticular formation in the medulla to the alpha motor neurons of the spinal cord.

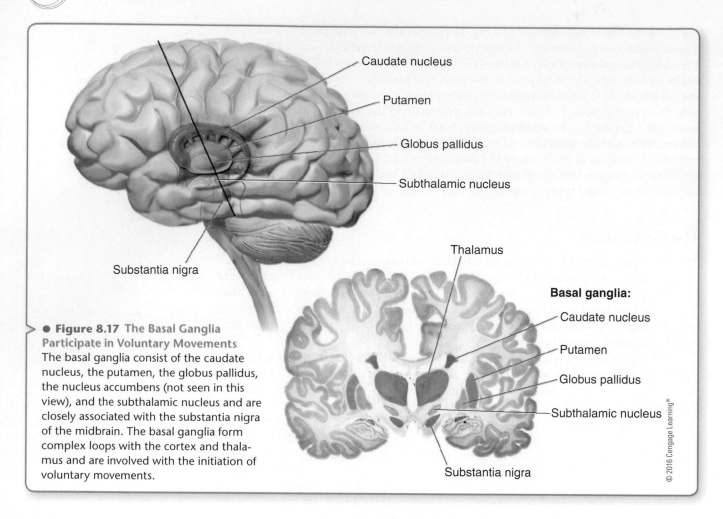

● **Figure 8.17 The Basal Ganglia Participate in Voluntary Movements** The basal ganglia consist of the caudate nucleus, the putamen, the globus pallidus, the nucleus accumbens (not seen in this view), and the subthalamic nucleus and are closely associated with the substantia nigra of the midbrain. The basal ganglia form complex loops with the cortex and thalamus and are involved with the initiation of voluntary movements.

© 2016 Cengage Learning®

are inhibited. In other words, the basal ganglia do not initiate movement, but without the "approval" of the basal ganglia, the cerebral cortex cannot send motor commands to lower levels of the system.

As we will see later in the chapter, a number of disorders result from abnormalities in the basal ganglia, including Parkinson's disease and Huntington's disease. These conditions feature motor activity that is either lower (Parkinson's) or higher (Huntington's) than normal. In addition to these two primarily motor disorders, the basal ganglia are implicated in a number of psychological disorders, including obsessive-compulsive disorder and attention deficit hyperactivity disorder (see Chapter 16). Like the cerebellum, the basal ganglia participate in a number of important cognitive functions in addition to their motor responsibilities, such as the formation and management of various types of implicit or unconscious memories (see Chapter 12).

The Motor Cortex

supplementary motor area (SMA) Motor area located in the gyrus rostral to the precentral gyrus; involved with managing complex sequences of movement.

premotor cortex A motor area located in the gyrus rostral to the precentral gyrus; this area participates in holding a motor plan until it can be implemented; formerly referred to as the premotor area (PMA).

Cortex located in the precentral (before the central sulcus) gyrus has been identified as primary motor cortex (M1), the main source of voluntary motor control. The primary motor cortex not only forms direct connections with the spinal alpha motor neurons, but it also influences the activity of the other motor pathways, including the rubrospinal, tectospinal, and reticulospinal pathways discussed earlier. In the gyrus just rostral to primary motor cortex, additional motor areas were identified by Wilder Penfield (Penfield & Rasmussen, 1950). Penfield named one the **supplementary motor area (SMA)** and the other the premotor area (PMA). The PMA is usually referred to today as **premotor cortex.**

THE ORGANIZATION OF PRIMARY MOTOR CORTEX Using stimulation techniques, we can map the primary motor cortex in the precentral gyrus. You can see an example of a motor cortex map, or homunculus, in ● Figure 8.18. In Chapter 7, we saw a similar map of the sensory cortex in the parietal lobe. The premotor and supplementary motor areas of the cortex also are organized as homunculi.

The first thing you might notice is that the homunculus is upside down. Neurons controlling voluntary movement of the head are found in the most ventral portions of the precentral gyrus, whereas neurons controlling the feet are located in the opposite direction. Neurons serving the feet are found where the gyrus has actually curved across the top of the hemisphere into the longitudinal fissure, which separates the two hemispheres.

As we observed in the case of the sensory homunculus (see ● Figure 7.20), the proportions of the homunculus are quite different from the proportions of our body. Once again, parts of the body that require delicate control are given a larger share of cortical territory. Face, lips, jaw, and tongue are given a great deal of space to manage the fine movements required by speech. Hands also get a disproportionate amount of cortical space, allowing for the many fine movements we need for tool use. In contrast, the torso gets very little space at all, especially considering the actual size of this body part. There isn't much to do with torsos other than maintain posture, bend, lift, and twist.

THE INITIATION AND AWARENESS OF MOVEMENT What happens when we decide to move? You might be thinking that this would be a good time to close your text and take a snack break (which is fine as long as you also decide to come back and reopen the book). We might like to believe that we are consciously aware of our intent to move, but the brain makes a commitment to a choice of movement as many as 10 seconds before we become aware of the decision (Soon, Brass, Heinze, & Haynes, 2008). In many cases, our conscious awareness of our movement might serve to "interpret," or make sense out of our own actions, rather than actually guiding these actions (Gazzaniga, 2011).

Imaging technologies such as PET and fMRI have been used to track the initiation of movement in human volunteers (Roland, 1993; Deiber et al., 1999).

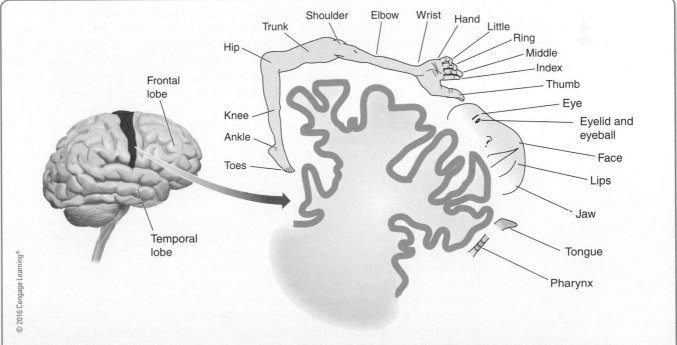

© 2016 Cengage Learning®

● **Figure 8.18** **The Motor Homunculus** Areas of the body requiring fine motor control have more than their fair share of cortical neurons. Large amounts of space in the human primary cortex are devoted to control of the hands, face, lips, jaw, and tongue, whereas relatively little space is given to the torso, arms, and legs. Compare this motor homunculus to the sensory homunculus in Figure 7.20.

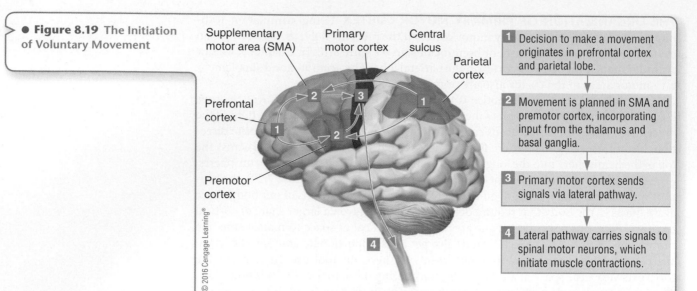

● Figure 8.19 The Initiation of Voluntary Movement

Supplementary motor area (SMA)

Primary motor cortex

Central sulcus

Parietal cortex

Prefrontal cortex

Premotor cortex

© 2016 Cengage Learning®

1 Decision to make a movement originates in prefrontal cortex and parietal lobe.

2 Movement is planned in SMA and premotor cortex, incorporating input from the thalamus and basal ganglia.

3 Primary motor cortex sends signals via lateral pathway.

4 Lateral pathway carries signals to spinal motor neurons, which initiate muscle contractions.

Participants were asked to carry out movements of the fingers from memory. As shown in ● Figure 8.19, the first areas to show increased activity were the frontal and parietal lobes. These areas might be viewed as the parts of the brain that actually "think" about the movement and its consequences before the movement is initiated.

Within the frontal lobe, several areas appear to be involved with motor control: the supplementary motor area (SMA), premotor cortex, and components of the anterior cingulate cortex (ACC). Planning of internally generated movements are associated with activity in SMA, while externally initiated and guided movements are associated with activity in the premotor cortex. The ACC appears to coordinate an organisms's history of reward with the selection of voluntary movement (Shima & Tanji, 1998).

Activity in the premotor cortex appears to hold a complex plan until it can be implemented. Weinrich and Wise (1982) taught monkeys to move their arms toward a target. The monkeys were given one signal that identified the location of the target, followed by another signal that told the monkey that it was time to respond. Premotor cortical neurons fired in response to the first signal and continued firing until the second signal came on, at which time the monkey initiated the correct arm movement. Premotor cortex activity helps us bridge delays between the planning and initiation of movement.

Premotor cortex and SMA are also the targets of input from the thalamus. We saw previously that the basal ganglia form connections with the thalamus. It is at this point in the sequence that the basal ganglia influence the choice of intentional behaviors. If input from the thalamus to the premotor cortex and SMA is not overly inhibited by the basal ganglia, the sequence will continue. If the input from the thalamus is inhibited, the sequence will be abandoned.

Premotor cortex and SMA activation is followed by activation in primary motor cortex. Inputs from the premotor cortex, SMA, and the thalamus converge on some very large cells located in Layer V of the primary motor cortex. These cells are referred to as **pyramidal cells** because of their pyramid shape, and the diameter of their cell bodies can be nearly 0.1 mm. Pyramidal cell axons are an important source of input to the brainstem and to spinal motor neurons. Once the motor cortex is activated, information flows down the lateral pathways to the spinal cord, either directly or through the red nucleus of the midbrain. The axons from the lateral pathways then synapse on the alpha motor neurons, which initiate the muscle contractions needed to carry out the descending commands.

What exactly is the primary motor cortex telling the alpha motor neurons in the spinal cord to do? Neurons in the primary motor cortex produce action potentials between 5 and 100 msec prior to any observable movement. This suggests that primary

pyramidal cell A large, pyramid-shaped neuron found in the output layers (Layers III and V) of the cerebral cortex, including primary motor cortex.

motor cortex commands are transmitted and implemented by the alpha motor neurons. Primary motor cortex input also transmits information about the amount of force needed for a movement (picking up a feather or a bowling ball), but it is up to the alpha motor neurons to adjust their rate of firing and extent of their recruitment to fit the requirements of this command.

THE CODING OF MOVEMENT In the case of vision, single-cell recording techniques can be used to discover the precise type of stimulus to which a particular cell will respond. Similar efforts to identify the responsibilities of single neurons in the primary motor cortex have produced curious results. Even though our movements are generally very precise, individual primary motor cortex neurons seem to be active during a wide range of movements. This finding led Apostolos Georgopoulos and his colleagues (Georgopoulos, Taira, & Lukashin, 1993) to propose the idea that movement is encoded by populations of motor neurons rather than by single cells.

In this research, monkeys were observed as they moved an arm in one of eight possible directions. Single cells in the monkey's primary motor cortex responded to a wide range of movement, but they responded most vigorously to a single preferred direction. The best predictor for whether the monkey's arm would move in a particular direction was a population vector, or the sum of the activity of the entire population of neurons in the area being observed. An example of the population vectors computed by Georgopoulos et al. (1993) is shown in ● Figure 8.20.

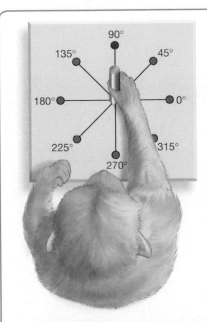
(a) The Monkey and Apparatus

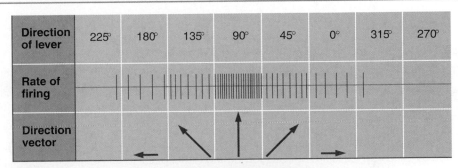
(b) Responses of a Single Cell

(c) Individual Direction Vectors and Population Vectors from Two Neurons

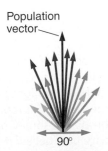
(d) Vector Representing Summed Activity from a Population of Neurons

● **Figure 8.20** **The Direction of Movement Is Encoded by Populations of Neurons** (a) Monkeys were trained to move a joystick in response to a small light moving around a circle. (b) Although single-cell recordings indicated that neurons responded most vigorously to a preferred direction, they also indicated that cells would respond to directions that varied as much as 45 degrees from the preferred direction. (c) Responses of single cells can be combined into population vectors. (d) The summed response of each population of neurons accurately predicts the direction of the monkey's movement. In other words, the population of cells essentially tallies up individual cell "votes" on the best direction to move.

© 2016 Cengage Learning®

mirror neuron A special motor neuron that responds to a particular action, whether that action is performed or simply observed.

This finding predicts that large numbers of motor cortex cells, rather than a small group, should be active during any type of movement. It also suggests that the direction of a movement represents the averaging of all inputs from the entire population of neurons.

MIRROR NEURONS Not only do motor neurons code for movement, but they might also help us understand the behavior of others. **Mirror neurons**, which are special premotor cortex neurons discovered by Giacomo Rizzolatti and his colleagues (1992), fire whenever an individual carries out an action, such as reaching, or simply watches another individual carry out the same act.

Although the exact functions of mirror neurons remain unknown, mirror neurons might form the basis for imitation, empathy, and theory of mind (TOM), the ability to predict and understand the thoughts of others (Fogassi et al., 2005). Mirror neuron activity might allow us to simulate others' thoughts subconsciously by literally putting ourselves mentally in another person's shoes (Gazzola, Aziz-Zadeh, & Keysers, 2006; Jabbi, Swart, & Keysers, 2007). Some researchers have suggested that mirror neuron function is disturbed in individuals with autism spectrum disorder, which might account for some of the lack of empathy and social awkwardness that often characterizes people with this disorder (Perkins, Stokes, McGillivray, & Bittar, 2010). Other researchers argue that a "broken mirror" explanation of social deficits in autism spectrum disorder is overly simplistic (Fan, Decety, Yang, Liu, & Cheng, 2010).

••• Connecting to **Research**

MIRROR NEURONS

During a routine single-cell recording experiment using a rhesus monkey, a group of Italian scientists led by Giacomo Rizzolatti noticed something rather peculiar. Certain neurons located in the inferior premotor cortex seemed to become especially active when the monkey performed certain actions, such as reaching for a peanut, but also became active when one of the researchers picked up the peanut (see ● Figure 8.21). In other words, the neurons seemed to be encoding "reaching for food" regardless of who or what did the reaching. The researchers dubbed these neurons "mirror neurons" (Di Pellegrino, Fadiga, Fogassi, Gallese, & Rizzolatti, 1992).

While we might take this finding for granted today, at the time of this report in 1992, the existence of mirror neurons was somewhat surprising. Previously, neuroscientists had believed that premotor neurons retrieved movements in response to sensory stimuli. In other words, when the monkey sees a peanut (visual stimulus), one appropriate motor action is to pick up the peanut. However, the mirror neurons apparently encoded the meaning of gestures by others toward the stimulus as well. The authors suggest that for a social species like the monkey, understanding actions performed by other monkeys could provide important guidance for the selection of appropriate movements.

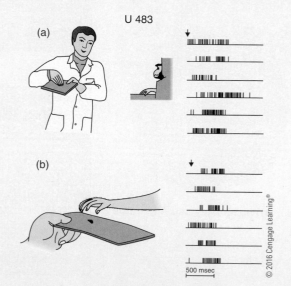

● **Figure 8.21** Recording a Mirror Neuron
Recordings of a single cell (U 483) in response to seeing an experimenter reach for a peanut (a) and in response to the monkey reaching for a peanut (b) are shown on the right. The arrow indicates the onset of reaching behavior. Data from Di Pellegrino, Fadiga, Fogassi, Gallese, and Rizzolatti (1992).

INTERIM SUMMARY 8.2

Summary Table: Central Motor Systems

Structure or Pathway	Location	Principal Connections	Functions
Lateral pathways	Lateral spinal cord	Motor cortex and red nucleus to spinal motor neurons	Voluntary fine movements of hands, feet, and outer limbs
Ventromedial pathways	Ventromedial spinal cord	Brainstem to spinal motor neurons	Maintain posture; carry out reflexive responses to sensory input
Cerebellum	Hindbrain	Spinal motor neurons, forebrain motor systems	Sequencing of complex movements, muscle tone, balance, and coordination
Basal ganglia	Forebrain	Motor cortex, thalamus	Choice and initiation of voluntary movements
Primary motor cortex	Precentral gyrus of the frontal lobe	Other cortical areas, basal ganglia, brainstem, spinal motor neurons	Initiation of voluntary movements
Premotor cortex	Rostral to the primary motor cortex	Thalamus, primary motor cortex	Managing movement strategies
Supplementary motor area (SMA)	Rostral to the primary motor cortex	Thalamus, primary motor cortex	Managing movement strategies
Anterior cingulate cortex	Rostral portion of the gyrus dorsal to the corpus callosum	Red nucleus and spinal motor neurons	Selection of voluntary movement based on prior reward

Summary Points

1. Monosynaptic reflexes, such as the myotatic reflex, require the interaction of only one sensory and one motor neuron. Polysynaptic reflexes involve more than one synapse. (LO4)

2. The lateral pathways connect the primary motor cortex and red nucleus with the spinal motor neurons and are responsible for voluntary movements. The ventromedial pathways originate in the brainstem and are responsible for reflexive movements. (LO5)

3. The cerebellum is involved with the timing and sequencing of complex movements. The basal ganglia form complex loops with the cortex and the thalamus and serve as a gate or filter for intentional activity. (LO5)

4. Cortical areas involved in the control of voluntary movement include the primary motor cortex, the supplementary motor area (SMA), the premotor cortex, and the anterior cingulate cortex (ACC). (LO5)

5. The initiation of voluntary movement is correlated with sequential activity in the prefrontal cortex and parietal cortex, followed by activity in the premotor cortex and SMA, and finally by activity in the pyramidal cells of the primary motor cortex. These primary motor neurons control movement as a function of cell population activity rather than as a function of single-cell activity. **(LO5)**

6. Special motor neurons known as mirror neurons are active when an individual either performs a movement or sees another individual perform the same movement, forming a basis for the understanding of the behavior of others. **(LO5)**

‖ Review Questions

1. What motor functions are carried out by reflexive or involuntary processes?

2. What steps lead to the initiation of a voluntary movement?

Disorders of Movement

We can learn a great deal about the neural control of movement by observing what goes wrong when the system is damaged. Because movement disorders obviously cause enormous human suffering, our further understanding might also lead to more effective treatments.

Toxins

A variety of toxic substances interfere with movement. Many of these toxins impact the neurochemical ACh, which is used by alpha motor neurons to communicate with muscle fibers at the neuromuscular junction. Toxins that are cholinergic agonists boost the activity of ACh at the neuromuscular junction, affecting muscle tone. For example, black widow spider venom overstimulates the release of ACh from the alpha motor neuron, causing the muscles to spasm in painful convulsions (see Chapter 4). In unusually severe cases, the alpha motor neuron runs out of ACh and can no longer signal the muscles to contract, leading to paralysis and possibly death.

Although large doses of cholinergic agonists are capable of producing death, cholinergic antagonists are generally far more dangerous and potent. These substances paralyze muscles, including those required for respiration. We observed the deadly actions of the cholinergic antagonists curare and botulinum toxin in Chapter 4. The venom of the Taiwanese cobra also binds tightly to the nicotinic ACh receptor and is nearly impossible to dislodge, leading rapidly to paralysis and death.

Sarin, a man-made chemical used as a bioweapon, is a colorless, odorless liquid that can evaporate into a gas (see ● Figure 8.22). Sarin acts as a neurotoxin by inhibiting acetylcholinesterase (AChE), the enzyme that normally breaks down ACh in the synaptic gap. In the presence of sarin, ACh continues to remain active, and muscles are continually stimulated. This produces rapid fatigue and respiratory failure, as new messages from the motor system to diaphragm muscles are unable to produce movement.

Myasthenia Gravis

myasthenia gravis An autoimmune condition caused by the degeneration of acetylcholine (ACh) receptors at the neuromuscular junction, resulting in muscle weakness and fatigue.

Myasthenia gravis results when a person's immune system, for reasons that are not well understood, produces antibodies that bind to the nicotinic ACh receptor (Engel, 1984). Over time, the ACh receptors degenerate and become less efficient, leading to extreme muscle weakness and fatigue. The degeneration usually affects the muscles of

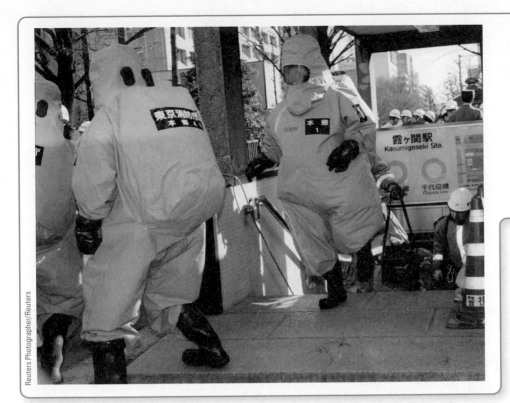

● **Figure 8.22** Neurotoxins Often Affect the Neuromuscular Junction Sarin was released on several trains by members of the Aum Shinrikyo cult in a Tokyo subway in 1995, killing 12 people and sickening thousands of others. Rescue workers wore special suits for protection against the deadly neurotoxin.

the head first, resulting in droopy eyelids and slurred speech. As the degeneration proceeds, the patient might experience difficulty swallowing and breathing.

Myasthenia gravis is typically treated with medications that suppress the immune system. This approach slows the production of the troublesome antibodies. Another approach is to administer medications that inhibit AChE, the enzyme that deactivates ACh at the synapse. Because the ability of AChE to break down ACh is reduced, more ACh remains active in the synaptic gap. Fortunately, most cases of myasthenia gravis have a positive long-term prognosis when these treatment regimens are adhered to carefully.

Muscular Dystrophy

Muscular dystrophy is not a single disease but, rather, a group of inherited diseases characterized by progressive muscle degeneration. These diseases are caused by abnormalities involving the protein dystrophin, which makes up part of the muscle fiber membrane. Dystrophin protects the membrane from injuries due to the force that occurs during normal movement. Muscular dystrophy is a sex-linked disorder, typically affecting males, because the gene responsible for encoding dystrophin is located on the X chromosome (see Chapter 5).

In the most severe type of muscular dystrophy, Duchenne muscular dystrophy, dystrophin is not produced at all (see ● Figure 8.23). Faulty dystrophin is present in cases of Becker muscular dystrophy. Without the protective action of dystrophin, muscles are damaged during normal activity. The muscle turns to scar tissue before gradually wasting away. This disorder eventually reduces mobility and results in a shortened life span.

Currently, there are no effective treatments for muscular dystrophy. However, gene therapy, in which faulty dystrophin genes are replaced with functioning genes have produced improvement in animal models of muscular dystrophy (Shin et al., 2013). Researchers are getting closer to conducting human trials using this approach.

muscular dystrophy A group of diseases characterized by extreme muscle development followed by muscle wasting, due to abnormalities in the protein dystrophin.

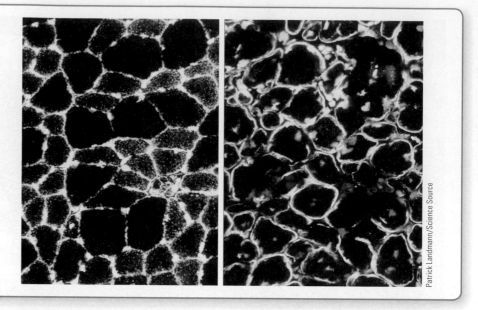

● **Figure 8.23** Cellular Changes in Muscular Dystrophy Healthy muscle cells are shown on the left, while cells unable to produce the protein dystrophin are shown on the right. Recent breakthroughs in gene therapy might eventually provide relief from some forms of muscular dystrophy.

Patrick Landmann/Science Source

Polio

Polio, or poliomyelitis, occurs only in human beings and is caused by a contagious virus that specifically targets and destroys spinal alpha motor neurons. *Polio* comes from the ancient Greek word for "gray," and refers to damage to the gray matter of the spinal cord. Symptoms can include muscle weakness and paralysis, usually of the legs. If the infection affects higher levels of the CNS, breathing can be impacted. This situation leads to the patient's reliance on assisted respiration, such as an "iron lung."

Following the development of effective vaccines, the last wild variety case of polio in the United States was reported in 1979, and worldwide eradication of the virus seems imminent. However, cases continue to occur in areas impacted by war and extreme poverty, such as Syria, Afghanistan, Nigeria, and Pakistan (Centers for Disease Control, 2012).

polio A contagious viral disease that attacks the spinal motor neurons, producing paralysis.

••• Building Better HEALTH   WHEN VACCINATION IS NOT ENOUGH

In the United States, we take it for granted that children will be immunized against polio and that the risk of contracting this disease is virtually zero. Other parts of the world are not so fortunate. Although vaccines are effective and available, war, poverty, and distrust of vaccination makes total eradication of polio challenging.

A key strategy for targeting vaccination efforts is careful surveillance (The Global Polio Eradication Initiative, 2014). India has been very successful at reducing polio rates by instructing parents and health care providers to report any evidence of paralysis, especially in children, that might be polio. In response to such reports, public health officials are able to test for the presence of the virus and plan vaccination programs accordingly. Egypt has been even more proactive. Due to its past history as a problem area for wild poliovirus strains, Egyptian scientists collect sewage samples and test for the virus even in the absence of any reports of paralysis in the population. Individuals carrying the virus are relatively likely to remain free from symptoms, although they can of course pass the virus to others. Proactive detection of the virus in 2012 led to waves of vaccination that kept the country polio free.

Accidental Spinal Cord Damage

The spinal cord can be accidentally damaged when the protective vertebrae surrounding the cord are broken and compress or sever the cord itself. These tragic accidents, such as that suffered by Hollywood actor Christopher Reeve (1952–2004) while horseback riding in 1995 and by approximately 8,000 Americans per year in automobile accidents, generally result in permanent paralysis of the muscles served by neurons below the level of damage. If the damage occurs in the cervical, or neck, region of the spinal cord, the person will experience quadriplegia, or the loss of movement in both arms and legs. If the damage occurs in the lumbar region of the lower back, the person will experience paraplegia, the loss of movement in the legs.

Until his death in 2004, Reeve lobbied for additional research funds for spinal cord damage and its treatment. Although a "cure" is still years away, progress is occurring. A combination of electrical stimulation, serotonin and dopamine agonists, and locomotor training (active walking as opposed to passive treadmill work, going up stairs, and avoiding obstacles) restored voluntary movement in rats with paralyzed hind legs (van den Brand et al., 2012). Treatments designed to enhance axon regeneration and sprouting in animal models appear encouraging (Zhao et al., 2013).

Emergency treatment immediately following an injury is becoming more successful in minimizing paralysis. In 2007, NFL football player Kevin Everett sustained a spinal injury during a game that his physician described as "catastrophic." Everett's doctors used steroids, surgery, and a controversial cooling technique to prevent swelling in his spinal cord (Cappuccino, 2008). Against all odds, Everett eventually regained nearly normal movement (see ● Figure 8.24).

Simon Bruty/Sports Illustrated/Getty Images

● **Figure 8.24** Emergency Treatment of Spinal Damage Is Improving In 2007, Buffalo Bills tight end Kevin Everett sustained a serious neck injury that left him paralyzed on the field. After his physicians performed a number of controversial treatments, including cooling his body, Everett made a remarkable recovery. Although treatment of existing spinal damage is still in the future, emergency care of spinal injuries is preventing more extensive damage.

●●● **Behavioral Neuroscience GOES TO WORK**   PHYSICAL THERAPY

Management of the remediation of movement disorders is primarily the domain of the physical therapist (PT). Physical therapists assess movement issues and administer remediation in the form of special exercises, education, manipulation, and other similar techniques.

Although the idea of treating movement problems with exercise dates back to ancient times, events occurring in the 20th century promoted the rapid acceptance of this practice. Polio outbreaks at the beginning of the 20th century led to the use of massage and remedial exercise as treatments. Soldiers recovering from injuries in World Wars I and II benefited from physical therapy techniques. Today, physical therapists not only treat patients with existing movement disorders but also attempt to prevent the development of movement disorders in vulnerable populations.

Physical therapists typically hold either a Doctor of Physical Therapy (DPT) or Master of Physical Therapy (MPT) degree and are licensed on a state-by-state basis in the United States (American Physical Therapy Association [APTA], 2013). The course of study is broad, from biomechanics to neuroscience to psychology and communication. Neuroscience, and in particular its contributions to the understanding of pain (see Chapter 7), has played an increasingly important role in the physical therapy profession.

Amyotrophic Lateral Sclerosis (ALS; Lou Gehrig's Disease)

Amyotrophic lateral sclerosis (ALS) is also known as Lou Gehrig's disease, after the outstanding baseball player of the 1930s whose life was ended by the disease. Physicist Stephen Hawking also suffers from ALS. ALS results from the degeneration of motor neurons in the spinal cord and brainstem. The muscles served by these motor neurons degenerate when their input ceases. Patients experience muscle weakness, but cognition remains unaffected in most cases. Only 4 percent of patients survive longer than 10 years after diagnosis, so Hawking's more than 50 years as an ALS patient is highly unusual.

The causes of ALS are still somewhat mysterious. Ninety percent of cases appear in people with no known family history of the disease, whereas approximately 10 percent of the cases run in families. Daniel Rosen and his colleagues (1993) found that about 15 to 25 percent of patients with familial ALS (FALS) had an abnormal version of a gene known as *SOD-1*. Over 100 mutant variations of *SOD-1* have been identified in patients with FALS (Selverstone, 2005). The mutant forms of *SOD-1* cause damage to motor neurons in multiple ways, including interference with the normal functions of mitochondria (Hervias et al., 2006).

Nikolaos Scarmeas and his colleagues (Scarmeas, Shih, Stern, Ottman, & Rowland, 2002) noted that people who develop ALS are much more likely than the general population to have always been lean and to have participated in college-level varsity athletics. Professional soccer players in Italy were found to have a much higher rate of ALS than members of the general public (Chio, Benzi, Dossena, Mutani, & Mora, 2005). Something related to extremely vigorous physical activity might trigger the disease in susceptible individuals. Obviously, there are thousands of lean university athletes who have never developed ALS, along with many non-athletes who have developed ALS, so the exact basis for this correlation remains unknown. The number of players in the NFL who have developed ALS has led to suggestions that head trauma can be a risk for the disease. In a large scale population study, ALS patients were found to be much more likely than healthy participants to report a history of head trauma (Pupillo et al., 2012). Other cases of ALS might be triggered by viral infections (Berger et al., 2000; Ravits, 2005). Although these correlational data are intriguing, further research is necessary to pinpoint the causes of ALS.

Currently, there are no "cures" for people with the disease. Riluzole, the only medication approved for the condition, extends life an average of two to three months (Miller, Mitchell, & Moore, 2012). Research continues in the effort to identify effective treatments. In particular, researchers are investigating the possible use of stem cell therapies (Teng et al., 2012).

Parkinson's Disease

Parkinson's disease is characterized by a progressive difficulty in all movements, muscular tremors in the resting hand, and frozen facial expressions. These symptoms were first observed and described by the English physician James Parkinson in the early 1800s.

Patients with Parkinson's disease experience enormous difficulty initiating voluntary movements, such as standing up from a chair. The disease produces a characteristically stooped posture. Patients' reflexive movements are also impaired, and they fall easily if they lose their balance. Parkinson's is often associated with drops in blood pressure, dizziness, and other symptoms of autonomic nervous system disorder (Goldstein, Holmes, Dendi, Bruce, & Li, 2002). Eventually, the condition leads to premature death. Normally, Parkinson's disease affects people after the age of 50 years. Men are twice as likely to develop the disorder, possibly due to some protection women gain from estrogen (Baldereschi et al., 2000; Leranth et al., 2000).

amyotrophic lateral sclerosis (ALS) A disease in which motor neurons of the spinal cord and brainstem progressively deteriorate, leading to death.

Parkinson's disease A degenerative disease characterized by difficulty in moving, muscular tremors, and frozen facial expressions.

The direct causes of Parkinson's disease are quite clear. This disease occurs when the dopaminergic neurons of the substantia nigra in the brainstem begin to degenerate. As we discussed previously, the substantia nigra forms close connections with the basal ganglia in the cerebral hemispheres. The end result of degeneration in the substantia nigra is a lack of typical dopaminergic activity in the basal ganglia. Because the basal ganglia are intimately involved with the production of voluntary movements, it should come as no surprise that the patients show great difficulties in voluntary movement.

The factors responsible for the degeneration of the substantia nigra remain unknown. Genetic mutations in fifteen genes directly cause some cases and increase risk factors in others (Bonifati, 2014; Singleton, Farrer, & Bonifati, 2013). In early-onset cases, genes encoding a substance known as alpha synuclein are abnormal (McCann, 2000). As a result, alpha synuclein forms filaments within neurons that interfere with axonal transport. This process might account for the degeneration of the dopaminergic axons originating in the substantia nigra.

Other cases appear to result from exposure to environmental toxins. Support for this hypothesis originated from an unfortunate accidental experiment involving young heroin addicts who suddenly developed symptoms of Parkinson's disease (Langston, 1985). The addicts had shared a homemade synthetic heroin, which contained a chemical known as MPTP. When MPTP binds with the enzyme monoamine oxidase, which is found in large quantities in the substantia nigra, it forms a very toxic substance known as MPP$^+$. MPP$^+$ is attracted to the pigment neuromelanin, which is also found in large quantities in the substantia nigra. You may recall that substantia nigra means "black substance" and that the structure is named in part because of its pigmentation. The affinity between MPP$^+$ and neuromelanin results in the accumulation of MPP$^+$ in the substantia nigra, leading to degeneration of the neurons.

Obviously, the vast majority of people with Parkinson's disease have never been exposed to heroin, synthetic or otherwise. However, similar toxins that act like MPTP are present in the environment. People who report having applied insecticides and herbicides on their home gardens or farms are significantly more likely to develop Parkinson's disease than relatives who do not have any direct pesticide exposure (Hancock et al., 2008). Exposure to commonly used solvents such as toluene differentiated between identical twins with and without Parkinson's disease (Goldman et al., 2012). These toxins bind to the neuromelanin of the substantia nigra, which initially has a protective effect. However, the neuromelanin appears to release the toxins under certain circumstances, allowing them to produce damage (Karlsson & Lindquist, 2013).

One of the strangest findings in the quest to understand Parkinson's disease is the fact that drinking caffeinated coffee reduces the odds of developing the disease (Chade, Kasten, & Tanner, 2006). G. Webster Ross and his colleagues (2000) reported that men who didn't drink any coffee at all were four to five times more likely to develop Parkinson's disease than were the heaviest coffee drinkers, who drank about five cups of coffee per day. Animal research suggests that caffeine might play a role in preventing neural degeneration resulting from a number of conditions, such as stroke, Parkinson's disease, and Alzheimer's disease (Sonsalla et al., 2012), but this should not inspire you to head immediately for your nearest coffee shop. These correlational data do not allow us to say that reduced risk for Parkinson's disease was *caused* by coffee consumption. More research is needed.

Not only does caffeine have a potential protective effect against the development of Parkinson's disease, but investigators have explored the possibility of its use as a treatment (Rivera-Oliver & Díaz-Ríos, 2014). Caffeine and other substances that block adenosine receptors (see Chapter 4), appear to improve movement in both human patients and animal models of the disease.

The traditional treatment for Parkinson's disease is the medication levodopa, or l-dopa. L-dopa is a precursor in the synthesis of dopamine (see Chapter 4), so additional l-dopa should help the neurons in the substantia nigra manufacture more of

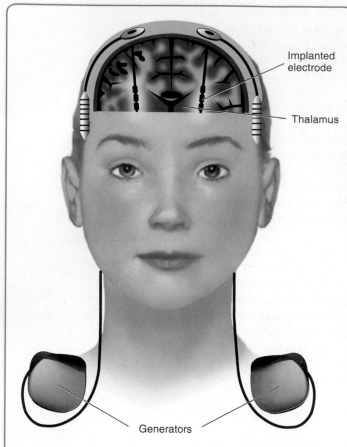

Implanted electrode

Thalamus

Generators

● **Figure 8.25 Deep Brain Stimulation Treatment for Parkinson's Disease** To date, thousands of patients with Parkinson's disease have been treated with this electricity-based technique that requires the insertion of two generators under the skin, usually near the collarbone. The generators, each about two inches in diameter, emit tiny electrical pulses that pass along wires, also under the skin, through electrodes implanted in select areas of the brain. Some patients experience a tingling sensation, but typically the stimulation pulses go unnoticed.

Images provided courtesy of Sanjiv Sam Gambhir, M.D., Ph.D., Stanford University.

the neurochemical. However, l-dopa loses its effectiveness as the numbers of substantia nigra neurons decrease and feedback loops inhibit the further production of dopamine. Because l-dopa affects all dopaminergic systems, not just those originating in the substantia nigra, it also has a variety of undesirable side effects. Increasing overall dopamine activity often results in psychotic behavior, including hallucination and delusional thinking. As we noted in Chapter 4, the increased activity of dopaminergic neurons associated with schizophrenia and with the abuse of dopamine agonists such as amphetamine can produce similar types of psychotic behaviors.

Surgery has also been used to treat advanced cases of Parkinson's disease. In a procedure known as a pallidotomy, a part of the globus pallidus of the basal ganglia is destroyed. Seventy-six percent of patients who underwent pallidotomy on both sides of the brain and 64 percent of the patients who underwent pallidotomy on only one side of the brain rated their outcomes as excellent or good in spite of side effects that included speech difficulties (Favre, Burchiel, Taha, & Hammerstad, 2000). Another surgical approach to Parkinson's is the thalamotomy, in which a small area of the thalamus is destroyed. These procedures, when successful, generally reduce unwanted muscle tension and tremor. An alternative to surgery is electrical stimulation, shown in ●Figure 8.25. Wires are surgically implanted in the thalamus and are connected to two pulse generators each implanted near the patient's collarbone. The generators maintain a steady electrical signal that interferes with signals that lead to tremor.

Transplantation of stem cells has restored movement in animal models (Rhee et al., 2011). Gene therapy might also lead to effective treatments, as initial experiments in human patients appear promising and relatively safe (LeWitt et al., 2011). More work needs to be done before this type of treatment is widely available, but the outlook is optimistic (Ganz, Lev, & Offen, 2014).

Huntington's Disease

Huntington's disease is a genetic disorder that usually strikes in middle age and produces involuntary, jerky movements. As the disease progresses, cognitive symptoms such as depression, hallucination, and delusion occur. Fifteen to 20 years after the onset of symptoms, the patient dies. There is no known cure for this disease, which affects about one person out of 1,000. The disease was first identified by George Huntington, a doctor on Long Island, in 1872. Eventually, Huntington's original patients were found to be part of one extended family going back to a pair of brothers who came to America from England in 1630. A number of family members were burned as witches in Salem in 1693, probably due to the odd behaviors associated with the disease (Ridley, 1999).

Huntington's disease A genetic disorder beginning in middle age that results in jerky, involuntary movements and progresses to psychosis and premature death.

The cause of Huntington's disease is simple and well understood. The *Huntingtin* gene on Chromosome 4, named after George Huntington, encodes the brain protein huntingtin. At the end of the *Huntingtin* gene is a codon, or sequence that encodes an amino acid, that can repeat between 6 and more than 100 times (see Chapter 5). Most people have between 10 and 15 repeats of this sequence. A person having fewer than 35 repeats will remain healthy, but a person with 39 or more repeats will develop Huntington's disease. Higher numbers of repeats are correlated with an earlier onset of symptoms (Gusella et al., 1996). To make matters worse, this gene is one of the few examples of a dominant gene for a disease. It doesn't help at all to have one normal *Huntingtin* gene. If you have one abnormal gene, you will have the disease. If one of your parents has the disease, then you have a 50 percent chance of developing the disease yourself. The identification of the *Huntingtin* gene in 1993 made genetic testing possible for those who are at risk for the disease (Gusella & McDonald, 1993).

How does the mutant huntingtin protein produce the symptoms of Huntington's disease? The version of the huntingtin protein produced by the abnormal gene appears to accumulate, particularly in the cells of the basal ganglia. This accumulation of abnormal proteins forms a sticky lump in the cells and triggers cellular suicide (apoptosis). A comparison of the basal ganglia from a healthy person and a patient with Huntington's disease is shown in ● Figure 8.26.

Currently, there are no effective treatments for Huntington's disease, in spite of the fact that the responsible gene has been recognized for quite a few years. Brain imaging shows that changes in brain volume begin to occur long before the appearance of symptoms leads to diagnosis (Ross et al., 2014). Investigation of these changes might lead to treatments that delay the onset of symptoms or slow the progression of the disease. For example, the administration of high doses of creatine has been explored in patients whose status is premanifest (genetically tested to show they have the disease, but no symptoms yet) and at risk (not tested but having a parent with the disease) (Rosas et al., 2014).

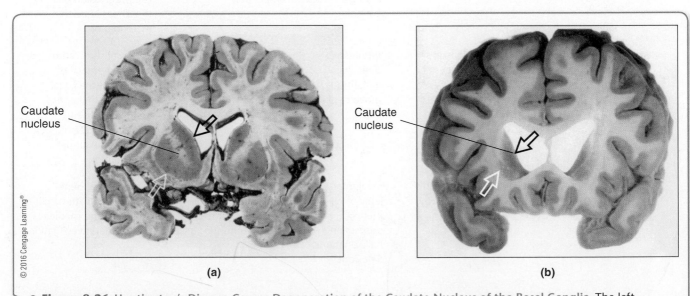

Caudate nucleus

Caudate nucleus

© 2016 Cengage Learning®

(a)

(b)

> ● **Figure 8.26** Huntington's Disease Causes Degeneration of the Caudate Nucleus of the Basal Ganglia The left image (a) shows a healthy human brain, whereas the right image (b) shows the brain of a person suffering from Huntington's disease. The arrows in both images indicate the boundaries of the caudate nucleus. In the brain of the person with Huntington's disease, the caudate nucleus is quite a bit smaller than normal, and the lateral ventricles have enlarged to take up the extra space.

INTERIM SUMMARY 8.3

|| Summary Table: Major Disorders of the Motor Systems

Disorder	Symptoms	Causes	Treatments
Myasthenia gravis	Muscle weakness, fatigue	Autoimmune damage to the nicotinic ACh receptor	Medications that inhibit the immune system or AChE
Muscular dystrophy	Progressive muscle degeneration	Abnormalities in the gene that encodes for the protein dystrophin	None currently approved; gene replacement and muscle cell replacement under investigation
Polio	Damage to spinal motor neurons leading to mild to severe muscle paralysis	Virus	Prevented by immunization
Accidental spinal cord damage	Paralysis in muscles served by the spinal cord areas below the point of damage	Compression or laceration of the spinal cord	None currently approved; stem cell therapy and methods for promoting axon regrowth are under investigation
Amyotrophic lateral sclerosis (ALS)	General weakness, muscle atrophy, cramps, muscle twitching	Possible link to genetic inheritance, possible link to viral infection	None currently approved; use of medications to slow the progression of the disease under investigation
Parkinson's disease	Progressive difficulty initiating movement	Genetic risk and exposure to toxins	Electrical stimulation, surgical removal of sections of the basal ganglia or thalamus, medication; gene therapy and stem cell implants under investigation
Huntington's disease	Involuntary, jerky movements; depression, hallucinations, delusions	Abnormalities in the gene that encodes for the protein huntingtin	Experimental gene replacement, stem cell implants, and medications under investigation

|| Summary Points

1. A number of toxins interfere with movement due to their action at the cholinergic neuromuscular junction. **(LO6)**

2. Myasthenia gravis is an autoimmune disease that produces extreme muscle weakness and fatigue due to the breakdown of ACh receptor sites at the neuromuscular

junction. Muscular dystrophy is a collection of diseases that produces extreme muscular development followed by muscular degeneration. Polio is a contagious viral disease that attacks spinal motor neurons, causing some degree of paralysis. Accidental spinal damage results in the loss of voluntary movement produced by nerves below the level of injury. **(LO6)**

3. Amyotrophic lateral sclerosis (ALS) is a degenerative condition resulting from the progressive loss of motor neurons in the spinal cord and brainstem. **(LO6)**

4. Parkinson's disease produces difficulty moving, tremor in resting body parts, frozen facial expressions, and reduced heart innervation. **(LO6)**

5. Huntington's disease is a genetic disorder characterized by involuntary movement and cognitive decline. **(LO6)**

‖ Review Questions

1. What effects do toxins have on the neuromuscular junction, and how does this affect movement?

2. What physical changes underlie the symptoms of Parkinson's disease?

Chapter Review

THOUGHT QUESTIONS

1. What advice would you give an elderly person who wanted to maintain or improve muscle strength?
2. Why do you think we evolved three types of muscle fibers?
3. Damage or abnormalities in the prefrontal cortex and basal ganglia might be responsible for some impulsive behavior. Using your knowledge of the initiation of movement, explain why abnormalities in these areas might lead to impulsivity.
4. If you had a parent with Huntington's disease, would you take the genetic screening? What factors would influence your decision?
5. At what levels of the motor system do we treat fine motor activities, such as speech and the movement of our fingers and hands, differently from gross motor activities, such as posture?

KEY TERMS

actin (p. 256)
alpha motor neuron (p. 260)
amyotrophic lateral sclerosis (ALS) (p. 282)
extensor (p. 266)
extrafusal muscle fiber (p. 262)
fast-twitch fiber (p. 257)
flexor (p. 266)
flexor reflex (p. 267)
gamma motor neuron (p. 263)
Golgi tendon organ (p. 263)

Huntington's disease (p. 284)
Ia sensory fiber (p. 262)
Ib sensory fiber (p. 263)
intrafusal muscle fiber (p. 262)
lateral pathway (p. 269)
mirror neuron (p. 276)
monosynaptic reflex (p. 262)
motor unit (p. 261)
muscle fiber (p. 255)
muscle spindle (p. 262)
muscular dystrophy (p. 279)

myasthenia gravis (p. 278)
myofibril (p. 256)
myosin (p. 256)
myotatic reflex (p. 262)
neuromuscular junction (p. 260)
Parkinson's disease (p. 282)
polio (p. 280)
polysynaptic reflex (p. 266)
premotor cortex (p. 272)
recruitment (p. 261)
sarcomeres (p. 256)

CHAPTER 9

Homeostasis and Motivation

LEARNING OBJECTIVES

L01 Differentiate between the terms *homeostasis*, *set point*, and *motivation*.

L02 Explain the behavioral and physical adaptations organisms use to regulate body temperature.

L03 Explain the mechanisms used to initiate and cease drinking.

L04 Explain the mechanisms leading to the initiation of feeding and to satiety.

L05 Differentiate between healthy eating and disordered eating.

CHAPTER OUTLINE

BUILDING BETTER HEALTH: Understanding the Benefits of Fever

CONNECTING TO RESEARCH: Swallowing Balloons and Growling Stomachs

BEHAVIORAL NEUROSCIENCE GOES TO WORK: Dieticians and Nutritionists

THINKING ETHICALLY: How Dangerous Is It to Be Overweight or Obese?

Homeostasis and Motivation

Without much conscious awareness or effort on our part, our bodies maintain **homeostasis**. Homeostasis, a term coined by psychologist Walter Cannon (1932), refers to an organism's ability to adjust its physiological processes to maintain a steady internal balance or equilibrium. To achieve homeostasis, regulatory systems actively defend certain values, or **set points**, for variables such as temperature, fluid levels, and body weight. The defense of these set points is similar to the thermostat of your home's heating system (see ● Figure 9.1). If the air temperature drops below the setting, the furnace is turned on. Once the desired temperature is reached, the furnace turns off again.

Deviations from the body's ideal states are rapidly assessed by the nervous system. Once deficits are recognized, the nervous system makes appropriate internal adjustments and motivates behavior designed to regain the ideal state. The process of **motivation** both activates and directs behavior toward a goal. When homeostasis has been compromised, the nervous system first activates behavior by generating tension and discomfort in the form of drive states such as thirst or hunger. Drive states arise in response to physiological needs and disappear again, usually with a sense of relief, when those needs are met. Once the organism is activated by a drive state, it will initiate behavior to solve the specific problem. The action chosen to reestablish homeostasis will not be random. We do not respond to hunger cues by getting a drink of water. Instead, the activity of the nervous system ensures that we will be motivated specifically to seek out food.

As demonstrated by the frequency of disordered eating, discussed in greater detail later in this chapter, the systems maintaining homeostasis are not foolproof. Regulatory systems can help us identify a problem, but our reaction to this information usually involves a complicated set of psychological and biological processes.

Psychologists study a wide range of motivated behavior, from basic needs like hunger and thirst to more cognitive motives for achievement and affiliation. This chapter will focus on model systems involved with the regulation of body temperature, thirst, and hunger.

Regulating Body Temperature

Temperature regulation involves all of the major features of a homeostatic system that we have discussed so far: a precisely defined set point, mechanisms for detecting deviations away from the set point, and, finally, internal and behavioral elements designed to regain the set point.

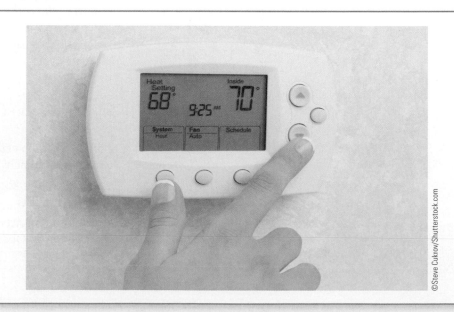

● **Figure 9.1 Set Points** Set points for many of our physiological systems work much like the setting on the thermostat of your home. Deviations from the set point initiate behaviors (turning the heat or air conditioning on) that return the system to homeostasis or equilibrium.

Animals inhabit niches that vary dramatically in external temperature, from the frozen Arctic to steamy equatorial jungles. Some bacteria exist in the hot volcanic vents in the ocean floor. Extreme temperatures limit life through their impact on the chemical properties of living cells. If temperatures are too low, ice crystals form within cells and damage the cell membrane. In high temperatures, the proteins necessary for carrying out cell functions become unstable. No matter where they live, animals must maintain an internal temperature that is ideal for the normal activity of their bodies' cells.

endotherm An animal that can use internal methods, such as perspiration or shivering, to maintain body temperature.

ectotherm An animal that relies on external methods, such as moving into the sun or shade, for maintaining body temperature.

Adaptations Maintain Temperature

Two solutions have evolved to help animals maintain an optimum body temperature in a varying environment. Mammals and birds are referred to as **endotherms** (*endon* is the Greek word for "within") due to their ability to maintain body temperature through internal metabolic activity. Amphibians, reptiles, and fish are referred to as **ectotherms** (*ektos* is the Greek word for "outside") because they rely on external factors, such as basking in the sunlight or retreating to the shade below a rock, to maintain ideal body temperature. The common terms warm-blooded and cold-blooded are misleading because the internal temperatures maintained by all animals fall within a few degrees of one another. Endotherms and ectotherms simply use different methods to maintain a standard body temperature.

The maintenance of body temperature is influenced by an animal's surface-to-volume ratio. The larger the overall volume of the body, the more heat is produced by metabolic activity. Heat is lost to the surrounding environment as a function of the animal's surface area. As shown in ● Figure 9.2, smaller animals have more surface

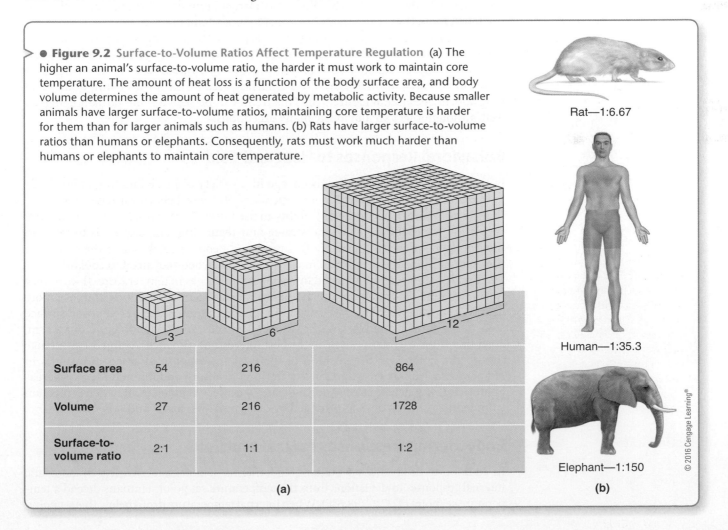

● **Figure 9.2 Surface-to-Volume Ratios Affect Temperature Regulation** (a) The higher an animal's surface-to-volume ratio, the harder it must work to maintain core temperature. The amount of heat loss is a function of the body surface area, and body volume determines the amount of heat generated by metabolic activity. Because smaller animals have larger surface-to-volume ratios, maintaining core temperature is harder for them than for larger animals such as humans. (b) Rats have larger surface-to-volume ratios than humans or elephants. Consequently, rats must work much harder than humans or elephants to maintain core temperature.

Rat—1:6.67

Human—1:35.3

Elephant—1:150

© 2016 Cengage Learning®

	3	6	12
Surface area	54	216	864
Volume	27	216	1728
Surface-to-volume ratio	2:1	1:1	1:2

(a)

(b)

● **Figure 9.3 Adaptations to Climate Occur within Species** Animals in warm climates disperse heat by having slim bodies and long appendages. Animals in cold climates conserve heat by having compact, stocky bodies and short legs, tails, and ears. These foxes are found in (left) warm, (center) temperate, and (right) Arctic climates.

area relative to the overall body volume than larger animals do, so small animals must use much more energy to maintain a constant body temperature.

Within a species, populations of animals evolve features that fit a particular environmental niche. In cold climates, surface area and heat loss are reduced in animals that have compact, stocky bodies and short legs, tails, and ears. To promote heat loss in warm climates, animals have greater surface area in the form of slim bodies and long appendages (see ● Figure 9.3). This trend can be seen among human beings as well, although there are obviously many exceptions.

Behavioral Responses to Heat and Cold

Both endotherms and ectotherms engage in a variety of behaviors to regulate body temperature. Ectotherms are more dependent on these behavioral devices because they do not share the endotherms' ability to use internal mechanisms for temperature regulation. One simple behavioral strategy for regulating temperature is to move to the right type of environment. Both snakes and people stretch out in the sun when they seek additional warmth and move to the shade when they need to cool off.

Body position can be adjusted in response to changes in temperature. If we're very warm, we tend to stretch out our bodies to increase our surface area and lose more heat. When we're very cold, we curl up in an attempt to reduce our exposed surface area. Social animals huddle together more when cold, so sitting too close to a warm, crackling fireplace might not be in the best interests of romance. Animals can change the weight, color, and composition of their fur in response to seasonal changes in temperature. Humans use dark, heavy clothing to absorb and maintain heat, whereas lighter clothing helps reflect and dissipate heat (see Chapter 6). Further protection from temperature changes is provided by dens, burrows, nests, and other shelters.

Endothermic Responses to Heat and Cold

In addition to behavioral adaptations, endotherms demonstrate a variety of automatic internal responses to deviations from the temperature set point. Humans defend a temperature set point of 37°C (98.6°F). When internal temperature drops below this set point,

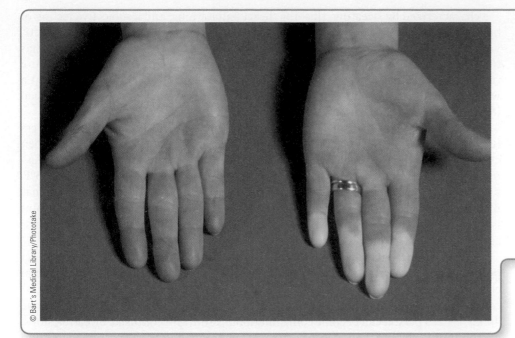

● **Figure 9.4** Raynaud's Disease Produces an Extreme Reaction to Cold Blood vessels normally constrict in response to cold. In Raynaud's disease, this constriction becomes extreme, leading to a lack of circulation in the affected digit. People with Raynaud's disease are cautioned to avoid sudden cold and to use gloves when removing food from their freezers.

© Bart's Medical Library/Phototake

we shiver. Shivering results from muscle twitches, which can be so intense that teeth chatter together. The muscle activity involved in shivering produces heat, but at the cost of a high expenditure of energy. Blood vessels constrict, keeping most of the blood away from the surface of the skin, where heat loss is greatest. In some cases, blood vessel constriction is too extreme, leading to a condition known as Raynaud's disease. This condition produces sudden spasms in arteries, particularly those in fingers and toes, in response to cold. As shown in ● Figure 9.4, the affected digit or digits lose feeling and appear white.

If cold conditions persist in spite of shivering, the thyroid gland increases the release of thyroid hormone. Higher levels of thyroid hormone are associated with greater overall metabolic activity, which warms the body. Deficits in thyroid activity are often diagnosed on the basis of the patient's lower-than-normal body temperature (Barnes & Galton, 1976). In human infants and small animals, the sympathetic nervous system responds to cold by stimulating greater metabolic activity in so-called brown fat cells. Brown fat cells are located primarily in the torso, close to the vital organs. The fat cells appear brown due to large numbers of mitochondria, the organelles responsible for energy production.

Very warm temperatures produce their own set of responses. Perspiration cools the skin through evaporation. Human beings have around 2.5 million sweat glands and lose an average of a liter (0.22 gallon) of sweat each day under average conditions (Stiefel Laboratories, 2001). Animals, such as dogs, which do not perspire much, pant or lick their fur. Licking the fur produces cooling by evaporation in much the same way that perspiration does. Blood vessels near the surface of the skin dilate in hot environments, allowing more heat loss to the external environment. As a result, people often become very red-faced in warm temperatures.

Deviations in Human Core Temperature

The body's core temperature refers to the temperature maintained for vital organs within the head and torso. Although we can survive drastic changes in the temperature of the body's outer shell, much smaller deviations in our core body temperature can have serious consequences.

Disturbances in the body's ability to maintain the normal core temperature set point can result in the hot flashes experienced by nearly 80 percent of women in the months or years surrounding menopause. Hot flashes last seconds to minutes and

fever A carefully controlled increase in the body's thermal set point that is often helpful in ridding the body of disease-causing organisms.

hyperthermia A life-threatening condition in which core body temperature increases beyond normal limits in an uncontrolled manner.

are characterized by sweating, flushing, heart palpitations, and a subjective feeling of being very warm. Hot flashes result from changes in sympathetic nervous system activation due to reduced estrogen levels (Freedman, 2013). The sympathetic activity has the effect of slightly raising core body temperature and narrowing the temperature range between shivering and sweating thresholds. Frequent hot flashes can impact a woman's quality of life, particularly since these episodes are correlated with poor sleep (Savolainen-Peltonen, Hautamäki, Tuomikoski, Ylikorkala, & Mikkola, 2014).

We all know how miserable a **fever** of only a few degrees feels, and very high fevers (in excess of 41°C/105.8°F) can cause brain damage. Fevers due to illness result when chemical byproducts of bacteria or viruses known as pyrogens enter the brain, causing the brain to increase the core temperature set point from 37°C to 39°C (98.6°F to 102.2°F). We'll see exactly how this occurs in the next section on brain mechanisms and temperature. Body temperature will rise gradually until the new set point is reached. Although uncomfortable, fever does have beneficial effects in fighting disease (Kluger, 1991; Roth, 2006).

A fever represents a carefully monitored increase in the body's temperature set point. In contrast, heat stroke, or **hyperthermia**, occurs when the body's normal compensations (such as sweating and dilating the blood vessels close to the skin) cannot keep core temperature within normal limits. If core temperature rises above 40°C/104°F, a person can become confrontational, faint, and confused. Sweating stops, compounding the problem of overheating. Heat stroke is a life-threatening condition and requires immediate medical assistance (Weinmann, 2003).

Heat stroke often results from engaging in strenuous physical activity or wearing heavy clothing in hot, humid environments, conditions that limit the body's ability to get rid of excess heat (see ● Figure 9.5). Although not typically the result of illness alone, heat stroke interacts with immune system functioning (Carter, Cheuvront, & Sawka, 2007; Lim & Mackinnon, 2006). People with existing infections are more likely to develop heat stroke during exercise. Special care should be taken by individuals who have existing infections when engaged in strenuous activities.

Many recreational and therapeutic drugs are capable of producing hyperthermia. Drugs can either increase production of heat, interfere with heat dissipation, or both (Hayes, Martinez, & Barrueto 2013). Stimulant drugs, including amphetamine, cocaine, and MDMA (Ecstasy), are particularly likely to interfere with normal temperature regulation. Antidepressants, including selective serotonin reuptake inhibitors (SSRIs), monoamine oxidase inhibitors (MAOIs), and tricyclic antidepressants, can

●●● Building Better HEALTH

UNDERSTANDING THE BENEFITS OF FEVER

Not only are fevers uncomfortable, but from an evolutionary point of view, they are expensive. Raising the core body temperature of an ectotherm requires about a 10 percent increase in metabolism. To support this cost across many different types of species, fever must provide substantial benefits.

Many disease-causing organisms can tolerate a much narrower temperature range than can the infected animal or person. Viruses have survival rates at 37°C/98.6°F that are 250 times higher than at 40°C/104°F. Raising the host's set point kills many of the invading organisms, assisting the immune system in its task of ridding the body of disease. Prevention of

fever through the use of sodium salicylate increased the death rate of animals infected with bacteria (Bernheim & Kluger, 1976).

Among the pathogens that are reduced by fever are the viruses responsible for many upper respiratory diseases and the bacteria responsible for gonorrhea and syphilis. Prior to the discovery of antibiotics, patients with syphilis were deliberately infected with malaria to induce fever (Bruetsch, 1949). Because of the potential benefits of fever, current medical practice suggests using medication to reduce a fever only if other health risk factors are present or when discomfort is excessive (World Health Organization, 1993).

● **Figure 9.5** Heat Stroke Heat stroke is a risk whenever people experience physical activity, warm weather, and heavy clothing. Military personnel often wear heavy protective gear that retains heat. This soldier is attempting to cool off in a village well in Afghanistan.

also disrupt body temperature. **Serotonin syndrome**, which produces muscular rigidity and hyperthermia, can result from the use of multiple types of antidepressants, overdose with antidepressants, or gradual increases in antidepressants intended to achieve therapeutic effects (Buckley, Dawson, & Isbister, 2014). The highest risk of serotonin syndrome occurs when medications act as agonists at the 5-HT2 serotonergic receptor. Medications that target other subtypes of serotonergic receptors or act as serotonin antagonists do not typically carry a risk of serotonin syndrome (Buckley et al., 2014).

Low core temperatures are also life threatening. **Hypothermia** (low core body temperature) has killed many stranded hikers and ocean swimmers. Hypothermia occurs when core body temperature drops below 35°C/95°F. Uncontrolled, intense shivering, slurred speech, pain, and discomfort occur. At core temperatures below 31°C/87.8°F, the pupils dilate, behavior resembles drunkenness, and consciousness is gradually lost (Search and Rescue Society of British Columbia, 1995).

Deliberately producing mild hypothermia has become a common method of reducing brain damage following cardiac arrest, stroke, or open heart surgery (Groysman, Emanuel, Kim-Tenser, Sung, & Mack, 2011; Nolan et al., 2003). Cooling can be achieved using a special mattress, intravenous fluids, or applications of ice. Although the mechanism by which cooling prevents damage is not completely understood, it is likely that cooling counteracts typical negative reactions to an interruption in the blood supply to the brain, such as the increased activity of free radicals, excitatory neurochemicals, and calcium (Greer, 2006). Not only can carefully induced hypothermia protect the brain from damage, but it also seems to promote regeneration after injury (Yenari & Han, 2013).

Brain Mechanisms for Temperature Regulation

Temperature regulation is too important for survival to be left to a single system. Instead, temperature regulation results from the activity of a structural hierarchy, beginning with the spinal cord and extending through the brainstem to the hypothalamus. Sensitivity to temperature change increases from the lower to the higher levels of this hierarchy. Lower levels, such as the spinal cord, do not respond to heat or cold until an animal's core temperature is as much as two to three degrees away from the set point. Patients with spinal cord damage, which prevents temperature regulation of the body by the brainstem and hypothalamus, frequently complain about their inability to manage temperature control of their arms and legs. Higher levels of the hierarchy act

serotonin syndrome A life-threatening condition characterized by hyperthermia and muscular rigidity caused by excess serotonin activity due to medication use.

hypothermia A potentially fatal core body temperature below 31°C/87.8°F.

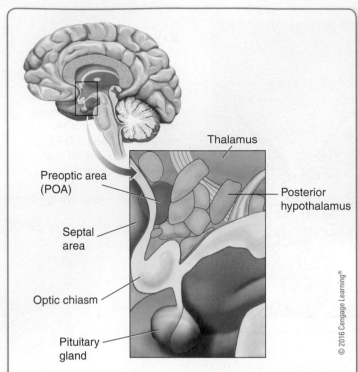

Thalamus

Preoptic area (POA)

Posterior hypothalamus

Septal area

Optic chiasm

Pituitary gland

© 2016 Cengage Learning®

● **Figure 9.6** The Hypothalamus Controls Temperature Regulation The preoptic area (POA) of the hypothalamus, along with adjacent areas of the anterior hypothalamus and septal area, coordinates incoming information from thermoreceptors with structures responsible for appropriate responses to higher core temperatures such as panting, sweating, and the dilation of blood vessels. The posterior hypothalamus is responsible for initiating responses to cooler core temperatures such as shivering and blood vessel constriction.

as much more precise thermostats. The hypothalamus initiates compensation whenever core temperature deviates as little as 0.01 degree from the ideal set point (Satinoff, 1978).

The **preoptic area (POA)** of the hypothalamus, shown in ●Figure 9.6, along with adjacent areas of the anterior hypothalamus and septum, coordinates incoming information from thermoreceptors with structures that trigger appropriate responses to higher core temperatures, such as panting, sweating, and the dilation of blood vessels. The posterior hypothalamus is responsible for initiating responses to cooler core temperatures, such as shivering and blood vessel constriction. In addition to receiving input from skin receptors and the spinal cord, the hypothalamus is sensitive to the body's core temperature as reflected by thermoreceptors within the hypothalamus itself.

The POA contains three types of neurons that contribute to the temperature set point: warm-sensitive, cold-sensitive, and temperature-insensitive (Boulant, 2000). Warm-sensitive neurons make up about 30 percent of the POA. In addition to receiving input from thermoreceptors in the skin and spinal cord, warm-sensitive neurons have receptors embedded in their membranes similar to those in the mouth that are sensitive to capsaicin, the ingredient in peppers that gives us the sensation of heat (see Chapter 7). These receptors respond directly to changes in the temperature of the brain and blood in their vicinity. Warm-sensitive neurons maintain a background level of activity that increases sharply when core temperatures surpass 37°C (98.6°F). Output from the warm-sensitive neurons travels to the paraventricular nucleus (PVN) and lateral nucleus of the hypothalamus, which in turn initiate parasympathetic activity designed to dissipate heat, such as sweating.

Cold-sensitive neurons make up about 5 percent of the POA, but larger numbers are also found in the posterior hypothalamus. These neurons receive input from thermoreceptors in the skin and spinal cord. However, unlike the warm-sensitive neurons, the cold-sensitive neurons do not have any special membrane receptors for sensing coldness in the nearby brain and blood. Instead, cold-sensitive neurons receive inhibitory input from the warm-sensitive neurons. As core temperature drops below 37°C (98.6°F), the reduced activity of the warm-sensitive neurons results in less inhibition of the cold-sensitive neurons, allowing them to increase their activity. Output from the cold-sensitive neurons to the PVN and the posterior hypothalamus results in activation of the sympathetic nervous system. Sympathetic activity generates and conserves heat by raising metabolism and constricting blood vessels at the surface of the skin.

Temperature-insensitive neurons make up about 60 percent of the POA and are also found in the posterior hypothalamus. These neurons maintain a fairly steady rate of responding under all temperature conditions, yet they do have a role to play in thermoregulation. Input from the temperature-insensitive neurons provides a baseline of activity in the cold-sensitive neurons that is modified by the amount of inhibition provided by the warm-sensitive neurons.

A series of clever experiments demonstrated that temperature sensors in the hypothalamus can override input from skin sensors. Rats can be taught to press a bar to obtain a brief puff of cool air (Corbit, 1973; Satinoff, 1964). The rate at which the rats press the bar corresponds to changes in either skin temperature or hypothalamic

preoptic area (POA) A part of the hypothalamus involved in a number of regulatory functions.

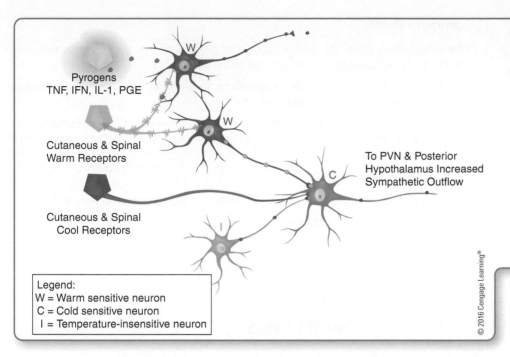

Pyrogens
TNF, IFN, IL-1, PGE

Cutaneous & Spinal
Warm Receptors

Cutaneous & Spinal
Cool Receptors

To PVN & Posterior
Hypothalamus Increased
Sympathetic Outflow

Legend:
W = Warm sensitive neuron
C = Cold sensitive neuron
I = Temperature-insensitive neuron

© 2016 Cengage Learning®

● **Figure 9.7** Pyrogens **Reset the Temperature Set Point in Fever** Pyrogens stimulate the release of prostaglandin E2 (PGE2), which binds to surface receptors on the warm-sensitive neurons of the POA, lowering their activity. In response to reduced inhibition from the warm-sensitive neurons, cold-sensitive cells increase their output, which results in a higher temperature set point.

temperature. Skin temperature mirrors changes in room temperature, whereas hypo-thalamic temperature can be manipulated by bathing the hypothalamus with warm or cool water applied through a surgically inserted micropipette. When either skin temperature or hypothalamic temperature is raised, the rat will press more frequently to obtain cool puffs of air. However, cooling the hypothalamus alone will reduce or suppress bar pressing even when the room (and hence the skin receptors) remains very warm (Kupfermann, Kandel, & Iverson, 2000).

As mentioned earlier, pyrogens entering the brain act to gradually increase the body's temperature set point, causing fever. Not surprisingly, the pyrogens' target in the brain is located in the hypothalamus. The blood–brain barrier is relatively weak near the POA, which allows pyrogens to exit the blood supply and enter the brain tissue. Once in the POA, pyrogens stimulate the release of prostaglandin E2, which in turn inhibits the firing rate of warm-sensitive neurons (Mackowiak & Boulant, 1996). This process is illustrated in ● Figure 9.7. Due to the reduced activity of these central thermoreceptors and the result-ing disinhibition of the cold-sensitive neurons, the hypothalamus responds by raising the temperature set point. Activity in the cold-sensitive neurons, which is usually associated with feeling colder rather than warmer, leads to greater production and retention of heat, leading to increased heart rate, shivering, and the other unpleasant symptoms of fever.

INTERIM SUMMARY 9.1

Summary Table: Strategies Used to Maintain Body Temperature Homeostasis

Temperature	Behavioral Strategies	Internal Strategies
Cold temperatures	• Move to a warmer place or shelter • Huddle with others to conserve heat • Curl up to decrease exposed surface area • Add more clothing, preferably dark colors	• Shivering • Constriction of blood vessels • Increased release of thyroid hormone to increase metabolic rate • Increased metabolism in brown fat stores
Warm temperatures	• Move to cooler, shadier place or shelter • Stretch out • Wear less clothing, preferably light colors	• Perspiration and panting • Dilation of blood vessels

solute A chemical dissolved in solution.

solution A fluid containing solutes.

electrolyte A substance that has broken up into ions in solution.

interstitial fluid A type of extracellular fluid surrounding the body's cells.

Summary Points

1. When deviations from set points occur, the process of motivation activates and directs behavior designed to remedy the situation. **(LO1)**

2. Endotherms can maintain body temperature through internal activity, whereas ectotherms rely on external behaviors. **(LO2)**

3. The hypothalamus, brainstem, and spinal cord produce a hierarchy of responses to changes in temperature, with the hypothalamus providing the most precise level of control. **(LO2)**

Review Questions

1. What are the mechanisms used by endotherms to regulate internal temperature?

2. What are the differences between fever and hyperthermia?

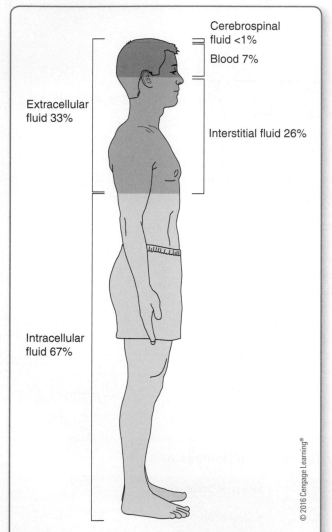

● **Figure 9.8** **The Body's Fluids Are Held in Three Compartments** About two thirds of the body's fluid is stored as intracellular fluid. The remaining third is stored as extracellular fluid, divided between the interstitial fluid surrounding cells (26 percent) and the blood supply (7 percent). The cerebrospinal fluid accounts for less than 1 percent of the body's fluids.

© 2016 Cengage Learning®

Thirst: Regulating the Body's Fluid Levels

As animals became more complex and moved out of the ocean environment onto dry land, they devised ways to incorporate part of their watery environment into their bodies. Maintaining appropriate fluid levels is essential to survival.

The fluids of the body contain many dissolved chemical molecules. Molecules that have been dissolved in a fluid are known as **solutes** and the fluid that contains the solutes is known as a **solution**. If a solute breaks into ions (see Chapter 3) when it is dissolved, it is referred to as an **electrolyte**. You might recognize this term from laboratory blood tests or from the advertising of sports drinks. Some of the important electrolytes involved in healthy body functioning include sodium, calcium, potassium, chloride, magnesium, and bicarbonate. As we will see shortly, sodium is the most important electrolyte for managing the body's fluid levels.

Intracellular and Extracellular Fluid Compartments

The body has three major compartments for storing water, illustrated in ● Figure 9.8. About two thirds of the body's water is contained within cells as intracellular fluid or cytoplasm. The remaining third is found in extracellular fluid, which is further divided into the blood supply (about 7 percent of the body's water total) and the **interstitial fluid** surrounding the body's cells (about 26 percent of the body's water total). Cerebrospinal fluid makes up an additional tiny fraction of a percentage of the extracellular fluid.

As we have seen previously in Chapter 3, the composition of extracellular and intracellular fluids is quite different. Extracellular fluid has higher concentrations of sodium and chloride, and intracellular fluid has higher concentrations of potassium. Even though the identity of the solutes in these two compartments is different, the relative concentration of total solutes is the same. Two solutions with equal concentrations of solutes are referred to as **isotonic**. Intravenous (IV) fluids provided in medical treatment are typically isotonic solutions containing sugars and sodium. In other words, the IV fluid has the same concentration of solutes as normal body fluids, although the exact identity of the solutes might be different. The body can absorb the fluids and solutes without requiring further adjustments to intracellular and extracellular fluid levels.

isotonic Having the same concentration of solutes as a reference solution.
osmosis The movement of water to equalize concentration on two sides of a membrane.

Osmosis Causes Water to Move

The balance found in the isotonic state reduces any movement of fluid into or out of the body's cells due to **osmosis**. Osmosis, illustrated in ● Figure 9.9, is the force that causes water to move from an area with lower concentration of solutes to an area with higher concentration of solutes. Osmosis is similar to diffusion in that both processes produce the movement of molecules. In diffusion, which we discussed in Chapter 3, solutes tend to spread themselves out equally in a space,

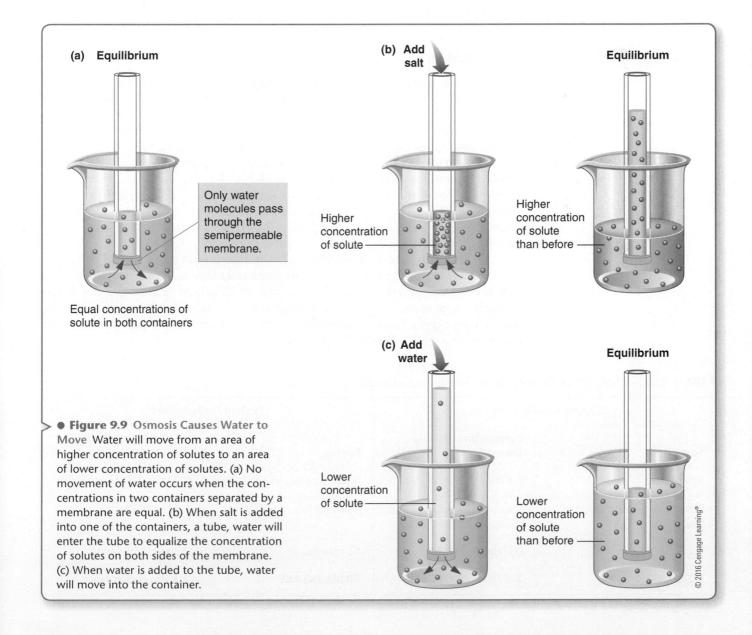

> ● **Figure 9.9** Osmosis Causes Water to Move Water will move from an area of higher concentration of solutes to an area of lower concentration of solutes. (a) No movement of water occurs when the concentrations in two containers separated by a membrane are equal. (b) When salt is added into one of the containers, a tube, water will enter the tube to equalize the concentration of solutes on both sides of the membrane. (c) When water is added to the tube, water will move into the container.

(a) **Equilibrium**

Only water molecules pass through the semipermeable membrane.

Equal concentrations of solute in both containers

(b) **Add salt**

Higher concentration of solute

Equilibrium

Higher concentration of solute than before

(c) **Add water**

Lower concentration of solute

Equilibrium

Lower concentration of solute than before

© 2016 Cengage Learning®

hypotonic Having a relatively lower concentration of solutes than a reference solution.

hypertonic Having a relatively higher concentration of solutes than a reference solution.

kidney One of a pair of structures located in the lower back responsible for maintaining fluid balance and for producing urine.

moving from areas of high to low concentration. In osmosis, it is the water that moves across a barrier, such as a cell membrane, to equalize concentrations of the solutes on either side.

Solutions that are lower in concentration of solutes than a reference solution are referred to as **hypotonic**, and solutions that are relatively higher in concentration of solutes are referred to as **hypertonic**. Hypotonic and hypertonic solutions have different effects on the body's fluid levels. Emergency treatment of people who nearly drown varies accordingly. In a freshwater near-drowning, the person often breathes in large amounts of fresh water. The extracellular fluid becomes highly hypotonic, or less concentrated than the intracellular fluid. In an effort to regain balance, osmotic pressure will drive water from the less concentrated extracellular fluid into the more concentrated cells, possibly rupturing cell membranes. In a saltwater near-drowning, the extracellular fluid becomes hypertonic, or more concentrated than the intracellular fluid. In this case, osmotic pressure will drive water out of the less concentrated intracellular fluid into the highly concentrated extracellular fluid. Exposed cells will rapidly dehydrate, disrupting their ability to carry out normal functions. In either case, damage is particularly prevalent in the lungs, further contributing to the lack of oxygen that has already occurred due to submersion (Shepherd & Martin, 2002).

The Kidneys

Given normal access to food and water, people usually consume more water and sodium than they really need to maintain fluid balances. However, livestock in the field are often provided with a salt lick, and athletes or soldiers engaging in high levels of physical activity in hot, humid conditions benefit from salt supplements.

Any excess sodium or water is excreted by the two **kidneys**, located in the lower back. Blood enters the kidneys, where it is filtered through a complex system made up of over a million structures known as nephrons. Impurities and excess water and sodium are removed by the nephrons and sent to the bladder for excretion as urine. The filtered blood returns to the circulation. In cases of kidney failure, patients must undergo regular sessions of kidney dialysis. Machines are used in an effort to duplicate the filtering normally performed by the kidneys.

In addition to urination, we lose water through several other normal body processes. Steaming breath on a cold day demonstrates that some water is lost during simple breathing or respiration. About 1 liter (0.22 gallon) of fluid per day is lost through perspiration. Evaporation through the skin and defecation also reduce the body's water supply. Table 9.1 shows the relative loss and intake of fluids from the body during normal daily activity.

TABLE 9.1 | Sources of Typical Daily Fluid Loss and Intake in Humans

Typical Daily Loss		Typical Daily Intake	
Source	**Approximate Daily Quantity**	**Source**	**Approximate Daily Quantity**
Urine	1.4 liters/4.928 cups*	Fluids from beverages	1.2 liters/4.224 cups
Perspiration, evaporation, respiration	0.9 liter/3.168 cups	Fluids contained in food	1.0 liter/3.52 cups
Feces	0.2 liter/0.704 cup	Plain water	0.3 liter/0.056 cup
TOTAL LOSS	**2.5 liters/8.8 cups**	**TOTAL INTAKE**	**2.5 liters/8.8 cups**

*1 cup = 8 ounces

The Sensation of Thirst

Animals vary in their need to take in water during the day. Some desert-dwelling species never seem to drink at all. Animals that spend a lot of time in the water are nearly always ingesting some. As shown in Table 9.1, humans need an average of about 2.5 liters (0.55 gallons) of water per day. This is roughly equivalent to the eight glasses of water a day that we are commonly advised to consume. No offense to mothers' advice or to corporations marketing bottled water, but there is nothing special about consuming plain water. Any source of fluid will do. As a matter of fact, we take in about half the fluids we need through the foods we eat without drinking any beverages at all, so following the eight-glasses-a-day rule is likely to provide an excess of fluids.

When a drop in the body's water supply is perceived, two processes are initiated. We experience the sensation of thirst, and our bodies begin to conserve whatever water we still have. Walter Cannon (1929) proposed that the sensation of a dry mouth was the critical stimulus responsible for feelings of thirst, which in turn leads to drinking. Cannon's hypothesis is quite wrong. Although the feelings of a dry, dusty mouth and throat certainly stimulate us to take a drink, these feelings are too quickly relieved to be trusted completely as a means of fluid regulation. As anyone with outdoors experience can relate, swirling a mouthful of water from a canteen is usually enough to make the dry-mouth sensation go away. Claude Bernard (1856) provided more direct evidence against the dry-mouth theory. Bernard surgically produced an opening, or fistula, in the esophagus of animals. As long as the fistula remained closed and all water consumed reached the stomach, the animals drank normally. However, when the fistula was open, allowing all of the consumed water to escape without reaching the stomach, Bernard's animals drank continuously. Their mouths were certainly quite wet, but this did not inhibit their drinking in any way.

Thirst actually occurs as a result of two more sophisticated processes. In the first case, **osmotic thirst** occurs in response to cellular dehydration resulting from drops in the intracellular fluid volume. In the second case, **hypovolemic** (low volume) **thirst** occurs in response to drops in blood volume. A double-depletion hypothesis suggests that a combination of these processes contributes to thirst. However, osmotic thirst appears to be the more common mechanism, whereas hypovolemic thirst serves as a less frequently used emergency backup system.

OSMOTIC THIRST You probably have some relevant experience with the most common cause of osmotic thirst: eating salty foods. After you eat and digest a salty meal, your blood becomes more concentrated with sodium. The higher salt content makes the blood hypertonic, or more concentrated, relative to the intracellular fluid. Osmotic pressure will move water out of the cells in an effort to regain the balanced, isotonic state. Receptors sense the lower volume of water in the cells, and you begin to feel very thirsty.

A similar process results in the overdrinking, or polydipsia, that is typical of untreated **diabetes mellitus**. We will discuss diabetes in more detail later in this chapter. People with untreated diabetes are unable to move sugars out of the blood supply, causing the blood to become hypertonic. The cells attempt to compensate by releasing water, and strong sensations of thirst result that lead to overdrinking. The combination of polydipsia and fluids moving from the cells into the blood supply provides an excess of fluids that stimulates urination. Urination further concentrates the blood supply, and the cycle continues. Strong sensations of thirst accompanied by frequent urination are early warning signs of diabetes mellitus.

Cellular dehydration is detected by specialized **osmoreceptors** located in the brain. Verney (1947) coined the term osmoreceptors and predicted that these specialized neurons might alter their firing rate when their intracellular fluid levels changed. An area located around the third ventricle, the **organum vasculosum of the lamina terminalis (OVLT)**, along with surrounding areas of the hypothalamus, has been implicated in the detection of cellular dehydration (Verbalis, 2007). The OVLT, shown

osmotic thirst Thirst produced by cellular dehydration.
hypovolemic thirst Thirst that results from a decrease in the volume of the extracellular fluid.
diabetes mellitus A disease characterized by insulin deficiency, resulting in hunger, excess sugar in blood and urine, and extreme thirst.
osmoreceptor A receptor that detects cellular dehydration.
organum vasculosum of the lamina terminalis (OVLT) An area located around the third ventricle in the brain that detects cellular dehydration.

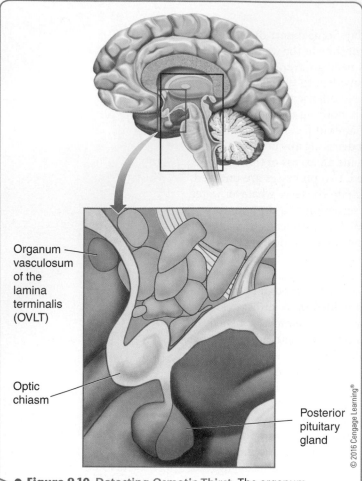

Organum vasculosum of the lamina terminalis (OVLT)

Optic chiasm

Posterior pituitary gland

© 2016 Cengage Learning®

● **Figure 9.10 Detecting Osmotic Thirst** The organum vasculosum of the lamina terminalis (OVLT), located near the third ventricle, contains osmoreceptors that detect osmotic thirst.

in ● Figure 9.10, is particularly well situated for a role in detecting blood solute levels because the blood–brain barrier (see Chapter 3) is weak in this area. A series of elegant experiments by Charles Bourque and his colleagues not only established the OVLT as a probable location for osmoreceptors but also provided insight as to how these neurons encode changes in the concentration of their surrounding fluids (Bourque & Oliet, 1997; Nissen, Bourque, & Renaud, 1993). OVLT cells from rats were kept alive in an artificial medium resembling interstitial fluid. If the surrounding fluid was made hypertonic, leading to loss of fluid from the cells, the OVLT cells increased their firing rates. When the surrounding fluid was made hypotonic, leading to movement of water into the cells, firing rates decreased.

HYPOVOLEMIC THIRST Hypovolemic thirst results when we experience a drop in the volume of interstitial fluid, blood, or both. The most obvious cause for hypovolemic thirst is the loss of blood due to internal bleeding or a severe injury.

Lower blood volume is sensed by receptors in the heart and kidneys. The wall of the heart muscle contains **baroreceptors** that measure blood pressure. As blood volume decreases, blood pressure decreases as well. The kidneys contain blood-flow receptors that also respond to changes in blood volume. When low blood volume is perceived, thirst is initiated, and the kidneys act to conserve remaining fluids.

RESPONDING TO THIRST When either cellular dehydration or hypovolemia is sensed, a sequence of hormone actions helps return fluid levels to their set point. As shown in ● Figure 9.11, both osmoreceptors and baroreceptors stimulate release of **antidiuretic hormone (ADH)**, also known as **vasopressin**, by the posterior pituitary gland located just below the hypothalamus. Diuretic medications promote water loss through urination, so an *anti*diuretic promotes water retention.

ADH has two major effects on the kidneys. First, ADH signals the kidneys to reduce urine production, which conserves fluid. Second, ADH stimulates the kidneys to release the hormone **renin** into the blood supply. Renin is also released in response to activity in the kidneys' blood-flow receptors. Once in the bloodstream, renin triggers the conversion of **angiotensinogen**, a blood protein, into **angiotensin II**. There is an angiotensin I, which is produced as a brief, interim step between the blood proteins and angiotensin II, but angiotensin II is the important, biologically active component. Angiotensin II constricts blood vessels, helping to maintain blood pressure. Angiotensin II also triggers the release of the hormone **aldosterone** from the adrenal glands, located above the kidneys. Aldosterone signals the kidneys to retain sodium rather than excrete it in the urine.

Levels of water and sodium are intricately bound together but are managed by different processes. ADH controls the retention of water, and aldosterone controls the retention of sodium. Sodium is essential to the maintenance of the extracellular fluid. Without sodium solutes, the extracellular fluid would become hypotonic, and too much water would move into the cells. When blood volume is lost, as in a serious injury, treatments designed to increase extracellular sodium levels prevent further loss of water into the cells and stimulate some release of water from cells into the blood supply.

baroreceptor A receptor in the heart and kidneys that measures blood pressure.

antidiuretic hormone (ADH) A hormone that promotes retention of fluid by signaling the kidneys to reduce urine production and by stimulating the release of renin. Also known as vasopressin.

vasopressin Another name for antidiuretic hormone (ADH).

renin A substance released by the kidneys that converts angiotensinogen into angiotensin II.

angiotensinogen A blood protein converted into angiotensin II by renin.

angiotensin II A hormone that constricts blood vessels to maintain blood pressure and triggers the release of aldosterone.

aldosterone A hormone that signals the kidneys to retain sodium.

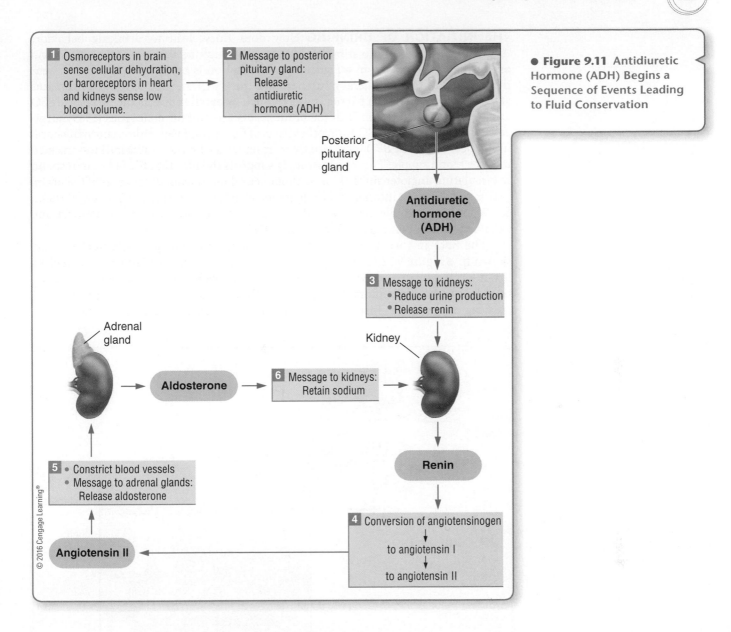

1 Osmoreceptors in brain sense cellular dehydration, or baroreceptors in heart and kidneys sense low blood volume.

2 Message to posterior pituitary gland: Release antidiuretic hormone (ADH)

Posterior pituitary gland

● **Figure 9.11** Antidiuretic Hormone (ADH) Begins a Sequence of Events Leading to Fluid Conservation

Antidiuretic hormone (ADH)

3 Message to kidneys:
• Reduce urine production
• Release renin

Kidney

Adrenal gland

Aldosterone

6 Message to kidneys: Retain sodium

Renin

5 • Constrict blood vessels
• Message to adrenal glands: Release aldosterone

4 Conversion of angiotensinogen ↓ to angiotensin I ↓ to angiotensin II

Angiotensin II

© 2016 Cengage Learning®

Low blood volume stimulates a specific hunger for sodium. Although it might seem odd that thirst and sodium craving can occur simultaneously (eating salty foods usually makes us more thirsty), this is exactly what happens during hypovolemia. There are a number of ways to induce hypovolemia experimentally without removing a quantity of blood. Injections of formalin (Rescorla & Freberg, 1978) or propylene glycol (Fitzsimons, 1961) can produce both excessive thirst and salt cravings in experimental animals. Once hypovolemia is artificially induced, animals will prefer a normally rejected hypertonic sodium solution to regular water (Fitzsimons, 1961).

Normal sodium levels represent a balance between dietary intake and excretion by the kidneys. If dietary consumption of sodium is high or excretion of sodium by the kidneys is inadequate, high blood pressure and its associated complications, such as stroke, often occur. Chronically high sodium levels in the blood promote the release of water from cells into the circulation due to osmosis. This higher blood volume increases blood pressure. Most medications for high blood pressure are diuretics because promoting urination is an effective way to reduce blood volume. Lower-than-normal sodium levels are also a risk to health. Vomiting and diarrhea due to illnesses can reduce sodium, and therefore blood volume and blood pressure, to dangerously low, life-threatening levels.

THE INITIATION OF DRINKING How does thirst lead to drinking behavior? Angiotensin II appears to stimulate drinking through its action on the **subfornical organ (SFO)**, illustrated in ● Figure 9.12. Its location is below (sub) the fornix, near the junction of the two lateral ventricles. Like the OVLT, the SFO is located in an area at which the blood–brain barrier is weak. Much research supports the role of the SFO as a target for angiotensin II in the brain. Kadekaro and his colleagues (1989) surgically disconnected the SFO from other parts of the brain. Even without normal neural input, neurons in the SFO increased their firing rates when angiotensin II was injected into the blood supply. This result strongly supports the idea that the SFO can respond to circulating angiotensin II alone, without neural input from other areas of the brain. Lesions of the SFO interfere with angiotensin-induced drinking (Simpson, Epstein, & Camardo, 1978). Electrical stimulation of the SFO produces immediate drinking behavior (Smith, Beninger, & Ferguson, 1995).

The SFO in turn forms connections with the **median preoptic nucleus**, also shown in ● Figure 9.12. Unlike the OVLT and the SFO, the median preoptic nucleus is not located in an area where the blood–brain barrier is weak. Although the structure does contain receptors for angiotensin II, it cannot respond to angiotensin circulating in the blood. Instead, it appears that angiotensin II can serve as a classical

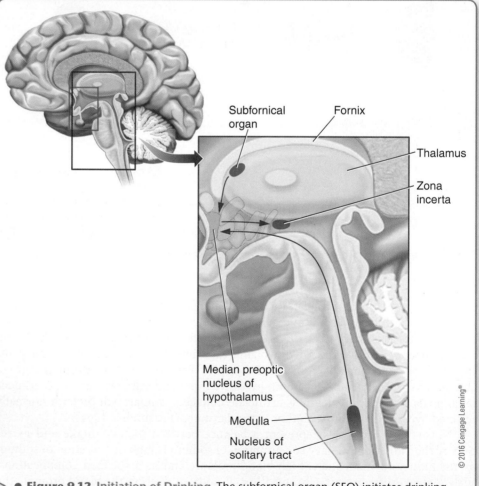

subfornical organ (SFO) An area of the brain located near the junction of the two lateral ventricles that regulates drinking.

median preoptic nucleus An area of the hypothalamus that is involved with drinking behavior.

● **Figure 9.12 Initiation of Drinking** The subfornical organ (SFO) initiates drinking in response to detection of angiotensin II. Along with the nucleus of the solitary tract, the SFO communicates with the median preoptic nucleus of the hypothalamus. The median preoptic nucleus communicates with the zona incerta by way of the lateral hypothalamus. The zona incerta connects with a number of motor areas responsible for drinking behavior.

© 2016 Cengage Learning®

neurotransmitter within the central nervous system (CNS), passing information between structures like the SFO and median preoptic nucleus (Fitzsimons, 1998; Lind & Johnson, 1982). The median preoptic nucleus also receives input from the **nucleus of the solitary tract (NST)**, which is located in the medulla. The NST in turn receives input from baroreceptors in the circulatory system and osmoreceptors located in the digestive tract. The median preoptic nucleus communicates with the **lateral hypothalamus (LH)**, which projects to the **zona incerta** of the midbrain. The zona incerta sends information to a number of motor regions, including the basal ganglia, the red nucleus, and the ventral horn of the spinal cord (Ricardo, 1981). Stimulation of the zona incerta produces drinking behavior, suggesting that this structure is responsible for initiating the motor components of drinking behavior.

WHY DOES DRINKING STOP? We typically stop drinking long before water levels in either the intracellular or extracellular compartments return to normal (Grossman, 2012). Although taking in excess water is not nearly as significant a problem as not having enough water to drink, because the excess can be excreted easily, drinking represents time, energy, and potential exposure to predators. It makes sense to assume that animals would be able to assess whether or not they required more water.

After 24 hours of fluid deprivation, humans consume about 75 percent of their fluid needs in the first 5–10 minutes in which fluid is available. Drinking slows at least 10 minutes before any real changes in sodium concentrations and cellular hydration occur. This suggests that animals have systems for the "oral metering" of fluid intake (Grossman, 2012). Fluid receptors have been identified in the mouth, throat, and at various levels of the digestive system. As we saw previously, having a "dry" mouth does not play a significant role in initiating drinking, but these receptors might be very important for deciding when to stop drinking. To test the effectiveness of this feedback, animals with esophageal fistulae have been shown to consume enough water to meet their exact needs, then stop. Stomach receptors also play a role. When the stomachs of experimental animals who have stopped drinking are drained, the animals immediately begin drinking again.

You might be wondering about a person's response to intravenous fluids, which bypass the "oral metering" system entirely. Rats can be trained to administer water intravenously by pressing a bar that activated a pump. Rats obtaining water this way only "consumed" about two-thirds of the amount of water they would drink under normal situations, yet they seemed perfectly healthy on this amount (Grossman, 2012). This suggests that some of our drinking behavior reflects an "oral need" as opposed to a true need to maintain homeostasis.

Overdrinking can be dangerous under certain conditions, resulting in **hyponatremia**, a condition in which extracellular sodium levels drop 10 percent or more below normal (Vellaichamy, 2001). Untreated hyponatremia results in nausea, vomiting, cramps, and disorientation. If the condition persists, seizures, coma (due to swelling of the brain), and death may follow. A large number of medical problems result in hyponatremia, including congestive heart failure, kidney failure, and some tumors. Recently, the condition has become more common due to the increased popularity of extreme endurance events (Rosner & Kirven, 2007) (see ● Figure 9.13).

Under normal circumstances, extracellular fluid levels are negatively correlated with sodium concentrations. When extracellular fluid levels are high, sodium concentrations are low, and vice versa. During extreme endurance activities, however, low extracellular fluid levels and low sodium concentrations can coexist. During a long race, an athlete might lose unusually high amounts of sodium and water through perspiration, vomiting, and urination. As a result, conflicting messages will be sent to the fluid regulation system. The release of ADH cannot simultaneously increase (in response to low extracellular fluid levels) and decrease (in response to low sodium concentrations). Because protecting blood volume enjoys a higher priority in terms of survival, the posterior pituitary gland will continue to pump out ADH under these circumstances. Water is retained due to ADH's inhibition of urination, even though

nucleus of the solitary tract (NST) A structure in the medulla that processes information from baroreceptors, osmoreceptors, glucoreceptors, and taste receptors.

lateral hypothalamus (LH) A part of the hypothalamus that participates in behavioral responses to thirst and in the initiation of feeding behavior.

zona incerta An area of the midbrain that participates in the initiation of drinking behavior.

hyponatremia A life-threatening condition in which sodium concentrations in the extracellular fluid are too low.

● **Figure 9.13 Extreme Sports and the Risk of Hyponatremia** The popularity of extreme sports has led to more frequent cases of hyponatremia. Athletes competing in the Sahara Race run 155 miles (250 km) over seven days while carrying 9 kilograms (20 pounds) of gear, food, and clothing. Temperatures during the race can reach 120 degrees Fahrenheit (49° C). The combination of heat and exertion places tremendous stress on the body's mechanisms for fluid regulation.

this further reduces the concentration of sodium (Hiller, 1989). As the extracellular fluid becomes increasingly hypotonic, water moves into the cells, generating a strong sensation of hypovolemic thirst. In response to these sensations, the athlete might drink large amounts of plain water during the race, further compounding the hyponatremia (Noakes, 1993). Current efforts at preventing hyponatremia focus on educating athletes to drink only when thirsty and not in large amounts (Rosner & Kirven, 2007). Consuming additional sodium or sports drinks to not seem to reduce an athlete's risk of hyponatremia (Rosner & Kirven, 2007).

INTERIM SUMMARY 9.2

‖ Summary Table: Brain Mechanisms for Initiating Drinking

Stimulus	Receptors	Step 1	Step 2	Step 3	Step 4	Step 5
Osmotic thirst	Osmoreceptors	OVLT	OVLT, NST, and SFO communicate with the median preoptic area.	Median preoptic area communicates with the lateral hypothalamus (LH).	LH communicates with the zona incerta.	Zona incerta initiates drinking through connections with the motor systems.
Hypovolemic thirst	Cardiac baroreceptors	Communicate with the NST via the vagus nerve				
	Kidney baroreceptors	Communicate with the SFO by stimulating increased angiotensin II				

Summary Points

1. Drops in intracellular fluid volume produce osmotic thirst, which is detected by osmoreceptors located in the organum vasculosum of the lamina terminalis (OVLT). **(LO3)**

2. Decreases in the volume of the extracellular fluid, such as blood, result in hypovolemic thirst. Baroreceptors located in the heart and kidneys detect drops in blood pressure. **(LO3)**

3. Both osmoreceptors and baroreceptors stimulate the release of antidiuretic hormone (ADH). ADH signals the kidneys to reduce urine production and initiates a sequence leading to increased production of angiotensin II. Angiotensin II constricts blood vessels to maintain blood pressure and triggers the release of aldosterone. Aldosterone signals the kidneys to retain sodium. **(LO3)**

4. Angiotensin II appears to stimulate drinking by its action on the subfornical organ (SFO). Drinking stops in response to receptors located in the mouth, throat, and digestive system. **(LO3)**

Review Questions

1. What are the differences between osmotic thirst and hypovolemic thirst?

2. Once thirst is perceived, what processes lead to drinking behavior?

Hunger: Regulating the Body's Supply of Nutrients

Emotions and learning exert more influence on our eating behaviors than they do on the regulatory behaviors of temperature control and thirst. Not only do we eat to obtain the energy and specific nutrients needed by our bodies, but we eat for pleasure as well. Complex cultural and psychological factors can overwhelm the body's natural regulatory mechanisms, leading to different patterns of disordered eating.

The Environment and Eating

Human beings take in a remarkable variety of nutrients. The traditional diet of the Inuit people who live in Arctic regions contains little vegetable matter at all, whereas people following a vegan diet eat only plant material. In spite of these differences, we somehow manage to consume the nutrients we need.

Some seemingly cultural differences in food intake have their roots in biology. Many American foods are based on dairy products, but this is not the case in every culture. Some people no longer produce the enzymes necessary to process fresh milk products after infancy, resulting in lactose intolerance. The use of dairy products correlates with the geographical distribution of lactose intolerance. As shown in ● Figure 9.14, the highest rates of lactose intolerance occur among Asians, whose consumption of dairy products is very low. Lactose intolerance is rare among people from Scandinavia and parts of the Middle East, where reliance on dairy products has been historically high (Rozin & Pelchat, 1988).

Learned food preferences begin at a surprisingly early point in life (Mennella & Beauchamp, 2005). Exposure to flavors through the amniotic fluid or breast milk appears to influence later food choices. When pregnant and nursing women consumed carrot juice rather than plain water, their infants ate much more cereal that was prepared with carrot juice than with water, and they were rated as appearing to enjoy the carrot cereal more (Mennella, Jagnow, & Beauchamp, 2001). This mechanism could promote learning about safe and available foods in very young children (Mennella, 2006).

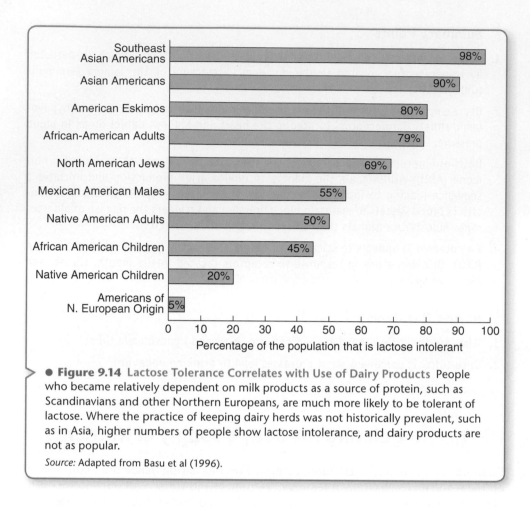

● **Figure 9.14** **Lactose Tolerance Correlates with Use of Dairy Products** People who became relatively dependent on milk products as a source of protein, such as Scandinavians and other Northern Europeans, are much more likely to be tolerant of lactose. Where the practice of keeping dairy herds was not historically prevalent, such as in Asia, higher numbers of people show lactose intolerance, and dairy products are not as popular.

Source: Adapted from Basu et al (1996).

The Process of Digestion

Foods are broken down into usable chemicals by the digestive tract, shown in ● Figure 9.15. Digestion begins in the mouth, where saliva is mixed with food. The water and enzymes contained in saliva begin the breakdown of food into a semi-liquid state that can then be swallowed. Saliva is automatically secreted when food enters the mouth, courtesy of the autonomic nervous system. However, Pavlov (1924) demonstrated conclusively that this process is quickly modifiable through experience. If you see or smell a delicious chocolate cake in the oven, you might experience anticipatory salivation based on your past experience with chocolate cakes.

After food is swallowed, it proceeds through the esophagus to the stomach, where it is mixed with hydrochloric acid and pepsin. These chemicals break down the food particles into even smaller pieces. The partially digested food is released periodically through the duodenum into the small intestine, where the process of digestion is completed. Indigestible material travels on to the large intestine, where water is reabsorbed and feces are formed.

During digestion, fats, proteins, and carbohydrates are absorbed into the blood supply and circulated to waiting tissues. Fats are either used for immediate energy or stored by adipose tissue (fat cells). The hormone **cholecystokinin (CCK)** is released when large quantities of fat are consumed. Proteins are broken down into amino acids and used by muscles and other tissues for growth and protein synthesis. Carbohydrates are broken into simple sugars, including **glucose**. Under normal circumstances, glucose is the exclusive source of energy for the brain, whereas the rest of the body can use both glucose and fatty acids. Excess glucose is stored as fat by adipose tissue or converted by the liver into a complex carbohydrate called **glycogen** for storage. If the body requires more energy than can be supplied by the glucose circulating in the blood, such

cholecystokinin (CCK) A gut hormone released in response to the consumption of fats that also acts as a central nervous system (CNS) neurochemical that signals satiety.

glucose A type of sugar found in foods that is a major source of energy for living organisms.

glycogen A complex carbohydrate used to store energy in the liver.

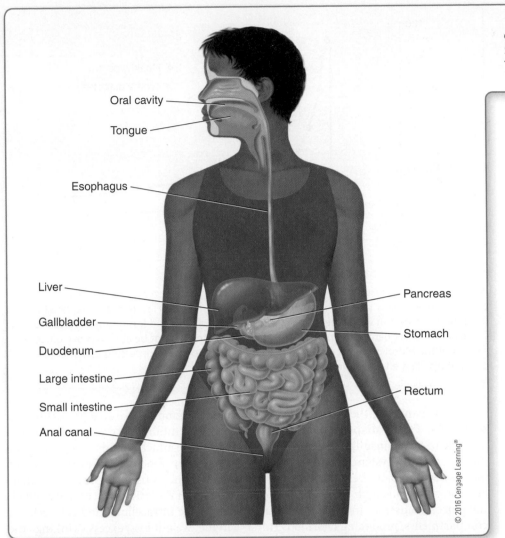

Oral cavity

Tongue

Esophagus

Liver

Gallbladder

Duodenum

Large intestine

Small intestine

Anal canal

Pancreas

Stomach

Rectum

© 2016 Cengage Learning®

● **Figure 9.15** The Major Structures of the Digestive Tract

as during a period of fasting, the liver converts stored glycogen back into readily available glucose. Consequently, we maintain a fairly steady level of blood glucose over time.

If continued fasting depletes stores of glycogen, all body structures except the brain begin to use fatty acids from adipose tissue for energy. Energy can be supplied by ketones, chemicals produced from stored fat by the liver. People following extremely low-carbohydrate diets, such as the Atkins diet, often rely on ketones for energy. In addition, fasting causes muscle tissue to break down, and the liver converts the resulting amino acids into glucose. This is a good reason for moderation in dieting. Even with the loss of two to three pounds per week on a sensible, balanced diet, approximately 25 percent of the weight lost will be from bone and muscle (Nunez et al., 1997).

The Pancreatic Hormones

The body's supply of energy from glucose is regulated in large part by two hormones, **glucagon** and **insulin**, that are manufactured by the pancreas. The pancreas, shown in ● Figure 9.15, is a large gland located behind the stomach. Glucagon converts stored glycogen back into glucose. Levels of glucagon increase during periods of fasting, as the body taps into its glycogen stores to maintain blood glucose levels. Insulin helps store glucose as glycogen and assists in moving glucose from the blood supply into body cells. As shown in ● Figure 9.16, levels of insulin normally increase after a meal, helping some glucose circulating in the blood supply to move into cells and the rest to be stored as glycogen. Insulin levels are lowest during long periods of fasting.

glucagon A pancreatic hormone that converts glycogen into glucose.

insulin A pancreatic hormone that facilitates the movement of sugars from the blood supply into the body's tissues.

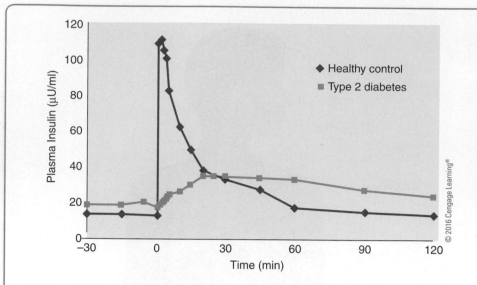

● **Figure 9.16** **Insulin Release Is Reduced in Type 2 Diabetes** Following a meal (time 0), a healthy person experiences a large spike in insulin levels in the circulation. In contrast, a person with type 2 diabetes has a much slower and less dramatic release of insulin. Consequently, the person with type 2 diabetes will not be able to move glucose out of the blood into cells requiring nutrients. The appetite-suppressing action of insulin is also less effective for a person with diabetes.

Disturbances in the activity of the pancreatic hormones have serious health consequences. **Type 1 diabetes mellitus** is diagnosed in childhood or young adulthood, and occurs when insulin-producing pancreatic cells are attacked and destroyed by the body's immune system. Without insulin, glucose from food circulates through the bloodstream without being absorbed or stored by the body's tissues. The cells are literally starving while high levels of glucose are excreted in the urine. The excess circulating glucose causes an imbalance of solutes between the intracellular and extracellular compartments, producing enormous thirst. Fatigue, weight loss, excess drinking, and excess urination are classic symptoms of untreated diabetes.

Type 2 diabetes mellitus is diagnosed when individuals produce insulin but their bodies either do not make sufficient amounts of insulin or do not use insulin efficiently—a condition known as insulin resistance. After a few years of insulin resistance, the amount of insulin produced by the pancreas begins to decline (NIDDK, 2002), and the person becomes diabetic. Approximately 12.3 percent of all American adults have diabetes (Centers for Disease Control and Prevention [CDC], 2014). Symptoms of type 2 diabetes are the same as in type 1. Obesity is a major risk factor for type 2 diabetes (Cruickshank, 2014). Unlike type 1 diabetes, type 2 usually can be prevented and treated by maintaining a healthy weight.

The Initiation of Eating

We respond to both external and internal cues that make us feel hungry. Among the external cues are factors such as time of day, the delightful sights and smells of favorite foods, or the social setting we are in when food is presented. These external cues often encourage us to eat when our bodies do not need nutrients or to eat more food than we require to meet our energy needs.

Internal hunger cues are generated when our body is genuinely short on nutrients. One internal sign of hunger occurs when our stomachs begin to rumble. However, we typically initiate eating long before our stomachs begin to growl, so other systems must also be involved in making us feel hungry.

Hunger can occur as a function of blood glucose levels. Glucose levels in the blood are high just following a meal. As glucose levels drop, a person begins to feel hungry

type 1 diabetes mellitus The form of diabetes that appears early in life and is characterized by insufficient production of insulin.

type 2 diabetes mellitus The form of diabetes generally diagnosed in middle-aged adults and characterized by resistance to insulin.

••• Connecting to **Research**

SWALLOWING BALLOONS AND GROWLING STOMACHS

In an early study on the role of stomach contractions in hunger, Walter Cannon persuaded his colleague A. L. Washburn to swallow a balloon attached to an air pump (Cannon & Washburn, 1912). The balloon allowed Washburn's stomach contractions to be monitored. Washburn couldn't speak due to the tube down his throat attached to the balloon, so he indicated hunger by tapping a telegraph key. Washburn's feelings of hunger did correlate with his stomach contractions, as shown in ● Figure 9.17.

Today, we know that in response to feedback from the enteric nervous system (see Chapter 2), our stomachs begin anticipatory contractions about two hours after the last meal, which clear out any remaining contents of the stomach in preparation for upcoming feeding. These waves of contractions, which Washburn likely perceived, last about 10 to 20 minutes and repeat about once every hour or two until feeding occurs again. What Cannon and Washburn did not know at the time is that stomach contractions happen frequently, both when we're hungry and when we're full. Contractions following a meal are very important to moving food along the gastrointestinal tract. We are simply more aware of the contractions when we're hungry, because an empty stomach makes more noise than a full one.

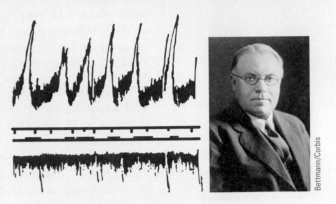

Bettmann/Corbis

● **Figure 9.17** Does a Growling Stomach Mean Hunger? To test their stomach contraction hypothesis, Walter Cannon (photo) and A. L. Washburn conducted an experiment in which Washburn swallowed a balloon connected to a recording device that measured contractions of the stomach. At the same time, Washburn tapped a telegraph key whenever he felt hunger. The upper tracing shows the recordings of stomach contractions while the lower tracing shows Washburn's key taps, which correlated with the stomach contractions over time.

again. Glucose levels are intimately tied to insulin levels. Insulin is normally released in response to eating or even to the anticipation of eating. Therefore, we would expect high levels of insulin and glucose to correspond to satiety, whereas low levels of insulin and glucose should correspond with fasting and feeling hungry. Unfortunately for our hypothesis, two observations are inconsistent with this simple approach. First of all, injections of insulin generally produce feelings of hunger instead of satiety (Vijande et al., 1990). Second, patients with diabetes experience substantial hunger in spite of high levels of circulating glucose. An improved glucose hypothesis suggests that it is not the total amount of circulating glucose that determines whether we feel hungry but the availability of that glucose to our cells (Mayer, 1955). In a healthy person, circulating glucose is the same as available glucose, and hunger will occur when blood glucose levels are low. However, in the person with diabetes, circulating glucose is not available to cells due to reduced insulin functioning. As a result, hunger occurs in spite of ample supplies of glucose. An injection of insulin drives circulating blood glucose into cells, reducing the amount of available glucose and producing sensations of hunger.

Another explanation for why we feel hungry is a "lipostatic theory" that suggests that hunger results from low fat supplies (Kennedy, 1953). A person of normal weight (see discussion of body mass index or BMI later in this chapter) generally maintains enough body fat to provide calories for five to six weeks of total starvation. Obesity obviously increases the amount of time an individual can survive without food. A man monitored by Stewart and Fleming (1973) survived a total fast of 382 days, while his weight went from 207 kilograms (455.4 pounds) to 81.6 kilograms (179.5 pounds). It is also likely that we have mechanisms for assessing levels of circulating amino acids. However, assessing these mechanisms experimentally would be difficult to do because

glucoreceptor A receptor that is sensitive to the presence of glucose.

depriving a research participant of these essential building blocks for proteins would affect much more than just hunger.

RECEPTORS AND HUNGER If hunger results from low levels of available glucose and fats, receptors must exist that can assess nutrient levels and communicate with areas of the brain that initiate feeding behavior. **Glucoreceptors** have been identified in the hindbrain, particularly in the medulla (Ritter, Li, Wang, & Dinh, 2011). Other receptors in the liver monitor levels of both glucose and fatty acids. Glucoreceptors in the liver influence the release of insulin from the pancreas.

BRAIN MECHANISMS FOR HUNGER Early research suggested that the lateral hypothalamus (LH) served as a hunger center (Anand & Brobeck, 1951) (see ● Figure 9.18). Rats with lesions in the LH would starve to death in the presence of food because they would not initiate eating. Human patients with tumors in the LH often lose considerable weight due to loss of appetite. Electrical stimulation of the LH produces immediate feeding.

Subsequent research raised doubts about a simplistic role for the LH as a feeding center. If rats with LH lesions were force-fed, they eventually began to initiate feeding on their own again. The LH probably participates in initiating eating, but other structures that will be described in the next section are also involved.

NEUROCHEMICALS AND HUNGER Feeding behavior is influenced by complex interactions among several neurochemicals. These interactions are outlined in ● Figure 9.19.

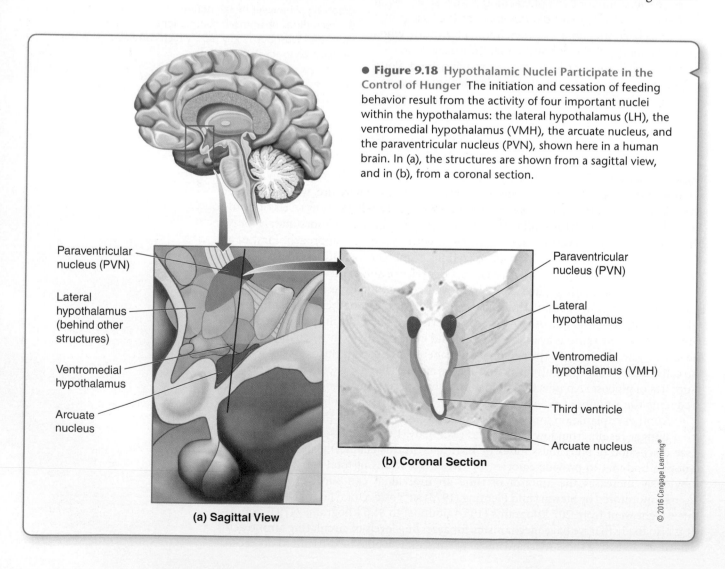

● **Figure 9.18** Hypothalamic Nuclei Participate in the Control of Hunger The initiation and cessation of feeding behavior result from the activity of four important nuclei within the hypothalamus: the lateral hypothalamus (LH), the ventromedial hypothalamus (VMH), the arcuate nucleus, and the paraventricular nucleus (PVN), shown here in a human brain. In (a), the structures are shown from a sagittal view, and in (b), from a coronal section.

Paraventricular nucleus (PVN)

Lateral hypothalamus (behind other structures)

Ventromedial hypothalamus

Arcuate nucleus

(a) Sagittal View

Paraventricular nucleus (PVN)

Lateral hypothalamus

Ventromedial hypothalamus (VMH)

Third ventricle

Arcuate nucleus

(b) Coronal Section

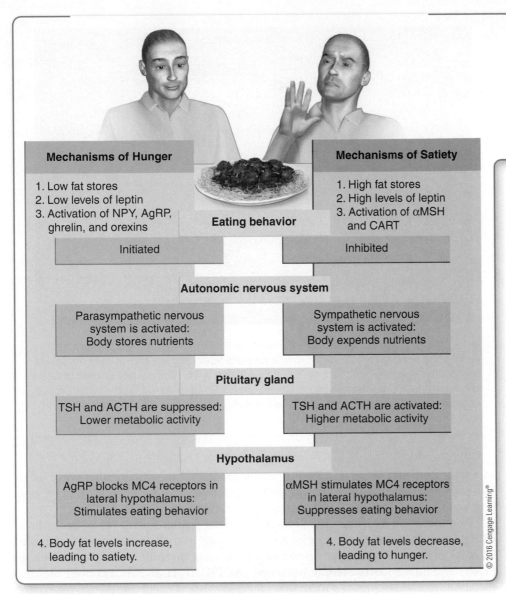

● **Figure 9.19**
Neurochemical Correlates of Hunger and Satiety Fat stores determine leptin levels, which in turn trigger a cascade of events leading to either hunger or satiety.

Fat cells produce and secrete a substance known as **leptin**, from *leptos*, the Greek word for "thin" (Zhang et al., 1994). When fat stores are low, levels of circulating leptin will also be low. Initial reports that administering additional leptin to obese rodents reduced their weight led many researchers to believe that leptin could be used to treat human obesity (see ● Figure 9.20). Unfortunately, obese humans already produce large amounts of leptin, but they seem to be resistant to its effects (Friedman & Halaas, 1998). Providing more leptin is unlikely to help obese individuals lose weight.

Leptin and insulin communicate with neurons in the **arcuate nucleus** of the hypothalamus, shown in ● Figure 9.18. When leptin and insulin levels are low, these cells release **neuropeptide Y (NPY)** and **agouti-related protein (AgRP)** to communicate with the LH and with the **paraventricular** (around the ventricle) **nucleus (PVN)** of the hypothalamus. In response to these signals, the parasympathetic division of the autonomic nervous system is activated, and feeding behavior is stimulated.

Experimental evidence supports a role for NPY and AgRP in the initiation of feeding. As food deprivation continues over time, NPY builds up within the arcuate nucleus. When NPY is applied directly to the hypothalamus, animals will begin eating immediately (Stanley, Magdalin, Seirafi, Thomas, & Leibowitz, 1993). If NPY receptors in the hypothalamus are blocked, animals will fail to eat following either food deprivation or NPY infusions (Myers, Wooten, Ames, & Nyce, 1995). AgRP acts

leptin A substance secreted by fat cells that helps the body regulate its fat stores.

arcuate nucleus A cluster of neurons involved with feeding located within the hypothalamus.

neuropeptide Y (NPY) A peptide neurochemical secreted by the arcuate nucleus of the hypothalamus that initiates eating.

agouti-related protein (AgRP) A small protein secreted by the arcuate nucleus that initiates eating.

paraventricular nucleus (PVN) A portion of the hypothalamus involved with the regulation of hunger.

● **Figure 9.20** **Leptin Knockout Rats Become Obese** Genetically engineered rats lacking the *obese* gene (*ob*) are unable to produce leptin and are enormously obese, like the rat on the left. When these obese rats are injected with leptin, they lose weight, like the rat on the right. Researchers have been disappointed to learn that the same process is unlikely to help obese humans, who are already producing large amounts of leptin but appear to be resistant to its effects.

as an antagonist at a special receptor site in the lateral hypothalamus known as an MC4 receptor. When MC4 receptors are blocked, feeding is initiated. We will see later how agonists at these same MC4 receptors inhibit feeding.

In addition to activating the parasympathetic nervous system (PNS) and stimulating eating behavior, the release of NPY and AgRP in the lateral hypothalamus and PVN suppresses the release of two pituitary hormones, **thyroid-stimulating hormone (TSH)** and **adrenocorticotropic hormone (ACTH)**. TSH and ACTH both increase metabolic rate, so suppressing them slows the body's use of energy, allowing some of the nutrients taken in during feeding to be used to replenish the fat stores. Parasympathetic activity, feeding behavior, and TSH/ACTH suppression work together to allow an animal to find, eat, and store nutrients. As fat stores return to normal levels, more leptin is released, NPY and AgRP are less active, and the feeding cycle tapers off.

Other neurons within the lateral hypothalamus communicate via yet another important peptide neurotransmitter, **melanin-concentrating hormone (MCH)**. These neurons project widely throughout the cerebral cortex and might provide the necessary link between the hypothalamus' recognition of hunger and higher-order motivated behaviors that lead to eating and the storage of nutrients. Mice genetically modified to be incapable of producing MCH burned energy faster, ate less, and had less body fat (Shimada, Tritos, Lowell, Flier, & Maratos-Flier, 1998). Unfortunately, these mice are also much more likely to die of starvation than normal mice.

The hormone **ghrelin** is produced primarily by the pancreas and the lining of the stomach, and receptors for ghrelin have been found in the arcuate nucleus and the ventromedial hypothalamus (Inui et al., 2004). Levels of ghrelin are highest during fasting and decrease following a meal. Not only does ghrelin appear to act as a short-term circulating hormone that stimulates hunger, but it also appears to affect feeding by acting on brain circuits involved with memory and reward (Olszewski, Schiöth, & Levine, 2008). Ghrelin activity might contribute to the rewarding feeling that is associated with feeding, especially when food deprivation has been more severe.

thyroid-stimulating hormone (TSH) A pituitary hormone that stimulates the growth and function of the thyroid gland, which in turn increases metabolic rate.

adrenocorticotropic hormone (ACTH) A pituitary hormone that stimulates the adrenal glands.

melanin-concentrating hormone (MCH) A hormone that interacts with leptin and plays a role in the regulation of eating.

ghrelin A hormone produced in the pancreas and in the stomach that stimulates feeding behavior.

Orexins, or hypocretins, are produced in the lateral hypothalamus (de Lecea et al., 1998; Sakurai et al., 1998). Injection of orexins into the hypothalamus results in increased eating in rats (Sakurai et al., 1998). Levels of both NPY and the orexins are higher following food deprivation (Sahu, Kalra, & Kalra, 1988). Cells releasing orexins are influenced by leptin levels. When leptin levels are high, indicating sufficient fat is stored, the orexin cells are inhibited, and feeding is reduced. When leptin levels are low, indicating fat stores are low, the orexin cells are active, orexins are released, and feeding is stimulated. Orexin cells are also stimulated by ghrelin, which again should lead to feeding. Neurons that release orexins, like those releasing MCH, project widely in the cerebral cortex as well as to regulatory centers in the midbrain and pons. These neurons play a more general role in linking internal homeostatic states to complex feeding behaviors (Sakurai, 2002). In addition, the discovery that orexins play an important role in the sleep disorder narcolepsy (Siegel, 1999) has led to interest in the connection between feeding, activity levels, and sleep (see Chapter 11).

orexin A peptide neurochemical produced in the lateral hypothalamus that stimulates eating. Also known as hypocretin.
satiety The sensation of being full, cessation of eating.
ventromedial hypothalamus (VMH) An area within the hypothalamus that participates in satiety.

Satiety

We use both external and internal cues to decide when to stop eating as well as when to start. Unfortunately, the current obesity epidemic shows that we are quite capable of overriding or ignoring these internal cues.

ASSESSING SATIETY **Satiety**, or fullness, occurs long before sufficient nutrients make their way into cells. Stomach fullness provides an early warning signal to tell us that we have eaten enough. In extreme cases of obesity, some people have a portion of their stomach stapled in hopes of feeling full faster and therefore eating less. The intestines also provide satiety signals. The duodenum, shown previously in ● Figure 9.15, joins the stomach and the small intestines. When duodenal glucoreceptors sense sugars, eating generally stops quickly. The arrival of foods containing fats and proteins at the duodenum signals the release of the peptide cholecystokinin (CCK) (Dockray, 2012). CCK promotes the release of insulin by the pancreas and contracts the gallbladder to release bile to help break down fats. CCK clearly contributes to feelings of satiety (Stacher, 1986), and injection with CCK antagonists increases eating (Cooper & Dourish, 1990). CCK limits meals by activating pathways connecting the gastrointestinal tract and the hindbrain (Blevins et al., 2009).

BRAIN MECHANISMS FOR SATIETY Early research suggested that the **ventromedial hypothalamus (VMH)**, shown in ● Figure 9.18, might serve as a satiety center. Lesions of the VMH in rats produced VMH syndrome, characterized by large weight gains and picky eating habits (Hoebel & Teitelbaum, 1966) (see ● Figure 9.21). If their food is mixed with quinine, which is quite bitter, VMH rats will eat much less than normal control rats (Sclafani, Springer, & Kluge, 1976).

As we found in the case of the LH and feeding, it is overly simplistic to view the VMH as a single center for satiety. Animals with VMH lesions do not continue to eat indefinitely. Instead they seem to establish a much higher set point, which is then defended in a somewhat normal manner. Lesions of the VMH not only destroy the VMH nucleus itself but also damage important adjacent fiber pathways. Among these pathways are fibers connecting the paraventricular nucleus (PVN) to the nucleus of the solitary tract (NST) in the brainstem. The NST receives information from glucoreceptors and taste receptors and participates in energy storage. Disruption of this pathway could easily produce abnormal eating patterns. VMH lesions also result in excess insulin production. Chronically low-circulating glucose levels due to excess insulin produce constant hunger and feeding.

● **Figure 9.21** **Weight Gain in VMH Syndrome** Lesions of the ventromedial hypothalamus (VMH) result in substantial weight gains. This rat is about three times heavier than a normal rat.

alpha melanocyte stimulating hormone (αMSH) A neurochemical originating in the arcuate nucleus, believed to inhibit feeding behavior.

cocaine- and amphetamine-regulated transcript (CART) A neurochemical, originating in the arcuate nucleus, believed to inhibit feeding behavior.

body mass index (BMI) A measure comparing height and weight that is used to determine underweight, healthy weight, overweight, and obesity.

obese The state of being extremely overweight, with a body mass index of 30 to 39.9, or a weight that is 20 percent higher than typical.

NEUROCHEMICALS AND SATIETY When body-fat levels are high, higher concentrations of leptin are found in the blood. High levels of circulating leptin interact with a second set of neurons in the arcuate nucleus, distinct from the neurons that respond to low levels of leptin. This second set of neurons is the source of two additional neuropeptides, **alpha melanocyte stimulating hormone (αMSH or alpha-MSH)** and **cocaine- and amphetamine-regulated transcript (CART)**. Projections from the arcuate nucleus neurons travel once again to the PVN, LH, and autonomic nervous system control centers in the brainstem and spinal cord. Alpha-MSH and CART cause the pituitary gland to release TSH and ACTH, raising body metabolic rates. Alpha-MSH and CART also activate the sympathetic division of the autonomic nervous system, increasing metabolism and body temperature and inhibiting feeding behavior.

In the lateral hypothalamus, αMSH competes directly with AgRP for activation of the MC4 receptors. Recall that AgRP initiated feeding behavior by blocking these receptors. Alpha-MSH serves as an agonist at the MC4 receptor. When the MC4 receptors are activated by αMSH, feeding is inhibited. When the MC4 receptors are blocked by AgRP, feeding is stimulated. In addition, high levels of circulating leptin discourage feeding by directly inhibiting the synthesis and release of NPY and AgRP (Howlett, 1996).

Healthy and Disordered Eating

Many people seem to have a great deal of difficulty maintaining a healthy body weight. Because our bodies evolved to survive with a limited, difficult-to-obtain food supply, we struggle for balance in modern cultures in which food is often amply available (Chakravarthy & Booth, 2004).

Defining Healthy Weight

What does it mean to be at a healthy weight? The medical standard for determining ideal weight is the computation of a **body mass index (BMI)**. The BMI is computed by dividing a person's weight in kilograms by the square of his or her height in meters. A BMI of between 18.5 and 24.9 is considered healthy, a BMI of 25 to 29.9 is defined as overweight, a BMI of 30 to 39.9 is **obese**, and a BMI of 40 or more is morbidly obese. You can check your own BMI using ● Figure 9.22.

BMI is a good starting point, but it is not a perfect system for assessing healthy weight. A major drawback to the BMI system is its blindness to factors of sex, skeletal

●●● **Behavioral Neuroscience GOES TO WORK**

DIETICIANS AND NUTRITIONISTS

Because of the complex physical, social, and psychological variables involved with healthy eating, professional dieticians and nutritionists must pull information from across many disciplines to help their patients and clients make the right food choices.

Many dieticians and nutritionists work in healthcare settings or in private practice, where they evaluate the diets of patients and clients and recommend changes designed to alleviate or prevent illnesses, such as type 2 diabetes. Other dieticians and nutritionists work to educate communities and plan meals, often on a large scale as for entire school districts. Still others work for food manufacturers.

Dieticians and nutritionists typically have a bachelor's degree, including internships. Most states in the United States require licensure as well (Academy of Nutrition and Dietetics, 2014).

Height (inches)	80	90	100	110	120	130	140	150	160	170	180	190	200	210	220	230	240	250
80	9	10	11	12	13	14	15	17	18	19	20	21	22	23	24	25	26	28
78	9	10	12	13	14	15	16	17	19	20	21	22	23	24	25	27	28	29
76	10	11	12	13	15	16	17	18	20	21	22	23	24	26	27	28	29	30
74	10	12	12	14	15	17	18	19	21	22	23	24	26	27	28	30	31	32
72	11	12	14	15	16	18	19	20	22	23	24	26	27	28	30	31	33	34
70	12	13	14	16	17	19	20	22	23	24	26	27	29	30	32	33	35	36
68	12	14	15	17	18	20	21	23	24	26	27	29	30	32	34	35	7	38
66	13	15	16	18	19	21	23	24	26	27	29	31	32	34	36	37	39	40
64	14	15	17	19	21	22	24	26	28	29	31	33	34	36	38	40	41	43
62	15	17	18	20	22	24	26	27	29	31	33	35	37	38	40	42	44	46
60	16	17	20	22	23	25	27	25	31	33	35	37	39	41	43	45	47	49
58	17	19	21	23	25	27	29	31	34	36	38	40	42	44	46	48	50	52
56	18	21	22	25	27	29	31	34	36	38	40	43	45	47	49	52	54	56
54	19	22	24	27	29	31	34	36	39	41	43	46	48	51	53	56	58	60
52	21	23	26	29	31	34	36	39	40	44	47	49	52	55	57	60	62	65
50	23	25	28	31	34	37	39	42	45	48	51	53	56	59	62	65	68	70
48	24	28	31	34	37	40	42	46	49	52	55	58	61	64	67	70	73	76

Weight (pounds)

☐ BMI under 18.5: Underweight   ☐ BMI between 30–39: Obese
☐ BMI between 18.5–24: Healthy weight   ☐ BMI over 40: Severely/morbidly obese
☐ BMI between 25–29: Overweight

© 2016 Cengage Learning®

● **Figure 9.22** Body Mass Index Provides a Measure of Ideal Weight Body mass index (BMI) is computed by dividing your weight in kilograms by the square of your height in meters. (We have converted the scale to inches and pounds.) BMIs between 18.5 and 24.9 are considered healthy. A person with a BMI of 25 to 29.9 is considered overweight, and a person with a BMI of 30 to 39.9 is obese. BMIs of 40 and above are considered morbidly obese.

structure, and musculature. By this measure, many of our most fit professional athletes would be considered overweight or obese. The BMI assumes that men and women of the same height should weigh similar amounts, in spite of the typically heavier muscle mass found in males. Although BMIs indicating overweight or obesity are correlated with increased risk of death, people with normal BMIs who have higher than normal waist circumference also experience increased risk of death (Koster et al., 2008).

Ideal weight can also be assessed by measuring body fat. One of the most accurate techniques for measuring body fat is the submersion test, illustrated in ● Figure 9.23, in which the person is submersed in a tank of water. Body fat of 32 percent or more for women and 25 percent or more for men is considered obese. Athletes can have very low levels of body fat (6 to 13 percent for men and 14 to 20 percent for women), but men with average fitness have body fat in the 18 to 24 percent range and women with average fitness have body fat between 25 and 31 percent. Females should not allow body fat to go below 12 percent, due to the negative impact this has on fertility, but men can sustain body fat of as little as 5 percent.

Obesity

In 1988, no state in the United States reported obesity rates greater than 15 percent. As shown in ● Figure 9.24, by 2012, no state had an obesity rate less than 20 percent. How can we account for this rapid change?

Human beings use energy very efficiently. When at rest, the average human body uses only about 12 calories (actually kcals) per pound per day. In other words, a person who weighs 150 pounds and spends most of his or her day watching television or sitting in front of the computer needs only about 1,800 calories of food. Considering that the typical fast-food meal of a hamburger, fries, and soda contains about 1,500 calories, it becomes easy to see why people are getting a lot heavier.

● **Figure 9.23** The Submersion Test of Body Composition The submersion test is considered one of the most accurate measures of body fat. The person's weight outside the tank is compared with the person's weight when completely submerged in water. Bone and muscle are more dense than water, and fat is less dense. Remember that fat floats. A person with a lot of bone and muscle will weigh more than a person with less bone and muscle when submersed. Standard formulas are used to compare the two weights, providing an estimate of body fat percentage.

© 2016 Cengage Learning®

● **Figure 9.24 Obesity Rates Continue to Rise** According to the Centers for Disease Control and Prevention (CDC), approximately 35 percent of American adults have BMIs greater than 30, which is the cutoff for defining obesity. No state reported an obesity rate of less than 20 percent in 2012, whereas no state reported an obesity rate ABOVE 15 percent in 1988. Complex interactions between biology and lifestyle factors contribute to these changes.

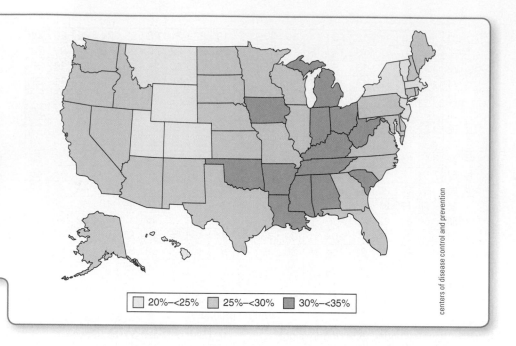

centers of disease control and prevention

☐ 20%–<25% ☐ 25%–<30% ☐ 30%–<35%

A large number of complex, interacting factors in our modern lifestyles contribute to obesity. Social factors, such as the acceptance of large body size, are reflected in the fact that having obese friends increases your risk of obesity by 57 percent, and having an obese spouse increases your risk of obesity by 37 percent (Christakis & Fowler, 2007). Stress alone and a high-fat diet alone do not necessarily lead to obesity, but the combination of the two appears to increase the release of NPY, which in turn increases appetite (Kuo et al., 2007).

Genetics appear to play an important role in a person's vulnerability to obesity. One twin study suggested that differences in adult women's body sizes could be predicted by their genes more than 50 percent of the time (Livshits, Kato, Wilson, & Spector, 2007). Genetic variations probably explain part of the reason why some people exposed to current lifestyles continue to maintain a healthy weight while others become obese. Large numbers of gene variations have been associated with obesity, each having small effects. However, a smaller number of single gene variations have been identified that might make more personalized treatments possible (El-Sayed Moustafa & Froguel, 2013)

The types of bacteria in a person's gut influence fat storage and obesity. When bacteria from obese mice were transplanted into typical mice, the typical mice increased their body fat 47 percent in two weeks (Turnbaugh et al., 2006). Manipulations of bacteria through the use of probiotics and antibiotics to promote weight gain in farm animals have been a staple in livestock management for decades. *Lactobacillus* species increase in humans who consume high-fat diets and are obese (Million & Raoult, 2013). In contrast, the gut concentrations of *Bifidobacterium* species are higher in lean humans (Million et al., 2013). It is possible that future treatments for obesity might involve methods that influence the relative frequency of various types of gut bacteria.

INTERVENTIONS FOR OBESITY All weight-loss diets work by reducing the number of calories consumed. Successful long-term weight loss requires lifestyle changes that are sustainable indefinitely. Popular diets tend to allow too few calories, triggering physiological responses aimed at avoiding starvation. The body lowers its metabolic rate, and the dieter might actually gain weight while eating less than before.

Current medications approved for treating obesity include orlistat, which reduces the absorption of consumed fats (Rucker, Padwal, Li, Curioni, & Lau, 2007), and lorcaserin, a serotonin agonist (O'Neil et al., 2012). Phentermine-topiramate is a combination of drugs that suppress appetite and make foods taste less appealing. Weight loss for those using these drugs is modest, in the range of 5 to 10 pounds in one year, and the benefits of this weight loss may not offset the drugs' side effects for many patients.

Many obese patients become discouraged with diets and medications and turn instead to a variety of surgical interventions, including stomach stapling and gastric bypass procedures. Although the weight loss from such procedures is typically significant, such as the average loss of 90 pounds within three months of gastric bypass (Maggard et al., 2005), these procedures represent major surgery, often result in complications, and should be considered carefully. We are still a long way from having an easy fix for obesity. In the meantime, moderate caloric restriction and increasing exercise still work, if people can be convinced to view these habits as a lifestyle change rather than as a temporary fix.

••• THINKING *Ethically*

HOW DANGEROUS IS IT TO BE OVERWEIGHT OR OBESE?

Just how dangerous is it to be overweight or obese? You have probably seen accounts in the popular media suggesting that lean, unfit people have a greater risk of dying than overweight, fit people, or that older adults who are slightly overweight enjoy better health than older adults who weigh less.

It is true that BMI should be viewed as a starting point for evaluating healthy weight, but by no means is BMI the only variable to consider. For example, time spent sitting down (Matthews et al., 2008) and large waist circumference (102 cm or 40 inches for men and 88 cm or 35 inches for women; Koster et al., 2008) are other powerful predictors of mortality. People who combine a healthy BMI with a large waist circumference are at higher risk than people with both a healthy BMI and a healthy waist circumference. At the same time, at least in a sample of 1.46 million white adults, the risk of all-cause mortality is lowest in people with a BMI between 20.0 and 24.9 (Berrington de Gonzalez et al., 2010). These conclusions hold even when smokers are excluded, as people who smoke tobacco products tend to be thinner than those who do not (see ● Figure 9.25). Other researchers have suggested that returning the U.S. population to a healthy weight range would produce about the same improvement in overall life expectancy as the total elimination of smoking would produce (Stewart, Cutler, & Rosen, 2009).

The general takeaway from these studies is that without extenuating circumstances, like your being an NFL lineman, we should not discount the ability of BMI to predict health. If your BMI is not within a healthy range, this might be something to discuss with your healthcare providers who are familiar with your individual case.

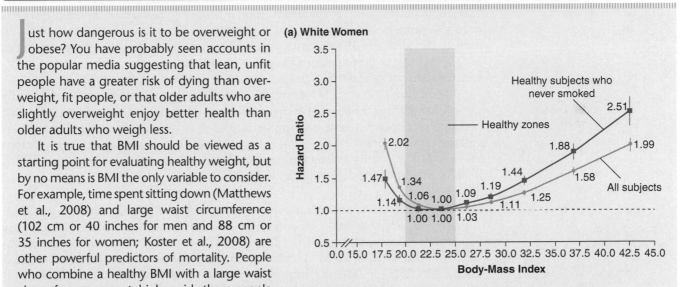

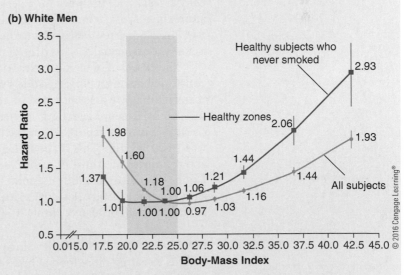

● **Figure 9.25** **Body Mass Index and Risk of Mortality** In an evaluation of 1.46 million white adults, a body mass index (BMI) between 20 and 25 was correlated with the lowest risk of death from all causes, even after variables such as socioeconomic status, education, alcohol intake, and smoking history had been controlled.

Disordered Eating

Feeding is essential to maintaining life, but distortions can occur in the finely regulated systems we have described so far. The *Diagnostic and Statistical Manual of Mental Disorders* (DSM-5; American Psychiatric Association [APA], 2013) describes a number of different types of feeding and eating disorders. Among these are anorexia nervosa (restricting and binge-eating/purging types), bulimia nervosa, and binge-eating disorder. The DSM-5 actively rejected the inclusion of obesity as a "mental disorder."

ANOREXIA NERVOSA Anorexia means "loss of appetite." In cases of **anorexia nervosa**, individuals maintain very low body weight, demonstrate intense fear of gaining weight, and experience a distorted image of their bodies as obese (APA, 2013). Individuals with the restricting subtype severely restrict food intake, exercise excessively, or both. Individuals with the binge-eating/purging subtype also engage in behaviors like induced vomiting and use of laxatives in efforts to lose weight. Severity based on a person's BMI ranges from "mild" (BMI of 17 to 18.4) to "severe" (BMI less than 15). Females with anorexia nervosa outnumber males by a factor of 10 to 1, and overall prevalence in the previous year among young females is 0.4 percent (APA, 2013). However, men who identify as gay or bisexual have greater risk for eating disorders than men who identify as heterosexual (Wooldridge & Lytle, 2012).

In addition to extremely low weight, females with anorexia nervosa will usually show amenorrhea (cessation of menstruation); dry or yellowed skin; fine downy hair (lanugo) on the face, trunk, and limbs; increased sensitivity to cold; and cardiovascular and gastrointestinal problems. This is one of the few psychological conditions that can kill; mortality among patients per decade is approximately 5 percent, which includes an elevated risk for suicide (APA, 2013).

BULIMIA NERVOSA **Bulimia nervosa** involves a cyclical pattern of binge eating followed by purging through compensatory methods, such as induced vomiting or use of laxatives. Patients with this disorder eat more food at a sitting than would be considered normal accompanied by a feeling of not being in control of how much food is eaten (APA, 2013). Episodes of binge eating and purging occur on a regular basis, typically at least once per week for a period of three months or more. As was the case with anorexia nervosa, females outnumber males with bulimia nervosa by a factor of 10 to 1 (APA, 2013). Prevalence during the past 12 months is approximately 1 to 1.5 percent among young females. This disorder typically peaks in young adulthood.

The extent of bingeing varies widely among patients, but estimates of the calories consumed during a binge episode shines an interesting spotlight on changes in eating patterns that are also reflected in contemporary obesity rates. An article published in 1986 by Rosen, Leitenberg, Fisher, and Khazam, prior to the onset of the current obesity epidemic, reported that the typical binge episode in cases of bulimia nervosa was 1,500 calories. This is about the equivalent of a typical fast-food lunch today, and about half to one-third of a meal served by some contemporary chain restaurants. Under laboratory conditions, contemporary individuals with bulimia nervosa typically consume 2,500 calories at a sitting, or enough to meet or exceed their entire day's caloric needs (Forbush & Hunt, 2014).

BINGE-EATING DISORDER **Binge-eating disorder** is similar to bulimia nervosa in regards to eating more food at one sitting than is normal and feeling a lack of control, but it does not include the compensatory behaviors such as vomiting and use of laxatives (APA, 2013). In addition to these main criteria, people with binge-eating disorder eat rapidly, eat until they are uncomfortably full, eat large amounts of food when they are not physically hungry, eat alone because of embarrassment about the amount eaten, and feel disgusted or depressed following a binge-eating episode. These episodes occur at least once per week for a period of three months or more. As a new disorder in the DSM-5, prevalence data are still preliminary. Estimates suggest that binge-eating disorder was

anorexia nervosa An eating disorder characterized by voluntary self-starvation and a grossly distorted body image.
bulimia nervosa An eating disorder characterized by cycles of bingeing and purging.
binge-eating disorder An eating disorder characterized by bingeing without purging.

experienced in the last 12 months by 1.6 percent of adult females and 0.8 percent of adult males. Compared to the other eating disorders, the difference between the numbers of men and women with binge-eating disorder is smaller.

CAUSES OF EATING DISORDERS There are obvious environmental factors associated with eating disorders, including exposure to excessively thin and glamorous models and actresses. In 1965, models were thinner than the average American woman, but only by 8 percent. Today, models are 23 percent thinner than the average American woman. In response to the deaths of several models from starvation and concerns about the messages being sent to young women, several European countries have banned fashion models whose BMI is less than 18.5. Fashion models, like the one shown in ● Figure 9.26, have an average BMI of 16.5.

Anne Becker and her colleagues chronicled the impact of American television on disordered eating in the South Pacific islands of Fiji (Becker, 2004; Becker et al., 2002). Becker reported that dieting was previously unknown in a culture that valued a "robust, well-muscled body" for both sexes (see ● Figure 9.27). Soon after the arrival of popular American television in 1995, with its frequent images of glamorous ultrathin actresses, 17 percent of adolescent girls reported having deliberately induced vomiting in an effort to control weight, whereas Becker reports only 3 percent doing so prior to 1995. Because Becker's data are correlational, we cannot conclude that watching TV directly produced the change in eating habits among young Fijians (Becker et al., 2011). However, these results strongly suggest that culture, in this case values transmitted through TV, plays a significant role in the development of body dissatisfaction and disordered eating habits.

● **Figure 9.26 Anorexia and Fashion Models** The average runway model has a BMI of 16.5. American fashion designers have complained that the 18.5 BMI standard set by some European countries would require a six-feet-tall model to "balloon" to 136 pounds. In contrast, a six-feet-tall model with a BMI of 16.5 weighs only 121 pounds.

● **Figure 9.27 External Influences Can Change Cultural Ideals of Beauty** Anne Becker's research into the eating habits of young Fijian women suggests that the introduction of American television programs led to higher rates of dieting and eating disorders. This Fijian woman meets the pretelevision Fijian ideal of beauty—a robust, well-muscled body.

The evidence for biological factors leading to eating disorders, however, is more difficult to interpret. Results of twin studies have been mixed; some authors have reported heritability for eating disorders in the typical range for most human traits of 48 to 88 percent, and others have found no evidence for a genetic base (Hinney & Volckmar, 2013). The search for candidate genes distinguishing people with eating disorders from the rest of the population has not been productive, especially compared to similar searches in the case of other types of psychological disorders (Trace, Baker, Peñas-Lledó, & Bulik, 2013). It is possible that the general personality characteristics that produce a vulnerability to the development of eating disorders, not the disorders themselves, are influenced by genetics.

Once established, however, eating disorders appear to be maintained at least in part by biological factors. Elevated CART levels have been observed in patients with anorexia nervosa, even after the patients reached normal weight during treatment (Stanley et al., 2003). You might recall that CART raises metabolic rates and inhibits feeding. CART might also reduce the rewarding aspects of eating through its actions in the nucleus accumbens, which participates in reward circuits implicated in addiction (Jean et al., 2007). CART's action in the nucleus accumbens is mediated by the activity of serotonin. Serotonin abnormalities have been implicated in both eating disorders and major depressive disorder, which might account for the higher risk for these disorders within the same families (Wade et al., 2000).

The binge-purge cycling of bulimia nervosa might involve processes similar to addiction (Hoebel, Patten, Colantuoni, & Rada, 2000). When food-deprived rats were given access to sugar water, they binged, or consumed large quantities. Bingeing rats, but not control rats, subsequently responded to the opiate antagonist naloxone with anxiety, agitation, and chattering teeth. These symptoms are identical to the responses of rats addicted to morphine when given naloxone. People who fast and then binge on sweets might be setting up a similar addictive process that would make it difficult for them to stop bingeing. This model provides a possible explanation for the higher incidence of substance abuse among family members of patients with bulimia nervosa (Lilenfeld, Ringham, Kalarchian, & Marcus, 2008).

TREATING EATING DISORDERS No medication to date has proved effective in alleviating anorexia nervosa (Berkman et al., 2006). The first priority when treating anorexia nervosa is keeping the patient alive, which usually requires a period of hospitalization and careful monitoring of food intake. Antidepressants, particularly selective serotonin reuptake inhibitors (SSRIs; see Chapters 4 and 16), are frequently useful in the management of bulimia nervosa.

Addressing the distorted body image that characterizes eating disorders is also an essential aspect of treatment. Standard treatments for eating disorders typically take the form of psychotherapy, and cognitive behavioral and interpersonal therapies in particular (Kass, Kolko, & Wilfley, 2013).

INTERIM SUMMARY 9.3

Summary Points

1. During the process of digestion, carbohydrates, proteins, and fats are broken down into components, which are either used immediately or stored for later use. (LO4)

2. Glucoreceptors in the lateral hypothalamus (LH) participate in the identification of hunger and the initiation of feeding behavior. Feeding behavior is also stimulated by a number of chemicals, including neuropeptide Y (NPY), agouti-related protein (AgRP), orexins, ghrelin, and melanin-concentrating hormone (MCH). (LO4)

3. The ventromedial hypothalamus, paraventricular nucleus, and the nucleus of the solitary tract appear to participate in satiety. High levels of leptin stimulate

the release of alpha melanocyte stimulating hormone (αMSH) and cocaine- and amphetamine-regulated transcript (CART), which inhibit feeding. **(LO4)**

4. Sensible diets and moderate exercise result in weight loss. Chemical and surgical interventions are popular, but there are no easy fixes available for treating obesity. **(LO5)**

5. Complex cultural and physical processes contribute to the development and course of anorexia nervosa, bulimia nervosa, and binge-eating disorder. **(LO5)**

‖ Review Questions

1. In what ways can the environment shape our eating habits?
2. How do leptin levels influence appetite and weight control?

Chapter Review

THOUGHT QUESTIONS

1. What adaptations might you expect to see in the body shapes of animals during an extended period of global warming?
2. If you were stranded in a hot place without a source of water, what automatic mechanisms might be activated to conserve your body's fluids? What behavioral solutions might you employ to conserve fluids?
3. What factors have contributed to the increase in obesity in America during the past few decades?
4. Which potential chemical intervention for obesity do you believe to be the most promising? Why?

KEY TERMS

agouti-related protein (AgRP) (p. 313)
aldosterone (p. 302)
alpha melanocyte stimulating hormone (αMSH) (p. 316)
angiotensin II (p. 302)
anorexia nervosa (p. 320)
antidiuretic hormone (ADH) (p. 302)
baroreceptor (p. 302)
binge-eating disorder (p. 320)
body mass index (BMI) (p. 316)
bulimia nervosa (p. 320)
cholecystokinin (CCK) (p. 308)
cocaine- and amphetamine-regulated transcript (CART) (p. 316)
diabetes mellitus (p. 301)
ectotherm (p. 291)
endotherm (p. 291)

ghrelin (p. 314)
glucoreceptor (p. 312)
homeostasis (p. 290)
hyperthermia (heat stroke) (p. 294)
hypothermia (p. 295)
hypovolemic thirst (p. 301)
insulin (p. 309)
lateral hypothalamus (LH) (p. 305)
leptin (p. 313)
median preoptic nucleus (p. 304)
melanin-concentrating hormone (MCH) (p. 314)
motivation (p. 290)
neuropeptide Y (NPY) (p. 313)
nucleus of the solitary tract (NST) (p. 305)

obesity (p. 316)
orexin (also known as hypocretin) (p. 315)
organum vasculosum of the lamina terminalis (OVLT) (p. 301)
osmoreceptor (p. 301)
osmosis (p. 299)
osmotic thirst (p. 301)
paraventricular nucleus (PVN) (p. 313)
preoptic area (POA) (p. 296)
satiety (p. 315)
set point (p. 290)
subfornical organ (SFO) (p. 304)
ventromedial hypothalamus (VMH) (p. 315)
zona incerta (p. 305)

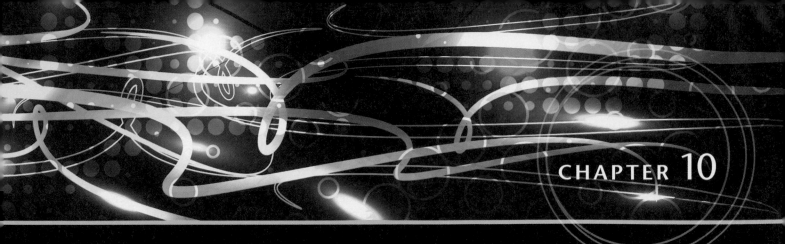

CHAPTER 10

Sexual Behavior

LEARNING OBJECTIVES

L01 Compare and contrast typical and atypical development of male and female gonads, internal organs, external genitalia, and secondary sex characteristics.

L02 Differentiate between the organizing and activating functions of sex hormones.

L03 Explain the significance of sexually dimorphic brain structures for behavior.

L04 Assess the biological contributions to sexual orientation.

L05 Describe the biological correlates of attraction, romantic love, sexual desire, and parenting.

L06 Explain the biological correlates of sexual dysfunction.

CHAPTER OUTLINE

BEHAVIORAL NEUROSCIENCE GOES TO WORK: How Do Therapists Treat Gender Dysphoria?

CONNECTING TO RESEARCH: Simon LeVay and INAH-3

THINKING ETHICALLY: Biology's Role in Explaining Gender and Sexual Orientation

BUILDING BETTER HEALTH: Treating Patients with Antidepressant-Induced Sexual Dysfunction

325

Sexual Development

The biology of sex interacts with complex environmental influences to produce the final male or female phenotype. In the following discussions, we will be using the term *sex* to refer to biological sex. The term *gender* is usually applied in situations that involve social, learned, and personal aspects. The biological and experiential aspects of sex and gender should not be construed as an either/or type of discussion. As we saw in the case of nature and nurture, our biology and experience typically intertwine in such a manner that they only rarely can be compartmentalized in useful ways (see ● Figure 10.1).

The Genetics of Sex

In 355 BCE, Aristotle argued that the sex of a child was the result of the temperature of semen at the time of conception. Hot semen resulted in males, and cool semen resulted in females. Today, we understand that an individual's genetic sex begins with sex chromosomes inherited from two parents. Mothers provide an **X chromosome** to all their offspring; fathers determine the offspring's sex by providing either another X (producing a female) or a **Y chromosome** (producing a male). The initial receipt of an XX or an XY genotype begins a cascade of hormonal, structural, and behavioral events. These pivotal sex chromosomes, along with the other 22 pairs of human chromosomes, are illustrated in ● Figure 10.2. This view of the chromosomes is known as a **karyotype**, which is the profile of chromosome number and appearance in the nucleus of a cell as seen under a light microscope.

In the vast majority of cases, the transmission of the sex chromosomes to a child is uneventful. However, variations in sex chromosomes occur that can illuminate the

X chromosome One of two types of sex chromosomes; individuals with two X chromosomes will usually develop into females.

Y chromosome One of two types of sex chromosomes; individuals with a Y chromosome will usually develop into males.

karyotype A profile of chromosome number and appearance in the nucleus of a cell as seen under a light microscope.

● **Figure 10.1** David Reimer and the Nature and Nurture of Sex and Gender On the advice of 1970s experts, who believed that socialization was more important than biology in the development of gender, David Reimer was raised as a girl following an accident during his circumcision. In contrast to the experts' claims, David never accepted a female role. By the age of 14, he chose to live as a male (above). He married and adopted his wife's children but, sadly, committed suicide in 2004.

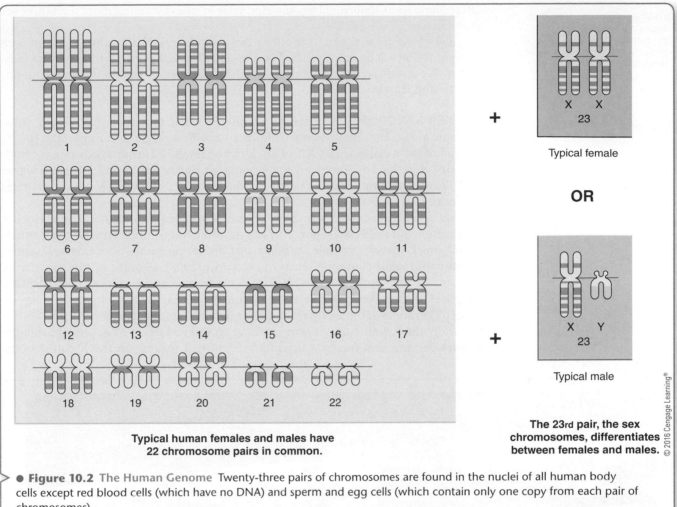

Typical female

OR

Typical male

The 23rd pair, the sex chromosomes, differentiates between females and males.

Typical human females and males have 22 chromosome pairs in common.

© 2016 Cengage Learning®

> ● **Figure 10.2** The Human Genome Twenty-three pairs of chromosomes are found in the nuclei of all human body cells except red blood cells (which have no DNA) and sperm and egg cells (which contain only one copy from each pair of chromosomes).

contributions of genetic sex to the adult phenotype. Most sex chromosome variations produce relatively mild differences, but others are more dramatic. One set of twins, one a phenotypical male and the other a phenotypical female, possessed the same exact karyotype (Maeda, Ohno, Matsunobu, Yoshihara, & Yabe, 1991). The twins shared a mosaic karyotype of 45, X/46,XY/47,XYY, with the number indicating the number of chromosomes in a cell and the X and Y indicating the presence of sex chromosomes within that number. Having a mosaic karyotype means that a single individual has cells with differing complements of chromosomes.

In comparison to genetic abnormalities like Down syndrome, in which an individual has three copies of the 21st chromosome, abnormalities due to a third sex chromosome appear to have relatively mild effects (Bender, Linden, & Harmon, 2001). In many cases, the effects are so mild that individuals with sex chromosome abnormalities do not get diagnosed (Boyd, Loane, Garne, Khoshnood, & Dolk, 2011). In conclusions drawn from a study of more than 13,000 newborns over a 13-year period, Nielsen and Wohlert (1991) found that none of the children with three sex chromosomes had intellectual disabilities and that all were in regular public school. There were no increases in criminal activity, mental disorders, or physical disorders relative to the population with typical sex chromosomes. IQ may be reduced approximately 10 to 20 points compared to siblings, but it remains within normal ranges in most cases (Boyd et al., 2011). Out of the possible combinations of three sex chromosomes, females with an XXX genotype experience the largest reduction in IQ (Boyd et al.,

Turner syndrome A condition caused by an XO genotype, characterized by frequent abnormalities of the ovaries and infertility.

2011). Significant abnormalities, however, arise in cases involving more than three sex chromosomes.

Reviewing these genetic variations can provide insight into the impact of each stage of the developmental process on the sexuality and gender of the mature individual. We are also reminded of the variability that extends beyond simple definitions of male and female.

TURNER SYNDROME We have no record of a viable organism that has a Y chromosome alone. However, when a child receives only a single X chromosome (45, X) instead of the usual pair (46, XX or 46, XY), the result is **Turner syndrome**, a condition first described by American endocrinologist Henry Turner in 1938 (see ● Figure 10.3). Turner syndrome occurs in about 1 out of 2,500 live births (National Institutes of Health [NIH], 2004).

Many individuals with Turner syndrome show chromosomal mosaicism (Hook & Warburton, 2014). In particular, Turner syndrome frequently features cryptic mosaicism, which involves complex mosaics that do not necessarily become apparent in karyotyping alone (Iourov, Vorsanova, & Yurov, 2008). Because of this mosaicism, outcomes among individuals with Turner syndrome can be quite variable. For the purposes of this discussion, we will examine the characteristics of simple, complete cases of Turner syndrome rather than cases involving mosaicism.

Individuals with Turner syndrome have typical female external genitalia, but the ovaries develop abnormally. Currently unidentified regions on the X chromosome

> ● **Figure 10.3** Turner Syndrome Individuals with Turner syndrome have normal female external appearance and genitalia but are usually infertile due to abnormally developing ovaries. This condition is also associated with short stature, skin folds in the neck, and difficulty with spatial relations tasks.

are responsible for the development of the ovaries, and having a single X appears to interfere in this process (Schlessinger et al., 2002). In most cases, the ovaries do not produce either eggs (ova) or normal levels of female hormones, leading to infertility. Women with Turner syndrome are relatively short, reaching an average height of 4'8", and they may have increased skin folds at the neck (National Institutes of Health [NIH], 2004). Intelligence is normal, but specific deficits in spatial relationships and memory can occur (National Institute of Child Health and Human Development [NICHHD], 2000). Human growth hormone, plastic surgery, female hormone replacement therapy, and assisted reproductive technologies can be used to address the issues of height, neck appearance, hormone production, and fertility respectively.

It is possible to identify the parent who contributes the X chromosome in cases of Turner syndrome. A number of studies have shown that cases in which the maternal X is passed to daughters outnumber cases in which the paternal X is passed along by a factor of three to one (Hook & Warburton, 2014). Although initial investigations indicated that the women with their paternal X chromosome had better social skills (Skuse et al., 1997), subsequent research did not support this conclusion (Lepage, Hong, Hallmayer, & Reiss, 2012). Having the paternal X was, however, associated with better visuospatial abilities (Lepage et al., 2012).

KLINEFELTER SYNDROME **Klinefelter syndrome**, first identified by Harry Klinefelter in 1942, is the most common genetic abnormality related to the sex chromosomes, occurring in 1.79 out of 1,000 male births (Morris, Alberman, Scott, & Jacobs, 2007). Klinefelter syndrome features a 47/XXY genotype. These individuals are phenotypically male, but they usually experience reduced fertility and require hormone treatment at puberty to promote the development of secondary male sex characteristics (facial hair, deeper voice, development of external genitalia) and to inhibit female characteristics such as breast development (Nielsen, Pelsen, & Sørensen, 1988). Other symptoms associated with having an extra X chromosome result from interference with the process of X-inactivation, in which one X chromosome in each female cell is randomly silenced (see Chapter 5).

Like Turner syndrome, Klinefelter syndrome is associated with normal intelligence that may be marked by mild cognitive difficulties and social awkwardness (Sørensen, 1987). In cases of Klinefelter syndrome, the cognitive difficulties usually take the form of delayed and reduced verbal skills. Left-handedness is more common among males with Klinefelter syndrome than in the general male population. These findings suggest that Klinefelter syndrome might affect brain lateralization or the localization of specific functions such as language in one hemisphere or the other (Ross et al., 2008).

47,XYY The existence of individuals with an 47, XYY genotype was first reported by Sandberg, Koepf, Ishiara, and Hauschka (1961). This variation occurs in about 1 out of 1,000 male births. The physical and behavioral correlates of the condition are typically subtle and generally do not prompt the parents to seek a postnatal genetic analysis (Abramsky & Chapple, 1997). The boys appear to be physically within typical limits, although they tend to be somewhat taller and leaner, suffer from acne, and have a higher risk for minor physical abnormalities of the eye, elbow, and chest. Average IQ scores are slightly below the average of males with typical 46, XY genotypes (Linden, Bender, & Robinson, 1996). Men with the 47, XYY genotype are fertile, but they are slightly more likely than typical men to produce sperm with sex chromosome abnormalities (Rives et al., 2003).

The relationship between the 47, XYY genotype and a higher likelihood of antisocial behavior has been the subject of considerable debate. An initial report suggested that XYY individuals were overrepresented in prisons (Casey, Segall, Street, & Blank, 1966). The popular press immediately embraced the hypothesis that an extra Y chromosome would produce a violent "super male." Gotz, Johnstone, and Ratcliffe (1999) followed the progress of 17 men identified as having the 47, XYY genotype at birth. These men did show a significantly higher rate of antisocial and criminal behavior than

Klinefelter syndrome A condition in males caused by an XXY genotype, characterized by frequent problems with fertility, secondary sex characteristics, and verbal skills.

control participants. However, the majority of the criminal behavior of 47, XYY men involved property crimes rather than violent crimes (Milunsky, 2004). Further analysis suggested that criminal and antisocial behavior was more closely associated with lower intelligence than with an atypical genotype. In addition, compared to control populations, 47, XYY men had fewer partners, were less likely to become parents, had lower income, and were not as well educated (Stochholm, Juul, & Gravholt, 2012). These socioeconomic variables might contribute to higher rates of antisocial behavior as well.

Three Stages of Prenatal Development

Development of male and female reproductive structures involves three distinct processes: the development of **gonads**, of internal organs, and of **external genitalia**. In the vast majority of cases, all three processes occur congruently to produce an unambiguous male or female. In rare conditions known as **intersex**, elements of both male and female development occur in the same fetus.

THE DEVELOPMENT OF THE GONADS Up until the sixth week after conception, both male and female embryos have identical primordial gonads that have the capacity to develop into either **ovaries**, the female gonads, or **testes**, the male gonads.

At about six weeks after conception, a gene on the short arm of the Y chromosome, known as the **sex-determining region of the Y chromosome**, or *SRY*, is expressed in male embryos (Berta et al., 1990; Jäger, Anvret, Hall, & Scherer, 1990). **Testis-determining factor**, the protein encoded by the *SRY* gene, switches on additional genes that cause the primordial gonads to develop into testes. In female embryos, which lack the *SRY* gene and its ability to produce testis-determining factor, alternate genes guide the development of the primordial gonad into ovaries (Sinclair et al., 1990). Chromosomally male mice genetically modified to lack the *SRY* gene develop ovaries, whereas female mice in which the *SRY* gene has been inserted develop testes (Goodfellow & Lovell-Badge, 1993).

DIFFERENTIATION OF THE INTERNAL ORGANS The differentiation of the internal organs, shown in ● Figure 10.4, follows the development of the gonads. Until about the third month of development in humans, both male and female embryos possess a male **Wolffian system** and a female **Müllerian system**. Advantages for this apparent duplication are not currently understood. In males, the Wolffian system will develop into the seminal vesicles, the vas deferens, and the prostate. In females, the Müllerian system will develop into the uterus, the upper portion of the vagina, and the fallopian tubes.

During the third month following conception, the male's relatively new testes begin to secrete two hormones, **testosterone** and **anti-Müllerian hormone**. Testosterone, one of several types of male hormone or **androgen**, promotes the development of the Wolffian system. Anti-Müllerian hormone initiates the degeneration of the Müllerian system. In the female fetus, no additional hormones are needed in this stage of development. Unlike the testes, the ovaries are not active during fetal development. In the absence of any androgens or anti-Müllerian hormone, the Müllerian system will develop in the typical female direction. In the absence of androgens, the Wolffian system regresses, although nonfunctional remnants can persist in adult females. No hormone analogous to the male anti-Müllerian hormone is needed to promote degeneration of the Wolffian system in females.

Androgen insensitivity syndrome (AIS) disrupts the normal development of the Wolffian system in males. In AIS, a defective gene produces abnormal androgen receptors (Gottlieb, Pinsky, Beitel, & Trifiro, 1999). As a result, the fetus's tissues are blind to the presence of androgens. Fetuses with AIS have an XY genotype and normal testes that remain undescended within the abdomen. The testes release androgens and anti-Müllerian hormone in a typical manner, but the lack of functional androgen receptors prevents the development of the Wolffian system. However, anti-Müllerian hormone still works normally, so the female Müllerian system also fails to develop.

gonads The internal organs, ovaries in females and testes in males, that produce reproductive cells (eggs and sperm) and secrete sex hormones.

external genitalia The external sexual organs, including the penis and scrotum in males and the labia, clitoris, and lower third of the vagina in females.

intersex A condition in which elements of both male and female development occur in the same fetus.

ovaries Female gonads; the source of ova and sex hormones.

testes Male gonads; source of sperm and sex hormones.

sex-determining region of the Y chromosome (*SRY*) A gene located on the short arm of the Y chromosome that encodes for testis-determining factor.

testis-determining factor A protein encoded by the *SRY* gene on the Y chromosome that turns the primordial gonads into testes.

Wolffian system The internal system that develops into seminal vesicles, vas deferens, and the prostate gland in males.

Müllerian system The internal system that develops into a uterus, fallopian tubes, and the upper two thirds of the vagina in the absence of anti-Müllerian hormone.

testosterone An androgen produced primarily in the testes.

anti-Müllerian hormone A hormone secreted by fetal testes that causes the degeneration of the Müllerian system.

androgen A steroid hormone that develops and maintains typically masculine characteristics.

androgen insensitivity syndrome (AIS) A condition in which a genetic male fetus lacks functional androgen receptors, which leads to the development of female external genitalia and typically female gender identity and sexual behavior.

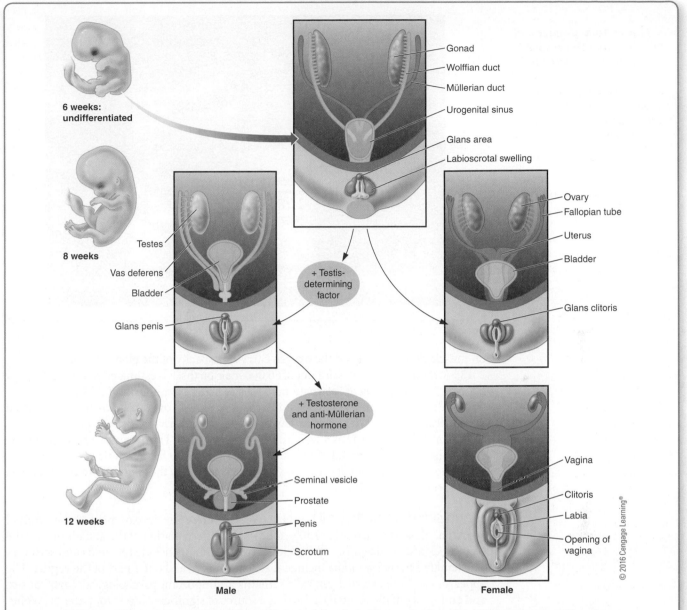

● **Figure 10.4** **Differentiation of Gonads and External Genitals** During the first six weeks after conception, the primordial gonads are undifferentiated. Subsequently, testis-determining factor encoded by the *SRY* gene on the Y chromosome will begin to turn the undifferentiated gonads into testes in males. The testes begin to release androgens, causing the external genitalia to develop into a penis and scrotum. Alternate genes guide the development of female gonads into ovaries. In the absence of androgens, the female external genitalia develop into clitoris, labia, and vagina.

Because the Müllerian system is responsible for the upper two thirds of the vagina and the female internal organs, the result is a shallow vagina and no ovaries, fallopian tubes, or uterus. Although adult individuals with AIS are infertile, their external appearance is quite typically female.

AIS provides a clear view of the difference between chromosomal sex and **gender identity**, our sense of being male or female. Individuals with AIS are genetic males but typically have female appearance and female gender identities. Many marry and engage in typical female sexual behavior (Morris, 1953).

Complete AIS is unlikely to confer any advantages to female athletes, but as we saw in the case of sex chromosome abnormalities, outcomes can be highly variable. Incomplete forms of AIS might be an advantage for women in sports due to the effects of androgens

gender identity The sense of being male or female, independent of genetic sex or physical appearance.

● **Figure 10.5** Gender and Sports Castor Semenya of South Africa was forced to undergo "gender verification" after observers complained about her "masculine appearance." Semenya's situation remains appropriately private, and she has been allowed to continue competition. Although some variations in sexual development provide advantages to female athletes, sports authorities view these as being among the variations that enhance athletic performance across the board.

Paul Kitagaki Jr./ZUMA Press, Inc./Alamy

on muscle development and the oxygen carrying capacity of the blood (Wood & Stanton, 2012). Although AIS occurs in 1 out of 60,000 male births, it is estimated that 1 out of every 500 women competing at international levels of sport have a form of AIS (Doig, Lloyd-Smith, Prior, & Sinclair, 1997). Most international sports organizations have eliminated genetic testing. The current philosophy in sports is that a person identifying and living as a woman should compete as a woman (see ● Figure 10.5). Transsexuals who have undergone gonadectomy (removal of testes or ovaries) and who have experienced appropriate hormone replacement for at least two years can compete in the Olympics in their adopted sex (Wood & Stanton, 2012).

DEVELOPMENT OF THE EXTERNAL GENITALIA The development of the external genitalia, illustrated in ● Figure 10.4, follows the differentiation of the gonads during the sixth week after conception. The male external genitalia include the penis and scrotum. The female external genitalia include the labia, clitoris, and outer part of the vagina. The appearance of the external genitalia remains an important psychological "sign" of sex, and ambiguity of the genitalia at birth is a source of significant stress for parents (Wolfe-Christensen et al., 2012). Healthcare providers typically use the Prader scale shown in ● Figure 10.6 to assess the relative masculinization of the external genitalia.

No hormonal activity is required to develop female external genitalia. However, hormonal stimulation is essential for the development of male external genitalia.

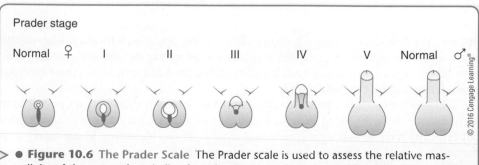

Prader stage

Normal ♀   I   II   III   IV   V   Normal ♂

© 2016 Cengage Learning®

● **Figure 10.6** The Prader Scale The Prader scale is used to assess the relative masculinity of the external genitalia of newborns. Example IV shows a hypospadia, in which the urethra of the male is not properly positioned relative to the penis.

A particular androgen, **5-alpha-dihydrotestosterone**, must be recognized by receptor sites for the male external genitalia to develop normally. A reaction between testosterone from the testes and the enzyme 5-alpha-reductase produces 5-alpha-dihydrotestosterone. We will see later in the chapter that the absence of 5-alpha-dihydrotestosterone leads the immature genitalia to develop in the direction of an ambiguous to female pattern.

If genetic females are exposed prenatally to excess androgens, their external genitalia become masculinized. **Congenital adrenal hyperplasia (CAH)** is a recessive heritable condition in which the fetus's adrenal glands release elevated levels of androgens during the second trimester of pregnancy, which is also when sexual differentiation is well underway. Males with CAH show few observable effects related to sexual development, because male fetuses are already typically exposed to high levels of circulating androgens. Females with CAH are exposed to about half the amount of androgens of a typical male and are born with ambiguous external genitalia, like the middle images in ●Figure 10.6. The clitoris is enlarged, the labia look similar to a scrotum, and in some cases, there is no vaginal opening.

Females with CAH more frequently describe themselves as tomboys, engage in more male-interest play, and are more likely than other women to engage in bisexual and lesbian behavior (Hines, Brook, & Conway, 2004; Meyer-Bahlburg, Dolezal, Baker, & New, 2008; Money, Schwartz, & Lewis, 1984). However, it is important to remember that the majority of women with CAH are heterosexual, and that the majority of bisexual and lesbian women do not have CAH or other similar conditions.

Development at Puberty

The prenatal development of gonads, internal organs, and external genitalia is only part of the sexual development story. At puberty, additional hormonal events lead to maturation of the genitals and the development of **secondary sex characteristics**. Secondary sex characteristics include facial hair and a deeper voice for males and wider hips and breast development for females.

TYPICAL AGE AT PUBERTY As shown in ●Figure 10.7 the average age of puberty has dropped dramatically over the past century and a half, from about 16 to about 12 years of age (Frisch, 1983; Herman-Giddings et al., 1997). Possible explanations for this drop in age at puberty include increased rates of childhood obesity (see

5-alpha-dihydrotestosterone An androgen secreted by the testes that masculinizes the external genitalia.
congenital adrenal hyperplasia (CAH) A condition in which a fetus is exposed to higher-than-normal androgens, resulting in masculinization of external genitalia and some cognitive behaviors in affected females.
secondary sex characteristics Characteristics related to sex that appear at puberty, including deepening voice and facial hair growth in males and widening hips and breast development in females.

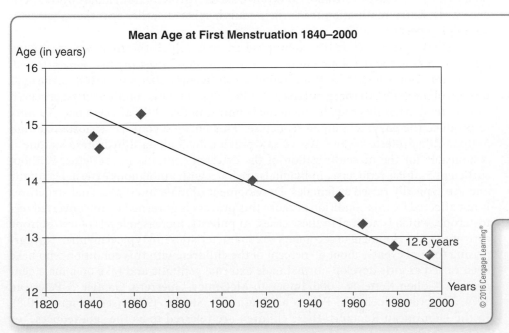

Mean Age at First Menstruation 1840–2000

● **Figure 10.7** Female Age at Puberty Since 1840, the average age of puberty has dropped from nearly 16 years to around 12 years (Ducros, 1978). Among the possible explanations for this drop are increased rates of obesity and exposure to estrogen-like chemicals from foods, plastics, and insecticides.

© 2016 Cengage Learning®

Chapter 9). Accumulation of enough body fat to support reproduction might serve as a signal for puberty. When body fat is abnormally low, as in anorexia nervosa, puberty is delayed.

Exposure to compounds similar to female hormones in meat and dairy products, shampoo, plastics, and insecticides might also trigger earlier puberty. All edible tissues from animals contain a type of **estrogen**, or female hormone, called **estradiol**, so we can assume that humans have always experienced some level of exposure to outside sources of sex hormones. However, many nations, including the United States, also permit the use of additional sex hormones to promote growth in livestock production. Consumption of treated meat can increase exposure to estrogens by nearly 40 percent (Aksglaede, Juul, Leffers, Skakkebaek, & Andersson, 2006). Because children are especially sensitive to small amounts of hormone, increased exposure from external sources is cause for concern (Aksglaede et al., 2006).

Exposure in utero to a number of endocrine disruptors, including phthalates, diethylstilbestrol (DES), and bisphenol A (BPA), might promote earlier puberty directly or by increasing obesity (Biro, Greenspan, & Galvez, 2012). Phthalate exposure appears to reduce the likelihood that boys will play with "masculine" toys, and phthalates also have been found to advance puberty in rats (Ge et al., 2007). Phthalates are released into air and fluid from plastic and cosmetic products and are found in measurable levels in most of the world's human population (Sathyanarayana et al., 2008).

HORMONE CHANGES AT PUBERTY At the onset of puberty, **gonadotropin-releasing hormone (GnRH)** is released by the hypothalamus. This hormone initiates the release of two hormones by the anterior pituitary gland, **follicle-stimulating hormone (FSH)** and **luteinizing hormone (LH)**. Both males and females release these same hormones, but with different effects. In response to stimulation by FSH and LH, the testes begin to produce additional testosterone, and the ovaries produce estradiol. The testes also produce small amounts of estrogens, including estradiol, and the ovaries produce small amounts of androgens, including testosterone.

In males, this burst of additional androgens stimulates muscular development, maturity of the external genitalia, facial hair, and enlargement of the larynx, which leads to a deeper voice. In conjunction with LH and FSH, testosterone begins to regulate the production of sperm. Testosterone also affects a male's hairline and can result in baldness later in adulthood. In females, estradiol produces breast growth, maturity of the external genitalia, maturity of the uterus, and changes in fat distribution and quantity. In both sexes, estradiol slows down skeletal growth. Individuals who experience early sexual maturation reach their adult heights at earlier ages than their later developing peers.

We have previously reviewed atypical cases in which the first two organizing steps, involving the development of gonads and internal sex organs, were affected. A rare condition known as **5-alpha-reductase deficiency** affects the last step, the maturation of the male external genitalia (see ● Figure 10.8). This condition, first observed in an extended family group living in the Dominican Republic, affects a male's ability to produce the enzyme 5-alpha-reductase. This enzyme converts testosterone into 5-alpha-dihydrotestosterone. As we saw previously, 5-alpha-dihydrotestosterone is responsible for the masculinization of the external genitalia in the fetus. Without sufficient 5-alpha-reductase, individuals are born with ambiguous external genitalia and are typically raised as females. Development of male internal sexual structures is not affected by this condition because this process is governed by unconverted testosterone, which is normal in these cases. At puberty, increased levels of testosterone activate the development of secondary sex characteristics in a typical manner. In a surprising turn of events, about 60 percent of the children with this condition who have been raised as girls develop normal male external genitalia and take on a male gender role (Cohen-Kettenis, 2005; Imperato-McGinley, Guerrero, Gautier, & Peterson, 1974; Imperato-McGinley, Peterson, Gautier, & Sturla, 1979) (see ● Figure 10.8). In the Dominican Republic, these children are referred to as the "guevedoces," or "eggs (testes) at 12."

estrogen A steroid hormone that develops and maintains typically female characteristics.

estradiol An estrogen hormone synthesized primarily in the ovaries.

gonadotropin-releasing hormone (GnRH) A hormone released by the hypothalamus that stimulates the release of luteinizing hormone (LH) and follicle-stimulating hormone (FSH) by the anterior pituitary gland.

follicle-stimulating hormone (FSH) A hormone released by the anterior pituitary that stimulates the development of eggs in the ovaries and sperm in the testes.

luteinizing hormone (LH) A hormone released by the anterior pituitary that signals the male testes to produce testosterone and that regulates the menstrual cycle in females.

5-alpha-reductase deficiency A rare condition in which a child is born with ambiguous genitalia but develops male secondary sex characteristics at puberty.

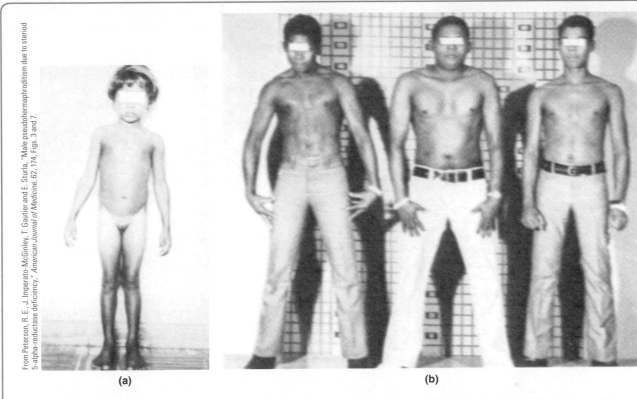

From Peterson, R. E., J. Imperato-McGinley, T. Gautier and E. Sturla, "Male pseudohermaphroditism due to steriod 5-alpha-reductase deficiency," *American Journal of Medicine*, 62, 174, Figs. 3 and 7.

(a)　　　　　(b)

● **Figure 10.8** **5-Alpha-Reductase Deficiency Changes External Appearance at Puberty** (a) Individuals born with 5-alpha-reductase deficiency are born with ambiguous external genitalia and are usually raised as girls. This child is 8 years old. (b) At puberty, unconverted testosterone, which is unaffected by the syndrome, produces male secondary sex characteristics. The male on the right is the normal brother of the male on the left, and the males on the left and in the center have 5-alpha-reductase deficiency.

●●● **Behavioral Neuroscience GOES TO WORK**

HOW DO THERAPISTS TREAT GENDER DYSPHORIA?

Gender dysphoria is defined as the "distress that may accompany the incongruence between one's experienced or expressed gender and one's assigned gender" (APA, 2013, p. 451). This term replaced the earlier term *gender identity disorder* used by psychiatrists and psychologists (APA, 2000). The change in terms resulted from a recognition that it is not the identity that is the problem requiring treatment, but rather the distress caused by the individual's perceptions of his or her situation.

The *Diagnostic and Statistical Manual of Mental Disorders* (DSM-5; APA, 2013) specifies criteria for diagnosis but does not make recommendations for treatment. In response to that lack, the authoring organization, the American Psychiatric Association, has begun work on treatment guidelines (Byne et al., 2012). The guidelines cover different age groups in detail, in recognition that gender dysphoria can be very different in a young child, an adolescent, and an adult.

In general, the guidelines for treatment call for appropriate diagnosis of gender concerns, evaluation of any coexisting psychological problems, psychotherapy to address discrimination and stereotyping, provision of complete education for the individual regarding medical and psychological options, evaluation for possible hormonal or surgical treatment, and education of family members and the community. Sex reassignment might alleviate the feelings of gender dysphoria, but this procedure also increases risk for suicide and psychological disorder (Dhejne et al., 2011). Continued monitoring and treatment following sex reassignment is frequently beneficial.

Although many generally trained psychologists and psychiatrists are probably well prepared to provide support and psychotherapy for individuals with gender dysphoria, it is also likely that therapists with significant experience and specialization in this area will best serve the needs of the individual. Evidence-based practice, where the best scientific research forms a basis for a clinician to combine his or her professional expertise with the goals of the client or patient, could help bring about the best outcomes.

INTERIM SUMMARY 10.1

Summary Table: Steps in Sexual Development

Chromosomes (determined at conception)	Gonads (6–8 weeks postconception)	Internal Structures (9–12 weeks postconception)	External Structures (6–12 weeks postconception)	Puberty (8–16 years)
XX	• By **6 weeks**, primordial gonads have developed but are undifferentiated relative to sex. • Alternate genes (not SRY) guide the development of the primordial gonads into ovaries.	• Müllerian system develops in the absence of androgens and anti-Müllerian hormone. • Primitive, non-functional Wolffian system is retained.	• In the absence of androgens such as testosterone, female external structures develop. • Female structures include labia, clitoris, and outer vagina.	• Gonadotropin-releasing hormone (GnRH) stimulates the release of LH and FSH by the pituitary. • LH and FSH signal the ovaries to begin releasing estradiol.
XY	• At **6 weeks**, primordial gonads are developed but are undifferentiated. • At **8 weeks**, testes-determining factor encoded by the *SRY* gene on the Y chromosome stimulates the development of primordial gonads into testes.	• Testosterone stimulates development of the Wolffian system. • Anti-Müllerian hormone stimulates the degeneration of the Müllerian system.	• 5-alpha-reductase converts testosterone to 5-alpha-dihydrotestosterone. • 5-alpha-dihydrotestosterone masculinizes the external structures into penis and scrotum.	• Gonadotropin-releasing hormone (GnRH) stimulates the release of LH and FSH by the pituitary. • LH and FSH stimulate the release of additional testosterone by the testes.

Summary Points

1. Sexual development begins with chromosomes. A person with two X chromosomes typically will be female, whereas a person with an X and a Y typically will be male. Variations in the number of sex chromosomes may lead to Turner syndrome (45, X), Kleinfelter syndrome (47, XXY), the 47, XYY male, among other conditions. **(LO1)**

2. Testis-determining factor turns the primordial gonads into testes. In the absence of testis-determining factor, ovaries will develop. Prenatal androgens promote the development of male internal organs and masculinize the external genitalia. Anti-Müllerian hormone prevents the development of female internal organs. **(LO1)**

3. At puberty, follicle-stimulating hormone (FSH) and luteinizing hormone (LH) promote the release of testosterone by the testes and estradiol by the ovaries, leading to the development of secondary sex characteristics. **(LO1)**

4. Variations in the development of internal organs, external genitalia, and secondary sex characteristics occur in androgen insensitivity syndrome, congenital adrenal hyperplasia, and 5-alpha-reductase deficiency. **(LO1)**

Review Questions

1. What processes must occur in order to develop male and female gonads, internal organs, and external genitalia?

2. What different pathways can occur in sexual development?

Sex Differences in Hormones, Brain Structure, and Behavior

The cascade of events begun by the actions of genes on the X and Y chromosomes is only the beginning of the story of sex and gender. Continued expression of genes on both X and Y chromosomes, especially in the brain, hormone effects, and epigenetics continue to push the individual in one of many possible directions.

The Organizing Role of Sex Hormones

Sex hormones are classified as steroids, chemicals that are synthesized from cholesterol in the gonads and in lesser amounts in the adrenal glands, brain, bone, and fat cells. The chemical structure of cholesterol and the synthesis of the major sex hormones are illustrated in ● Figure 10.9. Males and females both produce androgens and estrogens, but in different amounts. Females produce about 10 percent of the amount of androgens produced by males.

Sex hormones play both organizational and activating roles in development (see ● Figure 10.10). In prenatal and early postnatal development, sex hormones organize circuits in the brain that differ according to sex. **Organization** produces permanent changes in biological structures. These circuits are then activated by the sex hormones at the onset of puberty and throughout adulthood. **Activation** by hormones is reversible, although the effects of activation are constrained by the organizational effects that occurred earlier (McCarthy & Arnold, 2011).

ORGANIZATION DURING DEVELOPMENT Sex hormones play especially important roles at three points in early human development: between 6 and 24 weeks following conception (prenatal development), a period beginning shortly before birth and extending to the age of 6 to 12 months (a "mini-puberty"), and finally at puberty.

For males, these periods are times when testosterone levels are particularly high. During the first part of the prenatal organizing period, testosterone contributes to the development of the male reproductive system, as described earlier in this chapter. During the latter part of this period, testosterone influences both the reproductive systems and the brain, which contains androgen receptors (Hines, 2010). Estrogen receptors are also expressed in the prenatal brain. Estradiol plays a critical role in sexual development, but also influences apoptosis in both sexes (Wilson, Westberry, & Trout, 2011). As we will see later in this chapter, certain parts of the human brain are **sexually dimorphic**, or differ between males and females in structure and volume. These differences are likely the result of different prenatal hormonal environments. Gray matter volume in cortical areas known to be sexually dimorphic is consistent with individual variations in fetal testosterone levels (Lombardo et al., 2012).

In the absence of influence by substantial amounts of prenatal testosterone, the female brain will continue to develop by default in a female direction. As we saw earlier, the vast majority of genetic males with AIS, who are insensitive to circulating testosterone, cannot be distinguished from typical girls and women in terms of outward appearance, gender identity, or behavior. In contrast,

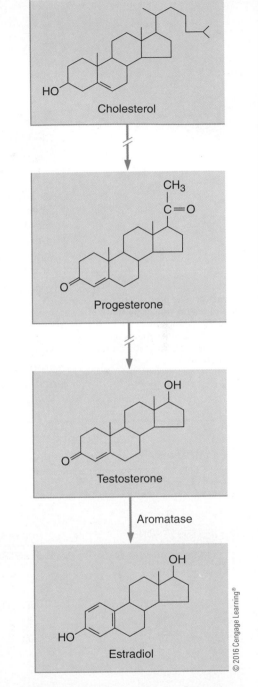

● **Figure 10.9 The Synthesis of Human Sex Hormones** Sex hormones are steroids derived from cholesterol. There are several chemical reactions, indicated by the broken arrows, that take place in the development of progesterone from cholesterol and testosterone from progesterone. However, there is only one step, aromatization, that is necessary to turn testosterone into estradiol.

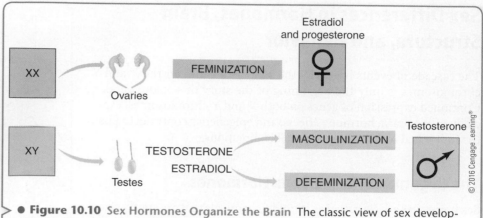

> ● **Figure 10.10** **Sex Hormones Organize the Brain** The classic view of sex development begins with the sex chromosomes, which in turn determine whether the fetus develops ovaries or testes. Production of sex hormones further organizes sexual dimorphism in the brain. In the presence of estradiol and progesterone, and in the absence of androgens, the brain develops in the female pattern. In males, testosterone promotes male-typical behavior, while estradiol suppresses female-typical behavior.

organization The permanent effects of sex hormones on body structures.

activation Reversible effects of sex hormones on body structures and functions.

females with CAH and children of women who are prescribed androgens for medical reasons during pregnancy demonstrate more male-typical behaviors than unaffected females, while children of women who use anti-androgen medications during pregnancy show less male-typical behaviors (Hines, 2010).

MARKERS OF PRENATAL HORMONE ENVIRONMENTS Ethical constraints certainly preclude the artificial manipulation of the prenatal hormonal environment in humans. To investigate the possible influences of the prenatal hormonal environment on outcomes in typical individuals, researchers have attempted to identify "markers" that are correlated with prenatal exposure to hormones. For example, testosterone levels in both maternal blood and in amniotic fluid are correlated with sex-typical behavior in offspring (Auyeung et al., 2009).

One area of interest has been the relative length of the digits (fingers) of the hand, and in particular, the relationship between the length of the index finger (2D, because the thumb is 1D) and the ring finger (4D). Dividing the length of 2D by the length of 4D provides the 2D:4D ratio, which is determined by the prenatal ratio of testosterone to estrogens (Manning, 2011; Zheng & Cohn, 2011) (see ● Figure 10.11). Male 2D:4D ratios, particularly in the right hand, are typically smaller than female 2D:4D ratios. This means that the female index and ring fingers are similar in length (ratio approaching 1.0), while male index fingers tend to be shorter than ring fingers (ratio of about .955). The 2D:4D ratio sex difference occurs in other mammals as well as humans. The 2D:4D ratio is negatively correlated with sports ability and competitive ability in general (such as financial trading) (Manning,

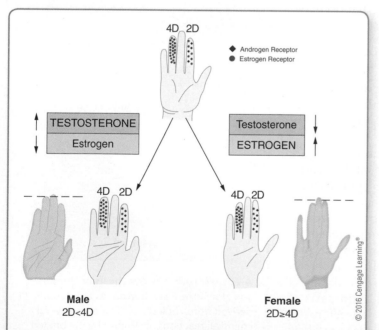

> ● **Figure 10.11** **Relationships between Prenatal Hormones and the 2D:4D Ratio** Androgen and estrogen receptors are present on both digits 2 and 4, but are more numerous on digit 4. The relationship between prenatal testosterone and estrogen levels determines the relative lengths of the digits. With higher testosterone and lower estrogen, the hand develops in the masculine pattern. With higher estrogen and lower testosterone, the hand develops in the female pattern.
> *Source:* This is Manning, 2011

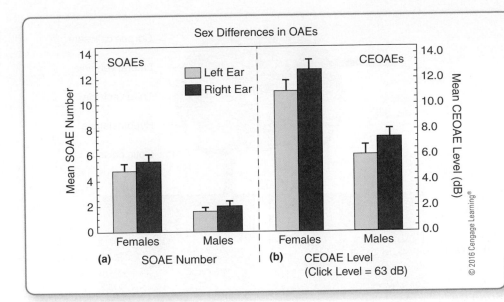

● **Figure 10.12** Otoacoustic Emissions Differ between Males and Females Recordings of otoacoustic emissions (OAEs) in both ears show that (a) females produce a higher number of spontaneous otoacoustic emissions (SOAEs) than males, and (b) females produce louder click-evoked OAEs (CEOAEs) than males. OAEs presumably indicate the influence of prenatal testosterone levels.

2011). In other words, evidence of higher prenatal testosterone predicts better sports performance and more competitive ability. Having a low 2D:4D ratio is also linked to left-handedness and autism spectrum disorder, and it predicts some sex-dependent diseases (Manning, 2011).

Another potential marker for prenatal hormonal exposure occurs in the inner ear, where you might think sex differences are unlikely. The cochlea of the inner ear (see Chapter 7) is capable of producing its own sounds, known as **otoacoustic emissions**. As shown in ● Figure 10.12, females produce louder and more frequent otoacoustic emissions (McFadden, 1993). These differences appear early in life and are possibly due to the amount of prenatal testosterone exposure experienced by an individual (McFadden, 2011). Like the digit ratios, sex differences in otoacoustic emissions also occur in other mammals. Experimental manipulation of prenatal testosterone in sheep produced differences in otoacoustic emissions consistent with these signals serving as a biomarker for prenatal testosterone exposure (McFadden, Pasanen, Valero, Roberts, & Lee, 2009).

What can we learn about sex and gender from studies about finger length and sounds from the inner ear? As we will see in a later section, variations in these patterns not only differentiate between men and women but also contribute to our understanding of sexual orientation.

Sexual Dimorphism in the Brain

While acknowledging the importance of social factors in gender differences, researchers have also observed differences in the brains and nervous systems of males and females. As we have observed, exposure to prenatal androgens masculinizes the brain as well as the internal and external reproductive systems. What exactly do we mean by "masculinizing" a brain or nervous system? First, we must identify features that are sexually dimorphic, which means to display structural differences between the sexes. Second, just as we observed in the masculinization of external genitalia, masculinizing the brain would result in the male pattern in any sexually dimorphic feature.

A number of sexually dimorphic brain structures have been identified. As shown in ● Figure 10.13, the **sexually dimorphic nucleus of the preoptic area (SDN-POA)**, located in the hypothalamus, is much larger in male rats than in female rats (Gorski, Gordon, Shryne, & Southam, 1978). The development of the SDN-POA reflects the early organizing effects of hormone exposure. In humans, most organizing effects occur prenatally. In rats, however, a critical window exists within a few days of birth in

otoacoustic emissions Sounds emitted by the cochlea of the inner ear that show sex differences.
sexually dimorphic nucleus of the preoptic area (SDN-POA) A nucleus in the preoptic area of the hypothalamus that is larger in male rats than in female rats.

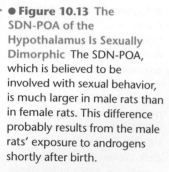

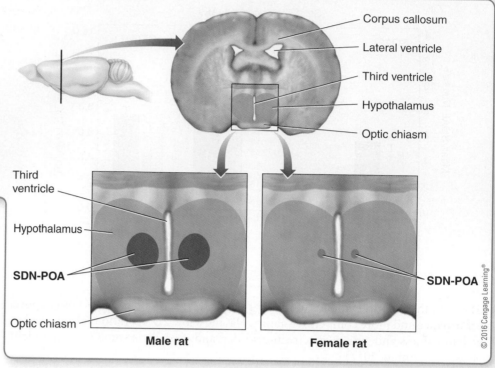

● **Figure 10.13** The **SDN-POA of the Hypothalamus Is Sexually Dimorphic** The SDN-POA, which is believed to be involved with sexual behavior, is much larger in male rats than in female rats. This difference probably results from the male rats' exposure to androgens shortly after birth.

Corpus callosum

Lateral ventricle

Third ventricle

Hypothalamus

Optic chiasm

Third ventricle

Hypothalamus

SDN-POA

Optic chiasm

SDN-POA

Male rat

Female rat

© 2016 Cengage Learning®

which exposure to androgens masculinizes the brain. At birth, the SDN-POA of rats is approximately the same size in males and females. Normally, the SDN-POA of the male begins to grow rapidly during the newborn period. If a newborn male rat is castrated, its SDN-POA is much smaller than normal. If a newborn female rat is injected with testosterone, its SDN-POA will be much larger than normal. Castration or injection of older animals does not change the size of the SDN-POA, indicating that this structure responds to early hormonal organization (Gorski, 1980). The precise function of the SDN-POA is not currently well understood, although lesions in this area of the hypothalamus generally reduce male sexual behavior (De Jonge et al., 1989).

The human equivalent of SDN-POA consists of a cluster of neurons in the preoptic area of the human hypothalamus known as the **interstitial nuclei of the anterior hypothalamus**, or INAH-1 (Bao & Swaab, 2011). Three additional clusters, INAH-2, INAH-3, and INAH-4 have been identified in the human brain. INAH-2 and INAH-3 are about twice as large in males as in females (Allen, Hines, Shryne, & Gorski, 1989). As we will see later, there is a connection between the size of these nuclei and a male's sexual orientation.

Additional structural differences between male and female brains have been discovered in the hypothalamus, thalamus, and in the white matter of the cerebral hemispheres (Breedlove, 1992; Hsu et al., 2008). Although it is likely that some of these differences, such as those in the hypothalamus, are related to sexual behavior, the significance of many of these differences remains unclear. Male and female patterns of performance on cognitive and emotional tasks might be related to some of these observed structural differences.

Sexual dimorphism has also been observed in the spinal cords of mammals. Male rats have more motor neurons in a structure known as the **spinal nucleus of the bulbocavernosus (SNB)** than do female rats. The male rat's SNB motor neurons innervate the bulbocavernosus muscles of the rat's penis. These muscles, or their equivalent, are missing in adult female rats. Prior to the rats' critical period of masculinization at birth, males and females both possess these muscles and about the same number of SNB cells (Rand & Breedlove, 1987). However, during the critical period, the low levels of androgens in female rats cause the muscles and most of the SNB neurons to die.

interstitial nuclei of the anterior hypothalamus A collection of four small nuclei in the anterior hypothalamus, two of which (INAH-2 and INAH-3) appear to be sexually dimorphic. The size of INAH-3 might be associated with male sexual orientation.

spinal nucleus of the bulbocavernosus (SNB) Motor neurons in the spinal cord that innervate the male rat's bulbocavernosus muscles in the penis.

Sex Differences in Behavior and Cognition

Undeniably, socialization plays a significant role in shaping male and female behavior, but recognizing the contributions of biology and the intricate interactions between biology and socialization enriches rather than diminishes our understanding of sex and gender.

PLAY BEHAVIOR Toy stores epitomize either/ or thinking about males and females. Male-typical toys include cars, trucks, and guns and the color blue while female-typical toys include dolls, tea sets, and cosmetics and the color pink. Neutral toys do exist, such as books, puzzles, and crayons. While socialization clearly plays a role in a child's choice of toy, what do we know about biological contributions to play behavior?

Returning to the example of CAH females, who experience unusually high levels of prenatal androgens, provides interesting insights into the effects of biology on toy choice. Parents act as key socializing agents early in childhood; but parents of CAH daughters seem to be even more determined than parents of typically developing girls to socialize their daughters in a feminine pattern. Despite these efforts, toy choices by girls with CAH are significantly more likely to be in the masculine direction than in the feminine direction (Hines, 2010) (see ● Figure 10.14). In a similar fashion, androgen exposure as measured in maternal blood or amniotic fluid is predictive of masculine toy interest in typically developing girls (Hines, 2010). Because the parents of this latter set of girls girls have no information about their daughters' prenatal hormone state, it is highly unlikely that differences in socialization could account for these results.

Children begin to prefer sex-typed toys between the ages of 12 and 18 months. At these same ages, children are unable to match sex-typed toys (vehicles and dolls) with male or female faces or voices, suggesting that they have not yet been socialized to think of toys as "male" or "female" (Serbin, Poulin-Dubois, Colburne, Sen, & Eichstedt, 2001). Socialization is even less likely to play a role in the toy choices of monkeys (see ● Figure 10.15). Young male monkeys spend more time with wheeled toys and balls, whereas young female monkeys prefer dolls, plush animals, and pots (Alexander & Hines, 2002; Hassett, Siebert, & Wallen, 2008; Swan et al., 2010).

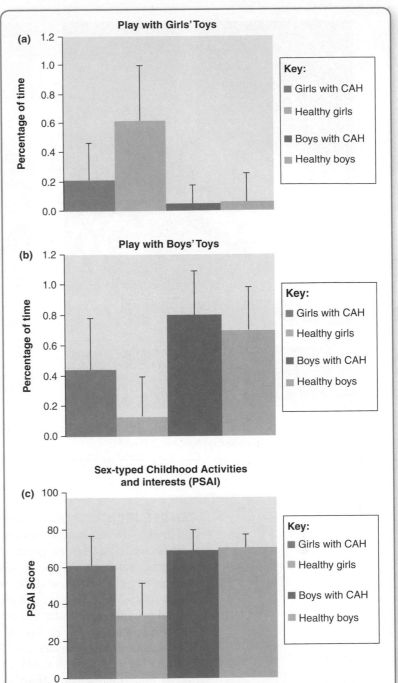

● **Figure 10.14** Prenatal Androgen Exposure and Play Behavior Typically developing boys are exposed prenatally to about 2.5 times the amount of androgens as typically developing girls. Girls with CAH are exposed to about half the amount of prenatal androgens as typically developing boys or about 25 percent more than typically developing girls. Boys with CAH are exposed to higher levels of androgens than typically developing boys, but because prenatal androgens are very high in both cases, this seems to have little behavioral effect. Time spent with girls' toys (a) is lower in girls with CAH than typically developing girls, but both are much higher than boys. Time spent with boys' toys (b) is higher in girls with CAH and typically developing unaffected girls, but is still lower than in boys. The PSAI score (c) results from subtracting scores for girl-typical items from boy-typical items on a 24-item, standardized measure. Higher scores reflect more male-typical behavior.

Source: Hines (2010)

● **Figure 10.15 Sex-typical Toy Preferences in Monkeys** Young vervet monkeys show preferences for sex-typical toys in the absence of any human-like gender socialization.

GENDER IDENTITY Gender identity is defined as a person's self-concept as male or female, and is usually viewed as the end product of years of socialization. In **transsexuality**, a person's gender identity is inconsistent with his or her biological sex and is often resolved with sex-reassignment surgery and hormonal treatment. Information about the contribution of social factors in the development of transsexuality is sparse. Research on the biological correlates of transsexuality might illuminate general principles of gender identity as a whole.

Transsexuality in biological females is rare, occurring in approximately .005 percent of women (Dessens, Slijper, & Drop, 2005). In contrast, approximately 3 percent of women with CAH, raised as girls, express a wish to live as men, a rate that is 600 times greater than in the general public. An additional 5 percent of CAH women express a general dissatisfaction with the female role (Bao & Swaab, 2011). Keep in mind that this still means that the vast majority of women with CAH (92 percent) are satisfied with their female gender identity.

Transsexuality might occur due to the prenatal timing of hormone influences on the reproductive systems and on the brain, with influences on the reproductive systems occurring first. If these two processes are separable due to different timing, the systems might not develop congruently (Bao & Swaab, 2011). In a sample of male-to-female transsexual individuals, two brain structures known to be sexually dimorphic (the central nucleus of the bed nucleus of the stria terminalis [BSTc] and INAH-3) were found to show the typical "female" pattern of volume. In a single case of a female-to-male transsexual individual, BSTc and INAH-3 both conformed to the "male" pattern. Complicating this analysis, however, is the fact that BSTc typically does not show sexual dimorphism before puberty, while many transsexual individuals express strong gender dissatisfaction at younger ages.

transsexuality Having a gender identity that is inconsistent with biological sex.

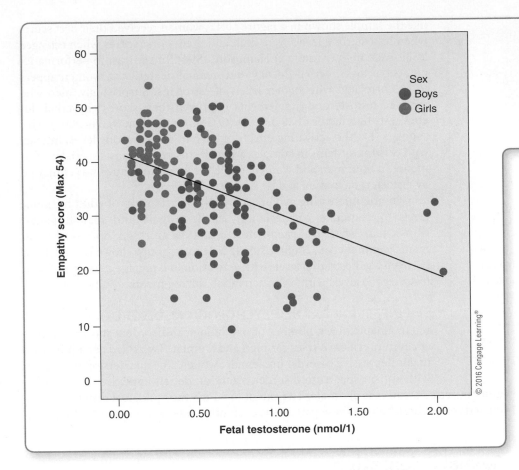

● **Figure 10.16** Fetal Testosterone and Empathy Levels of fetal testosterone are negatively correlated with children's scores on a standardized test of empathy.

© 2016 Cengage Learning®

PERSONALITY Early organization of the nervous system might influence later development across a number of sophisticated behavioral domains, while interacting, of course, with socialization at each step of the way.

In general, large numbers of studies have pointed to higher empathy in females and higher levels of physical aggression in males (see ● Figure 10.16). Consistent with the patterns we have already observed, females with CAH show decreased empathy and increased physical aggression relative to typically developing girls (Hines, 2010). Both boys and girls with high amniotic fluid levels of testosterone or prenatal exposure to androgen medications taken by their mothers show reduced empathy and higher levels of physical aggression. It is important to note that not all personality dimensions that show reliable differences between males and females, such as assertiveness, are related to prenatal testosterone exposure.

ADULT HORMONE LEVELS AND COGNITION Up to this point, we have largely focused on the organizing effects of sex hormones. As we have seen, prenatal hormone levels seem to have a significant impact in a number of different domains but do not explain all of the observed differences. The remaining differences could be environmental in origin, epigenetic, due to differences in activation rather than organization by hormones, or some combination of factors.

In a large body of research data, males (both human and nonhuman) have been shown to have a slight advantage in visuospatial tasks (Kimura, 1992), whereas females have a slight advantage in verbal tasks (see Chapter 13). Research results investigating these trends within CAH females are mixed, suggesting that the organizing role of prenatal hormones plays less of a part here than in the previously discussed behavioral domains.

The male advantage in visuospatial skills appears early in life. Visuospatial skills are correlated with current, not necessarily prenatal, testosterone levels in both men and women. Older men receiving testosterone supplements improved their performance on spatial tasks (Janowsky, Oviatt, & Orwell, 1994). On tests of mental figure rotations,

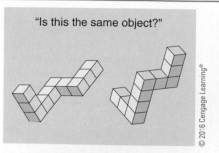

"Is this the same object?"

Figure Rotation

● **Figure 10.17** Gender Influences Cognition Women generally have a slight advantage in verbal tasks such as naming objects that have the same color and listing words that begin with a particular letter. Men have a slight advantage in visuo spatial tasks, such as this figure rotation task. When asked whether the two shapes are the same, males respond somewhat faster than females.

like the sample shown in ● Figure 10.17, women received their best scores when testosterone levels were high and their worst scores when estrogen levels were high (Kimura & Hampson, 1994). In contrast to performance on spatial tasks, verbal fluency and manual dexterity in women appear to be correlated with higher levels of estrogens. Surprisingly, men who received testosterone supplements improved their scores on verbal fluency tests by a factor of 20 percent (O'Connor, Archer, & Wu, 2000). This suggests that the activating effects of current sex hormone levels interact with existing systems in complex ways. Testosterone boosts spatial performance in both men and women, while verbal performance was enhanced by testosterone in men and by estrogens in women.

In one interesting exploration of the relationship of adult hormone levels to cognitive performance, female-to-male and male-to-female transsexuals were evaluated before and after cross-sex hormonal treatment (Sommer et al., 2008). Using fMRI, both groups showed correlations between their estradiol levels with activation in language centers and their testosterone levels with brain activation during mental rotation tasks.

SEX DIFFERENCES AND PSYCHOLOGICAL DISORDERS As we will see in Chapter 16, a number of psychological disorders show big differences in prevalence rates for men and women. Two thirds of adults with major depressive disorder are female, while three quarters of individuals with autism spectrum disorder, attention deficit hyperactivity disorder, and Tourette's syndrome are male. The extent to which the biological differences discussed so far contribute to these patterns is currently under active investigation.

Sexual Orientation

While the previous discussion of male and female prenatal hormonal environments, brain structure, and behavior is interesting in its own right, it also forms the foundation for understanding the biological correlates of sexual orientation.

Sexual orientation refers to a stable pattern of attraction to members of a particular sex. Approximately 1.8 percent of adult males and 1.5 percent of adult females identify themselves as gay or lesbian, and 0.4 percent of men and 0.9 percent of women describe themselves as bisexual (Ward, Dahlhamer, Galinsky, & Joestl, 2014) Sexual orientation is not synonymous with sexual behavior. Many people engage in same-sex behavior and fantasy while maintaining a strong heterosexual orientation. Stoller and Herdt (1985) described a tribal culture in which all adolescent males are expected to engage in same-sex behavior until they are married to women. In spite of this prior sexual experience, the sexual orientation of these males as adults was overwhelmingly heterosexual.

Hormones and Sexual Orientation

Early hormone exposure influences adult sexual behavior in animals and humans. As noted previously, male rats have a larger SDN-POA than female rats. Exposure to testosterone during a critical period accounts for this sexual dimorphism. If male rats do not receive exposure to testosterone during this critical period, their SDN-POA remains small, and their adult sexual behavior differs from rats receiving typical exposure to testosterone. Rats exposed to low testosterone are less likely to engage in sexual behavior with females and more likely to engage in sexual behavior with males than are rats exposed to normal testosterone levels (Matuszczyk, Fernandez-Guasti, & Larsen, 1988). In addition, exposure to testosterone during the critical period increases the size of SDN-POA in female rats and increases the likelihood that they will engage in sexual activity with females as adults. We have already seen that a typical conditions such as CAH, which involves prenatal exposure to androgens, can increase the likelihood that women

sexual orientation A stable pattern of attraction to members of a particular sex.

will engage in bisexual or lesbian behavior as adults. However, the majority of CAH women are heterosexual. Also, the majority of lesbian and bisexual women do not have a history of CAH or similar conditions.

Earlier, we described the differences between otoacoustic emissions in men and women and explored the likelihood that these differences served as a biomarker of prenatal androgen exposure. McFadden and Pasanen (1999) measured the otoacoustic emissions of lesbian, bisexual, and heterosexual women. As shown in ●Figure 10.18, the rate of the emissions in lesbian and bisexual women fell between the normal levels for heterosexual women and for men. McFadden and Pasanen suggested that exposure to prenatal androgens may have influenced both the ear structure and sexual orientation of the lesbian and bisexual women.

We also discussed another possible indicator of prenatal exposure to androgens, the 2D:4D ratio. Lesbians tended to show the more masculine pattern of finger length, suggesting that they might have experienced prenatal exposure to androgens (Kraemer et al., 2006). As shown in ●Figure 10.19, researchers do not find a systematic pattern of finger length among homosexual men as opposed to heterosexual men, however.

What could initiate the differences in prenatal hormonal environments associated with homosexuality? One interesting clue comes from the observation that birth order matters for homosexual men. Men who have older brothers are slightly more likely to be homosexual than men who have no siblings, younger siblings only, or older sisters (Blanchard, 1997; Cantor, Blanchard, Paterson, & Bogaert, 2002). The protein products of three genes located on the Y chromosome might provoke the mother's immune response, which should become greater with each successive pregnancy with a male fetus. A strong immune response from the mother could affect her fetus's brain while not affecting the gonads or genitals.

Brain Structure and Sexual Orientation

As we have seen previously, several brain structures are sexually dimorphic, especially INAH-3 in the hypothalamus. Building on these observations, Simon LeVay asked whether INAH-3 might be different in heterosexual and homosexual men. Lesions of INAH-3 in monkeys impairs heterosexual behavior but does not affect overall sex drive, as indicated by rates of masturbation. He found that INAH-3 was two to three times larger in heterosexual men than in homosexual men (LeVay, 1991). The size of INAH-3 among LeVay's homosexual subjects was not significantly different from the size observed in female subjects. ●Figure 10.20 shows the location of INAH-3, as well as heterosexual and homosexual examples from LeVay's research.

The anterior commissure, a small band of fibers connecting the two cerebral hemispheres, is also among the structures known to be sexually dimorphic in humans. Laura Allen and Roger Gorski (1992) reported that the size of

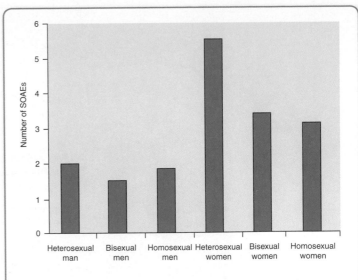

● **Figure 10.18 Sexual Orientation and Otoacoustic Emissions** Men typically emit lower numbers of spontaneous otoacoustic emissions (SOAEs) than women, which is believed to be the result of different exposure to prenatal testosterone. Bisexual and homosexual males do not show different rates of SOAEs than heterosexual males, but bisexual and homosexual women show rates that are midway between those found in heterosexual females and men.

Source: Adapted from McFadden and Pasanen, 1999.

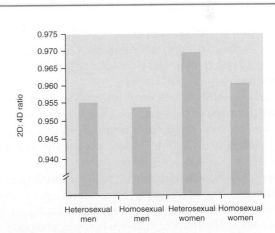

● **Figure 10.19 Sexual Orientation and 2D:4D Ratio** Lower 2D:4D ratios are related to exposure to prenatal testosterone. Heterosexual and homosexual males do not show different 2D:4D ratios, but the 2D:4D ratio of homosexual women falls midway between the ratios of heterosexual women and men, possibly indicating greater exposure to prenatal testosterone.

Source: Data from Williams et al. (2000).

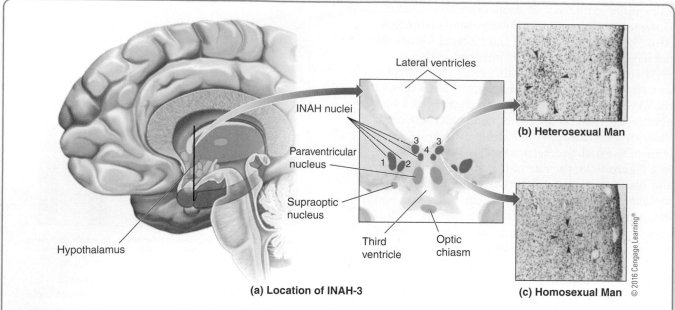

(a) Location of INAH-3

(b) Heterosexual Man

(c) Homosexual Man

© 2016 Cengage Learning®

> ● **Figure 10.20 INAH-3 Size Correlates with Sexual Orientation** Simon LeVay reported that INAH-3 is smaller among women and homosexual men than among heterosexual men. (a) This image shows the location of INAH-3. The micrograph in (b) is taken from a heterosexual man, whereas the micrograph in (c) is taken from a man who was homosexual.

the anterior commissure varies reliably between homosexual and heterosexual males. Unlike the hypothalamus, the anterior commissure has no direct role in sexual behavior. The observed differences in this structure might simply be an additional marker like otoacoustic emissions for the fetal hormone environment.

●●● Connecting to **Research**

SIMON LEVAY AND INAH-3

Today, it might not seem exactly revolutionary or earth-shattering to think that sexual orientation has a strong biological component, but the cultural environment of 1991, when Simon LeVay published his study on INAH-3, was very different. Prior to the 1990s, the term *sexual preference* was used more frequently by scientists than the current term, *sexual orientation*.

LeVay was cautious in interpreting his results. First of all, because INAH-3 is too small to observe in living participants with available imaging technologies, LeVay studied autopsied brains. This obviously prevented him from obtaining a detailed history of his subjects' sexual behavior. The homosexual men's medical records documented their sexual behavior, as this was relevant to their diagnosis of AIDS, but those of the presumed heterosexual men did not. The study could not be extended to the sexual orientation of women, because their medical records also lacked this information. In addition, LeVay raised the possibility that the AIDS condition, which affected his homosexual participants, could have caused shrinkage of INAH-3. However, he didn't give

this argument much credibility because INAH-3 in the heterosexual subjects with AIDS followed the heterosexual male pattern. Finally, critics have suggested that engaging in different types of sexual behavior might influence the size of INAH-3. LeVay again discounted this interpretation and suggested that the differences he observed were more logically the result of organizing prenatal factors.

Because this type of research is quite difficult to conduct with human participants, other researchers have investigated the correlation of brain structure and sexual behavior in animals. Among domestic sheep, 6 to 8 percent of rams (males) mate exclusively with other males. Kay Larkin and her colleagues (Larkin, Resko, Stormshak, Stellflug, & Roselli, 2002) studied SDN-POA (a non-primate equivalent of INAH) in rams who engaged in same-sex behavior, in rams that mated with ewes (females), and in ewes. SDN-POA in rams that engaged in same-sex behavior was about the same size as in ewes and differed from SDN-POA in rams that mated with ewes. These results provide a parallel to LeVay's findings in INAH-3.

Genes and Sexual Orientation

Genetics appear to influence sexual orientation, although the exact mechanisms are not well understood and are likely to be quite complex. It is currently unknown whether genetics can have direct effects on sexual orientation or indirect effects on prenatal androgen environments. The chances of a homosexual male twin having a homosexual brother are 20 to 25 percent for fraternal twins and about 50 percent for identical twins (Kirk, Bailey, & Martin, 2000). Compared with mothers with heterosexual sons, mothers of homosexual sons showed more extreme skewing, in which an X chromosome from one parent is much more likely to be inactivated than the X chromosome from the other parent (Bocklandt, Horvath, Vilain, & Hamer, 2006) (see Chapter 5).

Sexual Orientation and Cognition

We previously observed that males and females differed on visuospatial tasks and verbal tasks. Like the biomarkers and sexually dimorphic structures, will we see variations in performance of these tasks based on sexual orientation?

In one large-scale study using mental rotation tasks for assessing visuospatial skills, men consistently performed better than women, regardless of sexual orientation (Peters, Manning, & Reimers, 2007) (see ● Figure 10.21). Taking sexual orientation into account, heterosexual men outperformed homosexual men, with bisexual men scoring between these two groups. Homosexual and bisexual women scored at about equal levels, and both groups outperformed heterosexual women. Similar findings were reported for the results of three tests of verbal fluency. Homosexual men outperformed heterosexual women, but both of these groups outperformed heterosexual men and homosexual women, who performed at about the same level (Rahman, Abrahams, & Wilson, 2003).

Although the findings on visuospatial skills and verbal skills suggest a cognitive "reversal" occurs, in which homosexual individuals perform similarly to their opposite sex, it is overly simplistic and inaccurate to assume that a homosexual orientation is a gender inversion (LeVay, 2011). A large group of participants self-identified as homosexual male, heterosexual male, bisexual male, homosexual female, heterosexual female, and bisexual female, and then rated themselves on a seven-point masculinity–femininity scale with 1 being extremely feminine and 7 being extremely masculine (Lippa, 2008). As shown in ● Figure 10.22, all groups clustered between scores of 3 and slightly above 5. Heterosexual females and heterosexual males were farther away from

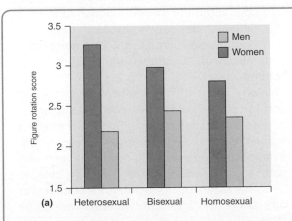

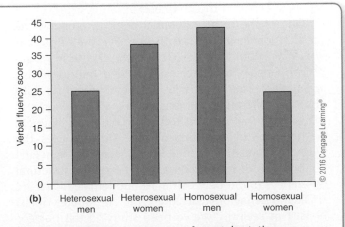

© 2016 Cengage Learning®

● **Figure 10.21 Sexual Orientation and Cognition** (a) Men typically outscore women on tests of mental rotation. Heterosexual men performed better on mental rotation tasks than homosexual men, with the performance of bisexual men falling between these two groups. Bisexual and homosexual women did not differ from one another, and both performed better than heterosexual women, but worse than all groups of men (Data from Peters et al., 2007). (b) Women typically outscore men on verbal tasks. Heterosexual women and homosexual men performed better on a set of verbal fluency tasks than did heterosexual men and homosexual women (Data from Rahman et al., 2003).

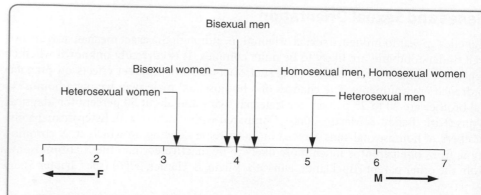

● **Figure 10.22 Self-identification of Masculinity/Femininity** Participants were asked to choose a number describing themselves on a scale from 1 (Very feminine) to 7 (Very masculine). The results do not support the idea of homosexuality as an inversion of gender, in which homosexual men were similar to heterosexual women and homosexual women were similar to heterosexual men.

Source: Data from Lippa (2008).

●●● THINKING *Ethically*

BIOLOGY'S ROLE IN EXPLAINING GENDER AND SEXUAL ORIENTATION

This chapter has explored research that focuses on biological aspects of gender, but at no time should we assume that these factors work in some fashion that is isolated from the influence of experience. At the same time, it can be equally misleading to assume that experience can operate in isolation without the influence of biology. Knowing that parents treat their sons and daughters quite differently from their day of birth, and that daughters are much more likely than sons to be reinforced for playing with dolls, interacts with but does not negate the biological influences on toy choice reviewed earlier in this chapter.

One of the most influential books promoting the socialization view of gender is Cordelia Fine's *Delusions of Gender,* published in 2010. Using the term *neurosexism,* Fine, who is herself a trained neuroscientist, argues that biology has little if anything to do with observed differences in male and female behavior, and that studies that purport to show biological influences on gender are inherently flawed. She dismisses the work of Laura Allen and Roger Gorski on the sexual dimorphism of INAH-3 by arguing that the structural differences found between male and female brains are small and behaviorally insignificant, and quotes Gorski himself as saying, "We've been studying this nucleus for 15 years, and we still don't know what it does" (Fine, 2010, p. 104).

The attentive reader might recall something else about INAH-3 besides its sexual dimorphism. This is the same structure that appeared to differ in size between Simon LeVay's samples of male heterosexual and homosexual men. In fact, LeVay selected INAH-3 for his study specifically because of Gorski and Allen's work on the structure's sexual dimorphism. When compared to the differences Gorski and Allen found in INAH-3 between men and women, LeVay's differences between homosexual and heterosexual men were smaller and showed greater overlap. If Gorski and Allen's observed differences are "small and behaviorally insignificant," LeVay's logically are more so. Nor does LeVay know any more than Gorski does about the specific function of INAH-3 in humans, although he reviews research regarding its functions in monkeys. Surprisingly, Fine completely omitted any discussion of the sexual orientation literature in her book.

The biology of gender differences provides the foundation for any argument in favor of a biological basis for sexual orientation, making these two research lines inseparable. To argue that observed gender differences have little to do with biology and everything to do with socialization absolutely requires one to make the same argument for sexual orientation, yet few if any contemporary neuroscientists would be comfortable with such a view. We return to the conclusion that human behavior represents complex interactions between biology and environment, and a balanced approach to both will provide us with the best answers.

4 (neutral) than the other groups. Bisexual women and men were just about at neutral, and homosexual men and women were slightly above neutral in the masculine direction. The point is that homosexual men did not see themselves as very feminine nor did homosexual women see themselves as very masculine, which would be required to support the gender inversion approach.

INTERIM SUMMARY 10.2

|| Summary Points

1. Prenatal exposure to testosterone masculinizes the brain, and in the absence of testosterone, the female brain will develop in a female-typical direction **(LO2)**.

2. A number of brain structures are sexually dimorphic, which means that their structure and volume differs between male and female brains **(LO3)**.

3. Some sex differences in behavior appear to be influenced by organizing effects of prenatal hormones, while others respond to activating effects of hormones later in life **(LO2)**.

4. Sexual orientation is associated with possible genetic and prenatal hormonal influences, leading to structural differences in the brain **(LO4)**.

|| Review Questions

1. What does it mean to masculinize the brain?

2. What evidence exists for a biological basis of sexual orientation?

Biological Influences on Adult Sexual Behavior

The activation of behavior by hormones is particularly important to sexual behavior beginning at puberty and extends throughout the remainder of the lifespan.

The Regulation of Sex Hormones

The hypothalamus exerts the most immediate control over the endocrine system, although, of course, it is receiving direction from other structures of the brain.

The hypothalamus manages the release of sex hormones through its secretion of gonadotropin-releasing hormone (GnRH). Light sensed by the retina increases GnRH secretion through its action on melatonin, a neurohormone implicated in the regulation of sleep and produced by the nearby pineal gland (see Chapter 11). Melatonin normally inhibits the release of GnRH, and light in turn inhibits melatonin, which is secreted primarily at night. Light, therefore, increases GnRH release by reducing the inhibition normally produced by melatonin.

In nonhuman species, this response of the hypothalamus to light provides means for producing offspring at the right time of year. Fertility can be timed according to the lengthening or shortening of daylight hours. Human beings show this same competition between GnRH and melatonin release, but the exact impact on sexual behavior is unknown. Like other mammals, human beings do show some evidence of seasonality in birth rates (Cummings, 2010). In countries such as Sweden, where there are strong contrasts between seasons in length of day, fertility is highest during the summer, leading to a spring-season baby boomlet (Rojansky, Brzezinski, & Schenker, 1992).

GnRH secreted by the hypothalamus travels to the anterior pituitary gland, shown in ●Figure 10.23. In response to GnRH, the anterior pituitary releases

● **Figure 10.23**
Hypothalamic Control of the Pituitary Gland By secreting GnRH, the hypothalamus stimulates the release of luteinizing hormone (LH) and follicle-stimulating hormone (FSH) by the anterior pituitary gland. In males, LH signals the testes to produce testosterone. Both testosterone and FSH are necessary for producing mature sperm. In females, LH and FSH control the menstrual cycle.

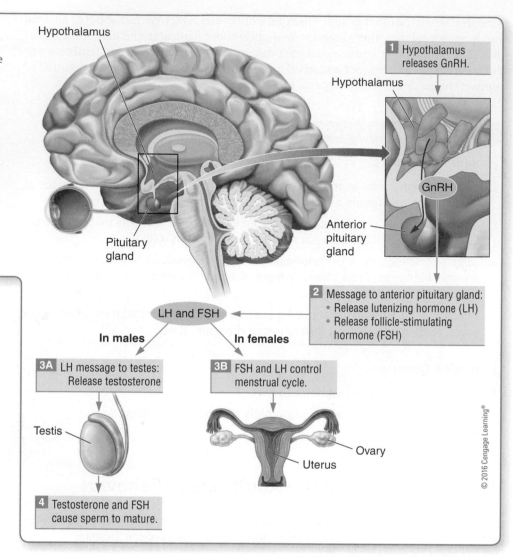

the gonadotropins, LH, and FSH. As we saw previously, the initial release of these hormones is associated with the onset of puberty. From puberty on, the gonadotropins continue to play a major role in fertility. In males, LH signals the testes to produce testosterone. Both testosterone and FSH are required for the maturation of sperm. In females, LH and FSH control the menstrual cycle.

The Menstrual Cycle and Female Fertility

As shown in ● Figure 10.24, the menstrual cycle represents a very stable and predictable fluctuation in events controlled by LH and FSH. On the first day of menstruation, the anterior pituitary gland increases secretion of FSH. When this hormone circulates to the ovaries, they respond by developing **follicles**, small clusters of cells that each contain an egg cell, or **ovum**. One follicle begins to develop more rapidly than the others, and it releases estrogens that inhibit the growth of competing follicles. If more than one follicle matures, and the ova are fertilized, fraternal (nonidentical) twins will develop. Commonly prescribed fertility drugs stimulate the development of follicles and ova and subsequently promote multiple births (Imaizumi, 2003). Estrogens from the follicle also provide feedback to the hypothalamus and pituitary gland, which respond by sharply increasing release of LH. Increased LH levels initiate the release of the ovum, or **ovulation**, about two weeks after the first day of the last menstruation. Estradiol

follicle One of several clusters of cells in the ovary, each of which contains an egg cell.
ovum A female reproductive cell, or egg.
ovulation The process of releasing a mature egg from the ovary.

released by the ovaries signals the uterus to thicken in anticipation of a fertilized embryo.

After the release of the ovum, the ruptured follicle is now called the **corpus luteum**, which means "yellow body." The corpus luteum releases estradiol and a new hormone, **progesterone**. Progesterone promotes pregnancy (gestation) by preventing the development of additional follicles and by further developing the lining of the uterus. If fertilization does not take place, the corpus luteum stops producing estradiol and progesterone. When levels of these hormones drop, the uterine lining cannot be maintained, menstruation will start, and the entire cycle will repeat.

MOOD, MENSTRUATION, AND CHILDBIRTH Approximately 5 to 8 percent of women experience **premenstrual syndrome** in response to shifts in the hormones that regulate the menstrual cycle (Yonkers, O'Brien, & Eriksson, 2008). Premenstrual syndrome is characterized by physical symptoms of bloating and breast enlargement and tenderness as well as psychological symptoms of depression and irritability. Severe cases of premenstrual mood changes are diagnosed as **premenstrual dysphoric disorder (PMDD)** (APA, 2013). Women with PMDD experience more depression, changes in appetite (consuming more calories total and more calories from fat), and impaired cognitive performance than women who do not suffer from this disorder (Reed, Levin, & Evans, 2008). These symptoms are consistent with a hypothesis linking serotonin dysfunction with PMDD, leading to the current treatment of medication with selective serotonin reuptake inhibitors (SSRIs) (ibid.)

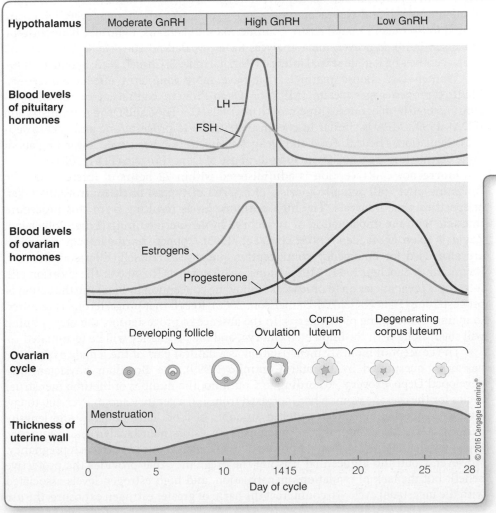

● **Figure 10.24** **The Human Menstrual Cycle** The menstrual cycle is tightly regulated by the release of GnRH from the hypothalamus, LH and FSH by the anterior pituitary gland, and estrogens and progesterone from the follicles and corpus luteum.

corpus luteum A yellow mass of cells in the ovary formed by a ruptured follicle that has released an egg.

progesterone A hormone produced in the corpus luteum that prevents the development of additional follicles and promotes the growth of the uterine lining.

premenstrual syndrome A condition in which some women experience physical and psychological symptoms immediately prior to the onset of menstruation.

premenstrual dysphoric disorder (PMDD) A condition in which premenstrual mood changes are unusually severe.

Within one year of the delivery of a baby, approximately 10 to 15 percent of women experience **postpartum depression** as hormones shift from the pregnant state back to normal monthly cycles (Centers for Disease Control [CDC], 2008). Postpartum depression appears to be quite mild in the vast majority of cases. Mothers at highest risk for postpartum depression are younger than 20 years of age, unmarried, less educated, and of lower socioeconomic status. A history of being physically abused or using tobacco during the last three months of pregnancy also increases risk (Centers for Disease Control [CDC], 2008). Cases of postpartum depression can be detected in nearly 90 percent of patients as early as the third trimester of pregnancy by evaluating sensitivity to estrogen signaling (Mehta et al., 2014). This predictive ability might lead to additional support for women judged to be at risk for this condition.

FEMALE CONTRACEPTION Women who are exclusively breast-feeding their infants (no water, juice, solid foods, or formula) and are not menstruating have less than a 1 to 6 percent chance of becoming pregnant (Gray et al., 1990; Li & Qiu, 2007). Breast-feeding suppresses GnRH, which in turn interferes with the pulse of LH associated with follicle growth and ovulation (McNeilly, 2001) (see ● Figure 10.24 above).

Oral contraceptives (birth control pills) work by providing hormones that interfere with normal ovulation. There are two types of commonly used oral contraceptives, the combination pill and the progestin-only pill. The combination pill contains two synthetic hormones, an estrogen and progestin (a hormone similar to progesterone). This pill prevents the maturation of follicles and ovulation. The progestin-only pill prevents the thinning of cervical mucus that typically accompanies ovulation. Subsequently, the passage of sperm into the uterus and fallopian tubes becomes less likely. Both types of pill also act to prevent fertilized eggs from implanting in the lining of the uterus. All oral contraceptives reduce a woman's testosterone levels, which are related to a woman's sexual desire (Zimmerman, Eijkemans, Bennink, Blankenstein, & Fauser, 2014). However, meta-analyses have revealed no consistent effects of oral contraceptives on female sexual interest (Pastor, Holla, & Chmel, 2013; Schaffir, 2006).

Women can choose methods that have more long-term effects on fertility. Medroxyprogesterone acetate (MPA or Depo-Provera contraceptive injection) is administered by injection at three-month intervals (U.S. Food and Drug Administration [FDA], 1993). MPA is similar in chemical structure to progesterone and acts to suppress ovulation. The U.S. Food and Drug Administration has issued a warning about bone density loss associated with long-term use of Depo-Provera (FDA, 2004).

Emergency contraception is administered within 72 hours of intercourse. The "morning after" pill actually consists of a series of typical birth control pills taken at specified time intervals. The high hormone levels resulting from this procedure interfere with the implantation of an embryo in the uterine lining (Ling, Robichaud, Zayid, Wrixon, & MacLeod, 1979; Ling et al., 1983). Copper-bearing intrauterine wires are also used for emergency contraception purposes (Trussell, Ellertson, Stewart, Raymond, & Shochet, 2004). Mifepristone, also known as RU-486 or the abortion pill, interrupts pregnancies up to nine weeks following conception by blocking the action of progesterone (Fiala & Gemzel-Danielsson, 2006). Recall that progesterone is required to maintain the lining of the uterus. In the absence of progesterone, the uterus lining will shed, along with the implanted embryo, and the pregnancy will be terminated.

The concept of monthly menstruation as a natural part of the female experience has been questioned by Elsimar Coutinho (1999), the Brazilian physician who developed Depo-Provera. According to Coutinho, the number of lifetime menstrual cycles for the average woman has increased from 100 a century ago to over 400 today. Due to frequent pregnancies, reduced amounts of food, later puberty, and lengthy periods of breastfeeding infants, our female ancestors menstruated less frequently. We know that the risk of many reproductive cancers is reduced with each pregnancy. However, Coutinho argues that it is not the pregnancy that provides the protective benefit but the lack of ovulation, menstruation, and high estrogen levels associated with the menstrual cycle. To counteract the harm of greater estrogen exposure, the use

postpartum depression A condition in which mothers who have recently given birth experience feelings of depression due to their rapidly changing hormonal environment.

of uninterrupted cycles of birth control pills to reduce the frequency of menstruation has become an accepted medical practice (Edelman et al., 2005; Kwiecien, Edelman, Nichols, & Jensen, 2003).

Male Contraception

Breakthroughs in the area of male contraception have been slowed by perceptions on the part of the pharmaceutical industry that little market exists for male contraceptive alternatives, especially those that are associated with side effects. However, others argue that men want additional "control" and wish to participate more in reproductive decisions (Harper, 2008).

Beginning in ancient times, marijuana has been used to reduce fertility. The active ingredients of marijuana lower LH levels, contributing to reductions in both testosterone secretion and sperm production in men (Fronczak, Kim, & Barqawi, 2012). However, given the number of marijuana-using fathers, this is hardly a recommended method. Currently, the only methods of contraception available to men are condoms, withdrawal, and vasectomies.

A number of additional options designed to prevent male fertility are under investigation (Brown & Sorbera, 2013). Among the approaches currently being explored are birth control pills for men containing progestin (also a key ingredient in birth control pills for women), an "Intra Vas" device that physically blocks the movement of sperm, gels that damage sperm moving through the vas deferens, and pills that reduce a man's vitamin A levels and, consequently, his fertility (Aaltonen et al., 2007). Other medications under investigation block ejaculation without preventing orgasm and impact the viability of sperm.

estrus A regularly occurring period of sexual desire and fertility in some mammals.

Hormones and Adult Sexual Behavior

In the females of species that undergo **estrus**, a period of hours or days in which the female is receptive to males, hormones play an important role in determining the timing and frequency of sexual behavior. Estrus coincides with ovulation in many species, making the likelihood of fertilization quite high. During nonestrus periods, a female will not only reject sexual overtures from males, but she is also likely to respond aggressively to his advances. Only humans and Old World primates experience menstrual cycles, and their sexual activity is quite different from species that have seasonal mating patterns or estrus (Rushton et al., 2001).

SEXUAL INTEREST IN HUMAN FEMALES The sexual activity of human females, who do not display estrus, is under little if any control of the hormones involved with ovulation. Menopause and the surgical removal of the ovaries both exert a dramatic influence on a woman's hormone levels yet have little effect on her sexual interest and activity (Galyer, Conaglen, Hare, & Conaglen, 1999). Human females show receptivity throughout the menstrual cycle, although some women report feeling slightly more interest in sex around the time of ovulation (Slob, Bax, Hop, Rowland, & van der Werff ten Bosch, 1996). As shown in ● Figure 10.25, women near ovulation assessed the sexual orientation of men more accurately but showed no comparable improvement in their ability to assess the sexual orientation of other women (Rule, Rosen, Slepian, & Ambady, 2011).

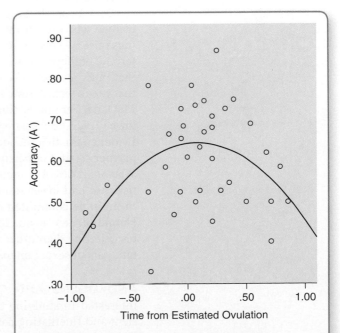

● **Figure 10.25** Accuracy in Judging Male Sexual Orientation as a Function of Fertility Status Women show the highest accuracy in detecting male sexual orientation when they are close to ovulation. There was no effect of the women's fertility status on their abilities to judge the sexual orientation of other women.

Source: Adapted from Rule et al. (2011).

A woman's testosterone levels have the greatest impact on her sexual activity. Women who receive standard estrogen replacement therapy following the surgical removal of their ovaries still report less satisfaction with their sex lives than before surgery (Kingsberg et al., 2007; Shifren et al., 2000). The estrogen therapy alone does not prevent negative changes in sexual interest. After the women were given testosterone through a skin patch, they reported having sex more frequently and enjoying it more. In addition, they scored higher on questionnaires of psychological well-being. Because women derive about half of their testosterone from the adrenal glands, adrenal disease can also have negative impacts on sexual behavior (Mazer, 2002). Not only do women show increased sexual interest when their testosterone levels are higher, but they also demonstrate a greater preference for "masculinity" in faces, voices, and behavioral displays (Welling et al., 2007).

SEXUAL INTEREST IN HUMAN MALES Male sexual frequency varies significantly from culture to culture, reminding us that hormones are just a part of the story. Subjective sexual well-being for both men and women depend on a number of factors, including relational satisfaction, relative equality between the sexes, mental and physical health, and the importance of sex to the individual (Laumann et al., 2006).

As long as a young human male's testosterone level falls within normal limits, it does not provide a strong predictor of his sexual frequency (Gray et al. 2005). However, the sexual frequency of older men is more closely correlated with their testosterone levels (ibid.). When testosterone is dramatically reduced below normal levels at any age, significant changes in male sexual behavior occur. MPA, or Depo-Provera, is used not only as a contraceptive method for women, but in larger and more frequent doses, as a form of chemical castration for male sex offenders (Berlin, 1997). MPA reduces circulating testosterone levels in men to pre-puberty levels, generally eliminating any sexual activity (Kravitz et al., 1995; Meyer, Cole, & Emory, 1992).

Men in stable, long-term marriages have lower testosterone levels than single men or men who are within a few years of divorce (Mazur & Michalek, 1998). These findings raise two possibilities. The first explanation is that being partnered reduces testosterone, perhaps due to lower levels of competition with other men for mates. The idea that one's reproductive situation impacts hormone levels is supported by the finding that men's testosterone levels drop significantly following the birth of a child (Gettler, McDade, Feranil, & Kuzawa, 2011). The second explanation suggests that men with lower levels of testosterone are more successful in maintaining stable relationships. Evidence for this second explanation was provided by a longitudinal study in which partnering and unpartnering did not impact men's testosterone levels (van Anders & Watson, 2006). A subsequent study found that men in a monogamous, committed relationship had lower testosterone levels than single men, and men who were involved in multiple committed relationships had the highest testosterone of all (van Anders, Hamilton, & Watson, 2007). Women in multiple committed relationships had higher testosterone than other women, emphasizing again that testosterone plays an important part in sexual interest for both males and females.

ANDROGENS AND COMPETITION One of the challenges facing researchers interested in studying the effects of adult sex hormones on behavior is their transient and fluctuating nature. Many environmental factors influence rapid changes in hormone levels.

Among both male and female collegiate athletes, testosterone levels appear to increase in anticipation of a competition (Booth, Shelley, Mazur, Tharp, & Kittok, 1989; Edwards & Casto, 2013). Following a competition, testosterone has been shown to increase further in the winners and decrease in the losers (Booth, Shelley, Mazur, Tharp, & Kittok, 1989). Simply observing a competition influences testosterone levels. Men cheering for the successful Brazilian soccer team at the 1994 World Cup competition experienced increases in testosterone, whereas men supporting the losing Italian team experienced a decrease (Bernhardt, Dabbs, Fielden, & Lutter, 1998).

Attraction, Romantic Love, Sexual Desire, and Parenting

Attraction is usually the territory of poets and artists, not neuroscientists. Although this might not be the most romantic approach to attraction that you have ever read, it will provide insight into why you swoon over Scarlett Johansson or Christian Bale. Viewing beautiful people appears to be quite rewarding. Young heterosexual men were observed with fMRI while looking at the faces of average men, average women, beautiful men, and beautiful women (Aharon et al., 2001). Viewing the faces of the beautiful women activated areas of the brain involved in pleasure and reward, including the nucleus accumbens, which also participates in addictive behavior (see Chapter 4). The men were also given the opportunity to press a lever to see pictures of beautiful women. The participants were willing to press the lever 6,000 times in an interval of 40 minutes, analogous to the amount of work rats are willing to do to obtain cocaine.

Cultures often have their own definitions of physical beauty, but this may not be the complete source of our opinions. A preference for beauty is evident at a very early age, before the media and other cultural factors have had a chance to influence perceptions. Judith Langlois and her colleagues (Langlois, Roggman, & Rieser-Danner, 1990) found that three- and six-month-old infants spend more time staring at faces adults had judged to be attractive than at faces judged to be unattractive.

Elements of Physical Attractiveness

What would these very young infants find so attractive? One possible factor is body symmetry, or the degree of similarity of one side of the face or body to the other (see ● Figure 10.26). Although some parts of our bodies are notably asymmetrical, such as the location of our heart toward the left side of our chest, most of our features are relatively symmetrical. Highly symmetrical bodies are generally healthier, and some researchers believe that we are programmed to select healthy mates. As a result, we view symmetry as attractive and beautiful. Symmetrical people have more opportunities for sexual activity (Thornhill & Gangestad, 1994). The influence of mating patterns in our preference for symmetry is supported by findings that symmetry appears to play a bigger role in the judgment of attractiveness in members of the opposite sex than in members of the same sex (Little, Jones, DeBruine, & Feinberg, 2008).

Beyond symmetry, we make distinctions in preferred features for males and females. The preference for these features could reflect a natural attraction to younger females, who are most likely to be fertile.

Women's responses to male features are not consistent. Some features are preferred in a short-term relationship (sexual desire) that are not preferred in long-term relationships (romantic love) (Diamond, 2004; Gonzaga, Turner, Keltner, Campos, & Altemus, 2006). Women seem to find masculine men, with their square jaws and other testosterone-related facial features, more attractive as "one night stands" than their less masculine counterparts. Evolutionary psychologists suggest that this attraction to masculine men results from the ability of women to recognize good genes. Testosterone is very hard on the immune system (Gaillard & Spinedi, 1998), so a man with features indicating high testosterone levels could not survive without an excellent immune system. In turn, this means that a woman's children would inherit an excellent immune system from such a father.

Balancing this attraction is women's association of negative characteristics with masculine features. Women believe that men with very masculine faces would be more dominant, less faithful, worse fathers, and have colder personalities than their more feminine looking counterparts (Boothroyd, Jones, Burt, & Perrett, 2007).

● **Figure 10.26** Attractive Faces Are Symmetrical People who are considered by others to be attractive, like actor Brad Pitt, typically have more symmetrical faces than people who have average looks. This photo of Pitt is overlaid with a mask based on the Fibonacci ratio, a mathematical principle that can be demonstrated in many living things that people see as beautiful. Although the mask doesn't fit exactly, it's close enough to help explain why Pitt is viewed as a handsome man.

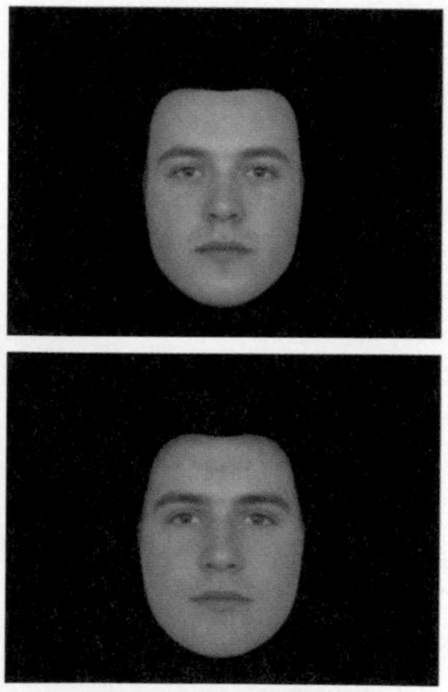

© DFree/Shutterstock.com

Detail from F. Moore et al, Figure 1, Composite male faces constructed to differ in levels of T and C, from the article "Evidence for the stress-linked immunocompetence handicap hypothesis in human male faces," Proc. R. Soc. B, March 7, 2011, © The Royal Society 2011

● **Figure 10.27** Female Preferences for Masculine Features Women prefer less masculine faces, like the one on the bottom, to more masculine faces, like the one on the top, when asked which man would make the best long-term partner.

major histocompatibility complex (MHC) gene A gene that encodes our immune system's ability to recognize intruders; might account for preferences for body odors.

Simply looking at photographs of men's faces, women were able to anticipate how a man would score on an infant interest questionnaire, a measure of how involved a father a man is likely to be (Penton-voak et al., 2007; Roney, Hanson, Durante, & Maestripieri, 2006). Consequently, women might prefer less masculine-looking men for long-term partnerships because these men are assumed to be less likely to be unfaithful and more willing to invest in parenting (see ● Figure 10.27). These findings are consistent with observations discussed earlier in the chapter that men with lower testosterone are more likely to be in long-term relationships.

Some attraction factors are less obvious than physical beauty. We might be programmed to prefer mates that smell a particular way. However, the use of floral and other pleasant scents by the perfume industry, not to mention the large deodorant industry, might be on the wrong track. Real sex appeal is probably based on sweat. McCoy and Pitino (2002) investigated the effects of underarm secretions of fertile, sexually active, heterosexual females. Compared with women wearing placebo scents, women who were wearing the underarm secretions reported significantly increased sexual activity. Wederkind and Füri (1997) asked participants to rate the smell of T-shirts worn over two consecutive nights according to sexiness, pleasantness, and intensity of smell. The participants showed distinct preferences for certain odors, especially those that reminded them of past or current lovers and that smelled distinctly different from their close relatives.

What accounts for these smell preferences? We seem to react to an aspect of the immune system that is reflected in body odor. **Major histocompatibility complex (MHC) genes** code for our immune system's ability to recognize intruders. It is to your advantage to find a mate whose MHC profile is as different as possible from your own because this will result in the best immune system possible for your children. Couples undergoing fertility treatment are more likely to have overlapping MHC profiles (Ho et al., 1994). This finding suggests that similar parental MHC profiles might interfere with conception or the viability of an embryo or fetus. As MHC profiles become more similar in young couples, women become less responsive to their partners, their number of extra-pair sexual partners increased, and their attraction to men other than their primary partners increased (Garver-Apgar, Gangestad, Thornhill, Miller, & Olp, 2006). Due to the reduction in sensitivity to odors in women using oral contraception, women using this method of contraception might be less capable of selecting partners on the basis of MHC profile (Roberts, Gosling, Carter, & Petrie, 2008).

Romantic Love and Sexual Desire

Particularly for adolescents and young adults, very few aspects of life reach the importance and confusion associated with romantic love, sexual activity, and long-term relationships. Romantic love involves the establishment and maintenance of long-term relationships, whereas sexual desire promotes mating and reproduction. A review of the fMRI literature pertaining to sexual desire and love suggests that they belong on a continuum, with the pleasant sensorimotor experiences associated with sexual desire leading to the development of more cognitive feelings of love (Cacioppo, Bianchi-Demicheli, Frum, Pfaus, & Lewis, 2012).

Romantic love produces characteristic patterns of activity in the human brain. While undergoing fMRI, participants were shown photographs of people they described as either friends or true loves (Bartels & Zeki, 2000). As shown in ● Figure 10.28, when participants viewed lovers, increased activity was observed in areas of the brain often associated with reward. Other areas became less active when participants viewed photographs of lovers. These areas are associated with negative emotions and social judgment. Consequently, "love" is not only rewarding, but it makes us less judgmental of the lover.

The bonding that is associated with romantic love is influenced by two closely related, yet sexually dimorphic pituitary hormones, **oxytocin** and vasopressin

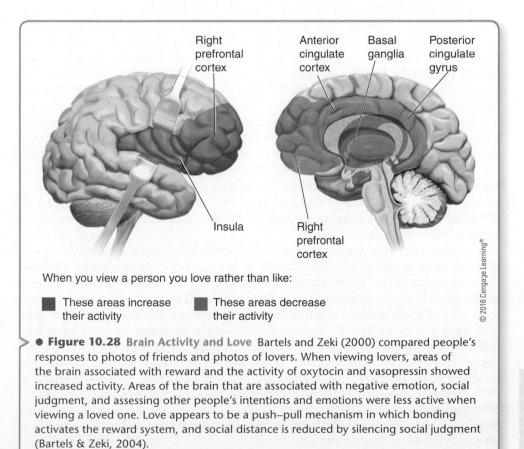

When you view a person you love rather than like:

■ These areas increase their activity   ■ These areas decrease their activity

© 2016 Cengage Learning®

● **Figure 10.28** Brain Activity and Love Bartels and Zeki (2000) compared people's responses to photos of friends and photos of lovers. When viewing lovers, areas of the brain associated with reward and the activity of oxytocin and vasopressin showed increased activity. Areas of the brain that are associated with negative emotion, social judgment, and assessing other people's intentions and emotions were less active when viewing a loved one. Love appears to be a push–pull mechanism in which bonding activates the reward system, and social distance is reduced by silencing social judgment (Bartels & Zeki, 2004).

oxytocin A hormone, released by the posterior pituitary gland, that stimulates uterine contractions, releases milk, and participates in social bonding, including romantic love and parenting behavior.

(also known as antidiuretic hormone or ADH; see Chapter 9). In addition to their effects elsewhere in the body, these hormones are active in the brain. Vasopressin is associated with mobilization and vigilance, while oxytocin is associated with immobility without fear (Carter & Porges, 2013). In the human brain, vasopressin receptors are expressed more by males and oxytocin receptors by females (Ishunina & Swaab, 1999; van Londen et al., 1997). For both sexes, oxytocin appears to enhance bonding. Reduced levels of oxytocin in people with autism spectrum disorder might account for the reduced sociability associated with this condition and might also explain why males with autism spectrum disorder vastly outnumber females (Marazziti & Dell'osso, 2008).

Oxytocin is released by the posterior pituitary gland into the circulation during orgasm for both sexes and during childbirth and breastfeeding in women. Women's oxytocin levels increase in response to a simple hug from their partners (Light, Grewen, & Amico, 2005). Couples with higher than average oxytocin levels report more physical intimacy and greater support from their partners (Gouin et al., 2010). When couples argued, oxytocin supplied in a nasal spray improved positive communication (Ditzen et al., 2009).

Reproduction and Parenting

Although it might seem unromantic, evolutionary psychologists maintain that an overriding goal of sexual behavior is the production of offspring who will survive to reproduce. According to this view, males and females, particularly among mammals, are subjected to different types of reproductive pressures. These pressures act to shape different sexual behaviors in males and females. Males are capable of producing many offspring over their lifespan, leading to overall reproductive strategies that reward behaving in less selective and more promiscuous ways. In terms of reproductive success, few men can compete with Genghis Khan (1162–1227). Approximately 16 million men living today, or about 0.5 percent of the world's population, are closely related to this Mongol emperor (Zerjal et al., 2003). The reproductive pressures on males to be promiscuous are offset by the advantages fathers provide by helping to raise offspring. To the extent that a father's exclusive presence provides a higher survival rate, we would expect more monogamous behavior from males.

For females, the costs of reproduction are quite high. Not only must she maintain a lengthy pregnancy, but the female also typically bears most of the responsibility for offspring until they are mature. As a result, we would expect females to be highly selective because the number of possible offspring is sharply limited by the amount of time and resources required to raise each to maturity. Females need to choose healthy mates to increase the chances that offspring will survive. **Monogamy**, the practice of having one mate at a time, would help the mother retain the protection and other benefits offered by a father.

To what extent are mating patterns and reproductive strategies biological in origin? For obvious ethical reasons, research on human beings in this area is difficult if not impossible to do. However, one clue comes from the study of the vole, a rather large rodent found in North America. Voles are useful in this context because they show very different mating patterns among similar species. The prairie vole (*Microtus ochrogaster*) is exclusively monogamous following a first mating experience, and males participate substantially in the raising of young. The very similar montane vole (*Microtus montanus*) is quite promiscuous, and the males do not interact with the offspring at all. Montane vole mothers are not very nurturant, either, and abandon their pups at a very early age. The key to these differences in vole behavior appears to be two hormones we met previously, oxytocin and vasopressin. Prairie voles have higher receptor densities in the brain for these hormones than do the montane voles, especially in the nucleus accumbens.

monogamy The custom of having one mate at a time or for life.

● **Figure 10.29** Maternal Oxytocin Levels Predict a Mother's Bonding to Her Infant A woman's oxytocin levels assessed in her second month of pregnancy reliably predict her later bonding behaviors directed at her infant, such as gazing, vocalizing, and touching (Feldman et al., 2007).

Epigenetic processes appear to account for the impact of mating on the prairie voles' monogamy (Wang, Duclot, Liu, Wang, & Kabbaj, 2013). Prairie voles housed together for six hours without the opportunity to mate were injected with drugs promoting the expression of genes for oxytocin and vasopressin receptors in the nucleus accumbens. The result was the same type of monogamous pair bonding found after the prairie voles mated. Mating activates the nucleus accumbens, leading to changes in oxytocin and vasopressin that enhance bonding.

Although much research must be done before we can generalize from voles to humans, researchers are moving in this direction (Bartz & Hollander, 2006). Interactions between oxytocin and vasopressin help parents to achieve a balance between care-taking and aggression designed to protect their young (Carter & Porges, 2013). A woman's oxytocin levels during pregnancy and following childbirth predicted maternal bonding behaviors, including gazing, affectionate touching of her infant, vocalizations, and positive mood (Feldman, Weller, Zagoory-Sharon, & Levine, 2007) (see ● Figure 10.29). In a circular fashion, the oxytocin levels of young adults who were not currently in romantic relationships were correlated with their reports of bonding to their parents (Gordon et al., 2008).

Sexual Dysfunction and Its Treatment

Sex therapists Masters and Johnson (1970) estimated that as many as half of all American couples experienced some type of sexual problem. Many of these difficulties are psychological in origin. However, in some other cases, the causes (and cures) are biological.

Many cases of sexual dysfunction in both men and women are associated with type 2 diabetes due to circulatory and neurological problems associated with the disease (Corona, Giorda, Cucinotta, Guida, & Nada, 2013; Cortelazzi et al., 2013). Due to the increases in cases of type 2 diabetes related to increasing obesity, this is becoming a more common problem. Rates of sexual dysfunction are also increasing due to the more frequent use of antidepressants (Taylor et al., 2013). One of the most common side effects of antidepressant medications is sexual dysfunction in both men and women.

Common forms of female sexual dysfunction include reduced sexual desire and orgasm problems. As mentioned previously, problems with sexual desire can be

●●● Building Better HEALTH

TREATING PATIENTS WITH ANTIDEPRESSANT-INDUCED SEXUAL DYSFUNCTION

Antidepressant use, particularly the use of selective serotonin reuptake inhibitors (SSRIs), negatively affects the entire sexual response cycle, from desire to arousal to orgasm (Strohmaier et al., 2011). The mechanisms through which SSRIs impact sexual dysfunction remain poorly understood. The numbers of patients affected by sexual dysfunction varies widely in published reports from 10 percent to 90 percent (Strohmaier et al., 2011). Because major depression itself (see Chapter 16) can lead to sexual dysfunction, it becomes challenging to know whether sexual dysfunction experienced by individual patients with depression being treated with SSRIs is due to the psychological disorder, the treatment, or some interaction between the two.

Researchers have attempted to find ways to address sexual dysfunction while maintaining good outcomes for the individual using an SSRI. An analysis of 23 studies using nearly 2,000 participants was conducted to compare pharmaceutical strategies for managing this situation (Taylor et al., 2013). Many of these studies suggested the addition of other medications, such as erectile dysfunction medications for men. Switching antidepressant medications appeared useful in a small number of cases. The authors noted that the literature in this area lacks randomized trials regarding the use of psychological or mechanical interventions or methods such as drug holidays. Given the importance of sexual satisfaction to overall well-being, additional research in this area would be very helpful.

alleviated by treatments that increase testosterone levels. A common type of sexual dysfunction in men is **erectile dysfunction**, which occurs when a man is unable to achieve an erection sufficient for satisfactory sexual activity. Approximately 30 million men in the United States experience some degree of erectile dysfunction, including about half the men between the ages of 40 and 70 years. Erections occur as a result of either direct stimulation or cognitive factors. Parasympathetic neurons in the sacral spinal cord respond to both mechanoreceptors in the genitals (direct stimulation) and descending input from the brain (cognitive factors). These parasympathetic neurons release acetylcholine (Ach) and nitric oxide (NO) into the spongy erectile tissues of the penis, which subsequently fill with blood. Medications used to treat erectile dysfunction promote erection by enhancing the effects of NO on the erectile tissues.

▌ INTERIM SUMMARY 10.3

▌ Summary Points

1. We may be preprogrammed to prefer certain physical characteristics in mates. **(LO5)**

2. Mating and parenting patterns are influenced by biological factors, including the activity of oxytocin and vasopressin. **(LO5)**

3. Sexual dysfunction results from a variety of situations, including relationship satisfaction, medical problems such as type 2 diabetes, and use of antidepressant medications **(LO6)**

▌ Review Questions

1. What physical features appear to be most attractive to males and to females, and how are these related to fertility and health?

2. What are the possible contributions of hormones to parenting behavior?

erectile dysfunction The inability to achieve and maintain an erection long enough for satisfactory sexual activity.

Chapter Review

THOUGHT QUESTIONS

1. If you were a physician who had just delivered a child with ambiguous external genitalia, how would you advise the child's parents?
2. Why do you think animals, including humans, would evolve a system in which their testosterone levels would fluctuate with winning and losing in competitive situations?

KEY TERMS

androgen (p. 330)

androgen insensitivity syndrome (AIS) (p. 330)

anti-Müllerian hormone (p. 330)

congenital adrenal hyperplasia (CAH) (p. 333)

estradiol (p. 334)

estrogen (p. 334)

external genitalia (p. 330)

5-alpha-reductase deficiency (p. 334)

follicle-stimulating hormone (FSH) (p. 334)

gender identity (p. 331)

gonadotropin-releasing hormone (GnRH) (p. 334)

gonads (p. 330)

intersex (p. 330)

interstitial nuclei of the anterior hypothalamus (INAH) (p. 340)

Klinefelter syndrome (p. 329)

luteinizing hormone (LH) (p. 334)

Müllerian system (p. 330)

ovaries (p. 330)

ovulation (p. 350)

oxytocin (p. 357)

progesterone (p. 351)

secondary sex characteristics (p. 333)

sex-determining region of the Y chromosome (SRY) (p. 330)

sexually dimorphic nucleus of the POA (SDN-POA) (p. 339)

testes (p. 330)

testis-determining factor (p. 330)

testosterone (p. 330)

Turner syndrome (p. 328)

Wolffian system (p. 330)

X chromosome (p. 326)

Y chromosome (p. 326)

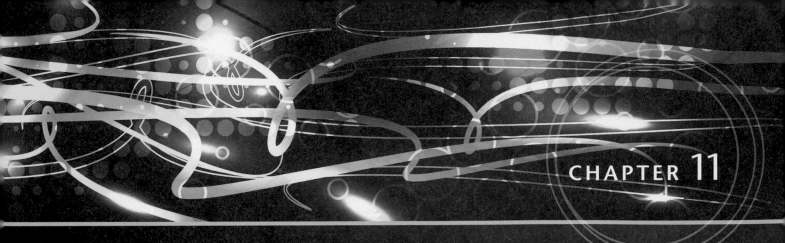

CHAPTER 11

Sleep and Waking

LEARNING OBJECTIVES

LO1 Differentiate between types of biological rhythms.

LO2 Describe the brain structures and neurochemicals that participate in the management of waking and sleep.

LO3 Analyze theories that explain the possible functions of sleep.

LO4 Describe the features, causes, and treatments of major types of sleep–wake disorders.

CHAPTER OUTLINE

CONNECTING TO RESEARCH: A Composite Scale of Morningness

THINKING ETHICALLY: Artificial Lighting and Circadian Rhythms

BUILDING BETTER HEALTH: Do Smartphone Sleep Apps Work?

BEHAVIORAL NEUROSCIENCE GOES TO WORK: Sleep Medicine

circadian rhythm A repeating cycle of about 24 hours.
ultradian cycle A cycle that occurs several times in a single day.
zeitgeber An external cue for setting biological rhythms.
free-running circadian rhythm A rhythm that is not synchronized to environmental time cues.
entrainment The resetting of internal biological clocks to the 24-hour cycle of the earth's rotation.

Biorhythms

Seasonal migrations, mating seasons, and the human menstrual cycle are just a few examples of behaviors that occur at regular intervals in response to internal, biological clocks. Our focus in this chapter is on the rhythms associated with sleep and waking (see ● Figure 11.1). Together, the interplay of sleep and waking cycles follow **circadian**, or daily, **rhythms**. The term *circadian* comes from the Latin words for "about a day." In addition, regular cycles of relative activation and quiet occur about every 90 to 120 minutes within the 24-hour day. These **ultradian cycles** are shown in ● Figure 11.2.

To establish and maintain these rhythms, internal biological clocks interact with stimuli known as **zeitgebers**. (*Zeit* means "time" in German; *geber* means "to give"; hence these are "time givers.") Light is the most important zeitgeber for human beings. In the absence of natural light, human **free-running circadian rhythms** last approximately 24.2 hours to 24.9 hours (Czeisler & Gooley, 2007; Sack, Brandes, Kendall, & Lewy, 2000). Exposure to sunlight each day helps reset, or **entrain**, the internal biological clock to the 24-hour cycle of the earth's rotation. Totally blind people and sailors on submarines experience free-running cycles that are longer than 24 hours, often resulting in severe sleep disruptions (Skene, Lockley, & Arendt, 1999; Kelly et al., 1999).

In addition to light, other zeitgebers include physical activity, feeding, body temperature, and sleep-related hormones discussed later in this chapter (Van Someren &

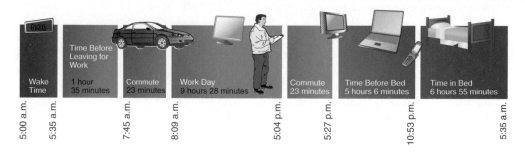

> ● **Figure 11.1 A Day in the Life of a Typical American Worker** Americans are believed to be somewhat sleep deprived because the average adult spends only 6 hours and 55 minutes in bed, which includes time needed to initiate sleep. Although people try to make up for lost sleep on weekends by sleeping longer, this is not a very effective solution.
>
> *Source:* Data from 2008 Omnibus Sleep in America Poll, National Sleep Foundation.

> ● **Figure 11.2 Ultradian Rhythms Characterize Wakefulness in Humans** Not only do our rapid eye movement (REM) cycles appear approximately every 90 to 120 minutes during sleep, but brain activity levels also ebb and flow in 90- to 120-minute intervals during wakefulness.
>
> *Source:* Adapted from Kaiser & Sterman (1994).

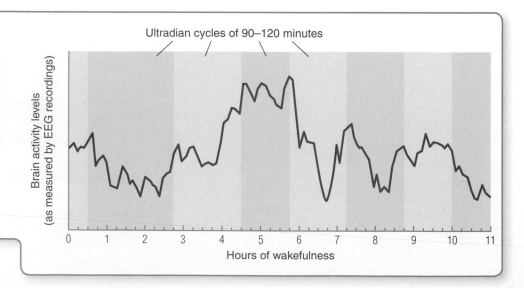

Riemersma-Van Der Lek, 2007; Whalley, 2013). When food is plentiful, light has the greatest impact on circadian rhythms, but when food is scarce, animals remain awake when food is available regardless of lighting conditions (Fuller, Lu, & Saper, 2008).

Individual Variations in Sleep Patterns

Do you have family members or roommates who wake up at the crack of dawn? Other people you know might have difficulty getting to sleep before midnight and struggle to awaken in time for work or school.

These individual sleep patterns result from different versions of the genes responsible for our internal clocks (Dijk & Lockley, 2002; Gottlieb, O'Connor, & Wilk, 2007). People who are most alert and productive in the morning have been referred to as "larks," whereas night people have been referred to as "night owls" (Akerstedt & Froberg, 1976). Many people fall somewhere between these two extremes. Adults with the lark pattern demonstrate more positive emotions and subjective well-being (Biss & Hasher, 2012).

••• Connecting to **Research**

A COMPOSITE SCALE OF MORNINGNESS

After reading about larks and owls, you might be curious about your own circadian status or "morningness." A number of morningness measures have been developed, but the following instrument is simple and widely cited (Smith, Reilly, & Midkiff, 1989). To complete the instrument, check the response that best describes you. When you're finished, add up the numbers next to your responses, and this will be your morningness score. We'll tell you how to interpret that score when you're finished.

1. Considering only your own "feeling best" rhythm, at what time would you get up if you were entirely free to plan your day?
   5:00–6:30 a.m. _____ (5)
   6:30–7:45 a.m. _____ (4)
   7:45–9:45 a.m. _____ (3)
   9:45–11:00 a.m. _____ (2)
   11:00 a.m.–12:00 (noon) _____ (1)

2. Considering your only "feeling best" rhythm, at what time would you go to bed if you were entirely free to plan your evening?
   8:00–9:00 p.m. _____ (5)
   9:00–10:15 p.m. _____ (4)
   10:15 p.m.–12:30 a.m. _____ (3)
   12:30–1:45 a.m. _____ (2)
   1:45–3:00 a.m. _____ (1)

3. Assuming normal circumstance, how easy do you find getting up in the morning? (Check one.)
   Not at all easy _____ (1)
   Slightly easy _____ (2)
   Fairly easy _____ (3)
   Very easy _____ (4)

4. How alert do you feel during the first half hour after having awakened in the morning? (Check one.)
   Not at all alert _____ (1)
   Slightly alert _____ (2)
   Fairly alert _____ (3)
   Very alert _____ (4)

5. During the first half hour after having awakened in the morning, how tired do you feel? (Check one.)
   Very tired _____ (1)
   Fairly tired _____ (2)
   Fairly refreshed _____ (3)
   Very refreshed _____ (4)

6. You have decided to engage in some physical exercise. A friend suggests that you do this one hour twice a week and the best time for him is 7:00–8:00 a.m. Bearing in mind nothing else but your own "feeling best" rhythm, how do you think you would perform?
   Would be in good form _____ (4)
   Would be in reasonable form _____ (3)
   Would find it difficult _____ (2)
   Would find it very difficult _____ (1)

7. At what time in the evening do you feel tired and, as a result, in need of sleep?
   8:00–9:00 p.m. _____ (5)
   9:00–10:15 p.m. _____ (4)
   10:15 p.m.–12:30 a.m. _____ (3)
   12:30–1:45 a.m. _____ (2)
   1:45–3:00 a.m. _____ (1)

8. You wish to be at your peak performance for a test that you know is going to be mentally exhausting and lasting for two hours. You are entirely free to plan your day, and considering only your own

(continued)

••• Connecting to **Research**

A COMPOSITE SCALE OF MORNINGNESS (*Continued*)

"feeling best" rhythm, which ONE of the four testing times would you choose?

8:00–10:00 a.m. _____ (4)
11:00 a.m.–1:00 p.m. _____ (3)
3:00–5:00 p.m. _____ (2)
7:00–9:00 p.m. _____ (1)

9. One hears about "morning" and "evening" types of people. Which ONE of these types do you consider yourself to be?

Definitely a morning type _____ (4)
More a morning than an evening type _____ (3)
More an evening than a morning type _____ (2)
Definitely an evening type _____ (1)

10. When would you prefer to rise (provided you have a full day's work—8 hours) if you were totally free to arrange your time?

Before 6:30 a.m. _____ (4)
6:30–7:30 a.m. _____ (3)
7:30–8:30 a.m. _____ (2)
8:30 a.m. or later _____ (1)

11. If you always had to rise at 6:00 a.m., what do you think it would be like?

Very difficult and unpleasant _____ (1)
Rather difficult and unpleasant _____ (2)
A little unpleasant but no great problem _____ (3)
Easy and not unpleasant _____ (4)

12. How long a time does it usually take before you "recover your senses" in the morning after rising from a night's sleep?

0–10 minutes _____ (4)
11–20 minutes _____ (3)
21–40 minutes _____ (2)
More than 40 minutes _____ (1)

13. Please indicate to what extent you are a morning or evening *active* individual.

Pronounced morning active (morning alert and evening tired) _____ (4)
To some extent, morning active _____ (3)
To some extent, evening active _____ (2)
Pronounced evening active (morning tired and evening alert) _____ (1)

TOTAL POINTS: _____

If you scored 22 or less, you are an evening type and if you scored 44 or more, you are a morning type. Scores of 23–43 are considered intermediate. Do you agree with your results? If not, what changes would you recommend for the instrument?

Nearly everyone acts like an owl during adolescence (Carskadon, Acebo, & Jenni, 2004; Crowley, Acebo, & Carskadon, 2007; Taylor, Jenni, Acebo, & Carskadon, 2005). Teen sleep patterns might reflect a dramatic drop in melatonin, one of the neurochemicals involved in the regulation of sleep patterns, at the onset of puberty (Molina-Carballo et al., 2007; Yun, Bazar, & Lee, 2004). Following adolescence, many temporary owls will revert to their previous state, possibly due to the maturation of neural systems that regulate sleep. In fact, some researchers view the return to a previous sleep pattern in young adulthood as a reliable indication that the brain is now fully mature (Roenneberg et al., 2005). Regardless of the origins of adolescent owl behavior, accommodations can be useful. Shifting from a 7:15 a.m. start time to an 8:40 a.m. start time improved both attendance and student grades at Minnesota high schools (Wahlstrom, 2003).

Shift Work, Jet Lag, and Daylight Saving Time

When demands of employment conflict with workers' natural circadian rhythms, the result can be poor health for the worker, and greater danger to the public served by the worker.

Some employees, such as those working in hospitals, in public safety, or in convenience stores, work evening or night shifts. Between 40 and 80 percent of workers on the 11 p.m. to 7:30 a.m. night shift experience disturbed sleep and a cluster of symptoms referred to as **shift maladaptation syndrome** (Wagner, 1996). These workers

shift maladaptation syndrome
A condition resulting in health, personality, mood, and interpersonal problems resulting from sleep disruption due to shift work.

obtain 1.5 hours less total sleep than workers on other shifts, leading to frequent health, personality, mood, and interpersonal problems. Accident rates in the 3 p.m. to 11:30 p.m. shift are higher than in the 7 a.m. to 3:30 p.m. day shift and higher still during the 11 p.m. to 7:30 a.m. shift (Hänecke, Tiedemann, Nachreiner, & Grzech-Sukalo, 1998). Night shift workers are more likely than other workers to develop breast cancer (Davis & Mirick, 2006; Kolstad, 2008).

Shift workers are not only a risk to themselves, but their errors also jeopardize the public. Hospital workers, such as nurses, are much more likely to make significant errors such as providing the wrong prescription or dose during evening or night shifts than during day shifts (Narumi et al., 1999). Response to shift work interacts with the individual differences discussed previously. Larks appear to be more disrupted by shift work than owls (Arendt, 2010), a fact that both employers and employees should consider.

Conflicts between internal clocks and external zeitgebers also result in the unsettling experience of **jet lag**. After crossing time zones, people often experience fatigue, irritability, and sleepiness. The travel itself is not to blame, because north–south travel of equal distance does not produce the symptoms of jet lag (Herxheimer & Waterhouse, 2003). Chronic jet lag might have more serious consequences. Airline flight attendants who crossed time zones at least once a week for four or more years had reduced reaction times and made 9 percent more mistakes on memory tasks than local crews who did not cross time zones (Cho, Ennaceur, Cole, & Suh, 2000).

Not all changes in time zone have equal effects. People adjust more readily when travel or changes in shift work require staying up later and sleeping later. In other words, it is easier to adjust to a phase-delay of our cycle (setting the clock to a later point) than to a phase-advance (setting the clock to an earlier point). As shown in ● Figure 11.3, a New Yorker traveling to Los Angeles goes to bed three hours later

jet lag Fatigue, irritability, and sleepiness resulting from travel across time zones.

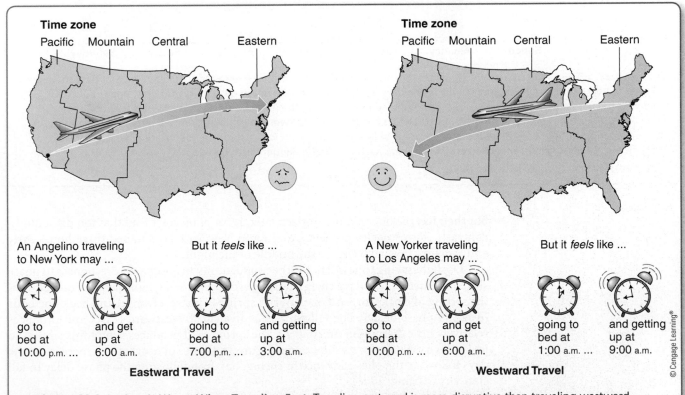

> ● **Figure 11.3** Jet Lag Is Worse When Traveling East Traveling eastward is more disruptive than traveling westward. The Los Angeles resident arriving in New York feels like he or she is going to bed three hours earlier than usual (7 p.m. Los Angeles time) and waking up in the middle of the night (3 a.m. Los Angeles time). The New Yorker traveling to Los Angeles has to stay up a little later (1 a.m. New York time) but then can sleep later to compensate (9 a.m. New York time). Most people find the latter scenario much easier.

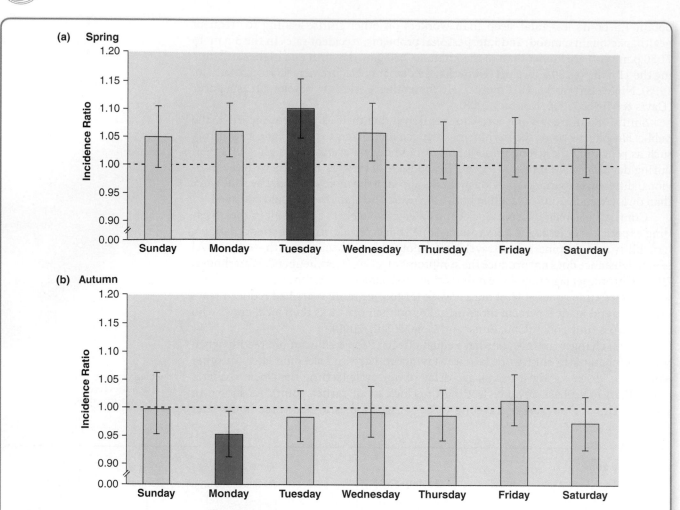

● **Figure 11.4 The Daylight Saving Change in Spring Correlates with More Heart Attacks** Fifteen years of data show that (a) rates of heart attack increase significantly in the days following the spring shift in daylight saving time, and (b) decrease following the fall shift. The "incidence ratio" is computed by comparing the number of heart attacks on the specified day following the shift to the mean number of heart attacks for the same day two weeks before and two weeks after the shift. An incidence ratio of 1.00 means there is no difference. The likely reason for the increase is sleep deprivation, which increases sympathetic nervous system activation and inflammation, which can be dangerous to people with existing health problems.

Source: Adapted from Janszky and Ljung (2008).

but then has the opportunity to sleep later. Most of us don't find that too difficult. In contrast, a Los Angeles resident traveling to New York goes to bed three hours early and awakens in what feels like the middle of the night.

Daylight saving time offers another opportunity to observe our responses to phase shifts. Created to help save energy during World War I, daylight saving time requires the setting of clocks forward one hour in spring (a phase advance) and back one hour in fall (a phase delay). The fall shift is equivalent to westward travel and produces relatively little disruption. In contrast, the spring shift produces symptoms similar to jet lag for a day or two. As shown in ● Figure 11.4, rates of heart attack increase in the days following the phase advance in spring, but drop following the phase delay in fall (Janszky & Ljung, 2008).

The Body's Internal Clocks Manage Circadian Rhythms

suprachiasmatic nucleus (SCN) An area of the hypothalamus located above the optic chiasm; responsible for maintaining circadian rhythms.

The body's internal master clock is the **suprachiasmatic nucleus (SCN)** in the hypothalamus, shown in ● Figure 11.5 (Moore & Eichler, 1972; Stephan & Zucker, 1972). The term *suprachiasmatic* comes from the structure's location above (*supra*) the

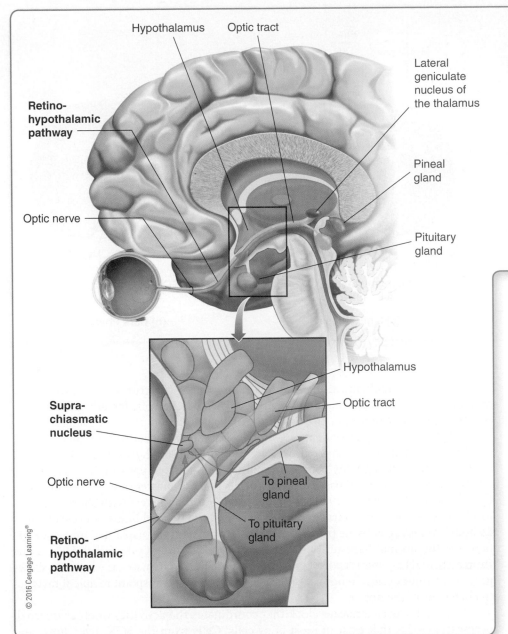

Hypothalamus   Optic tract

Lateral geniculate nucleus of the thalamus

Retino-hypothalamic pathway

Pineal gland

Optic nerve

Pituitary gland

Hypothalamus

Optic tract

Supra-chiasmatic nucleus

Optic nerve

To pineal gland

To pituitary gland

Retino-hypothalamic pathway

© 2016 Cengage Learning®

● **Figure 11.5** The Suprachiasmatic Nucleus The suprachiasmatic nucleus (SCN) is well situated to serve as the body's master internal clock. Its proximity to the optic nerves provides necessary information regarding environmental light. Its links to other parts of the hypothalamus and to the pituitary and pineal glands allow the SCN to influence rhythmic behaviors by controlling the release of hormones.

optic chiasm. Axons of special cells known as **intrinsically photosensitive retinal ganglion cells (ipRGCs)**, leave the optic nerve and project to the SCN, forming the **retinohypothalamic pathway** (Güler et al., 2008). Unlike other retinal ganglion cells (see Chapter 6), the ipRGCs do not process information about visual images. The ipRGCs contain a photopigment known as **melanopsin** that is related to, but different from, the other photopigments involved in vision (Brown & Robinson, 2004; Güler et al., 2008).

The SCN is active only during the day (Schwartz & Gainer, 1977; Schwartz, Reppert, Eagan, & Moore-Ede, 1983) (see ● Figure 11.6). This is true regardless of whether a species is diurnal (awake during the day), like monkeys, or nocturnal (awake at night), like rats. The SCN helps animals distinguish between day and night, but other structures dictate whether an animal is nocturnal or diurnal in its behavior. Activity in the human SCN produces a response in the sympathetic nervous system (see Chapter 2), which in turn communicates with the pineal gland (see ● Figure 11.5). As light decreases in the evening, the pineal gland synthesizes and releases more

intrinsically photosensitive retinal ganglion cells (ipRGC) Retinal cells that do not process information about visual images, but rather provide light information to the suprachiasmatic nucleus.

retinohypothalamic pathway A pathway leading from the retina of the eye to the hypothalamus; provides light information necessary for the maintenance of circadian rhythms.

melanopsin A photopigment used by ipRGCs.

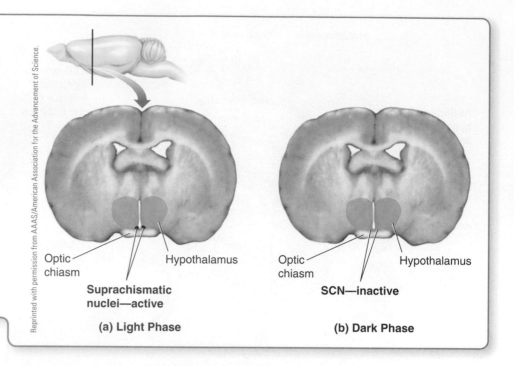

● **Figure 11.6** The SCN Is Active During the Day In the image on the left (a), the SCN (colored red) is active during the rat's light phase. These areas are not active in the image on the right (b), which represents the rat's dark phase. The SCN perceives the difference between day and night but does not dictate whether an animal is nocturnal or diurnal in its behavior.

Source: Schwartz and Gainer (1977). From "Suprachiasmatic nucleus: use of 14C-labeled deoxyglucose uptake as a functional marker," by W.J. Schwartz and H. Gainer, *Science* 1977 (197):1089–1091.

Reprinted with permission from AAAS/American Association for the Advancement of Science.

Optic chiasm   Hypothalamus

Suprachismatic nuclei—active

(a) Light Phase

Optic chiasm   Hypothalamus

SCN—inactive

(b) Dark Phase

melatonin, a neurochemical that modulates brainstem structures related to waking and sleep. The SCN also manages other sleep-related changes, including body temperature, hormone secretion, production of urine, and blood pressure changes.

The SCN is not dependent on input from other structures to maintain its rhythms. Isolated SCN tissue cultures continued to show rhythmic fluctuations in activity consistent with the source animal's previous day–night cycle (Ding et al., 1994). Transplants of SCN tissue also support its role as a master internal clock (Ralph, Foster, Davis, & Menaker, 1990). It is possible to breed hamsters with short free-running cycles of about 20 hours, in comparison with the normal hamster cycle of about 24 hours. When SCN tissue from a short-period hamster is transplanted into a normal hamster, the normal hamster shows the short free-running cycle. When SCN tissue from a normal hamster is transplanted into a short-period hamster, the hamster shows normal 24-hour cycles. In both cases, the behavior of the transplant recipient matches the behavior of the donor.

The SCN acts as a master clock that coordinates the activities of other internal, peripheral clocks that exist in most body cells. Cells from the SCN, liver, lung, and muscle of rats were observed following six-hour phase shifts in the rats' light–dark schedules (Yamazaki et al., 2000). The SCN adjusted to the new time after only one or two cycles of light and dark, but peripheral clocks in the other tissues were much slower to respond. Lung and muscle tissue required 6 cycles to adjust to the new time, and the liver required more than 16 cycles. The effects of phase shifts on muscles, lungs, and other tissues appear to last long after the initial discomfort is gone.

The rhythms of the SCN are heavily influenced by information about light provided by the retinohypothalamic pathway. In contrast, the peripheral clocks are more easily influenced by daily feeding cycles (Mendoza, 2007). Abrupt changes in feeding patterns, such as feeding nocturnal mice during the day only, can reset the animals' circadian rhythms by influencing these peripheral clocks (Hirota & Fukada, 2004). Many travelers attempt to compensate for jet lag by immediately adjusting their mealtimes to their current time zone.

melatonin An indoleamine secreted by the pineal gland that participates in the regulation of circadian rhythms.

THE CELLULAR BASIS OF CIRCADIAN RHYTHMS How can a structure like the SCN tell time? The answer lies in the oscillation of protein production and degradation within a cell, illustrated in ● Figure 11.7. The ebbing and flowing of special circadian

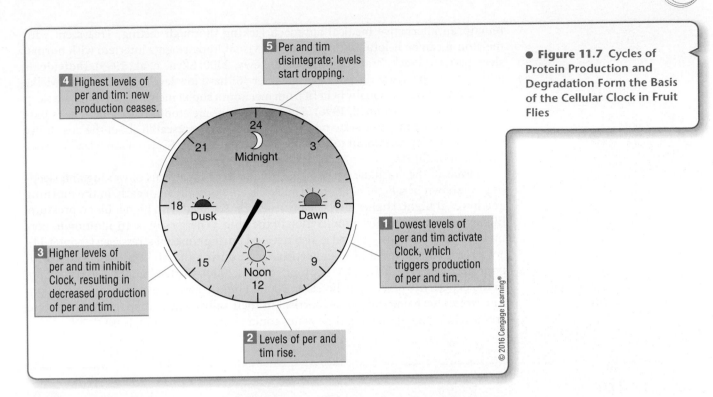

Figure 11.7 Cycles of Protein Production and Degradation Form the Basis of the Cellular Clock in Fruit Flies

5 Per and tim disintegrate; levels start dropping.

4 Highest levels of per and tim: new production ceases.

1 Lowest levels of per and tim activate Clock, which triggers production of per and tim.

3 Higher levels of per and tim inhibit Clock, resulting in decreased production of per and tim.

2 Levels of per and tim rise.

© 2016 Cengage Learning®

proteins require approximately 24 hours. Research with fruit flies (*Drosophila melanogaster*) has allowed researchers to identify three separate genes and their protein products that are involved with cellular circadian rhythms. These genes and their proteins are *per* (for *period*; Konopka & Benzer, 1971), *tim* (for *timeless*; Sehgal, Price, Man, & Young, 1994), and *Clock* (for *circadian locomotor output cycles kaput*; Vitaterna et al., 1994). Together, per and tim proteins inhibit the Clock protein, whereas the Clock protein promotes the production of more per and tim proteins. As levels of per and tim proteins increase, inhibition of the Clock protein ensures that no further per and tim proteins will be produced. When levels of per and tim proteins drop over time, the reduced inhibition of the Clock protein results in increased production of per and tim proteins. Neural activity reflects the oscillation of the levels of these internal proteins, providing a mechanism for communicating rhythms to other cells.

Similar processes involving additional circadian genes and proteins occur in mice and other mammals, including humans (Huang, Ramsey, Marcheva, & Bass, 2011; Paquet, Rey, & Naef, 2008). Clock genes in humans appear to be implicated in schizophrenia and depression (see Chapter 16; Kishi et al., 2009).

THE BIOCHEMISTRY OF CIRCADIAN RHYTHMS As we mentioned earlier, the SCN regulates the release of the hormone melatonin from the pineal gland. Lesions of the SCN abolish the circadian release of melatonin, demonstrating the dependence of the pineal gland on input from the SCN.

Melatonin levels are very low during the day, begin to rise in the hours before sleep, and usually peak at about 4 a.m., a time when nearly everybody finds it very difficult to stay awake (Aeschbach et al., 2003). Totally blind individuals experience a melatonin peak at a different time each day, often leading to sleep difficulties. People with pineal gland tumors or other medical conditions affecting melatonin report sleep problems (Haimov & Lavie, 1996). Melatonin release is suppressed by light (Lewy, Wehr, Goodwin, Newsome, & Markey, 1980). Although bright lights are more likely to suppress melatonin, dimmer lights typical of indoor lighting and electronic devices, including tablets and phones, also have the ability to suppress production and release (Duffy & Wright, 2005).

Melatonin supplements have been reported to improve cases of jet lag, shift maladaptation syndrome, and other sleep disorders (Hardeland et al., 2008). Adverse reactions to melatonin are rare, but we should recognize that melatonin supplements remain an alternative medical approach lacking thorough testing. Treatment with melatonin can be helpful in cases in which visual impairments interfere with normal sleep patterns (Sack, Brandes, Kendall, & Lewy, 2000; Skene et al., 1999). Individuals with autism spectrum disorder (see Chapter 16) have low levels of melatonin (Melke et al., 2007) and occasionally benefit from melatonin supplements to help regulate sleep patterns (Jan & O'Donnell, 1996). The existence of melatonin receptors in cells participating in the immune system has led to considerable research about the possibility of administering melatonin to improve immune function (Calvo, González-Yanes, & Maldonado, 2013).

Levels of the hormone **cortisol** also fluctuate with patterns of waking and sleeping. As shown in ● Figure 11.8, cortisol levels are normally high early in the morning and lower at night. Higher levels of cortisol are associated with higher blood pressure, higher heart rate, and the mobilization of the body's energy stores. In addition to normal daily fluctuations, cortisol is also released during times of stress (see Chapter 14). As a result, stress-induced high cortisol levels during the night are correlated with poor sleep quality (van Cauter, Leproult, & Plat, 2000). Cortisol might also contribute to the experience of jet lag (Cho et al., 2000). Flight crews who cross more than eight time zones have one third more cortisol in their saliva when compared with ground crews. The stress of crossing time zones could stimulate cortisol release.

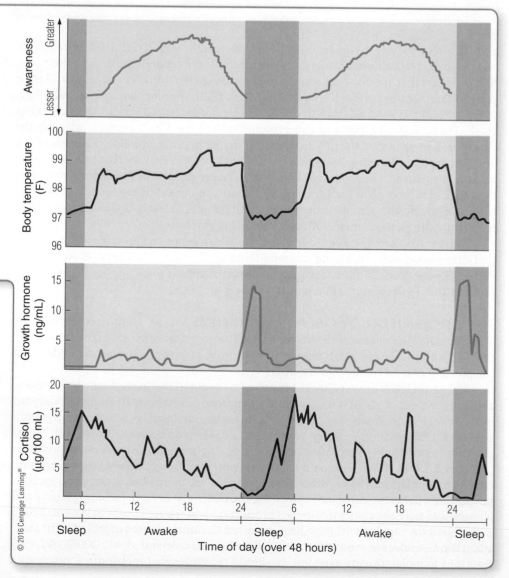

● **Figure 11.8** Body Temperature and Hormone Secretions Follow Circadian Rhythms Over the course of two days, we can see that body temperature and alertness are positively correlated. Growth hormone is released primarily during stages 3 and 4 of non-rapid eye movement (NREM) sleep, whereas cortisol levels are highest first thing in the morning and decrease during the day.

Source: Adapted from Coleman (1986).

cortisol A hormone released by the adrenal glands that promotes arousal.

••• THINKING *Ethically*

ARTIFICIAL LIGHTING AND CIRCADIAN RHYTHMS

Discovery of inexpensive, artificial light sources about 100 years ago changed the light environment for many of the earth's inhabitants. By 2001, 62 percent of the world's population, including 99 percent of the population of Europe and the United States, became exposed regularly to night light greater than nights with a full moon (Cinzano, Falchi, & Elvidge, 2001) (see ● Figure 11.9). Less than one hour of exposure to artificial lighting, especially the new forms featuring short-wave or blue light (including fluorescent lights and phone and tablet screens), can produce as much as a 50 percent reduction in circulating melatonin levels (Pauley, 2004). As you have learned in this chapter, melatonin provides one of the key signals for the maintenance of circadian rhythms.

Should we be worried? Changes in melatonin release have been implicated in coronary heart disease, oxidative stress, decreased immune function, and cancer in humans and animals (Navara & Nelson, 2007). In particular, breast cancer appears linked to exposure to artificial light (Schernhammer & Schulmeister, 2004). Night shift workers have higher rates of breast cancer than workers on other shifts. This effect probably arises from melatonin's contributions to immune system function and its ability to suppress estrogen synthesis (Dopfel, Schulmeister, & Schernhammer, 2007).

Given that we can hardly escape the constant night lighting of our environment, what steps can we take to minimize its potential for negative health consequences? Efforts to move back to more reddish (long wave) standard light bulbs, which have less impact on melatonin, from the popular energy-saving compact fluorescent lights, which emit more blue (short wave)

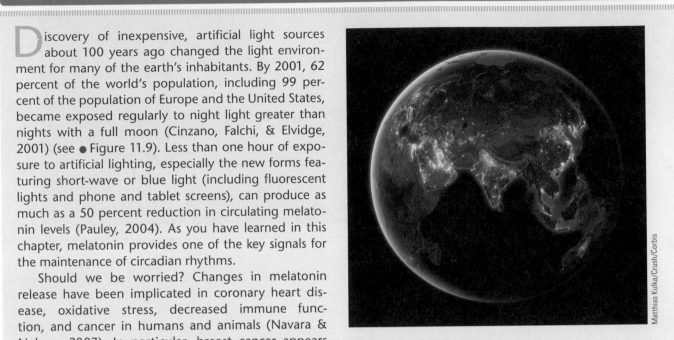

● **Figure 11.9 Artificial Light Seen from Space**
Exposure to artificial light is part of living in industrialized nations. The implications of this relatively recent invention for health are still not completely understood.

Matthias Kulka/Crush/Corbis

light, is unlikely due to concerns about climate change and energy costs. Fortunately, ongoing research points to other correlations between low melatonin levels and lifestyle factors that are, in fact, under our control. High body mass index (BMI; see Chapter 9) and smoking are also linked to low melatonin levels (Schernhammer, Kroenke, Dowsett, Folkerd, & Hankinson, 2006), suggesting that maintaining a healthy weight and avoiding smoking could be helpful in offsetting some negative effects of artificial lighting.

Major Depressive Disorder with Seasonal Pattern

During the winter months at higher latitudes (areas closer to the poles of the earth), the reduction in daylight hours can interfere with circadian rhythms leading to **major depressive disorder with seasonal pattern** (American Psychiatric Association, 2013). Prior to publication of the *Diagnostic and Statistical Manual of Mental Disorders* (DSM-5; APA, 2013), patients with this condition were diagnosed with seasonal affective disorder (SAD). Rates of seasonal depression vary from 1.4 percent in Florida to 9.7 percent in New Hampshire (Modell et al., 2005).

Several mechanisms appear to lead to seasonal depression. Serotonin levels typically drop in the fall and winter, and people vulnerable to seasonal depression might experience a greater than normal decrease, (Jepson, Ernst, & Kelly, 1999) (see Chapter 16). Seasonal depression might also be influenced by disruptions in melatonin release caused

major depressive disorder with seasonal pattern A type of depression that results from insufficient amounts of daylight during the winter months; formerly known as seasonal affective disorder (SAD).

● **Figure 11.10** Light Therapy Can Help Reset Circadian Rhythms Light therapy is available for free to travelers at Charles de Gaulle Airport in Paris, France. Although we don't know for certain if this will reduce jet lag, light therapy is a standard treatment for major depressive disorder with seasonal pattern.

Horizons WWP/Alamy

by uneven patterns of daily light (Levitan, 2007). Serotonin not only serves as a precursor for melatonin synthesis in the pineal gland, but its own synthesis is activated by light (Danilenko & Levitan, 2012). Variations in the genes that express melanopsin, the photopigment found in ipRGCs, appear to predispose individuals to seasonal depression (Roecklein et al., 2013). As a result of their melanopsin genes, some people are less sensitive to light in general. The paler light of winter is insufficient for maintaining their normal circadian patterns, leading to circadian disruption and depression.

Seasonal depression is treated by exposure to bright lights, with or without melatonin and antidepressants (see ●Figure 11.10). Although the light used in therapy (2,500 lux) is much stronger than what is normally experienced indoors (100 lux), it is more like the light on an overcast day than the light at the beach on an August afternoon (10,000 lux). Light therapy administered at dawn corrects cases in which people stay up too late, whereas light therapy in the evening helps people who are sleepy too early (Lewy, 2007).

Not all populations living at high latitudes experience seasonal depression frequently. Magnusson, Axelsson, Karlsson, and Oskarsson (2000) reported that Icelanders experience no more frequent or severe symptoms of depression during winter than during summer. The Icelanders might enjoy protective genetic influences. Compared to white Canadians living at the same latitudes, whose ancestors immigrated to Canada within the past 400 years or less, Icelanders experience lower rates of seasonal depression (Axelsson, Stefánsson, Magnússon, Sigvaldason, & Karlsson, 2002). Seasonal depression might be more prevalent among those who move from a location with more daylight to one with less, compared to people who experience constant low levels of light.

INTERIM SUMMARY 11.1

‖ Summary Points

1. Daily or circadian rhythms respond to both internal signals and external zeitgebers. Ultradian rhythms occur several times within a single day. **(LO1)**

2. The body's internal master clock is the suprachiasmatic nucleus (SCN), which receives information about light via the retinohypothalamic pathway. **(LO2)**

3. Some biochemicals, such as melatonin and cortisol, show circadian patterns of activity. **(LO2)**

Review Questions

1. How do shift work, jet lag, and daylight saving time affect our normal circadian rhythms?
2. What is the basis for the rhythmicity observed in the SCN?

Neural Correlates of Waking and Sleep

For many years, sleep was viewed as an absence of activity. Nothing could be further from the truth. Both waking and sleep are active processes that are carefully choreographed by the brain. These states are not simply the results of activity in "waking" or "sleep" centers but, rather, involve reciprocal circuits of excitation and inhibition. For example, waking not only results from excitation in some parts of the brain but also requires the active inhibition of sleep.

Electroencephalogram Recordings of Waking and Sleep

We can evaluate waking and sleep using electroencephalogram (EEG) recordings. As we observed in Chapter 1, the EEG provides a general measure of overall brain activity. **Desynchronous** brain activity arises from the relatively independent action of many neurons and is correlated with alertness. **Synchronous** activity occurs when neurons are firing more in unison and characterizes deep stages of sleep. Consider the contrast between a typical afternoon of activity at the community swimming pool (desynchronous) and the actions of a team of synchronized swimmers (synchronous).

As shown in ● Figure 11.11, recording the activity of sleeping people is not easy. Volunteers must sleep with scalp electrodes for EEG recordings. Sleep is also correlated with changes in muscle and autonomic nervous system activity. To capture these events, participants are outfitted with electrodes near their eyes to measure eye movement and additional electrodes to measure heart rate and muscular tension. They are observed and filmed through a two-way mirror. Fortunately, most sleep research has been done in university settings with student volunteers, and, apparently, students can manage to sleep under the most trying conditions.

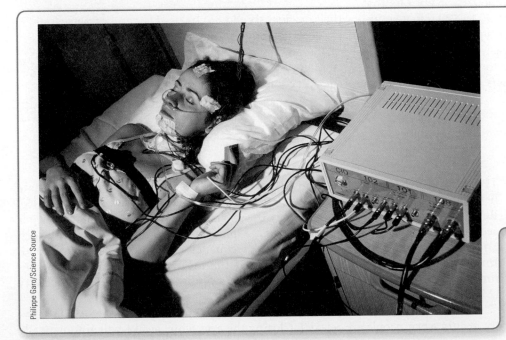

Philippe Garo/Science Source

● **Figure 11.11** Sleep Research Involves Multiple Measurements Participants in sleep experiments are wired with scalp electrodes for EEG, electrodes around the eyes to measure eye movement, and electrodes on their major postural muscles. As if that weren't enough, they are being observed and probably filmed through a two-way mirror by researchers.

desynchronous Brain activity associated with independent action of many neurons and alertness.
synchronous Brain activity associated with neurons firing in unison and deep sleep.

••• Building Better HEALTH

DO SMARTPHONE SLEEP APPS WORK?

You might have seen news reports or advertisements for apps for your smartphone that track your "sleep quality." Do these work? What exactly do they tell you?

The smartphone sleep quality apps take advantage of the built-in accelerometer technology contained in your phone (see ● Figure 11.12). These sensors tell the phone how it is being moved and tilted so that the screen display can shift appropriately from horizontal to vertical depending on how the phone is being held. On a small scale, this is the same technology that makes Nintendo's Wii controller work. Information about tilt and direction of movement are fed into the game console and translated into movements on the screen. Developers realized that they could take advantage of the accelerometer in the phones to track body movements during sleep.

When they were first released, the apps were marketed as a means to wake you up gently. Based on movement recordings, they would set off your alarm within a 30-minute window of time during periods where you appeared to be more lightly asleep. Eventually, the apps branched into measures of time in bed and sleep quality.

What is the "sleep quality" that is being measured? As you have seen in this chapter, movement does correlate with the differences between rapid eye movement or REM sleep (where you are paralyzed, but with slight twitches of the extremities) and non-rapid eye movement or NREM sleep (where your muscles become progressively more relaxed in deeper stages but you are capable of movement) (Krejcar, Jirka, & Janckulik, 2011). In samples shared by the developers, it appears that their trackings approximate the 90 to 120 minute ultradian cycles that we would expect to see during sleep.

A phone app is highly unlikely to substitute for the careful analysis performed in a formal sleep laboratory, however, and the app developers are careful to say that

● **Figure 11.12 Do Sleep Apps Work?** Sleep apps for smartphones take advantage of the built-in movement detectors the phones use to adjust your screen orientation as you move the phone in your hand. What can movement tell you about your stages of sleep and sleep quality?

their product should not be used in cases of pathological sleep. It would be interesting to compare the results of the app to a sleep analysis conducted in a formal laboratory to see more precisely what the phone apps can and cannot do.

---

beta wave A brain waveform having 14 to 30 cycles per second, associated with high levels of alertness during wakefulness.

alpha wave A brain waveform having 8 to 13 cycles per second, associated with less alertness and more relaxation than beta activity during wakefulness.

gamma band activity A brain waveform having more than 30 cycles per second, associated with the processing of sensory input.

THE EEG DURING WAKING During waking, EEG recordings typically alternate between **beta wave** and **alpha wave** patterns of brain activity (see ● Figure 11.13). Beta activity is characterized by highly desynchronized, rapid (14 to 30 cycles per second), irregular, low-amplitude waves. Alpha waves are slightly slower, larger, and more regular than beta waves, with a frequency of 8 to 13 cycles per second. Improvements in EEG technology provided the means to record waking waveforms that are faster than 30 cycles per second, known as **gamma band activity** (Miller, 2007).

Beta activity is correlated with alert, active information processing. Alpha activity occurs when people are relaxed. Closing the eyes while awake will automatically

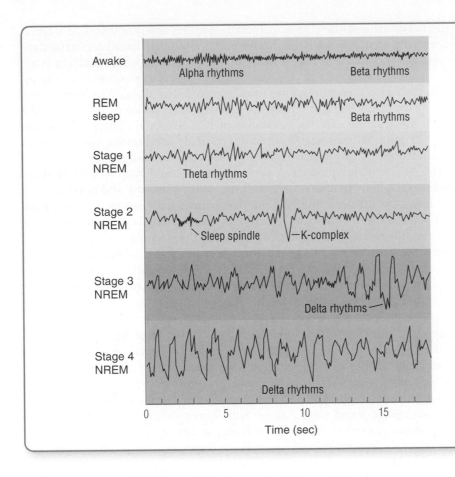

● **Figure 11.13** EEG Recordings Correlate with Waking and Sleep This image illustrates EEG patterns characteristic of waking, REM, and the four stages of NREM.

Source: Adapted from Horne (1998).

result in the initiation of alpha activity, although engaging in mathematical calculations with the eyes closed will reinstate beta rhythms. Alpha and beta activity alternate throughout periods of waking. As we mentioned previously, periods of high and low alertness follow ultradian cycles of 90 to 120 minutes in humans (Lavie & Kripke, 1981). We will see that this ultradian pattern continues into periods of sleep as well. Gamma band activity is particularly obvious during the processing of sensory input, and visual input in particular.

In children and young adults, EEG recordings during waking might also include brief moments of **theta wave** (4 to 7 cycles per second) frequencies, but organized and sustained theta waves during wakefulness is usually restricted to cases of brain damage or neurological disorder (Niedermeyer, 1999). Theta activity characterizes lighter stages of sleep, although it begins to intrude into the waking EEGs of sleep-deprived volunteers (Vyazovskiy & Tobler, 2005).

THE EEG DURING SLEEP Sleep consists of alternating periods of **rapid eye movement (REM) sleep** and **non-REM (NREM) sleep**. As shown in ● Figure 11.11, sleep typically begins when a person enters stage 1 of NREM. In stage 1, the EEG is difficult to distinguish from the waking EEG of a drowsy person. Some theta wave activity now occurs, and heart rate and muscle tension begin to decrease. This early stage of sleep is disturbed occasionally by a muscle jerk, usually in an arm or leg, referred to as **myoclonia**. This experience is often accompanied by a brief visual image, such as stumbling on the stairs or on a curb. Although myoclonia interrupts sleep, no harm is being done to the sleeper.

After 10 to 15 minutes, stage 1 gives way to stage 2 NREM, which accounts for about 50 percent of the night's entire sleep. Further reductions in heart rate and muscle tension occur. The EEG begins to show **sleep spindles**, short bursts of 12 to 14 cycle-per-second waves lasting about half a second that are generated by interactions

theta wave A brain waveform having 4 to 7 cycles per second found primarily in lighter stages of NREM sleep.

rapid eye movement (REM) sleep A period of sleep characterized by desynchronous brain activity, muscle paralysis, eye movement, and storylike dream behavior.

non-REM (NREM) sleep A period of sleep characterized by slow, synchronous brain activity, reductions in heart rate, and muscle relaxation.

myoclonia A muscle jerk occurring in early stages of sleep.

sleep spindle A short burst of 12 to 14 cycle-per-second waves observed during NREM sleep.

between the thalamus and the cortex. Although spindles are prominent in stage 2, they do occur in other stages of NREM. **K-complexes** also begin to appear in the stage 2 EEG recording. These waveforms are made up of single delta waves (Colrain et al., 2011), which are discussed later in this section. Although K-complexes occur spontaneously, they are also seen in response to unexpected stimuli, such as loud noises. Spindles and K-complexes might reflect the brain's efforts to keep us asleep while continuing to monitor the external environment (Colrain et al., 2011). We usually sleep through familiar stimuli, such as the hum of an air conditioner, but awaken in response to unexpected stimuli such as the sound of a door opening.

After about 15 minutes in stage 2, we enter stage 3 and stage 4 NREM sleep. During these stages, body temperature, breathing, blood pressure, and heart rate are at very low levels due to the activity of the parasympathetic nervous system. Both stage 3 and stage 4 feature **delta wave** activity, which is the largest, slowest (1 to 4 cycles per second), most synchronized waveform of the sleeping state. Stages 3 and 4 differ from each other in that a greater proportion of stage 4 (about half) consists of delta waves. Awakening from stage 4 is difficult and disorienting. You might have received a phone call about an hour after going to sleep, when you are likely to be in stage 4. If you hear the phone at all, it might take several seconds to locate the phone and wake up enough to have a decent conversation.

After approximately 90 minutes of NREM, a first period of REM sleep occurs. This stage is also referred to as *paradoxical* sleep, reflecting its combination of brain activity resembling waking with the external appearance of deep sleep. Vivid dreaming, which we will discuss later in more detail, generally occurs during this stage. The transition between stage 4 and REM is rather abrupt, but it usually involves brief passages through stage 3 and stage 2 sleep. Subsequent periods of REM sleep continue the ultradian cycles observed during waking, occurring at approximately 90- to 120-minute intervals. In eight hours of sleep, the average person typically experiences five periods of REM.

During REM, the EEG shows activity very similar to beta activity observed during waking, with occasional periods of theta activity as well (Gelisse & Crespel, 2008). The eyes make the periodic back-and-forth movements that give this stage its name. Some researchers believe that these rapid movements signify the scanning of visual images during dreaming (Leclair-Visonneau, Oudiette, Gaymard, Leu-Semenescu, & Arnulf, 2010). The sympathetic nervous system becomes very active. Heart rate, blood pressure, and breathing become rapid or irregular. Males experience erections, and females experience increased blood flow in the vicinity of the vagina (Hirshkowitz & Moore, 1996). At the same time, major postural muscles are completely inactive, effectively paralyzing the sleeper. Some smaller muscles, such as those in the fingers, retain the capacity to jerk or twitch during REM sleep. Cats' paws frequently twitch during a REM episode, leading to speculation that they are chasing mice in their dreams.

The cycling between NREM and REM sleep in humans follows a characteristic pattern over eight hours of sleep, as illustrated in ● Figure 11.12. The first four hours are characterized by longer periods of NREM and brief periods of REM. Stages 3 and 4 are especially dominant in the first half of the sleep cycle. REM is the principal stage seen in hours 5 through 8, and any NREM during this time remains in the lighter stages 1 and 2. Stages 3 and 4 are usually infrequent or absent altogether during the last four hours of sleep. We usually spend the last half hour or so of the night's sleep in REM and often wake up with the awareness that we have just been dreaming (see ● Figure 11.14).

Brain Networks Control Waking and Sleep

Circuits connecting the brainstem, hypothalamus, and basal forebrain play essential roles in the initiation and maintenance of stages of waking and sleep. These structures are shown in ● Figure 11.15 and their relationship to waking and sleep is outlined in Table 11.1.

K-complex A brief burst of brain activity consisting of single delta waves occurring during stage 2 NREM sleep.

delta wave A brain waveform having 1 to 4 cycles per second that occurs during stages 3 and 4 of NREM sleep.

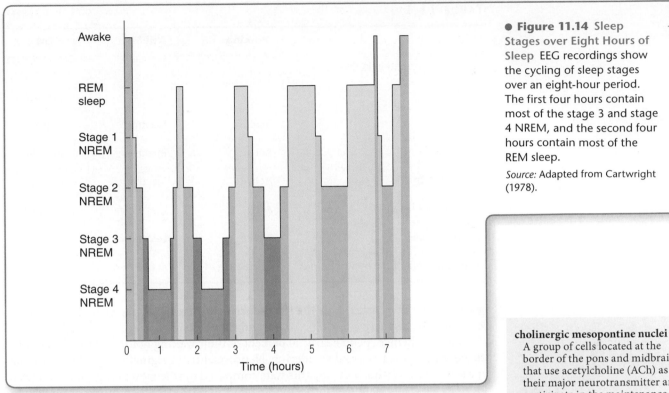

● **Figure 11.14** Sleep Stages over Eight Hours of Sleep EEG recordings show the cycling of sleep stages over an eight-hour period. The first four hours contain most of the stage 3 and stage 4 NREM, and the second four hours contain most of the REM sleep.

Source: Adapted from Cartwright (1978).

cholinergic mesopontine nuclei A group of cells located at the border of the pons and midbrain that use acetylcholine (ACh) as their major neurotransmitter and participate in the maintenance of waking. *Meso* refers to mesencephalon, or midbrain, and *pontine* refers to the pons.

NETWORKS MANAGING WAKING Staying awake requires the cooperation of a complex network of structures located in the brainstem and basal forebrain. No one structure is uniquely responsible for waking, and several of these structures participate in REM sleep as well.

Two pathways originating in the reticular formation of the medulla are essential to waking. One pathway proceeds from the medulla to the posterior hypothalamus and on to the basal forebrain. The other pathway projects to a group of cells in the midbrain reticular formation known as the **cholinergic mesopontine nuclei**, located at the junction of the pons and midbrain. These neurons project to the thalamus, which in turn influences the activity of the cerebral cortex and modulates the amount of sensory input the cortex receives.

In addition to these two pathways, the locus coeruleus of the pons also participates in waking through its rich connections to the thalamus, hippocampus, and cortex (see Chapter 2). The locus coeruleus, which is the source of most of the norepinephrine in the brain, provides a good example of how a single structure participates in diverse states of awareness. The locus coeruleus is most active when people are vigilant and alert, but is relatively less active when a person is relaxed. The locus coeruleus is quieter still during NREM sleep, and is totally silent during REM.

The anterior raphe nuclei also play important roles in managing sleep–waking cycles. These serotonergic nuclei communicate with the preoptic area and suprachiasmatic nucleus of the anterior hypothalamus as well as

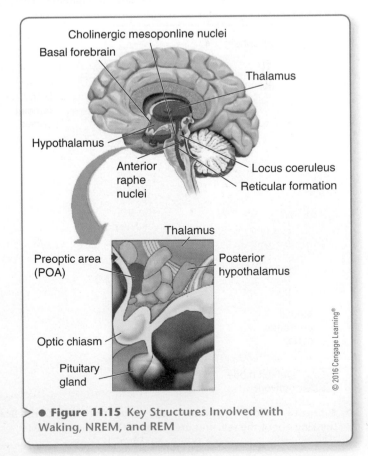

● **Figure 11.15** Key Structures Involved with Waking, NREM, and REM

© 2016 Cengage Learning®

TABLE 11.1

	Waking	NREM	REM
Reticular formation in the:			
Midbrain	Active	Inactive	Inactive
Pons	Inactive	Inactive	Active
Medulla	Active	Inactive	Inactive
Basal forebrain	Active	Inactive	Inactive
Locus coeruleus	Active	Less active	Inactive
Raphe nuclei	Active	Less active	Inactive
Preoptic area of the hypothalamus	Less active	Active	Inactive

with the cerebral cortex. Like the locus coeruleus, the raphe nuclei are active during wakefulness, less active during NREM, and silent during REM.

Human beings spend nearly 50 percent of their waking hours in a relatively unfocused state known as mind wandering. Neuroscientists originally expected to see that the brain was very quiet during this state compared to when it was engaged in focused, alert activity, but that does not seem to be the case. Instead, the brain uses only about 5 percent more energy when it is focused compared to when it is unfocused. These observations led to the identification of a **default mode network (DMN)**, shown in ● Figure 11.16, that consists of the medial prefrontal cortex, the medial parietal cortex, the lateral parietal cortex, and the lateral temporal cortex (Raichle & Snyder, 2011).

default mode network (DMN) A circuit that is active during periods of unfocused thought.

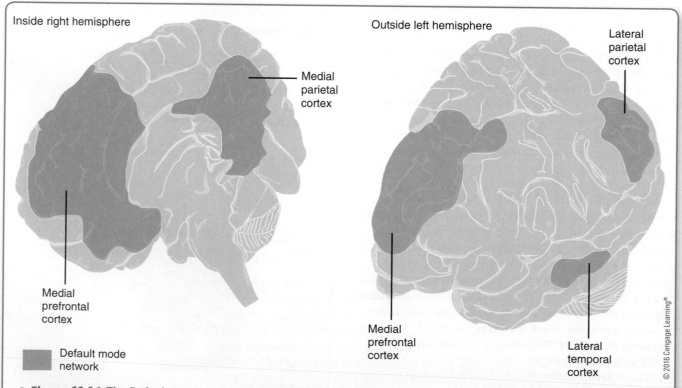

Inside right hemisphere

Outside left hemisphere

Medial parietal cortex

Lateral parietal cortex

Medial prefrontal cortex

Medial prefrontal cortex

Lateral temporal cortex

Default mode network

© 2016 Cengage Learning®

> ● **Figure 11.16** The Default Mode Network (DMN) of the Brain Activity of the DMN corresponds to "mind wandering," thinking about the self, and preparing for conscious thought.

Activity in the DMN is often associated with daydreaming and actually decreases when a person begins engaging in a conscious task like problem solving. Researchers were able to predict participants' mistakes during a computer test on the basis of observations of the DMN (Eichele et al., 2008). About 30 seconds before a mistake was made, but not when a correct answer was given, activity in the DMN would increase and displace activity in areas involved with focused attention, such as the anterior cingulate cortex and other parts of the prefrontal cortex. These types of observations have given rise to the idea of competing networks, where focused activity suppresses the DMN and DMN activity suppresses focused activity (Buckner, Andrews-Hanna, & Schacter, 2008).

NREM SLEEP NETWORKS Once waking has been initiated, it is maintained by ongoing activity in networks that manage waking as well as by incoming stimulation from the outside world. How then do we make a transition from waking to NREM sleep?

The preoptic area (POA) of the hypothalamus, which receives input from the anterior raphe nuclei, forms inhibitory feedback loops with waking pathways. These hypothalamic circuits appear to manage homeostatic control of wakefulness, sometimes referred to as **sleep debt**. In other words, these circuits keep track of the duration and intensity of waking and actually promote sleep after a certain period of time has passed. Continued activation of the POA by input from the raphe nuclei will eventually lead to inhibition of the circuits promoting waking, allowing sleep to occur (Gallopin et al., 2000). POA cells are often referred to as NREM-on cells because electrical stimulation of these cells produces immediate NREM sleep, and lesions result in insomnia. NREM-on cells are most active during NREM and relatively inactive during waking and REM.

Unless some pathology is present, such as in the case of narcolepsy described later in this chapter, the first segment of sleep is always NREM. Without input from circuits that manage waking, neurons in the thalamus begin to synchronize the activity of cortical neurons, eventually leading to the slow, large waves observed in the deeper stages of NREM sleep. As this synchronization progresses, the cortex becomes progressively less "tuned" to the outside world, and waking becomes more difficult to achieve. Electrical stimulation of the thalamus in waking animals produces NREM sleep.

The default mode network (DMN) described earlier also behaves somewhat differently during deep stages of NREM sleep compared to waking (Horovitz et al., 2009). During waking, activity in the medial prefrontal cortex is tightly correlated with the more posterior parts of the network. During NREM, however, the frontal parts of the network decouple from the posterior parts, and the correlations between the activity in these two areas become nonsignificant. It is possible that these changes in the DMN are associated with the relative reduction in consciousness experienced during deep sleep.

As NREM begins, activity in the locus coeruleus and the raphe nuclei gradually declines, preparing the brain for its first episode of REM sleep. During REM, these areas are virtually silent.

REM NETWORKS Some of the same areas of the brain are active during both waking and REM sleep, such as the cholinergic mesopontine nuclei mentioned previously. These neurons maintain high levels of activity during waking and REM, but are relatively quiet during NREM. Stimulation of this area produces desynchronous EEG activity due to its connections with circuits linking the thalamus and cortex.

REM-on areas are active during REM but not during waking, and REM-off areas are active during waking but not during REM. Most of the key REM-on areas are located in the pons (McCarley, 2007). In particular, parts of the rostral pontine reticular formation seem particularly important because lesions of this area selectively abolish REM sleep (Steriade & McCarley, 2005). These neurons are inactive during waking

sleep debt The homeostatic control of sleep, in which sleep promotion is related to the preceding duration and intensity of wakefulness.

and NREM sleep but are very active during REM. Critical REM-off components are the locus coeruleus and the raphe nuclei. As these structures reduce their activity during NREM, they disinhibit the activity of the rostral pontine reticular formation, allowing REM to occur (McCarley, 2007). After REM has occurred for about 30 minutes in human beings, the locus coeruleus and raphe nuclei reactivate, inhibiting the rostral pontine reticular formation and ending REM. Either waking or another cycle of NREM will follow.

Areas of the pons are responsible for several distinctive features of REM sleep, including muscular paralysis and the eye movements that give this stage its name. The purpose of rapid eye movements is unknown. The movements result in the absence of external visual input from activity in the pontine reticular formation. This area stimulates the superior colliculi of the midbrain, which coordinate the timing and direction of eye movements. The superior colliculi in turn communicate with a different part of the pontine reticular formation, resulting in the characteristic eye movements.

Each eye movement is accompanied by a characteristic waveform known as a **PGO wave**, illustrated in ● Figure 11.17. These waveforms originate in the pontine reticular formation (P) and travel to the lateral geniculate nucleus of the thalamus (G; the visual center of the thalamus) and the occipital lobe (O; the location of primary visual cortex). The muscular paralysis accompanying REM results from inhibitory messages traveling from the pontine reticular formation to the medulla and, from there, to the motor systems of the spinal cord. Although the primary motor cortex

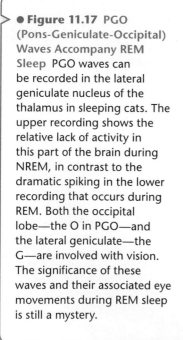

● Figure 11.17 PGO (Pons-Geniculate-Occipital) Waves Accompany REM Sleep PGO waves can be recorded in the lateral geniculate nucleus of the thalamus in sleeping cats. The upper recording shows the relative lack of activity in this part of the brain during NREM, in contrast to the dramatic spiking in the lower recording that occurs during REM. Both the occipital lobe—the O in PGO—and the lateral geniculate—the G—are involved with vision. The significance of these waves and their associated eye movements during REM sleep is still a mystery.

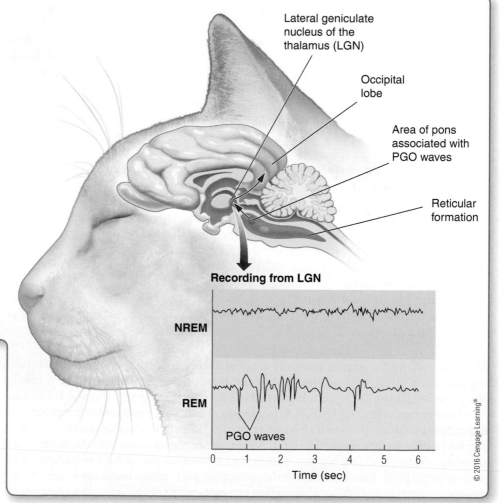

PGO wave An electrical waveform observed during REM sleep, originating in the pons and traveling to the thalamus and occipital lobe. Each PGO wave is associated with an eye movement.

© 2016 Cengage Learning®

of the brain is quite active during REM, the only muscles that are able to respond fully during REM are the eye muscles, muscles of the middle ear, and those involved with breathing.

Imaging studies of REM sleep indicate little activity in either the primary visual cortex of the occipital lobe (after all, the eyes are closed) or the frontal lobe (Maquet, 1999). However, there is significant activity in the secondary visual cortex. The inactivity of the frontal lobe, which participates in waking judgments, might account for the often bizarre, illogical, and socially inappropriate content of our dreams (see ● Figure 11.18). The hippocampus, in contrast, is quite active, possibly due to the suspected role in memory consolidation for REM sleep. The amygdala and anterior cingulate cortex are also quite active, perhaps leading to the rapidly changing, emotional quality of dreaming.

Biochemical Correlates of Waking and Sleep

A wide array of neurochemicals participates in the maintenance of our sleep–waking cycles.

Acetylcholine (ACh) release by the pons and basal forebrain is associated with both waking and REM sleep (Vazquez & Baghdoyan, 2001). Cholinergic agonists, such as nicotine, produce a high level of mental alertness. Similarly, glutamate activity in the frontal lobes is high during both waking and REM sleep, and it is likely that glutamate promotes REM-on processes (Datta, Spoley, & Patterson, 2001).

Some neurons in the thalamus and hypothalamus use histamine as their major neurochemical. These neurons project widely throughout the forebrain, and their activity is associated with alertness. Histamine activity is high during waking but relatively low during NREM and REM sleep. Traditional antihistamines (histamine antagonists) used for suppressing cold and allergy symptoms are known to produce drowsiness. Modern antihistamines do not cross the blood–brain barrier (see Chapter 3), thereby avoiding the side effect of drowsiness.

Activity of serotonin (from the raphe nuclei) and norepinephrine (from the locus coeruleus) is highest during waking, drops off during NREM sleep, and is very low during REM sleep. People with major depressive disorder (see Chapter 16) initiate REM too early and too frequently during the sleep cycle, possibly due to reduced serotonin activity. Antidepressant drugs boost serotonin activity and often suppress REM. Drugs that stimulate the release of norepinephrine, such as amphetamine, delay sleepiness (Siegel & Rogawski, 1988).

Caffeine keeps us awake by blocking receptors for adenosine, an ATP byproduct that has an inhibitory effect on many brain systems (see Chapter 4). When adenosine is inhibited, alertness is maintained. When artificially applied, adenosine induces sleep (Radulovacki, 1985). Adenosine accumulates throughout the day, and if sleep is postponed, concentrations continue to rise until sleep occurs (Porkka-Heiskanen, 1999). Adenosine specifically inhibits neurons releasing neurochemicals associated with waking, including acetylcholine (ACh), serotonin, and norepinephrine. During the night's sleep, adenosine levels once again drop, allowing waking to occur again in the morning.

For human beings, melatonin not only signals the onset of the dark cycle but also contributes to sleepiness. Most people experience an "opening of the sleep gate," or a period of time in which going to sleep becomes much more likely (Lavie, 1986). This opening of the sleep gate reflects both decreases in the signals maintaining waking and the action of melatonin (Gorfine & Zisapel, 2009). A reliable surge in melatonin release occurs two hours prior to the opening of the sleep gate.

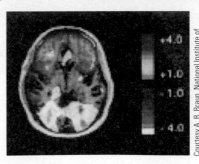

Courtesy A. R. Braun, National Institute of Deafness, NIH, Bethesda

● **Figure 11.18** Comparing Patterns of Brain Activity PET scans can be used to compare brain activity during two states, such as activity during REM versus activity during waking. Taking one PET scan of a brain during REM and another of a waking brain, a researcher compared their activity pixel by pixel and plotted the results on a composite image. The scale to the right of the image allows us to apply colors to represent the differences observed during the two states. Areas that are more active during REM sleep than during waking will be colored red or yellow (+1 to +4), areas that are about equally active during REM and waking will not be colored (0), and areas that are less active during REM than during waking will be colored blue or purple (–1 to –4). We can see that the secondary visual cortex, located toward the bottom of the image, is more active during REM than waking (yellow) and the frontal lobes, located toward the top of the image, are less active during REM than waking (purple).

INTERIM SUMMARY 11.2

Neurochemical	Locations at which Neurochemical Is Active Relative to Sleep–waking Cycles	Relation of Activity to Sleep and Waking	Effect of Agonists for Neurochemical	Effect of Antagonists for Neurochemical
Acetylcholine (ACh)	• Pons • Basal forebrain	• High during waking and REM • Low during NREM	• Increased arousal • Increased REM sleep	• Decreased arousal • Decreased REM sleep
Glutamate	Frontal lobe	• High during waking and REM • Low during NREM	• Increased waking • Suppression of NREM sleep	• Decreased REM sleep
Histamine	• Thalamus • Hypothalamus	• High during waking • Low during NREM and REM		• Increased drowsiness and sleep
Serotonin	Raphe nuclei	• High during waking • Low during NREM • No activity during REM	• Increased sleep time • Decreased REM	• Increased REM sleep • Increased arousal
Norepinephrine	Locus coeruleus	• High during waking • Low during NREM • No activity during REM	• Increased arousal • Decreased REM	• Increased REM sleep
Adenosine	Widely distributed areas in the brain	Accumulates in the brain during waking; probably helps induce sleep	Possibly promotes sleep	Inhibits sleep
Melatonin	Widely distributed areas of the brain	Probably helps induce sleep	Decreased sleep	Waking

‖ Summary Points

1. Activity in the basal forebrain, parts of the reticular formation, the raphe nuclei, and the locus coeruleus are associated with waking and vigilance. **(LO2)**

2. A default mode network (DMN) is active during unfocused thought and is inhibited by activity in the brain during focused thought. **(LO2)**

3. NREM becomes possible when the circuits managing waking are inhibited and activity in the raphe nuclei and locus coeruleus drops. **(LO2)**

4. Different aspects of REM sleep are controlled by parts of the reticular formation located in the pons. **(LO2)**

5. Neurochemicals associated with the regulation of sleep and waking include acetylcholine, glutamate, histamine, serotonin, norepinephrine, adenosine, and melatonin. **(LO2)**

‖ Review Questions

1. What can we learn from the EEG recordings taken from different stages of waking and sleep?

2. In what ways should sleep be considered an active, as opposed to a passive, process?

The Functions of Sleep

In 2007, Tony Wright, shown in ● Figure 11.19, went 266 hours without sleep in order to beat the standing record for sleep deprivation. Although Wright's experience shows that we can obviously survive extreme levels of sleep deprivation, the results of sleepiness can be serious indeed. Sleepiness contributed to the Three Mile Island nuclear meltdown in 1979, the Challenger space shuttle explosion in 1986, and the grounding of the oil tanker *Exxon Valdez* in 1989 (Coren, 1996a). Sleep deprivation has also been implicated in the 1984 chemical leak at a factory in Bhopal, India, that resulted in the deaths of 3,800 people (Kurzman, 1987). You can see just how sleepy you are right now by completing the Epworth Sleepiness Scale (Johns, 1991).

The adverse effects of sleep deprivation suggest that sleep is beneficial. Most animals show activity levels that follow circadian rhythms with at least one period of time in which they are relatively quiet and less responsive to external stimuli. Even the humble fruit fly takes a seven-hour rest each day (Shaw, Cirelli, Greenspan, & Giulio Tononi, 2000). What possible benefits do organisms receive from these periods of rest?

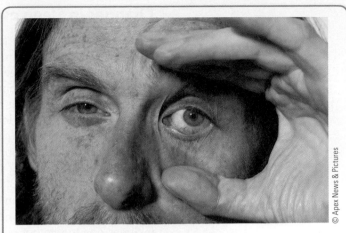

> ● **Figure 11.19** A New Sleep Deprivation Record Is Set The most recent record-breaking attempt for sleep deprivation was Tony Wright's 11 days, 2 hours, 4 minutes, and 8 seconds. Tony's efforts were chronicled by the BBC, and thousands of people watched him via webcam.

© Apex News & Pictures

EPWORTH SLEEPINESS SCALE

In contrast to just feeling tired, how likely are you to doze off or fall asleep in the following situations? (Even if you have not done some of these things recently, try to work out how they would have affected you.) Use the following scale to choose the most appropriate number for each situation.

0 = Would never doze
1 = Slight chance of dozing
2 = Moderate chance of dozing
3 = High chance of dozing

Situation	Chance of Dozing
Sitting and Reading	_____
Watching TV	_____
Sitting inactive in a public place (i.e., theatre)	_____
As a car passenger for an hour without a break	_____
Lying down to rest in the afternoon	_____
Sitting and talking to someone	_____
Sitting quietly after lunch without alcohol	_____
In a car, while stopping for a few minutes in traffic	_____

A score of greater than 10 is a definite cause for concern as it indicates significant excessive daytime sleepiness.

Changes in Sleep over the Lifetime

Hints about the possible functions of sleep can be gleaned from observing nightly sleep patterns as a function of age, as shown in ● Figure 11.20. Not only does the overall amount of sleep change, but the composition of sleep is altered as well.

Newborn infants spend as much as 14 to 16 hours per day in sleep. About half of the newborn's sleeping time is spent in REM sleep, in comparison with approximately 20 percent in adolescence and adulthood (McCarley, 2007). Babies born prematurely show even greater percentages of REM sleep than other infants. The more prematurely the child is born, the greater percentage of his or her sleep time is spent in REM. Babies born during the seventh month of pregnancy spend up to 80 percent of their sleeping time in REM. REM sleep can be recorded for the first time in the fetus at about this same point in development (Inoue et al., 1986).

By the age of one year, the child's sleep time has been reduced to 13 hours, which includes one to two hours of napping that will continue until about the age of three. Between the ages of one and five years, most children sleep approximately 8.7 hours (Acebo et al., 2005). The amount of delta wave (stages 3 and 4 NREM) activity is highest between the ages of three and six years. At puberty, there is a further slight decrease in REM and a substantial decrease in stages 3 and 4 sleep (Dahl, 1996). Teens often feel the need for increased amounts of sleep, possibly 9–10 hours per night, but they do not often have the opportunity to sleep this much (Carskadon et al., 1980).

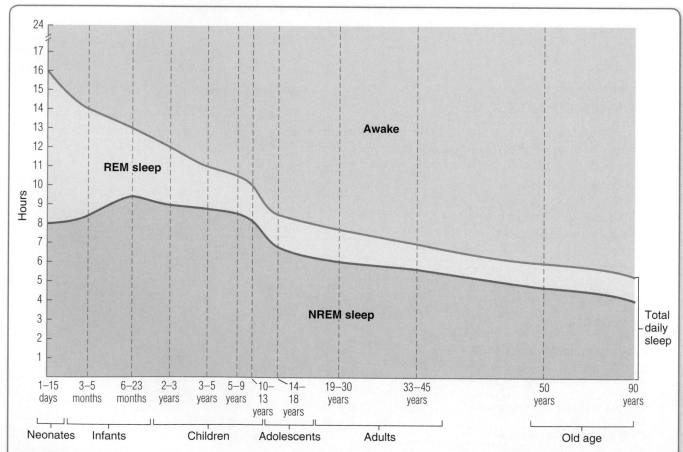

● **Figure 11.20** Sleep Patterns over the Lifespan Young children spend more time sleeping, and their sleep contains a disproportionately higher amount of REM. As we age, we experience a decrease in the total amount of sleep and in the amount of stages 3 and 4 NREM.

Source: Adapted from Roffwarg, Muzio, and Dement (1962).

NREM sleep declines further as people approach midlife. Time spent in stages 3 and 4 of NREM declines from 20 percent of the night in men under 25 years of age to less than 5 percent of the night for men over 35 (van Cauter, Leproult, & Plat, 2000). Around the age of 50, total sleep time begins to decrease by about 27 minutes per decade into a person's eighties. The pineal gland in older adults begins to calcify and produce smaller amounts of melatonin, which might result in fewer hours of sleep. Increased awakening accompanies a reduction in sleep spindles with age (Crowley, Trinder, Kim, Carrington, & Colrain, 2002). Drops in sex hormones associated with aging might be at least partly responsible for some of the age-related changes observed in sleeping patterns. Women approaching menopause frequently experience disruptions in sleep (Hollander et al., 2001). Kruijver and Swaab (2002) identified receptors for estrogen and progesterone in the human SCN, suggesting that sex hormones have a very direct role in the regulation of biorhythms. Although some age-related changes in sleep quality and quantity appear inevitable, healthy, mentally active seniors usually enjoy a better quality of sleep (Driscoll et al., 2008).

Possible Advantages of Sleep

"Sleep" seems to take many forms across different species, and it is unlikely that sleep serves a single purpose for all animals (Siegel, 2008). Functions requiring sleep in one species can be managed during waking in another. A number of theories have attempted to identify the possible functions of sleep in humans.

SLEEP KEEPS US SAFE Sleep prevents some animals from being active during parts of the day when they are least safe from predation. Being inactive, however, is not a safe thing to do unless you are in a secure location. Allison and Cicchetti (1976) were able to predict a species' sleep habits quite accurately on the basis of the animals' risk of predation and their access to shelter. For example, the horse is a heavily preyed upon animal in the wild, and it generally lives out in the open. Consequently, wild horses sleep as little as one to two hours per day. Rabbits are also frequent prey, but because they have burrows in which to hide, they sleep much more than the horse. Predators, such as lions, tend to sleep whenever and wherever they desire for lengthy periods of time (see ● Figure 11.21). A sample of different species and their average sleep times is shown in ● Figure 11.22.

SLEEP RESTORES OUR BODIES Sleep, particularly NREM, helps us restore our bodies and conserve energy. Sleep deprivation results in a number of negative physical consequences, including reduced immune system function (Zager, Andersen, Ruiz, Antunes, & Tufik, 2007), inability to heal (Murphy et al., 2007), and the inhibition of adult neurogenesis in the hippocampus (Mueller et al., 2008). Individuals who are deprived of NREM sleep will rebound, or attempt to make up for this deprivation during their next opportunity to sleep. Volunteers can be selectively deprived of stages 3 and 4 NREM by awakening them when their EEGs begin to show the characteristic delta waves. After a night of deprivation, volunteers typically complain of muscle and joint pain (Moldofsky & Scarisbrick, 1976). It is possible that some of the muscle and joint

● **Figure 11.21 Safety Predicts a Species' Sleep Habits** Like most large predators, lions don't have to worry too much about when and where to sleep.

● **Figure 11.22 Predation, Shelter, and Sleep Patterns** We can predict the amount of time an animal will sleep on the basis of its risk of predation and whether it has a den, burrow, or other safe place to sleep. Animals that are frequently preyed upon and that also sleep in the open, such as horses, sleep very little. Prey species with burrows sleep a lot, which keeps them out of danger. Predators tend to sleep well no matter what.

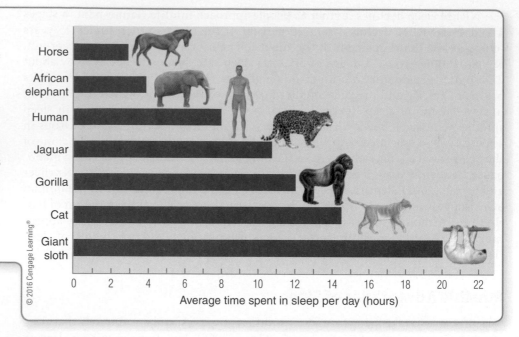

© 2016 Cengage Learning®

aches and pains experienced by older adults might arise from age-related reductions in stages 3 and 4 sleep.

Increased physical demands during the day correlate with a need for increased amounts of sleep the following night, reinforcing the role of NREM in the restoration of the body. Runners competing in ultramarathons (races that are twice the length of a marathon) add a surprisingly modest 20 to 30 minutes to their sleep the following night. However, most of this increase is in the form of NREM. When highly trained athletes skip a day of exercise, they experience a substitution of about 15 to 20 minutes of REM sleep for NREM (Hague, Gilbert, Burgess, Ferguson, & Dawson, 2003).

Small animals, which tend to have higher metabolic rates, generally sleep more than larger animals, whose metabolic rates are lower. Metabolism rates are positively correlated with the production of free radicals, which can be harmful to many tissues. During NREM sleep, lower body temperatures and rates of metabolism might provide an ideal environment for repairing the damage produced by free radicals during wakefulness (Siegel, 2005). Human forebrain metabolic activity is greatly reduced during NREM sleep compared to waking, contributing to an efficient use of energy (Siegel, 2008).

Most human **growth hormone (GH)** is released during stages 3 and 4 NREM (see ● Figure 11.8 earlier in the chapter). In childhood, GH is primarily responsible for physical growth, but throughout life, it contributes to building muscle and bone mass and maintaining immune system function. The release of growth hormone during NREM peaks around the onset of puberty and begins to drop by age 21 (Savine & Sonksen, 2000). Both growth hormone levels and healing of injuries are reduced by sleep deprivation (Murphy et al., 2007). Supplementation with GH increases lean muscle mass and bone mass in elderly participants (Brill et al., 2002).

MEMORIES ARE CONSOLIDATED DURING SLEEP The relationship between sleep and memory is complex and controversial. Originally, many neuroscientists believed that the positive role of sleep in memory formation resulted from a lack of interference. In other words, you were more likely to remember things you learned right before sleep because sleep limited the amount of new data entering the system. Today, researchers believe that sleep plays a more active role in the consolidation of memories. Staying up all night resulted in poor memory retention for a visual task, and two additional nights of sleep did not compensate for the initial deprivation (Stickgold, James, & Hobson, 2000). Memories for word pairs were stronger following a period

growth hormone (GH)
A hormone released during stages 3 and 4 of slow-wave sleep that promotes growth, increases in bone and muscle mass, and immune system function.

of NREM than following a period of waking (Gais & Born, 2004). Other research has indicated that REM sleep improves the retention of highly emotional material (Wagner et al., 2001; Wagner et al., 2002). Memories for procedures, such as how to solve a puzzle or ride a bicycle, are enhanced following stage 2 NREM sleep (Smith & MacNeill, 1994; Smith & Fazekas, 1997).

Sleep-related changes in memory might be different from the changes that occur when we learn something while awake (Stickgold & Walker, 2007). Learning during waking might be a simple matter of strengthening connections, whereas sleep-related memory processes might involve the reorganization of existing memory systems to accommodate new information. The day's memories can be reactivated during NREM and redistributed from the hippocampal circuits to the cerebral cortex (Diekelmann & Born, 2010). Memories now stored in the cerebral cortex can then be strengthened during REM, which will make the memories easier to recall during waking (Ribeiro & Nicolelis, 2004). Further research is needed to provide a clearer picture of the relationship between sleep and memory. Nonetheless, it is safe to say that students who wish to retain the material they have studied would benefit from a good night's sleep.

Special Benefits of REM Sleep

Only birds and mammals show true REM sleep. Researchers once believed that the echidna, shown in ● Figure 11.23, and its relative the platypus did not show true REM, but more recent reports indicate that even these primitive, egg-laying mammals are capable of REM (McCarley, 2007).

One consistent observation for both humans and animals is that REM sleep increases after learning has taken place, possibly due to the participation of sleep in the consolidation of memory mentioned earlier. On the other hand, individuals in whom REM sleep is regularly suppressed due to brain injury (Lavie, 1998) or medication retain an ability to learn. In one case, an Israeli soldier who suffered a brain wound that prevented either REM sleep or dreaming was still able to learn new information (Dement & Vaughan, 1999). Individuals taking SSRI medications (see Chapters 4 and 16) experience less REM sleep, yet are still able to learn (Pace-Schott et al., 2001). REM sleep is clearly not the only mechanism for consolidating new information in memory.

Changes in REM sleep over the lifespan suggest that REM sleep plays a role in brain development. The large proportion of REM sleep observed in the fetus and in young children correlates with periods of time in which the brain is undergoing great change (see Chapter 5). As we mature, the brain continues to change, although far less dramatically. As a result, the adult's need for REM sleep is reduced.

Although adults need less REM sleep than children do, and some individuals seem to do quite well without REM sleep at all, REM deprivation does produce changes in behavior. Dement (1960) awakened volunteers each time they entered REM sleep. As deprivation progressed, the deprived volunteers tried more and more frequently to enter REM sleep. After several days of deprivation, participants showed a phenomenon known as **REM rebound**. When allowed to sleep normally, they spent an unusually large amount of their sleep time in REM. The fact that we try to make up for lost REM sleep suggests that REM sleep does have a necessary function in the adult brain.

REM deprivation appears to have many of the same effects as overall loss of sleep, such as irritability and difficulty concentrating. On the other hand, it appears we can have too much of a good thing. As we will see in Chapter 16, people with major depressive disorder enter

REM rebound The increased amount of REM sleep following a period of REM deprivation.

● **Figure 11.23 The Echidna and REM Sleep** Researchers once believed that the echidna (*Tachyglossus aculeatus*), an egg-laying relative of the platypus native to Australia and New Guinea, did not show true REM sleep. More recent reports indicate that the echidna and platypus, like other mammals and birds, do experience REM sleep.

© Staffan Widstrand/CORBIS

REM sleep at earlier points in the sleep cycle and spend a greater proportion of their sleep time in REM. Many antidepressant medications suppress and delay REM sleep. Further research is needed to reconcile these data and develop a better understanding of the various roles and purposes of REM sleep.

The Possible Functions of Dreaming

Until the 1950s, the study of dreams was hampered by the inability of research participants to remember dreams very well upon awakening. The discovery that dreams are usually associated with REM sleep allowed researchers to awaken volunteers and assess the dream experience (Dement & Kleitman, 1957). Dreaming during REM sleep is correlated with activity in circuits that overlap with the DMN (Fox, Nijeboer, Solomonova, Domhoff, & Christoff, 2013). This suggests that daydreaming, which occurs during periods of DMN activity, and REM dreams exist on a continuum.

Dreaming behavior occurs during both REM sleep and NREM. However, dreams are more likely to be reported by volunteers awakened during REM sleep than during NREM. REM dreams are lengthy, complicated, vivid, and storylike, providing us with the sense of firsthand experience with the events taking place. In contrast, NREM dreams are short episodes characterized by logical single images and a relative lack of emotion. Otto Loewi (1873–1961) discovered the role of acetylcholine in the regulation of heart rhythms after dreaming about the perfect experiment. Unfortunately, even though he wrote down his "dream," he was unable to read his notes the next day. The next night, Loewi experienced the dream again, and this time, took no chances. He rushed immediately to his laboratory and conducted his famous experiment. It is most likely that the logical processes needed to design a Nobel Prize–caliber experiment would occur during NREM, as opposed to REM sleep.

Psychologists have found that most dreams appear to be rather ordinary. Calvin Hall (1951) reviewed the content of thousands of dreams collected from volunteers and found that most dreams occur in familiar places and involve routine activities. We participate as characters in our dreams only about 15 percent of the time, and imaginary strangers are more likely to appear in our dreams than familiar people.

Allen Hobson and Robert McCarley (1977) proposed an **activation-synthesis theory** of dreaming, in which they argue that the content of dreams reflects ongoing neural activity. When sleeping volunteers were sprinkled with water, they subsequently reported dreams of rain and other water-related themes. Dreams of being unable to move in a dangerous situation accurately mirror the muscle paralysis present during the REM state. Common dreams of flying or falling could be caused by the unusual activation of the vestibular system during REM sleep (Hunt, 1989). Dreams with sexual content are consistent with the physical sexual arousal that occurs during REM sleep.

Francis Crick and Graeme Mitchison (1983) proposed a computerized **neural network model** that sees dreaming as a way for the brain to forget irrelevant and unnecessary information. Jonathan Winson (1985) rejected both the Hobson-McCarley and Crick-Mitchison hypotheses in favor of a more evolutionary approach. In Winson's **evolutionary model**, animals evolved the ability to integrate sensory experience with stored memories during REM sleep rather than while awake. Dreaming, in this view, is just a window into the brain's processing of the day's events. In another evolutionary approach, the **threat simulation hypothesis**, dreaming is viewed as a way to simulate escape from threatening situations (Revonsuo, 2000). In other words, animals gain a survival advantage if they can "practice" dealing with threatening situations in their dreams. The advantages of dreaming could combine some or all of these proposed elements, and further research is needed to clarify the issue.

Although we often put our children to bed saying, "sweet dreams," it appears that about 70 percent of our dreams have negative emotional content (Hall & Van de Castle, 1966). Among the dreams most frequently reported by college students are those of being chased, falling, flying, appearing naked, being unable to find a restroom, being

activation-synthesis theory A theory suggesting that dream content reflects ongoing neural activity.

neural network model An approach to understanding the function of dreaming as a means for forgetting irrelevant information.

evolutionary model of dreaming A theory suggesting that dreaming provides the advantage of consolidating memories during sleep rather than during waking.

threat simulation hypothesis A theory suggesting that dreams provide practice for dealing with threats.

frozen with fright, and taking exams for which one is unprepared (Schredl, Ciric, Götz, & Wittmann, 2004). Men report more aggression in their dreams than do women (Schredl et al., 2004). Viewing upsetting entertainment or reports of natural disaster increases the likelihood of negative dreams. In the weeks following the 1989 earthquake in San Francisco, 40 percent of students in San Francisco universities reported dreaming about earthquakes, compared with 5 percent of students in Arizona (Wood, Bootzin, Kihlstrom, & Schacter, 1992).

When the content of a REM dream is especially upsetting, we refer to the experience as a **nightmare**. Nightmares first appear when children are between three and six years of age and tend to decrease in frequency as puberty approaches. Although adults experience nightmares, they are typically not as disturbed by them as children generally are. However, recurrent, disturbing nightmares occur in a number of psychological disorders such as post-traumatic stress disorder (PTSD; see Chapter 16). People troubled by nightmares can benefit from training in **lucid dreaming**, in which the dreamer is consciously aware that he or she is dreaming and uses this awareness to control or direct the content of the dream (Spoormaker & van den Bout, 2006).

Nightmares are often mistaken for **sleep terrors**, but they are very different phenomena (see ●Figure 11.24). Distinctions between these phenomena are outlined in Table 11.2. Nightmares are dreams that occur during REM, whereas sleep terrors occur during NREM, particularly during the first three hours of sleep. Somewhere between 1 and 4 percent of children will experience a sleep terror, usually between the ages of 4 and 12 years (Pagel, 2000). Most episodes begin with an abrupt scream, followed by sweating and an accelerated heartbeat. The sleeper sits upright in bed and stares forward but is not responsive. If awakened, the person shows the disorientation and confusion typically demonstrated when a sleeper is disturbed during very deep NREM. Mental imagery during sleep terrors is rare and, if present, tends to be of the

● **Figure 11.24 Nightmare or Sleep Terror?** Henry Fuseli (1741–1825) titled his painting *The Nightmare,* but the experience of feeling like a monster is sitting on the chest is more typical in a sleep terror than a true nightmare.

World History Archive/Image Asset Management Ltd/Alamy

TABLE 11.2 | A Comparison of Sleep Terrors and Nightmares

	Sleep Terrors	**Nightmares**
Time of night	Within four hours of bedtime	Late in sleep cycle
State on waking	Disoriented, confused	Upset, scared
Response to caregivers	Unaware of presence, not consolable	Comforted
Memory of events	None, unless fully awakened	Vivid recall of dream
Return to sleep	Usually rapid, unless fully awakened	Often delayed by fear
Sleep stage during which event occurs	Partial arousal from deep NREM sleep	REM sleep

nightmare A REM dream with disturbing content.
lucid dreaming Thoughtful dreaming; the dreamer is aware that he or she is dreaming and can manipulate the experience.
sleep terror An NREM episode in which the individual is partially aroused, disoriented, frightened, and inconsolable.

single-image variety characteristic of NREM dreams. Individuals often report feelings of pressure on the chest, which children interpret as a monster or bear sitting on them. There is usually no memory of the sleep terror the next day. A genetic predisposition appears to contribute to sleep terrors (APA, 2013). In addition, boys tend to experience sleep terrors more frequently than do girls. Fortunately, most children eventually outgrow their sleep terrors, although not fast enough for their weary family members. Adults who experience sleep terrors are more likely to have been diagnosed with some type of psychopathology, commonly anxiety or personality disorders (APA, 2013).

Sleep–Wake Disorders

The *Diagnostic and Statistical Manual of Mental Disorders* (DSM 5; APA, 2013) identifies a number of conditions related to the initiation, maintenance, timing, and quality of sleep. We will review the major types of these disorders.

Insomnia

The most common sleep–wake disorder is **insomnia**, in which a person has difficulty initiating or maintaining enough sleep to feel rested. Individual needs for sleep vary widely. In one case of "healthy insomnia," an elderly female participant slept only one hour per night without any apparent detrimental effects (Meddis, Pearson, & Langford, 1973).

Onset insomnia occurs when a person is unable to go to sleep. Sleep can be delayed by multiple factors, including stress, anxiety, and use of stimulant drugs. **Maintenance insomnia** occurs when sleep is frequently interrupted or early waking occurs. Frequent waking can result from stress, substance use, or psychopathology. As we'll see in Chapter 16, major depressive disorder often results in frequent waking. Drinking alcohol will put a person to sleep quickly, but early-morning waking often occurs as the alcohol effects wear off.

In any case of insomnia, diagnosis should be left to sleep experts. Occasionally, people overestimate the extent of their sleeplessness. Some people even dream that they are awake, a condition often referred to as *pseudoinsomnia* (Borkovec, Grayson,

●●● Behavioral
Neuroscience   **SLEEP MEDICINE**
GOES TO WORK

Years ago, it was nearly impossible for a person with a sleep–wake disorder to be evaluated outside a small, select group of university laboratories. Today, sleep centers are located in most geographical locations in the United States. Sleep evaluations used to mean that a person would need to sleep a minimum of one night at the center, but technology that is appropriate for home use is now available. In many ways, home evaluation more accurately captures the types of problems the patient is trying to resolve.

To maintain quality of treatment, the American Academy of Sleep Medicine (American Academy of Sleep Medicine [AASM], 2014) coordinates its certification programs with the American Board of Internal Medicine and the American Board of Psychiatry and Neurology, reflecting the interdisciplinary nature of sleep. Training involves reviewing real sleep records and seeing where a physician's evaluations of a record overlap or differ from a highly trained reviewer. The AASM also provides training and certification for sleep center staff leading to a sleep technologist certification.

As sleep gains more interest in the medical field as not just a symptom but a causal factor in some illnesses, it is likely that sleep evaluation will become a more routine part of a medical evaluation.

O'Brien, & Weerts, 1979). For minor cases of onset insomnia, behavioral adjustments are usually helpful. Keeping to a regular sleeping schedule, avoiding stimulants, and writing down "to do" lists prior to sleep may be all that's needed. If insomnia is associated with psychopathology, it should resolve along with the disorder during treatment.

Medications prescribed for insomnia include benzodiazepines and other sedatives. Sedatives speed up the onset of sleep by about 15 minutes and lengthen the night's sleep by perhaps a half hour (Buscemi et al., 2007). This small increase might not warrant the risk of dependence and other possible side effects of these medications. One of the more common medications prescribed for insomnia is zolpidem (Ambien), which acts as a GABA agonist, much like the benzodiazepines. Use of zolpidem has been associated with a number of troubling behaviors, including sleepwalking and binge eating or even driving while asleep (Dolder & Nelson, 2008). However, long-term sleep loss has its own risks. If behavioral treatment is ineffective, medications may be the only remaining option.

Narcolepsy

Probably the most dramatic of the sleep–wake disorders is **narcolepsy**. Narcolepsy consists of extreme levels of daytime sleepiness and "sleep attacks," in which aspects of REM sleep intrude into wakefulness (Dahl, Holttum, & Trubnick, 1994). These sleep attacks usually last from 10 to 20 minutes, although they can continue for as long as an hour. In a sleep attack, people with narcolepsy enter REM sleep immediately and awaken feeling refreshed. Sleepiness soon returns, however, with attacks occurring approximately every two to three hours. Narcolepsy might have affected Harriet Tubman, shown in ● Figure 11.25, who was one of the leaders of the Underground

Bettmann/Corbis

> ● **Figure 11.25 Narcolepsy Didn't Stop Harriet Tubman** In spite of her suspected narcolepsy, Harriet Tubman (1820–1913) helped hundreds of slaves escape through the Underground Railroad during the Civil War era. Tubman appears on the left in this photo with some of the former slaves whom she helped. Unfortunately, narcoleptic attacks are often brought on by stress. Tubman had a number of close escapes when she experienced sleep attacks while being pursued by Confederate troops and irate slave owners.

narcolepsy A sleep disorder characterized by the intrusion of REM sleep, and occasionally REM paralysis, into the waking state.

Railroad around the time of the American Civil War. Tubman had many close calls while aiding escaped slaves. The emotion of the escape might have triggered sleep attacks, which came at the most inconvenient times.

In addition to sleep attacks, other aspects of REM sleep can intrude into the waking periods of patients with narcolepsy. **Cataplexy** is a condition in which the muscle paralysis that is normally associated with REM sleep occurs when the person is completely awake. Cataplexy does not cause a loss of consciousness. The muscle paralysis can be fairly minor, affecting part of the face, for example, or large-scale enough to cause the person to collapse in a heap on the floor. Cataplexy is nearly always preceded by a strong emotional reaction or stress. Unfortunately, having sex is a common emotional trigger for the disorder.

Many patients with narcolepsy also experience **sleep paralysis**, or muscle paralysis that either precedes actual sleep or lingers once the person has awakened. In some patients, REM dreaming phenomena intrude into wakefulness in the form of **hypnogogic hallucinations** (preceding sleep) or **hypnopompic hallucinations** (upon awakening). The imagery in these hallucinations is similar to REM dreaming, but the person remains awake.

Narcolepsy results from disruptions in the synthesis of orexins (also known as hypocretins) or in their receptors. As we saw in Chapter 9, orexins also play a major role in appetite (Siegel, 1999, 2004). In general, orexins appear to monitor the internal and external states of the animal and adjust the level of arousal required for survival (Ohno & Sakurai, 2008). Orexins are typically found in the cerebrospinal fluid of people without narcolepsy but are absent or greatly reduced in patients with the disorder. In addition, cells in the hypothalamus that normally secrete orexins are missing or damaged in the brains of patients with narcolepsy (Thannickal et al., 2000). The genetic contribution to narcolepsy is demonstrated by the ability to breed dogs with the disorder (see ● Figure 11.26). However, the causes of narcolepsy in humans appears to be more complicated. Interactions between genetic vulnerabilities and autoimmune processes that attack orexin-producing cells in the brain provide a better explanation

cataplexy A feature of narcolepsy in which REM muscle paralysis intrudes into the waking state.

sleep paralysis A feature of narcolepsy in which REM muscle paralysis occurs preceding or following actual sleep.

hypnogogic hallucinations A REM-type dream that intrudes into the waking state prior to the onset of sleep.

hypnopompic hallucinations A REM-type dream that intrudes into the waking state upon awakening.

● **Figure 11.26 Narcolepsy Can Be Bred in Dogs** Sleep research Dr. William Dement is holding Tucker before (left) and after (right) a cataplexy attack. Although genetics play a big role in narcolepsy in dogs, human narcolepsy appears more complicated.

than simple genetics in human cases (Taheri & Mignot, 2002). Narcolepsy can be treated successfully with stimulant medications such as modafinil (Wise, Arand, Auger, Brooks, & Watson, 2007).

Breathing-Related Sleep Disorders

The breathing-related sleep disorders include obstructive sleep apnea hypopnea and central sleep apnea (APA, 2013). In **hypopnea**, the person experiences shallow breathing or a very low rate of breathing, while in **apnea**, breathing stops more completely. Obstructive sleep apnea hypopnea is typically caused by obstruction of the airways, while central sleep apnea is caused by deficits in the brain functions that maintain breathing during sleep.

It is not uncommon for people to stop breathing during sleep for very short periods, and breathing during REM sleep can be quite irregular. In apnea, breathing ceases for as long as a minute or two, resulting in reduced oxygen levels in the blood. The person awakens gasping for air, as if he or she had been underwater. Although sleep returns relatively quickly, apnea affects the quality of sleep enough to cause symptoms of sleep loss the next day. Possibly due to chronic sleep deprivation, apnea increases the risk for heart disease (Kendzerska, Gershon, Hawker, Leung, & Tomlinson, 2014).

Obstructive sleep apnea hypopnea often occurs in obese individuals who snore, indicating that airway obstructions might be the root of the problem. Losing weight or surgically correcting any obstructions in the airway can be helpful. In central sleep apnea, abnormalities occur in brainstem neurons responsible for the maintenance of breathing during sleep. Using machines to regulate airflow during sleep is an inconvenient but relatively effective solution.

Sudden Infant Death Syndrome (SIDS)

In **sudden infant death syndrome (SIDS)**, a basically healthy baby, usually between two and four months of age, dies while asleep. Sleeping position can play a major role in many cases of SIDS. At ages two to four months, babies are not very skilled at turning over. Between 1992 and 2003, SIDS rates in the United States dropped 50 percent after the American Academy of Pediatrics recommended putting infants to sleep on their backs instead of on their stomachs, as shown in ● Figure 11.27 (National Institute of Child Health and Human Development, [NICHHD] 2008; Malloy & Freeman, 2004). Rates of SIDS are lower among children who are breastfed, especially among those who are exclusively breastfed (Hauck, Thompson, Tanabe, Moon, & Vennemann, 2011). In spite of these improvements, SIDS remains the most common cause of death in the first six months of life in industrialized nations, yet its causes remain elusive (Krous, 2014).

No single factor appears to account for all cases of SIDS (Filiano & Kinney, 1994). In their triple-risk model of SIDS, Filiano and Kinney argue that SIDS involves a vulnerable infant in a critical period of development exposed to an external stressor. Among the vulnerabilities of infants are race, gender, and abnormalities in the serotonergic systems of the medulla (Paterson et al., 2006). African American babies are twice as likely to die from SIDS as white babies, and Native American infants are three times as likely to die from SIDS as white babies (NICHHD, 2002). Boys are at higher risk than girls (NICHHD, 2002). In addition to sleeping position, exposure to cigarette smoke (Klonoff-Cohen, Edelstein, & Lefkowitz, 1995) and sharing a bed with parents (Paterson et al., 2006) might act as external stressors.

hypopnea A reduction in airflow during sleep.
apnea The total absence of airflow for a period of time during sleep.
sudden infant death syndrome (SIDS) A syndrome in which an otherwise healthy infant stops breathing and dies during sleep.

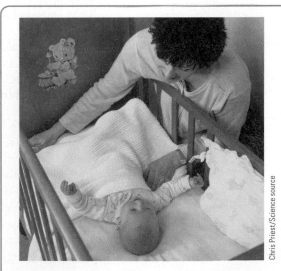

Chris Priest/Science source

● **Figure 11.27 Sleeping Position Helps Prevent SIDS** SIDS rates in the United States dropped 50 percent between 1992 and 2003 after the American Academy of Pediatrics (AAP) issued new recommendations for infant sleeping position. Unlike previous recommendations to put infants to sleep on their stomachs, the new AAP recommendations included putting babies to sleep on their backs with a blanket tucked in no higher than the chest. No pillows, stuffed animals, quilts, or other soft objects should be near the baby's face.

Sleep Talking and Sleep Walking

Sleep talking typically occurs in lighter stages of sleep of both REM and NREM. Sleep talking is most common in young people and diminishes with age. The talking person is often responsive to external stimuli. My college roommate and I were both frequent sleep talkers, and we would politely take our turns speaking. Eventually, the fact that my roommate's conversation had nothing to do with my own would wake me up. There is no support for the myth that people speak only the truth during sleep. Most of the time, the speaker's words don't seem to make much sense at all.

Sleepwalking is much more common in children than in adults; most sleepwalkers are between the ages of 4 and 12 years (Kryger, Roth, & Dement, 1994). At least 15 percent of children have one episode of sleepwalking, and 5 percent of children sleepwalk at least one time per week. During an episode, the child walks anywhere from a few seconds to 30 minutes. Body movements are typically uncoordinated and aimless rather than purposeful. As a result, sleepwalking can lead to physical injury from falling down stairs and similar accidents. Sleepwalking is probably a deep NREM phenomenon because episodes occur during the first three hours of sleep, awakened individuals show considerable disorientation, and the paralysis accompanying REM makes walking during this stage unlikely. Sleepwalking appears to run in families, with 80 percent of sleep walkers having a family history of sleepwalking or sleep terrors (APA, 2013). Episodes can be triggered by sleep deprivation, use of alcohol or other medications, stress, or fever (Pressman, 2007).

REM Sleep Behavior Disorder

In cataplexy, we observed the intrusion of REM paralysis into the waking state. In **REM sleep behavior disorder**, we see the absence of normal REM paralysis when it is supposed to occur. Instead of being paralyzed while dreaming, people with REM sleep behavior disorder act out their dreams, occasionally destroying furniture and injuring their sleeping partners and themselves. Schenck, Bundlie, Ettinger, and Mahowald (1986) describe a case study of a man who dreamed of playing football. During this episode, the man knocked everything off his dresser, hit his head against the wall, and hit his knee on the dresser.

REM sleep behavior disorder appears to be an inherited problem in most cases, but it can also result from brain damage, particularly in the pons (Culebras & Moore, 1989). As we discussed previously, structures within the pons are responsible for inhibiting motor movement during REM. When these areas are lesioned in cats, the cats behave as if they were acting out their dreams (Jouvet, 1972). REM sleep behavior disorder might also accompany or precede neurodegenerative diseases, especially Parkinson's disease (Fulda, 2011; Gugger & Wagner, 2007). REM sleep behavior disorder is usually treated with sedative medications, such as the benzodiazepines, or with melatonin (Gugger & Wagner, 2007).

Restless Leg Syndrome (RLS)

Restless leg syndrome (RLS) occurs when one of a person's limbs, usually a leg, experiences a sensation of tingling and moves at regular intervals of 15, 30, or 45 seconds. In the National Sleep Foundation (2009) Omnibus Sleep in America Poll, about 15 percent of the respondents reported symptoms of RLS. RLS occurs frequently in children and adults with attention deficit hyperactivity disorder (see Chapter 16; Wagner, Walters, & Fisher, 2004; Dement, 2000). Both conditions are characterized by atypical dopamine function (Taheri & Mignot, 2002). Other medical conditions, such as kidney disease, pregnancy, and anemia, might be at fault (Hening, Allen, Tenzer, & Winkelman, 2007). Treatment generally consists of massage, the application of heat or cold, avoidance of caffeine, and, if necessary, medication.

REM sleep behavior disorder
A sleep disorder in which the normal REM paralysis is absent.
restless leg syndrome (RLS)
A sleep disorder in which a limb, usually a leg, moves at regular intervals during sleep.

INTERIM SUMMARY 11.3

Name of Disorder	Major Features	Treatment (if any)
Insomnia	Difficulty initiating or maintaining sleep	• Avoidance of stimulants • Regular sleeping schedules • Treatment of underlying psychopathology (if present) • Medication
Narcolepsy	Inappropriate intrusions of sleep phenomena into normal waking	• Medication • Stress management
Breathing-related sleep disorders	Failure to maintain normal breathing patterns during sleep	• Weight loss • Surgical correction of airways • Mechanical regulation of airflow during sleep
Sudden infant death syndrome (SIDS)	Unexplained death of otherwise healthy infant during sleep	• Avoiding smoking in household with infants • Avoiding putting infant to sleep on stomach or with blankets or stuffed animals
Sleep talking	Speech during early stages of NREM and REM	None—appears to diminish with age
Sleepwalking	Walking during deep stages of NREM	None—appears to diminish with age
REM sleep behavior disorder	Lack of normal muscle paralysis during REM sleep	Medication
Restless leg syndrome	Regular movements of limbs during sleep	• Correction of any underlying medical conditions • Massage • Application of heat or cold • Medication

‖ Summary

1. Among the leading theories of the function of sleep are the ideas that sleep keeps us safe, sleep restores the body, and memories are consolidated during sleep. **(LO3)**

2. Several theories attempt to identify the functions of REM dreams, including the activation-synthesis theory, the Crick-Mitcheson forgetting theory, Winson's evolutionary theory, and the threat simulation theory. **(LO3)**

3. Sleep–wake disorders include insomnia, narcolepsy, breathing-related sleep disorders, nightmares, sleep terrors, sleep talking, sleepwalking, REM sleep behavior disorder, and restless leg syndrome (RLS). **(LO4)**

‖ Review Questions

1. Considering the benefits of sleep discussed in this section, what are the likely risks of all-nighters and sleep deprivation?

2. What treatments are available for sleep–wake disorders?

Chapter Review

THOUGHT QUESTIONS

1. A recent survey asked participants to rate their "highs," or experiences that made them feel especially wonderful. For middle-aged respondents, one of the top five highs was eight hours of uninterrupted sleep. Why do you think this item was reported as a high by people in this age group?
2. Describe the likely effects that being blind would have on your daily sleep–waking cycles. What advice would you give a blind person to improve the quality of his or her sleep?
3. Using the information you learned in this chapter, explain the relationship between low serotonin and the sleep disturbances characteristic of depression.

KEY TERMS

alpha wave (p. 376)
apnea (p. 000)
beta wave (p. 376)
breathing-related sleep disorder (p. 000)
cataplexy (p. 394)
circadian rhythm (p. 364)
cortisol (p. 372)
default mode network (DMN) (p. 380)
delta wave (p. 378)
gamma-band activity (p. 376)
growth hormone (GH) (p. 388)

insomnia (p. 392)
jet lag (p. 367)
K-complex (p. 378)
lucid dreaming (p. 391)
maintenance insomnia (p. 392)
major depressive disorder with seasonal pattern (p. 373)
melatonin (p. 370)
narcolepsy (p. 393)
nightmare (p. 391)
non-REM sleep (NREM) (p. 377)
onset insomnia (p. 392)
PGO wave (p. 382)

rapid-eye-movement (REM) sleep (p. 377)
REM sleep behavior disorder (p. 396)
restless leg syndrome (RLS) (p. 396)
retinohypothalamic pathway (p. 369)
sleep spindle (p. 377)
sleep terror (p. 391)
sudden infant death syndrome (SIDS) (p. 395)
suprachiasmatic nucleus (SCN) (p. 367)
theta wave (p. 377)
ultradian cycle (p. 364)
zeitgeber (p. 364)

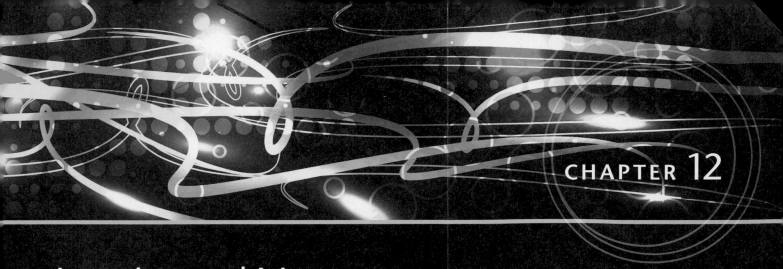

CHAPTER 12

Learning and Memory

LEARNING OBJECTIVES

LO1 Differentiate between reflexive behaviors, fixed action patterns, and learned behaviors.

LO2 Explain the correlations between changes in synaptic processing and brain activity that coincide with learning.

LO3 Differentiate between the major types of memory and their correlated brain structures and patterns of activity.

LO4 Identify major biochemical pathways associated with memory formation.

LO5 Explain the effects of stress and normal aging on learning and memory.

BEHAVIORAL NEUROSCIENCE GOES TO WORK: What Is Neuro Education?

CONNECTING TO RESEARCH: Karl Lashley's Search for the Engram

THINKING ETHICALLY: Should We Erase Traumatic Memories?

BUILDING BETTER HEALTH: Can We Avoid Age-Related Memory Deficits?

CHAPTER OUTLINE

reflex An involuntary response to a stimulus.

fixed action pattern (also known as instinct) A stereotyped pattern of behavior elicited by particular environmental stimuli.

learning A relatively permanent change in behavior or the capacity for behavior due to experience.

associative learning A type of learning that involves the formation of a connection between two elements or events.

Learning

In the ongoing challenge that is daily survival, organisms must have ways to respond to the fluid, ever-changing stimulus environment by producing appropriate patterns of behavior.

The behavior of organisms can be separated into three major categories: reflexes, fixed action patterns (instincts), and learned behaviors. **Reflexes** are inevitable, involuntary responses to stimuli. These behaviors are produced by prewired neural connections or reflex arcs. Reflexes have the advantage of producing rapid, reliable responses, but their inflexibility can be a disadvantage when the environment changes (see ●Figure 12.1).

Fixed action patterns, also known as instincts, are species-specific, inborn patterns of behavior elicited by specific environmental stimuli or "releasers." Like reflexes, fixed action patterns are automatic, unconscious responses to the environment, but their behavioral patterns are more complex. Once initiated in response to a releaser, the stereotypical fixed action pattern runs to completion. Most fixed action patterns involve mating or parenting behavior (Tinbergen, 1951). In the courtship display of the male peacock, the identification of an appropriate female partner initiates a chain of predictable, stereotyped behaviors. A possible example of a human fixed action pattern is contagious yawning, or yawning in response to seeing others yawn (Provine, 1986, 2005) (see ● Figure 12.2).

Learning, or a relatively permanent change in behavior (or the capacity for behavior) due to experience, provides organisms with the most flexible means for responding to the environment. Human beings occupy nearly every niche on the planet, from blazing equatorial environments to the frigid Arctic. Much of this adaptability stems from the remarkable human capacity for learned behavior. Our definition of learning specifies that only those behavioral changes that result from experience will be considered learned. This specification excludes changes in behavior that occur due to maturation or growth. The requirement that learning be "relatively permanent" excludes brief or unstable changes in behavior. Fatigue, boredom, illness, and mood all influence behavior, but in a temporary and transitory manner. Exactly how permanent memories really are is open to debate, as we will see later in this chapter.

Learning occurs in one of two ways. **Associative learning** occurs when an organism forms a connection between two features of its environment. Classical conditioning, which allows organisms to learn about signals that predict important events,

> ● **Figure 12.1** Reflexes Provide Fast, Reliable Responses If the frog had to calculate the distance and movement of its prey, it would very likely go hungry. Instead, a visual signal from the frog's retina indicating the presence of an insect elicits a reflexive tongue strike in the right direction. Reflexes, however, are not flexible. When the frog's eye is rotated (Sperry, 1945), the animal is unable to learn to correct the direction of its tongue strike.

Buddy Mays/Alamy

● **Figure 12.2 Contagious Yawning Might Be a Fixed Action Pattern** Although some scientists disagree, contagious yawning might represent a fixed action pattern for a number of species including our own. Puppies over the age of seven months were susceptible to contagious yawning (Provine, 1986).

Carolyn Brown/Science Source

and operant conditioning, in which a behavior's consequences change its subsequent frequency, fall into this category. **Nonassociative learning**, including the processes of habituation and sensitization, involves changes in the magnitude of responses to stimuli rather than the formation of connections between specific elements or events.

Habituation and Sensitization

Habituation occurs when an organism reduces its response to unchanging, harmless stimuli. You might sleep better the second night you spend in a hotel than the first, because you have habituated to all of the new sounds. **Sensitization** occurs when repeated exposure to a strong stimulus increases response to other environmental stimuli. For example, following major disasters such as earthquakes, people often experience exaggerated responses to movement, light, and noise. Increasing our overall level of responsiveness as a result of detecting one type of harmful stimulus makes us able to react more quickly to other sources of potential harm, even if the precise stimulus that signals danger changes. Why would we show habituation to some stimuli and sensitization to others? In general, habituation occurs in response to milder stimuli, like noises in a hotel, while sensitization occurs in response to stronger stimuli, like the shaking of an earthquake.

Classical Conditioning

In **classical conditioning**, organisms learn that stimuli act as signals that predict the occurrence of other important events. Credit for discovering and articulating the basic phenomena of classical conditioning goes to the famous Russian physiologist Ivan Pavlov (1927). Pavlov distinguished between conditioned and unconditioned stimuli and responses. The term *conditioned* refers to the presence of learning, whereas *unconditioned* refers to factors that are innate or unlearned. Therefore, a

nonassociative learning A type of learning that involves a change in the magnitude of responses to stimuli rather than the formation of connections between elements or events.

habituation A type of learning in which the response to a repeated, harmless stimulus becomes progressively weaker.

sensitization A type of learning in which the experience of one stimulus heightens response to subsequent stimuli.

classical conditioning A type of associative learning in which a neutral stimulus acquires the ability to signal the occurrence of a second, biologically significant event.

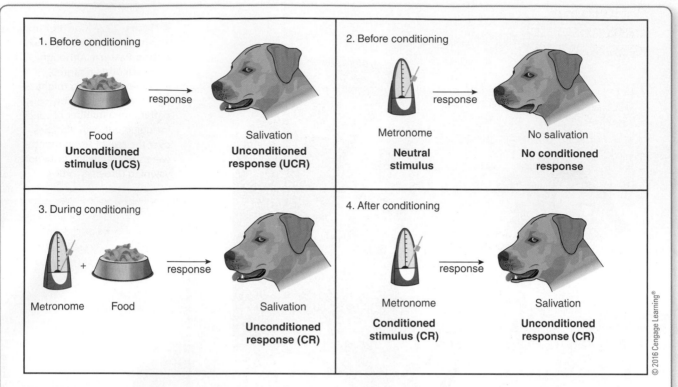

1. Before conditioning

response

Food
**Unconditioned
stimulus (UCS)**

Salivation
**Unconditioned
response (UCR)**

2. Before conditioning

response

Metronome
**Neutral
stimulus**

No salivation
**No conditioned
response**

3. During conditioning

Metronome + Food

response

Salivation
**Unconditioned
response (CR)**

4. After conditioning

response

Metronome
**Conditioned
stimulus (CR)**

Salivation
**Unconditioned
response (CR)**

© 2016 Cengage Learning®

● **Figure 12.3** **The Process of Classical Conditioning** Prior to training (1 and 2), the food (unconditioned stimulus) can elicit salivation (unconditioned response), but the dog shows no particular response to the sound of the ticking metronome. After the sound has been paired with the arrival of food (3), however, the sound (conditioned stimulus; 4) alone now gains the power to elicit salivation (conditioned response). The dog has learned that the sound is a reliable signal for the arrival of food.

conditioned stimulus (CS) refers to an environmental event whose significance is learned, whereas an **unconditioned stimulus (UCS)** has innate meaning to the organism. In many of Pavlov's classic experiments with his famous salivating dogs, diagrammed in ● Figure 12.3, a ticking metronome served as a conditioned stimulus, and food was used as the unconditioned stimulus. Dogs lack innate responses to ticking metronomes, but they generally are born knowing what to do with food.

Conditioned responses (CR) are those behaviors that must be learned, whereas **unconditioned responses (UCR)** appear without prior experience with a stimulus. Salivating in response to the presence of food in the mouth is unconditioned because the dog does this without prior experience with food. Salivating in response to a ticking metronome is a conditioned response because the dog does this only as a result of experience. The development of conditioned responses constitutes the change in behavior that tells us learning has occurred. Once learning has taken place, the organism not only responds to the unconditioned stimulus but now responds to stimuli that reliably predict its arrival. This ability to anticipate future events and prepare responses provides significant advantages to an organism in the struggle for survival.

Operant Conditioning

In **operant conditioning**, examined extensively by B. F. Skinner, organisms form connections between a behavior and its consequences that impact the subsequent frequency of that behavior. Reinforcing consequences increase the likelihood the behavior will be repeated, while punishing consequences reduce the likelihood that the behavior will be repeated. Unlike classical conditioning, which is an association between two stimuli (e.g., metronome and food), operant conditioning links a behavior and a stimulus (pressing a bar leads to food). Classical conditioning usually involves

conditioned stimulus (CS) In classical conditioning, an initially neutral event that takes on the ability to signal other biologically significant events.
unconditioned stimulus (UCS) In classical conditioning, an event that elicits a response without prior experience.
conditioned response (CR) In classical conditioning, a learned reaction to the conditioned stimulus.
unconditioned response (UCR) In classical conditioning, a spontaneous unlearned reaction to a stimulus without prior experience.
operant conditioning Learning that links behavior with its consequences, producing change in the subsequent frequency of the behavior.

Behavioral Neuroscience GOES TO WORK

WHAT IS NEURO EDUCATION?

As you will see in this chapter, cognitive neuroscientists have made significant progress in understanding how the brain processes learning and memory. This understanding is central to our efforts to enhance learning in educational settings, yet, traditionally, the fields of education and neuroscience have not held many conversations.

The isolated specializations that characterized academic life in the 20th century have begun to give way to more transdisciplinary, problem-based teamwork. For example, at Johns Hopkins, the School of Education is partnering with the School of Medicine, Kennedy-Krieger Institute, and the Brain Science Institute on a Neuro Education Initiative. Among the goals of the program are the pursuit of joint research projects and efforts to develop better lines of communication between educators and neuroscientists (Johns Hopkins School of Education, 2014).

As you work your way through the material in this chapter, try thinking about ways that our knowledge of learning and memory processes in the brain might be used to enhance the educational experience of students. How would elementary and secondary school teachers and your professors apply this information in the classroom?

relatively involuntary behaviors, such as fear or salivation, while operant conditioning usually affects voluntary behavior, like studying for an exam or waving to a friend.

Learning at the Synapse

We begin our exploration of the neuroscience of learning by zooming in to look at changes taking place at the level of the synapse. Much of our knowledge regarding the synaptic mechanisms of learning is the result of investigations using invertebrates. Invertebrates are not only capable of several types of learning, but their large-celled, simple, and, hence, easily observed nervous systems also make them ideal subjects. Some invertebrate learning research is bizarre, such as G. A. Horridge's (1962) demonstration that headless cockroaches can learn classically conditioned responses. More typically, researchers have relied on fruit flies or the sea slug, *Aplysia californica*, shown in ● Figure 12.4.

© Visual&Written SL/Alamy

● **Figure 12.4** *Aplysia californica* The sea slug, *Aplysia californica*, has been a useful subject in the search for the underlying neural mechanisms of habituation, sensitization, classical conditioning, and more recently, operant conditioning.

Aplysia californica An invertebrate sea slug frequently used as a subject of experiments on learning and memory.

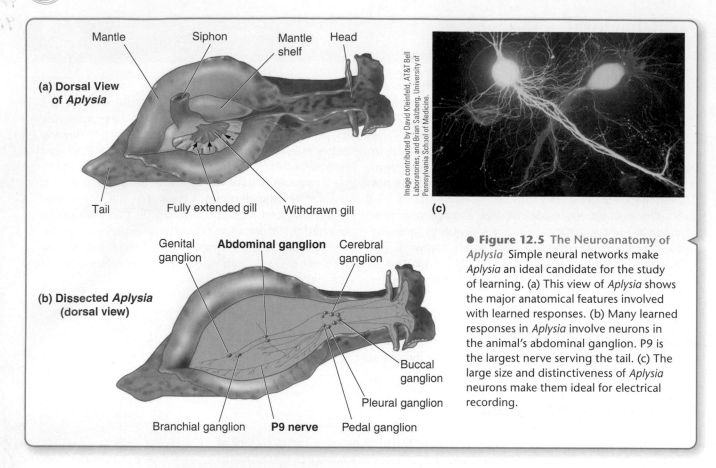

(a) Dorsal View of Aplysia

Mantle · Siphon · Mantle shelf · Head

Tail · Fully extended gill · Withdrawn gill

(b) Dissected Aplysia (dorsal view)

Genital ganglion · **Abdominal ganglion** · Cerebral ganglion

Buccal ganglion

Pleural ganglion

Branchial ganglion · **P9 nerve** · Pedal ganglion

(c)

Image contributed by David Kleinfeld, AT&T Bell Laboratories, and Brian Salzberg, University of Pennsylvania School of Medicine.

● **Figure 12.5** The Neuroanatomy of *Aplysia* Simple neural networks make *Aplysia* an ideal candidate for the study of learning. (a) This view of *Aplysia* shows the major anatomical features involved with learned responses. (b) Many learned responses in *Aplysia* involve neurons in the animal's abdominal ganglion. P9 is the largest nerve serving the tail. (c) The large size and distinctiveness of *Aplysia* neurons make them ideal for electrical recording.

To understand learning processes in *Aplysia*, it is helpful to know a bit about its anatomy, shown in ● Figure 12.5. On the dorsal surface of the animal, you can locate the gill, which the animal uses to breathe. The gill can be covered by a structure known as the mantle shelf. At one end of the mantle shelf is the siphon, a tube through which the animal releases waste and seawater. Touching the animal's siphon reliably produces a protective response known as the **gill-withdrawal reflex**, in which the gill is retracted. In addition to this natural defensive response, researchers interested in learning have also taken advantage of the animal's tendency to engage in spontaneous biting behavior.

Simple invertebrates such as *Aplysia* have neural nets as opposed to brains (see Chapter 2). Within these neural nets, ganglia, or collections of cell bodies, serve as major processing centers. The siphon is served by 24 touch receptors whose cell bodies are located in the animal's abdominal ganglion. In the *Aplysia* abdominal ganglion, the touch receptors form synapses with a number of excitatory and inhibitory inter-neurons as well as with the six motor neurons serving the gill.

Short-Term Habituation at the Synapse

When the *Aplysia* siphon is touched repeatedly, the gill-withdrawal reflex habituates, or weakens. Beginning in the 1960s, Eric Kandel and his colleagues began to trace the neural pathways responsible for the habituation of this reflex.

Kandel and his colleagues considered several possible hypotheses that might account for habituation within this simple network. With repeated stimulation, the sensory neurons serving the siphon might become less responsive. This possibility was discarded after recordings from the sensory neurons demonstrated steady, ongoing activity in response to touch, even after the gill-withdrawal reflex had become very weak. Another possibility was a reduction in the gill muscle's ability to react

gill-withdrawal reflex In Aplysia, a protective reflex in which the gill is retracted in response to touch.

in response to input from the motor neurons. This explanation was ruled out when electrical stimulation of the motor neurons reliably produced muscle contraction, even after habituation had occurred.

This leaves a final alternative. Repeated touching of the siphon might produce changes at synapses between the sensory neurons of the siphon and motor neurons that serve the gill muscles. Kandel successfully demonstrated that repeated touching of the siphon reduced the size of excitatory postsynaptic potentials (EPSPs; see Chapter 3) in relevant interneurons and motor neurons. As shown in ● Figure 12.6, a smaller amount of input to the motor neurons resulted in diminished activity between the motor neurons and gill muscles, which in turn produced a weak withdrawal reflex.

Kandel further demonstrated that the reduced activity at the synapse between the sensory and motor neurons in habituation was a direct result of the release of less neurotransmitter (Castelucci, Carew, & Kandel, 1978). The repeated stimulation depletes the amount of available neurotransmitter in the presynaptic sensory neuron, producing a type of short-term habituation now referred to as "within-session" habituation (Thompson, 2009).

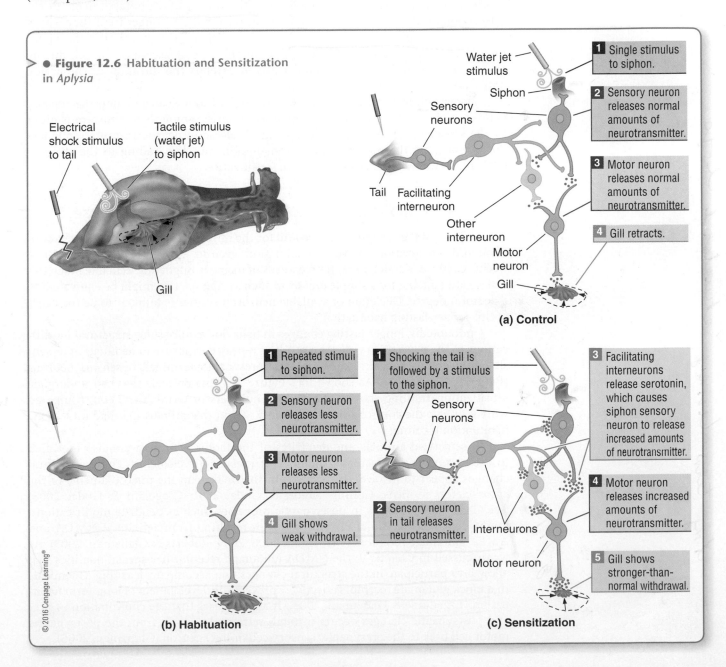

● **Figure 12.6** Habituation and Sensitization in *Aplysia*

Electrical shock stimulus to tail

Tactile stimulus (water jet) to siphon

Gill

Water jet stimulus

Siphon

Sensory neurons

Tail Facilitating interneuron

Other interneuron

Motor neuron

Gill

1 Single stimulus to siphon.

2 Sensory neuron releases normal amounts of neurotransmitter.

3 Motor neuron releases normal amounts of neurotransmitter.

4 Gill retracts.

(a) Control

1 Repeated stimuli to siphon.

2 Sensory neuron releases less neurotransmitter.

3 Motor neuron releases less neurotransmitter.

4 Gill shows weak withdrawal.

(b) Habituation

1 Shocking the tail is followed by a stimulus to the siphon.

Sensory neurons

2 Sensory neuron in tail releases neurotransmitter.

Interneurons

Motor neuron

3 Facilitating interneurons release serotonin, which causes siphon sensory neuron to release increased amounts of neurotransmitter.

4 Motor neuron releases increased amounts of neurotransmitter.

5 Gill shows stronger-than-normal withdrawal.

(c) Sensitization

© 2016 Cengage Learning®

Short-Term Sensitization at the Synapse

Habituation in *Aplysia* occurs in a single pathway connecting sensory input from the siphon to neurons controlling the movement of the gill. In sensitization, however, a stimulus gains the ability to influence more than one neural pathway. After *Aplysia* is sensitized by the administration of an electric shock to the head or tail, touching the siphon results in an enhanced gill-withdrawal response.

A diagram of the basic connections responsible for sensitization is shown in Figure 12.6. Shocking the animal's tail stimulates sensory neurons, which form excitatory synapses with a group of interneurons. These interneurons, in turn, form synapses with the sensory neurons serving the siphon. The synapses between the interneurons and sensory neurons are axo-axonic in form. In other words, the axon from the interneuron forms a facilitating synapse at the axon terminal of the sensory neuron (see Chapter 3). The interneurons release serotonin at these axo-axonic synapses (Brunelli, Castellucci, & Kandel, 1976). When receptors on the sensory axon terminal bind molecules of serotonin, a metabotropic process (see Chapter 4) closes potassium channels. With the closing of the potassium channels, action potentials reaching the sensory axon terminal last longer than they would in a typical response to a siphon touch. (Recall from Chapter 3 that the opening of potassium channels is responsible for the repolarization of the cell during an action potential. Delaying repolarization extends the duration of the action potential.)

Longer action potentials produce a greater influx of calcium into the sensory neuron, which in turn results in the release of larger amounts of neurotransmitter by the sensory axon terminal. The increased release of neurotransmitter enhances the response by the motor neurons and the gill muscles, leading to the stronger gill-withdrawal reflex that we observe in sensitization.

Long-Term Habituation and Sensitization at the Synapse

Adjustments at the synaptic level account for the immediate changes we see in habituation and sensitization. However, habituation, even in *Aplysia*, can last up to three weeks (Carew & Kandel, 1973). Three weeks of memory might not seem like much to a college student, but for a simple organism such as *Aplysia*, this might be equivalent to a doctoral degree. Depletion of available neurotransmitter is unlikely to be the cause of this longer-lasting habituation.

Undoubtedly, longer-lasting changes in behavior require some structural modifications to the neurons as well. As a result of repeated exposure to habituation or sensitization, changes occur in the number of presynaptic terminals of sensory neurons (Bailey & Chen, 1983). As shown in ● Figure 12.7, the animals that had undergone sensitization training showed the highest numbers of terminals, 2,800, compared with 1,300 for the control animals and only 800 in the animals that had undergone habituation training.

In sensitized animals, the dendrites of the motor neurons were also modified to accommodate the increased number of presynaptic elements. These structural changes appear to involve actin, a protein that makes up the microfilaments of the cytoskeleton (Colicos, Collins, Sailor, & Goda, 2001; Cingolani & Goda, 2008) (see Chapter 3). Changes in postsynaptic processes, such as dendrite modifications, might involve intracellular enzyme cascades resulting from activity at NMDA and AMPA glutamate receptors (Glanzman, 2006, 2009; Roberts & Glanzman, 2003). As we discussed in Chapter 4, the NMDA glutamate receptor has special qualities that allow it to participate in the structural changes that accompany learning. Chemicals that block glutamate receptors effectively prevent the development of long-term habituation (Ezzeddine & Glanzman, 2003). It also appears that the coordination of pre- and postsynaptic changes occurs through retrograde signals from the postsynaptic motor cell back to the presynaptic sensory cell or interneuron (Glanzman, 2006).

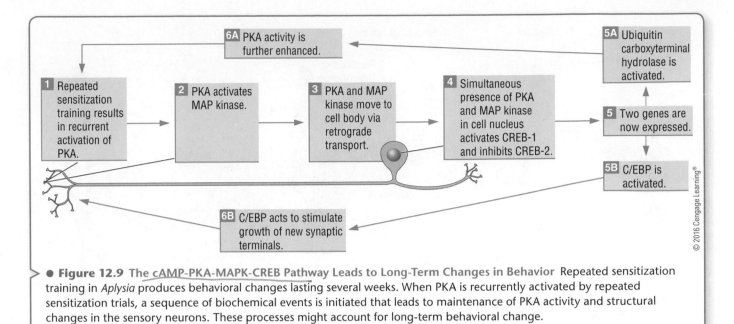

● **Figure 12.9** The **cAMP-PKA-MAPK-CREB Pathway Leads to Long-Term Changes in Behavior** Repeated sensitization training in *Aplysia* produces behavioral changes lasting several weeks. When PKA is recurrently activated by repeated sensitization trials, a sequence of biochemical events is initiated that leads to maintenance of PKA activity and structural changes in the sensory neurons. These processes might account for long-term behavioral change.

This enzyme allows PKA to be nearly continuously active. As a result, neurotransmitter release continues to be elevated long after training has ceased. The second activated gene encodes a protein known as **C/EBP**. C/EBP in turn activates other genes that stimulate the growth of new synaptic terminals on the sensory neuron. As we observed previously, *Aplysia* given repeated sensitization training show approximately twice the number of sensory neuron synaptic terminals as do control animals.

These biochemical and structural changes stimulated by the cAMP-PKA-MAPK-CREB pathway probably account for the long-term presynaptic changes observed following repeated sensitization training. Similar processes might underlie all long-term memory formation. The cAMP-PKA pathway also appears to be important to changes associated with learning and memory in the brains of mammals (Arnsten et al., 2005).

Classical Conditioning at the Synapse

In addition to their ability to display nonassociative learning, *Aplysia* are also capable of demonstrating associative learning in the form of classical conditioning. In a typical experiment, illustrated in ● Figure 12.10, a slight touch of the mantle shelf serves as the conditioned stimulus (CS^+), and an electrical shock to the tail serves as the unconditioned stimulus (UCS). This electrical shock to the tail reliably elicits the gill-withdrawal reflex (UCR). To provide a control stimulus that is not paired with shock, the siphon (CS^-) of the *Aplysia* is occasionally touched, but not frequently enough to produce habituation.

Prior to training, touching the mantle shelf produces little if any movement of the gill. After several pairings of the mantle shelf touch (CS^+) and the electrical shock to the tail (UCS), the mantle shelf touch is applied alone to see whether any learning has occurred. Typically, the mantle shelf by itself will now elicit a stronger gill-withdrawal reflex (CR). In contrast, no changes are observed in the animal's response to the siphon touch (CS^-), which has never been paired with shock (UCS). The change in the ability of the CS^+ to elicit strong gill-withdrawal reflexes meets our definition of classical conditioning.

As we observed in sensitization, change in the gill-withdrawal reflex parallels change in the amount of neurotransmitter released by the sensory neurons onto the motor neurons serving the gill muscles. The mantle shelf touch (CS^+) produces action potentials in a sensory neuron. When these action potentials reach the axon terminal, calcium (Ca^{2+}) enters the cell and determines the amount of neurotransmitter to be released onto the motor neuron controlling the gill-withdrawal reflex. The shock to the tail (UCS) results in the release of serotonin by an interneuron onto the sensory axon serving the mantle in the same manner that we observed in our discussion of

C/EBP A substance activated by CREB-1 that in turn activates genes related to synaptic growth.

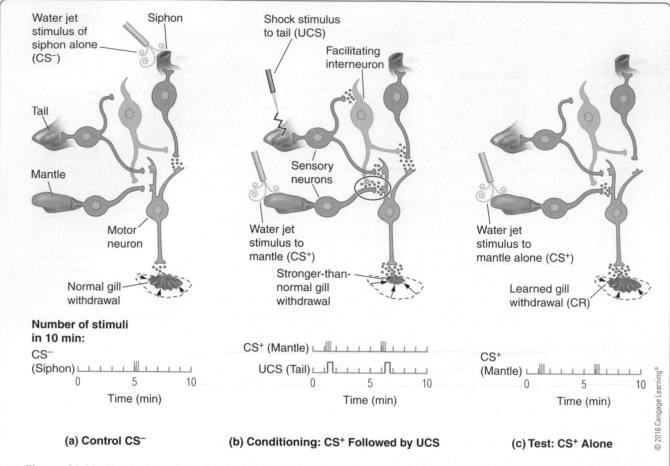

● **Figure 12.10 Classical Conditioning in *Aplysia*** (a) Touching the siphon (CS^-) is not paired with shock and serves as a control. (b) Touching the mantle (CS^+) is always followed by shock to the tail (UCS). (c) After several pairings of touching the mantle (CS^+) followed by shock (UCS), touching the mantle alone now triggers gill withdrawal (CR). In the circled area in (b), the mantle shelf sensory neurons are sequentially activated, first by touching the mantle shelf and then by input from interneurons serving the tail. This sequence produces increased presynaptic facilitation, leading to the recording of greater postsynaptic potentials in the motor neuron than those recorded prior to training.

sensitization. Once again, potassium channels close, increasing the amount of neurotransmitter that is released by the sensory neuron onto the motor neuron. Most importantly, we can see how the conditioned and unconditioned stimuli interact to boost the amount of neurotransmitter released by the sensory neuron. Whenever large concentrations of Ca^{2+} are present, the processes leading to potassium channel closing are enhanced (Abrams, Yovell, Onyike, Cohen, & Jarrad, 1998). The arrival of the signal from the CS^+ at the sensory axon terminal triggers the increase in Ca^{2+} necessary to enhance the effects of the serotonin released by the interneuron in response to the UCS. As in the cases of habituation and sensitization, postsynaptic mechanisms leading to structural change also contribute to classical conditioning (Antonov, Antonova, Kandel, & Hawkins, 2003; Antonov, Ha, Antonova, Moroz, & Hawkins, 2007).

Classical conditioning can occur to both rewarding unconditioned stimuli (food) and aversive conditioning stimuli (electric shock). Using another type of snail, the *Lymnaea*, the networks responsible for conditioning in these two different situations have been identified (Kemenes, O'Shea, & Benjamin, 2011). Amyl acetate (CS), commonly used to provide a fruity banana flavor to foods, was followed by either sucrose (reward UCS) or quinine (aversive UCS) unconditioned stimuli. Even though the CS was the same in either case, it promoted an increase in feeding when paired with sucrose and an inhibition of feeding when paired with quinine, which tastes bitter to us. This allowed the researchers to identify two separate networks: an excitatory network supporting the reward conditioning that uses dopamine and an inhibitory network supporting the aversive conditioning that uses octopamine, which is the sea snail equivalent of norepinephrine.

Operant Conditioning at the Synapse

Operant conditioning results when an organism's naturally occurring behavior becomes more or less frequent in response to its consequences. The previous section outlined some of the advances that have been made in our understanding of classical conditioning at the level of the synapse, but far less is known about the underlying mechanisms of operant conditioning. Discovering a way to study operant conditioning in simple animals has been hampered by their limited repertoire of spontaneous behavior. As described by learning researcher Bjorn Brembs, *Aplysia's* behavior is largely limited to eating and reproduction. Brembs and his colleagues cleverly increased the frequency of the animals' biting behavior (part of its feeding repertoire) by stimulating the esophageal nerve, which mimicked the arrival of food (Brembs, Lorenzetti, Reyes, Baxter, & Byrne, 2002). Evidence of operant conditioning of the biting behavior lasted at least 24 hours and could be attributed to changes in the animals' buccal ganglion neurons, shown earlier in Figure 12.5.

Not only can operant conditioning be observed in living animals, but it can also be demonstrated in single cells of the buccal ganglion in a cell culture (Lorenzetti, Baxter, & Byrne, 2008). In particular, buccal neuron 51 (B51) appears to be a decision-making neuron in the operant conditioning situation. When dopamine is applied to isolated B51 neurons at precisely the correct moment to mimic operant conditioning, these cells show higher excitability (Brembs et al., 2002). The eventual effects of operant conditioning on the action of the buccal neuron network appears to "fix" what had been a fairly random pattern of behavior into a more reliable, stereotyped pattern, as shown in ● Figure 12.11 (Nargeot & Simmers, 2011).

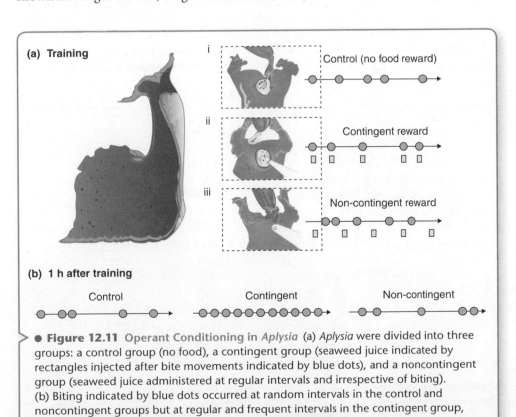

● **Figure 12.11 Operant Conditioning in** *Aplysia* (a) *Aplysia* were divided into three groups: a control group (no food), a contingent group (seaweed juice indicated by rectangles injected after bite movements indicated by blue dots), and a noncontingent group (seaweed juice administered at regular intervals and irrespective of biting). (b) Biting indicated by blue dots occurred at random intervals in the control and noncontingent groups but at regular and frequent intervals in the contingent group, indicating behavior had changed due to operant conditioning.

Source: Nargeot, R., & Simmers, J. (2011). Neural mechanisms of operant conditioning and learning-induced behavioral plasticity in Aplysia. *Cellular and Molecular Life Sciences, 68*(5), 803–816.

Brain Structures and Circuits Involved in Learning

Zooming out from the microscopic level of the synapse, progress has also been made in gaining further understanding about the brain structures and circuits involved in learning.

Classical Conditioning of Threat

Many emotional responses to environmental stimuli are learned by the process of classical conditioning, such as the nervousness students feel before a big exam or a child's fear of dogs following a dog bite. The underlying circuits for this type of classical conditioning are well understood. For the purposes of this discussion, it is important to distinguish between "fear" as a conscious feeling of being afraid and "threat," which is the unconscious mobilization of defensive behaviors (LeDoux, 2014).

The amygdala is a complex structure that plays an important role in the classical conditioning of emotional responses (Wilensky, Schafe, Kristensen, & LeDoux, 2006). Lesion studies, recording studies, and research involving the administration of NMDA antagonists all point to the importance of the amygdala in this type of learning (LeDoux, 1994; Quirk, Repa, & LeDoux, 1995; Gewirtz & Davis, 1997; Fanselow & LeDoux, 1999).

In a typical investigation of classically conditioned threat in rats, a stimulus such as a tone (CS) is followed by electrical shock to the feet (UCS). The conditioned response (CR) is a reduction in behaviors that are incompatible with threat, such as feeding. Following the pairing of a shock with a tone, the tone by itself will begin to serve as a danger signal that evokes defensive responses and inhibits feeding. As shown in ● Figure 12.12, information about the tone (CS) and the shock (UCS) converges in the lateral nucleus of the amygdala, while the central nucleus initiates the defensive response, which in this example would be freezing (Ciocchi et al., 2010; Wilensky, Schafe, Kristensen, & LeDoux, 2006). When the same cells are receiving input about both the CS and UCS within a short period of time, the resulting high influx of calcium triggers a cascade of events, similar to those observed in *Aplysia*, that

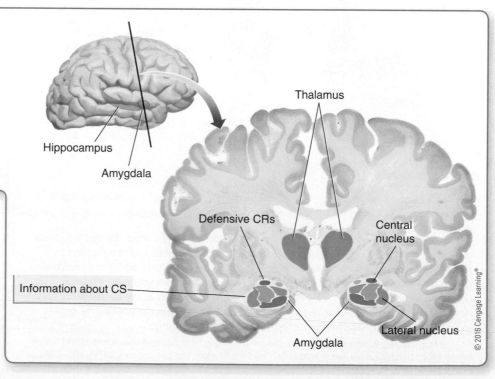

● **Figure 12.12** The Amygdala Participates in Threat Conditioning Sensory information about a conditioned stimulus (CS) converges on the lateral nucleus of the amygdala. Output from the central nucleus of the amygdala results in defensive behaviors (CRs) like freezing.

Hippocampus

Amygdala

Thalamus

Defensive CRs

Central nucleus

Information about CS

Amygdala

Lateral nucleus

© 2016 Cengage Learning®

result in protein synthesis and more sensitivity to subsequent CS input. Consequently, when the CS is presented alone, the newly conditioned circuits within the amygdala respond more strongly than before and are capable of generating the threat response.

Classical Conditioning of the Eyeblink

Additional insight into the brain structures associated with classical conditioning comes from investigations into conditioned eyeblinks in the rabbit by Richard Thompson and his colleagues (Christian & Thompson, 2003; Lee & Thompson, 2006; Thompson, Thompson, Kim, Krupa, & Shinkman, 1998). In this type of experiment, a tone (CS) is followed by a puff of air directed at the rabbit's eye (UCS), which causes movement of the rabbit's **nictitating membrane** (UCR), an additional inner eyelid found in some birds, fish, and mammals, but not in humans. After several pairings of the tone and puff, the tone alone will elicit the movement of the nictitating membrane (CR). Considerable evidence points to a role for the cerebellum in this type of classical conditioning (Woodruff-Pak & Disterhoft, 2008).

Thompson and his colleagues focused on a particular structure in the cerebellum known as the **interpositus nucleus**. Recordings from cells in the interpositus nucleus initially show little response to the tone CS. However, as learning proceeds, a steady increase in this structure's response occurs (Thompson, 1986). Further evidence for the importance of the interpositus nucleus in classical conditioning was demonstrated through a series of reversible lesion experiments, illustrated in ● Figure 12.13.

nictitating membrane An additional, moveable inner eyelid found in some birds, fish, and mammals, but not in humans.

interpositus nucleus A cerebellar nucleus thought to be essential to classical conditioning in vertebrates.

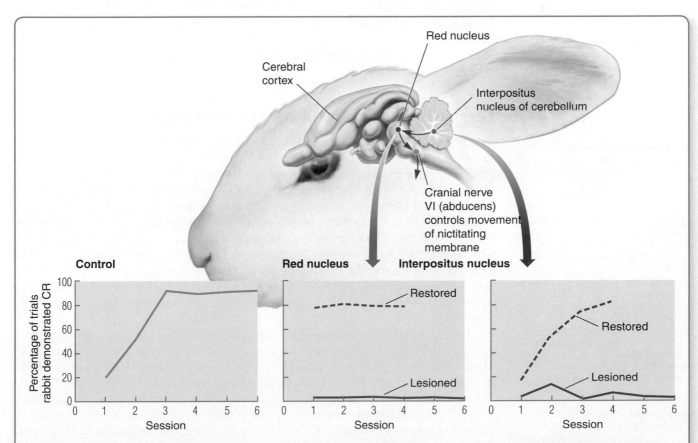

> ● **Figure 12.13** **The Role of the Interpositus Nucleus in Classical Conditioning** Temporarily disabling the red nucleus by cooling prevents conditioned responding by rabbits trained in a conditioned eyeblink paradigm. However, the response resumes immediately when the red nucleus recovers. In contrast, temporarily disabling the interpositus nucleus by cooling appears to prevent learning because these animals demonstrate the same subsequent learning curve as controls.

Source: Adapted from Krupa, Thompson & Thompson (1993).

Inactivating the interpositus nucleus by cooling it effectively prevents classical conditioning. When the cooling wears off, rabbits begin to learn the conditioned response as if they had had no prior experience at all.

When we lesion a structure, it is possible that behavior will change due to the loss of that structure. On the other hand, the changed behavior we observe might be due to a lack of information traveling via fibers that are also affected by the lesion. The red nucleus is a brainstem structure involved in motor control that receives substantial input from the cerebellum and is directly responsible for performance of the eyeblink response (Robleto & Thompson, 2008). If the interpositus nucleus has only an indirect effect on learning via its connections with other structures, inactivation of the red nucleus should also prevent learning. In fact, inactivation of the red nucleus by cooling prevents the nictitating-membrane response. However, when the red nucleus recovers, the animals produce strong conditioned responses (Krupa, Thompson, & Thompson, 1993). Learning did occur, although performance was suppressed while the red nucleus was inactivated. It appears, then, that the interpositus nucleus is primarily responsible for the formation of the classically conditioned response of the nictitating membrane in rabbits.

Evidence from human studies also points to a role for the cerebellum in classical conditioning (Cheng et al., 2013; Parker et al., 2012). Human participants do not have nictitating membranes, of course, but they can learn to blink in response to stimuli paired with a puff of air directed at the eye. Using PET scans, Logan and Grafton (1995) observed changes in the cerebellar activity of their human participants during classical conditioning. Individuals with cerebellar damage have a difficult time learning the conditioned eyeblink response (Woodruff-Pak, Papka, & Ivry, 1996). The degree of age-related shrinkage of the cerebellum is correlated with the speed of acquisition of conditioned blinking in elderly human volunteers (Woodruff-Pak et al., 2001).

Cerebellar Circuits and Classical Conditioning

The rather unusual anatomy of the cerebellum, shown in ● Figure 12.14, seems ideally designed to carry out classical conditioning. In the cerebellar cortex, large **Purkinje cells** receive inputs known as **climbing fibers** from neurons located in the inferior olive in the medulla. In addition, the Purkinje cells receive input from **parallel fibers** that originate in an adjacent layer of cerebellar cells known as **granule cells**. Cerebellar granule cells make up possibly half the neurons in the entire brain. These granule cells in turn receive input from **mossy fibers**, which originate from neurons in the pons. Integrating input from the parallel and climbing fibers, the Purkinje cells form inhibitory synapses on the output cells of the cerebellum, located in the **deep cerebellar nuclei**. As the result of this network, the Purkinje cells are perfectly situated to influence the output of the cerebellum.

James Albus (1971) suggested learning will occur if the climbing-fiber and parallel-fiber synapses onto a Purkinje cell are activated at the same time. Masao Ito (1984) provided support for Albus's predictions. Ito recorded EPSPs in the Purkinje cells in response to electrical stimulation of the parallel fibers. Subsequently, both climbing and parallel fibers were simultaneously stimulated. The paired stimulation produced a reduction in Purkinje cell EPSPs that lasted up to one hour. The reduced activity in the Purkinje cells is known as **long-term depression**, or LTD.

Further research showed that the reduction in EPSPs was due to a reduced responsiveness by the Purkinje cell to glutamate released by the parallel fibers. Activity in the climbing and parallel fibers produces three simultaneous events within the postsynaptic Purkinje cell. Calcium (Ca^{2+}) and sodium (Na^{2+}) flow into the cell. At the

Purkinje cell A cell in the cerebellum that influences the structure's activity by forming inhibitory synapses with the output cells in the deep cerebellar nuclei.

climbing fiber A fiber originating in the inferior olive of the brainstem that forms synapses on the large Purkinje cells of the cerebellar cortex.

parallel fiber A fiber originating in the granule cells of the cerebellum that synapses on the Purkinje cells.

granule cell A cell within the cerebellum that is the source of parallel fibers.

mossy fiber (cerebellum) A fiber connecting a neuron in the pons to the granule cells of the cerebellum.

deep cerebellar nuclei Structures that contain the major output cells of the cerebellum; recipients of input from the cerebellar Purkinje cells.

long-term depression A type of synaptic plasticity in which postsynaptic potentials in target cells is reduced.

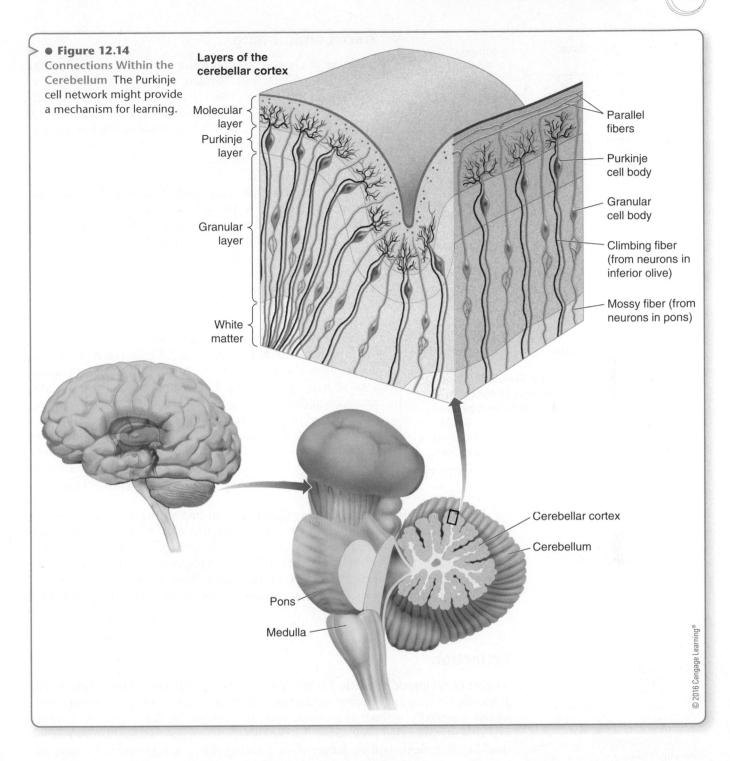

● Figure 12.14
Connections Within the Cerebellum The Purkinje cell network might provide a mechanism for learning.

Layers of the cerebellar cortex

Molecular layer

Purkinje layer

Granular layer

White matter

Parallel fibers

Purkinje cell body

Granular cell body

Climbing fiber (from neurons in inferior olive)

Mossy fiber (from neurons in pons)

Cerebellar cortex

Cerebellum

Pons

Medulla

© 2016 Cengage Learning®

same time, a second messenger known as **protein kinase C** is activated. Together, these three events produce a decrease in the number of available glutamate receptors found in the Purkinje cell membrane. As a result of having fewer receptors to activate, subsequent input produced LTD in the form of reduced EPSPs. Although it might seem difficult to see a connection between learning and LTD, which is a reduction in activity, LTD involving the inferior olive-climbing fiber system is recognized as essential for learning the eyeblink CR (Christian & Thompson, 2003; Woodruff-Pak & Disterhoft, 2008).

protein kinase C A second messenger found in the Purkinje cells of the cerebellum.

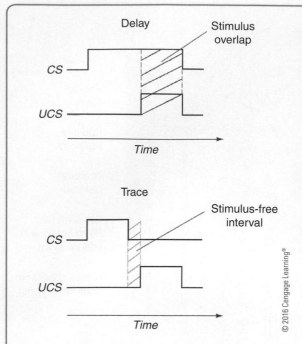

● **Figure 12.15 Delay Versus Trace Conditioning**
In delay conditioning, an example of nondeclarative or implicit learning, the onset of the UCS overlaps with the CS. In contrast, the CS and UCS do not overlap in trace conditioning, which is considered to be an example of declarative or explicit learning.

Trace Conditioning

The type of classical conditioning we have discussed so far in *Aplysia*, rabbits, and humans was described by Pavlov as **delay conditioning**. The CS in traditional delay conditioning overlaps the UCS somewhat, with no stimulus-free interval between the CS and UCS. In **trace conditioning**, diagrammed in ● Figure 12.15, a stimulus-free interval occurs, and bridging the interval requires more than just cerebellar activity alone.

The first clue that delay and trace conditioning were managed by different learning processes arose from research with mutant mice, whose abnormal cerebellums interfered with their delay conditioning but not their trace conditioning (Kishimoto et al., 2002; Kishimoto, Hirono et al., 2001; Kishimoto, Kawahara et al., 2001). Next, human patients with cerebellar lesions showed greater impairment in delay than in trace conditioning (Gerwig et al., 2008; Gerwig et al., 2006).

Subsequent research has demonstrated that bridging the time gap between the CS and UCS in trace conditioning requires the participation of forebrain areas, including areas of sensory cortex, the hippocampus, and the prefrontal cortex (Woodruff-Pak & Disterhoft, 2008). Instead of a direct projection of information about the CS to the cerebellum via nuclei in the pons, trace conditioning requires the forebrain structures to hold the CS information during the stimulus-free interval, after which the information is transmitted to the pons and cerebellum (Siegel, Kalmbach, Chitwood, & Mauk, 2012).

Why is this difference in conditioning paradigms important? As we will see later in this chapter, we can distinguish between declarative or conscious memory processes (also known as explicit learning) and nondeclarative or unconscious memory processes (also known as implicit learning). Trace conditioning in humans appears to require conscious, declarative processes (Clark, Manns, & Squire, 2001). Consequently, trace conditioning provides an excellent model for the study of declarative memories in many species.

Extinction

As part of his classic research, Pavlov described how conditioned responding would gradually decrease, or undergo **extinction**, when the conditioned stimulus was presented repeatedly without the unconditioned stimulus. In the conditioned threat experiments discussed previously, if a tone CS is no longer followed by an electric shock UCS, rodents will no longer show freezing (CRs) in response to hearing the tone. Can we identify the brain correlates of this extinction process?

One of the challenges of understanding extinction is that it is very context specific (Maren, Phan, & Liberzon, 2013). In other words, before any extinction training, a trained rat would freeze in response to hearing the CS tone whether it was in its home cage, the cage where it was trained, or any novel space. When extinction training reduces responding to the CS, the reduction in threat response does not generalize much outside the training context. The rat may no longer freeze in the context in which extinction training occurred, but it is very likely to continue to freeze elsewhere. It appears that circuits connecting the amygdala, hippocampus, and medial prefrontal cortex participate in matching the correct responses to their contexts following extinction training (Maren et al., 2013).

delay conditioning A type of classical conditioning in which CS onset precedes and overlaps UCS onset.

trace conditioning A type of classical conditioning in which the CS and UCS do not overlap in time.

extinction In classical conditioning, the reduction in conditioned responding that follows exposure to the conditioned stimulus alone, without the unconditioned stimulus.

INTERIM SUMMARY 12.1

Summary Table: Types of Learning

Type of Learning	Description	Possible Underlying Mechanisms in Invertebrates	Possible Underlying Mechanisms in Vertebrates
Habituation	A reduction in response to a repeated stimulus.	• Persistent changes in activity at the synapse between sensory neurons and either interneurons or motor neurons. • Postsynaptic structural changes in longer-lasting learning.	Currently unknown.
Sensitization	A type of learning in which experiencing one stimulus heightens the response to subsequent stimuli.	• Enhancement of activity at axo-axonic synapses between interneurons and sensory neurons • Postsynaptic structural changes in longer-lasting learning.	Currently unknown.
Classical conditioning	A type of associative learning in which a neutral stimulus acquires the ability to signal the occurrence of a second, biologically significant event.	Convergence of input from both the conditioned stimulus (CS) and the unconditioned stimulus (UCS) increases the amount of neurotransmitter released by the sensory neuron and stimulates postsynaptic changes in glutamate receptors.	• Participation of the amygdala in classically conditioned threat responses in rats. • Participation of circuits in the cerebellum, including the interpositus nucleus, in the conditioning of skeletal reflexes such as the eyeblink. • Participation of forebrain structures in trace conditioning and extinction.
Operant conditioning	A type of associative learning in which the consequences of a behavior influence the future frequency of the behavior.	Possibly changes in excitability in particular neurons, like the *Aplysia* B51.	• Currently unknown

Summary Points

1. Reflexes, fixed action patterns, and learning fall along a continuum of flexibility. Reflexes produce rigid patterns of response, whereas the flexibility of learned behaviors is well suited to rapidly changing environments. Major types of learning include habituation, sensitization, classical conditioning, and operant conditioning. (L01)

information processing models Theories of memory that seek to explain the management of information by the brain, from detection to storage to retrieval.

sensory memory An initial stage in memory formation in which large amounts of data can be held for very short periods.

short-term memory An intermediate memory store in which limited amounts of data can be held for a limited amount of time; without further processing, such information is permanently lost.

2. Research using *Aplysia* suggests that learning results from both pre- and postsynaptic changes. **(LO2)**

3. Classical conditioning in vertebrates involves the amygdala (emotional learning) and the cerebellum (skeletal reflexes). In addition to the cerebellum, trace conditioning and extinction require activity in the forebrain. **(LO2)**

‖ Review Questions

1. What cellular changes are associated with habituation, sensitization, and classical conditioning in invertebrates?

2. What brain structures are involved with learning in vertebrates?

Types of Memory

Although memory commonly refers to the storage and retrieval of information, there is no absolute boundary between the processes of learning and those of memory. Learning and memory are best viewed as occurring along a continuum of time that also includes processes like attention, sensation, and perception. Among the critical steps along the pathway of memory processing are encoding, consolidation, and retrieval. Encoding refers to the transformation of input into a form the brain can process further. Consolidation refers to the organization of memory information into more long-term storage. Retrieval, of course, is the recovery of the stored information. Some cognitive neuroscientists add an additional phase called reconsolidation. As we use memories, they are vulnerable to modification, and reconsolidation refers to the stabilizing of the used memory.

Information processing models of memory assume that information flows through a series of stages on its way to permanent storage in memory, as shown in ● Figure 12.16 (Atkinson & Shiffrin, 1968, 1971). Not only do these models provide a helpful framework for thinking about memory, but they also predict the participation of different brain structures in each stage of processing.

According to the Atkinson-Shiffrin model, any information sensed by an organism initially enters the **sensory memory**. This first memory stage can hold a large amount of data for a very brief period of time, on the order of a few seconds. From this initial set of data, we select information for further processing and move it to the next stage of memory, the **short-term memory**. This stage contains all the data about

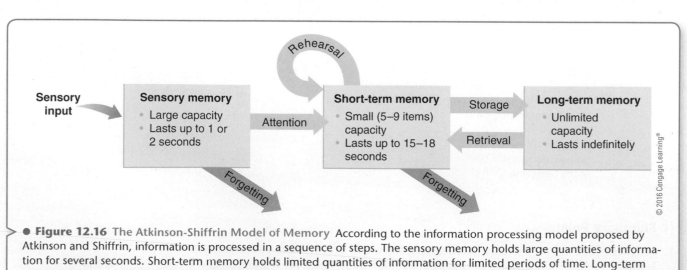

● Figure 12.16 The Atkinson-Shiffrin Model of Memory According to the information processing model proposed by Atkinson and Shiffrin, information is processed in a sequence of steps. The sensory memory holds large quantities of information for several seconds. Short-term memory holds limited quantities of information for limited periods of time. Long-term memory can hold unlimited amounts of information for unlimited periods of time. Information that does not move to the next stage for processing will be permanently lost.

© 2016 Cengage Learning®

which we are currently thinking. In an adaptation of the concept of short-term memory, information is sorted within a working memory into temporary storage areas or buffers for auditory, visual, or combined types of information, managed by a "central executive" process (Baddeley, 2000; Baddeley & Hitch, 1974).

Short-term memory has a very limited capacity, somewhere between five and nine unrelated items (Miller, 1956). When we try to add additional items, previous information is often lost. If somebody asks you the time while you're trying to remember the telephone number whispered by your attractive classmate, disaster can result. In addition to having a limited capacity, short-term memory is also notable for its temporary nature. Classic research by Peterson and Peterson (1959) showed that material in short-term memory was lost rapidly, in 15 to 18 seconds, but others believe that loss occurs in as little as 2 seconds (Sebrechts, Marsh, & Seamon, 1989).

The final destination for information in the Atkinson-Shiffrin model is **long-term memory**. Unlike short-term memory, long-term memory seems to have few, if any, limitations on capacity or duration. Elderly people still recall childhood memories of events that occurred many years in the past and retain the ability to learn and remember facts read in the morning news, in spite of the large quantity of information already stored from a lifetime of experience.

As illustrated in ●Figure 12.17, long-term memories can be either **declarative** (explicit or conscious) or **nondeclarative** (implicit or unconscious). Declarative memories are easy to "declare," or to discuss verbally, while nondeclarative memories are not. Declarative memories are further divided into semantic and episodic memories, which together form the basis of our autobiographical memories (Tulving, 1972, 1985, 1987, 1995). **Semantic memory** contains basic knowledge of facts and language. Using your semantic memory, you can answer questions such as "Who was the first president of the United States?" or "What is a bagel?" **Episodic memory** relates to your own personal experience. You use your episodic memory to remember the *episodes* of your life—what you ate for breakfast or the time you chose your first puppy.

Nondeclarative memories include processes such as classical conditioning, procedural memory, and priming. As we observed previously, however, trace conditioning (a type of classical conditioning) shares many similarities with declarative memory. **Procedural memory** stores information about motor skills and

long-term memory A memory store in which apparently unlimited amounts of data can be held for an unlimited amount of time.
declarative memory An explicit memory for semantic and episodic information that can easily be verbalized, or "declared."
nondeclarative memory An implicit memory that is accessed unconsciously and automatically.
semantic memory A type of declarative, explicit memory for facts and verbal information.
episodic memory A type of declarative, explicit memory for personal experience.
procedural memory A type of implicit memory for performing learned skills and tasks.

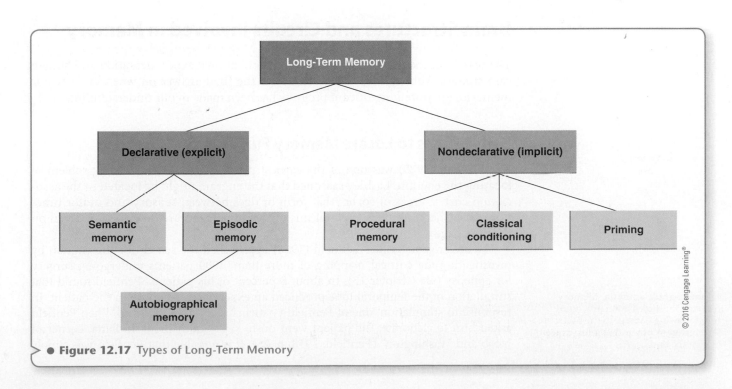

> ● **Figure 12.17** Types of Long-Term Memory

procedures such as riding a bicycle, using a software program, or cooking your favorite meal. In priming, exposure to a stimulus changes subsequent responding to another stimulus. For example, participants hearing rude words were more likely to interrupt a researcher than people who had heard polite words (Bargh, Chen, & Burrows, 1996).

In contrast to declarative memories, procedural memories are often quite difficult to describe verbally but are easy to demonstrate or perform (Squire, 1987). Writing an essay about how to ride a bicycle for someone who has never even seen a bicycle is much harder than showing the person how to ride. Declarative and procedural memories differ in one other important way. Declarative memories are typically recalled consciously or explicitly, whereas procedural memories are usually recalled unconsciously or implicitly. Learning a skill, such as driving a car, requires quite a bit of attention and conscious effort. Once mastered, however, a skill such as driving can become quite automatic.

The distinction between declarative and nondeclarative memories can be demonstrated in patients with a type of memory loss known as **anterograde amnesia**. In cases of anterograde amnesia, patients have good recall for events that occurred prior to the time of their brain damage, but they seem unable to remember anything they experience following their brain damage. However, the inability of these patients to remember the present, such as the name of the current president of the United States, is not due to a complete memory failure. Squire (1987) demonstrated that patients with anterograde amnesia were able to learn to solve the Tower of Hanoi puzzle, in which a stack of rings must be moved from one peg to another one at a time without placing a larger ring on top of a smaller ring. When asked about the puzzle, most patients could not recall seeing it before, and they certainly had no confidence that they could solve it. When given the opportunity, however, the patients solved the puzzle skillfully. In other words, their brain damage did not prevent them from forming nondeclarative, procedural memories of how to solve the puzzle, although it did prevent them from explicitly remembering that they knew how to solve it.

Where exactly are these memory functions located? To answer this question, psychologists have engaged in an extended search for the **engram**, or the physical representation of memory in the brain.

Brain Structures and Circuits Involved in Memory

The search for the elusive engram involved both animal experimentation and human case studies. Although we still do not have the final answer on where or how our memories are stored, significant progress has been made in our understanding.

Early Efforts to Locate Memory Functions

Karl Lashley (1929) was one of the earliest psychologists to tackle the problem of locating the engram. Lashley reasoned that the engram might be located in the association cortex, areas of cortex that form bridges between sensory and motor functions (see Chapter 2). His explorations of this hypothesis are described in detail on the next page.

Neurosurgeon Wilder Penfield (1958) approached the search for the engram by investigating the cortical mapping of more than 1,000 patients undergoing surgery for epilepsy (see Chapter 15). In about 8 percent of his patients, Penfield found that stimulation of the temporal lobe produced an experiential response in the patient. In response to stimulation, one of Penfield's patients said "street corner." When Penfield asked him to elaborate, the patient went on to say, "South Bend, Indiana, corner of Jacob and Washington" (Penfield, 1958, p. 25). It is possible that Penfield was simply

anterograde amnesia Memory loss for information processed following damage to the brain.
engram A physical memory trace in the brain.

••• Connecting to **Research**

KARL LASHLEY'S SEARCH FOR THE ENGRAM

To test his hypothesis about the engram's being located in the association cortex, Lashley (1929) performed a series of lesions on rats both before and after they were trained to run through mazes to find food. Rats that received cortical lesions prior to any training were slow to learn their way through the maze. Rats that received cortical lesions following their training seemed to have forgotten many of their previously learned behaviors.

Lashley's next task was to investigate the influence of the size and location of his lesions on the rats' maze performance. Surprisingly, Lashley reported that the location of his lesions didn't seem to matter much. Instead, the deficit in the rats' performance seemed due to the size of the lesion. As shown in ●Figure 12.18, larger lesions appeared to produce poorer performance, regardless of where the lesion was made. Lashley mistakenly concluded that all parts of the cortex make an equal contribution to learning and memory, a concept he referred to as equipotentiality. In other words, Lashley believed that the engram is distributed evenly across the cortex, such that no single area is more responsible for learning and memory than any other. He also believed that the parts of the cortex are basically interchangeable. As a result, the more cortex you have, the better your memory will be, a concept Lashley referred to as mass action.

Most contemporary neuroscientists believe Lashley's concept of equipotentiality is wrong. Why is Lashley's conclusion believed to be a mistake? First, as we will see shortly, more recent data suggest that all parts of the cortex are *not* equally likely to participate in memory. Lashley's lesions were huge. It is likely that lesions of this size would affect multiple aspects of maze-learning behavior. This makes the identification of parts of the brain responsible for a specific function a difficult, if not impossible, task. Second, maze learning is a complex task involving a number of sensory and motor processes. If a lesion affected a rat's sense of smell, for example, it is likely that the rat could compensate by

using its visual or tactile memories. Retained functions would allow the rat to perform similarly, regardless of the particular modality affected by a lesion, leading to the appearance of equipotentiality. We should not conclude, however, that Lashley's work was all in vain. Lashley's major contribution was his suggestion that memories are in fact distributed across the cortex rather than stored in one specific location. This conclusion stimulated further efforts to identify areas of the brain responsible for storing memory.

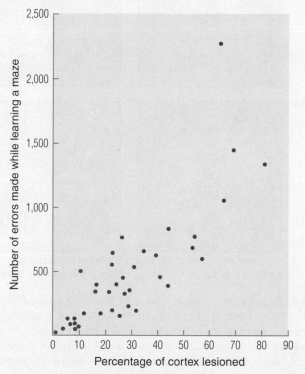

● **Figure 12.18** Karl Lashley Observed the Results of Brain Lesions on Maze-Learning Performance Lashley trained rats to run a maze and then performed brain lesions on them. As larger amounts of cortex were damaged, errors in running the maze increased.

Source: Adapted from Lashley (1929).

observing a side effect of epilepsy rather than some universal principle of memory storage in the brain. All of Penfield's patients suffered from epilepsy and only a small minority reported experiential responses to stimulation, limiting our ability to generalize from these findings to all typical participants. However, Penfield's work did focus the interests of other researchers on a possible role for the temporal lobe in the formation and retention of long-term memories.

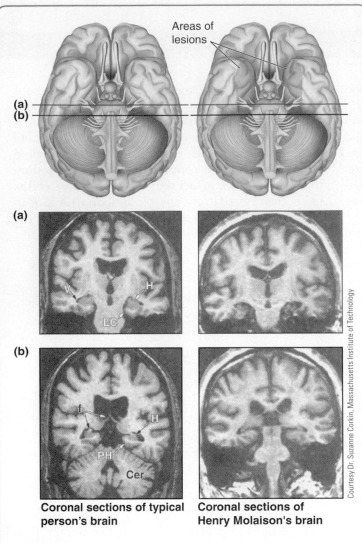

Coronal sections of typical person's brain

Coronal sections of Henry Molaison's brain

Courtesy Dr. Suzanne Corkin, Massachusetts Institute of Technology

● **Figure 12.19** **Surgical Removal of Henry Molaison's Temporal Lobe Tissue.** To control life-threatening seizures, Henry Molaison underwent surgery that removed the hippocampus, amygdala, and part of the association cortex from both temporal lobes. These MRI scans compare a typical control participant with Molaison. You can see that Molaison has some hippocampus (H) but no entorhinal cortex (EC). In this image, (V) refers to the lateral ventricle, (f) refers to the fornix, (PH) refers to the parahippocampal cortex, and (Cer) refers to the cerebellum.

Other investigators have presented evidence for very specific, localized memory storage, using single-cell recordings. Activity of single neurons in patients undergoing surgery for epilepsy corresponded to the type of information being processed (Ojemann, Schoenfield-McNeill, & Corina, 2002). Instead of generic memory neurons, Ojemann states that neurons "show statistically significant relationships to memory for a particular thing" (Neary, 2002). In a similar investigation discussed in Chapter 1, one participant had a single cell that responded selectively to several representations of the actress Halle Berry, including her photograph, a drawing of her, the word string of her name, and a photo of her in her *Catwoman* costume (Quian Quiroga, Reddy, Kreiman, Koch, & Fried, 2005).

The Temporal Lobe and Memory

The search for the engram received a boost from studies focused on the temporal lobe. Significant evidence of the temporal lobe's involvement in memory came from case studies of patients with anterograde amnesia. As mentioned earlier, patients suffering from anterograde amnesia appear to retain their newly acquired procedural, implicit memories while experiencing a dramatic deficit in their ability to form new explicit memories. One of the most thoroughly studied cases of anterograde amnesia is Henry Molaison (1926–2008), known in the literature as the amnesic patient H. M. Possibly as a result of a childhood bicycle accident in which he suffered brain damage, Molaison experienced severe seizures that required surgery when he was 27. As shown in ● Figure 12.19, the hippocampus, amygdala, and part of the association cortex of the temporal lobe were removed from both his right and left hemispheres (Corkin, Amaral, Gonzalez, Johnson, & Hyman, 1997). Had the surgery affected only one hemisphere, Molaison's behavioral changes would have been far less dramatic.

The good news for Molaison was that his seizure disorder was much improved and his personality, vocabulary, and above-average IQ appeared unchanged. He remembered most of the information he had acquired prior to surgery, but his anterograde amnesia was profound. He seemed completely unable to transfer any new information about people, places, events, and numbers from short-term memory to long-term memory. Brenda Milner (1966), followed by her student Suzanne Corkin, made an extensive study of Molaison's memory deficits and found that his surgery did not affect all types of memory equally. Molaison's short-term memory allowed him to engage in normal conversation as long as there were no big gaps between statements. Much to Milner's surprise, Molaison performed as well as typical control participants on procedural memory tasks. In one of Milner's tasks, shown in ● Figure 12.20, he was required to draw the shape of a star while looking at a sample star and his own hand in a mirror.

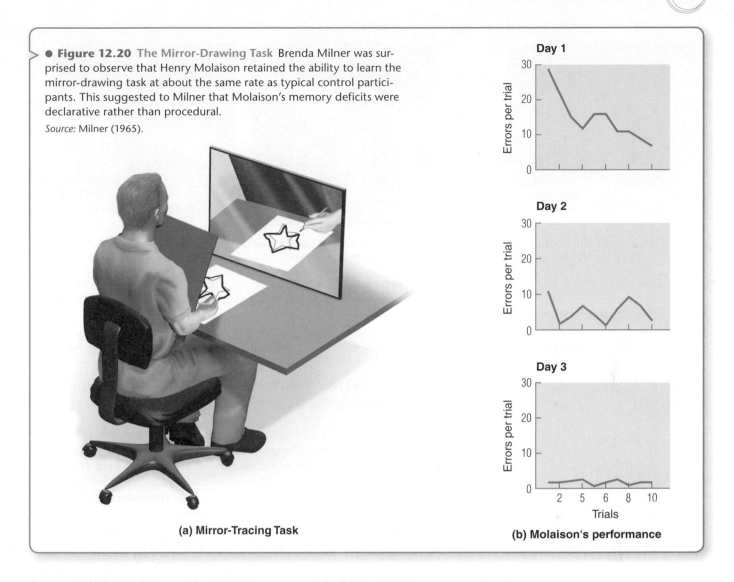

● **Figure 12.20** **The Mirror-Drawing Task** Brenda Milner was surprised to observe that Henry Molaison retained the ability to learn the mirror-drawing task at about the same rate as typical control participants. This suggested to Milner that Molaison's memory deficits were declarative rather than procedural.

Source: Milner (1965).

(a) Mirror-Tracing Task

(b) Molaison's performance

Molaison mastered the task and performed as well as typical controls (Milner, 1965). If asked, however, he would deny ever having performed the task, just as Squire's patients who also had anterograde amnesia could not recall seeing their puzzles previously.

Molaison's case provides further support for the differentiation of declarative and nondeclarative memories as well as for the stage approach to memory articulated by the Atkinson-Shiffrin model. Damage to the medial temporal lobes affects declarative but not nondeclarative memories. Molaison's damage did not affect long-term memories that had already been stored, but it did affect the transfer of new information from short-term to long-term memory. It is unlikely that the hippocampus itself is a storage location for the elusive engram. The fact that patients with anterograde amnesia still retain fairly stable memories dating from their presurgical lives suggests that the actual representations of these memories do not reside in the medial temporal lobe itself. Nor is the medial temporal lobe necessarily essential for the retrieval of stored memories.

Expanding on information from case studies such as Molaison's, researchers explored the results of temporal lobe lesions on the memory performance of rhesus monkeys using a memory task known as the **delayed nonmatching to sample (DNMS) task** (Mishkin & Appenzeller, 1987; Squire, 1987). In this task, illustrated in ● Figure 12.21, a monkey is presented with a single object that covers a food reward. After some period of time (the delay), the monkey is then presented with two objects. One of the objects is the one the animal saw prior to the delay. The other is new. The

delayed nonmatching to sample (DNMS) task A standard test of memory in which the subject must identify the novel member of a stimulus pair following a delay.

Variable
delay
(a few
seconds
to several
minutes)

(a) Sample: Food Found
Under an Object

(b) Test: Choose the Object That
Is New (Nonmatching)

(c) Food Found Under the
Nonmatching Object

© 2016 Cengage Learning®

● **Figure 12.21** The Delayed Nonmatching to Sample (DNMS) Task To find food successfully, monkeys must select the nonmatching (new) stimulus following a delay. Monkeys with medial temporal lobe damage appear to have difficulty forming new memories and subsequently perform poorly on the task.

monkey's task is to select the new object from the pair. The delays varied from a few seconds to several minutes. Solving the problem after a delay of minutes requires the use of long-term memory.

Monkeys with medial temporal lobe lesions in both hemispheres performed poorly on the DNMS task, especially as the delay period increased. Experienced control monkeys could select the correct stimulus about 90 percent of the time. Performance by the lesioned monkeys after a short delay of 8 to 10 seconds was nearly identical to the performance of control monkeys, supporting the view that the lesions did not compromise short-term memory. After a delay of 2 to 10 minutes, however, the lesioned monkeys performed correctly less than 60 percent of the time. Like Henry Molaison, these monkeys appeared to have difficulty forming new long-term memories.

Structures typically damaged by medial temporal lobe lesions include the amygdala, the hippocampus, and the surrounding areas of cortex known as the **parahippocampal cortex** and the **rhinal cortex**. In addition, the pathways connecting these structures to one another, as well as to other parts of the brain, are also damaged. The amygdala appears to play a role in processing emotional memories, but damage to the amygdala alone does not produce anterograde amnesia. As a result, attention has focused on the hippocampus and the surrounding parahippocampal and rhinal cortices as structures involved in the formation of long-term memories.

Long-Term Potentiation (LTP)

parahippocampal cortex An area of cortex ventral to the hippocampus.

rhinal cortex An area of cortex ventral to the hippocampus.

entorhinal A subdivision of the rhinal cortex.

perirhinal cortex A subdivision of the rhinal cortex.

fornix A pathway carrying information from the hippocampus to the hypothalamus.

Ammon's horn One of two major layers of neurons found in the hippocampus.

Beginning in the 1970s, researchers began to investigate neural mechanisms in the hippocampus that appear to provide a basis for learning and memory (Bliss and Lømo, 1973). To understand these mechanisms, we must first explore the major anatomical features of the hippocampus and surrounding structures, shown in ● Figure 12.22. The hippocampus consists of a gentle arc just medial to the lateral ventricle in each hemisphere. Ventral to the hippocampus are the parahippocampal cortex and the rhinal cortex, which in turn is made up of the **entorhinal** and **perirhinal cortices**. Input from the association areas of the cortex enters the parahippocampal and rhinal cortices, which in turn transmit the information to the hippocampus. Output from the area generally travels along the **fornix**, a pathway that terminates in the mammillary bodies of the hypothalamus. A closer look at the hippocampus shows us that it is a folded structure with two main layers of neurons. One layer is known as **Ammon's horn**, and

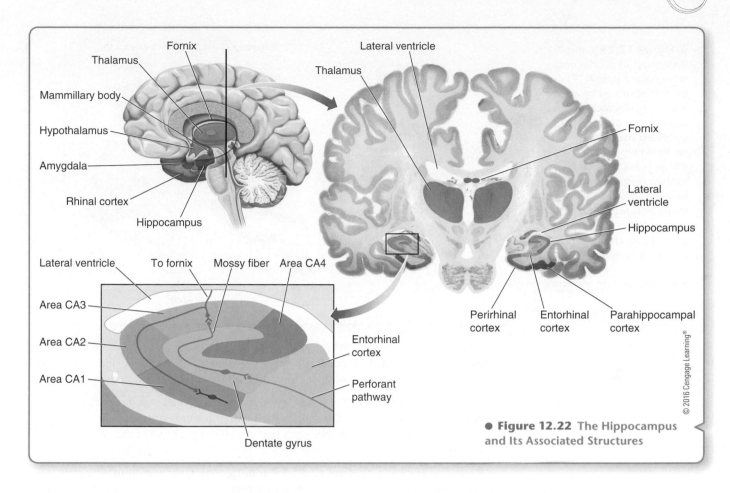

● **Figure 12.22** The Hippocampus and Its Associated Structures

© 2016 Cengage Learning®

the other layer is known as the **dentate gyrus**. Ammon's horn is further divided into four sections, named CA1 to CA4. (CA stands for the Latin term for Ammon's horn, *cornu Ammonis*.)

The pathways connecting the hippocampus to the rest of the brain, as well as the connections formed within the hippocampus itself, are also central to our understanding of the functions of this structure. Input from the rhinal cortex travels along the **perforant pathway**, whose axons form synapses on the cells of the dentate gyrus. Axons from the dentate gyrus, also known as **mossy fibers**, synapse on cells found in CA3 (the third division of Ammon's horn). Axons from CA3 form two branches. One branch, the **Schaffer collateral pathway**, synapses with the cells of CA1. The other branch exits the hippocampus as the fornix.

As demonstrated by Bliss and Lømo (1973), the application of a rapid series of electrical shocks to one of these pathways increases the postsynaptic potentials recorded in their target hippocampal cells. In other words, experience makes these synapses more efficient (see ● Figure 12.23). By a rapid series of shocks, we mean that somewhere between 50 and 100 stimuli are applied at a rate of 100 stimuli per second, a rate that is found among naturally firing axons. When stimuli are presented at a rate of 2 per second or less, synaptic change fails to occur. The change in responsiveness in the target cells after the rapid series of shocks is known as **long-term potentiation, or LTP**. LTP can be demonstrated in living animals as well as in isolated slices of hippocampus and other brain tissues. In the living animal, LTP might last indefinitely. In an isolated brain slice, LTP will last a period of several hours.

LTP AS A MEMORY MECHANISM Several factors point to LTP as an important memory device. First, the fact that LTP lasts a long time is important because we believe that some memories last throughout life. Second, it takes only seconds of input to produce LTP. In many cases, we are able to remember very brief exposures

dentate gyrus One of two major layers of neurons found in the hippocampus.

perforant pathway A pathway made up of axons originating in the rhinal cortex that form synapses in the dentate gyrus of the hippocampus.

mossy fiber (hippocampus) An axon from the dentate gyrus that synapses on cells found in CA3 of Ammon's horn.

Schaffer collateral pathway A pathway connecting CA3 to CA1 in Ammon's horn of the hippocampus.

long-term potentiation, or LTP A type of synaptic plasticity in which the application of a rapid series of electrical shocks to an input pathway increases the postsynaptic potentials recorded in target neurons.

● Figure 12.23 Long-Term Potentiation (LTP) Long-term potentiation (LTP) can be demonstrated by applying a series of electrical pulses (center) and observing the increased reactions of cells receiving input from the stimulated cells (right) compared to their previous untreated baseline (left). LTP shares many features with memory, such as being long-lasting and formed after a very brief exposure to stimuli.

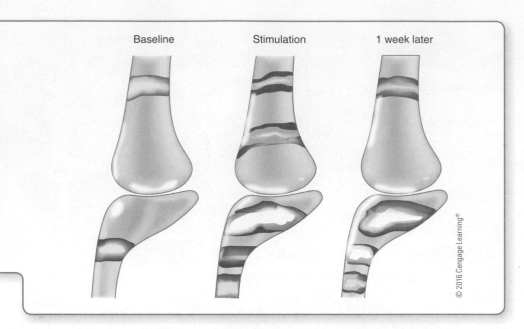

Baseline   Stimulation   1 week later

© 2016 Cengage Learning®

to stimuli. In addition, LTP occurs in ways predicted by the cellular learning model proposed by Canadian psychologist Donald Hebb in 1949. Hebb stated:

> When an axon of cell A is near enough to excite a cell B and repeatedly or persistently takes part in firing it, some growth process or metabolic change takes place in one or both cells such that A's efficacy, as one of the cells firing B, is increased. (p. 62)

Both the Hebbian synapse and LTP require relatively simultaneous firing, or **associativity**, in the pre- and postsynaptic neurons. In addition, only those synapses that are simultaneously active appear to be strengthened. LTP also requires **cooperativity**, which means that several synapses onto the target postsynaptic neuron must be simultaneously active. NMDA glutamate receptors, illustrated in ● Figure 12.24, are particularly well suited to facilitate both associativity and cooperativity. For glutamate from a presynaptic neuron to influence postsynaptic NMDA receptors, both pre- and postsynaptic neurons must be simultaneously active (associativity). The channel of the NMDA receptor is normally blocked by a molecule of magnesium $\left(Mg^{2+}\right)$ (see Chapter 4). Depolarization of the postsynaptic cell resulting from the binding of excitatory glutamate at nearby AMPA receptors acts to expel the Mg^{2+} from the channel. The activity of the AMPA receptors in conjunction with activity of NMDA receptors meets the requirement for cooperativity. When a molecule of glutamate is bound to the now unblocked NMDA receptor, both sodium $\left(Na^{2+}\right)$ and calcium $\left(Ca^{2+}\right)$ enter the cell. The entrance of Ca^{2+} stimulates several second messengers within the cell, which initiate the structural changes necessary to strengthen the synapse.

LTP that occurs within the first three hours of stimulation is referred to as early phase LTP, whereas subsequent LTP is known as late phase LTP. The two processes can be distinguished from one another along a variety of dimensions. In early LTP, the flow of calcium $\left(Ca^{2+}\right)$ into the postsynaptic cell results in new AMPA receptors being inserted into the post-synaptic neural membrane near the active synapses. The presence of these extra AMPA receptors will make the postsynaptic neuron more responsive to any future release of glutamate by the presynaptic neuron. Late-phase LTP results when incoming calcium activates transcription factors, such as CREB, that change the cell's gene expression, which in turn changes the quantities of certain proteins produced by the cell. More AMPA receptors are produced and inserted in the membrane. Proteins known as growth factors are also synthesized in greater quantities, leading to the formation of new synapses.

Learning models require the strengthening of particular synapses, not an indiscriminate strengthening of synapses on an entire postsynaptic cell. If the cell body increases its production of proteins required for strengthening synapses, how does the

associativity A condition believed necessary for learning in which the pre- and postsynaptic neurons are nearly simultaneously active.

cooperativity A condition for the formation of LTP in which several synapses onto the target postsynaptic neuron must be simultaneously active.

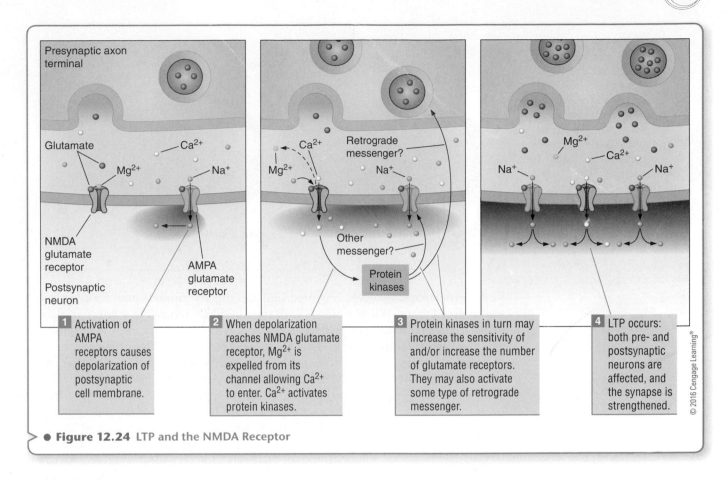

> ● **Figure 12.24** LTP and the NMDA Receptor

cell ensure that these go to the correct synapse? One solution to this problem is the process of synaptic tagging (Frey & Morris, 1997). Significant stimulation of a synapse produces temporary **synaptic tags** that somehow "capture" the newly produced proteins and insert them in the correct location.

LTP appears to be a general process of learning that "can be implemented by a variety of receptors and signaling systems" (Cooke & Bliss, 2006, p. 1,660). Presynaptic processes appear to be important to LTP in some locations, whereas postsynaptic processes predominate at others. Some synapses showing LTP involve the neurotransmitter glutamate, whereas others do not. Although LTP was originally observed in the hippocampus and remains important for the understanding of the role of the hippocampus in memory, the phenomenon has also been demonstrated throughout the central nervous system, from the cerebral cortex to the spinal cord (Cooke & Bliss, 2006).

LTP AND BEHAVIORAL MEMORY Studies of spatial memory, or an organism's ability to map a location, provide further evidence linking LTP to memory. O'Keefe and Dostrovsky (1971) demonstrated that mice use different patterns of activation in the hippocampus to represent their location in space. By using single-cell recordings, researchers have been able to conclude that hippocampal spatial maps are formed within minutes of entering a new environment. These maps remain stable for months. All of this should sound somewhat familiar to you by now—rapid formation and stability over time are features of both long-term memories and LTP.

Several research approaches have been used to investigate links between LTP and spatial memory. Genetic mutations can be produced in the chemical pathways responsible for LTP. Knocking out the gene that encodes a component of the NMDA receptor found in the cells of CA1 has a negative impact on LTP in the Schaffer collateral pathway (Tsien, Huerta, & Tonegawa, 1996). LTP is also negatively affected when genetic mutations affect the second messengers in CA1 cells (Mayford et al., 1996). Does this inability to produce normal LTP affect spatial memory? The answer to this question is yes, but not in the way you might have guessed. Animals with impaired LTP can still

synaptic tag Mechanism that allows newly produced proteins to be captured and inserted at an active synapse.

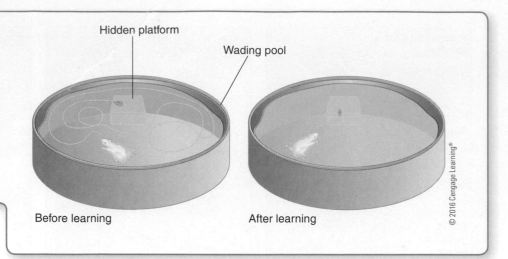

● **Figure 12.25 The Morris Water Maze Requires Spatial Memory** Rats are excellent swimmers, as evidenced by their abilities to board ships anchored in European harbors to travel to the New World. However, they cannot swim indefinitely. To solve the Morris Water Maze, the rat must recall the location of a submerged platform.

Hidden platform

Wading pool

Before learning

After learning

© 2016 Cengage Learning®

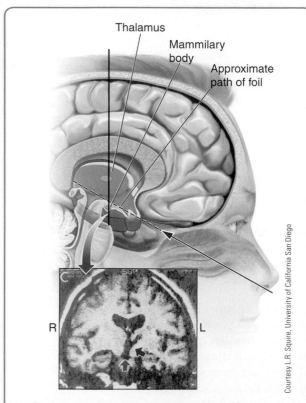

Thalamus

Mammillary body

Approximate path of foil

R   L

Courtesy L.R. Squire, University of California San Diego

● **Figure 12.26 Damage to the Diencephalon in Patient N. A.** The purple arrow in the illustration (above) traces the pathway of a fencing foil into the left hemisphere of patient N. A.'s brain. In the MRI image (below) the red and purple arrows indicate areas damaged by the foil. (Note that the mammillary body indicated in the illustration can no longer be seen in the MRI, as it was obliterated by the accident. Normally, it would appear near the tip of the red arrow.)

form spatial maps. However, impaired LTP prevents the animals from forming stable, well-defined maps. When a mouse with impaired LTP returns to a familiar place, it forms a new map instead of reactivating a previous one. In many ways, the mouse acts a lot like Henry Molaison, who is unable to learn the route to his postsurgery home.

Spatial learning in rodents can also be impaired by the application of NMDA receptor antagonists (Abraham & Mason, 1988; Morris, Anderson, Lynch, & Baudry, 1986). When these chemicals are applied to the hippocampus in rats, the rats are unable to learn the location of an underwater platform in the Morris water maze shown in ● Figure 12.25. At the same time, these drugs prevent the development of LTP in the hippocampus of these rats. However, the drugs do not have any effect on performance or LTP if they are applied after spatial learning has occurred (Morris et al., 1986).

Researchers have also demonstrated that LTP can account for learning in an inhibitory avoidance situation (Whitlock, Heynen, Shuler, & Bear, 2006). Inhibitory avoidance is demonstrated by placing a rat in an apparatus with a dark and light side. When the rat enters the dark side of the apparatus, it receives an electric foot shock. This produces single-trial avoidance learning, because the rat will not enter the dark side again. Once again, if LTP is to model real learning successfully, it must mimic the ability of single, brief experiences to change neural functioning. Following the training, analysis of the rats' CA1 area of the hippocampus showed the same changes in AMPA receptors observed following LTP. In addition, no further changes in the trained synapses could be produced using LTP methods of stimulation. Taken together, these results strongly suggest that LTP forms the basis for several types of behavioral memories.

The Diencephalon and Memory

The hippocampus and other areas of the temporal lobe are tightly connected to the thalamus. Disruption to these structures or to their connections results in amnesia (Gold & Squire, 2006).

Case studies of patients with diencephalic lesions support the role of this area in memory. Patient N. A. suffered brain damage as a result of a freak accident in which he was stabbed through the nostril with a miniature fencing foil (a long thin metal blade) held by one of his roommates. As shown in ● Figure 12.26, N. A.

suffered a lesion in his left dorsomedial thalamus, mammillary bodies, and mammillothalamic tract (Squire, Amaral, Zola-Morgan, & Kritchevsky, 1989). Patient N. A. experienced significant permanent anterograde amnesia as well as some retrograde amnesia, affecting memories from several years prior to his accident (Squire & Moore, 1979). In many ways, the memory loss experienced by N. A. was quite similar to that of Henry Molaison in spite of the anatomical differences between the damage experienced by these two men. N.A.'s intelligence and short-term memory were preserved, but even in the absence of hippocampal damage, he had difficulties forming new declarative (explicit) memories. The differences may not be as big as they look, however. It is likely that Henry Molaison experienced some transneuronal degeneration (see Chapter 5) that affected his mammilary bodies and thalamus (Weiskrantz, 1985).

Chronic alcoholics who develop **amnestic confabulatory** (Korsakoff's) **neurocognitive disorder** experience anterograde amnesia similar to that of Henry Molaison and patient N. A. Alcoholism often results in a deficiency of thiamine, also known as vitamin B1. Thiamine is important to nervous system functioning because it participates in the synthesis of the neurotransmitter acetylcholine. Untreated thiamine deficiencies lead to damage in the dorsomedial thalamus and mammillary bodies of the diencephalon (Mair, Warrington, & Wieskrantz, 1979), which are precisely the same areas affected by patient N.A.'s accident. In addition to their anterograde amnesia, patients with Korsakoff's syndrome usually experience severe retrograde amnesia, possibly due to lesions in the cerebellum, brainstem, and cortex as well as in the diencephalon. Animal research confirms observations made in these human case studies. Monkeys with lesions of the anterior and dorsomedial nuclei of the thalamus and of the mammillary bodies have great difficulty with the DNMS task (Parker, Eacott, & Gaffan, 1997).

Semantic Memory and the Cerebral Cortex

There appears to be considerable evidence that semantic knowledge, or our basic knowledge of facts and language, is widely distributed in the cortex. Different areas of association cortex are activated during semantic memory tasks based on the particular characteristics of the concept being processed. As shown in ● Figure 12.27, PET scans can be used to identify brain areas that participants activated while naming either animals or tools (Martin, Wiggs, Ungerleider, & Haxby, 1996). While naming animals but not tools, participants activated their left medial occipital lobes, which are involved in processing visual input. While naming tools but not animals, the participants activated the left premotor area and the left middle temporal gyrus. These latter areas are associated with concepts related to tool use, such as hand movements and the production of action words. The distribution of semantic knowledge is also supported by case studies of patients with damage to their association cortex. McCarthy and Warrington (1990) describe a patient who had substantial difficulty describing living things but who retained a perfect capacity for describing inanimate objects such as wheelbarrows.

Retrieving these distributed memories requires a coordinated effort (Damasio, 1989). Antonio Damasio suggests that this type of coordination might occur in a series of "convergence zones," or a particular location responsible for assembling separate aspects of a memory into a whole. Among the likely candidates for a convergence zone for semantic memories are areas along the left lateral inferior frontal gyrus (Hagoort, 2005; Hagoort, Hald, Bastiaansen, & Petersson, 2004). These areas became more active when rules of language or world knowledge were violated than when correct language usage or factual information was presented to participants (Hagoort et al., 2004).

Episodic Memory and the Cerebral Cortex

A number of former students have told me that they remember my teaching them that "rats can't barf." Not only did these students expand their semantic memories (accurately, by the way) with a fact about rats, but they formed episodic memories about when, where, and from whom they learned the fact.

amnestic confabulatory neurocognitive disorder Anterograde amnesia resulting from thiamine deficiency, typically found in chronic alcoholics; previously known as Korsakoff's syndrome.

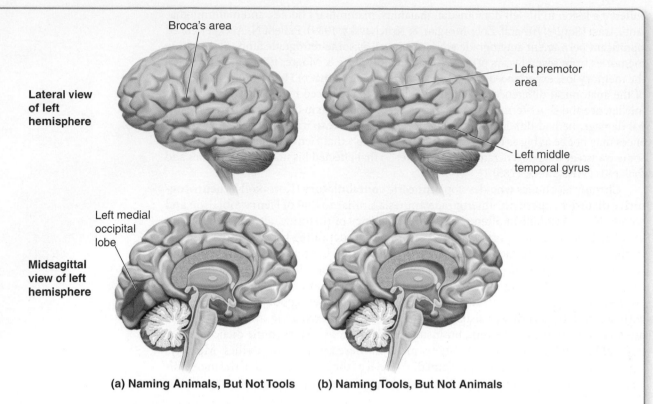

Broca's area

Left premotor area

Lateral view of left hemisphere

Left middle temporal gyrus

Left medial occipital lobe

Midsagittal view of left hemisphere

(a) Naming Animals, But Not Tools   **(b) Naming Tools, But Not Animals**

● **Figure 12.27 Semantic Memories Are Widely Distributed** Participants were scanned while silently naming animals or tools. Areas that became active in both conditions cancel each other out and are not highlighted. (a) Silently naming animals, but not tools, activated the left medial occipital lobe. (b) Naming tools, but not animals, activated the left premotor area and left middle temporal gyrus, areas associated with concepts and hand movements related to tool use. *Source:* Adapted from Martin et al. (1996).

Tulving's concept of an independent episodic memory store for our personal experiences is supported by case studies with patients with cortical damage. Patients who experience damage to the prefrontal areas of the cortex often experience a memory deficit known as **source amnesia**. These patients retain their semantic memories but are unable to remember how and when they learned a bit of information. Patient K. C. damaged his left frontal-parietal cortex and right parietal-occipital cortex as the result of a traffic accident (Tulving, 1989). In addition, this patient also experienced shrinkage of the hippocampus and the parahippocampal cortex (Rosenbaum et al., 2000). K. C. retains his general semantic knowledge, as evidenced by his knowledge of the rules of chess. However, he can't remember many facts from his past, such as how and when he learned to play chess.

Although the prefrontal areas are no doubt involved with the long-term management of episodic memories, the formation of episodic memories appears to be associated with activity in the hippocampus and the caudate nucleus of the basal ganglia (Ben-Yakov & Dudai, 2011). In particular, the hippocampus is essential in the binding of separate episodic elements into an integrated memory trace. For example, activity in the hippocampus was particularly noticeable when participants had to rank three words according to their "desirability" (Davachi & Wagner, 2002). Simply repeating the words without evaluating them relative to one another did not produce as much hippocampal activity.

We might use our episodic memories to distinguish between fantasy and reality. When participants were asked whether it would be possible to have a conversation with a real or fantasy person (George Bush or Cinderella), brain areas associated with declarative memories in general, such as the hippocampus and other medial

source amnesia Memory loss for the circumstances in which a particular fact or skill was learned.

temporal lobe structures, were activated (Abraham et al., 2008). However, other areas appear to be differentially active. When considering reality, structures associated with episodic memory, such as the prefrontal cortex and posterior cingulate cortex, were active. These results imply that we consult our personal experience to determine reality. In contrast, when considering fantasy, areas associated with semantic processing, such as the left inferior frontal gyrus (IFG) showed greater activity (ibid.). Recall that the IFG showed greater activation when semantic rules of language and world knowledge were violated (Hagoort et al., 2004), which of course they are when imagining a conversation with Cinderella. Disturbances in this distinction might form the basis for the delusions, or false beliefs, that characterize some psychological disorders (see Chapter 16).

Short-Term Memory and the Brain

According to the Atkinson-Shiffrin model, new information coming into the memory system, as well as information being recalled from long-term storage, is held for relatively brief periods of time in short-term memory. Baddeley (1974, 2000) divided his related model of working memory into four components: a central executive, the phonological loop, the visuo-spatial scratchpad, and an episodic buffer. Is it possible to locate these processes in the brain?

The dorsolateral prefrontal cortex (DLPFC) and the anterior cingulate cortex (ACC) are believed to provide the neural basis for the central executive (Kaneda & Osaka, 2008). These areas provide important attentional aspects of short-term memory. Human patients with prefrontal cortex lesions have significant difficulty with the Wisconsin card-sorting test (Barceló & Knight, 2002). The cards used in this test can be sorted according to several dimensions such as symbol, color, number, and shape. Patients with prefrontal lesions can learn a sorting rule—for example, "put all the cards with the same-colored objects together"—but they can't seem to adjust when the rule changes. They persevere with a previous rule (such as sorting by color) when they are prompted to switch to sorting by shape. The patients experience specific deficits in their ability to shift attention to the new sorting dimension.

Further evidence supporting a role for the prefrontal cortex in short-term memory comes from research on the development of memory. The short-term memories of young monkeys and of human infants can be assessed by an object permanence test, illustrated in ● Figure 12.28, in which a toy is hidden in one of

Doug Goodman/Science Source

> ● **Figure 12.28** Object Permanence The short-term memory abilities of a young child can be assessed by hiding a toy while the child is watching. After a delay, the child is allowed to search for the toy. Prior to the age of seven or eight months, most children are unable to use their memories of watching the toy being hidden to help them successfully locate it. Immaturity of the prefrontal cortex might account for these results.

two locations (with the subject watching). After a delay, the infant or young monkey can search for the toy. Human infants are unable to find the hidden toy until they are about seven or eight months old (Diamond & Goldman-Rakic, 1989). Prior to this age, the child will look for the toy in the location at which it was last found, whether or not this is the location at which the child most recently watched the toy being hidden. Diamond and Goldman-Rakic (1989) compared the performances of adult monkeys with prefrontal cortical lesions to those of adult monkeys with inferior parietal lesions on the object permanence task. The monkeys with the inferior parietal lesions performed normally on the task. However, the monkeys with the prefrontal lesions performed similarly to immature human infants. These data suggest that a certain level of maturity in the prefrontal cortex is necessary for short-term memory.

Evidence for an executive role for the anterior cingulate cortex (ACC) in short-term memory comes from comparisons of people with large or small short-term memory capacities for verbal information. People with large capacities show more activation of the ACC than people with smaller capacities (Osaka et al., 2003). The differing capacities were also associated with different memory strategies. People with smaller capacities used rehearsal, or simple repetition, to maintain information in short-term memory, whereas people with larger capacities were more likely to use semantic strategies, such as imagery and making stories (Osaka et al., 2003; Turley-Ames & Whitfield, 2003). These observations support a role for the ACC in the processing of verbal information in short-term memory.

The Striatum and Procedural Memory

The striatum, including the basal ganglia and nucleus accumbens, are involved with the formation of procedural memories (Barnes, Kubota, Hu, Jin, & Graybiel, 2005). As we saw in Chapter 2, the basal ganglia are part of our motor system, so it would seem logical that these structures would be involved in the learning and memory of motor patterns. The nucleus accumbens contributes an evaluation of emotion and reward to the learning of procedures (Arnsten, Ramos, Birnbaum, & Taylor, 2005). Within the striatum, a set of interneurons serve as a gate for both the learning and performance of procedural memories (Crossley, Ashby & Maddox, 2013). When reward is available, the gate opens, allowing the learning and performance of procedures to occur. As a result, the striatum allow organisms to match learning about procedures to their environmental context and likelihood of reward. Sitting in class and attending a football game require different procedures for speaking at the proper volume.

The role of the striatum in procedural, but not declarative, memories was demonstrated by observing the effects of lesions on rats trained in one of two different maze tasks (Packard, Hirsh, & White, 1989). In one task, the rats learned which arms of a radial maze, such as the one shown in ● Figure 12.29, contained food. This task is assumed to be a test of declarative memory because the rat must use its explicit episodic memories about arms that have been visited to perform successfully. The second task involves a maze in which food is located in arms that are lit by small lights. The rat does not need to remember much about the maze but must learn to associate light with the availability of food. Consequently, this light maze serves as an implicit procedural memory task. Different brain lesions affect performance in the two types of mazes. Lesions to structures associated with the hippocampus impaired performance on the declarative task (the standard maze), but performance on

© 2016 Cengage Learning®

● **Figure 12.29 The Radial Arm Maze** The radial arm maze can be modified to investigate declarative and procedural memories. The rat's task is to locate food as quickly as possible, which requires it to form representations of which arms have contained food and which arms have already been visited.

the procedural task (the light maze) remained normal. However, rats with lesions in the basal ganglia performed poorly on the procedural task but experienced little difficulty with the declarative task.

INTERIM SUMMARY 12.2

Summary Table: Brain Structures and Their Roles in Memory

Structure	Possible Role in Memory	Results of Damage
Temporal lobe (including the hippocampus and surrounding structures)	• Transfer of information from short-term to long-term memory • Management of declarative (explicit) memories	• Anterograde amnesia • Existing long-term memories are retained • Ability to form new procedural (implicit) memories is retained • Difficulty with formation of new long-term memories required to solve the DNMS task (monkeys) • Difficulty with the spatial learning tasks (rodents)
Diencephalon (including the thalamus and mammillary bodies)	• Transfer of information from short-term to long-term memory • Similar to temporal lobe because these areas are highly interconnected	• Anterograde amnesia • Some retrograde amnesia • Difficulty with DNMS task (monkeys)
Association cortex	• Semantic memory • Encoding long-term memory • Retrieval of long-term memory	• Naming difficulties, such as being able to name animals but not tools
Prefrontal cortex	• Episodic memory • Short-term memory	• Source amnesia • Difficulty shifting attention • Immature object permanence (monkeys)
Basal ganglia	• Procedural (implicit) memory	• Failure to learn new procedures and skills

Summary Points

1. Memory can be conceptualized as a series of stages, including sensory memory, short-term memory, and long-term memory. Long-term memory is further divided into declarative (explicit) and nondeclarative (implicit) memories. **(LO3)**

2. Patients with damage to the medial temporal lobes experience anterograde amnesia, the inability to form new declarative memories. **(LO3)**

3. Long-term potentiation (LTP), first observed in the hippocampus, might provide a basis for the changes necessary for forming long-term memories. **(LO3)**

4. Diencephalic structures also play a role in declarative memory formation. **(LO3)**

5. Semantic and episodic memories appear to be widely distributed in the cerebral cortex, yet tightly interconnected. The prefrontal cortex appears to play a significant role in short-term memory. Procedural memories are mediated by the striatum. **(LO3)**

Review Questions

1. How did the work of Lashley, Penfield, and Milner contribute to our understanding of memory?

2. What brain structures seem to be most involved with episodic, semantic, and procedural memories?

The Biochemistry of Memory

At this point in our discussion, we hope it has become obvious that "memory" is not a single entity, but rather a flexible process featuring different mechanisms (such as short- and long-term memory) and phases (encoding, consolidation, and retrieval). It would be naturally surprising, therefore, to find that a single biochemical process accounts for memory. The biochemistry of memory is as diverse and complex as its structural and functional features demand.

However, at the outset of scientific inquiry into the biochemistry of memory, one neurochemical did seem to stand apart from the crowd: acetylcholine (ACh). Many lines of research seemed to converge in the direction of identifying ACh as essential to memory functions. If you took medications that reduced cholinergic activity, you might expect to experience deficits in learning and memory (Atri et al., 2004). As we will see in Chapter 15, the loss of cholinergic neurons in the basal forebrain accompanies memory impairments in older adults, and this loss is especially dramatic in cases of Alzheimer's disease. Cholinergic agonists have been approved as treatments for Alzheimer's disease (Holzgrabe, Kapkova, Alptuzun, Scheiber, & Kugelmann, 2007). While these medications do not "cure" the disease, they reduce the pace at which deterioration of memory occurs.

More recently, the connections between cholinergic activity and learning and memory have been subject to further debate. The development of neurotoxins that selectively target cholinergic neurons in the basal forebrain showed that large decreases in the numbers of these cells seems to have relatively mild effects on learning and memory (Berger-Sweeney et al., 1994). Instead of a simple relationship between cholinergic activity and memory, it appears that cholinergic activity has different effects in different phases of memory. Increases of cholinergic activity in the hippocampus are associated with better encoding of new information, but consolidation and retrieval of memory appear to be impaired by high cholinergic activity (Micheau & Marighetto, 2011). The lower ACh levels found during NREM sleep (see Chapter 11) might facilitate the transfer of information from temporary storage in the hippocampus to permanent storage in the cerebral cortex (Diekelmann & Born, 2010).

In our earlier discussion of LTP, the importance of glutamate and its AMPA and NMDA receptors in learning and memory were emphasized. In particular, glutamate appears to be more critical in the encoding and consolidation phases than in the retrieval phases (Matus-Amat, Higgins, Sprunger, Wright-Hardesty, & Rudy, 2007). Glutamate activity, however, is modulated by dopamine (Papenberg et al., 2013). Blocking both NMDA and dopamine receptors produces larger impairments in memory than blocking the NMDA receptors alone. Dopamine agonists can offset some of the memory impairments caused by NMDA receptor antagonists.

The Effects of Stress and Healthy Aging on Learning and Memory

We tend to take the processes of learning and memory for granted until they suddenly fail us. Stress, or the state that accompanies the perception of threat, has effects on memory that most students find all too familiar. You might know the information on your exam very well, but somehow, retrieving the memories you need during an exam becomes challenging. Then as you leave the classroom, the answers to all of the test questions float effortlessly into your mind. In addition to stress, healthy aging also produces relatively mild but noticeable changes in the way memories are processed. The more dramatic disruption of memory function associated with neurocognitive disorders like Alzheimer's disease will be covered in Chapter 15.

Stress Effects on Memory

Stress prepares our bodies for dealing with immediate danger (see Chapter 14). Part of this preparation includes the release of a number of biochemicals that can have long-lasting effects on both the encoding of new memories and the retrieval of stored memories. The fast-acting sympathetic nervous system leads to the release of epinephrine (adrenalin) and norepinephrine from the adrenal glands into the blood supply (LeDoux, 1993; McGaugh, 1992). A slower system, the hypothalamus-pituitary-adrenal (HPA) axis (see Chapter 14) leads to the release of glucocorticoids, such as cortisol, from the adrenal glands. Glucocorticoids freely cross the blood–brain barrier and enter the brain to interact with their own receptor systems. Norepinephrine released by the adrenal glands into the blood supply cannot directly influence the brain, but does so indirectly via the vagus nerve (cranial nerve X). The joint action of norepinephrine and glucocorticoids can have a profound effect on the processing of new information by the brain.

BEHAVIORAL OBSERVATIONS OF STRESS EFFECTS ON MEMORY Neuroscientists have been puzzled over the years by contradictory findings about the effects of stress on memory. In some instances, stress seems to impair memory. Stress can also have beneficial effects by promoting subsequent survival by enhancing memories for events. If you were frightened by a near miss on the highway, an enhanced memory of those circumstances might help you cope better the next time you encounter a similar situation. In still other cases, stress is associated with the formation of especially vivid and detailed memories. In cases of posttraumatic stress disorder (PTSD; see Chapter 16), experiencing trauma can lead to intrusive, unwanted flashback memories of the traumatic event. Flashbulb memories for traumatic events include vivid details of the event alongside episodic memories for where you were and what you were doing when you became aware of the trauma (see ● Figure 12.30).

How can we reconcile these apparently conflicting outcomes of stress on memory? The critical variable determining the effects of stress on memory appears to be timing, similar to the observations about the actions of ACh discussed previously. Memories, as we observed using the Atkinson-Shiffrin model, pass through a series of stages during which they are relatively fragile and open to modification. At each stage, stress and its associated biochemical correlates can have unique effects on how information is encoded, stored, and retrieved. As shown in ● Figure 12.31, when stress coincides with learning, it tends to enhance learning, but when it is experienced outside the learning experience, it tends to impair learning (Joëls, 2006).

What happens when an individual is stressed prior to learning something new? Being in a stressed state, perhaps during a natural disaster or other emergency situation, can either enhance or impair memories depending on a number of variables, such as the amount of time separating the onset of stress and the encoding of important information (Diamond, Campbell, Park, Halonen, & Zoladz, 2007). If stress

● **Figure 12.30** Flashbulb Memories Seem More Vivid and Complete Few witnesses will ever forget the images of the terrorist attacks on the World Trade Center. It is possible that moderate levels of stress produce unusually clear memories, whereas more extreme stress begins to interfere with accurate memory encoding.

and learning coincide, as in the formation of a flashbulb memory, memory might be enhanced. However, stress produces a refractory period, during which subsequent information will be more difficult to encode. This effect of timing might protect important emotional memories from interference from the processing of subsequent information that might be less important to survival.

● **Figure 12.31** Stress Has Different Effects at Different Times in the Memory Process Stress prior to and following learning impairs memory, while stress that coincides with learning appears to enhance memory formation.

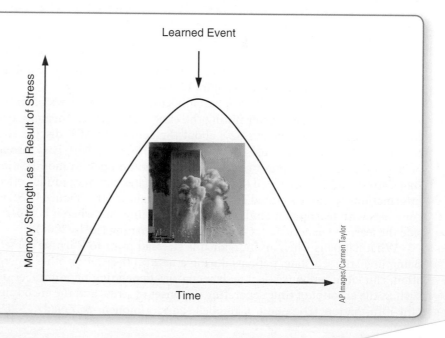

Learned Event

Memory Strength as a Result of Stress

Time

While we don't recommend that you do this deliberately, stress experienced shortly after learning improves memory, particularly memory for emotional events (Schwabe, Joëls, Roozendaal, Wolf, & Oitzl, 2012). After viewing emotional slides and neutral slides, participants who were stressed recalled more of the emotional slides than non-stressed participants (Cahill, Gorski, & Le, 2003). In animal research, administering glucocorticoids after training enhanced memory performance (Roozendaal, Okuda, Van der Zee, & McGaugh, 2006).

Stress or administration of glucocorticoids directly before the recall of a memory reduces retrieval performance (Schwabe et al., 2012). This effect is especially strong in the case of retrieval of emotional material. Finally, stress and the administration of glucocorticoids following retrieval can impair later recall of the same material. According to the Atkinson-Shiffrin model, we cannot access long-term memory directly. Instead, when we recall something from our long-term stores, we bring the material into short-term memory. Once reactivated this way, memories are subject to distortion (Loftus, 2005). To maintain the memory that has been retrieved, a recon-solidation process must take place, and this, too, seems subject to disruption by stress or glucocorticoid administration (Schwabe & Wolf, 2010).

EFFECTS OF NOREPINEPHRINE AND GLUCOCORTICOIDS ON MEMORY One of the targets for both norepinephrine and glucocorticoids released by the adrenal glands as a result of stress is the lateral nucleus of the amygdala, which we discussed previously in the context of conditioned threat. The emotional components of memory associated with activation in the amygdala can be dissociated from the declarative aspects of memory encoded by the hippocampus. In one case study, a man who was nearly buried alive in sand experienced damage to his hippocampus due to lack of oxygen. He remained constantly fearful during the day and troubled by nightmares at night, but he was unable to remember the details of his traumatic experience (Diamond et al., 2007). His intact amygdala, however, was able to initiate the encoding of the emotional aspects of the experience.

As shown in ● Figure 12.32, the stress-induced actions of norepinephrine and glucocorticoids in the amygdala initiate a "memory formation" state in the prefrontal

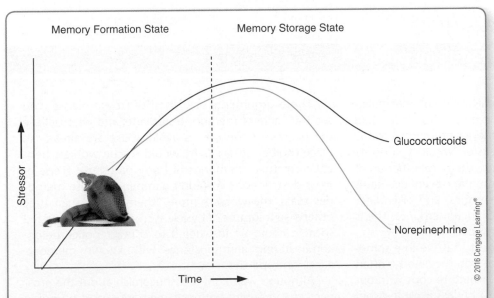

© 2016 Cengage Learning®

● **Figure 12.32 Effects of Glucocorticoids and Norepinephrine on Memories for Stressors** Stress-induced glucocorticoid and norepinephrine release signals the amygdala to engage the prefrontal cortex, hippocampus, and caudate nucleus in a "memory formation state." Subsequently, norepinephrine levels return to their prestress state, but glucocorticoids remain active longer. Glucocorticoids initiate changes in gene expression that shifts the brain into a "memory storage state."

cortex, the hippocampus, and the caudate nucleus (Schwabe et al., 2012). While in this mode, perception and attention are enhanced while the organism attempts to cope with the stressor and form memories about the experience. Any other ongoing information processing is inhibited. As time passes, norepinephrine levels return to normal. However, glucocorticoids remain active in the brain for a much longer time. In addition, glucocorticoids initiate enzyme cascades that result in changes in gene expression (Schwabe et al., 2012). This in turn shifts the brain from a memory formation mode into a "memory storage" mode in which processing of material unrelated to the stressful situation becomes less likely. Long-term storage of the important emotional event is enhanced, while interference from other information is suppressed.

So far, we have examined the effect of a single stressful episode on memory, but as we will see in Chapter 14, modern living is often the source of chronic, repeated exposure to stressful experiences. Repeated exposure to stress produces structural changes in several interconnected parts of the brain that are important to memory (Roozendaal, McEwen, & Chattarji, 2009). In the amygdala, repeated stress leads to dendritic growth and spine formation, which in turn makes the organism hyperresponsive to subsequent stressors. In the hippocampus, reversible atrophy of dendrites accompanied by reduced rates of neurogenesis contributes to an overall reduction in hippocampal volume. Finally, the medial prefrontal cortex also experiences reversible dendrite and spine loss, making this structure less responsive than under less stressful conditions.

Further understanding of these processes might help us prevent and treat traumatic memories. Propranolol, which blocks the effects of glucocorticoids in the brain, might prevent the formation of traumatic memories when administered immediately following a traumatic event (Miller, 2004; Pitman et al., 2002). By manipulating certain enzymes in animals, researchers are making progress in their ability to "erase" some long-term memories, raising the possibility of new approaches to the treatment of PTSD (Shema, Sacktor, & Dudai, 2007; Cao et al., 2008).

••• THINKING *Ethically*

SHOULD WE ERASE TRAUMATIC MEMORIES?

What are the ethical implications of manipulating a person's traumatic memories? If you had the chance to reduce your memories of a serious traffic accident, war, or a natural disaster, would you do it? As we discovered in this chapter, the administration of propranolol within hours of a traumatic event decreases the formation of traumatic memories, and taken later reduces the emotional impact of such memories. This is not science fiction, but rather modern fact.

On one side, ethicists suggest that we lose something of ourselves when we don't do the "work," often with the aid of a therapist, of learning to cope with our past experiences. We might also be less likely to avoid trauma, say in war, if we knew we could erase negative memories later on. A witness to a crime might not be able to recall sufficient information if he or she has undergone propranolol treatment.

These arguments are dismissed by ethicists who see the value of memory treatments and who believe the necessary controls to avoid abuse are already in place (Kolber, 2011). Why would rescue workers benefit from their memories of body parts at a scene of mass destruction? Wouldn't dampening these memories make the workers more "themselves" than they otherwise might be? Physicians treating a traumatized witness could be instructed to contact police before administering any substance with known memory-altering properties.

Although we might feel squeamish about the prospect of tampering with our memories, and by doing so manipulating our sense of self, the hardships faced by patients with PTSD might warrant a further look at the potential of memory-altering drugs (Sambataro et al., 2012).

The Effects of Healthy Aging on Memory

Some aspects of learning and memory undergo age-related changes, even in healthy older adults. For example, eyeblink conditioning, which we discussed earlier in this chapter, is more difficult and takes longer in older participants (Flaten & Friborg, 2005). Working memory functions, the ability to form new episodic memories, and reaction time all typically decline in healthy older adults. The deficits observed in healthy older adults might be the result of white matter deterioration (Charlton, Barrick, Markus, & Morris, 2013) and reduction in sleep quality associated with memory consolidation (Pace-Schott & Spencer, 2014). The older brain has a harder time clearing extracellular adenosine. Adenosine suppresses one of the signaling cascades involved in memory consolidation (Baudry, Bi, Gall, & Lynch, 2011).

However, most measures of cognitive ability in healthy older adults remain stable. This stability might arise from modifications in brain activity that compensate for age-related declines in brain function (Beason-Held, Kraut, & Resnick, 2008). As people age, decreased blood flow is observed in many parts of the brain essential to memory and cognition, especially in the frontal and temporal lobes. However, the aging brain also shows areas of increased activation. Beason-Held et al. (2008) suggest that these areas of increased activity represent a reorganization of the brain that allows cognitive performance to remain stable in spite of age-related deficits in brain function. In other words, an older person's brain activity correlated with memory and cognition shows less localization than a younger person's brain while engaged in the same task (Sambataro et al., 2012).

Comparisons of healthy young adults, healthy older adults, patients with Alzheimer's disease (see Chapter 15), and those at high risk for Alzheimer's disease provide further insight into the nature of aging effects on cognition (Sperling, 2007). Comparisons of young and older adults demonstrated no differences in hippocampal activation during the encoding of face–name pairs that were subsequently recalled successfully. However, young participants show reduced activation of the parietal lobe and the posterior cingulate cortex during successful encoding. High-performing older participants showed similar areas of deactivation, while lower-performing older participants did not. These lower-performing participants might be experiencing very early stages of dementia. Participants at risk for Alzheimer's disease, either because of their genetic vulnerability or evidence of mild cognitive impairment, actually demonstrate increased hippocampal activity during encoding compared to healthy older participants. This increased activity might provide another example of the brain's effort to compensate for decline observed by Beason-Held et al. (2008). Eventually, this compensation fails as dementia progresses, and activity in the hippocampus is reduced below that seen in healthy older controls (Sperling, 2007).

●●● Building Better
HEALTH

CAN WE AVOID AGE-RELATED MEMORY DEFICITS?

The idea of experiencing age-related memory problems holds little appeal. Is it possible to prevent or minimize such loss?

Schaie (1994) conducted a 35-year-long longitudinal study of more than 5,000 participants and identified several factors that are correlated with maintaining good cognitive function in old age. Attainment of above-average education, engaging in complex, nonroutine professions, and earning high income appear to protect against cognitive decline. Obviously, these factors are highly correlated with one another and would likely protect against many other health problems throughout the life span as well. Schaie's data also emphasize the importance of strong social relationships. People who maintain close family ties retain more cognitive function in their senior years. Schaie also reports that "being married to a spouse with high cognitive status" is also

(continued)

Building Better HEALTH

CAN WE AVOID AGE-RELATED MEMORY DEFICITS? *(Continued)*

good for your brain (p. 310). We must be cautious when interpreting Schaie's data. These lifestyle factors are typical of people with above-average intelligence. People who are intelligent experience a more gradual decline in cognitive abilities during aging, even when they are diagnosed with a degenerative condition such as Alzheimer's disease (Whalley et al., 2000).

With the large Baby Boom generation entering its senior years, concerns about maintaining cognitive health have spawned a whole new industry of "brain-improving" activities (see ● Figure 12.33). Nintendo is offering "Brain Age," and Cognifit's "Drive Fit" program is marketed to seniors concerned about diminishing driving skills. Sudoku and crossword puzzles have gained in popularity. While further research is necessary before we can conclude that these activities are helpful, some positive reports have been published. Elderly participants playing Nintendo's Brain Age for four weeks showed improvement in tests of executive function and processing speed (Nouchi et al., 2012). An entire journal, *Games for Health,* features research on the use of electronic games for improving cognition, among other health-related topics. A new term, *serious games,* is used to describe games used for health, whether designed for that specific purpose or designed for entertainment but also useful for improving health (McCallum & Boletsis, 2013).

● **Figure 12.33 Electronic Games and Healthy Aging** Until research establishes any significant benefits of electronic games for maintaining cognitive function in aging, we suggest that people who enjoy games play games without any unrealistic expectations.

Although the use of games is promising, it is important to ensure that marketing does not get ahead of neuroscience, promising results that cannot be delivered (Chancellor & Chatteriee, 2013). In the meantime, people who enjoy games should play games. Maintaining an overall healthy lifestyle, with good food, exercise, sleep, and lifetime learning remains an excellent strategy for maintaining good cognitive function.

INTERIM SUMMARY 12.3

‖ Summary Points

1. Acetylcholine, glutamate, norepinephrine, glucocorticoids, and dopamine play important roles in memory processing. **(LO4)**

2. Unusual memory phenomena, including repression, flashbacks associated with post-traumatic stress disorder, and flashbulb memories, might result from the effects of different levels of stress on the amygdala, hippocampus, and prefrontal cortex. **(LO5)**

3. In healthy aging, patterns of brain activity during memory processing might compensate for age-related changes to maintain cognitive function. **(LO5)**

‖ Review Questions

1. In which situations is the timing of neurochemical activity important to the understanding of memory functioning?

2. What memory changes are associated with normal, healthy aging?

Chapter Review

THOUGHT QUESTIONS

1. If researchers succeed in identifying chemicals that will enhance people's ability to learn and remember, what impact might that have on human society?
2. Most of us have had the experience of watching an event with a group of people, only to discover that our memory of the event is quite different from the memories formed by the other observers. What processes might be responsible for the individual nature of such memories?
3. Recent research suggests that neurogenesis in adulthood can erase prior memories. What implications does this research have for the use of neural stem cells to treat central nervous system damage?

KEY TERMS

anterograde amnesia (p. 420)
associative learning (p. 400)
associativity (p. 426)
classical conditioning (p. 401)
conditioned response (CR) (p. 402)
conditioned stimulus (CS) (p. 402)
cooperativity (p. 426)
declarative memory (p. 419)
delay conditioning (p. 416)
delayed nonmatching to sample (DNMS) task (p. 423)
dentate gyrus (p. 425)
engram (p. 420)

episodic memory (p. 419)
extinction (p. 416)
fixed action pattern (p. 400)
habituation (p. 401)
information processing models (p. 418)
learning (p. 400)
long-term memory (p. 419)
long-term depression (LTD) (p. 414)
long-term potentiation (LTP) (p. 425)
nonassociative learning (p. 401)
nondeclarative memory (p. 419)
operant conditioning (p. 402)

procedural memory (p. 419)
reflex (p. 400)
semantic memory (p. 419)
sensitization (p. 401)
sensory memory (p. 418)
short-term memory (p. 418)
source amnesia (p. 430)
trace conditioning (p. 416)
unconditioned response (UCR) (p. 402)
unconditioned stimulus (UCS) (p. 402)

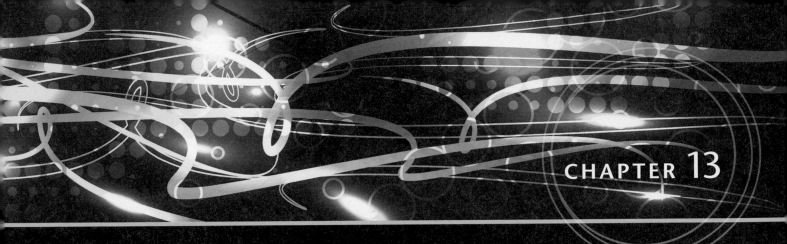

CHAPTER 13

Hemispheric Asymmetry, Language, and Intelligence

LEARNING OBJECTIVES

LO1 Evaluate theories accounting for the development of lateralization.

LO2 Interpret the correlations between lateralization, handedness, and behavior.

LO3 Describe the origins of human language and assess the evidence regarding the use of language by nonhuman species.

LO4 Explain the implications of multilingualism, American Sign Language, and communication disorders for our understanding of the brain processes underlying language abilities.

LO5 Evaluate the biological correlates of intelligence.

CHAPTER OUTLINE

CONNECTING TO RESEARCH: Savants and Laterality

BEHAVIORAL NEUROSCIENCE GOES TO WORK: Speech and Language Pathology

THINKING ETHICALLY: Performance-Enhancing Drugs for the Mind?

BUILDING BETTER HEALTH: Enriched Environments, Infectious Load, and IQ

lateralization The localization of a function in one hemisphere or the other.

hemispherectomy An operation in which the cerebral cortex is removed from one hemisphere.

Hemispheric Asymmetry and Its Behavioral Correlates

Organisms are not perfectly symmetrical. Most of us know that we need to try on both shoes before we purchase a pair because our feet are slightly different in size. This asymmetry extends to our brains as well. The right and left hemispheres are not just typically different in size; substantial evidence suggests that they differ in function as well. The localization of a function in one hemisphere or the other is known as **lateralization**.

Learning About Asymmetry

In Chapter 2, we saw that much was learned about localization of cognitive function from the behavior of Phineas Gage following his bizarre accident. So too, much of what we know about brain lateralization comes from studies of patients who have undergone surgery to reduce life-threatening seizures that could not be controlled with medication. More recently, however, imaging studies have been able to refine our understanding of the scope of lateralization in the brain.

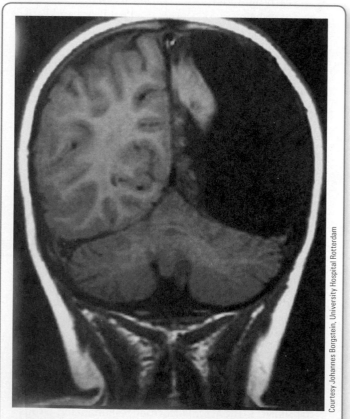

Courtesy Johannes Borgstein, University Hospital Rotterdam

> **Figure 13.1** Hemispherectomies Are Used to Treat Rasmussen's Syndrome In 2007, physicians at Johns Hopkins University diagnosed nine-year-old Cameron Mott with Rasmussen's Syndrome. In a seven-hour surgery, her right cerebral cortex was removed. After four weeks of physical therapy, Cameron walked out of the hospital. She has a slight limp but still dreams of being a ballerina.

HEMISPHERECTOMY Rasmussen's syndrome is a rare brain disorder that produces seizures in only one hemisphere of the brain. It usually affects children after the age of five years, and its causes are currently unknown. The seizures produced by Rasmussen's syndrome, unlike those in many other disorders, do not respond to medication or to more commonly performed surgeries, including the split brain procedure we discuss in a later section. The most effective treatment for Rasmussen's is a **hemispherectomy**, or the complete removal of the cortex from one entire cerebral hemisphere. The cortex of the frontal, parietal, temporal, and occipital lobes is removed, leaving the underlying white matter, basal ganglia, thalamus, and ventricles. Following surgery, the remaining cavity eventually fills with cerebrospinal fluid (see ● Figure 13.1).

What results might we expect from such a radical treatment? For about 75 to 80 percent of the patients, seizures are completely stopped, and for most others, seizure activity is greatly reduced. But what is the cost to the patient? In Chapter 2, we learned that each of the two cerebral hemispheres has special roles in behaviors such as movement and language. What impact might a hemispherectomy have on these behaviors? Rather than being completely paralyzed on one half of the body as we might expect, treated children move with a slight limp and perhaps an ankle brace. Language development is also surprisingly normal, although the removal of the dominant hemisphere impacts language to a greater extent than removal of the non-dominant hemisphere (Curtiss, de Bode, & Mathern, 2001; Varadkar et al., 2014). How is overall intelligence affected by the loss of half the cerebral cortex? Once again, the results are surprising (Vining et al., 1997). The procedure is associated with an average of a 10-point increase on intelligence tests, probably due to a reduced need for the sedative medications typically used to control seizures (see Chapter 15). In one case, a boy who underwent the procedure on his left hemisphere at age five eventually developed superior intelligence and language abilities, allowing him to complete graduate studies (Smith & Sugar, 1975).

The success of the hemispherectomy is related to the young age of the patients and would likely have more severe and detrimental effects in adults (Choi, Vining, Mori, & Bastian, 2010). The fact that we are capable of living with one hemisphere certainly does not imply that we don't need or use all parts of our brains. Instead, the two hemispheres appear to provide unique and distinct contributions to our highest levels of human cognitive functions.

THE SPLIT-BRAIN OPERATION   The **split-brain operation**, in which pathways connecting the right and left cerebral hemispheres are severed, is another treatment that has been used to reduce life-threatening seizures that cannot be controlled with medication. The operation involves severing some or all of the pathways, or commissures, that link the two hemispheres (see ● Figure 13.2). The largest of these is the corpus callosum. The anterior commissure links the two temporal lobes, and the **hippocampal commissure** links the right and left hippocampus. In animals and some humans, the **massa intermedia** forms a bridge between the right and left medial thalamus.

Although split-brain surgeries date back to the 1930s, the most thoroughly studied cases were performed in the 1960s by Joseph Bogen. Bogen severed all four commissures listed above in 16 patients who had been suffering uncontrollable seizures (Bogen, Schultz, & Vogel, 1988). By separating the two hemispheres, a seizure originating in one half of the brain is restricted to that half. Seizures result from abnormal electrical events, which in turn lead to observable clinical events such as convulsions

split-brain operation A treatment for seizure disorder in which the commissures linking the two cerebral hemispheres are severed.
hippocampal commissure A pathway linking the right and left hippocampal structures.
massa intermedia The connection between the right and left thalamic nuclei.

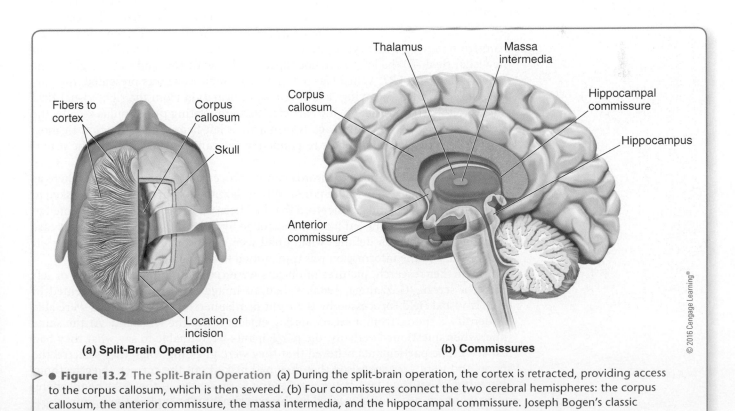

(a) Split-Brain Operation

(b) Commissures

© 2016 Cengage Learning®

> ● **Figure 13.2** The Split-Brain Operation (a) During the split-brain operation, the cortex is retracted, providing access to the corpus callosum, which is then severed. (b) Four commissures connect the two cerebral hemispheres: the corpus callosum, the anterior commissure, the massa intermedia, and the hippocampal commissure. Joseph Bogen's classic split-brain procedure involved severing all four.

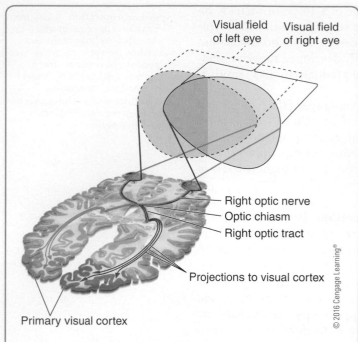

Visual field of left eye

Visual field of right eye

Right optic nerve
Optic chiasm
Right optic tract

Projections to visual cortex

Primary visual cortex

© 2016 Cengage Learning®

● **Figure 13.3** **The Relationship between the Visual Fields and the Right and Left Visual Cortices** Assuming that the eyes and head are stationary, information from the right visual field (blue) is processed in the left visual cortex. Conversely, information from the left visual field (red) is processed in the right visual cortex. In the patient with a split brain, this organization allows researchers to demonstrate differences between the properties of the right and left hemispheres.

(see Chapter 15). When the propagation of abnormal electrical activity is restricted to a single hemisphere, electrical disturbances still occur, but might not reach the thresholds required to produce observable clinical symptoms. Split-brain procedures reduce both the severity and overall frequency of seizures. Forty-one percent of the patients in one sample were completely free of seizures following surgery, and another 45 percent had seizures less than half as frequently as before surgery (Sorenson et al., 1997).

Surprisingly, Bogen's patients experienced no changes in personality, intelligence, or speech (Gazzaniga, 1970; Sperry, 1974). Roger Sperry, Michael Gazzaniga, and their colleagues conducted further explorations of the unique behavioral outcomes of this surgery. These investigations took advantage of the fact that the processing of certain types of information is lateralized. For example, we know that both sensation and motor control in the left half of the body are controlled by the right hemisphere of the brain. Similarly, as shown in ● Figure 13.3, information from the right half of a person's visual field is transmitted to the left visual cortex. This allows visual stimuli to be presented to one hemisphere of a split-brain patient but not the other, assuming the head is stationary.

In one typical experiment by Gazzaniga (1967), illustrated in ● Figure 13.4, participants who had previously undergone split-brain operations were instructed to focus on a dot located in the center of the visual field. This instruction prevents the participants from moving either eyes or head, ensuring that each hemisphere "sees" only half the visual field. To the left of the dot appeared the word *HE*, and to the right of the dot was the word *ART*. When Gazzaniga asked which word was presented, the participants responded by saying "art." Because information from the right visual field crosses to the left hemisphere, the participants were relating the stimulus seen by the left hemisphere. Because language is primarily a left-hemisphere function in most people, the verbal left hemisphere responded to Gazzaniga's question with the stimulus it had seen.

Numbers, letters, and short words can be processed by the right hemisphere as long as a nonverbal response is required. When Gazzaniga's participants were asked to point with their left hands to the word that had been seen, the participants pointed to the word *HE*. Because the left hand is controlled by the right hemisphere, in this case the right hemisphere is "telling" what it had seen. The word *HE* appeared in the left visual field, and the information was transmitted to the right hemisphere.

In further research, pictures of objects were flashed on either the right or left side of a screen (Gazzaniga, 1983). When an image of a spoon was presented in the left visual field (processed by the right hemisphere), the participants were able to identify a spoon from a set of similar objects using the left hand. At the same time, when questioned verbally, the participants were unable to say what they had just seen. The participants believed that they were guessing when they selected the spoon and were very surprised that they had picked out the correct object without "knowing" what they saw. If the word *stand* is presented to the right hemisphere, participants stand up. When asked by the experimenter to explain the action, a participant might reply that he or she needed to get up and stretch. The verbal left

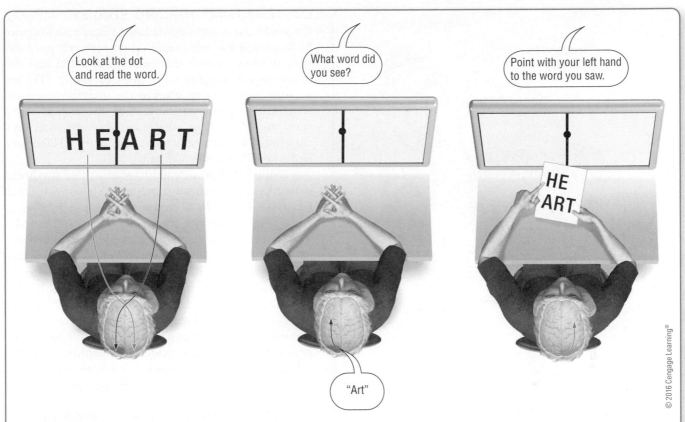

● **Figure 13.4** Differences in Language Capacities between the Two Hemispheres When the participant in a split-brain study was asked what she saw, she replied "art," the word seen by the verbal left hemisphere. When asked to point with the left hand to the word she saw, she pointed to HE, the word seen by the right hemisphere. The left hand is controlled by the right hemisphere.

© 2016 Cengage Learning®

hemisphere, observing the action of standing but being unaware of the command to stand, attempts to provide a reasonable explanation for the behavior. These observations led Gazzaniga (1988) to describe the left hemisphere as an "interpreter" that tries to make sense out of our actions.

In addition to differences in the localization of language, the two hemispheres appear to differ in the processing of other types of information. Logical, sequential information is processed more effectively by the left hemisphere, whereas emotional, intuitive information is processed by the right hemisphere. The processing of spatial relations, as in thinking about a three-dimensional figure, is superior in the right hemisphere. Although all of the participants studied by Sperry and Gazzaniga were right-handed, their ability to draw or copy a three-dimensional figure was superior when using the left hand, which is controlled by the right hemisphere.

We should interpret the behavior of patients after split-brain surgery with caution. Not only have these patients undergone extensive, invasive surgery, but the epilepsy that required surgery in the first place could have affected brain function and organization. Fortunately, other methods can be used to study lateralization in healthy, typical individuals. In the Wada test, named after its inventor, Juhn Wada, the anesthetic sodium amytal is applied to one cerebral hemisphere through a catheter inserted in the groin area and advanced into one of the carotid arteries in the neck. As a result of this procedure, illustrated in ● Figure 13.5, one cerebral hemisphere is literally put to sleep. If the patient has language localized to the anesthetized hemisphere, speech and most comprehension will be absent.

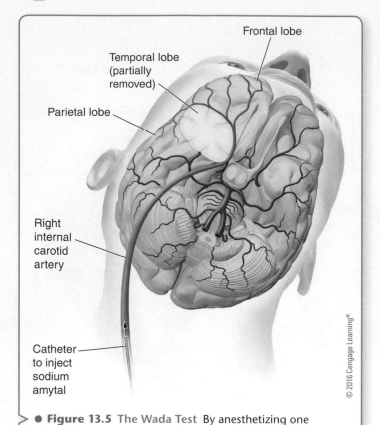

Frontal lobe

Temporal lobe
(partially
removed)

Parietal lobe

Right
internal
carotid
artery

Catheter
to inject
sodium
amytal

© 2016 Cengage Learning®

● **Figure 13.5 The Wada Test** By anesthetizing one hemisphere with an injection of sodium amytal, researchers can determine which hemisphere processes language. If the hemisphere that manages language is the one anesthetized, the patient will be unable to speak or comprehend.

CONTEMPORARY IMAGING STUDIES Although the Wada test is appropriate for medical patients prior to surgery, it has been replaced for research purposes with the less invasive combination of fMRI and diffusion tensor imaging (DTI; see Chapter 1). DTI has allowed researchers to observe the underlying microstructure of single pathways, like the corpus callosum, providing even greater insight into individual variations in hemisphere connectivity (Häberling, Badzakova-Trajkov, & Corballis, 2011).

Using fMRI, researchers have identified two broad networks for lateralized functions (Nielsen, Zielinski, Ferguson, Lainhart, & Anderson, 2013). As shown in Table 13.1, researchers located 20 lateralization hubs, 9 in the left-lateralized and 11 in the right-lateralized networks. The left-lateralized network includes language areas such as Broca's and Wernicke's areas, along with parts of the default mode network (DMN; see Chapter 11). The right-lateralized network includes three regions associated with attention to external stimuli and executive function. The left-lateralized network shows greater connectivity within the hemisphere, while the right-lateralized network involves connections between hubs in both hemispheres.

LATERALIZATION AND MICROSCOPIC ANALYSES In Chapter 5, we discussed neurogenesis and the migration of neurons to the cerebral cortex. Cortical asymmetries do not appear to be the result of death (apoptosis) among cells that have already migrated (Rosen, 1996).

TABLE 13.1 | Lateralization Hubs of the Left and Right Hemisphere

Left Hemisphere Hubs	Right Hemisphere Hubs
Broca's area (Br)	Right supplementary motor area (r-S)
Wernicke's area (We)	Mid insula (MI)
Inferior dorsolateral prefrontal cortex (DP)	Parietooccipital (PO)
Left supplementary motor area (l-S)	Lateral intraparietal sulcus (LI)
Lateral premotor cortex (LP)	Frontal eye fields (FE)
Medial prefrontal cortex (MP)	Dorsolateral prefrontal cortex (DL)
Medial superior frontal (SF)	Middle temporal area (MT)
Posterior cingulate cortex (PC)	Broca homologue (Bh)
Lateral temporoparietal junction (TP)	Mid cingulate cortex (MC)
	Superior medial intraparietal sulcus (IP)
	Anterior insula (AI)

© 2016 Cengage Learning®

A "hub" represents connections between regions that are significantly lateralized. Nine hubs in the left hemisphere and 11 hubs in the right were identified using fMRI. Left hemisphere networks connect language areas and parts of the default mode network (DMN), while right hemisphere networks connect regions involved with attention and executive function.

Instead, differences leading to the ultimate observed asymmetries in the cortex are likely to originate at earlier stages, such as the proliferation of progenitor cells.

The Evolution of Lateralization

Lateralization is not exclusive to human beings. Preferences for one hand (or paw) are generally accepted as indications of functional asymmetry in the brain. Paw preferences during reaching for food have been observed in mice, rats, cats, and dogs (Sun & Walsh, 2006). As shown in ● Figure 13.6, chimpanzees and other great apes show structural asymmetries in their brains that are similar to those in humans (Corballis, 2014).

What advantages might lateralization provide? In terms of natural selection (see Chapter 2), we must distinguish between the advantages of lateralization to an individual and the advantages of lateralization to a species (Rogers, 2002). Individual benefits of lateralization include enhanced skill performance and faster reaction time (Rogers, 2002). Population lateralization is more common among social species, where it may serve to coordinate responses to a predator (Rogers, 2002). If a school of fish or a flock of sheep turn in a coordinated fashion when a predator is detected, this could enhance survival. Even more sophisticated social cohesion might be made possible by lateralization. Individuals in many species attack another's left side, so approaching a member of the group on the individual's right sends a more peaceful message. Being lateralized similarly to the population makes behavior more predictable, which allows lateralized species to form stable hierarchies.

Rogers (2000) suggested that lateralization improves divided attention abilities, or the ability to split attention between different aspects of the environment. Chicks incubated in the dark do not lateralize some of their visually guided responses, and, therefore, they can serve as a control group for normally lateralized chicks incubated in the light. Compared with the dark-incubated, nonlateralized chicks, the light-incubated, normally lateralized chicks were more efficient in managing the dual tasks of identifying potential predators while feeding (see ● Figure 13.7). Lateralization also helped the chicks discriminate between grain and pebbles (Rogers, Andrew, & Johnston, 2007). These abilities would confer obvious advantages to the chicks' survival. Lateralization in human beings appears to provide similar benefits. When carrying out two simultaneous tasks, one processed by the left hemisphere and the other by the right, participants demonstrating typical lateralization performed better than those with weaker lateralization (Lust et al., 2011).

Lateralization might be directly related to language and language-like functions, which we discuss later in this chapter. Songbirds' song production is lateralized to their left hemispheres. Japanese macaque monkeys show evidence of a left-hemisphere advantage for processing sound. As we have seen, most humans lateralize language to the left hemisphere. Keeping language functions on one side of the brain might have been especially efficient as brain size increased (Toga & Thompson, 2003).

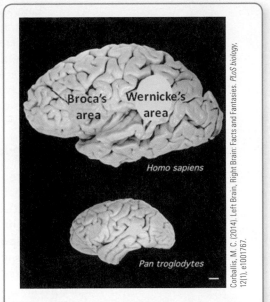

Corballis, M. C. (2014). Left Brain, Right Brain: Facts and Fantasies. *PLoS biology.* 12(11), e1001767.

● **Figure 13.6** Humans Are Not the Only Lateralized Species The chimpanzee shows similar left-lateralized development of areas of the brain corresponding to the human Broca's and Wernicke's language areas.

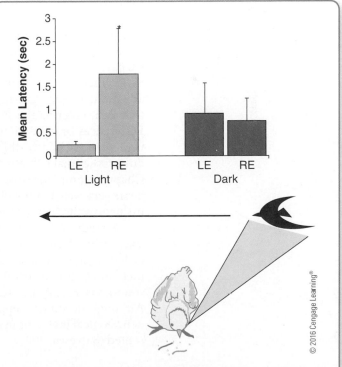

© 2016 Cengage Learning®

● **Figure 13.7** Lateralization and Multitasking Chicks raised in the light lateralize feeding and predator search behaviors, while chicks raised in the dark do not. The chick feeds while a model raptor moves in one visual field or the other. The latency, or time to detection, was noted for both the left eye (LE) and right eye (RE). Light-exposed chicks showed a much shorter latency to respond (by interrupting feeding and chirping) when the image of the predator impacted the left eye.

Lateralization of language may have grown from gesture. As we will see in a later section, most people are right-handed, and the right side of the body is controlled by the left hemisphere (see Chapter 8). Captive apes gesture with the right hand (Toga & Thompson, 2003). Lateralization of spoken language might represent an extension of the motor areas that provide fine control of the right hand for gesturing. Language, a relatively new invention, might have built upon brain structures already in place to make gesturing and fine motor control possible.

The Development of Lateralization

What produces lateralization in humans? Geschwind and Galaburda (1987) suggested that prenatal androgens play key roles in the lateralization of language and visuospatial skills. Prenatal testosterone might impact lateralization by enhancing pruning in the corpus callosum during brain development (see Chapter 5; Lust et al., 2010). Especially high levels of prenatal testosterone might lead to abnormal lateralization, supported by the finding that a higher proportion of males than females are left-handed (Mathews et al., 2004). Handedness, as we will see later in this chapter, is correlated with lateralization. Handedness has a strong genetic component (Llaurens, Raymond, & Faurie, 2009). Data from twin and adoption studies are much more consistent with genetic explanations of handedness than environmental accounts. What appears to be inherited is not right or left handedness itself, but rather whether the typical bias to right-handedness will be expressed or not (Corballis, 2014). However, the genetics of handedness are not simple. For example, maternal handedness has more of an effect on offspring handedness than paternal handedness.

The two hemispheres appear to develop along different timelines. The timing of the development of dendrites in left-hemisphere language areas, such as Broca's area, is different than in the analogous areas of the right hemisphere (Scheibel et al., 1985). The overall maturation of the left-hemisphere language areas lag behind the development of their right-hemisphere counterparts during the first year of life, then quickly surpass them (Scheibel et al., 1985).

Which environmental factors have been implicated in the development of lateralization? In the light-exposed chick, embryos are turned in the egg in such a way that light entering the shell stimulates the right eye, but not the left (Rogers, 2002). Differences in light stimulation produce asymmetrical development in visual pathways. Similarly, two-thirds of human fetuses maintain a position in the uterus during the final trimester in which their right side faces outward. As we discussed in Chapter 7, amniotic fluid is an excellent conductor of sound, and the fetus at this stage hears very well. It is possible that the asymmetry of auditory input due to fetal position influences the lateralization of the developing brain (Previc, 1991).

A study of 180,000 Swedish male military recruits suggested that routine ultrasounds conducted during their mothers' pregnancies resulted in higher numbers of left-handers (Kieler, Cnattingius, Haglund, Palmgren, &Axelsson, 2001). A later meta-analysis of nearly 9,000 children confirmed the finding that exposure to ultrasound has a small, but statistically significant effect on handedness (Salvesen, 2011). Although no studies support any relationship between prenatal ultrasound and later neurological problems in children, further research into this phenomenon seems warranted (Salvesen, 2007).

Implications of Asymmetry for Behavior

Roger Sperry (1982, p. 1225) observed, "The left-right dichotomy in cognitive mode is an idea with which it is very easy to run wild." What are the implications of lateralization in the typical intact brain?

One common assertion about hemisphere lateralization is the concept of a dominant hemisphere (Bakan, 1971; Zenhausen, 1978). People who are "left-brain dominant" are described as logical, verbal, and analytic. "Right-brained" people are supposed to be artistic and intuitive. Anecdotal data, such as the large number of left-handed statesmen, musicians, artists, and athletes, compared with a much smaller number of left-handed writers, contribute to popular beliefs about hemisphere dominance. However, experimental support for this notion is weak. Springer and Deutsch (1998) report no strong correlations between hemisphere dominance and occupational choice or artistic talent.

HANDEDNESS, LANGUAGE, AND HEMISPHERE LATERALIZATION One of the strongest correlations regarding hemisphere lateralization is the association between handedness and the localization of language. Handedness is surprisingly difficult to establish, but a common standard is the use of a preferred hand for writing (McManus, 1999). Using that standard, approximately equal use of both hands is quite rare, accounting for about 1 percent of the population (Corballis, Hattie, & Fletcher, 2008). Of the 90 percent of the population who are primarily right-handed, about 96 percent localize language primarily to the left hemisphere. Most of the remaining 4 percent localize language to the right, although there are a very small number of right-handed individuals who use both hemispheres for language. Among the 10 percent of people who are primarily left-handed, about 70 percent localize language to the left hemisphere, 15 percent localize language to the right hemisphere, and the remaining 15 percent use both hemispheres fairly equally for language (Corballis, 2003; Rasmussen & Milner, 1977).

Because they are relatively unusual, left-handers are traditionally excluded from many brain imaging studies. Neuroscientists have begun to call for increased inclusion of left-handers in imaging research, not just in studies of lateralization and asymmetry, but in all aspects of behavior (Willems, Van der Haegen, Fisher, & Francks, 2014). In particular, the routine exclusion of left-handers from studies of genetic contributions to cognitive processes might confound the results. Because left-handers represent a normal variation in human attributes, including them in research provides a more thorough snapshot of human phenomena.

Left-handedness is an advantage in forward-facing sports, such as fencing, tennis and baseball, but not in others, such as gymnastics (Faurie & Raymond, 2005). Judging from buried remains, left-handedness becomes more frequent in societies engaged in sustained wars (Faurie & Raymond, 2004). As shown in ●Figure 13.8, left-handedness is strongly correlated with homicide rates in nonindustrialized societies, ranging from 3 percent in the most peaceful groups to 27 percent in the most warlike (Faurie & Raymond, 2005). We are not saying that being left-handed makes you homicidal, but in violent circumstances, being left-handed might provide a survival advantage.

DICHOTIC LISTENING Much of the work by Sperry and Gazzaniga on the effects of split-brain surgeries focused on the processing of information by the visual cortex. However, listening tasks also provide insight into lateralization. Although information from one ear is processed by both cerebral hemispheres, it is processed more rapidly by the contralateral auditory cortex. In other words, information presented to the left ear is processed more rapidly by the right hemisphere, whereas information provided to the right ear is processed more rapidly by the left hemisphere.

To investigate the lateralization of auditory processing, Doreen Kimura used **dichotic listening** tasks, in which different sounds are presented

dichotic listening A task in which different sounds are presented simultaneously to the right and left ears.

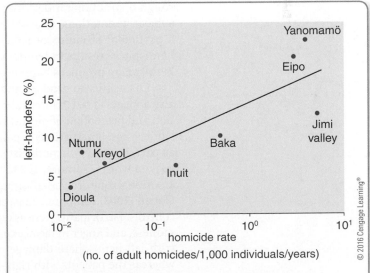

● **Figure 13.8** **Left-Handedness Rates Correlate with Homicides** Rates of homicide in nonindustrialized cultures show a strong positive correlation with left-handedness. Although it is true that males are more likely to be left-handed, and excess males in a population are associated with more violence, these indirect factors play a minor role in explaining these results.

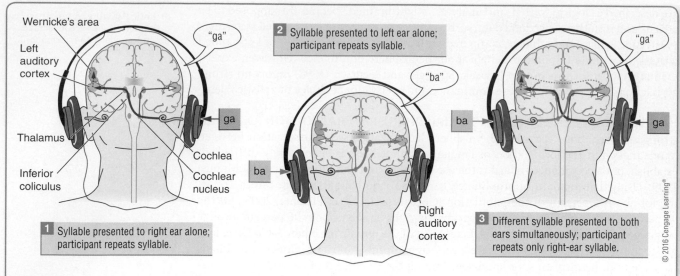

● **Figure 13.9** Dichotic Listening Is Related to Hemisphere Lateralization for Language When conflicting information is provided to the two ears, the person who has language lateralized to the left hemisphere will show a preference for the word heard by the right ear. The information presented to the right ear will reach Wernicke's area in the left hemisphere faster than information presented to the left ear.

simultaneously to the left and right ears (see ● Figure 13.9). If words reaching the two ears are different, most right-handers show a right-ear advantage, repeating the word they heard in the right ear (Kimura, 1973). This result suggests that language for these individuals is lateralized to the left hemisphere. As we will see in the next section, right-handers show a left-ear advantage, or right-hemisphere advantage, for emotional information.

THE LATERALIZATION OF EMOTION AND MUSICAL ABILITIES In most people, activity in the left hemisphere is correlated with positive emotions, whereas activity in the right hemisphere is correlated with negative emotions. This provides us with a rough distinction for deciding whether to approach (left hemisphere activity, positive subjective emotions) or avoid (right hemisphere activity, negative subjective emotions) a particular stimulus or situation (Davidson & Irwin, 1999). Anesthetizing the left hemisphere results in temporary feelings of depression, while anesthetizing the right hemisphere produces happiness (Lee et al., 2004).

Our ability to produce and detect emotional tone in language, known as **prosody**, also appears to be lateralized. Evidence for right-hemisphere participation in the production and perception of prosody comes from analyses of dichotic listening tasks, imaging studies, and observations of patients with right-hemisphere strokes (see Chapter 15). Just as participants in dichotic listening tasks showed a right-ear advantage for identifying spoken words (Kimura, 1973), they also show a left-ear advantage for determining the emotional tone of a verbal stimulus (Bryden, 1988). Charbonneau, Scherzer, Aspirot, and Cohen (2003) compared 22 patients with right- or left-hemisphere damage with healthy controls. Participants were asked to discriminate, imitate, and produce emotions of fear, sadness, and anger in facial expressions and in vocal expressions (prosody). The patients with left-hemisphere damage performed as well as the control group in most cases, whereas the patients with right-hemisphere damage showed deficits in processing both facial expressions and prosody. Studies using fMRI confirm that the right hemisphere participates in the evaluation of emotional tone in language (Wildgruber, Ackermann, Kreifelts, & Ethofer, 2006; Wildgruber et al., 2005). However, the situation is not simple. These researchers also note that the orbitofrontal cortex of both hemispheres contributes to the explicit, or conscious, evaluation of emotional tone in spoken language.

Researchers have also tried to evaluate the lateralization of musical abilities. Following a stroke that damaged his left hemisphere, composer Maurice Ravel retained his ability to judge pitch and to recognize a piece of music he heard. However, Ravel was unable

prosody The use of pitch and intonation in language to convey emotional tone and meaning.

to play the piano, recognize written music, or compose music. Ravel's outcomes show us that some musical abilities are lateralized to the right hemisphere but that a simple "language-on-the-left, music-on-the-right" model of hemispheric functioning is incorrect. The extent to which music is lateralized is still debatable. Some imaging studies suggest that music and language share overlapping brain resources (Brown, Martinez, & Parsons, 2006), which is not surprising given the processes' shared reliance on sound. A number of studies have indicated that musical training can provide advantages in using language, including the detection of prosody and rhythm (Slevc, 2012). Musical training might therefore have potential in programs designed to improve language skills and reading.

The brains of musicians with perfect pitch, or the ability to name a musical note that they hear, appear to be structurally different from those of nonmusicians or from those of musicians without perfect pitch, particularly in the left hemisphere areas responsible for processing sound (Schlaug, Jancke, Huang, & Steinmetz, 1995). The **planum temporale**, shown in ● Figure 13.10, is usually somewhat larger in the left hemisphere than in the right in most people. However, the difference between the left and right planum temporale was about twice as large in the musicians with perfect pitch as in the control participants. In more recent investigations using diffusion tensor imaging (DTI), the increased volume seen in the left hemisphere of musicians

planum temporale An area located posterior to the primary auditory cortex in the temporal lobes.

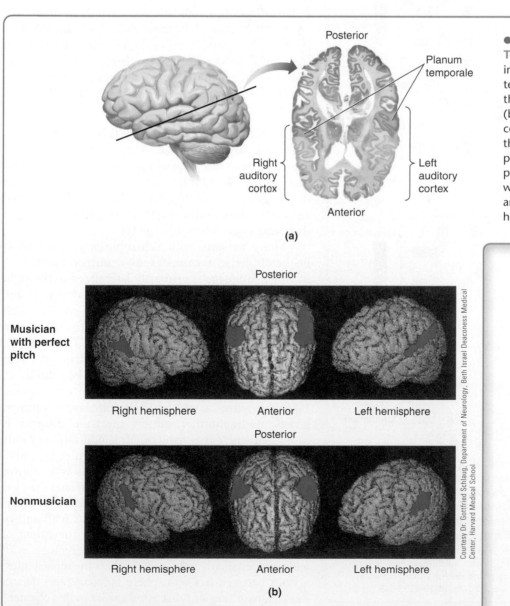

(a)

(b)

● **Figure 13.10 The Planum Temporale** (a) In most individuals, the left planum temporale is larger in the left than in the right hemisphere. (b) Gottfried Schlaug and his colleagues have found that this asymmetry is even more pronounced in musicians with perfect pitch, as compared with nonmusical participants and musicians who do not have perfect pitch.

Courtesy Dr. Gottfried Schlaug, Department of Neurology, Beth Israel Deaconess Medical Center, Harvard Medical School

with perfect pitch might be the result of "hyperconnectivity," or greater volume of white matter in the temporal lobe (Loui, Li, Hohmann, & Schlaug, 2010).

GENDER DIFFERENCES IN LATERALIZATION The prenatal hormone hypothesis discussed earlier predicts gender differences in lateralization, given the much higher exposure of the male fetus to prenatal androgens (see Chapter 10). In general, the male brain is more lateralized (more asymmetrical in structure and function) than the female brain (Shaywitz et al., 1995). Males are about twice as likely to be left-handers than females (Faurie & Raymond, 2004). Gender differences in lateralization have been proposed to explain observations of gender differences in language and visuospatial skills (see Chapter 10; Clements et al., 2006). Females typically show a slight advantage over males in language skills, while males show a slight advantage over females in visuospatial skills.

Such discrepancies could result from different degrees of functional asymmetry in the brains of males and females. Males performing a visuospatial task showed activity in the right hemisphere, whereas females performing the task showed activity in both hemispheres (Johnson, McKenzie, & Hamm, 2002). Although neuroscientists continue to debate the existence of gender differences in lateralization, a sophisticated analysis of functional connectivity showed stronger rightward lateralization in the male superior temporal lobe, which participates in spatial processing, and a stronger leftward lateralization in the female inferior frontal lobe areas associated with language processing (Tomasi & Volkow, 2012).

LATERALIZATION, PSYCHOLOGICAL DISORDERS, AND DISEASE A number of conditions are correlated with atypical asymmetry of the cerebral hemispheres. In addition to the reading and language disorders discussed in a later section, schizophrenia and autism spectrum disorder (see Chapter 16) involve differences in cerebral asymmetry.

Many patients with schizophrenia either show no hemispheric asymmetry or a mirror asymmetry in which language is primarily lateralized to the right hemisphere (Petty, 1999; Sommer, Ramsey, Kahn, Aleman, & Bouma, 2001). In addition, patients with schizophrenia are more likely than healthy controls to have a mixed or ambiguous handedness (Crow, 1997).

Diagnostic criteria for autism spectrum disorder include communication difficulties (APA, 2013). In many cases, language can be delayed or even absent. Like schizophrenia, with which it shares some common genetic underpinnings, autism spectrum disorder is associated with either reduced left lateralization or mirrored lateralization for language (Nielsen et al., 2014). As shown in ● Figure 13.11, individuals with autism spectrum disorder showed less evidence of lateralization compared to typical controls. The severity of communication and social deficits in individuals with autism spectrum disorder was correlated with the extent of abnormal lateralization. In addition, individuals with autism spectrum disorder did not show the typical interactions between left-hemisphere language and default mode network regions discussed earlier in this chapter.

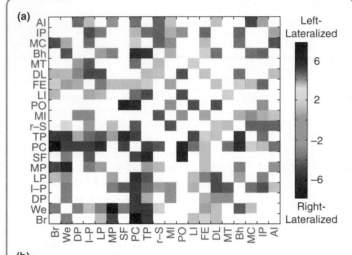

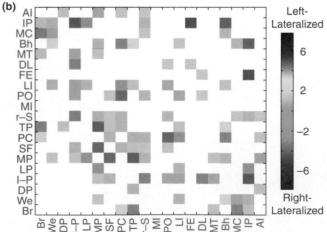

● **Figure 13.11 Atypical Lateralization in Autism Spectrum Disorder** Using the 20 lateralized hubs described previously and outlined in Table 13.1, researchers compared the connections in typical individuals (a) and in individuals with autism spectrum disorder (b). The comparison demonstrates the reduced lateralization found in cases of autism spectrum disorder.

Source: Nielsen, J. A., Zielinski, B. A., Fletcher, P. T., Alexander, A. L., Lange, N., Bigler, E. D., et al. (2014). Abnormal lateralization of functional connectivity between language and default mode regions in autism. *Molecular Autism*, 5(1), 8. doi: 10.1186/2040-2392-5-8

••• Connecting to **Research**

SAVANTS AND LATERALITY

Savant behaviors are exceptional skills and talents found in people whose intellectual functioning otherwise falls within the range of intellectual disability. Stephen Wiltshire, shown in ● Figure 13.12, is an adult male with autism spectrum disorder living in the UK. Stephen can take a one hour or less helicopter flight over a major city such as Rome or Tokyo and then draw from memory every street, building, and landmark with remarkable accuracy. Leslie Lemke, a patient who is blind and intellectually disabled, heard Tchaikovsky's Piano Concerto No.1 played one time on television. Several hours later, Lemke sat down at the piano, which he had never studied, and played the entire concerto without error (Treffert & Wallace, 2002). Such a task would be beyond the abilities of most talented, highly-trained, professional musicians. How can we account for such remarkable abilities in people whose general level of functioning is otherwise quite low?

Researchers have made a detailed case study of one 63-year-old male savant with autism spectrum disorder (Corrigan et al., 2012). This individual demonstrates a number of strong skills, including perfect pitch, proficiency in many musical instruments, conversational skills in 12 languages, remarkable imitation of sounds, and exceptional artistic abilities. To investigate the possible biological correlates of these skills, multiple methods were used, including high-resolution magnetic resonance imaging, diffusion tensor imaging, brain volumetrics, assessment of white matter bundle volumes, and neurochemical assays.

We have discussed the typical lateralization of the human brain in this section, and the case study subject

James Ambler/Barcroft USA/Getty Images

● **Figure 13.12** Savant Behavior Stephen Wiltshire is able to fly over a major city for a short period of time and then draw the cityscape in precise detail from memory. The biological correlates of savant behavior suggest a role for atypical laterality.

showed a number of differences in comparison with that model. His right cerebral hemisphere was 1.9 percent larger than the left, his right amygdala was 24 percent larger than the left, and his right caudate nucleus was 9.9 percent larger than the left. Fiber tract bundle volumes on the right were larger for the amygdala, hippocampus, frontal lobe, and occipital lobe. GABA and glutamate concentrations were greatly reduced in the parietal lobe.

We do not know how these variations map onto the savant behavior, but using the same techniques with multiple cases of savant behavior might highlight common elements.

INTERIM SUMMARY 13.1

|| Summary Table: Localization of Function in the Cerebral Hemispheres

Typically Greater Representation in the Left Hemisphere	Typically Greater Representation in the Right Hemisphere
Motor control of the right side of the body	Motor control of the left side of the body
• Processing of the right visual field • Right-ear advantage in dichotic listening tasks	• Processing of the left visual field • Left-ear advantage in dichotic listening tasks
• Language • Mathematics	• Prosody • Music
Logical processing	• Intuition • Spatial relations
	Art

savant behavior Exceptional skills and talents found in people whose intellectual functioning otherwise falls within the range of intellectual disability.

language A system of communicating thoughts and feelings using arbitrary signals, such as sounds, gestures, or written signals.

Summary Points

1. Research involving patients who had undergone surgery to treat life-threatening seizures led to an understanding that some functions are not symmetrically organized in the brain. **(LO1)**

2. Lateralization results from genetic influences, but understanding the exact processes responsible for its development requires further research. Lateralization appears to involve differential gene expression in the two hemispheres, differences in connectivity, and environmental influences. **(LO1)**

3. Handedness, language, spatial relations, dichotic listening, the processing of music and prosody, gender, and some psychological disorders correlate with patterns of lateralization. **(LO2)**

Review Question

1. What are the possible advantages of lateralization of functions in the cerebral hemispheres?

Language

Language has been defined as a system of communicating thoughts and feelings using arbitrary signals, such as sounds, gestures, or written signals. Table 13.2 outlines standard linguistic criteria used to assess communication and language (Aitchison, 1983).

TABLE 13.2 | Aitchison's Ten Criteria for Language

Feature	Definition	Example
1. Vocal-auditory canal	Use of vocalization to communicate	Speech and birdsong but not American Sign Language (ASL) or bee dances
2. Arbitrariness	No connection between symbol and what it signifies	Using the word *dog* to refer to the animal
3. Semanticity	Use of symbols to refer to objects and actions	*Chair* can be used to refer to all chairs
4. Cultural transmission	Handed down from generation to generation	We learn language from our families
5. Spontaneous usage	No training or force is necessary to make individuals communicate	Children exposed to language will use language freely
6. Turn-taking	Communication follows social rules	Birds will respond to another bird's song
7. Duality	Use of different sounds and orders of sounds to communicate	C, *A*, and *T* are meaningless until they are combined
8. Displacement	Ability to communicate about objects and events that are distant in time and place	Bee dances direct other bees to distant sources of food
9. Structure-dependence	Use of grammar, or structured "chunks"	Understanding that the "man in the hat" means the same as "he"
10. Creativity	Ability to create novel utterances	Humans and possibly signing apes can say things they have never heard before

The Origins of Language

Several lines of reasoning point to a biological origin for human language. No human culture on earth exists without language. In addition, learning spoken language seems to proceed differently than other types of learning. No specific instruction is needed, as it is with related skills for reading and writing. The fact that language learning does not always correlate with intelligence provides evidence for an independent "language module" in the brain. Some individuals with normal intelligence experience great difficulty learning language (Tallal, Ross, & Curtiss, 1989). In contrast, children with a genetic condition known as Williams syndrome typically score in the moderately intellectually disabled range on intelligence tests, but they are fluent speakers who develop very large vocabularies (Bellugi, Wang, & Jernigan, 1994).

The possible existence of mirror systems in the brain coupled with the emergence of bipedal movement might have spurred our eventual development of spoken language. Many linguists believe that spoken languages evolved from elaborate systems of gestures, which in turn were made possible by the existence of mirror systems in the primate brain (Corballis, 2009). Mirror systems could provide the understanding of another's behavior necessary for a system of gestures to work. Standing upright not only freed the hands to make gestures, but also prevented the nearly constant physical contact between mother and infant typical among other primates. A system of vocal signals might have developed to bridge this gap in contact (Falk, 2010).

How might these vocalizations have developed? Although most vertebrates have a system of gesture, assuming we include body language like that of a dog when threatening or playing, relatively few species are capable of learned vocalizations. Vocalization of language requires a phonological loop in the brain, or a mechanism for perceiving, understanding, and producing sounds. Pathways connecting auditory processing to the prefrontal lobe might have become strengthened in primate evolution (Aboitiz, 2012). In humans, this pathway might have included mirror systems that made imitation possible, and imitation is essential to learned vocalization. Together, simultaneous gesture and vocalization could be used to establish shared attention between two individuals (pointing and saying, "Look!") (Aboitiz, 2012). Gradually, just as in childhood, the efficiencies and complexities of vocalization compared to gesture began to make vocalization more dominant. In addition, vocalization requires far less energy than gestures (ask anyone you know who teaches courses in signing for the deaf), provides the opportunity to communicate at night or when hidden from sight, and frees the hands for tool use, all advantages that may have served our hunter-gatherer ancestors quite well (Corballis, 2009).

Researchers are getting closer to identifying the genes responsible for some aspects of language. One gene reliably associated with speech and language disorders is the forkhead box *P2* gene *(FOXP2),* located on chromosome 7 (Spiteri et al., 2007). Control of vocalization in nonhuman primates occurs at the subcortical level, and ancient mutations in the *FOXP2* gene might have resulted in the transfer of vocal control to the cortical level, Broca's area especially, in hominins (Corballis, 2009). Members of several generations of a particular family, called the KE family, show a mutation in the *FOXP2* gene accompanied by low-normal intelligence and severe difficulties in the production of language (Lai, Fisher, Hurst, Vargha-Khadem, & Monaco, 2001). A number of structural abnormalities have been identified in the KE family, particularly in the caudate nucleus of the basal ganglia (Watkins et al., 2002). The caudate nucleus was smaller in affected family members than in unaffected family members and in typical control participants. During brain development, *FOXP2* targets the basal ganglia and Broca's area (Spiteri et al., 2007). *FOXP2* is expressed differently in these areas of the human brain than in the chimpanzee brain (Corballis, 2009).

How might the earliest human languages have sounded? Click languages, used by African groups ranging from Tanzania to South Africa, might represent the earliest form of human language (see ● Figure 13.13).

● **Figure 13.13** Click Languages May Be Among the Earliest Human Languages Click languages include sounds made by clicking the tongue. Groups using click languages have been found to be genetically distinct, leading to conclusions that these languages are quite ancient.

Click languages use clicks made by the tongue to symbolize words. Studies of genetic relatedness among African groups using click languages show that the groups are highly distinct from one another (Knight et al., 2001). In spite of their common use of click languages, these groups have not had shared ancestors for between 15,000 and 35,000 years. This suggests that the origin of click languages occurred in a time long before human beings settled down to begin agriculture (Tishkoff et al., 2007).

Communication in Nonhuman Animals

The previous discussion of the origins of language characterized human language as an opportunistic development built upon existing systems for movement, hearing, and imitation. If such a system has evolved according to Darwinian concepts, animals other than humans should possess some language or language-like capabilities.

Many animals communicate with one another, often vocally and in complex ways. Communication, however, is not the same as language (Dronkers, Pinker, & Damasio, 2000). Some animals, like prairie dogs, have a fairly inflexible group of calls used for functions such as signaling danger and identifying territories. Others use signals that communicate magnitude, as in the case of bee dances that indicate the location of food. Finally, animals communicate through sequences of behavior, as in the case of birdsong. These animal behaviors, although clearly used for communication, do not match the flexibility and creativity of human language. Vocal learning, or the modification of vocalization, is an important aspect of human spoken language, yet is only found in a very small subset of nonhuman animals, including elephants, bats, whales, and some birds (Jarvis, 2006).

If we are to find an animal precursor to human language capability, the most logical place to start is with our nearest relatives, the great apes. As we have seen previously, chimpanzees and other nonhuman primates appear to share hemispheric asymmetries in areas related to language with humans.

Researchers have attempted to teach human-like languages to apes. In 1931, Winthrop N. Kellogg and his wife adopted a baby chimpanzee named Gua, but their attempts to teach him human speech were unsuccessful. This is not surprising. Neuroimaging studies have demonstrated that learning of speech sounds and spoken words in human infants requires strong reciprocal activation of circuits connecting Broca's and Wernicke's areas, and connections between analogous areas in nonhuman primates are relatively weak (Pulvermüller & Fadiga, 2010). Because apes are naturally proficient in gesturing, efforts to teach apes sign language have been more promising. Allen and Beatrice Gardner (1969) taught 132 different signs to a chimp named Washoe. The Gardners' work was followed by Francine Patterson (1978), who trained a gorilla named Koko to use signs. Sue Savage-Rumbaugh and her colleagues (Savage-Rumbaugh, Shanker, & Taylor, 1998) have successfully taught a pygmy chimpanzee named Kanzi to associate geometric symbols with words. Even before his own training began, Kanzi appeared to have learned 10 symbols simply by observing his mother's training sessions. Kanzi also seems to be able to understand some human speech. In response to 660 verbal requests, Kanzi behaved correctly 72 percent of the time. Savage-Rumbaugh is shown working with another one of her pupils in ● Figure 13.14.

Whether these animal behaviors constitute real language is the subject of debate. Herbert Terrace (1979) concluded that signing is just advanced imitation that lacks several major features of human language. Whereas human children build vocabularies spontaneously if they are exposed to language (Aitchison's criteria for cultural transmission and spontaneous usage), ape language must be taught laboriously. Word order (Aitchison's structure dependence) does not seem to matter too much to apes, although it has an essential role in human language. Terrace also questioned the objectivity of some observers. When Washoe signed "waterbird" while observing a swan, the Gardners concluded that she was making a new, creative observation. Washoe might simply have noticed a "bird" sitting on the "water" and made the corresponding

© Anna Clopet/CORBIS

● **Figure 13.14 Chimpanzees Can Learn Language-like Behaviors** Sue Savage-Rumbaugh of Georgia State University taught Panbanisha, a bonobo, chimpanzee to use a keyboard to produce grammatical sentences. Although apes can be taught to use symbols, linguists disagree over the issue of whether such behavior truly constitutes language.

signs. On the other hand, evidence of spontaneous signing has been observed among a group of trained chimps, who ask one another to chase, tickle, hug, or groom (Fouts & Bodamer, 1987).

Apes are not the only animals suspected of having language capabilities. Irene Pepperberg makes a strong case for her African grey parrots based on the birds' ability to communicate in ways that meet many of the criteria for language, such as arbitrariness and semanticity (Pepperberg, 2014). Others argue for language abilities for dolphins and whales (Caldwell & Caldwell, 1976; Lilly, 1967) and dogs (Bloom, 2004). Whether we believe in animal language or not, we are left with an enormous respect for both the complexity and intelligence of animal behavior and the remarkable sophistication of human language.

Multilingualism

Multilingualism refers to proficiency in more than one language. More than half of the world's population is **bilingual**, or proficient in two languages (Chertkow et al., 2010). Some individuals are remarkably proficient at using multiple languages, such as the 19th-century Italian Cardinal Mezzofanti, who allegedly spoke 50 languages (Della Rosa et al., 2013). How are multiple languages handled by the brain?

Research into the effects of strokes and other types of brain damage in multilingual patients provides some fascinating insights into the way the brain manages multiple languages. Several variables contribute to the extent of language deficits following a stroke. The fluency or ease of use that the patient achieved in each language, the order in which languages were learned (simultaneous vs. sequential), and how recently a language has been used are all factors that contribute to the patient's outcome. Typically, researchers find that languages learned early in life and languages in which the patient is highly fluent are retained better after brain damage than languages learned later in life or with less fluency. If the patient is equally fluent in two languages, both are affected at about the same level. Holding fluency constant, a language learned at a younger age is retained better than one learned at an older age (Neville et al., 1998). These findings suggest that multiple languages use some of the same areas of the brain but that the degree of overlap is not 100 percent.

bilingual Proficient in two languages.

Imaging research using healthy participants confirms the observations of patients with known brain damage. Kim, Relkin, Lee, and Hirsch (1998) report that participants who learn multiple languages at early ages do not show much spatial separation between areas of the frontal and temporal cortex that respond to each language. However, "late" language learners show greater spatial separation between areas that process each language in frontal regions, including Broca's area. Perani et al. (1998) argue that proficiency, not necessarily age of acquisition, influences the cortical representation of language. If a speaker is equally proficient in two languages regardless of age of learning, the cortical representations for the languages will overlap to a greater extent than they do in a person who is much more proficient in one language than in another. Even when proficiency is held constant, we still might be able to detect a neural bilingual signature, or a difference in activity, that indicates that the speaker uses more than one language. Participants who were highly proficient, early learners of English as a second language activated the same brain structures as monolingual English speakers, but showed greater activation of a portion of Broca's area (Kovelman, Baker, & Petitto, 2008).

If multiple languages have overlapping representations in the brain, how does the speaker keep them separated? This question has led to a search for the hypothetical "language switch." Hernandez, Martinez, and Kohnert (2000) used fMRI to investigate bilingual participants' reactions to picture-naming tasks. In a single-language task, participants were asked to name objects in one language only. In a mixed-language task, the participants were required to name objects in one of their languages or the other on different trials. During the mixed-language condition, reaction time was slower, and activation of the dorsolateral prefrontal cortex increased when compared with the single-language condition.

The language switch might simply be a function of general executive attentional systems of the brain, managed in part by the dorsolateral prefrontal cortex, which is an area of cortex anterior and superior to Broca's area. In addition, the left lower region of the parietal lobe participates in attentional processes related to a number of functions, including language. When this area is damaged by stroke, switching between languages is disrupted (Della Rosa et al., 2013). As shown in ● Figure 13.15, individuals with early bilingualism show increased gray matter density in this same area (Mechelli et al., 2004).

It is possible that the question of how the brain manages multiple languages "draws borders where there are none" (Reiterer, 2010, p. 309). If we assume that human language abilities have their roots in biology, there is no reason to assume that a second, third, or fourth language would be acquired by any different processes than the first. Instead of searching for unique changes in processing when additional languages are learned, we might better view bilingualism or multilingualism as being similar to expanding our vocabulary in a single language.

Bilingualism seems to be associated with a number of positive outcomes. Chinese-English, French-English, and Spanish-English speaking children all outperformed English monolinguals on tests of executive control (Barac & Bialystok, 2012). Bilingualism also contributes to "cognitive reserve," or protection against cognitive decline in older adults. Bilingualism is associated with a delay in the onset of dementia, possibly resulting from enhancement of executive control systems in the frontal and parietal lobes (Bialystok, Craik, & Luk, 2012).

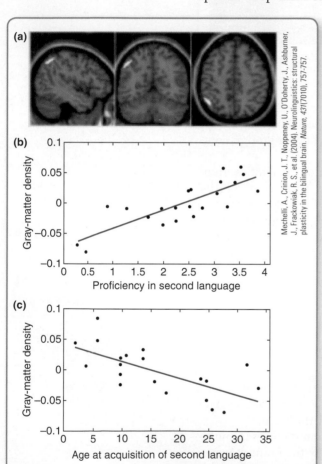

● **Figure 13.15** Bilingualism and Gray Matter Density The left inferior parietal region, displayed in yellow (a), shows increased gray matter density in bilinguals compared to monolinguals. The effect is enhanced in individuals with greater proficiency (b) who learned their second language at a young age (c).

Source: Mechelli, A., Crinion, J. T., Noppeney, U., O'Doherty, J., Ashburner, J., Frackowiak, R. S. et al. (2004). Neurolinguistics: Structural plasticity in the bilingual brain. *Nature*, 431(7010), 757-757.

American Sign Language (ASL)

American Sign Language (ASL) provides additional insights into the processing of language. ASL is a language not of sounds but of sight and movement (see ● Figure 13.16). As such, ASL provides an interesting contrast between language functions, generally lateralized to the left hemisphere, and spatial functions, generally lateralized to the right hemisphere.

Antonio Damasio and his colleagues (Damasio, Bellugi, Damasio, Poizner, & Gilder, 1986) documented the case of a young ASL interpreter who had her right temporal lobe removed to control her seizures. During a Wada test prior to surgery, anesthetizing the left hemisphere produced a number of deficits in both spoken English and ASL signing. Subsequent surgery on the patient's right temporal lobe, which might be assumed to affect her spatial processing, did not impair her ability to sign. In spite of the spatial nature of ASL, this case suggests that a language is still a language and that the left hemisphere is the likely place for that language to be processed. Damasio's clinical observations have been confirmed by fMRI studies. The same areas of the brain are activated during language tasks regardless of whether the person uses spoken English or ASL (Neville et al., 1998). The similarities between the processing of sign and spoken languages support the hypothesis that gesture might have been the natural precursor to spoken language (Corballis, 2009).

● **Figure 13.16** American Sign Language Insight into the brain's processing of language is provided by the study of people using American Sign Language (ASL), a language of sight and movement instead of sound.

AP Images/Tery Gilliam

aphasia A condition involving the loss of the ability to speak or to understand language.

Broca's aphasia A condition marked by the production of slow, laborious speech accompanied by good comprehension, poor repetition, and poor naming.

In an interesting twist, people who use ASL differ more from non-ASL users in their processing of human movement than in their processing of language (Corina et al., 2007). Hearing participants showed the same patterns of brain activity while watching a person drink from a cup, stretch, or use ASL, indicating the use of a single process for evaluating human movement. In contrast, deaf signers used different patterns of activity to distinguish between the linguistic movements of ASL and nonlinguistic movements.

Communication Disorders and Brain Mechanisms for Language

Earlier in the chapter, we saw how language perception was affected by the split-brain operation. Further clues to the localization of language functions have been obtained from case studies of individuals who lose some aspects of language due to strokes or other types of brain damage.

Paul Broca and Patient Tan

Broca's area is located in the left inferior frontal region adjacent to motor cortex and plays an important role in speech production. This area was named after Parisian physician Paul Broca, who made some of the earliest observations of the localization of language in the brain. In 1861, Broca began to study a 51-year-old man named Leborgne, who had been institutionalized for more than 20 years. Leborgne came to be referred to as "Tan" because when questioned, "tan" was one of a very few syllables he could produce. He apparently understood much of what was said to him, and he retained his ability to answer numerical questions by raising an appropriate number of fingers on his left hand (Herrnstein & Boring, 1965). Leborgne died shortly after Broca's examination of him, and Broca performed an autopsy on his patient's brain. Broca found significant damage to the patient's left inferior frontal region, which is believed to play a role in speech production.

Aphasia

Aphasia is defined as a total or partial loss of the ability to either produce or comprehend spoken language. Tan's aphasia resulted from brain damage caused by the sexually transmitted disease syphilis, but most modern aphasia results from strokes or head injuries (see Chapter 15). Careful observations of both language symptoms and areas of damage provide important insights into the localization of language. Modern researchers enjoy an advantage that Paul Broca would surely envy: with modern imaging technologies, it is not necessary to wait until the patient dies to determine which areas of the brain are damaged, and damage can be assessed much more accurately. Tan's preserved brain has been imaged using high-resolution MRI (Dronkers, Plaisant, Iba-Zizen, & Cabanis, 2007). Tan's lesions extended more deeply into the brain than Broca had suspected, and the areas described by Broca differ somewhat from our current delineation of Broca's area.

BROCA'S APHASIA Today, the symptoms of Broca's patient Tan are known as **Broca's aphasia**, or production aphasia. Damage in these cases affects Broca's area in the frontal lobe, along with associated subcortical regions. The locations of the major brain structures involved in language, including Broca's area, are illustrated in ● Figure 13.17.

The primary symptom of Broca's aphasia is difficulty in producing speech. Speech is very slow and requires significant effort, and errors occur in the pronunciation of some speech sounds. Although the speech produced generally makes sense, many expected modifying words and word endings are omitted, giving a telegraphic quality to the speech. Adjectives, words such as *both* or *all*, and word endings such as *-s* or *-ed* are often lacking. Broca's aphasia patients also typically show anomia, a difficulty retrieving the correct words for the ideas they wish to express, and are unable to repeat complex sentences. In some cases, patients retain the ability to curse, as with Tan's *"Sacre nom de Dieu!"* ("In the name of God!"), which he uttered in frustration when unable to make himself understood with gestures.

Howard Gardner (1976) conducted an interview with a 39-year-old male patient with Broca's aphasia:

> "Why are you in the hospital, Mr. Ford?"
>
> Ford looked at me a bit strangely, as if to say, Isn't it patently obvious? He pointed to his paralyzed arm and said, "Arm no good," then to his mouth and said, "Speech … can't say … talk, you see." (p. 61)

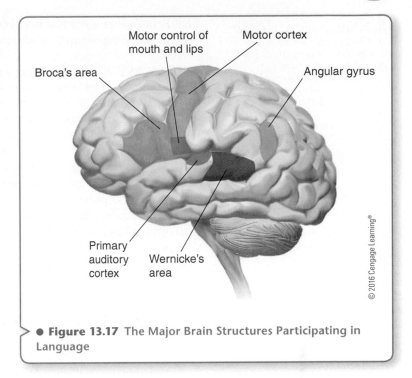

● **Figure 13.17** The Major Brain Structures Participating in Language

Although the primary deficit in Broca's aphasia is the ability to speak clearly, comprehension is affected as well. Patients with Broca's aphasia struggle with the meanings of sentences that depend on the same modifying words and endings that they often omit from their own speech. For example, most Broca's patients would be unable to comprehend the sentence, "The boy that the girl is chasing is tall" (Dronkers, Pinker, & Damasio, 2000, p. 1177). Comprehension of this sentence depends on a person's ability to process "that" and "is chasing" accurately. Otherwise, a person might depend on word order only, and make incorrect assumptions about who is tall and who is chasing whom.

There is additional evidence that Broca's aphasia is more than a simple motor deficit affecting the production of speech. Broca's patients can still sing songs they know well. Their writing is generally about as good as their speech and shows many of the same errors and omissions. If the damage to Broca's area affected motor control of the vocal apparatus only, one would expect that patients' written communication would not show the same deficits as their speech.

Broca's area might participate in the maintenance of verbal short-term memory through rehearsal. Patients with Broca's aphasia are unable to identify grammatical errors when the salient elements are widely spaced in a sentence. For example, Nina Dronkers and her colleagues (2000, p. 1179) point out that people with Broca's aphasia have no difficulty identifying the following sentence as ungrammatical: "John was finally kissed Louise." The verbal elements required to make the judgment appear near each other in the sentence (passive verb *was kissed* followed by object *Louise*). In contrast, the patients are unable to identify the following sentence as ungrammatical: "The woman is outside, isn't it?" The elements that don't agree grammatically, "woman" and "it," are separated by a "gap" in the sentence. Using PET scans, Dronkers and her colleagues showed that Broca's area is activated whenever healthy participants must comprehend a sentence with a long gap between related elements of a sentence as opposed to sentences containing a shorter gap. The inability to bridge verbal gaps is consistent with the patterns of impairment in the production and comprehension of speech experienced by patients with Broca's aphasia.

Patients with damage to Broca's area also show a specific deficit in understanding action-related verbs (Pulvermüller & Fadiga, 2010). They are unable to group action-related pictures together that are similar in meaning (jogging, running). This suggests

Wernicke's aphasia A condition in which speech is fluent, but comprehension, repetition, and naming are quite poor.

Wernicke's area An area of cortex adjacent to primary auditory cortex in the left hemisphere believed to be responsible for decoding speech sounds.

arcuate fasciculus A pathway connecting Broca's area and Wernicke's area.

conduction aphasia A condition characterized by fluent speech and good comprehension but poor repetition and naming; believed to result from damage to the arcuate fasciculus and underlying structures.

that Broca's area is not just important for speech production, but also for understanding the meaning of some words and concepts.

WERNICKE'S APHASIA Shortly after Paul Broca presented his revolutionary work on patient Tan, Carl Wernicke published his observations on another type of language deficit (Wernicke, 1874). In honor of his contributions, this syndrome is now referred to as **Wernicke's aphasia**, and the affected area of the brain is known as **Wernicke's area** (see ●Figure 13.18). Wernicke's area is located on the superior surface of the temporal lobe, adjacent to structures involved with audition (see Chapter 7).

The symptoms of Wernicke's aphasia are quite different from those of Broca's aphasia. In Broca's aphasia, speech is slow and laborious but generally meaningful. In Wernicke's aphasia, speech is rapid and fluent but virtually meaningless. Patients with Wernicke's aphasia seem totally unaware that they are not making sense, whereas patients with Broca's aphasia are typically frustrated by their inability to communicate.

Howard Gardner interviewed a patient, Mr. Gorgan, who had been diagnosed with Wernicke's aphasia (1976):

> "Thank you, Mr. Gorgan. I want to ask a few—"
> "Oh sure, go ahead, any old think you want. If I could I would. Oh, I'm taking the word the wrong way to say, all of the barbers here whenever they stop you it's going around and around, if you known what I mean, that is typing and tying for repucer, repuceration, well we were trying the best that we could while another time it was with the beds over the same thing ..." (p. 68)

If you don't pay attention to the content, the speech of patients with Wernicke's aphasia sounds rather normal, if slightly fast. Grammar is generally correct, but there appears to be a complete lack of meaning. Substitutions of sounds (*think* for *thing* and *repuceration* for *recuperation* in Gardner's excerpt) are common. Neologisms, or made-up words, are also frequent. Mr. Gorgan tells Dr. Gardner (1976, p. 68), "I have to run around, look it over, trebbin and all that sort of stuff." Mr. Gorgan alone seems to know what "trebbin" might mean.

The major deficit in Wernicke's aphasia is comprehension, usually for both the written and spoken word. These patients can neither repeat nor understand words or sentences that they hear. They are completely locked into a world without linguistic connection to other people, yet they do not seem overly aware of their circumstances nor are they in any apparent distress.

CONDUCTION APHASIA Wernicke correctly speculated that Broca's area and Wernicke's area must be intimately connected. A band of fibers known as the **arcuate fasciculus** connects the two areas. Furthermore, Wernicke believed that any compromise of this connection would produce a different type of aphasia from that seen in patients with either Broca's or Wernicke's aphasia. Once again, Wernicke was correct. Damage to the arcuate fasciculus and adjacent cortex, shown in ●Figure 13.18, results in **conduction aphasia**.

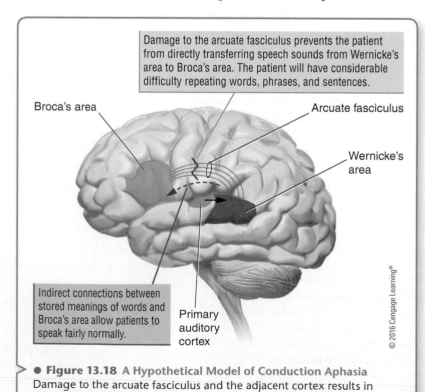

Damage to the arcuate fasciculus prevents the patient from directly transferring speech sounds from Wernicke's area to Broca's area. The patient will have considerable difficulty repeating words, phrases, and sentences.

Broca's area

Arcuate fasciculus

Wernicke's area

Indirect connections between stored meanings of words and Broca's area allow patients to speak fairly normally.

Primary auditory cortex

© 2016 Cengage Learning®

● **Figure 13.18 A Hypothetical Model of Conduction Aphasia** Damage to the arcuate fasciculus and the adjacent cortex results in conduction aphasia. These patients retain most of their abilities to produce and comprehend speech but have significant difficulties repeating sentences they hear.

In patients with conduction aphasia, speech remains fluent, and comprehension is fairly good. These patients are less impaired in language function than patients with either Wernicke's or Broca's aphasia. The nature of their aphasia becomes most obvious when they are asked to repeat a sentence, a task they find nearly impossible to do. They also struggle with a task known as "confrontation naming," in which they must verbally produce the names of pictures and objects. Finally, they seem to have difficulty assembling speech sounds into words, as shown by their frequent sound substitutions. It is common for these patients to say something like "treen" instead of "train." These symptoms probably result from impairments in the patients' ability to transfer information about speech sounds directly from Wernicke's area to Broca's area due to damage to the arcuate fasciculus.

GLOBAL APHASIA In **global aphasia**, patients lose essentially all language functions. This condition combines all of the deficits of Broca's, Wernicke's, and conduction aphasia. Abilities to speak, comprehend, read, and write are impaired to some extent, depending on the amount of damage the patient has experienced. Most patients are still able to curse, count, say the days of the week, and sing familiar songs. Comprehension is typically limited to a very small set of words.

The amount of cortex damaged in global aphasia is substantial. Both Broca's and Wernicke's areas, as well as much of the cortex and white matter between them, are affected. Most cases of global aphasia are caused by damage to the middle cerebral artery, which serves the language centers of the left hemisphere (see Chapter 2).

TRANSCORTICAL APHASIAS The **transcortical aphasias** result from damage to connections and cortical areas associated with the major language centers. You might think of the transcortical aphasias as isolating the main language areas from other parts of the brain. Patients with transcortical aphasias share some features with patients with either Broca's or Wernicke's aphasia. However, they retain the ability to repeat words that is lacking in these other aphasias. In most cases of **transcortical motor aphasia**, damage occurs in the dorsolateral prefrontal cortex. In other cases, damage is found in the supplementary motor area (SMA), located adjacent to primary motor cortex in the frontal lobe (see Chapter 8). Damage to the cortex at the intersection of the temporal, parietal, and occipital lobes results in the condition of **transcortical sensory aphasia**. These areas are shown in ● Figure 13.19.

As in cases of Broca's aphasia, patients with transcortical motor aphasia do not speak fluently. Unlike patients with Broca's aphasia, however, these patients are capable of accurate repetition of complex sentences. The damaged areas are probably responsible for the initiation of speech (supplementary motor area) and the ongoing executive control of speech (dorsolateral prefrontal cortex). Earlier, we discussed a role for the dorsolateral prefrontal area in language switching among bilingual speakers. Additional insight into the normal function of the dorsolateral prefrontal cortex in language comes from PET scans. This area shows activation when participants are asked to produce verbs related to particular nouns, such as *drive* in response to *car* (Dronkers et al., 2001). Participants with transcortical motor aphasia fail at this task, although they can accurately use the same words in normal conversation. As a result, we can think of transcortical motor aphasia as affecting some of the higher cognitive and attentional functions related to language production.

In transcortical sensory aphasia, the connections between the language centers and the parts of the brain responsible for word meaning are disrupted. Patients retain fluent, grammatical speech, but their comprehension is impaired. They experience great difficulty in naming tasks, but their repetition performance is excellent. They can even repeat words from unfamiliar foreign languages. As a result, we can conclude that these deficits affect the patients' ability to understand the meaning of words, although basic processing at the levels of speech sounds and grammar are spared.

global aphasia A condition in which all language functions are lost, including both language production and comprehension.

transcortical aphasias A language disorder resulting from damage to the connections and cortical areas associated with the major language centers.

transcortical motor aphasia A condition in which language is not fluent, but the ability to repeat is retained.

transcortical sensory aphasia A condition in which comprehension is poor, but the ability to repeat is retained.

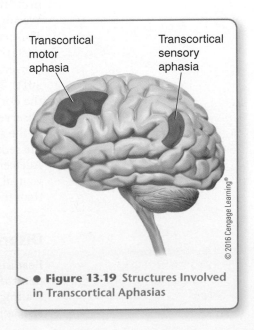

Transcortical motor aphasia

Transcortical sensory aphasia

© 2016 Cengage Learning®

> ● **Figure 13.19** Structures Involved in Transcortical Aphasias

LANGUAGE MODELS Based on his clinical observations of patients with various aphasias, Carl Wernicke developed a classic model to explain and predict the effects of damage to various areas on language performance. Norman Geschwind (1972) further developed the model, which now bears the names of both men. The Wernicke-Geschwind model emphasized the connections between various speech- and language-processing areas in the brain. According to the model, Broca's area was responsible for speech production, whereas Wernicke's area was responsible for speech comprehension. The arcuate fasciculus was believed to be a one-way pathway connecting Wernicke's area to Broca's area. Although Wernicke's and Broca's areas were believed to communicate with association cortex, they were viewed as having the primary responsibility for decoding, or extracting the meaning from, verbal information.

Although the Wernicke-Geschwind model succeeded in predicting most of the symptoms associated with the various types of aphasia, it is not completely consistent with the wealth of data from modern imaging investigations of language in healthy participants. First, researchers now believe that information travels in two directions, not just one, between Broca's area and Wernicke's area via the arcuate fasciculus. Second, much larger areas of cortex appear to be involved in the processing of language. These areas include sizable chunks of the frontal, temporal, and parietal lobes as well as of the cingulate cortex, the insula (in the lateral sulcus), and the basal ganglia.

A later model proposed three interacting language components (Dronkers, Pinker, & Damasio, 2000). The first is a language implementation system, made up of Broca's area, Wernicke's area, parts of the insula, and the basal ganglia. This system decodes incoming verbal information and produces appropriate verbal responses. Surrounding this implementation system is a mediational system made up of association cortex in the temporal, parietal, and frontal lobes. This system manages communication between the implementation system and the final component, a conceptual system. This third and final system, which is responsible for managing semantic knowledge (see Chapter 12), is located in higher-level association cortex areas. Further exploration using analysis of lesions, functional MRI, and investigations of white matter connectivity confirms that language functions are more accurately viewed as involving a vast network primarily but not exclusively located in the left hemisphere (Turken & Dronkers, 2011).

Dual stream models of language, like the one shown in ● Figure 13.20, identify a ventral and a dorsal pathway for language processing. The ventral pathway connects the superior temporal gyrus, which contains both primary auditory cortex and Wernicke's area, to Broca's area and the frontal operculum, a part of the frontal lobe. This pathway supports the conversion of sound to meaning. The dorsal pathway connects the superior temporal gyrus to premotor cortex and Broca's area, and supports the conversion of sound to motor movements involved in speech production (Friederici, 2011). The two pathways contribute to our processing of complex sentences, too, with the dorsal pathway assisting with the processing of nonadjacent elements. Earlier, we observed how patients with Broca's aphasia could not spot the grammatical trouble in the sentence "The woman is outside, isn't it?" but were able to identify problems in the sentence with adjacent ungrammatical items — "John was finally kissed Louise." Adjacent items in complex sentences, like the "Louise" sentence, are supported by the ventral pathway. This suggests that Broca's aphasia disrupts the dorsal pathway more than the ventral pathway.

Disorders of Reading and Writing

Reading and writing developed relatively recently in human history, probably at some point in the past 5,000 to 6,000 years. Unlike spoken language, people do not learn reading and writing simply through exposure. Once learned, however, these functions also appear to be localized in the brain.

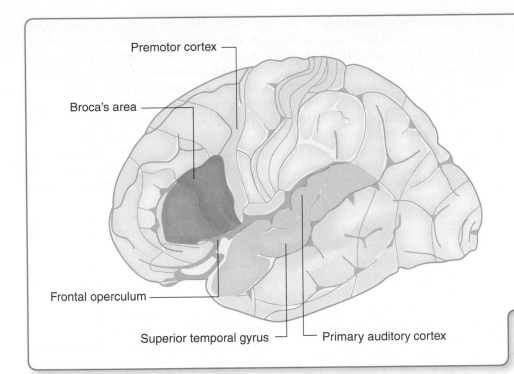

● **Figure 13.20 Dual Stream Language Models** Dual stream models propose a dorsal stream connecting the superior temporal gyrus and Broca's area and the frontal operculum that supports sound to meaning processing and a ventral stream connecting the superior temporal gyrus to pre-motor cortex and Broca's area that supports the conversion of sound to the movements necessary for speech.

Source: Friederici, A. D. (2011). The brain basis of language processing: from structure to function. *Physiological reviews*, *91*(4), 1357–1392.

Premotor cortex

Broca's area

Frontal operculum

Superior temporal gyrus

Primary auditory cortex

ALEXIA AND AGRAPHIA Deficits can occur in either reading (**alexia**) or writing (**agraphia**) or in both. For most people, reading and writing are localized in the same hemisphere as speech. Reading and writing are typically impaired in most cases of aphasia.

Patients with alexia, or pure word blindness, speak and understand the spoken word normally but are unable to read or to point to words and letters on command (Geschwind, 1970). Patients retain the ability to recognize words that are spelled out loud to them. Alexia appears to be the result of disruptions in pathways connecting cortex at the junction of the left occipital and temporal lobes, an area involved with the visual recognition of letters, to the language areas in the vicinity of the insula (Epelbaum et al., 2008).

Agraphia, or the inability to write, is a frequent side effect of damage to networks involved with spoken language, yet it is possible to experience problems with spoken but not written language and vice versa. Although as in spoken language, a rather wide network of cortical areas participates in writing, agraphia seems particularly likely when the supplementary motor area (SMA; see Chapter 8) is damaged (Scarone et al., 2009).

DYSLEXIA Dyslexia refers to an unexpected difficulty in reading fluently in spite of normal intelligence and exposure to normal teaching methods. Dyslexia is the most common form of learning disability, affecting between 5 to 17 percent of school children (Shaywitz, Morris, & Shaywitz, 2008). The first patient with dyslexia appearing in the medical literature, Percy F., was described by his physician as "quick at games, and in no way inferior to others of his age. His great difficulty has been … his inability to learn to read" (Shaywitz, 1996, p. 98). Earlier reports of sex differences in dyslexia (e.g., Tallal, 1991) might have exaggerated the differences between boys and girls. Boys are still somewhat more likely to have dyslexia but are also more likely than girls to be referred for remedial services due to their frequent disruptive behaviors (Shaywitz et al., 2008). Famous individuals who probably had dyslexia include Walt Disney, Winston Churchill, and Albert Einstein.

Dyslexia is strongly influenced by genetics. A parent with dyslexia has a 23 to 65 percent chance of producing a child with dyslexia, and 40 percent of the siblings of a

alexia A condition characterized by the ability to speak and understand the spoken word normally accompanied by an inability to read or to point to words and letters on command.

agraphia A condition characterized by the loss of the ability to write.

dyslexia A condition characterized by difficulty learning to read in spite of normal intelligence and exposure to standard instruction.

phonological awareness The ability to discriminate between rapidly presented speech sounds.

angular gyrus A region of the parietal lobe believed to participate in language and cognition.

child with dyslexia will also have the disorder (Gilger, Hanebuth, Smith, & Pennington, 1996). The genetics of dyslexia are complex, as shown by the greater heritability of dyslexia among individuals with higher IQs (Olson et al., 1999). However, in spite of the heavy genetic influences on dyslexia, children with this condition benefit substantially from remedial treatment begun prior to the third grade (Shaywitz et al., 2008).

Anatomical features of dyslexia include differences in hemispheric symmetry. The left planum temporale is usually larger in people whose language functions are located in the left hemisphere. Most researchers report less difference between the right and left planum temporale in participants with dyslexia (Beaton, 1997; Galaburda, Sherman, Rosen, Aboitiz, & Geschwind, 1985). People with dyslexia are slightly more likely to be left-handed or ambidextrous than people without dyslexia (Eglinton & Annett, 1994).

Most cases of dyslexia involve poor **phonological awareness**, or the ability to discriminate verbal information at the level of speech sounds, or phonemes, as evidenced by difficulties with words that rhyme. During a rhyming task, typically developing children, but not children with dyslexia, recruited the left dorsolateral prefrontal cortex (Kovelman et al., 2012). The left dorsolateral prefrontal cortex might play an important role in the development of phonological awareness of speech that forms the basis of reading. Dyslexia is also associated with difficulties in processing rapidly presented stimuli. Individuals with dyslexia seem to process speech sounds (Merzenich et al., 1996) and visual information more slowly than typical control participants (Dronkers et al., 2001). In addition, some individuals with dyslexia experience spatial problems, leading to reversals of letters such as *b* and *d*.

Overactivation of anterior language areas, including Broca's area, coupled with a lack of activation of posterior language areas, including Wernicke's area and the **angular gyrus**, occurs during reading by participants with dyslexia (Shaywitz et al., 1998; Hoeft et al., 2011). As shown in ● Figure 13.21, typical readers pass information from the visual cortex along the angular gyrus to Wernicke's area, with only slight

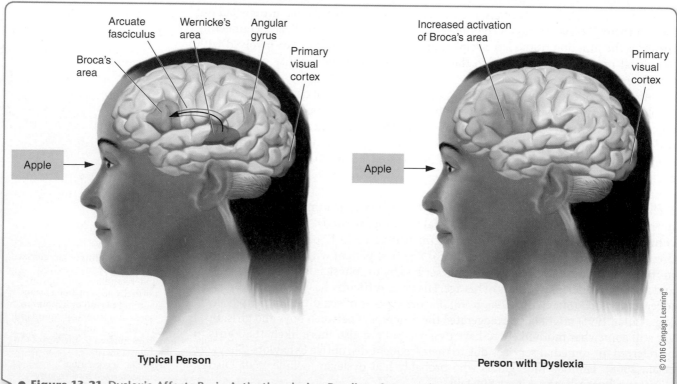

● **Figure 13.21 Dyslexia Affects Brain Activation during Reading** Compared with typical readers, people with dyslexia show little activation of the angular gyrus and Wernicke's area and increased activation of Broca's area while reading.

© 2016 Cengage Learning®

activation of Broca's area. In readers with dyslexia, the posterior language areas are hardly used at all. Instead, there is a much greater activation in the anterior language areas. Greater understanding of the processes underlying dyslexia has the potential to lead to more effective remedial strategies.

stutter To abnormally repeat or prolong speech sounds when speaking.

Stuttering

Nearly all children experience occasional fluency problems. However, approximately 5 percent of the population **stutters**, producing repetitions (*wa wa want*) or the prolonging of sounds (*n-ah-ah-ah-ow*) (Månsson, 2000). Children begin to stutter between the ages of two and seven years, with a peak onset at about five years of age. Males are two to five times as likely as females to stutter (Craig & Tran, 2005).

Stuttering appears to be primarily genetic in origin (Andrews, Morris-Yates, Howie, & Martin, 1991). Individuals who stutter have abnormal lateralization of some speech functions (De Nil, 1999; Van Borsel, Achten, Santens, Lahorte, & Voet, 2003). Typical individuals who do not stutter show strong left-hemisphere advantages for detecting differences in speech sounds compared to differences in prosody. Individuals who stutter, however, do not show this typical lateralization of sound detection and prosody (Sato et al., 2011).

As a result of this abnormal pattern of lateralization, both hemispheres try to control the vocal apparatus simultaneously, leading to conflict. This conflict is resolved to some extent when the stuttering person sings because singing activates right-hemisphere areas that are not otherwise involved in speech (Jeffries, Fritz, & Braun, 2003). Imaging studies also suggest that abnormally high activity in the basal ganglia and midbrain motor structures might be responsible for stuttering (Brown, Ingham, Ingham, Laird, & Fox, 2005; Giraud et al., 2008; Watkins, Smith, Davis, & Howell, 2008). Because these motor systems use dopamine as their major neurotransmitter, stuttering is improved by dopamine antagonists, such as haloperidol, and worsened by dopamine agonists such as l-dopa (levodopa; Watkins et al., 2008).

Current treatments for stuttering center on reducing the rate at which speech is produced and on the stress usually associated with the disorder. Other therapy programs involve the use of software programs that teach people to use special breathing techniques, soft voice onsets, and the prolongation of syllables (Giraud et al., 2008). Giraud and her colleagues also noted that these therapies normalized the abnormal basal ganglia and midbrain activity observed during stuttering.

●●● Behavioral Neuroscience GOES TO WORK

SPEECH AND LANGUAGE PATHOLOGY

Although we have seen that there are strong biological correlates involved in communication disorders, treatment can greatly enhance a patient's level of functioning. Speech-language pathologists (SLPs) assess, diagnose, and treat speech, language, cognitive-communication, and swallowing disorders in patients of all ages (American Speech-Language-Hearing Association, 2014).

Speech-language pathologists hold graduate degrees, and the PhD is desirable. Nearly half are also certified as audiologists, which allows them to assess and treat hearing disorders. Most SLPs work in educational settings, with another large group working in healthcare settings. Approximately 20 percent are employed in private practice.

Future trends affecting the profession are the larger numbers of older adults as the Baby Boom generation moves into that age group. Older adults are more likely to experience brain damage from strokes that result in language disorders. In addition, many states are now requiring auditory assessment of newborns and remediation if needed. Medical advances are increasing the survival rate of premature infants and individuals with stroke or traumatic brain injuries, who often require extensive rehabilitation.

INTERIM SUMMARY 13.2

Summary Table: The Major Aphasias

Type of Aphasia	Location of Damage	Ability to Produce Speech	Ability to Comprehend Meaning of Spoken Words	Does Person Exhibit Sound Substitutions?	Ability to Repeat Spoken Words Accurately	Ability to Name Objects
Broca's aphasia	Broca's area	Not fluent	Good	Not common	Poor	Poor
Wernicke's aphasia	Wernicke's area	Fluent	Poor	Common	Poor	Poor
Conduction aphasia	Arcuate fasciculus	Fluent	Good	Common	Poor	Poor
Global aphasia	Broca's area, Wernicke's area, and the arcuate fasciculus	Not fluent	Poor	Variable	Poor	Poor
Transcortical motor aphasia	Supplementary motor area, cortex adjacent to Broca's area	Not fluent	Good	Common	Good	Poor
Transcortical sensory aphasia	Cortex at the junction of temporal, parietal, and occipital lobes	Fluent	Poor	Common	Good	Poor

Summary Points

1. The evolution of language might have occurred as early humans formed cooperative societies and shared tool-making skills. (LO3)

2. Nonhuman animals clearly communicate, but controversy remains as to whether nonhuman animals truly possess the ability to use language. (LO3)

3. Multilingualism involves overlapping representations of multiple languages in the brain, and appears to be beneficial for cognitive functioning. In spite of the spatial nature of ASL, research evidence suggests that it is processed by the left hemisphere like other languages. (LO4)

4. The clinical study of aphasias, alexias, and agraphias has helped identify the major areas of the brain involved with the comprehension and production of language. (LO4)

5. Dyslexia and stuttering are developmental disorders in which an otherwise intelligent person experiences difficulty learning to read (dyslexia) or to articulate clearly (stuttering) when exposed to standard experience and instruction. (LO4)

Review Questions

1. What are the relationships between gesture, imitation, and language?

2. What does ASL teach us about the localization of language in the brain?

Intelligence

Intelligence refers to an individual's "ability to understand complex ideas, to adapt effectively to the environment, to learn from experience, to engage in various forms of reasoning, and to overcome obstacles" (Neisser et al., 1996, p. 77). Among the topics of interest to behavioral neuroscientists and psychologists, intelligence is possibly one of the most contentious, and the biological correlates of intelligence are especially so.

Assessing Intelligence

Interest in assessing intelligence arose from compulsory education laws passed during the 19th and early 20th centuries. In 1904, Alfred Binet was charged by the French government with devising an objective means to identify the potential of schoolchildren. Binet and his colleague, Théodore Simon, assumed that relatively bright children behaved cognitively like older children, whereas less intelligent children would behave like younger children. They devised items that they believed would indicate a child's "mental age" or "intelligence quotient" (IQ). Stanford professor Lewis Terman (1916) adapted Binet's test for use in the United States and named his revised version the Stanford-Binet.

The IQ tests used today, such as the Wechsler Adult Intelligence Scale-Revised (WAIS-R) or the Stanford-Binet, no longer use the concept of mental age introduced by Binet and Simon. Instead, test results are structured in such a way that they fall along a statistically normal curve. The average IQ score is 100, with a standard deviation of 15. Normal distributions follow a "68–95–99.7" rule. In other words, 68 percent of the population falls within one standard deviation of the mean, or in the case of IQ, between 85 and 115. Only 5 percent of the population will have IQs that are more than two standard deviations away from the mean (below 70 or above 130), and only 0.3 percent will be more than three standard deviations from the mean (below 55 or above 145). The table in Interim Summary 13.3 provides a breakdown of the approximate percentage of the population found within different ranges of IQ scores.

General Versus Specific Abilities

Psychologists are unable to agree on whether intelligence comprises a single underlying ability or some combination of separate abilities. Charles Spearman (1904) proposed a **general intelligence (g) factor**. In Spearman's view, all intelligent behavior arises from a single trait. Measurements of g are predictive of important outcomes, including educational attainment, occupational success, social mobility, health, illness, and survival (Deary et al., 2012). This type of intelligence is highly heritable beginning in adolescence and extending through old age (Deary et al., 2012).

Other psychologists are not so sure. Savant behaviors illustrate how certain abilities can be separated from others. Children with Williams syndrome, mentioned earlier in the chapter, generally score in the range of intellectual disability on intelligence tests, yet their verbal skills are quite good. Some athletes have exceptional physical skills but struggle to read. Howard Gardner (1983) interprets these and similar findings to mean that we have multiple, independent types of intelligence.

It is likely that both approaches are true to some extent. We seem to have separate abilities for different types of behavior. However, enough of these abilities are typically correlated within individuals to provide some support for Spearman's idea of a general intelligence factor.

Intelligence and Genetics

How much of the variation we see in human intelligence is determined by our genes? While asking this question, we want to avoid the either–or, nature *versus* nurture thinking that has plagued this type of discussion historically. Intelligence is surely the

intelligence An individual's ability to understand complex ideas, to adapt effectively to the environment, to learn from experience, to engage in various forms of reasoning, and to overcome obstacles.

general intelligence (g) factor Also known as "Spearman's g." A hypothesized single trait that predicts intelligent behavior.

end product of complex interactions between our biological heritage and our experiences and environment. The heritability of adult intelligence as measured by IQ tests is usually reported to be about .75 (Neisser et al., 1996). This means that scientists expect that about 75 percent of the variation in intelligence among humans can be attributed to genetic factors. It absolutely does *not* mean that 75 percent of an individual's intelligence is determined by his or her genes with the environment determining the remainder (see Chapter 5).

The complex interactions between genetics and environment can be illustrated by studies of the effects of breastfeeding on IQ. As a group, children who are breastfed have higher IQs than those who are not, and this result persists into adulthood (Caspi et al., 2007). However, the gain produced by breastfeeding interacts with genetics. Individuals with one form of a gene involved with the metabolism of fatty acids show no IQ benefit from breastfeeding, whereas those with another form of the gene gain as much as seven IQ points when breastfed compared to those with the same genotype who are not breastfed (Caspi et al., 2007).

Although many genes have been identified as responsible for intellectual disability, genes associated specifically with high intelligence have been far more elusive. It is likely that a large number of genes are involved in intelligence, each having a relatively small effect. For example, Robert Plomin and his colleagues (Plomin et al., 2004) report a 1.5-point difference in IQ resulting from a single gene. Analyses using DNA data for hundreds of thousands of SNPs (see Chapter 5) from unrelated individuals allow researchers to estimate the genetic influence on a trait (Plomin, 2012). Using this technique, researchers found a correlation of 0.62 between intelligence at age 11 years and in old age, suggesting that many of the same genetic elements account for intelligence across the lifespan (Deary et al., 2012).

Structural and Functional Correlates of Intelligence

How might the brains of highly intelligent people be different from those of more average people? Intelligence is a broad concept, so it is unlikely that we have "intelligence centers" in the brain. Instead, intelligent brains probably enjoy quick, efficient communication along networks. When working on the same problem, the brains of people

••• THINKING *Ethically*

PERFORMANCE-ENHANCING DRUGS FOR THE MIND?

News reports frequently feature athletes who are in trouble for the use of banned substances for enhancing athletic performance. Not only do such cases offend our general sense of fair play, but they confer economic, social, and health consequences to the user (Sternberg, 2014). What happens when we have drugs that provide similar advantages and disadvantages to individuals in intellectual activities?

Already, cognitive performance enhancement comes in the form of over-the-counter drugs like caffeine, which enhances both attention and retention of material (Borota et al., 2014). Prescription drugs used to treat attention deficit hyperactivity disorder (ADHD; see Chapter 16) increase focus and concentration whether a person has ADHD or not. Up to 16 percent of students on some college campuses use one of these prescription drugs, methylphenidate (Ritalin), to improve academic performance without having been diagnosed with ADHD (Farah et al., 2004). As treatments for cognitive decline become more sophisticated, they, too, have the potential to be used for enhancement of cognitive function in healthy individuals.

The time to consider the ethical implications of such practices is not down the road, but now (Sternberg, 2014). We have not found very satisfying solutions to the problem of performance-enhancing drugs in sports. Will we do better when considering performance enhancement of cognition?

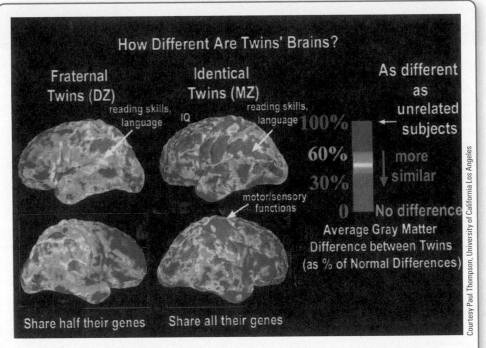

How Different Are Twins' Brains?

Fraternal Twins (DZ)

reading skills, language

Identical Twins (MZ)

IQ

reading skills, language

100%

60%

30%

0

As different as unrelated subjects

more similar

No difference

motor/sensory functions

Average Gray Matter Difference between Twins (as % of Normal Differences)

Share half their genes   Share all their genes

Courtesy Paul Thompson, University of California Los Angeles

● **Figure 13.22 Mass of Gray Matter Correlates with Intelligence and Heredity** Paul Thompson and his colleagues used MRI to measure the gray matter of dizygotic (fraternal) and monozygotic (identical) twins. These researchers concluded that the amount of gray matter in the brains of the identical twins was nearly the same, especially in the frontal lobe and language areas. Their findings suggest a strong association between genetics, brain structure, and some measures of cognitive function.

with high standard intelligence test scores do not work as hard as the brains of people with lower scores, although both groups eventually solve the problem (Haier, 1992).

Standard measures of intelligence correlate positively with overall brain volume, adjusted for body size (Deary, Penke, & Johnson, 2010). This adjustment is necessary because brain size is correlated with body size. Gray matter volume and cortical thickness in prefrontal and temporal association areas of the brain are especially highly correlated with cognitive ability (Narr et al., 2007) (see ● Figure 13.22). In adolescents studied over time, variations in verbal and nonverbal IQ performance were tightly correlated with gray matter increases in Broca's area and the cerebellum respectively (Ramsden et al., 2011). To a lesser extent, cognitive ability is associated with white matter volume as well (Achard, Salvador, Whitcher, Suckling, & Bullmore, 2006).

What can we learn from case studies of extremely intelligent individuals? Dahlia Zaidel (2001) examined slides made from Albert Einstein's brain after he died in 1955 at the age of 76. Zaidel noted that the neurons in Einstein's left hippocampus were much larger than neurons in the right hippocampus. She found this structural asymmetry to be quite different from the brains of 10 control participants with normal intelligence. Zaidel admits that it is not known whether this structural difference is at all related to Einstein's genius, but the participation of the hippocampus in memory makes Zaidel's observations quite intriguing. Sandra Witelson and her colleagues (Witelson, Kigar, & Harvey, 1999) found another apparent abnormality in Einstein's brain. Einstein's inferior parietal lobe, an area believed to be related to mathematical and abstract reasoning, was about 15 percent larger than comparable areas in the brains of control participants.

••• Building Better
HEALTH

ENRICHED ENVIRONMENTS, INFECTIOUS LOAD, AND IQ

In the context of a discussion of a human attribute from the behavioral neuroscience perspective, it is often easy to lose track of the fact that a trait that shows high heritability can be modified. A case in point is the highly heritable condition of phenylketonuria (PKU) that we discussed in Chapter 5. Without treatment, PKU produces intellectual disability. With a proper diet, however, individuals with PKU develop normally. Our discussion of the biological correlates of general intelligence should not imply that we should "give up" on anybody's intellectual development.

Over the last 100 years, worldwide measures of IQ have increased approximately 3 points per decade (Dickens & Flynn, 2001; Flynn, 2006). This increase, known as the "Flynn Effect," has happened far too quickly for any accounts based on genetic change. Instead, it is likely that improvements in health are likely to be responsible for the observed increases in IQ. A nation's burden from infectious disease is negatively correlated with the average IQ of its population (Eppig, Fincher, & Thornhill, 2010). As nations become wealthier and more capable of protecting their populations from disease, IQ increases.

Poverty in general continues to be a strong risk factor for low IQ. Good nutrition and access to mentally stimulating activities cost money, and these factors contribute to intellectual development. The vocabulary of U.S. three-year-olds from professional families is estimated to be twice as large as the vocabulary of children whose families receive government assistance (Hackman, Farah, & Meaney, 2010). Children from lower socioeconomic status (SES) families showed decreased specialization of language functions in the left hemisphere compared to children from wealthier families. Working memory and executive function also show relationships to SES.

As you know, we cannot use the magic word "cause" when discussing these types of correlational data, so the exact relationship between SES and intellect remains blurry. However, the level of cognitive stimulation in the home (books, computers, trips, parental communication) explains the bulk of variance in cognitive ability in children related to SES, even when maternal IQ, a very potent predictor of child IQ, has been controlled (Hackman et al., 2010). With our increasing understanding of epigenetic influences, we are beginning to understand how parental stress, nutrition, health, and cognitive stimulation can have dramatic influences on a child's intellectual development.

INTERIM SUMMARY 13.3

‖ Summary Table: Distribution of IQ Scores

IQ Score	Population with This Score (%)	Characteristics
130 or above	2	Gifted (academics should be easily mastered)
115–129	14	Above average (above-average academic performance)
85–114	68	Average (average academic performance)
70–84	14	Below average (average to poor academic performance)
50–69	1.7	Mild intellectual disability (can learn academic skills up to sixth grade)
35–49	0.2	Moderate intellectual disability (can learn academic skills up to second grade)

IQ Score	Population with This Score (%)	Characteristics
20–34	0.08	Severe intellectual disability (can learn to talk and to perform supervised work)
Below 20	less than 0.02	Profound intellectual disability (requires constant supervision)

▌ Summary Points

1. Psychologists do not agree on whether intelligence is a single entity or a combination of multiple abilities. **(LO5)**

2. A possible correlate of intelligence is the amount of gray matter in the brain, particularly in the frontal lobe and language areas. **(LO5)**

▌ Review Questions

1. Which structural features in the brain might be correlated with intelligence?

2. How might epigenetics affect cognitive development?

Chapter Review

THOUGHT QUESTIONS

1. Some linguists believe that we will go from having thousands of languages world-wide to fewer than a dozen within 100 years. What might be the implications of such a rapid change?
2. What might be the advantages to an animal of localizing functions to one hemisphere of the brain as opposed to distributing the functions over both hemispheres?
3. If being nonright-handed is associated with higher rates of learning disability and immune disease, why do you think nonright-handedness is maintained in the population?
4. We identify people with math and verbal difficulties as being learning disabled. Why don't we also have terms such as musically disabled or athletically disabled?

KEY TERMS

alexia (p. 467)
agraphia (p. 467)
angular gyrus (p. 468)
aphasia (p. 462)
arcuate fasciculus (p. 464)
bilingual (p. 459)
Broca's aphasia (p. 462)
conduction aphasia (p. 464)
dichotic listening (p. 451)
dyslexia (p. 467)

general intelligence (g) factor (p. 471)
global aphasia (p. 465)
hemispherectomy (p. 444)
hippocampal commissure (p. 445)
insula (p. 466)
intelligence (p. 471)
language (p. 456)
lateralization (p. 444)
massa intermedia (p. 445)
phonological awareness (p. 468)

planum temporale (p. 453)
prosody (p. 452)
savant behavior (p. 455)
split-brain operation (p. 445)
stutter (p. 469)
transcortical aphasia (p. 465)
transcortical motor aphasia (p. 465)
transcortical sensory aphasia (p. 465)
Wernicke's aphasia (p. 464)
Wernicke's area (p. 464)

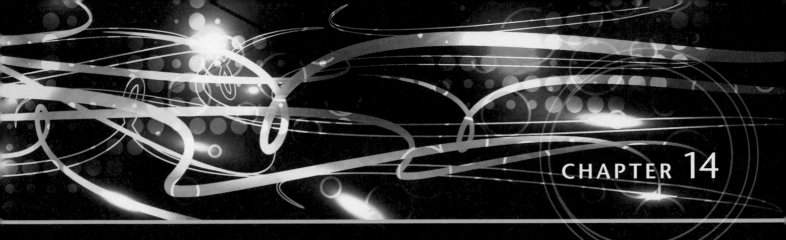

CHAPTER 14

Emotion, Reward, Aggression, and Stress

LEARNING OBJECTIVES

LO1 Interpret the contributions of biology and learning to emotional expression.

LO2 Differentiate between the leading theories of emotion.

LO3 Describe the nervous system structures involved in emotion.

LO4 Assess the biological correlates of feelings of reward and pleasure.

LO5 Explain the possible roles of genetics, brain damage, and biochemistry in aggression.

LO6 Evaluate the major physical and psychological responses to stress.

CHAPTER OUTLINE

Emotion

Whether we're feeling sad, scared, or euphoric, an **emotion** has two major components: a physical sensation, such as a rapid heartbeat, and a conscious, subjective experience or feeling, such as feeling scared. Emotions demonstrate **valence**, or a generally positive or negative quality. Emotions differ from moods, which are more general states that last a longer time than emotions. You can be in a generally good mood while experiencing different emotions, such as happiness, pride, and relief.

The Evolution and Adaptive Benefits of Emotion

Charles Darwin (1872) made a careful study of the facial expressions produced by humans and other primates and concluded that emotional expression must have evolved. Because evolution implies beneficial change, we might ask how emotions improved our ancestors' chances of survival.

One possible advantage of emotions is their contribution to general arousal. When the brain perceives a situation requiring action, emotions provide the arousal needed to trigger a response. A behaving animal probably stands a better chance of surviving than an animal that fails to react to a situation. Robert Yerkes and Donald Dodson (1908) observed that arousal interacts with the complexity of a task to predict performance. For simple tasks, such as outrunning a predator, greater arousal tends to lead to superior performance. For more complex tasks, however, we see deficits in performance when arousal levels are too high. Many of us have had the experience of performing badly on a difficult exam because we are too stressed or anxious.

In addition to contributing to general arousal, emotions manage our approach and withdrawal behaviors relative to particular environmental stimuli (Davidson & Irwin, 1999). The positive emotions associated with eating contribute to our seeking food when we are hungry, and the negative emotions elicited by observing a large snake or rotting food lead to avoidance, providing obvious advantages for survival. Individuals with brain damage affecting their emotional abilities often have difficulty making decisions (Damasio, 1994). Emotions form a bridge to past memories that can be used to decide how to respond to a stimulus like a snake.

In addition to contributing to general arousal and the management of approach/avoidance behaviors, emotions also enhance survival by helping us communicate. **Nonverbal communication**, consisting of facial expression and body language, provides an important source of social information. For example, body expressions of fear, illustrated in ● Figure 14.1, communicate important information in an immediate, arousing, and contagious manner (de Gelder, Snyder, Greve, Gerard, & Hadjikhani, 2004).

The Expression and Recognition of Emotion

Human adults usually express and interpret emotions accurately. In one experiment, observers correctly judged whether or not a teacher liked an off-camera student after watching only 10 seconds of a videotaped interaction (Babad, Bernieri, & Rosenthal, 1991). We might believe that we can hide our feelings, but the subtleties of emotional expression often give us away.

CONTROLLING FACIAL EXPRESSION Although we use our whole bodies to express emotion, humans pay the most attention to the face, and in particular to the eyes (Adolphs, 2007). Early in development, human infants prefer gazing at faces rather than at other types of visual stimuli.

Movement of the human face is controlled by two cranial nerves, the facial nerve (cranial nerve VII) and the trigeminal nerve (cranial nerve V). The facial nerve controls the superficial muscles attached to the skin, which are primarily responsible for facial expressions. The trigeminal nerve controls the deeper facial muscles attached to the bones of the head that are responsible for chewing food and speaking.

emotion A combination of physical sensations and the conscious experience of a feeling.

valence A positive (attractive) or negative (aversive) reaction to an object or event.

nonverbal communication The use of facial expressions, gestures, and body language to communicate ideas and feelings.

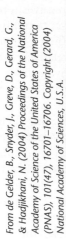

From de Gelder, B., Snyder, J., Greve, D., Gerard, G., & Hadjikhani, N. (2004) Proceedings of the National Academy of Science of the United States of America (PNAS), 101(47), 16701–16706. Copyright (2004) National Academy of Sciences, U.S.A.

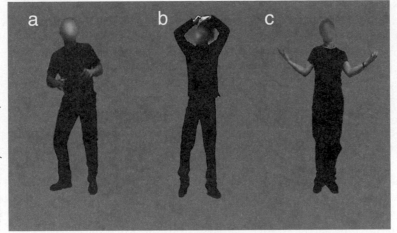

● **Figure 14.1 Emotional Expression Helps Us Communicate** Viewing full-body expressions of fear (a), compared to neutral (b) and happy (c) postures, produced strong, immediate activity in brain areas associated with the processing of fearful stimuli and the preparation of responses such as flight. Fearful postures, therefore, are likely to have had significant survival benefits to humans because the need to flee could be communicated rapidly to others without verbal explanation.

The facial nerve has five major branches, with each branch serving a different portion of the face. As shown in ● Figure 14.2, the facial nerves originate in the two **facial nuclei** located on either side of the midline in the pons. These nuclei do not communicate directly with each other. As we will see later in the chapter, this organization makes it possible for emotional expression to vary in intensity from one half of the face to the other. The facial nuclei receive input from the primary motor cortex located in the precentral gyrus of the frontal lobe as well as from several subcortical motor areas.

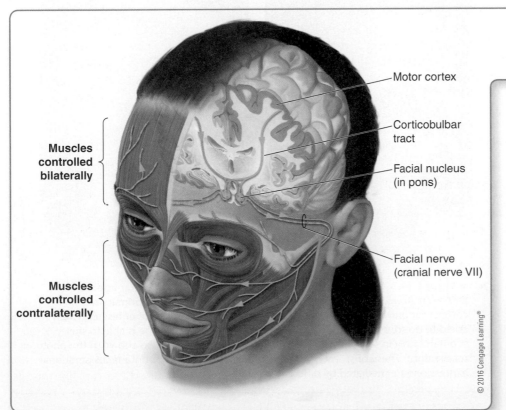

● **Figure 14.2** Innervation of the Facial Muscles

Motor cortex
Corticobulbar tract
Facial nucleus (in pons)
Facial nerve (cranial nerve VII)
Muscles controlled bilaterally
Muscles controlled contralaterally

facial nucleus A cranial nerve nucleus, located at the level of the pons, that controls the facial nerves.

The upper third of the face is controlled differently than the lower two thirds (Koff, Borod, & Strauss, 1985; Rinn, 1984). The upper third of the face receives input from both the ipsilateral and contralateral facial nerves, whereas the lower two thirds of the face are controlled primarily by the contralateral facial nerve. When a person suffers damage to the primary motor cortex of one hemisphere, there is relatively little impact on the muscle tone of the upper face, which continues to receive ipsilateral input from the healthy hemisphere. However, the contralateral lower face will be paralyzed and appear to sag.

Two major pathways control facial expression of emotion (Morecraft, Louie, Herrick, & Stilwell-Morecraft, 2001). One involves input from the primary motor cortex and is responsible for voluntary expression. The second is a subcortical system that is responsible for spontaneous expression. We all know that the smiles we make for our driver's license pictures look different from the spontaneous smiles a photographer catches in a candid photo. People with damage to the primary motor cortex, such as the young man shown in ● Figure 14.3, are unable to smile on command on the side of the mouth contralateral to their damage. However, when they hear a good joke, they can show some spontaneous smiling on the otherwise paralyzed side of the face. This condition is known as volitional (voluntary) facial paresis (paralysis) because the ability to express voluntary emotion is impaired. In contrast, people with Parkinson's disease, which involves subcortical motor structures including the substantia nigra and basal ganglia (see Chapters 2 and 8), lose the ability to smile spontaneously while retaining the ability to smile on command. This condition is referred to as emotional facial paresis because the ability to express spontaneous emotions is impaired.

BIOLOGICAL CONTRIBUTIONS TO EMOTIONAL EXPRESSION Darwin assumed that emotional expression had a strong biological basis. Supporting that view, major emotional expressions appear to be viewed very similarly across human cultures (Keltner & Ekman, 2000). These expressions include anger, sadness, happiness, fear,

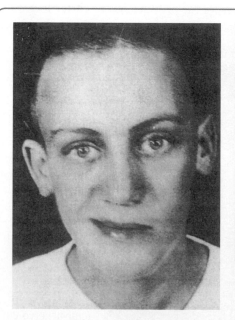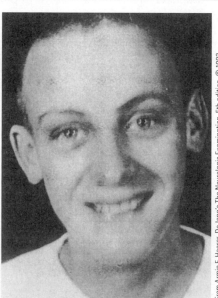

From Armin F. Haerer, DeJong's The Neurologic Examination, 5th edition, © 1992 J. B. Lippincott Company. Fig. 13-4. http://llww.com

> ● **Figure 14.3** Voluntary and Spontaneous Expressions Are Managed by Different Areas of the Brain This man has a tumor in his right primary motor cortex that prevents him from voluntarily smiling on the left side of his face when asked to do so, as shown in the photo on the left. In contrast, he is able to smile spontaneously in response to a genuine, involuntary emotion, as shown in the photo on the right. These observations suggest that voluntary and spontaneous emotional expressions are mediated by different networks the brain.

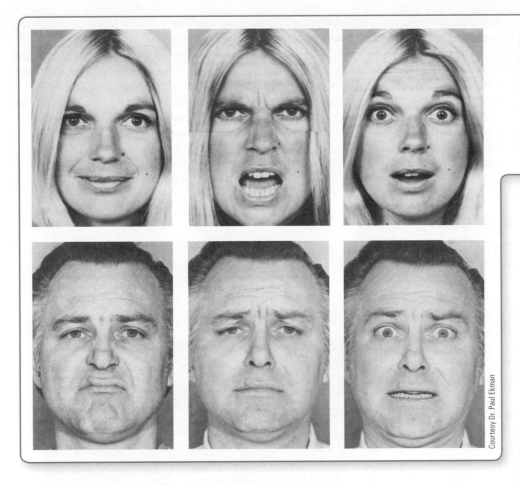

● **Figure 14.4** Major Facial Expressions Are Easily Recognized around the World These photos represent the possibly universal expressions of happiness, anger, surprise, disgust, sadness, and fear.

disgust, surprise, contempt, and embarrassment. Most people, regardless of culture, have little difficulty identifying the major emotional expressions shown in ● Figure 14.4.

Several other lines of reasoning support Darwin's view. Children's capacities for emotional expression and recognition develop according to a fairly regular timeline, with relatively little influence by experience. Infants who are blind from birth show a progression in the development of social smiling that is similar to that of sighted infants, in spite of being unable to learn by observing others (Freedman, 1964). As shown in ● Figure 14.5, a careful comparison of photographs from the 2004 Olympic and Paralympic Games demonstrated that all competitors, sighted or blind, displayed the same expressions in response to winning or losing (Matsumoto & Willingham, 2009). Monozygotic (identical) twins are more similar than dizygotic (fraternal) twins in the age at which they begin to show fear of strangers (Freedman, 1974). Rhesus monkeys raised in isolation still showed fear at the sight of pictures of other monkeys engaged in threatening behaviors. The development of their fear response was about the same as that of monkeys raised in normal social circumstances (Sackett, 1966).

ENVIRONMENTAL CONTRIBUTIONS TO EMOTIONAL EXPRESSION Although our basic emotional responses seem largely innate, the influences of culture and learning modify emotional expression (Jack, Garrod, Yu, Caldara, & Schyns, 2012; Matsumoto, Yoo, & Chung, 2010). These cultural modifications maintain social order in culturally relevant situations. For example, medical doctors undergo training to withhold emotions such as disgust that would be inappropriate to express to patients.

The presence of other people often influences the intensity of emotional expression. People make more intense facial expressions in response to odors when in a group as opposed to when they are alone (Jancke & Kaufmann, 1994). Cultures typically have different display rules, or norms that specify when, where, and how a person

Blind athlete

Sighted athlete

● **Figure 14.5** Blind and Sighted Athletes Produce Similar Emotional Expressions David Matsumoto and his colleagues carefully analyzed photographs of the facial expressions of athletes during the 2004 Olympic and Paralympic Games. The athletes responded very similarly to winning and losing, supporting a universal hypothesis of emotional expression.

should express emotion (Matsumoto, Willingham, & Olide, 2009). Japanese students watching an emotional film alone were more expressive than when they watched with unfamiliar peers. In contrast, the emotional expression of American students did not vary significantly depending on whether they viewed the film alone or in a group (Ekman, Friesen, & Ellsworth, 1972).

Cultures also influence the direction of attention to faces, which has an impact on the interpretation of facial expressions. Asian participants focused more on the eyes in order to interpret facial expression of emotion, while Western Caucasian participants focused more on the eyebrows and mouths of faces (Jack, Caldara, & Schyns, 2012). The picture emerging is one of innate, genetically determined emotional responses that immediately come under the influence of social and environmental feedback.

••• Connecting to **Research**

FACIAL EXPRESSIONS PREDICT ASSAULT

Later in this chapter, we will distinguish between impulsive and premeditated aggression. Do people communicate their intent to engage in aggression through their facial expressions? If so, law enforcement personnel and others who work with potentially violent individuals could benefit from training that alerts them to these signals.

David Matsumoto and Hyisung Hwang (2014) compared the reactions of law enforcement personnel in the United States and in Korea and American university students who had experienced an assault with students who did not report experiencing an assault. All participants responded to photos of a white professional actor recreating expressions produced by assailants found in security videos of actual assaults. The law enforcement personnel and the students who had experienced assault rated the photos similarly, and these groups differed in their responses from students who had not experienced assault. This finding suggested that the experience of assault was important in the identification of aggressive potential.

How did the faces of the aggressors look? The premeditated assault face was consistent with a person who was attempting to mask emotion. The person lowered his or her brows, raised the upper eyelid resulting in a stare, with a slight tightening of the lips (see ● Figure 14.6). Matsumoto and Hwang (2014) describe this face as that of an angry person who is determined and concentrating on the situation. The impulsively aggressive face indicates a loss of temper. The brows are slightly lowered, the eyelids are strongly raised resulting in a pronounced stare, and the lips are strongly tightened. This expression indicates high-intensity anger and loss of control of the mouth.

The fact that the experience of assault improved the ability to detect these signals suggests that training people to recognize an imminent assault would be useful. The similar reactions to these facial expressions in the United States and Korea supports the idea that aggressive facial displays are universal.

DI CROLLALANZA ARALDO/SIPA/Newscom

● **Figure 14.6** The Look of Premeditated Aggression Arnold Schwarzenegger demonstrates the classic expression of premeditated aggression in his iconic role in the Terminator movies. As reported by Matsumoto and Hwang (2014), premeditated aggression is preceded by controlled anger, concentration, and determination.

INDIVIDUAL DIFFERENCES IN EMOTIONAL EXPRESSION AND RECOGNITION

Individuals are quite different from one another in their overall intensity of emotional expression and their abilities to identify the emotions of others correctly. Individuals also vary in their overall emotional style, or positive or negative emotional tendencies (Davidson & Irwin, 1999).

Jerome Kagan (1997) found that newborn infants showed consistent levels of reactivity to an unpleasant odor. Infants who are highly reactive to environmental stimuli are at greater risk for anxiety and mood disorders later in life. Extremely low-reactive infants have a greater tendency toward antisocial behavior. A study of psychopaths incarcerated for murder indicated that these men showed low-reactivity. They responded much less than control participants to slides of pleasant, neutral, and unpleasant situations (Herpertz et al., 2001).

Correct identification of another person's facial expressions of emotion is critical to competent social functioning. Twin studies suggest the ability to interpret the emotional expressions of others is heavily influenced by genetics (Anokhin, Goglsheykin, & Heath, 2010). The ability to read emotion in others can be distorted by several psychological disorders. Individuals diagnosed with schizophrenia process facial features normally but perform worse than healthy controls on tasks requiring them to distinguish between different facial expressions (Kohler et al., 2003; Schneider et al., 2006). These patients are particularly likely to misinterpret all types of emotional stimuli, including facial expressions, as threatening, which might lead to delusions of persecution and paranoia (Phillips, Drevets, Rauch, & Lane, 2003) (see Chapter 16). People with autism spectrum disorder (Jones et al., 2011) and antisocial personality disorder have specific difficulties recognizing expressions of fear (Marsh & Blair, 2008) (see Chapter 16).

CAN WE SPOT A LIAR? In spite of our usually reliable ability to recognize emotions, we often find ourselves victimized by liars. Deception, or a false communication that benefits the communicator, along with the ability to detect deception have been shaped by natural selection (Bond & Robinson, 1988). Plants, fireflies, octopuses, and primates share the ability to deceive through the use of camouflage, mimickry, and in some cases, intentional deception. To avoid giving away their feelings of fear, expressed by the spontaneous baring of teeth, baboons turn their backs on others until the expression passes. Organisms that deceive successfully leave behind more offspring, making the ability to deceive more likely in successive generations (Dawkins & Krebs, 1979).

Paul Ekman (1996) suggests that deliberate lying is difficult to do successfully because it requires a great deal of short-term memory (see Chapter 12). As a result, people who are deliberately lying slip in predictable ways. The normally articulate person stumbles verbally, adding "um"s and "uh"s as he or she struggles to assemble a plausible lie. People who are lying tend to stiffen the head and upper body. They nod their heads less frequently and do not use hand gestures as much as when they're telling the truth. Inappropriate smiling and laughing can result from the nervousness caused by lying. In contrast to the stiffer upper body, the feet begin swinging. In the United States, lack of eye contact is interpreted as a sign of dishonesty, but in many other cultures, eye contact is viewed as an impolite expression of dominance.

An excellent signal that a person may be lying is a relative lack of detail in a story. Truthful people include 20 to 30 percent more detail to a story compared to liars (Colwell, Hiscock-Anisman, Memon, Rachel, & Colwell, 2007). Another effective strategy for detecting deception is to ask a person to tell a story backwards in time (Fisher & Geiselman, 2010). We are very dependent on timelines as cues for episodic memory retrieval (see Chapter 12). A person telling the truth can move easily from one event to the previous event, but constructing a false story backwards will overwhelm a person's memory for detail very quickly.

As difficult as lying might be, some individuals are quite capable of producing authentic-looking, yet fake emotional expressions (Gunnery, Hall, & Ruben, 2013).

polygraph A lie-detector test based on measures of autonomic arousal.

The Duchenne smile is typically viewed by scientists as genuine, and includes movement of the eye muscles that make "crow's feet" at the corner of the eye. Fake smiles do not produce this eye muscle movement. Sarah Gunnery and her colleagues found a substantial minority of their participants were capable of producing Duchenne smiles during role-play activities and when asked to imitate a Duchenne smile shown in a photograph. The ability of participants to appear authentic in role-play is probably similar to the abilities shown by skilled actors and actresses who portray believable emotions by "getting into the role."

Polygraph, or lie-detector, tests are widely used by both law enforcement and employers, in spite of their unreliability (Holden, 1986). In one study, illustrated in ● Figure 14.7, a panel of experts evaluated polygraph data and declared a third of the innocent people to be guilty, whereas a quarter of the guilty were deemed to be innocent (Kleinmuntz & Szucko, 1984). Polygraph data reflect arousal, and an innocent person might be aroused out of fear of being accused. The general lack of arousal often found in antisocial people, along with their failure to see lying as morally wrong, allows many guilty people to appear innocent. Because of these inaccuracies, polygraph results are typically not admitted to courtrooms in the United States.

New technologies might eventually provide more accurate means of assessing honesty (see Figure 14.7). Functional MRIs may be used in the future to detect changes in brain activation during lying (Spence, Kaylor-Hughes, Farrow, & Wilkinson, 2008; Holden, 2001). Laboratory studies have shown that deception can be detected using fMRI in law-abiding participants, as opposed to real criminals, who are lying about simple, concrete tasks such as which playing card is being held (Langleben, 2008). How well these laboratory demonstrations predict detection of real criminals lying about real crimes remains the subject of debate. The use of fMRI to detect deception raises a number of challenging ethical and privacy questions (Wolpe, Foster, & Langleben, 2010).

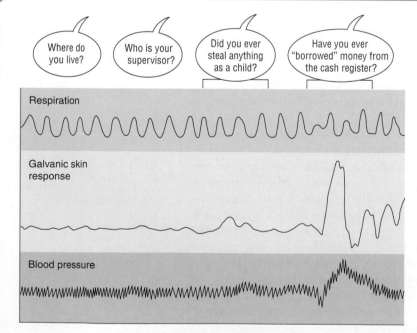

(a) Sample Questions and Responses

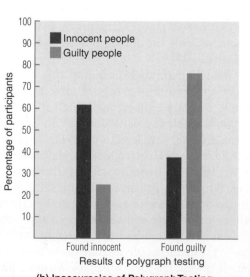

(b) Inaccuracies of Polygraph Testing

● **Figure 14.7** Polygraph Testing (a) Autonomic measures including respiration, galvanic skin response (an arousal measure using the electrical conductance of the skin), and blood pressure are taken during a series of neutral and emotional questions. (b) In Kleinmuntz and Szucko's experiment using polygraph tests, a panel of "experts" concluded that more than a third of the innocent participants were guilty, whereas a quarter of the guilty were judged to be innocent.

Source: Adapted from Kleinmuntz & Szucko (1984).

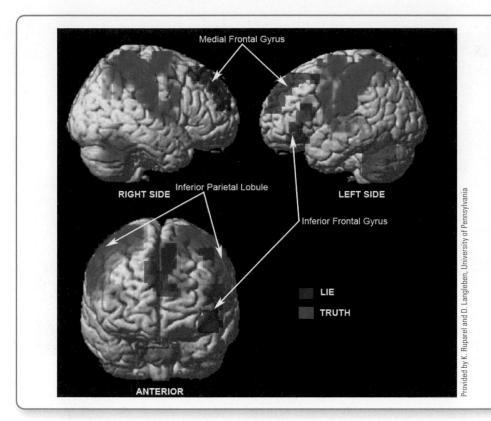

Medial Frontal Gyrus

RIGHT SIDE

LEFT SIDE

Inferior Parietal Lobule

Inferior Frontal Gyrus

LIE

TRUTH

ANTERIOR

Provided by K. Ruparel and D. Langleben, University of Pennsylvania

● **Figure 14.8** Can fMRI Detect Lying? Participants' brains showed different patterns of activity during a "Guilty Knowledge Test." Red areas were more active when the participant was lying, and blue areas were more active when the participant was telling the truth.

Theories of Emotion

In our original definition, we noted two components of emotion: a physiological experience and a conscious, subjective experience or feeling. Several theories have attempted to characterize the relationships between these components. In other words, what relationship, if any, does the feeling of having butterflies in your stomach have with your subjective sense of being afraid?

Theories of emotion differ in their emphasis on bottom-up and top-down processing. As we discussed in Chapter 6, bottom-up processing refers to building a perception of a situation from initial sensations, whereas top-down processing uses cognition, including memories and expectations, to organize incoming sensory information. Theories of emotion emphasizing bottom-up processing build the emotional experience from the physical sensations (my stomach is upset) up through the cognitive appraisal of the situation (I'm scared). Theories emphasizing top-down processing rely on cognitive appraisal of a situation (I'm standing on the winner's platform with a gold medal around my neck) to organize and interpret incoming physical sensations (my heart is beating fast).

THE JAMES-LANGE THEORY Both William James (1890) and Danish physiologist Carl Lange (1885/1912) independently developed similar theories about emotion. Consequently, the **James-Lange theory** bears the names of both men. This theory suggests that a sequence of events results in an emotional experience. An awareness of our physical state leads to the identification of a subjective feeling. The theory assumes that physical states related to each type of feeling (sadness and happiness, for instance) are highly distinct from one another and that we are capable of correctly labeling these distinct physical states as separate feelings. As James explained, "We feel sorry because we cry, angry because we strike, afraid because we tremble" (1890, p. 1066).

A variation of the James-Lange theory is the suggestion that our facial expressions affect the way we feel (Izard, 1972, 1977). Intentionally making facial movements can stimulate physical responses that are quite similar to spontaneous emotional

James-Lange theory A theory of emotion in which a person's physical state provides cues for the identification of an emotional state.

© Reuters/CORBIS

Focus New Zealand Photo Library

● **Figure 14.9 Expressing an Emotion Heightens Feelings** The New Zealand All Blacks, a rugby team, prepare for competition by borrowing moves from the Maori *haka*. By displaying fierce facial expressions and body movements, both warriors and rugby players get in the mood for battle.

expression (Levenson, Ekman, & Friesen, 1990). When participants were instructed to move their faces in a particular way (raise your eyebrows, etc.) without seeing their own faces or knowing they were modeling a particular emotion, they reported feeling the emotions they portrayed. These results have some useful practical implications. If people are feeling depressed or angry, engaging in activities that elicit smiling or laughing might help lift their moods. William James (1899, p. 153), who battled depression throughout his adult life, gave the following advice: "To feel cheerful, sit up cheerfully, look around cheerfully, and act as if cheerfulness were already there." A dramatic use of emotional expression to induce a particular state is the Maori *haka*, shown in ● Figure 14.9. Traditional Maori warriors preparing for battle engaged in stereotyped grimaces, vocalizations, and battle moves. A contemporary rugby team, the New Zealand All Blacks, uses hakas to prepare for games. Not only does this aid in their mental and physical preparation for the game ("psyching up"), but it no doubt intimidates the opposing team as well.

Imitating the facial expressions of others might contribute to **empathy**, the ability to understand another person's feelings. The early back-and-forth imitation of facial expressions that adults do with infants possibly signifies the beginning of this important capacity. The writer Edgar Allan Poe was apparently aware of the role of mimicry in judging the feelings of others:

> When I wish to find out how wise or how stupid or how good or how wicked is anyone, or what are his thoughts at the moment, I fashion the expression of my face, as accurately as possible, in accordance with the expression of his, and then wait to see what thoughts or sentiments arise in my mind or heart, as if to match or correspond with the expression. (From "The Purloined Letter," 1845, as quoted in Levenson et al., 1990.)

Levenson and Ruef (1992) confirmed Poe's observations by showing that people are most accurate in assessing the emotions of another person when their own emotions match those of the person they are observing.

It is clear that performing the haka not only elicits an emotional response in the rugby players but also raises the intensity of their emotions. The idea that the expression

empathy The ability to relate to the feelings of another person.

of an emotion increases its intensity might seem counterintuitive to you. Our commonsense notion is that having a good cry should make us feel better or that holding anger inside will somehow make it worse. In fact, the belief that the best way to reduce an emotion is to express it contributes to the popularity of playing violent video games (Bushman & Whitaker, 2010). These common sense ideas originate with the concept of **catharsis**, or "purging." The idea of catharsis dates back to Aristotle and has been promoted by psychoanalyst Sigmund Freud and ethologist Konrad Lorenz, among others. According to catharsis theory, emotions are viewed as filling a reservoir. When the reservoir is full, the emotions will "overflow," emptying the person of that emotion. Catharsis theorists recommend that people "let it all hang out" by expressing their emotions (Kennedy-Moore & Watson, 1999). Obviously, the example of the rugby players we reviewed in this section indicates otherwise. In many circumstances, expressing an emotion is more likely to enhance than reduce your feelings (Bushman, 2002).

The James-Lange theory is not without its flaws. One of the main assumptions of the theory is that we have very specific physical states that map onto recognizable emotional states. If I feel this set of physical sensations, I know I'm scared, but if I feel that other set, I must be angry. This is not always the case. Many emotional states are accompanied by overlapping physical sensations. In fairness, James expressed an interest in emotions "that have a distinct bodily expression" (1884, p. 189), which suggests he recognized the limitations of his own theory.

An example of a situation that made interpretation of physical states difficult was a study conducted with men crossing the Capilano Canyon bridge in British Columbia (Dutton & Aron, 1974). As shown in ● Figure 14.10, the bridge is 450 feet long with low handrails, and is suspended about 230 feet above rocks and rapids. Aron and Dutton stationed an attractive female researcher in the middle of the bridge. She stopped single men and asked them to participate in an interview, after which she provided them her phone number in case they had further questions about the experiment. Compared to men crossing a safer bridge upstream, the men crossing the frightening bridge provided much more sexual content during their interview and were four times more likely to call the researcher. Although the failure to randomly assign men to bridges might compromise the interpretation of the experiment (bold men who cross scary bridges might also be more likely to call women they just met), it appeared that the men were not able to distinguish very well between fear and sexual arousal. Instead of the bottom-up approach suggested by James-Lange, they appeared to be using top-down processing to interpret their situation: recognizing they were in the presence of an attractive person, they attributed their physical sensations to sexual attraction instead of fear.

● **Figure 14.10 The Capilano Canyon Bridge** Dutton and Aron (1974) found that men walking across this bridge were much more likely to be attracted to the female interviewer than men walking on a much safer bridge upstream. Apparently, it was difficult for the men to distinguish between the emotions of fear and sexual arousal.

catharsis The relief of tension through the expression of emotion.

THE CANNON-BARD THEORY The James-Lange theory was extensively criticized by Walter Cannon (1927), who proposed his own theory, later modified by Philip Bard (1934). The end product is known as the **Cannon-Bard theory**. Whereas the James-Lange theory proposes a sequence of events, from physical response to subjective feeling, the Cannon-Bard theory proposes that both the subjective and physical responses occur simultaneously and independently.

How are these theories different? Let's assume that you are innocently reading your textbook when a bear walks in the door of your room. According to the James-Lange theory, the sight of the bear would immediately set off physical responses that the brain would then interpret as fear. In the Cannon-Bard theory, the sight of the bear would immediately and simultaneously trigger an independent, subjective feeling of fear and the physiological fight-or-flight response. According to the Cannon-Bard theory, the central nervous system has the ability to produce an emotion directly, without needing feedback from the peripheral nervous system.

THE SCHACHTER-SINGER TWO-FACTOR THEORY Like the James-Lange theory, the **Schachter-Singer two-factor theory** (Schachter & Singer, 1962; Sinclair, Hoffman, Mark, Martin, & Pickering, 1994) assumes that emotions result from a sequence of events. However, unlike the James-Lange theory, the Schachter-Singer theory does not require a specific set of physical responses for each emotion. Instead, a stimulus first produces general arousal. Once aroused, we make a conscious, cognitive appraisal of our circumstances, which allows us to identify our subjective feelings. Arousal might lead to several interpretations, based on the way a person assesses his or her situation. Fans of two basketball teams watching the same game respond to the final score with very different emotions. Returning to our example of the bear entering your room, Schachter and Singer would predict that the sight of the bear would initiate general arousal. To identify the source of your arousal, you would cognitively assess your situation, attribute your arousal to the presence of a bear in your room, and identify your subjective feelings as fear. In other words, the Schachter-Singer theory uses more of a top-down approach.

One direct test of the Schachter-Singer two-factor theory involved injecting participants with epinephrine (adrenalin), which produces symptoms of physical arousal (Schachter & Singer, 1962). Participants were told that they were getting an injection of a vitamin and that their vision would be tested as soon as another person arrived to participate in the experiment. The other person was actually an actor employed by the researchers. In half of the trials, the actor behaved in a happy, silly manner, whereas in the other half, he acted angry and stomped out of the room. Participants who had received epinephrine and were exposed to the happy actor rated themselves as feeling happy, whereas participants exposed to the angry actor felt angry. Importantly, when the participants were accurately informed beforehand that they were getting a drug that would produce physiological arousal, the behavior of the actor did not influence their assessment of their emotions.

A later attempt to replicate this experiment did not succeed, throwing significant doubts on the results (Marshall & Zimbardo, 1979). An additional weakness of the Schachter-Singer theory is the assumption that physiological states are not uniquely associated with specific emotions. Many emotional states appear to be associated with distinct patterns of physiological arousal (Levenson et al., 1990). Nonetheless, Schachter and Singer provided considerable insight into how we identify our subjective feelings. In particular, the two-factor theory is helpful in explaining how general arousal can intensify an emotion. For example, exercising (producing physical arousal) can make people more angry or sexually aroused when they are subsequently exposed to relevant stimuli (Reisenzein, 1983).

● Figure 14.11 shows a comparison of the James-Lange, Cannon-Bard, and Schachter-Singer two-factor theories. Each of these classic theories offers important insights into our experience of emotion, yet none definitively resolves our question regarding the relationship of physical and subjective experiences.

Cannon-Bard theory A theory of emotion in which the simultaneous activation of physical responses and the recognition of subjective feelings occur independently.

Schachter-Singer two-factor theory A theory of emotion in which general arousal leads to cognitive assessment of the context, which in turn leads to the identification of an emotional state.

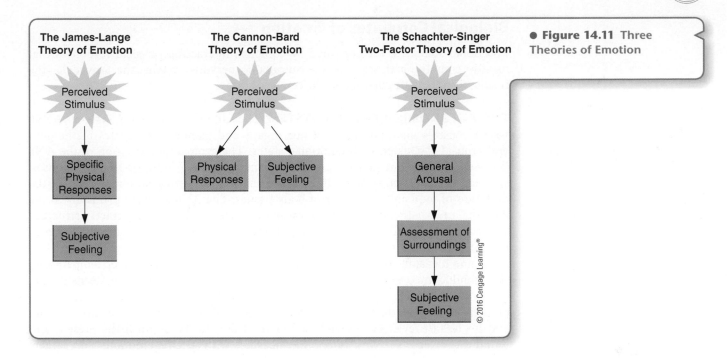

● **Figure 14.11** Three Theories of Emotion

CONTEMPORARY THEORIES OF EMOTION While the classic theories of emotion give us a good starting place for understanding the relationships between the physical and cognitive components of emotion, scientists have continued to explore and refine explanations of our emotional experiences.

Some contemporary theorists note that physical responses associated with an emotion may range from quite specific to quite ambiguous (Cacioppo, Berntson, & Klein, 1992). For example, the physical sensations associated with disgust may be more precise and recognizable than the physical sensations associated with pride. Emotional stimuli can produce overlapping physical responses such as anger or fear. The initial specificity of the physical response leads to different pathways and cognitive responses. A highly specific physical response leads to unambiguous recognition by the cerebral cortex in the manner proposed by James and Lange. At the other extreme, the least differentiated physical signals will produce general arousal, which will require significant cognitive processing and evaluation in a manner consistent with the Schachter-Singer two-factor theory. This contemporary model correctly predicts that emotional responses may range from immediate (fear) to delayed (pride) based on the amount of cognitive processing that is required (Cacioppo, Berntson, Larsen, Poehlmann, & Ito, 2000).

Clinical observations of people whose emotions are impacted by neurological damage provide the basis for a **somatic marker** explanation of emotion (Bechara, Damasio, & Damasio, 2000; Damasio, 1994). This explanation of emotional processing expands on the James-Lange theory to suggest that physical responses to stimuli not only contribute to subjective feelings, but also contribute to decision making (Reimann & Bechara, 2010). Remembered patterns of physical responses, the somatic markers, provide a way for the brain to map the external world by coloring situations as positive or negative based on prior experience. Patients with damage to the frontal lobes can easily describe graphic images of sex and violence that they are shown, but they are unable to tap into the somatic markers that would provide them with normal emotional responses to these stimuli (Bechara et al., 2000). It is the job of the ventromedial prefrontal cortex to form associations between somatic markers and facts about the situations that elicited them. This model helps to account for choices that are made on the basis of emotional responses (I like Macs better than PCs) rather than on the basis of cold, rational logic alone (the Mac has more features I need than the PC).

somatic marker An association formed between stimuli and resulting patterns of physical activation.

Biological Correlates of Emotion

Emotional states are accompanied by complex, interacting physical responses that usually combine activation of the autonomic nervous system, the amygdala, the insula, the cingulate cortex, and the cerebral cortex.

THE AUTONOMIC NERVOUS SYSTEM The autonomic nervous system (ANS), which controls many activities of our organs and glands, participates in the general arousal associated with emotional states. The sympathetic division of the ANS is responsible for our general arousal and more extreme fight-or-flight responses, whereas the parasympathetic division participates in resting activities such as the digestion of food and the repair of body tissues. The ANS answers primarily to the hypothalamus, either directly or by way of the nucleus of the solitary tract, a structure located in the medulla that receives input from the hypothalamus and participates in the control of the autonomic nervous system.

Some measures of autonomic function, such as heart rate, finger temperature, skin conductance, and muscle activity, appear to produce different patterns during different emotional states (Levenson et al., 1990). However, the degree and reliability of such differences remains in dispute. Cacioppo, Berntson, Larsen, Poehlmann, and Ito (2000) reviewed research conducted from the 1950s until the present and found that attempts to link autonomic measures with specific emotions were largely inconclusive. General differences, such as the correlation of autonomic measures and positive or negative emotions, are clear. Autonomic responses associated with negative emotions generally appear to be stronger than those associated with positive emotions (Cacioppo, Berntson, Norris, & Gollan, 2011). However, identifying differences in autonomic correlates between two positive states (such as happiness and hope) or between two negative states (such as anger and fear) is far more difficult.

THE AMYGDALA AND THE INSULA The amygdala and the insula, an area located within the fold at the junction of the frontal and temporal lobes, are associated with the identification of emotional stimuli and the arousal resulting from that identification.

One of the first clues to the importance of the amygdala to emotion resulted from an experiment in which Heinrich Klüver and Paul Bucy (1939) removed both temporal lobes, which include the amygdala, in rhesus monkeys. Following recovery, the previously difficult-to-handle adult rhesus monkeys were much tamer, and their emotions were far less intense. They seemed oblivious to normally fear-producing stimuli. They approached snakes repeatedly, even after being attacked, and allowed themselves to be picked up and stroked (something you definitely don't want to try with a normal adult rhesus). They made fewer fear-related grimaces and vocalizations. This set of symptoms, whether observed in monkeys or in humans, collectively became known as **Klüver-Bucy syndrome**.

What accounts for the emotional changes seen in Klüver and Bucy's monkeys? The evidence points to the amygdala. Because of the complexity of the amygdala, it is overly simplistic to describe it as a unitary structure with a single function. Different parts of the amygdala participate in a wide variety of processes, including emotion, reward, motivation, learning, memory, and attention (Murray, 2007). We discussed the contributions of the amygdala to learning and memory in Chapter 12.

Extending the findings of Klüver and Bucy, experimental data from studies in which the amygdala is lesioned support a role for this structure in both the identification and expression of emotion. Bilateral damage to the amygdala usually produces reduced emotionality. Fear, anxiety, and aggression appear to be particularly reduced. Following selective lesions in both amygdalas, rhesus monkeys are more likely to engage in social interactions with unfamiliar monkeys, which is normally a very dangerous thing to do in the strictly enforced social hierarchy that characterizes rhesus groups (Emery et al., 2001). Normal monkeys will show great reluctance to reach across a fake snake to

Klüver-Bucy syndrome
A collection of symptoms, including tameness, extreme sexual behavior, and oral exploration, that results from damage to the temporal lobes, and the amygdala in particular.

retrieve a food reward, but monkeys with lesioned amygdalas show little or no reaction to a fake snake (Izquierdo, Suda, & Murray, 2005; Murray, 2007; Murray & Izquierdo, 2007). Rats with damaged amygdalas fail to learn to fear a tone that reliably predicts the onset of electric shock (LeDoux, 2000).

Studies of human participants with amygdala damage parallel these animal results. Patient S. M., whose amygdalas were destroyed by a condition known as Urbach-Wiethe disease, was asked to draw pictures that represented the primary emotions. S.M.'s drawings, shown in ● Figure 14.12, demonstrate that she was able to effectively represent all emotions but fear. She complained to the researchers that "she did not know what an afraid face would look like and therefore could not draw the expression" (Adolphs, Tranel, Damasio, & Damasio, 1995, p. 5887; Adolphs, Tranel, & Damasio, 1998). When shown a series of faces in photographs, she was able to recognize the emotions of happiness, sadness, and disgust portrayed in the photographs. However, she had selective difficulty identifying anger and fear correctly. S.M.'s impaired abilities to process fear appear to result from her failure to look at the eye region of the faces she was asked to evaluate (Adolphs, 2007). Fear in another's face can be distinguished most effectively from other emotions by observing the eyes. When explicitly instructed to pay attention to the eyes of faces, patient S.M. was able to evaluate fear normally. Individuals with autism spectrum disorder (ASD) also seem to have serious difficulties identifying the emotions of other people, particularly fear (see Chapter 16). Not only do individuals with ASD fail to make eye contact with others beginning at early ages, but one of the consistent physical correlates of ASD is abnormality of the amygdala (Amaral, Schumann, & Nordahl, 2008). These findings suggest that the amygdala participates in the active exploration of the social environment as well as in the interpretation of the results of that exploration (Adolphs, 2007).

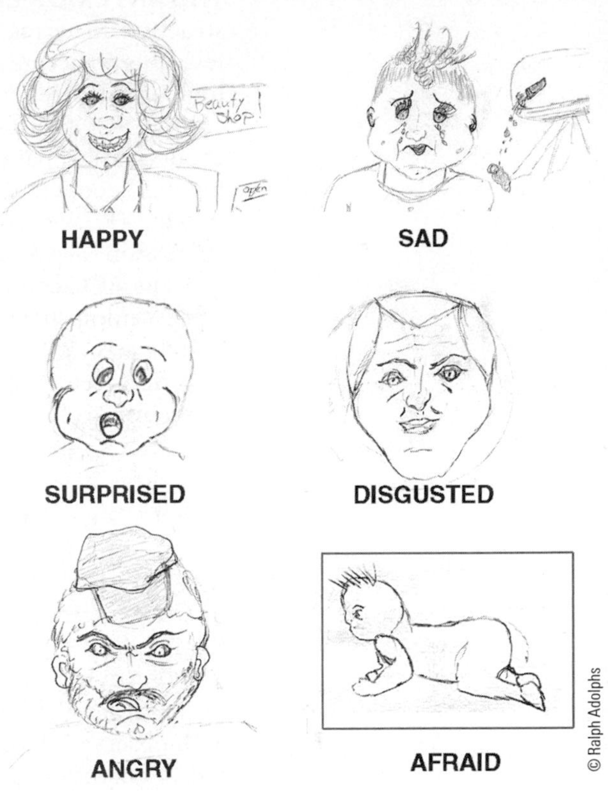

● **Figure 14.12 Damage to the Amygdala Affects the Processing of Fear** Patient S. M. experienced damage to both amygdalas as a result of a rare condition known as Urbach-Wiethe disease. When asked to draw pictures that represented the primary emotions, S.M. did well with all emotions except "afraid."
Source: Adolphs et al., 1995.

Although we have emphasized the role of the amygdala in fear and other negative emotional states, evidence for its participation in reward and positive emotional states also exists (Murray, 2007). In addition, several studies have demonstrated that the amygdala responds to stimuli that have no particular emotional value at all, but are simply unusual (Ousdal et al., 2008; Blackford, Buckholtz, Avery, & Zald, 2010). As a result, we might conclude that the amygdala's primary role is to process unexpected, unusual stimuli, especially those that might be important to safety and survival (Armony, 2012).

The amygdala is part of a tightly connected circuit that includes the frontal lobes of the cortex, the cingulate cortex (discussed on next page), and the insula. The behavior of individuals with damage to the insula suggests that this area participates in making the distinction between positive and negative stimuli (Berntson et al., 2011). Participants were asked to rate photos on a scale from very pleasant to very unpleasant while indicating how arousing each photo was. Participants with damage to the insula rated the photos as more neutral and as less arousing than control participants did. Participants with damage to the amygdala did not show differences in their ratings of positivity and negativity compared to controls, but they showed much less arousal in response to negative photos. These results suggest that the amygdala initiates arousal, especially in response to negative stimuli, while the insula helps us discriminate between positive and negative stimuli.

THE ANTERIOR CINGULATE CORTEX The cingulate cortex is a relatively ancient structure in terms of evolution as compared to the remainder of the cerebral cortex. This structure appears to serve as a major gateway between the amygdala, other limbic structures, and the frontal lobes of the cerebral cortex. The anterior cingulate cortex (ACC) participates in the brain's pain matrix, which processes information about physical pain. As we will see in subsequent sections on reward and aggression, the ACC cooperates with the orbitofrontal cortex in processing reward and decision-making (Rushworth, Behrens, Rudebeck, & Walton, 2007) and in the inhibition of aggression (Siever, 2008).

The ACC contributes to the more conscious, cognitive appraisals of threat (that's a frightening snake, but it's in a terrarium at the zoo) compared to the less conscious signals arising from the amygdala (Kalisch & Gerlicher, 2014). People with anxiety disorders (see Chapter 16) often exaggerate threat. During catastrophizing and worrying by people with anxiety disorders, researchers observed unusually high levels of activation in the ACC.

THE BASAL GANGLIA The basal ganglia participate in voluntary movement in general, including the coordination of movement in response to emotional stimuli. People who experience strokes that damage the basal ganglia experience an overall decrease in the experience of emotional intensity (Paradiso, Ostedgaard, Vaidya, Ponto, & Robinson, 2013).

Observing facial expressions of disgust seem a to produce considerable activity in the basal ganglia (Phan, Wager, Taylor, & Liberzon, 2002). These results are consistent with observations of individuals who have experienced damage to the basal ganglia, due to conditions such as Parkinson's disease. Although these patients can recognize facial expressions of other emotions, they seem uniquely impaired in their ability to recognize the facial expression of disgust (Hennenlotter et al., 2004).

THE CEREBRAL CORTEX When humans experience cortical damage, particularly in the frontal lobes, emotional disturbance often results. In Chapter 2, we discussed the case of Phineas Gage, the railroad worker whose frontal lobe was damaged in an accident. Frontal lobe damage is associated with a reduction in emotional feelings, especially those of fear and anxiety (Rolls, 2004).

Elliot Valenstein (1986) traced the history of medical efforts to influence emotional behavior through frontal lobe surgery. In 1935, John Fulton and Carlyle Jacobsen removed the frontal lobes from two chimpanzees and reported that the chimpanzees became much calmer. Egaz Moniz believed that Fulton and Jacobsen's technique would be beneficial for human patients suffering from a number of mental disorders. He advocated the use of the frontal lobotomy, or the surgical separation of the frontal lobes from the rest of the brain. Between 1939 and 1951, approximately 18,000 Americans were treated with frontal lobotomies for problems ranging from schizophrenia to depression to anxiety. Traveling across the United States in a vehicle he dubbed "the Lobotomobile," Walter Freeman popularized one version of the procedure, illustrated in ● Figure 14.13. In what was described as "ice pick surgery," a sharp instrument was inserted above the eye and then wiggled back and forth, severing the connections between the frontal lobe and the anterior cingulate cortex, in particular. In some cases, the procedure did reduce patients' anxiety. However, subsequent side effects, including seizures, lack of inhibition, impulsivity, or lack of initiative, often emerged. Frontal lobotomies were largely discontinued after the discovery of effective antipsychotic medications after World War II (see Chapter 16).

In addition to the specific roles of the frontal lobes in emotion, which we will discuss further in later sections on reward and aggression, we can distinguish between the contributions of the two cerebral hemispheres to emotion (see Chapter 13). In most people, left hemisphere activity is correlated with positive emotions, whereas right hemisphere activity is correlated with negative emotions. Participants viewing positive emotional stimuli showed increased activation in the left hemisphere prefrontal

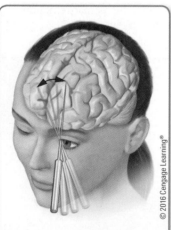

© 2016 Cengage Learning®

● **Figure 14.13** Frontal Lobotomy Between 1939 and 1951, about 18,000 Americans underwent frontal lobotomies for problems ranging from schizophrenia to depression to anxiety. Parts of the frontal lobes were surgically separated from the rest of the brain in what has been referred to as "ice pick surgery."

cortex, whereas viewing negative stimuli was correlated with increased activation of the right hemisphere prefrontal cortex (Davidson & Irwin, 1999). Patients who suffer damage exclusively to the left hemisphere are often quite depressed, especially if their damage is located in the left frontal lobe (Gainotti, 1972; Robinson, Kubos, Starr, Rao, & Price, 1984; Sackheim et al., 1982). Patients with right-hemisphere damage, however, are often surprisingly cheerful. These clinical observations are supported by results from the Wada test, in which one cerebral hemisphere at a time is anesthetized. Anesthetizing the left hemisphere generally results in a lingering feeling of depression, whereas anesthetizing the right hemisphere is associated with apparent happiness (Lee et al., 2004).

As we saw in the discussion of lateralization in Chapter 13, for many people, the right hemisphere plays a greater role than the left in processing emotion. Stimuli can be constructed in which half the face demonstrates one facial expression while the other half displays a second, different expression. If the person looks at a focal point in the center of the image, the visual information to the left of the focal point will be processed by the right hemisphere, and the visual information to the right of the focal point will be processed by the left hemisphere. In a patient who had undergone the split-brain operation (described in Chapter 13), the assessment of facial expression by the right hemisphere was superior to judgment by the left hemisphere (Stone, Nisenson, Eliassen, & Gazzaniga, 1996). In normal, healthy right-handed participants, the right hemisphere processes emotional facial expressions faster and more accurately than the left hemisphere (Bryden, 1982). You can see the effects of this hemisphere difference for yourself by evaluating the faces in ● Figure 14.14.

As you might recall from Chapters 10 and 13, dichotic listening tasks, in which different information is presented to each ear, are also used to assess the functioning of the two hemispheres. Information presented to the left ear is processed more rapidly by the right hemisphere, whereas information presented to the right ear is processed more rapidly by the left hemisphere. Ley and Bryden (1982) presented sentences with different emotional tones to each ear of their research participants. Participants did a better job recognizing the meaning of sentences when asked to pay attention to input from their right ears. In contrast, participants were more successful at identifying the emotional tone of the sentence when attending to their left ears. These findings are consistent with the concept that the meaningfulness of language is localized in the left hemisphere (right ear advantage) and emotional aspects of language are processed in the right hemisphere (left ear advantage).

Another clue to a difference between the hemispheres in emotional processing is the asymmetry of facial expression. As we mentioned earlier, the right and left facial nerves are relatively independent. This allows higher levels of control, including the cerebral cortex, to influence the intensity of emotions expressed on the right and left halves of the face. In general, the left side of the face (primarily controlled by the right hemisphere) is more expressive than the right side (primarily controlled by the left hemisphere). This is especially true of the lower two thirds of the face, which receives input from the contralateral hemisphere only.

Facial asymmetry can be observed by manipulating photos of faces, in a technique you can easily duplicate with most photo software. Divide the photo of a face in half, and combine each half with a mirror image of itself. In this way, you can construct one composite face made of two right halves and one made of two left halves. As Sackheim, Gur, and Saucy (1978) demonstrated, the results of this procedure will give you very different intensities of emotional expression (● Figure 14.15). When placed beside the original image, the composite made of two left halves of the face is usually judged as the most expressive while the composite of the two right halves of the face is considered the least expressive.

PATTERNS OF ACTIVATION AND EMOTION It is overly simplistic to look for specific areas of the brain that are activated during a particular type of emotional experience. We do not have "happy centers" and "sadness centers" in the brain. Widespread areas of the

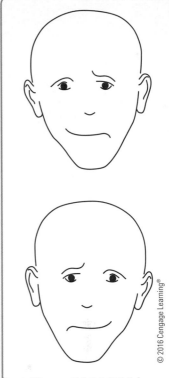

© 2016 Cengage Learning®

● **Figure 14.14** Which Face Is Happy? Which Face Is Sad? These faces are actually mirror images of each other, but you will probably perceive them as expressing different emotions. Because the left part of the visual field is processed by the emotional right hemisphere, the expression on the left side of the face is more likely to influence your judgment. Thus the face on top will look happy, whereas the face on the bottom will look sad. For left-handers and ambidextrous people, these results might vary.

● **Figure 14.15** Facial Expressions Are Not Symmetrical For most people, the left lower half of the face, controlled by the emotional right hemisphere, is more expressive than the right lower half of the face. The author's husband, Roger, agreed to demonstrate this phenomenon. Image (a) is a photo of Roger. Image (b) is a composite of the two left sides of his face, which clearly show more emotion than (c) the composite of his two right sides.

brain appear to be associated with each specific emotion, and areas associated with different emotions show considerable overlap. Antonio Damasio and his colleagues (Damasio et al., 2000) observed PET scans of 41 participants as they experienced anger, sadness, fear, and happiness. To generate the emotional response, participants were instructed to recall a specific event from their past associated with each emotion. While recalling the event, the participants were asked to attempt to re-create feelings. The results indicated that complex patterns of activity involving multiple regions of the brain characterized each emotion. Although the patterns for the four emotions were distinct from one another, single brain regions might participate in more than one of the emotional states.

INTERIM SUMMARY 14.1

Summary Table: Brain Damage with Emotional Consequences

Area Damaged	Emotional Consequences
Amygdala	Difficulty perceiving and experiencing negative emotions, particularly fear
Insula	Reduced response to negativity, positivity, and overall arousal
Basal ganglia	Difficulty perceiving disgust
Frontal lobe	Reduced fear and anxiety
Left cerebral hemisphere	Depression
Right cerebral hemisphere	Cheerful mood

Summary Points

1. Emotions promote survival by enhancing arousal, organizing approach and avoidance behaviors, and providing a means of communication. **(LO1)**

2. Facial expression is mediated by the facial nerve (cranial nerve VII). Voluntary expressions are controlled by the primary motor cortex, whereas spontaneous expressions are controlled by subcortical structures. **(LO1)**

3. Some basic emotional expressions appear to be universal, but environmental factors and learning influence the intensity and context for emotional expression. **(LO1)**

4. Three classic theories of emotion attempt to organize the relationships between physical reactions and subjective feelings. The James-Lange theory suggests that autonomic responses are used as cues for the recognition of emotional states. The Cannon-Bard theory suggests that both physical reactions and subjective feelings occur simultaneously and independently. The Schachter-Singer theory suggests that the physical reactions contribute to a general arousal, which leads to an assessment of subjective feelings based on context. Contemporary theories of emotion emphasize the complex interactions of physical and emotional states and the existence of learned somatic markers. **(LO2)**

5. The autonomic nervous system, amygdala, insula, anterior cingulate cortex, basal ganglia, and cerebral cortices play important roles in emotion. **(LO3)**

‖ Review Questions

1. What behaviors suggest that a person might be lying?

2. How do the three classic theories of emotion differ in their explanations of emotional behavior?

Pleasure and Reward

James Olds and Peter Milner (1954) discovered some of the first evidence that particular locations in the brain are involved with the positive emotions of pleasure and reward. They surgically implanted a wire electrode in the brain of a rat and allowed the animal to wander around a box. Whenever the rat entered a specified corner of the box, electricity was passed through the electrode. Fairly soon, the rat became reluctant to leave that corner of the box. Olds and Milner then added a lever that the rat could press to stimulate its own brain through the electrode, a procedure known as **electrical self-stimulation of the brain**, or **ESB**. The power of ESB to reward behavior is dramatic. Not only will rats learn bar-pressing behavior rapidly when ESB is used as a reward, but they also show very high rates of responding. Routtenberg and Lindy (1965) allowed rats access to two levers for one hour per day. Pressing one lever resulted in food and pressing the other resulted in rewarding ESB. Even though the rats had no access to food outside of this one-hour period per day, they chose ESB over food. Many starved to death as a result.

Rats are obviously unable to explain why the sensations produced by ESB are so compelling. However, electrode implants have also been used with human participants. Robert Heath (1963) reported his observations of two patients with implanted electrodes. One patient frequently activated an electrode located in the septal area, shown in ● Figure 14.16. He reported that stimulation of the site produced pleasurable sexual feelings, similar to those leading up to an orgasm. He pushed the button for this site frequently in hopes of achieving orgasm, but his efforts were unsuccessful. Heath's second patient also reported pleasant, sexual feelings from septal area stimulation. In addition, this patient frequently stimulated the medial thalamus, in spite of his report that this produced a feeling of irritation. Stimulation of this

electrical self-stimulation of the brain (ESB) A behavior engaged in willingly by research subjects that leads to electrical stimulation of certain parts of the brain.

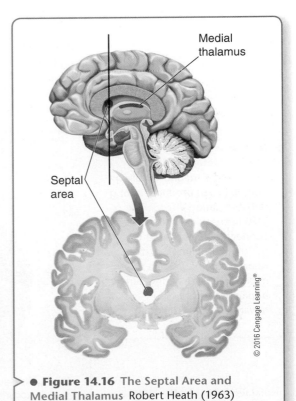

© 2016 Cengage Learning®

● **Figure 14.16** The Septal Area and Medial Thalamus Robert Heath (1963) reported that his human participants experienced pleasant sexual feelings when their septal areas were electrically stimulated. When the medial thalamus was stimulated, Heath's patient reported feeling irritated.

site gave the patient the feeling that he was about to remember something important. Heath's research reminds us that sites producing emotions other than pleasure can support self-stimulation.

The Mesostriatal Pathway

As we discussed in Chapter 4, the ventral portion of the mesostriatal pathway connects the substantia nigra with the nucleus accumbens, the olfactory cortex, the caudate nucleus, and the putamen. Together, the structures in this circuit respond to both reward and novelty (Bunzeck, Doeller, Dolan, & Duzel, 2012). The **medial forebrain bundle (MFB)**, shown in ● Figure 14.17, connects these structures. Electrical stimulation of the MFB produces extremely powerful reinforcement effects (Olds & Olds, 1963). Normal activation of this circuit might lead to exploration of the environment in search of rewards.

The mesostriatal pathway responds to many types of reward. According to Comings and Blum (2000), eating and sexual behaviors constitute "natural" situations for the activation of reward circuits in the brain. The same circuits, however, can also be activated by "unnatural" situations, including compulsive eating, compulsive sex, gambling, and the use of addictive drugs. Observing rats bar-pressing to the point of exhaustion or starvation to stimulate this circuit helps us capture the essence of compulsive and addictive behavior.

Most neurons in the mesostriatal system use dopamine as their primary neurochemical. As we observed in Chapter 4, many addictive substances act as dopamine agonists, particularly in the nucleus accumbens. When a rat obtains ESB in the ventral tegmentum, higher quantities of dopamine are released in the nucleus accumbens (Phillips et al., 1992). Drugs that block dopamine activity in the nucleus accumbens reduce the rewarding effects of ESB. Stellar, Kelley, and Corbett (1983) trained rats to run down the arm of a maze to obtain ESB. Following the injection of a dopamine antagonist, higher levels of stimulation were required to maintain the rats' running behavior.

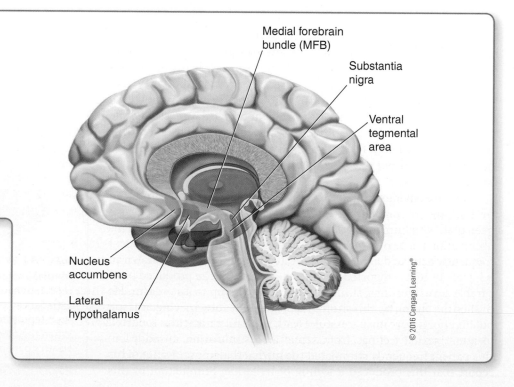

● **Figure 14.17 Connections of the Medial Forebrain Bundle** The medial forebrain bundle (MFB) produces strong self-stimulation effects. The MFB forms widely distributed connections between the midbrain and limbic system. Many of the neurons in this network use the neurochemical dopamine and function as a reward circuit in the brain.

Medial forebrain bundle (MFB)

Substantia nigra

Ventral tegmental area

Nucleus accumbens

Lateral hypothalamus

© 2016 Cengage Learning®

medial forebrain bundle (MFB) A fiber pathway that is a major site for electrical self-stimulation. The MFB connects the substantia nigra and ventral tegmental area with higher forebrain structures, including the hypothalamus and nucleus accumbens.

Reward and Decision Making

To survive, animals must make accurate approach or avoidance decisions. The mesostriatal system begins the process of responding to rewarding stimuli. Areas receiving input from the mesostriatal system provide further evaluation of the circumstances leading to reward. In response to input from the mesostriatal system and the amygdala, the orbitofrontal cortex (OFC) and ventromedial prefrontal cortex assign positive or negative value to situations (Goschke, 2014). An additional circuit provides attention to significant stimuli and involves the insula, anterior cingulate cortex (ACC), and the amygdala. To avoid making unwanted responses, a final circuit involving the lateral prefrontal cortex and the parietal cortex exerts impulse control. As we observed in Chapter 4, the balance of these circuits is distorted in addiction, leading to a weakening of impulse control and a dominance of pleasure seeking behavior.

University students spend a great deal of time and money to obtain a degree and must pass up immediate pleasures such as going to parties to ensure long-term success. The decision to stay in school requires the evaluation of the eventual rewards of graduation and the ability to delay gratification. Does the value of a reward offset the amount of effort required to obtain it? The ACC plays an important role in these types of cost-benefit decisions (Kennerley, 2012; Rushworth, 2008; Rushworth, Behrens, Rudebeck, & Walton, 2007). Rats in a T-maze typically will choose a larger reward over a smaller one, even when they must climb over a barrier to obtain the larger reward (Salamone, Cousins, & Bucher, 1994) but will fail to do so following lesions of the ACC. Is the reward likely to be immediate or delayed? Lesions of the OFC reverse the rats' normal preference for larger, delayed rewards over smaller, immediate rewards (Rudebeck, Walton, Smyth, Bannerman, & Rushworth, 2006).

Humans with damage to these cortical systems involved in evaluating reward can make remarkably poor decisions, showing very little regard for the likely consequences of their behaviors (Gläscher et al., 2012). Patient EVR experienced damage to his OFC during surgery for a tumor. Although he was previously considered a role model in his community, EVR's decision-making skills changed radically following his surgery. He lost his job, went bankrupt, divorced his wife, and married a prostitute (Eslinger & Damasio, 1985). It is not so much the loss of the functions of a given area that causes behavioral problems, but rather the failure of these executive systems to hold other more primitive reward systems in check.

Aggression and Violence

Aggressive behavior continues to plague the human species. We will use the term **aggression** to refer to the intentional initiation of hostile or destructive acts toward another individual. Predatory (cold) aggression is premeditated, or planned in advance, goal-directed, and relatively unemotional. In contrast, impulsive (hot) aggression occurs immediately in response to some provocative stimulus that produces anger or fear (Siever, 2008). Different patterns of brain activity appear to be involved in these two types of aggression (Mobbs, Lau, Jones, & Frith, 2007).

While recognizing the significant contributions of learning, culture, and other environmental influences to aggression, we can identify many biological correlates of violent aggressive behavior. Violent behavior will occur when subcortical structures, in particular the amygdala, respond strongly to provocative stimuli without sufficient inhibition from the prefrontal cortex and the anterior cingulate cortex (ACC; Siever, 2008). In other words, aggressive behavior will not occur as long as aggressive "drives" originating in subcortical areas experience top-down control by frontal cortical areas. When this top-down inhibition is insufficient, violence will result.

aggression The intentional initiation of a hostile or destructive act.

Genetics, Environment, Epigenetics, and Aggression

To what extent is human aggression rooted in our genetic heritage? Within-species aggression might have been incorporated into our genetic heritage as individuals competed with one another for food, territory, and mates. If more aggressive individuals survived, their offspring would inherit these aggressive tendencies. Most within-species aggression is confined to the establishment of dominance, and it is unusual for one animal to kill another. Typically, the "loser" need only withdraw to end the aggressive engagement. The only species in which groups of males systematically hunt and kill members of their own species are chimpanzees and humans (Wrangham & Peterson, 1996; Wright, 1994). Approximately 1,000 people a day are killed in local wars around the world (Miller, 2003). Be reassured that we have made some progress. In ancient societies, as many as one-quarter of all adult men were killed in warfare (LeBlanc, 2003). Even with the 50 million people killed in World War II alone, modern humans have not approached that 25 percent mark.

Aggression is certainly a trait that can be selectively bred in animals, as evidenced by the breeding of fighting bulls in Spain. Mice (Lagerspetz & Lagerspetz, 1983) and fruit flies (Diereck & Greenspan, 2006) can also be bred selectively for aggressiveness, allowing researchers to begin identifying particular genes that might be involved. Human twin studies indicate significant genetic influences on aggressiveness (Rushton, Fulker, Neale, Nias, & Eysenck, 1986). The heritability of impulsive aggression is particularly high, between 44 and 72 percent (Coccaro, Bergeman, Kavoussi, & Seroczynski, 1997; Seroczynski, Bergeman, & Coccaro, 1999).

It would be a considerable overstatement to suggest that we have "genes for" aggression, as any genetic predispositions interact in complex ways with a variety of environmental influences. Different alleles for the enzyme monoamine oxidase A (MAOA) interact with the presence or absence of child maltreatment to predict antisocial behavior in boys (Caspi et al., 2002). These findings were supported in a more recent 30-year longitudinal study (Fergusson, Boden, Horwood, Miller, & Kennedy, 2011). Boys with a low-activity version of the MAOA gene were unlikely to engage in antisocial behavior in the absence of child abuse and neglect, but extremely likely to engage in antisocial behavior when exposed to severe maltreatment.

Another way to illustrate the interactions between any natural predispositions toward violence and the social environment is to explore cross-cultural data on homicide rates. Although the average homicide rate worldwide (excluding wars) is 10 per 100,000 people, individual nations can show remarkably different homicide rates. As shown in Table 14.1, South Africa has a homicide rate of 59.9 per 100,000 while

TABLE 14.1 | Homicide rates in selected cities

Country	Homicides per 100,000 residents	Percent of victims killed by intimate partner or family member	Percent of victims killed during robbery
Australia	1.1	76% of women 27% of men	3%
Finland	2.0	74% of women 19% of men	1.8%
Singapore	0.2	33% of women 0% of men	6.3%
South Africa	59.9	n/a	n/a
United States	5.1	52% of women 10% of men	5%

Singapore has a homicide rate of 0.2 per 100,000 (United Nations Office on Drugs and Crime [UNODC], 2014). Even within the same country, wide variations occur, as shown by the fact that the homicide rate in Washington, D. C. is five times higher than the rate in New York City. Cross-cultural comparisons suggest different motives for homicide as well. In Australia, 76 percent of murdered women are killed by intimate partners or family members, whereas 33 percent of murdered women in Singapore are murdered by someone they know. Across all cultures, women are more likely than men to be killed by intimate partners or family members than they are by strangers, gangs, or robbers (United Nations Office on Drugs and Crime [UNODC], 2014).

These variations across cultures are likely caused by a host of variables, but sophisticated statistical analyses of 60 years of World Health Organization data have pointed to the breakdown of social institutions, and the rising divorce rate in particular, as being a key factor in predicting a country's homicide rates (Messner, Pearson-Nelson, Raffalovich, & Miner, 2011). All countries worldwide experienced a doubling of homicide rates following World War II, although their peak rates were reached at different times consistent with the timing of loosening legal restrictions on divorce. All countries then experienced some reduction in rates, possibly due to aging populations and the implementation of programs aimed at reducing crime, such as increased police visibility. These complex trends remind us that understanding our human propensity for violence is only a starting point.

Brain Structures and Aggression

Aggression is correlated with patterns of activity in several brain structures, including the hypothalamus, the amygdala, the anterior cingulate cortex, and the prefrontal cortex.

Early physiologists discovered that removal of the cerebral cortices produced violent rage on the part of previously docile cats and dogs. Because the animals' violence was provoked by ordinary circumstances, such as a pat on the head, it was referred to as **sham rage**. Further research suggested that the role of the cortices, in this case, was to inhibit the action of the hypothalamus and other subcortical structures. When the hypothalamus in cats is electrically stimulated, many of the behaviors seen in cases of sham rage are duplicated (Hess, 1928). The cat will arch its back, spit, and hiss. Its ears will lie flat and its tail will puff out. When the stimulation stops, all rage also stops, and the cat often curls up and goes to sleep. John Flynn (1967) duplicated the rage attack of Hess's cats with stimulation to the medial hypothalamus. With electrodes implanted in the cats' lateral hypothalamus, however, Flynn was able to elicit hunting behavior. Flynn's cats would attack and kill rats in their cages when the lateral hypothalamus was stimulated. Although such studies are ethically improbable in humans, abnormalities of hypothalamic function have been observed in antisocial, violent people (Raine et al., 2004).

Previously in this chapter, we observed the role of the amygdala in processing fear. It appears that the amygdala, primarily through its connections with the hypothalamus, plays a role in aggression as well. If the amygdala processes a situation as fearful and threatening, a person might respond aggressively. After all, the fight-or-flight response to the perception of a threat does include the fighting option. Many instances of impulsive aggression appear to be defensive, and unusually violent people might be more likely to perceive threat in situations when others do not, causing them to overreact (Siever, 2008). Men with reduced amygdala volume had a history of aggression and psychopathic traits in childhood and were found to engage in more violence at a three-year follow up point (Pardini, Raine, Erickson, & Loeber, 2014). Karl Pribram and his colleagues (Rosvold, Mirsky, & Pribram, 1954) observed a reduction in aggression when the amygdalas of male rhesus monkeys were removed. In a very small number of human patients, lesions of the amygdala reduced violence associated with temporal lobe seizures (Mark & Ervin, 1970).

Together, the anterior cingulate cortex and the orbitofrontal cortex inhibit aggressive behavior (Siever, 2008). As we observed previously, these areas participate in decision making by evaluating the anticipated consequences, both positive and negative, of

sham rage A violent reaction to normally innocuous stimuli following removal of the cerebral cortices.

••• THINKING *Ethically*

BRAIN DAMAGE AND THE CRIMINAL JUSTICE SYSTEM

The insanity defense, or finding a person "not guilty by reason of insanity," implies that some people have more control over their behavior than others. Understanding the role of biology in violent criminal behavior matters because decisions about a person's responsibility for his or her actions directly influence outcomes of incarceration or treatment. In particular, our approach to juvenile crime is likely to be affected by brain research. Parts of the brain responsible for our most sophisticated decision making are not mature until a person's mid-20s (Mobbs et al., 2007).

In 2005, these issues came very close to home in my little community of San Luis Obispo, California (population 45,000). Eighty-seven-year-old Jerry O'Malley was brutally murdered by a 13-year-old who bludgeoned O'Malley's head with his skateboard, carefully locked up his mobile home to cover up the crime, and stole his car for a joyride (Gumbel, 2005). During the boy's trial, Joseph Wu, director of the Brain Imaging Center at the University of California, Irvine, testified that the young murderer had "abnormally reduced activity in parts of his brain that govern a person's judgment" (Sneed, 2006, p. B1). The murderer told the police,

"I knew it was wrong; I just did it," but this statement was excluded for consideration by the judge (Griffy, 2006, p. B1).

How do we deal with such cases? How should we consider the findings of "abnormally reduced activity in parts of the brain that govern a person's judgment?" Is this a matter of incarceration to prevent further harm by this person or a case requiring treatment for a medical condition?

Although a greater understanding of brain correlates and violent behavior should be useful in understanding criminal behavior, we are reminded that not all criminals show evidence of brain damage, and not everyone with brain damage engages in criminal behavior (Mobbs et al., 2007). If you're wondering what became of our 13-year-old murderer, he was sentenced to a state juvenile corrections facility, from which he will automatically be freed at age 25 (Parrilla, 2006). In April of 2014, a three-member state panel voted unanimously to release the murderer, now aged 22, but the district attorney of San Luis Obispo successfully argued that he not be released just yet (Pemberton, 2014).

behaviors. Emerging evidence suggests that antisocial behavior leading to violence is associated with abnormalities in the orbitofrontal cortex (see Chapter 16). Individuals with damage to the orbitofrontal cortex were more likely to use physical intimidation and verbal threats in confrontations (Grafman et al., 1996). However, once again we see the importance of distinguishing between impulsive and premeditated, predatory aggression. Impulsive murderers show reduced frontal activation, whereas premeditating murderers do not (Raine et al., 1998).

Biochemistry and Aggression

Drug use, particularly alcohol use, is strongly associated with human aggression. Prison studies and police reports show that alcohol use is involved in 39–45 percent of murders, 32–40 percent of sexual assaults, 63 percent of intimate partner abuse, and 45–46 percent of physical assaults (Giancola, 2013). Alcohol is also associated with the majority of suicides. Alcohol contributes to violence by reducing the inhibition of aggression normally managed by the cingulate and frontal cortices. Unfortunately, the same genotypes we discussed earlier that are associated with violence in the presence of child maltreatment also increase the risk of alcohol dependence (Heinz, Beck, Meyer-Lindenberg, Sterzer, & Heinz, 2011).

Testosterone might influence aggression by increasing reactivity to threatening stimuli. Women who were given testosterone showed stronger subcortical reactions to images of angry faces (Hermans, Ramsey, & van Honk, 2008). Once again, if subcortical reactions are strong enough to overwhelm cortical inhibition, aggression is the likely outcome. Animal research has shown strong correlations between testosterone

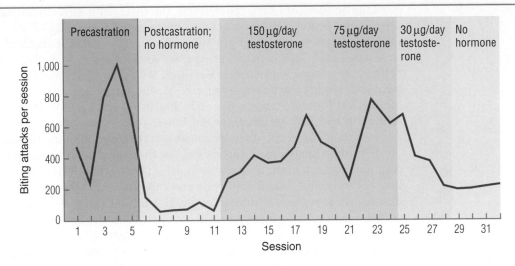

● **Figure 14.18** Testosterone Influences Biting Attacks by Mice Male mice demonstrate a significant drop in the number of biting attacks following castration. Administration of testosterone to castrated males reestablished biting behavior close to precastration levels.

Source: Adapted from Wagner, Beuving, & Hutchinson (1980).

levels and aggressive behavior. As shown in ● Figure 14.18, castration of mice reduced the incidence of biting attacks to nearly zero. However, administering testosterone to the castrated mice quickly reestablished normal male levels of biting behavior (Wagner, Beuving, & Hutchinson, 1980).

Prenatal exposure to testosterone is correlated with higher aggressiveness in humans. Reinisch, Ziemba-Davis, and Sanders (1991) observed children whose mothers had been given testosterone in an effort to prevent miscarriage. As shown in ● Figure 14.19, both boys and girls exposed prenatally to extra testosterone showed higher average physical aggression scores than their unexposed siblings of the same sex. As we discussed in Chapter 10, the ratio between a person's index and ring fingers (2D:4D) reflects prenatal androgen exposure. Men with greater 2D:4D ratios, indicating higher prenatal androgen exposure, were more likely to be physically aggressive (Bailey & Hurd, 2005). Another marker of prenatal testosterone exposure, the ratio of facial width to height, has also been suggested as a predictor of aggressiveness (Carré, McCormick, & Mondloch, 2009).

Levels of adult testosterone are not particularly well correlated with human aggression. However, Dabbs and Morris (1990) reported that testosterone levels that are on the high end of the typical range in teen and adult males were positively correlated with delinquency, drug abuse, and aggression. When levels are unusually high, due to factors such as the use of anabolic steroids, more aggression can be the result. Yates, Perry, and Murray (1992) reported that male weightlifters who used steroids were more hostile and aggressive than weightlifters who did not use steroids. Because these are correlational data, we don't know if steroid use causes greater aggression in this case or if aggressive athletes are more likely to choose to use steroids.

Higher testosterone levels among aggressive males might be the result of living in highly competitive, threatening environments rather than serving as the root cause of aggressive behavior. As we observed in Chapter 10, testosterone levels respond to competition. Athletes playing in front of the home crowd against bitter rivals showed the greatest increases in testosterone, leading to the suggestion that territoriality might influence testosterone levels in human males (Wolfson & Neave, 2002).

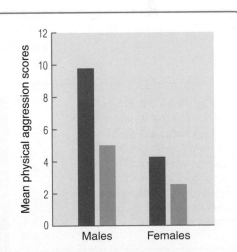

● **Figure 14.19** Prenatal Testosterone Contributes to Aggression Males and females exposed prenatally to high levels of testosterone exhibited higher levels of physical aggression than their unexposed same-sex siblings.

Source: Adapted from Reinisch, Ziemba-Davis & Sanders (1991).

Like testosterone, serotonin levels fluctuate with life circumstances and can predict aggression. Serotonin activity impacts the processing of aversive stimuli by the limbic system (Heinz et al., 2011). Decreased serotonin levels in the amygdala were associated with increases in aggressive behavior in male rats (Toot, Dunphry, & Ely, 2001). Raleigh, Brammer, McGuire, Pollack, and Yuwiler (1992) measured the serotonin levels of male rhesus monkeys, who form very precise social hierarchies. Monkeys at the bottom of the hierarchy had the lowest serotonin levels, whereas those at the top had high serotonin levels. Lower-ranking rhesus monkeys attempting to increase their status initiate more aggression than dominant monkeys.

Serotonin facilitates the activity of the prefrontal cortical regions, including the cingulate cortex and the orbitofrontal cortex (Heinz et al., 2011). Consequently, higher levels of serotonin should predict greater inhibition of the aggressive drive produced in subcortical regions. Serotonin might also inhibit violence against others by influencing empathy. Imagining harmful acts against others is correlated with activity in serotonin-rich areas of the brain (Siegel & Crockett, 2013). Atypical serotonin function has been implicated in the development of psychopathic traits, particularly callous-unemotional traits, in youth (Blair, 2013).

Individuals with histories of violent suicide attempts or impulsive violence show evidence of decreased serotonin activity (Siever, 2008). As we will see in Chapter 16, low serotonin levels in humans are also associated with feelings of depression, often described as aggression toward the self. Why low serotonin might promote aggression toward others in some cases, toward the self in other cases, and toward both the self and others, as in murder–suicides, remains unclear.

Stress

Stress is defined as an unpleasant and disruptive state resulting from the perception of danger or threat. The term **stressor** is often used to identify a source of stress. The critical term in our definition is *perception*. The experience of stress is highly variable from one person to the next. The source of one person's phobia can be another person's beloved, albeit slithery, pet. What matters is that an individual perceives him- or herself to be in some kind of dangerous or threatening situation (see ● Figure 14.20). Regardless of the nature of a stressor, once danger has been perceived and identified, a predictable series of reactions is set into motion.

● **Figure 14.20** Stress Is in the Eye of the Beholder The same experience, such as riding a roller coaster, can provoke very different responses in individuals. Some might find the experience very stressful, while others find it rewarding.

Paul A. Souders/CORBIS

stress An unpleasant and disruptive state resulting from the perception of danger or threat.
stressor A source of stress.

While you probably think of stress as a bad thing, it has its positive outcomes as well. Short-term stress, like the exercise we do at the gym, produces significant benefits. However, long-term, chronic stress can definitely take a toll on our performance and well-being. In a later chapter on psychological disorders, we will see how a diathesis-stress model explains the role of stress in the development of depression, schizophrenia, post-traumatic stress disorder, and other serious conditions.

Hans Selye and the General Adaptation Syndrome (GAS)

Modern research into stress began with observations by Walter Cannon (1929). Cannon was able to demonstrate that a variety of stressors, including extreme cold, lack of oxygen, and emotional experiences, have the capability of stimulating the sympathetic division of the autonomic nervous system (see Chapter 2). In response, the body prepares for what Cannon termed "fight or flight." Heart rate, blood pressure, and respiration all increase. Functions that are not essential during emergencies, such as digesting food, are inhibited. Stored energy is released, and blood vessels at the surface of the skin contract to drive blood from the surface (preventing excessive bleeding due to injury) and toward the skeletal muscles (preparing for exertion).

Hans Selye extended Cannon's findings during a career that spanned 40 years (1936–1976). Selye investigated the effects of various stressors on the amount of time rats were able to swim in a tank until they gave up, when they were rescued. Selye's stressors included cold water, cutting off the rats' whiskers, restraint, electric shock, and surgery. Regardless of the stressor used, Selye (1946) observed a consistent reaction, which he labeled the **General Adaptation Syndrome (GAS)**.

The GAS consisted of three stages, diagrammed in Figure 14.20. When the stressor is first perceived and identified, an **alarm reaction** is initiated. This is the same state that Cannon described as the fight-or-flight response. If you have had a close call on the highway, you know how this feels. Your heart beats rapidly, you're breathing quickly, your palms are sweaty, and you are highly alert. So far, the system is working well because this is the type of emergency the system was designed to manage.

If the stressful situation continues past this initial alarm stage, we enter into the **resistance stage**. This stage is less physiologically dramatic than the alarm reaction, but our bodies expend considerable energy coping with stress while also attempting to maintain our normal activities. During this stage, judgment and resistance to disease can deteriorate. If stress continues further, we enter the final **exhaustion stage**, in which strength and energy are at very low levels.

Exhaustion can lead to disorders such as depression (see Chapter 16). In rare cases, such as the stress of forced marches in time of war, exhaustion can lead to death. In 1942, Walter Cannon described the case of a young, apparently healthy African woman who apparently died of stress after learning that a fruit she had just eaten was spiritually forbidden. Cannon (1942/1957) referred to the case as a "voodoo" death. Robert Sapolsky (2001) studied the effects of chronic stress on baboons in Kenya. Normally, low-status male baboons avoid interacting with high-status males. One year, in response to fears about losing crops to the baboons, the local farmers caged many of the animals. While caged, the low-status males were unable to escape the high-status males, and many low-status males died as a result. They did not die, as you may have guessed, due to wounds from battle. Instead, they died from stress-related conditions such as ulcers and cardiovascular disease.

Responses to Stress

To manage emergencies successfully, physical, cognitive, and behavioral responses must be coordinated. Assume, for the sake of example, that a human ancestor is facing a hungry lion. The sympathetic division of the autonomic nervous system is preparing our ancestor either to escape or to fight. In a parallel process,

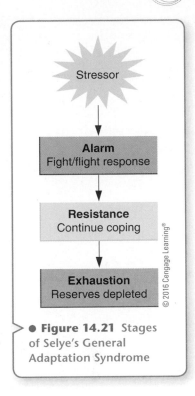

● **Figure 14.21** Stages of Selye's General Adaptation Syndrome

General Adaptation Syndrome (GAS) A three-stage model for describing the body's response to stress; developed by Hans Selye.

alarm reaction The first stage of Selye's General Adaptation Syndrome, characterized by activation of the sympathetic nervous system and mental alertness.

resistance stage The second stage in Selye's General Adaptation Syndrome, characterized by the person's efforts to maintain normal activities while coping with stress.

exhaustion stage The final stage of Selye's General Adaptation Syndrome, characterized by extremely low reserves of strength and energy.

the cognitive system becomes highly aroused and vigilant as the hypothalamus instructs the adrenal glands, via the pituitary gland, to release the hormone cortisol. Behaviorally, we would expect that our ancestor would try to escape the stressor rather than fight.

STRESS AND THE AMYGDALA We can trace the pathways that mediate these physical, cognitive, and behavioral responses. At the outset, the sensory systems detect the threatening stimulus (the lion). Connections with higher cortical processing centers identify the object as a lion and access memories of lion behaviors (including their eating habits). At the same time, sensory information travels from the thalamus to the amygdala.

The amygdala participates in a "threat circuit" that provides a very rapid assessment of a stimulus or situation as potentially dangerous (LeDoux, 2000, 2014). As we mentioned earlier in this chapter, if the amygdala is lesioned, animals no longer respond with conditioned fear to a stimulus (perhaps a tone or light) that had previously served as a conditioned stimulus predicting the arrival of electric shock. Animals with lesions in the amygdala are also unable to learn to respond appropriately to unfamiliar, dangerous stimuli (Wilensky, Schafe, Kristensen, & LeDoux, 2006).

Because sensory information travels separate pathways from the thalamus to the amygdala and from the thalamus to the cortex, you might find yourself frightened by stimuli that are not consciously viewed as dangerous (Knight, Nguyen, & Bandettini, 2003). You might feel anxious as you return to your parked car after an evening class without really knowing why you feel this way. In an interesting demonstration of the amygdala's ability to stimulate fear without full consciousness and understanding of a stimulus, a patient who is blind due to occipital lobe damage still demonstrates normal activation of the amygdala when he is shown faces expressing fear (Morris, DeGelder, Weiskrantz, & Dolan, 2001). The patient couldn't tell you whether he was viewing a face, a building, or a landscape, but his amygdala still knows that there is a source of danger in the environment.

STRESS, SAM, AND THE HPA AXIS Once a potential source of danger has been perceived, the amygdala communicates with the hypothalamus. The hypothalamus in turn mobilizes the body's resources for coping with the emergency by initiating activity in two systems—the sympathetic adrenal-medullary (SAM) system and the hypothalamic-pituitary-adrenal (HPA) axis, as illustrated in ● Figure 14.22.

Activation of the SAM system begins with messages from the hypothalamus, which controls the activity of the sympathetic division of the autonomic nervous system. Sympathetic activity leads to the release of adrenaline (also known as epinephrine) and norepinephrine from the adrenal glands (located above your kidneys in the lower back) into the bloodstream. These neurochemicals circulate to the brain and to other organs to produce many of the immediate, short-lived, fight-flight responses to stress, such as a pounding heart or rapid breathing.

Activation of the HPA axis begins when incoming messages from the amygdala reach the paraventricular nucleus (PVN) of the hypothalamus, which in turn makes connections with the locus coeruleus, the spinal cord, and the pituitary gland (Tausk, Elenkov, & Moynihan, 2008). The PVN releases **corticotrophin-releasing hormone (CRH)** and vasopressin (ADH, see Chapter 9), which act as chemical messengers between the hypothalamus and the anterior pituitary gland. In response to CRH and vasopressin, the pituitary gland releases another hormone, **adrenocorticotropic hormone**, or **ACTH**. ACTH diffused from the pituitary into the bloodstream will eventually reach the adrenal glands, where it stimulates the release of the glucocorticoid cortisol. CRH and ACTH are released in pulses, each of which accounts for approximately a 15-minute period of cortisol release. Cortisol remains in the bloodstream for about three hours before breaking down.

The amygdala is not the only structure regulating the HPA axis. The hippocampus is also involved in this process. Whereas the amygdala stimulates the release of

corticotrophin-releasing hormone (CRH) A hormone released by the hypothalamus that signals the release of ACTH by the anterior pituitary gland.
adrenocorticotropic hormone or **ACTH** A pituitary hormone that stimulates release of cortisol from the adrenal glands.

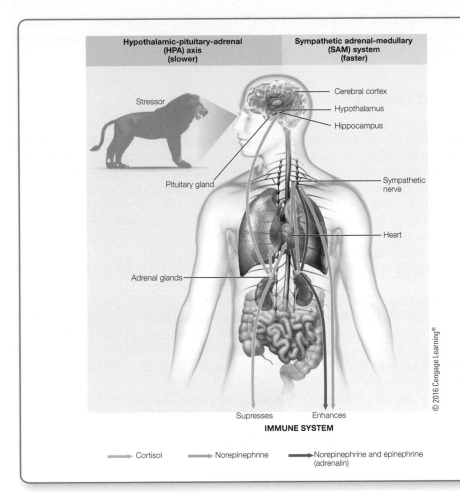

| Hypothalamic-pituitary-adrenal (HPA) axis (slower) | Sympathetic adrenal-medullary (SAM) system (faster) |

Stressor

Cerebral cortex

Hypothalamus

Hippocampus

Pituitary gland

Sympathetic nerve

Heart

Adrenal glands

Supresses   Enhances

IMMUNE SYSTEM

→ Cortisol   → Norepinephrine   → Norepinephrine and epinephrine (adrenalin)

© 2016 Cengage Learning®

● **Figure 14.22** Two Systems Respond to Stress The sympathetic adrenal-medullary (SAM) system responds very quickly to a stressor by releasing epinephrine (adrenalin) and norepinephrine from the adrenal glands into the circulation. The hypothalamic-pituitary-adrenal (HPA) axis results in the release of cortisol by the adrenal glands.

CRH by the hypothalamus, the hippocampus acts to inhibit CRH release. The hippocampus contains receptors for glucocorticoids, including cortisol. The hippocampus, therefore, acts as part of a feedback loop (Stokes, 1995). If cortisol levels reaching the hippocampus are too high, CRH release by the hypothalamus will be reduced, leading to less release of ACTH and cortisol.

Circulating cortisol boosts the energy available for dealing with a stressor. As we observed in Chapter 11, cortisol is also released in a circadian pattern, with highest levels associated with morning waking, reinforcing the idea that cortisol is associated with high levels of alertness. When cortisol reaches the brain via the bloodstream, it has the ability to bind with many types of neurons. Cortisol increases the amount of calcium entering neurons (Kerr, Campbell, Thibault, & Langfield, 1992), leading to an increase in the amount of neurochemical released by each affected neuron (see Chapter 3). This should produce the arousal and vigilance needed by our friend facing the hungry lion. Unfortunately, too much calcium can be toxic to neurons. When rats were given daily injections of the rat cortisol equivalent, corticosterone, dendrites on neurons with corticosterone receptors began to retract, and the neurons themselves began to die within a few weeks (Stein-Behrens, Mattson, Chang, Yeh, & Sapolsky, 1994). If the rats were stressed daily in lieu of receiving the injections, the same results occurred. Sapolsky's stressed baboons, mentioned earlier, experienced neural death particularly in the hippocampus. Cushing's disease, which results in unusually high cortisol levels, is associated with reduced hippocampal volume, memory problems, abnormal sleep patterns, and depression (Langenecker et al., 2012). Some patients diagnosed with posttraumatic stress disorder (see Chapter 16) have also been found to have a smaller-than-average hippocampus. Perhaps consistently high levels of cortisol overwhelm the hippocampal feedback loop that would normally lower cortisol levels. This would make individuals even more vulnerable to the negative outcomes of chronic stress.

Stress and Epigenetics

Psychologists have long believed that the care and nurture of children early in life had long-lasting results. Early researchers noticed that if infant rats were handled by humans, the rat mothers engaged in more licking and grooming (the rat equivalent of a hug) when the pups were returned to them. This maternal care was associated with the pups' showing stronger resistance to stress well into adulthood (Denenberg, 1964; Levine, 1970). Further investigations showed that the early grooming experience by the mothers changed the behavior of the pups' HPA axis. The pups showed a milder HPA axis response to stressors and their feedback loops controlling the action of cortisol were more sensitive (Liu et al., 1997).

Rat mothers can be placed in two categories: attentive (high levels of licking and grooming) and inattentive (low levels of licking and grooming). Michael Meaney and his colleagues (Francis, Diorio, Liu, & Meaney, 1999; Meaney, 2010) conducted a series of foster mother experiments in which they removed some of the pups soon after birth and placed them with mothers having the same or different attentiveness as their biological mothers. As shown in ● Figure 14.23, they discovered that the attentiveness of the mother raising the pup had more influence on the pups' later resilience to stress than the attentiveness of the biological mother.

Maternal care has an epigenetic effect on gene expression in the pups' hippocampus. Specifically, attentive mothers had offspring with high levels of expression of the gene for glucocorticoid receptors. Recall that cortisol is a type of glucocorticoid. Increased expression of glucocorticoid receptors is associated with lower hormonal and behavioral responses to stressors (Meaney, 2010).

● **Figure 14.23** Maternal Nurture Influences Pups' Resilience to Stress Infant rats raised by attentive mothers (high licking and grooming or Hi-LG) were more resilient to stress (time spent in the open) than rats raised by less attentive mothers (low licking and grooming or Low-LG), regardless of the attentiveness status of their biological mothers.

Exploration by Rat Pups Raised by High- and Low-Licking/Grooming Mothers. The amount of time a rat pup will stay out in the open is highly related to the type of nurture it received. All pups raised by an attentive mother (Hi-LG, or high licking and grooming) explored longer than pups raised by less attentive mothers (Low-LG, or low licking and grooming), regardless of the nurture style used by their biological mother. *Source:* Adapted from Francis, Diorio, Liu, and Meaney (1999).

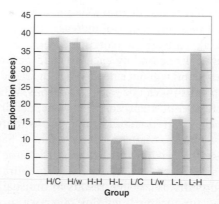

H/C = "High Control"; pups left undisturbed with their own Hi-LG mothers

H/w = "High Cross-fostered"; pups removed and put back with their own Hi-LG mothers

H-H = "High-High"; pups with Hi-LG mother fostered by Hi-LG mother

H-L = "High-Low"; pups with Hi-LG mother fostered by Low-LG mother

L/C = "Low Control"; pups left undisturbed with their own Low-LG mothers

L/w = "Low Cross-fostered"; pups removed and put back with their own Low-LG mothers

L-L = "Low-Low"; pups with Low-LG mother fostered by a Low-LG mother

L-H = "Low-High"; pups with Low-LG mother fostered by a Hi-LG mother

Stephen Dalton/Science Source

What would be the adaptive advantage of a system where maternal care translates into responsiveness to stress? Like most epigenetic processes, the impact of maternal care on stress prepares the offspring for their immediate environment. While being responsive to stress is unpleasant, it might save your life in dangerous circumstances. If a young mother lives in a dangerous place, and her own stress makes her inattentive to her children, they will enter the environment prepared to be highly reactive to any threats. In contrast, a mother living in a safer environment has the luxury of providing high levels of care to her children. Because of her safe environment, her children are likely to remain safe even if they are less responsive to threat. The mothers' level of care helps to match their children's responses to the environments they're likely to experience.

Stress, the Immune System, and Health

Short-term bursts of stress can have beneficial effects on many biological systems, including the **immune system**, the body's frontline defense against infection and cancer (Dhabhar, 2009).

However, the immune system does not fare so well in the face of long-term, chronic sources of stress. When faced with chronic stress, our stress response system prioritizes body functions. Functions that are not necessary for handling the stressor are taken offline. Unfortunately for those suffering chronic stress, one of those expendable systems is the immune system (Thornton, Andersen, Crespin, & Carson, 2007). The immune system produces two types of white blood cells, or **lymphocytes**, that protect us from invaders. The B lymphocytes, produced in bone marrow, release antibodies that destroy foreign substances of a type that the body has previously encountered. Routine immunizations activate B lymphocytes by providing them the opportunity to form antibodies against a variety of disease-causing organisms. T lymphocytes, produced by the thymus gland, directly attack cancer cells and other foreign substances. In addition, the T lymphocytes interact with the B lymphocytes by either boosting or suppressing their activity.

The action of stress hormones such as cortisol directly suppresses the activity of lymphocytes (Panesar, 2008). As a result, stress can lead to greater frequency and severity of illnesses. People experiencing chronic stress are more vulnerable to infectious diseases, such as colds or the flu (Cohen, Tyrrell, & Smith, 1991). Flare-ups of oral and genital herpes are more likely to occur during periods of stress (Cohen & Herbert, 1996), as is mononucleosis (Cacioppo & Berntson, 2011). HIV infection progresses more rapidly to AIDS in stressed individuals (Harper, 2006). Unfortunately, knowledge of these relationships can place an even greater burden on sick people, who may blame themselves for failure to manage their stress appropriately.

Much has also been written about the relationship between stress and heart disease. In particular, men exhibiting the highly competitive, workaholic "type A" personality, as opposed to the more mellow and relaxed "type B," were originally believed to be at higher risk for heart disease due to stress (Friedman & Rosenman, 1959, 1974). However, John Macleod and his colleagues (2002) compared self-reported levels of stress in more than 5,000 men with measures of their medical conditions taken 20 years later. Hospital records of heart disease were lowest among the men who described their stress as being at the highest levels (see ● Figure 14.24). Upon further study, a competitive drive does not seem to predict heart problems, but a pattern of hostility found among some type A's

immune system The system used by the body to defend against bacteria, viruses, and other foreign substances.
lymphocyte A white blood cell; an important feature of the immune system.

Jason O. Watson/Alamy

> ● **Figure 14.24 Competitive People and Health** Contrary to popular myth, not all competitive people, like college football coach Charlie Strong, experience negative health consequences. People who are hostile and angry are more vulnerable to health problems, probably because they alienate their social networks, who could otherwise help buffer their stress.

is definitely related to cardiac health. People most at risk for heart disease are frequently suspicious, angry, and resentful of others (Smith, 1992; Nabi et al., 2008). Although the exact mechanism linking hostility to heart disease remains unknown, hostility, anger, and depression are associated with increased levels of immune system proteins that appear to contribute to heart disease (Boyle, Jackson, & Suarez, 2007). Hostility might also damage the social relationships that we need in times of stress. Chronic stressors related to social roles (e.g., death of a loved one or divorce) produce the greatest suppression of the immune system (Segerstrom & Miller, 2004).

Stress can produce adverse effects on health by interfering with the quantity and quality of sleep, indirectly affecting a person's mood and appetite. As discussed in Chapter 11, cortisol is released according to circadian rhythms. Normally, cortisol release is highest in the morning and tapers off through the day. Release of cortisol due to a stressor can interfere with sleep onset and good sleep quality (Van Cauter, Leproult, & Plat, 2000). Not only is poor sleep quality correlated with depressed mood, but also with risk for obesity. Dieters who sleep well or sleep poorly lose the same amount of weight, but there is a difference in the composition of the weight that is lost (Nedeltcheva, Kilkus, Imperial, Schoeller, & Penev, 2010). Sleep-deprived dieters lose only about half as much fat as dieters sleeping well, and three-quarters of their weight loss consisted of precious bone and muscle tissue instead of fat.

Stress in modern life is inevitable, but if we otherwise pay good attention to health habits like exercising, following a healthy diet, getting a good night's sleep, and maintaining strong, positive social networks, our chances of rebounding from particularly stressful episodes should be enhanced.

••• Behavioral Neuroscience GOES TO WORK

PET THERAPY FOR STRESS

As Karen Allen (2003) has discovered, having a pet can enhance resilience to stress. Some people are unable to care for a pet but can benefit from interacting with a trained therapy pet. In particular, therapy dogs visit schools, day-care facilities, special education classrooms, hospitals, hospice care facilities, and assisted-care facilities. Shy children in libraries might read out loud to a dog when they refuse to read to an adult. A dog can encourage movement in an older adult during physical rehabilitation. In recognition of the growing trend to use dogs as therapy animals, the American Kennel Club (AKC) formally designates dogs as AKC therapy dogs (American Kennel Club [AKC], 2014).

While most therapy dog work is done by dedicated volunteers, crisis management professionals are beginning to recognize the benefits of animal therapy (see ● Figure 14.25). The military has designated stress-management dog handlers who visit deployed troops. Therapy dogs were used after the Newtown school shooting and following devastating tornados. To help in these intensely stressful situations, both dog and handler must have both the right temperament and

● **Figure 14.25** **Pet Therapy** The 98th Medical Combat Stress Control Detachment of the U.S. Army includes two canine members—Butch and Zack. Interacting with animals can help reduce stress and hopefully prevent further stress-related problems for deployed soldiers and veterans.

Erik de Castro/Reuters

training. It is likely that these roles will continue to become more formal and professional in the future.

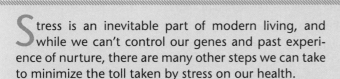

Building Better HEALTH

STRESS MANAGEMENT

Stress is an inevitable part of modern living, and while we can't control our genes and past experience of nurture, there are many other steps we can take to minimize the toll taken by stress on our health.

One critical variable in stress management is maintaining a sense of control. We can't wish cancer away, but we can control how we respond to a life-threatening disease by educating ourselves and participating actively in treatment decisions. Residents of nursing homes who make decisions about their daily routines and activities live longer than those who do not participate in decision making (Rodin, 1986).

Stress is intimately intertwined with our eating and sleeping habits. In response to stress hormones, fat cells grow more rapidly in both size and number (Kuo et al., 2009). High levels of cortisol interfere with sleep quality (Van Cauter et al., 2000). This should not come as a surprise, as we discussed the circadian fluctuations of cortisol in Chapter 11. We can't change the biology of these stress effects, but we can maintain the best eating and sleep habits possible. Stress depletes everyone's reserves, but if you have good health habits overall, your body can take more stress-related damage than someone who is already at a low level of reserves.

Regular aerobic exercise appears to be one of the best ways to not only promote health, but to buffer the negative impact of stress. Highly stressed heart patients who exercised as part of their rehabilitation program outlived those who did not (Milani & Lavie, 2009).

Finally, we are members of a very social species, and social networking has a highly beneficial effect on managing stress (Montpetit, Bergeman, Deboeck, Tiberio, & Boker, 2010). Highly stressed stockbrokers living alone who were being treated for high blood pressure were selected to choose a cat or dog from an animal shelter (Allen, 2003). When under stress, the pet owners experienced a reduced increase in blood pressure compared to people without pets.

One of the good pieces of news about stress is that we adapt to it. If you think about what stressed you in middle school, you might actually smile, as the stresses you face today probably seem much greater. This contrast demonstrates continued improvement in your stress management skills. By using the hints in this section, perhaps you can further improve your response to stress.

INTERIM SUMMARY 14.2

|| Summary Table: Structural and Biochemical Correlates of Increased and Decreased Aggression

	Increased Aggression	Decreased Aggression
Structural correlates	Removal of cerebral cortex	Damage to the amygdala
	Electrical stimulation of the hypothalamus	
	Damage to the orbitofrontal cortex	
Biochemical correlates	Alcohol use	
	High levels of testosterone	Low levels of testosterone (castrated males)
	Low levels of serotonin	

▌ Summary Points

1. Electrical self-stimulation (ESB) research suggests that some structures of the brain participate in a reward or pleasure circuit. **(LO4)**

2. Aggression is influenced by genetics, although aggressive behavior can be modified through culture and learning. **(LO5)**

3. The hypothalamus, amygdala, cingulate cortex, and orbitofrontal cortex are involved with aggression. **(LO5)**

4. Alcohol use, high testosterone levels, and low serotonin levels correlate with aggression. **(LO5)**

5. Selye described a three-stage General Adaptation Syndrome (GAS) that occurs in response to stress. The organism will experience alarm, resistance, and exhaustion as long as the source of stress continues to be present. **(LO6)**

6. Chronic stress suppresses immune system activity, leading to higher rates of illness. **(LO6)**

▌ Review Questions

1. What does the analysis of ESB tell us about the brain's processing of reward?

2. What are the effects of chronic stress on the immune system and on general health?

Chapter Review

THOUGHT QUESTIONS

1. Which of the theories of emotion presented in this chapter makes the most sense to you, and why?
2. If we discover that brain damage is responsible for most violent criminal acts, what changes, if any, would you propose in the criminal justice and prison systems?
3. Paul Ekman suggests that we aren't very good at detecting liars because "we often want to be misled, we collude in the lie unwittingly because we have a stake in not knowing the truth" (1996, p. 814). In what circumstances do you want to catch a liar? To what circumstances might Ekman be referring in this statement?
4. How might emotional expressiveness be different among those who do not localize language to the left hemisphere (see Chapter 13)?

KEY TERMS

aggression (p. 497)
alarm reaction (p. 503)
Cannon-Bard theory (p. 488)
catharsis (p. 487)
corticotrophin-releasing hormone (CRH) (p. 504)
electrical self-stimulation of the brain (ESB) (p. 495)
emotion (p. 478)

empathy (p. 486)
exhaustion stage (p. 503)
facial nucleus (p. 479)
General Adaptation Syndrome (GAS) (p. 503)
immune system (p. 507)
James-Lange theory (p. 485)
lymphocyte (p. 507)

medial forebrain bundle (MFB) (p. 496)
resistance stage (p. 503)
Schachter-Singer two-factor theory (p. 488)
somatic marker (p. 489)
stress (p. 502)
stressor (p. 502)
valence (p. 478)

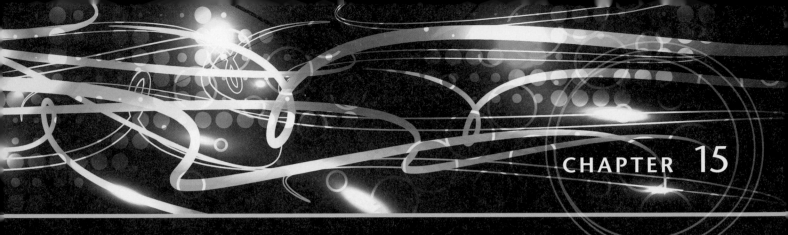

CHAPTER 15

Neuropsychology

LEARNING OBJECTIVES

LO1 Describe the responsibilities and assessment methods of the neuropsychologist.

LO2 Explain the major characteristics of Alzheimer's disease, vascular disease, traumatic brain injury, substance/medication-induced neurocognitive disorders, HIV-associated neurocognitive disorder, and prion diseases.

LO3 Describe the features of tumors, infections, epilepsy, multiple sclerosis, and migraine headaches.

LO4 Explain the basic principles that predict recovery from brain damage.

LO5 Describe the major methods used to treat neurocognitive disorders.

CHAPTER OUTLINE

BEHAVIORAL NEUROSCIENCE GOES TO WORK: Preparing to Be a Clinical Neuropsychologist

THINKING ETHICALLY: *APOE e⁴* in Younger Adults

BUILDING BETTER HEALTH: Recognizing the Signs of a Stroke

CONNECTING TO RESEARCH: Stanley Prusiner and the Prion

What Is Neuropsychology?

Neuropsychology is a specialty field within clinical psychology that seeks to understand and treat patients with cognitive impairments. Such impairments may be the result of factors such as aging, disease, or injury.

Who Are the Neuropsychologists?

Neuropsychology is carried out in the United States by licensed doctoral level clinical psychologists who complete specialized training as specified by the Houston Conference on Specialty Education and Training in Clinical Neuropsychology (1997). **Neuropsychologists** are expected to understand a broad range of relationships between the nervous system and behavior.

Neuropsychologists often work in collaboration with neurologists, who are medical doctors. The division of labor between these two professions can be described as follows: the neurologist assesses and treats the physical consequences of disease or injury, while the neuropsychologist assesses and treats the cognitive consequences of disease or injury. If a soldier experiences a concussion as the result of being near an explosion, the neurologist would address the physical challenges, such as potential bleeding and swelling in the brain. The neuropsychologist might work with the soldier to assess and provide rehabilitation for changes in attention span and short-term memory.

Neuropsychological Assessment

Similar to any psychological assessment, such as those involving personality or psychological disorders, neuropsychological assessments use standardized instruments to evaluate underlying behavior. The careful assessment of a patient's cognitive and behavioral strengths and weaknesses can lead to the development of an informed treatment plan.

The choice of standardized test, of course, will depend on the goals of the assessment and the condition of the patient (Lezak, 2004). In some cases, tests that compare an individual's score to the normal scores of a population are appropriate (see ● Figure 15.1). For example, a child who is having unusual difficulty learning to read might have either an intellectual disability or dyslexia, and a standardized IQ test would help the clinician make this distinction. In other cases, a standardized test will

●●● **Behavioral Neuroscience GOES TO WORK**

PREPARING TO BE A CLINICAL NEUROPSYCHOLOGIST

The training of a clinical neuropsychologist begins with a PhD or PsyD degree in clinical psychology and licensure to practice given by the appropriate government entity, usually at the state level in the United States.

Either during or after the doctoral studies are completed, the neuropsychologist must obtain a foundation in the neurosciences, including neurology, neuroanatomy, and neurophysiology. Following the awarding of the doctoral degree, the neuropsychologist completes a minimum of two years of supervised training in neuropsychology. It is conventional to specialize in either

child (pediatric) or adult neuropsychology, and two to three years of additional experience in this specialty area is expected prior to becoming eligible for the examinations leading to board certification as a clinical neuropsychologist (American Board of Professional Psychology [ABPP], n.d.).

This might sound like a very long road to take. However, if this is a field about which you can be passionate, the time spent on this journey will be more than offset by the satisfaction of helping people with neurocognitive disorders.

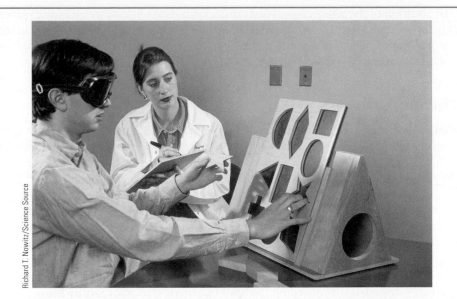

Richard T. Nowitz/Science Source

● **Figure 15.1**
Neuropsychological Testing
Standardized tests are an important part of a neuropsychological assessment.

be used to determine how an individual has been affected by an illness or injury. To accomplish this goal, performance on tests measuring abilities relevant to the injury or illness can be compared to performance on abilities believed to be unaffected by the injury or illness (Clare, 2011). For example, if we know that a patient's recent stroke affected his or her Broca's area, we would expect to see worse scores on tests of language production than on tests of visual perception.

In some cases, the neuropsychologist will select specific tests relevant to a particular individual's situation. In other cases, the neuropsychologist will administer comprehensive batteries of tests, such as the Halstead-Reitan battery, which includes tests of intellect, sensation, motor function, attention, and psychological disorder. The comprehensive batteries offer a good level of reliability, but they can take as much as a full day to administer, which might exceed the capabilities of badly injured patients. Computerized testing often produces more valid results than paper-and-pencil tests, particularly in the measurement of reaction time items (Graham et al., 2014). An obvious challenge to obtaining valid test results is the likelihood that the very condition for which the individual is being tested can impact his or her test performance (Graham, Rivara, Ford, & Spicer, 2014). Factors such as pain, fatigue, depression, test anxiety, medications, and motivation can easily distort results on standardized tests, such as IQ tests.

Neurocognitive Disorders

Despite the significant protection that the skull bones, the cerebrospinal fluid, and the blood–brain barrier provide to the brain, damage can occur due to interruptions in the brain's blood supply and from blows to the head. The abnormal electrical activity of seizures can also interrupt normal brain functioning. Like other parts of the body, the brain is also subject to tumor growth, infection, autoimmune disorders, and other challenges.

Most of these neurological conditions have important cognitive consequences, ranging from mild to major (American Psychiatric Association [APA], 2013). **Neurocognitive disorder** is diagnosed when a patient experiences a decline in functioning in one or more cognitive domains, such as attention, executive function, learning and memory, perception and movement, or social cognition as a result of a known challenge to the central nervous system. Major neurocognitive disorder is distinguished from minor neurocognitive disorder on the basis of whether the disorder interferes with independent living (APA, 2013).

neurocognitive disorder
A disorder characterized by a decline in function in cognition following a known challenge to the nervous system.

In addition to the neurocognitive disorders discussed below, we already explored Parkinson's disease and Huntington's disease in Chapter 8. To organize our further study of the wide variety of conditions that can cause neurocognitive disorder, we will follow the outline of the DSM-5 (APA, 2013).

Alzheimer's Disease

Alzheimer's disease is one of a number of degenerative conditions associated with aging that results in **dementia**, or the loss of normal cognitive and emotional function. Patients with Alzheimer's disease account for 60 to 90 percent of all patients with dementia (APA, 2013). Other forms of dementia include frontotemporal lobar degeneration and Lewy body disease. Frontotemporal lobar degeneration is characterized by a variety of symptoms, including disinhibition, apathy, lack of empathy, ritualistic behaviors, language difficulties, and dietary changes. Lewy body disease, named after the particular clumps of protein that form within neurons, can result in fluctuations of attention, visual hallucination, and Parkinson's disease-like motor disturbances (APA, 2013).

A definitive diagnosis of Alzheimer's disease requires an autopsy, but probable Alzheimer's disease is diagnosed on the basis of genetic testing or family history, clear evidence of learning and memory impairments, and a steady, gradual loss of cognitive function without plateaus (APA, 2013).

The risk of Alzheimer's disease typically increases with age, with rates of 5 to 10 percent in people between the ages of 60 and 74 years increasing to about 25 percent beyond the age of 74. For the majority of patients, the e^4 variant of the *APOE* gene, located on chromosome 19 and discussed in Chapter 5, is the most reliable genetic risk factor for Alzheimer's disease (Roses, 1997). The e^4 allele occurs in about 25 to 30 percent of the population, but is found in as many as 40 to 80 percent of individuals with Alzheimer's disease (Mahley, Weisgraber, & Huang, 2006). Individuals with one E^4 allele have three times the risk for developing Alzheimer's disease and those with two alleles experience 15 times the risk compared to those having other genotypes (Blennow, de Leon, & Zetterberg, 2006).

In a small percentage of patients, however, Alzheimer's disease is inherited as a dominant trait due to mutations in one of three genes: the genes for amyloid precursor protein (APP) on chromosome 21, presenilin 1 (PSEN1) on chromosome 14, or presenilin 2 (PSEN2) on chromosome 1 (Müller, Winter, & Graeber, 2013). Alois Alzheimer's first patient to develop the disease that now bears his name, a woman named Auguste Deter, has been found in recent evaluations of her preserved DNA to possess a PSEN1 mutation (Müller et al., 2013).

Behaviorally, Alzheimer's disease usually begins with mild memory loss. As the disease progresses, problem solving, language, and social behavior deteriorate. The patient begins to experience severe symptoms of hallucination and delusional thinking. Eventually, basic life skills begin to deteriorate, and the person needs careful supervision and care. Prior to death, many of these patients are unable to move or speak.

Alzheimer's disease is associated with atrophy of the cerebral cortex and a characteristic pattern of neural degeneration, shown in ●Figure 15.2. The emergence of abnormal structures known as **neurofibrillary tangles** is one of the hallmark features of the disease. Tangles result from the detachment of the tau protein, which normally holds structural microtubules in place (see Chapter 3). Without tau, the microtubules are not able to maintain their structure, and the neuron basically folds in on itself and collapses.

The disruption in tau might result from the action of another protein found in the neurons of patients with Alzheimer's disease called **beta amyloid**. Amyloids are misfolded proteins that form fibrous clumps. In Alzheimer's disease, beta amyloid contributes to the detachment of tau and the subsequent disruption of cell structure and function that we discussed in Chapter 3. In addition, beta amyloid collects in **plaques**, or abnormal patches, on axons of affected neurons and within blood vessels serving the brain. Individuals with Down syndrome, who have three copies of chromosome 21, frequently show this characteristic abnormality. Beta amyloid is formed from a larger molecule, the amyloid precursor protein (APP), which occurs in normally

Alzheimer's disease An age-related neurocognitive disorder resulting in gradual loss of cognitive function.

dementia A loss of normal cognitive and emotional function.

neurofibrillary tangles Abnormal structures resulting from the breakdown of microtubules in Alzheimer's disease.

beta amyloid The misfolded protein associated with Alzheimer's disease.

amyloid plaque Abnormal patches on cells formed by amyloid that disrupt normal function.

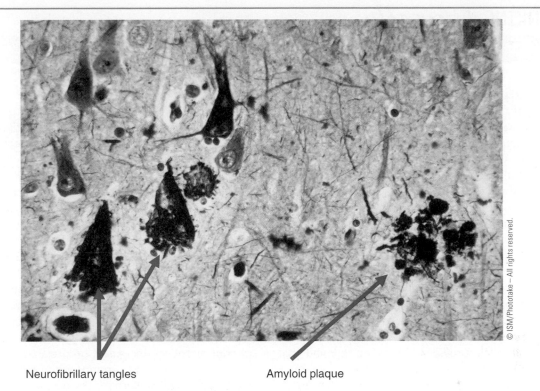

Neurofibrillary tangles   Amyloid plaque

> ● **Figure 15.2** **Alzheimer's Disease Produces Structural Abnormalities in Neurons** This image illustrates the abnormal structural effects of Alzheimer's disease on neurons. The cone-shaped elements are neurofibrillary tangles, and the brown clumps are amyloid plaques found in the brain of a patient who died from Alzheimer's disease.

functioning cells. Recall that the APP gene is located on chromosome 21. One function of the apolipoproteins (*APOE*) is to break down beta amyloid. *APOE4*, encoded by the e^4 allele associated with higher risk for Alzheimer's disease, does not perform this function as well as the other forms.

The damage to the brains of patients with Alzheimer's disease follows a characteristic pattern. As we observed in Chapter 5, death of a neuron can lead to deterioration among its postsynaptic connections through the process of transneuronal degeneration. This process spreads deterioration rapidly throughout the brain of the patient with Alzheimer's disease, leading to progressive loss of volume in both cortical and subcortical areas. To explain the impact of this damage, researchers have become more interested in the networks involved with Alzheimer's disease than in the correlations between individual structures and behavioral outcomes. Alzheimer's disease produces decreased strength in the connections of the default mode network (DMN), possibly leading to some of the observed deficits in the patients' episodic memory functions (Alexander-Bloch, Giedd, & Bullmore, 2013; Wang et al., 2013).

Currently, there are no treatments that reverse the course of Alzheimer's disease. At best, current medications slow the progression of the condition, but they do not reverse the damage already in place. Many institutionalized patients are treated with antipsychotic medications (see Chapter 16) to reduce aggressiveness and make them more manageable, but in a study of over 26,000 patients, this practice is associated with earlier death (Langballe et al., 2013).

Vascular Disease (Stroke)

The cells of the nervous system are unable to rely on stored supplies of oxygen, which is delivered to the brain by a rich network of blood vessels (see Chapter 2; see ● Figure 15.3). The circulation of blood to neural tissue can be interrupted by

••• THINKING *Ethically*

APOE E⁴ IN YOUNGER ADULTS

After reading this section, you might be wondering how your *APOE* genotype looks. Do you have one or two copies of the e^4 allele associated with Alzheimer's disease? Although the e^4 allele is considered a risk factor for late-onset Alzheimer's disease, identifying a person's genotype cannot reliably predict who will and who will not develop the disease. The *APOE* studies you're reading about involve large numbers of participants, and this does not provide much information about a single individual's risk. As a result, genetic testing for *APOE* is done for research purposes only.

You might also be wondering why an allele that puts people at risk for Alzheimer's disease (and for poor recovery outcomes following brain damage in general, as we'll see through the remainder of this chapter) would remain in the gene pool. What possible fitness could such an allele provide? First, keep in mind that Alzheimer's disease is not evident until most people are long past their reproductive years. As a result, Alzheimer's disease is unlikely to have any impact on a person's reproductive success. We observed a similar situation with Huntington's disease, discussed in Chapter 8. This disease strikes in midlife, often after people have produced children. As a result, short of testing embryos for the Huntington gene, there is no mechanism for removing the disease genes from the gene pool.

Many alleles, like the one that causes sickle cell anemia, have some good and bad contributions to make. If a person has one sickle cell allele and one healthy allele, he or she is more resistant to malaria without experiencing sickle cell anemia. It is only when a person has two sickle cell alleles that he or she experiences the disease. Is there possibly a similar offset for the e^4 *APOE* allele?

One group of researchers thinks so. Younger adults with an e^4 allele actually demonstrate superior cognitive performance than young adults with other genotypes (Rusted et al., 2013). The e^4 young adults demonstrated superior attention, increased task-related brain activation seen in fMRI, and superior white matter integrity as measured by DTI. Perhaps the cost some e^4 individuals pay for superior cognitive functioning in youth is a greater likelihood of cognitive decline in old age.

● **Figure 15.3 The Brain's Blood Supply** Due to the brain's enormous need for oxygen, it is supplied by a rich network of blood vessels. Interruptions to this supply produce rapid changes in brain function and, potentially, infarct and death.

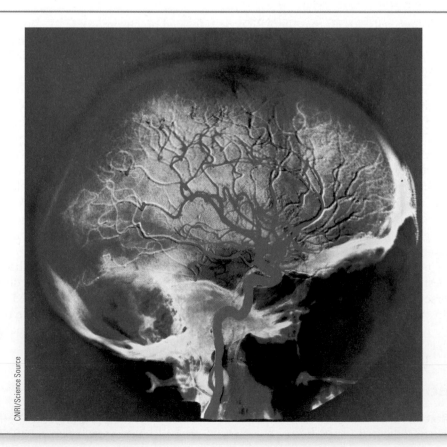

CNRI/Science Source

TABLE 15.1 | Characteristics of Types of Stroke

Type of Stroke	Causes	Outcomes
Hemorrhage (about 20% of cases)	High blood pressure Vascular abnormalities	Frequently fatal
Ischemia (about 80% of cases)	Arteriosclerosis Blood clots	Infarct of varying size Changes in consciousness, sensation, and movement

ruptures and blockages of the blood vessels serving the brain. Types and outcomes of these vascular accidents are summarized in Table 15.1.

A **stroke** occurs when the brain's blood supply is interrupted by either hemorrhage (bleeding) or by the sudden blockage of a blood vessel (Cotran, Kumar, Fausto, Robbins, & Abbas, 2005) (see ● Figure 15.4). Risk factors for stroke include age, hypertension (high blood pressure), smoking, diabetes, high cholesterol levels, obesity, and the use of alcohol, cocaine, amphetamines, heroin, and other drugs (American Heart Association, 2008). Risk is also increased when arteries are narrowed gradually by conditions such as arteriosclerosis, or hardening of the arteries. Nearly 800,000 strokes per year occur in the United States, or about one every 40 seconds (Hunsberger, Fessler, Elkahloun, & Chuang, 2012). Worldwide, stroke is the second most frequent cause of death and the leading cause of permanent disability (Albert-Weißenberger, Sirén, & Kleinschnitz, 2013).

Cerebral hemorrhage, or bleeding in the brain, generally results from hypertension or structural defects in the arteries serving the brain (Donnan, Fisher, Macleod, & Davis, 2008). Some hemorrhages occur due to the rupture of **aneurysms**, balloon-like bulges in the walls of arteries. Others result from blood diseases such as leukemia or exposure to toxic chemicals. Cerebral hemorrhages are frequently fatal due to the brain damage they produce by interfering with the blood supply to neurons and by flooding areas of the brain with salty blood that dehydrates and kills nearby neurons.

Blockages of blood vessels result in **ischemia**, or low oxygen levels. Cases of ischemia account for about 80 percent of all strokes (Donnan, Fisher, Macleod, & Davis, 2008). Ischemia often results in the death of neural tissue, producing an area known as an **infarct**. Infarcts can cause changes in consciousness, sensation, or the ability to move, depending on their size and location. **Transient ischemic attacks (TIAs)** produce brief episodes (24 hours or less) of stroke symptoms. Although these brief attacks do not cause permanent damage, they are strong predictors of subsequent stroke (Donnan et al., 2008).

Material causing the blockage of a blood vessel can be classified as either a **thrombosis** or an **embolism**. A thrombosis is a plug of blood or other material

stroke A type of brain damage caused by an interruption of the blood supply to the brain.
cerebral hemorrhage A condition caused by bleeding in the brain.
aneurysm A balloon-like bulge in the wall of an artery.
ischemia A condition in which inadequate blood flow results in insufficient quantities of oxygen being delivered to tissue.
infarct An area of dead tissue.
transient ischemic attack (TIA) A brief episode (of 24 hours or less) of stroke symptoms that does not cause permanent damage.
thrombosis A blockage that doesn't move from its point of origin in a blood vessel.
embolism A blood vessel blockage that originated elsewhere and traveled to its current location.

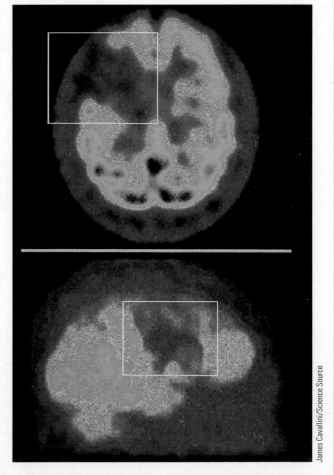

James Cavallini/Science Source

● **Figure 15.4 Brain Infarct** When an area of the brain is deprived of oxygen for a sufficient amount of time, cells begin to die. The area of dead tissue is referred to as an infarct. In this image, the patient suffered a fatal infarct in the right frontal lobe.

••• Building Better HEALTH

RECOGNIZING THE SIGNS OF A STROKE

Because treatment for stroke is much more effective within three hours of onset, it is important to know the outward signs of a stroke. The American Heart Association uses the FAST acronym: F is for face drooping, A is for arm weakness, S is for speech difficulty, and T is for time to call 9-1-1 to summon help. The observation of any of these symptoms, even if they pass quickly, should be viewed as a medical emergency. Additional symptoms include any sudden numbness or weakness of a limb, sudden onset of confusion, difficulty seeing out of one or both eyes, difficulty walking or maintaining balance, or a sudden, severe headache without a known cause.

that blocks a blood vessel without moving from its point of origin. If a plug passes into smaller and smaller blood vessels until it forms a blockage, we refer to it as an embolism. Blockages in small blood vessels are far less damaging than blockage of large arteries serving the brain. Nonetheless, multiple small strokes can produce significant damage.

Until the 1980s, it was generally assumed that most of the damage related to ischemia resulted from interruptions to the supplies of oxygen that reach neurons and glia served by the affected blood vessels (Zivin & Choi, 1991). However, autopsy results of patients who died following ischemia showed that only certain cells appeared to be damaged. In particular, cells in the middle layers of the cortex and in the hippocampus appeared to be the most vulnerable. If cell death occurred only because of a lack of oxygen, the damage should have been more widespread. Therefore, other processes must be involved in brain damage caused by ischemia.

In 1969, John Olney coined the term *excitotoxicity* to describe the ability of excess glutamate to kill neurons (see Chapter 4). Olney's hypothesis received further support from reports that glutaminergic antagonists had a protective effect on cells undergoing oxygen deprivation (Simon, Swan, Griffiths, & Meldrum, 1984). Rothman (1984) demonstrated that the presence of high concentrations of magnesium prevented cell death in cultures of rat hippocampal cells. Recall that magnesium blocks one type of glutamate receptor, the NMDA receptor (see Chapter 4). As a result, we now generally believe that cell death following strokes is largely caused by excess glutamate activity triggered by disruptions in the delivery of oxygen. Excess glutamate entering a neuron initiates a cascade of events leading to cell death. In response to unusual amounts of glutamate, abnormal calcium activity in the cell stimulates four "executioner" enzymes that damage the cell's energy stores, membranes, cytostructure, and DNA (Besancon, Guo, Lok, Tymianski, & Lo, 2008).

Currently, the only treatments approved for ischemic stroke in the United States involve the use of drugs that reduce blood clotting, which must be administered within three to four hours of a stroke for their benefits to offset their risk of producing hemorrhage (Hunsberger et al., 2012). Consequently, significant research efforts are focused on alternative methods of treatment. A number of tiny mechanical devices can be inserted into blood vessels, where they can be used to trap and remove blood clots. Histone deacetylase (HDAC) inhibitors, including the mood stabilizer valproic acid used to treat bipolar disorder (see Chapter 16), have shown considerable promise in reducing infarct size and promoting cognitive function (Baltan, Murphy, Danilov, Bachleda, & Morrison, 2011). Other methods, including surgery, preventing the formation of new thromboses and emboli, and reducing blood pressure remain standard medical practices for stroke (Donnan et al., 2008). Although some cells die immediately following a stroke, prompt medical attention can save many other neurons and glia in the ischemic **penumbra**, the area immediately surrounding an infarct (Donnan, Fisher, Macleod, & Davis, 2008; Lu et al., 2014). Physical activity, known to reduce stroke risk in the first place, also limits the damage produced by a stroke (Middleton et al., 2013).

Traumatic Brain Injury (TBI)

Traumatic brain injuries (TBI) are the result of physical damage to the brain. Traditionally, leading causes of TBI in the United States have included traffic accidents, gunshot wounds, and falls (Adekoya, Thurman, White, & Webb, 2002). More recently, increasing numbers of military personnel and civilians in war zones have experienced TBI as a result of blast injuries (Risdall & Menon, 2011).

> **penumbra** The area of tissue surrounding an infarct.
> **traumatic brain injury (TBI)** Physical damage to the brain.
> **open head injury** A head injury in which the brain is penetrated, as in a gunshot wound.
> **concussion** A head injury that results from a blow to the head without penetration of the brain or from a blow to another part of the body that results in force transmitted to the brain.

TYPES OF TBI Traumatic brain injuries can be divided into two categories. **Open head injuries** involve penetration of the skull, whereas **concussions**, or closed head injuries, do not. Open head injuries usually occur as a result of gunshot wounds or of fractures of the skull in which fragments of bone enter the brain. A projectile produces immediate damage to tissues in its pathway, which is compounded by the stretching and compression of the tissues that result from the shock waves produced by the projectile's movement (Risdall & Menon, 2011). The severity of the consequences of an open head injury is highly dependent on the areas of the brain that are affected. Injuries that involve damage to ventricles, both hemispheres, or multiple lobes of the brain are most likely to result in death (Martins, Siqueira, Santos, Zanon-Collange, & Moraes, 2003).

Approximately 7 percent of U.S. combat veterans serving in Iraq or Afghanistan between 2004 and 2009 have been diagnosed with TBI (Zollman, Starr, Kondiles, Cyborski, & Larson, 2014). The distribution of activities leading to military TBI are shown in ● Figure 15.5. Blast injuries resulting from terrorist activity can produce both open and closed head injuries. Blast pressures from an explosion can actually deform the skull, producing damage resembling physical impact, similar to the windshield of a car in an automobile accident (Moss, King, & Blackman, 2009). In addition, terrorists typically incorporate projectiles such as ball bearings, nails, rocks, or scrap metal into their explosive devices, leading to frequent open head injuries (Risdall & Menon, 2011). Blast injuries produce symptoms similar to those of other types of TBI, with a few major exceptions. Severe swelling, disruption of the blood–brain barrier (see Chapter 3), and major damage to the blood supply are more frequently observed in military as opposed to civilian cases of TBI.

A concussion occurs in response to a blow to the head or to another part of the body resulting in "impulsive" force transmitted to the brain (Aubry et al., 2002). Concussions can range from mild (no or very brief periods of unconsciousness) to severe (coma). Concussions produce damage in several ways, as illustrated in ● Figure 15.6. At the site of

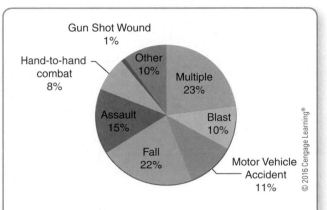

● **Figure 15.5 Sources of Military TBI** The 7 percent of U.S. combat veterans experiencing TBI as a result of serving in Iraq and Afghanistan between 2004 and 2009 were injured in a variety of situations.

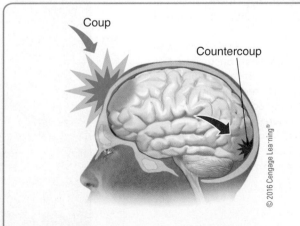

● **Figure 15.6 Coup and Countercoup** In concussions, the coup, shown here in blue, is an injury that occurs at the site of the blow. When the blow pushes the brain in the opposite direction, a second area of injury occurs, known as the countercoup, shown here in red.

coup An area of brain damage at the site of the blow to the head.

countercoup An area of brain damage that occurs on the opposite side of the head from the original site of the blow, or coup.

subdural hematoma A mass of clotted blood (like a bruise) that forms between the dura mater and arachnoid layers of the meninges following a head injury.

neurocognitive disorder due to traumatic brain injury A set of symptoms that follow concussion for a period of days to years, including headache, cognitive deficits, and emotional changes.

dementia pugilistica A severe form of traumatic brain injury often experienced by boxers.

a blow, known as the **coup**, the brain might be damaged by compression of the skull against the neural tissue. The force of the blow pushes the brain against the side of the skull opposite the coup, producing a second area of damage known as the **countercoup**. A severe coup or countercoup might be accompanied by bleeding, or **subdural** (under the dura mater) **hematoma**. White matter damage can also occur, due to twisting of the brain within the skull in response to the blow. Pressure exerted on the brain by the swelling of injured tissues produces additional damage or interruptions in normal functioning.

OUTCOMES OF TBI Behavioral and cognitive consequences of concussion vary widely. Cortical functions normally taking place at the location of the coup and countercoup are affected adversely. Resulting symptoms can include memory loss, dizziness, fatigue, irritability, disorientation and confusion, and evidence of neurological deficits. Although most individuals recover within a week or two, approximately 11–17 percent of patients demonstrate these symptoms three months after an injury (Iverson & Lange, 2011). When symptoms extend beyond the "acute" or immediate timeframe of the injury, the patient might be diagnosed with **neurocognitive disorder due to traumatic brain injury** (APA, 2013). Long-lasting symptoms seem to occur more frequently in patients with pre-injury psychological disorders, anxiety and depression in particular, accompanied by post-traumatic stress immediately following the injury (Meares et al., 2011).

Repeated TBI, often experienced by athletes, appears to be especially damaging (Guskiewicz et al., 2003). Professional boxers are subjected to repeated blows to the head over the course of their careers, possibly resulting in **dementia pugilistica**, or boxer's syndrome (Martland, 1928) (see ● Figure 15.7). Dementia pugilistica is a type of traumatic brain injury. Typically, dementia pugilistica is associated with slurred speech, memory impairment, personality changes, lack of coordination, and a Parkinson-like syndrome (see Chapter 8). Autopsy results of dementia pugilistica and Alzheimer's disease show similar patterns of degeneration (Jordan, 1998; Saing, Dick,

● **Figure 15.7** Boxers Risk Repeated Head Injuries
Boxer Jerry Quarry, shown on the left fighting Muhammad Ali, developed traumatic brain injury (TBI) as a result of repeated concussions. This type of TBI causes slurred speech, memory impairment, lack of coordination, personality changes, and a Parkinson-like syndrome.

AP Images

Nelson, Kim, Cribbs, & Head, 2012). Many boxers and American football players have experienced symptoms typical of these repeated injuries.

Not all boxers, even those with lengthy careers, are afflicted with dementia pugilistica (Jordan, 2000). George Foreman is one notable example of a boxer who escaped this disorder. Boxers who carry the E^4 variant of the *APOE* gene, which has been implicated in some cases of Alzheimer's disease, might be more likely to develop dementia pugilistica (Jordan et al., 1997; Zetterberg et al., 2009; Förstl, Haass, Hemmer, Meyer, & Halle, 2010). Boxers who had the E^4 variant and had participated in more than 12 professional bouts had greater neurological damage than those who did not carry the E^4 variant. All boxers in one sample who were considered severely impaired possessed the E^4 variant. The presence of the E^4 variant might make a person more vulnerable to the negative effects of brain injury (Crawford et al., 2009; Nathoo, Chetty, van Dellen, & Barnett, 2003). In another sample, 57 percent of patients with the E^4 variant experienced a negative outcome (death, vegetative state, severe disability) as a result of brain injury, compared with 27 percent of the patients without the allele (Teasdale, Nicoll, Murray, & Fiddes, 1997).

TREATING TBI The discovery of effective therapies for different types of brain injury has been complicated by the wide range of systems that can be affected and the need for more information about the cascade of destruction that often continues well past the time of the initial damage (Young, 2012).

Researchers have investigated a number of pharmacological approaches for reducing damage immediately following TBI. As in the case of treating stroke, efforts have centered on medications that inhibit the excitatory neurotransmitter glutamate. Not only is excess glutamate released during a brain injury, but this release can initiate changes in calcium levels within neurons that lead to a number of unwanted outcomes, including swelling and circulatory problems (Young, 2012). Progesterone and bradykinin receptor blockers have shown promise in the treatment of TBI, but further studies are needed to establish their efficacy.

During the more chronic phase of recovery from TBI, drugs that enhance dopamine activity, such as amphetamines and methylphenidate (Ritalin), are associated with short-term improvements, but their long-term benefits remain relatively unknown. Norepinephrine reuptake blockers, occasionally used to treat attention deficit hyperactivity disorder (ADHD; see Chapter 16), also appear useful in improving the cognitive performance and attention abilities of patients following TBI (Reid & Hamm, 2008).

Patient and family education regarding TBI appears to be helpful (Boussard et al., 2014). Although many clinicians advise both physical and cognitive rest after TBI, scientific evidence for benefits of this practice are lacking (Boussard et al., 2014). Additional rehabilitation methods, including the use of virtual reality (VR) are discussed later in this chapter.

Substance/Medication-Induced Neurocognitive Disorder

A number of recreational and therapeutic drugs produce symptoms of neurocognitive disorder outside the actual intoxication or withdrawal periods associated with a drug. The drugs that are particularly likely to result in neurocognitive disorder are alcohol (30 to 40 percent of individuals during their first two months of abstinence), cocaine, methamphetamine, opioids, phencyclidine (PCP), sedatives, hypnotics, and anti-anxiety drugs (33 percent or more with strong likelihood of persistence after extended abstinence), and solvents (APA, 2013).

People who abuse substances typically begin their use in adolescence and experience peak use during their 20s. Individuals who begin abstinence prior to age 50 years recover more effectively from neurocognitive disorder than those who persist in their drug use beyond that age.

Several types of drugs produce specific effects that are capable of independently producing neurocognitive deficits. For example, methamphetamine is associated with risk for vascular accidents, which produce their own set of issues as discussed previously. Methamphetamine also damages the blood–brain barrier, which in turn puts users at greater risk for HIV-associated neurocognitive disorder, discussed in the next section (O'Shea, Urrutia, Green, & Colado, 2014). Alcohol abuse is associated with nutritional deficits, which can produce cognitive symptoms in addition to the detrimental effects of chronic abuse of alcohol itself (see Chapter 12). For example, vitamin deficiencies common in alcohol abuse can lead to amnestic confabulatory (Korsakoff's) neurocognitive disorder (APA, 2013).

HIV-associated Neurocognitive Disorder (HAND)

Acquired immune deficiency syndrome (AIDS) is a set of symptoms and infections resulting from the damage to the human immune system caused by the human immunodeficiency virus (HIV). **HIV-associated neurocognitive disorder (HAND)**, previously referred to as AIDS Dementia Complex), is a collection of neurocognitive symptoms that results either directly from the actions of the HIV virus itself or from other opportunistic infections that can overwhelm the impaired immune system of the HIV patient. The initial symptoms of HAND are relatively mild and can easily be mistaken for depression (see Chapter 16). The patient might complain of difficulty concentrating, forgetfulness, decreased work productivity, low sex drive, social withdrawal, and general apathy. In more advanced cases, serious motor and cognitive problems begin to emerge. Imbalance, clumsiness, and weakness are followed by memory loss and language impairment. In children with HIV, HAND expresses itself primarily in a failure to reach normal developmental milestones. In children, HIV appears to affect the central nervous system from the outset of infection, whereas in adults, HAND usually occurs much later in the course of the disease.

The action of the HIV virus on neural cell death appears to be indirect. HIV directly invades macrophages (cells that are part of the immune system), microglia, astrocytes, and the vascular endothelial cells that line the blood vessels serving the brain. HIV does not, however, invade neurons themselves (Bowers, 1996). The infected cells release chemical messengers known as cytokines, which then damage neighboring neurons by inducing apoptosis, or programmed cell death (see Chapter 5). Additional damage occurs when a substance found in the external envelope of the HIV virus binds to NMDA receptors. Consequently, too much calcium enters the neuron, triggering neural death. As shown in ● Figure 15.8, viral particles form buds on infected cells, which frequently burst and continue the spread of the virus.

Although contemporary antiretroviral treatments have effectively diminished the prevalence and severity of the most severe cases of HAND, milder forms of HAND continue to be a problem for many patients (Spudich & González-Scarano, 2012).

HIV-associated neurocognitive disorder (HAND) Neurocognitive symptoms that result from the HIV virus itself or from opportunistic infections.

transmissible spongiform encephalopathy (TSE) A disease that can be transferred from one animal to another and that produces a fatal, degenerative condition characterized by dementia and motor disturbance.

bovine spongiform encephalopathy (BSE) A form of TSE that primarily affects cattle; mad-cow disease.

Prion Diseases

Among the most dramatic neurocognitive disorders are the **transmissible spongiform encephalopathies (TSEs)**, a group that includes **bovine spongiform encephalopathy (BSE)**, or so-called mad-cow disease. Human versions of TSEs include Creutzfeld-Jakob disease (CJD), kuru, and fatal familial insomnia. The symptoms common to this group of diseases are devastating: psychological disturbances, including paranoia, anxiety, and depression in humans and skittishness in herd animals; progressive loss of cognitive function; motor disturbances; and finally death. The brains of animals and people who died from TSEs show a spongelike appearance due to clustered cell death, which is the source of the word *spongiform* in the name of the disorders (see ● Figure 15.9).

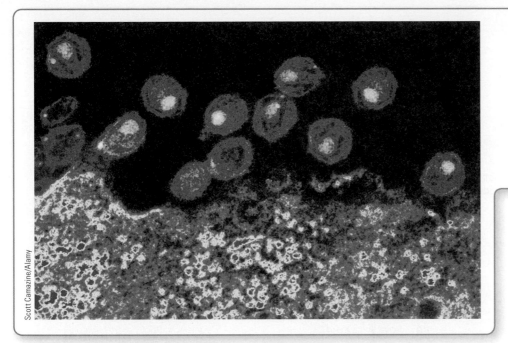

● **Figure 15.8** HIV Viral Particles Bud from an Infected Cell In cases of HAND, many cells containing the HIV virus can be observed. In the image shown here, the particles budding from an infected cell burst, leading to further spreading of the virus within the brain.

In the process of understanding TSEs and their cause, it was discovered that the infectious agent involved in TSEs acted in ways that were distinct from the behavior of any known viruses. The incubation period was unusually long, and there was no sign of the inflammation typically found in viral infections. The infectious agent seemed remarkably able to withstand hospital sterilization techniques. Stanley Prusiner (1982) proposed that TSEs were caused by a new type of infectious agent, a single protein, which he named a **prion**. The prion protein can exist in two forms, depending on how it's folded (Prusiner, 1995). The normal version became known as PrP^c (prion protein cellular), whereas the abnormal version involved in scrapie, the sheep version of TSE, became known as PrP^{sc} (prion protein scrapie).

Prusiner (1995) argued that the abnormal version of the protein, PrP^{sc}, is the cause of TSEs. If the abnormal protein somehow manages to get into the brain, it appears to

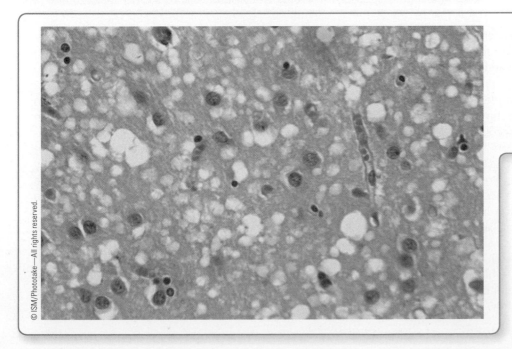

● **Figure 15.9** Bovine Spongiform Encephalopathy ("Mad-Cow" Disease) This image shows the characteristic damage to the brain that gives the TSEs the name *spongiform*.

prion A protein particle that lacks nucleic acid and is believed to be responsible for TSEs.

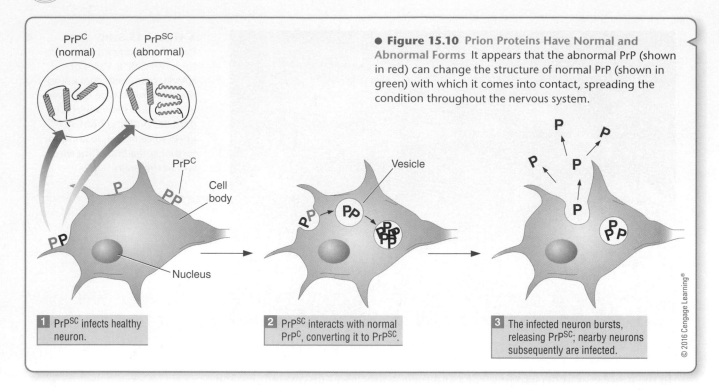

● **Figure 15.10 Prion Proteins Have Normal and Abnormal Forms** It appears that the abnormal PrP (shown in red) can change the structure of normal PrP (shown in green) with which it comes into contact, spreading the condition throughout the nervous system.

1 PrP^{SC} infects healthy neuron.

2 PrP^{SC} interacts with normal PrP^{C}, converting it to PrP^{SC}.

3 The infected neuron bursts, releasing PrP^{SC}; nearby neurons subsequently are infected.

© 2016 Cengage Learning®

convert normal PrP^c proteins into the abnormal form, as shown in ● Figure 15.10. In cell cultures, the PrP^{sc} filled neurons, eventually causing them to explode. The abnormal prions were then released to convert proteins in adjacent cells.

UNRAVELING THE TSE MYSTERY Our current understanding of TSEs began in 18th-century England. At that time, a disease known as scrapie was first identified

●●● Connecting to **Research**

STANLEY PRUSINER AND THE PRION

The work of Stanley Prusiner on prions and the eventual, albeit somewhat reluctant acceptance of his ideas by his scientific colleagues illustrates some of the finest aspects of science.

Initial descriptions of what we now call TSEs attributed their causes to "slow-acting" viruses. Scientists really had no other way to account for the long time frame from apparent infection to observable symptoms. But the idea of a virus just didn't fit the observations. Like many scientists, Prusiner "stood on the shoulder of giants," or in this case, built his hypotheses on the work of 1960s radiation biologist Tikvah Alper and physicist J. S. Griffith. While studying scrapie, Alper discovered that brain tissue of sick animals remained infectious even after she treated it with known methods for destroying RNA and DNA, which ruled out any type of virus. Griffith argued independently that a protein could misfold and then somehow make others do so as

well. This idea was in direct conflict with the molecular biology of the day, which maintained that information could only be transmitted from one generation to the next via nucleic acids.

Inspired by one of his patients with a human TSE, Creutzfeld-Jakob disease (CJD), Prusiner began working on TSEs. With painstaking work, he demonstrated that a protein existed in the brains of scrapie-infected hamsters than was not present in healthy animals. Additional work showed that mice lacking a healthy form of the prion were extra resistant to prion diseases.

In recognition of Prusiner's efforts, which he maintained in spite of often virulent criticism, he was awarded the Nobel Prize in physiology or medicine in 1997. He was only the 10th researcher to be named alone in one year in the preceding 50 years, and the first single awardee to be named in a decade.

● **Figure 15.11** **A Sheep with Scrapie** Scrapie, a TSE affecting sheep and goats, was first observed 300 years ago in England. The condition was named after the fact that afflicted sheep scraped themselves against other objects, removing much of their wool.

Creutzfeldt-Jakob disease (CJD) A human TSE that results in a progressively degenerative condition characterized by movement and cognitive disorder.

kuru A human TSE identified among the Fore of New Guinea, related to their practice of cannibalism.

among sheep and goats. The disease got its name from the fact that afflicted animals often developed intense itching in addition to other TSE symptoms, leading them to scratch repeatedly by scraping against something (Prusiner, 1995) (see ● Figure 15.11). Scrapie was not considered a threat because it appeared unable to infect humans who consumed meat from infected animals.

H. G. Creutzfeldt (1920) and A. Jakob (1921) published the first descriptions of patients with a human form of TSE. The condition described by these physicians became known as **Creutzfeldt-Jakob disease (CJD)**. CJD is quite rare, with only 0.5–1 case per million worldwide (UK Creutzfeldt-Jakob Disease Surveillance Unit, 2002). The causality of CJD was mixed, with some cases running in families and others resulting from spontaneous genetic mutation. A very small number of cases of CJD result from the transplanting of tissues or use of contaminated neurosurgical instruments. These cases demonstrated that the causal factors involved in infectious CJD are not destroyed by typical medical sterilization techniques.

Another piece of the TSE puzzle fell into place during the 1950s, when scholars investigated a disease known as **kuru**, which was identified among the Fore people of New Guinea (see ●Figure 15.12). Kuru produced symptoms that were very similar to CJD. Kuru initially appeared to be a genetic condition, but it was eventually traced to the Fore's practice of

● **Figure 15.12** **Kuru Occurred Among the Fore of New Guinea** This photograph of two Fore women with kuru was among Gadjusek's original field study photos taken in 1960. Both women required the use of a stick to stand, and they died within six months.

cannibalism of relatives that was part of their burial ritual (Gadjusek & Zigas, 1957). Following legislation outlawing cannibalism, kuru gradually disappeared.

Proof that kuru was transmissible came from research in which brain tissue from patients who died from the disease was injected into the brains of chimpanzees (Gadjusek, Gibbs, & Alpers, 1966). The infected chimpanzees developed symptoms of kuru, and their brains were found to contain the characteristic spongy tissue associated with a TSE. Monkeys injected with tissue from people who had died of Creutzfeldt-Jakob disease also developed a TSE (Gadjusek, 1973).

BSE AND NEW VARIANT CREUTZFELDT-JAKOB DISEASE (vCJD) In 1985, an outbreak of BSE (mad-cow disease) occurred, beginning in Great Britain. The BSE epidemic resulted from changes in procedures for producing animal feed. Ground meat and bone meal were included as a protein source in animal feed, allowing infected tissue to be included. Once steps were taken to resolve these feeding practices, the BSE epidemic began to abate, as shown in ● Figure 15.13.

The infectious agent responsible for BSE in cows caused a corresponding outbreak of **new variant Creutzfeldt-Jakob disease (vCJD)** in humans (Bruce et al. 1997; Hill et al. 1997). To date, one hundred seventy-six individuals in the UK have acquired vCJD from ingesting infected meat (Head & Ironside, 2012). The new variant CJD cases differed from classic CJD on a number of dimensions. Patients with vCJD were an average of 28 years old at diagnosis, whereas classic CJD patients were an average of 63 years old (USDA, 2002). Brain pathologies were similar, but vCJD showed greater concentration of prion protein plaques (USDA, 2002).

Efforts to contain BSE included bans on the use of mammal proteins in animal feed and limitations on cattle exports from infected countries. Hopefully, these precautions have made vCJD, like kuru before it, a thing of the past.

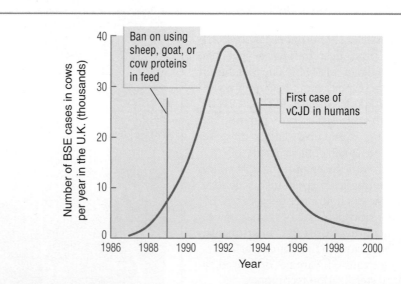

> ● **Figure 15.13 Time Course of the BSE Epidemic in the United Kingdom** Steps that have been taken against the BSE epidemic in the United Kingdom are working. The use of sheep, goats, or cattle in animal feed has been banned, and cattle exports to other countries ceased. These data reflect the long incubation periods of TSEs. The benefits of the new feeding practices did not show until several years had passed. In addition, the first related case of vCJD was diagnosed several years after the disease in cattle had been identified and addressed.

Source: Based on from BSE website at the University of Illinois, Urbana-Champaign.

new variant Creutzfeldt-Jakob disease (vCJD) A human TSE resembling classic CJD that results from consumption of beef products contaminated by BSE.

INTERIM SUMMARY 15.1

Summary Table: Major Types of Neurocognitive Disorder

Neurocognitive Disorder	Causes	Symptoms	Treatments
Alzheimer's disease	Age, genetic predisposition, and possible unknown environmental factors	• Cognitive decline • Emotional disturbance • Neurofibrillary tangles • Amyloid plaques	• None that reverse symptoms • Medications slow progression of disease
Vascular disease	Age, hypertension, smoking, obesity, diabetes, high cholesterol, use of some recreational substances	• Face drooping • Numbness or weakness of a limb • Speech difficulties • Confusion • Visual disturbances • Sudden, severe headache	• Medications to thin blood and discourage clotting • Surgery
Traumatic brain injury (TBI)	Open or closed head injury	• Cognitive problems related to location of injury • General problems with memory and cognition	• Medications that antagonize glutamate and enhance dopamine activity • Patient education • Virtual reality stimulation
Substance/ medication-induced neurocognitive disorder	Use of particular recreational or therapeutic chemicals	• Vascular accidents • Damage to blood-brain barrier • Cognitive deficits	• Abstention from substance
HIV-associated neurocognitive disorder (HAND)	HIV virus	• Depression • Motor disturbance • Cognitive disturbance	• Antiretroviral medications slow progression
Transmissible spongiform encephalopathy (TSE)	Prions	• Paranoia, anxiety, depression • Dementia • Motor disturbance	• None • Prevention by avoidance of contaminated medical instruments and food

Summary Points

1. Neuropsychologists are clinical psychologists with additional training who evaluate and plan treatment for patients with neurocognitive disorders. **(LO1)**

2. Alzheimer's disease is a major form of age-related dementia that results in a gradual loss of cognitive function. **(LO2)**

3. Vascular disease, or stroke, produces cognitive deficits as a result of brain damage. **(LO2)**

4. Traumatic brain injuries (TBI) are classified as open, in which the brain is penetrated, or closed, in which the brain is not penetrated. **(LO2)**

5. Many recreational and therapeutic substances have the capability of producing neurocognitive disorders after use of the substance is discontinued. **(LO2)**

6. HIV-associated Neurocognitive Disorder (HAND) results when the HIV virus affects the nervous system indirectly by allowing opportunistic infections to produce damage or directly through promoting apoptosis. **(LO2)**

7. Prion diseases, including transmissible spongiform encephalopathies (TSEs), are fatal, degenerative conditions characterized by paranoia, depression, dementia, and motor disturbance. **(LO2)**

Review Questions

1. How does the training and role of the neuropsychologist differ from that of the neurologist?

2. What is the role of the *APOE* gene in neurocognitive disorders?

Neurocognitive Disorders Due to Other Medical Conditions

In keeping with the organization of the neurocognitive disorder section of the DSM-5 (APA, 2013), we will now examine a number of disorders in the "due to other medical conditions" category. This category includes brain tumors, hydrocephalus (see Chapter 2), oxygen deficits following cardiac arrest, endocrine conditions, nutritional conditions, infectious diseases, immune disorders, kidney failure, metabolic conditions, epilepsy, and multiple sclerosis (APA, 2013). Of these, we will consider brain tumors, infectious diseases, epilepsy, and multiple sclerosis in detail. Although not listed in the DSM-5 under "other medical conditions," we will also explore migraine headaches in this section. Migraine headaches have an indirect relationship with neurocognitive disorder due to their increasing a person's risk for stroke.

Brain Tumors

After the uterus, the brain is the organ most likely to give rise to **tumors**, which are independent growths of new tissue that lack purpose. Primary tumors originate in the brain itself, while secondary tumors result from cells shed by tumors in other parts of the body, particularly in cases of lung, breast, skin, kidney, and colon cancers. Primary tumors of the brain remain rare (Porter, McCarthy, Freels, Kim, & Davis, 2010). The causes of primary tumors of the brain remain unknown, although ionizing radiation (including x-rays and nuclear energy) are known risk factors. The vast majority of brain tumors arise from glial cells and from the cells of the meninges. Smaller numbers of tumors originate in the cells lining the ventricles.

Some tumors are classified as **malignant tumors** because they lack distinct boundaries and are very likely to recur following surgical removal. In the process known as **metastasis**, malignant tumors shed cells, which travel to other sites of the body and start new tumors. Tumors that originate in the brain rarely metastasize, but when they do so, the shed cells travel through the cerebrospinal fluid to other parts of the nervous system, as opposed to traveling through the bloodstream to other organ Other tumors are classified as **benign tumors** because they are contained within t' own membrane, are unlikely to recur following removal, and do not metastasize does not imply that benign tumors do no harm. As we will see shortly, any

tumor An independent growth of tissue that lacks purpose.

malignant tumor A type of abnormal cell growth that, lacking boundaries, invades the surrounding tissue and is very likely to recur following surgical removal.

metastasis The migration of cancerous cells from one part of the body to another.

benign tumor An abnormal cell growth that develops within its own membrane and is unlikely to recur following surgery to remove it.

mass that occurs in the brain can disrupt normal function. If the benign tumor is not located where it can be surgically removed, it can be as life threatening as the malignant variety due to its disruption of nearby neural processes.

SYMPTOMS OF TUMORS Nearly all tumors, once they have attained sufficient size, produce general symptoms due to increased pressure within the skull. These symptoms include headache, vomiting, double vision, reduced heart rate, reduced alertness, and seizures (Chandana, Movva, Arora, & Singh, 2008). Specific disruptions related to the location of the tumor can also occur. For instance, a tumor of the occipital lobe would affect vision. Tumors in the frontal lobe produce changes in emotionality and the ability to plan behavior.

TYPES OF TUMORS Tumors are identified according to the tissue from which they arise. **Gliomas** develop in glial cells and account for more than 70 percent of brain tumors (Ohgaki, 2009). Gliomas arise in astrocytes, oligodendrocytes, or mixtures of the two types of cells. **Meningiomas** are tumors that arise within the tissues of the meninges (see Chapter 2). These tumors are typically benign. Because meningiomas compete with the brain for space, the pressure they exert can produce the headache, vomiting, double vision, and other symptoms of tumors discussed previously. Meningiomas are usually easy to remove surgically because they lie on the surface of the brain instead of invading the tissue within the brain (see ● Figure 15.14).

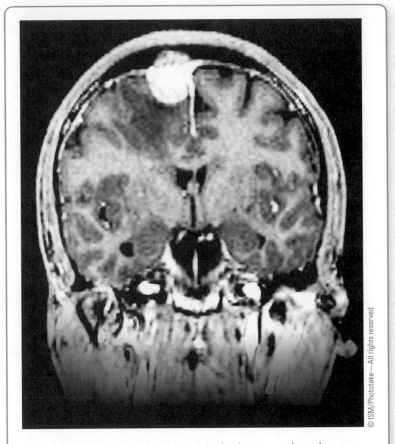

> ● **Figure 15.14** A Meningioma Meningiomas, such as the one shown in the light area of this image, are tumors that arise in the meninges surrounding the brain. Although typically benign, meningiomas can still disrupt brain functioning by the pressure they exert on adjacent tissues.

The World Health Organization (WHO) issued a classification system for describing central nervous system tumors, ranging from Grade I (least serious) to Grade IV (most serious) (Brat et al., 2008). Grade I tumors are benign, slow-growing, and respond well to surgery. Grade II tumors are malignant, have a higher likelihood of recurrence following surgery, but grow relatively slowly. Grade III tumors are malignant and require more aggressive therapies than Grade II tumors, and Grade IV tumors can be rapidly fatal. Survival rates following diagnosis can vary from decades to months, depending on the type of tumor.

TREATMENT FOR TUMORS The most common approach to brain tumors is surgical removal. In addition to surgery, or in cases in which surgery is very risky or impossible, whole brain radiation is used. The advent of stereotaxic radiosurgery (SRS) allows physicians to deliver radiation with pinpoint accuracy, which reduces damage to healthy brain tissue (Kalkanis et al., 2010). Ultrasound therapy, a noninvasive approach, allows physicians to use heat generated by acoustic energy to damage the tissue of the tumor (Jolesz & Hynynen, 2013).

Chemotherapy, in which chemicals that destroy tumor cells are applied via the bloodstream, has proven quite challenging for use with brain tumors because most chemotherapy agents do not cross the blood–brain barrier (see Chapter 4). Newer agents are being developed that either interfere with the blood–brain barrier or bypass it completely (Blakeley, 2008; Levin, 2002). Researchers have also implanted dissolving,

glioma A tumor that develops from glial cells.
meningioma A tumor arising from the tissue of the meninges.

chemotherapy-releasing wafers during surgery to remove tumors (Massachusetts General Hospital/Harvard Medical School, 2002). Another approach is the use of thalidomide to "starve" tumors by reducing the growth of blood vessels supplying them (Fine et al., 2007). Thalidomide became infamous during the 1950s and 1960s because when taken by pregnant women, it produces serious birth defects, such as undeveloped limbs. However, it is proving useful as a treatment of tumors in conjunction with surgery, radiation, and other types of chemotherapy (Gilbert et al., 2010). In animal models, anticancer genes inserted into stem cells, which are then delivered to a tumor, have produced encouraging results (Aboody, Najbauer, & Danks, 2008; Bexell, Scheding, & Bengzon, 2010).

Infections

Certain types of infections manage to circumvent the formidable protection surrounding the brain and nervous system. The neurocognitive consequences of such invasions are dramatic, and many of these disorders are life threatening.

PARASITES A variety of parasitic infections can affect the central nervous system, but the most common of these is **neurocysticercosis**. This condition, once considered a disease of the developing world, now affects 2 to 6 people out of each 10,000 residents of the United States or about 5,000 new cases per year (Serpa & Clinton White, 2012). Neurocysticercosis results from infection with the pork tapeworm, *Taenia solium*, through the ingestion of *T. solium* eggs in contaminated pork products or in fecal material from infected pigs or humans (Kossoff, 2001). The *T. solium* eggs hatch in the stomach, and the larvae penetrate the intestine and enter the bloodstream. The larvae lodge in soft tissue, notably the skin, muscle, eye, and brain (see ● Figure 15.15). When

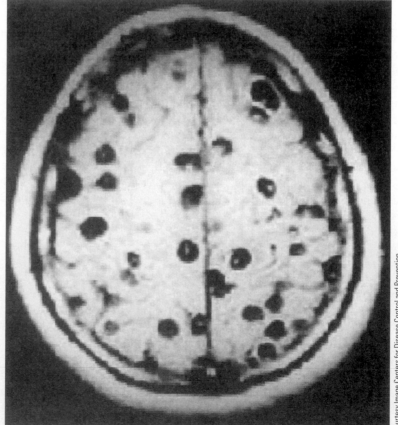

● **Figure 15.15** Complicated Neurocysticercosis Involves Multiple Infections in the Brain Simple neurocysticercosis usually involves a single cyst and is typical of cases that occur in areas of the world in which the condition is not well established. In the case depicted here, multiple cysts have occurred. These complicated cases usually occur in areas in which the condition is common.

Courtesy Image Centers for Disease Control and Prevention

neurocysticercosis A condition characterized by brain cysts resulting from parasitic infection by the pork tapeworm, *T. solium*.

this occurs, fluid-filled cysts, approximately 1 to 2 cm in diameter, form around the larvae. The infected person will not experience any symptoms until the encysted worm dies, which can take as long as five years (Kossoff, 2001). Prior to the death of the worm, the body's immune system generally does not recognize or attack it unless the infection involves very large numbers of the parasite. However, when the worm dies, the immune system does act, and inflammation will occur around the cyst. At this time, the most frequent symptom of infection in the brain is the sudden onset of partial seizures, discussed later in this chapter.

Treatment generally consists of medication for seizure control. If the cysts still harbor a live worm, treatment with antiworm (antihelminthic) medications can be useful (Jung, Cárdenas, Sciutto, & Fleury, 2008). If cysts cause uncontrollable seizures, surgery can be performed to remove them. Some progress has been made in preventing the infection through community hygiene education and the development of vaccines for pigs (García et al., 2007).

BACTERIAL, VIRAL, AND FUNGAL INFECTIONS Many kinds of bacteria, viruses, and fungi are capable of infecting the brain and meninges, and all have serious implications.

Encephalitis, from the Greek *enkephalos* for "brain" and *itis* for "inflammation," is an inflammation of the brain caused by viral infection. In some cases, symptoms are mild. In other cases, encephalitis can lead to convulsions, delirium, coma, and death. Some patients experience permanent impairments to memory, speech, muscle coordination, hearing, and vision. Two modes of infection produce encephalitis. Primary encephalitis occurs when a virus directly invades the central nervous system. This type of encephalitis frequently occurs as a result of infection with mosquito-borne viruses such as West Nile virus. Secondary encephalitis occurs following viral infection of other parts of the body.

There are several types of primary encephalitis in the United States, including the fairly common but not particularly deadly St. Louis encephalitis and the rare but deadly Eastern equine encephalitis. Probably the most famous type of encephalitis is caused by **West Nile virus**, which first appeared in the United States in 1999. Like many similar viruses, West Nile virus is transmitted to humans through mosquitoes that have fed on infected birds. Researchers tracking the disease in humans were surprised by both the rate of increase in the number of cases and the speed at which the disease spread geographically. However, it appears that rates of infection in the United States have leveled off (Snapinn et al., 2007).

Herpes simplex, the class of viruses responsible for cold sores and genital herpes, produces one of the most serious and likely fatal versions of secondary encephalitis. If a person has a weakened immune system, the herpes virus is able to reactivate and travel to the brain (Whitley, 2006). The damage caused by the virus in encephalitis is similar to that seen in Alzheimer's disease, leading some researchers to suspect a connection between prior herpes infection and subsequent dementia (Zambrano et al., 2008).

Meningitis, or inflammation of the meninges, can result from infection by bacteria, viruses, or fungi. Meningitis produces flulike symptoms, including high temperature, vomiting, diarrhea, and joint and muscle pains. However, meningitis can be distinguished from the flu by the presence of neck stiffness (the inability to touch the chin to the chest), aversion to bright lights, and drowsiness. In some cases, particularly in young children, the rapidly developing fever caused by meningitis stimulates seizures.

Bacterial meningitis can occur alone or in conjunction with septicemia, or blood poisoning. Bacterial meningitis is caused by several common classes of bacteria. In most people, the body's immune system keeps these bacteria in check, and carrying them actually contributes to the person's natural protection against developing this form of meningitis. Prolonged close contact, coughing, sneezing, and intimate kissing can spread the bacteria. However, the bacteria do not live very long outside the body,

encephalitis A condition characterized by inflammation of the brain.

West Nile virus An encephalitis-causing virus that is carried by birds and transmitted to humans via mosquitoes.

so they are not a threat in swimming pools, buildings, and the water supply. Although rare, these infections are considered a medical emergency, with fatality rates between 10 and 20 percent (Meningitis Trust, 2002). Those who recover might still suffer from deafness or brain injury. Following the development of effective vaccines for the more common types of meningitis in the late 1980s and 1990s, rates of bacterial meningitis in the United States plummeted (McIntyre, O'Brien, Greenwood, & van de Beek). These vaccines are routinely required or strongly recommended for incoming on-campus resident college students.

Viral meningitis is the most common form of meningitis, but it is generally considered the least dangerous type. Symptoms are similar to those of the bacterial forms of the disease. Many types of viruses can cause meningitis, but the most common are the coxsackie viruses and enteroviruses. Viral meningitis does not respond to antibiotics or to other medications. Headaches, fatigue, and depression can last for weeks or even months.

Some fungi have the ability to produce fungal meningitis. However, these cases are exceedingly rare. Normally, they occur only when a person's immune system has been seriously impaired. Patients with HIV/AIDS and those taking medications that suppress the immune system (organ transplant patients or cancer patients) are especially at risk. These cases are slow to develop, hard to diagnose, and difficult to treat.

Epilepsy

Seizures are uncontrolled electrical disturbances in the brain that are correlated with changes in consciousness. Seizures often occur as a result of brain injury, infection, or withdrawal from drugs, but other seizures appear without an obvious cause. When patients experience repeated, unprovoked seizures, they are diagnosed with **epilepsy** (Hauser & Beghi, 2008). To diagnose a seizure disorder reliably, electroencephalography (EEGs) and imaging (e.g., fMRI) are used to look for abnormalities in brain activity. However, not all individuals with a seizure disorder will demonstrate abnormal scans, nor do all people with abnormal scans experience seizures.

Some seizures appear to occur when the brain's balance between excitation and inhibition is disturbed. As we observed in Chapter 4, gamma-aminobutyric acid (GABA) is one of the primary inhibitory neurotransmitters in the brain. Changes in GABA activity can either produce or prevent seizures (Jacob, Moss, & Jurd, 2008). Drugs that inhibit GABA activity produce seizures (Butuzova & Kitchigina, 2008). Withdrawal from drugs that interact with GABA receptors, such as alcohol, also produces severe seizures (Ritvo & Park, 2007; Rogawski, 2005). Many medications used to control seizures enhance the action of GABA (Meldrum & Rogawski, 2007).

TYPES OF SEIZURES Seizures vary widely in terms of their causes, duration, and symptoms. Classification systems help physicians match treatment to the type of seizure (International League Against Epilepsy [ILAE], 2008). We can make an initial distinction between **partial seizures** and **generalized seizures**. Partial seizures originate in an identifiable part of the brain (the focus or focal area) and then spread outward. Generalized seizures do not appear to have a focus or clear point of origin and affect both sides of the brain symmetrically. Some partial seizures are preceded by an **aura**, or premonition of the impending seizure. In some cases, the aura involves sensory distortions, whereas in others, it is simply the sense that a seizure will occur soon. Generalized seizures typically are not accompanied by an aura.

Partial seizures are further divided into simple and complex seizures. **Simple partial seizures** cause movements or sensations appropriate to the location of the starting point, or focus, of the seizure activity. These seizures are not accompanied by changes in consciousness. An example of a simple partial seizure affecting the motor cortex is the **Jacksonian seizure**, named after John Hughlings Jackson, a 19th-century

seizure An uncontrolled electrical disturbance in the brain.

epilepsy A disorder characterized by repeated seizure activity in the brain.

partial seizure A seizure that has a clear area of origin, or focus.

generalized seizure A seizure that affects the brain symmetrically without a clear point of origin.

aura A subjective sensory or motor sensation that signals the onset of a seizure or migraine.

simple partial seizure A seizure with symptoms that relate to the functions of the focal area.

Jacksonian seizure A type of simple partial seizure originating in the motor cortex.

observer of seizure disorders whom we met in Chapter 1. In Jacksonian seizures, motor disturbance moves from one part of the body to the next in what is called the **Jacksonian march**, reflecting the representation of each body part in the motor cortex. For instance, if twitching began in a single finger, it might spread to adjacent fingers, the hand, the arm, and so on.

Complex partial seizures normally begin in the temporal lobes and are associated with alterations in consciousness. During the seizure, the patient is likely to be very confused and will often have no memory of the seizure. In some cases, the person has the sense that he or she is reexperiencing a past event. In others, there is a sense that his or her environment is oddly unknown or foreign.

During partial seizures, neurons within the seizure focus show a characteristic electrical response pattern known as the **paroxysmal depolarizing shift (PDS)**, which can be observed in an electroencephalogram (EEG) recording of the patient's brain activity (Westbrook, 2000). The PDS begins with a large, abrupt depolarization of affected neurons that triggers a train of action potentials and is followed by a period of hyperpolarization. This excitatory activity overwhelms the GABA-mediated inhibitory system, leading to high-frequency discharges of action potentials (Westbrook, 2000).

Generalized seizures symmetrically affect both sides of the brain and do not appear to have a focus, or clear point of origin. Generalized seizures appear to result from the activation of circuits connecting the thalamus with the cortex. The differences between the spread of abnormal activation in partial and generalized seizures are illustrated in ● Figure 15.16.

The two major categories of generalized seizure are the **tonic-clonic** (also known as grand mal) and **absence** (also known as petit mal) **seizures**. Tonic-clonic seizures begin with a **tonic phase** lasting several seconds which is characterized by loss of consciousness, cessation of breathing, and intense muscular contraction. This tonic phase gives way to a **clonic phase**, which lasts about one minute. In this phase, the body experiences violent, rhythmic contractions that often result in broken bones or other physical injuries. Urination and defecation can occur. Due to accompanying autonomic excitation, the person will sweat and salivate

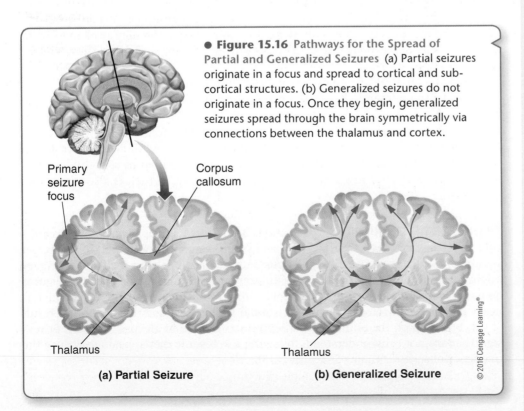

● **Figure 15.16** Pathways for the Spread of Partial and Generalized Seizures (a) Partial seizures originate in a focus and spread to cortical and subcortical structures. (b) Generalized seizures do not originate in a focus. Once they begin, generalized seizures spread through the brain symmetrically via connections between the thalamus and cortex.

Primary seizure focus

Corpus callosum

Thalamus

Thalamus

(a) Partial Seizure

(b) Generalized Seizure

© 2016 Cengage Learning®

Jacksonian march During some simple partial seizures, the progression of convulsions or twitches from body part to body part related to the organization of the primary motor cortex.

complex partial seizures A type of partial seizure originating in the temporal lobes.

paroxysmal depolarizing shift (PDS) A characteristic electrical pattern that occurs in neurons within a focus during a partial seizure.

tonic-clonic seizure A generalized seizure that results in violent convulsions; also known as a grand mal seizure.

absence seizure A mild type of generalized seizure in which the patient experiences a brief period of unconsciousness; also known as a petit mal seizure.

tonic phase The initial stage of a grand mal seizure, in which the patient experiences a loss of consciousness, cessation of breathing, and muscular contraction.

clonic phase The second phase of a grand mal seizure, characterized by violent, repetitious muscle contractions.

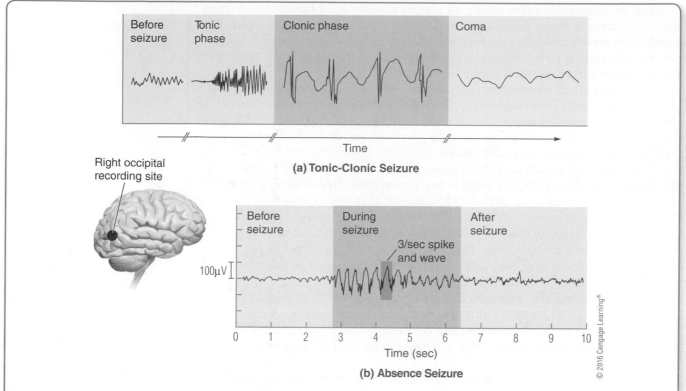

Figure 15.17 illustrating:
- (a) Tonic-Clonic Seizure: Before seizure, Tonic phase, Clonic phase, Coma — plotted against Time.
- Right occipital recording site.
- (b) Absence Seizure: Before seizure, During seizure, After seizure, with 3/sec spike and wave, 100µV, plotted against Time (sec) from 0 to 10.

© 2016 Cengage Learning®

● **Figure 15.17** **EEG Recordings During Generalized Seizures** In the upper image, we see recordings made during the stages of a tonic-clonic seizure. The lower image shows recordings made during an absence seizure. These recordings illustrate the characteristic "3/sec spike and wave" pattern that generally accompanies this type of seizure.

profusely. Cycling of tonic and clonic phases is followed by a period of **coma**, lasting about five minutes. The muscles relax, breathing resumes normally, but the person remains unconscious. Following the coma, the person may awaken or transition into sleep. An image of an EEG recording of a tonic-clonic seizure can be seen in ● Figure 15.17.

Absence seizures are much less violent than tonic-clonic seizures. For about 10 seconds, the person loses consciousness, and motor movements are limited to blinking, head turns, and eye movements. The person is unaware of his or her surroundings during the seizure. If the person happens to be standing or sitting, he or she does not fall over, in contrast to the complete loss of body control seen in a tonic-clonic seizure. Absence seizures are accompanied by a highly characteristic EEG pattern known as a "3/sec spike and wave," which is also illustrated in Figure 15.17.

TREATMENT FOR EPILEPSY Medications used to treat epilepsy are known as antiepileptic drugs, or AEDs. Many AEDs act as GABA agonists, although others target sodium and calcium channels (see Chapter 3). If medications are not effective, surgery might be indicated (see Chapter 13). Children ages 12 and younger whose seizures do not respond to medication often benefit from following a ketogenic diet, which is heavy in fats and low in carbohydrates, similar to the popular Atkins diet. As a result of this type of diet, the brain uses fat byproducts instead of glucose for fuel. For reasons that are not fully understood, following a ketogenic diet appears to reduce the frequency of seizures (Lutas & Yellen, 2013).

coma A deep, prolonged period of unconsciousness from which the person cannot be awakened.

Cognitive reserve plays a role in recovery from moderate to severe TBI. Educational attainment, which is one indicator of a person's cognitive reserve, was a strong predictor of a disability-free recovery after a period of one year (Schneider et al., 2014). Further, progressively greater amounts of education a person attained after high school indicated a higher likelihood of recovery. Cognitive reserve might predict a person's overall ability to adapt following neurological damage.

Rehabilitation for Neurocognitive Disorders

Rehabilitation literally means "to restore to good health." The considerable diversity among types of neurocognitive disorders and their respective symptoms makes a general approach to rehabilitation difficult. However, three factors that typically must be addressed include changes in cognitive abilities related to the disorder, emotional changes due to or in response to the disorder, and physical correlates, such as pain (O'Hara, 1988).

The development of effective rehabilitation is progressing rapidly. Patients with spinal cord injury have regained significant movement through the use of assisted motor training and epidural stimulation (Roy, Harkema, & Edgerton, 2012). These methods rely on the retraining of spinal circuits related to movement that can operate without input from motor systems in the brain (see Chapters 2 and 8). In one case, epidural stimulation allowed a patient to wiggle his toes on command, control some movement, and support 100 percent of his weight as he practices standing and stepping for a period of two hours.

Cognitive function can be improved through one of two methods (Giles, 2010). A cognitive approach (top-down) advocates stressing a particular cognitive function, like attention. By "practicing" good attention behavior, the patient experiences improvement. A functional approach focuses on specific tasks rather than cognitive skills. Following the cognitive approach, patients might engage in a variety of repetitive tasks that require attention, such as pressing a buzzer every time they see the number 3. In the functional approach, therapists might select a practical task in which attention is essential, such as driving a car, and specifically train the patient to relearn that task. A large meta-analysis indicated that both approaches are effective for patients over the long-term, but that the cognitive approach produced better short-term improvements in functioning (Vanderploeg et al., 2008).

Instead of receiving the enriched stimulus environment needed for optimum recovery, patients recovering from neurocognitive disorders often experience brain impoverishment because they are unable to provide themselves with the stimulation that could help regain some of their lost function. Tinson (1989) observed that hospitalized patients recovering from stroke spent 30 to 40 percent of their time "disengaged," with only 30 to 60 minutes per day of formal therapy. One commonly used solution to this problem is the use of virtual reality (VR), which allows the patient to participate in therapy for as long as he or she wishes without aid from expensive staff (Rose, Brooks, & Rizzo, 2005). Through virtual reality simulation, patients can experience moving through a building or up stairs or be exposed to whatever sensory stimulation might be most useful to address their specific deficits (Broeren et al., 2008; Deutsch & Mirelman, 2007). Imaging studies indicate that VR activates the same brain areas as a real interaction with the environment (Rose, Attree, Brooks, & Johnson, 1998; (Sorita et al., 2012). As this technology is refined, we can expect to see improvements in its use to treat patients with brain injuries.

Recent motion-sensitive technologies incorporated in entertainment games have made rehabilitation cost-effective and actually fun. Under the guidance of a healthcare professional, individuals recovering from neurocognitive conditions undergo "Wii-hab," using Nintendo's Wii gaming system (or Microsoft Kinect or Sony PlayStation Move) to augment their more formal physical therapy and other rehabilitation programs (see ● Figure 15.21).

rehabilitation A therapeutic process designed to restore function after illness or injury.

● **Figure 15.21** "Wii-hab" The use of commercial motion-sensing gaming systems allows people to augment their rehabilitation programs and have fun at the same time. This senior takes her tennis game very seriously.

SAUL LOEB/AFP/Getty Images

INTERIM SUMMARY 15.2

Characteristics of Partial and General Seizures

Type of Seizure	Subtype	Does Seizure Have a Focal Point?	Are Hemispheres Affected Symmetrically?	Major Features of This Type of Seizure
Partial seizures	Simple partial	Yes	No	Movements or sensations appropriate to the location of the focus; example: Jacksonian march
	Complex partial	Yes	No	Begin in temporal lobes; cause cognitive disturbances
Generalized seizures	Tonic-clonic (grand mal)	No	Yes	Tonic phase (loss of consciousness, muscular contraction, cessation of breathing) followed by clonic phase (violent muscular contractions), then coma
	Absence (petit mal)	No	Yes	Loss of consciousness; movements restricted to blinking, head turns, and eye movements

Summary Points

1. Although neurons usually do not form tumors, tumors can arise in the glial cells and meninges of the brain. **(LO3)**

2. Seizures are caused by a number of different conditions and are classified as partial or generalized. **(LO3)**

3. Multiple sclerosis is an autoimmune disorder in which the oligodendrocytes forming myelin in the central nervous system are damaged. **(LO3)**

4. Migraine, once believed to be the result of a vascular disorder, might arise due to neural events in a brainstem "migraine generator" that involves the neurochemical serotonin. **(LO3)**

5. The Kennard Principle states that recovery from brain damage is a function of developmental stage, but conflicting data exist. **(LO4)**

6. Rehabilitation in brain injury takes a multidisciplinary approach, addressing cognitive, emotional, and physical issues. **(LO4)**

‖ Review Questions

1. What are the major causes of seizures?

2. What is the relationship between age and recovery from brain injury?

3. What is cognitive reserve?

Chapter Review

THOUGHT QUESTIONS

1. Would you recommend genetic counseling for athletes who play contact sports that involve high rates of head injury? Why or why not?
2. TBI outcomes are influenced by other psychological conditions, including anxiety and depression. What are the implications for joint TBI and post-traumatic stress disorder among military personnel? How should this problem be addressed?

KEY TERMS

absence seizure (p. 533)
Alzheimer's disease (p. 514)
amyloid plaque (p. 514)
aneurysm (p. 517)
aura (p. 532)
bovine spongiform encephalopathy (BSE) (p. 522)
cerebral hemorrhage (p. 517)
cognitive reserve (p. 538)
complex partial seizure (p. 533)
concussion (p. 519)
countercoup (p. 520)
coup (p. 520)
Creutzfeldt-Jakob disease (CJD) (p. 525)
dementia (p. 514)
dementia pugilistica (p. 520)
encephalitis (p. 531)

epilepsy (p. 532)
generalized seizure (p. 532)
glioma (p. 529)
HIV-associated neurocognitive disorder (HAND) (p. 522)
infarct (p. 517)
ischemia (p. 517)
Kennard Principle (p. 537)
migraine (p. 536)
multiple sclerosis (p. 535)
neurocysticercosis (p. 530)
neuropsychologist (p. 512)
neuropsychology (p. 512)
neurocognitive disorder (p. 513)
neurocognitive disorder due to traumatic brain injury (p. 520)
neurofibrillary tangles (p. 514)

new variant Creutzfeldt-Jakob disease (vCJD) (p. 526)
open head injury (p. 519)
partial seizure (p. 532)
prion (p. 523)
rehabilitation (p. 539)
seizure (p. 532)
simple partial seizure (p. 532)
stroke (p. 517)
thrombosis (p. 517)
tonic-clonic seizure (p. 533)
transmissible spongiform encephalopathy (TSE) (p. 522)
transient ischemic attack (TIA) (p. 517)
traumatic brain injury (TBI) (p. 519)
tumor (p. 528)

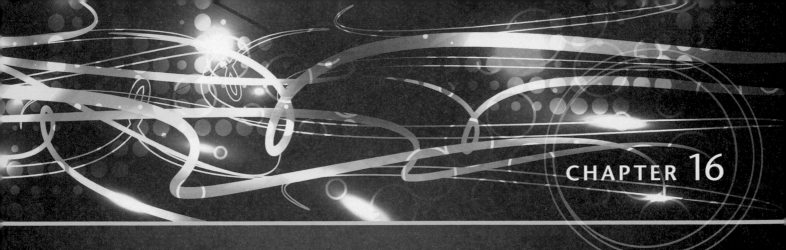

CHAPTER 16

Psychopathology

LEARNING OBJECTIVES

L01 Define mental disorder.

L02 Analyze the major symptoms and possible biological correlates of autism spectrum disorder and attention deficit hyperactivity disorder.

L03 Summarize the major biological correlates and treatments of schizophrenia.

L04 Compare and contrast the main features of bipolar disorder and major depressive disorder.

L05 Differentiate between the major features, causal factors, and treatments of panic disorder, post-traumatic stress disorder, and obsessive-compulsive disorder.

L06 Describe the biological correlates of antisocial personality disorder.

CONNECTING TO RESEARCH: Genetic Overlap in Five Disorders

BEHAVIORAL NEUROSCIENCE GOES TO WORK: Applied Behavior Analysis

BUILDING BETTER HEALTH: Diet and Bipolar Disorder

THINKING ETHICALLY: Are Psychopaths Legally Liable for Their Actions?

CHAPTER OUTLINE

mental disorder A syndrome characterized by clinically significant disturbance in an individual's cognition, emotion regulation, or behavior that reflects a dysfunction in the psychological, biological, or development processes underlying mental functioning.

What Does It Mean to Have a Mental Disorder?

Scientists and practitioners have a number of terms for the disorders described in this chapter, including behavior disorder, psychological disorder, and mental disorder. Because the organization of this chapter follows the diagnostic system put forward by the American Psychiatric Association, we will be consistent with this organization's terminology, using the term *mental disorder*. According to the *Diagnostic and Statistical Manual of Mental Disorders* (DSM-5, APA, 2013), a **mental disorder** is "a syndrome characterized by clinically significant disturbance in an individual's cognition, emotion regulation, or behavior that reflects a dysfunction in the psychological, biological, or development processes underlying mental functioning" (p. 20).

A course in behavioral neuroscience is not the place for a comprehensive description of all of the mental disorders classified by the DSM-5. Instead, our focus will be on disorders that feature substantial biological correlates, such as genetic vulnerability, structural differences in the brain, and biochemical differences that form the basis for biologically-based treatment approaches. Throughout this discussion, it is important to remember that we have few if any objective assessments that tell us whether someone has a particular condition or not. Unlike standard medicine, where a blood test or X-ray might provide definitive evidence of a disease, mental disorders are diagnosed purely through clinical observations of symptoms. As a result, the organization of the DSM-5 might not reflect the underlying biological causality of disorders. For example, five disorders that occupy very different categories in the DSM-5 based on their observable symptoms actually share overlapping genetic profiles. Schizophrenia, bipolar disorder, depression, attention deficit hyperactivity disorder, and autism spectrum disorder might have more in common than has previously been recognized (Cross-Disorder Group of the Psychiatric Genomics Consortium et al., 2013).

Although we still have much to learn, significant progress in our understanding and treatment of mental disorders has been made over the past six decades. Our previous understanding of mental disorders has not been the most enlightened aspect of human history. With the exception of bright spots of knowledge in ancient Egypt and Greece, people have typically accounted for unusual behaviors by using supernatural explanations. Medieval Europe experienced mass instances of "dance mania," in which individuals would move in unusual, uncontrollable ways that looked to observers like an odd dance. Their superstitious neighbors assumed that they were possessed and offered the "cure" of being burned at the stake. We now suspect that some "dancers" suffered from Sydenham's chorea, which is a rare consequence of strep infections. As medical knowledge progressed, we gained a greater understanding of the underlying biological causes of disorders. However, even as recently as the 1940s and 1950s, parents were blamed for causing disorders such as schizophrenia and autism spectrum disorder through bad child-rearing practices. Today, we combine our understanding of the interactions between biology and experience to explain and treat mental disorders.

A scientific understanding of mental disorders is urgent, given the large numbers of people affected by these disorders and the cost to society in the forms of lost days of work and treatment expenses. Approximately 26.2 percent of Americans over the age of 18 meet DSM criteria for a mental disorder in any given year, with anxiety disorders and mood disorders being the most frequent (Kessler, Chiu, Demler, & Walters, 2005) (see ● Figure 16.1).

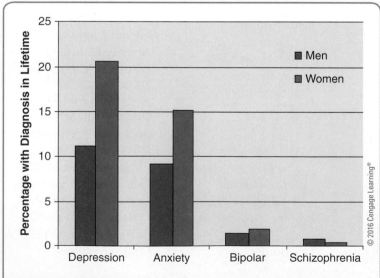

© 2016 Cengage Learning®

▶ ● **Figure 16.1 Mental Disorders Are Common** Significant numbers of adults in the United States report having been diagnosed with mental disorders at some time during their lives. Mental disorders account for more disability in developed countries than any other group of illnesses, including cancer and heart disease (CDC, 2011).

••• Connecting to **Research**

GENETIC OVERLAP IN FIVE DISORDERS

People can vary from one another genetically in many millions and possibly billions of ways. Out of all of these possible sources of variation, people diagnosed with schizophrenia, bipolar disorder, major depressive disorder, autism spectrum disorder, or attention deficit hyperactivity disorder shared variations in only four genes (Cross-Disorder Group of the Psychiatric Genomics Consortium, 2013). Two of these genes were linked with the process of moving calcium into cells. As we learned in Chapter 3, calcium plays a central role in the release of neurochemicals at the synapse.

The researchers in the Psychiatric Genomics Consortium found that out of the possible combinations of the five disorders, schizophrenia and bipolar disorder showed the greatest genetic overlap in heritability, at 15 percent. The overlap between bipolar disorder and depression was 10 percent, 9 percent between schizophrenia and depression, and 3 percent between schizophrenia and autism spectrum disorder.

Overall, common genetic variations explained 17 to 28 percent of the risk for the illnesses, so clearly other factors are at work. We will explore the individual factors believed to contribute to these and other psychological disorders in the remainder of this chapter.

Across entire lifetimes, it is possible that as many as 65 percent of the population experiences a disorder at least once (Moffitt et al., 2010). Worldwide, numbers of people with mental disorders are higher than in the United States because poverty, war, and other environmental factors contribute to increased prevalence (Kessler et al., 2007).

Following the ordering of disorders in the DSM-5 (APA, 2013), this chapter will feature a number of disorders that seem to have particularly important biological correlates.

Autism Spectrum Disorder (ASD)

The word *autism* literally means "within oneself." **Autism spectrum disorder (ASD)** is one of several neurodevelopmental disorders, which means that the onset of symptoms occurs during development (APA, 2013). This new category combines the previous categories of autism, Asperger's syndrome, and pervasive developmental disorder not otherwise specified (PDD-NOS). According to the DSM-5, ASD is characterized by deficits in two behavioral domains: social communication and interaction and restricted, repetitive patterns of behavior, interests, or activities (APA, 2013).

Autism is described as a spectrum of disorders because the severity of the observed deficits and the course of the disorder can vary widely from individual to individual. A few children make relatively normal adjustments, but 30–60 percent will be intellectually disabled (Amaral, Schumann, & Nordahl, 2008; Matson & Shoemaker, 2009). Most children with autism spectrum disorder show evidence of the disorder within the first 18 months of life, whereas 25–40 percent develop normally until about the age of 18–24 months, when they begin to regress (Werner & Dawson, 2005). It has become more common to diagnose ASD in school children after the age of seven years (Blumberg et al., 2013). It is possible that these time courses represent different sets of causal factors, although the behavioral outcomes are indistinguishable.

Recent estimates based on parent reports suggest that about 1 child in 50 (2%) between the ages of 6 and 17 years has been diagnosed with ASD (Blumberg et al., 2013). This represents a significant increase in prevalence relative to 2007, when prevalence was about 1 in 86 (1.16%; see ● Figure 16.2). This in turn represents a truly dramatic increase from the 3 to 6 children in 10,000 reported prior to 1990 (.03% to

autism spectrum disorder (ASD)
A lifetime disorder characterized by impairments in social interaction and communication and range of interests.

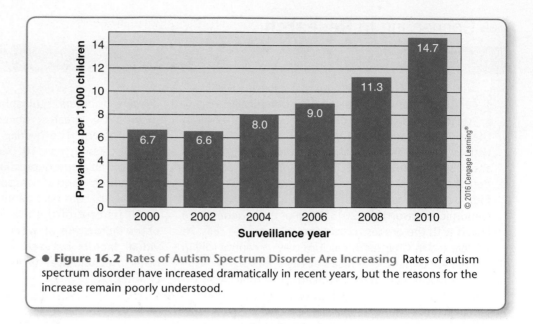

● **Figure 16.2** Rates of Autism Spectrum Disorder Are Increasing Rates of autism spectrum disorder have increased dramatically in recent years, but the reasons for the increase remain poorly understood.

.06%; Wing, 1993). It is unclear whether these rate increases reflect a genuine rise in the incidence of the disorder or a relaxation of diagnostic criteria or a combination of both factors (Barbaresi, Katusic, Colligan, Weaver, & Jacobsen, 2005). Among the growing number of cases diagnosed after the age of seven years, the vast majority are "mild," suggesting that some increases in the rates of diagnosis have resulted from greater awareness, changes in how diagnostic criteria are applied, or increased special education services (Blumberg et al., 2013).

ASD is one of the disorders that shows a strong gender difference in risk. School-aged boys are about four times as likely to be diagnosed with ASD than girls (3.23 percent compared to 0.70 percent) (Blumberg et al., 2013).

Causes of ASD

The exact causes of ASD remain unknown. There is strong evidence from family and twin studies that ASD is influenced by genetics (Frazier et al., 2014). Studies of identical twins suggest that the concordance rate (see Chapter 5) for ASD is approximately 76 to 88 percent (Ronald & Hoekstra, 2011). Relatives of people with ASD have elevated levels of autistic traits compared to those who do not have relatives with ASD (Constantino et al., 2009). This suggests that autistic traits are continuously distributed across the human population, and only reach the level of a diagnosable disorder in a relatively smaller group of individuals (Baron-Cohen, Wheelwright, Skinner, Martin, & Clubley, 2001).

Genes that seem most likely to participate in ASD are involved with the regulation of brain development (Yang & Gill, 2007) and specifically with synaptic changes (Persico & Bourgeron, 2006). As we observed earlier, some of the genetic risk factors for ASD overlap with risk factors for other types of disorders (Cross-Disorder Group of the Psychiatric Genomics Consortium, 2013). Given the diverse and complex systems of behavior affected by ASD, such as sociability and language, it should come as no surprise to learn that no single gene has been shown to contribute to a person's susceptibility to all aspects of ASD. However, one of the most reliable early signs of most cases of ASD is language delay, and studies comparing genetic vulnerability for both ASD and language have pinpointed a susceptibility gene on chromosome 7 for "age at first word" (Alarcón et al., 2008). Another candidate susceptibility gene, the *CNTNAP2* gene, is expressed in the cerebellum and impacts language. *CNTNAP2* is linked to both ASD and dyslexia, a developmental reading disorder which we discussed in Chapter 13 (Stoodley, 2014). Otherwise, general tendencies managed by large pools of genes are likely to be involved (Skafidas et al., 2012). For example, people with ASD are much more likely to have relatives who are engineers and scientists, whose thinking is highly systematic, than relatives who are artists and poets, whose thinking can be characterized as more emotional and empathic (Baron-Cohen & Belmonte, 2005; Alarcón et al., 2008; Persico & Bourgeron, 2006).

Genetic predispositions for ASD likely interact with multiple environmental factors (Happe, Ronald, & Plomin, 2006). Monozygotic (identical) twins are not 100 percent concordant for ASD, indicating that some additional factors can play a role. One of the environmental risk factors for ASD is perinatal complications, or complications surrounding the birth of the individual with ASD (Ronald & Hoekstra, 2011). As in all correlations, we do not know whether the birth complications contribute to the development of ASD, are caused by the genetic profile of the fetus, or result from some interaction between the two. Increased parental age also increases risk of producing a child with ASD, but the effect is rather small (Shelton, Tancredi, & Hertz-Picciotto, 2010). Exposure to infection, pesticides, and nutritional factors have also been implicated as possible risks for ASD (Hamlyn, Duhig, McGrath, & Scott, 2013; Rossignol, Genius, & Frye, 2014).

Researchers have examined the possibility that maternal use of selective serotonin reuptake inhibitors (SSRIs) during or prior to pregnancy might impact the likelihood of giving birth to a child with ASD. As we mentioned in Chapter 4, children with ASD often have abnormalities in their blood levels of serotonin, although the implications for this difference on the functioning of the nervous system is unknown. Boys with ASD were three times as likely as typically developing boys to have been exposed prenatally to SSRIs (Harrington, Lee, Crum, Zimmerman, & Hertz-Picciotto, 2014). The effect was largest when the SSRI exposure occurred during the first trimester of pregnancy.

Yet another possible risk for ASD is abnormal responses of the maternal immune system during pregnancy (Bauman et al., 2013). It is customary for maternal antibodies to cross the placenta to provide protection for the fetus. However, in approximately 12 percent of mothers with children with ASD but in no mothers with typically developing children, maternal antibodies that target fetal brain proteins have been identified. When these antibodies were administered to pregnant rhesus monkeys, their male offspring showed brain abnormalities and inappropriate social behaviors.

Brain Structure and Function in ASD

A leading theory of ASD suggests that brain development is abnormally accelerated through early childhood, producing first brain enlargement, then a period of deceleration (Amaral et al., 2008). Consistent with this view is the finding that infants eventually diagnosed with ASD have much higher levels of circulating neurotrophins than healthy infants within a few days of birth (Nelson et al., 2001). High levels of neurotrophins may lead to less apoptosis and larger brain size (see Chapter 5). This different developmental pathway appears to occur in children with a pattern of early symptom onset, but not in those with normal development followed by regression (Webb et al., 2007).

Larger head size at birth in children who will eventually be diagnosed with ASD might also be the result of excess cerebrospinal fluid (CSF; see Chapter 2) in the subarachnoid space. Excess CSF observed in an MRI at the age of six months was predictive of not only a diagnosis of ASD, but also the eventual severity of ASD symptoms (Shen et al., 2013).

An alternate view of brain anatomy in ASD suggests that the structure of minicolumns, representing the smallest units of processing in the prefrontal cortex, is different in individuals with ASD compared to healthy controls (Casanova, Switala, Trippe, & Fitzgerald, 2007; Casanova et al., 2006; Opris & Casanova, 2014) (see ● Figure 16.3). The number of neurons within each minicolumn in the brains of people with ASD is normal, but the distance between minicolumns is reduced (Opris & Casanova, 2014). These findings are consistent with differences in connectivity that favor local or detail-focused processing over global processing (Casanova et al., 2007; Casanova

● **Figure 16.3** Minicolumn Differences in Autism Spectrum Disorder Researchers have observed differences in the cortical minicolumn organization between people with autism spectrum disorder and healthy controls. The differences are consistent with more local, detailed processing rather than global processing.

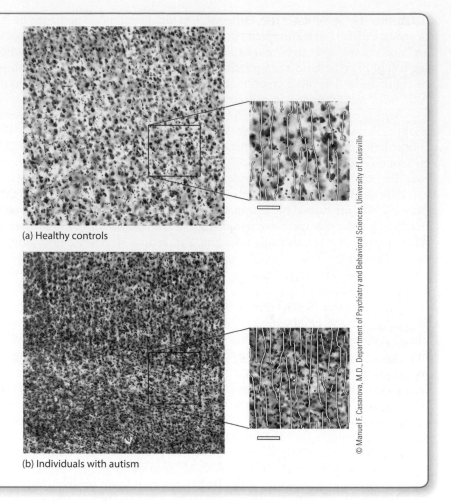

(a) Healthy controls

(b) Individuals with autism

© Manuel F. Casanova, M.D., Department of Psychiatry and Behavioral Sciences, University of Louisville

et al., 2006; Opris & Casanova, 2014). The additional finding that the brains of three distinguished scientists without deficits in language and sociability showed minicolumn structure similar to that found in patients with ASD suggests that minicolumn dimensions might account for the extreme focus of interests found in ASD and possibly savant behavior (Casanova, Switala, Trippe, & Fitzgerald, 2007).

Other brain structures associated with ASD include the cerebellum, amygdala, and hippocampus. Decreased cerebellar cortical volume is a very important biomarker for ASD (Stoodley, 2014). The degree of structural differences in the cerebellum compared to the brains of healthy control individuals is correlated with the severity of behavioral symptoms. Although earlier researchers have reported abnormalities in the development of the amygdala, a longitudinal comparison of children with ASD and normally developing controls found similar changes in amygdala volume over time (Barnea-Goraly et al., 2014). Within the ASD group, the volume of the right amygdala predicted the capability of making appropriate eye contact. The children with ASD did not differ from the healthy control participants in the volume of the left hippocampus, but their right hippocampus was relatively enlarged (Barnea-Goraly et al., 2014). Over the course of development, the children with ASD experienced normalization of their right hippocampal volume due to reductions that did not occur in the normally developing group.

Dysfunctions in mirror system function (see Chapter 8) have been proposed to account for a number of deficits in ASD because mirror system function has been implicated in empathy, imitation, and language (Iacoboni & Dapretto, 2006; Iacoboni & Mazziotta, 2007). However, a meta-analysis found no evidence of a global deficit in mirror functioning in ASD (Hamilton, 2013). A possible role for mirror system function in ASD continues to be debated (Gallese, Rochat, & Berchio, 2013).

Treatment of ASD

ASD is usually treated with intensive, early-childhood learning experiences provided during most of the child's waking hours (Newsom, 1998). For high-functioning children who have some spontaneous language prior to the age of 3 to 5 years, this aggressive intervention can produce nearly normal behavioral outcomes (Smith & Lovaas, 1998).

Efforts to use medications to improve core behavior problems (social relatedness and ritualistic behavior) in children with ASD have been ineffective (Buitelaar, 2003). Only two medications, both antipsychotic drugs to be used to reduce self-injurious behavior among the most severely affected individuals (McPheeters et al., 2011), have been approved in the United States for the treatment of ASD. Like all antipsychotics, both approved medications carry significant side effects in the form of sedation and weight gain. However, many additional medications are prescribed "off label," or without Federal Drug Administration approval for ASD, including antidepressants. A disturbing 35 percent of children with ASD in one sample had been prescribed at least one off-label drug, and 9 percent were taking three or more off-label drugs, in spite of the fact that none of these prescribed drugs had been approved for use in cases of ASD (Rosenberg et al., 2010).

Based on reports that people with ASD show evidence of excess peptides from gluten (found in wheat) and casein (found in dairy products), many families chose to exclude these food sources from the diets of children with ASD. However, controlled studies do not indicate that diet changes reduce core symptoms of ASD (Millward, Ferriter, Calver, & Connell-Jones, 2008).

••• Behavioral Neuroscience GOES TO WORK

APPLIED BEHAVIOR ANALYSIS

Early work by Ivar Lovaas and his colleagues at UCLA established the efficacy of applying basic principles of operant conditioning, or the pairing of consequences and target behaviors (see Chapter 12), to improve the language and social skills of children with ASD (Smith & Lovaas, 1998). Originally, such applications were known as "behavior modification." Eventually, the preferred term became *applied behavior analysis* or ABA. While not restricted to the treatment of children with ASD or other neurodevelopmental disorders, ABA is the major approach used in these situations (see ● Figure 16.4).

Board certification in ABA is available through the nonprofit Behavior Analyst Certification Board at different levels depending on an individual's attainment of a bachelor's, master's, or doctoral degree. Certification at the bachelor's degree level gives the person the title of board certified assistant behavior analyst and certification at the master's degree level gives the person the title of board certified behavior analyst (Behavior Analyst Certification Board [BACB], n.d.). Additional certification is available at the doctoral level. Approved university training is typically housed in either psychology or education departments.

Behavior analysts work with clients by using learning principles to change the frequency of behaviors, such as increasing language output or decreasing unwanted, self-stimulation behaviors such as rocking, hand flapping, and head banging. The analyst considers the circumstances in which the target behavior occurs and possible rewarding mechanisms already in place that may be maintaining the behavior and designs a plan to change the frequency of the target behavior. In the case of autism spectrum disorder, teams of analysts take turns working with a child through most of the child's waking day.

● **Figure 16.4 Autism Spectrum Disorder Is Treated with Applied Behavior Analysis** In the absence of medications that improve the core symptoms of autism spectrum disorder, the only effective method for treating this disorder remains applied behavior analysis (ABA).

Attention Deficit Hyperactivity Disorder

Also found in the neurodevelopmental disorder category of the DSM-5 (APA, 2013) is **attention deficit hyperactivity disorder (ADHD)**. In 2011, 11 percent of children between the ages of 4 and 17 years had been diagnosed with ADHD in the United States, an increase of 42 percent over rates of ADHD in 2003 (Visser et al., 2014). In some cases, symptoms of ADHD continue beyond childhood, affecting approximately 4 percent of adults (Kessler et al., 2007). Symptoms of ADHD include inattentiveness, impulsivity, and hyperactivity (APA, 2013). Individuals can be diagnosed with inattentiveness alone without impulsivity/hyperactivity (although there is no official ADD designation), impulsivity/hyperactivity alone without inattentiveness, or combined inattentiveness and impulsivity/hyperactivity. ADHD is diagnosed at least twice as frequently in males as in females, and females are more likely to exhibit inattention without impulsivity and hyperactivity (APA, 2013).

Accurate diagnosis of ADHD is challenging because many of the criteria for the disorder seem to involve very normal behaviors (see ● Figure 16.5). For example, the criteria include "often avoids, dislikes, or is reluctant to engage in tasks that require sustained mental effort (such as schoolwork or homework; for older adolescents and adults, preparing reports, completing forms, reviewing lengthy papers)" (APA, 2013, p. 59). Few of us have not shared that dislike or reluctance on occasion. The criteria do specify that symptoms must "interfere with, or reduce the quality of, social, academic, or occupational functioning" (APA, 2013, p. 60). Nonetheless, it is easy to see how normal child behavior might be mistaken for ADHD. Angold, Erkanli, Egger, and Costello (2000) found that more than half of the children in a large sample who were prescribed stimulant medications for ADHD did not meet even relaxed diagnostic criteria for the disorder. When vignettes describing case studies were sent to 1,000 child psychologists, psychiatrists, and social workers, 17 percent of the clinicians diagnosed

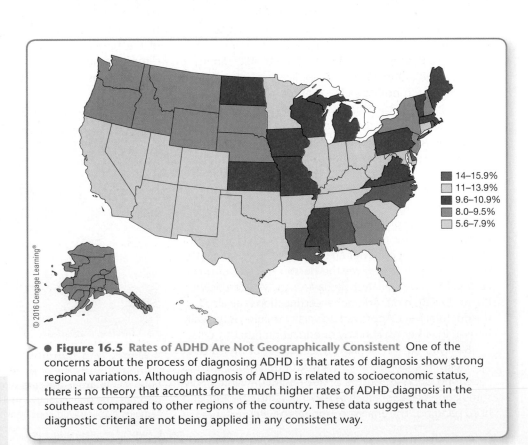

© 2016 Cengage Learning®

> ● **Figure 16.5** Rates of ADHD Are Not Geographically Consistent One of the concerns about the process of diagnosing ADHD is that rates of diagnosis show strong regional variations. Although diagnosis of ADHD is related to socioeconomic status, there is no theory that accounts for the much higher rates of ADHD diagnosis in the southeast compared to other regions of the country. These data suggest that the diagnostic criteria are not being applied in any consistent way.

attention deficit hyperactivity disorder (ADHD) A disorder first diagnosed in childhood, characterized by inattention, hyperactivity, or both.

ADHD incorrectly in healthy children (Bruchmüller, Margraf, & Schneider, 2012). Clinicians continue to debate, however, whether ADHD is overdiagnosed or even underdiagnosed (Sciutto & Eisenberg, 2007).

Causes of ADHD

The heritability of ADHD has been estimated to be around 70 percent or possibly higher (Faraone & Mick, 2010). The mechanism for this genetic influence is currently unknown, and it is very likely that multiple genes are involved.

Dopaminergic systems are a logical place for researchers to look. Brain structures consistently implicated in ADHD, such as the basal ganglia and prefrontal cortex, are rich in dopaminergic neurons. Traditional medications used for ADHD, which include **methylphenidate (Ritalin)**, **dextroamphetamine (Dexedrine** or **Dextrostat)**, and mixed amphetamine salts (**Adderall**), are known dopamine agonists. Research has therefore focused on genes associated with dopamine, including dopamine transporter genes (Albrecht et al., 2014; Spencer et al., 2013).

Although genetic influences on ADHD are substantial, environmental factors alone or in conjunction with susceptibility genes contribute to the prevalence of the disorder. Among environmental risk factors for ADHD are lead contamination, low birth weight, and prenatal exposure to tobacco, alcohol, and other drugs (Banerjee, Middleton, & Faraone, 2007).

Brain Structure and Function in ADHD

Brain structures implicated in ADHD include the prefrontal cortex, the basal ganglia, and the circuits that connect these two areas. The fact that people with known frontal lobe damage behave in ways that are similar to those with ADHD led to interest in the frontal lobes as a possible area responsible for ADHD symptoms. Specifically, both groups have problems with organization, impulsivity, emotional behavior, and sustained attention.

Some researchers have argued that the frontal lobes, and the prefrontal areas in particular, seem to mature differently in children with ADHD compared to healthy controls (Shaw et al., 2007; Vaidya, 2012). Peak cortical thickness, a measure of brain maturation, occurred in healthy controls around age 7.5 years but not until age 10.5 years in the children with ADHD. Other researchers view differences in cortical thickness between patients with ADHD and typical control participants to be the result of abnormal development rather than maturity, as these differences are also observed in adults (Almeida Montes et al., 2012). As we noted in Chapter 5, cortical thickening followed by some degree of thinning is a normal part of adolescent brain development. Cases in which symptoms of ADHD persisted into adulthood were correlated with an increased rate of cortical thinning compared to healthy controls, while individuals whose symptoms disappeared as they matured experienced either cortical thickening or minimal thinning during adolescence (Shaw et al., 2013).

A number of researchers have reported smaller volume of the caudate nucleus, a part of the basal ganglia, associated with ADHD (Castellanos et al., 1994; Filipek et al., 1997; Mataro et al., 1997; Swanson, Castellanos, Murias, LaHoste, & Kennedy, 1998). However, this difference between individuals with and without ADHD disappears by the age of 16 years (Krain & Castellanos, 2006), lending further support to the view of ADHD as a problem of maturation in many cases.

Although all cases of ADHD appear to involve the prefrontal areas and basal ganglia, subtypes of ADHD might be differentially affected by problems in these two areas. ADHD with hyperactivity might represent a central problem with the basal ganglia, whereas inattentive ADHD without hyperactivity is more likely to result from problems in the prefrontal cortex (Diamond, 2007).

Behavioral neuroscience continues to move in the direction of considering networks, like the default mode network (DMN; see Chapter 11) rather than

methylphenidate (Ritalin) A close relative of amphetamine that is prescribed to treat attention deficit hyperactivity disorder.

dextroamphetamine (Dexedrine or Dextrostat) A dopamine agonist used to treat some cases of attention deficit hyperactivity disorder.

Adderall A combination of amphetamine salts prescribed to treat attention deficit hyperactivity disorder.

abnormalities in specific structures or regions of the brain as the source of abnormal behavior. Although network analysis in cases of ADHD has produced inconsistent results so far, improved methods are likely to soon highlight differences in connectivity and patterns of network activity related to some symptoms (Konrad & Eickhoff, 2010).

Treatment of ADHD

Children with a diagnosis of ADHD are treated primarily with medication, either alone or in combination with behavioral therapy similar to that used to treat ASD. The use of medication for ADHD in the United States, which is five times greater than in any other nation, has been the subject of considerable criticism. Nonetheless, medication provides benefits for the majority of children with ADHD (Faraone & Buitelaar, 2010).

The use of stimulant medication to treat ADHD resulted from an accidental discovery. In 1937, Charles Bradley administered the stimulant Benzedrine, a type of dextroamphetamine, to children referred to him for learning and behavior problems. Bradley (1937) observed that the children responded with spectacular improvement in school performance while becoming emotionally subdued.

The most commonly prescribed drugs for ADHD are the closely related stimulants methylphenidate (Ritalin), dextroamphetamine, and amphetamine salts (Adderall). The amphetamine drugs act as dopamine and norepinephrine reuptake inhibitors and increase the release of these neurotransmitters. Methylphenidate acts as a dopamine reuptake inhibitor (see Chapter 4). The positive outcomes resulting from the use of dopamine agonists has led to the suggestion that ADHD is associated with lower levels of dopamine activity (Volkow et al., 2009). Although most patients tolerate these medications well, serious side effects, including loss of appetite and sleep disturbance can occur (Ogrim, Hestad, Brunner, & Kropotov, 2013). For patients who do not respond to stimulants, or who experience unacceptable levels of side effects, nonstimulant drugs such as atomoxetine (Strattera), a norepinephrine reuptake inhibitor, might be helpful (Prasad & Steer, 2008). However, atomoxetine has been the subject of a public health advisory by the U.S. Food and Drug Administration due to its association with increased suicidal thoughts (FDA, 2013).

A recent and troubling trend in the treatment of ADHD has been to prescribe antipsychotic medications in addition to stimulant medications (Bussing & Winterstein, 2012). Antipsychotic medications usually produce either a direct or indirect suppression of dopamine function, which is not consistent with the stimulant medications' agonistic effect on dopamine (Bussing & Winterstein, 2012) or with a hypothesis implicating inadequate dopamine activity as the source of ADHD symptoms.

INTERIM SUMMARY 16.1

‖ Summary Points

1. A mental disorder is defined as "a syndrome characterized by clinically significant disturbance in an individual's cognition, emotion regulation, or behavior that reflects a dysfunction in the psychological, biological, or development processes underlying mental functioning." **(LO1)**

2. Autism spectrum disorder (ASD) is heavily influenced by genetics and is correlated with abnormal development in the limbic system and cerebellum. Early, intense behavioral intervention is the typical treatment for ASD. **(LO2)**

3. Attention deficit hyperactivity disorder (ADHD) is characterized by short attention span and high levels of motor activity. Abnormal functioning of the frontal

lobe and basal ganglia might contribute to ADHD. ADHD is typically treated with stimulant medication with or without behavioral therapy. **(LO3)**

‖ Review Questions

1. What are the leading hypotheses for explaining the causes of ASD and ADHD?
2. What structural and functional brain correlates characterize ASD and ADHD?

Schizophrenia

When people think of mental disorders, **schizophrenia** comes readily to mind. The word *schizophrenia* is Greek for "split mind," but this should not be confused with a condition characterized by multiple personalities, currently referred to as dissociative identity disorder (APA, 2013). Instead, the split in schizophrenia represents a discrepancy between emotion and thought. Schizophrenia dramatically disrupts many of the basic capacities that are central to human experience—perception, reason, emotion, movement, and social engagement. The DSM-5 places schizophrenia in a general category for schizophrenia spectrum and other psychotic disorders (APA, 2013). A diagnosis of schizophrenia requires at least two of the following to be present most of the time during a single one-month period: **delusions** (unrealistic thoughts), **hallucinations** (false perceptions), disorganized speech, grossly disorganized or catatonic behavior, and negative symptoms (diminished emotional expression or avolition) (APA, 2013).

These symptoms of schizophrenia can be divided into categories of positive and negative symptoms. **Positive symptoms** of schizophrenia are behaviors that are not expected to occur normally, such as hallucinations and delusions. Instances of these behaviors are frequently referred to as "psychotic episodes." **Negative symptoms**, such as diminished emotional expression and avolition (lack of motivation), occur when normal and expected behaviors are missing. Healthy people are typically emotionally expressive (see Chapter 14) and motivated (see Chapter 9), so the disruptions to these aspects of behavior seen in schizophrenia represent the absence of normal behavior. Although the distinction between positive and negative symptoms may appear arbitrary, these symptoms appear to differ in their underlying causes and responses to treatment.

Schizophrenia strikes people of all nationalities at about the same rate—0.5 to 1 percent of the population (Shaner, Miller, & Mintz, 2004). Most cases of schizophrenia are diagnosed for the first time in individuals between the ages of 18 and 25 years of age, although a sizable minority of cases appear for the first time after age 40 (Howard et al., 2000). About 60 percent of patients with schizophrenia are male (McGrath, Saha, Chant, & Welham, 2008).

Genetic Contributions to Schizophrenia

Substantial evidence exists for a genetic predisposition for schizophrenia. In schizophrenia, the concordance rate is about 50 percent in identical twins and about 17 percent in fraternal twins (Gottesman, 1991). As shown in ● Figure 16.6, the odds that a person will develop schizophrenia increase as more closely related family members are diagnosed with the disorder. Results of adoption studies also support a large role for genetics in schizophrenia (Kety, Rosenthal, Wender, & Schulsinger, 1968). Genes are not the entire story, however, as shown by the case of the Genain sisters, identical quadruplets diagnosed with schizophrenia (DeLisi et al., 1984; Mirsky et al., 1984). Although all four sisters had schizophrenia, their outcomes differed substantially. One sister graduated from a two-year business college, married,

---

schizophrenia A disorder characterized by hallucination, delusion, cognitive impairment, mood disturbance, and social withdrawal.

delusion A false belief or opinion that is strongly held in spite of conclusive, contradictory evidence.

hallucinations A false or distorted perception of objects or events.

positive symptom An abnormal behavior, such as hallucination and delusion, that does not occur in healthy individuals but occurs in people with schizophrenia.

negative symptom A normal and expected behavior that is absent due to schizophrenia.

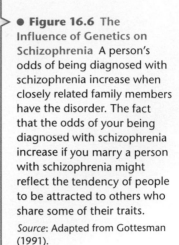

● **Figure 16.6** The Influence of Genetics on Schizophrenia A person's odds of being diagnosed with schizophrenia increase when closely related family members have the disorder. The fact that the odds of your being diagnosed with schizophrenia increase if you marry a person with schizophrenia might reflect the tendency of people to be attracted to others who share some of their traits.

Source: Adapted from Gottesman (1991).

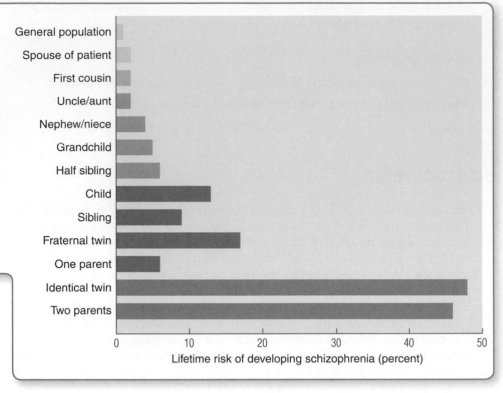

and had two children, while her sisters' social functioning was described as "grossly inadequate."

The hunt to identify the genes responsible for schizophrenia is an active area of research. A large number of genes might function abnormally in the brains of people with schizophrenia (Owen, Craddock, & Jablensky, 2007; Mirnics, Middleton, Marquez, Lewis, & Levitt, 2000). Susceptibility genes for schizophrenia overlap with those implicated in bipolar disorder, a type of mood disorder we discuss in a later section (Owen, Craddock, & Jablensky, 2007). In one case of identical triplets, two were diagnosed with schizophrenia, whereas the third was diagnosed with bipolar disorder (McGuffin, Reveley, & Holland, 1982). Susceptibility genes for schizophrenia also overlap with those of autism spectrum disorder (Cross-Disorder Group of the Psychiatric Genomics Consortium, 2013; Gejman, Sanders, & Kendler, 2011).

A majority of individuals with schizophrenia, as well as about 45 percent of their healthy family members, share an abnormality of eye movement that might serve as a useful genetic marker, or indicator of a genetic predisposition, to schizophrenia (Ettinger et al., 2004; Holzman, Levy, & Proctor, 1976). When we track a moving object, such as a ball's trajectory during a game of tennis, our eyes make characteristic smooth-pursuit movements. For other tasks, such as reading, our eyes jump from one fixation point to the next in jerky movements known as **saccades**. As shown in ● Figure 16.7, patients with schizophrenia and some of their family members show intrusions of saccades during smooth-pursuit tasks. These abnormal eye movements might represent deficits in executive cognitive functions, normally carried out by the frontal lobes, and in goal-related behavior in particular (Reuter & Kathmann, 2004; Thakkar, Schall, Boucher, Logan, & Park, 2011). These irregular eye movement patterns might also be related to abnormal corollary discharges in the brains of people with schizophrenia (Pack, 2014). Corollary discharges are neural responses that signal intention to move. In the case of eye movements like saccades, corollary discharges allow individuals to estimate their own eye position, a task that proves very difficult for people with schizophrenia.

saccades The rapid eye movement that occurs when an individual is visually tracking a moving stimulus.

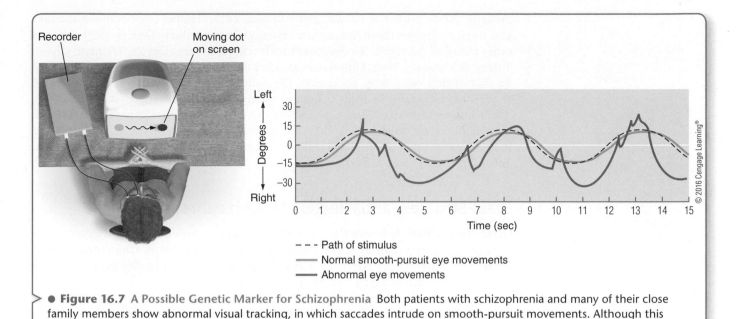

● Figure 16.7 A Possible Genetic Marker for Schizophrenia Both patients with schizophrenia and many of their close family members show abnormal visual tracking, in which saccades intrude on smooth-pursuit movements. Although this behavior helps us evaluate the genetic basis of schizophrenia, we do not know its exact underlying cause.

Environmental Influences on Schizophrenia

The fact that concordance rates among identical twins fall short of 100 percent points to a contribution by environmental factors in the development of schizophrenia. These environmental factors interact with genetic vulnerability for schizophrenia. In other words, if you do not have a family history of schizophrenia or related conditions, it is less likely that experiencing these situations will increase your risk for developing the disorder.

Rates of schizophrenia are somewhat higher in urban environments (Van Os, 2004). Schizophrenia is five times more likely in lower than in middle or higher socio-economic groups (Robins & Regier, 1991), although it is not clear how much of this effect is causal and how much reflects the inability of people with schizophrenia to remain employed. Some of this environmental influence may arise from poverty, poor nutrition, and the stress related to racism (Boydell et al., 2001; Boydell & Murray, 2003). Another possible explanation is that living in an urban environment raises the likelihood of using marijuana, which in turn appears to interact with an individual's genetic predisposition to psychosis (Fergusson, Horwood, & Ridder, 2005; Henquet et al., 2005; Onwuameze et al., 2013). Marijuana use might represent the efforts of an individual to self-medicate for schizophrenia, but it has also been shown to be used more frequently by those with the disorder who experience relapses of psychotic symptoms (Linszen, 1994).

Prenatal environmental factors might play a role in the development of schizophrenia. The eventual development of schizophrenia in offspring is correlated with mothers' difficulties during pregnancy (bleeding and diabetes), abnormal fetal development (low birth weight and small head circumference), and birth complications (emergency caesarean section, lack of oxygen) (Cannon, Jones, & Murray, 2002). It is possible that the experience of a difficult birth triggers schizophrenia, infants vulnerable to schizophrenia possess characteristics that predispose them to difficult prenatal and birth processes, some combination of the two occurs, or the existence of a third, currently unknown variable leading to both schizophrenia and birth complications might account for these correlations.

A mother's exposure to famine or viral infection during her pregnancy can contribute to the development of schizophrenia in her offspring (Brown, 2006; Kyle &

Pichard, 2006; Penner & Brown, 2007; Brown, 2012). People born between January and April (in the northern hemisphere) are slightly more likely than people born in at other times of the year to be diagnosed with schizophrenia (Davies, Welham, Chant, Torrey, & McGrath, 2003; Hultman et al., 1999). One explanation of this finding might be that during the winter flu season, the patients' pregnant mothers were exposed to viruses, especially in colder climates (Cannon, Kendell, Susser, & Jones, 2003). Additional evidence of a role for viral infection in schizophrenia is the observation that people recently diagnosed with schizophrenia have higher levels of viral enzymes in their brains and cerebrospinal fluid (CSF) than healthy controls (Yolken, Karlsson, Yee, Johnston-Wilson, & Torrey, 2000).

Brain Structure and Function in Schizophrenia

Given the dramatic behavioral deficits found in schizophrenia, we might expect associated brain abnormalities to be obvious and easy to document. Unfortunately, it is difficult to separate the effects of schizophrenia from other possible causes of brain abnormalities such as aging and medication history.

Many patients with schizophrenia have enlarged ventricles, as shown in ● Figure 16.8. The presence of enlarged lateral ventricles distinguishes between an identical twin who has schizophrenia and the twin who is healthy (McNeil, Cantor-Graae, & Weinberger, 2000). Having enlarged ventricles is not associated with any particular behaviors because the ventricles are only fluid-filled spaces. However, enlarged ventricles represent a loss of neurons in adjacent areas. In particular, the hippocampus has been found to be smaller than normal in some individuals with schizophrenia (Morgan et al., 2007; Lawrie, Whalley, Job, & Johnstone, 2003; Schulze et al., 2003). In addition, the hippocampus shows an unusual disorganization in some cases of schizophrenia (Kovelman & Scheibel, 1984). The cells of the hippocampus are normally lined up rather neatly in rows. In the hippocampus of some patients with schizophrenia, the cells are in relative disarray. Given the importance of the hippocampus in memory and cognition, this lack of organization might account for some of the deficits in reasoning and thought found in schizophrenia. The role of the hippocampus in stress (see Chapter 14) could explain observed associations between the onset and course of schizophrenia and stress levels.

● **Figure 16.8** Schizophrenia Is Associated with Enlarged Ventricles MRI images of the brains of a pair of identical twins show the discrepancy between normal ventricles and the enlargement of ventricles found in some people who have schizophrenia. The twin on the left is healthy; the twin on the right suffers from schizophrenia.

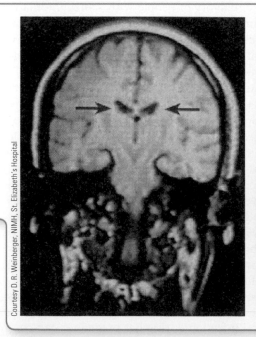
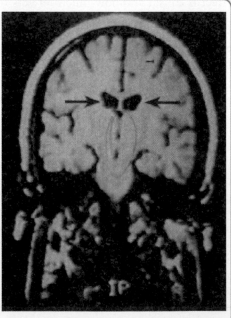

Courtesy D. R. Weinberger, NIMH, St. Elizabeth's Hospital

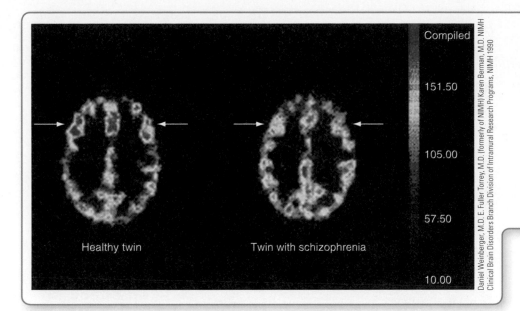

Daniel Weinberger, M.D. E. Fuller Torrey, M.D. (formerly of NIMH) Karen Berman, M.D. NIMH Clinical Brain Disorders Branch Division of Intramural Research Programs, NIMH 1990

● **Figure 16.9**
Hypofrontality Frontal lobe activity (toward the top of the page) appears to be reduced in people with schizophrenia when compared with their healthy identical twins engaged in the same tasks. Active regions of the brain appear red or yellow, and inactive areas are green, blue, violet, and black.

Lower activity in the frontal lobes, or hypofrontality, is associated with some of the negative symptoms of schizophrenia, such as mood disturbance and social withdrawal (Andreasen, Rezai, Alliger, Swayze, Flaum et al., 1992). As shown in ●Figure 16.9, measures of glucose metabolism indicate that people with schizophrenia show lower levels of frontal lobe activity than healthy controls both during rest and during difficult cognitive tasks (Weinberger, Aloia, Goldberg, & Berman, 1994). Differences in frontal lobe activity can be used to distinguish between an identical twin with schizophrenia and the healthy member of the pair (Berman, Torrey, Daniel, & Weinberger, 1992). The abnormality of frontal lobe activity in patients with schizophrenia might result from a more widespread problem in their default mode network (DMN; see Chapter 11). Activity in the DMN appears to be markedly abnormal in patients with schizophrenia, and the degree to which their DMN activity differs from healthy control participants correlates with the severity of their positive symptoms (Garrity et al., 2007; Pomarol-Clotet et al., 2008).

Brains of people with schizophrenia are more symmetrical in structure and function than brains of healthy individuals, and people with schizophrenia are more likely to have ambiguous handedness as opposed to being clearly right-handed or left-handed (Crow, 1997). Based on these observations, Berlim, Mattevi, Belmonte-de-Abreu, and Crow (2003) suggested that schizophrenia arose in conjunction with cerebral lateralization and the development of language in our species' past (see Chapter 13). Schizophrenia, according to this view, could be considered as an occasional failure of normal brain lateralization.

One of the puzzles surrounding schizophrenia has been its typical onset in late adolescence and early adulthood. If susceptibility genes interact with environmental factors, especially those that involve prenatal development, why does it take so long for observable symptoms to occur? One possible solution to this dilemma lies in observations of brain development during the teen years (see Chapter 5). Teens typically experience a burst of cortical gray matter growth at puberty followed by a period of cortical thinning extending into their early twenties. As shown in ●Figure 16.10, healthy teens experience relatively little loss of gray matter, whereas teens diagnosed with schizophrenia experience a loss that has been likened to a "forest fire" (Thompson et al., 2001). This finding pushes back the beginning of observable changes from young adulthood to puberty, and might provide cues for locating changes occurring even earlier in brain development.

● **Figure 16.10**
Schizophrenia Is Associated with Larger Losses of Gray Matter in Adolescence Teens typically experience a burst of cortical gray matter growth at puberty followed by a wave of gray matter thinning that extends into their early twenties. Compared with their healthy peers, teens diagnosed with schizophrenia lose far more gray matter.
Source: Thompson et al. (2001).

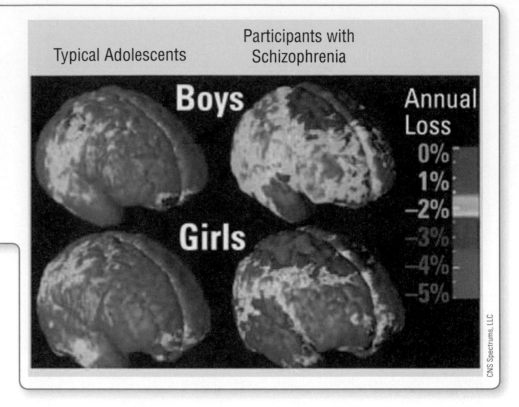

Discovering the causes for the increased loss of gray matter in schizophrenia will require further research. One clue comes from research showing that continued cannabis use, but not tobacco use, appears to produce greater amounts of gray matter loss in patients with schizophrenia (Van Haren, Cahn, Hulshoff Pol, & Kahn, 2012).

The Biochemistry of Schizophrenia

The dopamine hypothesis of schizophrenia has been an influential model for many years. This model rests on observations of psychosis resulting from higher levels of dopamine activity along with the efficacy of dopamine antagonists in treating schizophrenia. As noted in Chapter 4, amphetamine, cocaine, and L-dopa (used to treat Parkinson's disease) are potent dopamine agonists. Over time, these drugs often produce behaviors similar to the positive symptoms of schizophrenia, including hallucinations and paranoid delusions (Goetz, Leurgans, Pappert, Raman, & Stemer, 2001). It is very difficult to make a clinical distinction between a person with schizophrenia and a person who has chronically abused stimulant drugs such as amphetamine or cocaine (Brady, Lydiard, Malcolm, & Ballenger, 1991). The dopamine antagonists used to treat schizophrenia, also known as **typical antipsychotic medications**, act primarily by blocking the D_2 dopamine receptor (see Chapter 4) and reduce psychotic symptoms that result from either schizophrenia or stimulant abuse.

To summarize evidence for the dopamine hypothesis, illustrated in ● Figure 16.11, increases in dopamine activity are associated with psychosis, and decreases in dopamine activity are associated with a reduction in psychosis. However, the dopamine hypothesis is probably too simplistic. About one-quarter of all patients with schizophrenia fail to respond favorably to treatment with dopamine antagonists such as the **phenothiazines** (Kane & Freeman, 1994). In addition, **atypical antipsychotic medications** provide relief from schizophrenia by acting on

typical antipsychotic medication A dopamine antagonist that is used to treat schizophrenia or psychosis.

phenothiazine One of a major group of dopamine antagonists used in the treatment of psychosis.

atypical antipsychotic medication One of several newer medications used to treat schizophrenia that are not dopamine antagonists.

neurotransmitters other than dopamine. For example, the atypical antipsychotic clozapine has a greater effect on serotonin systems than on dopamine systems (Syvalahti, 1994).

If the dopamine hypothesis cannot account for all schizophrenia phenomena, what other neurochemicals might be involved? A disturbance in glutamate systems might provide the large-scale effects that would account for the wide range of positive symptoms in schizophrenia (Matosin & Newell, 2013). Patients with schizophrenia show evidence of reduced numbers of glutamate receptors in their brains (Konradi & Heckers, 2003). Patients with schizophrenia experience a greater drop in glutamate activity in the brain as a result of aging compared to healthy controls (Marsman et al., 2013).

Glutamate and dopamine systems often interact in the brain, and increasing dopamine or decreasing glutamate should result in similar behavioral outcomes. If psychotic symptoms are associated with higher dopamine sensitivity, they might also be related to reductions in glutamate activity. Glutamate's important roles in the normal functioning of the hippocampus and frontal lobes, areas of the brain where abnormalities occur in schizophrenia, also make it an attractive candidate as an underlying mechanism for the disorder. The drug phencyclidine (PCP or "angel dust") provides a useful model for this process (Jentsch & Roth, 1999; Moghaddam & Adams, 1998). PCP is capable of producing several schizophrenia-like symptoms, including auditory hallucinations. PCP not only stimulates dopamine release but also blocks the NMDA glutamate receptor. Psychosis due to PCP use responds favorably to treatment with dopamine antagonists (Jentsch et al., 1997).

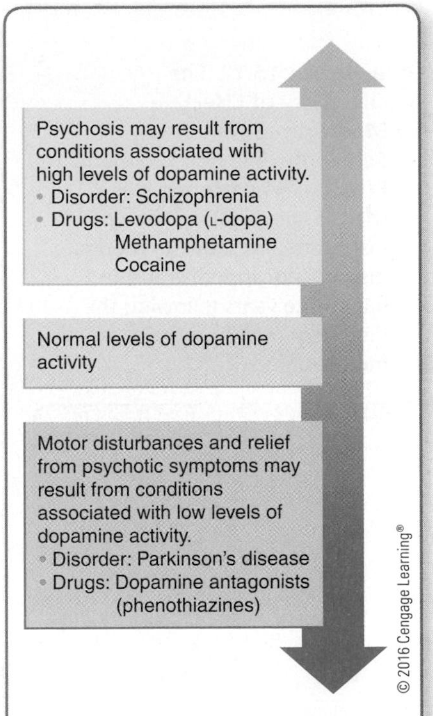

Treating Schizophrenia

Prior to the 1950s, effective treatment for schizophrenia was virtually nonexistent. Treatment for schizophrenia was revolutionized with the discovery of the typical antipsychotics in the 1950s. The first of these to be used were the phenothiazines, including **chlorpromazine** (Thorazine). French surgeon Henri Laborit was so impressed by the calming effects of phenothiazines on his surgical patients that he encouraged his colleagues in psychiatry to experiment with the drugs for treating psychosis. Subsequent research led to the discovery that phenothiazines were effective in treating the symptoms of schizophrenia. Typical antipsychotics primarily benefit patients with schizophrenia by reducing positive symptoms. Negative symptoms, such as social withdrawal and emotional disturbances, do not appear to respond much to these medications (Carpenter, Conley, Buchanan, Breier, & Tamminga, 1995). However, the discovery of the typical antipsychotics allowed many patients, who previously required institutionalization, to resume relatively normal lives. As shown in ● Figure 16.12, the introduction of typical antipsychotics in the 1950s coincided with a dramatic reduction in the number of mental patients who were institutionalized.

Unfortunately, the typical antipsychotics are not specific in their choice of target. They block dopamine receptors in multiple systems, including those controlling movement. **Tardive dyskinesia** is a common and troubling side effect of these drugs. (Tardive refers to "slow," and dyskinesia means "difficulty moving.") Patients with tardive dyskinesia, like the patient shown in ●Figure 16.13, experience tremors and involuntary movements, especially in the face and tongue. Even when medication is discontinued, movement difficulties often persist permanently. The exact causes of tardive dyskinesia remain elusive. Hypersensitivity to dopamine, disturbances of balances between dopamine and acetylcholine, interference with GABA-dependent inhibition in pathways linking the substantia nigra to the basal ganglia, and excitotoxicity (see Chapter 15) have all been suggested as possible mechanisms (Kulkarni & Naidu, 2003).

Psychosis may result from conditions associated with high levels of dopamine activity.
• Disorder: Schizophrenia
• Drugs: Levodopa (L-dopa)
         Methamphetamine
         Cocaine

Normal levels of dopamine activity

Motor disturbances and relief from psychotic symptoms may result from conditions associated with low levels of dopamine activity.
• Disorder: Parkinson's disease
• Drugs: Dopamine antagonists (phenothiazines)

© 2016 Cengage Learning®

● **Figure 16.11** Correlations Between Dopamine Activity Levels and Behavior Situations that lead to higher than normal levels of dopamine activity are associated with psychosis, while situations that lead to lower levels of dopamine activity are associated with movement difficulties.

chlorpromazine A commonly prescribed dopamine antagonist, also known as Thorazine.
tardive dyskinesia A chronic disorder, characterized by involuntary, jerky movements, that occurs as the result of long-term treatment with antipsychotic medications.

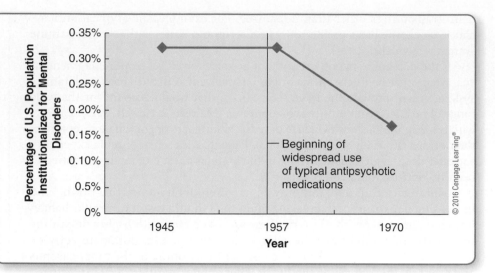

● **Figure 16.12** The Discovery of Effective Medications for Schizophrenia Had Dramatic Effects The percentage of the U.S. population that was institutionalized due to mental disorders dropped almost in half in the years following the discovery of antipsychotic medications.

Because of the serious side effects associated with typical antipsychotics, along with the lack of response in some patients, more than half of all patients today are treated with newer atypical antipsychotic medications such as olanzapine, clozapine, and rispiridone (Meltzer, 2000). As mentioned earlier, clozapine has a stronger effect on serotonin receptors than on dopamine receptors. An advantage of these newer medications is a reduction in negative symptoms, as well as in positive symptoms, in some patients (Rivas-Vazquez, Blais, Rey, & Rivas-Vazquez, 2000). However, these newer medications are not necessarily safer than the typical antipsychotics. They produce weight gain and diabetes in many patients and still carry the risk of producing tardive dyskinesia (Haddad & Dursun, 2008; Henderson, 2008). Side effects of

● **Figure 16.13** Tardive Dyskinesia Can Occur as a Side Effect of Treatment with Antipsychotic Medications Antipsychotics can produce tardive dyskinesia, characterized by intrusive, involuntary movements and tremors.

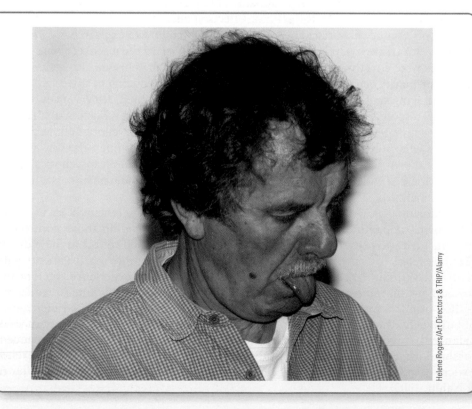

medication can be avoided in most cases with careful monitoring, but many patients receive poor medication management, indicated by doses above the recommended range and failure to adjust doses based on observed behaviors (Young, Sullivan, Burnam, & Brook, 1998).

In addition to medication, psychosocial rehabilitation can be helpful in cases of schizophrenia (Mueser, Deavers, Penn, & Cassisi, 2013). Much to the embarrassment of Western medical practitioners, the World Health Organization (WHO) published research suggesting that patients with schizophrenia in developing countries, such as Nigeria, India, and Colombia, were recovering more frequently than patients in wealthier countries, such as the United States and European nations (Sartorius et al., 1986). Improved outcomes occur when patients are given work and social skills training, education about schizophrenia and the importance of medication, affordable housing linked to services, and information about symptom management.

Bipolar Disorder

Bipolar disorders, also known as manic-depressive disorders, have been described as a "bridge" between the psychotic disorders, such as schizophrenia, and depressive disorders in respect to their symptoms, family histories, and genetics (APA, 2013, p. 123). Of the several types of bipolar disorders described in the DSM-5, we will focus our discussion on cases of classic Bipolar Idisorder.

Bipolar disorder is characterized by at least one lifetime episode of mania, which is often preceded or followed by a period of depression. **Mania** consists of "a distinct period of abnormally and persistently elevated, expansive, or irritable mood, abnormally and persistently increased goal-directed activity or energy, lasting at least one week and present most of the day, nearly every day (or any duration if hospitalization is necessary)" (APA, 2013, p. 124). Further symptoms include inflated self-esteem, decreased need for sleep, higher-than-normal verbal output, flight of ideas, distractibility, increased goal-directed activity, and excessive involvement in activities that have a high potential for negative consequences (such as buying sprees or risky sexual encounters).

Many people with bipolar disorder experience depression as well as mania, although is no longer required for a diagnosis of bipolar disorder, In these cases, the symptoms of depression are the same as those found in major depressive disorder (APA, 2013), which we discuss in more detail later in this chapter. A major depressive episode occurs when a person experiences five or more symptoms of depression within the same two-week period. One of the symptoms must be either depressed mood or loss of pleasure. Additional symptoms include changes in appetite, abnormal sleeping patterns, restlessness or feeling slowed down, fatigue, feelings of worthlessness or guilt, difficulty concentrating, and recurrent thoughts of death (APA, 2013).

In a single year, approximately 2.6 percent of adults in the United States meet the diagnostic criteria for bipolar disorder (Kessler, Chiu, Demler, & Walters, 2005). Women are more likely to be diagnosed with bipolar disorder than men, but the ratio of 3:2 in bipolar is less extreme than the 2:1 female-to-male ratio seen in major depressive disorder (CDC, 2011). The average age of onset for bipolar disorder is 25 years (NIMH, 2013). Children and youth under the age of 18 years with symptoms of bipolar disorder are diagnosed with disruptive mood dysregulation disorder (APA, 2013).

Bipolar disorder has been linked to enhanced creativity. Kay Jamison (1993) argues that artists are at greater risk for bipolar disorder than other people, and she includes the poet William Blake, composers Handel and Mahler, and visual artists Michelangelo and van Gogh on her list of people whose behavior might fit the profile of bipolar disorder. Many noted actors and actresses, including comedian Russell

bipolar disorder A disorder featuring at least one lifetime episode of mania, which is often preceded or followed by a period of depression.

mania An unrealistically elevated, expansive, or irritable mood accompanied by unusually high levels of goal-directed behavior or energy that lasts about 1 week.

© Jaguar PS/Shutterstock.com

● **Figure 16.14** Is Bipolar Disorder More Common Among Artists? Comedian Russell Brand is one of many creative, artistic people who have been diagnosed with bipolar disorder.

Brand (see ● Figure 16.14), Carrie Fisher (*Star Wars*), and Vivien Leigh (*Gone With the Wind*), have been formally diagnosed with bipolar disorder. A controlled study comparing patients with bipolar disorder, patients with major depressive disorder, and healthy controls participating in creative or noncreative disciplines lends some support to these observations. The patients with bipolar disorder scored similarly on tests of creativity to the healthy controls in creative disciplines and higher than either those with major depressive disorder or controls in noncreative disciplines (Santosa et al., 2007).

Genetics and Bipolar Disorder

Genes appear to play a significant role in bipolar disorder. Concordance rates among identical twins are often reported to be as high as 40 to 70 percent (Craddock & Sklar, 2013). Adoption studies also support a powerful role of genetics in the development of bipolar disorder (Taylor, Faraone, & Tsuang, 2002). As mentioned previously in this chapter, a significant overlap in the susceptibility genes for bipolar disorder and schizophrenia exists.

Brain Structure and Function in Bipolar Disorder

Similar brain structure abnormalities are observed in both schizophrenia and bipolar disorder (De Peri et al., 2012; Pol et al., 2012). Both conditions are associated with smaller white matter volume, a thinner parahippocampus, a thinner right orbitofrontal cortex, and thicker temporoparietal and left superior motor cortices (Pol et al., 2012). These overlapping structural features are consistent with the shared genetic profiles for these two disorders. However, bipolar disorder differs from schizophrenia in its association with larger than normal intracranial volume, which is a measure of all tissue and fluid within the skull.

Biochemistry and Treatment of Bipolar Disorder

Bipolar disorder is related to oxidative stress, or an imbalance between the production of free radicals and the body's defenses against them. In particular, bipolar disorder causes oxidative damage to the DNA of brain cells, which in turn can lead to apoptosis (Soeiro-de-Souza et al., 2013). Higher amounts of DNA damage were correlated with the number of lifetime manic episodes experienced by patients.

Lithium salts, a major form of treatment for bipolar disorder, produce antioxidant effects in animal models of mania (Jornada et al., 2011), and are likely to produce relief from symptoms in humans through this same means. Lithium salts also appear to promote adult neurogenesis in the hippocampus (Quiroz, Machado-Vieira, Zarate, & Manji, 2010). The toxicity and unpleasant side effects of lithium salts often lead patients to abandon the drug. In these cases, other medications available for treating bipolar disorder with varying levels of success include SSRIs, benzodiazepines (e.g., Valium), antipsychotics, and anticonvulsant mood stabilizers.

Consistent with observations of increased oxidative stress, bipolar disorder features changes that are consistent with accelerated aging (Rizzo et al., 2014). Human beings progressively lose their ability to respond physically to stress after the age of

lithium A simple salt that appears to stabilize serotonin and norepinephrine levels in cases of bipolar disorder.

••• Building Better HEALTH

DIET AND BIPOLAR DISORDER

Among the many possible environmental factors that interact with susceptibility genes for bipolar disorder is diet. Compared to our hypothesized ancestral diet, contemporary Western diets are heavy in omega-6 fatty acids and deficient in omega-3 fatty acids, which are essential for the development of the brain and retina (Simopoulos, 2011). Diets high in omega-3 fatty acids, generally found in fish, might provide some protection from bipolar disorder (Noaghiul & Hibbeln, 2003). As shown in ● Figure 16.15, prevalence rates for bipolar disorder are highest in countries where fish is rarely consumed (such as Germany) and lowest in countries where fish is an important diet staple (such as Iceland). Patients diagnosed with bipolar disorder show reduced levels of one type of omega-3 fatty acid, DHA (Pomponi et al., 2013). Administration of omega-3 supplements reduced the development of psychosis in people at very high risk for psychotic disorders in a randomized, placebo-controlled experiment (Amminger et al., 2010). However, attempts to improve symptoms in patients with bipolar disorder with omega-3 supplementation have produced mixed results (Murphy et al., 2012; Stahl, Begg, Weisinger, & Sinclair, 2008).

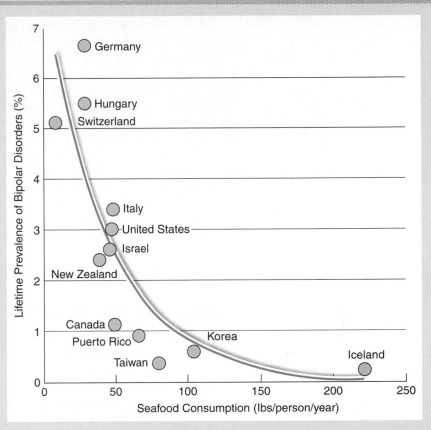

● **Figure 16.15 Diet May Influence the Prevalence of Bipolar Disorder** Nations with heavy seafood consumption, such as Iceland, have lower rates of bipolar disorder than nations where seafood consumption is less typical, such as Switzerland and Hungary. Omega-3 fatty acids have been suggested as a possible protective factor, but further research is needed to confirm a causal relationship.

Source: Noaghiul & Hibbeln (2003).

35 years. Similar changes in inflammation, amyloid, and neurotrophin activity are observed in both patients with bipolar disorder and individuals with dementia (Rizzo et al., 2014). Individuals with bipolar disorder experience earlier onset and higher rates of many diseases, including cardiovascular disease, cancer, and autoimmune diseases (Rizzo et al., 2014).

Major Depressive Disorder (MDD)

The DSM-5 defines major depressive episodes as periods of pervasive sadness that last for at least two weeks (APA, 2013). In addition, people with **major depressive disorder (MDD)** often withdraw from activities they previously found rewarding, including hobbies and sex. Major depressive disorder also affects eating habits, energy levels,

major depressive disorder (MDD)
A disorder in which intense feelings of sadness, hopelessness, and worthlessness persist a minimum of two weeks.

sleep, and cognition. People report difficulty concentrating and often experience thoughts of hopelessness, guilt, worthlessness, and suicide.

MDD affects approximately 7 percent of the adult population each year (APA, 2013). Rates of MDD drop with age, with people in the 18–29 year old age group having rates that are three times higher than people over the age of 60 years.

MDD, like several of the other disorders discussed in this chapter, differs as a function of gender. Prior to adolescence, rates of MDD for boys and girls are approximately equal. However, rates for boys and girls begin to diverge between ages 13 and 15 (Hankin et al., 1998; Nolen-Hoeksema & Girgus, 1994). As shown in ● Figure 16.16, adult women are nearly twice as likely as men to be diagnosed with MDD (Culbertson, 1997; Broquet, 1999; Kessler et al., 2003). This discrepancy between rates of depression in men and women has been observed independent of demographic factors such as race and ethnicity, social class, and country of residence (Strickland, 1992; Üstün, Ayuso-Mateos, Chatterji, Mathers, & Murray, 2004), suggesting a biological basis. A number of mood disturbances appear to be either caused or made worse by changes in female hormones, including premenstrual syndrome (PMS), premenstrual dysphoric disorder (PMDD), postpartum depression, and mood disturbances experienced by women undergoing menopause (Rapkin, Mikacich, Moatakef-Imani, & Rasgon, 2002) (see Chapter 10). Many of the same medications used for MDD appear to be effective for treating these conditions (Steiner et al., 2003).

Genetic Contributions to MDD

Genes appear to play a moderate role in the development of MDD. Based on analyses of twins, the heritability of depression appears to be around 40 percent (Shi et al., 2011). Adoption studies also support a role for genes in the development of depression (Shih, Belmonte, & Zandi, 2004; Wender et al., 1986). A number of genes have been implicated in depression, including those involved with serotonin reuptake (Wurtman, 2005) and the genes that regulate circadian rhythms (McClung, 2007) (see Chapter 11).

Genome-wide association studies have not identified specific single nucleotide polymorphisms (SNPs; see Chapter 5) correlated with MDD (Shi et al., 2011). Assessing the heritability of MDD is complicated by the strong interactions observed between genetic predispositions and environmental factors in this disorder. Variations in the serotonin transporter gene, which comes in both long and short forms, do not by

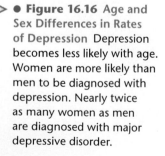

● **Figure 16.16** Age and Sex Differences in Rates of Depression Depression becomes less likely with age. Women are more likely than men to be diagnosed with depression. Nearly twice as many women as men are diagnosed with major depressive disorder.

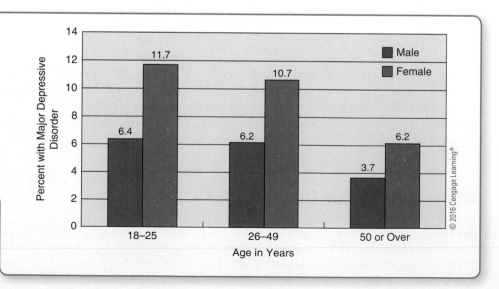

© 2016 Cengage Learning®

themselves predict the development of MDD. However, among individuals who experience stressful life events, those with one or two copies of the short form of the gene were much more likely to develop depression than those with two copies of the long form (Caspi et al., 2003). In the absence of stressful life events, having a short copy was not sufficient to cause depression.

Environmental Influences on MDD

As with schizophrenia, prenatal events might contribute to a vulnerability to MDD. Mothers who were in their third trimester of pregnancy during a famine known as the "Dutch Hunger Winter" of 1944–1945 not only gave birth to more offspring with schizophrenia, but were also more likely to give birth to individuals who subsequently required hospitalization for MDD (Brown, van Os, Driessens, Hoek, & Susser, 2000).

Stress often serves as a trigger for depressive episodes (see Chapter 14). Stader and Hokanson (1998) asked participants to list daily stressors, such as having an argument with a friend. These self-reports were then correlated with the participants' moods. Depressive episodes were often preceded by significant stressors. Stress might lead to depression by leading to a larger and prolonged release of cortisol (see Chapter 14), particularly in people with short versions of the serotonin transporter gene discussed previously (Gotlib, Joormann, Minor, & Hallmayer, 2008). As we will see in a later section, cortisol regulation appears to be impaired in some people with MDD.

Brain Structure and Function in MDD

Differences between people with MDD and healthy control participants have been observed in several structures and patterns of brain activity, but whether these represent the causes or results of the disorder remains unknown (Wagner et al., 2008). Reduced volumes in the hippocampus (Videbech & Ravnkilde, 2004) and the orbitofrontal cortex (Bremner et al., 2002) have been observed in the brains of patients with MDD. During decision-making tasks, patients with MDD showed abnormal activation in the anterior cingulate cortex (ACC) relative to healthy controls (Wagner et al., 2008). Differences in the volume and activity of these structures in cases of MDD are consistent with the important role they play in emotional regulation (see Chapter 14).

As we discussed in Chapters 13 and 14, the right and left hemispheres participate differently in positive and negative emotions (Davidson, 1998; Maxwell & Davidson, 2007). Typically, happy moods are associated with greater activity in the left cerebral hemisphere. Depression is correlated with reduced activity in the left frontal lobe and increased activity in the right frontal lobe (Schaffer, Davidson, & Saron, 1983; Hecht, 2010). Damage to the left frontal lobe from a stroke or another pathological condition typically produces a profound depression in the patient, whereas damage to the right frontal lobe appears to have less impact on mood (Shimoda & Robinson, 1999).

Correlations between sleep patterns and depressed mood reflect a larger disturbance in circadian rhythms (Wehr, Sack, Rosenthal, Duncan, & Gillin, 1983; Soria et al., 2010). As we discovered in Chapter 11, some people experience major depressive disorder with seasonal pattern, formerly known as seasonal affective disorder (SAD), in which seasonal variations in light interfere with circadian rhythms. Both sleeping more than normal (more than nine hours) and sleeping less than normal (less than seven hours) are symptoms of depression. As shown in ● Figure 16.17, some people who are depressed enter their first cycle of REM sleep after approximately 45 minutes of sleep rather than the normal 90 minutes. Stages 3 and 4 of NREM sleep are reduced, and the lighter stages 1 and 2 are more prominent. Because it is much easier to awaken during REM or during NREM stages 1 and 2, frequent waking during the night is a common complaint associated with depression. Further evidence for a relationship between sleep and depression comes from the effects of selective REM deprivation

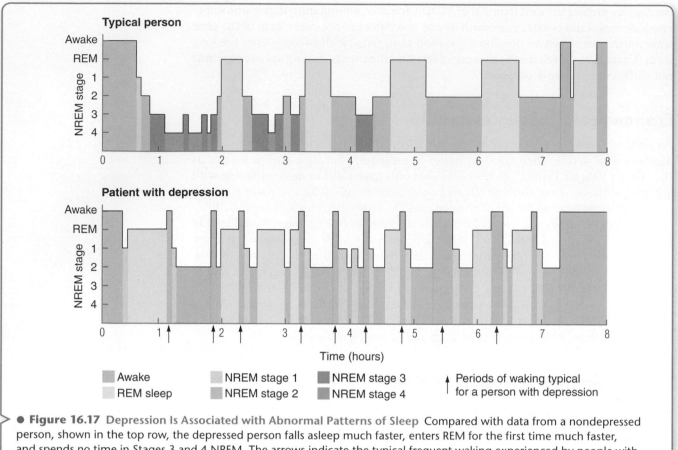

Typical person

Patient with depression

Time (hours)

| Awake | NREM stage 1 | NREM stage 3 | ↑ Periods of waking typical |
| REM sleep | NREM stage 2 | NREM stage 4 | for a person with depression |

● **Figure 16.17 Depression Is Associated with Abnormal Patterns of Sleep** Compared with data from a nondepressed person, shown in the top row, the depressed person falls asleep much faster, enters REM for the first time much faster, and spends no time in Stages 3 and 4 NREM. The arrows indicate the typical frequent waking experienced by people with depression.

Source: Adapted from Gillin & Borbely (1985).

on mood. When people are awakened each time they enter REM sleep, they report a significant reduction in depression (Vogel, Vogel, McAbee, & Thurmond, 1980). In addition, most antidepressants reduce REM to some extent (Pace-Schott et al., 2001) (see Chapter 11).

Although earlier work suggested that people with depression were experiencing a circadian phase advance (Wirz-Justice, 2006), more recent work makes this less clear. Other researchers have reported that phase delays seem more prevalent among individuals with MDD (Robillard et al., 2013). As we discussed in Chapter 11, a phase advance occurs when a person attempts to sleep earlier than normal, as in eastward travel or moving the clock an hour ahead in the spring for daylight savings. A phase delay occurs when a person sleeps later than normal, as in westward travel or moving the clock an hour later in the fall for daylight savings. Depression possibly results from irregular circadian rhythms, as opposed to an orderly shift forward or backward (Koenigsberg et al., 2004).

Biochemistry of MDD

Several lines of research support abnormalities in monoamine activity, and serotonin activity in particular, as a basis for depression. As we observed in Chapter 4, the drug reserpine interferes with the storage of monoamines in vesicles, reducing the amount of these neurochemicals available for release. Although reserpine has been used for centuries in Indian folk medicine to treat heart disease, it is rarely used today due to its ability to produce profound depression (Webster & Koch, 1996). **Selective serotonin reuptake inhibitors (SSRIs)**, frequently used to treat depression, act to increase the availability of serotonin at the synapse.

Suicidal behavior typically occurs in the context of deep depression. People who commit suicide have lower concentrations of serotonin and its byproducts in the brain (Asberg, 1986) and in cerebrospinal fluid (Linnoila & Virkkunen, 1992). People who used more violent methods, such as guns, to commit suicide were found to have lower concentrations of serotonin in the prefrontal cortex than did those who used less violent means, such as taking pills (Oquendo et al., 2003).

In addition to its other duties, serotonin acts as a neurotrophic factor that stimulates both neurogenesis and the release of brain-derived neurotrophic factor (BDNF) (Moylan, Maes, Wray, & Berk, 2013). Lower levels of serotonin activity linked with MDD might result in less overall neurogenesis. Antiserotonin antibodies are more prevalent in people with MDD than in healthy controls (Moylan et al., 2013). This autoimmune response might interfere with serotonin signaling, resulting in the lower levels of serotonin activity that accompany MDD. The more depressive episodes a person experiences, the stronger this autoimmune response appears to be, which might account for the recurrent nature of MDD in many patients.

In addition to serotonin abnormalities, altered norepinephrine function is strongly associated with MDD. People who die as a result of suicide show abnormal density and sensitivity of norepinephrine receptors in the prefrontal cortex (Moylan et al., 2013). MDD is associated with reduced axonal density in neurons releasing norepinephrine, a state that is reversed by the use of antidepressants (Moylan et al., 2013).

A monoamine hypothesis of depression is also consistent with the circadian hypotheses discussed previously because monoamines play essential roles in the regulation of sleep and waking cycles (see Chapter 11). Systems using serotonin and norepinephrine are very active during wakefulness, less active during NREM sleep, and silent during REM sleep.

Cortisol is one of several glucocorticoids released by the adrenal glands in response to both circadian rhythms and stress-related activity in the hypothalamic-pituitary-adrenal (HPA) axis (see Chapter 14). Because cortisol levels increase in response to stress, this system could provide a link between stressful life events, circadian disruption, and the development of depression. Abnormalities in glucocorticoid metabolism can be tested directly by using the dexamethasone suppression test (DST). When dexamethasone is injected into healthy participants, cortisol secretion is suppressed. When the test is administered to adults diagnosed with depression, about 75 percent fail to show the expected levels of cortisol suppression (Aihara et al., 2007). Following successful treatment with medication, these patients respond normally to the DST.

Patients diagnosed with MDD have lower levels of a major byproduct of dopamine, which suggests that dopamine activity is also reduced in this disorder. It is possible that repeated stress and the associated release of cortisol and other glucocorticoids change the responses of the dopaminergic reward pathways originating in the midbrain (Moylan et al., 2013) (see Chapters 4 and 14). The extent of binding of dopamine to the D2 receptors in the striatum, which includes the nucleus accumbens, distinguishes between patients who respond well to SSRIs and those who do not (Moylan et al., 2013).

Treatment of MDD

Treatment for major depressive disorder takes a number of pathways. The most common route is the prescription of some type of antidepressant medication, particularly an SSRI. Effective antidepressant medications appear to share the ability to stimulate neurogenesis in the hippocampus (Perera et al., 2007). In animal studies, drugs that block neurogenesis also prevent the therapeutic effects of antidepressants (ibid.).

selective serotonin reuptake inhibitors (SSRI) A type of medication, used to treat major depressive disorder and related conditions, that interferes with the reuptake of serotonin at the synapse.

SSRIs have significant side effects, and only about 30–35 percent of patients with MDD treated with SSRIs meet criteria for complete remission, leading to the need to find alternate or complementary therapies (Trivedi et al., 2006). Blumenthal et al. (1999) reported that a brisk 30-minute walk or jog three times a week produced the same relief from major depression as typical treatment with antidepressant medications. Cognitive-behavioral therapy (CBT), combining behavioral, cognitive, and self-control therapies, is about as effective as antidepressant therapy alone. A combination of antidepressant and cognitive-behavioral therapy typically produces the best long-term outcomes for patients with depression (Broquet, 1999).

Electroconvulsive therapy (ECT), illustrated in ● Figure 16.18, can produce significant relief for depressed patients who do not respond to medication or CBT (UK ECT Group, 2003). In ECT, the patient is anesthetized and given a muscle relaxant while seizures are induced by electricity applied through electrodes on the head. Six to 12 treatments are given, typically at a rate of three per week. Although the exact mode of action for ECT remains unknown, the procedure does appear to affect responsiveness to dopamine and norepinephrine. In addition, like antidepressant medications, ECT appears to stimulate neurogenesis in the hippocampus (Perera et al., 2007). Largely due to the way ECT was depicted in Ken Kesey's novel *One Flew Over the Cuckoo's Nest*, and the movie of the same title, many people have a highly negative view of the procedure. Some patients undergoing the procedure have experienced associated memory problems, but the procedure is generally considered as safe as minor surgery under general anesthesia (American Psychiatric Association [APA], 2003). There is no evidence that the procedure produces permanent brain damage (Weiner, 1984).

Patients who do not respond to conventional therapies for major depressive disorder might benefit from deep brain stimulation. In this procedure, stimulating electrodes are surgically implanted in the white matter of the cingulate cortex of both hemispheres, and stimulation is delivered constantly. In one study, the majority of patients achieved remission of their depressive symptoms after two years of stimulation (Holtzheimer et al., 2012). Considering that these patients had been nonresponders to more conventional treatment, this improvement is impressive.

● **Figure 16.18**
Electroconvulsive Therapy (ECT) A patient is shown being prepared for treatment with ECT for serious depression. The patient is given muscle relaxants and anesthesia before shocks are applied through electrodes to induce seizures. The treatments are given over a course of several weeks.

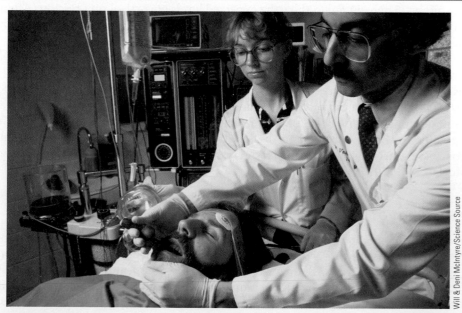

Will & Deni McIntyre/Science Source

electroconvulsive therapy (ECT)
A treatment for depression in which convulsions are produced by the passage of an electric current through the brain.

Summary Table: Comparison of Positive and Negative Symptoms of Schizophrenia

Type of Symptom	Examples	Possible Causes	Responds to Medication?
Positive	• Hallucinations • Delusions • Disorganized speech • Disorganized behavior	• Hippocampal disarray • Possible dopamine and/or glutamate disturbances	Yes
Negative	• Mood disturbance • Social withdrawal	• Brain damage • Enlarged ventricles • Hypofrontality	Better response to atypical than to typical antipsychotics

Summary Points

1. Schizophrenia is a disorder characterized by the presence of hallucinations, delusions, disorganized thinking, social withdrawal, and mood disturbances. **(LO3)**

2. A genetic vulnerability to schizophrenia appears to interact with a variety of environmental factors, including birth complications, prenatal exposure to viruses, marijuana use, and stress, to produce symptoms of the disorder. **(LO3)**

3. Schizophrenia is usually treated with medication, although the addition of psychosocial rehabilitation is quite useful. **(LO3)**

4. Bipolar disorder serves as a "bridge" between the psychotic disorders and depression, and features unrealistically elevated mood states known as mania. **(LO4)**

5. Major depressive disorder (MDD) is characterized by a constant state of depressed mood and loss of pleasure in normally enjoyable activities. **(LO4)**

6. Genes appear to play a role in both major depressive disorder and bipolar disorder, but the genetic influence on bipolar disorder appears to be the stronger. **(LO4)**

7. Monoamine imbalances contribute to both major depressive disorder and bipolar disorder. **(LO4)**

8. Major depressive disorder is treated with medication, cognitive-behavioral therapy, or ECT. Increased aerobic activity is also quite helpful. Bipolar disorder is treated primarily with medication. **(LO4)**

Review Questions

1. What are the advantages and disadvantages of the use of medications to treat schizophrenia?

2. What are the major similarities and differences between schizophrenia, bipolar disorder, and major depressive disorder?

Anxiety Disorders

As many as 30 percent of all Americans experience one or more anxiety disorders during their lifetimes (Kessler, Chiu, Demler, & Walters, 2005). Anxiety disorders take many forms, but all share the core element of anxiety, a strong negative emotion arising from the anticipation of danger (Barlow, 1988). Under normal circumstances, a reasonable amount of anxiety is a good thing. Without sufficient anxiety, we might spend far too much money with our credit cards or engage in risky sexual practices. When anxiety becomes overwhelming and unrealistic, however, we cross the line into disordered behavior. Of the various types of anxiety disorders, we will focus our discussion on panic disorder because this disorder raises especially interesting and representative biological questions. Before addressing this specific anxiety disorder, we will explore the biological correlates of this group of disorders in general.

Twin and adoption studies support a genetic predisposition for anxiety disorders (Andrews, Steward, Allen, & Henderson, 1990). However, the specific type of anxiety disorder will vary among family members. In other words, a vulnerability to anxiety disorder appears to be inherited, but related people will not necessarily experience the same type of anxiety disorder (DiLalla, Kagan, & Reznick, 1994). Families in which anxiety disorders are common are also more likely to have members with MDD because these disorders appear to share an underlying genetic basis (Weissman, Warner, Wickramaratne, Moreau, & Olfson, 1997). Nearly two-thirds of adult patients with MDD also meet criteria for at least one anxiety disorder (Mathew, Pettit, Lewinsohn, Seeley, & Roberts, 2011).

Brain structure and activity appear to contribute to the experience of anxiety. We have seen previously how pathways connecting the brainstem, the amygdala and related subcortical structures, and the decision-making areas of the frontal lobes are involved with generating fear in the face of danger (see Chapter 14). Disordered levels of anxiety are often accompanied by distortions in the operation of these pathways. Anxiety disorders might also involve abnormalities in the HPA axis, resulting in disruptions in responding to stressful stimuli.

A number of neurochemicals participate in the management of anxiety, including serotonin, norepinephrine, and GABA (Taylor, Fricker, Devi, & Gomes, 2005; Barlow & Durand, 1995), and abnormalities in their activity is correlated with anxiety disorders. GABA agonists reduce the subjective experience of anxiety and the activity of the locus coeruleus, a major source of norepinephrine in the brain (Kalueff & Nutt, 2007). Alcohol and benzodiazepines probably achieve their antianxiety results by enhancing the inhibitory effects of GABA at the synapse. Benzodiazepine receptors are particularly common in areas of the brain that participate in the assessment of potential danger, including the hippocampus, the amygdala, and the cerebral cortex. Without appropriate levels of GABA-induced inhibition, a person might overreact to perceived threats in the environment.

Treatment for anxiety disorders typically combines medication with cognitive-behavioral therapy (CBT) to help the person learn to manage reactions to anxiety-producing stimuli. The most commonly prescribed medications include SSRIs, serotonin-norepinephrine reuptake inhibitors (SNRIs) (Dell'Osso, Buoli, Baldwin, & Altamura, 2010), and benzodiazepines (American Psychiatric Association [APA], 2006; Velosa & Riddle, 2000). Exposure therapy, an application of classical conditioning principles, gradually exposes an individual to a fear-inducing stimulus until the fear abates. Ironically, because antianxiety medications typically reduce arousal, they may actually interfere with memory formation required in effective cognitive-behavioral approaches, especially exposure therapy (Otto, McHugh, & Kantak, 2010).

Anxiety is especially acute in cases of panic. In a **panic attack**, a person experiences "intense fear or discomfort" accompanied by strong sympathetic arousal leading to heart palpitations, sweating, trembling, and shortness of breath (APA, 2013, p. 208). **Panic disorder** is diagnosed when repeated panic attacks are followed by at least one month of worrying about having another attack or changing behavior in an effort to avoid another attack. Single panic attacks are relatively common, with one-quarter to one-third of college students reporting experiencing one attack in the previous year (Asmundson & Norton, 1993). Panic disorder is much less common than single panic attacks, affecting between 2 and 3 percent of the population (Kessler et al., 2007).

panic attack The experience of intense feelings of impending doom and the need to escape accompanied by strong sympathetic arousal, including heart palpitations, sweating, trembling, and shortness of breath.

panic disorder A condition characterized by repeated panic attacks and worries about having panic attacks.

About half of all patients with panic disorder also suffer from MDD or a second type of anxiety disorder (Kearney, Albano, Eisen, Allan, & Barlow, 1997).

Panic attacks can be artificially generated in patients suffering from panic disorder by administering sodium lactate (Papp et al., 1993). The sodium lactate appears to provoke panic through its action on the hypothalamus and adjacent areas, which in turn mobilize the sympathetic nervous system for fight or flight (Johnson, Truitt, Fitz, Lowry, & Shekhar, 2008). Imaging research suggests that a circuit including the hippocampus, orbitofrontal cortex, and cingulate cortex also participates in the panic response (Bystritsky et al., 2001). Treatment for panic disorder generally consists of either antidepressant medication, cognitive-behavioral therapy, or a combination of the two (van Apeldoorn et al., 2008).

Obsessive-Compulsive Disorder (OCD)

Individuals with **obsessive-compulsive disorder (OCD)** are haunted by repetitive, intrusive thoughts (**obsessions**), the need to carry out repetitive behaviors (**compulsions**) such as hand washing or counting objects, or both (APA, 2013). Adults with OCD realize that their obsessions and compulsions are unrealistic and excessive but are unable to inhibit these thoughts and behaviors. The obsessions and compulsions can be so frequent and disruptive that normal activities are impaired. Between 2 and 3 percent of the American public experiences OCD during their lifetimes (Ruscio, Stein, Chiu, & Kessler, 2010).

Typical obsessions include thoughts of germs and disease, fear for the safety of the self or others, symmetry, and religious or moral concerns. Common compulsions include washing, checking, touching, counting, and arranging. Compulsions appear to be efforts to ward off the anxiety produced by the obsessions. For example, people obsessed with germs and disease often compulsively wash their hands hundreds of times per day.

OCD often features exaggerations of normal behaviors, including the use of ritual to deal with stress, territoriality, and grooming (Rapoport, 1989). The checking behavior of patients with OCD, in which a person might check door and window locks repeatedly, might be an extreme version of the normal presleep routines of our hunter-gatherer ancestors. The idea that OCD represents exaggerations of natural behavior is supported by observations of similar problems in other species. Dogs occasionally develop an exaggerated grooming version of OCD, in which they repeatedly lick and chew their front paws to the point of causing extensive tissue damage. This behavior can be managed with the same medications used to treat OCD in humans (Seksel & Lindeman, 2001).

OCD is characterized by substantial concordance rates (63–87 percent) among monozygotic twins (Menzies et al., 2008). However, it is likely that significant gene–environment interactions occur in OCD (Grisham, Anderson, & Sachdev, 2008). Symptoms of OCD can arise following head trauma, encephalitis, and seizure disorder. Birth complications and streptococcal infections have also been implicated in the development of OCD in young children (Swedo et al., 1997).

OCD is associated with abnormalities in circuits connecting the thalamus, basal ganglia, and orbitofrontal cortex (Saxena, 2003; Szeszko et al., 2004), although other circuits might also participate, including connections to the amygdala and anterior cingulate cortex (Menzies et al., 2008; Milad & Rauch, 2012). Relative to people with anxiety disorders, people with OCD have increased gray matter in the basal ganglia and reduced gray matter in the cingulate cortices (Radua, van den Heuvel, Surguladze, & Mataix-Cols, 2010). Imaging studies indicate that the basal ganglia are abnormally active in cases of OCD (Guehl et al., 2008), and medications that successfully reduce the symptoms of OCD also reduce the activity of these structures. In one study of brain activity, patients with OCD and their healthy family members demonstrated

obsessive-compulsive disorder (OCD) A disorder characterized by repetitive, intrusive thoughts and the need to engage in certain behaviors to control anxiety.
obsession An intrusive thought, feeling, or emotion with which a person is preoccupied; characteristic of obsessive-compulsive disorder.
compulsion An irresistible, repeated, impulse to perform an action; characteristic of obsessive-compulsive disorder.

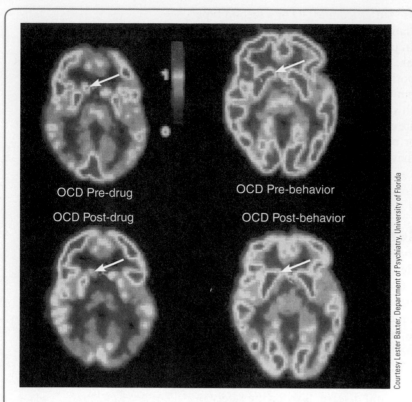

OCD Pre-drug

OCD Post-drug

OCD Pre-behavior

OCD Post-behavior

Courtesy Lester Baxter, Department of Psychiatry, University of Florida

● **Figure 16.19 OCD and Behavioral Treatment** Lewis Baxter and his colleagues (1992) compared PET scans of patients with OCD both before and after either drug treatment or behavioral treatment. In particular, both types of treatment reduced activity in the caudate nucleus, indicated by the arrow.

underactivity in the orbitofrontal cortex relative to healthy controls without a family history of OCD (Chamberlain et al., 2008). This was especially true during a task that required the participant to adjust to changing rules, suggesting that lower activity in the orbitofrontal cortex might be responsible for some of the rigid, ritualistic behavior observed in OCD.

OCD is typically treated with antidepressant medications and SSRIs in particular (Soomro, Altman, Rajagopal, & Oakley-Browne, 2008). The most severe cases of OCD occur in patients with the lowest serotonin levels (Piacentini & Graae, 1997), making serotonin function a logical target for treatment. Medication is not the only effective treatment available to reduce OCD symptoms. Not only is cognitive-behavioral therapy effective in some cases of OCD, but it also produces some of the same changes in the basal ganglia as are observed during treatment with medication (Baxter et al., 1992). ● Figure 16.19 shows PET scans of patients with OCD both before and after drug treatment or behavioral treatment. The results of both types of treatment appear similar. Patients who respond best to SSRIs appear to have different patterns of frontal lobe gray matter than patients who respond best to cognitive-behavioral therapy (Hoexter et al., 2013). Still other patients experience relief from severe OCD symptoms with deep brain stimulation of the basal ganglia (Guehl et al., 2008).

Posttraumatic Stress Disorder (PTSD)

Posttraumatic stress disorder (PTSD) is the current term for a condition that was known previously as "shell shock" or "battle fatigue." Combat experience is a common trigger for PTSD, but exposure to natural disasters, accidents, assaults, and abuse can also result in the disorder (APA, 2013). In PTSD, people exposed to trauma undergo "re-experiencing" in the form of recurrent dreams about the traumatic event and unusually vivid and intrusive memories (flashbacks) of the incident. Active avoidance of stimuli associated with the trauma, hyperarousal, high levels of vigilance, and persistent negative mood and cognitions are common, leading to frequent impairments in daily functioning (APA, 2013). PTSD is unique in the DSM system in that it is the only disorder for which a definite cause (experience of trauma) is identified.

PTSD usually affects between 3 and 4 percent of American adults in a given year (Kessler et al., 2007), although more than 12 percent of lower Manhattan residents developed the disorder as a consequence of the terrorist attacks of 9/11 (DiGrande et al., 2008). Twice as many women as men develop PTSD. Children appear more vulnerable than adults, with 25 percent of children as opposed to 15 percent of their parents developing PTSD following automobile accidents in which they suffer

posttraumatic stress disorder (PTSD) An disorder arising in response to an extremely stressful event, characterized by intrusive memories, recurrent dreams, avoidance of stimuli associated with the stressful event, and heightened arousal.

injuries (de Vries et al., 1999). Combat continues to be one of the most common experiences related to the development of PTSD. About 16 percent of soldiers who have served in Iraq or Afghanistan show symptoms of PTSD (Hoge, Terhakopian, Castro, Messer, & Engel, 2007).

Hypotheses regarding the brain mechanisms underlying PTSD have focused on gray matter volume decreases, particularly in the hippocampus and anterior cingulate cortex. Imaging studies show that the hippocampus is smaller in patients with PTSD than in healthy controls (Bossini et al., 2008; Bremner et al., 1995). Stress-related elevations of circulating glucocorticoids, including cortisol, could reduce hippocampal size (Sapolsky, Krey, & McEwen, 1985). The length of time that had elapsed since the triggering traumatic event predicted the amount of decrease in hippocampal volume in a sample of combat-exposed veterans with PTSD (Chao, Yaffe, Samuelson, & Neylan, 2014). This suggests that ongoing PTSD continues to damage the hippocampus over time. In a study of pairs of identical twins in which only one member of each pair was combat exposed, an interaction between the volume of the anterior cingulate cortex and combat exposure was found (Kasai et al., 2008). As shown in ● Figure 16.20, combat-exposed twins with PTSD had lower anterior cingulate cortex volume compared to their own non-exposed twins and to combat-exposed twins without PTSD and their non-exposed co-twins. Taken together, these results suggest that PTSD has a neurotoxic effect on the hippocampus and anterior cingulate cortex.

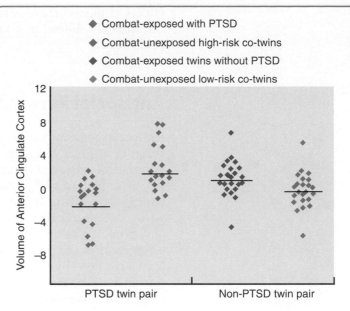

● **Figure 16.20 Combat Experience Interacts with Diagnosis of PTSD to Predict Anterior Cingulate Cortex Volume** Lower gray matter volume in people diagnosed with PTSD could be either a risk factor for PTSD, a result of PTSD, or both. Vietnam veterans diagnosed with PTSD had lower volume in the anterior cingulate cortex compared to their own combat-unexposed twins, or combat veterans without PTSD and their combat-unexposed twins.

Source: Kasai, K., Yamasue, H., Gilbertson, M. W., Shenton, M. E., Rauch, S. L., & Pitman, R. K. (2008). Evidence for acquired pregenual anterior cingulate gray matter loss from a twin study of combat-related posttraumatic stress disorder. *Biological Psychiatry, 63*(6), 550–556.

Comparisons of combat veterans with and without PTSD have demonstrated that the veterans with PTSD experience higher levels of spontaneous activity in the amygdala, anterior cingulate cortex, and orbitofrontal cortex, while also experiencing lower levels of spontaneous activity in the prefrontal cortex and thalamus (Yan et al., 2013). The extent of re-experiencing the traumatic event, or flashbacks, was negatively correlated with spontaneous activity of the thalamus.

Many of these structural and functional changes interact with experience, including experience prior to the traumatic event that might predispose an individual to develop PTSD in response to that event. Exposure to childhood trauma may produce changes in the amygdala and anterior cingulate cortex that increase a person's vulnerability to PTSD in response to later exposure to combat trauma (Woodward, Kuo, Schaer, Kaloupek, & Eliez, 2013).

Animal research suggests that stress produces a decrease in benzodiazepine receptor binding in the frontal cortex (Fukumitsu, Tsuchida, Ogi, Uchiyama, & Mori, 2002). Similar reductions in benzodiazepine activity have been observed in the brains of veterans with combat-related PTSD (Geuze et al., 2008; Bremner et al., 2000). Because benzodiazepine medications, such as Valium, have a tranquilizing effect, reductions in benzodiazepine activity could produce high levels of vigilance characteristic of PTSD.

Treatment for PTSD typically consists of cognitive-behavioral therapy with or without antianxiety or antidepressant medication. Newer therapies might prevent PTSD from developing at all (see Chapter 12). Propranolol, which blocks the effects of glucocorticoids in the brain, might prevent PTSD when administered immediately following a traumatic event (Pitman & Delahanty, 2005; Pitman et al., 2002).

Antisocial Personality Disorder (ASPD)

Antisocial behavior, or the deliberate harming of others, continues to plague human societies at great cost. Many of those who exhibit such behavior meet the DSM criteria for **antisocial personality disorder (ASPD)**, which is characterized by "a pervasive pattern of disregard for and violation of the rights of others" (APA, 2013 p. 659). People with ASPD are described as egocentric, lacking empathy, manipulative, deceitful, callous, and hostile. They may also be irresponsible, impulsive, and prone to taking unnecessary risks (APA, 2013). Between 0.2 percent and 3.3 percent of the population experiences ASPD within a given year (APA, 2013). Men are more likely to demonstrate ASPD than women (Alegria et al., 2013; National Collaborating Centre for Mental Health, 2010). Individuals with ASPD often meet diagnostic criteria for bipolar disorder, major depressive disorder, or substance use disorders as well (Glenn, Johnson, & Raine, 2013).

The DSM-5 version of ASPD and the related concept of **psychopathy** are now defined in more similar terms, although this has not been true in previous versions of the DSM, which focused more on criminality. Many criminals are not psychopaths, and not all psychopaths are criminals. Psychopaths typically lack guilt, empathy, and normal emotional responses while callously using others to achieve their personal goals (Hare, 1993). A triarchic theory of psychopathy argues that three dimensions of disinhibition, boldness, and meanness characterize psychopaths (Patrick, Fowles, & Krueger, 2009).

We can distinguish between reactive aggression, in which an individual responds aggressively, impulsively, and emotionally to a perceived threat, from instrumental aggression, in which a person uses aggression to meet his or her goals in a calculating, unemotional fashion (see Chapter 14). Instrumental aggression appears to have more in common with predation among animals, although unlike humans, animals rarely engage in this type of behavior within their own species (see Chapter 14). The psychopath often engages in both types of aggression but is more likely than other antisocial individuals to engage in instrumental aggression.

Genetics and ASPD

ASPD shows complex interactions between genes and environment. In one study, the extent of child maltreatment, a known risk factor for later antisocial behavior, interacted with a single gene, MAOA (Caspi et al., 2002). Variations in the MAOA gene had been implicated in aggression in studies with animals. However, variations in the MAOA gene do not by themselves predict human antisocial behavior (Moffitt, 2005). It was only when gene–environment interactions were examined that the variations in the MAOA gene had significant effects. Eighty-five percent of boys with the low-activity version of the MAOA gene who experienced severe maltreatment later engaged in some forms of antisocial behavior. In contrast, boys with the higher activity version of the MAOA gene were not likely to engage in antisocial behavior, even when exposed to severe maltreatment.

Using assessments that target the emotional aspects of psychopathy, as opposed to observations of antisocial behavior, twin studies have indicated substantial heritability (46 to 67 percent) for psychopathic traits such as fearless dominance, impulsive antisociality, and callousness (Blair, Peschardt, Budhani, Mitchell, & Pine, 2006). These results suggest relatively significant genetic influence on the core characteristics of psychopathy. Although child maltreatment appears to interact with genetic

antisocial personality disorder (ASPD) A personality disorder diagnosed in adults, characterized by a pervasive pattern of disregard for and violation of the rights of others.

psychopathy A condition characterized by an abnormal lack of remorse and empathy, often leading to the exploitation of others to meet personal goals.

predispositions in producing criminal behavior, it is unlikely to produce the emotional "flattening" that characterizes the psychopath (Blair et al., 2006).

Brain Structure and Function in ASPD

In our discussion of aggression in Chapter 14, we proposed a model in which limbic activation, particularly in the amygdala, provides aggressive drive that is normally held in check by inhibitory influences provided by the orbitofrontal cortex and anterior cingulate cortex. According to this view, impulsive aggressive violence will result from limbic overstimulation, insufficient frontal inhibition, or both. Not too surprisingly, abnormalities in these structures and their functions have been implicated in antisocial behavior. Lower amygdala volume is associated with childhood aggression, early psychopathic traits, and later violence in males (Pardini, Erickson, Loeber, & Raine, 2014).

Understanding the callousness that characterizes the psychopath is more difficult. Kiehl et al. (2001) reported that criminal psychopaths showed less activity in several limbic structures than noncriminal controls when exposed to stimuli that normally elicit an emotional response, such as the word *torture*. Blair et al. (2002) reported that criminal psychopaths were especially impaired in identifying fear in a person's voice. These impairments in empathy, mediated by circuits involving the amygdala and by levels of oxytocin and vasopressin, could interfere with some of the normal controls that prevent us from hurting one another (Patrick, Drislane, & Strickland, 2012).

Another possible source of interpersonal callousness might arise from a simple deficit in the psychopath's ability to understand his or her own physical state. Following a task that normally elicits an emotional response, nonpsychopathic control participants demonstrated a match between their subjective verbal description of their physical state and actual measures of heart rate reactivity. The psychopaths did not show this match (Gao, Raine, & Schug, 2012). As described in Chapter 14, the James-Lange theory of emotion suggests that assessing our own physical reactions leads to an understanding of our subjective state. If psychopaths are unable to do this for their own personal emotional experiences, it becomes highly unlikely that they could assess the states of other people accurately.

Anderson, Bechara, Damasio, Tranel, and Damasio (1999) reported that antisocial behavior appears to be related to damage to the orbitofrontal cortex, illustrated in ● Figure 16.21. They described two adult participants who had been raised in stable, middle-class homes but had experienced damage to the orbitofrontal cortex before the age of 16 months. As adults, these individuals engaged in stealing, lying, aggressive behavior, poor parenting, and an inability to understand the consequences of their

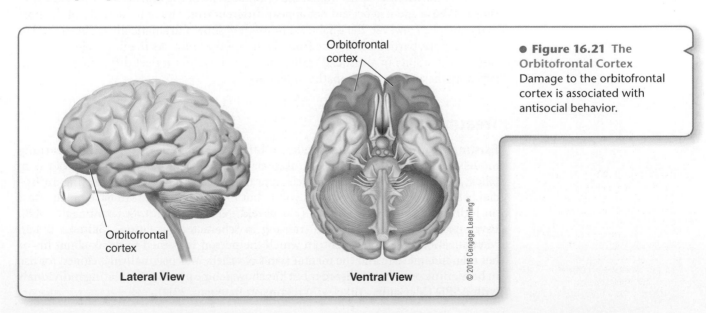

Orbitofrontal cortex

Orbitofrontal cortex

Lateral View

Ventral View

© 2016 Cengage Learning®

● **Figure 16.21** The Orbitofrontal Cortex Damage to the orbitofrontal cortex is associated with antisocial behavior.

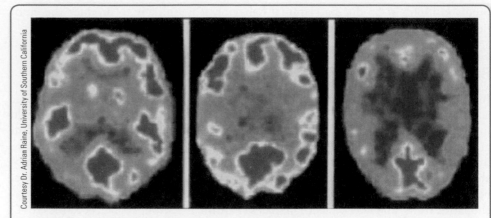

Courtesy Dr. Adrian Raine, University of Southern California

● **Figure 16.22** Brain Activity among Murderers Adrian Raine and his colleagues (1998) compared PET scans of normal control participants (left), murderers who had a history of abuse and neglect (middle), and murderers who had not experienced deprivation, abuse, or neglect (right). The brain activity of the abused murderers looks quite similar to that of the normal participants. In contrast, the brain activity of the unabused murderers is unusually low, especially in the frontal lobes.

behavior. Davidson, Putnam, and Larson (2000) identified frequent orbitofrontal dysfunctions in murderers, people with aggressive impulsive personality disorder, and people diagnosed with antisocial personality disorder. Kip Kinkel, who was accused of murdering his parents and two students in a subsequent school shooting in 1998, was found to have lesions in his orbitofrontal cortex.

Consistent with current trends in neuroscience to identify circuits rather than focusing on the activity of parts of the brain, researchers noted that psychopaths show different patterns of connectivity involving the frontal lobes when compared to typical control participants (Sundram et al., 2012; Yang et al., 2012). In addition, the typical controls used the inferior frontal cortices and orbitofrontal cortices as information "hubs," while the psychopaths used the superior frontal cortices for this function.

Researchers have investigated the interactions of nature and nurture in brain activity related to antisocial behavior. In addition to comparing PET scans of the brains of nonviolent offenders and murderers, Raine, Stoddard, Bihrle, and Buchsbaum (1998) assessed such environmental factors as neglect, poverty, and physical and sexual abuse. As shown in ● Figure 16.22, the brain activity of the murderers who had experienced abuse and neglect did not appear different from the brain activity of the normal controls. However, the unabused murderers show a dramatically reduced level of brain activity, particularly in the frontal lobes of the brain. As in our previous discussion of heritability of antisocial traits, these results might reflect differences between psychopaths and nonpsychopathic offenders.

Treatment of ASPD

Existing treatment programs for violent offenders are frequently based on learning models that emphasize anger control, social skills, and moral reasoning (Goldstein, Glick, & Gibbs, 1998). These models appear modestly effective in reducing antisocial behaviors among children and youth, but they do not appear to have much effect on individuals with psychopathy (Hornsveld, Nijman, Hollin, & Kraaimaat, 2008). Psychopathy requires additional training in "character formation" (Salmon, 2004). Mentalization-based treatment, in which the person is trained to think about his or her own mental state and the mental states of others, was originally developed for use in borderline personality disorder but has shown some promise in treating individuals with ASPD (McGauley, Yakeley, Williams, & Bateman, 2011).

••• THINKING *Ethically*

ARE PSYCHOPATHS LEGALLY LIABLE FOR THEIR ACTIONS?

Psychopaths have been a puzzle to law enforcement officials for centuries. While many of the crimes they commit are horrific, psychopaths seem like relatively normal people in many respects. This paradox led to the use of the term "moral insanity" to describe the psychopath's behavior. While the psychopath did not appear to be outwardly "insane" in the sense of the way the term was used in the 18th and 19th centuries, his or her actions were morally deranged in the eyes of society.

Adrian Raine (1999), who helped conduct several of the studies included in the section on antisocial personality disorder, asked a provocative question: "If brain deficits make a person more likely to commit violent crime, and if the cause of the brain deficits was not under that person's control, then should he be held fully responsible for his crimes?"

This question reaches far beyond psychology into the realms of scholars who discuss free will. As Raine describes, theologians are likely to think that our actions, criminal or otherwise, are completely under our free will and control. In contrast, Raine notes the thoughts of Francis Crick, who suggested that free will resulted from the activity of collections of neurons, and that it was feasible that a machine could be built someday that demonstrated free will.

Raine describes his own position as being somewhere in the middle of this debate. He sees the ability to control one's actions as lying along a continuum instead of in all-or-nothing terms. He cites the example of placing a beer in front of an alcoholic and a nonalcoholic. While it is true that the absolute decision to pick up that glass of beer or not rests with the individual, it is also likely that the abilities of these two people to resist picking up the glass have been shaped differently by genetic, biological, and environmental influences from the past.

While this might seem like a very philosophical discussion for a biological psychology textbook, Raine (2013) pointed out that our society is already poised to act. Brain imaging studies have indicated that prisoners about to be released are twice as likely to be re-arrested in the next three years if activity in their anterior cingulate cortex is lower than normal. A similar study indicated that prisoners with small amygdala volume were three times as likely to reoffend. While these types of studies might have practical implications for law enforcement and public safety, Raine cautions that acting on these studies could lead to ethically challenged efforts to scan the entire population for "risk" of criminal behavior. This might sound like something out of a science fiction film, but the reality and means to conduct these types of assessments are squarely here in the present.

INTERIM SUMMARY 16.3

|| Summary Points

1. Anxiety disorders share a core element of unrealistic and counterproductive anxiety. In cases of panic disorder, regular panic attacks are accompanied by worry about further attacks and avoidance of situations associated with attacks. (LO5)

2. Obsessive-compulsive disorder (OCD) combines intrusive, anxiety-producing thoughts and ritualistic, repetitive behaviors. (LO5)

3. Posttraumatic stress disorder (PTSD) is characterized by intrusive flashbacks, hypervigilance, and avoidance of stimuli associated with the experience of trauma. (LO5)

4. Antisocial personality disorder (ASPD) is diagnosed in people who show a callous disregard of the rights of others, lack of empathy, and lack of remorse. (LO6)

|| Review Questions

1. What biological changes appear to accompany the experience of anxiety and trauma?

2. How would you rate the efficacy of treatment methods for ASPD?

Chapter Review

THOUGHT QUESTIONS

1. Why do you think rates of diagnosed autism spectrum disorder and attention deficit hyperactivity disorder continue to increase?
2. What parallels do you see between major depressive disorder and the anxiety disorders in terms of genetics, brain structure and function, and biochemistry?
3. Why is bipolar disorder considered to be a "bridge" between schizophrenia and major depressive disorder?
4. Which of the disorders discussed in this chapter are influenced by gender? Why do you think this is the case?

KEY TERMS

antisocial personality disorder (ASPD) (p. 574)

attention deficit hyperactivity disorder (ADHD) (p. 550)

autism spectrum disorder (ASD) (p. 545)

bipolar disorder (p. 561)

compulsion (p. 571)

delusion (p. 553)

electroconvulsive therapy (ECT) (p. 568)

hallucination (p. 553)

lithium (p. 562)

major depressive disorder (MDD) (p. 563)

mania (p. 561)

mental disorder (p. 544)

negative symptom (p. 553)

obsession (p. 571)

obsessive-compulsive disorder (OCD) (p. 571)

panic attack (p. 570)

panic disorder (p. 570)

positive symptom (p. 553)

posttraumatic stress disorder (PTSD) (p. 572)

psychopathy (p. 574)

schizophrenia (p. 553)

selective serotonin reuptake inhibitor (SSRI) (p. 567)

tardive dyskinesia (p. 559)

References

Aaltonen, P., Amory, J. K., Anderson, R. A., Behre, H. M., Bialy, G., Blithe, D., ... Zitzmann, M. (2007). 10th Summit Meeting consensus: Recommendations for regulatory approval for hormonal male contraception. *Journal of Andrology, 28*(3), 362–363. doi:10.2164/jandrol.106.002311

Aboitiz, F. (2012). Gestures, vocalizations, and memory in language origins. *Frontiers in Evolutionary Neuroscience, 4*(2). doi:10.3389/fnevo.2012.00002

Aboody, K. S., Najbauer, J., & Danks, M. K. (2008). Stem and progenitor cell-mediated tumor selective gene therapy. *Gene Therapy, 15,* 739–752. doi:10.1038/gt.2008.41

Abraham, A., von Cramon, D. Y., & Schubotz, R. I. (2008). Meeting George Bush versus meeting Cinderella: The neural response when telling apart what is real from what is fictional in the context of our reality. *Journal of Cognitive Neuroscience, 20*(6), 965–976. doi:10.1162/jocn.2008.20059

Abraham, W. C., & Mason, S. E. (1988). Effects of the NMDA receptor/channel antagonists CPP and MK801 on hippocampal field potentials and long-term potentiation in anesthetized rats. *Brain Research, 462*(1), 40–46.

Abrams, T. W., Yovell, Y., Onyike, C. U., Cohen, J. E., & Jarrad, H. E. (1998). Analysis of sequence-dependent interactions between transient calcium and transmitter stimuli in activating adenylyl cyclase in *Aplysia*: Possible contribution to CS–US sequence requirement during conditioning. *Learning and Memory, 4,* 496–509.

Abramsky, L., & Chapple, J. (1997). 47, XXY (Klinefelter syndrome) and 47, XYY: Estimated rates of and indication for postnatal diagnosis with implications for prenatal counseling. *Prenatal Diagnosis, 17,* 363–368.

Academy of Nutrition and Dietetics. (2014). Commission on dietetic registration. http://cdrnet.org/default.cfm

Acebo, C., Sadeh, A., Seifer, R., Tzischinsky, O., Hafer, A., & Carskadon, M. A. (2005). Sleep/wake patterns derived from activity monitoring and maternal report for healthy 1- to 5-year-old children. *Sleep, 28*(12), 1568–1577.

Achard, S., Salvador, R., Whitcher, B., Suckling, J., & Bullmore, E. (2006). A resilient, low-frequency, small-world human brain functional network with highly connected association cortical hubs. *The Journal of Neuroscience, 26*(1), 63–72. doi:10.1523/JNEUROSCI.3874-05.2006

Addams, R. (1964). An account of a peculiar optical phaenomenon. In W. Dember (Ed.), *Visual perception: The nineteenth century* (pp. 81–83). New York: Wiley. (Original work published 1934.)

Adekoya, N., Thurman, D. J., White, D. D., & Webb, K. W. (2002). Surveillance for traumatic brain injury deaths: United States, 1989–1998.

MMWR Surveillance Summaries: Morbidity and mortality weekly report, 51(10), 1–14.

Adolphs, R. (2007). Looking at other people: Mechanisms for social perception revealed in subjects with focal amygdala damage. *Novartis Foundation Symposium, 278,* 146–159; discussion 160–144, 216–121.

Adolphs, R., Tranel, D., & Damasio, A. R. (1998). The human amygdala in social judgment. *Nature, 393,* 470–474.

Aeschbach, D., Sher, L., Postolache, T. T., Matthews, J. R., Jackson, M. A., & Wehr, T. A. (2003). A longer biological night in long sleepers than in short sleepers. *The Journal of Clinical Endocrinology & Metabolism, 88*(1), 26–30.

Afraz, S.-R., Kiani, R., & Esteky, H. (2006). Microstimulation of inferotemporal cortex influences face categorization. *Nature, 442*(7103), 692–695.

Agrawal, Y., Platz, E. A., & Niparko, J. K. (2008). Prevalence of hearing loss and differences by demographic characteristics among US adults: Data from the National Health and Nutrition Examination Survey, 1999–2004. *Archives of Internal Medicine, 168*(14), 1522–1530. doi:10.1001/archinte.168.14.1522

Aharon, I., Etcoff, N., Ariely, D., Chabris, C. F., O'Connor, E., & Breiter, H. C. (2001). Beautiful faces have variable reward value: fMRI and behavioral evidence. *Neuron, 32,* 537–551.

Ahlstrom, R., Berglund, R., Berglund, U., Engen, T., & Lindvall, T. (1987). A comparison of odor perception in smokers, nonsmokers, and passive smokers. *American Journal of Otolaryngology, 8,* 1–6.

Aihara, M., Ida, I., Yuuki, N., Oshima, A., Kumano, H., Takahashi, K., et al. (2007). HPA axis dysfunction in unmedicated major depressive disorder and its normalization by pharmacotherapy correlates with alteration of neural activity in prefrontal cortex and limbic/paralimbic regions. *Psychiatry Research, 155*(3), 245–256.

Aitchison, J. (1983). *The articulate mammal: An introduction to psycholinguistics.* London, UK: Hutchinson.

Akerstedt, T., & Froberg, J. (1976). Interindividual differences in circadian pattern of catecholamine excretion, body temperature, performance, and subjective arousal. *Biological Psychology, 4,* 277–292.

Aksglaede, L., Juul, A., Leffers, H., Skakkebaek, N. E., & Andersson, A.-M. (2006). The sensitivity of the child to sex steroids: Possible impact of exogenous estrogens. *Human Reproduction Update, 12*(4), 341–349.

Alais, D., & Burr, D. (2004). The ventriloquist effect results from near-optimal bimodal integration. *Current Biology, 14*(3), 257–262. doi:10.1016/j.cub.2004.01.029

Alarcón, M., Abrahams, B. S., Stone, J. L., Duvall, J. A., Perederiy, J. V., Bomar, J. M., Geschwind, D. H. (2008). Linkage, association, and gene-expression analyses identify *CNTNAP2* as an autism-susceptibility gene. *The American Journal of Human Genetics, 82*(1), 150–159. doi:10.1016/j.ajhg.2007.09.005

Albert-Weißenberger, C., Sirén, A.-L., & Kleinschnitz, C. (2013). Ischemic stroke and traumatic brain injury: The role of the kallikrein–kinin system. *Progress in Neurobiology, 101–102,* 65–82. doi:10.1016/j.pneurobio.2012.11.004

Albrecht, B., Brandeis, D., von Sandersleben, H. U., Valko, L., Heinrich, H., Xu, X., ... Banaschewski, T. (2014). Genetics of preparation and response control in ADHD: The role of DRD4 and DAT1. *Journal of Child Psychology and Psychiatry, 55*(8), 914–923. doi:10.1111/jcpp.12212

Albus, J. S. (1971). A theory of cerebellar function. *Mathematical Biosciences, 10,* 25–61.

Alegria, A. A., Blanco, C., Petry, N. M., Skodol, A. E., Liu, S.-M., Grant, B., & Hasin, D. (2013). Sex differences in antisocial personality disorder: Results from the National Epidemiological Survey on Alcohol and Related Conditions. *Personality Disorders: Theory, Research, and Treatment, 4*(3), 214. doi:10.1037/a0031681

Alexander-Bloch, A., Giedd, J. N., & Bullmore, E. (2013). Imaging structural co-variance between human brain regions. *Nature Reviews Neuroscience, 14*(5), 322–336. doi:10.1038/nrn3465

Alexander, G. M., & Hines, M. (2002). Sex differences in response to children's toys in nonhuman primates (*Cercopithecus aethiops sabaeus*). *Evolution and Human Behavior, 23,* 467–479.

Alexander, G. M., Carden, W. B., Mu, J., Kurukulasuriya, N. C., McCool, B. A., Nordskog, B. K., Godwin, D. W. (2006). The native T-type calcium current in relay neurons of the primate thalamus. *Neuroscience, 141*(1), 453–461.

Alexander, G. M., Kurukulasuriya, N. C., Mu, J., & Godwin, D. W. (2006). Cortical feedback to the thalamus is selectively enhanced by nitric oxide. *Neuroscience 142*(1), 223–234.

Allen, K. (2003). Are pets a healthy pleasure? The influence of pets on blood pressure. *Current Directions in Psychological Science, 12,* 236–239. doi:10.1046/j.0963-7214.2003.01269.x

Allen, L. S., & Gorski, R. A. (1992). Sexual orientation and the size of the anterior commissure in the human brain. *Proceedings of the National Academy of Sciences of the United States of America (PNAS), 89,* 7191–7202.

Allen, L. S., Hines, M., Shryne, J. E., & Gorski, R. A. (1989). Two sexually dimorphic cell groups in the human brain. *Journal of Neuroscience, 9,* 497–506.

Allison, T., & Cicchetti, D. (1976). Sleep in mammals: Ecological and constitutional correlates. *Science, 194,* 732–734.

Allman, J. M., Tetreault, N. A., Hakeem, A. Y., Manaye, K. F., Semendeferi, K., Erwin, J. M. …, Hof, P. R. (2011). The von Economo neurons in the frontoinsular and anterior cingulate cortex. *Annals of the New York Academy of Sciences, 1225,* 59–71. doi:10.1111/j.1749-6632.2011.06011.x

Allman, J. M., Watson, K. K., Tetreault, N. A., & Hakeem, A. Y. (2005). Intuition and autism: A possible role for Von Economo neurons. *Trends in Cognitive Science, 9*(8), 367–373.

Almeida Montes, L. G., Prado Alcántara, H., Martíncz García, R. B., De La Torre, L. B., Ávila Acosta, D., & Duarte, M. G. (2012). Brain cortical thickness in ADHD: Age, sex, and clinical correlations. *Journal of Attention Disorders.* doi:10.1177/1087054711434351

Alonso, A., & Hernan, M. A. (2008). Temporal trends in the incidence of multiple sclerosis: A systematic review. *Neurology, 71*(2), 129–135.

Amaral, D. G., Schumann, C. M., & Nordahl, C. W. (2008). Neuroanatomy of autism. *Trends in Neurosciences, 31*(3), 137–145. doi:10.1016/j.tins.2007.12.005

American Academy of Sleep Medicine (AASM). (2014). Maintenance of certification for sleep medicine physicians. www.aasmnet.org/moc/

American Board of Genetics Counseling (ABGC). (2008). Genetic counseling programs—US. http://www.abgc.net/english/view.asp?x=1643

American Board of Professional Psychology (ABPP). (n.d.). Clinical neuropsychology FAQ's. http://www.abpp.org/i4a/pages/index.cfm?pageid=3405

American Heart Association. (2008). Stroke risk factors. http://www.americanheart.org/presenter.jhtml?identifi er=4716.

American Kennel Club (AKC). (2014). Therapy dog organizations. https://www.akc.org/akctherapydog/organizations.cfm

American Optometric Association (2014). *Diet and nutrition.* http://www.aoa.org/patients-and-public/caring-for-your-vision/diet-and-nutrition?sso=y

American Physical Therapy Association (APTA). (2013). Physical therapist (PT) education overview. http://www.apta.org/PTEducation/Overview/

American Psychiatric Association (APA). (2003). *Electroconvulsive therapy (ECT).* http://www.psych.org/public_info/ect‑1.cfm.

American Psychiatric Association (APA). (2006). *Practice guidelines for the treatment of psychiatric disorders: Compendium 2006.* Washington, DC: American Psychiatric Publishing.

American Psychiatric Association (APA). (2013). *Diagnostic and Statistical Manual of Mental Disorders (DSM-5).* Washington, DC: Author.

American Psychological Association (APA). (1992, December 1). *Ethical principles of psychologists and code of conduct.* Retrieved from the American Psychological Association Web site: http://www.apa.org/ethics/code.html.

American Psychological Association (APA). (1997). *The Houston Conference on Specialty Education and Training in Clinical Neuropsychology.* http://www.theaacn.org/position_papers/houston_conference.pdf

American Psychological Association (APA). (2014). *Guidelines for ethical conduct in the care and use of nonhuman animals in research.* http://www.apa.org/science/leadership/care/guidelines.aspx

American Speech-Language-Hearing Association. (2014). Careers in speech-language pathology. http://www.asha.org/careers/professions/careers-in-speech-language-pathology/americas/

californian-idyll-shocked-by-skateboard-murder-of-87yearold-527617.html

Ames, E. (1997). *The development of Romanian orphanage children adopted to Canada.* Human Resources Development. Burnaby, British Columbia, Canada: Simon Fraser University.

Amminger, G., Schäfer, M. R., Papageorgiou, K., et al. (2010). Long-chain ω-3 fatty acids for indicated prevention of psychotic disorders: A randomized, placebo-controlled trial. *Archives of General Psychiatry, 67*(2), 146–154. doi:10.1001/archgenpsychiatry.2009.192

Anand, B., & Brobeck, J. R. (1951). Hypothalamic control of food intake in rats and cats. *Yale Journal of Biology and Medicine, 24,* 123–140.

Andersen, J. L., Schjerling, P., & Saltin, B. (2000). Muscle, genes and athletic performance. *Scientific American, 283,* 48–55.

Anderson, S. W., Bechara, A., Damasio, H., Tranel, D., & Damasio, A. R. (1999). Impairment of social and moral behavior related to early damage in human prefrontal cortex. *Nature Neuroscience, 2,* 1032–1037.

Andreasen, N. C., Rezai, K., Alliger, R., Swayze, V. W., II, Flaum, M., et al. (1992). Hypofrontality in neuroleptic-naive patients and in patients with chronic schizophrenia: Assessment with xenon 133 single-photon emission computed tomography and the Tower of London. *Archives of General Psychiatry, 49,* 943–958.

Andrews, G., Morris-Yates, A., Howie, P., & Martin, N. G. (1991). Genetic factors in stuttering confirmed. *Archives of General Psychiatry, 48,* 1034–1035.

Andrews, G., Steward, G., Allen, B., & Henderson, A. S. (1990). The genetics of six neurotic disorders: A twin study. *Journal of Affective Disorders, 19,* 23–29.

Angold, A., Erkanli, A., Egger, H. L., & Costello, E. J. (2000). Stimulant treatment for children: A community perspective. *Journal of the American Academy of Child and Adolescent Psychiatry, 39,* 975–984.

Anokhin, A. P., Golosheykin, S., & Heath, A. C. (2010). Heritability of individual differences in cortical processing of facial affect. *Behavior Genetics, 40*(2), 178–185. doi:10.1007/s10519-010-9337-1

Antonov, I., Antonova, I., Kandel, E. R., & Hawkins, R. D. (2003). Activity-dependent presynaptic facilitation and Hebbian LTP are both required and interact during classical conditioning in Aplysia. *Neuron, 37*(1), 135–147.

Antonov, I., Ha, T., Antonova, I., Moroz, L. L., & Hawkins, R. D. (2007). Role of nitric oxide in classical conditioning of siphon withdrawal in *Aplysia. Journal of Neuroscience, 27*(41), 10993–11002.

Antonucci, F., Rossi, C., Gianfranceschi, L., Rossetto, O., & Caleo, M. (2008). Long-distance retrograde effects of botulinum neurotoxin A. *The Journal of Neuroscience, 28*(14), 3689–3696. doi:10.1523/jneurosci.0375-08.2008

Anway, M. D., & Skinner, M. K. (2006). Epigenetic transgenerational actions of endocrine disruptors. *Endocrinology, 147*(6), s43–s49. doi:10.1210/en.2005-1058

Apostolova, G., & Dechant, G. (2009). Development of neurotransmitter phenotypes in sympathetic neurons. *Autonomic Neuroscience, 151*(1), 30–38. doi:10.1016/j.autneu.2009.08.012

Arendt, J. (2010). Shift work: Coping with the biological clock. *Occupational Medicine, 60*(1), 10–20. doi:10.1093/occmed/kqp162

Armony, J. L. (2012). Current emotion research in behavioral neuroscience: The role(s) of the amygdala. *Emotion Review.* doi:10.1177/1754073912457208

Arnsten, A. F. T., Ramos, B. P., Birnbaum, S. G., & Taylor, J. R. (2005). Protein kinase A as a therapeutic target for memory disorders: Rationale and challenges. *Trends in Molecular Medicine, 11*(3), 121–128.

Aronson, S. M. (2007). Galen and the causes of disease. *Medicine and Health, Rhode Island, 90*(12), 375.

Arzy, S., Seeck, M., Ortigue, S., Spinelli, L., & Blanke, O. (2006). Induction of an illusory shadow person. *Nature, 443*(7109), 287.

Asberg, M. (1986). Biochemical aspects of suicide. *Clinical Neuropharmacology, 9*(Suppl. 4), 374–376.

Asmundson, G. J. G., & Norton, G. R. (1993). Anxiety sensitivity and its relationship to spontaneous and cued panic attacks in college students. *Behavior Research and Therapy, 31,* 199–201.

Atkinson, R. C., & Shiffrin, R. M. (1968). Human memory: A proposed system and its control processes. In K. W. Spence & J. T. Spence (Eds.), *The psychology of learning and motivation: Vol. 2. Advances in research and theory* (pp. 89–195). New York: Academic Press.

Atkinson, R. C., & Shiffrin, R. M. (1971). The control of short-term memory. *Scientific American, 225,* 82–90.

Atri, A., Sherman, S., Norman, K. A., Kirchhoff, B. A., Nicolas, M. M., Grecius, M. D. …, Stern, C. E. (2004). Blockade of central cholinergic receptors impairs new learning and increases proactive interference in a word paired-associate memory task. *Behavioral Neuroscience, 118,* 223–236. doi:10.1037/0735-7044.118.1.223

Aubry, M., Cantu, R., Dvorak, J., Graf-Baumann, T., Johnston, K., Kelly, J., et al. (2002). Summary and agreement statement of the First International Conference on Concussion in Sport, Vienna 2001. Recommendations for the improvement of safety and health of athletes who may suffer concussive injuries. *British Journal of Sports Medicine, 36*(1), 6–10.

Auyeung, B., Baron-Cohen, S., Ashwin, E., Knickmeyer, R., Taylor, K., Hackett, G., & Hines, M. (2009). Fetal testosterone predicts sexually differentiated childhood behavior in girls and in boys. *Psychological Science, 20*(2), 144–148.

Axelsson, J., Stefansson, J. G., Magnusson, A., Sigvaldason, H., & Karlsson, M. M. (2002). Seasonal affective disorders: Relevance of Icelandic and Icelandic-Canadian evidence to etiologic hypotheses. *Canadian Journal of Psychiatry, 47*(2), 153–158.

Baas, P. W., & Qiang, L. (2005). Neuronal microtubules: When the MAP is the roadblock. *Trends in Cell Biology, 15*(4), 183–187.

Babad, E., Bernieri, F., & Rosenthal, R. (1991). Students as judges of teachers' verbal and nonverbal behavior. *American Educational Research Journal, 28,* 211–234.

Baddeley, A. D. (2000). The episodic buffer: A new component of working memory? *Trends in Cognitive Sciences, 4,* 417–423.

Baddeley, A. D., & Hitch, G. J. (1974). Working memory. In G. Bower (Ed.), *The psychology of learning and motivation* (Vol. 8, pp. 47–89). New York: Academic Press.

Bailey, A. A., & Hurd, P. L. (2005). Finger length ratio (2D:4D) correlates with physical aggression in men but not in women. *Biological Psychology, 68*(3), 215–222.

Bailey, C. H., & Chen, M. C. (1983). Morphological basis of longterm habituation and sensitization in *Aplysia. Science, 220,* 91–93.

Baird, A. A., Gruber, S. A., Fein, D. A., Maas, L. C., Steingard, R. J., Renshaw, P. F. . . ., Yurgelun-Todd, D. A. (1999). Functional magnetic resonance imaging of facial affect recognition in children and adolescents. *Journal of the American Academy of Child and Adolescent Psychiatry, 38*(2), 195–199.

Bakan, P. (1971, August). The eyes have it. *Psychology Today,* 64–69.

Baker, K. G., Halliday, G. M., Hornung, J. P., Geffen, L. B., Cotton, R. G., & Törk, I. (1991). Distribution, morphology and number of monoamine-synthesizing and substance P-containing neurons in the human dorsal raphe nucleus. *Neuroscience, 42*(3), 757–775.

Bakker, R., Steegers, E. A., Obradov, A., Raat, H., Hofman, A., & Jaddoe, V. W. (2010). Maternal caffeine intake from coffee and tea, fetal growth, and the risks of adverse birth outcomes: The Generation R Study. *The American Journal of Clinical Nutrition, 91*(6), 1691–1698. doi:10.3945/ajcn.2009.28792

Baldereschi, M., Di Carlo, A., Rocca, W. A., Vanni, P., Maggi, S., Perissinotto, E., Grigoletto, F., Amaducci, L., & Inzitari, D. (2000). Parkinson's disease and parkinsonism in a longitudinal study: Twofold higher incidence in men. *Neurology, 55,* 1358–1363.

Baldini, S., Restani, L., Baroncelli, L., Coltelli, M., Franco, R., Cenni, M. C. . . ., Berardi, N. (2013). Enriched early life experiences reduce adult anxiety-like behavior in rats: A role for insulin-like growth factor 1. *The Journal of Neuroscience, 33*(28), 11715–11723. doi:10.1523/JNEUROSCI.3541-12.2013

Baltan, S., Murphy, S. P., Danilov, C. A., Bachleda, A., & Morrison, R. S. (2011). Histone deacetylase inhibitors preserve white matter structure and function during ischemia by conserving ATP and reducing excitotoxicity. *The Journal of Neuroscience, 31*(11), 3990–3999. doi:10.1523/jneurosci.5379-10.2011

Baltimore Longitudinal Study of Aging. (2000, March 12). *Welcome to the BLSA.* Retrieved from the Baltimore Longitudinal Study of Aging Web site: http://www.grc.nia.nih.gov/branches/blsa/blsanew.htm.

Bami, M., Episkopou, V., Gavalas, A., & Gouti, M. (2011). Directed neural differentiation of mouse embryonic stem cells is a sensitive system for the identification of novel Hox gene effectors. *PLoS ONE, 6*(5), e20197. doi:10.1371/journal.pone.0020197

Banerjee, T. D., Middleton, F., & Faraone, S. V. (2007). Environmental risk factors for attention-deficit hyperactivity disorder. *Acta Paediatrica, 96*(9), 1269–1274.

Bao, A.-M., & Swaab, D. F. (2011). Sexual differentiation of the human brain: Relation to gender identity, sexual orientation and neuropsychiatric disorders. *Frontiers in Neuroendocrinology, 32*(2), 214–226. doi:http://dx.doi.org/10.1016/j.yfrne.2011.02.007

Barac, R., & Bialystok, E. (2012). Bilingual effects on cognitive and linguistic development: Role of language, cultural background, and education. *Child development, 83*(2), 413–422. doi:10.1111/j.1467-8624.2011.01707.x

Barbaresi, W. J., Katusic, S. K., Colligan, R. C., Weaver, A. L., & Jacobsen, S. J. (2005). The incidence of autism in Olmsted County, Minnesota, 1976–1997: Results from a population-based study. *Archives of Pediatric and Adolescent Medicine, 159,* 37–44.

Barbaro, N. M. (1988). Studies of PAG/PVG stimulation for pain relief in humans. *Progress in Brain Research, 77,* 165–173.

Barcelo, F., & Knight, R. T. (2002). Both random and perseverative errors underlie WCST deficits in prefrontal patients. *Neuropsychologia, 40,* 349–356.

Bargh, J. A., Chen, M., & Burrows, L. (1996). Automaticity of social behavior: Direct effects of trait construct and stereotype activation on action. *Journal of Personality and Social Psychology, 71*(2), 230–244. doi:10.1037/0022-3514.71.2.230

Barlow, D. (1988). *Anxiety and its disorders: The nature and treatment of anxiety and panic.* New York: Guilford Press.

Barlow, D. H., & Durand, V. M. (1995). *Abnormal psychology: An integrative approach.* Pacific Grove, CA: Brooks/Cole.

Barnea-Goraly, N., Frazier, T. W., Piacenza, L., Minshew, N. J., Keshavan, M. S., Reiss, A. L., & Hardan, A. Y. (2014). A preliminary longitudinal volumetric MRI study of amygdala and hippocampal volumes in autism. *Progress in Neuro-Psychopharmacology and Biological Psychiatry, 48,* 124–128. doi:10.1016/j.pnpbp.2013.09.010

Barnea, A., & Nottebohm, F. (1994). Seasonal recruitment of hippocampal neurons in adult free-ranging black-capped chickadees. *Proceedings of the National Academy of Sciences of the United States of America (PNAS), 91,* 11217–11221.

Barnes, T. D., Kubota, Y., Hu, D., Jin, D. Z., & Graybiel, A. M. (2005). Activity of striatal neurons reflects dynamic encoding and recoding of procedural memories. *Nature, 437*(7062), 1158–1161.

Baron-Cohen, S., & Belmonte, M. K. (2005). Autism: A window onto the development of the social and the analytic brain. *Annual Review of Neuroscience, 28,* 109–126.

Baron-Cohen, S., Wheelwright, S., Skinner, R., Martin, J., & Clubley, E. (2001). The autism-spectrum quotient (AQ): Evidence from Asperger syndrome/high-functioning autism, males and females, scientists and mathematicians. *Journal of Autism and Developmental Disorders, 31*(1), 5–17. doi:10.1023/A:1005653411471

Barr, A. M., Panenka, W. J., Macewan, G. W., Thornton, A. E., Lang, D. J., Honer, W. G., & Lecomte, T. (2006). The need for speed: An update on methamphetamine addiction. *Journal of Psychiatry and Neuroscience, 31*(5), 301–313.

Bartels, A., & Zeki, S. (2004). The neural correlates of maternal and romantic love. *NeuroImage, 21,* 1155–1166.

Barton, J. J. (2003). Disorders of face perception and recognition. *Neurologic Clinics, 21*(2), 521–548.

Bartoshuk, L. M. (2000). Comparing sensory experiences across individuals: Recent psychophysical advances illuminate genetic variation in taste perception. *Chemical Senses, 25,* 447–460.

Bassett, A. S., Scherer, S. W., & Brzustowicz, L. M. (2010). Copy number variations in schizophrenia: Critical review and new perspectives on concepts of genetics and disease. *American Journal of Psychiatry, 167,* 899–914.

Bateman, B. T., Hernandez-Diaz, S., Rathmell, J. P., Seeger, J. D., Doherty, M., Fischer, M. A., & Huybrechts, K. F. (2014). Patterns of opioid utilization in pregnancy in a large cohort of commercial insurance beneficiaries in the United States. *Anesthesiology, 120*(5), 1216–1224. doi:10.1097/ALN.0000000000000172

Baudry, M., Bi, X., Gall, C., & Lynch, G. (2011). The biochemistry of memory: The 26 year journey of a "new and specific hypothesis." *Neurobiology of Learning and Memory, 95*(2), 125–133. doi:10.1016/j.nlm.2010.11.015

Bauman, M., Iosif, A., Ashwood, P., Braunschweig, D., Lee, A., Schumann, C., . . . Amaral, D. G. (2013). Maternal antibodies from mothers of children with autism alter brain growth and social behavior development in the rhesus monkey. *Translational Psychiatry, 3*(7), e278. doi:10.1038/tp.2013.47

Baxter, L. R., Jr., Schwartz, J. M., Bergman, K. S., Szuba, M. P., Guze, B. H., Mazziotta, J. C., et al. (1992). Caudate glucose metabolic rate changes with both drug and behavior therapy for obsessive-compulsive disorder. *Archives of General Psychiatry, 49,* 681–689.

Baylor, D. A. (1987). Photoreceptor signals and vision. Proctor lecture. *Investigative Ophthalmology and Visual Science, 28*(1), 34–49.

Beason-Held, L. L., Kraut, M. A., & Resnick, S. M. (2008). I. Longitudinal changes in aging brain function. *Neurobiology of Aging, 29*(4), 483–496.

Beaton, A. A. (1997). The relation of planum temporale asymmetry and morphology of the corpus callosum to handedness, gender, and dyslexia: A review of the evidence. *Brain and Language, 60,* 252–322.

Bechara, A., Damasio, H., & Damasio, A. R. (2000). Emotion, decision making and the orbitofrontal cortex. *Cerebral Cortex, 10*(3), 295–307.

Becker, A. E. (2004). Television, disordered eating, and young women in Fiji: Negotiating body image and identity during rapid social change. *Culture, Medicine, and Psychiatry, 28*(4), 533–559.

Becker, A. E., Burwell, R. A., Herzog, D. B., Hamburg, P., & Gilman, S. E. (2002). Eating behaviours and attitudes following prolonged exposure to television among ethnic Fijian adolescent girls. *British Journal of Psychiatry, 180,* 509–514.

Becker, A. E., Fay, K. E., Agnew-Blais, J., Khan, A. N., Striegel-Moore, R. H., & Gilman, S. E. (2011). Social network media exposure and adolescent eating pathology in Fiji. *The British Journal of Psychiatry, 198*(1), 43–50. doi:10.1192/bjp.bp.110.078675

Behavior Analyst Certification Board (BACB). (n.d.). Eligibility standards. http://www.bacb.com/index.php?page=53

Belliveau, J. W., Kennedy, D. N., Jr., McKinstry, R. C., Buchbinder, B. R., Weisskopf, R. M., Cohen, M. S., et al. (1991). Functional mapping of the human visual cortex by magnetic resonance imaging. *Science, 254,* 716–719.

Bellugi, U., Wang, P. P., & Jernigan, T. L. (1994). Williams syndrome: An unusual neuropsychological profile. In S. H. Broman & J. Grafman (Eds.), *Atypical cognitive deficits in developmental disorders: Implications for brain function* (pp. 23–56). Hillsdale, NJ: Erlbaum.

Ben-Yakov, A., & Dudai, Y. (2011). Constructing realistic engrams: Poststimulus activity of hippocampus and dorsal striatum predicts subsequent episodic memory. *The Journal of Neuroscience, 31*(24), 9032–9042. doi:10.1523/JNEUROSCI.0702-11.2011

Bender, B. G., Linden, M. G., & Harmon, R. J. (2001). Life adaptation in 35 adults with sex chromosome abnormalities. *Genetics in Medicine, 3*(3), 187–191.

Bennett, M. V., & Zukin, R. S. (2004). Electrical coupling and neuronal synchronization in the mammalian brain. *Neuron, 41*(4), 495–511.

Berardi, N., Pizzorusso, T., & Maffei, L. (2000). Critical periods during sensory development. *Current Opinion in Neurobiology, 10,* 138–145.

Berger-Sweeney, J., Heckers, S., Mesulam, M.-M., Wiley, R. G., Lappi, D. A., & Sharma, M. (1994). Differential effects on spatial navigation of immunotoxin-induced cholinergic lesions of the medial septal area and nucleus basalis magnocellularis. *The Journal of Neuroscience, 14*(7), 4507–4519.

Berger, M. M., Kopp, N., Vital, C., Redl, B., Aymard, M., & Lina, B. (2000). Detection and cellular localization of enterovirus RNA sequences in spinal cord of patients with ALS. *Neurology, 54,* 20–25.

Berkman, N. D., Bulik, C. M., Brownley, K. A., Lohr, K. N., Sedway, J. A., Rooks, A., et al. (2006). Management of eating disorders. *Evidence Report/Technology Assessment, 135,* 1–166.

Berlim, M. T., Mattevi, B. S., Belmonte-de-Abreu, P., & Crow, T. J. (2003). The etiology of schizophrenia and the origin of language: Overview of a theory. *Comprehensive Psychiatry, 44*(1), 7–14.

Berlin, F. S. (1997). "Chemical castration" for sex offenders. *New England Journal of Medicine, 336*(14), 1030.

Berman, K. F., Torrey, E. F., Daniel, D. G., & Weinberger, D. R. (1992). Regional cerebral blood flow in monozygotic twins discordant and concordant for schizophrenia. *Archives of General Psychiatry, 49,* 927–934.

Bernard, C. (1856). *Leçons de physiologie expérimentale appliqué à la medicine faites au College de France* (Vol. 2). Paris: Balliere.

Bernhardt, P. C., Dabbs, J. M., Jr., Fielden, J. A., & Lutter, C. D. (1998). Testosterone changes during vicarious experiences of winning and losing among fans at sporting events. *Physiology and Behavior, 65,* 59–62.

Bernheim, H., & Kluger, M. (1976). Fever: Effect of drug-induced antipyresis on survival. *Science, 193*(4249), 237–239. doi:10.1126/science.935867

Berns, G. S., Chappelow, J., Cekic, M., Zink, C. F., Pagnoni, G., & Martin-Skurski, M. E. (2006). Neurobiological substrates of dread. *Science, 312*(5774), 754–758.

Bernstein, H.-G., Becker, A., Keilhoff, G., Grecksch, G., & Bogerts, B. (2011). Schizophrenia and the nitric oxide controversy: Do all things fall into place now? *Synapse, 65*(6), 545–546. doi:10.1002/syn.20871

Berntson, G. G., Norman, G. J., Bechara, A., Bruss, J., Tranel, D., & Cacioppo, J. T. (2011). The insula and evaluative process. *Psychological Science, 22*(1), 80–86. doi:10.1177/0956797610391097

Berrington de Gonzalez, A., Hartge, P., Cerhan, J. R., Flint, A. J., Hannan, L., MacInnis, R. J. ... Thun, M. J. (2010). Body-mass index and mortality among 1.46 million white adults. *New England Journal of Medicine, 363*(23), 2211–2219. doi:10.1056/NEJMoa1000367

Berta, P., Hawkins, J. R., Sinclair, A. H., Taylor, A., Griffiths, B. L., Goodfellow, P. N., & Fellous, M. (1990). Genetic evidence equating SRY and the testis determining factor. *Nature, 348,* 448–450.

Besancon, E., Guo, S., Lok, J., Tymianski, M., & Lo, E. H. (2008). Beyond NMDA and AMPA glutamate receptors: Emerging mechanisms for ionic imbalance and cell death in stroke. *Trends in Pharmacological Sciences, 29*(5), 268–275.

Bewernick, B. H., Hurlemann, R., Matusch, A., Kayser, S., Grubert, C., Hadrysiewicz, B., ... Schlaepfer, T. E. (2010). Nucleus accumbens deep brain stimulation decreases ratings of depression and anxiety in treatment-resistant depression. *Biological Psychiatry, 67*(2), 110–116. doi:10.1016/j.biopsych.2009.09.013

Bexell, D., Scheding, S., & Bengzon, J. (2010). Toward brain tumor gene therapy using multipotent mesenchymal stromal cell vectors. *Molecular Therapy, 18*(6), 1067–1075. doi:10.1038/mt.2010.58

Beyreuther, K., Biesalski, H. K., Fernstrom, J. D., Grimm, P., Hammes, W. P., Heinemann, U., ... Walker, R. (2007). Consensus meeting: Monosodium glutamate—An update. *European Journal of Clinical Nutrition 61*(3), 304–313.

Bialystok, E., Craik, F. I., & Luk, G. (2012). Bilingualism: Consequences for mind and brain. *Trends in Cognitive Sciences, 16*(4), 240–250. doi:10.1016/j.tics.2012.03.001

Biederman, I. (1987). Recognition-by-components: A theory of human image understanding. *Psychological Review, 94*(2), 115–147.

Bierut, L. J., Agrawal, A., Bucholz, K. K., Doheny, K. F., Laurie, C., Pugh, E., ... Rice, J. P. (2010). A genome-wide association study of alcohol dependence. *Proceedings of the National Academy of Sciences of the United States of America (PNAS), 107*(11), 5082–5087. doi:10.1073/pnas.0911109107

Biezonski, D. K., & Meyer, J. S. (2011). The nature of 3, 4-Methylenedioxymethamphetamine (MDMA)-induced serotonergic dysfunction: Evidence for and against the neurodegeneration hypothesis. *Current Neuropharmacology, 9*(1), 84–90. doi:10.2174/157015911795017146

Birnbaumer, L., Abramowitz, J., & Brown, A. M. (1990). Receptor-effector coupling by G proteins. *Biochimica et Biophysica Acta (BBA) - Reviews on Biomembranes, 1031*(2), 163–224. doi:10.1016/0304-4157(90)90007-y

Biro, F. M., Greenspan, L. C., & Galvez, M. P. (2012). Puberty in girls in the 21st century. *Journal of Pediatric and Adolescent Gynecology, 25*(5), 289–294. doi:http://dx.doi.org/10.1016/j.jpag.2012.05.009

Biss, R. K., & Hasher, L. (2012). Happy as a lark: Morning-type younger and older adults are higher in positive affect. *Emotion, 12*(3), 437–441. doi:10.1037/a0027071

Blackford, J. U., Buckholtz, J. W., Avery, S. N., & Zald, D. H. (2010). A unique role for the human amygdala in novelty detection. *NeuroImage, 50*(3), 1188–1193. doi:http://dx.doi.org/10.1016/j.neuroimage.2009.12.083

Blair, R. J. R. (2013). The neurobiology of psychopathic traits in youths. *Nature Reviews Neuroscience, 14*(11), 786–799. doi:10.1038/nrn3577

Blair, R. J., Mitchell, D. G., Richell, R. A., Kelly, S., Leonard, A., Newman, C., & Scott, S. K. (2002). Turning a deaf ear to fear: Impaired recognition of vocal affect in psychopathic individuals. *Journal of Abnormal Psychology, 111,* 682–686.

Blair, R. J., Peschardt, K. S., Budhani, S., Mitchell, D. G., & Pine, D. S. (2006). The development of psychopathy. *Journal of Child Psychology and Psychiatry, 47*(3–4), 262–276.

Blakeley, J. (2008). Drug delivery to brain tumors. *Current Neurology and Neuroscience Reports, 8*(3), 235–241.

Blanchard, R. (1997). Birth order and sibling sex ratio in homosexual versus heterosexual males and females. *Annual Review of Sex Research, 8,* 27–67.

Blasdel, G. G. (1992). Orientation selectivity, preference, and continuity in monkey striate cortex. *Journal of Neuroscience, 12,* 3139–3161.

Blennow, K., de Leon, M. J., & Zetterberg, H. (2006). Alzheimer's disease. *The Lancet, 368*(9533), 387–403. doi:10.1016/S0140-6736(06)69113-7

Blevins, J. E., Morton, G. J., Williams, D. L., Caldwell, D. W., Bastian, L. S., Wisse, B. E., ... Baskin, D. G. (2009). Forebrain melanocortin signaling enhances the hindbrain satiety response to CCK-8. *American Journal of Physiology - Regulatory, Integrative and Comparative Physiology, 296*(3), R476–R484. doi:10.1152/ajpregu.90544.2008

Bliss, T. V. P., & Lømo, T. (1973). Long-lasting potentiation of synaptic transmission in the dentate gyrus of the anesthetized rabbit following stimulation of the perforant path. *Journal of Physiology, 232,* 331–356.

Bloom, P. (2004). Can a dog learn a word? *Science, 304,* 1605–1606.

Blumberg, S. J., Bramlett, M. D., Kogan, M. D., Schieve, L. A., Jones, J. R., & Lu, M. C. (2013). Changes in prevalence of parent-reported autism spectrum disorder in school-aged US children: 2007 to 2011–2012. *National Health Statistics Reports, 65,* 1–11.

Blumenthal, J. A., Babyak, M. A., Moore, K. A., Craighead, W. E., Herman, S., Khatri, P., et al. (1999). Effects of exercise training on older patients with major depression. *Archives of Internal Medicine, 159,* 2349–2356.

Bocklandt, S., Horvath, S., Vilain, E., & Hamer, D. H. (2006). Extreme skewing of X chromosome inactivation in mothers of homosexual men. *Human Genetics, 118*(6), 691–694.

Bogen, J. E., Schultz, D. H., & Vogel, P. J. (1988). Completeness of callosotomy shown by magnetic resonance imaging in the long term. *Archives of Neurology, 45,* 1203–1205.

Bond, C., Jr., & Robinson, M. (1988). The evolution of deception. *Journal of Nonverbal Behavior, 12*(4), 295–307. doi:10.1007/BF00987597

Bonifati, V. (2014). Genetics of Parkinson's disease—State of the art, 2013. *Parkinsonism & Related Disorders, 20,* S23–S28.

Booth, A., Shelley, G., Mazur, A., Th arp, G., & Kittok, R. (1989). Testosterone, and winning and losing in human competition. *Hormones and Behavior, 23,* 556–571.

Boothroyd, L. G., Jones, B. C., Burt, D. M., & Perrett, D. I. (2007). Partner characteristics associated with masculinity, health and maturity in male faces. *Personality and Individual Differences, 43*(5), 1161–1173.

Borkovec, T. D., Grayson, J. B., O'Brien, G. T., & Weerts, T. C. (1979). Relaxation treatment of pseudoinsomnia and idiopathic insomnia: An electroencephalographic evaluation. *Journal of Applied Behavior Analysis, 12,* 37–54.

Borota, D., Murray, E., Keceli, G., Chang, A., Watabe, J. M., Ly, M., ... Yassa, M. A. (2014). Post-study caffeine administration enhances memory consolidation in humans. *Nature Neuroscience, 17*(2), 201–203. doi:10.1038/nn.3623

Bossini, L., Tavanti, M., Calossi, S., Lombardelli, A., Polizzotto, N. R., Galli, R., et al. (2008). Magnetic resonance imaging volumes of the hippocampus in drug-naive patients with post-traumatic stress disorder without comorbidity conditions. *Journal of Psychiatric Research, 42*(9), 752–762.

Bossong, M. G., Jansma, J. M., van Hell, H. H., Jager, G., Oudman, E., Saliasi, E., ... Ramsey, N. F. (2012). Effects of δ9-tetrahydrocannabinol on human working memory function. *Biological Psychiatry, 71*(8), 693–699. doi:10.1016/j.biopsych.2012.01.008

Bouchard, T., Jr. (1994). Genes, environment, and personality. *Science, 264,* 1700–1701.

Bouchard, T., Jr., Lykken, D. T., McGue, M., Segal, N. L., & Tellegen, A. (1990). Sources of human psychological differences: The Minnesota Study of Twins Reared Apart. *Science, 250,* 223–228.

Boulant, J. A. (2000). Role of the preoptic-anterior hypothalamus in thermoregulation and fever. *Clinical Infectious Diseases, 31,* S57–61.

Bourque, C. W., & Oliet, S. H. R. (1997). Osmoreceptors in the central nervous system. *Annual Review of Physiology, 59,* 601–619.

Boussard, C. N.-d., Holm, L. W., Cancelliere, C., Godbolt, A. K., Boyle, E., Stålnacke, B.-M., … Borg, J. (2014). Nonsurgical interventions after mild traumatic brain injury: A systematic review. Results of the International Collaboration on Mild Traumatic Brain Injury Prognosis. *Archives of Physical Medicine and Rehabilitation, 95*(3), S257–S264. doi:10.1016/j.apmr.2013.10.009

Bowery, N., Enna, S. J., & Olsen, R. W. (2004). Six decades of GABA. *Biochemical Pharmacology, 68*(8), 1477–1478.

Bowman, R. M., & McLone, D. G. (2010). Neurosurgical management of spina bifida: Research issues. *Developmental Disabilities Research Reviews, 16*(1), 82–87. doi:10.1002/ddrr.100

Boyd, P. A., Loane, M., Garne, E., Khoshnood, B., & Dolk, H. (2011). Sex chromosome trisomies in Europe: Prevalence, prenatal detection and outcome of pregnancy. *European Journal of Human Genetics, 19*(2), 231–234.

Boydell, J., & Murray, R. (2003). Urbanization, migration and risk of schizophrenia. In R. M. Murray, P. B. Jones, E. Susser, J. van Os, & M. Cannon (Eds.), *The epidemiology of schizophrenia* (pp. 49–67). Cambridge, UK: Cambridge University Press.

Boydell, J., van Os, J., McKenzie, K., Allardyce, J., Goel, R., McCreadie, R. G., et al. (2001). Incidence of schizophrenia in ethnic minorities in London: Ecological study into interactions with environment. *British Medical Journal, 323,* 1336–1338.

Boyden, E. S. (2011). A history of optogenetics: The development of tools for controlling brain circuits with light. *Biology Reports, 3*(11). doi:10.3410/B3-11

Boyle, S. H., Jackson, W. G., & Suarez, E. C. (2007). Hostility, anger, and depression predict increases in C3 over a 10-year period. *Brain, Behavior, and Immunity, 21*(6), 816–823.

Bozarth, M. A., & Wise, R. A. (1986). Involvement of the ventral tegmental dopamine system in opioid and psychomotor stimulant reinforcement. *NIDA Research Monograph, 67,* 190–196.

Bradley, C. (1937). The behavior of children receiving Benzedrine. *American Journal of Psychiatry, 94,* 577–585.

Bradley, R. (1979). Effects of aging on the sense of taste: Anatomical considerations. In S. S. Han & D. H. Coons (Eds.), *Special senses in aging: A current biological assessment* (pp. 3–8). Ann Arbor: University of Michigan, Institute of Gerontology.

Brady, K. T., Lydiard, R. B., Malcolm, R., & Ballenger, J. C. (1991). Cocaine-induced psychosis. *Journal of Clinical Psychiatry, 52,* 509–512.

Brandt, R. (2001). Cytoskeletal mechanisms of neuronal degeneration. *Cell and Tissue Research, 305,* 255–265.

Brat, D. J., Parisi, J. E., Kleinschmidt-DeMasters, B. K., Yachnis, A. T., Montine, T. J., Boyer, P. J., et al. (2008). Surgical neuropathology update: A review of changes introduced by the WHO classification of tumours of the central nervous system, 4th edition. *Archives of Pathology and Laboratory Medicine, 132*(6), 993–1007.

Braun, S. M. G., & Jessberger, S. (2014). Review: Adult neurogenesis and its role in neuropsychiatric disease, brain repair and normal brain function. *Neuropathology and Applied Neurobiology, 40*(1), 3–12. doi:10.1111/nan.12107

Breasted, J. H. (1930). *Edwin Smith Surgical Papyrus.* Chicago, IL: University of Chicago Press.

Breedlove, S. M. (1992). Sexual differentiation of the brain and behavior. In J. Becker, S. M. Breedlove, & D. Crews (Eds.), *Behavioral endocrinology* (pp. 39–70). Cambridge, MA: MIT Press.

Breiter, H. C., Aharon, I., Kahneman, D., Dale, A., & Shizgal, P. (2001). Functional imaging of neural responses to expectancy and experience of monetary gains and losses. *Neuron, 30*(2), 619–639. doi:10.1016/s0896-6273(01)00303-8

Brembs, B., Lorenzetti, F. D., Reyes, F. D., Baxter, D. A., & Byrne, J. H. (2002). Operant reward learning in *Aplysia*: Neuronal correlates and mechanisms. *Science, 296,* 1706–1709. doi:10.1126/science.1069434

Bremner, J. D., Innis, R. B., Southwick, S. M., Staib, L., Zoghbi, S., & Charney, D. D. (2000). Decreased benzodiazepine receptor binding in prefrontal cortex in combat-related post-traumatic stress disorder. *American Journal of Psychiatry, 157,* 1120–1126.

Bremner, J. D., Vythilingam, M., Vermetten, E., Nazeer, A., Adil, J., Khan, S., et al. (2002). Reduced volume of orbitofrontal cortex in major depression. *Biological Psychiatry, 51*(4), 273–279.

Brill, K. T., Weltman, A. L., Gentili, A., Patrie, J. T., Fryburg, D. A., Hanks, J. B., et al. (2002). Single and combined effects of growth hormone and testosterone administration on measures of body composition, physical performance, mood, sexual function, bone turnover, and muscle gene expression in healthy older men. *Journal of Clinical Endocrinology and Metabolism, 87,* 5649–5657.

Bristow, D., Frith, C., & Rees, G. (2005). Two distinct neural effects of blinking on human visual processing. *NeuroImage, 27*(1), 136–145.

Brock, D. W. (2011). Behavioral genetics and equality. In E. Parens, A. R. Chapman & N. Press (Eds.), *Wrestling with behavioral genetics: Science, ethics, and public conversation* (pp. 199–219). Baltimore, MD: The Johns Hopkins University Press.

Brodmann, K. (1909/1994). *Localisation in the cerebral cortex by Korbinian Brodmann* (L. J. Garey, Trans.). London: Smith-Gordon.

Broeren, J., Bjorkdahl, A., Claesson, L., Goude, D., Lundgren-Nilsson, A., Samuelsson, H., et al. (2008). Virtual rehabilitation after stroke. *Studies in Health Technology and Informatics, 136,* 77–82.

Brookes, J. C., Hartoutsiou, F., Horsfield, A. P., & Stoneham, A. M. (2007). Could humans recognize odor by phonon assisted tunneling? *Physical Review Letters, 98*(3), 038101.

Broquet, K. (1999). Status of treatment of depression. *Southern Medical Journal, 92*(9), 848–858.

Brown, A. S. (2006). Prenatal infection as a risk factor for schizophrenia. *Schizophrenia Bulletin, 32*(2), 200–202.

Brown, A. S. (2012). Epidemiologic studies of exposure to prenatal infection and risk of schizophrenia and autism. *Developmental Neurobiology, 72*(10), 1272–1276. doi:10.1002/dneu.22024

Brown, A. S., van Os, J., Driessens, C., Hoek, H. W., & Susser, E. S. (2000). Further evidence of relation between prenatal famine and major affective disorder. *American Journal of Psychiatry, 157,* 190–195.

Brown, A., & Sorbera, L. (2013). Therapeutic targets for male contraception. *Drugs of the Future, 38*(7), 499–511.

Brown, R. L., & Robinson, P. R. (2004). Melanopsin—Shedding light on the elusive circadian photopigment. *Chronobiology International, 21*(2), 189–204.

Brown, S., Ingham, R. J., Ingham, J. C., Laird, A. R., & Fox, P. T. (2005). Stuttered and fluent speech production: An ALE meta-analysis of functional neuroimaging studies. *Human Brain Mapping, 25*(1), 105–117.

Brown, S., Martinez, M. J., & Parsons, L. M. (2006). Music and language side by side in the brain: A PET study of the generation of melodies and sentences. *European Journal of Neuroscience, 23*(10), 2791–2803.

Bruce, M. E., Will, R. G., Ironside, J. W., McConnell, I., Drummond, D., Suttie, A., et al. (1997). Transmissions to mice indicate that "new variant" CJD is caused by the BSE agent. *Nature, 389,* 498–501.

Bruchmüller, K., Margraf, J., & Schneider, S. (2012). Is ADHD diagnosed in accord with diagnostic criteria? Overdiagnosis and influence of client gender on diagnosis. *Journal of Consulting and Clinical Psychology, 80*(1), 128. doi:10.1037/a0026582

Bruetsch, W. L. (1949). Why malaria cures general paralysis. *Journal of the Indiana State Medical Association Journal, 42,* 211–216.

Brunelli, M., Castellucci, V., & Kandel, E. R. (1976). Synaptic facilitation and behavioral sensitization in *Aplysia*: Possible role of serotonin and cyclic AMP. *Science, 194*(4270), 1178–1181.

Bryden, M. P. (1982). *Laterality: Functional asymmetry in the intact brain.* New York: Academic Press.

Bryden, M. P. (1988). An overview of the dichotic listening procedure and its relation to cerebral organization. In K. Hugdahl (Ed.), *Handbook of dichotic listening* (pp. 1–44). Chichester, England: John Wiley.

Buck, L. B., & Axel, R. (1991). A novel multi-gene family may encode odorant receptors: A molecular basis for odor recognition. *Cell, 65,* 175–187.

Buckley, N. A., Dawson, A. H., & Isbister, G. K. (2014). Serotonin syndrome. *BMJ: British Medical Journal, 348,* g1626.

Buckner, R. L., Andrews-Hanna, J. R., & Schacter, D. L. (2008). The brain's default network. *Annals of the New York Academy of Sciences, 1124*(1), 1–38.

Buitelaar, J. K. (2003). Why have drug treatments been so disappointing? *Novartis Foundation Symposium, 251,* 235–244; discussion 245–239, 281–297.

Bunzeck, N., Doeller, C. F., Dolan, R. J., & Duzel, E. (2012). Contextual interaction between novelty and reward processing within the mesolimbic system. *Human Brain Mapping, 33*(6), 1309–1324. doi:10.1002/hbm.21288

Burr, D. (2005). Vision: In the blink of an eye. *Current Biology, 15*(14), R554–556.

Buscemi, N., Vandermeer, B., Friesen, C., Bialy, L., Tubman, M., Ospina, M., et al. (2007). The efficacy and safety of drug treatments for chronic insomnia in adults: A meta-analysis of RCTs. *Journal of General Internal Medicine, 22*(9), 1335–1350.

Bushman, B. J. (2002). Does venting anger feed or extinguish the flame? Catharsis, rumination, distraction, anger and aggressive responding. *Personality & Social Psychology Bulletin, 28*(6), 724–731.

Bushman, B. J., & Whitaker, J. L. (2010). Like a magnet: Catharsis beliefs attract angry people to violent video games. *Psychological Science, 21*(6), 790–792. doi:10.1177/0956797610369494

Bussing, R., & Winterstein, A. (2012). Polypharmacy in attention deficit hyperactivity disorder treatment: Current status, challenges and next steps. *Current Psychiatry Reports, 14*(5), 447–449. doi:10.1007/s11920-012-0295-6

Butuzova, M. V., & Kitchigina, V. F. (2008). Repeated blockade of GABA(A) receptors in the medial septal region induces epileptiform activity in the hippocampus. *Neuroscience Letters, 434*(1), 133–138.

Buxbaum, J., & Baron-Cohen, S. (2010). Molecular autism: Accelerating and integrating research into neurodevelopmental conditions. *Molecular Autism, 1*(1), 1.

Byne, W., Bradley, S. J., Coleman, E., Eyler, A. E., Green, R., Menvielle, E. J., ... American Psychiatric Association Task Force on Treatment of Gender Identity Disorder. (2012). Report of the American Psychiatric Association task force on treatment of gender identity disorder. *Archives of Sexual Behavior, 41*(4), 759–796.

Bystritsky, A., Pontillo, D., Powers, M., Sabb, F. W., Craske, M. G., & Bookheimer, S. Y. (2001). Functional MRI changes during panic anticipation and imagery exposure. *Neuroreport, 12,* 3953–3957.

Cacioppo, J. T., & Berntson, G. G. (2011). The brain, homeostasis, and health: Balancing demands of the internal and external milieu. In H. S. Friedman (Ed.), *The Oxford handbook of health psychology* (pp. 73–91). New York: Oxford University Press.

Cacioppo, J. T., Berntson, G. G., & Klein, D. J. (1992). What is an emotion? The role of somatovisceral afference, with special emphasis on somatovisceral "illusions." *Review of Personality and Social Psychology, 14,* 63–98.

Cacioppo, J. T., Berntson, G. G., Larsen, J. T., Poehlmann, K. M., & Ito, T. A. (2000). The psychophysiology of emotion. In M. Lewis & J. M. Haviland-Jones (Eds.), *Handbook of emotions* (Vol. 2, pp. 173–191). New York: Guilford Press.

Cacioppo, J. T., Berntson, G. G., Norris, C. J., & Gollan, J. K. (2011). The evaluative space model. In P. Van Lange, A. Kruglanski, & E. T. Higgins (Eds.), *Handbook of theories of social psychology* (Vol. 1, pp. 50–72). Thousand Oaks, CA: Sage.

Cacioppo, S., Bianchi-Demicheli, F., Frum, C., Pfaus, J. G., & Lewis, J. W. (2012). The common neural bases between sexual desire and love: A multilevel kernel density fMRI analysis. *Journal of Sexual Medicine, 9*(4), 1048–1054. doi:10.1111/j.1743-6109.2012.02651.x

Cacioppo, S., Frum, C., Asp, E., Weiss, R. M., Lewis, J. W., & Cacioppo, J. T. (2013). A quantitative meta-analysis of functional imaging studies of social rejection. *Scientific Reports, 3.* doi:10.1038/srep02027

Caggiano, V., Rizzolatti, G., Pomper, J. K., Thier, P., Giese, M. A., & Casile, A. (2011). View-based encoding of actions in mirror neurons of area f5 in macaque premotor cortex. *Current Biology, 21*(2), 144–148.

Cahill, L., Gorski, L., & Le, K. (2003). Enhanced human memory consolidation with postlearning stress: Interaction with the degree of arousal at encoding. *Learning & Memory, 10*(4), 270–274. doi:10.1101/lm.62403

Caldwell, D. F., & Caldwell, M. C. (1976). Cetaceans. In T. A. Sebeok (Ed.), *How animals communicate* (pp. 794–808). Bloomington: Indiana University.

Calvin, W. H. (2004). *A brief history of the mind: From apes to intellect and beyond.* Oxford, UK: Oxford University Press.

Calvo, J. R., González-Yanes, C., & Maldonado, M. D. (2013). The role of melatonin in the cells of the innate immunity: A review. *Journal of Pineal Research, 55*(2), 103–120. doi:10.1111/jpi.12075

Cannon, M., Jones, P. B., & Murray, R. M. (2002). Obstetric complications and schizophrenia: Historical and meta-analytic review. *American Journal of Psychiatry, 159,* 1080–1092.

Cannon, M., Kendell, R., Susser, E., & Jones, P. (2003). Prenatal and perinatal risk factors for schizophrenia. In R. M. Murray, P. B. Jones, E. Susser, J. van Os, & M. Cannon (Eds.), *The epidemiology of schizophrenia* (pp. 74–99). Cambridge, UK: Cambridge University Press.

Cannon, W. (1927). The James-Lange theory of emotions: A critical examination and an alternative theory. *American Journal of Psychology, 39,* 106–124.

Cannon, W. (1929). *Bodily changes in pain, hunger, fear and rage* (2nd ed.). New York: Harper & Row.

Cannon, W. (1932). *The wisdom of the body.* New York: Norton.

Cannon, W. B. (1957). "Voodoo" death. *Psychosomatic Medicine, 19,* 182–190. (Original work published 1942.)

Cannon, W., & Washburn, A. L. (1912). An explanation of hunger. *American Journal of Physiology, 29,* 441–454.

Cantor, J. M., Blanchard, R., Paterson, A. D., & Bogaert, A. F. (2002). How many gay men owe their sexual orientation to fraternal birth order? *Archives of Sexual Behavior, 31*(1), 63–71.

Cao, X., Wang, H., Mei, B., An, S., Yin, L., Wang, L. P., et al. (2008). Inducible and selective erasure of memories in the mouse brain via chemical-genetic manipulation. *Neuron, 60*(2), 353–366.

Cappuccino, A. (2008). Moderate hypothermia as treatment for spinal cord injury. *Orthopedics, 31*(3), 243–246.

Carew, T. J., & Kandel, E. R. (1973). Acquisition and retention of long-term habituation in *Aplysia:* Correlation of behavioral and cellular processes. *Science, 182*(4117), 1158–1160.

Carpenter, W. T., Jr., Conley, R. R., Buchanan, R. W., Breier, A., & Tamminga, C. A. (1995). Patient response and resource management: Another view of clozapine treatment of schizophrenia. *American Journal of Psychiatry, 152,* 827–832.

Carré, J. M., McCormick, C. M., & Mondloch, C. J. (2009). Facial structure is a reliable cue of aggressive behavior. *Psychological Science, 20*(10), 1194–1198. doi:10.1111/j.1467-9280.2009.02423.x

Carskadon, M. A., Acebo, C., & Jenni, O. G. (2004). Regulation of adolescent sleep: Implications for behavior. *Annals of the New York Academy of Sciences, 1021*(1), 276–291.

Carskadon, M. A., Harvey, K., Duke, P., Andres, T. F., Litt, I. F., & Dement, W. C. (1980). Pubertal changes in daytime sleepiness. *Sleep, 2,* 453–460.

Carter, C. S., & Porges, S. W. (2013). The biochemistry of love: An oxytocin hypothesis. *EMBO reports, 14*(1), 12–16.

Carter, R., 3rd, Cheuvront, S. N., & Sawka, M. N. (2007). A case report of idiosyncratic hyperthermia and review of U.S. Army heat stroke hospitalizations. *Journal of Sport Rehabilitation, 16*(3), 238–243.

Casanova, M. F., Switala, A. E., Trippe, J., & Fitzgerald, M. (2007). Comparative minicolumnar morphometry of three distinguished scientists. *Autism, 11*(6), 557–569. doi:10.1177/1362361307083261

Casanova, M. F., van Kooten, I. A., Switala, A. E., van Engeland, H., Heinsen, H., Steinbusch, H. W., ... Schmitz, C. (2006). Minicolumnar abnormalities in autism. *Acta Neuropathologica, 112*(3), 287–303. doi:10.1212/WNL.58.3.428

Casey, M. D., Segall, L. J., Street, D. R., & Blank, C. E. (1966). Sex chromosome abnormalities in two state hospitals for patients requiring special security. *Nature, 209,* 641–642.

Caspi, A., McClay, J., Moffitt, T. E., Mill, J., Martin, J., Craig, I. W., ... Poulton, R. (2002). Role of genotype in the cycle of violence in maltreated children. *Science, 297*(5582), 851–854. doi:10.1126/science.1072290

Caspi, A., Sugden, K., Moffitt, T. E., Taylor, A., Craig, I. W., Harrington, H., et al. (2003). Influence of life stress on depression: Moderation by a polymorphism in the 5-HTT gene. *Science, 301*(5631), 386–389.

Caspi, A., Williams, B., Kim-Cohen, J., Craig, I. W., Milne, B. J., Poulton, R., et al. (2007). Moderation of breastfeeding effects on the IQ by genetic variation in fatty acid metabolism. *Proceedings of the National Academy of Sciences of the United States of America (PNAS), 104,* 18860–18865.

Castellanos, F. X., Giedd, J. N., Eckburg, P., Marsh, W. L., Vaituzia, A. C., Kaysen, D., et al. (1994). Quantitative morphology of the caudate nucleus in attention deficit hyperactivity disorder. *American Journal of Psychiatry, 151,* 1791–1796.

Castelucci, V. F., Carew, T. J., & Kandel, E. R. (1978). Cellular analysis of long-term habituation of the gill-withdrawal reflex in *Aplysia californica. Science, 202,* 1306–1308.

Caterina, M. J., Leffler, A., Malmberg, A. B., Martin, W. J., Trafton, J., Petersen-Zeitz, K. R., et al. (2000). Impaired nociception and pain sensation in mice lacking the capsaicin receptor. *Science, 220,* 306–313.

Caterina, M. J., Schumacher, M. A., Tominaga, M., Rosen, T. A., Levine, J. D., & Julius, D. (1997). The capsaicin receptor: A heat-activated ion channel in the pain pathway. *Nature, 389*(6653), 816–824. doi:10.1038/39807

Ceccarelli, B., Hurlbut, W. P., & Mauro, A. (1973). Turnover of transmitter and synaptic vesicles at the frog neuromuscular junction. *The Journal of Cell Biology, 57*(2), 499–524. doi:10.1083/jcb.57.2.499

Center for Science, Technology, and Congress. (2001, June). NBAC proposes human subjects reforms. Retrieved from the American Association for the Advancement of Science Web site: http://www.aaas.org/spp/cstc/stc/stc01/01-06/nbac.htm.

Centers for Disease Control and Prevention (CDC). (2008). Prevalence of self-reported postpartum depressive symptoms: 17 states, 2004–2005. *Morbidity and Mortality Weekly Report, 57*(14), 361–366.

Centers for Disease Control and Prevention (CDC). (2012). *Polio.* http://www.cdc.gov/polio/

Centers for Disease Control and Prevention (CDC). (2011). 2011 national diabetes fact sheet. http://www.cdc.gov/diabetes/pubs/estimates11.htm

Centers for Disease Control and Prevention. (2011). Vital signs: Current cigarette smoking among adults aged ≥18 years—United States, 2005–2010. *Morbidity and Mortality Weekly Report.* http://www.cdc.gov/mmwr/pdf/wk/mm60e0906.pdf

Centers for Disease Control and Prevention (CDC) (2013). *Tetanus.* http://www.cdc.gov/tetanus/

Chade, A. R., Kasten, M., & Tanner, C. M. (2006). Nongenetic causes of Parkinson's disease. *Journal of Neural Transmission. Supplementum,* (70), 147–151.

Chakravarthy, M. V., & Booth, F. W. (2004). Eating, exercise, and "thrift y" genotypes: Connecting the dots toward an evolutionary understanding of modern chronic diseases. *Journal of Applied Physiology, 96*(1), 3–10.

Chamberlain, S. R., Menzies, L. A., Hampshire, A., Fineberg, N. A., del Campo, N., Craig, K., et al. (2008). Orbitofrontal dysfunction in patients with obsessive-compulsive disorder and their unaffected relatives. *Science, 321,* 3131.

Champagne, F., Francis, D. D., Mar, A., & Meaney, M. J. (2003). Naturally-occurring variations in maternal care in the rat as a mediating influence for the effects of environment on the development of individual differences in stress reactivity. *Physiology & Behavior, 79,* 359–371.

Chan, W. Y., Lorke, D. E., Tiu, S. C., & Yew, D. T. (2002). Proliferation and apoptosis in the developing human neocortex. *The Anatomical Record, 267*(4), 261–276. doi:10.1002/ar.10100

Chancellor, B., & Chatterjee, A. (2013). Brain training. In A. Chatterjee & M. J. Farah (Eds.), *Neuroethics in Practice* (pp. 57–68). New York: Oxford University Press.

Chandana, S. R., Movva, S., Arora, M., & Singh, T. (2008). Primary brain tumors in adults. *American Family Physician, 77*(10), 1423–1430.

Changeux, J. P., & Danchin, A. (1976). Selective stabilisation of developing synapses as a mechanism for the specification of neuronal networks. *Nature, 264,* 705–712.

Chao, L. L., Yaffe, K., Samuelson, K., & Neylan, T. C. (2014). Hippocampal volume is inversely related to PTSD duration. *Psychiatry Research: Neuroimaging, 222*(3), 119–123. doi:10.1016/j.pscychresns.2014.03.005

Chapman, S., & MacKenzie, R. (2010). The global research neglect of unassisted smoking cessation: Causes and consequences. *PLoS Medicine, 7*(2): e1000216. doi:10.1371/journal.pmed.1000216

Charbonneau, S., Scherzer, B. P., Aspirot, D., & Cohen, H. (2003). Perception and production of facial and prosodic emotions by chronic CVA patients. *Neuropsychologia, 41,* 605–613.

Charlton, R. A., Barrick, T. R., Markus, H. S., & Morris, R. G. (2013). Verbal working and long-term episodic memory associations with white matter microstructure in normal aging investigated using tract-based spatial statistics. *Psychology and Aging, 28*(3), 768–777. doi:10.1037/a0032668

Charvet, C. J., & Finlay, B. L. (2012). Embracing covariation in brain evolution: Large brains, extended development, and flexible primate social systems. In M. A. Hofman & D. Falk (Eds.), *Progress in brain research* (Vol. 195, pp. 71–87). New York, NY: Elsevier.

Cheng, D. T., Meintjes, E. M., Stanton, M. E., Desmond, J. E., Pienaar, M., Dodge, N. C., … Jacobson, S. W. (2013). Functional MRI of cerebellar activity during eyeblink classical conditioning in children and adults. *Human Brain Mapping, 35*(4), 1390–1403.

Chertkow, H., Whitehead, V., Phillips, N., Wolfson, C., Atherton, J., & Bergman, H. (2010). Multilingualism (but not always bilingualism) delays the onset of Alzheimer disease: Evidence from a bilingual community. *Alzheimer Disease & Associated Disorders, 24*(2), 118–125. doi:110.1097/WAD.1090b1013e3181ca1221

Chio, A., Benzi, G., Dossena, M., Mutani, R., & Mora, G. (2005). Severely increased risk of amyotrophic lateral sclerosis among Italian professional football players. *Brain: A Journal of Neurology, 128,* 472–476.

Cho, K., Ennaceur, A., Cole, J. C., & Suh, C. K. (2000). Chronic jet lag produces cognitive deficits. *Journal of Neuroscience, 20,* RC66.

Choi, J. T., Vining, E. P., Mori, S., & Bastian, A. J. (2010). Sensorimotor function and sensorimotor tracts after hemispherectomy. *Neuropsychologia, 48*(5), 1192–1199. doi:10.1016/j.neuropsychologia.2009.12.013

Christian, K. M., & Thompson, R. F. (2003). Neural substrates of eyeblink conditioning: Acquisition and retention. *Learning and Memory, 10*(6), 427–455.

Chung, J. H., Des Roches, C. M., Meunier, J., & Eavey, R. D. (2005). Evaluation of noise-induced hearing loss in young people using a web-based survey technique. *Pediatrics, 115*(4), 861–867.

Cicero, T. J., Ellis, M. S., & Surratt, H. L. (2012). Effect of abuse-deterrent formulation of OxyContin. *New England Journal of Medicine, 367*(2), 187–189. doi:10.1056/NEJMc1204141

Cingolani, L. A., & Goda, Y. (2008). Actin in action: The interplay between the actin cytoskeleton and synaptic efficacy. Nature Reviews. *Neuroscience, 9*(5), 344–356.

Cinzano, P., Falchi, F., & Elvidge, C. D. (2001). The first World Atlas of the artificial night sky brightness. *Monthly Notices of the Royal Astronomical Society, 328*(3), 689–707.

Ciocchi, S., Herry, C., Grenier, F., Wolff, S. B. E., Letzkus, J. J., Vlachos, I., … Lüthi A. (2010). Encoding of conditioned fear in central amygdala inhibitory circuits. *Nature, 468*(7321), 277–282. doi:10.1038/nature09559

Clark, R. E., Manns, J. R., & Squire, L. R. (2001). Trace and delay eyeblink conditioning: Contrasting phenomena of declarative and nondeclarative memory. *Psychological Science, 12*(4). 304–308.

Clements, A. M., Rimrodt, S. L., Abel, J. R., Blankner, J. G., Mostofsky, S. H., Pekar, J. J., … Cutting, L. E. (2006). Sex differences in cerebral laterality of language and visuospatial processing. *Brain and Language, 98,* 150–158. doi:10.1016/j.bandl.2006.04.007

Clower, W. T., & Finger, S. (2001). Discovering trepanation: The contribution of Paul Broca. *Neurosurgery, 49*(6), 1417–1425; discussion 1425–1416.

Coccaro, E. F., Bergeman, C. S., Kavoussi, R. J., & Seroczynski, A. D. (1997). Heritability of aggression and irritability: A twin study of the Buss-Durkee aggression scales in adult male subjects. *Biological Psychiatry, 41*(3), 273–284.

Cohen–Kettenis. P. T. (2005). Gender change in 46,XY persons with 5α-reductase-2 deficiency and 17β-hydroxysteroid dehydrogenase-3 deficiency. *Archives of Sexual Behavior, 34*(4), 399–410.

Cohen, D. (1972). Magnetoencephalography: Detection of the brain's electrical activity with a superconducting magnetometer. *Science, 175*(22), 664–666.

Cohen, M. S., & Bookheimer, S. Y. (1994). Localization of brain function using magnetic resonance imaging. *Techniques in Neuroscience, 17,* 268–277.

Cohen, S., & Herbert, T. B. (1996). Health psychology: Psychological factors and physical disease from the perspective of human psychoneuroimmunology. *Annual Review of Psychology, 47,* 113–142. doi:10.1146/annurev.psych.47.1.113

Cohen, S., Levi-Montalcini, R., & Hamburger, V. (1954). A nerve growth stimulating factor isolated from sarcomas 37 and 180. *Proceedings of the National Academy of Sciences of the United States of America (PNAS), 40,* 1014–1018.

Cohen, S., Tyrrell, D. A., & Smith, A. P. (1991). Psychological stress and susceptibility to the common cold. *New England Journal of Medicine, 325*(9), 606–612. doi:10.1056/NEJM199108293250903

Colicos, M. A., Collins, B. E., Sailor, M. J., & Goda, Y. (2001). Remodeling of synaptic actin induced by photoconductive stimulation. *Cell, 107,* 605–616.

Colón-Ramos, D. A., & Shen, K. (2008). Cellular conductors: Glial cells as guideposts during neural circuit development. *PLoS Biol, 6*(4), e112. doi:10.1371/journal.pbio.0060112

Colrain, I. M., Sullivan, E. V., Rohlfing, T., Baker, F. C., Nicholas, C. L., Padilla, M. L., … Pfefferbaum, A. (2011). Independent contributions of cortical gray matter, aging, sex and alcoholism to K-complex amplitude evoked during sleep. *Sleep, 34*(6), 787–795.

Colwell, K., Hiscock-Anisman, C., Memon, A., Rachel, A., & Colwell, L. (2007). Vividness and spontaneity of statement detail characteristics as predictors of witness credibility. *American Journal of Forensic Psychology, 25*(1), 5–30.

Comings, D. E., & Blum, K. (2000). Reward deficiency syndrome: Genetic aspects of behavioral disorders. *Progress in Brain Research, 126,* 325–341.

Compton, M. T., McKenzie Mack, L., Esterberg, M. L., Bercu, Z., Kryda, A. D., Quintero, L., et al. (2006). Associations between olfactory identification and verbal memory in patients with schizophrenia, first-degree relatives, and non-psychiatric controls. *Schizophrenia Research, 86*(1–3), 154–166.

Constantino, J. N., Abbacchi, A. M., Lavesser, P. D., Reed, H., Givens, L., Chiang, L., … Todd, R. D. (2009). Developmental course of autistic social impairment in males. *Development and Psychopathology, 21*(01), 127–138. doi:10.1017/S095457940900008X

Cooke, S. F., & Bliss, T. V. P. (2006). Plasticity in the human central nervous system. *Brain, 129*(7), 1659–1673.

Cooper, S. J., & Dourish, C. T. (1990). Multiple cholecystokinin (CCK) receptors and CCK-monoamine interactions are instrumental in the control of feeding. *Physiology and Behavior, 48,* 849–857.

Corballis, M. C. (2003). From mouth to hand: Gesture, speech, and the evolution of right-handedness. *Behavioral & Brain Sciences, 26*(2), 199–260.

Corballis, M. C. (2009). The evolution of language. *The Year in Cognitive Neuroscience, 1156,* 19–43. doi:10.1111/j.1749-6632.2009.04423.x

Corballis, M. C. (2014). Left brain, right brain: Facts and fantasies. *PLoS Biology, 12*(1), e1001767. doi:10.1371/journal.pbio.1001767

Corballis, M. C., Hattie, J., & Fletcher, R. (2008). Handedness and intellectual achievement: An even-handed look. *Neuropsychologia, 46*(1), 374–378.

Corbit, J. D. (1973). Voluntary control of hypothalamic temperature. *Journal of Comparative and Physiological Psychology, 83*, 394–411.

Coren, S. (1996a). *Sleep thieves.* New York: Free Press.

Coren, S. (1996b). Daylight savings time and traffic accidents. *New England Journal of Medicine, 334*, 924.

Corina, D., Chiu, Y.-S., Knapp, H., Greenwald, R., San Jose-Robertson, L., & Braun, A. (2007). Neural correlates of human action observation in hearing and deaf subjects. *Brain Research, 1152*, 111–129.

Corkin, S., Amaral, D. G., Gonzalez, R. G., Johnson, K. A., & Hyman, B. T. (1997). H. M.'s medial temporal lobe lesion: Findings from magnetic resonance imaging. *Journal of Neuroscience, 17*, 3964–3979.

Corkin, S., Milner, B., & Rasmussen, T. (1970). Somatosensory thresholds. *Archives of Neurology, 23*, 41–58.

Cornish, J. L., Hunt, G. E., Robins, L., & McGregor, I. S. (2012). Regional c-Fos and FosB/ΔFosB expression associated with chronic methamphetamine self-administration and methamphetamine-seeking behavior in rats. *Neuroscience, 206*, 100–114. doi:10.1016/j.neuroscience.2012.01.004

Corona, G., Giorda, C., Cucinotta, D., Guida, P., & Nada, E. (2013). The SUBITO-DE study: Sexual dysfunction in newly diagnosed type 2 diabetes male patients. *Journal of Endocrinological Investigation, 36*(10), 864–868. doi:10.3275/8969

Corrao, G., Rubbiati, L., Bagnardi, V., Zambon, A., & Poikolainen, K. (2000). Alcohol and coronary heart disease: A meta-analysis. *Addiction, 95*(10), 1505–1523. doi:10.1046/j.1360-0443.2000.951015056.x

Corrigan, N. M., Richards, T. L., Treffert, D. A., & Dager, S. R. (2012). Toward a better understanding of the savant brain. *Comprehensive Psychiatry, 53*(6), 706–717. doi:10.1016/j.comppsych.2011.11.006

Cortelazzi, D., Marconi, A., Guazzi, M., Cristina, M., Zecchini, B., Veronelli, A., … Pontiroli, A. E. (2013). Sexual dysfunction in pre-menopausal diabetic women: Clinical, metabolic, psychological, cardiovascular, and neurophysiologic correlates. *Acta Diabetologica, 50*(6), 911–917.

Cotran, R. S., Kumar, V., Fausto, N., Robbins, S. L., & Abbas, A. K. (2005). *Robbins and Cotran pathologic basis of disease.* St. Louis, MO: Elsevier Saunders.

Coutinho, E. (1999). *Is menstruation obsolete? How suppressing menstruation can help women who suffer from anemia, endometriosis, or PMS.* New York: Oxford University Press.

Cowey, A., & Stoerig, P. (1991). The neurobiology of blindsight. *Trends in Neurosciences, 14*, 140–145.

Cox, J. J., Reimann, F., Nicholas, A. K., Thornton, G., Roberts, E., Springell, K., … Woods, C. G. (2006). An SCN9A channelopathy causes congenital inability to experience pain. *Nature, 444*(7121), 894–898. doi:10.1038/nature05413

Craddock, N., & Sklar, P. (2013). Genetics of bipolar disorder. *The Lancet, 381*(9878), 1654–1662.

Craig, A., & Tran, Y. (2005). The epidemiology of stuttering: The need for reliable estimates of prevalence and anxiety levels over the lifespan. *Advances in Speech–Language Pathology, 7*(1), 41–46. doi:10.1080/14417040500055060

Crawford, F., Wood, M., Ferguson, S., Mathura, V., Gupta, P., Humphrey, J., … Mullan, M. (2009). Apolipoprotein E-genotype dependent hippocampal and cortical responses to traumatic brain injury. *Neuroscience, 159*(4), 1349–1362. doi:http://dx.doi.org/10.1016/j.neuroscience.2009.01.033

Creutzfeldt, H. G. (1920). Uber eine eigenartige herdfornige erkrankung des zentralnervensystems. [On a particular focal disease of the central nervous system.] vorlaufi ge mitteilung [A preliminary report]. *Zeitschrift für die gesamte Neurologie und Psychiatrie, 57*, 1–18.

Crick, F., & Mitchison, G. (1983). The function of dream sleep. *Nature, 304*, 111–114.

Cross-Disorder Group of the Psychiatric Genomics Consortium. (2013). Genetic relationship between five psychiatric disorders estimated from genome-wide SNPs. *Nature Genetics, 45*(9), 984–994. doi:10.1038/ng.2711

Cross-Disorder Group of the Psychiatric Genomics Consortium (2013). Identification of risk loci with shared effects on five major psychiatric disorders: A genome-wide analysis. *The Lancet, 381*(9875), 1371–1379. doi:10.1016/S0140-6736(12)62129-1

Crossley, M. J., Ashby, F. G., & Maddox, W. T. (2013). Erasing the engram: The unlearning of procedural skills. *Journal of Experimental Psychology: General, 142*(3), 710–741. doi:10.1037/a0030059

Crow, T. J. (1997). Schizophrenia as failure of hemispheric dominance for language. *Trends in Neurosciences, 20*(8), 339–343.

Crowley, K., Trinder, J., Kim, Y., Carrington, M., & Colrain, I. M. (2002). The effects of normal aging on sleep spindle and K complex production. *Clinical Neurophysiology, 113*, 1615–1622.

Crowley, S. J., Acebo, C., & Carskadon, M. A. (2007). Sleep, circadian rhythms, and delayed phase in adolescence. *Sleep Medicine, 8*(6), 602–612.

Cruickshank, J. (2014). The unholy alliance between obesity, type-2 diabetes, the sympathetic nervous system, and hypertension in young/middle-aged subjects. *Journal of Molecular and Genetic Medicine*, S1:016. doi:10.4172/1747-0862.S1-016

Culbertson, F. M. (1997). Depression and gender: An international review. *American Psychologist, 52*, 25–31.

Culebras, A., & Moore, J. T. (1989). Magnetic resonance findings in REM sleep behavior disorder. *Neurology, 39*, 1519–1523.

Cummings, D. R. (2010). Human birth seasonality and sunshine. *American Journal of Human Biology, 22*(3), 316–324. doi:10.1002/ajhb.20987

Cursiefen, C., Chen, L., Saint-Geniez, M., Hamrah, P., Jin, Y., Rashid, S., … Dana, R. (2006). Nonvascular VEGF receptor 3 expression by corneal epithelium maintains avascularity and vision. *Proceedings of the National Academy of Sciences of the United States of America (PNAS), 103*(30), 11405–11410.

Curtiss, S., de Bode, S., & Mathern, G. W. (2001). Spoken language outcomes after hemispherectomy: Factoring in etiology. *Brain and Language, 79*(3), 379–396. doi:10.1006/brln.2001.2487

Czeisler, C. A., & Gooley, J. J. (2007). Sleep and circadian rhythms in humans. *Cold Spring Harbor Symposia on Quantitative Biology, 72*(1), 579–597.

Dabbs, J. M., Jr., & Morris, R. (1990). Testosterone, social class, and antisocial behavior in a sample of 4,462 men. *Psychological Science, 1*, 209–211.

Dahl, R. (1996). The regulation of sleep and arousal: Development and psychopathology. *Development and Psychopathology, 8*, 3–27.

Dahl, R. E., Holttum, J., & Trubnick, L. (1994). A clinical picture of child and adolescent narcolepsy. *Journal of the American Academy of Child and Adolescent Psychiatry, 33*, 834–841.

Damasio, A. R. (1989). Time-locked multiregional retroactivation: A systems-level proposal for the neural substrates of recall and recognition. *Cognition, 33*(1–2), 25–62.

Damasio, A. R. (1994). *Descartes' error: Emotion, reason, and the human brain.* New York: G.P. Putnam's Sons.

Damasio, A., Bellugi, U., Damasio, H., Poizner, H., & Gilder, J. V. (1986). Sign language aphasia during left-hemisphere amytal injection. *Nature, 322*, 363–365.

Damasio, H., Grabowski, T., Frank, R., Galaburda, A., & Damasio, A. (1994). The return of Phineas Gage: Clues about the brain from the skull of a famous patient. *Science, 264*(5162), 1102–1105. doi:10.1126/science.8178168

Damsma, G., Day, J., & Fibiger, H. C. (1989). Lack of tolerance to nicotine-induced dopamine release in the nucleus accumbens. *European Journal of Pharmacology, 168*(3), 363–368. doi:10.1016/0014-2999(89)90798-x

Dani, J. A. (2001). Overview of nicotinic receptors and their roles in the central nervous system. *Biological Psychiatry, 49*(3), 166–174.

Dani, J. A., & Harris, R. A. (2005). Nicotine addiction and comorbidity with alcohol abuse and mental illness. *Nature Neuroscience, 8*(11), 1465–1470. doi: 10/1038/nn1580

Danilenko, K. V., & Levitan, R. D. (2012). Seasonal affective disorder. In T. E. Schlaepfer & C. B. Nemeroff (Eds.), *Handbook of clinical neurology: Neurobiology of psychiatric disorders* (Vol. 106, pp. 279–289). Amsterdam, The Netherlands: Elsevier.

Dartnall, H. J. A., Bowmaker, J. K., & Mollon, J. D. (1983). Human visual pigments: Microspectrophotometric results from the eyes of seven persons. *Proceedings of the Royal Society of London. Series B. Biological Sciences, 220*(1218), 115–130. doi:10.1098/rspb.1983.0091

Darwin, C. (1859). *On the origin of species by means of natural selection, or the preservation of favoured races in the struggle for life.* London, UK: John Murray.

Datta, S., Spoley, E. E., & Patterson, E. H. (2001). Microinjection of glutamate into the pedunculo-pontine tegmentum induces REM sleep and wakefulness in the rat. *American Journal of Physiology, 280*, R752–R759.

Davachi, L., & Wagner, A. D. (2002). Hippocampal contributions to episodic encoding: Insights from relational and item-based learning. *Journal of Neurophysiology, 88*(2), 982–990.

Davidson, C., Gow, A. J., Lee, T. H., & Ellinwood, E. H. (2001). Methamphetamine neurotoxicity: Necrotic and apoptotic mechanisms and relevance to human abuse and treatment. *Brain Research Reviews, 36*(1), 1–22. doi:10.1016/s0165-0173(01)00054-6

Davidson, R. J. (1998). Anterior electrophysiological asymmetries, emotion, and depression: Conceptual and methodological conundrums. *Psychophysiology, 35*(5), 607–614.

Davidson, R. J., & Irwin, W. (1999). The functional neuroanatomy of emotion and affective style. *Trends in Cognitive Sciences, 3*(1), 11–21. doi:http://dx.doi.org/10.1016/S1364-6613(98)01265-0

Davidson, R. J., Putnam, K. M., & Larson, C. L. (2000). Dysfunction in the neural circuitry of emotion regulation: A possible prelude to violence. *Science, 289,* 591–594.

Davies, G., Welham, J., Chant, D., Torrey, E. F., & McGrath, J. (2003). A systematic review and meta-analysis of Northern Hemisphere season of birth studies in schizophrenia. *Schizophrenia Bulletin, 29*(3), 587–593.

Davies, J., Huang, C., Proschel, C., Noble, M., Mayer-Proschel, M., & Davies, S. (2006). Astrocytes derived from glial-restricted precursors promote spinal cord repair. *Journal of Biology, 5*(3), 7.

Davis, S., & Mirick, D. K. (2006). Circadian disruption, shift work and the risk of cancer: A summary of the evidence and studies in Seattle. *Cancer Causes Control, 17*(4), 539–545.

Dawkins, R. (1982). *The extended phenotype: The long reach of the gene.* Oxford: Oxford University Press.

Dawkins, R., & Krebs, J. R. (1979). Arms races between and within species. *Proceedings of the Royal Society of London: B. Biological Sciences, 205,* 489–512. doi:10.1098/rspb.1979.0081

Daxinger, L., & Whitelaw, E. (2010). Transgenerational epigenetic inheritance: More questions than answers. *Genome Research, 20*(12), 1623–1628. doi:10.1101/gr.106138.110

de Gelder, B., Snyder, J., Greve, D., Gerard, G., & Hadjikhani, N. (2004). Fear fosters flight: A mechanism for fear contagion when perceiving emotion expressed by a whole body. *Proceedings of the National Academy of Science of the United States of America (PNAS), 101*(47), 16701–16706.

de Graaf, G., Vis, J. C., Haveman, M., van Hove, G., de Graaf, E. A. B., Tijssen, J. G. P., & Mulder, B. J. M. (2011). Assessment of prevalence of persons with Down syndrome: A theory-based demographic model. *Journal of Applied Research in Intellectual Disabilities, 24*(3), 247–262. doi:10.1111/j.1468-3148.2010.00593.x

De Jonge, F. H., Louwerse, A. L., Ooms, M. P., Evers, P., Endert, E., & van de Poll, N. E. (1989). Lesions of the SDN-POA inhibit sexual behavior of male Wistar rats. *Brain Research Bulletin, 23,* 483–492.

de Lecea, L., Kilduff , T. S., Peyron, C., Gao, X. B., Foye, P. E., Danielson, P. E., et al. (1998). The hypocretins: Hypothalamus-specific peptides with neuroexcitatory activity. *Proceedings of the National Academy of Sciences of the United States of America (PNAS), 95*(1), 322–327.

De Nil, L. F. (1999). Stuttering: A neurophysiological perspective. In N. B. Ratner & C. Healey (Eds.), *Current perspectives in stuttering: Nature and treatment* (pp. 85–102). Mahwah, NJ: Erlbaum.

De Peri, L., Crescini, A., Deste, G., Fusar-Poli, P., Sacchetti, E., & Vita, A. (2012). Brain structural abnormalities at the onset of schizophrenia and bipolar disorder: A meta-analysis of controlled magnetic resonance imaging studies. *Current Pharmaceutical Design, 18*(4), 486–494. doi:10.2174/138161212799316253

De Valois, R. L., & De Valois, K. K. (1980). Spatial vision. *Annual Review of Psychology, 31,* 309–341.

de Vries, A. P., Kassam-Adams, N., Cnaan, A., Sherman-Slate, E., Gallagher, P. R., & Winston, F. K. (1999). Looking beyond the physical injury: Posttraumatic stress disorder in children and parents after pediatric traffic injury. *Pediatrics, 104,* 1293–1299.

Deakin, C. T., Alexander, I. E., & Kerridge, I. (2009). Accepting risk in clinical research: Is the gene therapy field becoming too risk-averse? *Molecular Therapy, 17*(11), 1842–1848. doi:10.1038/mt.2009.223

Deary, I. J., Penke, L., & Johnson, W. (2010). The neuroscience of human intelligence differences. *Nature Reviews Neuroscience, 11,* 201–211. doi:10.1038/nrn2793

Deary, I. J., Yang, J., Davies, G., Harris, S. E., Tenesa, A., Liewald, D., … Visscher, P. M. (2012). Genetic contributions to stability and change in intelligence from childhood to old age. *Nature, 482*(7384), 212–215. doi:10.1038/nature10781

DeChiara, T. M., Bowen, D. C., Valenzuela, D. M., Simmons, M. V., Poueymirou, W. T., Thomas, S., … Yancopoulos, G. D. (1996). The receptor tyrosine kinase MuSK is required for neuromuscular junction formation in vivo. *Cell, 85*(4), 501–512. doi:10.1016/s0092-8674(00)81251-9

Deems, D. A., Doty, R. L., Settle, R. G., Moore-Gillon, V., Shaman, P., Mester, A. F., et al. (1991). Smell and taste disorders, a study of 750 patients from the University of Pennsylvania Smell and Taste Center. *Archives of Otolaryngology— Head and Neck Surgery, 117,* 519–528.

Deiber, M.-P., Honda, M., Ibanez, V., Sadato, N., & Hallett, M. (1999). Mesial motor areas in self-initiated versus externally triggered movements examined with fMRI: Effect of movement type and rate. *Journal of Neurophysiology, 81*(6), 3065–3077.

DeLisi, L. E., Mirsky, A. F., Buchsbaum, M. S., van Kammen, D. P., Berman, K. F., Phelps, B. H., et al. (1984). The Genain quadruplets 25 years later: A diagnostic and biochemical follow-up. *Psychiatry Research, 13,* 59–76.

Dell'Osso, B., Buoli, M., Baldwin, D. S., & Altamura, A. C. (2010). Serotonin norepinephrine reuptake inhibitors (SNRIs) in anxiety disorders: A comprehensive review of their clinical efficacy. *Human Psychopharmacology: Clinical and Experimental, 25*(1), 17–29. doi:10.1002/hup.1074

Della Rosa, P., Videsott, G., Borsa, V., Canini, M., Weekes, B. S., Franceschini, R., & Abutalebi, J. (2013). A neural interactive location for multilingual talent. *Cortex, 49*(2), 605–608. doi:10.1016/j.cortex.2012.12.001

Dement, W. (1960). The effect of dream deprivation. *Science, 131,* 1705–1707.

Dement, W. (2000, February 21). *Sleep deprivation: The national nightmare.* WebMD Web site: http://my.webmd.com/content/article/1707.50296

Dement, W., & Kleitman, N. (1957). The relation of eye movements during sleep to dream activity: An objective method for the study of dreaming. *Journal of Experimental Psychology, 53,* 339–346.

Dement, W., & Vaughan, C. (1999). *The promise of sleep: A pioneer in sleep medicine explains the vital connection between health, happiness, and a good night's sleep.* New York: Delacourt Press.

Denenberg, V. H. (1964). Critical periods, stimulus input, and emotional reactivity: A theory of infantile stimulation. *Psychological Reviews, 71,* 335–351. doi:10.1037/h0042567

Dessens, A. B., Slijper, F. M., & Drop, S. L. (2005). Gender dysphoria and gender change in chromosomal females with congenital adrenal hyperplasia. *Archives of Sexual Behavior, 34*(4), 389–397.

Deutsch, J. E., & Mirelman, A. (2007). Virtual reality–based approaches to enable walking for people poststroke. *Topics in Stroke Rehabilitation, 14*(6), 45–53.

Devane, W. A., Hanuš, L., Breuer, A., Pertwee, R. G., Stevenson, L. A., Griffin, G., … Mechoulam, R. (1992). Isolation and structure of a brain constituent that binds to the cannabinoid receptor. *Science, 258*(5090), 1946–1949.

Dhabhar, F. S. (2009). Enhancing versus suppressive effects of stress on immune function: Implications for immunoprotection and immunopathology. *Neuroimmunomodulation, 16*(5), 300–317. doi:10.1159/000216188

Dhejne C, Lichtenstein P, Boman M, Johansson ALV, Långström N., & Landén, M. (2011) Long-term follow-up of transsexual persons undergoing sex reassignment surgery: Cohort study in Sweden. *PLoS ONE, 6*(2): e16885. doi:10.1371/journal.pone.0016885

Di Pellegrino, G., Fadiga, L., Fogassi, L., Gallese, V., & Rizzolatti, G. (1992). Understanding motor events: A neurophysiological study. *Experimental Brain Research, 91*(1), 176–180.

Diamond, A. (2007). Consequences of variations in genes that affect dopamine in prefrontal cortex. *Cerebral Cortex, 17,* 1161–1170.

Diamond, A., & Goldman-Rakic, P. S. (1989). Comparison of human infants and rhesus monkeys on Piaget's AB task: Evidence for dependence on dorsolateral prefrontal cortex. *Experimental Brain Research, 74,* 24–40.

Diamond, D. M., Campbell, A. M., Park, C. R., Halonen, J., & Zoladz, P. R. (2007). The temporal dynamics model of emotional memory processing: A synthesis on the neurobiological basis of stress-induced amnesia, flashbulb and traumatic memories, and the Yerkes-Dodson law. *Neural Plasticity, 2007,* 60803. doi:10.1155/2007/60803

Diamond, L. M. (2004). Emerging perspectives on distinctions between romantic love and sexual desire. *Current Directions in Psychological Science, 13*(3), 116–119.

Dickens, W. T., & Flynn, J. R. (2001). Heritability estimates versus large environmental effects: The IQ paradox resolved. *Psychological Review, 108,* 346–369. doi:10.1037/0033-295X.108.2.346

Dickens, W. T., & Flynn, J. R. (2006). Black Americans reduce the racial IQ gap: Evidence from standardization samples. *Psychological Science, 17*(10), 913–920. doi:10.1111/j.1467-9280.2006.01802.x

Diekelmann, S., & Born, J. (2010). The memory function of sleep. *Nature Reviews Neuroscience, 11*(2), 114–126. doi:10.1038/nrn2762

Diereck, H. A., & Greenspan, R. J. (2006). Molecular analysis of flies selected for aggressive behavior. *Nature Genetics, 38,* 1023–1031.

DiGrande, L., Perrin, M. A., Thorpe, L. E., Thalji, L., Murphy, J., Wu, D., et al. (2008). Posttraumatic stress symptoms, PTSD, and risk factors among lower Manhattan residents 2–3 years after the September 11, 2001, terrorist attacks. *Journal of Traumatic Stress, 21*(3), 264–273.

Dijk, D. J., & Lockley, S. W. (2002). Integration of human sleep-wake regulation and circadian rhythmicity. *Journal of Applied Physiology, 92*(2), 852–862.

Dijkstra, H. P., Pollock, N., Chakraverty, R., & Alonso, J. M. (2014). Managing the health of the elite athlete: A new integrated performance health management and coaching model. *British Journal of Sports Medicine, 48*(7), 523–531. doi:10.1136/bjsports-2013-093222

DiLalla, L. F., Kagan, J., & Reznick, J. S. (1994). Genetic etiology of behavioral inhibition among 2-year-old children. *Infant Behavior and Development, 17,* 405–412.

DiLella, A., & Woo, S. L. C. (1987). Molecular basis of phenylketonuria and its clinical applications. *Biology and Medicine, 4,* 183–192.

Ding, J. M., Chen, D., Weber, E. T., Faiman, L. E., Rea, M. A., & Gillette, M. U. (1994). Resetting the biological clock: Mediation of nocturnal circadian shifts by glutamate and NO. *Science, 266*, 1713–1717.

Ditzen, B., Schaer, M., Gabriel, B., Bodenmann, G., Ehlert, U., & Heinrichs, M. (2009). Intranasal oxytocin increases positive communication and reduces cortisol levels during couple conflict. *Biological Psychiatry, 65*(9), 728–731. doi:10.1016/j.biopsych.2008.10.011

Dobrucki, A. B., Kin, M. J., & Kruk, B. (2013). Preliminary study on the influence of headphones for listening music on hearing loss of young people. *Archives of Acoustics, 38*(3), 383–387.

Dockray, G. J. (2012). Cholecystokinin. *Current Opinion in Endocrinology, Diabetes and Obesity, 19*(1), 8–12. doi:10.1097/MED .1090b1013e32834eb32877d

Doig, P., Lloyd-Smith, R., Prior, J. C., & Sinclair, D. (1997). *Sex testing (gender verification) in sport.* Retrieved from the Canadian Academy of Sport Medicine Web site: http://www.casm-acms. org/PositionStatements/GendereVerifEng.pdf

Dolder, C. R., & Nelson, M. H. (2008). Hypnosedative-induced complex behaviours: Incidence, mechanisms and management. *CNS Drugs, 22*(12), 1021–1036 doi:1010.2165/0023210-200822120-200800005

Dolinoy, D. C., Huang, D., & Jirtle, R. L. (2007). Maternal nutrient supplementation counteracts bisphenol A-induced DNA hypomethylation in early development. *Proceedings of the National Academy of Sciences of the United States of America (PNAS), 104*, 13056–13061. doi: 10.1073/pnas.0703739104

Donnan, G. A., Fisher, M., Macleod, M., & Davis, S. M. (2008). Stroke. *Lancet, 371*(9624), 1612–1623. doi:10.1016/S0140-6736(08)60694-7

Dopfel, R. P., Schulmeister, K., & Schernhammer, E. S. (2007). Nutritional and lifestyle correlates of the cancer-protective hormone melatonin. *Cancer Detection and Prevention, 31*(2), 140–148.

Doty, R. L., Yousem, D. M., Pham, L. T., Kreshak, A. A., Geckle, R., & Lee, W. W. (1997). Olfactory dysfunction in patients with head trauma. *Archives of Neurology, 54*(9), 1131–1140.

Driscoll, H. C., Serody, L., Patrick, S., Maurer, J., Bensasi, S., Houck, P. R., et al. (2008). Sleeping well, aging well: A descriptive and cross-sectional study of sleep in "successful agers" 75 and older. *American Journal of Geriatric Psychiatry, 16*(1), 74–82.

Dronkers, N. F., Pinker, S., & Damasio, A. (2000). Language and the aphasias. In E. R. Kandel, J. H. Schwartz, & T. M. Jessell (Eds.), *Principles of neural science* (4th ed., pp. 1169–1185). New York: McGraw-Hill.

Dronkers, N. F., Plaisant, O., Iba-Zizen, M. T., & Cabanis, E. A. (2007). Paul Broca's historic cases: High resolution MR imaging of the brains of Leborgne and Lelong. *Brain, 130*(Pt 5, 1432–1441.

Duffy, J. F., & Wright, K. P., Jr. (2005). Entrainment of the human circadian system by light. *Journal of Biological Rhythms, 20*(4), 326–338. doi:10.1177/0748730405277983

Dunwiddie, T. V., & Masino, S.A. (2001). The role and regulation of adenosine in the central nervous system. *Annual Review of Neuroscience, 24*, 31–55.

Durand, J. B., Nelissen, K., Joly, O., Wardak, C., Todd, J. T., Norman, J. F., et al. (2007). Anterior regions of monkey parietal cortex process visual 3D shape. *Neuron, 55*(3), 493–505.

Dutton, D. G., & Aron, A. P. (1974). Some evidence for heightened sexual attraction under conditions of high anxiety. *Journal of Personality and Social Psychology, 30*, 510–517.

Edelman, A. B., Gallo, M. F., Jensen, J. T., Nichols, M. D., Schulz, K. F., & Grimes, D. A. (2005). Continuous or extended cycle vs. cyclic use of combined oral contraceptives for contraception. *Cochrane Database of Systematic Reviews, 20*(3), CD004695.

Edin, B. (2001). Cutaneous afferents provide information about knee joint movements in humans. *Journal of Physiology, 531*, 289–297.

Edvardsen, J., Torgersen, S., Røysamb, E., Lygren, S., Skre, I., Onstad, S., et al. (2008). Heritability of bipolar spectrum disorders. Unity or heterogeneity. *Journal of Affective Disorders, 106*(3), 229–240.

Edwards, D. A., & Casto, K. V. (2013). Women's intercollegiate athletic competition: Cortisol, testosterone, and the dual-hormone hypothesis as it relates to status among teammates. *Hormones and Behavior, 64*(1), 153–160.

Egan, J. M., & Margolskee, R. F. (2008). Taste cells of the gut and gastrointestinal chemosensation. *Molecular Interventions, 8*(2), 78–81. doi:10.1124/mi.8.2.5

Eglinton, E., & Annett, M. (1994). Handedness and dyslexia: A meta-analysis. *Perceptual Motor Skills, 79*, 1611–1616.

Ehlert, F. J., Roeske, W. R., & Yamamura, H. I. (1995). Molecular biology, pharmacology, and brain distribution of subtypes of the muscarinic receptor. In F. E. Bloom & D. J. Kupfer (Eds.), *Psychopharmacology: The fourth generation of progress* (pp. 111–124). Baltimore, MD: Lippincott, Williams, & Wilkins.

Eichele, T., Debener, S., Calhoun, V. D., Specht, K., Engel, A. K., Hugdahl, K., … Ullsperger, M. (2008). Prediction of human errors by maladaptive changes in event-related brain networks. *Proceedings of the National Academy of Sciences of the United States of America (PNAS), 105*(16), 6173–6178. doi:10.1073/ pnas.0708965105

Eisenberger, N. I., Lieberman, M. D., & Williams, K. D. (2003). Does rejection hurt? An fMRI study of social exclusion. *Science, 302*, 290–292.

Ekman, P. (1996). Why don't we catch liars? *Social Research, 63*, 801–817.

Ekman, P., Friesen, W. V., & Ellsworth, P. (1972). *Emotion in the human face: Guidelines for research and an integration of findings.* London: Pergamon Press.

El-Sayed Moustafa, J. S., & Froguel, P. (2013). From obesity genetics to the future of personalized obesity therapy. *Nature Reviews Endocrinology, 9*(7), 402–413. doi:10.1038/ nrendo.2013.57

Emery, N. J., Capitanio, J. P., Mason, W. A., Machado, C. J., Mendoza, S. P., & Amaral, D. G. (2001). The effects of bilateral lesions of the amygdala on dyadic social interactions in rhesus monkeys (*Macaca mulatta*). *Behavioral Neuroscience, 115*, 515–544.

Enard, W., Khaitovich, P., Klose, J., Zollner, S., Heissig, F., Giavalisco, P., et al. (2002). Intra- and interspecific variation in primate gene expression patterns. *Science, 296*(5566), 340–343.

Epelbaum, S., Pinel, P., Gaillard, R., Delmaire, C., Perrin, M., Dupont, S., … Cohen, L. (2008). Pure alexia as a disconnection syndrome: New diffusion imaging evidence for an old concept. *Cortex, 44*(8), 962–974. doi:10.1016/j. cortex.2008.05.003

Eppig, C., Fincher, C. L., & Thornhill, R. (2010). Parasite prevalence and the worldwide distribution of cognitive ability. *Proceedings of the Royal Society B: Biological Sciences, 277*(1701), 3801–3808. doi:10.1098/rspb.2010.0973

Eroglu, C., & Barres, B. A. (2010). Regulation of synaptic connectivity by glia. *Nature, 468*(7321), 223–231. doi: 10.1038/nature09612

Eslinger, P. J., & Damasio, A. R. (1985). Severe disturbance of higher cognition after bilateral frontal lobe ablation: Patient EVR. *Neurology, 35*, 1731–1741.

Ettinger, U., Kumari, V., Crawford, T. J., Corr, P. J., Das, M., Zachariah, E., et al. (2004). Smooth pursuit and antisaccade eye movements in siblings discordant for schizophrenia. *Journal of Psychiatric Research, 38*, 177–184.

Eugenin, E., & Berman, J. (2011). HIV infection of human astrocytes disrupts blood-brain barrier integrity by a gap junction-dependent mechanism. *Journal of Neuroscience, 31*(26), 9456–9465. Doi:10.1523/JNEUROSCI.1460-11.2011

Evans, E. (1982). Functional anatomy of the auditory system. In H. B. Barlow & J. D. Mollon (Eds.), *The senses* (pp. 251–306). Cambridge, UK: Cambridge University Press.

Ezzeddine, Y., & Glanzman, D. L. (2003). Prolonged habituation of the gill-withdrawal reflex in *Aplysia* depends on protein synthesis, protein phosphatase activity, and postsynaptic glutamate receptors. *Journal of Neuroscience, 23*(29), 9585–9594.

Falk, D. (2010). *Finding our tongues: Mothers, infants and the origins of language.* New York: Basic Books.

Fan, Y.-T., Decety, J., Yang, C.-Y., Liu, J.-L., & Cheng, Y. (2010). Unbroken mirror neurons in autism spectrum disorders. *Journal of Child Psychology and Psychiatry, 51*(9), 981–988. doi:10.1111/j.1469-7610.2010.02269.x

Fanselow, M. S., & LeDoux, J. E. (1999). Why we think plasticity underlying Pavlovian fear conditioning occurs in the basolateral amygdala. *Neuron, 23*, 229–232.

Farah, M. J., Illes, J., Cook-Degan, R., Gardner, H., Kandel, E., King, P., et al. (2004). Neurocognitive enhancement: What can we do and what should we do? *Nature Reviews Neuroscience, 5*, 421–425.

Faraone, S. V., & Buitelaar, J. K. (2010). Comparing the efficacy of stimulants for ADHD in children and adolescents using meta-analysis. *European Child & Adolescent Psychiatry, 19*(4), 353–364. doi:10.1007/s00787-009-0054-3

Faraone, S. V., & Mick, E. (2010). Molecular genetics of attention deficit hyperactivity disorder. *The Psychiatric Clinics of North America, 33*(1), 159. doi: 10.1016/j.psc.2009.12.004

Farber, N. B., Newcomer, J. W., & Olney, J. W. (1998). The glutamate synapse in neuropsychiatric disorders. Focus on schizophrenia and Alzheimer's disease. *Progress in Brain Research, 116*, 421–437.

Farrer, C., Franck, N., Frith, C. D., Decety, J., Georgieff, N., d'Amato, T., & Jeannerod, M. (2004). Neural correlates of action attribution in schizophrenia. *Psychiatry Research, 131*(1), 31–44.

Faurie, C., & Raymond, M. (2004). Handedness frequency over more than ten thousand years. *Proceedings of the Royal Society B, 271*(Suppl 3), S43-45. doi:10.1098/rsbl.2003.0092

Faurie, C., & Raymond, M. (2005). Handedness, homicide and negative frequency-dependent selection. *Proceedings of the Royal Society B, 272*, 25–28. doi:10.1098/rspb.2004.2926

Favre, J., Burchiel, K. J., Taha, J. M., & Hammerstad, J. (2000). Outcome of unilateral and bilateral pallidotomy for Parkinson's disease: Patient assessment. *Neurosurgery, 46,* 344–353.

Feero, W. G., Guttmacher, A. E., & Collins, F. S. (2010). Genomic medicine—An updated primer. *New England Journal of Medicine, 362,* 2001–2011.

Feldman, R., Weller, A., Zagoory-Sharon, O., & Levine, A. (2007). Evidence for a neuroendocrinological foundation of human affiliation: Plasma oxytocin levels across pregnancy and the postpartum period predict mother–infant bonding. *Psychological Science, 18*(11), 965–970.

Fellin, T., Sul, J. Y., D'Ascenzo, M., Takano, H., Pascual, O., & Haydon, P. G. (2006). Bidirectional astrocyte-neuron communication: The many roles of glutamate and ATP. *Novartis Foundation Symposium, 276,* 208–217; discussion 217–221, 233–207, 275–281.

Fergusson, D. M., Boden, J. M., Horwood, L. J., Miller, A. L., & Kennedy, M. A. (2011). MAOA, abuse exposure and antisocial behaviour: 30-year longitudinal study. *The British Journal of Psychiatry, 198*(6), 457–463. doi:10.1192/bjp.bp.110.086991

Fergusson, D. M., Horwood, L. J., & Ridder, E. M. (2005). Tests of causal linkages between cannabis use and psychotic symptoms. *Addiction Research and Theory, 100,* 354–366.

Fesenko, E. E., Kolesnikov, S. S., & Lyubarsky, A. L. (1985). Induction by cyclic GMP of cationic conductance in plasma membrane of retinal rod outer segment. *Nature, 313,* 310–313.

Fiala, C., & Gemzel-Danielsson, K. (2006). Review of medical abortion using mifepristone in combination with a prostaglandin analogue. *Contraception, 74*(1), 66–86.

Filiano, J. J., & Kinney, H. C. (1994). A perspective on neuropathologic findings in victims of the sudden infant death syndrome: The triple-risk model. *Biology of the Neonate, 65*(3–4), 194–197.

Filipek, P. A., Semrud-Clikeman, M., Steingard, J. F., Renshaw, P. F., Kennedy, D. N., & Beiderman, J. (1997). Volumetric MRI analysis comparing subjects having attention-deficit hyperactivity disorder with controls. *Neurology, 48,* 589–601.

Fine, C. (2010). *Delusions of gender: How our minds, society, and neurosexism create difference.* New York: Norton.

Fine, H. A., Kim, L., Albert, P. S., Duic, J. P., Ma, H., Zhang, W., et al. (2007). A phase I trial of lenalidomide in patients with recurrent primary central nervous system tumors. *Clinical Cancer Research, 13*(23), 7101–7106.

Finniss, D. G., Kaptchuk, T. J., Miller, F., & Benedetti, F. (2010). Biological, clinical, and ethical advances of placebo effects. *The Lancet, 375*(9715), 686–695.

Fischetto, G., & Bermon, S. (2013). From gene engineering to gene modulation and manipulation: Can we prevent or detect gene doping in sports? *Sports Medicine, 43*(10), 965–977. doi:10.1007/s40279-013-0075-4

Fisher, P. A., Van Ryzin, M. J., & Gunnar, M. R. (2011). Mitigating HPA axis dysregulation associated with placement changes in foster care. *Psychoneuroendocrinology, 36*(4), 531–539. doi:10.1016/j.psyneuen.2010.08.007

Fisher, R. P., & Geiselman, R. E. (2010). The cognitive interview method of conducting police interviews: Eliciting extensive information and promoting therapeutic jurisprudence. *International Journal of Law and Psychiatry, 33*(5–6), 321–328. doi:10.1016/j.ijlp.2010.09.004

Fitzpatrick, R. C., Butler, J. E., & Day, B. L. (2006). Resolving head rotation for human bipedalism. *Current Biology, 16*(15), 1509–1514.

Fitzsimons, J. T. (1998). Angiotensin, thirst, and sodium appetite. *Physiological Reviews, 78*(3), 583–686.

Flaten, M. A., & Friborg, O. (2005). Impaired classical eyeblink conditioning in elderly human subjects: The role of unconditioned response magnitude. *Aging Clinical and Experimental Research, 17*(6), 449–457.

Flynn, J. P. (1967). The neural basis of aggression in cats. In D. C. Glass (Ed.), *Neurophysiology and emotion* (pp. 40–60). New York: Rockefeller University Press.

Flynn, J. R. (2006). Efeito Flynn: Repensando a inteligência e seus efeitos [The Flynn Effect: Rethinking intelligence and what affects it]. In C. Flores-Mendoza & R. Colom (Eds.), *Introdução à Psicologia das Diferenças Individuais* (pp. 387–411). Porto Alegre, Brazil: ArtMed.

Fogassi, L., Ferrari, P. F., Gesierich, B., Rozzi, S., Chersi, F., & Rizzolatti, G. (2005). Parietal lobe: From action organization to intention understanding. *Science, 308*(5722), 662–667. doi:10.1126/science.1106138

Forbush, K. T., & Hunt, T. K. (2014). Characterization of eating patterns among individuals with eating disorders: What is the state of the plate? *Physiology & Behavior 134,* 92–109. doi:http://dx.doi.org/10.1016/j.physbeh.2014.02.045

Förstl, H., Haass, C., Hemmer, B., Meyer, B., & Halle, M. (2010). Boxing—Acute complications and late sequelae: From concussion to dementia. *Deutsches Ärzteblatt International, 107*(47), 835–839. doi:10.3238/arztebl.2010.0835

Fouts, R. S., & Bodamer, M. (1987). Chimpanzee intrapersonal signing. *Friends of Washoe, 7,* 4–12.

Fraga, M. F., Ballestar, E., Paz, M. F., Ropero, S., Setien, F., Ballestar, M. L., ... Esteller, M. (2005). Epigenetic differences arise during the lifetime of monozygotic twins. *Proceedings of the National Academy of Sciences of the United States of America (PNAS), 102*(30), 10604–10609. doi: 10.1073/pnas.0500398102

Francis, D., Diorio, J., Liu, D., & Meaney, M. J. (1999). Nongenomic transmission across generations of maternal behavior and stress responses in the rat. *Science, 286*(5442), 1155–1158. doi:10.1126/science.286.5442.1155

Frazier, T. W., Thompson, L., Youngstrom, E. A., Law, P., Hardan, A. Y., Eng, C., & Morris, N. (2014). A twin study of heritable and shared environmental contributions to autism. *Journal of Autism and Developmental Disorders, 44*(8), 1–13. doi:10.1007/s10803-014-2081-2

Freedman, D. G. (1964). Smiling in blind infants and the issue of innate vs. acquired. *Journal of Child Psychology and Psychiatry, 47,* 171–184.

Freedman, R. R. (2013). Menopausal hot flashes: Mechanisms, endocrinology, treatment. *The Journal of Steroid Biochemistry and Molecular Biology, 142,* 115–120. doi:http://dx.doi.org/10.1016/j.jsbmb.2013.08.010

Freud, S. (1885). *Über Coca.* Vienna, Austria: Verlag von Moritz Perles.

Frey, U., & Morris, R. G. (1997). Synaptic tagging and long-term potentiation. *Nature, 385*(6616), 533–536. doi:10.1038/385533a0

Frey, W. H., 2nd, DeSota-Johnson, D., Hoffman, C., & McCall, J. T. (1981). Effect of stimulus on the chemical composition of human tears. *American Journal of Ophthalmology, 92*(4), 559–567.

Friederici, A. D. (2011). The brain basis of language processing: From structure to function. *Physiological Reviews, 91*(4), 1357–1392. doi:10.1152/physrev.00000.2011

Friedman, M., & Rosenman, R. H. (1959). Association of specific overt behavior patterns with blood and cardiovascular findings: Blood cholesterol level, blood clotting time, incidence of arcus senilis, and clinical coronary artery disease. *Journal of the American Medical Association (JAMA), 169,* 1286–1296.

Friedman, M., & Rosenman, R. H. (1974). *Type A behavior and your heart.* New York: Knopf.

Frisch, R. E. (1983). Fatness, menarche, and fertility. In S. Golub (Ed.), *Menarche: The transition from girl to woman* (pp. 5–20). Lexington, MA: Lexington Books.

Friedland, R. (2014). Healthy brain aging and the multiple reserve hypothesis. *Neurobiology of Aging, 35*(3), 717. doi:http://dx.doi.org/10.1016/j.neurobiolaging.2013.10.045

Froehlich, J. C., Harts, J., Lumeng, L., & Li, T. K. (1987). Naloxone attenuation of voluntary alcohol consumption. *Alcohol and Alcoholism Supplement, 1,* 333–337.

Fronczak, C. M., Kim, E. D., & Barqawi, A. B. (2012). The insults of illicit drug use on male fertility. *Journal of Andrology, 33*(4), 515–528. doi:10.2164/jandrol.110.011874

Fukumitsu, N., Tsuchida, D., Ogi, S., Uchiyama, M., & Mori, Y. (2002). 125I-iomazenil-benzodiazepine receptor binding during psychological stress in rats. *Annals of Nuclear Medicine, 16,* 231–235.

Fulda, S. (2011). Idiopathic REM sleep behavior disorder as a long-term predictor of neurodegenerative disorders. *The EPMA Journal, 2*(4), 451–458. doi:10.1007/s13167-011-0096-8

Fuller, P. M., Lu, J., & Saper, C. B. (2008). Differential rescue of light- and food-entrainable circadian rhythms. *Science, 320*(5879), 1074–1077. doi:10.1126/science.1153277

Fulop, T., & Smith, C. (2006). Physiological stimulation regulates the exocytic mode through calcium activation of protein kinase C in mouse chromaffin cells. *The Biochemical Journal, 399*(1), 111–119.

Furchgott, R., & Vanhoutte, P. (1989). Endothelium-derived relaxing and contracting factors. *The FASEB Journal, 3*(9), 2007–2018.

Fuster, J. M. (1997). *The prefrontal cortex: Anatomy, physiology, and neuropsychology of the frontal lobe.* New York: Raven Press.

Gadjusek, D. C. (1973). Kuru and Creutzfeldt-Jakob disease: Experimental models of noninflammatory degenerative slow virus disease of the central nervous system. *Annals of Clinical Research, 5,* 254–261.

Gadjusek, D. C., & Zigas, V. (1957). Degenerative disease of the central nervous system in New Guinea: The endemic occurrence of kuru in the native population. *New England Journal of Medicine, 257,* 974–978.

Gadjusek, D. C., Gibbs, C. J., & Alpers, M. (1966). Experimental transmission of a kuru-like syndrome to chimpanzees. *Nature, 209,* 794–796.

Gage, F. (2000, November). *Neurogenesis in the adult brain and spinal cord.* Paper presented at the meeting of the Society for Neuroscience, New Orleans, LA.

Gaillard, R. C., & Spinedi, E. (1998). Sex-and stress-steroids interactions and the immune system: Evidence for a neuroendocrine-immunological sexual dimorphism. *Domestic Animal Endocrinology, 15,* 345–352.

Gainotti, G. (1972). Emotional behavior and hemispheric side of lesion. *Cortex, 8,* 41–55.

Gais, S., & Born, J. (2004). Declarative memory consolidation: Mechanisms acting during human sleep. *Learning and Memory, 11*(6), 679–685.

Galaburda, A. M., Sherman, G. F., Rosen, G. D., Aboitiz, F., & Geschwind, N. (1985). Developmental dyslexia: Four consecutive patients with cortical anomalies. *Annals of Neurology, 18*(2), 222–223.

Gallese, V., Rochat, M. J., & Berchio, C. (2013). The mirror mechanism and its potential role in autism spectrum disorder. *Developmental Medicine & Child Neurology, 55*(1), 15–22. doi:10.1111/j.1469-8749.2012.04398.x

Gallopin, T., Fort, P., Eggermann, E., Cauli, B., Luppi, P., Rossier, J., et al. (2000). Identification of sleep-promoting neurons in vitro. *Nature, 404,* 992–995.

Galvan, A., Hare, T., Voss, H., Glover, G., & Casey, B. J. (2007). Risk-taking and the adolescent brain: Who is at risk? *Developmental Science, 10*(2), F8–F14. doi:10.1111/j.1467-7687.2006.00579.x

Galyer, K. T., Conaglen, H. M., Hare, A., & Conaglen, J. V. (1999). The effect of gynecological surgery on sexual desire. *Journal of Sex and Marital Therapy, 25,* 81–88.

Ganz, J., Lev, N., & Offen, D. (2014). Stem cells as a source for cell therapy in Parkinson's disease. In G. L. Dunbar (Ed.), *Stem cells and neurodegenerative diseases* (pp. 1–19). Boca Raton, FL: CRC Press.

Gao, Y., Raine, A., & Schug, R. A. (2012). Somatic aphasia: Mismatch of body sensations with autonomic stress reactivity in psychopathy. *Biological Psychology, 90*(3), 228–233. doi:http://dx.doi.org/10.1016/j.biopsycho.2012.03.015

Garcia, H. H., Gonzalez, A. E., Del Brutto, O. H., Tsang, V. C., Llanos-Zavalaga, F., Gonzalvez, G., et al. (2007). Strategies for the elimination of taeniasis/cysticercosis. *Journal of the Neurological Sciences, 262*(1–2), 153–157.

Gardner, H. (1968). *Fundamentals of neurology.* Philadelphia: Saunders.

Gardner, H. (1976). *The shattered mind: The person after brain damage.* New York: Knopf.

Gardner, H. (1983). *Frames of mind: The theory of multiple intelligences.* New York: Basic Books.

Gardner, R. A., & Gardner, B. I. (1969). Teaching sign language to a chimpanzee. *Science, 165,* 664–672.

Garrity, A., Pearlson, G., McKiernan, K., Lloyd, D., Kiehl, K., & Calhoun, V. (2007). Aberrant "default mode" functional connectivity in schizophrenia. *American Journal of Psychiatry, 164*(3), 450–457. doi:10.1176/appi.ajp.164.3.450

Garstecki, D. (2005). Possible perils of mp3 player headphones. Retrieved from http://www.northwestern.edu/univ-relations/broadcast/2005/12/players.html

Garver-Apgar, C. E., Gangestad, S. W., Thornhill, R., Miller, R. D., & Olp, J. J. (2006). Major histocompatibility complex alleles, sexual responsivity, and unfaithfulness in romantic couples. *Psychological Science, 17*(10), 830–835. doi:10.1111/j.1467-9280.2006.01789.x

Gazzaniga, M. S. (1967). The split brain in man. *Scientific American, 217,* 24–29.

Gazzaniga, M. S. (1970). *The bisected brain.* New York: Appleton-Century-Crofts.

Gazzaniga, M. S. (1983). Right hemisphere language following brain bisection: A 20-year perspective. *American Psychologist, 38,* 525–537.

Gazzaniga, M. S. (1988). *Mind matters.* Boston: Houghton Mifflin.

Gazzaniga, M. S. (2005). Forty-five years of split-brain research and still going strong. *Nature Reviews Neuroscience, 6*(8), 653–659. doi:10.1038/nrn1723

Gazzaniga, M. S. (2011). *Who's in charge? Free will and the science of the brain.* New York, NY: Ecco.

Gazzola, V., Aziz-Zadeh, L., & Keysers, C. (2006). Empathy and the somatotopic auditory mirror system in humans. *Current Biology, 16*(18), 1824–1829. doi:http://dx.doi.org/10.1016/j.cub.2006.07.072

Ge, R.-S., Chen, G.-R., Dong, Q., Akingbemi, B., Sottas, C. M., Santos, M., et al. (2007). Biphasic effects of postnatal exposure to diethylhexylphthalate on the timing of puberty in male rats. *Journal of Andrology, 28*(4), 513–520.

Gejman, P. V., Sanders, A. R., & Kendler, K. S. (2011). Genetics of schizophrenia: New findings and challenges. *Annual Review of Genomics and Human Genetics, 12*(1), 121–144. doi:10.1146/annurev-genom-082410-101459

Gelisse, P., & Crespel, A. (2008). Slow alpha variant during REM sleep. *Neurophysiologie Clinique, 38*(1), 3–8.

Georgieva, S. S., Todd, J. T., Peeters, R., & Orban, G. A. (2008). The extraction of 3D shape from texture and shading in the human brain. *Cerebral Cortex, 18*(10), 2416–2438.

Georgopoulos, A. P., Taira, M., & Lukashin, A. (1993). Cognitive neurophysiology of the motor cortex. *Science, 260,* 47–52.

Gerwig, M., Eßer, A., Guberina, H., Frings, M., Kolb, F., Forsting, M., et al. (2008). Trace eyeblink conditioning in patients with cerebellar degeneration: Comparison of short and long trace intervals. *Experimental Brain Research, 187*(1), 85–96.

Gerwig, M., Haerter, K., Hajjar, K., Dimitrova, A., Maschke, M., Kolb, F., et al. (2006). Trace eyeblink conditioning in human subjects with cerebellar lesions. *Experimental Brain Research, 170*(1), 7–21.

Geschwind, N. (1970). The organization of language and the brain. *Science, 170,* 940–944.

Geschwind, N. (1972). Language and the brain. *Scientific American, 226,* 76–83.

Geschwind, N., & Galaburda, A. (1987). *Cerebral lateralization: The genetical theory of natural selection.* Oxford, UK: Clarendon Press.

Gettler, L. T., McDade, T. W., Feranil, A. B., & Kuzawa, C. W. (2011). Longitudinal evidence that fatherhood decreases testosterone in human males. *Proceedings of the National Academy of Sciences of the United States of America (PNAS), 108*(39), 16194–16199. doi:10.1073/pnas.1105403108

Geuze, E., van Berckel, B. N., Lammertsma, A. A., Boellaard, R., de Kloet, C. S., Vermetten, E., et al. (2008). Reduced GABAA benzodiazepine receptor binding in veterans with post-traumatic stress disorder. *Molecular Psychiatry, 13*(1), 74–83, 73.

Gewirtz, J. C., & Davis, M. (1997). Second-order fear conditioning prevented by blocking NMDA receptors in amygdala. *Nature, 388,* 471–474.

Giancola, P. R. (2013). *Alcohol and aggression: Theories and mechanisms.* Chichester, UK: Wiley-Blackwell.

Giedd, J. N., Blumenthal, J., Jeffries, N. O., Castellanos, F. X., Liu, H., Zijdenbos, A., ... Rapoport, J. L. (1999). Brain development during childhood and adolescence: A longitudinal MRI study. *Nature Neuroscience, 2*(10), 861–863. doi:10.1038/13158

Gilad, Y., Wiebe, V., Przeworski, M., Lancet, D., & Pääbo, S. (2004). Loss of olfactory receptor genes coincides with the acquisition of full trichromatic vision in primates. *PLoS Biology, 2*(1), e5. doi: 10.1371/journal.pbio.0020005

Gilbert, M. R., Gonzalez, J., Hunter, K., Hess, K., Giglio, P., Chang, E., ... Yung, W. K. (2010). A phase I factorial design study of dose-dense temozolomide alone and in combination with thalidomide, isotretinoin, and/or celecoxib as postchemoradiation adjuvant therapy for newly diagnosed glioblastoma. *Neuro-Oncology, 12*(11), 1167–1172. doi:10.1093/neuonc/noq100

Gilbertson, M. W., Shenton, M. E., Ciszewski, A., Kasai, K., Lasko, N. B., Orr, S. P., & Pitman, R. K. (2002). Smaller hippocampal volume predicts pathologic vulnerability to psychological trauma. *Nature Neuroscience, 5,* 1242–1247.

Giles, G. M. (2010). Cognitive versus functional approaches to rehabilitation after traumatic brain injury: Commentary on a randomized controlled trial. *AJOT: American Journal of Occupational Therapy, 64*(1), 182–185. doi:10.5014/ajot.64.1.182

Gilger, J. W., Hanebuth, E., Smith, S. D., & Pennington, B. F. (1996). Differential risk for developmental reading disorders in the offspring of compensated versus noncompensated parents. *Reading and Writing, 8*(5), 407–417.

Giraud, A. L., Neumann, K., Bachoud-Levi, A. C., von Gudenberg, A. W., Euler, H. A., Lanfermann, H., et al. (2008). Severity of dysfluency correlates with basal ganglia activity in persistent developmental stuttering. *Brain and Language, 104*(2), 190–199.

Glanzman, D. L. (2006). The cellular mechanisms of learning in Aplysia: Of blind men and elephants. *The Biological Bulletin, 210*(3), 271–279.

Glanzman, D. L. (2009). Habituation in aplysia: The Cheshire cat of neurobiology. *Neurobiology of Learning and Memory, 92*(2), 147–154. doi:10.1016/j.nlm.2009.03.005

Gläscher, J., Adolphs, R., Damasio, H., Bechara, A., Rudrauf, D., Calamia, M., ... Tranel, D. (2012). Lesion mapping of cognitive control and value-based decision making in the prefrontal cortex. *Proceedings of the National Academy of Sciences of the United States of America (PNAS), 109*(36), 14681–14686. doi:10.1073/pnas.1206608109

Gläscher, J., Rudrauf, D., Colom, R., Paul, L. K., Tranel, D., Damasio, H., & Adolphs, R. (2010). Distributed neural system for general intelligence revealed by lesion mapping. *Proceedings of the National Academy of Sciences of the United States of America (PNAS), 107*(10), 4705–4709. doi:10.1073/pnas.0910397107

Glasper, E. R., & Gould, E. (2013). Sexual experience restores age-related decline in adult neurogenesis and hippocampal function. *Hippocampus, 23*(4), 303–312. doi:10.1002/hipo.22090

Glenn, A. L., Johnson, A. K., & Raine, A. (2013). Antisocial personality disorder: A current review. *Current Psychiatry Reports, 15*(12), 1–8. doi:10.1007/s11920-013-0427-7

Godement, P., Wang, L. C., & Mason, C. A. (1994). Retinal axon divergence in the optic chiasm: Dynamics of growth cone behavior at the midline. *The Journal of Neuroscience, 14*(11), 7024–7039.

Goetz, C. G., Leurgans, S., Pappert, E. J., Raman, R., & Stemer, A. B. (2001). Prospective longitudinal assessment of hallucinations in Parkinson's disease. *Neurology, 57,* 2078–2082.

Gold, J. J., & Squire, L. R. (2006). The anatomy of amnesia: Neurohistological analysis of three new cases. *Learning and Memory, 13*(6), 699–710.

Goldman-Rakic, P. S., & Rakic, P. (1984). Experimentally modified convolutional patterns in nonhuman primates: Possible relevance of connections to cerebral dominance in humans. In N. S. Geschwind & A. M. Galaburda (Eds.), *Cerebral dominance: The biological foundations* (pp. 179–194). Cambridge, MA: Harvard University Press.

Goldman, S. M., Quinlan, P. J., Ross, G. W., Marras, C., Meng, C., Bhudhikanok, G. S., … Tanner, C. M. (2012). Solvent exposures and Parkinson disease risk in twins. *Annals of Neurology, 71*(6), 776–784. doi:10.1002/ana.22629

Goldstein, A. P., Glick, B., & Gibbs, J. C. (1998). *Aggression replacement training: A comprehensive intervention for aggressive youth.* Champaign, IL: Research Press.

Goldstein, D. S., Holmes, C., Li, S.-T., Bruce, S., Metman, L. V., & Cannon, R. O. (2000). Cardiac sympathetic denervation in Parkinson's disease. *Annals of Internal Medicine, 133,* 338–347.

Gonzaga, G. C., Turner, R. A., Keltner, D., Campos, B., & Altemus, M. (2006). Romantic love and sexual desire in close relationships. *Emotion, 6*(2), 163–179.

González-Maeso, J., Ang, R. L., Yuen, T., Chan, P., Weisstaub, N. V., Lopez-Gimenez, J. F., … Sealfon, S. C. (2008). Identification of a serotonin/glutamate receptor complex implicated in psychosis. *Nature, 452*(7183), 93–97. doi:10.1038/nature06612

González-Maeso, J., Weisstaub, N. V., Zhou, M., Chan, P., Ivic, L., Ang, R., … Gingrich, J. A. (2007). Hallucinogens recruit specific cortical 5-HT(2A) receptor-mediated signaling pathways to affect behavior. *Neuron, 53*(3), 439–452. doi:http://dx.doi.org/10.1016/j.neuron.2007.01.008

Goodale, M. A., & Humphrey, G. K. (2001). Separate visual systems for action and perception. In E. B. Goldstein (Ed.), *Blackwell handbook of perception* (pp. 311–343). Oxford, UK: Blackwell.

Goodale, M. A., & Milner, A. D. (1992). Separate visual pathways for perception and action. *Trends in Neurosciences, 15*(1), 20–25.

Goodfellow, P. N., & Lovell-Badge, R. (1993). SRY and sex determination in mammals. *Annual Review of Genetics, 27,* 71–92.

Gordon, I. T., & Whelan, P. J. (2006). Deciphering the organization and modulation of spinal locomotor central pattern generators. *The Journal of Experimental Biology, 209,* 2007–2014.

Gordon, I., Zagoory–Sharon, O., Schneiderman, I., Leckman, J. F., Weller, A., & Feldman, R. (2008). Oxytocin and cortisol in romantically unattached young adults: Associations with bonding and psychological distress. *Psychophysiology, 45*(3), 349–352.

Gorfine, T., & Zisapel, N. (2009). Late evening brain activation patterns and their relation to the internal biological time, melatonin, and homeostatic sleep debt. *Human Brain Mapping, 30*(2), 541–552. doi:10.1002/hbm.20525

Gorski, R. (1980). Sexual differentiation in the brain. In D. T. Krieger & J. C. Hughes (Eds.), *Neuroendocrinology* (pp. 215–222). Sunderland, MA: Sinauer.

Gorski, R. A., Gordon, J. H., Shryne, J. E., & Southam, A. M. (1978). Evidence for a morphological sex difference within the medial preoptic area of the rat brain. *Brain Research, 148,* 333–346.

Goschke, T. (2014). Dysfunctions of decision-making and cognitive control as transdiagnostic mechanisms of mental disorders: Advances, gaps, and needs in current research. *International Journal of Methods in Psychiatric Research, 23*(S1), 41–57. doi:10.1002/mpr.1410

Gotlib, I. H., Joormann, J., Minor, K. L., & Hallmayer, J. (2008). HPA axis reactivity: A mechanism underlying the associations among 5-HTTLPR, stress, and depression. *Biological Psychiatry, 63*(9), 847–851.

Gottesman, I. I. (1991). *Schizophrenia genesis: The origins of madness.* New York: Freeman.

Gottlieb, B., Pinsky, L., Beitel, L. K., & Trifiro, M. (1999). Androgen insensitivity. *American Journal of Medical Genetics, 89,* 210–217.

Gottlieb, D. J., O'Connor, G. T., & Wilk, J. B. (2007). Genome-wide association of sleep and circadian phenotypes. *BMC Medical Genetics, 8*(Suppl 1), S9.

Gotz, M. J., Johnstone, E. C., & Ratcliffe, S. G. (1999). Criminality and antisocial behaviour in unselected men with sex chromosome abnormalities. *Psychological Medicine, 29,* 953–962.

Gouin, J.-P., Carter, C. S., Pournajafi-Nazarloo, H., Glaser, R., Malarkey, W. B., Loving, T. J., … Kiecolt-Glaser, J. K. (2010). Marital behavior, oxytocin, vasopressin, and wound healing. *Psychoneuroendocrinology, 35*(7), 1082–1090. doi:10.1016/j.psyneuen.2010.01.009

Gould, E., Reeves, A. J., Graziano, M. S., & Gross, C. G. (1999). Neurogenesis in the neocortex of adult primates. *Science, 286,* 548–552.

Grafman, J., Schwab, K., Warden, D., Pridgen, A., Brown, H. R., & Salazar, A. M. (1996). Frontal lobe injuries, violence, and aggression: A report of the Vietnam Head Injury Study. *Neurology, 46*(5), 1231–1238.

Graham, R., Rivara, F. P., Ford, M. A., & Spicer, C. M. (2014). Treatment and management of prolonged symptoms and post-concussion syndrome. In Institute of Medicine and National Research Council, *Sports-related concussions in youth: Improving the science, changing the culture* (pp. 181–202). Washington, DC: The National Academies Press.

Grant, P. (2001). A tale of histone modifications. *Genome Biology, 2*(4), reviews0003.1 - reviews0003.6. doi:10.1186/gb-2001-2-4-reviews0003

Gray, P. B., Singh, A. B., Woodhouse, L. J., Storer, T. W., Casaburi, R., Dzekov, J., et al. (2005). Dose-dependent effects of testosterone on sexual function, mood, and visuospatial cognition in older men. *Journal of Clinical Endocrinology and Metabolism, 90*(7), 3838–3846.

Gray, R. H., Campbell, O. M., Apelo, R., Eslami, S. S., Zacur, H., Ramos, R. M., et al. (1990). Risk of ovulation during lactation. *Lancet, 335*(8680), 25–29.

Green, V. A., Pituch, K. A., Itchon, J., Choi, A., O'Reilly, M., & Sigafoos, J. (2006). Internet survey of treatments used by parents of children with autism. *Research in Developmental Disabilities, 27*(1), 70–84. doi:http://dx.doi.org/10.1016/j.ridd.2004.12.002

Greer, D. M. (2006). Hypothermia for cardiac arrest. *Current Neurology and Neuroscience Reports, 6*(6), 518–524.

Gresch, P. J., Smith, R. L., Barrett, R. J., & Sanders-Bush, E. (2005). Behavioral tolerance to lysergic acid diethylamide is associated with reduced serotonin-2A receptor signaling in rat cortex. *Neuropsychopharmacology, 30*(9), 1693–1702. doi:10.1038/sj.npp.1300711

Griffy, L. (2006). Suspect's words won't be considered. *The Tribune,* B1.

Griffin, D. (1959). *Echoes of bats and men.* New York: Doubleday/Anchor.

Grillner, S., Ekeberg, O., El Manira, A., Lansner, A., Parker, D., Tegner, J., & Wallen, P. (1998). Intrinsic function of a neuronal network: A vertebrate central pattern generator. *Brain Research Reviews, 26,* 184–197.

Grisham, J. R., Anderson, T. M., & Sachdev, P. S. (2008). Genetic and environmental influences on obsessive-compulsive disorder. *European Archives of Psychiatry and Clinical Neuroscience, 258*(2), 107–116.

Grossman, S. (2012). *Thirst and sodium appetite: Physiological basis.* New York: Elsevier.

Groysman, L. I., Emanuel, B. A., Kim-Tenser, M. A., Sung, G. Y., & Mack, W. J. (2011). Therapeutic hypothermia in acute ischemic stroke. *Neurosurgical Focus, 30*(6), E17. doi:10.3171/2011.4.FOCUS1154

Grueter, B. A., Rothwell, P. E., & Malenka, R. C. (2011). Integrating synaptic plasticity and striatal circuit function in addiction. *Current Opinion in Neurobiology, 22*(3), 545–551. doi:10.1016/j.conb.2011.09.009

Gu, Y., Huang, C.-S., Inoue, T., Yamashita, T., Ishida, T., Kang, K.-M., et al. (2010). Drinking hydrogen water ameliorated cognitive impairment in senescence-accelerated mice. *Journal of Clinical Biochemistry and Nutrition, 46*(3), 269–276. doi:10.3164/jcbn.10-19

Guehl, D., Benazzouz, A., Aouizerate, B., Cuny, E., Rotge, J. Y., Rougier, A., et al. (2008). Neuronal correlates of obsessions in the caudate nucleus. *Biological Psychiatry, 63*(6), 557–562.

Gugger, J. J., & Wagner, M. L. (2007). Rapid eye movement sleep behavior disorder. *Annals of Pharmacotherapy, 41*(11), 1833–1841. doi:10.1345/aph.1H587

Güler, A. D., Ecker, J. L., Lall, G. S., Shafiqul, H., Altimus, C. M., Hsi-Wen, L., … Hattar, S. (2008). Melanopsin cells are the principal conduits for rod–cone input to non-image-forming vision. *Nature, 453*(7191), 102–105. doi:10.1038/nature06829

Gumbel, A. (2005). California idyll shocked by "skateboard murder" of 87-year-old. http://www.independent.co.uk/news/world/

Gunnery, S. D., Hall, J. A., & Ruben, M. A. (2013). The deliberate Duchenne smile: Individual differences in expressive control. *Journal of Nonverbal Behavior, 37*(1), 29–41. doi:10.1007/s10919-012-0139-4

Gusella, J. F., & McDonald, M. E. (1993). Hunting for Huntington's disease. *Molecular Genetic Medicine, 3,* 139–158.

Gusella, J. F., McNeil, S., Persichetti, F., Srinidhi, J., Novelletto, A., Bird, E., Faber, P., Vonsattel, J.-P., Myers, R. H., & MacDonald, M. E. (1996). Huntington's disease. *Cold Spring Harbor Symposia on Quantitative Biology, 61,* 615–626.

Guskiewicz, K. M., McCrea, M., Marshall, S. W., Cantu, R. C., Randolph, C., Barr, W., et al. (2003). Cumulative effects associated with recurrent concussion in collegiate football players: The NCAA Concussion Study. *Journal of the American Medical Association (JAMA), 290*(19), 2549–2555.

Guyton, A. (1991). *Textbook of medical physiology* (8th ed.). Philadelphia: Saunders.

Häberling, I. S., Badzakova-Trajkov, G., & Corballis, M. C. (2011). Callosal tracts and patterns of hemispheric dominance: A combined fMRI and DTI study. *Neuroimage, 54*(2), 779–786. doi:10.1016/j.neuroimage.2010.09.072

Hackman, D. A., Farah, M. J., & Meaney, M. J. (2010). Socioeconomic status and the brain: Mechanistic insights from human and animal research. *Nature Reviews Neuroscience, 11*(9), 651–659. doi:10.1038/nrn2897

Haddad, P. M., & Dursun, S. M. (2008). Neurological complications of psychiatric drugs: Clinical features and management. *Human Psychopharmacology, 23* (Suppl.1), 15–26.

Hagoort, P. (2005). On Broca, brain, and binding: A new framework. *Trends in Cognitive Sciences, 9*(9), 416–423.

Hagoort, P., Hald, L., Bastiaansen, M., & Petersson, K. M. (2004). Integration of word meaning and world knowledge in language comprehension. *Science, 304*(5669), 438–441.

Hague, J. F., Gilbert, S. S., Burgess, H. J., Ferguson, S. A., & Dawson, D. (2003). A sedentary day: Effects on subsequent sleep and body temperatures in trained athletes. *Physiology and Behavior, 78*, 261–267.

Haier, R. J., Siegel, B. V., Jr., MacLachlan, A., Soderling, E., Lottenberg, S., & Buchsbaum, M. S. (1992). Regional glucose metabolic changes after learning a complex visuospatial/motor task: A positron emission tomographic study. *Brain Research, 570*, 134–143. doi:10.1016/0006-8993(92)90573-R

Haimov, I., & Lavie, P. (1996). Melatonin: A soporific hormone. *Current Directions in Psychological Science, 5*, 106–111.

Hall, C. (1951). What people dream about. *Scientific American, 184*, 60–63.

Hall, C., & Van de Castle, R. (1966). *The content analysis of dreams*. New York: Appleton-Century-Crofts.

Halpern, J. H., & Pope, H. G., Jr. (2003). Hallucinogen persisting perception disorder: What do we know after 50 years? *Drug and Alcohol Dependence, 69*(2), 109–119. doi:10.1016/s0376-8716(02)00306-x

Hamburger, V. (1975). Cell death in the development of the lateral motor column of the chick embryo. *Journal of Comparative Neurology, 169*, 535–546.

Hamel, E. (2007). Serotonin and migraine: Biology and clinical implications. *Cephalalgia, 27*(11), 1293–1300.

Hamilton, A. F. (2013). Reflecting on the mirror neuron system in autism: A systematic review of current theories. *Developmental Cognitive Neuroscience, 3*, 91–105. doi:http://dx.doi.org/10.1016/j.dcn.2012.09.008

Hamlyn, J., Duhig, M., McGrath, J., & Scott, J. (2013). Modifiable risk factors for schizophrenia and autism—Shared risk factors impacting on brain development. *Neurobiology of Disease, 53*, 3–9. doi:http://dx.doi.org/10.1016/j.nbd.2012.10.023

Hancock, D. B., Martin, E. R., Mayhew, G. M., Stajich, J. M., Jewett, R., Stacy, M. A., et al. (2008). Pesticide exposure and risk of Parkinson's disease: A family-based case-control study. *BMC Neurology, 8*, 6.

Hanecke, K., Tiedemann, S., Nachreiner, F., & Grzech-Sukalo, H. (1998). Accident risk as a function of hour at work and time of day as determined from accident data and exposure models for the German working population. *Scandinavian Journal of Work, Environment and Health, 24*, 43–48.

Hankin, B. L., Abramson, L. Y., Moffitt, T. E., Silva, P. A., McGee, R., & Andell, K. E. (1998). Development of depression from preadolescence to young adulthood: Emerging gender differences in a 10-year longitudinal study. *Journal of Abnormal Psychology, 107*, 128–140.

Hanson, D. R., & Fearn, R. W. (1975). Hearing acuity in young people exposed to pop music and other noise. *Lancet, 2*, 203–205.

Happe, F., Ronald, A., & Plomin, R. (2006). Time to give up on a single explanation for autism. *Nature Neuroscience, 9*(10), 1218–1220.

Harata, N. C., Aravanis, A. M., & Tsien, R. W. (2006). Kiss-and-run and full-collapse fusion as modes of exo-endocytosis in neurosecretion. *Journal of Neurochemistry, 97*(6), 1546–1570. doi: 10.1111/j.1471-4159.2006.03987.x

Harauzov, A., Spolidoro, M., DiCristo, G., De Pasquale, R., Cancedda, L., Pizzorusso, T., … Maffei, L. (2010). Reducing intracortical inhibition in the adult visual cortex promotes ocular dominance plasticity. *The Journal of Neuroscience, 30*(1), 361–371. doi:10.1523/jneurosci.2233-09.2010

Hardeland, R., Poeggeler, B., Srinivasan, V., Trakht, I., Pandi-Perumal, S. R., & Cardinali, D. P. (2008). Melatonergic drugs in clinical practice. *Arzneimittelforschung, 58*(1), 1–10.

Hare, R. D. (1993). *Without conscience: The disturbing world of psychopaths among us*. New York: Pocket Books.

Harkema, S., Gerasimenko, Y., Hodes, J., Burdick, J., Angeli, C., Chen, Y., … Grossman, R. G. (2011). Effect of epidural stimulation of the lumbosacral spinal cord on voluntary movement, standing, and assisted stepping after motor complete paraplegia: A case study. *The Lancet, 377*(9781), 1938–1947. doi: 10.1016/S0140-6736(11)60547-3

Harper, C., & Matsumoto, I. (2005). Ethanol and brain damage. *Current Opinion in Pharmacology, 5*(1), 73–78. doi: 10.1016/j.coph.2004.06.011

Harper, F. K., Schmidt, J. E., Beacham, A. O., Salsman, J. M., Averill, A. J., Graves, K. D., & Andrykowski, M. A. (2006). The role of social cognitive processing theory and optimism in positive psychosocial and physical behavior change after cancer diagnosis and treatment. *Psychooncology, 16*, 79–91. doi:10.1002/pon.1068

Harper, J. (2008). Breakthrough claimed in male contraceptives. From http://www.washingtontimes.com/apps/pbcs.dll/article?AID=/20080326/NATION/657226903/1002

Harrington, R. A., Lee, L.-C., Crum, R. M., Zimmerman, A. W., & Hertz-Picciotto, I. (2014). Prenatal SSRI use and offspring with autism spectrum disorder or developmental delay. *Pediatrics, 133*(5), e1241–e1248. doi:10.1542/peds.2013-3406

Hartline, H. K. (1938). The response of single optic nerve fibers of the vertebrate eye to illumination of the retina. *American Journal of Physiology—Legacy Content, 121*(2), 400–415.

Hassett, J. M., Siebert, E. R., & Wallen, K. (2008). Sex differences in rhesus monkey toy preferences parallel those of children. *Hormones and Behavior, 54*(3), 359–364. doi: 10.1016/j.yhbeh.2008.03.008

Hauck, F. R., Thompson, J. M. D., Tanabe, K. O., Moon, R. Y., & Vennemann, M. M. (2011). Breastfeeding and reduced risk of sudden infant death syndrome: A meta-analysis. *Pediatrics, 128*(1), 103–110. doi:10.1542/peds.2010-3000

Hauser, W. A., & Beghi, E. (2008). First seizure definitions and worldwide incidence and mortality. *Epilepsia, 49*(Supplement 1), 8–12.

Hawkins, R. A. (2009). The blood-brain barrier and glutamate. *The American Journal of Clinical Nutrition, 90*(3), 867S–874S. doi:10.3945/ajcn.2009.27462BB

Hayes, B. D., Martinez, J. P., & Barrueto, F., Jr. (2013). Drug-induced hyperthermic syndromes: Part I. Hyperthermia in overdose. *Emergency Medicine Clinics of North America, 31*(4), 1019–1033. doi: 10.1016/j.emc.2013.07.004

Head, M. W., & Ironside, J. W. (2012). Review: Creutzfeldt–Jakob disease: Prion protein type, disease phenotype and agent strain. *Neuropathology and Applied Neurobiology, 38*(4), 296–310. doi:10.1111/j.1365-2990.2012.01265.x

Heath, R. G. (1963). Electrical self-stimulation of the brain in man. *American Journal of Psychiatry, 120*, 571–577.

Hebb, D. O. (1949). *The organization of behavior: A neuropsychological theory*. New York: Wiley.

Hecht, D. (2010). Depression and the hyperactive right-hemisphere. *Neuroscience Research, 68*(2), 77–87. doi:10.1016/j.neures.2010.06.013

Hecht, S., Shlaer, S., & Pirenne, M. H. (1942). Energy, quanta, and vision. *Journal of General Physiology, 25*(6), 819–840.

Heidelberger, R., Heinemann, C., Neher, E., & Matthews, G. (1994). Calcium dependence of the rate of exocytosis in a synaptic terminal. *Nature, 371*(6497), 513–515. doi:10.1038/371513a0

Heinz, A. J., Beck, A., Meyer-Lindenberg, A., Sterzer, P., & Heinz, A. (2011). Cognitive and neurobiological mechanisms of alcohol-related aggression. *Nature Reviews Neuroscience, 12*(7), 400–413. doi:10.1038/nrn3042

Henderson, D. C. (2008). Managing weight gain and metabolic issues in patients treated with atypical antipsychotics. *Journal of Clinical Psychiatry, 69*(2), e4.

Hening, W., Allen, R. P., Tenzer, P., & Winkelman, J. W. (2007). Restless legs syndrome: Demographics, presentation, and differential diagnosis. *Geriatrics, 62*(9), 26–29.

Henneman, E. (1991). The size principle and its relation to transmission failure in Ia projections to spinal motoneurons. *Annals of the New York Academy of Sciences, 627*, 165–168.

Hennenlotter, A., Schroeder, U., Erhard, P., Haslinger, B., Stahl, R., Weindl, A., et al. (2004). Neural correlates associated with impaired disgust processing in presymptomatic Huntington's disease. *Brain, 127*(6), 1446–1453. doi:10.1093/brain/awh165

Henquet, C., Di Forti, M., Morrison, P., Kuepper, R., & Murray, R. M. (2008). Gene-environment interplay between cannabis and psychosis. *Schizophrenia Bulletin, 34*(6), 1111–1121. doi:10.1093/schbul/sbn108

Hering, E. (1878). *On the theory of sensibility to light. (Zur Lehre vom Lichtsinn)* Vienna: G.A. Agoston.

Herman-Giddens, M. E., Slora, E. J., Wasserman, R. C., Bourdony, C. J., Bhapkar, M. V., Koch, G. G., et al. (1997). Secondary sexual characteristics and menses in young girls seen in office practice: A study from the pediatric research in office settings network. *Pediatrics, 99*, 505–512.

Hermans, E. J., Ramsey, N. F., & van Honk, J. (2008). Exogenous testosterone enhances responsiveness to social threat in the neural circuitry of social aggression in humans. *Biological Psychiatry, 63*(3), 263–270.

Hernandez, A. E., Martinez, A., & Kohnert, K. (2000). In search of the language switch: An fMRI study of picture naming in Spanish-English bilinguals. *Brain and Language, 73*, 421–431.

Herpertz, S. C., Werth, U., Lukas, G., Qunaibi, M., Schuerkens, A., Kunert, H. J., et al. (2001). Emotion in criminal offenders with psychopathy and borderline personality disorder. *Archives of General Psychiatry, 58*, 737–745.

Herrnstein, R. J., & Boring, E. G. (1965). *A source book in the history of psychology*. Cambridge, MA: Harvard University Press.

Hervias, I., Beal, M. F., & Manfredi, G. (2006). Mitochondrial dysfunction and amyotrophic lateral sclerosis. *Muscle and Nerve, 33*(5), 598–608.

Herxheimer, A., & Waterhouse, J. (2003). The prevention and treatment of jet lag. *British Medical Journal, 326*, 296–297.

Hill, A. F., Desbruslais, M., Joiner, S., Sidle, K. C., Gowland, I., Collinge, J., Doey, L. J., & Lantos, P. (1997). The same prion strain causes vCJD and BSE. *Nature, 389*, 448–450, 526.

Hiller, W. D. (1989). Dehydration and hyponatremia during triathlons. *Medicine and Science in Sports and Exercise, 21*, S219–S221.

Hines, D. J., & Haydon, P. G. (2013). Inhibition of a SNARE-sensitive pathway in astrocytes attenuates damage following stroke. *The Journal of Neuroscience, 33*(10), 4234–4240. doi:10.1523/jneurosci.5495-12.2013

Hines, M. (2010). Sex-related variation in human behavior and the brain. *Trends in Cognitive Sciences, 14*(10), 448–456. doi: 10.1016/j.tics.2010.07.005

Hines, M., Brook, C., & Conway, G. S. (2004). Androgen and psychosexual development: Core gender identity, sexual orientation and recalled childhood gender role behavior in women and men with congenital adrenal hyperplasia (CAH). *Journal of Sex Research, 41*(1), 75–81.

Hinney, A., & Volckmar, A.-L. (2013). Genetics of eating disorders. *Current Psychiatry Reports, 15*(12), 1–9. doi: 10.1007/s11920-013-0423-y

Hirota, T., & Fukada, Y. (2004). Resetting mechanism of central and peripheral circadian clocks in mammals. *Zoological Science, 21*, 359–368.

Hirshkowitz, M., & Moore, C. A. (1996). Sleep-related erectile activity. *Neurological Clinics, 14*, 721–737.

Ho, H. N., Yang, Y. S., Hsieh, R. P., Lin, H. R., Chen, S. U., Huang, S. C., et al. (1994). Sharing of human leukocyte antigens in couples with unexplained infertility affects the success of in vitro fertilization and tubal embryo transfer. *American Journal of Obstetrics and Gynecology, 170*, 63–71.

Hobson, J., &. McCarley, R. W. (1977). The brain as a dream state generator: An activation-synthesis hypothesis of the dream process. *American Journal of Psychiatry, 134*, 1335–1348.

Hodgkin, A. L., & Huxley, A. F. (1952). A quantitative description of membrane current and its application to conduction and excitation in nerve. *Journal of Physiology, 117*, 500–544.

Hoebel, B. G., & Teitelbaum, P. (1966). Effects of forcefeeding and starvation on food intake and body weight in a rat with ventromedial hypothalamic lesions. *Journal of Comparative and Physiological Psychology, 61*, 189–193.

Hoebel, B. G., Patten, C. S., Colantuoni, C., & Rada, P. V. (2000, November). *Sugar withdrawal causes symptoms of anxiety and acetylcholine release in the nucleus accumbens*. Paper presented at the meeting of the Society for Neuroscience, New Orleans, LA.

Hoeft, F., McCandliss, B. D., Black, J. M., Gantman, A., Zakerani, N., Hulme, C., ... Gabrieli, J. D. E. (2011). Neural systems predicting long-term outcome in dyslexia. *Proceedings of the National Academy of Sciences of the United States of America (PNAS), 108*(1), 361–366. doi:10.1073/pnas.1008950108

Hoekstra, R. A., Bartels, M., Verweij, C. J. H., & Boomsma, D. I. (2007). Heritability of autistic traits in the general population. *Archives of Pediatric and Adolescent Medicine, 161*(4), 372–277. doi:10.1001/archpedi.161.4.372

Hoexter, M. Q., Dougherty, D. D., Shavitt, R. G., D'Alcante, C. C., Duran, F. L., Lopes, A. C., ... Miguel, E. C. (2013). Differential prefrontal gray matter correlates of treatment response to fluoxetine or cognitive-behavioral therapy in obsessive–compulsive disorder. *European Neuropsychopharmacology, 23*(7), 569–580. doi:10.1016/j.euroneuro.2012.06.014

Hoffman, E. J., Phelps, M. E., Mullani, N. A., Higgins, C. S., & Ter-Pogossian, M. M. (1976). Design and performance characteristics of a whole-body positron transaxial tomograph. *Journal of Nuclear Medicine, 17*, 493–502.

Hoffman, R. E., Hawkins, K. A., Gueorguieva, R., Boutros, N. N., Rachid, F., Carroll, K., & Krystal, J. H. (2003). Transcranial magnetic stimulation of left temporoparietal cortex and medication-resistant auditory hallucinations. *Archives of General Psychiatry, 60*(1), 49–56. doi:10.1001/archpsyc.60.1.49

Hofman, P. M., Van Riswick, J. G. A., & Van Opstal, A. J. (1998). Relearning sound localization with new ears. *Nature Neuroscience, 1*(5), 417–421. doi:10.1038/1633

Hoge, C. W., Terhakopian, A., Castro, C. A., Messer, S. C., & Engel, C. C. (2007). Association of posttraumatic stress disorder with somatic symptoms, health care visits, and absenteeism among Iraq war veterans. *American Journal of Psychiatry, 164*(1), 150–153.

Holden, C. (1986). Days may be numbered for polygraphs in the private sector. *Science, 232*, 705.

Holgers, K. M., & Pettersson, B. (2005). Noise exposure and subjective hearing symptoms among school children in Sweden. *Noise Health, 7*(27), 27–37.

Hollander, L. E., Freeman, E. W., Sammel, M. D., Berlin, J. A., Grisso, J. A., & Battistini, M. (2001). Sleep quality, estradiol levels, and behavioral factors in late reproductive age women. *Obstetrics and Gynecology, 98*, 391–397.

Holtzheimer, P. E., Kelley, M. E., Gross, R. E., Filkowski, M. M., Garlow, S. J., Barrocas, A., ... Mayberg, H. S. (2012). Subcallosal cingulate deep brain stimulation for treatment-resistant unipolar and bipolar depression. *Archives of General Psychiatry, 69*(2), 150–158. doi:10.1001/archgenpsychiatry.2011.1456

Holzgrabe, U., Kapkova, P., Alptuzun, V., Scheiber, J., & Kugelmann, E. (2007). Targeting acetylcholinesterase to treat neurodegeneration. *Expert Opinion on Therapeutic Targets 11*(2), 161–179. doi:10.1517/14728222.11.2.161

Holzman, P., Levy, D., & Proctor, L. (1976). Smooth pursuit eye movements, attention, and schizophrenia. *Archives of General Psychiatry, 33*, 1415–1420.

Hook, E. B., & Warburton, D. (2014). Turner syndrome revisited: Review of new data supports the hypothesis that all viable 45, X cases are cryptic mosaics with a rescue cell line, implying an origin by mitotic loss. *Human Genetics, 133*(4), 417–424. doi:10.1007/s00439-014-1420-x

Hornsveld, R. H., Nijman, H. L., Hollin, C. R., & Kraaimaat, F. W. (2008). Aggression control therapy for violent forensic psychiatric patients: Method and clinical practice. *International Journal of Offender Therapy and Comparative Criminology, 52*(2), 222–233.

Horovitz, S. G., Braun, A. R., Carr, W. S., Picchioni, D., Balkin, T. J., Fukunaga, M., & Duyn, J. H. (2009). Decoupling of the brain's default mode network during deep sleep. *Proceedings of the National Academy of Sciences of the United States of America (PNAS), 106*(27), 11376–11381. doi: 10.1073/pnas.0901435106

Horridge, G. (1962). Learning of leg position by the ventral nerve cord in headless insects. *Proceedings of the Royal Society of London, B, Biological Science, 157*, 33–52.

Howard, R., Rabins, P. V., Seeman, M. V., Jeste, D. V., & the International Late-Onset Schizophrenia Group. (2000). Late-onset schizophrenia and very-late-onset schizophrenia-like psychosis: An international consensus. *American Journal of Psychiatry, 157*, 172–178.

Howlett, R. (1996). Prime time for neuropeptide Y. *Nature, 382*, 113.

Hsu, J. L., Leemans, A., Bai, C. H., Lee, C. H., Tsai, Y. F., Chiu, H. C., et al. (2008). Gender differences and age–related white matter changes of the human brain: A diffusion tensor imaging study. *NeuroImage, 39*(2), 566–577.

Huang, A. L., Chen, X., Hoon, M. A., Chandrashekar, J., Guo, W., Trankner, D., et al. (2006). The cells and logic for mammalian sour taste detection. *Nature, 442*(7105), 934–938.

Huang, W., Ramsey, K. M., Marcheva, B., & Bass, J. (2011). Circadian rhythms, sleep, and metabolism. *The Journal of Clinical Investigation, 121*(6), 2133. doi: 10.1172/JCI46043

Huang, Y., Zheng, L., Halliday, G., Dobson-Stone, C., Wang, Y., Tang, H.-D., ... Chen, S. D. (2011). Genetic polymorphisms in sigma-1 receptor and apolipoprotein E interact to influence the severity of Alzheimers disease. *Current Alzheimer Research, 8*(7), 765–770. doi:10.2174/156720511797633232

Hubel, D. H., & Livingstone, M. S. (1987). Segregation of form, color, and stereopsis in primate area 18. *Journal of Neuroscience, 7*, 3378–3415.

Hubel, D. H., & Wiesel, T. N. (1962). Receptive fields, binocular interaction and functional architecture in the cat's visual cortex. *The Journal of Physiology, 160*(1), 106.

Hubel, D. H., & Wiesel, T. N. (1965). Binocular interaction in striate cortex kittens reared with artificial squint. *Journal of Neurophysiology, 288*, 1041–1059. (Figure 5.29.)

Hubel, D. H., & Wiesel, T. N. (1977). Ferrier lecture: Functional architecture of macaque monkey visual cortex. *Proceedings of the Royal Society of London, B, Biological Science, 198*, 1–59.

Huckfeldt, R. M., & Bennett, J. (2014). Promising first steps in gene therapy for choroideremia. *Human Gene Therapy, 25*(2), 96–97. doi: 10.1089/hum.2014.2503

Hudspeth, A. (1983). The hair cells of the inner ear. *Scientific American, 248*, 54–64. doi:10.1038/scientificamerican0183-54.

Hughes, J., Kosterlitz, H. W., & Smith, T. W. (1977). The distribution of methionine—enkephalin and leucine-enkephalin in the brain and peripheral tissues. *British Journal of Pharmacology, 61*, 639–647.

Hughes, J., Smith, T. W., Kosterlitz, H., Fothergill, L. A., Morgan, B. A., & Morris, H. R. (1975). Identification of two related pentapeptides from the brain with potent opiate agonist activity. *Nature, 258*, 577–579.

Hulka, B. S., & Moorman, P. G. (2002). Breast cancer: Hormones and other risk factors. *Maturitas, 42*(Suppl. 1), S95-105. doi: http://dx.doi.org/10.1016/S0378-5122(00)00196-1

Hultman, C. M., Sparen, P., Takei, N., Murray, R. M., & Cnattingius, S. (1999). Prenatal and perinatal risk factors for schizophrenia, affective psychosis, and reactive psychosis of early onset: Case control study. *British Medical Journal, 318,* 421–426.

Hulshoff Pol, H. E. van Baal, G. C. M., Schnack, H. G., Brans, R. G., van der Schot, A. C., Brouwer, R. M., ... Kahn, R. S. (2012). Overlapping and segregating structural brain abnormalities in twins with schizophrenia or bipolar disorder. *Archives of General Psychiatry, 69*(4), 349–359. doi:10.1001/archgenpsychiatry.2011.1615

Human Rights Watch. (2006). Lethal injection drugs. http://hrw.org/reports/2006/us0406/4.htm#_Toc133042054

Humphreys, G. W., & Riddoch, M. J. (1987). *To see but not to see: A case of visual agnosia.* London: Erlbaum.

Hunsberger, J. G., Fessler, E. B., Elkahloun, A. B., & Chuang, D.-M. (2012). Post-insult valproic acid-regulated microRNAs: Potential targets for cerebral ischemia. *American Journal of Translational Research, 4*(3), 316–332.

Hurvich, L. (1981). *Color vision.* Sunderland, MA: Sinauer.

Husky, M. M., Mazure, C. M., Paliwal, P., & McKee, S. A. (2008). Gender differences in the comorbidity of smoking behavior and major depression. *Drug and Alcohol Dependence, 93*(1–2), 176–179. doi: 10.1016/j.drugalcdep.2007.07.015

Huttenlocher, P. (1994). Synaptogenesis in human cerebral cortex. In G. Dawson & K. W. Fischer (Eds.), *Human behavior and the developing brain* (pp. 137–152). New York: Guilford Press.

Huybrechts, K. F., Palmsten, K., Mogun, H., Kowal, M., Avorn, J., Setoguchi-Iwata, S. et al. (2013). National trends in antidepressant medication treatment among publicly insured pregnant women. *General Hospital Psychiatry, 35*(3), 265–271. doi:http://dx.doi.org/10.1016/j.genhosppsych.2012.12.010

Iacoboni, M., & Dapretto, M. (2006). The mirror neuron system and the consequences of its dysfunction. *Nature Reviews Neuroscience, 7*(12), 942–951.

Iacoboni, M., & Mazziotta, J. C. (2007). Mirror neuron system: Basic findings and clinical applications. *Annals of Neurology, 62*(3), 213–218.

Imaizumi, Y. (2003). A comparative study of zygotic twinning and triplet rates in eight countries, 1972–1999. *Journal of Biosocial Science, 35,* 287–302.

Imperato-McGinley, J., Guerrero, L., Gautier, T., & Peterson, R. E. (1974). Steroid 5alpha-reductase deficiency in man: An inherited form of male pseudohermaphroditism. *Science, 186*(4170), 1213–1215.

Imperato-McGinley, J., Peterson, R. E., Gautier, T., & Sturla, E. (1979). Male pseudohermaphroditism secondary to 5 alpha-reductase deficiency— A model for the role of androgens in both the development of the male phenotype and the evolution of a male gender identity. *Journal of Steroid Biochemistry, 11*(1B), 637–645.

Inoue, M., Koyanagi, T., Nakahara, H., Hara, K., Hori, E., & Nakano, H. (1986). Functional development of human eye movement in utero assessed quantitatively with real time ultrasound. *American Journal of Obstetrics and Gynecology, 155,* 170–174.

International League Against Epilepsy (ILAE). (2008). Seizure types. http://www.ilae-epilepsy.org/Visitors/Centre/ctf/seizure_types.cfm.

Inui, A., Asakawa, A., Bowers, C. Y., Mantovani, G., Laviano, A., Meguid, M. M., et al. (2004). Ghrelin, appetite, and gastric motility: The emerging role of the stomach as an endocrine organ. *The FASEB Journal, 18*(3), 439–456.

Iourov, I. Y., Vorsanova, S. G., & Yurov, Y. B. (2008). Chromosomal mosaicism goes global. *Molecular Cytogenetics, 1*(1), 26. doi:10.1186/1755-8166-1-26

Ishunina, T. A., & Swaab, D. F. (1999). Vasopressin and oxytocin neurons of the human supraoptic and paraventricular nucleus: Size changes in relation to age and sex. *Journal of Clinical Endocrinology & Metabolism, 84*(12), 4637–4644.

Islam, T., Gauderman, W. J., Cozen, W., & Mack, T. M. (2007). Childhood sun exposure influences risk of multiple sclerosis in monozygotic twins. *Neurology, 69*(4), 381–388.

Ito, M. (1984). *The cerebellum and neural control.* New York: Raven.

Iverson, G. L., & Lange, R. T. (2011). Post-concussion syndrome. In M. R. Schoenberg & J. G. Scott (Eds.), *The little black book of neuropsychology: A syndrome-based approach* (pp. 745–763). New York: Springer.

Izard, C. E. (1972). *Patterns of emotions: A new analysis of anxiety and depression.* New York: Academic Press.

Izard, C. E. (1977). *Human emotions.* New York: Plenum.

Izquierdo, A., Suda, R. K., & Murray, E. A. (2005). Comparison of the effects of bilateral orbital prefrontal cortex lesions and amygdala lesions on emotional responses in rhesus monkeys. *Journal of Neuroscience, 25*(37), 8534–8542.

Jabbi, M., Swart, M., & Keysers, C. (2007). Empathy for positive and negative emotions in the gustatory cortex. *NeuroImage, 34,* 1744–1753.

Jack, R. E., Caldara, R., & Schyns, P. G. (2012). Internal representations reveal cultural diversity in expectations of facial expressions of emotion. *Journal of Experimental Psychology: General, 141*(1), 19–25. doi:10.1037/a0023463

Jack, R. E., Garrod, O. G., Yu, H., Caldara, R., & Schyns, P. G. (2012). Facial expressions of emotion are not culturally universal. *Proceedings of the National Academy of Sciences of the United States of America (PNAS), 109*(19), 7241–7244. doi:10.1073/pnas.1200155109

Jacob, T. C., Moss, S. J., & Jurd, R. (2008). GABA(A) receptor trafficking and its role in the dynamic modulation of neuronal inhibition. *Nature Reviews Neuroscience, 9*(5), 331–343.

Jager, R. J., Anvret, M., Hall, K., & Scherer, G. (1990). A human XY female with a frame shift mutation in the candidate testis—determining gene SRY. *Nature, 348,* 452–454.

Jagust, W. (2013). Vulnerable neural systems and the borderland of brain aging and neurodegeneration. *Neuron, 77*(2), 219–234. doi:http://dx.doi.org/10.1016/j.neuron.2013.01.002

Jakob, A. (1921). Uber eigenartige Erkrankungen des Zentralnervernsystems mit bemerkenswerten anatomischen Befunde (spastische Pseudosklerose- Encephalomyelopathie mit disseminierten Denerationsherden). Vorlaufi ge Mitteilung. [About strange illnesses of the central nervous system with remarkable anatomical findings (spastic pseudosclerosis-encephalomyopathy with disseminated (Denerationsherden) A preliminary report] *Deutsche Zeitschrift für Nervenheilkunde, 70,* 132–146.

James, W. (1884). What is an emotion? *Mind, 9,* 188–205. doi:10.1093/mind/os-IX.34.188

James, W. (1890). *The principles of psychology.* New York: Holt.

James, W. (1899). *Talks to teachers.* New York, NY: Henry Holt and Company.

Jamison, K. (1993). *Touched with fire: Manic-depressive illness and the artistic temperament.* New York: Free Press.

Jan, J. E., & O'Donnell, M. E. (1996). Use of melatonin in the treatment of paediatric sleep disorders. *Journal of Pineal Research, 21,* 193–199.

Jancke, L., & Kaufmann, N. (1994). Facial EMG responses to odors in solitude and with an audience. *Chemical Senses, 19,* 99–111.

Janowsky, J. S., Oviatt, S. K., & Orwell, E. S. (1994). Testosterone influences spatial cognition in older men. *Behavioral Neuroscience, 108,* 325–332.

Janszky, I., & Ljung, R. (2008). Shifts to and from daylight saving time and incidence of myocardial infarction. *New England Journal of Medicine, 359*(18), 1966–1968. doi: 10.1056/NEJMc0807104

Janusonis, S. (2008). Origin of the blood hyperserotonemia of autism. *Theoretical Biology and Medical Modelling, 5,* 10. doi:10.1186/1742-4682-5-10

Jarvis, E. D. (2006). Selection for and against vocal learning in birds and mammals. *Ornithological Science, 5*(1), 5–14. doi:10.2326/osj.5.5

Jean, A., Conductier, G., Manrique, C., Bouras, C., Berta, P., Hen, R., et al. (2007). Anorexia induced by activation of serotonin 5-HT4 receptors is mediated by increases in CART in the nucleus accumbens. *Proceedings of the National Academy of Sciences of the United States of America (PNAS), 104*(41), 16335–16340.

Jeffries, K. J., Fritz, J. B., & Braun, A. R. (2003). Words in melody: An H215O PET study of brain activation during singing and speaking. *Neuroreport, 14,* 749–754.

Jegalian, K., & Lahn, B. T. (2001). Why the Y is so weird. *Scientific American, 284,* 56–61.

Jentsch, J. D., & Roth, R. H. (1999). The neuropsychopharmacology of phencyclidine: From NMDA receptor hypofunction to the dopamine hypothesis of schizophrenia. *Neuropsychopharmacology, 20,* 201–225.

Jepson, T., Ernst, M. E., & Kelly, M. W. (1999). Perspectives on the management of seasonal affective disorder. *Journal of the American Pharmaceutical Association, 39,* 822–829.

Jha, P., & Peto, R. (2014). Global effects of smoking, of quitting, and of taxing tobacco. *New England Journal of Medicine, 370*(1), 60–68. doi:10.1056/NEJMra1308383

Jin, Y. H., Nishioka, H., Wakabayashi, K., Fujita, T., & Yonehara, N. (2006). Effect of morphine on the release of excitatory amino acids in the rat hind instep: Pain is modulated by the interaction between the peripheral opioid and glutamate systems. *Neuroscience, 138*(4), 1329–1339.

Joëls, M. (2006). Corticosteroid effects in the brain: U-shape it. *Trends in Pharmacological Sciences, 27*(5), 244–250. doi:10.1016/j.tips.2006.03.007

Jog, M. S., Kubota, Y., Connolly, C. I., Hillegaart, V., & Graybiel, A. M. (1999). Building neural representations of habits. *Science, 286*(5445), 1745–1749. doi:10.1126/science.286.5445.1745

Joghataie, M. T., Roghani, M., Negahdar, F., & Hashemi, L. (2004). Protective effect of caffeine against neurodegeneration in a model of Parkinson's disease in rat: Behavioral and histochemical evidence. *Parkinsonism & Related*

Disorders, 10(8), 465–468. doi: http://dx.doi.org/10.1016/j.parkreldis.2004.06.004

Johns Hopkins School of Education. (2014). Neuro Education Initiative. http://education.jhu.edu/research/nei/

Johnson, B. W., McKenzie, K. J., & Hamm, J. P. (2002). Cerebral asymmetry for mental rotation: Effects of response hand, handedness and gender. *Neuroreport, 13*, 1929–1932.

Johnson, E. M., & Deckwerth, T. L. (1993). Molecular mechanisms of developmental neuronal death. *Annual Review of Neuroscience, 16*(1), 31–46. doi:10.1146/annurev.ne.16.030193.000335.

Johnson, P. L., Truitt, W. A., Fitz, S. D., Lowry, C. A., & Shekhar, A. (2008). Neural pathways underlying lactate-induced panic. *Neuropsychopharmacology, 33*(9), 2093–2107.

Johnston, L. D., O'Malley, P. M., Bachman, J. G., & Schulenberg, J. E. (2011). *Monitoring the Future national survey results on drug use, 1975-2010. Volume I: Secondary school students*. Ann Arbor, MI: Institute for Social Research, The University of Michigan.

Johnston, V. (2000). Female facial beauty: The fertility hypothesis. *Pragmatics and Cognition, 8*, 107–122.

Jolesz, F. A., & Hynynen, K. H. (2013). *MRI-guided focused ultrasound surgery*. CRC Press.

Jones, C. R. G., Pickles, A., Falcaro, M., Marsden, A. J. S., Happé, F., Scott, S. K., … Charman, T. (2011). A multimodal approach to emotion recognition ability in autism spectrum disorders. *Journal of Child Psychology and Psychiatry, 52*(3), 275–285. doi:10.1111/j.1469-7610.2010.02328.x

Jordan, B. D. (1998). Genetic susceptibility to brain injury in sports: A role for genetic testing in athletes. *The Physician and Sports Medicine, 26*(2). http://www.physsportsmed.com/issues/1998/02feb/jordan.htm.

Jordan, G., Deeb, S. S., Bosten, J. M., & Mollon, J. D. (2010). The dimensionality of color vision in carriers of anomalous trichromacy. *Journal of Vision, 10*(8), 12. doi:10.1167/10.8.12

Jornada, L. K., Valvassori, S. S., Steckert, A. V., Moretti, M., Mina, F., Ferreira, C. L., … Quevedo, J. (2011). Lithium and valproate modulate antioxidant enzymes and prevent ouabain-induced oxidative damage in an animal model of mania. *Journal of Psychiatric Research, 45*(2), 162–168. doi:10.1016/j.jpsychires.2010.05.011

Jouvet, M. (1972). The role of monoamines and acetylcholine containing neurons in the regulation of the sleep-waking cycle. *Ergebnesse der Physiologie, 64*, 166–307.

Jung, C. K. E., & Herms, J. (2014). Structural dynamics of dendritic spines are influenced by an environmental enrichment: An in vivo imaging study. *Cerebral Cortex, 24*(2), 377–384. doi:10.1093/cercor/bhs317

Jung, H., Cardenas, G., Sciutto, E., & Fleury, A. (2008). Medical treatment for neurocysticercosis: Drugs, indications and perspectives. *Current Topics in Medicinal Chemistry, 8*(5), 424–433.

Jurynec, M. J., Riley, C. P., Gupta, D. K., Nguyen, T. D., McKeon, R. J., & Buck, C. R. (2003). TIGR is upregulated in the chronic glial scar in response to central nervous system injury and inhibits neurite outgrowth. *Molecular and Cellular Neuroscience, 23*(1), 69–80. doi:10.1016/s1044-7431(03)00019-8

Kaas, S. H., Nelson, R. H., Sur, M., & Merzenich, M. M. (1981). Organization of somatosensory cortex in primates. In F. O. Schmitt, F. G. Worden,

G. Adelman, & S. G. Dennis (Eds.), *The organization of the cerebral cortex* (pp. 237–262). Cambridge, MA: MIT Press.

Kadekaro, M., Cohen, S., Terrell, M. L., Lekan, H., Gary, J., & Eisenberg, H. M. (1989). Independent activation of subfornical organ and hypothalamoneurohypophysial system during administration of angiotensin II. *Peptides, 10*, 423–429.

Kagan, J. (1997). Temperament and the reactions to unfamiliarity. *Child Development, 68*, 139–143.

Kalant, H. (2010). What neurobiology cannot tell us about addiction. *Addiction, 105*(5), 780–789. doi: 10.1111/j.1360-0443.2009.02739.x

Kalisch, R., & Gerlicher, A. M. V. (2014). Making a mountain out of a molehill: On the role of the rostral dorsal anterior cingulate and dorsomedial prefrontal cortex in conscious threat appraisal, catastrophizing, and worrying. *Neuroscience & Biobehavioral Reviews, 42*, 1–8. doi:http://dx.doi.org/10.1016/j.neubiorev.2014.02.002

Kalkanis, S., Kondziolka, D., Gaspar, L., Burri, S., Asher, A., Cobbs, C., … Linskey, M. E. (2010). The role of surgical resection in the management of newly diagnosed brain metastases: A systematic review and evidence-based clinical practice guideline. *Journal of Neuro-Oncology, 96*(1), 33–43. doi:10.1007/s11060-009-0061-8

Kalueff , A. V., & Nutt, D. J. (2007). Role of GABA in anxiety and depression. *Depression and Anxiety, 24*(7), 495–517.

Kandel, E. R. (1995). Synaptic integration. In E. R. Kandel, J. H. Schwartz, & T. M. Jessel (Eds.), *Essentials of neural science and behavior* (pp. 219–242). Norwalk, CT: Appleton & Lange.

Kandel, E. R., & Siegelbaum, S. (1995). An introduction to synaptic transmission. In E. R. Kandel, J. H. Schwartz & T. M. Jessel (Eds.), *Essentials of neural science and behavior* (pp. 161–178). Norwalk, CT: Appleton & Lange.

Kandel, E. R., & Wurtz, R. H. (2000). Constructing the visual image. In E. R. Kandel, J. H. Schwartz, & T. M. Jessell (Eds.), *Principles of Neural Science* (4th ed., pp. 492–506). New York: McGraw-Hll.

Kaneda, M., & Osaka, N. (2008). Role of anterior cingulate cortex during semantic coding in verbal working memory. *Neuroscience Letters, 436*(1), 57–61.

Kant, I. (1978). *Anthropology from a pragmatic point of view* (H. H. Rudnick, Ed.; V. L. Dodwell, Trans.). Carbondale, IL: Southern Illinois University Press. (Original work published 1798.)

Karlsson, O., & Lindquist, N. (2013). Melanin affinity and its possible role in neurodegeneration. *Journal of Neural Transmission. Supplementa, 120*(12), 1623–1630. doi:10.1007/s00702-013-1062-5

Kasai, K., Yamasue, H., Gilbertson, M. W., Shenton, M. E., Rauch, S. L., & Pitman, R. K. (2008). Evidence for acquired pregenual anterior cingulate gray matter loss from a twin study of combat-related posttraumatic stress disorder. *Biological Psychiatry, 63*(6), 550–556. doi:http://dx.doi.org/10.1016/j.biopsych.2007.06.022

Kass, A. E., Kolko, R. P., & Wilfley, D. E. (2013). Psychological treatments for eating disorders. *Current Opinion in Psychiatry, 26*(6), 549–555. doi: 10.1097/YCO.0b013e328365a30e

Kazek, B., Jamroz, E., Kajor, M., Grzybowska-Chlebowczyk, U., Ciupińska-Kajor, M., & Woś, H. (2013). The content of serotonin cells in duodenal biopsies of autistic patients. *Pediatria Polska, 88*(3), 230–235. doi:http://dx.doi.org/10.1016/j.pepo.2013.03.005

Kearney, C. A., Albano, A. M., Eisen, A. R., Allan, W. D., & Barlow, D. H. (1997). The phenomenology of panic disorder in youngsters: An empirical study of a clinical sample. *Journal of Anxiety Disorders, 11*, 49–62.

Keenan, K., Bartlett, T. Q., Nijland, M., Rodriguez, J. S., Nathanielsz, P. W., & Zürcher, N. R. (2013). Poor nutrition during pregnancy and lactation negatively affects neurodevelopment of the offspring: Evidence from a translational primate model. *The American Journal of Clinical Nutrition, 98*(2), 396–402. doi:10.3945/ajcn.112.040352

Kelly, T. L., Neri, D. F., Grill, J. T., Ryman, D., Hunt, P. D., Dijk, D. J., et al. (1999). Nonentrained circadian rhythms of melatonin in submariners scheduled to an 18-hour day. *Journal of Biological Rhythms, 14*, 190–196.

Keltner, D., & Ekman, P. (2000). Facial expression of emotion. In M. Lewis & J. M. Haviland-Jones (Eds.), *Handbook of emotions* (2nd ed., pp. 236–250). New York: Guilford Press.

Kemenes, I., O'Shea, M., & Benjamin, P. R. (2011). Different circuit and monoamine mechanisms consolidate long-term memory in aversive and reward classical conditioning. *European Journal of Neuroscience, 33*(1), 143–152. doi:10.1111/j.1460-9568.2010.07479.x

Kendzerska, T., Gershon, A. S., Hawker, G., Leung, R. S., & Tomlinson, G. (2014). Obstructive sleep apnea and risk of cardiovascular events and all-cause mortality: A decade-long historical cohort study. *PloS Medicine, 11*(2), e1001599. doi:10.1371/journal.pmed.1001599

Kennard, M. A. (1936). Age and other factors in motor recovery from precentral lesions in monkeys. *Journal of Neurophysiology, 1*, 477–496.

Kennard, M. A. (1942). Cortical reorganization of motor function. *Archives of Neurological Psychiatry, 48*, 227–240.

Kennedy-Moore, E., & Watson, J. C. (1999). *Expressing emotion: Myths, realities, and therapeutic strategies*. New York. The Guilford Press.

Kennedy, G. C. (1953). The role of depot fat in the hypothalamic control of food intake in the rat. *Proceedings of the Royal Society of London, B, Biological Science, 140*, 578–592.

Kennerknecht, I., Grueter, T., Welling, B., Wentzek, S., Horst, J., Edwards, S., et al. (2006). First report of prevalence of non-syndromic hereditary prosopagnosia (HPA). *American Journal of Medical Genetics, Part A, 140*(15), 1617–1622.

Kennerley, S. W. (2012). Is the reward really worth it? *Nature Neuroscience, 15*(5), 647–649. doi:10.1038/nn.3096

Kerr, S., Campbell, L. W., Thibault, O., & Langfield, P. (1992). Hippocampal glucocorticoid receptor activation enhances voltage-dependent Ca2+ conductances: Relevance to brain aging. *Proceedings of the National Academy of Sciences of the United States of America (PNAS), 89*, 8527–8531.

Kessler, R. C., Angermeyer, M., Anthony, J. C., De Graaf, R., Demyttenaere, K., Gasquet, I., et al. (2007). Lifetime prevalence and age-of-onset distributions of mental disorders in the World Health Organization's World Mental Health Survey Initiative. *World Psychiatry, 6*(3), 168–176.

Kessler, R. C., Berglund, P., Demler, O., Jin, R., Koretz, D., Merikangas, K. R., et al. (2003). The epidemiology of major depressive disorder: Results from the National Comorbidity Survey Replication (NCS-R). *Journal of the American Medical Association (JAMA), 289*(23), 3095–3105.

Kessler, R. C., Chiu, W. T., Demler, O., & Walters, E. E. (2005). Prevalence, severity, and comorbidity of twelve-month DSM-IV disorders in the National Comorbidity Survey Replication. *Archives of General Psychiatry, 62*(6), 617–627. doi:10.1001/archpsyc.62.6.617

Kety, S. S., Rosenthal, D., Wender, P. H., & Schulsinger, F. (1968). The types and prevalence of mental illness in the biological and adoptive families of adopted schizophrenics. In D. Rosenthal & S. S. Kety (Eds.), *The transmission of schizophrenia* (pp. 345–362). Oxford, UK: Pergamon Press.

Kiehl, K. A., Smith, A. M., Hare, R. D., Mendrek, A., Forster, B. B., Brink, J., et al. (2001). Limbic abnormalities in affective processing by criminal psychopaths as revealed by functional magnetic resonance imaging. *Biological Psychiatry, 50*(9), 677–684.

Kieler, H., Cnattingius, S., Haglund, B., Palmgren, J., & Axelsson, O. (2001). Sinistrality—A side effect of prenatal sonography: A comparative study of young men. *Epidemiology, 12,* 618–623.

Kim, K. H., Relkin, N. R., Lee, K. M., & Hirsch, J. (1998). Distinct cortical areas associated with native and second languages. *Nature, 388,* 171–174.

Kim, Y. S., & Joh, T. H. (2006). Microglia, major player in the brain inflammation: their roles in the pathogenesis of Parkinson's disease. *Experimental and Molecular Medicine, 38*(4), 333–347. doi:10.1038/emm.2006.40

Kimura, D. (1973). The asymmetry of the human brain. *Scientific American, 228,* 70–78.

Kimura, D. (1992). Sex differences in the brain. *Scientific American, 267,* 119–125.

Kimura, D., & Hampson, E. (1994). Cognitive pattern in men and women is influenced by fluctuations in sex hormones. *Current Directions in Psychological Science, 3,* 57–61.

Kingsberg, S., Shifren, J., Wekselman, K., Rodenberg, C., Koochaki, P., & DeRogatis, L. (2007). Evaluation of the clinical relevance of benefits associated with transdermal testosterone treatment in postmenopausal women with hypoactive sexual desire disorder. *The Journal of Sexual Medicine, 4*(4i), 1001–1008.

Kirk, K. M., Bailey, J. M., & Martin, N. G. (2000). Etiology of male sexual orientation in an Australian twin sample. *Psychology, Evolution & Gender, 2*(3), 301–311.

Kishi, T., Kitajima, T., Ikeda, M., Yamanouchi, Y., Kinoshita, Y., Kawashima, K., … Iwata, N. (2009). Association study of clock gene (CLOCK) and schizophrenia and mood disorders in the Japanese population. *European Archives of Psychiatry and Clinical Neuroscience, 259*(5), 293–297. doi:10.1007/s00406-009-0869-4

Kishimoto, Y., Fujimichi, R., Araishi, K., Kawahara, S., Kano, M., Aiba, A., et al. (2002). mGluR1 in cerebellar Purkinje cells is required for normal association of temporally contiguous stimuli in classical conditioning. *European Journal of Neuroscience, 16*(12), 2416–2424.

Kishimoto, Y., Hirono, M., Sugiyama, T., Kawahara, S., Nakao, K., Kishio, M., et al. (2001). Impaired delay but normal trace eyeblink conditioning in PLCbeta4 mutant mice. *Neuroreport, 12*(13), 2919–2922.

Kishimoto, Y., Kawahara, S., Fujimichi, R., Mori, H., Mishina, M., & Kirino, Y. (2001). Impairment of eyeblink conditioning in GluRdelta2-mutant mice depends on the temporal overlap between conditioned and unconditioned stimuli. *European Journal of Neuroscience, 14*(9), 1515–1521.

Kleinmuntz, B., & Szucko, J. J. (1984). A field study of the fallibility of polygraph lie detection. *Nature, 308,* 449–450.

Kloner, R. A., & Rezkalla, S. H. (2007). To drink or not to drink? That is the question. *Circulation, 116*(11), 1306–1317. doi: 10.1161/CIRCULATIONAHA.106.678375

Klonoff-Cohen, H. S., Edelstein, S. L., & Lefkowitz, E. S. (1995). The effect of passive smoking and tobacco exposure through breast milk on sudden infant death syndrome. *Journal of the American Medical Association (JAMA), 273,* 795.

Kluger, M. J. (1991). Fever: Role of pyrogens and cryogens. *Physiological Reviews, 71*(1), 93–127.

Klüver, H., & Bucy, P. C. (1939). Preliminary analysis of functions of the temporal lobes in monkeys. *Archives of Neurological Psychology, 42,* 979–1000.

Knight, C. A., & Kamen, G. (2007). Modulation of motor unit firing rates during a complex sinusoidal force task in young and older adults. *Journal of Applied Physiology, 102*(1), 122–129.

Knight, D. C., Nguyen, H. T., & Bandettini, P. A. (2003). Expression of conditional fear with and without awareness. *Proceedings of the National Academy of Sciences of the United States of America (PNAS), 100*(25), 15280–15283. doi:10.1073/pnas.2535780100

Koelega, H. S., & Koster, E. P. (1974). Some experiments on sex differences in odor perception. *Annals of the New York Academy of Sciences, 237,* 234–246.

Koenigsberg, H. W., Teicher, M. H., Mitropoulou, V., Navalta, C., New, A. S., Trestman, R., et al. (2004). 24-h monitoring of plasma norepinephrine, MHPG, cortisol, growth hormone and prolactin in depression. *Journal of Psychiatric Research, 38*(5), 503–511.

Koff, E., Borod, J., & Strauss, E. (1985). Development of hemiface size asymmetry. *Cortex, 21*(1), 153–156.

Kohler, C. G., Turner, T. H., Bilker, W. B., Brensinger, C. M., Siegel, S. J., Kanes, S. J., … Gur, R. C. (2003). Facial emotion recognition in schizophrenia: Intensity effects and error pattern. *The American Journal of Psychiatry, 160*(10), 1768–1774. doi:10.1176/appi.ajp.160.10.1768

Kolber, A. (2011). Give memory-altering drugs a chance. *Nature, 426,* 275–276. doi:10.1038/476275a

Konopka, R. J., & Benzer, S. (1971). Clock mutants of *Drosophila melanogaster. Proceedings of the National Academy of Sciences of the United States of America, 68,* 2112–2116.

Konrad, K., & Eickhoff, S. B. (2010). Is the ADHD brain wired differently? A review on structural and functional connectivity in attention deficit hyperactivity disorder. *Human Brain Mapping, 31*(6), 904–916. doi:10.1002/hbm.21058

Konradi, C., & Heckers, S. (2003). Molecular aspects of glutamate dysregulation: Implications for schizophrenia and its treatment. *Pharmacology and Therapeutics, 97*(2), 153–179.

Kopsida, E., Mikaelsson, M. A., & Davies, W. (2011). The role of imprinted genes in mediating susceptibility to neuropsychiatric disorders. *Hormones and Behavior, 59*(3), 375–382. doi:10.1016/j.yhbeh.2010.04.005

Kossoff, E. H. (2001). *Neurocysticercosis.* Retrieved from http://www.emedicine.com/ped/topic1573.htm.

Koster, A., Leitzmann, M. F., Schatzkin, A., Mouw, T., Adams, K. F., van Eijk, J. T., … Harris, T. B. (2008). Waist circumference and mortality. *American Journal of Epidemiology, 167*(12), 1465–1475. doi:10.1093/aje/kwn079

Kovelman, I., Baker, S. A., & Petitto, L. A. (2008). Bilingual and monolingual brains compared: A functional magnetic resonance imaging investigation of syntactic processing and a possible "neural signature" of bilingualism. *Journal of Cognitive Neuroscience, 20*(1), 153–169.

Kovelman, I., Norton, E. S., Christodoulou, J. A., Gaab, N., Lieberman, D. A., Triantafyllou, C., … Gabrieli, J. D. (2012). Brain basis of phonological awareness for spoken language in children and its disruption in dyslexia. *Cerebral Cortex, 22*(4), 754–764. doi:10.1093/cercor/bhr094

Kovelman, J., & Scheibel, A. B. (1984). A neurohistological correlate of schizophrenia. *Biological Psychiatry, 19,* 1601.

Kraemer, B., Noll, T., Delsignore, A., Milos, G., Schnyder, U., & Hepp, U. (2006). Finger length ratio (2D:4D) and dimensions of sexual orientation. *Neuropsychobiology, 53*(4), 210–214.

Krain, A. L., & Castellanos, F. X. (2006). Brain development and ADHD. *Clinical Psychology Review, 26*(4), 433–444.

Kravitz, H. M., Haywood, T. W., Kelly, J., Wahlstrom, C., Liles, S., & Cavanaugh, J. L., Jr. (1995). Medroxyprogesterone treatment for paraphiliacs. *Bulletin of the American Academy of Psychiatry and the Law, 23,* 19–33.

Krech, D., Rosenzweig, M. R., & Bennett, E. L. (1960). Effects of environmental complexity and training on brain chemistry. *Journal of Comparative and Physiological Psychology, 53,* 509–519. doi: http://dx.doi.org/10.1037/h0041137

Kreisel, S. H., Hennerici, M. G., & Bazner, H. (2007). Pathophysiology of stroke rehabilitation: The natural course of clinical recovery, use-dependent plasticity and rehabilitative outcome. *Cerebrovascular Diseases, 23*(4), 243–255.

Krejcar, O., Jirka, J., & Janckulik, D. (2011). Use of mobile phones as intelligent sensors for sound input analysis and sleep state detection. *Sensors, 11*(6), 6037–6055. doi:10.3390/s110606037

Krous, H. (2014). Sudden infant death syndrome (SIDS), sudden unexpected death in infancy (SUDI), and sudden unexplained death in childhood (SUDC). *Forensic Pathology of Infancy and Childhood,* 193–206. doi: 10.1007/978-1-61779-403-2_32

Kruijver, F. P., & Swaab, D. F. (2002). Sex hormone receptors are present in the human suprachiasmatic nucleus. *Neuroendocrinology, 75,* 296–305.

Krupa, D. J., Thompson, J. K., & Thompson, R. F. (1993). Localization of a memory trace in the mammalian brain. *Science, 260,* 989–991.

Kryger, M. H., Roth, T., & Dement, W. C. (1994). *Principles and practice of sleep medicine* (2nd ed.). Philadelphia: Saunders.

Kulkarni, S. K., & Naidu, P. S. (2003). Pathophysiology and drug therapy of tardive dyskinesia: Current concepts and future perspectives. *Drugs of Today, 39*(1), 19–49.

Kuo, L. E., Czarnecka, M., Kitlinska, J. B., Tilan, J. U., Kvetňanský, R., & Zukowska, Z. (2009). Chronic stress, combined with a high-fat/high-sugar diet, shifts sympathetic signaling toward neuropeptide Y and leads to obesity and the metabolic syndrome. *Annals of the New York Academy of Sciences, 1148,* 232–237. doi:10.1196/annals.1410.035

Kuo, L. E., Kitlinska, J. B., Tilan, J. U., Li, L., Baker, S. B., Johnson, M. D., et al. (2007). Neuropeptide Y acts directly in the periphery on fat tissue and mediates stress-induced obesity and metabolic syndrome. *Nature Medicine, 13*(7), 803–811.

Kupfermann, I., Kandel, E. R., & Iverson, S. (2000). Motivational and addictive states. In E. R. Kandel, J. H. Schwartz, & T. M. Jessell (Eds.), *Principles of neural science* (4th ed., pp. 998–1013). New York: McGraw-Hill.

Kurzman, D. (1987). *A killing wind: Inside Union Carbide and the Bhopal catastrophe.* New York: McGraw-Hill.

Kwiecien, M., Edelman, A., Nichols, M. D., & Jensen, J. T. (2003). Bleeding patterns and patient acceptability of standard or continuous dosing regimens of a lowdose oral contraceptive: A randomized trial. *Contraception, 67,* 9–13.

Kyle, U. G., & Pichard, C. (2006). The Dutch Famine of 1944–1945: A pathophysiological model of long-term consequences of wasting disease. *Current Opinion in Clinical Nutrition and Metabolic Care, 9*(4), 388–394.

Lagerspetz, K. M. J., & Lagerspetz, K. Y. H. (1983). Genes and aggression. In E. C. Simmel, M. E. Hahn, & J. K. Walters (Eds.), *Aggressive behavior: Genetic and neural approaches* (pp. 89–102). Hillsdale, NJ: Erlbaum.

Lai, C. S., Fisher, S. E., Hurst, J. A., Vargha-Khadem, F., & Monaco, A. P. (2001). A forkhead-domain gene is mutated in a severe speech and language disorder. *Nature, 413,* 519–523.

Lalwani, A. K., Liu, Y.-H., & Weitzman, M. (2011). Secondhand smoke and sensorineural hearing loss in adolescents. *Archives of Otolaryngology—Head & Neck Surgery, 137*(7), 655–662. doi:10.1001/archoto.2011.109

Land, E. (1959). Experiments in color vision. *Scientific American, 200,* 84–94, 96, 99.

Landis, S. C. (1990). Target regulation of neurotransmitter phenotype. *Trends in Neurosciences, 13*(8), 344–350. doi:10.1016/0166-2236(90)90147-3

Landisman, C. E., Long, M. A., Beierlein, M., Deans, M. R., Paul, D. L., & Connors, B. W. (2002). Electrical synapses in the thalamic reticular nucleus. *The Journal of Neuroscience, 22*(3), 1002–1009.

Langballe, E. M., Engdahl, B., Nordeng, H., Ballard, C., Aarsland, D., & Selbæk, G. (2013). Short-and long-term mortality risk associated with the use of antipsychotics among 26,940 dementia outpatients: A population-based study. *The American Journal of Geriatric Psychiatry, 22*(4), 321–331. doi:10.1016/j.jagp.2013.06.007

Langenecker, S. A., Weisenbach, S. L., Giordani, B., Briceño, E. M., Guidotti Breting, L. M., Schallmo, M.-P., ... Starkman, M. N. (2012). Impact of chronic hypercortisolemia on affective processing. *Neuropharmacology, 62*(1), 217–225. doi:10.1016/j.neuropharm.2011.07.006

Langleben, D. D. (2008). Detection of deception with fMRI: Are we there yet? *Legal and Criminological Psychology, 13*(1), 1–9. doi:10.1348/135532507x251641

Langleben, D. D., Willard, D. F. X., & Moriarty, J. C. (2012). Brain imaging of deception. In J. R. Simpson (Ed.), *Neuroimaging in forensic psychiatry: From clinic to the courtroom* (pp. 217–236). New York: Wiley.

Langlois, J. H., Roggman, L. A., & Rieser-Danner, L. A. (1990). Infants' differential social responses to attractive and unattractive faces. *Developmental Psychology, 26,* 153–160.

Langston, J. W. (1985). MPTP and Parkinson's disease. *Trends in Neurosciences, 8,* 79–83.

Larkin, K., Resko, J. A., Stormshak, F., Stellflug, J. N., & Roselli, C. E. (2002, November). Neuroanatomical correlates of sex and sexual partner preference in sheep. (Program No. 383.1.) Retrieved from Society for Neuroscience, *2002 Abstract Viewer/Itinerary Planner* Web site: http://sfn.scholarone.com/itin2002/index.html.

Larkin, M. (1997). *The role of serotonin in migraine.* Retrieved from the American Medical Association Web site: http://www.ama-assn.org/special/migraine/newsline/briefing/serotoni.htm.

Lashley, K. (1929). *Brain mechanisms and intelligence.* Chicago: University of Chicago Press.

Laumann, E. O., Paik, A., Glasser, D. B., Kang, J.-H., Wang, T., Levinson, B., et al. (2006). A cross-national study of subjective sexual well-being among older women and men: Findings from the global study of sexual attitudes and behaviors. *Archives of Sexual Behavior, 35*(2), 145(117).

Lavie, P. (1986). Ultrashort sleep-waking schedule. III. "Gates" and "forbidden zones" for sleep. *Electroencephalography and Clinical Neurophysiology, 63,* 414–425.

Lavie, P. (1998). *The enchanted world of sleep.* New Haven, CT: Yale University Press.

Lavie, P., & Kripke, D. F. (1981). Ultradian circa 1.5-hour rhythms: A multioscillatory system. *Life Sciences, 29,* 2445–2450.

Lawrie, S. M., Whalley, H. C., Job, D. E., & Johnstone, E. C. (2003). Structural and functional abnormalities of the amygdala in schizophrenia. *Annals of the New York Academy of Sciences, 985,* 445–460.

Le Bihan, D., & Breton, E. (1985). Imagerie de diffusion in vivo par resonance magnetique nucleaire. *Comptes-Rendus de l'Academie des Sciences, 93*(5), 27–34.

LeBlanc, S. A. (2003). *Constant battles: The myth of the peaceful, noble savage.* New York: St. Martin's Press.

Leclair-Visonneau, L., Oudiette, D., Gaymard, B., Leu-Semenescu, S., & Arnulf, I. (2010). Do the eyes scan dream images during rapid eye movement sleep? Evidence from the rapid eye movement sleep behaviour disorder model. *Brain, 133*(6), 1737–1746. doi:10.1093/brain/awq110

LeDoux, J. (1994). Emotion, memory and the brain. *Scientific American, 270,* 50–57.

LeDoux, J. E. (2000). Emotion circuits in the brain. *Annual Review of Neuroscience, 23,* 155–184. doi:10.1146/annurev.neuro.23.1.155

LeDoux, J. E. (2014). Coming to terms with fear. *Proceedings of the National Academy of Sciences of the United States of America (PNAS), 111*(8), 2871–2878. doi:10.1073/pnas.1400335111

Lee, G. P., Meador, K. J., Loring, D. W., Allison, J. D., Brown, W. S., Paul, L. K., et al. (2004). Neural substrates of emotion as revealed by functional magnetic resonance imaging. *Cognitive and Behavioral Neurology, 17*(1), 9–17.

Lee, K. H., & Thompson, R. F. (2006). Multiple memory mechanisms in the cerebellum? *Neuron, 51*(6), 680–682.

Leonard, B. E. (1992). Sub-types of serotonin receptors: Biochemical changes and pharmacological consequences. *International Clinical Psychopharmacology, 7*(1), 13–21.

Lepage, J.-F., Hong, D. S., Hallmayer, J., & Reiss, A. L. (2012). Genomic imprinting effects on cognitive and social abilities in prepubertal girls with Turner syndrome. *The Journal of Clinical Endocrinology & Metabolism, 97*(3), E460-E464. doi: 10.1210/jc.2011-2916

Leranth, C., Roth, R. H., Elswoth, J. D., Naftolin, F., Horvath, T. L., & Redmond, D. E. (2000). Estrogen is essential for maintaining nigrostriatal dopamine neurons in primates: Implications for Parkinson's disease and memory. *Journal of Neuroscience, 20,* 8604–8609.

Leuner B, Gould E (2010) Structural plasticity and hippocampal function. *Annual Review of Psychology* 61:111-140, C1-3.

LeVay, S. (1991). A difference in hypothalamic structure between heterosexual and homosexual men. *Science, 253,* 1034–1037.

LeVay, S. (2011). *Gay, straight, and the reason why: The science of sexual orientation.* New York, NY: Oxford University Press.

Levenson, R. W., & Ruef, A. M. (1992). Empathy: A physiological substrate. *Journal of Personality and Social Psychology, 63,* 234–246.

Levenson, R. W., Ekman, P., & Friesen, W. V. (1990). Voluntary facial action generates emotion-specific autonomic nervous system activity. *Psychophysiology, 27,* 363–384.

Levin, E. D., & Rose, J. E. (1995). Acute and chronic nicotinic interactions with dopamine systems and working memory performance. *Annals of the New York Academy of Sciences, 757*(1), 245–252. doi:10.1111/j.1749-6632.1995.tb17481.x

Levin, L. I., Munger, K. L., Rubertone, M. V., Peck, C. A., Lennette, E. T., Spiegelman, D., et al. (2005). Temporal relationship between elevation of Epstein-Barr virus antibody titers and initial onset of neurological symptoms in multiple sclerosis. *Journal of the American Medical Association (JAMA), 293*(20), 2496–2500.

Levin, M. (2002). *Chemotherapy for brain tumors.* http://virtualtrials.com/levin1.cfm.

Levine, A., Huang, Y., Drisaldi, B., Griffin, E. A., Pollak, D. D., Xu, S., ... Kandel, E. R. (2011). Molecular mechanism for a gateway drug: Epigenetic changes initiated by nicotine prime gene expression by cocaine. *Science Translational Medicine, 3*(107), 107ra109. doi:10.1126/scitranslmed.3003062

Levine, S. (1970). The pituitary–adrenal system and the developing brain. *Progress in Brain Research, 32,* 79–85. doi:10.1016/S0079-6123(08)61521-6

Levitan, R. D. (2007). The chronobiology and neurobiology of winter seasonal affective disorder. *Dialogues in Clinical Neuroscience, 9*(3), 315–324.

LeWitt, P. A., Rezai, A. R., Leehey, M. A., Ojemann, S. G., Flaherty, A. W., Eskandar, E. N., ... Feigin, A. (2011). AAV2-GAD gene therapy for advanced Parkinson's disease: A double-blind, sham-surgery controlled, randomised trial. *The Lancet Neurology, 10*(4), 309–319. doi:10.1016/s1474-4422(11)70039-4

Lewy, A. J. (2007). Melatonin and human chronobiology. *Cold Spring Harbor Symposia on Quantitative Biology, 72,* 623–636.

Lewy, A. J., Wehr, T. A., Goodwin, F. K., Newsome, D. A., & Markey, S. P. (1980). Light suppresses melatonin secretion in humans. *Science, 210*(4475), 1267–1269.

Ley, R., & Bryden, M. P. (1982). A dissociation of right and left hemispheric effects for recognizing emotional tone and verbal content. *Brain and Cognition, 1,* 3–9.

Lezak, M. D. (2004). *Neuropsychological assessment.* New York, NY: Oxford University Press.

Li, D., Zhao, H., & Gelernter, J. (2011). Strong protective effect of the aldehyde dehydrogenase gene (ALDH2) 504lys (*2) allele against alcoholism and alcohol-induced medical diseases in Asians. *Human Genetics, 131*(5), 725–737. doi:10.1007/s00439-011-1116-4

Li, S., & Tator, C. H. (2000). Action of locally administered NMDA and AMPA/kainate receptor antagonists in spinal cord injury. *Neurological Research, 22,* 171–180.

Li, W., & Qiu, Y. (2007). Relation of supplementary feeding to resumptions of menstruation and ovulation in lactating postpartum women. *Chinese Medical Journal, 120*(10), 868–870.

Light, K. C., Grewen, K. M., & Amico, J. A. (2005). More frequent partner hugs and higher oxytocin levels are linked to lower blood pressure and heart rate in premenopausal women. *Biological Psychology, 69*(1), 5–21.

Lilenfeld, L., Ringham, R., Kalarchian, M., & Marcus, M. (2008). A family history study of binge-eating disorder. *Comprehensive Psychiatry, 49*(3), 247–254.

Lilly, I. C. (1967). *The mind of the dolphin.* New York: Doubleday.

Lim, C. L., & Mackinnon, L. T. (2006). The roles of exercise-induced immune system disturbances in the pathology of heat stroke: The dual pathway model of heat stroke. *Sports Medicine, 36*(1), 39–64.

Lin, Y., Shea, S. D., & Katz, L. C. (2006). Representation of natural stimuli in the rodent main olfactory bulb. *Neuron, 50*(6), 937–949.

Lind, R. W., & Johnson, A. K. (1982). Subfornical organ-median preoptic connections and drinking and pressor responses to angiotensin II. *The Journal of Neuroscience, 2*(8), 1043–1051.

Linden, M. G., Bender, B. G., & Robinson, A. (1996). Intrauterine diagnosis of sex chromosome aneuploidy. *Obstetrics and Gynecology, 87,* 468–475.

Ling, W. Y., Robichaud, A., Zayid, I., Wrixon, W., & MacLeod, S. C. (1979). Mode of action of dl-norgestrel and ethinylestradiol combination in postcoital contraception. *Fertility and Sterility, 32,* 297–302.

Ling, W. Y., Wrixon, W., Zayid, I., Acorn, T., Popat, R., & Wilson, E. (1983). Mode of action of dl-norgestrel and ethinylestradiol combination in postcoital contraception: II. Effect of postovulatory administration on ovarian function and endometrium. *Fertility and Sterility, 39,* 292–297.

Linszen, D. H., Dingemans, P. M., & Lenior, M. E. (1994). Cannabis abuse and the course of recent-onset schizophrenic disorders. *Archives of General Psychiatry, 51,* 273–279.

Lippa, R. A. (2008). Sex differences and sexual orientation differences in personality: Findings from the BBC internet survey. *Archives of Sexual Behavior, 37*(1), 173–187. doi: 10.1007/s10508-007-9267-z

Little, A. C., Jones, B. C., DeBruine, L. M., & Feinberg, D. R. (2008). Symmetry and sexual dimorphism in human faces: Interrelated preferences suggest both signal quality. *Behavioral Ecology, 19*(4), 902–908. doi:10.1093/beheco/arn049

Liu, D., Diorio, J., Tannenbaum, B., Caldji, C., Francis, D., Freedman, A., … Meaney, M. J. (1997). Maternal care, hippocampal glucocorticoid receptors, and hypothalamic-pituitary-adrenal responses to stress. *Science, 277*(5332), 1659–1662. doi:10.1126/science.277.5332.1659

Livingstone, M. S., & Hubel, D. H. (1984). Anatomy and physiology of a color system in the primate visual cortex. *Journal of Neuroscience, 4,* 309–356.

Livshits, G., Kato, B. S., Wilson, S. G., & Spector, T. D. (2007). Linkage of genes to total lean body mass in normal women. *Journal of Clinical Endocrinology and Metabolism, 92*(8), 3171–3176.

Llaurens, V., Raymond, M., & Faurie, C. (2009). Why are some people left-handed? An evolutionary perspective. *Philosophical Transactions of the Royal Society B: Biological Sciences, 364*(1519), 881–894. doi:10.1098/rstb.2008.0235

Loeb, G. E., & Ghez, C. (2000). The motor unit and muscle action. In E. R. Kandel, J. H. Schwartz, & T. M. Jessell (Eds.), *Principles of neural science* (4th ed., pp. 674–694). New York: McGraw-Hill.

Loewi, O. (1953). *From the workshop of discoveries.* Lawrence, KS: University of Kansas Press.

Loftus, E. (2005). Planting misinformation in the human mind: A 30-year investigation of the malleability of memory. *Learning and Memory, 12,* 361–366.

Logan, C. G., & Grafton, S. T. (1995). Functional anatomy of human eyeblink conditioning determined with regional cerebral glucose metabolism and positronemission tomography. *Proceedings of the National Academy of Sciences of the United States of America (PNAS), 92,* 7500–7504.

Lombardo, M. V., Ashwin, E., Auyeung, B., Chakrabarti, B., Taylor, K., Hackett, G., … Baron-Cohen, S. (2012). Fetal testosterone influences sexually dimorphic gray matter in the human brain. *The Journal of Neuroscience, 32*(2), 674–680. doi: 10.1523/JNEUROSCI.4389-11.2012

Lombion-Pouthier, S., Vandel, P., Nezelof, S., Haffen, E., & Millot, J. L. (2006). Odor perception in patients with mood disorders. *Journal of Affective Disorders, 90*(2–3), 187–191.

Lorenz, K. (1952). *King Solomon's ring.* New York: Crowell.

Lorenzetti, F. D., Baxter, D. A., & Byrne, J. H. (2008). Molecular mechanisms underlying a cellular analog of operant reward learning. *Neuron, 59*(5), 815–828. doi:10.1016/j.neuron.2008.07.019

Loui, P., Li, H. C., Hohmann, A., & Schlaug, G. (2010). Enhanced cortical connectivity in absolute pitch musicians: A model for local hyperconnectivity. *Journal of Cognitive Neuroscience, 23*(4), 1015–1026. doi:10.1162/jocn.2010.21500

Lu, A. Y., Ansari, S. A., Nyström, K. V., Damisah, E. C., Amin, H. P., Matouk, C. C., … Bulsara, K. R. (2014). Intra-arterial treatment of acute ischemic stroke: The continued evolution. *Current Treatment Options in Cardiovascular Medicine, 16*(2), 1–10. doi:10.1007/s11936-013-0281-2

Lust, J. M., Geuze, R. H., Van de Beek, C., Cohen-Kettenis, P. T., Bouma, A., & Groothuis, T. G. G. (2011). Differential effects of prenatal testosterone on lateralization of handedness and language. *Neuropsychology, 25*(5), 581–589. doi:10.1037/a0023293

Lust, J. M., Geuze, R. H., Van de Beek, C., Cohen-Kettenis, P. T., Groothuis, A. G. G., & Bouma, A. (2010). Sex specific effect of prenatal testosterone on language lateralization in children. *Neuropsychologia, 48*(2), 536–540. doi:10.1016/j.neuropsychologia.2009.10.014

Lutas, A., & Yellen, G. (2013). The ketogenic diet: Metabolic influences on brain excitability and epilepsy. *Trends in Neurosciences, 36*(1), 32–40. doi:http://dx.doi.org/10.1016/j.tins.2012.11.005

MacArthur, D. G., & North, K. N. (2007). ACTN3: A genetic influence on muscle function and athletic performance. *Exercise and Sport Sciences Reviews, 35*(1), 30–34.

Mackowiak, P. A., & Boulant, J. A. (1996). Fever's glass ceiling. *Clinical Infectious Diseases, 22*(3), 525–536.

Macleod, J., Davey Smith, G., Heslop, P., Metcalfe, C., Carroll, D., & Hart, C. (2002). Psychological stress and cardiovascular disease: Empirical demonstration of bias in a prospective observational study of Scottish men. *British Medical Journal, 324,* 1247.

Maeda, T., Ohno, M., Matsunobu, A., Yoshihara, K., & Yabe, N. (1991). A cytogenetic survey of 14,835 consecutive liveborns. *Japanese Journal of Human Genetics, 36*(1), 117–129.

Maggard, M. A., Shugarman, L. R., Suttorp, M., Maglione, M., Sugerman, H. J., Livingston, E. H., et al. (2005). Meta-analysis: Surgical treatment of obesity. *Annals of Internal Medicine, 142*(7), 547–559.

Magnusson, A., Axelsson, J., Karlsson, M. M., & Oskarsson, H. (2000). Lack of seasonal mood change in the Icelandic population: Results of a cross-sectional study. *American Journal of Psychiatry, 157,* 234–238.

Mahley, R. W., Weisgraber, K. H., & Huang, Y. (2006). Apolipoprotein E4: A causative factor and therapeutic target in neuropathology, including Alzheimer's disease. *Proceedings of the National Academy of Sciences of the United States of America (PNAS), 103*(15), 5644–5651. doi:10.1073/pnas.0600549103

Maier, N., Morris, G., Schuchmann, S., Korotkova, T., Ponomarenko, A., Böhm, C., et al. (2011). Cannabinoids disrupt hippocampal sharp wave-ripples via inhibition of glutamate release. *Hippocampus, 22*(6), 1350–1362. doi:10.1002/hipo.20971

Mair, W. G. P., Warrington, E. K., & Wieskrantz, L. (1979). Memory disorder in Korsakoff 's psychosis. *Brain, 102,* 749–783.

Malberg, J. E., Eisch, A. J., Nestler, E. J., & Duman, R. S. (2000). Chronic antidepressant treatment increases neurogenesis in adult rat hippocampus. *The Journal of Neuroscience, 20*(24), 9104–9110.

Malloy, M. H., & Freeman, D. H. (2004). Age at death, season, and day of death as indicators of the effect of the back to sleep program on sudden infant death syndrome in the United States, 1992–1999. *Archives of Pediatric and Adolescent Medicine, 158,* 359–365.

Manning, J. T. (2011). Resolving the role of prenatal sex steroids in the development of digit ratio. *Proceedings of the National Academy of Sciences of the United States (PNAS), 108*(39), 16143–16144. doi:10.1073/pnas.1113312108

Månsson, H. (2000). Childhood stuttering: Incidence and development. *Journal of Fluency Disorders, 25*(1), 47–57. doi:10.1016/s0094-730x(99)00023-6

Mantyh, P. W., Rogers, S. D., Honore, P., Allen, B. J., Ghilardi, J. R., Li, J., et al. (1997). Inhibition of hyperalgesia by ablation of lamina I spinal neurons expressing the substance P receptor. *Science, 278,* 275–279.

Maquet, P. (1999). Brain mechanisms of sleep: Contribution of neuroimaging techniques. *Journal of Psychopharmacology, 13*(4) Suppl 1, S25–28.

Marazziti, D., & Dell'osso, M. C. (2008). The role of oxytocin in neuropsychiatric disorders. *Current Medicinal Chemistry, 15*(7), 698–704.

Marder, E., & Bucher, D. (2001). Central pattern generators and the control of rhythmic movements. *Current Biology, 11*(23), R986–R996. doi: 10.1016/S0960-9822(01)00581-4

Maren, S., Phan, K. L., & Liberzon, I. (2013). The contextual brain: Implications for fear conditioning, extinction and psychopathology. *Nature Reviews Neuroscience, 14*(6), 417–428. doi:10.1038/nrn3492

Mark, V. H., & Ervin, F. R. (1970). *Violence and the brain.* New York: Harper & Row.

Marner, L., Nyengaard, J. R., Tang, Y., & Pakkenberg, B. (2003). Marked loss of myelinated nerve fibers in the human brain with age. *Journal of Comparative Neurology, 462*(2), 144–152. doi: 10.1002/cne.10714

Marr, D. (1969). A theory of cerebellar cortex. *The Journal of Physiology, 202,* 437–471.

Marsh, A. A., & Blair, R. J. R. (2008). Deficits in facial affect recognition among antisocial populations: A meta-analysis. *Neuroscience & Biobehavioral Reviews, 32*(3), 454–465. doi:10.1016/j.neubiorev.2007.08.003

Marshall, G. D., & Zimbardo, P. G. (1979). Affective consequences of inadequately explained physiological arousal. *Journal of Personality and Social Psychology, 37*(6), 970–988. doi:10.1037/0022-3514.37.6.970

Marsman, A., van den Heuvel, M. P., Klomp, D. W. J., Kahn, R. S., Luijten, P. R., & Hulshoff Pol, H. E. (2013). Glutamate in schizophrenia: A focused review and meta-analysis of 1H-MRS Studies. *Schizophrenia Bulletin, 39*(1), 120–129. doi:10.1093/schbul/sbr069

Martin, A., Wiggs, C. L., Ungerleider, L. G., & Haxby, J. V. (1996). Neural correlates of category-specific knowledge. *Nature, 379,* 649–652.

Martinez-Marcos, A. (2001). Controversies on the human vomeronasal system. *European Journal of Anatomy, 5,* 47–53.

Martins, R. S., Siqueira, M. G., Santos, M. T., Zanon-Collange, N., & Moraes, O. J. (2003). Prognostic factors and treatment of penetrating gunshot wounds to the head. *Surgical Neurology, 60*(2), 98–104; discussion, 104.

Martland, H. W. (1928). Punch drunk. *Journal of the American Medical Association, 91,* 1103–1107.

Mason, W. A., Capitanio, J. P., Machado, C. J., Mendoza, S. P., & Amaral, D. G. (2006). Amygdalectomy and responsiveness to novelty in rhesus monkeys (*Macaca mulatta*): Generality and individual consistency of effects. *Emotion, 6*(1), 73–81.

Massachusetts General Hospital/Harvard Medical School. (2002). *Malignant brain tumors and neuro-oncology resources.* http://neurosurgery. mgh.harvard.edu/nonc-hp.htm.

Masters, W. H., & Johnson, V. E. (1970). *Human sexual inadequacy.* Boston: Little, Brown.

Mataro, M. (1997). Magnetic resonance imaging measurement of the caudate nucleus in adolescents with attention-deficit hyperactivity disorder and its relationship with neuropsychological and behavioral measures. *Journal of the American Medical Association (JAMA), 278,* 1720.

Mathew, A., Pettit, J., Lewinsohn, P., Seeley, J., & Roberts, R. (2011). Co-morbidity between major depressive disorder and anxiety disorders: Shared etiology or direct causation? *Psychological Medicine, 41*(10), 2023–2034. doi:10.1017/S0033291711000407

Matosin, N., & Newell, K. A. (2013). Metabotropic glutamate receptor 5 in the pathology and treatment of schizophrenia. *Neuroscience & Biobehavioral Reviews, 37*(3), 256–268. doi:10.1016/j.neubiorev.2012.12.005

Matson, J. L., & Shoemaker, M. (2009). Intellectual disability and its relationship to autism spectrum disorders. *Research in Developmental Disabilities, 30*(6), 1107–1114. doi:http://dx.doi.org/10.1016/j.ridd.2009.06.003

Matsumoto, D., & Willingham, B. (2009). Spontaneous facial expressions of emotion of congenitally and noncongenitally blind individuals. *Journal of Personality and Social Psychology, 96*(1), 1–10. doi:10.1037/a0014037

Matsumoto, D., Willingham, B., & Olide, A. (2009). Sequential dynamics of culturally moderated facial expressions of emotion. *Psychological Science, 20*(10), 1269–1274. doi:10.1111/j.1467-9280.2009.02438.x

Matsumoto, D., Yoo, S., & Chung, J. (2010). The expression of anger across cultures. In M. Potegal, G. Stemmler, & C. Spielberger (Eds.), *International handbook of anger* (pp. 125–137). New York: Springer.

Matthes, H. W., Maldonalo, R., Simonin, R., Valverde, O., Slowe, S., Kitchen, I., et al. (1996). Loss of morphine induced analgesia, reward effect and withdrawal symptoms in mice lacking the mu-opioid-receptor gene. *Nature, 383,* 819–823.

Matthews, C. E., Chen, K. Y., Freedson, P. S., & Troiano, R. P. (2008). Amount of time spent in sedentary behaviors in the United States, 2003–2004. *American Journal of Epidemiology, 167,* 875–881. doi: 10.1093/aje/kwm390

Matus-Amat, P., Higgins, E. A., Sprunger, D., Wright-Hardesty, K., & Rudy, J. W. (2007). The role of dorsal hippocampus and basolateral amygdala NMDA receptors in the acquisition and retrieval of context and contextual fear memories. *Behavioral Neuroscience, 121*(4), 721–731. doi:10.1037/0735-7044.121.4.721

Matuszczyk, J. V., Fernandez-Guasti, A., & Larsen, K. (1988). Sexual orientation, proceptivity, and receptivity in the male rat as a function of neonatal hormonal manipulation. *Hormones and Behavior, 22,* 362–378.

Maxwell, J. S., & Davidson, R. J. (2007). Emotion as motion: Asymmetries in approach and avoidant actions. *Psychological Science, 18*(12), 1113–1119.

Mayer, J. (1955). Regulation of energy intake and the body weight: The glucostatic theory and the lipostatic hypothesis. *Annals of the New York Academy of Sciences, 63,* 15–43.

Mayford, M., Bach, M. E., Huang, Y.-Y., Wang, L., Hawkins, R. D., & Kandel, E. R. (1996). Control of memory formation through regulated expression of a CaMKII transgene. *Science, 274,* 1678–1683.

Mazer, N. A. (2002). Testosterone deficiency in women: Etiologies, diagnosis, and emerging treatments. *International Journal of Fertility and Women's Medicine, 47,* 77–86.

Mazur, A., & Michalek, J. (1998). Marriage, divorce and male testosterone. *Social Forces, 77,* 315–331.

McCallum, S., & Boletsis, C. (2013). Dementia games: A literature review of dementia-related serious games. In M. Ma, M. Oliveira, S. Petersen, & J. Hauge (Eds.), *Serious games development and applications* (Vol. 8101, pp. 15–27). Berlin Heidelberg: Springer.

McCann, J. (2000, September 18). Movement disorders: Less of a black box. *Scientist, 14,* 14.

McCarley, R. W. (2007). Neurobiology of REM and NREM sleep. *Sleep Medicine, 8*(4), 302–330.

McCarthy, M. M., & Arnold, A. P. (2011). Reframing sexual differentiation of the brain. *Nature Neuroscience, 14*(6), 677–683. doi: 10.1038/nn.2834

McCarthy, R. A., & Warrington, E. K. (1990). *Cognitive neuropsychology: A clinical introduction.* San Diego, CA: Academic Press.

McCarthy, S. E., Makarov, V., Kirov, G., Addington, A. M., McClellan, J., Yoon, S., … Sebat, J. (2009). Microduplications of 16p11.2 are associated with schizophrenia. *Nature Genetics, 41,* 1223–1227. doi: 10.1038/ng.474

McClung, C. A. (2007). Circadian genes, rhythms and the biology of mood disorders. *Pharmacology and Therapeutics, 114*(2), 222–232.

McCoy, N., & Pitino, L. (2002). Pheromonal influences on sociosexual behavior in young women. *Physiology and Behavior, 75,* 367–375.

McEwen, B. S., & Grafstein, B. (1968). Fast and slow components in axonal transport of protein. *The Journal of Cell Biology, 38*(3), 494–508. doi:10.1083/jcb.38.3.494

McFadden, D. (1993). A speculation about the parallel ear asymmetries and sex differences in hearing sensitivity and otoacoustic emissions. *Hearing Research, 68*(2), 143–151. doi:http://dx.doi.org/10.1016/0378-5955(93)90118-K

McFadden, D. (2011). Sexual orientation and the auditory system. *Frontiers in Neuroendocrinology, 32*(2), 201–213. doi:http://dx.doi.org/10.1016/j.yfrne.2011.02.001

McFadden, D., Pasanen, E. G., Valero, M. D., Roberts, E. K., & Lee, T. M. (2009). Effect of prenatal androgens on click-evoked otoacoustic emissions in male and female sheep (*Ovis aries*). *Hormones and Behavior, 55*(1), 98–105. doi: 10.1016/j.yhbeh.2008.08.013

McGaugh, J. L. (1992). Neuromodulatory regulation of memory: Role of the amygdaloid complex. *International Journal of Psychology, 27,* 403.

McGauley, G., Yakeley, J., Williams, A., & Bateman, A. (2011). Attachment, mentalization and antisocial personality disorder: The possible contribution of mentalization-based treatment. *European Journal of Psychotherapy & Counselling, 13*(4), 371–393. doi:10.1080/13642537.2011.629118

McGrath, J., Saha, S., Chant, D., & Welham, J. (2008). Schizophrenia: A concise overview of incidence, prevalence, and mortality. *Epidemiologic Reviews, 30*(1), 67–76. doi:10.1093/epirev/mxn001

McGuffin, P., Reveley, A., & Holland, A. (1982). Identical triplets: Non-identical psychosis? *British Journal of Psychiatry, 140,* 1–6.

McIntyre, P. B., O'Brien, K. L., Greenwood, B., & van de Beek, D. (2012). Effect of vaccines on bacterial meningitis worldwide. *The Lancet, 380*(9854), 1703–1711. doi:http://dx.doi.org/10.1016/S0140-6736(12)61187-8

McKetin, R., McLaren, J., Lubman, D. I., & Hides, L. (2006). The prevalence of psychotic symptoms among methamphetamine users. *Addiction, 101*(10), 1473–1478. doi: 10.1111/j.1360-0443.2006.01496.x

McManus, C. (1999). Handedness, cerebral lateralization, and the evolution of handedness. In M. C. Corballis & S. E. G. Lea (Eds.), *The descent of mind* (pp. 194–217). Oxford, UK: Oxford University Press.

McNeil, T. F., Cantor-Graae, E., & Weinberger, D. R. (2000). Relationship of obstetric complications and differences in size of brain structures in monozygotic twin pairs discordant for schizophrenia. *American Journal of Psychiatry, 157,* 203–212.

McNeilly, A. S. (2001). Neuroendocrine changes and fertility in breast-feeding women. *Progress in Brain Research, 133,* 207–214.

McPheeters, M. L., Warren, Z., Sathe, N., Bruzek, J. L., Krishnaswami, S., Jerome, R. N., & Veenstra-Vanderweele, J. (2011). A systematic review of medical treatments for children with autism spectrum disorders. *Pediatrics, 127*(5), e1312-1321. doi:10.1542/peds.2011-0427

McQueeny, T., Schweinsburg, B. C., Schweinsburg, A. D., Jacobus, J., Bava, S., Frank, L. R., & Tapert, S. F. (2009). Altered white matter integrity in adolescent binge drinkers. *Alcoholism: Clinical and Experimental Research, 33*(7), 1278–1285. doi:10.1111/j.1530-0277.2009.00953.x

Meaney, M. J. (2010). Epigenetics and the biological definition of gene x environment interactions. *Child Development, 81*(1), 41–79. doi:10.1111/j.1467-8624.2009.01381.x

Meares, S., Shores, E. A., Taylor, A. J., Batchelor, J., Bryant, R. A., Baguley, I. J., … Marosszeky, J. E. (2011). The prospective course of postconcussion syndrome: The role of mild traumatic brain injury. *Neuropsychology, 25*(4), 454–465. doi:10.1037/a0022580

Mechelli, A., Crinion, J. T., Noppeney, U., O'Doherty, J., Ashburner, J., Frackowiak, R. S., & Price, C. J. (2004). Neurolinguistics: Structural plasticity in the bilingual brain. *Nature, 431*(7010), 757–757. doi:10.1038/431757a

Meddis, R., Pearson, A., & Langford, G. (1973). An extreme case of healthy insomnia. *Electroencephalography and Clinical Neurophysiology, 35,* 213–214.

Medini, P., & Pizzorusso, T. (2008). Visual experience and plasticity of the visual cortex: A role for epigenetic mechanisms. *Frontiers in Bioscience, 138,* 3000–3007.

Mehta, D., Newport, D. J., Frishman, G., Kraus, L., Rex-Haffner, M., Ritchie, J. C. … Binder, E. B. (2014). Early predictive biomarkers for postpartum depression point to a role for estrogen receptor signaling. *Psychological Medicine, 44*(11), 2309–2322. doi:10.1017/S0033291713003231

Meldrum, B. S., & Rogawski, M. A. (2007). Molecular targets for antiepileptic drug development. *Neurotherapeutics, 4*(1), 18–61.

Melke, J., Goubran Botros, H., Chaste, P., Betancur, C., Nygren, G., Anckarsater, H., et al. (2007). Abnormal melatonin synthesis in autism spectrum disorders. *Molecular Psychiatry, 13*(1), 90–98.

Meltzer, H. Y. (2000). Side effects of antipsychotic medications: Physician's choice of medication and patient compliance. *Journal of Clinical Psychiatry, 61,* 3–4.

Melzack, R., & Wall, P. D. (1983). *The challenge of pain.* New York: Basic Books.

Mendoza, J. (2007). Circadian clocks: Setting time by food. *Journal of Neuroendocrinology, 19*(2), 127–137.

Meningitis Trust. (2002). *What is meningitis?* Retrieved from the Meningitis Trust Web site: http://www.meningitis-trust.org.uk/frame.htm.

Mennella, J. A. (2006). Development of food preferences: Lessons learned from longitudinal and experimental studies. *Food Quality and Preference, 17*(7-8), 635–637. doi:10.1016/j.foodqual.2006.01.008

Mennella, J. A., & Beauchamp, G. K. (2005). Understanding the origin of flavor preferences. *Chemical Senses, 30, Supplement 1,* i242–i243.

Mennella, J. A., Jagnow, C. P., & Beauchamp, G. K. (2001). Prenatal and postnatal flavor learning by human infants. *Pediatrics, 107,* E88.

Menzies, L., Chamberlain, S. R., Laird, A. R., Thelen, S. M., Sahakian, B. J., & Bullmore, E. T. (2008). Integrating evidence from neuroimaging and neuropsychological studies of obsessive-compulsive disorder: The orbitofronto-striatal model revisited. *Neuroscience and Biobehavioral Reviews, 32*(3), 525–549. doi:10.1016/j.neubiorev.2007.09.005

Merzenich, M. M., Jenkins, W. M., Johnston, P., Schreiner, C., Miller, S. L., & Tallal, P. (1996). Temporal processing deficits of language-learning impaired children ameliorated by training. *Science, 271,* 77–81.

Messner, S. F., Pearson-Nelson, B., Raffalovich, L. E., & Miner, Z. (2011). Cross-national homicide trends in the latter decades of the twentieth century: Losses and gains in institutional control? In W. Heitmeyer, H. Haupt, A. Kirschner, & S. Malthaner (Eds.), *Control of violence: Historical and international perspectives on violence in modern societies* (pp. 65–89). New York: Springer.

Meyer-Bahlburg, H. F., Dolezal, C., Baker, S. W., & New, M. I. (2008). Sexual orientation in women with classical or non-classical congenital adrenal hyperplasia as a function of degree of prenatal androgen excess. *Archives of Sexual Behavior, 37*(1), 85–99.

Meyer, W. J., III, Cole, C., & Emory, E. (1992). Depo Provera treatment for sex offending behavior: An evaluation of outcome. *Bulletin of the American Academy of Psychiatry and the Law, 20,* 249–259.

Micheau, J., & Marighetto, A. (2011). Acetylcholine and memory: A long, complex and chaotic but still living relationship. *Behavioural Brain Research, 221*(2), 424–429. doi:10.1016/j.bbr.2010.11.052

Middleton, L. E., Corbett, D., Brooks, D., Sage, M., MacIntosh, B. J., McIlroy, W. E., & Black, S. E. (2013). Physical activity in the prevention of ischemic stroke and improvement of outcomes: A narrative review. *Neuroscience & Biobehavioral Reviews, 37*(2), 133–137. doi:http://dx.doi.org/10.1016/j.neubiorev.2012.11.011

Migeon, B. R. (2007). Why females are mosaics, X-chromosome inactivation, and sex differences in disease. *Gender Medicine, 4*(2), 97–105. doi: 10.1016/S1550-8579(07)80024-6

Milad, M. R., & Rauch, S. L. (2012). Obsessive-compulsive disorder: Beyond segregated cortico-striatal pathways. *Trends in Cognitive Sciences, 16*(1), 43–51. doi:10.1016/j.tics.2011.11.003

Milani, R. V., & Lavie, C. J. (2009). Reducing psychosocial stress: A novel mechanism of improving survival from exercise training. *The American Journal of Medicine, 122*(10), 931–938. doi:10.1016/j.amjmed.2009.03.028

Milgram, S. (1963). Behavioral study of obedience. *Journal of Abnormal and Social Psychology, 67,* 371–378.

Millecamps, M., Centeno, M., Berra, H., Rudick, C., Lavarello, S., Tkatch, T., et al. (2007). d-Cycloserine reduces neuropathic pain behavior through limbic NMDA-mediated circuitry. *Pain, 132*(1–2), 108–128.

Miller, A. D., & Leslie, R. A. (1994). The area postrema and vomiting. *Frontiers in Neuroendocrinology, 15*(4), 301–320. doi:10.1006/frne.1994.1012

Miller, F. G., & Wertheimer, A. (2010). *The ethics of consent: Theory and practice.* New York, NY: Oxford University Press.

Miller, G. (2004). Forgetting and remembering. Learning to forget. *Science, 304*(5667), 34–36.

Miller, G. A. (1956). The magical number seven, plus or minus two: Some limits on our capacity for processing information. *Psychological Review, 63,* 81–97.

Miller, I. J., Jr., & Reedy, F. E. (1990). Variations in human taste bud density and taste intensity perception. *Physiology and Behavior, 47,* 1213–1219.

Miller, J. J. (2003, May 20). War of all against all. *The Wall Street Journal.* http://online.wsj.com/article_email/0,,SB105339612755716900-H9jeoNplaZ2m52tZH6I baWHm4,00.html.

Miller, R. (2007). Theory of the normal waking EEG: From single neurones to waveforms in the alpha, beta and gamma frequency ranges. *International Journal of Psychophysiology, 64*(1), 18–23. doi:http://dx.doi.org/10.1016/j.ijpsycho.2006.07.009

Miller, R. G., Mitchell, J. D., & Moore, D. H. (2012). Riluzole for amyotrophic lateral sclerosis (ALS)/motor neuron disease (MND). *Cochrane Database of Systematic Reviews* (3), CD001447. doi:10.1002/14651858.CD001447.pub3.

Miller, S. L., & Maner, J. K. (2011). Ovulation as a male mating prime: Subtle signs of women's fertility influence men's mating cognition and behavior. *Journal of Personality and Social Psychology, 100*(2), 295–308. doi:10.1037/a0020930

Million, M., & Raoult, D. (2013). The role of the manipulation of the gut microbiota in obesity. *Current Infectious Disease Reports, 15*(1), 25–30. doi:10.1007/s11908-012-0301-5

Million, M., Angelakis, E., Maraninchi, M., Henry, M., Giorgi, R., Valero, R., … Raoult, D. (2013). Correlation between body mass index and gut concentrations of *Lactobacillus reuteri, Bifidobacterium animalis, Methanobrevibacter smithii* and *Escherichia coli. International Journal of Obesity, 37*(11), 1460–1466. doi:10.1038/ijo.2013.20

Millward, C., Ferriter, M., Calver, S., & Connell-Jones, G. (2008). Gluten- and casein-free diets for autistic spectrum disorder. *Cochrane Database of Systematic Reviews,* (2): CD003498. doi: 10.1002/14651858.CD003498.pub3

Milner, A. D., & Goodale, M. A. (1995). *The visual brain in action.* New York: Oxford University Press.

Milner, B. (1966). Amnesia following operation on the temporal lobes. In C. W. M. Whitty & O. L. Zangwill (Eds.), *Amnesia* (pp. 109–133). London: Butterworth.

Milunsky, A. (2004). *Genetic disorders and the fetus: Diagnosis, prevention and treatment* (5th ed.). Baltimore, MD: The Johns Hopkins University Press.

Min, R., & Nevian, T. (2012). Astrocyte signaling controls spike timing-dependent depression at neocortical synapses. *Nature Neuroscience, 15*(5), 746–753. doi: 10.1038/nn.3075

Mirnics, K., Middleton, F. A., Marquez, A., Lewis, D. A., & Levitt, P. (2000). Molecular characterization of schizophrenia viewed by microarray analysis of gene expression in prefrontal cortex. *Neuron, 28,* 53.

Mirsky, A. F., DeLisi, L. E., Buchsbaum, M. S., Quinn, O. W., Schwerdt, P., Siever, L. J., et al. (1984). The Genain quadruplets: Psychological studies. *Psychiatry Research, 13,* 77–93.

Mishkin, M., & Appenzeller, T. (1987). The anatomy of memory. *Scientific American, 256,* 80–89.

Mithoefer, M. C., Wagner, M. T., Mithoefer, A. T., Jerome, L., & Doblin, R. (2011). The safety and efficacy of ±3,4-methylenedioxymethamphetamine-assisted psychotherapy in subjects with chronic, treatment-resistant posttraumatic stress disorder: The first randomized controlled pilot study. *Journal of Psychopharmacology, 25*(4), 439–452. doi:10.1177/0269881110378371

Mobbs, D., Lau, H. C., Jones, O. D., & Frith, C. D. (2007). Law, responsibility, and the brain. *PLOS Biology, 5*(4), 0693–0700.

Modell, J. G., Rosenthal, N. E., Harriett, A. E., Krishen, A., Asgharian, A., Foster, V. J., et al. (2005). Seasonal affective disorder and its prevention by anticipatory treatment with bupropion XL. *Biological Psychiatry, 58*(8), 658–667.

Moffitt, T. E., Caspi, A., Taylor, A., Kokaua, J., Milne, B. J., Polanczyk, G., & Poulton, R. (2010). How common are common mental disorders? Evidence that lifetime prevalence rates are doubled by prospective versus retrospective ascertainment. *Psychological Medicine, 40*(6), 899–909. doi:10.1017/S0033291709991036

Moghaddam, B., & Adams, B. W. (1998). Reversal of phencyclidine effects by a group II metabotropic glutamate receptor agonist in rats. *Science, 281*, 1349–1352.

Moldofsky, H., & Scarisbrick, P. (1976). Induction of neurasthenic musculoskeletal pain syndrome by selective sleep stage deprivation. *Psychosomatic Medicine, 38*, 35–44.

Molina-Carballo, A., Fernandez-Tardaquila, E., Uberos-Fernandez, J., Seiquer, I., Contreras-Chova, F., & Munoz-Hoyos, A. (2007). Longitudinal study of the simultaneous secretion of melatonin and leptin during normal puberty. *Hormone Research, 68*(1), 11–19.

Money, J., Schwartz, M., & Lewis, V. G. (1984). Adult erotosexual status and fetal hormonal masculinization and demasculinization: 46,XX congenital virilizing adrenal hyperplasia and 46,XY androgen–insensitivity syndrome compared. *Psychoneuroendocrinology, 9*, 405–414.

Montpetit, M. A., Bergeman, C. S., Deboeck, P. R., Tiberio, S. S., & Boker, S. M. (2010). Resilience-as-process: Negative affect, stress, and coupled dynamical systems. *Psychology and Aging, 25*(3), 631–640. doi:10.1037/a0019268

Moog, J. S., Geers, A. E., Gustus, C., & Brenner, C. (2011). Psychosocial adjustment in adolescents who have used cochlear implants since preschool. *Ear and Hearing, 32*(1 Suppl), 75S. doi:10.1097/AUD.0b013e3182014c76

Moore, R., & Eichler, V. B. (1972). Loss of circadian adrenal corticosterone rhythm following suprachiasmatic lesions in the rat. *Brain Research, 42*, 201–206.

Morecraft , R. J., Louie, J. L., Herrick, J. L., & Stilwell-Morecraft , K. S. (2001). Cortical innervation of the facial nucleus in the non-human primate: A new interpretation of the effects of stroke and related subtotal brain trauma on the muscles of facial expression. *Brain, 124*(Pt. 1), 176–208.

Morgan, K. D., Dazzan, P., Orr, K. G., Hutchinson, G., Chitnis, X., Suckling, J., et al. (2007). Grey matter abnormalities in first-episode schizophrenia and affective psychosis. *British Journal of Psychiatry*, Supplement, *51*, s111–116.

Morris, J. K., Alberman, E., Scott, C., & Jacobs, P. (2007). Is the prevalence of Klinefelter syndrome increasing? *European Journal of Human Genetics, 16*(2), 163–170.

Morris, J. M. (1953). The syndrome of testicular feminization in male pseudohermaphrodites. *American Journal of Obstetric Gynecology, 65*, 1192–1211.

Morris, J. S., DeGelder, B., Weiskrantz, L., & Dolan, R. J. (2001). Differential extrageniculostriate and amygdala responses to presentation of emotional faces in a cortically blind field. *Brain Research, 124*(6), 1241–1252. doi:10.1093/brain/124.6.1241

Morris, R. G., Anderson, E., Lynch, G. S., & Baudry, M. (1986). Selective impairment of learning and blockade of long-term potentiation by an N-methyl-D-aspartate receptor antagonist, AP5. *Nature, 319*(6056), 774–776.

Moseley, M. E., Cohen, Y., Kucharczyk, J., Mintorovitch, J., Asgari, H. S., Wendland, M. F., ... Norman, D. (1990). Diffusion-weighted MR imaging of anisotropic water diffusion in cat central nervous system. *Radiology, 176*(2), 439–445. doi: http://dx.doi.org/10.1148/radiology.176.2.2367658

Moss, W. C., King, M. J., & Blackman, E. G. (2009). Skull flexure from blast waves: A mechanism for brain injury with implications for helmet design. *Physical Review Letters, 103*(10), 108702. doi:10.1103/PhysRevLett.103.108702

Mosso, A. (1881). *Ueber den Kreislauf des Blutes im menschlichen Gehirn.* Leipzig: Viet.

Mountcastle, V. (1978). An organizing principle for cerebral function: The unit model and the distributed system. In G. M. Edelman & V. B. Mountcastle (Ed.), *The mindful brain* (pp. 7–50). Cambridge, MA: MIT Press.

Moylan, S., Maes, M., Wray, N., & Berk, M. (2013). The neuroprogressive nature of major depressive disorder: Pathways to disease evolution and resistance, and therapeutic implications. *Molecular Psychiatry, 18*(5), 595–606. doi:10.1038/mp.2012.33

Mueller, A. D., Pollock, M. S., Lieblich, S. E., Epp, J. R., Galea, L. A. M., & Mistlberger, R. E. (2008). Sleep deprivation can inhibit adult hippocampal neurogenesis independent of adrenal stress hormones. *American Journal of Physiology. Regulatory, Integrative and Comparative Physiology, 294*(5), R1693–1703.

Mueser, K. T., Deavers, F., Penn, D. L., & Cassisi, J. E. (2013). Psychosocial treatments for schizophrenia. *Annual Review of Clinical Psychology, 9*(1), 465–497. doi:10.1146/annurev-clinpsy-050212-185620

Müller, U., Winter, P., & Graeber, M. B. (2013). A presenilin 1 mutation in the first case of Alzheimer's disease. *The Lancet Neurology, 12*(2), 129–130. doi:10.1016/S1474-4422(12)70307-1

Mulloy, A., Lang, R., O'Reilly, M., Sigafoos, J., Lancioni, G., & Rispoli, M. (2010). Gluten-free and casein-free diets in the treatment of autism spectrum disorders: A systematic review. *Research in Autism Spectrum Disorders, 4*(3), 328–339. doi:http://dx.doi.org/10.1016/j.rasd.2009.10.008

Münte, T. F., Altenmüller, E., & Jäncke, L. (2002). The musician's brain as a model of neuroplasticity. *Nature Reviews Neuroscience, 3*, 473–478. doi:10.1038/nrn843

Murphy, B. L., Stoll, A. L., Harris, P. Q., Ravichandran, C., Babb, S. M., Carlezon, W. A., Jr., & Cohen, B. M. (2012). Omega-3 fatty acid treatment, with or without cytidine, fails to show therapeutic properties in bipolar disorder: A double-blind, randomized add-on clinical trial. *Journal of Clinical Psychopharmacology, 32*(5), 699–703. doi:10.1097/JCP.0b013e318266854c

Murphy, K. D., Rose, M. W., Chinkes, D. L., Meyer, W. J., 3rd, Herndon, D. N., Hawkins, H. K., et al. (2007). The effects of gammahydroxybutyrate on hypermetabolism and wound healing in a rat model of large thermal injury. *Journal of Trauma, 63*(5), 1099–1107.

Murray, E. A. (2007). The amygdala, reward and emotion. *Trends in Cognitive Sciences, 11*(11), 489–497.

Murray, E. A., & Izquierdo, A. (2007). Orbitofrontal cortex and amygdala contributions to affect and action in primates. *Annals of the New York Academy of Sciences, 1121*, 273–296.

Myers, R. D., Wooten, M. H., Ames, C. D., & Nyce, J. W. (1995). Anorexic action of a new potential neuropeptide Y antagonist [D-Tyr27, 36, D-Th r32]-NPY (27–36) infused into the hypothalamus of the rat. *Brain Research Bulletin, 37*, 237–245.

Nabi, H., Kivimaki, M., Zins, M., Elovainio, M., Consoli, S. M., Cordier, S., et al. (2008). Does personality predict mortality? Results from the GAZEL French prospective cohort study. *International Journal of Epidemiology, 37*(2) 386–396.

Nadarajah, B., & Parnavelas, J. G. (2002). Modes of neuronal migration in the developing cerebral cortex. *Nature Reviews Neuroscience, 3*(6), 423–432. doi:10.1038/nrn845

Nadeau, S. E., Lu, X., Dobkin, B., Wu, S. S., Dai, Y. E., Duncan, P. W., & LEAPS Investigative Team (2012). A prospective test of the late effects of potentially antineuroplastic drugs in a stroke rehabilitation study. *International Journal of Stroke, 9*(4), 449–456. doi:10.1111/j.1747-4949.2012.00920.x

Nakase-Richardson, R., Whyte, J., Giacino, J. T., Pavawalla, S., Barnett, S. D., Yablon, S. A. et al. (2012). Longitudinal outcome of patients with disordered consciousness in the NIDRR TBI Model Systems Programs. *Journal of Neurotrauma, 29*(1), 59–65. doi:10.1089/neu.2011.1829

Nargeot, R., & Simmers, J. (2011). Neural mechanisms of operant conditioning and learning-induced behavioral plasticity in Aplysia. *Cellular and Molecular Life Sciences, 68*(5), 803–816. doi:10.1007/s00018-010-0570-9

Narr, K. L., Woods, R. P., Thompson, P. M., Szeszko, P., Robinson, D., Dimtcheva, T., et al. (2007). Relationships between IQ and regional cortical gray matter thickness in healthy adults. *Cerebral Cortex, 17*(9), 2163–2171.

Narumi, J., Miyazawa, S., Miyata, H., Suzuki, A., Kohsaka, S., & Kosugi, H. (1999). Analysis of human error in nursing care. *Accident: Analysis and Prevention, 31*, 625–629.

Nathans, J. (1989). The genes for color vision. *Scientific American, 260*, 42–49.

Nathoo, N., Chetty, R., van Dellen, J. R., & Barnett, G. H. (2003). Genetic vulnerability following traumatic brain injury: The role of apolipoprotein E. *Molecular Pathology, 56*(3), 132–136. doi:10.1136/mp.56.3.132

National Collaborating Centre for Mental Health (UK). (2010). *Antisocial personality disorder: Treatment, management, and prevention.* Leicester, UK: British Psychological Society.

National Institute of Child Health and Human Development. (2000). *Clinical features of Turner syndrome.* Retrieved from the National Institutes of Health Web site: http://turners.nichd.nih.gov/ClinFrIntro.html.

National Institute of Child Health and Human Development. (2002). *Babies sleep safest on their backs: Reduce the risk of sudden infant death syndrome.* Retrieved April 24, 2003, from the National Institutes of Health Web site: http://www.nichd.nih.gov/sids/reduce_infant_risk.htm

National Sleep Foundation. (2009). Restless legs syndrome (RLS) and sleep. Retrieved from http://www.sleepfoundation.org/article/sleep-related-problems/restless-legs-syndrome-rls-and-sleep

Navara, K. J., & Nelson, R. J. (2007). The dark side of light at night: Physiological, epidemiological, and ecological consequences. *Journal of Pineal Research, 43*, 215–224.

Neary, W. (2002, January). *Individual neurons reveal complexity of memory within the brain*. Retrieved from http://www.eurekalert.org/pub_releases/2002-01/uow-inr010302.php.

Nedeltcheva, A. V., Kilkus, J. M., Imperial, J., Schoeller, D. A., & Penev, P. D. (2010). Insufficient sleep undermines dietary efforts to reduce adiposity. *Annals of Internal Medicine, 153,* 435–441. doi:10.7326/0003-4819-153-7-201010050-00006

Neigh, G. N., Gillespie, C. F., & Nemeroff, C. B. (2009). The neurobiological toll of child abuse and neglect. *Trauma, Violence, & Abuse, 10*(4), 389–410. doi:10.1177/1524838009339758

Neisser, U., Boodoo, G., Bouchard, T. J., Boykin, A. W., Brody, N., Ceci, S. J., et al. (1996). Intelligence: Knowns and unknowns. *American Psychologist, 51*(2), 77–101. doi:10.1037/0003-066X.51.2.77

Nelson, K. B., Grether, J. K., Croen, L. A., Dambrosia, J. M., Dickens, B. F., Jelliffe, L. L., … Phillips, T. M. (2001). Neuropeptides and neurotrophins in neonatal blood of children with autism or mental retardation. *Annals of Neurology, 49*(5), 597–606. doi:10.1002/ana.1024

Neumeyer, C. (2012). Color vision in goldfish and other vertebrates. In O. F. Lazareva, T. Shimizu, & E. A. Wasserman (Eds.), *How animals see the world: Comparative behavior, biology, and evolution of vision* (pp. 25–42). Oxford, UK: Oxford University Press.

Neville, H. J., Bavelier, D., Corina, D., Rauschecker, J., Karni, A., Lalwani, A., et al. (1998). Cerebral organization for language in deaf and hearing subjects: Biological constraints and effects of experience. *Proceedings of the National Academy of Sciences of the United States of America (PNAS), 95,* 922–929.

Newsom, C. (1998). Autistic disorder. In E. J. Mash & R. A. Barkley (Eds.), *Treatment of childhood disorders* (pp. 416–467). New York: Guilford Press.

NIDCD. (2014). Healthy Hearing 2010. Retrieved from http://www.nidcd.nih.gov/health/healthyhearing/what_hh/pages/objectives.aspx

Niedermeyer, E. (1999). The normal EEG of the waking adult. In E. Niedermeyer & F. Lopes da Silva (Eds.), *Electroencephalography: Basic principles, clinical applications and related fields* (pp. 149–173). Baltimore, MD: Lippincott, Williams, & Williams.

Nielsen, J. A., Zielinski, B. A., Ferguson, M. A., Lainhart, J. E., & Anderson, J. S. (2013). An evaluation of the left-brain vs. right-brain hypothesis with resting state functional connectivity magnetic resonance imaging. *PloS ONE, 8*(8), e71275. doi:10.1371/journal.pone.0071275

Nielsen, J. A., Zielinski, B. A., Fletcher, P. T., Alexander, A. L., Lange, N., Bigler, E. D., … Anderson, J. S. (2014). Abnormal lateralization of functional connectivity between language and default mode regions in autism. *Molecular Autism, 5*(1), 8. doi:10.1186/2040-2392-5-8

Nielsen, J., Pelsen, B., & Sørensen, K. (1988). Follow-up of 30 Klinefelter males treated with testosterone. *Clinical Genetics 33,* 262–269.

Nimchinsky, E. A., Gilissen, E., Allman, J. M., Perl, D. P., Erwin, J. M., & Hof, P. R. (1999). A neuronal morphologic type unique to humans and great apes. *Proceedings of the National Academy of Sciences of the United States of America (PNAS), 96,* 5268–5273. doi: 10.1073/pnas.96.9.5268

Nimmerjahn, A., Kirchhoff, F., & Helmchen, F. (2005). Resting microglial cells are highly dynamic surveillants of brain parenchyma

in vivo. *Science, 308*(5726), 1314–1318. doi: 10.1126/science.1110647

Nishimaru, H., Restrepo, C. E., Ryge, J., Yanagawa, Y., & Kiehn, O. (2005). Mammalian motor neurons corelease glutamate and acetylcholine at central synapses. *Proceedings of the National Academy of Sciences of the United States of America (PNAS), 102*(14), 5245–5249. doi:10.1073/pnas.0501331102

Nishimoto, S., Vu, An T., Naselaris, T., Benjamini, Y., Yu, B., & Gallant, J. L. (2011). Reconstructing visual experiences from brain activity evoked by natural movies. *Current Biology, 21*(19), 1641–1646. doi:10.1016/j.cub.2011.08.031

Nissen, R., Bourque, C. W., & Renaud, L. P. (1993). Membrane properties of organum vasculosum lamina terminalis neurons recorded in vitro. *American Journal of Physiology, 264,* R811–R815.

Noakes, T. (1993). Fluid replacement during exercise. *Exercise and Sport Sciences Reviews, 21,* 297–330.

Noaghiul, S., & Hibbeln, J. R. (2003). Cross-national comparisons of seafood consumption and rates of bipolar disorders. *American Journal of Psychiatry, 160,* 2222–2227.

Noakes, T. (1993). Fluid replacement during exercise. *Exercise and Sport Sciences Reviews, 21,* 297–330.

Noël, X., Brevers, D., & Bechara, A. (2013). A neurocognitive approach to understanding the neurobiology of addiction. *Current Opinion in Neurobiology, 23*(4), 632–638. doi:http://dx.doi.org/10.1016/j.conb.2013.01.018

Nolan, J. P., Morley, P. T., Vanden Hoek, T. L., Hickey, R. W., Kloeck, W. G. J., Billi, J., … Atkins, D. (2003). Therapeutic hypothermia after cardiac arrest: An advisory statement by the Advanced Life Support Task Force of the International Liaison Committee on Resuscitation. *Circulation, 108*(1), 118–121. doi:10.1161/01.cir.0000079019.02601.90

Nolen-Hoeksema, S., & Girgus, J. S. (1994). The emergence of gender differences in depression during adolescence. *Psychological Bulletin, 115,* 424–443.

Nouchi, R., Taki, Y., Takeuchi, H., Hashizume, H., Akitsuki, Y., Shigemune, Y., … Kawashima, R. (2012). Brain training game improves executive functions and processing speed in the elderly: A randomized controlled trial. *PloS ONE, 7*(1), e29676. doi:10.1371/journal.pone.0029676

Nunez, C., Beyer, J., Strain, G., Zumoff, B., Kovera, A., Gallagher, D., & Heymsfield, S. D. (1997). *Composition of weight-loss while dieting: A comparison of research and clinically based methods.* Retrieved from http://www.healthchecksystems.com/tdiet.htm.

O'Neil, P. M., Smith, S. R., Weissman, N. J., Fidler, M. C., Sanchez, M., Zhang, J., … Shanahan, W. R. (2012). Randomized placebo-controlled clinical trial of Lorcaserin for weight loss in type 2 diabetes mellitus: The BLOOM-DM Study. *Obesity, 20*(7), 1426–1436. doi: 10.1038/oby.2012.66

O'Shea, E., Urrutia, A., Green, A. R., & Colado, M. I. (2014). Current preclinical studies on neuroinflammation and changes in blood–brain barrier integrity by MDMA and methamphetamine. *Neuropharmacology.* doi:10.1016/j.neuropharm.2014.02.015

O'Connor, D. B., Archer, J., & Wu, F. C. W. (2000). Does testosterone affect cognitive function in normal men? *Proceedings of the British Psychological Society, 8,* 40–41.

O'Hara, C. (1988). Emotional adjustment following minor head injury. *Cognitive Rehabilitation, 6,* 26–33.

O'Keefe, J., & Dostrovsky, J. (1971). The hippocampus as a spatial map: Preliminary evidence from unit activity in the freely-moving rat. *Brain Research, 34,* 171–175.

O'Leary, C., Leonard, H., Bourke, J., D'Antoine, H., Bartu, A., & Bower, C. (2013). Intellectual disability: Population-based estimates of the proportion attributable to maternal alcohol use disorder during pregnancy. *Developmental Medicine & Child Neurology, 55*(3), 271–277. doi:10.1111/dmcn.12029

Ogawa, S., Lee, T. M., Kay, A. R., & Tank, D. W. (1990). Brain magnetic resonance imaging with contrast dependent on blood oxygenation. *Proceedings of the National Academies of Science of the USA, 87,* 9868-9872.

Ogrim, G., Hestad, K. A., Brunner, J. F., & Kropotov, J. (2013). Predicting acute side effects of stimulant medication in pediatric attention deficit/hyperactivity disorder: Data from quantitative electroencephalography, event-related potentials, and a continuous-performance test. *Neuropsychiatric Disease and Treatment, 9,* 1301. doi:10.2147/NDT.S49611

Ohgaki, H. (2009). Epidemiology of brain tumors. In M. Verma (Ed.), *Methods of molecular biology, cancer epidemiology* (Vol. 472, pp. 323–342). Totowa, NJ: Humana Press.

Ohno, K., & Sakurai, T. (2008). Orexin neuronal circuitry: Role in the regulation of sleep and wakefulness. *Frontiers in Neuroendocrinology, 29*(1), 70–87.

Ojemann, G., Schoenfield-McNeill, J., & Corina, D. P. (2002). Anatomic subdivisions in human temporal cortical neuronal activity related to recent verbal memory. *Nature Neuroscience, 5,* 64–71.

Oksenberg, J. R., Baranzini, S. E., Sawcer, S., & Hauser, S. L. (2008). The genetics of multiple sclerosis: SNPs to pathways to pathogenesis. *Nature Reviews Genetics, 9*(7), 516–526.

Olds, J., & Milner, P. (1954). Positive reinforcement produced by electrical stimulation of septal areas and other regions of the rat brain. *Journal of Comparative and Physiological Psychology, 47,* 419–427.

Olds, M. E., & Olds, J. (1963). Approach-avoidance analysis of rat diencephalon. *Journal of Comparative and Physiological Psychology, 120,* 259–295.

Olney, J. W. (1994). New mechanisms of excitatory transmitter neurotoxicity. *Journal of Neural Transmission Supplementa, 43,* 47–51.

Olson, R. K., Datta, H., Gayan, J., DeFries, J. C., Klein, R. M., & McMullen, P. A. (1999). A behavioral-genetic analysis of reading disabilities and component processes. In R. M. Klein & P. A. McMullen (Eds.), *Converging methods for understanding reading and dyslexia.* (pp. 133–151). Cambridge, MA: MIT Press.

Olszewski, P. K., Schioth, H. B., & Levine, A. S. (2008). Ghrelin in the CNS: From hunger to a rewarding and memorable meal? *Brain Research Reviews, 58*(1), 160–170.

Ölveczky, B. P., Baccus, S. A., & Meister, M. (2003). Segregation of object and background motion in the retina. *Nature, 423* (6938), 401–408. doi:10.1038/nature01652

Onwuameze, O. E., Nam, K. W., Epping, E. A., Wassink, T. H., Ziebell, S., Andreasen, N. C., & Ho, B. C. (2013). MAPK14 and CNR1 gene variant interactions: Effects on brain volume deficits in schizophrenia patients with marijuana misuse. *Psychological Medicine, 43*(03), 619–631. doi:10.1017/S0033291712001559

Opris, I., & Casanova, M. F. (2014). Prefrontal cortical minicolumn: From executive control to disrupted cognitive processing. *Brain, 137*(7), 1863–1875. doi:10.1093/brain/awt359

Oquendo, M. A., Placidi, G. P., Malone, K. M., Campbell, C., Keilp, J., Brodsky, B., et al. (2003). Positron emission tomography of regional brain metabolic responses to a serotonergic challenge and lethality of suicide attempts in major depression. *Archives of General Psychiatry, 60,* 14–22.

Osaka, M., Osaka, N., Kondo, H., Morishita, M., Fukuyama, H., Aso, T., et al. (2003). The neural basis of individual differences in working memory capacity: An fMRI study. *Neuroimage, 18*(3), 789–797.

Otto, M. W., McHugh, R. K., & Kantak, K. M. (2010). Combined pharmacotherapy and cognitive-behavioral therapy for anxiety disorders: Medication effects, glucocorticoids, and attenuated treatment outcomes. *Clinical Psychology: Science and Practice, 17*(2), 91–103. doi:10.1111/j.1468-2850.2010.01198.x

Ousdal, O. T., Jensen, J., Server, A., Hariri, A. R., Nakstad, P. H., & Andreassen, O. A. (2008). The human amygdala is involved in general behavioral relevance detection: Evidence from an event-related functional magnetic resonance imaging Go-NoGo task. *Neuroscience, 156*(3), 450–455. doi:http://dx.doi.org/10.1016/j.neuroscience.2008.07.066

Owen, M. J., Craddock, N., & Jablensky, A. (2007). The genetic deconstruction of psychosis. *Schizophrenia Bulletin, 33*(4), 905–911.

Paabo, S. (2001, April 25). *A comparative approach to human origins.* Paper presented at the Human Genome Meeting, Edinburgh, Scotland.

Pace-Schott, E. F., & Spencer, R. M. (2014). Sleep-dependent memory consolidation in healthy aging and mild cognitive impairment. In *Current Topics in Behavioral Neurosciences* (pp. 1–24). Berlin; Heidelberg: Springer. doi:10.1007/7854_2014_300

Pace-Schott, E. F., Gersh, T., Silvestri, R., Stickgold, R., Salzman, C., & Hobson, J. A. (2001). SSRI treatment suppresses dream recall frequency but increases subjective dream intensity in normal subjects. *Journal of Sleep Research, 10*(2), 129–142.

Pack, C. C. (2014). Eye movements as a probe of corollary discharge function in schizophrenia. *ACS Chemical Neuroscience 5*(5), 326–328. doi:10.1021/cn5000869

Packard, M. G., Hirsh, R., & White, N. M. (1989). Differential effects of fornix and caudate nucleus lesions on two radial maze tasks: Evidence for multiple memory systems. *Journal of Neuroscience, 9,* 1465–1472.

Pagel, J. (2000). Nightmares and disorders of dreaming. *American Family Physician, 61,* 2037–2042.

Palade, G. E., & Palay, S. L. (1954). Electron microscope observations of interneuronal and neuromuscular synapses. *Anatomical Record, 118,* 335–336.

Pan, H.-L., Wu, Z.-Z., Zhou, H.-Y., Chen, S.-R., Zhang, H.-M., & Li, D.-P. (2008). Modulation of pain transmission by G-protein-coupled receptors. *Pharmacology & Therapeutics, 117*(1), 141–161. doi: 10.1016/j.pharmthera.2007.09.003

Papenberg, G., Li, S.-C., Nagel, I. E., Nietfeld, W., Schjeide, B.-M., Schröder, J., … Bäckman, L. (2013). Dopamine and glutamate receptor genes interactively influence episodic memory in old age. *Neurobiology of Aging, 35*(5), 1213e3–1213e8. doi:10.1016/j.neurobiolaging.2013.11.014

Papp, L. A., Klein, D. F., Martinez, J., Schneier, F., Cole, R., Liebowitz, M. R., et al. (1993). Diagnostic and substance specificity of carbon-dioxideinduced panic. *American Journal of Psychiatry, 150,* 250–257.

Paquet, E. R., Rey, G., & Naef, F. (2008). Modeling an evolutionary conserved circadian cis-element. *PLoS Computational Biology, 4*(2), e38. doi: 10.1371/journal.pcbi.0040038

Paradiso, S., Ostedgaard, K., Vaidya, J., Ponto, L. B., & Robinson, R. (2013). Emotional blunting following left basal ganglia stroke: The role of depression and fronto-limbic functional alterations. *Psychiatry Research: Neuroimaging, 211*(2), 148–159. doi:http://dx.doi.org/10.1016/j.pscychresns.2012.05.008

Pardini, D. A., Raine, A., Erickson, K., & Loeber, R. (2014). Lower amygdala volume in men is associated with childhood aggression, early psychopathic traits, and future violence. *Biological Psychiatry, 75*(1), 73–80. doi:10.1016/j.biopsych.2013.04.003

Parker, A., Eacott, M. J., & Gaffan, D. (1997). The recognition memory deficit caused by mediodorsal thalamic lesion in non-human primates: A comparison with rhinal cortex lesion. *European Journal of Neuroscience, 9*(11), 2423–2431.

Parker, K., Andreasen, N., Liu, D., Freeman, J., Ponto, L., & O'Leary, D. (2012). Eyeblink conditioning in healthy adults: A positron emission tomography study. *The Cerebellum,* 1–11. doi:10.1007/s12311-012-0377-3

Parnas, H., Segel, L., Dudel, J., & Parnas, I. (2000). Autoreceptors, membrane potential and the regulation of transmitter release. *Trends in Neurosciences, 23*(2), 60–68. doi:10.1016/s0166-2236(99)01498-8

Parrilla, L. (2006). O'Malley killer begins his sentence. *The Tribune,* p. B2.

Parrott, A. C. (2007). The psychotherapeutic potential of MDMA (3,4-methylenedioxymethamphetamine): An evidence-based review. *Psychopharmacology, 191*(2), 181–198. doi: 10.1007/s00213-007-0703-5

Pascual-Leone, A., & Hamilton, R. (2001). The metamodal organization of the brain. *Progress in Brain Research, 134,* 427–446.

Pascual-Leone, A., & Torres, F. (1993). Plasticity of the sensorimotor cortex representation of the reading finger in Braille readers. *Brain, 116*(1), 39–52. doi:10.1093/brain/116.1.39

Pastor, Z., Holla, K., & Chmel, R. (2013). The influence of combined oral contraceptives on female sexual desire: A systematic review. *The European Journal of Contraception and Reproductive Health Care, 18*(1), 27–43. doi: 10.3109/13625187.2012.728643

Patel, N. S., Rhinn, M., Semprich, C. I., Halley, P. A., Dollé, P., Bickmore, W. A., & Storey, K. G. (2013). FGF signalling regulates chromatin organisation during neural differentiation via mechanisms that can be uncoupled from transcription. *PLoS Genetics, 9*(7), e1003614. doi:10.1371/journal.pgen.1003614

Paterson, D. S., Trachtenberg, F. L., Thompson, E. G., Belliveau, R. A., Beggs, A. H., Darnall, R., et al. (2006). Multiple serotonergic brainstem abnormalities in sudden infant death syndrome. *The Journal of the American Medical Association (JAMA), 296*(17), 2124–2132.

Patrick, C. J., Fowles, D. C., & Krueger, R. F. (2009). Triarchic conceptualization of psychopathy: Developmental origins of disinhibition, boldness, and meanness. *Development and Psychopathology, 21*(Special Issue 03), 913–938. doi:10.1017/S0954579409000492

Patrick, C., Drislane, L. E., & Strickland, C. (2012). Conceptualizing psychopathy in triarchic terms: Implications for treatment. *International Journal of Forensic Mental Health, 11*(4), 253–266. doi:10.1080/14999013.2012.746761

Patterson, F. (1978, October). Conversations with a gorilla. *National Geographic,* 438–465.

Pauley, S. M. (2004). Lighting for the human circadian clock: Recent research indicates lighting has become a public health issue. *Medical Hypotheses, 63,* 588–596.

Pavlov, I. P. (1927). *Conditioned reflexes* (G. V. Annep, Trans.). London: Oxford University Press.

Pearson, R., Barber, A., Rizzi, M., Hippert, C., Xue, T., West, E., … Azam, S. (2012). Restoration of vision after transplantation of photoreceptors. *Nature, 485*(7396), 99–103. doi:10.1038/nature10997

Pemberton, P. S. (2014). Release looms for man who, at 13, killed 87-year-old with skateboard, *The Tribune.* http://www.sanluisobispo.com/2014/03/27/2993482/gerald-omalley-murder-skateboard.html

Pembrey, M. E., Bygren, L. O., Kaati, G., Edvinsson, S., Northstone, K., Sjostrom, M., … ALSPAC Study Team (2005). Sex-specific, male-line transgenerational responses in humans. *European Journal of Human Genetics, 14*(2), 159–166. doi:10.1038/sj.ejhg.5201538

Penfield, W. (1958). Some mechanisms of consciousness discovered during electrical stimulation of the brain. *Proceedings of the National Academy of Sciences of the United States of America (PNAS), 44*(2), 51–66.

Penfield, W., & Rasmussen, T. (1950). *The cerebral cortex of man: A clinical study of localization of function.* New York, NY: Macmillan.

Penner, J. D., & Brown, A. S. (2007). Prenatal infectious and nutritional factors and risk of adult schizophrenia. *Expert Review of Neurotherapeutics, 7*(7), 797–805.

Penton-voak, I. S., Cahill, S., Pound, N., Kempe, V., Schaeffler, S., & Schaeffler, F. (2007). Male facial attractiveness, perceived personality, and child–directed speech. *Evolution and Human Behavior, 28*(4), 253–259.

Pepperberg, I. (2014). Interspecies communication with grey parrots: A tool for examining cognitive processing. In G. Witzany (Ed.), *Biocommunication of animals* (pp. 213–232). Amsterdam: Springer Netherlands.

Perani, D., Paulesu, E., Galles, N. S., Dupoux, E., Dehaene, S., Bettinardi, V., et al. (1998). The bilingual brain: Proficiency and age of acquisition of the second language. *Brain, 121,* 1841–1852.

Perera, T. D., Coplan, J. D., Lisanby, S. H., Lipira, C. M., Arif, M., Carpio, C., et al. (2007). Antidepressant-induced neurogenesis in the hippocampus of adult nonhuman primates. *Journal of Neuroscience, 27*(18), 4894–4901.

Perkins, T., Stokes, M., McGillivray, J., & Bittar, R. (2010). Mirror neuron dysfunction in autism spectrum disorders. *Journal of Clinical Neuroscience, 17*(10), 1239–1243. doi:10.1016/j.jocn.2010.01.026

Persico, A. M., & Bourgeron, T. (2006). Searching for ways out of the autism maze: Genetic, epigenetic and environmental clues. *Trends in Neurosciences, 29*(7), 349–358. doi:http://dx.doi.org/10.1016/j.tins.2006.05.010

Pert, C. B., Snowman, A. M., & Snyder, S. H. (1974). Localization of opiate receptor binding in synaptic membranes of rat brain. *Brain Research, 70,* 184–188.

Peters, A., Palay, S., & Webster, H. d. F. (1991). *The fine structure of the nervous system: Neurons and their supporting cells.* New York: Oxford University Press.

Peters, M., Manning, J. T., & Reimers, S. (2007). The effects of sex, sexual orientation, and digit ratio (2D: 4D) on mental rotation performance. *Archives of Sexual Behavior, 36*(2), 251–260. doi: 10.1007/s10508-006-9166-8

Peterson, L. R., & Peterson, M. J. (1959). Short-term retention of individual verbal items. *Journal of Experimental Psychology, 58,* 193–198.

Petit, F., Minns, A. B., Dubernard, J. M., Hettiaratchy, S., & Lee, W. P. (2003). Composite tissue allotransplantation and reconstructive surgery: First clinical applications. *Annals of Surgery, 237*(1), 19–25. doi: 10.1097/01.SLA.0000041228.23111.30

Petty, R. G. (1999). Structural asymmetries of the human brain and their disturbance in schizophrenia. *Schizophrenia Bulletin, 25,* 121–139.

Pfrieger, F. W., & Barres, B. A. (1997). Synaptic efficacy enhanced by glial cells in vitro. *Science, 277*(5332), 1684–1687. doi:10.1126/science.277.5332.1684

Phan, K. L., Wager, T., Taylor, S. F., & Liberzon, I. (2002). Functional neuroanatomy of emotion: A meta-analysis of emotion activation studies in PET and fMRI. *NeuroImage, 16,* 331–348. doi:10.1006/nimg.2002.1087

Phelps, M . E., Hoffman, E., Mullani, N., Higgins, C. S., Ter-Pogossian, M. M. (1976). Design considerations for a positron emission transaxial tomography (PETT III). *IEEE Transactions on Nuclear Science, NS-23,* 516–522.

Phillips, A. G., Coury, A., Fiorino, D., LePiane, F. G., Brown, E., & Fibiger, H. C. (1992). Self-stimulation of the ventral tegmental area enhances dopamine release in the nucleus accumbens: A microdialysis study. *Annals of the New York Academy of Sciences, 654,* 199–206.

Phillips, M. L., Drevets, W. C., Rauch, S. L., & Lane, R. (2003). Neurobiology of emotion perception II: Implications for major psychiatric disorders. *Biological Psychiatry, 54*(5), 515–528.

Piacentini, J., & Graae, F. (1997). Childhood OCD. In E. Hollander & D. Stein (Eds.), *Obsessive-compulsive disorders: Diagnosis, etiology, treatment* (pp. 23–46). New York: Dekker.

Pilgrim, J. L., Gerostamoulos, D., & Drummer, O. H. (2011). Deaths involving MDMA and the concomitant use of pharmaceutical drugs. *Journal of Analytical Toxicology, 35*(4), 219–226. doi: 10.1093/anatox/35.4.219

Pitman, R. K., & Delahanty, D. L. (2005). Conceptually driven pharmacologic approaches to acute trauma. *CNS Spectrums, 10*(2), 99–106.

Plailly, J., Delon-Martin, C., & Royet, J.-P. (2012). Experience induces functional reorganization in brain regions involved in odor imagery in perfumers. *Human Brain Mapping, 33*(1), 224–234. doi:10.1002/hbm.21207

Plomin, R. (2012). Genetics: How intelligence changes with age. *Nature, 482*(7384), 165–166. doi:10.1038/482165a

Plomin, R., Turic, D. M., Hill, L., Turic, D. E., Stephens, M., Williams, J., et al. (2004). A functional polymorphism in the succinate-semialdehyde dehydrogenase (aldehyde dehydrogenase 5 family, member A1) gene is associated with cognitive ability. *Molecular Psychiatry, 9*(6), 582–586.

Pomarol-Clotet, E., Salvador, R., Sarro, S., Gomar, J., Vila, F., Martinez, A. et al. (2008). Failure to deactivate in the prefrontal cortex in schizophrenia: Dysfunction of the default mode network? *Psychological Medicine, 38*(8), 1185–1194. doi:10.1017/S0033291708003565

Pomponi, M., Janiri, L., La Torre, G., Di Stasio, E., Di Nicola, M., Mazza, M., ... Pomponi, M. F. (2013). Plasma levels of n-3 fatty acids in bipolar patients: Deficit restricted to DHA. *Journal of Psychiatric Research, 47*(3), 337–342. doi:http://dx.doi.org/10.1016/j.jpsychires.2012.11.004

Pope, C., Karanth, S., & Liu, J. (2005). Pharmacology and toxicology of cholinesterase inhibitors: uses and misuses of a common mechanism of action. *Environmental Toxicology and Pharmacology, 19*(3), 433–446. doi:10.1016/j.etap.2004.12.048

Porkka-Heiskanen, T. (1999). Adenosine in sleep and wakefulness. *Annals of Medicine, 31,* 125–129.

Porter, K. R., McCarthy, B. J., Freels, S., Kim, Y., & Davis, F. G. (2010). Prevalence estimates for primary brain tumors in the United States by age, gender, behavior, and histology. *Neuro-Oncology, 12*(6), 520–527. doi:10.1093/neuonc/nop066

Prasad, S., & Steer, C. (2008). Switching from neurostimulant therapy to atomoxetine in children and adolescents with attention-deficit hyperactivity disorder: Clinical approaches and review of current available evidence. *Paediatric Drugs, 10*(1), 39–47.

Pressman, M. R. (2007). Factors that predispose, prime and precipitate NREM parasomnias in adults: Clinical and forensic implications. *Sleep Medicine Reviews, 11*(1), 5–30; discussion 31–33.

Previc, F. H. (1991). A general theory concerning the prenatal origins of cerebral lateralization in humans. *Psychological Review, 98*(3), 299. doi:10.1037/0033-295X.98.3.299

Provine, R. R. (1986). Yawning as a stereotyped action pattern and releasing stimulus. *Ethology, 72,* 109–122. doi:10.1111/j.1439-0310.1986.tb00611.x

Provine, R. R. (2005). Yawning. *American Scientist, 93*(6), 532–539. doi: 10.1511/2005.6.532

Prusiner, S. B. (1982). Novel proteinaceous infectious particles cause scrapie. *Science, 216,* 136–144.

Prusiner, S. B. (1995). The prion diseases. *Scientific American, 272,* 48–56.

Prusiner, S. B., Groth, D. F., Bolton, D. C., Kent, S. B., & Hood, L. E. (1984). Purification and structural studies of a major scrapie prion protein. *Cell, 38,* 127–134.

Pulvermüller, F., & Fadiga, L. (2010). Active perception: Sensorimotor circuits as a cortical basis for language. *Nature Reviews Neuroscience, 11*(5), 351–360. doi:10.1038/nrn2811

Pupillo, E., Messina, P., Logroscino, G., Zoccolella, S., Chiò, A., Calvo, A., ... EURALS Consortium. (2012). Trauma and amyotrophic lateral sclerosis: A case–control study from a population-based registry. *European Journal of Neurology, 19*(12), 1509–1517. doi:10.1111/j.1468-1331.2012.03723.x

Quan, H.-T., Barkowsky, M., & Le Callet, P. (2011). The importance of visual attention in improving the 3D TV viewing experience: Overview and new perspectives. *Broadcasting, IEEE Transactions on, 57*(2), 421–431. doi:10.1109/TBC.2011.2128250

Quian Quiroga, R., Reddy, L., Kreiman, G., Koch, C., & Fried, I. (2005). Invariant visual representation by single neurons in the human brain. *Nature, 435,* 1102–1107. doi:10.1038/nature03687

Quirk, G. J., Repa, J. C., & LeDoux, J. E. (1995). Fear conditioning enhances shortlatency auditory responses of lateral amygdala neurons: Parallel recordings in the freely behaving rat. *Neuron, 15,* 1029–1039.

Quiroz, J. A., Machado-Vieira, R., Zarate, J. C. A., & Manji, H. K. (2010). Novel insights into lithium's mechanism of action: Neurotrophic and neuroprotective effects. *Neuropsychobiology, 62*(1), 50–60. doi:10.1159/000314310

Radua, J., van den Heuvel, O. A., Surguladze, S., & Mataix-Cols, D. (2010). Meta-analytical comparison of voxel-based morphometry studies in obsessive-compulsive disorder vs other anxiety disorders. *Archives of General Psychiatry, 67*(7), 701–711. doi:10.1001/archgenpsychiatry.2010.70

Radulovacki, M. (1985). Role of adenosine in sleep in rats. *Reviews in Clinical and Basic Pharmacology, 5*(3–4), 327–339.

Rahman, Q., Abrahams, S., & Wilson, G. D. (2003). Sexual-orientation-related differences in verbal fluency. *Neuropsychology, 17*(2), 240. doi: http://dx.doi.org/10.1037/0894-4105.17.2.240

Raichle, M. E., & Snyder, A. Z. (2011). Intrinsic brain activity and consciousness. In S. Laureys and G. Tononi (Eds.), *The neurology of consciousness: Cognitive neuroscience and neuropathology* (pp. 79, 81–88). New York: Elsevier.

Raine, A., Ishikawa, S. S., Arce, E., Lencz, T., Knuth, K. H., Bihrle, S., et al. (2004). Hippocampal structural asymmetry in unsuccessful psychopaths. *Biological Psychiatry, 55*(2), 185–191.

Raine, A., Meloy, J. R., Bihrle, S., Stoddard, J., LaCasse, L., & Buchsbaum, M. S. (1998). Reduced prefrontal and increased subcortical brain functioning assessed using positron emission tomography in predatory and affective murderers. *Behavioral Sciences and the Law, 16*(3), 319–332.

Raine, A., Stoddard, J., Bihrle, S., & Buchsbaum, M. S. (1998). Prefrontal glucose deficits in murderers lacking psychosocial deprivation. *Neuropsychiatry, Neuropsychology, and Behavioral Neurology, 11,* 1–7.

Rainville, P., Duncan, H. G., Price, D. D., Carrier, B., & Bushnell, M. C. (1997). Pain affect encoded in human anterior cingulate but not somatosensory cortex. *Science, 277,* 968–971.

Rajnicek, A. M., Foubister, L.E., & McCaig, C.D. (2006). Growth cone steering by a physiological electric field requires dynamic microtubules, microfilaments and Rac-mediated filopodial asymmetry. *Journal of Cell Science, 119,* 1736–1745. doi: 10.1242/jcs.02897

Rakic, P. (1988). Specification of cerebral cortical areas. *Science, 241*(4862), 170–176. doi:10.1126/science.3291116

Raleigh, M. J., Brammer, G. L., McGuire, M. T., Pollack, D. B., & Yuwiler, A. (1992). Individual differences in basal cisternal cerebrospinal fluid F0HIAA and HVA in monkeys: The effects of gender, age, physical characteristics, and matrilineal influences. *Neuropsychopharmacology, 7,* 295–304.

Ralph, M. R., Foster, R. G., Davis, F. C., & Menaker, M. (1990). Transplanted suprachiasmatic nucleus determines circadian period. *Science, 247,* 975–978.

Ramachandran, V. S. (2005). Plasticity and functional recovery in neurology. *Clinical Medicine, 5*(4), 368–373. doi: 10.7861/clinmedicine.5-4-368

Ramachandran, V. S., & Hirstein, W. (1997). Three laws of qualia: What neurology tells us about the biological functions of consciousness. *Journal of Consciousness Studies, 4*(5-6), 5–6.

Ramachandran, V. S., & Rogers-Ramachandran, D. (2000). Phantom limbs and neural plasticity. *Archives of Neurology, 57*(3), 317–320. doi:10-1001/pubs.Arch Neurol.-ISSN-0003-9942-57-3-nnr8257

Ramsden, S., Richardson, F. M., Josse, G., Thomas, M. S. C., Ellis, C., Shakeshaft, C., … Price, C. J. (2011). Verbal and non-verbal intelligence changes in the teenage brain. *Nature, 479*(7371), 113–116. doi:10.1038/nature10514

Rand, M. N., & Breedlove, S. M. (1987). Ontogeny of functional innervation of bulbocavernosus muscles in male and female rats. *Brain Research, 430,* 150–152.

Rapkin, A. J., Mikacich, J. A., Moatakef-Imani, B., & Rasgon, N. (2002). The clinical nature and formal diagnosis of premenstrual, postpartum, and perimenopausal affective disorders. *Current Psychiatry Reports, 4,* 419–428.

Rapoport, J. (1989). *The boy who couldn't stop washing: The experience and treatment of obsessive-compulsive disorder.* New York: Dutton.

Rapoport, J. L., Giedd, J. N., Blumenthal, J., Hamburger, S., Jeffries, N., Fernandez, T., … Evans, A. (1999). Progressive cortical change during adolescence in childhood-onset schizophrenia: A longitudinal magnetic resonance imaging study. *Archives of General Psychiatry, 56*(7), 649–654. doi:10.1001/archpsyc.56.7.649

Rasband, M. N., & Shrager, P. (2000). Ion channel sequestration in central nervous system axons. *The Journal of Physiology, 525*(1), 63–73. doi:10.1111/j.1469-7793.2000.00063.x

Rashid, A. J., & Josselyn, S. A. (2012). Regulation of synaptic plasticity and long-term memory by CREB: Implications for targeting memory disorders including Alzheimer's disease and Rubinstein-Taybi syndrome. In B. C. Albensi (Ed.), *Transcription factors CREB and NF-kB: Involvement in synaptic plasticity and memory formation.* (pp. 3–21). Oak Park, IL: Bentham Science Publishers.

Rasmussen, T., & Milner, B. (1977). The role of early left-brain injury in determining lateralization of cerebral speech functions. *Annals of the New York Academy of Sciences, 299,* 355–369.

Ratajczak, H. V. (2011). Theoretical aspects of autism: Biomarkers—A review. *Journal of Immunotoxicology, 8*(1), 80–94. doi:10.3109/1547691x.2010.538749

Rauschecker, J. P. (2011). An expanded role for the dorsal auditory pathway in sensorimotor control and integration. *Hearing Research, 271*(1–2), 16–25. doi:10.1016/j.heares.2010.09.001

Rauschecker, J. P., & Tian, B. (2000). Mechanisms and streams for processing of "what" and "where" in auditory cortex. *Proceedings of the National Academy of Sciences of the United States of America (PNAS), 97*(22), 11800–11806. doi: 10.1073/pnas.97.22.11800

Ravits, J. (2005). Sporadic amyotrophic lateral sclerosis: A hypothesis of persistent (non-lytic) enteroviral infection. *Amyotrophic lateral sclerosis and other motor neuron disorders: Official publication of the World Federation of Neurology, Research Group on Motor Neuron Diseases, 6*(2), 77–87.

Rawson, N. E. (2006). Olfactory loss in aging. *Science of Aging Knowledge Environment, 2006*(5), pe6.

Reed, S. C., Levin, F. R., & Evans, S. M. (2008). Changes in mood, cognitive performance and appetite in the late luteal and follicular phases of the menstrual cycle in women with and without PMDD (premenstrual dysphoric disorder). *Hormones and Behavior, 54*(1), 185–193.

Regan, C. (2000). *Intoxicating minds.* London: Weidenfeld & Nicolson.

Reid, W. M., & Hamm, R. J. (2008). Post-injury atomoxetine treatment improves cognition following experimental traumatic brain injury. *Journal of Neurotrauma, 25*(3), 248–256. doi:10.1089/neu.2007.0389

Reimann, M., & Bechara, A. (2010). The somatic marker framework as a neurological theory of decision-making: Review, conceptual comparisons, and future neuroeconomics research. *Journal of Economic Psychology, 31*(5), 767–776. doi:10.1016/j.joep.2010.03.002

Reinisch, J. M., Ziemba-Davis, M., & Sanders, S. A. (1991). Hormonal contributions to sexually dimorphic behavioral development in humans. *Psychoneuroendocrinology, 16,* 213–278.

Reisenzein, R. (1983). The Schachter theory of emotion: Two decades later. *Psychological Bulletin, 94,* 239–264. doi:10.1037/0033-2909.94.2.239

Reiterer, S. (2010). The cognitive neuroscience of second language acquisition and bilingualism. In M. Kail & M. Hickmann (Eds.), *Language acquisition across linguistic and cognitive systems* (pp. 307–322). Amsterdam, The Netherlands: John Benjamins Publishing Company.

Rescorla, R. A., & Freberg, L. (1978). Extinction of within compound flavor associations. *Learning and Motivation, 9,* 411–427.

Reuter, B., & Kathmann, N. (2004). Using saccade tasks as a tool to analyze executive dysfunctions in schizophrenia. *Acta Psychologia, 115*(2–3), 255–269.

Revonsuo, A. (2000). The reinterpretation of dreams: An evolutionary hypothesis of the function of dreaming. *The Behavioral and Brain Sciences, 23*(6), 877–901; discussion 904–1121.

Rhee, Y.-H., Ko, J.-Y., Chang, M.-Y., Yi, S.-H., Kim, D., Kim, C.-H., … Lee, S.-H. (2011). Protein-based human iPS cells efficiently generate functional dopamine neurons and can treat a rat model of Parkinson disease. *The Journal of Clinical Investigation, 121*(6), 2326–2335. doi: 10.1172/JCI45794

Ribeiro, S., & Nicolelis, M. A. (2004). Reverberation, storage, and postsynaptic propagation of memories during sleep. *Learning and Memory, 11*(6), 686–696.

Ricardo, J. A. (1981). Efferent connections of the subthalamic region in the rat: II. The zona incerta. *Brain Research, 214,* 43–60.

Richardson, G. A., Larkby, C., Goldschmidt, L., & Day, N. L. (2013). Adolescent initiation of drug use: Effects of prenatal cocaine exposure. *Journal of the American Academy of Child and Adolescent Psychiatry, 52*(1), 37–46. doi:10.1016/j.jaac.2012.10.011

Ridley, M. (1999). *Genome: The autobiography of a species in 23 chapters.* New York: HarperCollins.

Riedel, G., & Davies, S. N. (2005). Cannabinoid function in learning, memory and plasticity. *Handbook of Experimental Pharmacology,168,* 445–477. doi: 10.1007/3-540-26573-2_15

Rinn, W. E. (1984). The neuropsychology of facial expression: A review of the neurological and psychological mechanisms for producing facial expressions. *Psychological Bulletin, 95*(1), 52–77.

Risdall, J. E., & Menon, D. K. (2011). Traumatic brain injury. *Philosophical Transactions of the Royal Society B: Biological Sciences, 366*(1562), 241–250. doi:10.1098/rstb.2010.0230

Ritter, S., Li, A.-J., Wang, Q., & Dinh, T. T. (2011). Minireview: The value of looking backward: The essential role of the hindbrain in counterregulatory responses to glucose deficit. *Endocrinology, 152*(11), 4019–4032. doi:10.1210/en.2010-1458

Ritvo, J. I., & Park, C. (2007). The psychiatric management of patients with alcohol dependence. *Current Treatment Options in Neurology, 9*(5), 381–392.

Rivas-Vazquez, R. A., Blais, M. A., Rey, G. J., & Rivas-Vazquez, A. (2000). Atypical antipsychotic medications: Pharmacological profiles and psychological implications. *Professional Psychology: Research and Practice, 31,* 628–640.

Rivera-Oliver, M., & Díaz-Ríos, M. (2014). Using caffeine and other adenosine receptor antagonists and agonists as therapeutic tools against neurodegenerative diseases: A review. *Life Sciences, 101*(1–2), 1–9. doi:http://dx.doi.org/10.1016/j.lfs.2014.01.083

Rives, N., Simeon, N., Milazzo, J. P., Barthelemy, C., & Mace, B. (2003). Meiotic segregation of sex chromosomes in mosaic and non-mosaic XYY males: Case reports and review of the literature. *International Journal of Andrology, 26,* 242–249.

Rivkin, M. J., Davis, P. E., Lemaster, J. L., Cabral, H. J., Warfield, S. K., Mulkern, R. V., … Frank, D. A. (2008). Volumetric MRI study of brain in children with intrauterine exposure to cocaine, alcohol, tobacco, and marijuana. *Pediatrics, 121*(4), 741–750. doi: 10.1542/peds.2007-1399

Rizzo, L. B., Costa, L. G., Mansur, R. B., Swardfager, W., Belangero, S. I., Grassi-Oliveira, R. et al. (2014). The theory of bipolar disorder as an illness of accelerated aging: Implications for clinical care and research. *Neuroscience & Biobehavioral Reviews, 42,* 157–169. doi:http://dx.doi.org/10.1016/j.neubiorev.2014.02.004

Rizzo, M., Nawrot, M., & Zihl, J. (1995). Motion and shape perception in cerebral akinetopsia. *Brain, 118*(5), 1105–1127. doi:10.1093/brain/118.5.1105

Rizzolatti, G., Fadiga, L., Gallese, V., & Fogassi, L. (1996). Premotor cortex and the recognition of motor actions. *Brain Research. Cognitive Brain Research, 3*(2), 131–141.

Roberts, A. C., & Glanzman, D. L. (2003). Learning in Aplysia: Looking at synaptic plasticity from both sides. *Trends in Neurosciences, 26*(12), 662–670. doi:10.1016/j.tins.2003.09.014

Roberts, M., & Scanlan, L. (1999). *The man who listens to horses.* New York: Ballantine Books.

Roberts, S. C., Gosling, L. M., Carter, V., & Petrie, M. (2008). MHC-correlated odour preferences in humans and the use of oral contraceptives. *Proceedings of the Royal Society B: Biological Sciences, 275*(1652), 2715–2722. doi: 10.1098/rspb.2008.0825

Robillard, R., Naismith, S. L., Rogers, N. L., Ip, T. K. C., Hermens, D. F., Scott, E. M., … Hickie, I. B. (2013). Delayed sleep phase in young people with unipolar or bipolar affective disorders. *Journal of Affective Disorders, 145*(2), 260–263. doi:http://dx.doi.org/10.1016/j.jad.2012.06.006

Robins, L. N., & Regier, D. A. (Eds.). (1991). *Psychiatric disorders in America: The Epidemiologic Catchment Area Study.* New York: The Free Press.

Robins, L. N., Helzer, J. E., & Davis, D. H. (1975). Narcotic use in Southeast Asia and afterward: An interview study of 898 Vietnam returnees. *Archives of General Psychiatry, 32*(8), 955–961. doi:10.1001/archpsyc.1975.01760260019001

Robinson, R. G., Kubos, K. L., Starr, L. B., Rao, K., & Price, T. R. (1984). Mood disorders in stroke patients: Importance of location of lesion. *Brain, 107*(1), 81–93.

Robison, A. J., & Nestler, E. J. (2011). Transcriptional and epigenetic mechanisms of addiction. *Nature Reviews Neuroscience, 12*(11), 623–637. doi:10.1038/nrn3111.

Robleto, K., & Thompson, R. F. (2008). Extinction of a classically conditioned response: Red nucleus and interpositus. *Journal of Neuroscience, 28*(10), 2651–2658.

Rodin, J. (1986). Aging and health: Effects of the sense of control. *Science, 233*, 1271–1276. doi:10.1126/science.3749877

Roecklein, K. A., Wong, P. M., Miller, M. A., Donofry, S. D., Kamarck, M. L., & Brainard, G. C. (2013). Melanopsin, photosensitive ganglion cells, and seasonal affective disorder. *Neuroscience & Biobehavioral Reviews, 37*(3), 229–239. doi:http://dx.doi.org/10.1016/j.neubiorev.2012.12.009

Roenneberg, T., & Merrow, M. (2005). Circadian clocks—The fall and rise of physiology. *Nature Reviews Molecular Cell Biology, 6*(12), 965–971. doi: 10.1038/nrm1766

Rogawski, M. A. (2005). Update on the neurobiology of alcohol withdrawal seizures. *Epilepsy Currents, 5*(6), 225–230.

Rogers, L. J. (2000). Evolution of hemispheric specialization: Advantages and disadvantages. *Brain and Language, 73*, 236–253.

Rogers, L. J. (2002). Advantages and disadvantages of lateralization. In L. J. Rogers & R. J. Andrew (Eds.), *Comparative vertebrate lateralization* (pp. 126–154). Cambridge: Cambridge University Press.

Rogers, L. J., Andrew, R. J., & Johnston, A. N. B. (2007). Light experience and the development of behavioural lateralization in chicks: III. Learning to distinguish pebbles from grains. *Behavioural Brain Research, 177*(1), 61–69.

Rojansky, N., Brzezinski, A., & Schenker, J. G. (1992). Seasonality in human reproduction: An update. *Human Reproduction, 7*, 735–745.

Roland, P. (1993). *Brain activation*. New York: Wiley-Liss.

Rolls, E. T. (2004). The functions of the orbitofrontal cortex. *Brain and Cognition, 55*(1), 11–29.

Ronald, A., & Hoekstra, R. A. (2011). Autism spectrum disorders and autistic traits: A decade of new twin studies. *American Journal of Medical Genetics Part B: Neuropsychiatric Genetics, 156*(3), 255–274. doi:10.1002/ajmg.b.31159

Roney, J. R., Hanson, K. N., Durante, K. M., & Maestripieri, D. (2006). Reading men's faces: Women's mate attractiveness judgments track men's testosterone and interest in infants. *Proceedings of the Royal Society, B: Biological Sciences, 273*(1598), 2169–2175.

Roozendaal, B., McEwen, B. S., & Chattarji, S. (2009). Stress, memory and the amygdala. *Nature Reviews Neuroscience, 10*(6), 423–433. doi:10.1038/nrn2651

Roozendaal, B., Okuda, S., Van der Zee, E. A., & McGaugh, J. L. (2006). Glucocorticoid enhancement of memory requires arousal-induced noradrenergic activation in the basolateral amygdala. *Proceedings of the National Academy of Sciences of the United States of America (PNAS), 103*(17), 6741–6746. doi:10.1073/pnas.0601874103

Rosas, H. D., Doros, G., Gevorkian, S., Malarick, K., Reuter, M., Coutu, J.-P., ... Salat, D. H. (2014). PRECREST: A phase II prevention

and biomarker trial of creatine in at-risk Huntington disease. *Neurology, 82*(10), 850–857. doi: 10.1212/WNL.0000000000000187

Rose, F. D., Brooks, B. M., & Rizzo, A. A. (2005). Virtual reality in brain damage rehabilitation: Review. *Cyberpsychology and Behavior, 8*(3), 241–262. doi:10.1089/cpb.2005.8.241

Rosen, D. R., Siddique, T., Patterson, D., Figlewicz, D. A., Sapp, P., Hentati, A., et al. (1993). Mutations in Cu/Zn superoxide dismutase gene are associated with familial amyotrophic lateral sclerosis. *Nature, 362*, 59–62.

Rosen, G. D. (1996). Cellular, morphometric, ontogenetic and connectional substrates of anatomical asymmetry. *Neuroscience & Biobehavioral Reviews, 20*(4), 607–615. doi:10.1016/0149-7634(95)00073-9

Rosen, J. C., Leitenberg, H., Fisher, C., & Khazam, C. (1986). Binge-eating episodes in bulimia nervosa: The amount and type of food consumed. *International Journal of Eating Disorders, 5*, 255–257.

Rosenbaum, R. S., Priselac, S., Kohler S., Black, S. E., Gao, F., Nadel, L., & Moscovitch, M. (2000). Remote spatial memory in an amnesic person withextensive bilateral hippocampal lesions. *Nature Neuroscience, 3*, 1044–1048.

Roses, A. D. (1997). A model for susceptibility polymorphisms for complex diseases: Apolipoprotein E and Alzheimer disease. *Neurogenetics, 1*(1), 3–11. doi: 10.1007/s100480050001

Rosner, M. H., & Kirven, J. (2007). Exercise-associated hyponatremia. *Clinical Journal of the American Society of Nephrology, 2*(1), 151–161. doi:10.2215/cjn.02730806

Ross, C. A., Aylward, E. H., Wild, E. J., Langbehn, D. R., Long, J. D., Warner, J. H., ... Paulsen, J. S. (2014). Huntington disease: Natural history, biomarkers and prospects for therapeutics. *Nature Reviews Neurology, 10*, 204–216. doi:10.1038/nrneurol.2014.24

Ross, G. W., & Petrovitch, H. (2001). Current evidence for neuroprotective effects of nicotine and caffeine against Parkinson's disease. *Drugs and Aging, 18*(11), 797–806.

Ross, G. W., Abbott, R. D., Petrovitch, H., Morens, D. M., Grandinetti, A., Tung, K. H., et al. (2000). Association of coffee and caffeine intake with the risk of Parkinson disease. *Journal of the American Medical Association (JAMA), 283*, 2674–2679.

Ross, J. L., Roeltgen, D. P., Stefanatos, G., Benecke, R., Zeger, M. P. D., Kushner, H., et al. (2008). Cognitive and motor development during childhood in boys with Klinefelter syndrome. *American Journal of Medical Genetics, 146A*(6), 708–719.

Rossignol, D. A., Genuis, S. J., & Frye, R. E. (2014). Environmental toxicants and autism spectrum disorders: A systematic review. *Translational Psychiatry,4*(2), e360. doi:10.1038/tp.2014.4

Rosvold, H. E., Mirsky, A. F., & Pribram, K. (1954). Influence of amygdalectomy on social behavior in monkeys. *Journal of Comparative Physiology and Psychology, 47*, 173–178.

Roth, J. (2006). Endogenous antipyretics. *Clinica Chimica Acta, 371*(1–2), 13–24.

Rothman, S. M. (1984). Synaptic release of excitatory amino acid neurotransmitter mediates anoxic neuronal death. *Journal of Neuroscience, 4*, 1884–1891.

Routtenberg, A., & Lindy, J. (1965). Effects of the availability of rewarding septal and

hypothalamic stimulation on bar-pressing for food under conditions of deprivation. *Journal of Comparative and Physiological Psychology, 60*, 158–161.

Roy, C. S., & Sherrington, C. S. (1890). On the regulation of the blood supply of the brain. *Journal of Physiology (London), 11*, 85–108.

Roy, R. R., Harkema, S. J., & Edgerton, V. R. (2012). Basic concepts of activity-based interventions for improved recovery of motor function after spinal cord injury. *Archives of Physical Medicine and Rehabilitation, 93*(9), 1487–1497. doi:http://dx.doi.org/10.1016/j.apmr.2012.04.034

Rozin, P., & Pelchat, M. L. (1988). Memories of mammaries: Adaptations to weaning from milk. *Progress in Psychobiology and Physiological Psychology, 13*, 1–29.

Ruano, D., Abecasis, G. R., Glaser, B., Lips, E. S., Cornelisse, L. N., de Jong, A. P. H., ... Posthuma, D. (2010). Functional gene group analysis reveals a role of synaptic heterotrimeric G proteins in cognitive ability. *The American Journal of Human Genetics, 86*(2), 113–125. doi:10.1016/j.ajhg.2009.12.006

Rubenstein, J. L. R., Anderson, S., Shi, L., Miyashita-Lin, E., Bulfone, A., & Hevner, R. (1999). Genetic control of cortical regionalization and connectivity. *Cerebral Cortex, 9*, 524–532. doi: 10.1093/cercor/9.6.524

Rucker, D., Padwal, R., Li, S. K., Curioni, C., & Lau, D. C. (2007). Long term pharmacotherapy for obesity and overweight: Updated meta-analysis. *British Medical Journal, 335*(7631), 1194–1199.

Rudebeck, P. H., Walton, M. E., Smyth, A. N., Bannerman, D. M., & Rushworth, M. F. (2006). Separate neural pathways process different decision costs: *Nature Neuroscience, 9*(9), 1161–1168.

Rule, N. O., Rosen, K. S., Slepian, M. L., & Ambady, N. (2011). Mating interest improves women's accuracy in judging male sexual orientation. *Psychological Science, 22*(7), 881–886. doi:10.1177/0956797611412394

Ruscio, A., Stein, D., Chiu, W., & Kessler, R. (2010). The epidemiology of obsessive-compulsive disorder in the National Comorbidity Survey Replication. *Molecular Psychiatry, 15*(1), 53–63. doi:10.1038/mp.2008.94

Rushton, D. H., Dover, R., Sainsbury, A. W., Norris, M. J., Gilkes, J. J., & Ramsey, I. D. (2001). Why should women have lower reference limits for haemoglobin and ferritin concentrations than men? *British Medical Journal, 322*, 1355–1357.

Rushton, J. P., Fulker, D. W., Neale, M. C., Nias, D. K. B., & Eysenck, H. J. (1986). Altruism and aggression: The heritability of individual differences. *Journal of Personality and Social Psychology, 50*, 1192–1198.

Rushton, W. A. H. (1961). Rhodopsin measurement and dark-adaptation in a subject deficient in cone vision. *The Journal of Physiology, 156*(1), 193–205.

Rushworth, M. F. (2008). Intention, choice, and the medial frontal cortex. *Annals of the New York Academy of Sciences, 1124*, 181–207. doi:10.1196/annals.1440.014

Rushworth, M. F., Behrens, T. E., Rudebeck, P. H., & Walton, M. E. (2007). Contrasting roles for cingulate and orbitofrontal cortex in decisions and social behaviour. *Trends in Cognitive Sciences, 11*(4), 168–176. doi:http://dx.doi.org/10.1016/j.tics.2007.01.004

Rusted, J. M., Evans, S. L., King, S. L., Dowell, N., Tabet, N., & Tofts, P. S. (2013). APOE e4 polymorphism in young adults is associated with improved attention and indexed by distinct neural signatures. *NeuroImage, 65,* 364–373. doi:http://dx.doi.org/10.1016/j.neuroimage.2012.10.010

Saalmann, Y. B., & Kastner, S. (2011). Cognitive and perceptual functions of the visual thalamus. *Neuron, 71*(2), 209–223. doi:10.1016/j.neuron.2011.06.027

Sacco, K. A., Termine, A., & Seyal, A. (2005). Effects of cigarette smoking on spatial working memory and attentional deficits in schizophrenia: Involvement of nicotinic receptor mechanisms. *Archives of General Psychiatry, 62*(6), 649–659.

Sachar, E. J., & Baron, M. (1979). The biology of affective disorders. *Annual Review of Neuroscience, 2*(1), 505–518. doi:10.1146/annurev.ne.02.030179.002445

Sack, R. L., Brandes, R. W., Kendall, A. R., & Lewy, A. J. (2000). Entrainment of free-running circadian rhythms by melatonin in blind people. *New England Journal of Medicine, 343*(15), 1070–1077.

Sackheim, H. A., Greenberg, M. S., Weiman, A. L., Gur, R. C., Hungerbuhler, J. P., & Geschwind, N. (1982). Hemispheric asymmetry in the expression of positive and negative emotions: Neurologic evidence. *Archives of Neurology, 39,* 210–218.

Sackett, G. P. (1966). Monkeys reared in isolation with pictures as visual input: Evidence for an innate releasing mechanism. *Science, 154,* 1468–1473.

Sackheim, H. A., Gur, R. C., & Saucy, M. C. (1978). Emotions are expressed more intensely on the left side of the face. *Science, 202,* 434–436.

Sacks, O. (1985). *The man who mistook his wife for a hat, and other clinical tales.* New York: Summit Books.

Sahu, A., Kalra, P. S., & Kalra, S. P. (1988). Food deprivation and ingestion induce reciprocal changes in neuropeptide Y concentration in the paraventricular nucleus. *Peptides, 9,* 83–86.

Saing, T., Dick, M., Nelson, P. T., Kim, R. C., Cribbs, D. H., & Head, E. (2012). Frontal cortex neuropathology in dementia pugilistica. *Journal of Neurotrauma, 29*(6), 1054–1070. doi:10.1089/neu.2011.1957

Sakai, K., Yamamoto, A., Matsubara, K., Nakamura, S., Naruse, M., Yamagata, M., ... Ueda, M. (2012). Human dental pulp-derived stem cells promote locomotor recovery after complete transection of the rat spinal cord by multiple neuro-regenerative mechanisms. *Journal of Clinical Investigation, 122*(1), 80–90. doi:10.1172/JCI59251

Sakai, Y., Dobson, C., Diksic, M., Aube, M., & Hamel, E. (2008). Sumatriptan normalizes the migraine attack-related increase in brain serotonin synthesis. *Neurology, 70*(6), 431–439.

Sakurai, T. (2002). Roles of orexins in feeding and wakefulness. *Neuroreport, 13,* 987–995.

Sakurai, T., Amemiya, A., Ishii, M., Matsuzaki, I., Chemelli, R. M., Tanaka, H., et al. (1998). Orexins and orexin receptors: A family of hypothalamic neuropeptides and G protein-coupled receptors that regulate feeding behavior. *Cell, 92*(4), 573–585

Salamone, J. D., Cousins, M. S., & Bucher, S. (1994). Anhedonia or anergia? Effects of haloperidol and nucleus accumbens dopamine depletion on instrumental response selection in a T-maze cost/benefit procedure. *Behavioral Brain Research, 65*(2), 221–229.

Salio, C., Lossi, L., Ferrini, F., & Merighi, A. (2006). Neuropeptides as synaptic transmitters. *Cell Tissue Research, 326*(2), 583–598. doi: 10.1007/s00441-006-0268-3

Salmon, S. (2004). The PEACE curriculum: Expanded aggression replacement training. In A. P. Goldstein, R. Nensen, B. Daleflod, & M. Kalt (Eds.), *New perspectives on aggression replacement training* (pp. 171–188). Chichester, UK: Wiley.

Salvesen, K. A. (2007). Epidemiological prenatal ultrasound studies. *Progress in Biophysics and Molecular Biology, 93,* 295–300.

Salvesen, K. Å. (2011). Ultrasound in pregnancy and non-right handedness: meta-analysis of randomized trials. *Ultrasound in Obstetrics & Gynecology, 38*(3), 267–271. doi:10.1002/uog.9055

Sambataro, F., Safrin, M., Lemaitre, H. S., Steele, S. U., Das, S. B., Callicott, J. H., Mattay, V. S. (2012). Normal aging modulates prefrontoparietal networks underlying multiple memory processes. *European Journal of Neuroscience, 36*(11), 3559–3567. doi:10.1111/j.1460-9568.2012.08254.x

Sandberg, A. A., Koepf, G. F., Ishiara, T., & Hauschka, T. S. (1961). An XYY human male. *Lancet, 2,* 488–489.

Santosa, C. M., Strong, C. M., Nowakowska, C., Wang, P. W., Rennicke, C. M., & Ketter, T. A. (2007). Enhanced creativity in bipolar disorder patients: A controlled study. *Journal of Affective Disorders, 100*(1–3), 31–39.

Sapolsky, R. (2001). *A primate's memoir.* New York: Scribner.

Sapolsky, R. M., Krey, L. C., & McEwen, B. S. (1985). Prolonged glucocorticoid exposure reduces hippocampal neuron number: Implications for aging. *Journal of Neuroscience, 5,* 1222–1227.

Sartorius, N., Jablensky, A., Korten, A., Ernberg, G., Anker, M., Cooper, J. E., et al. (1986). Early manifestations and first-contact incidence of schizophrenia in different cultures. A preliminary report on the initial evaluation phase of the WHO Collaborative Study on determinants of outcome of severe mental disorders. *Psychological Medicine, 16,* 909–928.

Sathyanarayana, S., Karr, C. J., Lozano, P., Brown, E., Calafat, A. M., Liu, F., et al. (2008). Baby Care products: Possible sources of infant phthalate exposure. *Pediatrics, 121*(2), e260–268.

Satinoff, E. (1964). Behavioral thermoregulation in response to local cooling of the rat brain. *American Journal of Physiology, 206,* 1389–1394.

Satinoff, E. (1978). Neural organization and evolution of thermal regulation in mammals. *Science, 201,* 16–22.

Sato, Y., Mori, K., Koizumi, T., Minagawa-Kawai, Y., Tanaka, A., Ozawa, E., ... Mazuka, R. (2011). Functional lateralization of speech processing in adults and children who stutter. *Frontiers in Psychology, 2.* doi:10.3389/fpsyg.2011.00070

Savage-Rumbaugh, S., Shanker, S. G., & Taylor, T. J. (1998). *Apes, language, and the human mind.* New York: Oxford University Press.

Savine, R., & Sonksen, P. (2000). Growth hormone: Hormone replacement for the somatopause? *Hormone Research, 53*(Suppl. 3), 37–41.

Savolainen-Peltonen, H., Hautamäki, H., Tuomikoski, P., Ylikorkala, O., & Mikkola, T. S. (2014). Health-related quality of life in women with or without hot flashes: A randomized placebo-controlled trial with hormone therapy. *Menopause, 21*(7), 732–739. doi:10.1097/GME.0000000000000120.

Saxena, S. (2003). Neuroimaging and the pathophysiology of obsessive compulsive disorder (OCD). In C. H. Y. Fu, C. Senior, T. Russell, D. Weinberger, & R. Murray (Eds.), *Neuroimaging in psychiatry* (pp. 191–224). London, UK: Martin Dunitz.

Sbordone, R. J., Liter, J. C., & Pettler-Jennings, P. (1995). Recovery of function following severe traumatic brain injury: A retrospective 10-year follow-up. *Brain Injury, 9,* 285–299.

Scarmeas, N., Shih, T., Stern, Y., Ottman, R., & Rowland, L. P. (2002). Premorbid weight, body mass, and varsity athletics in ALS. *Neurology, 59*(5), 773–775.

Scarone, P., Gatignol, P., Guillaume, S., Denvil, D., Capelle, L., & Duffau, H. (2009). Agraphia after awake surgery for brain tumor: New insights into the anatomo-functional network of writing. *Surgical Neurology, 72*(3), 223–241. doi:10.1016/j.surneu.2008.10.074

Schachter, S., & Singer, J. (1962). Cognitive, social and physiological determinants of emotional state. *Psychological Review, 69,* 379–399.

Schaffer, C. E., Davidson, R. J., & Saron, C. (1983). Frontal and parietal electroencephalogram asymmetry in depressed and nondepressed subjects. *Biological Psychiatry, 18,* 753–762.

Schaffir, J. (2006). Hormonal contraception and sexual desire: A critical review. *Journal of Sex and Marital Therapy, 32*(4), 305–314. doi: 10.1080/00926230600666311

Schaie, K. W. (1994). The course of adult intellectual development. *American Psychologist, 49,* 304–313.

Scheibel, A., Paul, L., Fried, I., Forsythe, A., Tomiyasu, U., Wechsler, A., ... Slotnick, J. (1985). Dendritic organization of the anterior speech area. *Experimental Neurology, 87*(1), 109–117. doi:10.1016/0014-4886(85)90137-2

Schenck, C. H., Bundlie, S. R., Ettinger, M. G., & Mahowald, M. W. (1986). Chronic behavioral disorders of human REM sleep: A new category of parasomnia. *Sleep, 9,* 293–308.

Schernhammer, E. S., & Schulmeister, K. (2004). Melatonin and cancer risk: Does light at night compromise physiologic cancer protection by lowering serum melatonin levels? *British Journal of Cancer, 90*(5), 941–943.

Schernhammer, E. S., Kroenke, C. H., Dowsett, M., Folkerd, E., & Hankinson, S. E. (2006). Urinary 6-sulfatoxymelatonin levels and their correlations with lifestyle factors and steroid hormone levels. *Journal of Pineal Research, 40*(2), 116–124.

Schlaug, G., Jancke, L., Huang, Y., & Steinmetz, H. (1995). In vivo evidence of structural brain asymmetry in musicians. *Science, 267,* 699–701.

Schlessinger, D., Herrera, L., Crisponi, L., Mumm, S., Percesepe, A., Pellegrini, M., et al. (2002). Genes and translocations involved in POF. *American Journal of Medical Genetics, 111*(3), 328–333.

Schmahmann, J. (2010). The role of the cerebellum in cognition and emotion: Personal reflections since 1982 on the dysmetria of thought hypothesis, and its historical evolution from theory to therapy. *Neuropsychology Review, 20*(3), 236–260. doi:10.1007/s11065-010-9142-x

Schmolesky, M. T., Wang, Y., Pu, M., & Leventhal, A. G. (2000). Degradation of stimulus selectivity of visual cortical cells in senescent rhesus monkeys. *Nature Neuroscience, 3,* 384–390.

Schneider, E. B., Sur, S., Raymont, V., Duckworth, J., Kowalski, R. G., Efron, D. T., ... Stevens, R. D. (2014). Functional recovery after moderate/severe traumatic brain injury A role for cognitive reserve? *Neurology, 82*(18), 1636–1642. doi:10.1212/WNL.0000000000000379

Schneider, F., Gur, R. C., Koch, K., Backes, V., Amunts, K., Shah, N. J., ... Habel, U. (2006). Impairment in the specificity of emotion processing in schizophrenia. *The American Journal of Psychiatry, 163*(3), 442–447. doi:10.1176/appi.ajp.163.3.442

Schredl, M., Ciric, P., Gotz, S., & Wittmann, L. (2004). Typical dreams: Stability and gender differences. *Journal of Psychology, 138*(6), 485–494.

Schulze, K., McDonald, C., Frangou, S., Sham, P., Grech, A., Toulopoulou, T., et al. (2003). Hippocampal volume in familial and nonfamilial schizophrenic probands and their unaffected relatives. *Biological Psychiatry, 53*, 562–570.

Schwab, M. E., Suda, K., & Thoenen, H. (1979). Selective retrograde transsynaptic transfer of a protein, tetanus toxin, subsequent to its retrograde axonal transport. *Journal of Cell Biology, 82*(3), 798–810. doi:10.1083/jcb.82.3.798

Schwabe, L., & Wolf, O. T. (2010). Learning under stress impairs memory formation. *Neurobiology of Learning and Memory, 93*(2), 183–188. doi:10.1016/j.nlm.2009.09.009

Schwabe, L., Joëls, M., Roozendaal, B., Wolf, O. T., & Oitzl, M. S. (2012). Stress effects on memory: An update and integration. *Neuroscience & Biobehavioral Reviews, 36*(7), 1740–1749. doi:10.1016/j.neubiorev.2011.07.002

Schwartz, J. H. (2000). Neurotransmitters. In E. R. Kandel, J. H. Schwartz & T. M. Jessell (Eds.), *Principles of neural science* (4th ed., pp. 280–297). New York: McGraw-Hill.

Schwartz, W., & Gainer, H. (1977). Suprachiasmatic nucleus: Use of 14C-labelled deoxyglucose uptake as a functional marker. *Science, 197*, 1089–1091.

Schwartz, W., Reppert, S. M., Eagan, S. M., & Moore-Ede, M. C. (1983). In vivo metabolic activity of the suprachiasmatic nuclei: A comparative study. *Brain Research, 274*, 184–187.

Sciutto, M. J., & Eisenberg, M. (2007). Evaluating the evidence for and against the overdiagnosis of ADHD. *Journal of Attention Disorders, 11*(2), 106–113. doi:10.1177/1087054707300094

Sclafani, A., Springer, D., & Kluge, L. (1976). Effects of quinine adulteration on the food intake and body weight of obese and nonobese hypothalamic hyperphagic rats. *Physiology and Behavior, 16*, 631–640.

Scott, J. A., Schumann, C. M., Goodlin-Jones, B. L., & Amaral, D. G. (2009). A comprehensive volumetric analysis of the cerebellum in children and adolescents with autism spectrum disorder. *Autism Research, 2*(5), 246–257. doi:10.1002/aur.97

Scott, W., Stevens, J., & Binder–Macleod, S. A. (2001). Human skeletal muscle fiber type classifications. *Physical Therapy, 81*(11), 1810–1816.

Search and Rescue Society of British Columbia. (1995). *Hypothermia: Physiology, signs, symptoms, and treatment considerations.* Retrieved from the Search and Rescue Society of British Columbia Web site: http://www.sarbc.org/hypo1.html.

Sears, C. L. (2005). A dynamic partnership: Celebrating our gut flora. *Anaerobe, 11*(5), 247–251. doi: 10.1016/j.anaerobe.2005.05.001

Sebat, J., Lakshmi, B., Malhotra, D., Troge, J., Lese-Martin, C., Walsh, T., ... Wigler, M. (2007). Strong association of de novo copy number mutations with autism. *Science, 316*, 445–449.

Sebrechts, M. M., Marsh, R. L., & Seamon, J. G. (1989). Secondary memory and very rapid forgetting. *Memory & Cognition, 17*, 693–700.

Seeley, W. W., Merkle, F. T., Gaus, S. E., Craig, A. D., Allman, J. M., & Hof, P. R. (2012). Distinctive neurons of the anterior cingulate and frontoinsular cortex: A historical perspective. *Cerebral Cortex, 22*, 245–250. doi:10.1093/cercor/bhr005

Segerstrom, S. C., & Miller, G. E. (2004). Psychological stress and the human immune system: A meta-analytic study of 30 years of inquiry. *Psychological Bulletin, 130*, 601–630. doi:10.1037/0033-2909.130.4.601

Sehgal, A., Price, J. L., Man, B., & Young, M. W. (1994). Loss of circadian behavioral rhythms and per RNA oscillations in the *Drosophila* mutant timeless. *Science, 263*, 1603–1606.

Seksel, K., & Lindeman, M. J. (2001). Use of clomipramine in treatment of obsessive-compulsive disorder, separation anxiety and noise phobia in dogs: A preliminary, clinical study. *Australian Veterinary Journal, 79*, 252–256.

Selverstone, V. J., Doucette, P. A., & Zittin, P. S. (2005). Copper-zinc superoxide dismutase and amyotrophic lateral sclerosis. *Annual Review of Biochemistry, 74*, 563–593.

Selye, H. (1936). A syndrome produced by diverse nocuous agents. *Nature, 138*, 32.

Selye, H. (1946). The general adaptation syndrome and the diseases of adaptation. *Journal of Clinical Endocrinology, 6*, 177–231.

Selye, H. (1976). *The stress of life.* New York: McGraw-Hill.

Sen, N., & Snyder, S. H. (2010). Protein modifications involved in neurotransmitter and gasotransmitter signaling. *Trends in Neurosciences, 33*(11), 493–502. doi:10.1016/j.tins.2010.07.004

Serbin, L. A., Poulin-Dubois, Colburne, K. A., Sen, M. G., & Eichstedt, J. A. (2001). Gender stereotyping in infancy: Visual preferences for and knowledge of gender-stereotyped toys in the second year. *International Journal of Behavioral Development, 25*(1), 7–15.

Sereno, M. I., & Tootell, R. B. H. (2005). From monkeys to humans: What do we now know about brain homologies? *Current Opinion in Neurobiology, 15*, 135–144. doi: 10.1016/j.conb.2005.03.014

Seroczynski, A. D., Bergeman, C. S., & Coccaro, E. F. (1999). Etiology of the impulsivity/aggression relationship: Genes or environment? *Psychiatry Research, 86*(1), 41–57.

Serpa, J. A., & Clinton White, A. (2012). Neurocysticercosis in the United States. *Pathogens and Global Health, 106*(5), 256–260. doi:10.1179/2047773212y.0000000028

Shaner, A., Miller, G., & Mintz, J. (2004). Schizophrenia as one extreme of a sexually selected fitness indicator. *Schizophrenia Research, 70*, 101–109.

Shaw, P. J., Cirelli, C., Greenspan, R. J., & Giulio Tononi, G. (2000). Correlates of sleep and waking in *Drosophila melanogaster*. *Science, 287*, 1834–1837.

Shaw, P., Eckstrand, K., Sharp, W., Blumenthal, J., Lerch, J. P., Greenstein, D., ... Rapoport, J. L. (2007). Attention-deficit/hyperactivity disorder is characterized by a delay in cortical maturation. *Proceedings of the National Academy of Sciences of the United States of America (PNAS), 104*(49), 19649–19654. doi:10.1073/pnas.0707741104

Shaw, P., Malek, M., Watson, B., Greenstein, D., de Rossi, P., & Sharp, W. (2013). Trajectories of cerebral cortical development in childhood and adolescence and adult attention-deficit/hyperactivity disorder. *Biological Psychiatry, 74*(8), 599–606. doi:10.1016/j.biopsych.2013.04.007

Shaywitz, B. A., Shaywitz, S. E., Pugh, K. R., Constable, R. T., Skudlarski, P., Fulbright, R. K., ... Gore, J. C. (1995). Sex differences in the functional organization of the brain for language. *Nature, 373*(6515), 607–609. doi:10.1038/373607a0

Shaywitz, S. E., Morris, R., & Shaywitz, B. A. (2008). The education of dyslexic children from childhood to young adulthood. *Annual Review of Psychology, 59*, 451–475.

Shelton, J. F., Tancredi, D. J., & Hertz-Picciotto, I. (2010). Independent and dependent contributions of advanced maternal and paternal ages to autism risk. *Autism Research, 3*(1), 30–39. doi:10.1002/aur.116

Shema, R., Sacktor, T. C., & Dudai, Y. (2007). Rapid erasure of long-term memory associations in the cortex by an inhibitor of PKM zeta. *Science, 317*(5840), 951–953.

Shen, M. D., Nordahl, C. W., Young, G. S., Wootton-Gorges, S. L., Lee, A., Liston, S. E., ... Amaral, D. G. (2013). Early brain enlargement and elevated extra-axial fluid in infants who develop autism spectrum disorder. *Brain, 136*(9), 2825–2835. doi:10.1093/brain/awt166

Shen, X., Orson, F. M., & Kosten, T. R. (2011). Anti-addiction vaccines. *F1000 Medical Reports, 3*(20). doi:10.3410/M3-20

Sheng, H.-W. (2000). Sodium, chloride, and potassium. In M. Stipanuk (Ed.), *Biochemical and physiological aspects of human nutrition* (pp. 686–710). Philadelphia, PA: Saunders.

Shepherd, S., & Martin, J. M. (2002). *Submersion injury, near drowning.* Retrieved from http://www.emedicine.com/emerg/topic744.htm.

Sherman, S. M., & Guillery, R. W. (2002). The role of the thalamus in the flow of information to the cortex. *Philosophical Transactions of the Royal Society B: Biological Sciences, 357*, 1695–1708. doi:10.1098/rstb.2002.1161

Shi, J., Potash, J., Knowles, J., Weissman, M., Coryell, W., Scheftner, W., ... Levinson, D. F. (2011). Genome-wide association study of recurrent early-onset major depressive disorder. *Molecular Psychiatry, 16*(2), 193–201. doi:10.1038/mp.2009.124

Shi, L., Butt, B., Ip, F. C. F., Dai, Y., Jiang, L., Yung, W.-H. et al. (2010). Ephexin1 is required for structural maturation and neurotransmission at the neuromuscular junction. *Neuron, 65*(2), 204–216. doi:10.1016/j.neuron.2010.01.012

Shifren, J. L., Braunstein, G. D., Simon, J. A., Casson, P. R., Buster, J. E., Redmond, G. P., et al. (2000). Transdermal testosterone treatment in women with impaired sexual function after oophorectomy. *New England Journal of Medicine, 343*(10), 682–688.

Shih, R. A., Belmonte, P. L., & Zandi, P. P. (2004). A review of the evidence from family, twin and adoption studies for a genetic contribution to adult psychiatric disorders. *International Review of Psychiatry, 16*(4), 260–283.

Shima, K., & Tanji, J. (1998). Role for cingulate motor area cells in voluntary movement selection based on reward. *Science, 282*(5392), 1335–1338.

Shimada, M., Tritos, N. A., Lowell, B. B., Flier, J. S., & Maratos-Flier, E. (1999). Mice lacking melanin-concentrating hormone are hypophagic and lean. *Nature, 396*, 670–674.

Shimoda, K., & Robinson, R. G. (1999). The relationship between poststroke depression and lesion location in long-term follow-up. *Biological Psychiatry, 45*, 187–192.

Shin, J.-H., Pan, X., Hakim, C. H., Yang, H. T., Yue, Y., Zhang, K., ... Duan, D. (2013). Microdystrophin ameliorates muscular dystrophy in the canine model of Duchenne muscular dystrophy. *Molecular Therapy, 21*(4), 750–757. doi: 10.1038/mt.2012.283

Siegel, J. J., Kalmbach, B., Chitwood, R. A., & Mauk, M. D. (2012). Persistent activity in a cortical-to-subcortical circuit: Bridging the temporal gap in trace eyelid conditioning. *Journal of Neurophysiology, 107*(1), 50–64. doi:10.1152/jn.00689.2011

Siegel, J. M. (1999). Narcolepsy: A key role for hypocretins (orexins). *Cell, 98*(4), 409–412.

Siegel, J. M. (2004). Hypocretin (orexin): Role in normal behavior and neuropathology. *Annual Review of Psychology, 55*, 125–148.

Siegel, J. M. (2005). Clues to the functions of mammalian sleep. *Nature, 437*(7063), 1264–1271.

Siegel, J. M. (2008). Do all animals sleep? *Trends in Neurosciences, 31*(4), 208–213.

Siegel, J. M., & Rogawski, M. A. (1988). A function for REM sleep: Regulation of noradrenergic receptor sensitivity. *Brain Research Review, 13*, 213–233.

Siegel, J. Z., & Crockett, M. J. (2013). How serotonin shapes moral judgment and behavior. *Annals of the New York Academy of Sciences, 1299*(1), 42–51. doi:10.1111/nyas.12229

Siegel, S., Hinson, R. E., Krank, M. D., & McCully, J. (1982). Heroin "overdose" death: Contribution of drug-associated environmental cues. *Science, 216*(4544), 436–437. doi: http://dx.doi.org/10.1126/science.7200260

Siever, L. J. (2008). Neurobiology of aggression and violence. *The American Journal of Psychiatry, 165*(4), 429–442.

Silvanto, J. (2008). A re-evaluation of blindsight and the role of striate cortex (V1) in visual awareness. *Neuropsychologia, 46*(12), 2869–2871.

Simon, R. P., Swan, J. H., Griffi ths, T., & Meldrum, B. S. (1984). Blockage of N-methyl-D-aspartate receptors may protect against ischemic damage in the brain. *Science, 226*, 850–852.

Simopoulos, A. P. (2011). Evolutionary aspects of diet: The omega-6/omega-3 ratio and the brain. *Molecular Neurobiology, 44*(2), 203–215. doi:10.1007/s12035-010-8162-0

Simpson, J. B., Epstein, A. N., & Camardo, J. S. (1978). The localization of dipsogenic receptors for angiotensin II in the subfornical organ. *Journal of Comparative and Physiological Psychology, 92*, 581–608.

Sinclair, A. H., Berta, P., Palmer, M. S., Hawkins, J. R., Griffi ths, B. L., Smith, M. J., et al. (1990). A gene from the human sex-determining region encodes a protein with homology to a conserved DNA binding motif. *Nature, 346*, 240–244.

Sinclair, R. C., Hoff man, C., Mark, M. M., Martin, L. L., & Pickering, T. L. (1994). Construct accessibility and the misattribution of arousal. *Psychological Science, 5*, 15–19.

Singleton, A. B., Farrer, M. J., & Bonifati, V. (2013). The genetics of Parkinson's disease: Progress and therapeutic implications. *Movement Disorders, 28*(1), 14–23. doi:10.1002/mds.25249

Skafidas, E., Testa, R., Zantomio, D., Chana, G., Everall, I., & Pantelis, C. (2012). Predicting the diagnosis of autism spectrum disorder using gene pathway analysis. *Molecular Psychiatry, 19*, 504–510. doi:10.1038/mp.2012.126

Skene, D. J., Lockley, S. W., & Arendt, J. (1999). Use of melatonin in the treatment of phase shift and sleep disorders. *Advances in Experimental Medicine and Biology, 467*, 79–84.

Skuse, D., James, R., Bishop, D., Coppin, B., Dalton, P., Aamodt-Leeper, G., ... Jacobs, P. A. (1997). Evidence from Turner's syndrome of an imprinted X-linked locus affecting cognitive function. *Nature, 387*(6634), 705–708.

Slevc, L. R. (2012). Language and music: Sound, structure, and meaning. *WIREs Cognitive Science 3*, 483–492. doi:10.1002/wcs.1186

Slob, A. K., Bax, C. M., Hop, W. C., Rowland, D. L., & van der Werff ten Bosch, J. J. (1996). Sexual arousability and the menstrual cycle. *Psychoneuroendocrinology, 21*, 545–558.

Slotema, C. W., Blom, J. D., Koek, H. W., & Sommer, I. E. C. (2010). Should we expand the toolbox of psychiatric treatment methods to include repetitive transcranial magnetic stimulation (rTMS)? A meta-analysis of the efficacy of rTMS in psychiatric disorders. *Journal of Clinical Psychiatry, 71*(7), 873–884. doi:10.4088/JCP.08m04872gre

Smith, A., & Sugar, O. (1975). Development of above normal language and intelligence 21 years after left hemispherectomy. *Neurology, 25*(9), 813–818.

Smith, C., & Fazekas, A. (1997). Amounts of REM sleep and stage 2 sleep required for efficient learning. *Sleep Research, 26*, 960.

Smith, C., & MacNeill, C. (1994) Impaired motor memory for a pursuit rotor task following Stage 2 sleep loss in college students. *Journal of Sleep Research, 3*(4), 206–213.

Smith, C. S., Reilly, C., & Midkiff, K. (1989). Evaluation of three circadian rhythm questionnaires with suggestions for an improved measure of morningness. *Journal of Applied Psychology, 74*(5), 728–738. doi:10.1037/0021-9010.74.5.728

Smith, P. M., Beninger, R. J., & Ferguson, A. V. (1995). Subfornical organ stimulation elicits drinking. *Brain Research Bulletin, 38*, 209–213.

Smith, T. W. (1992). Hostility and health: Current status of a psychosomatic hypothesis. *Health Psychology, 11*, 139–150.

Smith, T., & Lovaas, I. (1998). Intensive early behavioral intervention with autism: The UCLA Young Autism Project. *Infants and Young Children, 10*, 67–78.

Snapinn, K. W., Holmes, E. C., Young, D. S., Bernard, K. A., Kramer, L. D., & Ebel, G. D. (2007). Declining growth rate of West Nile virus in North America. *Journal of Virology, 81*(5), 2531–2534.

Sneed, D. (2006). Teen murder suspect's judgment could be impaired, says doctor. *The Tribune,* p. B1.

Snowdon, D. (1997). Aging and Alzheimer's disease: Lessons from the nun study. *Gerontologist, 37*, 150–156.

Snyder, A., Bahramali, H., Hawker, T., & Mitchell, D.J. (2006). Savant-like numerosity skills revealed in normal people by magnetic pulses. *Perception, 35*(6), 837–845.

Snyder, J. S., Radik, R., Wojtowicz, J. M., & Cameron, H. A. (2009). Anatomical gradients of adult neurogenesis and activity: Young neurons in the ventral dentate gyrus are activated by water maze training. *Hippocampus, 19*(4), 360–370. doi:10.1002/hipo.20525

Snyder, J. S., Soumier, A., Brewer, M., Pickel, J., & Cameron, H. A. (2011). Adult hippocampal neurogenesis buffers stress responses and depressive behaviour. *Nature, 476*(7361), 458–461. doi: 10.1038/nature10287

Snyder, S. H., & Dawson, T.M.. (2000). Nitric oxide and related substance as neural messengers. *Psychopharmacology: The fourth generation of progress.* Nashville, TN: American College of Neuropsychopharmacology.

Sobel, N., Prabhakaran, V., Zhao, Z., Desmond, J. E., Glover, G. H., Sullivan, E. V., et al. (2000).

Time course of odorant—induced activation in the human primary olfactory cortex. *Journal of Neurophysiology, 83*, 537–551.

Society for Neuroscience. (2012). About membership. http://www.sfn.org/index.cfm?pagename=membership_AboutMembership&section=membership

Soeiro-de-Souza, M. G., Andreazza, A. C., Carvalho, A. F., Machado-Vieira, R., Young, L. T., & Moreno, R. A. (2013). Number of manic episodes is associated with elevated DNA oxidation in bipolar I disorder. *The International Journal of Neuropsychopharmacology, 16*(7), 1505–1512. doi:10.1017/S1461145713000047

Sommer, I. E. C., Cohen-Kettenis, P. T., van Raalten, T., Vd Veer, A. J., Ramsey, L. A., Gooren, L. J., ... Ramsey, N. F. (2008). Effects of cross-sex hormones on cerebral activation during language and mental rotation: An fMRI study in transsexuals. *European Neuropsychopharmacology: The Journal of the European College of Neuropsychopharmacology, 18*(3), 215–221.

Sommer, I., Ramsey, N., Kahn, R., Aleman, A., & Bouma, A. (2001). Handedness, language lateralisation and anatomical asymmetry in schizophrenia: Meta-analysis. *The British Journal of Psychiatry, 178*(4), 344–351. doi:10.1192/bjp.178.4.344

Sonsalla, P. K., Wong, L.-Y., Harris, S. L., Richardson, J. R., Khobahy, I., Li, W., ... German, D. C. (2012). Delayed caffeine treatment prevents nigral dopamine neuron loss in a progressive rat model of Parkinson's disease. *Experimental Neurology, 234*(2), 482–487. doi:10.1016/j.expneurol.2012.01.022

Soomro, G. M., Altman, D., Rajagopal, S., & Oakley-Browne, M. (2008). Selective serotonin re-uptake inhibitors (SSRIs) versus placebo for obsessive compulsive disorder (OCD). *Cochrane Database of Systematic Reviews* 2008(1): CD001765.

Soon, C. S., Brass, M., Heinze, H.-J., & Haynes, J.-D. (2008). Unconscious determinants of free decisions in the human brain. *Nature Neuroscience, 11*(5), 543–545. doi: 10.1038/nn.2112

Sørensen, K. (1987). *Klinefelter's syndrome in childhood, adolescence and youth: A genetic, clinical, developmental, psychiatric and psychological study.* Chippenham, UK: Parthenon.

Sorenson, J. M., Wheless, J. W., Baumgartner, J. E., Thomas, A. B., Brookshire, B. L., Clifton, G. L., & Willmore, L. J. (1997). Corpus callosotomy for medically intractable seizures. *Pediatric Neurosurgery, 27*, 260–267.

Soria, V., Martinez-Amoros, E., Escaramis, G., Valero, J., Perez-Egea, R., Garcia, C., ... Urretavizcaya, M. (2010). Differential association of circadian genes with mood disorders: CRY1 and NPAS2 are associated with unipolar major depression and CLOCK and VIP with bipolar disorder. *Neuropsychopharmacology, 35*(6), 1279–1289. doi:10.1038/npp.2009.230

Sorita, E., N'Kaoua, B., Larrue, F., Criquillon, J., Simion, A., Sauzéon, H., ... Mazaux, J. M. (2012). Do patients with traumatic brain injury learn a route in the same way in real and virtual environments? *Disability and Rehabilitation, 35*(16), 1371–1379. doi:10.3109/09638288.2012.738761

Sorokowski, P., Sorokowska, A., & Witzel, C. (2014). Sex differences in color preferences transcend extreme differences in culture and ecology. *Psychonomic Bulletin & Review, 21*(5), 1195–1201. doi: 10.3758/s13423-014-0591-8.

Sowell, E. R., Thompson, P. M., Holmes, C. J., Jernigan, T. L., & Toga, A. W. (1999). In vivo evidence for post-adolescent brain maturation in frontal and striatal regions. *Nature Neuroscience, 2*(10), 859–861. doi:10.1038/13154

Sparrow, R. (2005). Defending deaf culture: The case of cochlear implants. *Journal of Political Philosophy, 13*(2), 135–152. doi: 10.1111/j.1467-9760.2005.00217.x

Spearman, C. E. (1904). "General intelligence" objectively determined and measured. *American Journal of Psychology, 5,* 201–293. doi:10.2307/1412107

Spehr, M., & Munger, S. D. (2009). Olfactory receptors: G protein-coupled receptors and beyond. *Journal of Neurochemistry, 109*(6), 1570–1583. doi:10.1111/j.1471-4159.2009.06085.x

Spence, S. A., Kaylor-Hughes, C., Farrow, T. F., & Wilkinson, I. D. (2008). Speaking of secrets and lies: The contribution of ventrolateral prefrontal cortex to vocal deception. *NeuroImage, 40*(3), 1411–1418.

Spencer, T. J., Biederman, J., Faraone, S. V., Madras, B. K., Bonab, A. A., Dougherty, D. D., … Fischman, A. J. (2013). Functional genomics of attention-deficit/hyperactivity disorder (ADHD) risk alleles on dopamine transporter binding in ADHD and healthy control subjects. *Biological Psychiatry, 74*(2), 84–89. doi:10.1016/j.biopsych.2012.11.010

Sperling, R. (2007). Functional MRI studies of associative encoding in normal aging, mild cognitive impairment, and Alzheimer's disease. *Annals of the New York Academy of Sciences, 1097,* 146–155.

Sperry, R. W. (1974). Lateral specialization in the surgically separated hemispheres. In F. O. Schmitt & F. G. Worden (Eds.), *The neurosciences: Third study program* (pp. 5–20). Cambridge, MA: MIT Press.

Sperry, R. W. (1982). Some effects of disconnecting the cerebral hemispheres. *Science, 217,* 1223–1226.

Spina Bifida Association of America. (2001). *Facts about spina bifida.* Retrieved from the Spina Bifida Association of America Web site: http://www.sbaa.org/html/sbaa_facts.html.

Spoormaker, V. I., & van den Bout, J. (2006). Lucid dreaming treatment for nightmares: A pilot study. *Psychotherapy and Psychosomatics, 75*(6), 389–394.

Springer, S. P., & Deutsch, G. (1998). *Left brain, right brain* (5th ed.). New York: Freeman.

Spudich, S., & González-Scarano, F. (2012). HIV-1-related central nervous system disease: Current issues in pathogenesis, diagnosis, and treatment. *Cold Spring Harbor Perspectives in Medicine, 2*(6). doi:10.1101/cshperspect.a007120

Squire, L. R. (1987). *Memory and the brain.* New York: Oxford University Press.

Squire, L. R., & Moore, R. Y. (1979). Dorsal thalamic lesion in a noted case of chronic memory dysfunction. *Annals of Neurology, 6,* 503–506.

Squire, L. R., Amaral, D. G., Zola-Morgan, S., & Kritchevsky, M. P. G. (1989). Description of brain injury in the amnesic patient N. A. based on magnetic resonance imaging. *Experimental Neurology, 105,* 23–35.

Stacher, G. (1986). Effects of cholecystokinin and caerulein on human eating behavior and pain sensation: A review. *Psychoneuroendocrinology, 11,* 39–48.

Stader, S. R., & Hokanson, J. E. (1998). Psychosocial antecedents of depressive symptoms: An evaluation using daily experiences methodology. *Journal of Abnormal Psychology, 107,* 17–26.

Stahl, L. A., Begg, D. P., Weisinger, R. S., & Sinclair, A. J. (2008). The role of omega-3 fatty acids in mood disorders. *Current Opinion in Investigational Drugs, 9*(1), 57–64.

Stanley, B. G., Magdalin, W., Seirafi , A., Thomas, W. J., & Leibowitz, S. F. (1993). The perifornical area: The major focus of (a) patchily distributed hypothalamic neuropeptide Y-sensitive feeding system(s). *Brain Research, 604,* 304–317.

Stanley, S. A., Connan, F., Small, C. J., Murphy, K. G., Todd, J. F., Ghatei, M., et al. (2003). Elevated circulating levels of cocaine- and amphetamine-regulated transcript (CART) in anorexia nervosa. *Endocrine Abstracts, 5,* OC30.

Stein-Behrens, B., Mattson, M. P., Chang, I., Yeh, M., & Sapolsky, R. (1994). Stress exacerbates neuron loss and cytoskeletal pathology in the hippocampus. *Journal of Neuroscience, 14,* 5373–5380.

Steiner, M., Brown, E., Trzepacz, P., Dillon, J., Berger, C., Carter, D., et al. (2003). Fluoxetine improves functional work capacity in women with premenstrual dysphoric disorder. *Archives of Women's Mental Health, 6,* 71–77.

Steinhausen, H.-C., Willms, J., & Spohr, H.-L. (1993). Long-term psychopathological and cognitive outcome of children with fetal alcohol syndrome. *Journal of the American Academy of Child and Adolescent Psychiatry, 32,* 990–994. doi: 10.1111/j.1530-0277.1998.tb03657.x

Stella, N., Schweitzer, P., & Piomelli, D. (1997). A second endogenous cannabinoid that modulates long-term potentiation. *Nature, 388*(6644), 773–778. doi: 10.1038/42015

Stellar, J. R., Kelley, A. E., & Corbett, D. (1983). Effects of peripheral and central dopamine blockade on lateral hypothalamic self-stimulation: Evidence for both reward and motor deficits. *Pharmacology, Biochemistry, and Behavior, 18,* 433–442.

Stephan, F. K., & Zucker, I. (1972). Circadian rhythms in drinking behavior and locomotor activity of rats are eliminated by hypothalamic lesions. *Proceedings of the National Academy of Sciences of the United States of America (PNAS), 69,* 1583–1586.

Steriade, M., & McCarley, R. W. (2005). *Brain control of sleep and wakefulness.* New York: Kluwer Academic Press.

Stern, Y. (2013). *Cognitive reserve: Theory and applications.* East Sussex, UK: Psychology Press.

Sternberg, R. J. (2014). Intelligence as trait—and state? *Journal of Intelligence, 2*(1), 4–5. doi:10.3390/jintelligence2010004

Sternberg, W. F., Bailin, D., Grant, M., & Gracely, R. H. (1998). Competition alters the perception of noxious stimuli in male and female athletes. *Pain, 76*(1–2), 231–238. doi: 10.1016/S0304-3959(98)00050-5

Stevens, S. S. (1960). Psychophysics of sensory function. *American Scientist, 48,* 226–252. doi: http://dx.doi.org/10.7551/mitpress/9780262518420.003.0001

Stewart, S. T., Cutler, D. M., & Rosen, A. B. (2009). Forecasting the effects of obesity and smoking on U.S. life expectancy. *New England Journal of Medicine, 361*(23), 2252–2260. doi:10.1056/NEJMsa0900459

Stewart, W. K., & Fleming, L. W. (1973). Features of a successful therapeutic fast of 382 days' duration. *Postgraduate Medical Journal, 49,* 203–209.

Stickgold, R., & Walker, M. P. (2007). Sleep-dependent memory consolidation and reconsolidation. *Sleep Medicine, 8*(4), 331–343.

Stickgold, R., James, L., & Hobson, J. A. (2000). Visual discrimination learning requires sleep after training. *Nature Neuroscience, 3,* 1237–1238.

Stiefel Laboratories. (2001). *Excessive perspiration.* Retrieved from the Stiefel Laboratories Web site: http://www.oilatum.co.uk/consumer/perspiration/about.html.

Stochholm, K., Juul, S., & Gravholt, C. H. (2012). Socioeconomic factors affect mortality in 47, XYY syndrome—A comparison with the background population and Klinefelter syndrome. *American Journal of Medical Genetics Part A, 158*(10), 2421–2429. doi: 10.1002/ajmg.a.35539

Stokes, P. E. (1995). The potential role of excessive cortisol induced by HPA hyperfunction in the pathogenesis of depression. *European Neuropsychopharmacology, 5,* 77–82. doi: http://dx.doi.org/10.1016/0924-977X(95)00039-R

Stoller, R. J., & Herdt, G. H. (1985). Theories of origins of male homosexuality. A cross-cultural look. *Archives of General Psychiatry, 42,* 399–404.

Stone, V. E., Nisenson, L., Eliassen, J. C., & Gazzaniga, M. S. (1996). Left hemisphere representations of emotional facial expressions. *Neuropsychologia, 34,* 23–29.

Stoodley, C. (2014). Distinct regions of the cerebellum show grey matter decreases in autism, ADHD and developmental dyslexia. *Frontiers in Systems Neuroscience, 8,* 92. doi:10.3389/fnsys.2014.00092

Stovner, L. J., Zwart, J. A., Hagen, K., Terwindt, G. M., & Pascual, J. (2006). Epidemiology of headache in Europe. *European Journal of Neurology, 13*(4), 333–345.

Streissguth, A. P., Aase, J. M., Clarren, S. K., Randels, S. P., LaDue, R. A., & Smith, D. F. (1991). Fetal alcohol syndrome in adolescents and adults. *The Journal of the American Medical Association (JAMA), 265*(15), 1961–1967. doi:10.1001/jama.1991.03460150065025

Strickland, B. R. (1992). Women and depression. *Current Directions in Psychological Science, 1,* 132–135.

Strohmaier, J., Wüst, S., Uher, R., Henigsberg, N., Mors, O., Hauser, J., … Rietschel, M. (2011). Sexual dysfunction during treatment with serotonergic and noradrenergic antidepressants: Clinical description and the role of the 5-HTTLPR. *World Journal of Biological Psychiatry, 12*(7), 528–538.

Sugden, K., Arseneault, L., Harrington, H., Moffitt, T. E., Williams, B., & Caspi, A. (2010). Serotonin transporter gene moderates the development of emotional problems among children following bullying victimization. *Journal of the American Academy of Child and Adolescent Psychiatry, 49*(8), 830–840. doi:10.1016/j.jaac.2010.01.024

Sundram, F., Deeley, Q., Sarkar, S., Daly, E., Latham, R., Craig, M., … Murphy, D. G. (2012). White matter microstructural abnormalities in the frontal lobe of adults with antisocial personality disorder. *Cortex, 48*(2), 216–229. doi:10.1016/j.cortex.2011.06.005

Swan, S. H., Liu, F., Hines, M., Kruse, R. L., Wang, C., Redmon, J. B., … Weiss, B. (2010). Prenatal phthalate exposure and reduced masculine play in boys. *International Journal of Andrology, 33*(2), 259–269. doi:10.1111/j.1365-2605.2009.01019.x

Swanson, J., Castellanos, F. X., Murias, M., LaHoste, G., & Kennedy, J. (1998). Cognitive neuroscience of attention deficit hyperactivity disorder and hyperkinetic disorder. *Current Opinion in Neurobiology, 8,* 263–271.

Sweatt, J. D. (2009). Experience-dependent epigenetic modifications in the central nervous system. *Biological Psychiatry, 65*(3), 191–197. doi: 10.1016/j.biopsych.2008.09.002

Swedo, S. E., Leonard, H. L., Mittleman, B. B., Allen, A. J., Rapoport, J. L., Dow, S. P., et al. (1997). Identification of children with pediatric autoimmune neuropsychiatric disorders associated with streptococcal infections by a marker associated with rheumatic fever. *American Journal of Psychiatry, 154,* 110–112.

Syvalahti, E. K. G. (April 1994). I. The theory of schizophrenia: Biological factors in schizophrenia. *British Journal of Psychiatry Supplement, 164,* 9–14.

Szeszko, P. R., MacMillan, S., McMeniman, M., Chen, S., Baribault, K., Lim, K. O., et al. (2004). Brain structural abnormalities in psychotropic drug-naive pediatric patients with obsessive-compulsive disorder. *American Journal of Psychiatry, 161*(6), 1049–1056.

Taheri, S., & Mignot, E. (2002). The genetics of sleep disorders. *The Lancet Neurology, 1*(4), 242–250. doi:10.1016/S1474-4422(02)00103-5

Tallal, P. (1991). Hormonal influences in developmental learning disabilities. *Psychoneuroendocrinology, 16,* 203–211.

Tallal, P., Ross, R., & Curtiss, S. (1989). Familial aggregation in Specific Language Impairment. *Journal of Speech and Hearing Disorders, 54,* 167–171.

Tanaka, K., & Saito, H. (1989). Analysis of motion of the visual field by direction, expansion/contraction, and rotation cells clustered in the dorsal part of the medial superior temporal area of the macaque monkey. *Journal of Neurophysiology, 62,* 626–641.

Tausk, F., Elenkov, I., & Moynihan, J. (2008). Psychoneuroimmunology. *Dermatologic Therapy, 21*(1), 22–31.

Taylor, C., Fricker, A. D., Devi, L. A., & Gomes, I. (2005). Mechanisms of action of antidepressants: From neurotransmitter systems to signaling pathways. *Cellular Signaling, 17*(5), 549–557.

Taylor, D. J., Jenni, O. G., Acebo, C., & Carskadon, M. A. (2005). Sleep tendency during extended wakefulness: Insights into adolescent sleep regulation and behavior. *Journal of Sleep Research, 14*(3), 239–244.

Taylor, J., Faraone, S. V., & Tsuang, M. T. (2002). Family, twin, and adoption studies of bipolar disease. *Current Psychiatry Reports, 4,* 130–133.

Taylor, M., Rudkin, L., Bullemor-Day, P., Lubin, J., Chukwujekwu, C., & Hawton, K. (2013). Strategies for managing sexual dysfunction caused by antidepressants. *Cochrane Database of Systematic Reviews, 5,* CD003382. doi:10.1002/14651858.CD003382.pub3

Taylor, S. F., Martis, B., Fitzgerald, K. D., Welsh, R. C., Abelson, J. L., Liberzon, I., ... Gehring, W. J. (2006). Medial frontal cortex activity and loss-related responses to errors. *Journal of Neuroscience, 26*(15), 4063–4070. doi: 10.1523/JNEUROSCI.4709-05.2006

Teasdale, G. M., Nicoll, J. A. R., Murray, G., & Fiddes, M. (1997). Association of apolipoprotein E polymorphism with outcome after head injury. *Lancet, 350,* 1069–1071.

Tecuapetla, F., Patel, J. C., Xenias, H., English, D., Tadros, I., Shah, F., ... Koos, T. (2010). Glutamatergic signaling by mesolimbic dopamine neurons in the nucleus accumbens. *The Journal of Neuroscience, 30*(20), 7105–7110. doi:10.1523/jneurosci.0265-10.2010

Teng, Y. D., Benn, S. C., Kalkanis, S. N., Shefner, J. M., Onario, R. C., Cheng, B., ... Snyder, E. Y. (2012). Multimodal actions of neural stem cells in a mouse model of ALS: A meta-analysis. *Science Translational Medicine, 4*(165), 165ra164. doi:10.1126/scitranslmed.3004579

Terman, L. (1916). *The measurement of intelligence.* Boston: Houghton Mifflin.

Terrace, H. S. (1979, November). How Nim Chimpsky changed my mind. *Psychology Today,* 65–76.

Thakkar, K. N., Schall, J. D., Boucher, L., Logan, G. D., & Park, S. (2011). Response inhibition and response monitoring in a saccadic countermanding task in schizophrenia. *Biological Psychiatry, 69*(1), 55–62. doi:10.1016/j.biopsych.2010.08.016

Thannickal, T. C., Moore, R. Y., Nienhuis, R., Ramanathan, L., Gulyani, S., Aldrich, M., et al. (2000). Reduced number of hypocretin neurons in human narcolepsy. *Neuron, 27,* 469–474.

The Global Polio Eradication Initiative. (2014). The ins and outs of polio surveillance. Retrieved from http://www.polioeradication.org/tabid/488/iid/357/Default.aspx

Thomasson, H. R., Edenberg, H. J., Crabb, D. W., Mai, X. L., Jerome, R. E., Li, T. K., ... Yin, S. J. (1991). Alcohol and aldehyde dehydrogenase genotypes and alcoholism in Chinese men. *American Journal of Human Genetics, 48*(4), 677–681. doi: 10.1007/BF01067417

Thompson, M. A., Callaghan, P. D., Hunt, G. E., Cornish, J. L., & McGregor, I. S. (2007). A role for oxytocin and 5-HT(1A) receptors in the prosocial effects of 3,4 methylenedioxymethamphetamine ("ecstasy"). *Neuroscience, 146*(2), 509–514. doi: 10.1016/j.neuroscience.2007.02.032

Thompson, P. M., Vidal, C., Giedd, J. N., Gochman, P., Blumenthal, J., Nicolson, R., et al. (2001). Mapping adolescent brain change reveals dynamic wave of accelerated gray matter loss in very early-onset schizophrenia. *Proceedings of the National Academy of Science of the United States of America (PNAS), 98,* 11650–11655.

Thompson, R. F. (1986). The neurobiology of learning and memory. *Science, 233,* 941–947.

Thompson, R. F. (2009). Habituation: A history. *Neurobiology of Learning and Memory, 92,* 127–134. doi:10.1016/j.nlm.2008.07.011

Thompson, R. F., Thompson, J. K., Kim, J. J., Krupa, D. J., & Shinkman, P. G. (1998). The nature of reinforcement in cerebellar learning. *Neurobiology of Learning and Memory, 70*(1–2), 150–176.

Thornhill, R., & Gangestad, S. W. (1994). Human Fluctuating Asymmetry and Sexual Behavior. *Psychological Science, 5*(5), 297–302. doi:10.1111/j.1467-9280.1994.tb00629.x

Thornton, L. M., Andersen, B. L., Crespin, T. R., & Carson, W. E. (2007). Individual trajectories in stress covary with immunity during recovery from cancer diagnosis and treatments. *Brain, Behavior, and Immunity, 21*(2), 185–194. doi:10.1016/j.bbi.2006.06.007

Tinbergen, N. (1951). *The study of instinct.* Oxford, UK: Clarendon Press.

Tinson, D. J. (1989). How stroke patients spend their days: An observational study of the treatment regimen offered to patients with movement disorders in hospitals following stroke. *International Disability Studies, 11,* 45–49.

Tishkoff, S. A., Gonder, M. K., Henn, B. M., Mortensen, H., Knight, A., Gignoux, C., et al. (2007). History of click-speaking populations of Africa inferred from mtDNA and Y chromosome genetic variation. *Molecular Biology and Evolution, 24*(10), 2180–2195.

Toga, A. W., & Thompson, P. M. (2003). Mapping brain asymmetry. *Nature Reviews Neuroscience, 4*(1), 37–48. doi:10.1038/nrn1009

Tomasi, D., & Volkow, N. D. (2012). Laterality patterns of brain functional connectivity: Gender effects. *Cerebral Cortex, 22*(6), 1455–1462. doi:10.1093/cercor/bhr230

Tong, F., & Pratte, M. S. (2012). Decoding patterns of human brain activity. *Annual Review of Psychology, 63*(1), 483–509. doi:10.1146/annurev-psych-120710-100412

Toot, J., Dunphry, G., & Ely, D. (2001, October). *Sex differences in brain monoamines and aggression.* Paper presented at the meeting of the American Physiological Society, Pittsburgh, PA.

Tostes, M. H. F. S., Teixeira, H. C., Gattaz, W. F., Brandão, M. A. F., & Raposo, N. R. B. (2012). Altered neurotrophin, neuropeptide, cytokines and nitric oxide levels in autism. *Pharmacopsychiatry, 45*(6), 241–243. doi:10.1055/s-0032-1301914

Trace, S. E., Baker, J. H., Peñas-Lledó, E., & Bulik, C. M. (2013). The genetics of eating disorders. *Annual Review of Clinical Psychology, 9,* 589–620. doi: 10.1146/annurev-clinpsy-050212-185546

Treffert, D. A., & Wallace, G. L. (2002). Islands of genius. *Scientific American, 286,* 76–85.

Trivedi, M. H., Greer, T. L., Grannemann, B. D., Church, T. S., Galper, D. I., Sunderajan, P., et al. (2006). TREAD: TReatment with exercise Augmentation for Depression: Study rationale and design. *Clinical Trials, 3*(3), 291–305.

Trotier, D. (2011). Vomeronasal organ and human pheromones. *European Annals of Otorhinolaryngology, Head and Neck Diseases, 128*(4), 184–190. doi:10.1016/j.anorl.2010.11.008

Trussell, J., Ellertson, C., Stewart, F., Raymond, E. G., & Shochet, T. (2004). The role of emergency contraception. *American Journal of Obstetrics and Gynecology, 190*(4, Supplement 1), S30–S38.

Tsien, J. Z., Huerta, P. T., & Tonegawa, S. (1996). The essential role of hippocampal CA1 NMDA receptor-dependent synaptic plasticity in spatial memory. *Cell, 87,* 1327–1338.

Tulving, E. (1972). Episodic and semantic memory. In E. Tulving & W. Donaldson (Eds.), *Organization and memory* (pp. 381–402). New York: Academic Press.

Tulving, E. (1985). How many memory systems are there? *American Psychologist, 40,* 385–398.

Tulving, E. (1987). Multiple memory systems and consciousness. *Human Neurobiology, 6,* 67–80.

Tulving, E. (1989). Memory: Performance, knowledge, and experience. *European Journal of Cognitive Psychology, 1,* 3–26.

Tulving, E. (1995). Organization of memory: Quo vadis? In M. S. Gazzaniga (Ed.), *The cognitive neurosciences* (pp. 839–853). Cambridge, MA: MIT Press.

Tulving, E. (1998). Brain/mind correlates of human memory. In M. Sabourin, F. Craik, & M. Robert (Eds.), *Advances in psychological science: Vol. 2. Biological and cognitive aspects* (pp. 441–460). Hove, UK: Psychology Press.

Turin, L. (2002). A method for the calculation of odor character from molecular structure. *Journal of Theoretical Biology, 216*(3), 367–385. doi:10.1006/jtbi.2001.2504

Turken, A. U., & Dronkers, N. F. (2011). The neural architecture of the language comprehension network: Converging evidence from lesion and connectivity analyses. *Frontiers in Systems Neuroscience, 5, 1.* doi:10.3389/fnsys.2011.00001

Turley-Ames, K. J., & Whitfield, M. M. (2003). Strategy training and working memory task performance. *Journal of Memory and Language, 49,* 446–468.

Turnbaugh, P. J., Ley, R. E., Mahowald, M. A., Magrini, V., Mardis, E. R., & Gordon, J. I. (2006). An obesity-associated gut microbiome with increased capacity for energy harvest. *Nature, 444*(7122), 1027–1031.

Turner, C. E., Byblow, W. D., Stinear, C. M., & Gant, N. (2014). Carbohydrate in the mouth enhances activation of brain circuitry involved in motor performance and sensory perception. *Appetite, 80,* 212–219. doi:http://dx.doi.org/10.1016/j.appet.2014.05.020

U.S. Department of Agriculture. (2002). *Bovine spongiform encephalopathy (BSE). Retrieved from* http://www.aphis.usda.gov/oa/bse/.

U.S. Food and Drug Administration. (1993). 3-month contraceptive injection approved. *FDA Medical Bulletin, 23,* 6–7.

U.S. Food and Drug Administration. (2004). Black box warning added concerning long-term use of Depo–Provera contraceptive injection. Retrived from http://www.fda.gov/bbs/topics/ANSWERS/2004/ANS01325.

U.S. Food and Drug Administration (FDA). (2010). FDA approves new formulation for OxyContin. Retrieved from http://www.fda.gov/NewsEvents/Newsroom/PressAnnouncements/ucm207480.htm

U.S. Food and Drug Administration (FDA). (2011). Food ingredients and colors. Retrieved from http://www.fda.gov/Food/FoodIngredientsPackaging/ucm094211.htm

U.S. Food and Drug Administration (FDA). (2013). Public health advisory: Suicidal thinking in children and adolescents being treated with Strattera (atomoxetine). Retrieved from http://www.fda.gov/Drugs/DrugSafety/PostmarketDrugSafetyInformationforPatientsandProviders/DrugSafetyInformationforHeathcareProfessionals/PublicHealthAdvisories/ucm051733.htm

UK Creutzfeldt-Jakob Disease Surveillance Unit. (2002). *Creutzfeldt-Jakob disease.* Retrieved from http://www.cjd.ed.ac.uk/intro.htm.

UK ECT Review Group. (2003). Efficacy and safety of electroconvulsive therapy in depressive disorders: A systematic review and meta-analysis. *Lancet, 361,* 799–808.

Ullian, E. M., Sapperstein, S. K., Christopherson, K. S., & Barres, B. A. (2001). Control of synapse number by glia. *Science, 291*(5504), 657–661. doi:10.1126/science.291.5504.657

Ungerleider, L. G., & Mishkin, M. (1982). Two cortical visual systems. In D. J. Ingle, M. A. Goodale, & R. J. Mansfield (Eds.), *Analysis of visual behavior* (pp. 549–580). Cambridge, MA: MIT Press.

Ungless, M. A., Whistler, J. L., Malenka, R. C., & Bonci, A. (2001). Single cocaine exposure in vivo induces long-term potentiation in dopamine neurons. *Nature, 411*(6837), 583–587. doi:10.1038/35079077.

United Nations Office on Drugs and Crime. (2010). World drug report. Retrieved from http://www.unodc.org/documents/wdr/WDR_2010/1.2_The_global_heroin_market.pdf

United Nations Office on Drugs and Crime (UNODC). (2014). UNODC homicide statistics 2013. Retrieved from https://www.unodc.org/gsh/en/data.html

University of California Los Angeles (2008). *The field of neuroscience.* Retrieved from http://www.neurosci.ucla.edu/index.asp.

University of Washington PKU Clinic. (2000). *What is the diet for PKU?* Retrieved from the University of Washington Web site: http://depts.washington.edu/pku/diet.html.

Üstün, T. B., Ayuso-Mateos, J. L., Chatterji, S., Mathers, C., & Murray, C. J. L. (2004). Global burden of depressive disorders in the year 2000. *The British Journal of Psychiatry, 184*(5), 386–392. doi:10.1192/bjp.184.5.386

Vaidya, C. (2012). Neurodevelopmental abnormalities in ADHD. In C. Stanford & R. Tannock (Eds.), *Behavioral neuroscience of attention deficit hyperactivity disorder and its treatment* (Vol. 9, pp. 49–66). Springer Berlin Heidelberg.

Valenstein, E. S. (1986). *Great and desperate cures.* New York: Basic Books.

Valla, J., Berndt, J. D., & Gonzalez-Lima, F. (2001). Energy hypometabolism in posterior cingulate cortex of Alzheimer's patients: Superficial laminar cytochrome oxidase associated with disease duration. *Journal of Neuroscience, 21*(13), 4923–4930.

van Anders, S. M., & Watson, N. V. (2006). Relationship status and testosterone in North American heterosexual and non–heterosexual men and women: Cross–sectional and longitudinal data. *Psychoneuroendocrinology, 31*(6), 715–723.

van Apeldoorn, F. J., van Hout, W. J., Mersch, P. P., Huisman, M., Slaap, B. R., Hale, W. W., 3rd, et al. (2008). Is a combined therapy more effective than either CBT or SSRI alone? Results of a multicenter trial on panic disorder with or without agoraphobia. *Acta Psychiatrica Scandinavica, 117*(4), 260–270.

Van Borsel, J., Achten, E., Santens, P., Lahorte, P., & Voet, T. (2003). fMRI of developmental stuttering: A pilot study. *Brain and Language, 85,* 369–376.

Van Cauter, E., Leproult, R., & Plat, L. (2000). Age-related changes in slow wave sleep and REM sleep and relationship with growth hormone and cortisol levels in healthy men. *Journal of the American Medical Association (JAMA), 284*(7), 861–868. doi:10.1001/jama.284.7.861

van den Brand, R., Heutschi, J., Barraud, Q., DiGiovanna, J., Bartholdi, K., Huerlimann, M., …Courtine, G. (2012). Restoring voluntary control of locomotion after paralyzing spinal cord injury. *Science, 336*(6085), 1182–1185. doi:10.1126/science.1217416

van der Gronde, T., de Hon, O., Haisma, H. J., & Pieters, T. (2013). Gene doping: An overview and current implications for athletes. *British Journal of Sports Medicine, 47*(11), 670–678. doi:10.1136/bjsports-2012-091288

van der Knaap, L. J., & van der Ham, I. J. M. (2011). How does the corpus callosum mediate interhemispheric transfer? A review. *Behavioural Brain Research, 223*(1), 211–221. doi:10.1016/j.bbr.2011.04.018

Van Haren, N. E., Cahn, W., Hulshoff Pol, H. E., & Kahn, R. S. (2012). Confounders of excessive brain volume loss in schizophrenia. *Neuroscience & Biobehavioral Reviews, 37*(10), 2418–2423. doi:http://dx.doi.org/10.1016/j.neubiorev.2012.09.006

Van Horn, J. D., Irimia, A., Torgerson, C. M., Chambers, M. C., Kikinis, R., & Toga, A. W. (2012). Mapping connectivity damage in the case of Phineas Gage. *PLoS ONE, 7*(5), e37454. doi:10.1371/journal.pone.0037454

van Londen, L., Goekoop, J. G., van Kempen, G. M. J., Frankhuijzen-Sierevogel, A. C., Wiegant, V. M., van der Velde, E. A., et al. (1997). Plasma levels of arginine vasopressin elevated in patients with major depression. *Neuropsychopharmacology, 17,* 284–292.

Van Os, J. (2004). Does the urban environment cause psychosis? *British Journal of Psychiatry, 184*(4), 287–288.

Van Someren, E. J., & Riemersma-Van Der Lek, R. F. (2007). Live to the rhythm, slave to the rhythm. *Sleep Medicine Reviews, 11*(6), 465–484. doi:http://dx.doi.org/10.1016/j.smrv.2007.07.003

Vandenburgh, H., Chromiak, J., Shansky, J., Del Tatto, M., & Lemaire, J. (1999). Space travel directly induces skeletal muscle atrophy. *FASEB Journal, 13,* 1031–1038.

Vanderploeg, R. D., Schwab, K., Walker, W. C., Fraser, J. A., Sigford, B. J., Date, E. S., … Defense and Veterans Brain Injury Center Study Group. (2008). Rehabilitation of traumatic brain injury in active duty military personnel and veterans: Defense and Veterans Brain Injury Center randomized controlled trial of two rehabilitation approaches. *Archives of Physical Medicine and Rehabilitation, 89*(12), 2227–2238. doi:10.1016/j.apmr.2008.06.015

Varadkar, S., Bien, C. G., Kruse, C. A., Jensen, F. E., Bauer, J., Pardo, C. A., … Cross, J. H. (2014). Rasmussen's encephalitis: clinical features, pathobiology, and treatment advances. *The Lancet Neurology, 13*(2), 195–205. doi:10.1016/S1474-4422(13)70260-6

Vassoler, F. M., Byrnes, E. M., & Pierce, R. C. (2014). The impact of exposure to addictive drugs on future generations: Physiological and behavioral effects. *Neuropharmacology, 76, Part B,* 269–275. doi:http://dx.doi.org/10.1016/j.neuropharm.2013.06.016

Vazquez, J., & Baghdoyan, H. A. (2001). Basal forebrain acetylcholine release during REM sleep is significantly greater than during waking. *American Journal of Physiology. Regulatory, Integrative and Comparative Physiology, 280*(2), R598–601.

Vecchia, D., & Pietrobon, D. (2012). Migraine: a disorder of brain excitatory–inhibitory balance? *Trends in Neurosciences, 35*(8), 507–520. doi:http://dx.doi.org/10.1016/j.tins.2012.04.007

Vellaichamy, M. (2001). Hyponatremia. *eMedicine Journal, 4*(1). Retrieved from http://author.emedicine.com/PED/topic1124.htm.

Velosa, J. F., & Riddle, M. A. (2000). Pharmacologic treatment of anxiety disorders in children and adolescents. *Child and Adolescent Psychiatry Clinics of North America, 9,* 119–133.

Verbalis, J. G. (2007). How does the brain sense osmolality? *Journal of the American Society of Nephrology, 18*(12), 3056–3059. doi:10.1681/asn.2007070825

Verdejo-Garcia, A., Clark, L., & Dunn, B. D. (2012). The role of interoception in addiction: A critical review. *Neuroscience & Biobehavioral Reviews, 36*(8), 1857–1869. doi: 10.1016/j.neubiorev.2012.05.007

Verney, E. B. (1947). The antidiuretic hormone and the factors which determine its release. *Proceedings of the Royal Society of London, B, Biological Science, 135,* 25–106.

Videbech, P., & Ravnkilde, B. (2004). Hippocampal volume and depression: A meta-analysis of MRI studies. *American Journal of Psychiatry, 161*(11), 1957–1966.

Vijande, M., Lopez-Sela, P., Brime, J. I., Bernardo, R., Diaz, F., Costales, M., & Marin, B. (1990). Insulin stimulation of water intake in humans. *Appetite, 15,* 81–87.

Vining, E. P., Freeman, J. M., Pillas, D. J., Uematsu, S., Carson, B. S., Brandt, J., et al. (1997). Why would you remove half a brain? The outcome of 58 children after hemispherectomy: The Johns Hopkins experience: 1968 to 1996. *Pediatrics, 100*(2) Pt 1, 163–171.

Viscusi, E. R., & Schechter, L. N. (2006). Patient-controlled analgesia: Finding a balance between cost and comfort. *American Journal of Health-System Pharmacy, 63*(8 Suppl 1), S3-13; quiz S15-16. doi: 10.2146/ajhp060011

Visser, S. N., Danielson, M. L., Bitsko, R. H., Holbrook, J. R., Kogan, M. D., Ghandour, R. M., … Blumberg, S. J. (2014). Trends in the parent-report of health care provider-diagnosed and medicated attention-deficit/hyperactivity disorder: United States, 2003-2011. *Journal of the American Academy of Child & Adolescent Psychiatry, 53*(1), 34–46. doi:10.1016/j.jaac.1013.09.001

Vitaterna, M. H., King, D. P., Chang, A. M., Kornhauser, J. M., Lowrey, P. L., McDonald, J. D., et al. (1994). Mutagenesis and mapping of a mouse gene, Clock, essential for circadian behavior. *Science, 278,* 38–39.

Vogel, G. W., Vogel, F., McAbee, R. S., & Thurmond, A. J. (1980). Improvement of depression by REM sleep deprivation: New findings and a theory. *Archives of General Psychiatry, 37,* 247–253.

Vogt, B. A., Finch, D. M., & Olson, C. R. (1992). Functional heterogeneity in cingulate cortex: The anterior executive and posterior evaluative regions. *Cerebral Cortex, 2*(6), 435–443. doi:10.1093/cercor/2.6.435-a

Volkow, N. D., Fowler, J. S., & Wang, G. -J. (2004). Dopamine in drug abuse and addiction: Results from imaging studies and treatment implications. *Molecular Psychiatry, 9*(9), 557–569.

Volkow, N. D., Wang, G.-J., Kollins, S. H., Wigal, T. L., Newcorn, J. H., Telang, F., … Swanson, J. M. (2009). Evaluating dopamine reward pathway in ADHD: Clinical implications. *Journal of the American Medical Association (JAMA), 302*(10), 1084–1091. doi:10.1001/jama.2009.1308

von Economo, C., & Koskinas, G. N. (1929). *The cytoarchitectonics of the human cerebral cortex.* London: Oxford University Press.

Von Gersdorff, H., & Mathews, G. (1994). Dynamics of synaptic vesicle fusion and membrane retrieval in synaptic terminals. *Nature, 367*(6465), 735–739. doi: 10.1038/367735a0

Voyer, D. (1996). On the magnitude of laterality effects and sex differences in functional lateralities. *Laterality, 1,* 51–84. doi:10.1080/713754209

Vunjak-Novakovic, G., & Scadden, D. T. (2011). Biomimetic platforms for human stem cell research. *Cell Stem Cell, 8*(3), 252–261. doi:10.1016/j.stem.2011.02.014

Vyazovskiy, V. V., & Tobler, I. (2005). Theta activity in the waking EEG is a marker of sleep propensity in the rat. *Brain Research, 1050*(1–2), 64–71. doi:http://dx.doi.org/10.1016/j.brainres.2005.05.022

Wade, T. D., Bulik, C. M., Neale, M., & Kendler, K. S. (2000). Anorexia nervosa and major depression: Shared genetic and environmental risk factors. *American Journal of Psychiatry, 157*(3), 469–471.

Wagner, D. R. (1996). Disorders of the circadian sleep-wake cycle. *Neurological Clinics, 14,* 651–670.

Wagner, G., Koch, K., Schachtzabel, C., Reichenbach, J. R., Sauer, H., & Schlosser Md, R. G. (2008). Enhanced rostral anterior cingulate cortex activation during cognitive control is related to orbitofrontal volume reduction in unipolar depression. *Journal of Psychiatry and Neuroscience, 33*(3), 199–208.

Wagner, M. L., Walters, A. S., & Fisher, B. C. (2004). Symptoms of attention-deficit/hyperactivity disorder in adults with restless legs syndrome. *Sleep, 27*(8), 1499–1504.

Wagner, U., Fischer, S., & Born, J. (2002). Changes in emotional responses to aversive pictures across periods rich in slow-wave sleep versus rapid eye movement sleep. *Psychosomatic Medicine, 64*(4), 627–634.

Wagner, U., Gais, S., & Born, J. (2001). Emotional memory formation is enhanced across sleep intervals with high amounts of rapid eye movement sleep. *Learning and Memory, 8*(2), 112–119.

Wahlstrom, K. L. (2003). Changing times: Findings from the first longitudinal study of later high school start times. *Bulletin of the National Association of Secondary School Principals (NASSP), 86,* 3–21.

Wald, G., & Brown, P. K. (1958). Human rhodopsin. *Science, 127*(3292), 222–249. doi:10.1126/science.127.3292.222

Wang, H., Duclot, F., Liu, Y., Wang, Z., & Kabbaj, M. (2013). Histone deacetylase inhibitors facilitate partner preference formation in female prairie voles. *Nature Neuroscience, 16*(7), 919–924. doi:10.1038/nn.3420

Wang, J.-F., Li, Y., Song, J.-N., & Pang, H.-G. (2014). Role of hydrogen sulfide in secondary neuronal injury. *Neurochemistry International, 64,* 37–47. doi:http://dx.doi.org/10.1016/j.neuint.2013.11.002

Wang, J., Zuo, X., Dai, Z., Xia, M., Zhao, Z., Zhao, X., … He, Y. (2013). Disrupted functional brain connectome in individuals at risk for Alzheimer's disease. *Biological Psychiatry, 73*(5), 472–481. doi:10.1016/j.biopsych.2012.03.026

Wang, X., Merzenich, M. M., Sameshima, K., & Jenkins, W. M. (1995). Remodelling of hand representation in adult cortex determined by timing of tactile stimulation. *Nature, 378*(6552), 71–75. doi:10.1038/378071a0

Ward, B. W., Dahlhamer, J. M., Galinsky, A. M., & Joestl, S. S. (2014). Sexual orientation and health among U.S. adults: National Health Interview Survey, 2013. Retrieved from www.cdc.gov/nchs/data/nhsr/nhsr077.pdf

Watkins, K. E., Smith, S. M., Davis, S., & Howell, P. (2008). Structural and functional abnormalities of the motor system in developmental stuttering. *Brain, 131*(1), 50–59.

Watkins, K. E., Vargha-Khadem, F., Ashburner, J., Passingham, R. E., Connelly, A., Friston, K. J., et al. (2002). MRI analysis of an inherited speech and language disorder: Structural brain abnormalities. *Brain, 127,* 465–478.

Webb, S. J., Nalty, T., Munson, J., Brock, C., Abbott, R., & Dawson, G. (2007). Rate of head circumference growth as a function of autism diagnosis and history of autistic regression. *Journal of Child Neurology, 22*(10), 1182–1190.

Webster, J., & Koch, H. F. (1996). Aspects of tolerability of centrally acting antihypertensive drugs. *Journal of Cardiovascular Pharmacology, 27* (Suppl. 3), S49–54.

Wederkind, C., & Furi, S. (1997). Body odour preferences in men and women: Do they aim for specific MHC combinations or simple heterogeneity? *Proceedings of the Royal Society of London, B, Biological Science, 264,* 1471–1479.

Wehr, T., Sack, D., Rosenthal, N., Duncan, W., & Gillin, J. C. (1983). Circadian rhythm disturbances in manic-depressive illness. *Federation Proceedings, 42,* 2809–2814.

Weiller, C., May, A., Limmroth, V., Juptner, M., Kaube, H., Schayck, R. V., et al. (1995). Brainstem activation in spontaneous human migraine attacks. *Nature Medicine, 1,* 658–660.

Weinberger, D. R., Aloia, M. S., Goldberg, T. E., & Berman, K. F. (1994). The frontal lobes and schizophrenia. *Journal of Neuropsychiatry and Clinical Neurosciences, 6,* 419–427.

Weiner, R. D. (1984). Does ECT cause brain damage? *Brain and Behavior Science, 7,* 153.

Weinmann, M. (2003). Hot on the inside. *Emergency Medical Services, 32*(7), 34.

Weinrich, M., & Wise, S. P. (1982). The premotor cortex of the monkey. *Journal of Neuroscience, 2,* 1329–1345.

Weiskrantz, L. (1985). On issues and theories of the human amnesic syndrome. In N. M. Weinberger, J. L. McGaugh, & G. S. Lynch (Eds.), *Memory systems in the brain* (pp. 380–415). New York: Guilford Press.

Weissman, M. M., Warner, V., Wickramaratne, P., Moreau, D., & Olfson, M. (1997). Offspring of depressed parents: 10 years later. *Journal of Affective Disorders, 15,* 269–277.

Weissman, T., Noctor, S. C., Clinton, B. K., Honig, L. S., & Kriegstein, A. R. (2003). Neurogenic radial glial cells in reptile, rodent and human: From mitosis to migration. *Cerebral Cortex, 13*(6), 550–559. doi:10.1093/cercor/13.6.550

Welling, L. L. M., Jones, B. C., DeBruine, L. M., Conway, C. A., Law Smith, M. J., Little, A. C., … Al-Dujaili, E. A. (2007). Raised salivary testosterone in women is associated with increased attraction to masculine faces. *Hormones and Behavior, 52*(2), 156–161. doi:10.1016/j.yhbeh.2007.01.010

Wender, P. H., Kety, S. S., Rosenthal, D., Schulsinger, F., Ortmann, J., & Lunde, I. (1986). Psychiatric disorders in the biological and adoptive families of adopted individuals with affective disorders. *Archives of General Psychiatry, 43,* 923–929.

Werner, E., & Dawson, G. (2005). Validation of the phenomenon of autistic regression using home videotapes. *Archives of General Psychiatry, 62*(8), 889–895.

Wernicke, C. (1874). *Der aphasische symptomenkomplex.* Breslau, Germany: Cohn & Weigart.

Westbrook, G. (2000). Seizures and epilepsy. In E. R. Kandel, J. H. Schwartz, & T. M. Jessell (Eds.), *Principles of neural science* (pp. 910–935). New York: McGraw-Hill.

Whalley, K. (2013). Circadian rhythms: Temperature training. *Nature Reviews Neuroscience, 14*(6), 380–380. doi:10.1038/nrn3510

Whalley, L. J., Starr, J. M., Athawes, R., Hunter, D., Pattie, A., & Deary, I. J. (2000). Childhood mental ability and dementia. *Neurology, 55,* 1455–1459.

Whitley, R. J. (2006). Herpes simplex encephalitis: Adolescents and adults. *Antiviral Research, 71*, 141–148.

Whitlock, J. R., Heynen, A. J., Shuler, M. G., & Bear, M. F. (2006). Learning induces long-term potentiation in the hippocampus. *Science, 313*(5790), 1093–1097. doi:10.1126/science.1128134

Wildgruber, D., Ackermann, H., Kreifelts, B., & Ethofer, T. (2006). Cerebral processing of linguistic and emotional prosody: fMRI studies. *Progress in Brain Research, 156*, 249–268.

Wildgruber, D., Riecker, A., Hertrich, I., Erb, M., Grodd, W., Ethofer, T., et al. (2005). Identification of emotional intonation evaluated by fMRI. *NeuroImage, 24*(4), 1233–1241.

Wilensky, A. E., Schafe, G. E., Kristensen, M. P., & LeDoux, J. E. (2006). Rethinking the fear circuit: The central nucleus of the amygdala is required for the acquisition, consolidation, and expression of Pavlovian fear conditioning. *Journal of Neuroscience, 26*(48), 12387–12396. doi:10.1523/JNEUROSCI.4316-06.2006

Wilkinson, L. S., Davies, W., & Isles, A. R. (2007). Genomic imprinting effects on brain development and function. *Nature Reviews Neuroscience, 8*(11), 832–843. doi:10.1038/nrn2235

Willems, R. M., Van der Haegen, L., Fisher, S. E., & Francks, C. (2014). On the other hand: Including left-handers in cognitive neuroscience and neurogenetics. *Nature Reviews Neuroscience, 15*, 193–201. doi:10.1038/nrn3679

Williams, S. (2006). Direct-to-consumer genetic testing: Empowering or endangering the public? Retrieved from http://www.dnapolicy.org/policy.issue.php?action=detail&issuebrief_id=32

Wilson, M. E., Westberry, J. M., & Trout, A. L. (2011). Estrogen receptor-alpha gene expression in the cortex: Sex differences during development and in adulthood. *Hormones and Behavior, 59*(3), 353–357. doi: 10.1016/j.yhbeh.2010.08.004

Wing, L. (1993). The definition and prevalence of autism: A review. *European Child and Adolescent Psychiatry, 2*(2), 61–74. doi:10.1007/BF02098832

Winson, J. (1985). *Brain and psyche.* Garden City, NY: Anchor Press/Doubleday.

Wirz-Justice, A. (2006). Biological rhythm disturbances in mood disorders. *International Clinical Psychopharmacology, 21*(Suppl. 1), s11–15.

Wise, M. S., Arand, D. L., Auger, R. R., Brooks, S. N., & Watson, N. F. (2007). Treatment of narcolepsy and other hypersomnias of central origin. *Sleep, 30*(12), 1712–1727.

Witelson, S. F., Kigar, D. L., & Harvey, T. (1999). The exceptional brain of Albert Einstein. *Lancet, 353*(9170), 2149–2153.

Wolfe-Christensen, C., Fedele, D. A., Kirk, K., Phillips, T. M., Mazur, T., Mullins, L. L., ... Wisniewski, A. B. (2012). Degree of external genital malformation at birth in children with a disorder of sex development and subsequent caregiver distress. *The Journal of Urology, 188*(4, Supplement), 1596–1600. doi:http://dx.doi.org/10.1016/j.juro.2012.02.040

Wolfson, S., & Neave, N. (2002). Testosterone surge linked to sports home advantage. *New Scientist.* Retrieved from http://www.newscientist.com/news/news.jsp?id=ns99992050.

Wolpe, P. R., Foster, K. R., & Langleben, D. D. (2010). Emerging neurotechnologies for lie-detection: Promises and perils. *American Journal of Bioethics, 10*(10), 40–48. doi:10.1080/15265161.2010.519238

Wong-Riley, M. T. (1989). Cytochrome oxidase: an endogenous metabolic marker for neuronal activity. *Trends in Neurosciences, 12*(3), 94–101.

Wood, J. M., Bootzin, R. R., Kihlstrom, J. F., & Schacter, D. L. (1992). Implicit and explicit memory for verbal information presented during sleep. *Psychological Science, 3*, 236–239.

Wood, R. I., & Stanton, S. J. (2012). Testosterone and sport: Current perspectives. *Hormones and Behavior, 61*(1), 147–155. doi:http://dx.doi.org/10.1016/j.yhbeh.2011.09.010

Woodruff-Pak, D. S., & Disterhoft , J. F. (2008). Where is the trace in trace conditioning? *Trends in Neurosciences, 31*(2), 105–112.

Woodruff-Pak, D. S., Papka, M., & Ivry, R. B. (1996). Cerebellar involvement in eyeblink classical conditioning in humans. *Neuropsychology, 10*, 443–458.

Woodruff-Pak, D. S., Vogel, R. W., 3rd, Ewers, M., Coffey, J., Boyko, O. B., & Lemieux, S. K. (2001). MRI-assessed volume of cerebellum correlates with associative learning. *Neurobiology of Learning and Memory, 76*(3), 342–357.

Woods, B. T., & Teuber, H. L. (1973). Early onset of complementary specialization of cerebral hemispheres in man. *Transactions of the American Neurological Association, 98*, 113–117.

Woodward, S. H., Kuo, J. R., Schaer, M., Kaloupek, D. G., & Eliez, S. (2013). Early adversity and combat exposure interact to influence anterior cingulate cortex volume in combat veterans. *NeuroImage: Clinical, 2*, 670–674. doi:http://dx.doi.org/10.1016/j.nicl.2013.04.016

Wooldridge, T., & Lytle, P. P. (2012). An overview of anorexia nervosa in males. *Eating Disorders, 20*(5), 368–378. doi: 10.1080/10640266.2012.715515

World Health Organization. (2008). *WHO report on the global tobacco epidemic, 2008: The MPOWER package.* Geneva, Switzerland: World Health Organization.

World Health Organization. (1993). *The management of fever in young children with acute respiratory infections in developing countries.* Retrieved February 3, 2003, from the World Health Organization Web site: http://www.who.int/childadolescent-health/New_Publications/CHILD_HEALTH/WHO_ARI_93.30.htm-2.%20UNDERSTANDING%20FEVER.

World Health Organization (2013). *Tobacco.* www.who.int./topics/tobacco/en/

World Health Organization (WHO) (2014). *Tetanus.* http://www.who.int/topics/tetanus/en/

Wrangham, R. W., & Peterson, D. (1996). *Demonic males: Apes and the origins of human violence.* Boston: Houghton Mifflin.

Wright, R. (1994). *The moral animal: The new science of evolutionary psychology.* New York: Pantheon Books.

Wurtman, R. J. (2005). Genes, stress, and depression. *Metabolism, 54*(5), Supplement 1, 16–19.

Wurtman, R. J., Wurtman, J. J., Regan, M. M., McDermott, J. M., Tsay, R. H., & Breu, J. J. (2003). Effects of normal meals rich in carbohydrates or proteins on plasma tryptophan and tyrosine ratios. *American Journal of Clinical Nutrition, 77*(1), 128–132.

Xiao, Y., Richter, J. A., & Hurley, J. H. (2008). Release of glutamate and CGRP from trigeminal ganglion neurons: Role of calcium channels and 5-HT1 receptor signaling. *Molecular Pain, 4*, 12.

Xu, K., Xu, Y. H., Chen, J. F., & Schwarzschild, M. A. (2010). Neuroprotection by caffeine: Time course and role of its metabolites in the MPTP model of Parkinson's disease. *Neuroscience, 167*(2), 475–481. doi:10.1016/j.neuroscience.2010.02.020

Yamazaki, S. (2000). Resetting central and peripheral circadian oscillators in transgenic rats. *Science, 288*, 682–685.

Yan, X., Brown, A. D., Lazar, M., Cressman, V. L., Henn-Haase, C., Neylan, T. C., ... Marmar, C. R. (2013). Spontaneous brain activity in combat related PTSD. *Neuroscience Letters, 547*(8), 1–5. doi:http://dx.doi.org/10.1016/j.neulet.2013.04.032

Yang, B.-Z., Zhang, H., Ge, W., Weder, N., Douglas-Palumberi, H., Perepletchikova, F., ... Kaufman, J. (2013). Child abuse and epigenetic mechanisms of disease risk. *American Journal of Preventive Medicine, 44*(2), 101–107. doi:10.1016/j.amepre.2012.10.012

Yang, M. S., & Gill, M. (2007). A review of gene linkage, association and expression studies in autism and an assessment of convergent evidence. *International Journal of Developmental Neuroscience, 25*(2), 69–85.

Yang, Y., Raine, A., Joshi, A. A., Joshi, S., Chang, Y.-T., Schug, R. A., ... Narr, K. L. (2012). Frontal information flow and connectivity in psychopathy. *The British Journal of Psychiatry, 201*(5), 408–409. doi:10.1192/bjp.bp.111.107128

Yates, W. R., Perry, P., & Murray, S. (1992). Aggression and hostility in anabolic steroid users. *Biological Psychiatry, 31*, 1232–1234.

Yenari, M., & Han, H. (2013). Influence of therapeutic hypothermia on regeneration after cerebral ischemia. *Frontiers of Neurology and Neuroscience, 32*, 122–128. doi:10.1159/000346428

Yerkes, R. M., & Dodson, J. D. (1908). The relation of strength of stimulus to rapidity of habit-formation. *Journal of Comparative Neurology and Psychology, 18*, 459–482.

Yolken, R. H., Karlsson, H., Yee, F., Johnston-Wilson, N. L., & Torrey, E. F. (2000). Endogenous retroviruses and schizophrenia. *Brain Research Review, 31*, 193–199.

Young, A. S., Sullivan, G., Burnam, M. A., & Brook, R. H. (1998). Measuring the quality of outpatient treatment for schizophrenia. *Archives of General Psychiatry, 55*, 611–617.

Young, J. A. (2012). Pharmacotherapy for traumatic brain injury: Focus on sympathomimetics. *Pharmacology & Therapeutics, 134*(1), 1–7. doi:http://dx.doi.org/10.1016/j.pharmthera.2011.08.003

Yun, A. J., Bazar, K. A., & Lee, P. Y. (2004). Pineal attrition, loss of cognitive plasticity, and onset of puberty during the teen years: Is it a modern maladaptation exposed by evolutionary displacement? *Medical Hypotheses, 63*(6), 939–950.

Zager, A., Andersen, M. L., Ruiz, F. S., Antunes, I. B., & Tufik, S. (2007). Effects of acute and chronic sleep loss on immune modulation of rats. *American Journal of Physiology. Regulatory, Integrative and Comparative Physiology, 293*(1), R504–509.

Zaidel, D. (2001). Neuron soma size in the left and right hippocampus of a genius. *Proceedings of the Society for Neuroscience, 27.* Retrieved from http://cogprints.soton.ac.uk/documents/disk0/00/00/19/27/index.html.

Zambelli, H., Carelli, E., Honorato, D., Marba, S., Coelho, G., Carnevalle, A., et al. (2007). Assessment of neurosurgical outcome in children prenatally diagnosed with myelomeningocele and development of a protocol for fetal surgery to prevent hydrocephalus. *Child's Nervous System, 23*(4), 421–425.

Zambrano, A., Solis, L., Salvadores, N., Cortes, M., Lerchundi, R., & Otth, C. (2008). Neuronal cytoskeletal dynamic modification and neurodegeneration induced by infection with herpes simplex virus type 1. *Journal of Alzheimer's Disease, 14*(3), 259–269.

Zeis, T., & Schaeren-Wiemers, N. (2008). Lame ducks or fierce creatures? The role of oligodendrocytes in multiple sclerosis. *Journal of Molecular Neuroscience, 35*(1), 91–100.

Zeki, S. (1983). Color coding in the cerebral cortex: The responses of wavelength-selective and color coded cells in monkey visual cortex to changes in wavelength composition. *Neuroscience, 9,* 767–781.

Zelman, S. (1973). Correlation of smoking history with hearing loss. *Journal of the American Medical Association (JAMA), 223,* 920.

Zenhausen, R. (1978). Imagery, cerebral dominance and style of thinking: A unified field model. *Bulletin of the Psychonomic Society, 12,* 381–384.

Zerjal, T., Xue, Y., Bertorelle, G., Wells, R. S., Bao, W., Zhu, S., et al. (2003). The genetic legacy of the Mongols. *American Journal of Human Genetics, 72*(3), 717–721.

Zetterberg, H., Tanriverdi, F., Unluhizarci, K., Selcuklu, A., Kelestimur, F., & Blennow, K. (2009). Sustained release of neuron-specific enolase to serum in amateur boxers. *Brain Injury, 23*(9), 723–726. doi:10.1080/02699050903120399

Zhang, Y., Proenca, R., Maffei, M., Barone, M., Leopold, L., & Friedman, J. M. (1994). Positional cloning of the mouse obese gene and its human homologue. *Nature, 372,* 425–432.

Zhao, R.-R., Andrews, M. R., Wang, D., Warren, P., Gullo, M., Schnell, L., … Fawcett, J. W. (2013). Combination treatment with anti-Nogo-A and chondroitinase ABC is more effective than single treatments at enhancing functional recovery after spinal cord injury. *European Journal of Neuroscience, 38*(6), 2946–2961. doi:10.1111/ejn.12276

Zheng, Z., & Cohn, M. J. (2011). Developmental basis of sexually dimorphic digit ratios. *Proceedings of the National Academy of Sciences of the United States of America (PNAS), 108*(39), 16289–16294. doi:10.1073/pnas.1108312108

Zimmer, C. (2009). On the origin of tomorrow. *Science, 326,* 1334–1336. doi: 10.1126/science.326.5958.1334

Zimmerman, Y., Eijkemans, M., Bennink, H. C., Blankenstein, M., & Fauser, B. (2014). The effect of combined oral contraception on testosterone levels in healthy women: A systematic review and meta-analysis. *Human Reproduction Update, 20*(1), 76–105. doi: 10.1093/humupd/dmt038

Zito, K. A., Vickers, G., & Roberts, D. C. S. (1985). Disruption of cocaine and heroin self-administration following kainic acid lesions of the nucleus accumbens. *Pharmacology Biochemistry and Behavior, 23*(6), 1029–1036. doi:10.1016/0091-3057(85)90110-8

Zivin, J. A., & Choi, D. W. (1991). Stroke therapy. *Scientific American, 265,* 56–63.

Zollman, F. S., Starr, C., Kondiles, B., Cyborski, C., & Larson, E. B. (2014). The Rehabilitation Institute of Chicago Military Traumatic Brain Injury Screening Instrument: Determination of sensitivity, specificity, and predictive value. *The Journal of Head Trauma Rehabilitation, 29*(1), 99–107. doi:10.1097/HTR.0b013e318294dd37

Zubieta, J.-K., Smith, Y. R., Bueller, J. A., Xu, Y., Kilbourn, M. R., Jewett, D. M., et al. (2001). Regional mu opioid receptor regulation of sensory and affective dimensions of pain. *Science, 293,* 311–315.

Zuscho, H. (1983). Posttraumatic anosmia. *Archives of Otolaryngology, 4,* 252–256.

Name Index

Cholinergic mesopontine nuclei A group of cells located at the border of the pons and midbrain that use acetylcholine (ACh) as their major neurotransmitter and participate in the maintenance of waking., 379

Cholinergic neurons, 105–106, 105f

Chordates The phylum of animals that possess true brains and spinal cords. Also known as vertebrates., 59, 59f

Choroid plexus The lining of the ventricles, which secretes the cerebrospinal fluid (CSF)., 29

Cilia Microscopic hair-like projections from a cell., 220f, 221, 222, 223f

Cingulate cortex A segment of older cortex just dorsal to the corpus callosum that is part of the limbic system., 41f, 43, 44t

Circadian rhythm A repeating cycle of about 24 hours., 364–365, 371–373
  artificial lighting and, 373, 374f
  biochemistry of, 371–372, 372f
  cellular basis of, 370–371, 371f
  free-running, 364
  zeitgebers and, 364, 365

CJD. *See* Creutzfeldt-Jakob disease (CJD)

Classical conditioning A type of associative learning in which a neutral stimulus acquires the ability to signal the occurrence of a second, biologically significant event., 401
  cerebellar circuits and, 414–415, 415f, 416
  extinction and, 416
  of eyeblink, 413–414, 413f
  learning and, 401–402, 402f
  learning at the synapse and, 409–411, 410f
  of threat, 412–413, 412f
  trace conditioning and, 416, 416f

Climbing fiber A fiber originating in the inferior olive of the brainstem that forms synapses on the large Purkinje cells of the cerebellar cortex., 414

Clonic phase The second phase of a grand mal seizure, characterized by violent, repetitious muscle contractions., 533

CNS. *See* Central nervous system (CNS)

CNVs. *See* Copy-number variation (CNVs)

Cocaine A powerful, addictive dopamine agonist derived from the leaves of the coca plant of South America., 128–130, 129f

Cocaine- and amphetamineregulated transcript (CART) A neurochemical, originating in the arcuate nucleus, believed to inhibit feeding behavior., 316

Coccygeal nerve The most caudal of the spinal nerves., 34, 34f, 55f

Cochlea The fluid-filled structure of the inner ear containing auditory receptors., 219f, 220–221, 220f

Cochlear duct The middle of three chambers of the cochlea., 220f, 221, 222f

Cochlear nucleus A nucleus found in the pons that receives information about sound from the inner ear., 36f, 37, 39t

Cochlear prosthetics Electrode arrays inserted in the cochlea to treat hearing loss due to damaged inner ear hair cells., 228, 229, 229f

Codeine An opium derivative used medicinally for cough suppression and pain relief., 131

Codons, 140

Cognition
  sexual behavior and, 341–344, 344f
  sexual orientation and, 347–349, 347f, 348f

Cognitive reserve A proposed basis for individual differences in responses to brain injury either due to brain size, synapse number, or flexible use of cognitive networks., 538–539

Cold
  behavioral responses to, 292
  endothermic responses to, 292–293
  See also Temperature regulation

Collateral One of the branches near the end of the axon closest to its targets., 72

Color, encoding, 205–208, 205f
  color constancy and, 208
  color contrast and, 207, 207f
  color deficiency and, 207
  opponent process theory and, 205–206, 206f
  trichromatic theory and, 205, 205f

Color constancy The concept that an object's color looks the same regardless of the type of light falling on the object., 208

Color contrast The fact that colors can look different depending on the surrounding colors., 207, 207f

Color deficiency, 207

Coma A deep, prolonged period of unconsciousness from which the person cannot be awakened., 534

Complex cortical cell A cortical interneuron that shows a preferred stimulus size and orientation, and in some cases direction of movement, but not location within the visual field., 195

Complex partial seizures A type of partial seizure originating in the temporal lobes., 533

Compulsion An irresistible, repeated, impulse to perform an action; characteristic of obsessive-compulsive disorder., 571

Computational neuroscience, 2, 2f

Computerized tomography (CT) An imaging technology in which computers are used to enhance X-ray images., 9, 9f

COMT. *See* Catechol-O-methyl-transferase (COMT)

Concentration gradient An unequal distribution in the concentration of molecules across a cell membrane., 77

Concordance rate The statistical probability that two cases will agree; usually used to predict the risk of an identical twin for developing a condition already diagnosed in his or her twin., 17, 546, 553, 555, 562, 571

Concussion A head injury that results from a blow to the head without penetration of the brain or from a blow to another part of the body that results in force transmitted to the brain., 519–520

Conditioned response (CR) In classical conditioning, a learned reaction to the conditioned stimulus., 402, 409–411, 410f

Conditioned stimulus (CS) In classical conditioning, an initially neutral event that takes on the ability to signal other biologically significant events., 402, 409–411, 410f

Conduction aphasia A condition characterized by fluent speech and good comprehension but poor repetition and naming; believed to result from damage to the arcuate fasciculus and underlying structures., 464–465, 464f

Conduction loss Hearing loss due to problems in the outer or middle ears; treated with the use of hearing aids., 228

Cone A photoreceptor that operates in bright conditions and responds differentially to color., 184–188, 185f, 186t
  photopic vision and, 185, 186t
  rods and, differences in, 187–188, 188f
  See also Photoreceptor

Confrontation naming, 465

Congenital adrenal hyperplasia (CAH) A condition in which a fetus is exposed to higher-than-normal androgens, resulting in masculinization of external genitalia and some cognitive behaviors in affected females., 333, 338, 341–345

Connectome, 49–50

Contraception
  female, 352–353
  male, 353

Contralateral A directional term referring to structures on opposite sides of the midline., 27

Contrast sensitivity function (CSF) The mapping of an individual's thresholds for contrast over a range of frequencies., 201, 202–203, 203f

Cooperativity A condition for the formation of LTP in which several synapses onto the target postsynaptic neuron must be simultaneously active., 426

Copy-number variation (CNVs) Mutation resulting from duplication or deletion of sections of DNA., 144

Cornea The transparent outer layer of the eye., 180

Coronal section An anatomical section dividing the brain front to back, parallel to the face; also known as a frontal section., 27, 27f

Corpus callosum A wide band of axons connecting the right and left cerebral hemispheres., 46, 47, 47f

Corpus luteum A yellow mass of cells in the ovary formed by a ruptured follicle that has released an egg., 351

Corpus striatum, 40

Cortex. *See* Cerebral cortex

Cortical columns, 197

Cortical mapping, 193f, 195, 198

Cortical module A unit of primary visual cortex containing two sets of ocular dominance columns, 16 blobs, and two hypercolumns., 197, 197f, 198

Cortical receptive fields, 195–196, 196f

Corticospinal tract A pathway connecting the motor cortex to alpha motor neurons in the spinal cord., 269

Corticotrophin-releasing hormone (CRH) A hormone released by the hypothalamus that signals the release of ACTH by the anterior pituitary gland., 504–505

Cortisol A hormone released by the adrenal glands that promotes arousal., 372

Countercoup An area of brain damage that occurs on the opposite side of the head from the original site of the blow, or coup., 519f, 520

Coup An area of brain damage at the site of the blow to the head., 519f, 520

CR. *See* Conditioned response (CR)

Cranial nerves Twelve pairs of nerves that exit the brain as part of the peripheral nervous system (PNS)., 51–52, 52f, 55f

CREB (cAMP Response Element Binding protein), 407–409

CREB-1 A protein that activates genes that might be responsible for structural changes associated with long-term memory., 408–409

CREB-2 A protein that normally inhibits the transcription of genes associated with structural changes in long-term memory., 408–409

Creutzfeldt-Jakob disease (CJD) A human TSE that results in a progressively degenerative condition characterized by movement and cognitive disorder., 522, 524, 525

CRH. *See* Corticotrophin-releasing hormone (CRH)

Critical period A period of time during development in which experience is influential and after which experience has little to no effect., 160

Crossing over A process occurring during meiosis in which chromosomes exchange equivalent segments of DNA., 142–143, 142f

CS. *See* Conditioned stimulus (CS)

CSF. *See* Cerebrospinal fluid (CSF); Contrast sensitivity function (CSF)

CT. *See* Computerized tomography (CT)

Curare A substance derived from Amazonian plants that causes paralysis by blocking the nicotinic acetylcholine (ACh) receptor., 118

Cyclic AMP (cAMP) A second messenger that participates in processes such as changes that occur as a result of learning and the responses of photoreceptors to light., 407

Cyclic guanosine monophosphate (cGMP) A second messenger within photoreceptors that is responsible for maintaining the dark current by opening sodium channels., 186

Cytochrome oxidase blobs An area of primary visual cortex rich in the enzyme cytochrome oxidase that responds to color., 197

Cytokines, 522

Cytoskeleton A network of filaments that provides the internal structure of a neuron., 69–70, 70f, 71f

Dark current The steady depolarization maintained by photoreceptors when no light is present., 186, 187

Daylight saving time, 367–368, 368f

dB. *See* Decibel (dB)

Deception, 483–484, 484f, 485f

Decibel (dB) A unit used to express a difference in intensity between two sounds, equal to 20 times the common logarithm of the ratio of the two levels., 218

Decision making, reward and, 497

Declarative memory An explicit memory for semantic and episodic information that can easily be verbalized, or "declared.," 419–420, 419f

Deep brain stimulation, 14–15, 15f, 284, 284f

Deep cerebellar nuclei Structures that contain the major output cells of the cerebellum; recipients of input from the cerebellar Purkinje cells., 414

Synaptic tag Mechanism that allows newly produced proteins to be captured and inserted at an active synapse., 427

Synaptic vesicles A small structure in the axon terminal that contains neurochemicals., 72

Synchronous Brain activity associated with neurons firing in unison and deep sleep., 375

Tardive dyskinesia A chronic disorder, characterized by involuntary, jerky movements, that occurs as the result of long-term treatment with antipsychotic medications., 559

Taste buds Structures that contain taste receptors., 248–249, 249f

Tau protein, 70, 71f

TBI. *See* Traumatic brain injury (TBI)

Tectorial (roof) membrane A membrane that covers the Organ of Corti., 221

Tectospinal tract A ventromedial pathway connecting the tectum of the midbrain to the alpha motor neurons in the spinal cord., 271

Tectum The "roof," or dorsal half, of the midbrain., 38, 38f

Tegmentum The "covering," or ventral half of the midbrain., 38, 38f

Telencephalon A division of the prosencephalon that develops into the bulk of the cerebral hemispheres., 39, 151

Temperature regulation, 290–297
  adaptations for maintaining, 291–292, 291f, 292f
  behavioral responses to heat and cold and, 292
  brain mechanisms for, 295–297
  endothermic responses to heat and cold and, 292–293
  human core temperature and, deviations in, 293–294
  surface-to-volume ratio and, 291–292, 291f

Temporal lobe The lobe of the cerebral cortex lying ventral and lateral to the frontal and parietal lobes and rostral to the occipital lobe., 40f, 44, 46f
  memory and, 422–424, 422f

Temporal summation Neural integration in which excitation from one active synapse is sufficient to initiate the formation of an action potential., 97

Temporal theory For frequencies below 4000 Hz, the pattern of neural firing matches the frequency of a sound., 225

Testes Male gonads; source of sperm and sex hormones., 57, 330

Testis-determining factor A protein encoded by the *SRY* gene on the Y chromosome that turns the primordial gonads into testes., 330

Testosterone An androgen produced primarily in the testes., 330, 500–502, 501f

Tetanus The point at which a muscle cannot contract further., 95, 261

Tetrahydrocannabinol (THC) The major psychoactive ingredient of cannabis., 132

Thalamus A structure in the diencephalon that processes sensory information, contributes to states of arousal, and participates in learning and memory., 36f, 39, 40f, 41f
  intralaminar nuclei of, 238f, 242, 242f
  medial dorsal nucleus of, 247f, 248
  medial geniculate nucleus of, 224
  olfaction and, 247f, 248

pain perception and, 241–244, 242f, 243f
  somatosensory areas of, 237–238, 238f
  ventral posterior medial nucleus of, 249–250, 250f
  ventral posterior nucleus of, 233, 237f, 238, 242f

THC. *See* Tetrahydrocannabinol (THC)

Theta wave A brain waveform having 4 to 7 cycles per second found primarily in lighter stages of NREM sleep., 377

Thirst, 298–307
  compartments for storing water and, 298–299, 298f
  drinking behavior and, 304–306, 304f
  hypovolemic, 301, 302
  kidneys and, 300, 300t
  osmosis and, 299–300, 299f
  osmotic, 301–302, 302f
  responding to, 302–303, 303f
  sensation of, 301–306

Thoracic nerve One of twelve spinal nerves that serve the torso., 34, 34f, 55f

Thorazine. *See* Chlorpromazine

Threat simulation hypothesis A theory suggesting that dreams provide practice for dealing with threats., 390

3D animation, 204

3/sec spike and wave pattern, 534, 534f

Threshold The level of depolarization at which an action potential is initiated., 81

Thrombosis A blockage that doesn't move from its point of origin in a blood vessel., 517, 518

Thyroid gland, 57

Thyroid-stimulating hormone (TSH) A pituitary hormone that stimulates the growth and function of the thyroid gland, which in turn increases metabolic rate., 314

TIA. *See* Transient ischemic attack (TIA)

Timbre Distinct quality of a sound due to combinations of frequencies., 218

Tolerance The process in which more of a drug is needed to produce the same effect., 123

Tonic-clonic seizure A generalized seizure that results in violent convulsions; also known as a grand mal seizure., 533

Tonic phase The initial stage of a grand mal seizure, in which the patient experiences a loss of consciousness, cessation of breathing, and muscular contraction., 533

Tonotopic Organization Neurons responding to one frequency are located next to neurons responding to similar frequencies., 225

Top-down processing The use of knowledge and expectation to interpret meanings., 177, 201

Touch, 233–244
  mechanoreceptors, 233–235, 233f, 234t, 235f
  pathways, 235–238, 236f, 237f
  plasticity of, 238, 239
  somatosensory cortex and, 238, 239f
  somatosensory disorders and, 239–240, 240f, 241f
  See also Pain

Toxins. *See* Environment

Trace conditioning A type of classical conditioning in which the CS and UCS do not overlap in time., 416, 416f

Transcortical aphasias A language disorder resulting from damage to the connections and cortical areas associated with the major language centers., 465–466, 465f

Transcortical motor aphasia A condition in which language is not fluent, but the ability to repeat is retained., 465–466, 465f

Transcortical sensory aphasia A condition in which comprehension is poor, but the ability to repeat is retained., 465

Transcription factor A chemical that controls gene expression., 407

Transduce To transform sensory information into neural signals., 176

Transduction by photoreceptor, 186, 187f

Transient ischemic attack (TIA) A brief episode (of 24 hours or less) of stroke symptoms that does not cause permanent damage., 517

Transmissible spongiform encephalopathy (TSE) A disease that can be transferred from one animal to another and that produces a fatal, degenerative condition characterized by dementia and motor disturbance., 522–526
  bovine spongiform encephalopathy and, 522, 523f, 526, 526f
  Creutzfeldt-Jakob disease and, 522, 524, 525
  fatal familial insomnia and, 522
  kuru and, 522, 525–526, 525f
  scrapie and, 523, 524–525, 525f

Transporter A receptor in the presynaptic membrane that recaptures released molecules of neurochemical in the process of reuptake., 93

Transsexuality Having a gender identity that is inconsistent with biological sex., 342

Transverse An anatomical section that divides the brain from top to bottom., 27f, 28

Traumatic brain injury (TBI) Physical damage to the brain., 519–521, 519f
  military, 519, 519f
  neurocognitive disorder due to, 520
  outcomes of, 520–521
  repeated, 520–521, 520f
  treating, 521
  types of, 519–520

Trephining or trepanation, 3–4, 4f

Trichromatic theory The theory that suggests human color vision is based on our possessing three different color photopigments., 205, 205f

Trigeminal lemniscus A pathway for pain information from the head and neck that connects the spinal trigeminal nucleus and the thalamus., 241, 242

Trigeminal nerve (V) A cranial nerve that controls chewing movements and provides feedback regarding facial expression., 51, 52, 52f

Trigeminovascular system The network formed by the trigeminal nerves, meninges, and blood vessels believed to participate in migraine headache., 536

Triptan One of a new class of highly specific serotonin agonists used to treat migraine headache., 536

Trisomy 21. *See* Down syndrome

Trochlear nerve (IV) A cranial nerve that controls the muscles of the eye., 51, 52f

Troponin The protein covering an actin molecule that prevents the molecule from binding with myosin when a muscle is in the resting state., 256

TSE. *See* Transmissible spongiform encephalopathy (TSE)

TSH. *See* Thyroid-stimulating hormone (TSH)

Tumor An independent growth of tissue that lacks purpose., 528–530, 529f
  symptoms of, 529
  treatment for, 529–530
  types of, 529

Turner syndrome A condition caused by an XO genotype, characterized by frequent abnormalities of the ovaries and infertility., 328–329, 328f

Twin studies, 17, 570

Twitch The contraction of a single muscle fiber., 256

2-AG. *See* Sn-2 arachidonylglycerol (2-AG)

Two-point discrimination test, 234, 235f

Tympanic canal The lower chamber of the cochlea., 220, 220f, 221, 222f

Tympanic membrane The membrane separating the outer and middle ears; also known as the eardrum., 219, 219f

Type 1 diabetes mellitus The form of diabetes that appears early in life and is characterized by insufficient production of insulin., 310

Type 2 diabetes mellitus The form of diabetes generally diagnosed in middle-aged adults and characterized by resistance to insulin., 310, 310f

Typical antipsychotic medication A dopamine antagonist that is used to treat schizophrenia or psychosis., 558

Ubiquitin carboxyterminal hydrolase An enzyme that allows PKA to be rather continuously active, possibly contributing to long-term memory., 408

UCR. *See* Unconditioned response (UCR)

UCS. *See* Unconditioned stimulus (UCS)

Ultradian cycle A cycle that occurs several times in a single day., 364, 364f

Ultrasound Sound at frequencies above the range of human hearing, or higher than about 20,000 Hz., 218

Umami A proposed taste category associated with the presence of proteins., 248

Unconditioned response (UCR) In classical conditioning, a spontaneous unlearned reaction to a stimulus without prior experience., 402, 409–411, 410f

Unconditioned stimulus (UCS) In classical conditioning, an event that elicits a response without prior experience., 402, 409–411, 410f

Unipolar neuron A neuron with one branch that extends a short distance from the cell body then splits into two branches., 74, 75f

Urbach-Wiethe disease, 491, 491f

Utricle One of the structures making up the otolith organs., 231

V1. *See* Primary visual cortex

V2, 198

V4, 198

Vaccination efforts, 280

Vagus nerve (X) A cranial nerve that serves the heart, liver, and digestive tract., 52, 52f, 55f

Vagusstoff, 103

Valence A positive (attractive) or negative (aversive) reaction to an object or event., 478